90 0957773 4

WITHDRAWN
FROM
UNIVERSITY OF PLYMOUTH
LIBRARY SERVICES

KU-214-884

Cases & Materials on International Law

Cases & Materials on
International Law

Sixth Edition

Martin Dixon

Professor of the Law of Real Property, University of Cambridge
Fellow of Queen's College, University of Cambridge

Robert McCorquodale

Director, British Institute of International and Comparative Law
Professor of International Law and Human Rights, University of Nottingham

Sarah Williams

Associate Professor, Faculty of Law, University of New South Wales

OXFORD
UNIVERSITY PRESS

OXFORD

UNIVERSITY PRESS

Great Clarendon Street, Oxford, OX2 6DP,
United Kingdom

Oxford University Press is a department of the University of Oxford.
It furthers the University's objective of excellence in research, scholarship,
and education by publishing worldwide. Oxford is a registered trade mark of
Oxford University Press in the UK and in certain other countries

© Martin Dixon, Robert McCorquodale, and Sarah Williams 2016

The moral rights of the authors have been asserted

Third edition 2000
Fourth edition 2003
Fifth edition 2011

Impression: 1

All rights reserved. No part of this publication may be reproduced, stored in
a retrieval system, or transmitted, in any form or by any means, without the
prior permission in writing of Oxford University Press, or as expressly permitted
by law, by licence or under terms agreed with the appropriate reprographics
rights organization. Enquiries concerning reproduction outside the scope of the
above should be sent to the Rights Department, Oxford University Press, at the
address above

You must not circulate this work in any other form
and you must impose this same condition on any acquirer

Public sector information reproduced under Open Government Licence v3.0
(http://www.nationalarchives.gov.uk/doc/open-government-licence/open-government-licence.htm)

Published in the United States of America by Oxford University Press
198 Madison Avenue, New York, NY 10016, United States of America

British Library Cataloguing in Publication Data
Data available

Library of Congress Control Number: 2016942486

ISBN 978–0–19–872764–4

Printed in Great Britain by
Bell & Bain Ltd., Glasgow

Links to third party websites are provided by Oxford in good faith and
for information only. Oxford disclaims any responsibility for the materials
contained in any third party website referenced in this work.

PLYMOUTH UNIVERSITY

9 00957773 4

OUTLINE CONTENTS

WITHDRAWN
FROM
UNIVERSITY OF PLYMOUTH
LIBRARY SERVICES

DETAILED CONTENTS

PREFACE TO SIXTH EDITION

If the daunting challenges now facing the world are to be overcome, it must be in important part through the medium of rules, internationally agreed, internationally implemented and, if necessary, internationally enforced. That is what the rule of law requires in the international order.

Lord Bingham, *The Rule of Law* (2010)

The clarification of international law is an essential part of the maintenance and promotion of the rule of law in the international system, as shown by Lord Bingham, who was the pre-eminent British judge of his generation. It is our intention to provide in this book the key cases and materials on current international law in an accessible manner, so that the international rules agreed, implemented and enforced are able to be applied by governments, lawyers and others everywhere, especially as the rule of law affects the daily lives of people around the world.

In this book, the relevant cases and materials are presented within the context of the development of international law over time and the changing understanding of the nature of international law. We have also attempted to respond to readers' comments and we continue to welcome constructive responses. This edition is fully revised and updated from the previous edition, which had been updated to October 2010, to reflect the amazing array of international legal activity over this time. Sarah Williams has undertaken the majority of the revisions, with Robert McCorquodale doing the other chapters, and then both reviewed each other's revisions. Martin Dixon was unable to assist with this edition.

We have been fortunate to have some very good research assistance in preparing this edition. We thank especially Jansen Calamita, Marine Corhay, Joseph Crampin and Souheir Edelbi and the support of the British Institute of International and Comparative Law and the University of New South Wales. We also thank Oxford University Press and all the various staff there, in particular, Tom Randall, Henry Cockburn and Fiona Tatham, who have been very helpful and patient.

Above all, we have been blessed with understanding partners and children. Our love and thanks go to Kate, Rory, Ella and Flora; and Jamie, Isobel and Lucy.

The materials in this book are generally current as at March 2016.

Robert McCorquodale
Sarah Williams
July 2016

ACKNOWLEDGEMENTS

Grateful acknowledgement is made to all the authors and publishers of copyright material which appears in this book, and in particular to the following for permission to reprint material from the sources indicated:

Extracts from House of Lords case reports (UKHL, UKSC) are Parliamentary copyright and are reproduced by permission of the Controller of OPSI on behalf of Parliament.

Extracts from the reports of the European Court of Justice and Court of First Instance (ECR) are taken from www.curia.europa.eu. These are unauthenticated reports and are reproduced free of charge. The definitive versions are published in *Reports of Cases before the Court of Justice* or the *Official Journal of the European Union*.

ABC-CLIO LLC: extract from Allen L Springer: *The International Law of Pollution—Protecting the Global Environment in a World of Sovereign States* (Quorum Books/Greenwood Press, 1983), copyright © Allen L Springer, 1983.

African Commission of Human Rights and Peoples' Rights: extract from The Social and Economic Rights Action Center and the Center for Economic and Social Rights v Nigeria, African Commission on Human and Peoples' Rights Communication 155/96, 27 May 2002.

Philip Allott: extracts from *Eunomia: New Order for a New World* (OUP, 1990).

American Law Institute: extract from Restatement (Third) Foreign Relations Law of the United States (1987).

American Society of Comparative Law: extracts from *American Journal of Comparative Law*: J Scott: 'Extraterritoriality and Territorial Extension in EU Law' in 62 AJCL 87 (2014).

American Society of International Law via Copyright Clearance Center: extracts from *American Journal of International Law*: D Akande: 'International Immunities and the International Criminal Court', (2004) 98 AJIL 407 (2004); D Bowett: 'Reprisals Involving Recourse to Armed Force', 66 AJIL 1(1972); E Brown-Weiss: Our Rights and Obligations to Future Generations for the Environment, 84 AJIL 198 (1990); J Charney: 'Universal International Law', 87 AJIL 529 (1993); C Chinkin: 'Third Party Intervention before the ICJ', 80 AJIL 495 (1986); L Dickinson: 'The Promise of Hybrid Courts', 97 AJIL 295 (2003); Clipperton Island Arbitration (*France* v *Mexico*) 2 RIAA 1105 (1932) transl. in 26 AJIL 390; D Donovan and A Roberts: 'The Emerging Recognition of Universal Civil Jurisdiction', 100 AJIL 142 (2006); T Franck: 'Who Killed Article 2 (4)?', 64 AJIL (1970) 809; T Franck: 'What Happens Now? The United Nations after Iraq', 97 AJIL 607 (2003); L Henkin: 'The Reports of the Death of Article 2 (4) are Greatly Exaggerated', 65 AJIL 544 (1971); D Leebron: 'Linkages', 96 AJIL 5 (2002); J Jackson: 'Sovereignty-Modern: A New Approach to an Outdated Concept' in 97 AJIL 782 (2003); H Kelsen: 'Collective Security and Collective Self-Defence under the Charter of the United Nations' in 42 AJIL 783 (1948); A Lowenfeld: note re Hartford Fire Insurance Company California, US Supreme Court, 113 S Ct. 2891 (1993), 89 AJIL 42 (1995); Ambassador Malone, Statement before the Subcommittee on Oceanography of the House of Representatives Committee on Merchant Marine and Fisheries, United States Congress, 28 April 1981, 76 AJIL (1981); S D Murphy: 'Aerial Incident off the Coast of China', 95 AJIL 630 (2002); S D Murphy (ed): 'Contemporary Practice of the United States Relating to International Law', 96 AJIL 236 (2002) and 97 AJIL 419 (2003); S Ratner: 'Belgium's War Crimes Statute: A Postmortem', 97 AJIL 888 (2003); M Reisman: 'The Past and Future of the Claim of Preemptive Self-Defense', 100 AJIL 525 (2007); E Rostow: 'Until What? Enforcement Action or Collective Self-Defence?', 85 AJIL 506 (1991); D Scheffer: 'The United States and the International Criminal Court', 93 AJIL 12 (1999); Carsten Stahn, 'Responsibility to

Protect: Political Rhetoric or Emerging Legal Norm?', 101 AJIL 99 (2007); S Talmon: 'The Security Council as World Legislature', 99 AJIL 175 (2000); P Weil: 'Towards relative normativity in International law', 77 AJIL 413 (1983); R Wilde: 'From Danzig to East Timor and Beyond: The Role of International Territorial Administration', 95 AJIL 583 (2001); US-Iran Claims Tribunal: note re Shahin Shane Ebrahimi v Government of the Islamic Republic of Iran, noted at 89 AJIL 385 (1995); 'The Security Council as World Legislature', 99 AJIL 175 (2005); and Vienna Convention on Succession of States in Respect of Treaties 1978, 72 AJIL 971 (1978); extract from the *Federal Supplement: United States* v *Yunis* in 681 F. Sup 896 (1988); and extracts from *International Legal Materials*, all copyright © American Society of International Law.

American University International Law Review: extracts from J Oloka-Onyango: 'Reinforcing Marginalized Rights in an Age of Globalization: International Mechanisms, Non-state Actors, and the Struggle for Peoples' Rights in Africa', 18 *American University International Law Review* 851 (2003).

Australian National University, College of Law, Centre for International and Public Law, and the authors: extracts from *Australian Year Book of International Law:* David Feldman: 'Monism, Dualism and Constitutional Legitimacy', 20 AYBIL (1999), and Y. Ghai: extract from 'Human Rights and Governance: The Asia Debate', 15 AYBIL (1994).

Brill Academic Publishers: extracts from *Recueil de Cours* (Hague Academy of International Law): J de Arechega: 'General Course in Public International Law', 159 RC 9 (1978); D Bowett: 'Contemporary developments in legal techniques in the Settlement of Disputes', 180 RC (1983); G Fitzmaurice: 'The General Principles of International Law Considered from the Standpoint of the Rule of Law', 92 RC 5(1957-II); and O Schachter: 'General Course in International Law', 179 RC (1982); via Copyright Clearance Center: extracts from F Orrega-Vicuña: 'Of contracts and treaties in the Global Market', 8 *Max-Planck Yearbook of United Nations Law* 341 (2004); and from G Fitzmaurice: 'Some Problems Regarding the Formal Sources of International Law' from *Symbolae Verzijl* 153 (M Nijhoff, 1958).

British Institute of International and Comparative Law: extract from K Starmer and T Christou: *Human Rights Manual and Sourcebook for Africa* (BIICL, 2005).

Brooklyn Journal of International Law and the author: extract from Kern Alexander: 'Global Financial Standard Setting, the G10 Committees, and the International Economic Law', 34 *Brooklyn Journal of International Law*, 861 (2008–9).

Brown Journal of World Affairs: extract from D Rothwell: 'The Arctic in International Affairs: Time for a New Regime?', XV *BJWA* 241 (2008).

Cambridge University Press and the authors: extracts from Yoram Dinstein: *War, Aggression, and Self-Defence* (4th edition, CUP, 2005); Martti Koskenniemi: *From Apology to Utopia; The Structure of International Legal Argument* (CUP, 2005); Susan Marks: 'Exploitation as an International Legal Concept' in S Marks (ed.): *International Law on the Left: Re-examining Marxist Legacies* (CUP, 2008); Gerry Simpson: *Great Powers and Outlaw States: Unequal Sovereigns in the International Legal Order* (CUP, 2004); and Carsten Stahn: *The Law and Practice of International Territorial Administration: Versailles to Iraq and Beyond* (CUP, 2005); and extracts from *Leiden Journal of International Law*: R McCorquodale: 'An Inclusive International Legal System' in 17 *LJIL* 477; H Thirlway: 'Human Rights in Customary Law: An Attempt to Define some of the Issues' in 28 LJIL 495 (2015); from *Asian Journal of International Law*: M. Wood: 'What is Public International Law? The Need for Clarity about Sources' in 1 AJIL 205 (2011); from *International and Comparative Law Quarterly* (ICLQ) on behalf of the British Institute of International and Comparative Law: Michael Akehurst 'Equity and General Principles of Law', 25 (4) ICLQ 801 (1976); D H Anderson: 'Further Efforts to Ensure Universal Participation in the United Nations Convention on The Law of the Sea', 43

ICLQ 886 (1994), and 'Legal Implications of the Entry into Force of the UN Convention on the Law of the Sea', 44 ICLQ 313 (1995); Paul Arnell: 'The Case for Nationality Based Jurisdiction', 50 (4) ICLQ 955 (2001); James Crawford & Simon Olleson: '*The Continuing Debate on a UN Convention on State Responsibility*', 54 (4) ICLQ 959 (2005); Eileen Denza: 'The 2004 UN Convention on State Immunity in Perspective', 55 ICLQ 395 (2006); Hazel Fox: 'In Defence of State Immunity: Why the UN Convention on State Immunity is important', 55 ICLQ 399 (2006); Douglas Guilfoyle 'Piracy off Somalia: UN Security Council Resolution 1816 and IMO Regional Counter-Piracy Efforts', 57 ICLQ 690 (2008); Rosalyn Higgins: 'A Babel of judicial voices? Ruminations from the Bench', 55 ICLQ 791 (2006); Pieter Kooijmans: 'The ICJ in the 21st Century: Judicial Restraint, Judicial Activism, or Proactive Judicial Policy?', 56 ICLQ (2007); A Vaughan Lowe: 'US Extra territorial Jurisdiction: The Helms-Burton and D'Amato Acts', 46 (2) ICLQ 378 (1997); Robert McCorquodale 'Self-Determination: A Human Rights Approach', 43 (4) ICLQ 857 (1994); Sean D Murphy: 'Democratic Legitimacy and the Recognition of States and Governments', 48 (3) ICLQ 545 (1999); B Simma: 'Foreign Investment Arbitration: A Place for Human Rights?' in 60 ICLQ 573 (2011); James A Sweeney: 'Margins of Appreciation: Cultural Relativity and the European Court of Human Rights in the Post-Cold War Era', 54 (2) ICLQ 459 (2005); Colin Warbrick, 'British Policy and the National Transitional Council of Libya', 61 ICLQ 247 (2012); Colin Warbrick: 'The Governance of Britain', 57 (1) ICLQ 209 (2008): Colin Warbrick & Dominic McGoldrick: 'Kosovo: The Declaration of Independence', 57 (3) ICLQ 675 (2008); and Colin Warbrick & Zeray W Yihdego: 'Ethiopia's Military Action Against the Union of Islamic Courts and Others in Somalia: Some Legal Implications', 56 (3) ICLQ 666 (2007); and from *International Law Reports* (ILR): *Attorney-General of the Government of Israel* v *Eichmann* in 36 ILR (1961); *Rainbow Warrior Arbitration (New Zealand* v *France)* 82 ILR 499 (1990); *Sei Fuji* v *State of California* 19 ILR 312 (1952).

Council of Europe, for the Venice Commission 'Opinion on the International legal obligations of Council of Europe member States in respect of secret detention facilities and inter-state transport of prisoners', March 2006 and for *European Court of Human Rights* Case Reports.

Edward Elgar Publishing: extract from E Crawford and R Rayfuse: 'Climate Change and Statehood' in R Rayfuse and S Scott (eds): *International Law in the Era of Climate Change* (2012).

Fordham Environmental Law Review: A Boyle: 'Human Rights or Environmental Rights? A Reassessment', 18 *Fordham Environmental Law Review* 471 (2007).

Harvard University/Law School via Copyright Clearance Center: extracts from *Harvard International Law Journal*: P Allott: 'State Responsibility and the unmaking of International Law', 29 HILJ (1988): A Orford: 'Locating the International: Military and Monetary Interventions after the Cold War', 38 HILJ (1997); and J Trachtman: 'The Domain of WTO Dispute Resolution', 40 HILJ (1999); all copyright © Harvard University/Law School.

Human Rights Law Centre, Nottingham University: extracts from *International Human Rights Reports* (IHR).

Incorporated Council of Law Reporting: extracts from the *Law Reports: Appeal Cases* (AC), *Queen's Bench Division* (QB), and *Weekly Law Reports* (WLR).

International Criminal Tribunal for the Former Yugoslavia (ICTY): extracts from Case Reports: Case No. IT-95-17/1-T, *The Prosecutor v Furundzija, Judgment* (1998) and *The Prosecutor v Kunurac et al, Judgement* (2002).

John H Jackson: extract from 'International Law: reflections on the "Boiler room" of International Relations' in Charlotte Ku and Paul F Diehl (eds.): *International Law: Classic and Contemporary Readings* (Lynne Reinner Publishers, 1998).

Martti Koskenniemi: extracts from *From Apology to Utopia; The Structure of International Legal Argument* (Cambridge University Press, 2005), from 'International Lawyers' in P Cane and J Conaghan (eds): *New Oxford Companion to Law* (OUP, 2008), and from 'Human Rights Mainstreaming as a Project of Power' (Institute for International Law and Justice, New York University, 2006).

LexisNexis: extract from *Journal of International Banking and Financial Law*: M Mendelson and M Paparinskis: 'Bail-Ins and the International Investment Law of Expropriation: In and Beyond Cyprus' in 28 JIBFL 475 (2013).

LexisNexis New Zealand: extracts from *New Zealand Law Reports*.

Manchester University Press: extracts from Hilary Charlesworth and Christine Chinkin: *The Boundaries of International Law: A Feminist Perspective* (Manchester University Press, 2000).

Melbourne Journal of International Law: extract from M Kirby: 'Transnational Judicial Dialogue, Internationalisation of Law and Australian Judges', 9 *Melbourne Journal of International Law* 171 (2008).

Michigan Journal of International Law and the author: extracts from R Wilde: 'Legal Black Hole'? Extra-territorial State Action and International Treaty Law', 26 *Michigan Journal of International Law* 739 (2005).

Oxford University Press: extracts from P Alston and R Goodman: *International Human Rights* (2012); M Anderson: 'Human Rights approaches to environmental protection' in Alan E Boyle and Michael R Anderson (eds.): *Human Rights Approaches to Environmental Protection* (Clarendon Press, 1996); M Baderin: *International Human Rights and Islamic Law* (2003); A Bianchi: 'State Responsibility and Criminal Liability of Individuals' in A Cassese (ed): *Oxford Companion to International Criminal Law* (OUP, 2009); A Boyle and C Chinkin: *The Making of International Law* (OUP, 2007); J L Brierly: *The Law of Nations* (1st edition, 1928, and 6th edition, edited by H Waldock, 1963); Antonio Cassese: *International Law* (2nd edition, 2005); A Cassese: 'For an Enhanced Role of Jus Cogens' in A Cassese (ed): *Realizing Utopia: The Future of International Law* (2012); A Clapham: *Human Rights Obligations of Non-State Actors* (OUP, 2006); James Crawford: *The Creation of States in International Law* (2nd edition, OUP, 2006); M B Dembour, 'Critiques' in D Moeckli, S Shah, & S Sivakumaran (eds): *International Human Rights* (2nd edition, 2014); H Fox: 'International Law and the Restraints on the Exercise of Jurisdiction by National Courts of States' in M Evans (ed) *International Law* (4th edition, 2014); H Fox: *The Law of State Immunity* (OUP, 2004); G Goodwin-Gill & J McAdam: *The Refugee in International Law* (3rd edition, OUP, 2007); C Gray: *International Law and the Use of Force* (3rd edition, OUP 2008); R Jennings and A Watts (eds): *Oppenheim's International Law*, (9th edition, Longman, 1992); C Redgwell: 'International Environmental Law' in Malcolm D Evans: *International Law* (3rd edition, 2010); Adam Roberts and Benedict Kingsbury: *United Nations, Divided World: The UN's Role in International Relations* (2nd edition, 1993); Dinah Shelton: 'International Law and Relative Normativity' in Malcolm D Evans (ed.): *International Law* (3rd edition, OUP, 2010); J Shestack: 'The Jurisprudence of Human Rights' in Theodor Meron (ed.): *Human Rights in International Law* (1984); and Heather A Wilson: *International Law and the Use of Force by National Liberation Movements* (OUP, 1989); and extracts from *British Yearbook of International Law* (BYBIL) on behalf of the Royal Insitute of International Affairs (RIIA): M Akehurst: 'Custom as a source of International Law', 47 BYBIL (1974–5); L Doswald Beck: 'The Legal Validity of Military Intervention by Invitation of the Government', 56 BYBIL 189 (1985); I Brownlie: 'Recognition in Theory and Practice', 53 BYBIL 197 (1982); J Charney: 'The Persistent Objector Rule and the Development of Customary International Law', 56 BYBIL 1 (1985): M Evans: 'Delimitation and the Common Maritime Boundary', 64 BYBIL 283 (1994); C Gray and B Kingsbury, 'Developments in Dispute Settlement: Inter-State Arbitration since 1945' in 63 BYIL 97 (1992); B Sloan: 'General Assembly Resolutions

Revisited', 58 BYBIL 93 (1987): and 'Challenge for the New Century', Speech by the UK Foreign Secretary, 1 BYBIL 646 (2000); Debate on the second reading in the House of Commons of the Jurisdiction (Conspiracy and Incitement) Bill, the Parliamentary Under Secretary of State, Home Office, Mr Timothy Kirkhope, 68 BYBIL 575 (1997); and United Kingdom Rules regarding the taking Up of International Claims by Her Majesty's Government, July 1983, 54 BYBIL 520 (1983).

Oxford University Press Journals: extracts from *Journal of Conflict and Security Law*: C Stahn: 'Between Law-breaking and Law-making: Syria, Humanitarian Intervention, and "What the Law Ought to Be"' in 19 JCSL 25 (2014); *Journal of International Criminal Justice*: P Akhavan: 'The Rise, and Fall, and Rise of International Criminal Justice' in 11 JICJ 527 (2013); M Bothe: 'Security Council's Targeted Sanctions against Presumed Terrorists', 6 JICJ (2008).

R Zacklin: 'The Failings of Ad Hoc International Tribunals', 2 JICJ 541 (2004); from *Journal of International Economic Law*: T Cottier: 'Challenges Ahead in International Economic Law', 12 JIEL 1 (2009); C Henckels: 'Protecting Regulatory Autonomy Through Greater Precision of Investment Treaties: The TTP, CETA and TTIP' in 19 JIEL (2016); and from *European Journal of International Law*: A Bianchi: 'International Law and US Courts: The Myth of Lohengrin Revisited', 15 (4) EJIL751 (2004); M Craven: 'Legal differentiation and the concept of the Human Rights Treaty in International Law', 11 EJIL 459 (2000); A Llamzon: 'Jurisdiction and Compliance in Recent Decisions of the International Court of Justice', 18 EJIL 815 (2007); M Milanovic and L A Sicilianos, 'Reservations to Treaties: An Introduction' in 24 EJIL 1055 (2013); S Talmon: 'Determining Customary International Law: The ICJ's Methodology between Induction, Deduction, and Assertion', 26 EJIL 417 (2015); C Tams: 'The Use of Force against Terrorists', 20 EJIL 359 (2002); and T Treves: 'Piracy, Law of the Sea, and Use of Force: Developments off the Coast of Somalia', 20 EJIL 399 (2009).

Palgrave Macmillan: extract from M C Davis: *Constitutional Confrontation in Hong Kong* (Macmillan, 1989).

Permanent Court of Arbitration (PCA): extract from Eritrea Ethiopia Claims Commission, Final Award, 17 August 2009 (Ethiopia's Damages Claims).

Princeton University Press: extract from R McCorquodale: 'International Law, Boundaries and Imagination' in D Miller and S Hashmi (eds.): *Boundaries and Justice* (2001), copyright © 2001 by Princeton University Press.

Reed Elsevier (UK) Ltd trading as LexisNexis: extracts from *All England Law Reports* (All ER).

The Royal Institute of International Affairs (RIIA), Chatham House: extracts from *British Yearbook of International Law* (BYBIL): M Akehurst: Enforcement Action by Regional Agencies with special reference to the Organization of American States', 42 BYBIL (1967); R Baxter: 'Multilateral Treaties as Evidence of Customary International Law', 41 BYBIL (1965).

Issa G Shivji: extract from *The Concept of Human Rights in Africa* (CODESRIA, 1989).

Sir Ian Sinclair: extract from *The Vienna Convention on the Law of Treaties* (2e, Manchester University Press, 1984).

Southern California Law Review: extract from Christopher D. Stone: 'Should Trees have Standing? Towards Legal Rights for Natural Objects', 45 *Southern California Law Review* (1972).

Sweet & Maxwell Ltd: extract from H Lauterpacht: *International Law and Human Rights* (1950).

Taylor & Francis: extract from *International Journal of Human Rights*: F Mégret: 'The Disabilities Convention: Towards a Holistic Concept of Rights' in 12 IJHL 274 (2008).

Thomson Reuters (Professional) Australia Ltd, www.thomsonreuters.com.au: extracts from *Commonwealth Law Reports* (CLR) and from M Pryles, J Waincymer and M Davies: *International Trade Law: Cases and Materials* (Lawbook Co, 1996).

University of Pennsylvania Press: extracts from Hilary Charlesworth: 'What are Women's International Rights?' in R Cook (ed): *Human Rights of Women* (1994); and *Humanity*: M Koskenniemi 'Human Rights Mainstreaming as a Project of Power' in 1 *Humanity* 47 (2010), reprinted with permission of the University of Pennsylvania Press.

Virginia Journal of International Law via Copyright Clearance Center: extracts from *Virginia Journal of International Law*: Makauwa Mutua: 'The Banjul Charter and the African Cultural Fingerprint: An Evaluation of the Language of Duties', 35 VJIL (1995); and F. Téson: 'International Human Rights and Cultural Relativism', 25 VJIL (1985).

John Wiley & Sons Ltd: extracts from *Modern Law Review*: A Cassese: 'Reflections on International Criminal Justice', 61 *MLR* 1 (1998); and R McCorquodale & P Simons: 'Responsibility Beyond Borders: State Responsibility for Extraterritorial Violations by Corporations of International Human Rights Law', 70 *MLR* 598 (2007).

World Trade Organization: extracts from *General Agreement on Tariffs and Trade* (GATT) 1947 and 1994, and from Reports, Decisions and Declarations of the WTO.

Although we have made every effort to trace and contact all copyright holders before publication this has not been possible in all cases. If notified, the publisher will rectify any errors or omissions at the earliest opportunity.

TABLE OF CASES

TABLE OF LEGISLATION

TABLE OF STATUTES OF THE INTERNATIONAL COURTS

TABLE OF THE RULES OF THE INTERNATIONAL COURTS

TABLE OF INTERNATIONAL SECONDARY LEGISLATION

TABLE OF TREATIES AND CONVENTIONS

TABLE OF OTHER DOCUMENTS

1

The Nature of the International Legal System

INTRODUCTORY NOTE

Open a newspaper, listen to the radio or watch television, and you will be confronted with events that have significance in international law. United Nations' resolutions and peacekeeping forces; the claims for independence by groups around the world; conferences on the environment and on trade; the changing political and social situation in Africa, Asia and Europe; allegations of human rights abuses in many States; attempts to control terrorism and drugs; debates concerning the future of the United Nations; and the increasing impact of European laws on the member States of the European Union, are but a few examples. Overall, there is an increased interdependence in the international community.

It is these events and this interdependence that international law addresses by analysing the legal principles arising from interactions between States, actions by States and certain actions by individuals, corporations, international organisations and other actors on the international plane. International law has effects on, and is affected by, international relations, political thought and communications, as well as by the awareness of women and men in every State that they are among those addressed by the United Nations Charter as being 'We, the Peoples of the United Nations'.

International law is really a description of an entire legal system: the international legal system. It is an international legal system by which legal rules are created in order to structure and organise societies and relationships. It acknowledges the influence of political, economic, social and cultural processes upon the development of legal rules. Within this international legal system are, for example, constitutional laws, property laws, criminal laws and laws about obligations, although these terms are not normally used. It is this extensive array of laws within the international legal system that is included under the name 'international law'.

SECTION 1: THE RELEVANCE OF INTERNATIONAL LAW

International law is law and has relevance to our daily lives. For example, international law enables international telephone calls to be made, overseas mail to be delivered and travel by air, sea and land to occur relatively easily. Fear of enforcement of law is rarely the sole reason why law is obeyed, but the behaviour of States and people often is modified depending on the substance of the law and its aspirational and inspirational aspects. International law does affect the actions of States and others in the international community.

H. Waldock, *J. Brierly's The Law of Nations*

(6th edn, 1963)

Violations of the law are rare in all customary systems, and they are so in international law....[That] the law is normally observed...receives little notice because the interest of most people in international law is not in the ordinary routine of international legal business, but in the occasions, rare but generally sensational, on which it is flagrantly broken. Such breaches generally occur either when some great political issue has arisen between states, or in that part of the system which professes to regulate the conduct of war. But our diagnosis of what is wrong with the system will be mistaken if we fail to realize that the laws of peace and the great majority of treaties are on the whole regularly observed in the daily intercourse of states....If we fail to understand this, we are likely to assume, as many people do, that all would be well with international law if we could devise a better system for enforcing it....It is not the existence of a police force that makes a system of law strong and respected, but the strength of the law that makes it possible for a police force to be effectively organized. The imperative character of law is felt so strongly and obedience to it has become so much a matter of habit within a...state that national law has developed a machinery of enforcement which generally works smoothly, though never so smoothly as to make breaches impossible. If the imperative character of international law were equally strongly felt, the institutions of definite international sanctions would easily follow.

   Whether from a review of all these shortcomings we ought to conclude that international law is a failure depends upon what we assume to be its aim. It has not failed to serve the purposes for which states have chosen to use it; in fact it serves these purposes reasonably well. The layman hears little of international law as a working system, for most of its practice goes on within the walls of foreign offices, which on principle are secretive; and even if the foreign offices were inclined to be more communicative the layman would not find what they could tell him very interesting, any more than he would normally be interested in the working of a solicitor's office. For in fact the practice of international law proceeds on much the same lines as that of any other kind of law, with the foreign offices taking the place of the private legal adviser and exchanging arguments about the facts and the law, and later, more often than is sometimes supposed, with a hearing before some form of international tribunal. The volume of this work is considerable, but most of it is not sensational, and it only occasionally relates to matters of high political interest. That does not mean that the matters to which it does relate are unimportant in themselves; often they are very important to particular interests or individuals. But it means that international law is performing a useful and indeed a necessary function in international life in enabling states to carry on their day-to-day intercourse along orderly and predictable lines. That is the role for which states have chosen to use it and for that it has proved a serviceable instrument. If we are dissatisfied with this role, if we believe that it can and should be used, as national law has begun to be used, as an instrument for promoting the general welfare in positive ways, and even more if we believe that it ought to be a powerful means of maintaining international peace, then we shall have to admit that it has so far failed. But it is only fair to remember that these have not been the purposes for which states have so far chosen to use it.

L. Henkin, *How Nations Behave*

(2nd edn, 1979)

[International] law works. Although there is no one to determine and adjudge the law with authoritative infallibility, there is wide agreement on the content and meaning of law and agreements, even in a world variously divided. Although there is little that is comparable to executive law enforcement in a domestic society, there are effective forces, internal and external, to induce general compliance. Nations recognize that the observance of law is in their interest, and that every violation may also bring particular undesirable consequences. It is the unusual case in which policymakers believe that the advantages of violation outweigh those of law observance, or where domestic pressures compel a government to violation even against the perceived national interest. The important violations are of political law and agreements, where basic interests of national security or independence are involved, engaging passions, prides and prejudices, and where rational calculation of cost and advantage is less likely to occur and difficult to make. Yet, as we have seen, the most important principle of law today is commonly observed: nations have not been going to war, unilateral uses of force have been only occasional, brief, limited. Even the uncertain law against intervention, seriously breached in several instances, has undoubtedly deterred intervention in many other instances. Where political law has not deterred action it has often postponed or limited action or determined a choice among alternative actions.

None of this argument is intended to suggest that attention to law is the paramount or determinant motivation in national behavior, or even that it is always a dominant factor. A norm or obligation brings no guarantee of performance; it does add an important increment of interest in performing the obligation. Because of the requirements of law or of some prior agreement, nations modify their conduct in significant respects and in substantial degrees. It takes an extraordinary and substantially more important interest to persuade a nation to violate its obligations. Foreign policy, we know, is far from free; even the most powerful nations have learned that there are forces within their society and, even more, in the society of nations that limit their freedom of choice. When a contemplated action would violate international law or a treaty, there is additional, substantial limitation on the freedom to act.

R. Jennings and A. Watts, *Oppenheim's International Law*

(9th edn, vol. 1, 1992)

International law is sometimes referred to as 'public international law' to distinguish it from private international law. Whereas the former governs the relations of states and other subjects of international law amongst themselves, the latter consists of the rules developed by states as part of their domestic law to resolve the problems which, in cases between private persons which involve a foreign element, arise over whether the court has jurisdiction and over the choice of the applicable law: in other terms, public international law arises from the juxtaposition of states, private international law from the juxtaposition of legal systems. Although the rules of private international law are part of the internal law of the state concerned, they may also have the character of public international law where they are embodied in treaties. Where this happens the failure of a state party to the treaty to observe the rule of private international law prescribed in it will lay it open to proceedings for breach of an international obligation owed to another party. Even where the rules of private international law cannot themselves be considered as rules of public international law, their application by a state as part of its internal law may directly involve the rights and obligations of the state as a matter of public international law, for example where the matter concerns the property of aliens or the extent of the state's jurisdiction....

There is…increasing acceptance that the rules of international law are the foundation upon which the rights of states rest, and no longer merely limitations upon states' rights which, in the absence of a rule of law to the contrary, are unlimited. Although there are extensive areas in which international law accords to states a large degree of freedom of action (for example, in matters of domestic jurisdiction), it is important that freedom is derived from a legal right and not from an assertion of unlimited will, and is subject ultimately to regulation within the legal framework of the international community. In the *Military and Paramilitary Activities* (*Nicaragua* v *United States*) case the International Court of Justice upheld the essential justiciability of even those disputes raising issues of the use of force and collective self-defence.

Furthermore international law may now properly be regarded as a complete system. By this is meant not that there is always a clear and specific legal rule readily applicable to every international situation, but that every international situation is capable of being determined *as a matter of law*, either by the application of specific legal rules where they already exist, or by the application of legal rules derived, by the use of known legal techniques, from other legal rules or principles.

S. Scott, 'International Law as Ideology: Theorizing the Relationship between International Law and International Politics'

5 *European Journal of International Law* 313 (1994)

The realist paradigm in international relations is unable to explain the nature and degree of the significance of international law to the system of international politics. Although international law appears to play a political role, that role cannot be conceptualized within a paradigm that posits power as the prime determinant of political outcomes and yet does not theorize the relationship between international law and power....

It has been suggested that the idea of international law is integral to the international distribution of power and that it actually sustains the structure of the international political order. In political terms it does not matter whether or not the ideology is true; it is not the verity of an ideology that matters but its acceptance by international actors as a basis for interaction. Legal debate is the process of ostensibly establishing a concrete law-non-law boundary and a set of objective, applicable rules to deal with all political issues. In order for the ideology to operate successfully, lawyers must continue to find ways of demonstrating the practicality of the image of international law portrayed by the ideology. Legal discourse is founded on an assumption of legal objectivity.

This conceptualization of the relationship of international law to international politics means that many previously asked questions regarding international law have been superseded. For example, the questions as to whether and why States 'obey' international law are no longer meaningful. It can now be seen that States neither obey nor disobey international law; they simply act so as to demonstrate acceptance of the ideology of international law. While States might be concerned that international law develops in their favour, this interest is indirect; favourable terms means that the State can more readily uphold the notion of the binding quality of international law.

T. Bingham, *The Rule of Law*

(2010)

If I am right that the invasion of Iraq [in March 2003] by the US, the UK and some other states was unauthorised by the Security Council there was, of course, a serious violation of international law and of the rule of law. For the effect of acting unilaterally was to undermine the foundation on which the post-1945 consensus had been constructed....The moment that a state treats the rules of international law as binding on others but not on itself, the compact on which the law rests is broken. 'It is', as has been said [by V. Lowe, *Austrian Review of International and European Law* 2003], 'the difference between the role of world policeman and world vigilante'....Particularly disturbing to proponents of the rule of law is the cynical lack of concern for international legality among some top officials in the Bush administration [2000–2008]....

[M]ost transactions governed by international law proceed smoothly and routinely on the strength of known and accepted rules. I have perhaps dwelt disproportionately on the non-compliant tip of the iceberg, illustrated by events in Iraq and elsewhere. But those events highlight what seem to me to be the two most serious deficiencies of the rule of law in the international order. The first is the willingness of some states in some circumstances to rewrite the rules to meet the perceived exigencies of the political situation, as the UK did in relation to the Suez crisis of 1956. The second is the consensual basis of the jurisdiction of the International Court of Justice.

If events in Iraq and elsewhere highlight some of the deficiencies of international law, they may nonetheless yield a public benefit in the longer term....While prophecy is always perilous, it is perhaps unlikely that states chastened by their experience in Iraq will be eager to repeat it. While they have not been hauled before the ICJ or any other tribunal to answer for their actions, they have been arraigned at the bar of world opinion, and been judged unfavourably, with resulting damage to their standing and influence. If the daunting challenges now facing the world are to be overcome, it must be through the medium of rules, internationally agreed, internationally implemented and, if necessary, internationally enforced. That is what the rule of law requires in the international order.

NOTES

1. While international law is of a different nature to national law in its sources, institutions and development, international law is 'law' in that it seeks to ensure that there is order and structure in the international community. This order enables the members of the international community to interact together with a reasonable degree of confidence and ensures that changes in rules generally occur by a coherent and consistent process.

2. States do still generally comply with international law. As Henkin and Scott suggest, international law can—and does—modify behaviour, particularly of States. Just as in national law, political considerations can also determine much of the content of international law. Even economically powerful States, such as the United States of America, have been affected by the pressure of international law and international relations to be pulled towards compliance with international law, such as with their unlawful detainment of people at Guantanamo Bay.

3. Tom Bingham (who was the most senior judge in the UK at the time of the Iraq war), notes the broad impact today across the international and national communities of an armed conflict that is contrary to international law and he stresses the importance of a rule of law in the international legal system. The core elements of an international rule of law would be essentially the

same as for a national rule of law, being legal order and stability, equality of application of the law, protection of human rights and settlement of disputes before an independent legal body. This is important in terms of international peace and security, transparency, good governance, justice and accountability in the international system.

SECTION 2: THE INTERNATIONAL COMMUNITY AND INTERNATIONAL LAW

The United Nations system is central to the international community and to international law. While international law lacks a consistently effective centralised system for the determination and enforcement of international law, the United Nations offers the possibility of some centralised action. It has some of the institutional structures—a body comprising some nominal representative of nearly all States (the General Assembly); a body with executive powers (the Security Council); and a court (the International Court of Justice)—but the limitations on the powers of these institutions mean that they cannot be considered as an effective equivalent to national institutions.

A. Roberts and B. Kingsbury, 'The UN's Roles in International Society since 1945'
in A. Roberts and B. Kingsbury (eds), *United Nations, Divided World* (2nd edn, 1993)

The first blueprints for the UN were drafted by the USA, the UK, the USSR, and their allies during World War II, reflecting their conceptions of the post-war international order. The Charter was finally adopted by fifty states meeting at San Francisco in June 1945. Although the nature and work of the UN has evolved considerably, the Charter has remained virtually unchanged. The UN was formally established on 24 October 1945, when its basic constitutive instrument, the UN Charter, entered into force.

In the years since 1945 the number of member states of the UN has steadily increased, due mainly to the effects of successive waves of decolonization and disintegration of states. In 1945 the UN had fifty-one original members; by the end of 1960, one hundred; by the end of 1984, one hundred and fifty-nine; and by July 1993, one hundred and eighty-four. Throughout its history, the UN has had as members the great majority of states. Despite trends towards regional integration, there have only exceptionally been enduring cases of UN member states unifying to form a single larger state: Tanzania (1964), Yemen (1990), and Germany (1990).

The most conspicuous case of non-membership was the People's Republic of China from the revolution in 1949 until 1971, during which period China was represented by the regime in Taiwan. Since 1971 the UN's claims to near-universalism have had real substance. Its members include virtually all the states of the contemporary world. No member state has ever left the UN. However, during 1950 the USSR refused to participate in the Security Council in protest against the UN's refusal to accept the government of the People's Republic of China as representative of China; and in 1965–6 Indonesia temporarily withdrew from the UN. In some cases the credentials of particular authorities to represent their state have not been accepted; and the Federal Republic of Yugoslavia (Serbia and Montenegro) was advised in 1992 by the Security Council and by the General Assembly that it could not continue the membership of the former Socialist Federal Republic of Yugoslavia, although it was able to continue participation in some UN bodies.

Six 'principal organs' of the UN were established by the Charter: the General Assembly, the Security Council, the Secretariat, the International Court of Justice (ICJ), the Trusteeship Council, and the Economic and Social Council (ECOSOC).

The *General Assembly* as the plenary body controls much of the work of the UN. It meets in regular session for approximately the last quarter of every year (with sessions spilling over well into the new year), and occasionally holds special or emergency sessions to consider specific issues. The General Assembly approves the budget, adopts priorities, calls international conferences, superintends the operations of the Secretariat and of numerous committees and subsidiary organs, and debates and adopts resolutions on diverse issues. It played a major role in supervising European decolonization, and has also become involved in human rights supervision and election-monitoring in independent countries. The many subsidiary bodies created by the General Assembly include the United Nations Children's Fund (UNICEF), the Office of the United Nations High Commissioner for Refugees (UNHCR), the United Nations Conference on Trade and Development (UNCTAD), the United Nations

Development Programme (UNDP), and the United Nations Environment Programme (UNEP). Much of the work of the General Assembly is done in permanent or *ad hoc* committees responsible for particular fields of UN activity or deliberation. The General Assembly's agenda also includes many areas of activity in which states prefer rhetoric to real action.

The fifteen-member *Security Council* is dominated by its five Permanent Members (China, France, Russia, the UK, and the USA), each of which has power to veto any draft resolution on substantive matters. The ten non-permanent members (six until a Charter amendment came into force in 1965) are elected for two-year periods by the General Assembly. The Security Council has primary responsibility for the maintenance of international peace and security, and unlike the General Assembly is able to take decisions which are supposed to be binding on all members of the UN. It meets almost continuously throughout the year, mainly to consider armed conflicts and other situations or disputes where international peace and security are threatened. It is empowered to order mandatory sanctions, call for cease-fires, and even to authorize military action on behalf of the UN.

The Security Council has also had a central role in the development of the institution of UN peacekeeping forces, which were not envisaged at all in the Charter. The blue berets or helmets worn by members of national military units working in the service of the UN have become a well-known symbol. UN peacekeeping forces, ranging from small observer units to larger forces for purposes of interposition, policing, and humanitarian assistance, have been established by the Security Council in numerous countries....

The Charter provision that the Council must operate on the basis of unanimity of its Permanent Members was not the product of impractical idealism: the memoirs of some of those who helped frame the Charter confirm that they knew what they were doing in this as in many other respects. The provision, which has been interpreted in practice to mean that any one of the Permanent Members has to vote against a resolution in order to veto it, reflects a highly realistic belief that UN action will not be possible if one of the great powers seriously dissents from it.

The UN system extends beyond the six UN organs created by the Charter, and the various subsidiary bodies established subsequently by the UN, to include also a host of specialized agencies with their own separate constitutions, memberships, and budgets. These agencies constitute a distinct part of the UN system. In the words of Article 57 of the UN Charter they are 'established by intergovernmental agreement' and have 'wide international responsibilities, as defined in their basic instruments, in economic, social, cultural, educational, health, and related fields'. There are sixteen such specialized agencies associated with the UN: apart from the financial agencies—the main ones being the International Monetary Fund (IMF) and the World Bank (IBRD)—the 'big four' are the International Labour Organization (ILO); the Food and Agriculture Organization (FAO); the United Nations Educational, Scientific and Cultural Organization (UNESCO); and the World Health Organization (WHO). Other intergovernmental organizations closely associated with the UN include the International Atomic Energy Agency (IAEA) and the General Agreement on Tariffs and Trade (GATT) [now the World Trade Organization]....

It is not easy to evaluate the performance of the UN separately from that of the member states. The UN is, as former US Secretary of State Dean Rusk observed, a political institution whose members 'are pursuing their national interests as they see them'. It was created by governments, and it can do little without the assent of at least the majority of them. This view is a necessary antidote to the widespread misapprehension that the UN is in the course of superseding the states system, and that the UN can and ought to take strong action on its own initiative irrespective of the views of states. But the UN cannot be adequately understood as simply the sum of its parts. Like all institutions, whatever their origins and power base, it has developed a life and an ethos of its own. The UN framework influences states' perceptions of their interests, the ordering of their priorities and preferences, and the possibilities they see of best advancing their interests. The UN has also come to embody a limited sense of a collective interest, distinct in specific cases from the particular interests of individual states. In these respects the UN has specific functions or roles against which its performance may be evaluated, even while responsibility for the quality of this performance may lie in great part with member states as well as with individual functionaries or with features of institutional design....

The UN has become, over the course of its first half century, an established part of the firmament of international relations. It is involved in a huge range of activities, many of them central to the functioning of international society. The UN is best seen, not as a vehicle for completely restructuring or replacing the system of sovereign states, so much as ameliorating the problems spawned by its imperfections, and managing processes of rapid change in many distinct fields. The UN finds roles for itself in those areas of activity which are more appropriately tackled either on a truly multilateral basis, or by individuals representing, not a particular state, but the collectivity of states. To the extent that the UN is involved in the transformation of international society, it is not by creating a new and conceptually simple supranational structure, but by participating in a more general process whereby a management of different problems is allocated to different, albeit overlapping and fluctuating, levels.

'The tents have been struck, and the great caravan of humanity is once more on the march.' So said Jan Christian Smuts in 1918, at the time of the planning of the League of Nations. It is tempting to dismiss such views as merely part of the inflated rhetoric which international organizations seem so often to attract. But in our still divided world, there remains a need for an institution which can in some way, however imperfectly, articulate the twin ideas of a universal society of states and the cosmopolitan universality of humankind.

K. Annan, Report of the Secretary General of the United Nations to the General Assembly, *In Larger Freedom: Towards Development, Security and Human Rights for All*
UN Doc A/59/2005, 21 March 2005

6. In the Millennium Declaration [an agreement containing eight international development goals adopted by 189 states in September 2000], world leaders were confident that humanity could, in the years ahead, make measurable progress towards peace, security, disarmament, human rights, democracy and good governance. They called for a global partnership for development to achieve agreed goals by 2015. They vowed to protect the vulnerable and meet the special needs of Africa. And they agreed that the United Nations needed to become more, not less, actively engaged in shaping our common future....

8. Much has happened since the adoption of the Millennium Declaration to compel such an approach. Small networks of non-State actors—terrorists—have, since the horrendous attacks of 11 September 2001, made even the most powerful States feel vulnerable. At the same time, many States have begun to feel that the sheer imbalance of power in the world is a source of instability. Divisions between major powers on key issues have revealed a lack of consensus about goals and methods. Meanwhile, over 40 countries have been scarred by violent conflict. Today, the number of internally displaced people stands at roughly 25 million, nearly one third of whom are beyond the reach of United Nations assistance, in addition to the global refugee population of 11 to 12 million, and some of them have been the victims of war crimes and crimes against humanity.

9. Many countries have been torn apart and hollowed out by violence of a different sort. HIV/AIDS, the plague of the modern world, has killed over 20 million men, women and children and the number of people infected has surged to over 40 million. The promise of the Millennium Development Goals still remains distant for many. More than one billion people still live below the extreme poverty line of one dollar per day, and 20,000 die from poverty each day. Overall global wealth has grown but is less and less evenly distributed within countries, within regions and in the world as a whole. While there has been real progress towards some of the Goals in some countries, too few Governments—from both the developed and developing world—have taken sufficient action to reach the targets by 2015. And while important work has been done on issues as diverse as migration and climate change, the scale of such long-term challenges is far greater than our collective action to date to meet them.

10. Events in recent years have also led to declining public confidence in the United Nations itself, even if for opposite reasons. For instance, both sides of the debate on the Iraq war feel let down by the Organization—for failing, as one side saw it, to enforce its own resolutions, or as the other side saw it, for not being able to prevent a premature or unnecessary war. Yet most people who criticize the United Nations do so precisely because they think the Organization is vitally important to our world. Declining confidence in the institution is matched by a growing belief in the importance of effective multilateralism....

16. Not only are development, security and human rights all imperative; they also reinforce each other. This relationship has only been strengthened in our era of rapid technological advances, increasing economic interdependence, globalization and dramatic geopolitical change. While poverty and denial of human rights may not be said to "cause" civil war, terrorism or organized crime, they all greatly increase the risk of instability and violence. Similarly, war and atrocities are far from the only reasons that countries are trapped in poverty, but they undoubtedly set back development. Again, catastrophic terrorism on one side of the globe, for example an attack against a major financial centre in a rich country, could affect the development prospects of millions on the other by causing a major economic downturn and plunging millions into poverty. And countries which are well governed and respect the human rights of their citizens are better placed to avoid the horrors of conflict and to overcome obstacles to development.

17. Accordingly, we will not enjoy development without security, we will not enjoy security without development, and we will not enjoy either without respect for human rights. Unless all these causes are advanced, none will succeed. In this new millennium, the work of the United Nations must move our world

closer to the day when all people have the freedom to choose the kind of lives they would like to live, the access to the resources that would make those choices meaningful and the security to ensure that they can be enjoyed in peace.

18. In a world of interconnected threats and challenges, it is in each country's self-interest that all of them are addressed effectively. Hence, the cause of larger freedom can only be advanced by broad, deep and sustained global cooperation among States. Such cooperation is possible if every country's policies take into account not only the needs of its own citizens but also the needs of others. This kind of cooperation not only advances everyone's interests but also recognizes our common humanity....

21. We also need agile and effective regional and global intergovernmental institutions to mobilize and coordinate collective action. As the world's only universal body with a mandate to address security, development and human rights issues, the United Nations bears a special burden. As globalization shrinks distances around the globe and these issues become increasingly interconnected, the comparative advantages of the United Nations become ever more evident. So too, however, do some of its real weaknesses. From overhauling basic management practices and building a more transparent, efficient and effective United Nations system to revamping our major intergovernmental institutions so that they reflect today's world and advance the priorities set forth in the present report, we must reshape the Organization in ways not previously imagined and with a boldness and speed not previously shown....

220. At no time in human history have the fates of every woman, man and child been so intertwined across the globe. We are united both by moral imperatives and by objective interests. We can build a world in larger freedom—but to do it we must find common ground and sustain collective action. This task can seem daunting, and it is easy to descend into generalities or stray into areas of such deep disagreement that differences are reinforced not overcome....

222. To make the right choice, leaders will need what United States President Franklin D. Roosevelt, whose vision was so central to the founding of the United Nations, called 'the courage to fulfil [their] responsibilities in an admittedly imperfect world'. They will also need the wisdom to transcend their differences. Given firm, clear-sighted leadership, both within States and among them, I am confident that they can. I am also certain that they must. What I have called for here is possible. It is within reach. From pragmatic beginnings could emerge a visionary change of direction in our world. That is our opportunity and our challenge.

NOTES

1. As at March 2016, there are 193 members of the United Nations. The member States of the United Nations are set out in the Appendix.

2. The United Nations is an institution comprised of States and governed by the United Nations Charter. While it does have some functions in addition to those given to it by States under the United Nations Charter (see Chapter 5 and the *Reparations for Injuries* Opinion, ICJ Rep 1949 174), it is limited in its activities to those that are allowed by its member States. The activities that the United Nations undertakes do change over time. For example, it now considers issues such as the environment, women's rights, HIV/AIDS and globalization.

3. There is some involvement of entities other than States in the United Nations. For example, non-governmental organisations, such as the International Committee of the Red Cross, have 'observer' status at the United Nations. A number of the United Nations agencies (for example, the International Labour Organization) have members who are individuals or non-governmental organisations.

4. Since the end of the Cold War, there has been a considerable change in the international community. One consequence has been pressure to change the membership and powers of the Security Council in order to reflect the present reality of international society. In particular, proposals have been put for permanent, semi-permanent or non-veto power permanent membership of the Security Council for Germany and Japan (which are major financial contributors to the United Nations) and for some regional powers, such as Brazil and India. These proposals face the difficult task of needing to be approved by the present permanent members of the Security Council. So far, all these proposals have not prospered and so the Security Council remains largely as it was established in 1945, though the Peoples' Republic of China and Russia have replaced the Republic of China and the Union of Soviet Socialist Republics respectively as permanent members of the Security Council. These replacements were made without any

amendment to the relevant provision (Article 23) of the United Nations Charter. In addition, the role of the International Court of Justice in reviewing the powers of the Security Council has been raised. This is discussed in Chapter 16.

SECTION 3: THEORIES OF INTERNATIONAL LAW

In order for the principles of international law (or the rest of this book!) to be understood fully, it is important for its underlying assumptions to be made clear. This is particularly necessary with international law, as many of the assumptions about who is subject to international law and the rights and obligations arising from international law must be analysed before the substance of international law itself can be determined. As Susan Marks notes: 'What you hold to be true about the world depends on what you take into account, and what you take into account depends on what you think matters' (Susan Marks, *The Riddle of All Constitutions* (2000), p. 121). Consequently, in many of the chapters of this book some aspects of the theories underlying the substantive law will be given. A number of the major theories are briefly described here.

J. Brierly, *The Law of Nations*
(1st edn, 1928)

The two views which may be regarded as in the orthodox tradition of international legal theory are...(1) a naturalist view, holding that the principles of the law or at least the most fundamental of them can be deduced from the essential nature of state-persons; and (2) a positivist view which regards the law merely as the sum of the rules by which these state-persons have consented to be bound....The former of these two doctrines holds that every state, by the very fact that it is a state, is endowed with certain fundamental, or inherent, or natural, rights. Writers differ in enumerating what these rights are, but generally five rights are claimed, namely, self-preservation, independence, equality, respect, and intercourse. It is obvious that the doctrine of fundamental rights is merely the old doctrine of the natural rights of man transferred to states....The positivist doctrine...attempts to explain the binding force of these rules [of international law] as arising from the supposed fact that states have consented to be bound by them.

H.L.A. Hart, *The Concept of Law*
(1961)

[The] absence of an international legislature, courts with compulsory jurisdiction, and centrally organized sanctions have inspired misgivings, at any rate in the breasts of legal theorists. The absence of these institutions means that the rules for states resemble that simple form of social structure, consisting only of primary rules of obligation, which, when we find it among societies of individuals, we are accustomed to contrast with a developed legal system. It is indeed arguable, as we shall show, that international law not only lacks the secondary rules of change and adjudication which provide for legislature and courts, but also a unifying rule of recognition specifying 'sources' of law and providing general criteria for the identification of its rules. These differences are indeed striking and the question 'Is international law really law?' can hardly be put aside.

A. Boyle and C. Chinkin, *The Making of International Law*
(2007)

The origins of contemporary international law are rooted in natural law thinking categorized by Van Hoof under the umbrella of 'legal idealism'. While many versions of natural law have been influential, especially (but by no means exclusively) in Western thought over many centuries, its 'constant factor has been the appeal to something superior to positive law, whether this superior factor was seen as directive [rooted in religious doctrine, or secular appeal to reason] or as a guide to positive law'. This 'superior law' offered universal principles for the determination of relations between states, but natural law cannot offer any blueprint for its derivation, verification or guidance for detailed regulation....

The legal positivist seeking rules deriving from state consent will tend to adhere to recognizable sources of authority, treaties and custom, and will give weight to those sources identified in the Statute of the ICJ, Article 38(1). The positivists are less willing to accept the normative effect of non-legal instruments such as GA resolutions or the final documents of global summit meetings, seeing any concept of so-called soft law as seeking 'unprecedented expansion of the concept of law into areas of normative regulation which have never been considered as belonging to the law proper....'

The adherent to the New Haven (Yale) policy science approach to international law focuses not on rules but explicitly on the processes by which legal decisions and policies are made. The method of analysis involves first the identification of the observer's standpoint to allow disengagement and objectivity, second consciousness of conceptual categories used by the observer to analyse particular situations, and third an understanding of the process used to influence particular outcomes. The constitutive process therefore requires identification of trends in decision-making with reliance on past decisions in the light of their contexts (conditioning factors) and the desired outcome, thereby incorporating policy objectives and values... For the New Haven school the over-riding and determinative value is the promotion of human dignity....

Critical legal scholars have used the form of legal argument to expose the indeterminacy of and contradictions in international (and national) legal rules and processes and thereby to challenge the view that law is rational, neutral, objective and principled. They emphasise that law is premised on substantive political or other values. David Kennedy, for example, has shown how positivists who adhere to treaties as the 'quintessential' form of hard law through their basis in state consent must fall back on the 'soft' principle of *pacta sunt servanda* as their justification for holding states bound in some situations where they have not consented. ['The Sources of International Law', 2 *American University Journal of International Law and Policy* (1987)]

S. Marks, 'Exploitation as an International Legal Concept'
in S. Marks (ed), *International Law on the Left* (2008)

Marx considers that exploitation is a feature of all modes of production based around a social division of classes. Thus, under capitalism, it is the fact the ruling class owns the means of production, while the working class owns nothing but its own labour-power, that enables the ruling class to extract surplus-value. Workers are induced to undertake surplus labour for their employers because they know that if they don't, there are others waiting on the sidelines—the 'reserve army' of the unemployed—who will. What, for Marx, is distinctive about capitalism compared to other class-based modes of production, such as slavery and feudalism, is that in the capitalist mode of production exploitation is masked. As Anwar Shaikh explains, the 'historical specificity of capitalism arises from the fact that its relations of exploitation are almost completely hidden behind the surface of its relations of exchange' [A. Shaikh, 'Exploitation' in K. Nielsen and R. Ware *Exploitation* (1997) pp. 70–73]. Whereas in slave-owning and feudal societies the exploitation of labour is readily apparent, in capitalist society labour is paid for and regulated according to a contract negotiated between two seemingly free and equal parties. It is only when we look behind, or beneath, that contract at the relations of production that we find 'a world of hierarchy and inequality, of orders and obedience, of bosses and subordinates.' We find a world in which the working class works to support the ruling class, and hence to 'reproduce the very conditions of their [the former's] own subordination'....

What is important for present purposes, however, is that the issue in these arenas [international trade law, international human rights and international law of indigenous peoples' rights] is almost never exploitation (in the pejorative sense) as such. Rather, it is non-sustainability, environmental degradation, expropriation of indigenous property, unfair trade, or the abuse of human rights. Thus, for instance, the TRIPs agreement [Agreement on Trade-Related Aspects of Intellectual Property] has been subjected to sustained criticism for its impact on access to drugs needed to treat HIV-AIDS. But while the point is undoubtedly in the background that the shareholders of pharmaceutical companies are being enabled to prosper at the expense of—quite literally, to drain life from—people infected with this disease, this point remains in the background. Front and centre are instead questions to do with the human rights of those infected and the measures that may be taken by governments in poor countries (compulsory licensing, etc.) to make the drugs available. Those who have benefited from patent revenues remain comfortably out of view....

What then would this new engagement with the problem of exploitation entail? It would place at the centre of international law the question of beneficiaries. International law has long been preoccupied with victims—victims of human rights abuse, victims of discrimination, victims of war crimes. In recent years, with developments in the sphere of international criminal law, it has also become much preoccupied with perpetrators.... [Yet] beyond victims and perpetrators there are also beneficiaries.... The category of 'beneficiary' refers less to a particular group of people than to a particular facet of human experience. To place the question this facet of experience at the centre of international law is to move onto the international legal agenda issues that include, but also go far beyond, those currently subsumed under the topic of exploitation....

At the same time, a more adequate engagement with the problem of exploitation would also bring out the connections between these issues and orient international law to a vision of the world as a structured totality. Quite obviously, exploitation is only one of many critical concepts that can be deployed to throw light on the asymmetrical distribution of advantage within countries and across the globe. Social exclusion and human rights are two alternative concepts that have particular currency today.

M. Koskenniemi, *From Apology to Utopia: The Structure of International Legal Argument*

(2005)

[M]y argument is that international law is singularly useless as a means for justifying or criticizing international behavior. Because it is based on contradictory premises it remains both over- and underlegitimizing: it is overlegitimizing as it can be ultimately invoked to justify any behaviour (apologism), it is underlegitimzing because it is incapable of providing a convincing argument on the legitimacy of any practices (utopianism)...

No coherent normative practice arises from the assumptions on which we identify international law. However, neither the demand for concreteness nor the requirement of normativity can be rejected without at the same time rejecting the idea that law is different from politics by being more 'objective' than this. My suggestion will not be to develop a 'more determinate' system of legal argument. Quite the contrary, I believe that lawyers should admit that if they wish to achieve justifications, they have to take a stand on political issues without assuming that there exists a privileged rationality which solves such issues for them. Before any meaningful attempt at reform may be attempted, however, the idea of legal objectivity—and with it the conventional distinction between law, politics and morality (justice) needs to be rethought.

F. Tesón, 'The Kantian Theory of International Law'

92 Columbia Law Review 53 (1992)

This Article defends the view, first developed by Immanuel Kant, that international law and domestic justice are fundamentally connected. Despite the recent prominence of the international law of human rights, the dominant discourse in international law fails to recognize the important normative status of the individual. Traditional international legal theory focuses upon the rights and duties of states and rejects the contention that the rights of states are merely derivative of the rights and interests of the individuals who reside in them. Accordingly, international legitimacy and sovereignty are a function of whether the government politically controls the population, rather than whether it justly represents its people. This statist conceptualization of international law argues for a dual paradigm for the ordering of individuals: one domestic, the other international. Justice and legitimacy are conceptually separate. It may well be that domestic systems strive to promote justice; but international systems only seek order and compliance.

International law thus conceived, however, is incapable of serving as the normative framework for present or future political realities. While it is understandably hard for lawyers to forsake the statist assumptions of classic international legal discourse, new times call for fresh conceptual and ethical language. A liberal theory [i.e. a theory of politics founded upon individual freedom, respect for individual preferences and individual autonomy] of international law can hardly be reconciled with the statist approach. Liberal theory commits itself instead to *normative individualism*, to the premise that the primary normative unit is the individual, not the state. The end of states and governments is to benefit, serve, and protect their components, human beings; and the end of international law must also be to benefit, serve, and protect human beings, and not its components, states and governments. Respect for states is merely derivative of respect for persons. In this way, the notion of state sovereignty is redefined: the sovereignty of the state is dependent upon the state's domestic legitimacy; and therefore the principles of international justice must be congruent with the principles of internal justice.

P. Allott, *Eunomia: New Order for a New World*

(1990)

20.20. International society had to find its own theory. It chose to see itself as a collection of state-societies turned inside-out, like a glove. It chose to be an unsocial society creating itself separately from the development of its subordinate societies, ignoring the idea and the ideal of democracy, depriving itself of the possibility of using social power, especially legal relations, to bring about the survival and prospering of the whole human race.... International society is the self-ordering of the whole human race and of all subordinate societies...

20.24. International law has been the primitive law of an unsocial international society. Itself a by-product of that unsocialization, it has contributed to holding back the development of international society as society. Failing to recognize itself as a society, international society has not known that it has a constitution. Not knowing its own constitution, it has ignored the generic principles of a constitution....

20.26. State-societies, like all other members of international society, have social power, including legal power, to serve the purposes of international society, to will and act for its survival and prospering, that is to say, for the survival and prospering of the whole human race. They are socially and legally accountable for the exercise of their powers and the carrying out of their obligations. Non-statal societies, including industrial and commercial and financial enterprises of all kinds, exercise social power and carry out obligations on the same conditions.

20.27. The new international law will be as dynamic and as rich as the law of any subordinate society, organizing human willing and acting in every field which concerns the survival and prospering of the society of which it is the law.

H. Charlesworth and C. Chinkin, *The Boundaries of International Law: A Feminist Analysis*

(2000)

Feminist analysis of international law has two major roles. One is deconstruction of the explicit and implicit values of the international legal system, challenging their claim to objectivity and rationality because of the limited base on which they are built. All tools and categories of international legal analysis become problematic when the exclusion of women from their construction is understood. The 'international', the canon purports to represent is, in Elizabeth Grosz's words, in fact a 'veiled representation and projection of a masculine which takes itself as the unquestioned norm, the ideal representative without any idea of the violence that this representational positioning does to its others' [*Volatile Bodies* (1994) p. 188]. Investigating the silences of international law is another way of discovering its gendered nature: why are some activities considered capable of international legal regulation while others are not? Deconstruction has transformative potential because it reduces the imaginative grip of the traditional theories. In this sense, all feminist theories are subversive strategies. They are 'forms of guerrilla warfare, striking out at points of patriarchy's greatest weakness, its blindspots'. They reveal the 'partial and partisan instead of the universal or representative position of patriarchal discourse'....

The second role of feminist analysis of international law is that of reconstruction. This does not mean a strategy of simply increasing international legal regulation, making 'public' all that the legal system deems 'private'. It requires rebuilding the basic concepts of international law in a way that they do not support or reinforce the domination of women by men. The benefits of such a reconstruction would not be limited to women. Non-domination of women would allow the major aims of the UN Charter—the maintenance of international peace and security, the self-determination of peoples and the protection of fundamental human rights—to be defined in new, inclusive, ways....

Liberal feminists typically accept the language and aims of the existing domestic order, couching many of their arguments in terms of individual rights...They work for reform of the law, dismantling legal barriers to women being treated like men in the public sphere, and criticise any legal recognition of 'natural' differences between women and men....

Cultural feminism is concerned with the identification and rehabilitation of qualities and perspectives identified as particular to women...it is a 'standpoint' theory in that it emphasises the importance of knowledge based upon experience and asserts that women's subjugated position allows them to formulate a more complete and accurate accounts of nature and social life—'morally and scientifically preferable' to those produced by men....

Radical feminism explains women's inequality as the product of domination of women by men—inequality is presented as political and sexual in nature...Qualities such as caring and conciliation have been foisted on women, radical feminists contend, by the structure of patriarchal societies and are based on a male view of personhood....[T]he law should support freedom from systematic subordination because of sex rather than freedom to be treated without regard to sex.

Prosecutor v *Tadić* (*Jurisdictional Phase*), **International Criminal Tribunal for the Former Yugoslavia**
35 *International Legal Materials* 35 (1996)

97. The impetuous development and propagation in the international community of human rights doctrines... has brought about significant changes in international law, notably in the approach to problems besetting the world community,....[Thus a] state-sovereignty-oriented approach has been gradually supplanted by a human-being-oriented approach. Gradually the maxim of Roman law *hominum causa omne jus constitutum est* (all law is created for the benefit of human beings) has gained a firm foothold in the international community as well.

A. Anghie, *Imperialism, Sovereignty, and the Making of International Law*
(2004)

My argument, then, is that what passes now as the defining dilemma of the discipline, the problem of order amongst states, is a problem which, from the time of its origins, has been peculiar to the specificities of European history. And, further, that the extension and universalization of this European experience, which is achieved by transmuting it into the major theoretical problem of the discipline, has the effect of suppressing and subordinating other histories of international law and the peoples to whom it has applied....The universalization of international law was principally a consequence of the imperial expansion which took place towards the end of the 'long nineteenth century'....

International lawyers over the centuries maintained this basic dichotomy between the civilized and the uncivilized, even while refining and elaborating their understanding of each of these terms. Having established this dichotomy, furthermore, jurists continually developed techniques for overcoming it by formulating legal doctrines directed towards civilizing the uncivilized world. I use the term 'dynamic of difference' to denote, broadly, the endless process of creating a gap between two cultures, demarcating one as 'universal' and civilized and the other as 'particular' and uncivilized, and seeking to bridge the gap by developing techniques to normalize the aberrant society....

The more alarming and likely possibility is that the civilizing mission is inherent in one form or another in the principal concepts and categories, which govern our existence: ideas of modernity, progress, development, emancipation and rights....

I have argued that because sovereignty was shaped by the colonial encounter, its existence often reproduces the inequalities inherent in that encounter. But the further and broader point is that sovereignty is a flexible instrument which readily lends itself to the powerful imperatives of the civilizing mission, in part because it is through engagement with that mission that sovereignty extends and expands its reach and scope. This is why the essential structure of the civilizing mission may be reconstructed in the very contemporary vocabulary of human rights, governance and economic liberalization.

R. McCorquodale, 'An Inclusive International Legal System'
17 *Leiden Journal of International Law* 477 (2004)

Despite a range of cogent critiques, the conceptual approach of a solely State-based international legal system still dominates much of international law thinking today. Much of this system is still largely developed by male, urban elites and does not include important parts of the daily lives of people....The increasing role of international organisations, such as the World Bank and the World Trade Organisation, the impact of globalisation, particularly the activities of transnational corporations, as well as actions by civil society, and the development of international environmental, criminal, humanitarian and human rights law, all have effects on the international legal system....

One new conceptual language needed is to move away from the rigid framework of conceiving entities in terms of 'subjects' or 'objects' of the international legal system. This binary opposition between 'subject' and 'object' has been rightly criticised, not least because it privileges the voices of States, as all potential participants are compared to States, and it silences alternative voices....As the international community, which includes both States and non-States as the ICJ acknowledged, changes and the 'requirements of international life' [ICJ *Reparations Opinion*], or the areas governed by international law develop, then so will participation in the international legal system. This means that actual actions are given acknowledgement in terms of their impact on this system, rather than there being a prior, State-based, determination as to what actions will be taken into account....Indeed, the notion of participation is a valuable framework to explore involvement in the international legal system, and thus as a means to determine the extent to which that system has become inclusive....

'We the Peoples of the United Nations' [being the opening words of the United Nations Charter] were determined to establish new values and methods to create the international society after 1945. The current dominant concept of the international legal system has stifled these values and ignored the reality of the participation of non-State actors in this system. It has even fostered conflict at times by resisting claims by non-State actors, by limiting the dialogue between participants in the system and by fostering a limited view of how international law is created.

An inclusive conceptual approach to the international legal system would acknowledge that non-State actors have values, identities and roles distinct from the geographic limitations of States and that these are reflected both in their daily lives and in the international legal system [and enable a more critical reflection on what is "international law"]. States have a role - a primary role at the moment - but it is not an exclusive role in that system. The participants in the international legal system are no longer just States. Non-State actors have distinct and independent international rights and responsibilities and an ability to bring claims, as well as a clear role in the creation, development and enforcement of international law separate to that of States. This participation will expand throughout the 21st century, particularly as the 'requirements of international life' demand it.

It is the role of international lawyers to develop concepts and practices consistent with this trend, rather than being, to use Philip Alston's phrase, 'handmaidens' to States. There is great power in the language of international law and a pull towards compliance with it. International lawyers have the ability to conceptualise and interpret the international legal system in a way that changes perceptions. Whilst a 'belief in the virtue and omnipresence of the sovereign State supports and no doubt tends to generate a particular understanding of [international] law' [N. MacCormick, 'Beyond the Sovereign State' 56 *Modern Law Review* (1993), pp. 1, 16], a belief in the virtue of inclusive participation of State and non-States offers an alternative and, it is argued, more accurate interpretation of the international legal system. Such an interpretation will enable non-State actors to be heard as active participants in a more inclusive and decentralised international legal system, which [as the UN Charter states] 'exists for, and serves, the needs and hopes of people everywhere'.

NOTES
1. Theories on the nature of the international legal system have often been placed in categories. For example, 'natural law' theories, in which law embodied principles which were in accordance with nature and morals (and often religious experience); 'positivist' theories, such as Hart's, where the legal system is made up solely of clear rules enacted by governments and is relatively divorced from moral concepts; as well as 'new stream' (see Koskenniemi); 'feminist' (see Charlesworth and Chinkin); and 'third world' (see Anghie), in which law is shown to be neither neutral nor objective and has a bias in its impact across the world, as well as other theories such as the decolonisation of international law (see Pahuja, *Decolonizing International Law*, 2011). Positivist theories, particularly liberal positivism, in which international law is a body of rules, remain the dominant theories in international law today, though they are under challenge by the new stream theories as the latter reflect a more nuanced, diverse and dynamic approach to the international legal system. A broader explanation of the theories on the nature of international law is found in G. Simpson (ed), *The Nature of International Law* (2001).

2. The events of 11 September 2001, and the response of the international community to them, have highlighted the changing nature of the international legal system. No longer can it be seen as a system in which only States are actors (see McCorquodale in this section and Chapter 5) or in which States can only take action against other States (see Chapter 15). The continuing development of international law, particularly in regard to the extension of its application beyond States alone, means that its nature has changed over time, and will continue to change. This is reflected in the decisions of both national and international judicial bodies, and in State and non-State practice.

SECTION 4: THE PRACTICE OF INTERNATIONAL LAW

M. Koskenniemi, 'International Lawyers'

Erik Castrén Institute of International Law and Human Rights, University of Helsinki (2007), http://www.helsinki.fi/eci/Publications/Koskenniemi/MKINTERNATIONAL%20LAWYERS-07b.pdf

From Hugo Grotius to the International Criminal Court, international law has been a *project* carried out by international lawyers. It has been sometimes a religious, sometimes a secular humanitarian project, a project for order, civilization, peace, security, development, rule of law and so on. Most of the time it has been a project by which European or European-origined lawyers or intellectuals have advanced their universalist ideals so as to substitute new rules and institutions for the present political or diplomatic world.

But international lawyers have never been a fully homogeneous group. They have also disagreed on how the world ought to be and, thus, just what direction their project should take. Such disagreements have reflected political preferences, cultural backgrounds, as well as professional experiences and ambitions. In most periods, mainstream views and assumptions have been juxtaposed by typical challenges: right of sovereignty vs. the interests of an "international community"; international security vs. cosmopolitan justice; self-determination and national autonomy vs. international rules on human rights, development and environment. Reform has proceeded through critique of earlier generations as either excessively utopian or then ignorant of the realities of an inter-sovereign world.

H. Charlesworth, 'International Law: A Discipline of Crisis'

65 Modern Law Review 377 (2002)

International lawyers grasped at the NATO campaign in the Federal Republic of Yugoslavia as an event that, properly unpacked and legally theorised, could rejuvenate our often overlooked discipline. Kosovo offered questions about sovereignty and self-determination, grave human rights abuses and expulsions, condemnation by international institutions, failed peace negotiations, military intervention by a regional alliance, international peace keeping and the role of the international criminal tribunals. It was a contemporary Cuban missile crisis. Kosovo gave international lawyers a sense of relevance, of being exhilaratingly close to the heart of grand and important issues of our time....

A concern with crises skews the discipline of international law. Through regarding 'crisis' as its bread and butter and the engine of progressive development of international law, international law becomes simply a source of justification for the status quo...One way forward is to refocus international law on issues of structural justice that underpin everyday life. What might an international law of everyday life look like?...An international law of everyday life would require a methodology to consider the perspectives of non-elite groups. For example, we should be able to study 'humanitarian intervention' from the perspective of the people on whose behalf the intervention took place. International lawyer accounts of humanitarian intervention prompted by Kosovo do not take the views of the objects of intervention into account....

What if we were to change the type of questions we ask? For example, David Kennedy ['When Renewal Repeats: Thinking against the Box' (2000) 32 *NYJIL* 346] has pointed out that the work of international lawyers typically focuses on humanitarian objectives (such as environmental protection or protection of human rights). We could begin from the opposite end and examine what international law has to offer to the person who wants to pollute the environment or violate human rights.

G. Simpson, *Great Powers and Outlaw States*
(2004)

The United States and the United Kingdom…were not constrained (in the strong sense) from making war on Iraq in 2003, and yet there was law and, most of all, there was the promise of law *and* constraint.…[L]aw was a powerful language through which argument was made and remade, butted and rebutted. The illegality of the war provoked mass protests, and may have contributed to the fall of at least one governing party (in Spain). Law shaped the way in which the debate about international society and the use of force was conducted. The [UK] Blair Government worked hard on a lengthy legitimacy strategy part of which required a full commitment to arguing a legal case. Admiral Boyce, then [UK] Chief of Defence Staff, was so worried about the ambiguous nature of the legal advice prior to war that he insisted on a clear legal mandate before committing ground forces to war. As Boyce stated in March 2004: 'I required a piece of paper saying it was lawful.…[I]f that caused them to go back saying we need our advice tightened up then I don't know' [*Guardian Weekly*, 11–17 March 2004]. The United States' failure to do likewise may have its costs in international credibility, operational legitimacy and a degradation in other forms of legal constraint. And international law on the use of force came home. International law was relied upon by the defendants in various criminal prosecutions brought in the United Kingdom against those who committed criminal acts in order to oppose the war. The prosecution of Katherine Gun under the *Official Secrets Act* case was dropped after Ms Gun's lawyers demanded to see the Attorney General's full, unpublished advice to the Prime Minster. When the Prime Minister of the United Kingdom said, as he was quoted as saying in the *CND v. Blair* case, '[w]e always act in accordance with international law,' [U.K., H.C., *Official Report*, col 482 WA (14 March 2003)] he created a series of expectations about the war, and about the role of law in international affairs. The *Sunday Telegraph* in an editorial disparaging international law as marginal reasoned that '[i]f a solid majority of the British people can be persuaded that the war was right and just, then Mr Blair's problems will be at an end'[*Sunday Telegraph* (29 February 2004) 24]. But it is hard, as the Prime Minister has discovered, to persuade people that illegal wars are just and right.

International law, in the end, is enforced in all sorts of ways. It is 'a kind of furnace' and many 'identities and fates' are shaped and buckled by it. For example, perhaps, the Prime Minister is now viewed as no longer a plausible multilateralist but a misadventurer willing to spurn international institutions. Meanwhile, the United States may have finally lost its claim to be the guardian of the San Francisco Consensus.

Wars are the outcome of arguments, armies move by the force of ideas. And law is a powerful idea. It is the power of this idea that ought to provide the inspiration for collaborative work between international lawyers and [international relations] scholars.

J. Klabbers, A. Peters and G. Ulfstein, *The Constitutionalization of International Law*
(2011)

It is a truism to state, or so it seems, that international law is increasingly starting to look like the sort of legal order we are familiar with from our domestic legal systems. Many international lawyers have made the somewhat panicky observation that international law is engaged in a process of fragmentation: the various aspects of the international legal regime are branching out and gaining some form of quasi-independence, often misleadingly labelled 'self-containment'. The label may be deceptive, but the underlying sentiment is not: just as in domestic law criminal lawyers have little or no time for tax law, and company lawyers by and large do not grapple with environmental law or administrative procedure, so too in international law the various sub-disciplines are increasingly leading a life of their own. And in much the same way as domestic systems are held together by constitutional law (the one area of domestic law which can hardly be practised), so too these various branches of international law are increasingly seen as having some form of constitutional law hovering over it: a general body of rules which, much like domestic law, does not really lend itself to legal practice in quite the same ways as contract law or tax law or criminal law do, but which nonetheless is vital for indicating how the branches hang together. In a justly famous metaphor probably first coined with by Oscar Schachter, general international law provides the highways between the otherwise isolated villages of international environmental, international criminal law, international trade law, etc.

NOTES
1. There are now many areas of international law, from international environmental law to European law, from international trade law to international criminal law and human rights law. This has raised questions about whether international law is becoming so fragmented that it will

lose coherence (see M. Koskenniemi, *Fragmentation of International Law: Difficulties arising from the Diversification and Expansion of International Law* (International Law Commission, 2006). However, as Charlesworth notes, it is also important not to focus solely on areas of crisis or difficulty when considering the impact of international law and for international lawyers not to chase the sources of political power or to simplify the history and other issues behind a conflict.

2. The expansion of international law has opened many opportunities for legal practice (see A. Smit and C. Waters, *A Guide to International Law Careers* (British Institute of International and Comparative Law, 2nd edn, 2015). International lawyers are now found in many corporations, working in refugee camps, managing international financial organisations, on government trade missions, in transactional and litigation areas of law firms, deciding human rights cases, drafting tax legislation, advising environmental non-governmental organisations, enthusing students at universities and doing a wide variety of other legal and non-legal jobs. Part of the role of an international lawyer is to clarify, declare and uphold international law. Yet it could be more than this, as Allott (in Allott and others (eds), *Theory and International Law: An Introduction* (British Institute of International and Comparative Law, 1991) has proclaimed: 'The function of the international lawyer is to change the course of human history'.

2

Sources of International Law

INTRODUCTORY NOTE

Like the rules of other legal systems, the rules of international law come from many different 'sources'. However, given that international law currently lacks both a universal legislative body—such as a Parliament—and a universal mechanism for the interpretation of laws—such as a compulsory court structure—the 'doctrine of the sources' of international law assumes an importance that is not openly expressed in national legal systems. The *relative* absence of international legal institutions having universal competence among the members of the international community requires an articulated and stable concept of the sources of international law. In general terms, an examination of these sources may focus on the role that a particular source plays in the international legal system—for example, does the source actually *create* the law or does it *identify* the content of the law—as well as an analysis of the often quite detailed rules about how legal rules come into existence. The usual starting place is to analyse the list of matters that the International Court of Justice must consider when deciding a case before it and these are to be found in Article 38 of its Statute (see Section 2). This lists customary international law, conventions (i.e. treaties), general principles, judicial decisions and the writings of 'highly qualified publicists' (e.g. academics). Although it is now recognised that this is not a complete list of the 'sources', it does provide the foundation stone for any credible discussion of the relevant principles.

It is also important to appreciate that the particular 'source' of a rule of international law may have an impact on the way it is applied or interpreted by an international tribunal or international organisation. For example, rules of international law derived from 'general principles of law' tend to be interpreted more flexibly than rules derived from a bilateral treaty. This is a reflection both of the content of the rule and of the manner in which it was created. Again, on one level, the 'sources' of international law explain why the rules of the international legal system are properly regarded as 'rules of law', as was considered in Chapter 1. On another level, as noted above, 'sources' means the methods by which those rules of law are created and, on another, the way in which those rules and the specific rights or obligations they stipulate can be identified.

SECTION 1: THE IMPORTANCE OF SOURCES

O. Schachter, 'General Course in International Law'
179 Receuil des Cours 9 (1982)

The principal intellectual instrument in the last century for providing objective standards of legal validation has been the doctrine of sources. That doctrine which became dominant in the nineteenth century and continues to prevail today lays down verifiable conditions for ascertaining and validating legal prescriptions. The conditions are the observable manifestations of the 'wills' of States as revealed in the *processes* by which norms are formed—namely, treaty and State practice accepted as law. (These are the principal processes; Article 38 of the Statute of the Court expands them to include general principles of law.) The emphasis in this doctrine on criteria of law applied solely on the basis of observable 'positive' facts can be linked to those intellectual currents of the nineteenth century that extolled inductive science....

The doctrine of sources was more than a grand theoretical conception. It also provided the stimulus for a methodology of international law that called for detailed 'inductive' methods for ascertaining and validating law. If sources were to be used objectively and scientifically, it was necessary to examine in full detail the practice and related legal convictions (*opinio juris*) of States. Most of the major treatises in international law purported to follow this methodology though they varied considerably in their fidelity to the ideal of positivist doctrine. The favoured instruments of the positivist methodology were the national digests of State practice prepared by, or in close association with, the government of the State concerned. These digests were widely lauded and strongly encouraged by the profession....

Thus, the doctrine of sources together with the digests of practice and similar material met, in principle at least, the requirement of a 'positive science of international law' based on the verifiable manifestation of the wills of the States concerned. The theory appeared realistic and practical. By and large, it seemed to be the dominant theory accepted by governments in their legal arguments, by tribunals and, to a large degree, by international lawyers. However, a closer look at the argumentation and the supporting materials indicates that there were significant deviations from the doctrine and its methodology. These deviations suggest that the idea of an inductive, factual positive science of international law may be characterized more as myth than as reality.

H. Charlesworth and C. Chinkin, *The Boundaries of International Law: A Feminist Perspective*

(2000)

The sources of law define how new rules are made and existing rules are repealed or abrogated. Analysis of them traditionally commences with article 38(1) of the Statute of the ICJ which lists as sources: international conventions, whether general or particular; international custom; general principles of law; judicial decisions and the teachings of the most highly qualified publicists.

International conventions are binding upon parties to them. Although the expression 'law-making treaties' is often used to describe multilateral agreements, a treaty creates rights and duties for third parties only in specified circumstances, for example when it declares or generates customary international law. Customary international law, binding upon all states, has two components: uniform and consistent state practice and *opinio juris sive necessitatis* (states' belief that the behaviour is required by law). Both requirements operate at a high level of generality. Decision-makers identifying the operative rules of customary international law must choose from among the many daily activities and statements made in the name of states, those that they regard as evidence of state practice. Emphasis is given to the official acts of government: statements and claims made by political leaders in local, regional and global public fora; diplomatic communications; judicial and administrative decisions. The chain of claim and counter-claim that typically constitutes evidence of state practice may be affected by acquiescence or silence or by 'persistent objection' to an activity. *Opinio juris* is also derived from the behaviour of a state's ruling elite.

Despite their separate categorisation in article 38(1), treaties and customary international law do not operate in isolation from each other. Customary international law is not codified in the same manner as a negotiated treaty text. However, the articulation of states' positions in negotiations can contribute to the generation of customary international law. Drafts, position papers and preliminary studies can clarify stances that may be incorporated within the text, or become part of future state practice. Customary international law that is created in this way shares some characteristics with treaty law....

The content of the category of 'general principles of law recognised by all civilised nations' is controversial. When drafted as part of the Statute of the PCIJ, article 38(1)(c) was a compromise between those who regarded general principles as derived from natural law and those who saw them as drawn from national law. It is now widely accepted that article 38(1)(c) applies to principles of both international and domestic law. The concept incorporates maxims normally found within state domestic law, including procedural principles, good faith and *res judicata*. It does not, however, contemplate the incorporation of municipal law principles 'lock, stock and barrel' into international law. The drafters of the Statute of the PCIJ suggested that general principles would form a safety net to avert the danger of a *non liquet* if neither custom nor treaty law provided an answer to the question before the Court. General principles can also be used in interpreting treaties and articulating customary law.

Judicial decisions and the writings of well-known publicists are subsidiary sources of international law. Although there is no formal doctrine of precedent in international law, the articulation of principles by the ICJ, or other international adjudicators, can clarify customary international law and treaty provisions. Decisions of regional and domestic tribunals, notably state supreme courts, may also be used by decision-makers when determining the requirements of customary international law.

The traditional schema of sources in article 38(1) preserves state control over what is deemed law, but is an incomplete reflection of the realities of contemporary international law-making. Other important modalities of law-making have been identified, for example through the resolutions of international organisations, such as the General Assembly of the UN, the practice of international organisations and international codes of conduct. An important feature of the international legal scene in the 1990s was global summits on broad, interlocking issues of international concern that have culminated in declarations and strategies for state and intergovernmental and non-governmental institutional action. Despite the high level of preparations, the often intense negotiations and the large number of participating states, traditional international legal doctrine denies the status of formally binding law to the conclusions of these conferences.

Although article 38(1) was drafted over seventy years ago to guide the PCIJ, it remains widely cited as the authoritative list of the sources of international law. However, it has also generated considerable debate. Certain questions have been consistently addressed. These include the requirements for establishing a rule of customary international law; the weight to be accorded to what a state says rather than what it does; the possibility of 'instant' custom; the effect of treaties on third parties; and the content of general principles of law.

Since the decolonisation era of the 1960s, other aspects of the sources of international law have become more controversial, for example the ways in which sources are manipulated to preserve the control over substantive principle by those states that had previously dominated the international legal system. Such issues include how and why a newly emergent state is bound by the customary international law in existence at the time of its acquiring statehood; how 'law-breaking' by dissentient states transforms into new customary international law; how the requirement of uniformity applies in the generation of customary international law when the numerical majority of states dissents from the practice of the minority of economically and politically powerful states; the law-making effect of a multilateral treaty; which treaties bind a successor state, and whether it is critical that the new state came into being through decolonisation rather than secession from, or union with, an existing state. The hierarchy of sources of international law has also prompted debate, in particular the relationship between treaty and customary international law. Perhaps the most significant aspect of the debate on hierarchy is over the concept of *jus cogens* which limits state sovereignty by asserting the fundamental values of the international legal system, including those based on the integrity of the human person.

Underlying this discussion are questions about the nature of international law and the impact of power relations on the making of international law. Does individual state consent (voluntarism) remain the basis of legal obligation, as was forcefully asserted in *The Lotus Case*, or has there been a shift towards a type of international 'democracy' in which a broader notion of the international community creates law? Could this type of system embrace the views of non-state actors? The notion of consent itself has been challenged as a basis for legal, as distinct from political, obligation....

The deficiencies of international law-making have been particularly highlighted in fields of international law where exclusive state interests may conflict more directly with those of non-state actors. Examples include human rights, international economic law and environmental law. Traditional international law-making assumes a monolithic state voice that silences individuals and other non-elite groups in the international arena, except insofar as their interests are championed by states. International law nevertheless has an impact upon individuals. It may be directly applicable within domestic legal systems, and domestic law in turn may influence the development of international law.

M. Wood, 'What is Public International Law? The Need for Clarity about Sources'

1 *Asian Journal of International Law* 205 (2011)

Why is clarity in public international law important? All law, to be worthy of its name, should be as clear as possible. Is clarity a particular issue for international law?

There are a number of reasons why it is important. First, international law is often seen among the public, including the well-informed public, and even among lawyers, as highly subjective, even political. They sometimes question whether it is law at all, or whether with the general absence of courts or enforcement, it needs to be obeyed.

A second reason why clarity is important is this. With the great expansion of the scope of public international law, more and more lawyers who are not specialists in the field are called upon to apply it. Nowadays, judges in the domestic courts, in England and elsewhere (including in Luxembourg), are frequently faced with arguments based on public international law. There is a tendency to "use"—or abuse—international law, or what is said to be international law, to bolster arguments, especially in judicial review cases. Sometimes the arguments based on international law are hardly respectable. It is thought right to present to the judge resolutions of international bodies, such as the UN General Assembly, or documents of human rights organs or non-governmental organizations, without any serious attempt to explain what weight, or lack of weight, they have for the formation or evidence of international law. The number, importance, and complexity of cases involving public international law have grown hugely in England, Europe, and elsewhere, over the last decade. Correspondingly, practitioners in many areas of domestic law cannot properly advise or represent their clients without knowing at least some international law; obvious fields are human rights, the environment, investment protection, state and diplomatic immunity, international criminal law, and the laws of war. Lawyers working for the government who do not specialize in public international law increasingly need to advise on questions of international law. Lawyers working for multinational corporations, such as the defence industries and 'private military companies', have to understand UN, regional, and domestic sanctions regimes and much else besides. Lawyers working for non-governmental organizations must keep up with international law relevant to their fields of activity, such as refugee law or human rights. Academic lawyers in many fields that are essentially domestic need to understand the international law aspects of their subject. Not all such non-specialists can be expected to master general international law to the same level as a specialist. Yet they definitely need a sound, if not detailed, grasp of general international law, and particularly of its sources.

NOTES

1. The first two extracts explain in general terms what is meant by a 'doctrine of sources' and identify how such a doctrine can be developed. As they illustrate, the way in which the 'sources' of international law are viewed as an abstract legal phenomenon may have consequences for the substance of the rules of international law that are generated by those sources. Note, however, that, as Schachter points out in a later work, 'customary law, new and old, are products of political aims and conditions' ('New Custom: Power, *Opinio Juris* and Contrary Practice' in *Theory of International Law at the Threshold of the 21st Century* (1996)). This at least is a reminder that a theory of the sources of international law ultimately is helpful only if it reflects the reality of how rules of law come into existence.

2. The extract from Charlesworth and Chinkin is a succinct statement of how Article 38 of the Statute of the ICJ is perceived to be the foundation for a discussion of the sources of international law at the concrete level. The extract is in fact part of a general critique of a masculine conception of international law. However, as they also point out, Article 38 has generated much debate, especially as it appears to exclude the role of non-State actors from the law creation process (see Chapter 5 on Personality). Whether such actors—e.g. individuals, multinational corporations, pressure groups, terrorists/freedom fighters, non-governmental organisations—*should* have such a role would be disputed by some academics and certainly by many States. Much of the international community and those who comment on it are still State-centred. For example, only States may be members of the United Nations, although many other groups do have Observer status. Indeed, even accepting that non-State actors do have a role (and this seems unarguable if we actually examine the reality of international life) *how* can such a role be effective to counter the largely self-interested motivation of States that pervades the law creation process? Of course, the international community is no longer the cosy preserve of 50 or so like-minded States that together could effectively run the international system. That may have been the case (if ever) back in 1945. Not only has the number of States increased (on which see Chapter 5), but also non-State actors now fulfil roles that once were the preserve of States—for example, in the field of the development and enforcement of human rights standards. Yet, the doctrine of the sources of international law has yet to include these participants effectively. The increasing scope of international law and the number of actors involved in making and applying international law renders a proper understanding of the sources of international law essential, as highlighted in the extract from Wood.

SECTION 2: STATUTE OF THE INTERNATIONAL COURT OF JUSTICE 1945

Article 38

1. The Court, whose function is to decide in accordance with international law such disputes as are submitted to it, shall apply:
    (a) international conventions, whether general or particular, establishing rules expressly recognized by the contesting states;
    (b) international custom, as evidence of a general practice accepted as law;
    (c) the general principles of law recognized by civilised nations;
    (d) subject to the provisions of Article 59, judicial decisions and the teachings of the most highly qualified publicists of the various nations, as subsidiary means for the determination of rules of law. 2. This provision shall not prejudice the power of the Court to decide a case *ex aequo et bono*, if the parties agree thereto.

NOTES

1 Although Article 38 is actually a direction to the International Court of Justice (and the Permanent Court of International Justice before it) in respect of what matters it must consider when deciding a case before it, we have noted already that it is treated as a statement of the most important of the sources of international law. This should be no surprise: after all, the ICJ is the principal judicial organ of the United Nations and we might expect that it would decide cases according to binding rules of international law! However, Article 38 is not meant to exclude other matters that may be said to give rise to international rights and obligations, such as binding resolutions of international bodies (e.g. the Security Council of the United Nations) or the unilateral acts of States. Indeed, whether the Article represents a complete list of the sources of international law rather depends on one's definitional perspective.

2. It will be noted that Article 38(2) of the Statute gives the Court the power, at the request of the parties to a dispute before it, to decide a case *ex aequo et bono*. This rarely invoked provision allows the parties to request the Court to reach a decision based not only on strict rules of law, but on general conceptions of fairness, good judgement and equality. Of course, these ideals should be found liberally sprinkled among the rules of law, but Article 38(2) could be useful if the parties were bound by a rule of international law (of a non-fundamental nature) that on the particular unusual facts of a case would produce an undesirable solution for both parties. It might then be disapplied by mutual consent.

SECTION 3: TREATIES

Treaties are now the most important source of international law. They offer States a deliberate method by which to create binding international law. The efforts of the International Law Commission (ILC) and the United Nations have produced a number of significant multilateral treaties, such as the Vienna Convention on Diplomatic Relations 1961 and the Law of the Sea Convention 1982, and such multinational treaties are designed to set global standards within particular areas of activity. Indeed, such treaties are ideal if the aim is to establish universal standards that would not be achieved if States were left to their own devices. However, it must not be forgotten that much of the law binding a State will take the form of a bilateral treaty between it and one other State or treaties open only to a limited group of States, such as the European Convention on State Immunity. Such bilateral or limited participation treaties, although often technical, are absolutely vital to the operation of the international legal system. In order to understand fully the role of treaties as a source of law it is necessary to be aware of the rules concerning the creation and operation of treaties. These are examined in Chapter 3.

Vienna Convention on the Law of Treaties 1969
1155 UNTS 331

Article 6

Every State possesses capacity to conclude treaties.

Article 26

Every treaty in force is binding upon the parties to it and must be performed by them in good faith.

Article 34

A treaty does not create either obligations or rights for a third state without its consent.

G. Fitzmaurice, 'Some Problems Regarding the Formal Sources of International Law'
Symbolae Verzijl 153 (1958)

The sources of law are commonly classified as 'formal' and 'material'. Side by side with these there are the 'evidences' or records of law. Thus, if State practice, for instance, is a source of law, it would be incorrect to regard such things as documents embodying diplomatic representations, notes of protest, etc., as constituting sources of law. They are evidences of it because they demonstrate certain attitudes on the part of States, but it is the State practice so evidenced which is the source of law.

Accepting this classification, it is of course possible to use other terms to describe the formal and material sources. Thus they may be described as, respectively, the legal sources and the historical sources, as direct and indirect, as proximate or immediate, and remote or ultimate, and so on. Or, as has been suggested, the material sources might better be described as the 'origins' of law. But whatever the terminology used, the essence of the distinction remains the same. Material, historical, indirect sources represent, so to speak, the stuff out of which the law is made. It is they which go to form the *content* of the law. These are the sources to which the lawgiver goes, so to speak, in order to obtain ideas, or to decide what the law is to consist of, and this is broadly true whether the lawgiver be conceived of as a national legislature, or as the international community evolving customary rules through State practice. The formal, legal, and direct sources consist of the acts or facts whereby this content, whatever it may be and from whatever material source it may be drawn, is clothed with legal validity and obligatory force. The essence of the distinction therefore is between the thing which inspires the content of the law, and the thing which gives that content its obligatory character as law.

Considered in themselves, and particularly in their inception, treaties are, formally, a source of obligation rather than a source of law. In their contractual aspect they are no more a source of law than an ordinary private law contract; which simply creates rights and obligations. Such instruments (as also, on the international plane, a commercial treaty, for example) create obligations and rights, not law. In this connexion, the attempts which have been made to ascribe a law-making character to *all* treaties irrespective of the character of their content or the number of the parties to them, by postulating that some treaties create 'particular' international law and others 'general', is of extremely dubious validity. There is really no such thing as 'particular' international treaty law, though there are particular international treaty rights and obligations. The only 'law' that enters into these is derived, not from the treaty creating them—or from any treaty—but from the principle *pacta sunt servanda*—an antecedent general principle of law. The law is that the obligation must be carried out, but the obligation is not, in itself, law. A genuine law may of course be applicable only to certain particular subjects of the legal system, but if so it is usually as members of a class, not as individuals. For instance, a law relating to married women obviously applies only to women who are married. But it applies automatically and *ipso facto* to *all* such women, not merely to those individual women who have set their hands to some particular instrument. In the latter event there would be rights or obligations for the women concerned, but not law—or if law, it would be something extraneous to the right or obligation, and general, not particular—i.e. that all rights and obligations thus arising must be honoured. A statute is always, *from its inception*, law: a treaty may reflect, or lead to, law, but, *particularly* in its inception, is not, as such, 'law'. So called treaty law is really pseudo-law—*a droit fainéant*. In itself, the treaty and the 'law' it contains only applies to the parties to it. True, where it reflects (e.g. codifies) existing law, non-parties may conform to the same rules, but they do so by virtue of the rules of general law thus reflected in the treaty, not by virtue of the treaty itself. In that sense, the treaty may be an instrument in which the law is conveniently stated, and evidence of what it is, but it is still not itself the law—it is still formally not a source of law but only evidence of it. Where a treaty is, or rather becomes, a *material* source of law, because the rules it contains come to be generally regarded as representing rules of universal applicability, it will nevertheless be the case that when non-parties apply or conform to these rules, this will be because the rules are or have become rules of general law: it is in the application of this general law, not of the treaty, that non-parties will act. For them, the rules are law; but the treaty is not the law, though it may be both the material source of it, and correctly state it.

NOTES

1. The running order of Article 38 of the Statute of the International Court of Justice suggests that treaties take precedence over the other 'sources' which follow. However, if 'international law' is to have credibility as a system of law, there is much to be said for the view that the sources of international law are not hierarchical in this way but are necessarily complementary and inter-related. This seems to have been the view of the majority of the International Court of Justice in *Nicaragua* v *USA* ICJ Rep 1986 14 (see Section 4), although it is true that rules of *jus cogens*, being customary rules of a fundamental nature, always take priority over treaty obligations. In the *Danube Dam Case* (see Chapter 3) the Court confirmed that *in general*, the law applicable to a treaty is the law in force when the treaty itself comes into operation, even if customary international law has developed further since then. However, the Court did recognise that the treaty itself might permit evolving customary international law rules to be relevant to its interpretation and operation. Once again this seems to be an attempt to introduce a coherence to the law irrespective of the source of any particular obligation.

2. As explained in Chapter 3, a fundamental rule in the law of treaties (with only limited exceptions) is that only States which are parties to a treaty are bound by it. With this in mind, the alleged distinction between 'law creating' and 'obligation creating' treaties may have reduced significance when trying to decide the precise obligations of a State in a real life situation. This is because, absent one of the special 'territorial status treaties', the only meaningful questions are whether the treaty has entered into force for the State concerned and, if not, whether the treaty mirrors existing rules of customary international law by which the State is otherwise bound. Consequently, to describe a treaty as 'multilateral' or 'lawmaking', as opposed to 'bilateral' or 'obligation making', may not describe their legal effect, but their purpose. Multilateral treaties may well be intended to lay down general rules for the community at large (i.e. *intended* to be 'lawmaking') but only the parties to them are bound. Bilateral treaties may be *intended* to create 'obligations' for only two States, but in reality for those two States the treaty *is* 'the law' on the particular issue.

3. Many texts, and the occasional case, refer to the alleged distinction between 'formal' and 'material' sources of international law, as discussed by Fitzmaurice. This distinction is best understood as an attempt to clarify the purpose that any given source plays in the evolution of rules of international law. To describe a source as 'formal' indicates that the source is law-creating, in that it is the method by which legally binding rules come into existence. Customary international law, and sometimes treaties and general principles of law, are said to be formal sources. A 'material' source is a source which identifies the substance of a legal obligation rather than expressing its role as a creator of law. Material sources may include judicial decisions and, for some commentators, treaties. There is considerable debate as to whether it is possible, necessary or even desirable to classify sources in this way.

4. Questions concerning the interpretation of treaties are more fully considered in Chapter 3. However, materials that aid the implementation or understanding of a treaty might also be regarded as a 'source' of international law. In *R* v *Secretary of State for the Home Department, ex parte Robinson* [1997] 3 WLR 1162 Lord Woolf MR noted, in connection with the Convention relating to the Statutes of Refugees 1951, that 'there is no international court charged with the interpretation and implementation of the Convention, and for this reason the UNHCR

Handbook on Procedures and Criteria for Determining Refugee Status (1979) is particularly helpful as a guide to what is the international understanding of the Convention obligations, as worked out in practice'.

A: General considerations

Customary international law derives from the practice of States. There has been considerable discussion of the elements of customary international law and these are discussed in the extracts below. In particular, State practice may give rise to customary international law when that practice is uniform, consistent and general, and if it is coupled with a belief that the practice is obligatory rather than habitual (the *opinio juris*). There is, in addition, some debate as to why State practice can give rise to binding international law at all and as to whether a State's continued objection to an emerging rule can absolve it from the scope of the rule (the problem of the 'persistent objector').

M. Akehurst, 'Custom as a Source of International Law'
47 British Yearbook of International Law 53 (1974–75)

1. Customary international law is created by State practice. State practice means any act or statement by a State from which views about customary law can be inferred; it includes physical acts, claims, declarations *in abstracto* (such as General Assembly resolutions), national laws, national judgments and omissions. Customary international law can also be created by the practice of international organizations and (in theory, at least) by the practice of individuals.

2. As regards the quantity of practice needed to create a customary rule, the number of States participating is more important than the frequency or duration of the practice. Even a practice followed by a few States, on a few occasions and for a short period of time, can create a customary rule, provided that there is no practice which conflicts with the rule, and provided that other things are equal; but other things are seldom completely equal, because there are various presumptions (e.g. the presumption in favour of the liberty of State action) which need to be taken into account.

3(a) Major inconsistencies in State practice prevent the creation of a customary rule; such inconsistencies cannot be explained away by saying that one type of practice is more important than another or that the practice of some States is more important than the practice of others.

3(b) A State is not bound by a customary rule if it has consistently opposed that rule from its inception. However, a new State is bound by rules which were well established before it became independent.

3(c) Special (e.g. regional) customs can co-exist with general customs. Apart from the number of States bound by the customs, there is little difference between special and general customs; where the number of States following one practice is roughly the same as the number of States following another practice, it may be difficult to say which is the special custom and which is the general custom.

4. *Opinio juris* is necessary for the creation of customary rules; State practice, in order to create a customary rule, must be accompanied by (or consist of) statements that certain conduct is permitted, required or forbidden by international law (a claim that conduct is permitted can be inferred from the mere existence of such conduct, but claims that conduct is required or forbidden need to be stated expressly). It is not necessary that the State making such statements believes them to be true; what is necessary is that the statements are not challenged by other States.

5. Treaties are part of State practice and can create customary rules if the requirements of *opinio juris* are met, e.g. if the treaty or its *travaux préparatoires* contain a claim that the treaty is declaratory of pre-existing customary

law. Sometimes a treaty which is not accompanied by *opinio juris* may nevertheless be imitated in subsequent practice; but in such cases it is the subsequent practice (accompanied by *opinio juris*), and not the treaty, which creates customary rules.

North Sea Continental Shelf Cases (*Federal Republic of Germany* v *Denmark; FRG* v *The Netherlands*)

ICJ Rep 1969 3, International Court of Justice

By two Special Agreements, the FRG and Denmark, and the FRG and The Netherlands, submitted a dispute over the delimitation of their shared Continental Shelf to the International Court of Justice. One of the Court's tasks was to identify the rules which bound these States, and in so doing the judgments shed considerable light on the circumstances in which customary international law can be created. The ICJ found that the delimitation of the continental shelf between these States (and hence giving access to the valuable oil deposits beneath them) had to be decided according to customary international law because the relevant treaty (the Continental Shelf Convention 1958) had not entered into force for all parties to the dispute.

75. The Court must now consider whether State practice in the matter of continental shelf delimitation has, subsequent to the Geneva Convention [on the Continental Shelf 1958], been of such a kind as to satisfy this requirement....

77. The essential point in this connection—and it seems necessary to stress it—is that even if these instances of action by non-parties to the Convention were much more numerous than they in fact are, they would not, even in the aggregate, suffice in themselves to constitute the *opinio juris*; for, in order to achieve this result, two conditions must be fulfilled. Not only must the acts concerned amount to a settled practice, but they must also be such, or be carried out in such a way, as to be evidence of a belief that this practice is rendered obligatory by the existence of a rule of law requiring it. The need for such a belief, i.e., the existence of a subjective element, is implicit in the very notion of the *opinio juris sive necessitatis*. The States concerned must therefore feel that they are conforming to what amounts to a legal obligation. The frequency, or even habitual character of the acts is not in itself enough. There are many international acts, e.g., in the field of ceremonial and protocol, which are performed almost invariably, but which are motivated only by considerations of courtesy, convenience or tradition, and not by any sense of legal duty....

79. Finally, it appears that in almost all of the cases cited, the delimitations concerned were median-line delimitations between opposite States, not lateral delimitations between adjacent States.... [The Court] simply considers that they are inconclusive, and insufficient to bear the weight sought to be put upon them as evidence of such a settled practice, manifested in such circumstances, as would justify the inference that delimitation according to the principle of equidistance amounts to a mandatory rule of customary international law,—more particularly where lateral delimitations are concerned....

81. The Court accordingly concludes that if the Geneva Convention was not in its origins or inception declaratory of a mandatory rule of customary international law enjoining the use of the equidistance principle for the delimitation of continental shelf areas between adjacent States, neither has its subsequent effect been constitutive of such a rule; and that State practice up-to-date has equally been insufficient for the purpose....

83. The legal situation therefore is that the Parties are under no obligation to apply either the 1958 Convention, which is not opposable to the Federal Republic, or the equidistance method as a mandatory rule of customary law, which it is not....

In sum, the general practice of States should be recognized as *prima facie* evidence that it is accepted as law. Such evidence may, of course, be controverted—even on the test of practice itself, if it shows 'much uncertainty and contradiction' (*Asylum, Judgment*...). It may also be controverted on the test of *opinio juris* with regard to 'the States in question' or the parties to the case.

Military and Paramilitary Activities in and against Nicaragua (*Nicaragua* v *United States*)

Merits, ICJ Rep 1986 14, International Court of Justice

In 1984, Nicaragua brought a claim against the United States alleging certain unlawful military and paramilitary activities against Nicaraguan territory, including the mining of Nicaraguan ports and support for Nicaraguan rebels, the Contras. The United States claimed that the Court had no jurisdiction because, inter alia, they had entered a reservation to the jurisdiction of the ICJ excluding a matter from the Court if the dispute concerned the application of a multilateral treaty. The relevant treaty here was the UN Charter itself, particularly Article 2(4) on the non-use of force. Nicaragua argued, however, that the Court had jurisdiction because its claim against the US was also based on rules of customary international law, which although similar in content to the law of the UN Charter, had not been suspended by it.

183. [T]he Court has next to consider what are the rules of customary international law applicable to the present dispute. For this purpose, it has to direct its attention to the practice and *opinio juris* of States…In this respect the Court must not lose sight of the Charter of the United Nations and that of the Organization of American States, notwithstanding the operation of the multilateral treaty reservation. Although the Court has no jurisdiction to determine whether the conduct of the United States constitutes a breach of those conventions, it can and must take them into account in ascertaining the content of the customary international law which the United States is also alleged to have infringed.

184. The Court notes that there is in fact evidence, to be examined below, of a considerable degree of agreement between the Parties as to the content of the customary international law relating to the non-use of force and non-intervention. This concurrence of their views does not however dispense the Court from having itself to ascertain what rules of customary international law are applicable. The mere fact that States declare their recognition of certain rules is not sufficient for the Court to consider these as being part of customary international law, and as applicable as such to those States. Bound as it is by Article 38 of its Statute to apply, *inter alia*, international custom 'as evidence of a general practice accepted as law', the Court may not disregard the essential role played by general practice. Where two States agree to incorporate a particular rule in a treaty, their agreement suffices to make that rule a legal one, binding upon them; but in the field of customary international law, the shared view of the Parties as to the content of what they regard as the rule is not enough. The Court must satisfy itself that the existence of the rule in the *opinio juris* of States is confirmed by practice.

185. In the present dispute, the Court, while exercising its jurisdiction only in respect of the application of the customary rules of non-use of force and non-intervention, cannot disregard the fact that the Parties are bound by these rules as a matter of treaty law and of customary international law. Furthermore, in the present case, apart from the treaty commitments binding the Parties to the rules in question, there are various instances of their having expressed recognition of the validity thereof as customary international law in other ways. It is therefore in the light of this 'subjective element'—the expression used by the Court in its 1969 Judgment in the *North Sea Continental Shelf* cases (*ICJ Rep 1969*, p. 44)—that the Court has to appraise the relevant practice.

186. It is not to be expected that in the practice of States the application of the rules in question should have been perfect, in the sense that States should have refrained, with complete consistency, from the use of force or from intervention in each other's internal affairs. The Court does not consider that, for a rule to be established as customary, the corresponding practice must be in absolutely rigorous conformity with the rule. In order to deduce the existence of customary rules, the Court deems it sufficient that the conduct of States should, in general, be consistent with such rules, and that instances of State conduct inconsistent with a given rule should generally have been treated as breaches of that rule, not as indications of the recognition of a new rule. If a State acts in a way prima facie incompatible with a recognized rule, but defends its conduct by appealing to exceptions or justifications contained within the rule itself, then whether or not the State's conduct is in fact justifiable on that basis, the significance of that attitude is to confirm rather than to weaken the rule.

J. Charney, 'Universal International Law'
87 American Journal of International Law 529 (1993)

Traditional textbook accounts of customary international lawmaking describe an amorphous process in which a pattern of behavior developed by states acting in their self-interest over a long period of time is coupled with opinions that the practice reflects a legal obligation (*opinio juris*). Treaties may codify the practice in normative terms. Eventually, it becomes well established that new international law on the subject has emerged. The judgments in the *Paquete Habana, Lotus* and *North Sea* cases epitomize this process. Traditional customary law formation may have sufficed when both the scope of international law and the number of states were limited. Today, however, the subject matter has expanded substantially into areas that were traditionally the preserve of states' domestic jurisdiction. In addition, the number of states has dramatically increased, together with their diversity. The relatively exclusive ways of the past are not suitable for contemporary circumstances. While customary law is still created in the traditional way, that process has increasingly given way in recent years to a more structured method, especially in the case of important normative developments.

Rather than state practice and *opinio juris*, multilateral forums often play a central role in the creation and shaping of contemporary international law. Those forums include the United Nations General Assembly and Security Council, regional organizations, and standing and ad hoc multilateral diplomatic conferences, as well as international organizations devoted to specialized subjects. Today, major developments in international law often get their start or substantial support from proposals, reports, resolutions, treaties or protocols debated in such forums. There, representatives of states and other interested groups come together to address important international problems of mutual concern. Sometimes these efforts result in a consensus on solving the problem and express it in normative terms of general application. At other times, the potential new law is developed through the medium of international relations or the practices of specialized international institutions and at later stages is addressed in international forums. That process draws attention to the rule and helps to shape and crystallize it.

The authoritativeness of the debates at these multilateral forums varies, depending upon many factors. Among the first is how clearly it is communicated to the participating states that the rule under consideration reflects a refinement, codification, crystallization or progressive development of international law. Of crucial importance is the amount of support given to the rule under consideration. Adoption of the rule by the forum in accordance with its procedures for decision making may not be necessary or even sufficient. On the other hand, unanimous support is not required. Consensus, defined as the lack of expressed objections to the rule by any participant, may often be sufficient. The absence of objections, of course, amounts to tacit consent by participants that do not explicitly support the norm. Even opposition by a small number of participating states may not stop the movement of the proposed rule toward law. The effect of the discussion depends upon the number of objecting states, the nature of their objections, the importance of the interests they seek to protect and their geopolitical standing relative to the states that support the proposed rule. Moreover, when objections are expressed, it must be determined whether they go to the heart of the norm under consideration or to subsidiary issues. Also relevant is whether the support for the norm is widespread and encompasses all interest groups. Do the objections demonstrate that an important group of states is not supportive, precluding the widespread support of the international community, or are relatively isolated states alone raising objections?

The discussions to such forums are necessarily communicated to all states and other interested parties. According to some customary law analysts, the work and products of those forums may be characterized as state practice or *opinio juris*. Certainly, the forums may move the solutions substantially toward acquiring the status of international law. Those solutions that are also positively received by the international community through state practice or other indications of support will rapidly be absorbed into international law, notwithstanding the technical legal status of the form in which they emerged from the multilateral forum. While this process may not conform to traditional customary lawmaking, nothing in the foundations of the international legal system bars such an evolution in the international lawmaking process. The international community itself holds the authority to make changes in this process and did so through the United Nations Charter and the system that evolved from it.

Letter from John Bellinger III, Legal Adviser, US Department of State, and William J Haynes, General Counsel, US Department of Defense, to Dr Jakob Kellenberger, President, International Committee of the Red Cross, Regarding Customary International Law Study

46 *International Legal Materials* 514 (2007)

The International Committee of the Red Cross (ICRC) prepared the Customary International Law Study after extensive consultation with governments and experts.

The Study set out a number of rules of customary international law, together with commentary and a study of State practice.

State practice

Although the Study's introduction describes what is generally an appropriate approach to assessing State practice, the Study frequently fails to apply this approach in a rigorous way.

- First, for many rules proffered as rising to the level of customary international law, the State practice cited is insufficiently dense to meet the 'extensive and virtually uniform' standard generally required to demonstrate the existence of a customary rule.
- Second, the United States is troubled by the type of practice on which the Study has, in too many places, relied. The initial U.S. review of the State practice volumes suggests that the Study places too much emphasis on written materials, such as military manuals and other guidelines published by States, as opposed to actual operational practice by States during armed conflict. Although manuals may provide important indications of State behavior and *opinio juris*, they cannot be a replacement for a meaningful assessment of operational State practice in connection with actual military operations. The United States also is troubled by the extent to which the Study relies on nonbinding resolutions of the General Assembly, given that States may lend their support to a particular resolution, or determine not to break consensus in regard to such a resolution, for reasons having nothing to do with a belief that the propositions in it reflect customary international law.
- Third, the Study gives undue weight to statements by non-governmental organizations and the ICRC itself, when those statements do not reflect whether a particular rule constitutes customary international law accepted by States.
- Fourth, although the Study acknowledges in principle the significance of negative practice, especially among those States that remain non-parties to relevant treaties, that practice is in important instances given inadequate weight.
- Finally, the Study often fails to pay due regard to the practice of specially affected States. A distinct but related point is that the Study tends to regard as equivalent the practice of States that have relatively little history of participation in armed conflict and the practice of States that have had a greater extent and depth of experience or that have otherwise had significant opportunities to develop a carefully considered military doctrine. The latter category of States, however, has typically contributed a significantly greater quantity and quality of practice.

Opinio juris

The United States also has concerns about the Study's approach to the *opinio juris* requirement. In examining particular rules, the Study tends to merge the practice and *opinio juris* requirements into a single test. In the Study's own words, 'it proved very difficult and largely theoretical to strictly separate elements of practice and legal conviction. More often than not, one and the same act reflects both practice and legal conviction....When there is sufficiently dense practice, an *opinio juris* is generally contained within that practice and, as a result, it is not usually necessary to demonstrate separately the existence of an *opinio juris*.'

The United States does not believe that this is an appropriate methodological approach. Although the same action may serve as evidence both of State practice and opinio juris, the United States does not agree that *opinio juris* simply can be inferred from practice. Both elements instead must be assessed separately in order to determine the presence of a norm of customary international law. For example, Additional Protocols I and II to the Geneva Conventions contain far-reaching provisions, but States did not at the time of their adoption believe that all of those instruments' provisions reflected rules that already had crystallized into customary international law; indeed, many provisions were considered ground-breaking and gap-filling at the time. One therefore must be cautious in drawing conclusions as to opinio juris from the practice of States that are parties to conventions, since their actions often are taken pursuant to their treaty obligations, particularly inter se, and not in contemplation of independently binding customary international law norms. Even if one were to accept the merger of these distinct requirements, the Study fails to articulate or apply any test for determining when state practice is 'sufficiently dense' so as to excuse the failure to substantiate *opinio juris*, and offers few examples of evidence that might even conceivably satisfy that burden.

The United States is troubled by the Study's heavy reliance on military manuals. The United States does not agree that *opinio juris* has been established when the evidence of a State's sense of legal obligation consists predominately of military manuals. Rather than indicating a position expressed out of a sense of a customary legal obligation, in the sense pertinent to customary international law, a State's military manual often (properly) will recite requirements applicable to that State under treaties to which it is a party. Reliance on provisions of military manuals designed to implement treaty rules provides only weak evidence that those treaty rules apply as a matter of customary international law in non-treaty contexts. Moreover, States often include guidance in their military manuals for policy, rather than legal, reasons....

A more rigorous approach to establishing *opinio juris* is required. It is critical to establish by positive evidence, beyond mere recitations of existing treaty obligations or statements that as easily may reflect policy considerations as legal considerations, that States consider themselves legally obligated to follow the courses of action reflected in the rules. In this regard, the practice volumes generally fall far short of identifying the level of positive evidence of *opinio juris* that would be necessary to justify concluding that the rules advanced by the Study are part of customary international law and would apply to States even in the absence of a treaty obligation.

S. Talmon, 'Determining Customary International Law: The ICJ's Methodology between Induction, Deduction and Assertion'

26 *European Journal of International Law* 417 (2015)

Methodology is probably not the strong point of the International Court of Justice (ICJ) or, indeed, of international law in general. Unlike its approach to methods of treaty interpretation, the Court has hardly ever stated its methodology for determining the existence, content and scope of the rules of customary international law that it applies. There are only isolated references in the ICJ's jurisprudence to the inductive and deductive method of law determination. In the *Gulf of Maine* case, a Chamber of the Court stated that 'customary international law ... comprises a set of customary rules whose presence in the *opinio juris* of States *can be* tested by *induction* based on the analysis of a sufficiently extensive and convincing practice and not by *deduction* from preconceived ideas' [para 111]. The use of the words 'can be', rather than 'is', implies that customary international law rules can also be discovered deductively. That deduction is part of the Court's methodological arsenal is demonstrated by the fact that in the *North Sea Continental Shelf* cases five judges used the deductive method in their separate or dissenting opinions. For example, Judge Lachs stated that in 'the event that the customary law character of the principle of equidistance cannot be proved, there exists another reason which seems more cogent for recognizing this character. That is the deduction of the necessity of this principle from the fundamental concept of the continental shelf.' In the while the *Jurisdictional Immunities of the State* case is regarded as a prime example of the Court using the inductive method....

The methods of determining the rules of international law must be distinguished from the methods of application of these rules in a specific case. The application of a rule of international law is a second step following its determination. It is with this narrower meaning that the terms 'induction' and 'deduction' usually are used.

For the purpose of determining the existence of rules of customary international law by the ICJ, the inductive method may be defined as inference of a general rule from a pattern of empirically observable individual instances of State practice and *opinio juris*. Induction is a process of going from the specific to the general. It is a systematic process of observation and empirical generalization. The deductive method, on the other hand, may be defined as inference, by way of legal reasoning, of a specific rule from an existing and generally accepted (but not necessarily hierarchically superior) rule or principle. Deduction is a process of going from the general to the specific.

Any examination of the methods used by the ICJ when determining rules of customary international law is complicated by its inconsistent and non-technical use of induction and deduction....There is widespread agreement that customary international law is, as a rule, ascertained by induction....The reason for the use of the inductive method is not that all states have to comply with the rules of customary international law, or that it is necessitated by the sovereign equality of states and the requirement of the unity of the international legal order, but, rather, due to the fact that the two elements of customary international law are, of necessity, gathered in an empirical and inductive way....

The Court cannot freely choose between induction and deduction when ascertaining rules of customary international law. However, there are certain situations in which the inductive method is impossible to use. Four such situations may be identified. In the first, state practice is non-existent because a question is too new....Second, state practice is conflicting or too disparate and thus inconclusive....Third, the *opinio juris* of states cannot be established....Fourth, there is a discrepancy between state practice and *opinio juris*.

NOTES

1. In the *Fisheries Jurisdiction Case* ICJ Rep 1973 3, a Joint Opinion by five Judges held that 'State practice must be common, consistent and concordant' (at p. 50). However, it is implicit in the extracts cited above that the degree of consistency, generality and uniformity of State practice necessary for the formation of customary international law may vary from situation to situation. The practice of States specially affected by a rule is of particular importance—see *North Sea Continental Shelf Case*, para. 74—as is the requirement of *opinio juris*, for this is what distinguishes 'law' from 'habit'. In the *North Sea Continental Shelf Case*, the members of the Court adopted different approaches to finding *opinio juris*, although it seems that a rather more relaxed view of the necessary proof of *opinio juris* was favoured by the majority in *Nicaragua* v *USA*. In the *Danube Dams Case* the Court adopted the ILC's formulation concerning the scope of the customary international law on the 'defence' of necessity with no analysis of State practice and no attempt to identify sufficient *opinio juris*.

2. Likewise, in the *Maritime Delimitation and Territorial Questions Between Qatar and Bahrain Case* (*Qatar* v *Bahrain*) ICJ Rep 2001 40, Qatar and Bahrain accepted that the relevant Articles of the Law of the Sea Convention 1982 represented customary international law and thus should form the basis of the Court's judgment even though that treaty was not in force between them. The point is not that the 1982 Convention might be said to represent customary international law (many commentators and States would not disagree), but rather that the Court was prepared to accept the parties' agreement that the treaty did indeed represent customary international law without any substantial analysis of the point. In other words, the Court seems prepared to allow the parties to choose *in effect* to be governed by a treaty (even if neither or only one is a party to it) by the simple device of accepting the parties' agreement that it represents customary international law. Once again, the context in which it is necessary to determine the validity of a particular 'source' of a rule of international law affects how the issue is dealt with.

3. It is obvious that many types of acts and omissions may amount to 'State practice' for the formation of customary international law. There has been considerable comment on this point, with various academics arguing in favour of, or against, the inclusion in 'State practice' of such matters as verbal statements, discussions in international fora, votes in international organs, government position papers and diplomatic exchanges. There is also disagreement as to what role is to be given to so-called 'negative' practice, the absence of any practice contrary to a purported rule, and the role of 'specially affected states'. Once again, Charney reminds us that any attempt to define the nature of customary international law should take account of the realities of the way international affairs are conducted and Charlesworth and Chinkin note that there is more to 'international' practice rather than 'State' practice.

4. The extract from the US comments on the ICRC customary humanitarian law study demonstrates the difficulties in obtaining evidence of State practice and *opinio juris*. It is also interesting as a rare statement from a State as to its understanding as to the formation of customary international law. For the response of the ICRC to the US criticisms, see 46 ILM 959 (2007). The views of the ICRC concerning international humanitarian law have been recognised as having special relevance and influence, with the institutional views of the ICRC qualifying as a secondary source of international law, as 'the teachings of the most highly qualified publicists': see, for example, *Serdar Mohammed and others* v *Secretary of State for Defence*, Court of Appeal, [2015] EWCA Civ 843, para. 171.

5. The extract from Talmon highlights the question of *how* the ICJ (and other courts, bodies and states) determine customary international law and the absence of any clearly defined methodology in international law. For a response to that analysis by Omri Sender and Sir Michael Wood, see *EJIL Talk*, 30 November 2015.

6. In 2012 the ILC placed the topic 'Identification of customary international law' on its long-term programme of work and appointed Sir Michael Wood (UK) as Special Rapporteur for the topic. Through a process of debate and informal consultation, the Special Rapporteur produced a set of draft conclusions aimed at developing a practical guide on the formative elements of customary international law. The Special Rapporteur drew the interim conclusion that: 'There was general support among members of the Commission for the "two-element" approach, that is to say, that the identification of a rule of customary international law requires an assessment of both general practice and acceptance of that

practice as law. … At the same time, it was recognized that the two elements may sometimes be "closely entangled", and that the relative weight to be given to each may vary according to the circumstances'.

B: Local customary international law

Asylum Case (Colombia v Peru)
ICJ Rep 1950 266, International Court of Justice

Following an unsuccessful coup in Peru in 1948, the leader of the rebel movement sought refuge and 'diplomatic asylum' in the Colombian Embassy in Lima, the Peruvian capital. The Peruvian government subsequently refused safe conduct for the rebel leader and the dispute was referred by agreement to the ICJ. One issue was whether a 'local custom' existed in Latin America permitting one State to grant political asylum and thereby offer consequential protection to the asylum seeker.

The Colombian Government has … relied on an alleged regional or local custom peculiar to Latin-American States.

The Party which relies on a custom of this kind must prove that this custom is established in such a manner that it has become binding on the other Party. The Colombian Government must prove that the rule invoked by it is in accordance with a constant and uniform usage practised by the States in question, and that this usage is the expression of a right appertaining to the State granting asylum and a duty incumbent on the territorial State. This follows from Article 38 of the Statute of the Court, which refers to international custom 'as evidence of a general practice accepted as law'. In support of its contention concerning the existence of such a custom, the Colombian Government has referred to a large number of … treaties …

Finally, the Colombian Government has referred to a large number of particular cases in which diplomatic asylum was in fact granted and respected. But it has not shown that the alleged rule … was invoked or—if in some cases it was in fact invoked—that it was, apart from conventional stipulations, exercised by the States as a duty incumbent on them and not merely for reasons of political expediency. The facts brought to the knowledge of the Court disclose so much uncertainty and contradiction, so much fluctuation and discrepancy in the exercise of diplomatic asylum and in the official views expressed on various occasions, there has been so much inconsistency in the rapid succession of conventions on asylum, ratified by some States and rejected by others, and the practice has been so much influenced by considerations of political expediency in the various cases, that it is not possible to discern in all this any constant and uniform usage, accepted as law, with regard to the alleged rule of unilateral and definitive qualification of the offence.

The Court cannot therefore find that the Colombian Government has proved the existence of such a custom. But even if it could be supposed that such a custom existed between certain Latin-American States only, it could not be invoked against Peru which, far from having by its attitude adhered to it, has, on the contrary, repudiated it by refraining from ratifying the Montevideo Conventions of 1933 and 1939, which were the first to include a rule concerning the qualification of the offence in matters of diplomatic asylum.

NOTE: In the *Asylum Case*, the Court found against the existence of local customary international law because of lack of evidence. However, the possibility that local customary international law could exist in an appropriate case was confirmed in the *Rights of Passage over Indian Territory Case*, ICJ Rep 1960 6, where the Court observed that:

[w]ith regard to Portugal's claim of a right of passage as formulated by it on the basis of local custom, it is objected on behalf of India that no local custom could be established between only two states. It is difficult to see why the number of states between which a local custom may be established on the basis of long practice must necessarily be larger than two. The Court sees no reason why long continued practice between two States accepted by them as regulating their relations should not form the basis of mutual rights and obligations between the two states.

C: Persistent objector

J. Charney, 'The Persistent Objector Rule and the Development of Customary International Law'
56 *British Yearbook of International Law* 1 (1985)

The role of the dissenting State in the development of customary international law is difficult to identify. The positivists clearly held that no rule of international law could be binding on a State without its consent. Most modern theories of international law do not require that express consent be found before a rule of customary international law can be held to be binding on a State. Many authorities argue that a State can be bound by a rule of customary international law even though the State neither expressly nor tacitly consented to the rule....No authority would permit a State unilaterally to opt out of an existing rule of customary international law, and few would permit new States to choose to exempt themselves from such rules.

Even though most authorities recognize that a State is not required to have expressly consented to be bound by a rule of customary international law, virtually all authorities maintain that a State which objects to an *evolving* rule of general customary international law can be exempted from its obligations....The International Court decision that writers primarily rely upon to support this rule is the *Anglo-Norwegian Fisheries* case. In that judgment the International Court of Justice made an alternative finding that a coastline delimitation rule put forward by the United Kingdom 'would appear to be inapplicable as against Norway, in as much as she has always opposed any attempt to apply it to the Norwegian coast'.

When the question of consent is directly addressed, most writers argue that States do not have the free will to decide whether or not to be bound by rules of international law. The obligation to conform to rules of international law is not derived from the voluntary decision of a State to accept or reject the binding force of a rule of law. Rather, it is the societal context which motivates States to have an international law and obligates them to conform to its norms....

If it is the societal context that is the source of the obligation to conform to specific rules of international law, then consent, either express or tacit, is irrelevant to the obligation. It may also appear to follow that if the societal context is the source, then an objection at any time, persistent or not, is irrelevant to the binding effect of a rule of law. If this is true, there is no place in international law for the persistent objector rule. A similar conclusion that the rule has no place in international law is reached if one maintains that consent is the basis of obligation. In that case, a particular persistent objector rule is redundant.

Only if one actually believes in the reality of the tacit consent theory of international legal obligation might there be any room for the persistent objector rule. In that case, it is difficult to limit its application only to overt dissent commenced at the formative stages of law development....

At this point it might be wise to conclude that regardless of one's theory of international law, the persistent objector rule has no legitimate basis in the international legal system. Not only is the rule hard to reconcile with the current theories of international law, but the evidence which might be produced to support the rule is weak indeed. This conclusion does not explain why so many reputable international law authorities explicitly report the existence of the rule. Perhaps its *raison d'être* can be found in the dynamics of international law development....

Customary international law is not static. It changes as the patterns of State behaviour change and *opinio juris* evolves to reflect current realities of obligation. Extant rules of law are subjected to change. Nations forge new law by breaking existing law, thereby leading the way for other nations to follow. Ultimately, new patterns of behaviour and obligation develop.

In the early stages a number of States may object to the new behaviour, but over time social pressures and modern realities will cause those reluctant States to conform to the new norm. On the other hand, some will seek to retain the traditional rule. The persistent objector rule becomes directly relevant when those resisting States continue to dissent from the new norm after it has replaced the old norm. At this stage the persistent objector rule promotes disharmony and discord in international relations. The international community will exert pressure to force the objector to conform to the new normative standard....In fact, the two International Court of Justice cases which appear to support the persistent objector rule both arose in circumstances in which the new rule itself was in substantial doubt. Thus, it was significantly easier for the objector to maintain its status. No case is cited for a circumstance in which the objector effectively maintained its status after the rule became well accepted in international law. In fact, it is unlikely that such a status could be maintained in light of the realities of the international legal system. This is certainly the plight that befell the US, the UK and Japan in the law of the sea.

Their objections to expanded coastal State jurisdiction were ultimately to no avail, and they have been forced to accede to 12-mile territorial seas and 200-mile exclusive economic zones.

It appears, therefore, that the persistent objector rule, if it really exists, focuses more on the process of law development than on the status of a State under stable international law. Its utility, if any, is to provide the State which objects to the evolution of a new rule of law with a tool it may use over the short term in its direct and indirect negotiations with the proponents of a new rule. The objecting State is armed with the theoretical right to opt out of the new rule. The proponents of the new rule are, as a consequence, encouraged to accommodate the objecting State or to utilize greater power to turn the objecting State to their will. At the same time, the persistent objector rule serves to soften the threat that the force of 'law' will impose a new and objectionable rule on the State that is content with the status quo. The persistent objector rule permits the objecting State to feel secure that it is not directly threatened, in an overt legal way, by changes in the law which it opposes. The legal system thereby appears to be fair and to permit an accommodation of views in the evolution of rules of law. It will be the political and social realities of the new status quo that will force the objecting State to conform to the new rule of law or the rest of the international community to accept on the basis of prescription the dissenter's unique status. It will not be a formal rule of uniform obligation that will procure conformity.

Viewed in this light, the persistent objector rule may be seen to be closely linked to the doctrine that in order to determine whether a rule of international law exists, one must examine the views and practices of the States whose interests are particularly affected. If the particularly affected States have not behaved in ways that conform to the purported rule of law, the International Court of Justice will be reluctant to hold in favour of that rule.

If any State will be the persistent objector, it will be the particularly affected State. Such a State will have interests directly at stake in the matter that is the subject of the rule of law under study. If it finds that the new rule is contrary to its interests, it will oppose the rule and will work for its rejection. As a particularly affected State, it will have leverage in determining the evolution of the applicable rule of law and will have the theoretical option of invoking the persistent objector rule. Thus both of these rules have one purpose, to force an accommodation of interests in the international community with respect to the evolution of new rules of law....

In conclusion, it appears that the persistent objector rule is, at best, only of temporary or strategic value in the evolution of rules of international law. It cannot serve a permanent role, unless, of course, one really does believe that States have the independence freely to grant or withhold their consent to rules of customary international law.

NOTES

1. In the *Anglo-Norwegian Fisheries Case*, ICJ Rep 1951 116, referred to by Charney, the United Kingdom objected to the delimitation of the territorial sea carried out by Norway by two Royal Decrees of 1935 and 1937. Part of the UK's objection rested on the fact that there was a customary rule of international law that 'closing lines' along the mouths of bays could be no longer than 10 nautical miles. As well as deciding that such a rule did not exist in general customary international law, due to inconsistent State practice, the Court also observed that '[i]n any event the ten mile rule would appear to be inapplicable as against Norway as she has always opposed any attempt to apply it to the Norwegian coast'.

2. The theory of the persistent objector clearly has a role within the international legal system: the difficulty is to identify its true effect. In reality it is difficult for an objector to remain outside the rule indefinitely. Likewise, some types of contrary conduct are not regarded as 'objections' at all, but 'violations' to be condemned. Perhaps it is a mistake to suppose that persistent objection/violation has the same effect irrespective of the content of the customary international law rule. The *Namibia Opinion* ICJ Rep 1971, 16 indicates that it would be impossible to be a persistent objector to a rule of *jus cogens* (see Chapter 3).

D: The relationship of customary international law and treaty law

Generally a treaty only binds the parties to it, whilst a rule of customary international law binds all States unless there is some local customary international law or persistent and effective objection. The two sources will interact and will occasionally come into conflict.

R. Baxter, 'Multilateral Treaties as Evidence of Customary International Law'

41 *British Yearbook of International Law* 275 (1965)

1. If reliance is to be placed on a multilateral treaty as evidence of customary international law, it is first necessary to establish whether the treaty was intended to be declaratory of existing customary international law or constitutive of new law. The silence of the treaty, which may necessitate resort to the *travaux préparatoires*, can make this a task of great difficulty.

2. If the treaty on its face purports to be declaratory of customary international law or if it can be established that such was the intent of its draftsmen, the treaty may be accepted as valid evidence of the state of customary international law. The weight it will carry varies in proportion to the number of parties and is also affected by the amount of consistent or inconsistent evidence of the state of customary international law available from other sources, such as judicial decisions or diplomatic correspondence.

If it can be established that a treaty that purports to be declaratory of international law actually lays down new law—a burden which must be sustained by the opponent of the proffered evidence—the impact of the treaty may be weakened. It nevertheless remains that if a State declares that what is apparently new law is actually part of existing law, that very assertion counts in favour of the rule's incorporation into customary international law.

The clear formulation of rules in a codification treaty and the assent of a substantial number of States may have the effect of arresting change and flux in the state of customary international law. Although the treaty 'photographs' the state of the law as at the time of its entry into force as to individual States, it continues, so long as States remain parties to it, to speak in terms of the present....

3. Early in the life of a treaty that is declaratory of customary law but has not yet entered into force, it carries weight as evidence of the state of the law. With the passage of time, its evidentiary force weakens. There still often remains a certain ambiguity about whether the lack of ratifications or accessions comes as the consequence of the fact that States disagree with the treaty or because the treaty has been so warmly received into customary international law that ratification of the treaty or accession to it would be supererogatory.

4. If a treaty was at the time of its adoption constitutive of new law, then the person or entity relying on the treaty as evidence of customary law has the burden of establishing that the treaty has subsequently been accepted into custom, either by express reference to this process by States and other authorities or by proof that the rule of the treaty is identical with customary law in the absence of the treaty.... Humanitarian treaties may, by reason of their special character, be an exception to this general rule. The adhesion of the great majority of the important States of the world to such an agreement may act in such a way as to impose the standards of the treaty on non-parties. But that view...requires acceptance of the notion that there is such a thing as true international legislation, by which the majority binds the dissenting or passive minority.

5. The advantage of the employment of a treaty as evidence of customary international law, as it was at the time of the adoption of the treaty or as it has come to be, is that it provides a clear and uniform statement of the rule to which a number of States subscribe. There is no problem of reconciling ambiguous and inconsistent State practice of varying antiquity and varying authority. The treaty speaks with one voice as of one time.

6. The convenience of reliance on the multilateral treaty is such that it may have a certain centripetal force, whether the agreement was initially declaratory or constitutive of the law. Inertia may lead advocates or decision-makers to drop other evidence of the law and to defer to the treaty because it speaks loudly and clearly. Thus the four elements of statehood listed in the Montevideo Convention on the Rights and Duties of States have become a standard expression of the definition of a State.

7. The passage of the rule of a treaty into customary international law may have certain consequences for the parties as well as non-parties. For example, if the treaty is accepted as a sound statement of customary international law, denunciation of the treaty by a party cannot absolve that State from its obligation to observe the rules of customary international law, proof of the existence of which is to be found in the treaty....

8. Reliance on a multilateral treaty as evidence of customary international law is not conditional on any demonstration that the signatory States have actually observed the norms of the treaty for any length of time. The process of establishing the state of customary international law is one of demonstrating what States consider to be the measure of their obligations. The actual conduct of States in their relations with other nations is only a subsidiary means whereby the rules which guide the conduct of States are ascertained. The firm statement by the State of what it considers to be the rule is far better evidence of its position than what can be pieced together from the actions of that country at different times and in a variety of contexts.

North Sea Continental Shelf Cases (Federal Republic of Germany v Denmark; FRG v The Netherlands)

ICJ Rep 1969 3, International Court of Justice

The facts of this case are set out in Section 4A.

70. The Court must now proceed to the last stage in the argument put forward on behalf of Denmark and the Netherlands. This is to the effect that even if there was at the date of the Geneva Convention [on the Continental Shelf 1958] no rule of customary international law in favour of the equidistance principle, and no such rule was crystallized in Article 6 of the Convention, nevertheless such a rule has come into being since the Convention, partly because of its own impact, partly on the basis of subsequent State practice,—and that this rule, being now a rule of customary international law binding on all States, including therefore the Federal Republic, should be declared applicable to the delimitation of the boundaries between the Parties' respective continental shelf areas in the North Sea.

71. In so far as this contention is based on the view that Article 6 of the Convention has had the influence, and has produced the effect, described, it clearly involves treating that Article as a norm-creating provision which has constituted the foundation of, or has generated a rule which, while only conventional or contractual in its origin, has since passed into the general *corpus* of international law, and is now accepted as such by the *opinio juris*, so as to have become binding even for countries which have never, and do not, become parties to the Convention. There is no doubt that this process is a perfectly possible one and does from time to time occur: it constitutes indeed one of the recognized methods by which new rules of customary international law may be formed. At the same time this result is not lightly to be regarded as having been attained.

72. It would in the first place be necessary that the provision concerned should, at all events potentially, be of a fundamentally norm-creating character such as could be regarded as forming the basis of a general rule of law....

73. With respect to the other elements usually regarded as necessary before a conventional rule can be considered to have become a general rule of international law, it might be that, even without the passage of any considerable period of time, a very widespread and representative participation in the convention might suffice of itself, provided it included that of States whose interests were specially affected....

74. As regards the time element, the Court notes that it is over ten years since the Convention was signed, but that it is even now less than five since it came into force in June 1964, and that when the present proceedings were brought it was less than three years, while less than one had elapsed at the time when the respective negotiations between the Federal Republic and the other two Parties for a complete delimitation broke down on the question of the application of the equidistance principle. Although the passage of only a short period of time is not necessarily, or of itself, a bar to the formation of a new rule of customary international law on the basis of what was originally a purely conventional rule, an indispensable requirement would be that within the period in question, short though it might be, State practice, including that of States whose interests are specially affected, should have been both extensive and virtually uniform in the sense of the provision invoked;—and should moreover have occurred in such a way as to show a general recognition that a rule of law or legal obligation is involved.

Military and Paramilitary Activities in and against Nicaragua (Nicaragua v USA)

Merits, ICJ Rep 1986 14, International Court of Justice

The facts of this case are set out in Section 4A.

174. The Court would observe that, according to the United States argument, it should refrain from applying the rules of customary international law because they have been 'subsumed' and 'supervened' by those of international treaty law, and especially those of the United Nations Charter. Thus the United States apparently takes the view that the existence of principles in the United Nations Charter precludes the possibility that similar rules might exist independently in customary international law, either because existing customary rules had been incorporated into the Charter, or because the Charter influenced the later adoption of customary rules with a corresponding content.

175. The Court does not consider that, in the areas of law relevant to the present dispute, it can be claimed that all the customary rules which may be invoked have a content exactly identical to that of the rules contained in the treaties which cannot be applied by virtue of the United States reservation....

177. But…even if the customary norm and the treaty norm were to have exactly the same content, this would not be a reason for the Court to hold that the incorporation of the customary norm into treaty-law must deprive the customary norm of its applicability as distinct from that of the treaty norm. The existence of identical rules in international treaty law and customary law has been clearly recognized by the Court in the *North Sea Continental Shelf cases*. To a large extent, those cases turned on the question whether a rule enshrined in a treaty also existed as a customary rule, either because the treaty had merely codified the custom, or caused it to 'crystallize', or because it had influenced its subsequent adoption. The Court found that this identity of content in treaty law and in customary international law did not exist in the case of the rule invoked, which appeared in one article of the treaty, but did not suggest that such identity was debarred as a matter of principle: on the contrary, it considered it to be clear that certain other articles of the treaty in question 'were…regarded as reflecting, or as crystallizing, received or at least emergent rules of customary international law' (*ICF Rep 1969*, p. 39, para. 63). More generally, there are no grounds for holding that when customary international law is comprised of rules identical to those of treaty law, the latter 'supervenes' the former, so that the customary international law has no further existence of its own.

178. There are a number of reasons for considering that, even if two norms belonging to two sources of international law appear identical in content, and even if the States in question are bound by these rules both on the level of treaty-law and on that of customary international law, these norms retain a separate existence. This is so from the standpoint of their applicability. In a legal dispute affecting two States, one of them may argue that the applicability of a treaty rule to its own conduct depends on the other State's conduct in respect of the application of other rules, on other subjects, also included in the same treaty.…But if the two rules in question also exist as rules of customary international law, the failure of the one State to apply the one rule does not justify the other State in declining to apply the other rule. Rules which are identical in treaty law and in customary international law are also distinguishable by reference to the methods of interpretation and application. A State may accept a rule contained in a treaty not simply because it favours the application of the rule itself, but also because the treaty establishes what that State regards as desirable institutions or mechanisms to ensure implementation of the rule. Thus, if that rule parallels a rule of customary international law, two rules of the same content are subject to separate treatment as regards the organs competent to verify their implementation, depending on whether they are customary rules or treaty rules.…

179. It will therefore be clear that customary international law continues to exist and to apply, separately from international treaty law, even where the two categories of law have an identical content. Consequently, in ascertaining the content of the customary international law applicable to the present dispute, the Court must satisfy itself that the Parties are bound by the customary rules in question; but the Court is in no way bound to uphold these rules only in so far as they differ from the treaty rules which it is prevented by the United States reservation from applying in the present dispute.

JUDGE JENNINGS (Dissenting Opinion): Let us look first, therefore, at the relationship between customary international law, and Article 2, paragraph 4, and Article 51 of the United Nations Charter. The proposition, however, that, after the Charter, there exists alongside those Charter provisions on force and self-defence, an independent customary law that can be applied as an alternative to Articles 2, paragraph 4, and 51 of the Charter, raises questions about how and when this correspondence came about, and about what the differences, if any, between customary law and the Charter provisions, may be.

A multilateral treaty may certainly be declaratory of customary international law…It could hardly be contended that these provisions of the Charter were merely a codification of the existing customary law. The literature is replete with statements that Article 2, paragraph 4,—for example in speaking of 'force' rather than war, and providing that even a 'threat of force' may be unlawful—represented an important innovation in the law.… Even Article 51, though referring to an 'inherent' and therefore supposedly pre-existing, right of self-defence, introduced a novel concept in speaking of 'collective self-defence'.…

If, then, the Charter was not a codification of existing custom about force and self-defence, the question must then be asked whether a general customary law, replicating the Charter provisions, has developed as a result of the influence of the Charter provisions, coupled presumably with subsequent and consonant States' practice.… But there are obvious difficulties about extracting even a scintilla of relevant 'practice' on these matters from the behaviour of those few States which are not parties to the Charter; and the behaviour of all the rest, and the *opinio juris* which it might otherwise evidence, is surely explained by their being bound by the Charter itself.

There is, however, a further problem: the widely recognized special status of the Charter itself. This is evident from paragraph 6 of Article 2, that:

> The Organization shall ensure that States which are not Members of the United Nations act in accordance with these Principles so far as may be necessary for the maintenance of international peace and security.

This contemplates obligations for non-members arising immediately upon the coming into operation of the Charter, which obligations could at that time only be derived, like those for Members, directly from the Charter itself. Even 'instant' custom, if there be such a thing, can hardly be simultaneous with the instrument from which it develops. There is, therefore, no room and no need for the very artificial postulate of a customary law paralleling these Charter provisions....

Vienna Convention on the Law of Treaties 1969

Article 38

Nothing...precludes a rule set forth in a treaty from becoming binding upon a third State as a customary rule of international law, recognised as such.

Article 53

A treaty is void if, at the time of its conclusion, it conflicts with a peremptory norm of general international law. For the purposes of the present Convention, a peremptory norm of general international law is a norm accepted and recognized by the international community of States as a whole as a norm from which no derogation is permitted and which can be modified only by a subsequent norm of general international law having the same character.

Article 64

If a new peremptory norm of international law emerges, any existing treaty which is in conflict with that norm becomes void and terminates.

NOTE: The relationship between conventional (i.e. treaty law) and customary international law is dealt with at length in the above extracts, and in this regard the majority opinion in *Nicaragua* v *USA* offers important guidance. It must be remembered, however, as Judge Jennings points out in that case, that 'particular' rules between two or more States will take precedence over general obligations, save where the latter constitute rules of *jus cogens* (see further Section 9 and Chapter 3).

SECTION 5: GENERAL PRINCIPLES OF LAW

There are many different interpretations of Article 38(1)(c) of the ICJ Statute, and some international lawyers argue that its inclusion adds nothing to the totality of rights and duties already existing in international law. Certainly, however, 'general principles' have been referred to by the ICJ on a number of occasions, both as a source of substantive rules and as the reason why considerations of 'equity' may be used in the determination of disputes involving questions of international law.

G. von Glahn, *Law Among Nations*
(6th edn, 1986)

General principles of law form the third source of international law. The meaning of 'general principles of law recognized by civilized nations' has been the subject of extensive discussion. Two major opinions prevail: one holds that the phrase embraces such general principles as pervade domestic jurisprudence and can be applied to international legal questions. Such principles might include the concept that both sides in a dispute should have a fair hearing, that no one should sit in judgment on his own case, and so on. The other view asserts that the phrase refers to general principles of law linked to natural law as interpreted during recent centuries in the Western world, that is, the transformation of broad universal principles of a law applicable to all of mankind into specific rules of international law. It must be assumed, however, that from a legal point of view, the law of nature represents at best a vague and ill-defined source of international law. Most modern writers appear to regard general principles of law as a secondary source of international law, infrequently used in practice but possibly helpful on occasion.

The former view concerning general principles of law is the one prevailing today. When this source of the law was written into the Statute of the Permanent Court of International Justice, the 1920 Committee of Jurists offered several interpretations of the source's meaning. It may well have been their purpose to avoid having an international court not hand down a decision because no 'positive applicable rule' existed. The phrase 'general principles' does enable a court, however, to go outside the generally accepted rules of international law and resort to principles common to various domestic legal systems. In fact, a number of court decisions and several law-making treaties refer to the general principles concept…

From a theoretical point of view, the acceptance of using general principles in fleshing out the body of international law means repudiating the extreme positivist doctrine that only rules created by means of the formal treaty process or a reliance on general custom are valid.

Thus it appears that, as yet, many international lawyers and diplomats doubt the validity of the claim that 'general principles' represent a truly usable source of international law.

International Status of South West Africa Case

Advisory Opinion, ICJ Rep 1950 128, International Court of Justice

In 1950, the General Assembly requested the ICJ to give an Advisory Opinion on the status of South West Africa (now Namibia) and its relationship with the Mandate power (South Africa), following the dissolution of the League of Nations in April 1946.

JUDGE MCNAIR: What is the duty of an international tribunal when confronted with a new legal institution the object and terminology of which are reminiscent of the rules and institutions of private law? To what extent is it useful or necessary to examine what may at first sight appear to be relevant analogies in private law systems and draw help and inspiration from them? International law has recruited and continues to recruit many of its rules and institutions from private systems of law. Article 38(1)(c) of the Statute of the Court bears witness that this process is still active, and it will be noted that this article authorizes the Court to 'apply…(c) the general principles of law recognized by civilized nations'. The way in which international law borrows from this source is not by means of importing private law institutions 'lock, stock and barrel', ready-made and fully equipped with a set of rules. It would be difficult to reconcile such a process with the application of 'the general principles of law'. In my opinion, the true view of the duty of international tribunals in this matter is to regard any features or terminology which are reminiscent of the rules and institutions of private law as an indication of policy and principles rather than as directly importing these rules and institutions.

River Meuse Case (Netherlands v Belgium)

PCIJ Ser A/B, (1937) No 70, Permanent Court of International Justice

JUDGE HUDSON (Individual Opinion): What are widely known as principles of equity have long been considered to constitute a part of international law, and as such they have often been applied by international tribunals…. A sharp division between law and equity, such as prevails in the administration of justice in some States, should find no place in international jurisprudence; even in some national legal systems, there has been a strong tendency towards the fusion of law and equity. Some international tribunals are expressly directed by the *compromis* which control them to apply 'law and equity'….Of such a provision, a special tribunal of the Permanent Court of Arbitration said in 1922 that 'the majority of international lawyers seem to agree that these words are to be understood to mean general principles of justice as distinguished from any particular systems of jurisprudence'….Numerous arbitration treaties have been concluded in recent years which apply to differences 'which are justifiable in their nature by reason of being susceptible of decision by the application of the principles of law or equity'. Whether the reference in an arbitration treaty is to the application of 'law and equity' or to justiciability dependent on the possibility of applying 'law or equity', it would seem to envisage equity as a part of law.

The Court has not been expressly authorized by its Statute to apply equity as distinguished from law. Nor, indeed, does the Statute expressly direct its application of international law, though as has been said on several occasions the Court is 'a tribunal of international law'….Article 38 of the Statute expressly directs the application of 'general principles of law recognized by civilized nations', and in more than one nation principles of equity have an established place in the legal system. The Court's recognition of equity as a part of international law is in no way restricted by the special power conferred upon it 'to decide a case *ex aequo et bono*, if the parties agree thereto'....It must be concluded, therefore, that under Article 38 of the Statute, if not independently of that Article, the Court has some freedom to consider principles of equity as part of the international law which it must apply.

M. Akehurst, 'Equity and General Principles of Law'

25 *International and Comparative Law Quarterly* 801 (1976)

The three functions of equity

Despite occasional statements to the contrary, the absence of an express authorisation to apply equity does not necessarily mean that an international tribunal is forbidden to apply equity....

Equity can perform three functions—it can be used to adapt the law to the facts of individual cases (equity *infra legem*); it can be used to fill gaps in the law (equity *praeter legem*); and it can be used as a reason for refusing to apply unjust laws (equity *contra legem*). These functions merge into one another to some extent; in particular, equity *infra legem* can be used in a wide number of situations, ranging from cases which differ only slightly from a strict application of the letter of the law, through cases where the spirit of the law is made to prevail over its letter, to cases where equitable exceptions are inferred into a rule of law. Consequently, a judge who wishes not to apply a rule of law can say that application of the letter of the law would be contrary to its spirit or that the legislator must have intended that there should be exceptions to the letter of the law (equity *infra legem*), or that the law does not apply to the case and that the judge can fill the resulting gap by recourse to equity (equity *praeter legem*) or that the law is unjust and should not be applied (equity *contra legem*). Not surprisingly, therefore, some (but not all) of the decisions of international tribunals are hard to fit into any one of the three classifications.

Is equity a source of international law?

The fact that tribunals often invoke equity does not necessarily mean that equity is a formal source of law. Counsel and judges in national courts frequently appeal to considerations of equity and justice when the law is uncertain, but this does not lead to equity being regarded as a source of national law. When deciding a doubtful case, a judge may point out that the rule he is laying down is just; he may also point out that it is a workable rule, which will be easy to apply and will yield predictable results in future cases. In both national and international law, similar appeals are often made to other extra-legal factors—religion, morality, good manners, neighbourliness, logic, reason, reasonableness, common sense, convenience, and political, economic, socio-logical, geographical and scientific factors. These factors are material sources of law; they are not formal sources. The same may well be true of equity....

However, it would be unwise to make too much of this argument. The fact that international law is less developed institutionally than municipal law means that the difference between formal sources and material sources is less clear in international law than in municipal law. To a large extent the question whether equity is a formal source of international law is a purely verbal question; whichever way the question is answered, it is an undeniable fact that international tribunals often apply equity.

Dangers of applying equity

The fact that international tribunals often apply equity does not necessarily mean that it is desirable that they should apply equity.

One of the dangers of applying equity arises from the fact that equity provides exceptions to general rules....

Normally States are deterred from breaking international law by fear of creating a precedent which can be used against them in subsequent cases. This fear is removed if one can invent an equitable exception to a rule; in such cases a State can continue to pay lip-service to the rule, while disregarding it and hoping that the precedent will not be copied by other States in other contexts. Such a state of affairs might not matter if compulsory judicial settlement existed in international law, but at present judicial settlement is optional and seldom used. In these circumstances there is a great danger that States will invoke equitable considerations as an exception to rules of law whenever obedience to the rules of law would be irksome...; the concept of equity could be used to give an aura of respectability to such exceptions, even though the States invoking them will probably refuse to allow the validity of the exceptions to be tested by an international tribunal. What makes this process particularly dangerous is that ideas of equity often vary according to the interests and culture of the State concerned.

The result is not only that respect for international law is weakened, but also that the rules of international law themselves become uncertain. Although it is desirable that rules of law should be just, it is perhaps even more desirable that they should be certain, clear and predictable.

The other main danger of applying equity lies in the fact that equity is subjective....

Even in a national society, equity can sometimes 'vary with the length of the Chancellor's foot.' The problem is far more acute in the international society, where political, ethical and cultural values are far more heterogeneous than in a national society...One of the problems about equity is that it can often be defined only by reference to a particular ethical system. Consequently, although references to equity are meaningful in a national society which can be presumed to hold common ethical values, the position is entirely different in the international arena, where the most mutually antagonist philosophies meet in head-on conflict. Moreover, many of the issues which come before international tribunals are so complex and raise such finely-balanced points of conflicting interests that an equitable solution does not exactly leap to the eye, to put it mildly.

It is sometimes said to be a general principle of law that a judge can apply equity. Even if such a general principle exists, it cannot be transplanted into international law, because the homogeneity of values, which is the condition precedent for such a principle in municipal law, simply does not exist in international law.

In a legal system where there is no compulsory judicial settlement, the subjectiveness of equity is very dangerous. States will base claims on considerations which seem equitable to them but which do not seem equitable to their opponents; disputes will become not only more frequent, but harder to settle.

It is also dangerous for an international tribunal to base its decisions on equity. A judgment which seems equitable to the winning party may not seem equitable to the losing party, who will be tempted to accuse the tribunal of being biased and acting *ultra vires* and to refuse to execute the judgment. Moreover, if...the unpredictability of judicial decisions is a major reason for the reluctance of States to accept the jurisdiction of international tribunals, it is likely that the number of cases submitted to international tribunals will vary in inverse proportion to the reliance on equity by judges and arbitrators.

This may explain why international tribunals often couple references to equity with a simultaneous invocation of general principles of law, customary law, treaties...or previous arbitral decisions.

Frontier Dispute Case (Burkina Faso v *Mali)*

ICJ Rep 1985 6, International Court of Justice

In 1983, Burkina Faso and Mali agreed to submit their frontier dispute to a Chamber of the ICJ. In the light of submissions by both States, the Chamber considered the application of 'principles of equity' and its relationship to the ability of the Court to decide a case *ex aequo et bono* under Article 38(2) of the Statute.

27. In their pleadings and oral arguments, the two Parties have advanced conflicting views on the question whether equity can be invoked in the present case. They both agree that no use should be made of the Chamber's power, under Article 38 of the Statute, to decide the case *ex aequo et bono* if they had agreed to this. However, Mali urges that account should be taken of 'that form of equity which is inseparable from the application of international law', which it sees as equivalent to equity *infra legem*. Although it did not object to this concept being resorted to, Burkina Faso considered that it was far from clear what the practical implications would be in this case. It emphasized that in the field of territorial boundary delimitation there is no equivalent to the concept of 'equitable principles' so frequently referred to by the law applicable in the delimitation of maritime areas. Mali did not question this statement; it explained that what it had in mind was simply the equity which is a normal part of the due application of law.

28. It is clear that the Chamber cannot decide *ex aequo et bono* in this case. Since the Parties have not entrusted it with the task of carrying out an adjustment of their respective interests, it must also dismiss any possibility of resorting to equity *contra legem*. Nor will the Chamber apply equity *praeter legem*. On the other hand, it will have regard to equity *infra legem*, that is, that form of equity which constitutes a method of interpretation of the law in force, and is one of its attributes. As the Court has observed: 'It is not a matter of finding simply an equitable solution, but an equitable solution derived from the applicable law' (*Fisheries Jurisdiction*...). How in practice the Chamber will approach recourse to this kind of equity in the present case will emerge from its application throughout this Judgment of the principles and rules which it finds to be applicable.

NOTES
1. The use of concepts found in most legal systems would seem to be within the spirit of 'general principles'. In the *Factory at Chorzów Case* PCIJ Rep Ser A (1928) No. 17 the Court observed 'that it is a principle of international law, and even a general conception of law, that any breach of an engagement involves an obligation to make reparation'. If this view of Article 38(1)(c) is correct, it is not clear whether general principles of national law can be regarded as 'formal' or 'material' sources of international law. However, in practice, they are designed to give efficacy and substance to international law and perhaps that is enough to warrant their inclusion in Article 38.
2. The use of equity and its relationship to the *ex aequo et bono* power of Article 38 was also discussed in the *Rann of Kutch Arbitration* 50 ILR (1968) 2 where the Tribunal confirmed that 'equity forms part of International Law; therefore the Parties are free to present and develop their cases with reliance on principles of equity', but that an 'International Tribunal will have the wider power to adjudicate a case *ex aequo et bono*, and thus go outside the bounds of law, only if such power has been conferred on it by mutual agreement between the Parties'. A similar view was put forward by the arbitrators in *AMCO* v *Indonesia* 89 ILR 365. Certain institutions are expressly prohibited from adjudicating a case *ex aequo et bono* (for example, Article 4(2) of the agreement establishing the Eritrea-Ethiopia Claims Commission).

SECTION 6: JUDICIAL DECISIONS AND THE WRITINGS OF PUBLICISTS

International law is a system of law, so considerable importance must attach to judicial decisions that purport to apply that law. This is so even though decisions of the ICJ are formally binding only between the parties to a dispute and are not to be taken as creating a system of precedent (Article 59, Statute of the ICJ, below). Whether a system of precedent does exist in fact is a matter of some debate, as the Court's decisions can have a considerable impact on the international community (see Chapter 16). In addition, although there is a tendency to focus on the ICJ, in practice arbitration awards and decisions of other courts (including national courts) may be crucial in determining rights and duties under international law.

Statute of the International Court of Justice 1945

Article 59

The decision of the Court has no binding force except between the parties and in respect of that particular case.

The Paquete Habana
175 US SC Rep (1900) 677, United States Supreme Court

In 1898, two fishing vessels, *The Lola* and *The Paquete Habana*, were seized by the United States Navy as Spanish prize during the Spanish-American War. One of the issues before the US Supreme Court was whether international law permitted the seizure of *bona fide* fishing vessels as prize. The case is an example of how decisions of national courts can be relevant in determining rules of international law; in this case the customary law of prize.

JUSTICE GRAY: International law is part of our law, and must be ascertained and administered by the courts of justice of appropriate jurisdiction as often as questions of right depending upon it are duly presented for their determination. For this purpose, where there is no treaty and no controlling executive or legislative act or judicial decision, resort must be had to the customs and usages of civilized nations, and, as evidence of these, to the works of jurists and commentators who by years of labor, research, and experience have made themselves peculiarly well acquainted with the subjects of which they treat. Such works are resorted to by judicial tribunals, not for the speculations of their authors concerning what the law ought to be, but for trustworthy evidence of what the law really is....

Wheaton places among the principal sources of international law 'text-writers of authority, showing what is the approved usage of nations, or the general opinion respecting their mutual conduct, with the definitions and modifications introduced by general consent.' As to these he forcibly observes:

> Without wishing to exaggerate the importance of these writers, or to substitute, in any case, their authority for the principles of reason, it may be affirmed that they are generally impartial in their judgment. They are witnesses of the sentiments and usages of civilized nations, and the weight of their testimony increases every time that their authority is invoked by statesmen, and every year that passes without the rules laid down in their works being impugned by the avowal of contrary principles. [Wheaton, *International Law* (8th edn), para. 15.]

NOTES

1. Article 38 describes judicial decisions as 'a subsidiary means' for the determination of rules of law and Article 59 attempts to deny a system of precedent. However, the Court itself frequently uses its previous decisions as authority in later cases. Cases such as the *North Sea Continental Shelf Cases* show how the Court can contribute significantly to the development of customary law. It has been suggested that, 'in connection with the jurisprudence of the Court on maritime delimitation...that the tendency of the Court to follow and apply earlier decisions rather than to investigate the practice of States supposedly creative of custom had led to a situation in which it might be said that maritime delimitation law was judge-made law rather than customary law' (Thirlway, *British Yearbook of International Law* 116 (2005), p. 116). In other areas, Thirlway suggests that there are signs that the Court prefers to cite its own previous decisions in support of findings of customary international law than to refer to the State practice. The Court has also relied on its own previous decisions (and those of the PCIJ) when considering questions of interpretation of a treaty with similar, but not identical, provisions: *Certain Property (Lichtenstein* v *Germany)* ICJ Rep 6 2005.

2. The impact of decisions of national courts on the content and role of international law should not be underestimated. The series of *Pinochet* cases in the United Kingdom continue to exert considerable influence over the way in which human rights obligations and principles of sovereign immunity interact (see further Chapter 9). Even if the *Pinochet* cases do not establish *as a matter of international law* the primacy of human rights law over principles of sovereign immunity, there is no doubt that the judgments have been used as a source of principles for the determination of this pressing and difficult issue in similar cases, see for example the reference to these cases by the ICJ in the *Case concerning the Arrest Warrant of 11 April 2000* (2002) ICJ Rep 22, para. 58), albeit as part of a study of relevant State practice. National courts, in applying international law, affect not only the law within the State but, as national court decisions form part of 'State practice', they can also affect the direction of customary international law more generally.

3. As the number of international courts and tribunals has grown, the likelihood of tribunals, including the ICJ, having overlapping jurisdiction and being required to pronounce on the same or similar points of law has also increased. While other international tribunals are generally deferential to decisions of the ICJ, the ICTY has departed from the findings of the ICJ on the question of attribution to a State of the acts of paramilitary groups (see Chapter 11). The overlap between the jurisdictions of these two institutions was also apparent in the *Bosnia Genocide Case* (see Chapter 11) and may also be an issue for the International Criminal Court (see Chapter 14).

4. The impact of writers on the *corpus* of international law is, of course, never capable of scientific analysis. For example, the degree to which judges of the ICJ rely on published works (other than their own!) is rarely made clear, as the practice of the Court is not to cite the views of scholars in decisions, although legal representatives before the Court frequently refer to publicists in their arguments. Greater reference to legal publicists is made in national courts when considering international law, as in the *Paquete Habana* case, and, it appears, in the international criminal tribunals (Chapter 14).

SECTION 7: **RESOLUTIONS OF INTERNATIONAL ORGANISATIONS**

United Nations Charter 1945

Article 10

The General Assembly may discuss any questions or any matters within the scope of the present Charter or relating to the powers and functions of any organs provided for in the present Charter, and, except as provided for in Article 12, may make recommendations to the Members of the United Nations or to the Security Council or to both on any such questions or matters.

Article 18

1. Each Member of the General Assembly shall have one vote.

2. Decisions of the General Assembly on important questions shall be made by two-thirds majority of the Members present and voting. These questions shall include: recommendations with respect to the maintenance of international peace and security, the election of the non-permanent members of the Security Council, the election of the members of the Economic and Social Council, the election of the members of the Trusteeship Council…, the admission of new members to the United Nations, the suspension of the rights and privileges of membership, the expulsion of Members, questions relating to the operation of the trusteeship system, and budgetary questions.

3. Decisions on other questions, including the determination of additional categories of questions to be decided by a two-thirds majority, shall be made by a majority of the Members present and voting.

Article 25

The Members of the United Nations agree to accept and carry out the decisions of the Security Council in accordance with the present Charter.

B. Sloan, 'General Assembly Resolutions Revisited'

58 *British Yearbook of international Law* 93 (1987)

Decisions

By virtue of powers expressly or impliedly authorized by the Charter, inherent in its nature or acquired through practice, the General Assembly may take decisions having binding force or operative effect. While these decisions concern mainly budgetary and internal organizational matters, some have direct and many have indirect external effects affecting obligations of States….

Some decisions (budgetary resolutions under Article 17) are directly binding on members, while decisions having operative effect are 'action' to which, under Article 2(5), is appended a duty to give 'every assistance'. Determinations and interpretations involved in decisions are binding for the particular case and create precedents for the future.

The binding force and operative effect of decisions applies to all such resolutions validly adopted by the majorities specified in Article 18 of the Charter. The size of the vote is legally irrelevant, although a decision taken against strong opposition may result in a refusal of some States to co-operate. Thus from a practical point of view agreement or acceptance may be material even with respect to legally binding decisions.

Recommendations

Those resolutions of the General Assembly which are recommendations *stricto sensu*, granted that normally they are non-binding, nevertheless carry with them obligations of co-operation and good faith….Whether recommendations are 'action' within the meaning of Article 2(5) may be debatable, but those resolutions which recommend action should entail the duty of assistance provided for in that article or at the very least an obligation not to interfere with action being taken by other States in accordance with the recommendation.

The foregoing obligations of co-operation, good faith and assistance apply to all validly adopted recommendations, without special regard to the size of the vote. The hortatory effect of recommendations will be strengthened by unanimity or near unanimity. Recommendations will also have value as precedents and may gain binding force through acceptance or estoppel.

Declarations

Declarations are a species of General Assembly resolutions based on established practice outside the express provisions of Chapter IV of the Charter. The practice of adopting declarations is consistent, universally accepted and 'immemorial' in the sense that it goes back to the very beginning of the UN. While the effect of declarations remains controversial, they are not recommendations and are not to be evaluated as such....Where, however, there is an intent to declare law, whether customary, general principles or instant, spontaneous or new law, and the resolution is adopted by a unanimous or nearly unanimous vote or by genuine consensus, there is a presumption that the rules and principles embodied in the declaration are law. This presumption could only be overcome by evidence of substantial conflicting practice supported by an *opinio juris* contrary to that stated or implied in the resolution. If the declaration is adopted by a majority vote its evidentiary value is to be weighed in the light of all relevant factors. It would in any event be part of the material sources of customary law and would constitute an expression of *opinio juris*, or a lack of *opinio juris* for conflicting norms, of those States voting for the resolution.

Determinations, interpretations and agreement

As noted previously determinations, interpretations and agreement may be involved in any of the preceding categories of resolutions.

Determinations include findings of fact and characterizations. Such determinations will normally enjoy the weight of the resolution in which they are found. If embodied in a decision they will be binding for the purpose of that decision and will have precedential value in other situations. Determinations contained in a recommendatory resolution are entitled as a minimum to the same respect as the recommendation, but as findings and characterizations they may have greater or at least a different effect. They may justify States in accepting and acting on the determinations in situations not covered by the recommendation and in expecting other States to respect their action. Determinations in declarations confirming rules and principles as existing law will carry special evidentiary weight. Moreover, determinations, whether in decisions, recommendations or declarations, will have precedential value as a part of State practice.

Interpretations of the Charter, and sometimes of other treaties and of general international law, will also be found in all three categories of resolution. Interpretations involved in decisions are binding for that case. The binding force of interpretations for other situations, whether they are found in decisions, recommendations or declarations, depends on their general acceptability....

Agreement in one form or another may also be involved in all three categories of resolution. Acceptance of a recommendation may convert a resolution into a binding agreement, or the status of a declaration may be confirmed by agreement. Even with respect to operative decisions, agreement may be necessary concerning certain aspects. For example, a resolution will through its own force establish a subsidiary organ, but the operation of that organ within the territory of a State may still depend on that State's acceptance or agreement.

Jus cogens and general principles

Special note should be taken of the role which General Assembly resolutions have played as a vehicle for expressing acceptance and recognition by the international community of States as a whole of norms of *jus cogens* and the similar role which they might play in recognizing other general principles of law in the sense of Article 38(1)(c) of the Statute of the International Court of Justice.

Legality of the Threat or Use of Nuclear Weapons
Advisory Opinion, ICJ Rep 1996 254, International Court of Justice

This advisory opinion was to consider the legality in international law of the use or the threat of the use of nuclear weapons.

68. According to certain States, the important series of Assembly resolutions, beginning with resolution 1653 (XVI) of 24 November 1961, that deal with nuclear weapons and that affirm, with consistent regularity, the illegality of nuclear weapons, signify the existence of a rule of international customary law which prohibits recourse to those weapons. According to other States, however, the resolutions in question have no binding character on their own account and are not declaratory of any customary rule of prohibition of nuclear weapons; some of these States have also pointed out that this series of resolutions not only did not meet with the approval of all of the nuclear-weapon States but of many other States as well.

69. States which consider that the use of nuclear weapons is illegal indicated that those resolutions did not claim to create any new rules, but were confined to a confirmation of customary law relating to the prohibition of means or methods of warfare which, by their use, overstepped the bounds of what is permissible in the conduct of hostilities. In their view, the resolutions in question did no more than apply to nuclear weapons the existing rules of international law applicable in armed conflict; they were no more than the 'envelope' or *instrumentum* containing certain pre-existing customary rules of international law. For those States it is accordingly of little importance that the *instrumentum* should have occasioned negative votes, which cannot have the effect of obliterating those customary rules which have been confirmed by treaty law.

70. The Court notes that General Assembly resolutions, even if they are not binding, may sometimes have normative value. They can, in certain circumstances, provide evidence important for establishing the existence of a rule or the emergence of an *opinio juris*. To establish whether this is true of a given General Assembly resolution, it is necessary to look at its content and the conditions of its adoption; it is also necessary to see whether an *opinio juris* exists as to its normative character. Or a series of resolutions may show the gradual evolution of the *opinio juris* required for the establishment of a new rule.

71. Examined in their totality, the General Assembly resolutions put before the Court declare that the use of nuclear weapons would be 'a direct violation of the Charter of the United Nations'; and in certain formulations that such use 'should be prohibited'. The focus of these resolutions has sometimes shifted to diverse related matters; however, several of the resolutions under consideration in the present case have been adopted with substantial numbers of negative votes and abstentions; thus, although those resolutions are a clear sign of deep concern regarding the problem of nuclear weapons, they still fall short of establishing the existence of an *opinio juris* on the illegality of the use of such weapons.

S. Talmon, 'The Security Council as World Legislature'
99 American Journal of International Law 175 (2005)

The term 'international legislation' has been used in a variety of ways by writers. They have employed it in a broad sense to cover 'both the process and the product of the conscious effort to make additions to, or changes in, the law of nations.' [International Legislation: A Collection of Texts of Multipartite International Instruments of General Interest, Manley O. Hudson 1931, xiii] They have also used it to describe the conclusion of lawmaking treaties (i.e., multilateral treaties on matters of general interest), the making of customary international law, and the adoption of binding decisions by international organizations. Security Council resolutions that established the United Nations Compensation Commission and the two ad hoc war crimes tribunals for Yugoslavia and Rwanda, imposed disarmament obligations on Iraq, determined the Kuwait-Iraq border, declared the applicability of the Fourth Geneva Convention to the occupied Palestinian territories, and, generally, imposed any economic sanctions have been termed international legislation or legislative acts in the literature. States, on the other hand, used the term for the first time in connection with Resolution 1373, and, more recently, Resolution 1540.

State practice seems to follow Krzysztof Skubiszewski, who suggested that international legislation should mean lawmaking that, in its basic features, remains identical with national legislation. But what are the basic features, the hallmarks, of international legislation? At the outset, it should be noted that international legislation does not necessarily require any legislative activity on the part of member states. International legislation is not to be equated with legislative agenda setting by the Council. It should be recalled that most resolutions imposing economic sanctions require some kind of legislative activity by the member states to make them applicable to individuals. The nature of the measures in these resolutions as mainly aimed at individuals and not at states is not the distinguishing feature of international legislation, either. By the mid-1990s, the Council had already turned to 'targeted' or 'smart' sanctions and aimed its measures specifically against certain persons or groups of persons deemed to bear particular responsibility for a threat to the peace. It primarily used financial sanctions and travel bans for this purpose. The hallmark of any international legislation is the general and abstract character of the obligations imposed. These may well be triggered by a particular situation, conflict, or event, but they are not restricted to it. Rather, the obligations are phrased in neutral language, apply to an indefinite number of cases, and are not usually limited in time. Thus, while Resolution 1390 provides that 'all States shall…[f]reeze without delay the funds and other financial assets or economic resources' of Osama bin Laden, members of Al Qaeda, and the Taliban, and other individuals, groups, undertakings, and entities associated with them, Resolution 1373 states in identical terms, but generally, that 'all States shall…[f]reeze without delay funds and other financial assets or economic resources of persons who commit, or attempt to commit, terrorist acts or participate in or facilitate the commission of terrorist acts.' The basic characteristic of this new type of legislative or generic resolution is, as the Colombian delegate to the Security Council put it, that it 'does not name a single country, society or group of people.' To that extent, the obligations imposed in such resolutions are akin to obligations entered into by states in international agreements. There is thus a basic difference between the classic individualized resolutions and the new legislative or generic resolutions; only the latter should be referred to as international legislation....

On the basis of the criteria for international legislation just established, the Security Council has legislated on four occasions so far. In Resolution 1373, adopted unanimously, the Council set out a range of abstract measures for all states to undertake in combating terrorism. These included the obligations to prevent and suppress the financing of terrorist acts, freeze the resources of terrorists, and criminalize the perpetration of terrorist acts. Several provisions were almost identical to provisions in the International Convention for the Suppression of the Financing of Terrorism, which was not yet in force. The representative of Angola declared in the Council debate on April 22, 2004: 'By adopting resolution 1373 (2001), the Security Council took the unprecedented step of bringing into force legislation binding on all States on the issue of combating terrorism.' The adoption of Resolution 1373 was widely welcomed by the UN member states. It was hailed as a 'groundbreaking resolution,' a 'landmark decision,' a 'historic event,' and even 'one of the most important resolutions in [the] history [of the Council].' During the debate on threats to international peace and security caused by terrorist acts, on January 18, 2002, representatives of thirty-seven states and the observer for Palestine spoke on the implementation of Resolution 1373. No speaker expressed concerns that the Council was legislating in that resolution for the international community, although some Council members, it seems, had expected such concerns. Even Mexico, which had objected to the creation of the ad hoc international criminal tribunals by the Council as exceeding its powers under Article 41, did not raise any objections to Resolution 1373.

The next, often overlooked, example of Security Council legislation was the adoption of Resolutions 1422 and 1487 on the International Criminal Court (ICC). In these resolutions the Council addressed a general request to the ICC to defer, for a twelve-month period, investigation or prosecution of any case involving current or former officials or personnel from a contributing state not a party to the Rome Statute of the ICC, over acts or omissions relating to a United Nations-established or authorized operation. The Council also obliged member states not to take any action inconsistent with this request or with their international obligations. While the initial resolution received unanimous support, on renewal it was adopted by only 12 votes to 3. The resolutions were widely criticized by member states for not specifying a threat to the peace as a precondition for Chapter VII action. States also disagreed on whether Article 16 of the Rome Statute allowed for such a general request. However, they did not object to the power of the Council to impose obligations of an abstract and general character.

The most recent example of Security Council legislation, Resolution 1540 [2004], was adopted unanimously. In that resolution the Council imposed a range of general obligations on all states to keep weapons of mass destruction and their means of delivery out of the hands of non-state actors. This resolution for the first time prompted several member states to voice their 'basic concerns over the increasing tendency of the Council in recent years to assume new and wider powers of legislation on behalf of the international community, with its resolutions binding on all States.' Others denied the Council any 'legislative authority' and claimed that the enactment of global legislation 'is not consistent with the provisions of the United Nations Charter.'

NOTES

1. Resolutions of international organisations, of which the United Nations is the most significant, must be considered in two respects. First, there is the question whether such resolutions are binding in law on the members of the organisations, and there is agreement that the great majority are not. Second, there is the separate issue as to whether such resolutions, irrespective of whether they are internally binding or not, have given rise to international law in another way, such as through the development of customary international law or the elucidation of general principles.

2. The 'decisions' of the Security Council are formally binding, although the Council instead often uses its general power to make recommendations. The extract from Talmon above suggests that the Security Council has engaged in a more legislative role in recent years. Resolution 1373 is discussed in greater detail in Chapter 15.

3. While resolutions of the General Assembly are generally accepted to be non-binding, resolutions regulating the internal affairs of the UN (which includes all the 'important questions' in Article 18 of the UN Charter except recommendations with respect to international peace and security) will in fact create situations that members of the UN cannot disregard, such as the election to various committees and matters of finance.

4. As noted in the extract from the *Nuclear Weapons Advisory Opinion,* General Assembly resolutions may provide evidence of the current state of the law and provide valuable guidance as to

the meaning and interpretation of legal texts. Moreover, such resolutions may contribute to the development of customary international law. In each case the circumstances surrounding the resolution should be considered before according any legal significance to it. Reference should also be made to the ICJ's reliance on General Assembly resolutions as establishing *opinio juris* in *Nicaragua v USA* (see extract in Chapter 15). In the *Advisory Opinion Concerning Legal Consequences of the Construction of a Wall in the Occupied Palestinian Territory* (ICJ Rep 2004 3, paras 87–88), the Court took note of General Assembly resolutions concerning the illegal acquisition of territory by force and the principle of self-determination. In addition, in determining whether the Fourth Geneva Convention, to which Israel is a party, was applicable in the Occupied Territories, the ICJ referred to several resolutions of the General Assembly and the Security Council, all of which supported the application of the Convention.

SECTION 8: SOFT LAW

A. Boyle and C. Chinkin, *The Making of International Law*
(2007)

'Soft law' is a frequently misunderstood phenomenon, although evidence of its importance as an element in modern international law-making is abundant, most notably in the declarations or resolutions adopted by states in international conferences or in the United Nations General Assembly. While the relationship between treaty and custom is well understood, the interplay between soft law and treaties, custom, or general principles of law is less often appreciated, but it is no less important, and has great practical relevance to the law-making and regulatory work of international organizations.

Perhaps the most important point to make at the outset is that some of the forms of 'soft law' under consideration here are potentially law-making in much the same way that multilateral treaties are potentially law-making. The proposition is not that non-binding declarations or resolutions of the General Assembly or any other soft law instrument are invariably law *per se*, but that they may be evidence of existing law, or formative of the *opinio juris* or state practice that generates new law....Moreover, widespread acceptance of soft law instruments will tend to legitimise conduct and make it harder to sustain the legality of opposing positions. They may additionally acquire binding legal character as elements of a treaty-based regulatory regime, or constitute a 'subsequent agreement between the parties regarding the interpretation of the treaty or the application of its provisions', or otherwise assist in the development and application of general international law'.

NOTE: As the extract from Weil (see Section 9) makes clear, the international legal system is imperfect and immature, at least by the standards of the national legal system. So-called 'soft law' is said to be a by-product of these deficiencies. Soft law may govern the conduct of certain situations without legal obligation, though it can lead to legal obligations or even, as Boyle and Chinkin suggest, soft law can have normative quality.

SECTION 9: A HIERARCHY OF SOURCES?

P. Weil, 'Towards Relative Normativity in International Law'
77 American Journal of international Law 413 (1983)

The structural weaknesses

3. As everyone knows, the international normative system, given the specific structure of the society it is called on to govern, is less elaborate and more rudimentary than domestic legal orders—which, of course, does not mean that it is their inferior or less 'legal' than they: it is just different.

Some of its structural weaknesses are too familiar to require lengthy treatment here: not only the inadequacy of its sanction mechanisms, but also the mediocrity of many of its norms. In regard to certain points, international law knows no norm at all, but a lacuna. As for others, the substance of the rule is still too controversial for it effectively to govern the conduct of states. On yet other points, the norm has remained at the stage of abstract general standards on which only the—necessarily slow—development of international law can confer concrete substance and precise meaning.

For some time, however, writers have been apt to point out a further weakness: alongside 'hard law,' made up of the norms creating precise legal rights and obligations, the normative system of international law comprises, they note, more and more norms whose substance is so vague, so uncompelling, that A's obligation and B's right all but elude the mind. One does not have to look far for examples of this 'fragile,' 'weak,' or 'soft law,' as it is dubbed at times: the 1963 Moscow Treaty banning certain nuclear weapon tests, Article I of which provides, *inter alia*, that 'each Party shall in exercising its national sovereignty have the right to withdraw from the Treaty if it decides that extraordinary events, related to the subject matter of this Treaty, have jeopardized the supreme interests of its country'; the numerous treaty provisions whereby the parties undertake merely to consult together, to open negotiations, to settle certain problems by subsequent agreement; and the purely hortatory or exhortatory provisions whereby they undertake to 'seek to,' 'make efforts to,' 'promote,' 'avoid,' 'examine with understanding,' 'act as swiftly as possible,' 'take all due steps with a view to,' etc. While particularly common in economic matters, there 'precarious' norms are similarly encountered in the political field, as witness, apart from the above-quoted Moscow Treaty provision, a recent Advisory Opinion of the International Court of Justice including obligations 'to co-operate in good faith' and 'to consult together' among the 'legal principles and rules' governing the relations between an international organization and a host country. Whether a rule is 'hard' or 'soft' does not, of course, affect its normative character. A rule of treaty or customary law may be vague, 'soft'; but, as the above examples show, it does not thereby cease to be a legal norm. In contrast, however definite the substance of a non-normative provision—certain clauses of the Helsinki Final Act, say, or of the Charter of Economic Rights and Duties of States—that will not turn it into a legal norm. Yet the fact remains that the proliferation of 'soft' norms, of what some also call 'hortatory' or 'programmatory' law, does not help strengthen the international normative system.

The conceptual weaknesses

4. Alongside those structural weaknesses—which a jurist may observe but is powerless to modify—the international normative system also suffers from failings that must rather be ascribed to a certain slackness in intellectual grasp. This time, it is not a question of inherent flaws but of conceptual weaknesses that jurists can strive to remove. One is already familiar and need not be dwelt upon, namely, the lack of rigor too often shown nowadays in handling the distinction between the non-normative and the normative. The other is more recent, and to it we shall devote our attention: it is the conception of variable normativity for which certain theories now in process of elaboration are paving the way.

The blurring of the normativity threshold

5. The acts accomplished by subjects of international law are so diverse in character that it is no simple matter for a jurist to determine what may be called the normativity threshold: *i.e.*, the line of transition between the non-legal and the legal, between what does not constitute a norm and what does. At what point does a 'nonbinding agreement' turn into an international agreement, a promise into a unilateral act, fact into custom? Of course, this problem of the transition from non-law to law occurs in all legal systems, in particular under the guise of the distinction between moral and legal obligation. But the multiplicity of the forms of action secreted by the needs of international intercourse has rendered it more acute in that field than in any other, since in the international order neither prenormative nor normative acts are as clearly differentiated in their effects as in municipal systems. While prenormative acts do not create rights or obligations on which reliance may be placed before an international court of justice or of arbitration, and failure to live up to them does not give rise to international responsibility, they do create expectations and exert on the conduct of states an influence that in certain cases may be greater than that of rules of treaty or customary law. Conversely, the sanction visited upon the breach of a legal obligation is sometimes less real than that imposed for failure to honor a purely moral or political obligation.

D. Shelton, 'International Law and Relative Normativity'
in M. Evans (ed), *International Law* (4th edn, 2014)

'Relative normativity' is a question of hierarchy of norms and the definition of law. As such, it concerns the nature, structure, and content of the international legal system. In practice issues of relative normativity arise in determining whether a legal rule exists to govern a problem, and in deciding whether priority must be given to a specific rule or interpretation among several that may be applicable to a legal matter or dispute.

Systems of law usually establish a hierarchy of norms based on the particular source from which the norms derive. In national legal systems, it is commonplace for the fundamental values of society to be given constitutional status and afforded precedence in the event of a conflict with norms enacted by legislation or adopted by administrative regulation; administrative rules themselves must conform to legislative mandates, while written law usually takes precedence over unwritten law and legal norms prevail over non-legal (political or moral) rules. The mode of legal reasoning applied in practice is thus naturally hierarchical, establishing relationships and order among normative statements and levels of authority (Koskenniemi, 1997).

The question of hierarchy or relative normativity in international law is unsettled and controversial. There has been growing attention paid to the issue in the two decades since a seminal article highly critical of the concept appeared in 1983 (Weil, 1983). In practice, conflicts among norms and their interpretation are probably inevitable in the present, largely decentralized international legal system where each State is entitled initially and equally to interpret for itself the scope of its obligations and the means of implementation such obligations require. The interpretations or determinations of applicable rules may vary considerably, making all international law somewhat relative, in the absence of institutions competent to render authoritative interpretations binding on all States.

Conceptual problems abound in determining relative normativity, in part because almost every purported principle of precedence (eg, *lex specialis derogate lex generali*) has exceptions and no rule establishes when to apply the principle and when to apply the expectation. There appears to be a fundamental supremacy of process over content, however, because the identification of legal norms and their relative normativity occurs only through consideration of the procedural norms that allow recognition of substantive rules. Some scholars argue from the ICJ Statute and from the sovereign equality of States that no hierarchy exists and logically there can be none: international rules are equivalent, sources are equivalent, and procedures are equivalent (Dupuy, 1995, pp 14–16) all deriving from the will of States. Others point to the concept of the community of States as a whole, expressed in Article 53 of the Vienna Convention on the Law of Treaties (VCLT) as an emerging limit on unilateral relativism (Salcedo, 1997, p 588)....

Legal regulation, however, has become perhaps the most prevalent response to social problems during the last century…but recent evolution in the international legal system has fostered a burgeoning interest in the issue. These developments appear particularly important. The first development centres on the role of consent in determining legal obligation. International law has traditionally been defined as a system of equal and sovereign States whose actions are limited only by rules freely accepted as legally binding. The emergence of global resource crises such as the widespread depletion of commercial fish stocks, destruction of the stratospheric ozone layer, and anthropogenic climate change, has produced growing concern about the 'free rider', the holdout State that benefits from legal regulation accepted by others while enhancing its own profits through continued utilization of the resource or by on-going production and sale of banned substances. The traditional consent-based international legal regime lacks a legislature to override the will of dissenting States, but efforts to affect their behavior are being made, first through the doctrine of peremptory norms applicable to all States, and, secondly, through expanding the concept of international law to include 'soft law'. The same approach may be taken with States seeking to denounce or acting to violate multilateral agreements that reflect widely and deeply held values, such as human rights or humanitarian law.

In respect to 'soft law', States inside and outside international organizations now often place normative statements and agreements in non-legally binding or political instruments such as declarations, resolutions, and programmes of action. These instruments may make it easier to press dissenting States into conforming behaviour because international law permits States to use political pressure to induce others conform to legal norms the latter have not accepted. Non-binding commitments may be entered into precisely to reflect the will of international community to resolve a pressing global problem over the objections of the one or few States causing the problem, while avoiding the doctrinal barrier of their lack of consent to be bound by the norm.

The second development that spurs consideration of relative normativity is substantial expansion of international law. Until the twentieth century, treaties were nearly all bilateral and the subject matter of international legal regulation mostly concerned diplomatic relations, the seas and other international waterways, trade, and extradition. Today, the number of international instruments has grown substantially, multilateral regulatory treaties are common, the topics governed by international law have proliferated and non-State actors are increasingly part of the system. This complexity demands consideration and development of means to reconcile conflicts of norms within a treaty or given subject area, for example, the law of the sea, as well as across competing regimes, such as free trade and environmental protection.

New topics of regulation also require innovative means of rule-making with respect to non-State actors, who generally are not parties to treaties or involved in the creation of customary international law. The emergence of codes of conduct and other 'soft law' reflects this development....

Third, the emergence of international criminal law has led to considering the nature of international crimes and the relationship of this body of law to doctrines of obligations *jus cogens*, discussed below, and obligations *erga omnes*. The ICJ was the first to identify the category of obligations *erga omnes* in dicta in the *Barcelona Traction* case. Unlike obligations arising in respect to specific injured States (eg, in the field of diplomatic protection), obligations *erga omnes* are owed to the international community as a whole. The broad nature of the obligation could be based upon the fact that such obligations generally aim at regulating the internal behaviour of a State, such as in the field of human rights, and thus there are likely to be no States materially affected by a breach. The principle of effectiveness thus supports broad standing, because without it violations could not be challenged. However, the rationale stated by the ICJ for recognizing this category of obligations appears more substantive: that 'in view of the importance of the rights involved, all States can be held to have a legal interest in their protection'. This statement suggests that obligations *erga omnes* have specific and broad procedural consequences because of the substantive importance of the norms they enunciate. In addition, the fact that all States can complain of a breach may make it more likely that a complaint will be made following commission of a wrongful act, suggesting a higher priority accorded these norms even if they are not considered substantively superior. The ICJ's examples of such obligations included the outlawing of aggression and genocide and the protection from slavery and racial discrimination.

Like obligations *erga omnes*, international crimes are so designated because the acts they sanction are deemed of such importance to the international community that individual criminal responsibility should result from their commission. Unlike obligations *erga omnes*, however, international criminal norms can pose problems of relative normativity. It has been clear since the Nuremburg Trials that conforming to or carrying out domestic law is no excuse for breach of international criminal law; it would seem plausible as well, if unlikely to arise in practice that a defence would fail based on carrying out norms of international law, such as those contained in a liberal treaty, if those norms contradict the requirements of criminal law. In this respect, norms of criminal law could be given supremacy over other international law in practice.

Other aspects of the inter-relationship of these categories of norms and the sources that create them should be noted. First, neither the designation of international crimes or obligations *erga omnes* involves a purported new source of law; crimes are created and defined through the conclusion of treaties; obligations *erga omnes* through treaty and customary international law. Secondly, it appears logical that all international crimes are obligations *erga omnes* because the international community as a whole identifies and may prosecute and punish the commission of such crimes. The reverse is not the case, however. Not all obligations *erga omnes* have been designated as international crimes. Racial discrimination, for example, is cited as an obligation *erga omnes*, but is not included among international crimes.

A. Cassese, 'For an Enhanced Role of *Jus Cogens*'

in A. Cassese (ed) *Realizing Utopia: The Future of International Law* (2012)

In sum, how could the role of *jus cogens*, a concept so crucial to the new international society, be enhanced in the next decades?

I think that *three paths* could be taken. First, international and national courts should increasingly rely on this notion, so as to contribute to the consolidation of existing peremptory norms and to the identification and recognition of emerging or incipient norms. As states and other international legal subjects are unlikely to insist on the notion or invoke it in international disputes, one should perforce turn to courts for this important action. Areas where promising developments are likely include human rights, humanitarian law (where the banning of cruel weapons causing unnecessary suffering, and the urgent need to step up the protection of civilians are likely to lead sooner or later to the formation of *jus cogens*) as well as international criminal law (where the norms banning and penalizing war crimes and crimes against humanity, and attributing universal jurisdiction over such crimes, can be considered as nascent peremptory norms in need of consolidation and specification) as well as environmental law.

Another crucial area is that of state immunity and immunity for state agents. State immunity and functional immunity of state agents are concepts belonging to the old international society. International dealings broke down into bilateral relationships, consequently there was a need to protect states from interference in domestic or international affairs by other states, and no collective body existed representing the whole membership of the society and proclaiming universal and non-derogable values. The world order is now different. Universal values have emerged, and the concept of accountability has firmly established itself. There is now no longer a need for the safeguards...

Also the area of treaty-making can be affected or influenced by *jus cogens*. For instance, reservations should increasingly be subjected to the scrutiny of imposed by peremptory norms, with the consequence that any reservation inconsistent with such a norm should be held to be inadmissible. Furthermore, *jus cogens* should be taken into account when interpreting treaties or other international instruments such as resolutions adopted by international organizations. If one of the various possible constructions runs counter to a peremptory norm, it should be rejected and another interpretation should be preferred that would be consistent with that norm.

The second avenue that should be taken relates to the domestic implementation of peremptory norms...the best way of ensuring national respect for those norms lies in passing national legislation imposing compliance with those norms. As noted, for such legislation to have a realistic chance of being passed, it would be necessary both to refer specifically in it to a set of peremptory norms that have widely been accepted in the world community and to provide that, with regard to any other norm of *jus cogens* asserted by a party, the ICJ must have the final say.

Finally, international civil society might play a significant role in prodding states and other international subjects as well as national courts increasingly to proclaim and comply with fundamental values upheld in *jus cogens* rules. This role should not be underestimated. Non-governmental organizations, as well as distinguished scholars and practitioners could underline the crucial importance of *jus cogens* for the new reality of the world community. Given the importance of the 'acceptance' of those principles and the way in which such 'acceptance' may take shape those organizations could stimulate international intergovernmental organizations and other international entities to pronounce on such principles. They could stress that a core of constitutional principles has revolutionized the mere 'contractual dimension' of the international law of the past and now yields sway in the world society, setting standards that no one, not even the UN Security Council, may shun. These principles, besides restraining the previous unfettered normative autonomy of sovereign states, also have a crucial impact of the daily conduct of states in international dealings and in their own domestic legal systems. To consolidate and expand them means to strengthen the collective will of the international community and make universal values override short-term national interests.

NOTES

1. Article 38(1) of the ICJ Statute does not provide a hierarchy of legal norms and there is no 'constitutional' court within the legal community to which such questions can be addressed (see further Chapter 16). The extract from Shelton discusses the question of whether there is a hierarchy of norms in the international legal order, as well as noting important changes, such as *erga omnes* obligations and peremptory (or *jus cogens*) norms, that have occurred.

2. States now accept that a limited number of international legal principles have attained the status of *jus cogens* norms, or peremptory norms from which no derogation is permitted. This concept, which originated in the law of treaties (see further Chapter 3), clearly impacts other areas of international law, such as recognition of States (Chapter 5), human rights (Chapter 6), state immunity (Chapter 9) and international criminal law (Chapter 14). Yet there is no consensus as to how to identify the existence or emergence of a *jus cogens* norm, and the content and force of a particular *jus cogens* norm, particularly where there is a possible 'clash' of norms. Despite—or perhaps because of—the role of *jus cogens* norms in elevating 'community values' over the self-interest of states, the concept is not often asserted by States or only used rarely by international or national courts to 'strike down' or sanction inconsistent norms or conduct. The extract from Cassese suggests ways in which the force and effect of *jus cogens* norms could be enhanced. In 2015, the ILC decided to include the topic of *jus cogens* in its programme of work.

SECTION 10: CODIFICATION AND DEVELOPMENT OF INTERNATIONAL LAW

UK Statement to the Sixth Committee of the General Assembly, 12 November 1996
67 British Yearbook of International Law 703 (1996)

'Codification' is a process designed to pin down the unique 'right solution' which represents what the law is at the given moment. 'Progressive development', on the other hand, necessarily entails an element of choice as to how the law *should* develop; various solutions are possible, none uniquely right, even if one seems (to the Commission) better than others. It is quite possible that over the years the Commission, in eliding the distinction, has been guilty of disguising this element of choice. Policy choices have been presented in the language of codification, as if they were uniquely right solutions, or at least uniquely preferable solutions. It would seem far better for the Commission to acknowledge the element of choice, indeed to go out of its way to identify the choices and explain the criteria. To provide guidance in this way would not only make the entire process of choice and recommendation more transparent, it would also be of positive benefit to Governments in their responses if the Commission guided them on their way, possibly by pointing out the consequences foreseen from making one choice rather than another. This would not prevent, or even inhibit, the Commission from stating what its own preference would be.

A. Boyle and C. Chinkin, *The Making of International Law*

(2007)

There remains outstanding a number of important empirical and theoretical questions. The most relevant is whether non-state actors (and in particular social and business sector NGOs in light of their ECOSOC consultative status) play an independent law-making role or whether they merely exert influence on governments. While there is undoubtedly an ever-growing number of international NGOs, many of which are exceedingly active in promoting international law-making, and there has certainly been a greater NGO presence at institutional meetings, expert groups, diplomatic conferences, prepcoms, meetings of states parties and other crucial meetings, the actual influence they have had on the development of international law is empirically uncertain. NGOs do have a catalytic effect. They bring issues onto the international agenda, make recommendations in their own name at international meetings, and wording emanating from NGOs has found its way into texts. However their participation is determined by the treaty or particular Rules of Procedure and invariably their accreditation excludes voting. Their precise influence on a final text can be difficult to gauge after what might have been a long and complex negotiation process....Nevertheless there are examples where it is safe to say that a treaty (or other instrument) would not have been adopted, or would not have been adopted in the particular form or at that time, without NGO action....NGOs have been most influential in law-making in special issue areas, notably human rights, environmental matters and international humanitarian law (the last through the unique position of the ICRC). These are areas of international regulation that impact directly upon individuals, which may explain the high level of NGO involvement compared with, for example, the law of the sea and the WTO....As is apparent from the examples where NGOs pushed for a international treaty where there was no governmental interest, it is not crucial at the initial stages to have the support of a major government, although not engaging the active opposition of important military, political or economic interests might be...

Nevertheless, despite the multiple NGO activities...and their often forceful presence, states retain a tight grip on the formal law-making processes, even in those areas where NGOs have had greatest impact. States control the agenda and access to the international arenas relevant for hard and soft law-making, in particular through accreditation to consultative status with ECOSOC and to meetings. Other devices such as imposing high admission fees, limiting space, ticket allocations and speaking time all reduce the effectiveness of NGO attendance at particular meetings. NGOs may be excluded from crucial stages of negotiations and states have the final word in the adoption of the text. The participation of NGOs throughout all the preparatory stages of the negotiation of the Rome Statute did not prevent the Conference Chair preparing the final text as a package that he thought would be an acceptable compromise for states, with some NGOs disappointed with some aspects of the outcome. States retain the final word through adoption, accession and ratification procedures and the power in some cases to make reservations. Soft measures of enforcement may also minimise changes sought by NGOs.

NOTES

1. The ILC was established by the General Assembly in 1947 to promote the codification and progressive development of international law. It consists of 34 members ('eminent jurists') sitting in an individual capacity and not as representatives of States. It holds two regular sessions each year and reports annually to the Sixth Committee of the General Assembly. The ILC has a close relationship to member States, which comment regularly on its work and provide input into the projects selected by the Commission. However, ultimately, the ILC tends to adopt a balanced position, 'reflecting its nature as an independent body of experts rather than representatives of States, but a body whose clients, to whom it reports and who can give life to its work product, are States': R. Rosenstock, 'The ILC and State Responsibility' 96 AJIL 792 (2002), p. 793.

2. The ILC routinely has a number of projects in hand. Current projects include treaties over time and the impact of subsequent agreements and practice on the interpretation of treaties, provisional application of treaties, the most-favoured-nation clause and the identification of customary international law (see Section 4). The work of the ILC would qualify as a work of the 'most highly qualified publicists' under Article 38(1)(d) of the ICJ Statute.

3. ILC proposals may well go on to form the basis of an international treaty. A good example is the Statute of the International Criminal Court (see Chapter 14). In addition, the ILC may produce a set of Draft Articles. These Articles might codify customary international law or aid in its development. For example, the Articles on State Responsibility (see Chapter 11) have been cited by the ICJ and several international tribunals. It is often difficult to determine which parts of a set of Draft Articles represent customary international law as it is now as opposed to the law as the ILC would like it to be.

4. Other United Nations bodies may also be involved in codification. The General Assembly can establish ad hoc committees, which are monitored by the Sixth Committee. In particular, the Ad Hoc Committee on Terrorism has been responsible for drafting various conventions concerning measures on international terrorism, including the yet to be finalised Comprehensive Convention against International Terrorism.

5. Non-governmental organisations, transnational corporations and individuals all contribute in various ways to the sources of international law, as is discussed in the extract from Boyle and Chinkin. While such entities do not have the same relationship with States as the ILC, they may make important contributions to many areas of international law (see Chapter 5).

3

The Law of Treaties

INTRODUCTORY NOTE

Treaties are evidence of the express consent of States to regulate their interests according to international law. They are an important source of international law, as seen in Chapter 2, and are used with increasing frequency to codify, to crystallise and to develop international law. They are particularly useful when States need to change or reorganise their obligations under international law rapidly, sometimes to reflect the changed reality of international society. The majority of international legal relationships between States are now governed by treaties.

The law of treaties is often equated by those unfamiliar with the subject with the national law of contracts. However, most analogies with contract law are misleading, particularly when analysing multilateral treaties, being treaties between more than two parties. With multilateral treaties, the rights and obligations of each party in respect of each of the other parties may vary significantly, especially due to 'reservations' to the terms of the treaty made by each party. In this sense, a multilateral treaty (being a treaty between many States) provides both a framework for basic principles binding on all parties and a mechanism whereby the precise relationships between individual parties can be adjusted to meet particular requirements. Treaties can also appear to have a legislative role in that they may establish a standard for all parties that creates universal or near universal international law. The 1982 Law of the Sea Convention, regulating much about the seas, is of this nature (see Chapter 10).

As the number of treaties increased, it became necessary for rules to be developed that governed the obligations of States in relation to the treaty process itself; for example, rules about how treaties are formed, how they are interpreted and the consequences for breaching them. These rules, which essentially establish a procedural framework for all the parties to a treaty, are most useful if they establish rules applicable to all types of treaty, whether they be bilateral (a treaty between two States) or multilateral and irrespective of their subject matter. The 'law of treaties' concerns these rules, and includes such matters as the initial process of the formation of treaties, their entry into force, principles of treaty interpretation, the procedures for invalidating and terminating treaties as well as the limitations (e.g. reservations) that States may place on their consent to be bound by a treaty.

SECTION 1: DEFINITION OF A TREATY

The primary reason for determining whether certain agreements, statements or other actions constitute a treaty, is that rights and obligations may then arise to which the law of treaties is applicable. Most treaties are concluded once the express consent of all the parties has been reached and usually there is little doubt that 'a treaty' has been concluded. However, occasionally it is not clear whether the contact between States has given rise to a treaty and in some circumstances it seems that even unilateral statements by State representatives may be regarded as being binding on that State in its dealings with other States.

A: General definition of a treaty

Vienna Convention on the Law of Treaties 1969
1158 UNTS 331

Article 2 Use of Terms
1. For the purposes of the present Convention:
    (a) 'treaty' means an international agreement concluded between States in written form and governed by international law, whether embodied in a single instrument or in two or more related instruments and whatever its particular designation

Case concerning Maritime Delimitation and Territorial Questions between Qatar and Bahrain (Qatar v Bahrain)
ICJ Rep 1994 112, International Court of Justice (Jurisdiction—First Phase)

This dispute related to competing claims of sovereignty over islands, shoals and maritime areas situated between the two States. The first aspect of the dispute to be considered by the Court was whether it had jurisdiction to decide the case. The basis of jurisdiction revolved around whether exchanges of letters between the Heads of each State—by which it was agreed to submit the dispute to the Court—were 'treaties' and so binding in international law. The Court held that it had jurisdiction.

22. The Parties agree that the exchanges of letters of December 1987 constitute an international agreement with binding force in their mutual relations. Bahrain however maintains that the Minutes of 25 December 1990 were no more than a simple record of negotiations, similar in nature to the Minutes of the Tripartite Committee; that accordingly they did not rank as an international agreement and could not, therefore, serve as a basis for the jurisdiction of the Court.

23. The Court would observe, in the first place, that international agreements may take a number of forms and be given a diversity of names [see] Article 2, paragraph (1)(a), of the Vienna Convention on the Law of Treaties of 23 May 1969…Furthermore, as the Court said, in a case concerning a joint communiqué, 'it knows of no rule of international law which might preclude a joint communiqué from constituting an international agreement to submit a dispute to arbitration or judicial settlement' (Aegean Sea Continental Shelf, Judgment, ICJ Reports 1978, p. 39, para. 96). In order to ascertain whether an agreement of that kind has been concluded, 'the Court must have regard above all to its actual terms and to the particular circumstances in which it was drawn up' (ibid.).

25. Thus the 1990 Minutes include a reaffirmation of obligations previously entered into; they entrust King Fahd with the task of attempting to find a solution to the dispute during a period of six months; and lastly, they address the circumstances under which the Court could be seised after May 1991.…Accordingly, and contrary to the contentions of Bahrain, the Minutes are not a simple record of a meeting, similar to those drawn up within the framework of the Tripartite Committee; they do not merely give an account of discussions and summarize points of agreement and disagreement. They enumerate the commitments to which the Parties have consented. They thus create rights and obligations in international law for the Parties. They constitute an international agreement.…

27. The Court does not find it necessary to consider what might have been the intentions of the Foreign Minister of Bahrain or, for that matter, those of the Foreign Minister of Qatar. The two Ministers signed a

text recording commitments accepted by their Governments, some of which were to be given immediate application. Having signed such a text, the Foreign Minister of Bahrain is not in a position subsequently to say that he intended to subscribe only to a 'statement recording a political understanding', and not to an international agreement....

29. The Court would observe that an international agreement of treaty that has not been registered with the Secretariat of the United Nations may not, according to the provisions of Article 102 of the Charter, be invoked by the parties before any organ on the United Nations. Non-registration or late registration, on the other hand, does not have any consequence for the actual validity of the agreement, which remains no less binding upon the parties.

30. The Court concludes that the Minutes of 25 December 1990, like the exchanges of letters of December 1987, constitute an international agreement creating rights and obligations for the Parties.

NOTES

1. There are many designations used other than 'treaty' to refer to an agreement binding in international law. These include, for example, 'convention', 'protocol', 'declaration', 'charter', 'covenant', 'agreement' and 'concordat'. The term 'treaty' is thus a generic description of the legal instrument by which States (and, in principle, other competent international legal persons) create binding international obligations.

2. Article 2(1)(a) of the Vienna Convention on the Law of Treaties 1969 (Vienna Convention) confirms that it is the *effect* of an agreement, rather than the nomenclature attributed to it, that is relevant. In *Qatar* v *Bahrain*, the International Court of Justice indicated that an exchange of letters can constitute an international agreement binding between those States. In *Land and Maritime Boundary (Cameroon* v *Nigeria)* ICJ Rep 2002 303, the Court found that a Joint Communiqué issued at the end of a summit meeting, which had been signed by the Heads of State of the two States, constituted an international agreement that had entered into force immediately.

3. Article 80 of the Vienna Convention provides that after a treaty enters into force, the treaty must be registered with the Secretariat of the United Nations. While an 'unregistered' treaty remains legally binding between the parties and fully operative in international law, by virtue of Article 102 of the United Nations Charter, an unregistered treaty may not be invoked before the ICJ or any UN organ.

4. The Vienna Convention applies only to treaties between States (Article 1). However, this does not affect the legality of agreements between States and other subjects of international law (Article 3). Indeed, it is possible to have treaties between a State and an international organisation and between international organisations, to which the law of treaties applies—see the Vienna Convention on the Law of Treaties Between States and International Organisations 1986, 25 ILM 543 (1986), Article 1. The capacity of international organisations to conclude treaties is governed by the constituent instrument or rules of that organisation, as the organisation may have treaty-making capacity only for some purposes.

5. There are an increasing number of agreements between States and private entities, mainly dealing with commercial matters. The ICJ has indicated that the law of treaties does not apply to these agreements, because these agreements do 'not regulate in any way the relations between... Governments' (*Anglo-Iranian Oil Case (United Kingdom* v *Iran) (Preliminary Objection)* ICJ Rep 1952 93, at p. 112). However, in *Texaco Overseas Petroleum Company* v *The Libyan Arab Republic* 53 ILR (1977) 389, the view was taken that private entities may be able to take advantage of general rules of international law in areas such as nationalisation and expropriation in order to invoke rights which result from the agreement with the State (see Chapter 13). There are also multilateral treaties (usually between States) which govern the legal aspects of these agreements between States and private entities; for example, the Convention on the Settlement of Investment Disputes Between States and Nationals of Other States 1966.

6. Some international agreements are intended not to be legally binding, and not to be 'governed by international law' as Article 2 of the Vienna Convention envisages. A prominent example is the Final Act of the Helsinki Conference on Security and Co-operation in Europe 1975 (15 ILM 1292 (1975)), although the terms of this agreement might be used as evidence of State practice.

B: Unilateral statements

Sometimes a State can be legally bound under international law even though it has acted unilaterally through its representatives.

Nuclear Test Cases (Australia v France and New Zealand v France)
Merits, ICJ Rep 1974 253, International Court of Justice

Australia and New Zealand brought proceedings against France arising from nuclear tests conducted by France in the South Pacific. Before the Court had an opportunity to hear in full the merits of the case, statements were made by French authorities indicating that France would no longer conduct atmospheric nuclear tests. The Court held by nine votes to six that, due to these statements by France, the claim of Australia and New Zealand no longer had any purpose and so the Court did not have to decide the issues in the case.

43. It is well recognized that declarations made by way of unilateral acts, concerning legal or factual situations, may have the effect of creating legal obligations. Declarations of this kind may be, and often are, very specific. When it is the intention of the State making the declaration that it should become bound according to its terms, that intention confers on the declaration the character of a legal undertaking, the State being thenceforth legally required to follow a course of conduct consistent with the declaration. An undertaking of this kind, if given publicly, and with an intent to be bound, even though not made within the context of international negotiations, is binding. In these circumstances, nothing in the nature of a *quid pro quo* nor any subsequent acceptance of the declaration, nor even any reply or reaction from other States, is required for the declaration to take effect, since such a requirement would be inconsistent with the strictly unilateral nature of the juridical act by which the pronouncement by the State was made....

45. With regard to the question of form, it should be observed that this is not a domain in which international law imposes any special or strict requirements. Whether a statement is made orally or in writing makes no essential difference, for such statements made in particular circumstances may create commitments in international law, which does not require that they should be couched in written form. Thus the question of form is not decisive....

46. One of the basic principles governing the creation and performance of legal obligations, whatever their source, is the principle of good faith. Trust and confidence are inherent in international co-operation, in particular in an age when this co-operation in many fields is becoming increasingly essential. Just as the very rule of *pacta sunt servanda* in the law of treaties is based on good faith, so also is the binding character of an international obligation assumed by unilateral declaration. Thus interested States may take cognizance of unilateral declarations and place confidence in them, and are entitled to require that the obligation thus created be respected....The Court must however form its own view of the meaning and scope intended by the author of a unilateral declaration which may create a legal obligation, and cannot in this respect be bound by the view expressed by another State which is in no way a party to the text.

49. Of the statements by the French Government now before the Court, the most essential are clearly those made by the President of the Republic. There can be no doubt, in view of his functions, that his public communications or statements, oral or written, as Head of State, are in international relations acts of the French State. His statements, and those of members of the French Government acting under his authority, up to the last statement made by the Minister of Defence (of 11 October 1974), constitute a whole. Thus, in whatever form these statements were expressed, they must be held to constitute an engagement of the State, having regard to their intention and to the circumstances in which they were made.

50. The unilateral statements of the French authorities were made outside the Court, publicly and *erga omnes*, even though the first of them was communicated to the Government of Australia. As was observed above, to have legal effect, there was no need for these statements to be addressed to a particular State, nor was acceptance by any other State required. The general nature and characteristics of these statements are decisive for the evaluation of the legal implications, and it is to the interpretation of the statements that the Court must now proceed. The Court is entitled to presume, at the outset, that these statements were not made *in vacuo*,

but in relation to the tests which constitute the very object of the present proceedings, although France has not appeared in the case.

51. In announcing that the 1974 series of atmospheric tests would be the last, the French Government conveyed to the world at large, including the Applicant, its intention effectively to terminate these tests. It was bound to assume that other States might take note of these statements and rely on their being effective. The validity of these statements and their legal consequences must be considered within the general framework of the security of international intercourse, and the confidence and trust which are so essential in the relations among States. It is from the actual substance of these statements, and from the circumstances attending their making, that the legal implications of the unilateral act must be deduced. The objects of these statements are clear and they were addressed to the international community as a whole, and the Court holds that they constitute an undertaking possessing legal effect. The Court considers that the President of the Republic, in deciding upon the effective cessation of atmospheric tests, gave an undertaking to the international community to which his words were addressed. It is true that the French Government has consistently maintained, for example in a Note dated 7 February 1973 from the French Ambassador in Canberra to the Prime Minister and Minister for Foreign Affairs of Australia, that it 'has the conviction that its nuclear experiments have not violated any rule of international law', nor did France recognize that it was bound by any rule of international law to terminate its tests, but this does not affect the legal consequences of the statements examined above. The Court finds that the unilateral undertaking resulting from these statements cannot be interpreted as having been made in implicit reliance on an arbitrary power of reconsideration. The Court finds further that the French Government has undertaken an obligation the precise nature and limits of which must be understood in accordance with the actual terms in which they have been publicly expressed.

NOTE: It is very rare that a Court will find that a unilateral statement will bind a State. In *Frontier Dispute Case (Burkina Faso* v *Mali)* 1986 ICJ Rep 554, a Chamber of the ICJ held that a statement made by the President of Mali at a press conference did *not* create legal obligations on Mali. The Chamber took the view that 'it has a duty to show even greater caution when it is a question of a unilateral declaration not directed to any particular recipient' (para. 39). Similarly, in *Case Concerning Armed Activities on the Territory of the Congo (New Application 2002)* (2006), the Court found that a statement made by the Rwandan Minister of Justice concerning the withdrawal of Rwandan reservations to various human rights instruments (see extract in Section 3A) did not constitute a unilateral declaration with binding legal effect, as the statement was of an indeterminate nature, with no precise time-scale for withdrawal; at most 'it can be interpreted as a declaration of intent, very general in scope' (para. 52). However, in *Questions Relating to the Seizure and Detention of Certain Documents (East Timor* v *Australia)* (Order), ICJ Rep 2014 147, the ICJ seemingly accepted that Australia's Attorney-General could bind Australia through his statements, even though that role does not fall within the category of persons presumed to be capable of binding the State (see Article 7(2) of the Vienna Convention).

C: Nature of a treaty

M. Craven, 'Legal Differentiation and the Concept of the Human Rights Treaty in International Law'

11 *European Journal of International Law* 489 (2000)

In their simplest form, treaties are conceived primarily in terms of an analogy with contracts in municipal law—that is, as consensual arrangements instituting, through the medium of legal rights and duties, a reciprocal exchange of goods or benefits. If that is the case the claim to non-reciprocity on the part of certain human rights treaties suggests that they are either an entirely novel form of treaty, or perhaps not treaties at all. Such a conclusion, however, is dependent upon the extent to which reciprocity is understood as a critical element of treaty law, and upon how that reciprocity is conceptualized.... [T]here seems no doubt that, according to the [Vienna] Convention [on the Law of Treaties], the 'agreement' is constituted in a mutual expression of consent.... In this context, the principle *pacta sunt servanda* [see Section 3C] must mean not just that 'promises shall be kept', as is so often assumed, but more specifically and literally, that 'agreements shall be followed'. It is, in other words, the multi-party, or relational, dimension of *pactum* that is central to the assumption of obligations in treaty law.

If treaties can only really be understood as 'agreements' between mutually consenting parties, it does not necessarily follow that they are to be regarded as 'reciprocal'. Indeed, it is apparent that as explanatory mediums the concepts of reciprocity and consent do not necessarily pull in the same direction.…Whilst theoretically distinct, each account of obligation exposes the incompleteness of the other: an emphasis on consent will potentially lead to one being bound by terms that are unfair; and an emphasis on reciprocity will potentially lead one to being bound in ways that one did not choose.…Consent and reciprocity are not, in that sense, mutually reinforcing, and indeed may supplant one another for the purposes of determining the presence of obligation in particular circumstances.…

Indeed, it is clear that the [Vienna] Convention does not invoke any concept of 'consideration' or 'cause' for the purpose of determining the obligatory effect of treaties. Such an understanding is reflected in general doctrine: it is possible after all, to conceive of treaties in which one state simply agrees to do something with no substantive or formal *quid pro quo*. The unconditional cession of territory from one state to another by means of a treaty might be a good example, as indeed may be the conclusion of a treaty of peace.…

Whilst it may be concluded, therefore, that treaties are not necessarily marked by any form of 'reciprocal exchange' of goods or benefits, the importance placed upon the 'mutuality' of consent suggest that some form of reciprocity might nevertheless be relevant.…Reciprocity [can be considered to be material exchange and psychological agreement as well as being] expressive of a mutual, but conditional, exchange of legal obligations in which the possession of rights and obligations of one party are linked to (and perhaps dependent upon) those of the other party.…The logic of reciprocity, however, derives not so much from the nature of treaty relations, *per se*, but from the apparent imperatives of the decentralized international system.…It is only by reason of reciprocity, therefore, that states will be able to participate in international relations without exposing themselves unduly to the risks involved with non-compliance on the part of other states: it provides the means, in other words, by which states may effectively 'police' those obligations by means of self-help.

N. White, 'The United Nations System: Conference, Contract or Constitutional Order?'
4 *Singapore Journal of International and Comparative Law* 281 (2000)

Attempts have been made, mainly since the adoption of the League of Nations Covenant in 1919 to suggest that there is a considerable distinction to be drawn between ordinary 'contractual' bilateral or multilateral treaties and 'constitutional' multilateral treaties. Such a suggestion was quite a radical departure from the view that international law was in essence private law between consenting states acting as equals, rather than any form of public law.…If we move from the post-1919 world order to the post-1945 order, the picture…is one of societal values shaping, informing and regulating the operation of a complex set of institutions, within a system framed by legal instruments of foundational significance. It is clear that the UN system is not governed by a series of treaties, but is governed by a complex constitution, with the UN Charter at its heart.…It is arguable that in 1945 the UN Charter was constructed as a constitutional document and not simply as an international treaty, a fact indicated by the opening words of the UN Charter—'We the Peoples of the United Nations'. What is clear is that the Charter has become a constitution, indeed is the foundational constitutional document in the UN system.

NOTES
1. Treaties may be categorised and compared in a number of ways: by extent of participation (bilateral/multilateral, regional/global); by subject matter (environment, law of the sea, trade, human rights); by structure (combinations of treaties/single treaty); and function. A treaty is both a procedural instrument and a source of obligation, with most of the law of treaties dealing with the former (e.g. formation, entry into force and termination).
2. As was noted in the introduction to this chapter, treaties are sometimes considered to be similar to contracts, sometimes to legislation and sometimes to constitutions. As is seen in the two extracts above, the nature of a treaty will often depend on the subject matter, the parties to the treaty and the effect of the treaty. Therefore it is arguable that, at least in relation to some treaties, the requirement that parties must demonstrate real consent has not been 'frontally assaulted but cunningly outflanked' (P. Weil, 'Towards Relative Normativity in International Law' 77 *American Journal of International Law* 413 (1983), 438).

3. Craven notes that two of the key elements of a treaty are consent and reciprocity but these do not always operate coherently. He concludes that because human rights treaties 'not only serve to place certain limits upon the nature and scope of governmental authority but also contribute to the development of a justifiable basis for that authority (albeit in no unproblematic manner), they cannot therefore simply be regarded as the accidental data of an otherwise disinterested legal system' and so are not 'only treaties' (p. 519). See further Chapter 6.

SECTION 2: VIENNA CONVENTION ON THE LAW OF TREATIES 1969

The Vienna Convention on the Law of Treaties 1969 ('the Vienna Convention') is the principal source of law for 'the law of treaties'. It entered into force on 27 January 1980, upon the deposit of the 35th instrument of ratification (pursuant to Article 84). As of 31 March 2016 there were 114 parties to the Vienna Convention. As its Preamble states, it was intended to codify and to develop the law of treaties.

A: General principles

I. Sinclair, *The Vienna Convention on the Law of Treaties*
(2nd edn, 1984)

Having regard to the significance of treaties as a primary source of international law, and having regard equally to the range and complexity of the law of treaties, it may be permissible to express satisfaction that this major enterprise in the field of codification and progressive development of international law—an enterprise which was embarked upon by the International Law Commission as early as 1949—has achieved finality, and has achieved it in the form of a Convention which has, albeit after more than ten years, attracted sufficient support from States to bring it into force. But satisfaction must be tempered with realism. The Convention is the product of many conflicting interests and viewpoints and has the customary vices of compromise. Among these is a tendency to overcome points of difficulty by expressing rules at a level of generality and abstraction sufficient to hide the underlying disagreements.

B: Customary international law

A. Aust, *Modern Treaty Law and Practice*
(3rd edn, 2013)

When law of treaty questions arise during negotiations, whether for a new treaty or about one concluded before the entry into force of the [Vienna] Convention, the rules set forth in the Convention are invariably relied upon even when the states are not parties to it. This author [who was for many years an experienced legal adviser in the British Foreign and Commonwealth Office] can recall at least three bilateral treaty negotiations when he had to respond to arguments of the other side which relied heavily on specific articles of the Convention, even though the other side had not ratified it....

Whether a particular rule in the Convention represents customary international law is only likely to be an issue if the matter is litigated, and even then the Court or tribunal will take the Convention as its starting—and normally also its finishing—point. This is certainly the approach taken by the International Court of Justice, as well as other courts and tribunals, international and national.... There has as yet been no case where the

Court has found that the Convention does not reflect customary law. This is not surprising. Despite what some critics of the Convention may assert, any codification of the law will inevitably reduce the scope for judicial law making. For most practical purposes treaty questions are resolved by applying the rules of the Convention. To attempt to determine whether a particular substantive provision of the Convention represents customary international law is now a rather futile task.... [T]he modern law of treaties is now authoritatively set out in the Convention.

NOTE: The application of the Vienna Convention itself is limited in theory. The Convention (being a treaty) is binding only on its parties, and as such is unlikely to apply directly to multilateral agreements because not all parties to the multilateral treaty are likely also to be parties to the Vienna Convention. However, as a codification of customary international law, the application of the Convention can be extended to all other treaties, including treaties between non-parties to the Convention and to treaties made prior to the Convention entering into force. Indeed, those provisions of the Vienna Convention which are not declaratory of customary international law may constitute evidence of emerging rules of international law.

SECTION 3: FORMATION AND APPLICATION OF TREATIES

A: Formation

Vienna Convention on the Law of Treaties 1969

Article 6 Capacity of States to conclude treaties
Every State possesses capacity to conclude treaties.

Article 7 Full powers
1. A person is considered as representing a State for the purpose of adopting or authenticating the text of a treaty or for the purpose of expressing the consent of the State to be bound by a treaty if:
    (a) he produces appropriate full powers [these are defined in Article 2(1) (c)]; or
    (b) it appears from the practice of the States concerned or from other circumstances that their intention was to consider that person as representing the State for such purposes and to dispense with full powers.

Article 8 Subsequent confirmation of an act performed without authorisation
An act relating to the conclusion of a treaty performed by a person who cannot be considered under article 7 as authorised to represent a State for that purpose is without legal effect unless afterwards confirmed by that State.

Article 11 Means of expressing consent to be bound by a treaty
The consent of a State to be bound by a treaty may be expressed by signature, exchange of instruments constituting a treaty, ratification, acceptance, approval or accession, or by any other means if so agreed.

Article 12 Consent to be bound by a treaty expressed by signature
1. The consent of a State to be bound by a treaty is expressed by the signature of its representative when:
    (a) the treaty provides that signature shall have that effect;
    (b) it is otherwise established that the negotiating States were agreed that signature should have that effect; or
    (c) the intention of the State to give that effect to the signature appears from the full powers of its representative or was expressed during the negotiation.

Article 14 Consent to be bound by a treaty expressed by ratification, acceptance or approval
1. The consent of a State to be bound by a treaty is expressed by ratification when:
    (a) the treaty provides for such consent to be expressed by means of ratification;

> (b) it is otherwise established that the negotiating States were agreed that ratification should be required;
> (c) the representative of the State has signed the treaty subject to ratification; or
> (d) the intention of the State to sign the treaty subject to ratification appears from the full powers of its representative or was expressed during the negotiation.
>
> 2. The consent of a State to be bound by a treaty is expressed by acceptance or approval under conditions similar to those which apply to ratification.
>
> **Article 15 Consent to be bound by a treaty expressed by accession**
>
> The consent of a State to be bound by a treaty is expressed by accession when:
> (a) the treaty provides that such consent may be expressed by that State by means of accession;
> (b) it is otherwise established that the negotiating States were agreed that such consent may be expressed by that State by means of accession; or
> (c) all the parties have subsequently agreed that such consent may be expressed by that State by means of accession.

Case Concerning Armed Activities on the Territory of the Congo
(New Application: 2002) (Democratic Republic of the Congo v Rwanda)
ICJ Rep 2006 6, International Court of Justice (Jurisdiction and Admissibility)

The Court was required to consider the legal effect of a statement made by the Minister of Justice of Rwanda, regarding the proposed withdrawal of Rwandan reservations to various human rights treaties, including the Genocide Convention.

> 46. The Court will begin by examining Rwanda's argument that it cannot be legally bound by the statement in question inasmuch as a statement made not by a Foreign Minister or a Head of Government 'with automatic authority to bind the State in matters of international relations, but by a Minister of Justice, cannot bind the State to lift a particular reservation'.... [I]t is a well-established rule of international law that the Head of State, the Head of Government and the Minister for Foreign Affairs are deemed to represent the State merely by virtue of exercising their functions, including for the performance, on behalf of the said State, of unilateral acts having the force of international commitments. The Court moreover recalls that, in the matter of the conclusion of treaties, this rule of customary law finds expression in Article 7, paragraph 2, of the Vienna Convention on the Law of Treaties....
>
> 47. The Court notes, however, that with increasing frequency in modern international relations other persons representing a State in specific fields may be authorized by that State to bind it by their statements in respect of matters falling within their purview. This may be true, for example, of holders of technical ministerial portfolios exercising powers in their field of competence in the area of foreign relations, and even of certain officials.
>
> 48. In this case, the Court notes first that Ms Mukabagwiza spoke before the United Nations Commission on Human Rights in her capacity as Minister of Justice of Rwanda and that she indicated *inter alia* that she was making her statement 'on behalf of the Rwandan people'. The Court further notes that the questions relating to the protection of human rights which were the subject of that statement fall within the purview of a Minister of Justice. It is the Court's view that the possibility cannot be ruled out in principle that a Minister of Justice may, under certain circumstances, bind the State he or she represents by his or her statements. The Court cannot therefore accept Rwanda's argument that Ms Mukabagwiza could not, by her statement, bind the Rwandan State internationally, merely because of the nature of the functions that she exercised.

NOTES
1. Care must be taken to distinguish between States that sign a treaty and those that ratify it. Most international treaties are made at international conferences where the text is adopted and often signed, but legally binding consent to the treaty usually is conditional upon subsequent ratification or accession (Articles 14, 15 of the Vienna Convention but see Article 18, set out in Section 3B).

2. Generally a State will be legally bound by a treaty only when it has ratified the treaty or has otherwise signified its consent to be bound and 'signing' the treaty does not usually amount to such consent. Ratification may depend on certain internal political (and sometimes legal) processes being observed, such as approval by a parliament or similar. The precise requirements will, of course, vary from State to State. States which were not original signatories to the treaty indicate their consent to be legally bound by 'accession' rather than 'ratification' (Article 15).

3. As an exception to the normal practice, a State may be legally bound by a treaty upon the signature of the treaty by the State (i.e. by its representative), but only if the treaty so provides, or if it is the intention of the State or if the parties to the treaty decide that signature amounts to binding consent (Article 11).

4. There is a distinction between ratification and compliance. A State may ratify a treaty but if it does not comply with it then it is in breach of its international obligations under that treaty (see Chapter 11 on the law of State responsibility).

B: Entry into force

Vienna Convention on the Law of Treaties 1969

Article 18 Obligation not to defeat the object and purpose of a treaty prior to its entry into force

A State is obliged to refrain from acts which would defeat the object and purpose of a treaty when:
   (a) it has signed the treaty or has exchanged instruments constituting the treaty subject to ratification, acceptance or approval, until it shall have made its intention clear not to become a party to the treaty; or
   (b) it has expressed its consent to be bound by the treaty, pending the entry into force of the treaty and provided that such entry into force is not unduly delayed.

Article 24 Entry into force

1. A treaty enters into force in such manner and upon such date as it may provide or as the negotiating States may agree.

2. Failing any such provision or agreement, a treaty enters into force as soon as consent to be bound by the treaty has been established for all the negotiating States.

3. When the consent of a State to be bound by a treaty is established on a date after the treaty has come into force, the treaty enters into force for that State on that date, unless the treaty otherwise provides.

4. The provisions of a treaty regulating the authentication of its text, the establishment of the consent of States to be bound by the treaty, the manner or date of its entry into force, reservations, the functions of the depositary and other matters arising necessarily before the entry into force of the treaty apply from the time of the adoption of its text.

Article 25 Provisional application

1. A treaty or part of a treaty is applied provisionally pending its entry into force if:
   (a) The treaty itself so provides; or
   (b) The negotiating States have in some other manner so agreed.

2. Unless the treaty otherwise provides or the negotiating State have otherwise agreed, the provisional application of a treaty or a part of a treaty with respect to a State shall be terminated if that State notifies the other States between which the treaty is being applied provisionally of its intention not to become a party to the treaty.

Article 28 Non-retroactivity of treaties

Unless a different intention appears from the treaty or is otherwise established, its provisions do not bind a party in relation to any act or fact which took place or any situation which ceased to exist before the date of the entry into force of the treaty with respect to that party.

Letter to the UN Secretary-General from the Under Secretary of State for Arms Control and International Security of the United States of America, 6 May 2002

Dear Mr. Secretary-General:

This is to inform you, in connection with the Rome Statute of the International Criminal Court adopted on July 17, 1998, that the United States does not intend to become a party to the treaty. Accordingly, the United States has no legal obligations arising from its signature on December 31, 2000. The United States requests that its intention not to become a party, as expressed in this letter, be reflected in the depositary's status lists relating to this treaty.

Sincerely,
John R. Bolton

International Law Commission, Provisional Application of Treaties

Second Report on the Provisional Application of Treaties (2014) UN Doc. A/CN.4/675

[An] emblematic case in relation to the legal effects of provisional application and, in particular, to the obligations arising from such application is the accession by the Syrian Arab Republic to the Convention on the Prohibition of the Development, Production, Stockpiling and Use of Chemical Weapons and on Their Destruction. The Syrian Arab Republic deposited its instrument of accession to this international treaty on 14 September 2013, and the treaty entered into force for that State on 14 October 2013. However, upon depositing its instrument of accession, the Syrian Arab Republic informed the United Nations Secretary-General, as depositary of the treaty, that it 'shall comply with the stipulations contained [in the Convention] and observe them faithfully and sincerely, applying the Convention provisionally pending its entry into force for the Syrian Arab Republic'....It was on this basis that the Executive Council of the Organization for the Prohibition of Chemical Weapons adopted its decision entitled 'Destruction of Syrian Chemical Weapons', in which it affirmed that 'the provisional application of the Convention gives immediate effect to its provisions with respect to the Syrian Arab Republic'.

NOTES
1. Many multilateral treaties provide that a certain number of States must have ratified (or acceded to) the treaty before the treaty enters into force. For example, the International Covenant on Civil and Political Rights provides in Article 49 that it will 'enter into force three months after the date of deposit with the Secretary-General of the United Nations of the thirty-fifth instrument of ratification or instrument of accession'.
2. Given that a multilateral treaty may take many years to enter into force, Article 18 of the Vienna Convention is an important provision as it obliges States not to defeat the object and purpose of the treaty between giving their consent to be bound and the entry into force of the treaty. Even if a treaty is not in force, the fact that many States have given their consent to be bound may be evidence of such a generality of State practice so as to amount to customary international law (see Chapter 2).
3. The United States of America's action in announcing that its signature to the Rome Statute that created the International Criminal Court (see Chapter 14) was to have no legal effect is consistent with Article 18(a) of the Vienna Convention in that a State does *not* have the obligation not to defeat the object and purpose of a treaty if it has 'made its intention clear not to become a party to the treaty'. This action was expressly said not to be an 'unsigning' or 'de-signing' of a treaty (if such can occur).
4. A treaty can be amended by agreement between the parties, though a separate treaty (often known as a 'protocol') is the usual method for changing the provisions of a treaty. The rules governing amendments are set out in Articles 39–41 of the Vienna Convention.
5. The ICJ seemingly referred to the existence of an obligation to negotiate in good faith when forming a treaty, when it stated that '[o]ne of the basic principles governing creation...of legal obligations, whatever their source, is the principle of good faith' (*Nuclear Tests Case (Australia v France)* [46] (see Section 1B)).

6. The report by the ILC indicates that the provisional application of treaties has become a frequently resorted to aspect of treaty application. See also the discussion in Chapter 15 about the possible use of force in regard to the alleged use by the Syrian government of chemical weapons.

C: *Pacta sunt servanda*

Vienna Convention on the Law of Treaties 1969

Article 26 *Pacta sunt servanda*
Every treaty in force is binding on the parties to it and must be performed by them in good faith.

Report of the International Law Commission to the General Assembly
Yearbook of the International Law Commission (1966) vol II, 172

(1) *Pacta sunt servanda*—the rule that treaties are binding on the parties and must be performed in good faith—is the fundamental principle of the law of treaties. Its importance is underlined by the fact that it is enshrined in the Preamble to the Charter of the United Nations. As to the Charter itself, paragraph 2 of Article 2 expressly provides that Members are to 'fulfil in good faith the obligations assumed by them in accordance with the present Charter'.

(2) There is much authority in the jurisprudence of international tribunals for the proposition that in the present context the principle of good faith is a legal principle which forms an integral part of the rule *pacta sunt servanda*. Thus, speaking of certain valuations to be made under articles 95 and 96 of the Act of Algeciras, the Court said in the *Case concerning Rights of Nationals of the United States of America in Morocco* (Judgment of 27 August 1954): 'The power of making the valuation rests with the Customs authorities, but it is a power which must be exercised reasonably and in good faith'. Similarly, the Permanent Court of International Justice, in applying treaty clauses prohibiting discrimination against minorities, insisted in a number of cases, that the clauses must be so applied as to ensure the absence of discrimination in fact as well as in law; in other words, the obligation must not be evaded by a merely literal application of the clauses. Numerous precedents could also be found in the jurisprudence of arbitral tribunals. To give only one example, in the *North Atlantic Coast Fisheries* arbitration the Tribunal dealing with Great Britain's right to regulate fisheries in Canadian waters in which she had granted certain fishing rights to United States nationals by the Treaty of Ghent, said; 'from the Treaty results an obligatory relation whereby the right of Great Britain to exercise its right of sovereignty by making regulations is limited to such regulations as are made in good faith, and are not in violation of the Treaty.'

NOTE: The principle of *pacta sunt servanda* is considered to be the primary explanation of why there is compliance with treaty obligations. The principle derives from the consent of States and is a principle of customary international law and possibly an example of a *jus cogens* obligation (see Chapter 2).

D: Impact of treaties on third States (non-parties)

Vienna Convention on the Law of Treaties 1969

Article 34 General rule regarding third States
A treaty does not create either obligations or rights for a third State without its consent.

Article 35 Treaties providing for obligations for third States

An obligation arises for a third State from a provision of a treaty if the parties to the treaty intend the provision to be the means of establishing the obligation and the third State expressly accepts that obligation in writing.

Article 36 Treaties providing for rights for third States

1. A right arises for a third State from a provision of a treaty if the parties to the treaty intend the provision to accord that right either to the third State, or to a group of States to which it belongs, or to all States, and the third State assents thereto. Its assent shall be presumed so long as the contrary is not indicated, unless the treaty otherwise provides.

2. A State exercising a right in accordance with paragraph 1 shall comply with the conditions for its exercise provided for in the treaty or established in conformity with the treaty.

Article 37 Revocation or modification of obligations or rights of third States

1. When an obligation has arisen for a third State in conformity with article 35, the obligation may be revoked or modified only with the consent of the parties to the treaty and of the third State, unless it is established that they had otherwise agreed.

2. When a right has arisen for a third State in conformity with article 36, the right may not be revoked or modified by the parties if it is established that the right was intended not to be revocable or subject to modification without the consent of the third State.

Article 38 Rules in a treaty becoming binding on third States through international custom

Nothing in articles 34 to 37 precludes a rule set forth in a treaty from becoming binding upon a third State as a customary rule of international law, recognized as such.

NOTES

1. While the Vienna Convention principles with regard to third party States' rights and obligations apply only to parties to the Vienna Convention itself, this rule is considered to represent customary international law—see *Free Zones of Upper Savoy and the District of Gex Case (France* v *Switzerland)*, PCIJ Rep, Ser A/B (1932), No. 46. Of course, where a treaty codifies existing customary international law, then the third State would be bound by that law in the normal way (see Chapter 2), subject to issues of immunity (see Chapters 9 and 14).

2. The special nature of the United Nations Charter (which is a treaty) may create obligations for the (few) non-parties to that treaty. Article 2(6) of the Charter provides that: 'The [United Nations] Organization shall ensure that States which are not Members of the United Nations act in accordance with [its] Principles so far as may be necessary for the maintenance of international peace and security'. In practice non-parties do act in accordance with these principles. For example, Switzerland, which was not then a party to the Charter (and so not a member of the UN), acted consistently with Security Council resolutions, imposing economic sanctions against Iraq during the first Gulf War (see Chapter 14). See also the *Reparations of Injuries Case* (Chapter 5), which dealt with the international personality of the UN in its dealing with States that were not members.

3. As a result of the United Nations Charter obligation on State parties to 'accept and carry out the decisions of the Security Council' (Article 26), the Security Council has been able to impose obligations that are substantively identical to those contained within a treaty on States that are not party to it (see also discussion of the Security Council as a legislature in Chapter 2). This was the case with Resolution 1373, which reproduces, almost verbatim, certain provisions of the International Convention for the Suppression of the Financing of Terrorism. The Security Council has also created legal obligations from a non-legally binding instrument, including for States that were not involved in the instrument's drafting. A Joint Comprehensive Plan of Action (JCPOA) was adopted in October 2015 regarding Iran's nuclear programme. Although this was largely perceived as a political, rather than legal, commitment, the Security Council effectively made this into a legal instrument by requiring that '[a]ll States shall comply with [certain] provisions' of the JCPOA (Resolution 2231). A similar example could be the actions of the Security Council when referring cases to the International Criminal Court (see Chapter 14).

E: State succession to treaties

Vienna Convention on Succession of States in Respect of Treaties 1978
1946 UNTS 3

This Convention entered into force on 6 November 1996 and, as of March 2016, 22 States had ratified it.

Article 2 Use of terms

(b) 'succession of States' means the replacement of one State by another in the responsibility for the international relations of territory;…

(f) 'newly independent State' means a successor State the territory of which immediately before the date of the succession of States was a dependent territory for the international relations of which the predecessor State was responsible;

Article 5 Obligations imposed by international law independently of a treaty

The fact that a treaty is not considered to be in force in respect of a State by virtue of the application of the present Convention shall not in any way impair the duty of that State to fulfil any obligation embodied in the treaty to which it is subject under international law independently of the treaty.

Article 6 Cases of succession of States covered by the present Convention

The present Convention applies only to the effects of a succession of States occurring in conformity with international law and, in particular, the principles of international law embodied in the Charter of the United Nations.

Article 8 Agreements for the devolution of treaty obligations or rights from a predecessor State to a successor State

1. The obligations or rights of a predecessor State under treaties in force in respect of a territory at the date of a succession of States do not become the obligations or rights of the successor State towards other States parties to those treaties by reason only of the fact that the predecessor State and the successor State have concluded an agreement providing that such obligations or rights shall devolve upon the successor State.

2. Notwithstanding the conclusion of such an agreement, the effects of a succession of States on treaties which, at the date of that succession of States, were in force in respect of the territory in question are governed by the present Convention.

Article 9 Unilateral declaration by a successor State regarding treaties of the predecessor State

1. Obligations or rights under treaties in force in respect of a territory at the date of a succession of States do not become the obligations or rights of the successor State or of other States parties to those treaties by reason only of the fact that the successor State has made a unilateral declaration providing for the continuance in force of the treaties in respect of its territory.

2. In such a case, the effects of the succession of States on treaties which, at the date of that succession of States, were in force in respect of the territory in question are governed by the present Convention.

Article 10 Treaties providing for the participation of a successor State

1. When a treaty provides that, on the occurrence of a succession of States, a successor State shall have the option to consider itself a party to the treaty, it may notify its succession in respect of the treaty in conformity with the provisions of the treaty or, failing any such provisions, in conformity with the provisions of the present Convention.

2. If a treaty provides that, on the occurrence of a succession of States, a successor State shall be considered as a party to the treaty, that provision takes effect as such only if the successor State expressly accepts in writing to be so considered.

3. In cases falling under paragraph 1 or 2, a successor State which establishes its consent to be a party to the treaty is considered as a party from the date of the succession of States unless the treaty otherwise provides or it is otherwise agreed.

Article 11 Boundary régimes

A succession of States does not as such affect:
- (a) a boundary established by a treaty; or
- (b) obligations and rights established by a treaty and relating to the régime of a boundary.

Article 12 Other territorial régimes

1. A succession of States does not as such affect:
    - (a) obligations relating to the use of any territory, or to restrictions upon its use, established by a treaty for the benefit of any territory of a foreign State and considered as attaching to the territories in question;
    - (b) rights established by a treaty for the benefit of any territory and relating to the use, or to restrictions upon the use, of any territory of a foreign State and considered as attaching to the territories in question.

2. A succession of States does not as such affect:
    - (a) obligations relating to the use of any territory, or to restrictions upon its use, established by a treaty for the benefit of a group of States or of all States and considered as attaching to that territory;
    - (b) rights established by a treaty for the benefit of a group of States or of all States and relating to the use of any territory, or to restrictions upon its use, and considered as attaching to that territory.

3. The provisions of the present article do not apply to treaty obligations of the predecessor State providing for the establishment of foreign military bases on the territory to which the succession of States relates.

Article 13 The present Convention and permanent sovereignty over natural wealth and resources

Nothing in the present Convention shall affect the principles of international law affirming the permanent sovereignty of every people and every State over its natural wealth and resources.

Article 15 Succession in respect of part of territory

When part of the territory of a State, or when any territory for the international relations of which a State is responsible, not being part of the territory of that State, becomes part of the territory of another State:
- (a) treaties of the predecessor State cease to be in force in respect of the territory to which the succession of States relates from the date of the succession of States; and
- (b) treaties of the successor State are in force in respect of the territory to which the succession of States relates from the date of the succession of States, unless it appears from the treaty or is otherwise established that the application of the treaty to that territory would be incompatible with the object and purpose of the treaty or would radically change the conditions for its operation.

Article 16 Position in respect of the treaties of the predecessor State

A newly independent State is not bound to maintain in force, or to become a party to, any treaty by reason only of the fact that at the date of the succession of States the treaty was in force in respect of the territory to which the succession of States relates.

Case Concerning the Arbitral Award of 31 July 1989 (Guinea-Bissau v Senegal)
83 ILR 1 (1992), Special Arbitration Tribunal

By a treaty in 1985, Guinea-Bissau and Senegal agreed to submit to international arbitration a dispute over their maritime boundaries. At the core of the dispute was whether an agreement in 1960 between Portugal and France (the former colonial powers over the relevant territories) was binding on Guinea-Bissau and Senegal as the successor States. The majority of the Tribunal held that the 1960 agreement was valid and binding.

33. A successor State can invoke before a tribunal all grounds of claim or objection which could have been invoked by the State to which it has succeeded. Consequently, Guinea-Bissau, as a successor State, is entitled to invoke before the Tribunal all the grounds of nullity which could have been raised by Portugal regarding the 1960 Agreement. Guinea-Bissau can also submit to the Tribunal any reasons for non-opposability to it of the Agreement, which in its view exclude succession to that Agreement. Similarly, Senegal can likewise invoke before the Tribunal all the grounds which, in its view, support the existence and validity of the Agreement and its effect in the present case.

Application of the Genocide Convention (Bosnia and Herzegovina v Yugoslavia (Serbia and Montenegro))

ICJ Rep 1993 325, International Court of Justice (Indication of Provisional Measures)

The facts are set out in Chapter 16. One of the key issues was whether each new State that arose from the former Yugoslavia could succeed to the Genocide Convention, which the former Yugoslavia had ratified. The Court did not have to make a final decision on this matter at the provisional measures stage but Judge Weeramantry gave a Separate Opinion that dealt with the matter of succession to human rights treaties.

JUDGE WEERAMANTRY (Separate Opinion): The principle that a new State ought not in general to be fettered with treaty obligations which it has not expressly agreed to assume after it has attained statehood (the clean slate principle) is of considerable historical and theoretical importance. New States ought not, in principle, to be burdened with treaty-based responsibilities without their express consent. With the sudden advent into the international community of nearly eighty newly independent States in the late fifties and early sixties, there was a realization among them, in the words of Julius Stone, that: 'their authority or their territory or both are burdened with debts, concessions, commercial engagements of various kinds or other obligations continuing on from the earlier colonial regime' [Julius Stone, 'A common law for mankind?', 1 *International Studies*, pp. 430–432 (1960)]. . . .

Theoretically, the clean slate principle can be justified on several powerful bases: the principle of individual State autonomy, the principle of self-determination, the principle of *res inter alios acta*, and the principle that there can be no limitations on a State's rights, except with its consent. Newly independent States should not have to accept as a *fait accompli* the contracts of predecessor States, for it is self-evident that the new State must be free to make its own decisions on such matters. The clean slate principle could also be described as an important corollary to the principle of self determination, which is of cardinal importance in modern international law. The principle of self determination could be emptied of an important part of its content if prior treaties automatically bind the new State. . . . Basic concepts of State sovereignty also require that any curtailment of the sovereign authority of a State requires the express consent of the State. If there is to be, in a given case, a deviation from the clean slate principle, sufficiently cogent reasons should exist to demonstrate that the new State's sovereignty is not being thereby impaired. The question needs therefore to be examined as to whether there is any impairment of State sovereignty implicit in the application of the principle of automatic succession to any given treaty.

Human rights and humanitarian treaties involve no loss of sovereignty or autonomy of the new State, but are merely in line with general principles of protection that flow from the inherent dignity of every human being which is the very foundation of the United Nations Charter. At the same time, it is important that the circle of exceptions should not be too widely drawn. Conceivably some human rights treaties may involve economic burdens, such as treaties at the economic end of the spectrum of human rights. It is beyond the scope of this Opinion to examine whether all human rights and humanitarian treaties should be exempted from the clean slate principle. It is sufficient for the purposes of this Opinion to note a variety of reasons why it has been contended that human rights and humanitarian treaties in general attract the principle of automatic succession. These reasons apply with special force to treaties such as the Genocide Convention or the Convention against Torture, leaving no room for doubt regarding automatic succession to such treaties. The international community has a special interest in the continuity of such treaties. . . . [He then sets out ten reasons why human rights and humanitarian treaties are exceptions to the general clean slate principle]

If the principle of continuity in relation to succession of States, adopted in Article 34(1) in the 1978 Vienna Convention on Succession of States in Respect of Treaties, is to apply to any treaties at all, the Genocide Convention must surely be among such treaties. . . . All of the foregoing reasons combine to create what seems to me to be a principle of contemporary international law that there is automatic State succession to so vital a human rights convention as the Genocide Convention. Nowhere is the protection of the quintessential human right—the right to life—more heavily concentrated than in that Convention. Without automatic succession to such a Convention, we would have a situation where the worldwide system of human rights protections continually generates gaps in the most vital part of its framework, which open up and close, depending on the break up of the old political authorities and the emergence of the new. The international legal system cannot condone a principle by which the subjects of these States live in a state of continuing uncertainty regarding the most fundamental of their human rights protections. Such a view would grievously tear the seamless fabric of international human rights protections, endanger peace, and lead the law astray from the Purposes and Principles of the United Nations, which all nations, new and old, are committed to pursue.

A. Rasulov, 'Revisiting State Succession to Humanitarian Treaties: Is There a Case for Automaticity?'

14 *European Journal of International Law* 141 (2003)

A critical review of state practice in the 1990s [finds that] the treaties of humanitarian character are not subject to automatic succession. Apart from one unique case, no successor state has acted as if succession to a humanitarian treaty could occur regardless of its will....[Nevertheless] [i]n the *German Settlers* case, the Permanent Court of International Justice pronounced that private property rights acquired by individuals did not cease simply by virtue of a change of sovereignty, but continued under the successor regime until modified according to regular procedures. Although 'acquired rights' and 'human rights' are not identical notions, reasonable analogies can be drawn here. After all, 'an acquired right is any right which, were there no territorial changes, would be protected by the courts in a lawful State'. History provides several examples of situations where human rights were treated on the basis of an 'acquisition logic'....Although extending the 'acquired rights' doctrine to humanitarian treaties would not necessarily make the treaties themselves automatically inheritable, such a measure could undoubtedly improve the overall legal environment.

NOTES

1. The issue of succession of States to treaties was important during the decolonisation era after the Second World War. It became a live issue again with the break-up of the federal republics of the Soviet Union and Yugoslavia: see, for example, the Agreement on Succession Issues between the five successor States of the Former Yugoslavia (41 ILM 1 (2002)).

2. In its judgment on the preliminary objections in the *Application of the Genocide Convention* (*Bosnia and Herzegovina* v *Yugoslavia* (*Serbia and Montenegro*) (*Preliminary Objections*) ICJ Rep 1996, the Court determined that Bosnia-Herzegovina was a party to the Genocide Convention. The Court declined to rule whether this was because of 'automatic succession' when it became independent from the former Yugoslavia (called the Socialist Federal Republic of Yugoslavia (SFRY)) (because of the special status of human rights treaties) or because it had deposited a Notice of Succession. Either way, it was a party at the relevant time. The Federal Republic of Yugoslavia (Serbia and Montenegro) did not dispute its status as a party to the Genocide Convention (as it asserted itself to be the successor State to the SFRY), and the Court held that it was also bound by the Convention.

3. In 2003, the Federal Republic of Yugoslavia (Serbia and Montenegro) applied for revision of the preliminary objections judgment on the basis that it had not been recognised as the successor State to the SFRY, and so was not bound by the Genocide Convention at the relevant time. The Court rejected this application, finding that new facts that warranted a revision of the judgment had not been presented: *Application for Revision of the Judgment of 11 July 1996 in the Case concerning Application of the Convention on the Prevention and Punishment of the Crime of Genocide (Bosnia and Herzegovina* v *Yugoslavia), Preliminary Objections (Yugoslavia* v *Bosnia and Herzegovina)* ICJ Rep 2003 (see Chapter 16). In its judgments on the merits in *Application of the Genocide Convention (Bosnia and Herzegovina* v *Yugoslavia* (*Serbia and Montenegro*) ICJ Rep 2007 and its decision in 2015 between Croatia and Serbia, the Court noted that Serbia cannot now contend that she is not 'Yugoslavia' for the purpose of the hearing as this objection was not raised during the 1996 hearings.

4. The Vienna Convention on Succession of States in Respect of Treaties 1978 reinforces the principle that a new State enters the international community with a 'clean slate'. This principle has some significant limitations—for example, a boundary treaty must be accepted—which are necessary for international peace and security (see Chapter 7). The Vienna Convention on Succession of States in Respect of Treaties 1978 also recognises limitations to this principle for boundary and territorial regimes (Articles 11–12). Judge Weeramantry (above) raises the possibility of other limitations to this principle, such as human rights and humanitarian law treaties. Generally, a new State will quickly become a party to many treaties in order to participate effectively as a member of the international community. Indeed, new States may well rush to join existing multilateral treaty regimes as a way of demonstrating that they have achieved full international personality.

SECTION 4: **RESERVATIONS TO TREATIES**

Reservations are the means whereby States accept as many of the rights and obligations under a treaty as possible, while expressly stating that there are some provisions of the treaty which they cannot accept. They are a useful and pragmatic device for ensuring that treaties do enter into force. However, reservations can have the effect of excluding altogether the legal effect of a particular provision of a treaty, or modifying or qualifying the extent of a provision.

A: General principles

Advisory Opinion Concerning Reservations to the Convention on the Prevention and Punishment of the Crime of Genocide
ICJ Rep 1951 15, International Court of Justice

The General Assembly sought an advisory opinion from the Court on the following questions:

In so far as concerns the Convention on the Prevention and Punishment of the Crime of Genocide, in the event of a State ratifying or acceding to the Convention subject to a reservation made either on ratification or on accession, or on signature followed by ratification:

I.   Can the reserving State be regarded as being a party to the Convention while still maintaining its reservation if the reservation is objected to by one or more of the parties to the Convention but not by others?

II. If the answer to Question I is in the affirmative, what is the effect of the reservation as between the reserving State and:

(a) The parties which object to the reservation?

(b) Those which accept it?

III. What would be the legal effect as regards the answer to Question I if an objection to a reservation is made:

(a) By a signatory which has not yet ratified?

(b) By a State entitled to sign or accede but which has not yet done so?

[As regards Question I]: It is well established that in its treaty relations a State cannot be bound without its consent, and that consequently no reservation can be effective against any State without its agreement thereto. It is also a generally recognized principle that a multilateral convention is the result of an agreement freely concluded upon its clauses and that consequently none of the contracting parties is entitled to frustrate or impair, by means of unilateral decisions or particular agreements, the purpose and *raison d'être* of the convention. To this principle was linked the notion of the integrity of the convention as adopted, a notion which in its traditional concept involved the proposition that no reservation was valid unless it was accepted by all the contracting parties without exception, as would have been the case if it had been stated during the negotiations....

It must also be pointed out that although the Genocide Convention was finally approved unanimously, it is nevertheless the result of a series of majority votes. The majority principle, while facilitating the conclusion of multilateral conventions, may also make it necessary for certain States to make reservations. This observation is confirmed by the great number of reservations which have been made of recent years to multilateral conventions.

In this state of international practice, it could certainly not be inferred from the absence of an article providing for reservations in a multilateral convention that the contracting States are prohibited from making certain reservations. Account should also be taken of the fact that the absence of such an article or even the decision not to insert such an article can be explained by the desire not to invite a multiplicity of reservations. The character of a multilateral convention, its purpose, provisions, mode of preparation and adoption, are factors which must be considered in determining, in the absence of any express provision on the subject, the possibility of making reservations, as well as their validity and effect....

The object and purpose of the Genocide Convention imply that it was the intention of the General Assembly and of the States which adopted it that as many States as possible should participate. The complete exclusion from the Convention of one or more States would not only restrict the scope of its application, but would detract from the authority of the moral and humanitarian principles which are its basis. It is inconceivable that the contracting parties readily contemplated that an objection to a minor reservation should produce such a result. But even less could the contracting parties have intended to sacrifice the very object of the Convention in favour of a vain desire to secure as many participants as possible. The object and purpose of the Convention thus limit both the freedom of making reservations and that of objecting to them. It follows that it is the compatibility of a reservation with the object and purpose of the Convention that must furnish the criterion for the attitude of a State in making the reservation on accession as well as for the appraisal by a State in objecting to the reservation. Such is the rule of conduct which must guide every State in the appraisal which it must make, individually and from its own standpoint, of the admissibility of any reservation....

It results from the foregoing considerations that Question I, on account of its abstract character, cannot be given an absolute answer. The appraisal of a reservation and the effect of objections that might be made to it depend upon the particular circumstances of each individual case.

[As regards Question II]: The considerations which form the basis of the Court's reply to Question I are to a large extent equally applicable here. As has been pointed out above, each State which is a party to the Convention is entitled to appraise the validity of the reservation, and it exercises this right individually and from its own standpoint. As no State can be bound by a reservation to which it has not consented, it necessarily follows that each State objecting to it will or will not, on the basis of its individual appraisal within the limits of the criterion of the object and purpose stated above, consider the reserving State to be a party to the Convention.

Vienna Convention on the Law of Treaties 1969

Article 2 Use of terms

(d) For the purposes of the present Convention ... 'reservation' means a unilateral statement, however phrased or named, made by a State, when signing, ratifying, accepting, approving or acceding to a treaty, whereby it purports to exclude or to modify the legal effect of certain provisions of the treaty in their application to that State.

Article 19 Formulation of reservations

A State may, when signing, ratifying, accepting, approving or acceding to a treaty, formulate a reservation unless:

(a) the reservation is prohibited by the treaty;
(b) the treaty provides that only specified reservations, which do not include the reservation in question, may be made; or
(c) in cases not falling under sub-paragraphs (a) and (b), the reservation is incompatible with the object and purpose of the treaty.

Article 23 Procedure regarding reservations

1. A reservation, an express acceptance of a reservation and an objection to a reservation must be formulated in writing and communicated to the contracting States and other States entitled to become parties to the treaty.

2. If formulated when signing the treaty subject to ratification, acceptance or approval, a reservation must be formally confirmed by the reserving State when expressing its consent to be bound by the treaty. In such a case the reservation shall be considered as having been made on the date of its confirmation.

3. An express acceptance of, or an objection to, a reservation made previously to confirmation of the reservation does not itself require confirmation.

4. The withdrawal of a reservation or of an objection to a reservation must be formulated in writing.

Belilos v Switzerland

ECHR Ser A (1988) Vol 132, European Court of Human Rights

Belilos claimed that she had not been given a fair trial in Switzerland in contravention of Article 6 of the European Convention on Human Rights. Switzerland objected to the case proceeding on the basis that, when it ratified the Convention, it had made an 'interpretative declaration' concerning Article 6. The Court held that the Swiss 'interpretative declaration' was in reality a reservation. However, it was not a valid reservation (being too broad in scope) within the requirements of Article 64 (which set out the requirements for a valid reservation). The Court then upheld the applicant's claim against Switzerland.

47. The [Swiss] Government derived an additional argument from the fact that there had been no reaction from the Secretary General of the Council of Europe or from the States Parties to the Convention.... The Swiss Government inferred that it could in good faith take the declaration as having been tacitly accepted for the purposes of Article 64. The Court does not agree with that analysis. The silence of the depository and the Contracting States does not deprive the Convention institutions of the power to make their own assessment....

48....Like the Commission and the Government, the Court recognises that it is necessary to ascertain the original intention of those who drafted the declaration. In its view, the documents show that Switzerland originally contemplated making a formal reservation but subsequently opted for the term 'declaration'....

49. The question whether a declaration described as 'interpretative' must be regarded as a 'reservation' is a difficult one, particularly—in the instant case—because the Swiss Government has made both 'reservations' and 'interpretative declarations' in the same instrument of ratification. More generally, the Court recognises the great importance, rightly emphasised by the Government, of the legal rules applicable to reservations and interpretative declarations made by States Parties to the Convention. Only reservations are mentioned in the Convention, but several States have also (or only) made interpretative declarations, without always making a clear distinction between the two.

In order to establish the legal character of such a declaration, one must look behind the title given to it and seek to determine the substantive content. In the present case, it appears that Switzerland meant to remove certain categories of proceedings from the ambit of Article 6(1) and to secure itself against an interpretation of that Article which it considered to be too broad. However, the Court must see to it that the obligations arising under the Convention are not subject to restrictions which would not satisfy the requirements of Article 64 as regard reservations. Accordingly, it will examine the validity of the interpretative declaration in question, as in the case of a reservation, in the context of this provision....

60. In short, the declaration does not satisfy two of the requirements of Article 64 of the Convention, with the result that it must be held to be invalid. At the same time, it is beyond doubt that Switzerland is, and regards itself as, bound by the Convention irrespective of the Validity of the declaration. Moreover, the Swiss Government recognised the Court's competence to determine the latter issue.

NOTES

1. The *Belilos* case shows that the status of the 'declaration' depends on an assessment of what it seeks to achieve, which is made by interpreting the text of the declaration and its legal effect (see Section 4B). If its effect is to make the State's consent to the treaty conditional upon the acceptance of the content of the declaration, rather than merely offering an interpretation of the treaty, the declaration will be treated as a reservation.

2. The rules in the Vienna Convention on reservations are based on the fundamental rule that all States that are parties to a treaty should be subject to the same rights and obligations under it. This is always the case with bilateral treaties, in which instance a reservation is better considered as a counter-offer which the other party can accept or refuse, resulting in either the conclusion or rejection of the treaty as drafted. However, where a multilateral treaty is concerned, a State may decide, for a variety of political, social and legal reasons, to restrict the extent to which it is bound by all of the treaty's obligations. This is usually done by making

a written reservation to the treaty when signing, ratifying, accepting, approving or acceding to the treaty. Reservations can be withdrawn at any time. Most treaties today have some provision regarding reservations, in which case that specific provision will apply instead of the rules of the Vienna Convention.

3. The extent to which reservations to treaties should be allowed is a question of considerable importance. On the one hand, there is a desire to preserve the 'integrity' of a treaty so that all parties are equally bound by the same obligations. On the other hand, there is the goal of securing wide participation in treaties even if all parties do not accept every detail of every obligation. The latter is particularly the case where a treaty may be regarded as 'standard-setting', such as many human rights treaties (see Chapter 6) and the Law of the Sea Convention 1982 (see Chapter 10). International tribunals recognise that reservations are an expression of a State's limitation on its consent to be bound, but they are also astute to prevent a reservation from compromising the central object and purpose of a treaty.

4. The Articles in the Vienna Convention concerning reservations are generally in line with the conclusions reached by the ICJ in the Advisory Opinion Concerning Reservations to the Genocide Convention. This part of the Vienna Convention is considered to reflect customary international law.

5. A reservation may be made unless the treaty prohibits it, or the reservation is not among the list of specified permissible reservations (given by the treaty itself) or it is incompatible with the object and purpose of the treaty: see Article 19 of the Vienna Convention.

B: The legal effect of reservations

Vienna Convention on the Law of Treaties 1969

Article 20 Acceptance of and objection to reservations

1. A reservation expressly authorized by a treaty does not require any subsequent acceptance by the other contracting States unless the treaty so provides.

2. When it appears from the limited number of negotiating States and the object and purpose of a treaty that the application of the treaty in its entirety between all the parties is an essential condition of the consent of each one to be bound by the treaty, a reservation requires acceptance by all the parties.

3. When a treaty is a constituent instrument of an international organization and unless it otherwise provides, a reservation requires the acceptance of the competent organ of that organization.

4. In cases not falling under the preceding paragraphs and unless the treaty otherwise provides:
    (a) acceptance by another contracting State of a reservation constitutes the reserving State a party to the treaty in relation to that other State if or when the treaty is in force for those States;
    (b) an objection by another contracting State to a reservation does not preclude the entry into force of the treaty as between the objecting and reserving States unless a contrary intention is definitely expressed by the objecting State;
    (c) an act expressing a State's consent to be bound by the treaty and containing a reservation is effective as soon as at least one other contracting State has accepted the reservation.

5. For the purposes of paragraphs 2 and 4 and unless the treaty otherwise provides, a reservation is considered to have been accepted by a State if it shall have raised no objection to the reservation by the end of a period of twelve months after it was notified of the reservation or by the date on which it expressed its consent to be bound by the treaty, whichever is later.

Article 21 Legal effects of reservations and of objections to reservations

1. A reservation established with regard to another party in accordance with articles 19, 20 and 23:
    (a) modifies for the reserving State in its relations with that other party the provisions of the treaty to which the reservation relates to the extent of the reservation; and
    (b) modifies those provisions to the same extent for that other party in its relations with the reserving State.

2. The reservation does not modify the provisions of the treaty for the other parties to the treaty *inter se*.

3. When a State objecting to a reservation has not opposed the entry into force of the treaty between itself and the reserving State, the provisions to which the reservation relates do not apply as between the two States to the extent of the reservation.

Article 22 Withdrawal of reservations and of objections to reservations

1. Unless the treaty otherwise provides, a reservation may be withdrawn at any time and the consent of a State which has accepted the reservation is not required for its withdrawal.

2. Unless the treaty otherwise provides, an objection to a reservation may be withdrawn at any time.

3. Unless the treaty otherwise provides, or it is otherwise agreed:
   (a) the withdrawal of a reservation becomes operative in relation to another contracting State only when notice of it has been received by that State;
   (b) the withdrawal of an objection to a reservation becomes operative only when notice of it has been received by the State which formulated the reservation.

Case Concerning Armed Activities on the Territory of the Congo (New Application: 2002) (Democratic Republic of the Congo v Rwanda)
ICJ Rep 6 (2006), International Court of Justice (Jurisdiction and Admissibility)

When considering whether the Court had jurisdiction, the Court had to consider whether Rwanda's reservation to the Genocide Convention was valid. It concluded that it was, as it was a reservation to a dispute resolution clause only (see Chapter 16). The Court's conclusion on this issue caused several judges to issue a separate opinion on the issue of reservations.

JUDGES HIGGINS, KOOIJMANS, ELARABY, OWADA AND SIMMA (SEPARATE OPINION)

4. In recent years there has been a tendency for some States, and certain commentators, to view the Court's 1951 Advisory Opinion on *Reservations to the Convention on the Prevention and Punishment of the Crime of Genocide* as stipulating a régime of inter-State *laissez-faire* in the matter of reservations, in the sense that while the object and purpose of a convention should be borne in mind both by those making reservations and those objecting to them, everything in the final analysis is left to the States themselves.

5. In our view a proper reading of the 1951 Advisory Opinion suggests that this conclusion is too sweeping. The Court in 1951 was answering certain specific questions put to it by the General Assembly; what it said has to be understood against that background....

9. The Court in 1951 was clearly not unaware of the hazards inherent in its answers, in the sense that they would entail a veritable web of diverse reciprocal commitments within the framework of a multilateral convention....

10. In the event, the problems which the Court could already envisage in 1951 have turned out to be vastly greater than it could have foreseen. The Genocide Convention stood virtually alone in the sphere of human rights in 1951. Since then it has been added to by a multitude of multilateral conventions, to which States have not hesitated to enter a plethora of reservations—often of a nature that gives serious concern as to compatibility with the object and purpose of the treaty concerned. And the vast majority of States, who the Court in 1951 envisaged would scrutinize and object to such reservations, have failed to engage in this task.

11. The assumption of the Court in 1951 that 'it is the compatibility of a reservation with the object and purpose of the Convention that must furnish the criterion for the attitude of a State in making the reservation on accession as well as for the appraisal by a State in objecting to the reservation' (p. 24), with a view to balancing the freedom to make reservations and the scrutiny and objections of other States, has turned out to be unrealized: a mere handful of States do this. For the great majority, political considerations would seem to prevail.

12. The Court itself was not in 1951 asked to pronounce on the compatibility of particular reservations to the Genocide Convention with its object and purpose—nor indeed whether its answers as to the role of States in making and responding to reservations precluded it from doing so. Since 1951 many other issues relating to reservations have emerged, that equally were not and could not have been before the Court at that time. Among

them are whether, in particular, a role as regards assessment of compatibility with object and purpose is to be assigned to monitoring bodies established under United Nations multilateral human rights treaties. Another related question not asked of the Court in 1951 concerns the scope of powers given to courts at the centre of great human rights treaties, such as the Inter-American Court on Human Rights, the European Court of Human Rights, and, for the future, the African Court on Human and Peoples' Rights. The Court in 1951 had no occasion to address the application of the law of treaties to issues of severability in the context of reservations to human rights treaties. And the Vienna Convention on the Law of Treaties, concluded in 1969, is not wholly unambiguous on these points especially in its Article 19. There are many other issues concerning reservations that were not covered by the Court's Advisory Opinion in 1951, either because they had not been put to the Court or because they had not yet arisen in State practice.

English Channel Arbitration (*United Kingdom* v *France*)

54 ILR 6 (1977), Special Court of Arbitration

The case concerned the continental shelf boundary in the English Channel. Both States were parties to the Geneva Convention on the Continental Shelf 1958. However, France had entered reservations to Article 6 (regarding the 'equidistance principle') which were objected to by the United Kingdom. Consequently, the Court of Arbitration had first to determine the law applicable to the dispute.

59. The Court considers that the answer to the question of the legal effect of the French reservations lies partly in the contentions of the French Republic and partly in those of the United Kingdom. Clearly, the French Republic is correct in stating that the establishment of treaty relations between itself and the United Kingdom under the Convention depended on the consent of each State to be mutually bound by its provisions; and that when it formulated its reservations to Article 6 it made its consent to be bound by the provisions of that Article subject to the conditions embodied in the reservations. There is, on the other hand, much force in the United Kingdom's observation that its rejection was directed to the reservations alone and not to Article 6 as a whole. In short, the disagreement between the two countries was not one regarding the recognition of Article 6 as applicable in their mutual relations but one regarding the matters reserved by the French Republic from the application of Article 6. The effect of the United Kingdom's rejection of the reservations is thus limited to the reservations themselves.…

61. In a more limited sense, however, the effect of the rejection may properly, in the view of the Court, be said to render the reservations non-opposable to the United Kingdom. Just as the effect of the French reservations is to prevent the United Kingdom from invoking the provisions of Article 6 except on the basis of the conditions stated in the reservations, so the effect of their rejection is to prevent the French Republic from imposing the reservations on the United Kingdom for the purpose of invoking against it as binding a delimitation made on the basis of the conditions contained in the reservations. Thus, the combined effect of the French reservations and their rejection by the United Kingdom is neither to render Article 6 inapplicable *in toto*, as the French Republic contends, nor to render it applicable *in toto*, as the United Kingdom primarily contends. It is to render the Article inapplicable as between the two countries to the extent, but only to the extent, of the reservations; and this is precisely the effect envisaged in such cases by Article 21, paragraph 3 of the Vienna Convention on the Law of Treaties and the effect indicated by the principle of mutuality of consent.

62. The fact that Article 6 is not applicable as between the Parties to the extent that it is excluded by the French reservations does not mean that there are no legal rules to govern the delimitation of the boundary in areas where the reservation operates. On the contrary, as the International Court of Justice observed in the *North Sea Continental Shelf* cases, 'there are still rules and principles of law to be applied' (ICJ Rep 1969, para 83); and these are the rules and principles governing delimitation of the continental shelf in general international law.

D. Bowett, 'Reservations to Non-Restricted Multi-Lateral Treaties'

48 *British Yearbook of International Law* 67 (1976)

6. The question of 'permissibility' is always a question to be resolved as a matter of construction of the treaty and does *not* depend on the reactions of the Parties. Therefore, though each Party may have to determine whether it regards a reservation as permissible, in the absence of any 'collegiate' system it must do so on the basis of

whether the treaty permits such a reservation. The issue of 'permissibility' is thus entirely separate from the issue of 'opposability', that is to say whether a Party accepts or does not accept a reservation which is permissible.

7. Parties may not accept an impermissible reservation.

8. As to permissible reservations, with non-restricted multilateral treaties, a reservation which is expressly authorized…requires no acceptance and takes effect with the reserving State's acceptance of the treaty. That apart, permissible reservations may meet with the following three reactions from other Parties:

(i)   acceptance of the reservation: the effect is that the treaty is in force and the reservation takes full effect between the reserving and accepting States, on a reciprocal basis;

(ii) objection to the reservation: the effect is that the treaty is in force, but *minus* the provision affected by the reservation *to the extent of the reservation*. The reservation is not 'opposable' to the objecting State;

(iii) objection to the reservation and an express objection to the treaty's entering into force: the effect is that the reserving and objecting States are not in any treaty relationship. Neither the treaty nor the reservation is 'opposable' to the objecting State.

9. The objecting State, exercising either of the last two options set out in conclusion 8 above, is free to object on any ground: that is to say, its objection is not confined to the ground of 'incompatibility' with the object and purpose of the treaty.

NOTES

1. While there is no need for a State to object to an impermissible reservation, the extract from Bowett (above) sets out the three options available to a State when considering how to react to a permissible reservation. Note, however, that some reservations require the approval of *all* State parties to the treaty in question. If a State makes no express response to a reservation then it may be bound by virtue of Article 20(5) of the Vienna Convention (though it is debatable whether this subsection represents customary international law).

2. A valid reservation accepted by a party to the treaty modifies the treaty between it and the re-serving State, but does not affect the treaty relations between the accepting party and any other State. Where a party has objected to a reservation (but not to the entry into force of the treaty between it and the reserving State) then the treaty is inapplicable between the party and the reserving State *to the extent of the reservation*. The *English Channel Arbitration* extract notes that the consequence of this position is that there is no express agreement between the two States concerning the issues covered by the reservation, but that other rules of international law may still apply.

3. The practical effect of the rules on reservations in respect of multilateral treaties is that they become, in effect, a series of bilateral treaties between States with the parties' precise legal rela-tions being dependent on how each State has reacted to other States' reservations. The judges in the Separate Opinion extract above are critical of the failure of a State to analyse the legality of various reservations and to respond accordingly.

4. While the Vienna Convention is silent as to the effect of an impermissible reservation, the fol-lowing section provides some useful clarifications on the matter.

C: Reservations to human rights treaties

General Comment on Issues Relating to Reservations UN Human Rights Committee, General Comment No 24

2 IHRR 10 (1995), UN Human Rights Committee

This General Comment was made in response to concerns that the large number and broad range of reservations to the International Covenant on Civil and Political Rights ('the Covenant') might undermine the effectiveness of the Covenant, as well as con-cerns about the general effect of the application of the Vienna Convention to reserva-tions to human rights treaties.

4. The possibility of entering reservations may encourage States which consider that they have difficulties in guaranteeing all the rights in the Covenant nonetheless to accept the generality of obligations in that instrument. Reservations may serve a useful function to enable States to adapt specific elements in their laws to the inherent rights of each person as articulated in the Covenant. However, it is desirable in principle that States accept the full range of obligations, because the human rights norms are the legal expression of the essential rights that every person is entitled to as a human being....

8. Reservations that offend peremptory norms would not be compatible with the object and purpose of the Covenant. Although treaties that are mere exchanges of obligations between States allow them to reserve *inter se* application of rules of general international law, it is otherwise in human rights treaties, which are for the benefit of persons within their jurisdiction. Accordingly, provisions in the Covenant that represent customary international law (and *a fortiori* when they have the character of peremptory norms) may not be the subject of reservations....

11. The Covenant consists not just of the specified rights, but of important supportive guarantees. These guarantees provide the necessary framework for securing the rights in the Covenant and are thus essential to its object and purpose. Some operate at the national level and some at the international level. Reservations designed to remove these guarantees are thus not acceptable....

13.... A reservation cannot be made to the Covenant through the vehicle of the Optional Protocol but such a reservation would operate to ensure that the State's compliance with that obligation may not be tested by the Committee under the first Optional Protocol....

17. [I]t is the Vienna Convention on the Law of Treaties that provides the definition of reservations and also the application of the object and purpose test in the absence of other specific provisions. But the Committee believes that its provisions on the role of State objections in relation to reservations are inappropriate to address the problem of reservations to human rights treaties. Such treaties, and the Covenant specifically, are not a web of inter-State exchanges of mutual obligations. They concern the endowment of individuals with rights. The principle of inter-State reciprocity has no place, save perhaps in the limited context of reservations to declarations on the Committee's competence under article 41. And because the operation of the classic rules on reservations is so inadequate for the Covenant, States have often not seen any legal interest in or need to object to reservations. The absence of protest by States cannot imply that a reservation is either compatible or incompatible with the object and purpose of the Covenant.

18. It necessarily falls to the Committee to determine whether a specific reservation is compatible with the object and purpose of the Covenant. This is in part because, as indicated above, it is an inappropriate task for States parties in relation to human rights treaties, and in part because it is the task that the Committee cannot avoid in the performance of its functions.... Because of the special character of a human rights treaty, the compatibility of a reservation with the object and purpose of the Covenant must be established objectively, by reference to legal principles, and the Committee is particularly well placed to perform this task. The normal consequence of an unacceptable reservation is not that the Covenant will not be in effect at all for a reserving party. Rather, such a reservation will generally be severable, in the sense that the Covenant will be operative for the reserving party without benefit of the reservation.

Rawle Kennedy v *Trinidad and Tobago*
7 IHRR 315 (2000), UN Human Rights Committee

Trinidad and Tobago had initially ratified the Optional Protocol to the Covenant (which allows individuals to bring complaints ('communications') to the UN Human Rights Committee) and then denounced it (i.e. withdrew from the Covenant) after a series of cases against it, especially in relation to Trinidad and Tobago's use of the death penalty. Trinidad and Tobago re-acceded to the Optional Protocol but this time included a reservation. The reservation stated:

'[T]he Human Rights Committee shall not be competent to receive and consider communications relating to any prisoner who is under sentence of death in respect of any matter relating to his prosecution, his detention, his trial, his conviction, his sentence or the carrying out of the death sentence on him and any matter connected therewith'.

In this case the Committee had to consider the effect of this reservation in relation to a complaint about the death penalty against Trinidad and Tobago. It decided that the complaint was admissible despite the reservation.

6.7. The present reservation, which was entered after the publication of General Comment No. 24, does not purport to exclude the competence of the Committee under the Optional Protocol with regard to any specific provision of the Covenant, but rather to the entire Covenant for one particular group of complainants, namely prisoners under sentence of death. This does not, however, make it compatible with the object and purpose of the Optional Protocol. On the contrary, the Committee cannot accept a reservation which singles out a certain group of individuals for lesser procedural protection than that which is enjoyed by the rest of the population. In the view of the Committee, this constitutes a discrimination which runs counter to some of the basic principles embodied in the Covenant and its Protocols, and for this reason the reservation cannot be deemed compatible with the object and purpose of the Optional Protocol. The consequence is that the Committee is not precluded from considering the present communication under the Optional Protocol.

International Law Commission, *Guide to Practice on Reservations to Treaties*
UN Doc. A/66/10/Add.1 (2011)

The divergent approach to reservations to human rights treaties was seen by some as an unjustifiable one which was fragmenting, and thus risking the coherence of, international law. This, alongside the existing gaps within the Vienna Convention, such as the effect of an impermissible reservation and the effect of such a determination on the reserving State's party status, led to the ILC seeking to identify an alternative approach, while also addressing some of the related uncertainties.

3.2 Assessment of the permissibility of reservations
The following may assess, within their respective competences, the permissibility of reservations to a treaty formulated by a State or an international organization:

- contracting States or contracting organizations;
- dispute settlement bodies;
- treaty monitoring bodies....

4.5.1 Nullity of an invalid reservation
A reservation that does not meet the conditions of formal validity and permissibility...is null and void, and therefore devoid of any legal effect.

4.5.2 Reactions to a reservation considered invalid
1. The nullity of an invalid reservation does not depend on the objection or the acceptance by a contracting State or a contracting organization.

2. Nevertheless, a State or an international organization which considers that a reservation is invalid should formulate a reasoned objection as soon as possible.

4.5.3 Status of the author of an invalid reservation in relation to the treaty
1. The status of the author of an invalid reservation in relation to a treaty depends on the intention expressed by the reserving State or international organization on whether it intends to be bound by the treaty without the benefit of the reservation or whether it considers that it is not bound by the treaty. Unless the author of the invalid reservation has expressed a contrary intention or such an intention is otherwise established, it is considered a contracting State or a contracting organization without the benefit of the reservation.

2. Notwithstanding paragraphs 1 and 2, the author of the invalid reservation may express at any time its intention not to be bound by the treaty without the benefit of the reservation.

3. Notwithstanding paragraphs 1 and 2, the author of the invalid reservation may express at any time its intention not to be bound by the treaty without the benefit of the reservation. If a treaty monitoring body expresses the view that a reservation is invalid and the reserving State or international organization intends not to be bound by the treaty without the benefit of the reservation, it should express its intention to that effect within a period of twelve months from the date at which the treaty monitoring body made its assessment.

M. Milanovic and L.A. Sicilianos, 'Reservations to Treaties: An Introduction'

24 *European Journal of International Law* 1055 (2013)

The [ILC's] Guide's perhaps most important contribution is its examination of the criteria for the validity of reservations and the consequences of invalid reservations. Here we not only have a meticulous analysis of a technical topic, but nothing short of an existential story of international law as a unified system as opposed to a set of fragmented sub-regimes. How so? When one reads Articles 19–22 VCLT [Vienna Convention], particularly in light of the ICJ's *Reservations to the Genocide Convention* opinion, one cannot avoid the impression that the process of determining whether a reservation was invalid as being contrary to the object and purpose of a treaty was meant to be more or less inter-subjective: each state should determine for itself whether a given reservation was compatible with the treaty's object and purpose, and if it was not it should make an objection to that effect.

But such an inter-subjective approach looks remarkably unappealing from the perspective of major multilateral normative treaties, particularly in the human rights context.... Many governments were less than pleased with what they saw as a power-grab by human rights bodies and a usurpation of their sovereign prerogatives.... [Also], [h]ow could international law survive as a coherent, unified system if more of its branches followed the human rights example and asserted that because they were special they needed special rules, rather than the outdated Vienna framework[?].... Fragmentation beckoned, and it needed to be resisted.... [A]ccording to the Guide, Article 19 VCLT should be regarded as laying down objective criteria for the validity of reservations. Secondly, Articles 20–23 VCLT deal with only those reservations which are objectively valid under Article 19; they do not mention or pertain to reservations which are in fact invalid. Thirdly, while states may object to reservations that they consider invalid, this is merely persuasive evidence of invalidity. In fact, objections have real legal effect only if they are made against reservations which are objectively valid; the objecting state may object for any reason whatsoever, simply because it does not want to accept the modified treaty bargain that the reserving state is offering. Fourthly, while the VCLT does not say what are the consequences of an invalid reservation, the only sensible option is to accept that such a reservation is null and void. Fifthly, however, saying that an invalid reservation is a nullity does not resolve the issue of the reserving state's status as a party to the treaty. That will depend on the intention of the reserving state, which has a choice—either stay on as a party to the treaty without the benefit of the invalid reservation, or say that it no longer considers itself bound by the treaty. In the absence of a clearly expressed position in this regard, there is a rebuttable presumption that the reserving state intends to remain a party.

Whether this is really the Vienna regime, 'Vienna-plus', or something else entirely will, we imagine, be the object of some debate. But what seems to be beyond debate is that the Guide's approach to the invalidity of reservation accommodates most of the human rights-inspired critique of Vienna without giving any ground to the idea of speciality. This is a general regime applying to all treaties, but it still moves from the inter-subjective approach in which state objections are paramount, it treats invalid reservations as a nullity, and it allows them to be severed. Yet they can be severed only if the reserving state does not actively oppose its continued status as a party to the treaty. The Guide even acknowledges that human rights bodies have the competence to assess the validity of reservations, but that this does not empower them to do more than they otherwise could, i.e., it would not suddenly make the Human Rights Committee's views binding or formally equal to a judgment of the European Court of Human Rights. The Guide further strengthens the presumption that the reserving state intends to remain a party to the treaty without the benefit of its invalid reservation by indicating that the state should make its intentions known within a year of a treaty body expressing its views that the reservation is invalid. From silence, which would probably be more common than active opposition, one could infer acquiescence in the reservation's demise. This is, in short, a remarkable compromise. What remains to be seen, however, is whether the actors on all sides of the debate will be willing to go along with it.

NOTES

1. The drive to ensure that as many States as possible undertake treaty obligations in respect of human rights has meant that there are many States which ratify such treaties but, for political, social, economic or cultural reasons, make reservations to some provisions. The Human Rights Committee (HRC) has tended to interpret such reservations very narrowly. Indeed, its General Comment 24 (above) affirms the European Court of Human Rights' decision in *Belilos* v *Switzerland* (above) that a reservation was invalid despite the lack of objections by any other States that were parties to that treaty.

2. Following the HRC's General Comment 24, many States, while recognising the different obligations imposed by various types of treaties, have expressed a preference for the maintenance of a

universal reservations regime rather than the creation of a dual regime. The Vienna Convention, by striking a balance between the interests of States and individuals, is said to provide a flexible system promoting universality of participation rather than hindering ratification. The Comment has also been criticised for the role it envisages for the HRC in the determination of the permissibility of reservations (para. 18 above). States including the United Kingdom, the United States, France and Libya have argued that monitoring bodies (such as the HRC) should not be able to decide if a reservation is permissible, and that their role should be confined to making recommendations to States, though others disagree with this limited interpretation of the HRC's role.

3. The HRC applied its General Comment 24 in the *Rawle Kennedy Case* (above). As a consequence, Trinidad and Tobago denounced the Optional Protocol again and did not re-accede. There is now no opportunity for any person in Trinidad and Tobago to bring a complaint to the HRC. While this is an undesirable consequence, the HRC would consider that it has made it clear that a State that makes a reservation that is incompatible with the object and purpose of a human rights treaty is attempting to avoid meaningful legal obligations and thus the purported reservation should not stand.

4. The reason why the HRC has taken this stance is because human rights treaties are not of the same nature as other treaties as there are usually no reciprocal obligations between States in such treaties (see Chapter 6). The obligations are to preserve the rights of individuals, rather than the rights of States. Accordingly, there may be no incentive by a State to object to reservations made by other States, whether those reservations are permissible or not (see para. 17 of the General Comment and the separate opinion extracts above). It therefore seems entirely appropriate that the organisation given the responsibility of ensuring compliance with a human rights treaty should determine the status and effect of reservations to that treaty, even if this means States lose an element of their control over the treaty process. While this may seem to be contrary to a concept of international law based on States' consent, it is consistent with a broader view of the nature of international law generally (i.e. that some elements are not derived from State consent—see Chapter 1) and of international human rights law in particular.

5. The ILC's Guide to Practice gave further weight to the view that treaty bodies can assess the validity of reservations. It also clarified that an impermissible reservation is null and void but nevertheless created a presumption that the reserving State intends to be bound by the treaty. While this ultimately defers to State sovereignty, it makes it more difficult for States to denounce their treaty obligations. This approach is considered applicable to all treaties, thereby losing the differentiation between human rights and other treaties. Nevertheless, concerns remain over whether (and how) States will adopt this approach.

SECTION 5: INTERPRETATION OF TREATIES

The way in which an international tribunal interprets the terms of a treaty can have a significant impact on the extent of the rights and obligations of the parties to that treaty.

G. Fitzmaurice, 'The Law and Procedure of the International Court of Justice: Treaty Interpretation and Certain other Treaty Points'
28 British Yearbook of International Law 1 (1951)

There are today three main schools of thought on the subject, which could conveniently be called the 'intentions of the parties' or 'founding fathers' school; the 'textual' or 'ordinary meaning of the words' school; and the 'teleological' or 'aims and objects' school. The ideas of these three schools are not necessarily exclusive of one another, and theories of treaty interpretation can be constructed (and are indeed normally held) compounded of all three. However, each tends to confer the primacy on one particular aspect of treaty interpretation, if not to the exclusion, certainly to the subordination of the others. Each, in any case, employs a different approach. For the 'intentions' school, the prime, indeed the only legitimate, object is to ascertain and give effect to the intentions, or presumed intentions, of the parties: the approach is therefore to discover what these were, or must be taken to have been. For the 'meaning of the text' school, the prime object is to establish what the text means according to the ordinary or apparent signification of its terms: the approach is therefore through the study and analysis of the text. For the 'aims and objects' school, it is the general purpose of the treaty itself that counts, considered to some extent as having, or as having come to have, an existence of its own, independent of the original intentions of the framers. The main object is to establish this general purpose, and construe the particular clauses in the light of it: hence it is such matters as the general tenor and atmosphere of the treaty, the circumstances in which it was made, the place it has come to have in international life, which for this school indicate the approach to interpretation. It should be added that this last, the teleological, approach has its sphere of operation almost entirely in the field of general multilateral conventions, particularly those of the social, humanitarian, and law-making type. All three approaches are capable, in a given case, of producing the same result in practice; but equally (even though the differences may, on analysis, prove to be more of emphasis and methodology than principle) they are capable of leading to radically divergent results.

Vienna Convention on the Law of Treaties 1969

Article 31 General rule of interpretation

1. A treaty shall be interpreted in good faith in accordance with the ordinary meaning to be given to the terms of the treaty in their context and in the light of its object and purpose.

2. The context for the purpose of the interpretation of a treaty shall comprise, in addition to the text, including its preamble and annexes:
    (a) any agreement relating to the treaty which was made between all the parties in connexion with the conclusion of the treaty;
    (b) any instrument which was made by one or more parties in connexion with the conclusion of the treaty and accepted by the other parties as an instrument related to the treaty.

3. There shall be taken into account, together with the context:
    (a) any subsequent agreement between the parties regarding the interpretation of the treaty or the application of its provisions;
    (b) any subsequent practice in the application of the treaty which establishes the agreement of the parties regarding its interpretation;
    (c) any relevant rules of international law applicable in the relations between the parties.

4. A special meaning shall be given to a term if it is established that the parties so intended.

Article 32 Supplementary means of interpretation

Recourse may be had to supplementary means of interpretation, including the preparatory work of the treaty and the circumstances of its conclusion, in order to confirm the meaning resulting from the application of article 31, or to determine the meaning when the interpretation according to article 31:
    (a) leaves the meaning ambiguous or obscure; or
    (b) leads to a result which is manifestly absurd or unreasonable.

Article 33 Interpretation of treaties authenticated in two or more languages

1. When a treaty has been authenticated in two or more languages, the text is equally authoritative in each language, unless the treaty provides or the parties agree that, in case of divergence, a particular text shall prevail.

2. A version of the treaty in a language other than one of those in which the text was authenticated shall be considered an authentic text only if the treaty so provides or the parties so agree.

3. The terms of the treaty are presumed to have the same meaning in each authentic text.

4. Except where a particular text prevails in accordance with paragraph 1, when a comparison of the authentic texts discloses a difference of meaning which the application of articles 31 and 32 does not remove, the meaning which best reconciles the texts, having regard to the object and purpose of the treaty, shall be adopted.

M. Koskenniemi, *From Apology to Utopia: The Structure of International Legal Argument*

(1989)

According to a subjective approach treaties bind because they express consent. An objective approach assumes that they bind because considerations of teleology, utility, reciprocity, good faith or justice require this. The history of the doctrine of treaty interpretation is the history of the contrast between these two approaches.

Doctrinal expositions and case-law on treaty interpretation usually start out by emphasizing that a text must first be so construed as to give effect to its 'normal', 'natural', 'ordinary' or 'usual' meaning. This seems supported both by the subjective as well as the objective understanding. 'Natural' meaning seems relevant as the most reliable guide to what the parties had consented to as well as what justice requires. But this position is not really a rule of interpretation at all. It assumes what was to be proved; that the expression has a certain meaning instead of another one. The doctrine of 'normal' meaning singularly fails to deal with the fact that already the ascertainment of the 'normal' requires interpretation and that the very emergence of the dispute conclusively proves this....

It is often held that the principal goal of interpretation is to give effect to (subjective) party intentions. But it is virtually impossible to ascertain real, subjective party intent. In particular, doctrine lacks means to oppose its conception of party intent on a deviating conception proposed by the party itself. Besides, sometimes intent may seem like a relatively minor matter—peace treaties or human rights instruments being the obvious examples. The important point is, however, that if intent is to be the *goal* of interpretation, it cannot be used as a *means* for attaining it....

But moving into the objective approach provides no solution. How can we know which interpretation (which behaviour, which teleology) manifests consent? The problem-solver should be capable of justifying his view about what it is that the text (party behaviour, contractual equilibrium) requires. Inasmuch he cannot justify it by referring to intent (because the argument started from the assumption that intent was not known) he must refer to some non-subjective criterion. The irony is, of course, that the system simultaneously denies there to be such a thing as an 'objective normality' or any other non-subjective criterion by which the contractual relationship could be evaluated. It tells us only that we cannot proceed beyond our subjective views about such matters and that nobody has any duty to defer to another's subjective views. By this simple assumption—the rejection of natural law and intelligible essences—the liberal system of treaty interpretation deconstructs itself....

The fusion of the subjective and objective understandings in this way resembles the tacit consent strategy. The subjective theory seems necessary to preserve the treaty's legitimacy. The objective view is needed to preserve the treaty's binding force. Neither can be maintained alone. Intent can be known only in its manifestations— which manifestations (text, behaviour, teleology etc.) count depends on whether they express intent. The subjective argument can be supported only by moving into an objective position. The objective argument can be held only on subjective premises. The argument is hopelessly circular....

The problems of treaty interpretation lie deeper than the unclear character of treaty language. They lie in the contradiction between the legal principles available to arrive at an interpretation.

Territorial Dispute Case (*Libyan Arab Jamahiriya* v *Chad*)

ICJ Rep 1994 6, International Court of Justice

The dispute revolved around whether a boundary between Libya and Chad had been settled by a treaty in 1955 between Libya and France (the former colonial power in Chad). The Court held, by 16 votes to 1, that the 1955 treaty did indeed define the boundary. In reaching this conclusion it noted (at para. 41) that Article 31 of the Vienna Convention reflected customary international law.

51. The parties could have indicated the frontiers by specifying in words the course of the boundary, or by indicating it on a map, by way of illustration or otherwise; or they could have done both. They chose to proceed in a different manner and to establish, by agreement, the list of international instruments from which the frontiers resulted, but the course for which they elected presents no difficulties of interpretation. That being so, the Court's task is clear:

> Having before it a clause which leaves little to be desired in the nature of clearness, it is bound to apply this clause as it stands, without considering whether other provisions might with advantage

have been added to or substituted for it. (*Acquisition of Polish Nationality*, Advisory Opinion, 1923, PCIJ, Series E. No. 7, p. 20.)

The text of Article 3 [of the 1955 treaty] clearly conveys the intention of the parties to reach a definitive settlement of the question of their common frontiers. Article 3 and Annex I are intended to define frontiers by reference to legal instruments which would yield the course of such frontiers. Any other construction would be contrary to one of the fundamental principles of interpretation of treaties, consistently upheld by international jurisprudence, namely that of effectiveness.

Case Concerning the Territorial and Maritime Dispute (Nicaragua v Colombia)

Preliminary Objections, ICJ Rep 2007 832, International Court of Justice

A 1928 Treaty concerning Territorial Questions between the States recognised the sovereignty of Colombia over various islands, islets and cays and thus resolved a territorial dispute between the States. The question for the ICJ was whether a 1930 Protocol to the treaty settled the dispute concerning the maritime delimitation between the States in respect of these islands. If it did, the ICJ would be unable to exercise jurisdiction.

115. The Court considers that, contrary to Colombia's claims, the terms of the Protocol, in their plain and ordinary meaning, cannot be interpreted as effecting a delimitation of the maritime boundary between Colombia and Nicaragua....

116. In the Court's view, a careful examination of the pre-ratification discussions of the 1928 Treaty by and between the Parties confirms that neither Party assumed at the time that the Treaty and Protocol were designed to effect a general delimitation of the maritime spaces between Colombia and Nicaragua....

117. Contrary to Colombia's assertion, the Court does not consider it significant that in the preamble of the Treaty, the Parties express their desire to put an end to the '*territorial dispute* pending between them' (emphasis added) whereas in the Protocol they refer 'to the *dispute* between both republics' (emphasis added). In the Court's view, the difference between the language of the Treaty and that of the Protocol cannot be read to have transformed the territorial nature of the Treaty into one that was also designed to effect a general delimitation of the maritime spaces between the two States. This conclusion is apparent from the full text of the aforementioned phrase in the Protocol, where the Parties state that the 1928 Treaty was concluded 'with a view to putting an end to the dispute between both republics concerning the San Andrés and Providencia Archipelago and the Nicaraguan Mosquito Coast'. In other words, the 'dispute' to which the Protocol refers relates to the Mosquito Coast along with the San Andrés Archipelago; it does not refer, even by implication, to a general maritime delimitation.

Case Concerning the Dispute Regarding Navigational and Related Rights (Costa Rica v Nicaragua)

13 July 2009, International Court of Justice

In determining the types of navigation conferred on Costa Rica by the 1958 Treaty of Limits between the States, the ICJ was required to interpret the phrase '*con objetos de comercio*' in the treaty. Nicaragua argued for a narrow interpretation of the phrase, so that navigation rights only extended to vessels carrying commercial objects, as opposed to journeys for the purpose of commerce.

48....the Court is not convinced by Nicaragua's argument that Costa Rica's right of free navigation should be interpreted narrowly because it represents a limitation of the sovereignty over the river conferred by the Treaty on Nicaragua, that being the most important principle set forth by Article VI. While it is certainly true that limitations of the sovereignty of a State over its territory are not to be presumed, this does not mean that treaty provisions establishing such limitations, such as those that are in issue in the present case, should for this reason be interpreted *a priori* in a restrictive way. A treaty provision which has the purpose of limiting the sovereign powers of a State must be interpreted like any other provision of a treaty, i.e. in accordance with the intentions of its authors as reflected by the text of the treaty and the other relevant factors in terms of interpretation.

A simple reading of Article VI shows that the Parties did not intend to establish any hierarchy as between Nicaragua's sovereignty over the river and Costa Rica's right of free navigation, characterized as 'perpetual', with each of these affirmations counter-balancing the other. Nicaragua's sovereignty is affirmed only to the extent that it does not prejudice the substance of Costa Rica's right of free navigation in its domain, the establishment of which is precisely the point at issue; the right of free navigation, albeit 'perpetual', is granted only on condition that it does not prejudice the key prerogatives of territorial sovereignty. There are thus no grounds for supposing, a priori, that the words 'libre navegación…con objetos de comercio' should be given a specially restrictive interpretation, any more than an extensive one.…

50. It is now appropriate to consider the issue of the meaning of the phrase 'con objetos de' as used in Article VI of the 1858 Treaty, specifically whether it means 'for the purposes of'—as Costa Rica contends—or 'with articles of'—as Nicaragua contends.

51. It should first be observed that the Spanish word 'objetos' can, depending on its context, have either of the two meanings put forward. Thus, the context must be examined to ascertain the meaning to be ascribed here. The two meanings—one concrete and the other abstract—are sufficiently different that examination of the context will generally allow for a firm conclusion to be reached.

52. Having conducted this examination, the Court is of the view that the interpretation advocated by Nicaragua cannot be upheld. The main reason for this is that ascribing the meaning 'with goods' or 'with articles' to the phrase 'con objetos' results in rendering meaningless the entire sentence in which the phrase appears. The part of Article VI which is relevant in this connection reads: 'Costa Rica tendrá…los derechos perpetuos de libre navegación…, con objetos de comercio, ya sea con Nicaragua ó al interior de Costa Rica.' If Nicaragua's interpretation were to be accepted, there would be no intelligible relationship between the clause following the phrase 'con objetos de comercio', i.e., 'ya sea con Nicaragua ó al interior de Costa Rica' ('whether with Nicaragua or with the interior of Costa Rica'), and the preceding part of the sentence.
Either the words 'with Nicaragua' would relate to 'objetos de comercio', which would hardly make sense, since it would not be meaningful to speak of 'goods (or articles) of trade with Nicaragua'; or these words relate to 'navegación' and that would make even less sense, because the expression 'navegación…con Nicaragua' would simply be incomprehensible.
By contrast, Costa Rica's interpretation of the words 'con objetos' allows the entire sentence to be given coherent meaning. If the phrase means 'purposes of commerce', then the immediately following clause, 'ya sea con Nicaragua…', plainly relates to 'comercio' ('for the purposes of commerce with Nicaragua…'), and the sentence then conveys a perfectly comprehensible idea. Thus, in the present instance a literal analysis of the sentence containing the words requiring interpretation leads to one of the proposed meanings being preferred over the other…

62. In respect of the narrow interpretation advanced by Nicaragua, the Court observes that it is supported mainly by two arguments: the first is based on the Respondent's interpretation of the phrase 'con objetos', which has just been rejected; the second is based on the assertion that 'commerce' should be given the narrow meaning it had when the Treaty was entered into.

63. The Court does not agree with this second argument. It is true that the terms used in a treaty must be interpreted in light of what is determined to have been the parties' common intention, which is, by definition, contemporaneous with the treaty's conclusion. That may lead a court seised of a dispute, or the parties themselves, when they seek to determine the meaning of a treaty for purposes of good-faith compliance with it, to ascertain the meaning a term had when the treaty was drafted, since doing so can shed light on the parties' common intention. The Court has so proceeded in certain cases requiring it to interpret a term whose meaning had evolved since the conclusion of the treaty at issue, and in those cases the Court adhered to the original meaning…

64. This does not however signify that, where a term's meaning is no longer the same as it was at the date of conclusion, no account should ever be taken of its meaning at the time when the treaty is to be interpreted for purposes of applying it. On the one hand, the subsequent practice of the parties, within the meaning of Article 31 (3) *(b)* of the Vienna Convention, can result in a departure from the original intent on the basis of a tacit agreement between the parties. On the other hand, there are situations in which the parties' intent upon conclusion of the treaty was, or may be presumed to have been, to give the terms used or some of them a meaning or content capable of evolving, not one fixed once and for all, so as to make allowance for, among other things, developments in international law. In such instances it is indeed in order to respect the parties' common intention at the time the treaty was concluded, not to depart from it, that

account should be taken of the meaning acquired by the terms in question upon each occasion on which the treaty is to be applied....

70. The Court concludes from the foregoing that the terms by which the extent of Costa Rica's right of free navigation has been defined, including in particular the term 'comercio', must be understood to have the meaning they bear on each occasion on which the Treaty is to be applied, and not necessarily their original meaning.

Thus, even assuming that the notion of 'commerce' does not have the same meaning today as it did in the mid-nineteenth century, it is the present meaning which must be accepted for purposes of applying the *Treaty*.

China Measures Affecting Imports of Automobile Parts
AB-2008–10, Report of the WTO Appellate Body, 15 December 2008

The Appellate Body was called upon to consider the context in interpreting a treaty, in this case whether a description and coding system under another treaty could be taken into account as part of the context of the treaty.

151. We have already stated that the task of the treaty interpreter is to ascertain the meaning of particular treaty terms using the tools set out in Articles 31 and 32 of the *Vienna Convention*. The realm of context as defined in Article 31(2) is broad. 'Context' includes all of the text of the treaty—in this case, the *WTO Agreement*—and may also extend to 'any agreement relating to the treaty which was made between all the parties in connection with the conclusion of the treaty' and 'any instrument which was made by one or more parties in connection with the conclusion of the treaty and accepted by the other parties as an instrument related to the treaty'. Yet context is *relevant* for a treaty interpreter to the extent that it may shed light on the interpretative issue to be resolved, such as the meaning of the term or phrase at issue. Thus, for a particular provision, agreement or instrument to serve as *relevant* context in any given situation, it must not only fall within the scope of the formal boundaries identified in Article 31(2), it must also have some pertinence to the language being interpreted that renders it capable of helping the interpreter to determine the meaning of such language. Because WTO Members' Schedules of Concessions were constructed using the nomenclature of the Harmonized System, the Harmonized System is apt to shed light on the meaning of terms used in these Schedules. It does not, however, automatically follow that the Harmonized System was context relevant to the interpretative question faced by the Panel in its analysis of the threshold issue in this dispute.

Oil Platforms (Islamic Republic of Iran v United States of America)
Merits, ICJ Rep 2003 161, International Court of Justice

The facts of this case are set out in Chapter 15. In interpreting the 1955 Treaty of Friendship between the States, the Court relied on Article 31(3)(c) of the Vienna Convention to enable it to refer to general principles on the use of force. This was necessary, as the Court otherwise did not have jurisdiction to consider violations of the Charter provisions on the use of force.

41. It should not be overlooked that Article 1 of the 1955 Treaty...declares that 'There shall be firm and enduring peace and sincere friendship between the United States of America and Iran.'...It is hardly consistent with Article 1 to interpret Article XX, paragraph 1 (d), to the effect that the 'measures' there contemplated could include even an unlawful use of force by one party against the other. Moreover, under the general rules of treaty interpretation, as reflected in the 1969 Vienna Convention on the Law of Treaties, interpretation must take into account 'any relevant rules of international law applicable in the relations between the parties' (Art. 31, para. 3 (c)). The Court cannot accept that Article XX, paragraph 1 (d), of the 1955 Treaty was intended to operate wholly independently of the relevant rules of international law on the use of force, so as to be capable of being successfully invoked, even in the limited context of a claim for breach of the Treaty, in relation to an unlawful use of force. The application of the relevant rules of international law relating to this question thus forms an integral part of the task of interpretation entrusted to the Court.

NOTES

1. The principle of *pacta sunt servanda* (see Section 3C) necessarily provides a basic rule of treaty interpretation. For a comprehensive account of the current law of treaty interpretation, see R. Gardiner, *Treaty Interpretation* (2015).

2. According to the ILC, since treaties constitute 'embodiments of the common will of their parties ...interpretation must seek to identify the intention of the parties' (ILC, UN Doc. A/68/10).

3. Article 31 of the Vienna Convention combines all of the major schools of treaty interpretation (identified in the extract by Fitzmaurice) into one rule. In relation to the 'intentions of the parties' approach, it is the *common intentions* of the parties that are relevant and not the individual intentions of each party. Indeed, an approach emphasising the subjective intentions of the negotiators of the treaty may be appropriate with a bilateral treaty, for example one concerning trade and commerce between two States. However, an objective approach based on the language used is generally applicable when multilateral treaties are in issue. Koskenniemi points out (above), that it is necessary to combine the subjective and objective approaches to treaty interpretation, as each by itself cannot provide a legally coherent solution. Indeed, one of the approaches that is being used more frequently is that of 'effectiveness' (see the *Territorial Dispute Case* above).

4. The extract from *Costa Rica* v *Nicaragua* demonstrates that the ICJ will adhere to the primacy of the text in treaty interpretation, in order to identify the parties' intention. The Court noted (para. 48) that provisions establishing restrictions on the sovereignty of States are not to be interpreted restrictively. The case also highlights that the text of a treaty does not remain frozen in time, and that in interpreting a treaty, it may be necessary to have regard to the usage of terms in contemporary times, rather than the intention of the drafters of the treaty. This approach accords an important role to international courts in interpreting older treaties. However, this approach is not always followed (see E. Bjorge, *The Evolutionary Interpretation of Treaties* (2014)). Similarly, when courts adopt a teleological approach, they can also play a significant role, particularly in standard-setting treaties (e.g. *Application of the Convention on the Prevention and Punishment of the Crime of Genocide (Bosnia and Herzegovina v Serbia and Montenegro)* (Merits) ICJ Rep 2007 43, [166]; *Questions relating to the Obligation to Prosecute or Extradite (Belgium v Senegal)* (Merits) ICJ Rep 2012 422, [114]).

5. Other extracts show the role of the context of the treaty, as well as the possible reliance on general principles of international law in the interpretation of a treaty.

6. The principles of treaty interpretation found in Article 31 have been applied to disputes other than those between States. In the arbitral award *Veteran Petroleum Limited* v *the Russian Federation* in November 2009, the arbitral panel applied Article 31 in deciding that there was no need to resort to the *travaux préparatoires* of the Energy Charter Treaty 1994 because the meaning of the words was unambiguous.

7. Article 32 allows recourse to the *travaux préparatoires* of a treaty to resolve ambiguities and absurdities, although what constitutes 'preparatory work' is not defined in the Vienna Convention. Some tribunals have required a high threshold before allowing recourse to the preparatory works. For example, the ICSID Annulment Committee has noted that while there may be possible problems with a particular interpretation of a treaty provision, 'this in itself does not make the interpretation of the BIT [Bilateral Investment Treaty]..."ambiguous or obscure" or "manifestly absurd or unreasonable" within the meaning of Article 32': *Azurix Corp* v *The Argentine Republic*, Decision on the Application for Annulment of the Argentine Republic, 1 September 2009, para. 114. However, some international courts and tribunals resort to the *travaux préparatoires* to confirm a particular interpretation, even if the term is not considered ambiguous or absurd *(Case Concerning the Territorial Dispute (Libyan Arab Jamahirya v Chad)* (Judgment) [1994] ICJ 6, [55]; and *Application of the International Convention on the Elimination of All Forms of Racial Discrimination (Georgia v Russian Federation)* (Preliminary Objections) ICJ Rep 2011 70 [147].

8. Many treaties are drawn up in more than one language. Where two versions of a treaty possess equal authority, but one version appears to have a wider meaning than the other, a court must adopt the interpretation that is in conformity with both versions as this may properly reflect the intention of the parties—see the *Mavrommatis Palestine Concessions Case* PCIJ Rep, Ser A, (1926) No. 2.

9. The more parties to a treaty, the more difficult it can be to apply the principles set out in Articles 31 and 32 of the Vienna Convention. For example, consistent 'subsequent practice' may be hard to find (see, for example, *Whaling in the Antarctic (Australia v Japan: New Zealand intervening)*,

Merits, Judgment of 31 March 2014, [83]); the initial object and purpose may be unclear; the original intentions of the parties may now be irrelevant; and the *travaux préparatoires* may shed no real light on the intentions of parties which were not involved in the initial negotiations. Accordingly, international tribunals are adept at adopting a flexible approach to treaty interpretation, though it is also true that in many cases they are not explicit about the approach they have adopted or the reasons why.

10. In order to determine a treaty's object and purpose, the ICJ has previously considered its title, preamble and substantive provisions. (*Case Concerning Rights of Nationals of the USA in Morocco (France v USA)* (Judgment) [1952] ICJ 176, 196; *Case Concerning the Territorial Dispute (Libyan Arab Jamahirya v Chad)* (Judgment) ICJ Rep 1994 6, 25–26; *Case of Certain Norwegian Loans (France v Norway)* (Judgment) ICJ Rep 1957 9, 24; and *Whaling in the Antarctic (Australia v Japan: New Zealand Intervening)* (Judgment) ICJ Rep 2014 158 [58]). Ascertaining the treaty's object and purpose is relevant not only for the obligation not to defeat the object and purpose before the treaty's entry into force, it is also relevant for treaty interpretation (Articles 31(1), (4) Vienna Convention), for determining a reservation's permissibility (Article 19(c) Vienna Convention), whether parties to a multilateral treaty can modify the agreement (Article 41(1)(b)(ii) Vienna Convention) or suspend it (Article 58(1)(b)(ii) Vienna Convention) and whether a material breach of a treaty has occurred (Article 60(3)(b) Vienna Convention).

SECTION 6: INVALIDITY OF TREATIES

A treaty that complies with all the formal procedural aspects discussed earlier concerning entry into force etc., may still be unenforceable if it is 'invalid'. However, even if there are grounds for invalidity, a party to a treaty can still agree to allow the treaty to remain in force in its relations with other parties. Discussion of the grounds of invalidity is rare as most treaties are not invalid, although there has been some analysis of 'error' (Article 48) and contravention of *jus cogens* (Articles 53 and 64).

A: General principles

Vienna Convention on the Law of Treaties 1969

Article 42 Validity and continuance in force of treaties

1. The validity of a treaty or of the consent of a State to be bound by a treaty may be impeached only through the application of the present Convention.

2. The termination of a treaty, its denunciation or the withdrawal of a party, may take place only as a result of the application of the provisions of the treaty or of the present Convention. The same rule applies to suspension of the operation of a treaty.

Article 43 Obligations imposed by international law independently of a treaty

The invalidity, termination or denunciation of a treaty, the withdrawal of a party from it, or the suspension of its operation, as a result of the application of the present Convention or of the provisions of the treaty shall not in any way impair the duty of any State to fulfil any obligation embodied in the treaty to which it would be subject under international law independently of the treaty.

Article 44 Separability of treaty provisions

1. A right of a party, provided for in a treaty or arising under article 56, to denounce, withdraw from or suspend the operation of the treaty may be exercised only with respect to the whole treaty unless the treaty otherwise provides or the parties otherwise agree.

2. A ground for invalidating, terminating, withdrawing from or suspending the operation of a treaty recognized in the present Convention may be invoked only with respect to the whole treaty except as provided in the following paragraphs or in article 60.

3. If the ground relates solely to particular clauses, it may be invoked only with respect to those clauses where:
   (a) the said clauses are separable from the remainder of the treaty with regard to their application;
   (b) it appears from the treaty or is otherwise established that acceptance of those clauses was not an essential basis of the consent of the other party or parties to be bound by the treaty as a whole; and
   (c) continued performance of the remainder of the treaty would not be unjust.

4. In cases falling under articles 49 and 50 the State entitled to invoke the fraud or corruption may do so with respect either to the whole treaty or, subject to paragraph 3, to the particular clauses alone.

5. In cases falling under articles 51, 52 and 53, no separation of the provisions of the treaty is permitted.

Article 45 Loss of a right to invoke a ground for invalidating, terminating, withdrawing from or suspending the operation of a treaty

A State may no longer invoke a ground for invalidating, terminating, withdrawing from or suspending the operation of a treaty under articles 46 to 50 or articles 60 and 62 if, after becoming aware of the facts:
   (a) it shall have expressly agreed that the treaty is valid or remains in force or continues in operation, as the case may be; or
   (b) it must by reason of its conduct be considered as having acquiesced in the validity of the treaty or in its maintenance in force or in operation, as the case may be.

Article 46 Provisions of internal law regarding competence to conclude treaties

1. A State may not invoke the fact that its consent to be bound by a treaty has been expressed in violation of a provision of its internal law regarding competence to conclude treaties as invalidating its consent unless that violation was manifest and concerned a rule of its internal law of fundamental importance.

2. A violation is manifest if it would be objectively evident to any State conducting itself in the matter in accordance with normal practice and in good faith.

Article 47 Authority of representative to conclude treaties

If the authority of a representative to express the consent of a State to be bound by a particular treaty has been made subject to a specific restriction, his omission to observe that restriction may not be invoked as invalidating the consent expressed by him unless the restriction was notified to the other negotiating States prior to his expressing such consent.

Article 48 Error

1. A State may invoke an error in a treaty as invalidating its consent to be bound by the treaty if the error relates to a fact or situation which was assumed by that State to exist at the time when the treaty was concluded and formed an essential basis of its consent to be bound by the treaty.

2. Paragraph 1 shall not apply if the State in question contributed by its own conduct to the error or if the circumstances were such as to put that State on notice of a possible error.

3. An error relating only to the wording of the text of a treaty does not affect its validity; article 79 then applies.

Article 49 Fraud

If a State has been induced to conclude a treaty by the fraudulent conduct of another negotiating State, the State may invoke the fraud as invalidating its consent to be bound by the treaty.

Article 50 Corruption of a representative of a State

If the expression of a State's consent to be bound by a treaty has been procured through the corruption of its representative directly or indirectly by another negotiating State, the State may invoke such corruption as invalidating its consent to be bound by the treaty.

Article 51 Coercion of a representative of a State

The expression of a State's consent to be bound by a treaty which has been procured by the coercion of its representative through acts of threats directed against him shall be without any legal effect.

Article 52 Coercion of a State by the threat or use of force

A treaty is void if its conclusion has been procured by the threat or use of force in violation of the principles of international law embodied in the Charter of the United Nations.

Article 53 Treaties conflicting with a peremptory norm of general international law (*jus cogens*)

A treaty is void if, at the time of its conclusion, it conflicts with a peremptory norm of general international law. For the purposes of the present Convention, a peremptory norm of general international law is a norm accepted and recognized by the international community of States as a whole as a norm from which no derogation is permitted and which can be modified only by a subsequent norm of general international law having the same character.

Article 64 Emergence of a new peremptory norm of general international law (*jus cogens*)

If a new peremptory norm of general international law emerges, any existing treaty which is in conflict with that norm becomes void and terminates.

NOTES

1. The main grounds for impugning the validity of a treaty are those that affect the capacity of a party to consent (Articles 46 and 47); those that affect the reality of consent itself (Articles 48–52); and those that affect the lawfulness of the treaty (Articles 53 and 64).
2. It is uncertain whether the grounds set out in the Vienna Convention are the only grounds of invalidity under customary international law. However, due to the fact that a treaty is usually negotiated by two or more States at arm's length, it could be argued that all grounds for invalidity must be interpreted narrowly. See, however, the discussion in Section 6E concerning so-called 'unequal treaties'.
3. Article 103 of the United Nations Charter may also limit the ability of a State to comply with its obligations under a treaty. It provides that 'in the event of a conflict between the obligations of the Members of the United Nations under the present Charter and their obligations under any other international agreement, their obligations under the present Charter shall prevail'. However, as the European Court of Human Rights stated in *Al-Jedda* v *the United Kingdom* (7 July 2011) (see Chapter 4) '"[P]revail" does not grammatically imply that the lower-ranking provision would become automatically null and void, or even suspended…Article 103 says literally that in case of a conflict, the State in question should fulfil its obligation under the Charter and perform its duties under other agreements in as far as compatible with obligations under the Charter. This also accords with the drafting materials of the Charter….In the event of any ambiguity in the terms of a United Nations Security Council resolution, the Court must therefore choose the interpretation which is most in harmony with the requirements of the Convention and which avoids any conflict of obligations.' In other words, the European Court of Human Rights implicitly employed a rule of treaty interpretation (Article 31(3)(c) Vienna Convention) in order to avoid finding that a Security Council Resolution (which, under the United Nations Charter, States have to comply with and give priority to) had limited European Union States' ability to comply with their human rights obligations.
4. A later treaty on the same subject matter overrides an earlier treaty between the same States parties (Article 30 Vienna Convention).

B: Inconsistency with domestic law and coercion

Case concerning the Territorial and Maritime Dispute (Nicaragua v Colombia)
ICJ Rep 2007 832, International Court of Justice

The facts of this case are set out in Section 5. Before interpreting the treaty, the ICJ had to consider an argument by Nicaragua that the treaty was invalid.

75. With respect to the validity of the 1928 Treaty, Nicaragua contends that the Treaty is invalid for two reasons. It argues first that the Treaty was 'concluded in manifest violation of the Nicaraguan Constitution

of 1911 that was in force in 1928'. In this regard, Nicaragua considers that the conclusion of the 1928 Treaty contravened Articles 2 and 3 of its 1911 Constitution which remained in force until 1939. Article 2 stipulated, inter alia, that 'treaties may not be reached that oppose the independence and integrity of the nation or that in some way affect her sovereignty…'. Article 3 provided that '[p]ublic officials only enjoy those powers expressly granted to them by Law. Any action of theirs that exceeds these [powers] is null.' Its second argument is that at the time the Treaty was concluded, Nicaragua was under military occupation by the United States and was precluded from concluding treaties that ran contrary to the interests of the United States and from rejecting the conclusion of treaties that the United States demanded it to conclude. Nicaragua submits that Colombia was aware of this situation and 'took advantage of the US occupation of Nicaragua to extort from her the conclusion of the 1928 Treaty'. Nicaragua claims that it remained under the influence of the United States even after the withdrawal of the last United States troops at the beginning of 1933.

78. … The Court notes that there is no evidence that the States parties to the Pact of Bogotá of 1948, including Nicaragua, considered the 1928 Treaty to be invalid. On 25 May 1932, Nicaragua registered the Treaty and Protocol with the League of Nations as a binding agreement, pursuant to Article 18 of the Covenant of the League, Colombia having already registered the Treaty on 16 August 1930.

79. The Court recalls that Nicaragua advanced 'the nullity and lack of validity' of the 1928 Treaty for the first time in an official declaration and White Paper published on 4 February 1980. … The Court thus notes that, for more than 50 years, Nicaragua has treated the 1928 Treaty as valid and never contended that it was not bound by the Treaty, even after the withdrawal of the last United States troops at the beginning of 1933. At no time in those 50 years, even after it became a Member of the United Nations in 1945 and even after it joined the Organization of American States in 1948, did Nicaragua contend that the Treaty was invalid for whatever reason, including that it had been concluded in violation of its Constitution or under foreign coercion. On the contrary, Nicaragua has, in significant ways, acted as if the 1928 Treaty was valid. …

80. The Court thus finds that Nicaragua cannot today be heard to assert that the 1928 Treaty was not in force in 1948.

A. Mills, 'The Formalism of State Sovereignty in Territorial and Maritime Disputes

67 *Cambridge Law Journal* 443 (2008)

If a State disputes the validity of a treaty on the grounds of foreign coercion, it seems somewhat unreasonable to hold against it the fact that it failed to raise the objection while a degree of influence or coercion continued. Such an approach reflects a formalistic application of the principle of sovereign independence and equality— Nicaragua [in *Nicaragua* v *Colombia*], as a sovereign State, was held to be bound by its treaty obligations and subsequent State practice regardless of their historical context.

C: Error

Temple of Preah Vihear Case (Cambodia v Thailand)

Merits, ICJ Rep 1962 6, International Court of Justice

The facts of this case are set out in Chapter 7.

It is an established rule of law that the plea of error cannot be allowed as an element vitiating consent if the party advancing it contributed by its own conduct to the error, or could have avoided it, or if the circumstances were such as to put that party on notice of a possible error. The Court considers that the character and qualifications of the persons who saw the Annex I map on the Siamese side would alone make it difficult for Thailand to plead error in law. These persons included the members of the very Commission of Delimitation within whose competence this sector of the frontier had lain. But even apart from this, the Court thinks that there were other circumstances relating to the Annex I map which make the plea of error difficult to receive.

An inspection indicates that the map itself drew such pointed attention to the Preah Vihear region that no interested person, nor anyone charged with the duty of scrutinizing it, could have failed to see what the map was purporting to do in respect of that region....The Siamese authorities knew it was the work of French topographical officers to whom they had themselves entrusted the work of producing the maps. They accepted it without any independent investigation, and cannot therefore now plead any error vitiating the reality of their consent. The Court concludes therefore that the plea of error has not been made out.

D: *Jus cogens*

Report of the International Law Commission to the General Assembly
Yearbook of the International Law Commission (1966) vol II, 172

(1) The view that in the last analysis there is no rule of international law from which States cannot at their own free will contract out has become increasingly difficult to sustain, although some jurists deny the existence of any rules of *jus cogens* in international law, since in their view even the most general rules still fall short of being universal. The Commission pointed out that the law of the Charter concerning the prohibition of the use of force in itself constitutes a conspicuous example of a rule in international law having the character of *jus cogens*. Moreover, if some Governments in their comments have expressed doubts as to the advisability of this article unless it is accompanied by provision for independent adjudication, only one questioned the existence of rules of *jus cogens* in the international law of today. Accordingly, the Commission concluded that in codifying the law of treaties it must start from the basis that today there are certain rules from which States are not competent to derogate at all by a treaty arrangement, and which may be changed only by another rule of the same character.

(2) The formulation of the article [i.e. Article 53] is not free from difficulty, since there is no simple criterion by which to identify a general rule of international law as having the character of *jus cogens*. Moreover, the majority of the general rules of international law do not have that character, and States may contract out of them by treaty. It would therefore be going much too far to state that a treaty is void if its provisions conflict with a rule of general international law. Nor would it be correct to say that a provision in a treaty possesses the character of *jus cogens* merely because the parties have stipulated that no derogation from that provision is to be permitted, so that another treaty which conflicted with that provision would be void. Such a stipulation may be inserted in any treaty with respect to any subject-matter for any reasons which may seem good to the parties. The conclusion by a party of a later treaty derogating from such a stipulation may, of course, engage its responsibility for a breach of the earlier treaty. But the breach of the stipulation does not, simply as such, render the treaty void...It is not the form of a general rule of international law but the particular nature of the subject-matter with which it deals that may, in the opinion of the Commission, give it the character of *jus cogens*.

(3) The emergence of rules having the character of *jus cogens* is comparatively recent, while international law is in process of rapid development. The Commission considered the right course to be to provide in general terms that a treaty is void if it conflicts with a rule of *jus cogens* and to leave the full content of this rule to be worked out in State practice and in the jurisprudence of international tribunals. Some members of the Commission felt that there might be advantage in specifying, by way of illustration, some of the most obvious and best settled rules of *jus cogens* in order to indicate by these examples the general nature and scope of the rule contained in the article. Examples suggested included (a) a treaty contemplating an unlawful use of force contrary to the principles of the Charter, (b) a treaty contemplating the performance of any other act criminal under international law, and (c) a treaty contemplating or conniving at the commission of acts, such as trade in slaves, piracy or genocide, in the suppression of which every State is called upon to co-operate. Other members expressed the view that, if examples were given, it would be undesirable to appear to limit the scope of the article to cases involving acts which constitute crimes under international law; treaties violating human rights, the equality of States or the principle of self-determination were mentioned as other possible examples. The Commission decided against including any examples of rules of *jus cogens* in the article for two reasons. First, the mention of some cases of treaties void for conflict with a rule of *jus cogens* might, even with the most careful drafting, lead to misunderstanding as to the position concerning other cases not mentioned in the article. Secondly, if the

Commission were to attempt to draw up, even on a selective basis, a list of the rules of international law which are to be regarded as having the character of *jus cogens*, it might find itself engaged in a prolonged study of matters which fall outside the scope of the present articles.

I. Sinclair, *The Vienna Convention on the Law of Treaties*

(2nd edn, 1984)

What conclusions can we draw so far from this analysis of the controversy surrounding the admissibility and application of the concept of *jus cogens* in international law? Perhaps one should stress at the outset that the 'great debate' on this issue involves taking a view on some of the fundamental and basic underpinnings of international law in general. It is no accident that some of the more vigorous Western proponents of *jus cogens* base their case largely upon private law analogies and upon concepts deriving from natural law. It is, equally, no accident that those who deny the existence of *jus cogens* found their denial in part upon considerations relating to State sovereignty and independence, and in part upon an analysis of the evidence of State practice; these are, of course, some of the hallmarks of the positivist approach. As de Visscher rightly points out the controversy surrounding *jus cogens* constitutes a renewal, in different terms, of the ancient doctrinal dispute between naturalists and positivists.

But there is a paradox here, particularly if one notes the enthusiasm of Soviet and other Eastern European publicists and official representatives for an extended application of the concept of *jus cogens* in international law. For those attached to Marxist-Leninist teachings there can be no place for any seed-bed of natural law in which *jus cogens* might take root. Equally, it might be thought unnatural that Soviet representatives, traditionally supporting some of the more exaggerated notions of State sovereignty, should come down in favour of a concept which postulates the existence of a superior international legal order....

Whatever their doctrinal point of departure, the majority of jurists would no doubt willingly concede to the sceptics that there is little or no evidence in positive international law for the concept that nullity attaches to a treaty concluded in violation of *jus cogens*. But they would be constrained to admit that the validity of a treaty between two States to wage a war of aggression against a third State or to engage in acts of physical or armed force against a third State could not be upheld; and, having made this admission, they may be taken to have accepted the principle that there may exist norms of international law so fundamental to the maintenance of an international legal order that a treaty concluded in violation of them is a nullity.

Some (among whom may be counted the present author) would be prepared to go this far, but would immediately wish to qualify this acceptance of the principle involved by sketching out the limits within which it may be operative in present-day international law. In the first place, they would insist that, in the present state of international society, the concept of an 'international legal order' of hierarchically superior norms binding all States is only just beginning to emerge. Ideological differences and disparities of wealth between the individual nation States which make up the international community, combined with the contrasts between the objectives sought by them, hinder the development of an overarching community consensus upon the content of *jus cogens*. Indeed, it is the existence of these very differences and disparities which constitute the principal danger implicit in an unqualified recognition of *jus cogens*, for it would be only too easy to postulate as a norm of *jus cogens* a principle which happened neatly to serve a particular ideological or economic goal. In the second place, they would test any assertion that a particular rule constitutes a norm of jus cogens by reference to the evidence for its acceptance as such by the international community as a whole, and they would require that the burden of proof should be discharged by those who allege the *jus cogens* character of the rule.

NOTES

1. There is disagreement about the concept of *jus cogens* and its role in the law of treaties (see Chapter 2). Some parties to the Vienna Convention have expressed hesitation in accepting the principle at all. Given that the effect of the rule is that a treaty will be void if it conflicts with a rule of *jus cogens*, this appears to compromise a State's ability to create international obligations through express consent. Nevertheless, there appears to be broad acceptance of the concept of *jus cogens* (if not about which rules qualify as being *jus cogens*) and so it must follow that treaties which conflict with those rules are void. The concept of *jus cogens* has also been applied outside the treaty context to State responsibility more generally (see Chapter 11).

2. There are few examples of a treaty being declared, or even claimed, to be void on the ground of it being inconsistent with *jus cogens*, though this claim was made in the *East Timor Case (Portugal v Australia)* (see Chapter 6). The reality is that States are likely to refrain from making these treaties in the first place.

E: Unequal treaties

P. Wesley-Smith, *Unequal Treaty 1898–1997: China, Great Britain and Hong Kong's New Territories*
(1980)

There is no doubt that the Convention of Peking 1898 [concerning the New Territories of Hong Kong] is an unequal treaty and is so considered by the Peoples' Republic of China: the circumstances in which it was negotiated were inconsistent with the sovereignty and equality of both contracting parties and its burdens and advantages are non-reciprocal. This does not necessarily mean, however, that it is invalid according to modern international law. Although duress has been recognized, both in the 1969 Vienna Convention on the Law of Treaties and by the International Court of Justice, as a factor which might vitiate a treaty, it is a concept which must be very restrictively interpreted, and it is doubtful that the Convention of Peking 1898, which arguably was not brought about by force or even the explicit threat of force, can be considered invalid on this ground. The doctrine of changed circumstances (*rebus sic stantibus*) was frequently relied upon by nationalistic Chinese polemicists in the first decades of this century, and the Chinese delegation to Paris in 1919 specifically referred to the complete change in the balance of power since 1898 to justify 'retrocession' of leased territories. But this too has been approached cautiously by the international community and is of dubious application to the New Territories convention.

The notion is gradually developing, however, that inequality may itself be a sufficient ground for disputing the validity of a treaty. First, an unequal treaty could be void from the beginning (*ab initio*), without any effect in international law at any time; such a treaty would be incapable of abrogation or repudiation, for it has never subsisted as an agreement between the parties. Secondly, an unequal treaty could be not void but voidable, able to be annulled because of its inherent defects yet effective until annulment. In this second case it must further be determined who may abrogate the voidable unequal treaty, in what circumstances, and how.

NOTE: There is no international consensus that 'inequality' is a ground of invalidity of a treaty.

F: Procedure for invoking the invalidity of a treaty

Vienna Convention on the Law of Treaties 1969

Article 65 Procedure to be followed with respect to invalidity, termination, withdrawal from or suspension of the operation of a treaty

1. A party which, under the provisions of the present Convention, invokes either a defect in its consent to be bound by a treaty or a ground for impeaching the validity of a treaty, terminating it, withdrawing from it or suspending its operation, must notify the other parties of its claim. The notification shall indicate the measure proposed to be taken with respect to the treaty and the reasons therefore.

2. If, after the expiry of a period which, except in cases of special urgency, shall not be less than three months after the receipt of the notification, no party has raised any objection, the party making the notification may carry out in the manner provided in article 67 the measure which it has proposed.

3. If, however, objection has been raised by any other party, the parties shall seek a solution through the means indicated in Article 33 of the Charter of the United Nations....

5. Without prejudice to article 45, the fact that a State has not previously made the notification prescribed in paragraph 1 shall not prevent it from making such notification in answer to another party claiming performance of the treaty or alleging its violation.

Article 69 Consequences of the invalidity of a treaty

1. A treaty the invalidity of which is established under the present Convention is void. The provisions of a void treaty have no legal force.

2. If acts have nevertheless been performed in reliance on such a treaty:
   (a) each party may require any other party to establish as far as possible in their mutual relations the position that would have existed if the acts had not been performed;
   (b) acts performed in good faith before the invalidity was invoked are not rendered unlawful by reason only of the invalidity of the treaty.

3. In cases falling under articles 49, 50, 51 or 52, paragraph 2 does not apply with respect to the party to which the fraud, the act of corruption or the coercion is imputable.

4. In the case of the invalidity of a particular State's consent to be bound by a multilateral treaty, the foregoing rules apply in the relations between that State and the parties to the treaty.

Article 71 Consequences of the invalidity of a treaty which conflicts with a peremptory norm of general international law

1. In the case of a treaty which is void under article 53 the parties shall:
   (a) eliminate as far as possible the consequences of any act performed in reliance on any provision which conflicts with the peremptory norm of general international law; and
   (b) bring their mutual relations into conformity with the peremptory norm of general international law.

2. In the case of a treaty which becomes void and terminates under article 64, the termination of the treaty:
   (a) releases the parties from any obligation further to perform the treaty;
   (b) does not affect any right, obligation or legal situation of the parties created through the execution of the treaty prior to its termination; provided that those rights, obligations or situations may thereafter be maintained only to the extent that their maintenance is not in itself in conflict with the new peremptory norm of general international law.

SECTION 7: TERMINATION OF TREATIES

In some situations, the breach of a treaty obligation may allow the party or parties affected by the breach to terminate the treaty. The Vienna Convention sets out a number of grounds for termination as a result of breach, though these can be waived by the party affected (Article 45).

Vienna Convention on the Law of Treaties 1969

Article 45 Loss of a right to invoke a ground for invalidating, terminating, withdrawing from or suspending the operation of a treaty

A State may no longer invoke a ground for invalidating, terminating, withdrawing from or suspending the operation of a treaty under Articles 46 to 50 or Articles 60 and 62 if, after becoming aware of the facts:
   (a) it shall have expressly agreed that the treaty is valid or remains in force or continues in operation, as the case may be; or
   (b) it must by reason of its conduct be considered as having acquiesced in the validity of the treaty or in its maintenance in force or in operation, as the case may be.

Article 54 Termination of or withdrawal from a treaty under its provisions or by consent of the parties

The termination of a treaty or the withdrawal of a party may take place:
   (a) in conformity with the provisions of the treaty; or
   (b) at any time by consent of all the parties after consultation with the other contracting States.

Article 56 Denunciation of or withdrawal from a treaty containing no provision regarding termination, denunciation or withdrawal

1. A treaty which contains no provision regarding its termination and which does not provide for denunciation or withdrawal is not subject to denunciation or withdrawal unless:
    (a) it is established that the parties intended to admit the possibility of denunciation or withdrawal; or
    (b) a right of denunciation or withdrawal may be implied by the nature of the treaty.

2. A party shall give not less than twelve months' notice of its intention to denounce or withdraw from a treaty under paragraph 1.

Article 57 Suspension of the operation of a treaty under its provisions or by consent of the parties

The operation of a treaty in regard to all the parties or to a particular party may be suspended:
    (a) in conformity with the provisions of the treaty; or
    (b) at any time by consent of all the parties after consultation with the other contracting States.

Article 59 Termination or suspension of the operation of a treaty implied by conclusion of a later treaty

1. A treaty shall be considered as terminated if all the parties to it conclude a later treaty relating to the same subject-matter and:
    (a) it appears from the later treaty or is otherwise established that the parties intended that the matter should be governed by that treaty; or
    (b) the provisions of the later treaty are so far incompatible with those of the earlier one that the two treaties are not capable of being applied at the same time.

2. The earlier treaty shall be considered as only suspended in operation if it appears from the later treaty or is otherwise established that such was the intention of the parties.

Article 60 Termination or suspension of the operation of a treaty as a consequence of its breach

1. A material breach of a bilateral treaty by one of the parties entitles the other to invoke the breach as a ground for terminating the treaty or suspending its operation in whole or in part.

2. A material breach of a multilateral treaty by one of the parties entitles:
    (a) the other parties by unanimous agreement to suspend the operation of the treaty in whole or in part or to terminate it either:
        (i) in the relations between themselves and the defaulting State, or
        (ii) as between all the parties;
    (b) a party specially affected by the breach to invoke it as a ground for suspending the operation of the treaty in whole or in part in the relations between itself and the defaulting State;
    (c) any party other than the defaulting State to invoke the breach as a ground for suspending the operation of the treaty in whole or in part with respect to itself if the treaty is of such a character that a material breach of its provisions by one party radically changes the position of every party with respect to the further performance of its obligations under the treaty.

3. A material breach of a treaty, for the purpose of this article, consists in:
    (a) a repudiation of the treaty not sanctioned by the present Convention; or
    (b) the violation of a provision essential to the accomplishment of the object or purpose of the treaty.

4. The foregoing paragraphs are without prejudice to any provision in the treaty applicable in the event of a breach.

5. Paragraphs 1 to 3 do not apply to provisions relating to the protection of the human person contained in treaties of a humanitarian character, in particular to provisions prohibiting any form of reprisals against persons protected by such treaties.

Article 61 Supervening impossibility of performance

1. A party may invoke the impossibility of performing a treaty as a ground for terminating or withdrawing from it if the impossibility results from the permanent disappearance or destruction of an object indispensable for the execution of the treaty. If the impossibility is temporary, it may be invoked only as a ground for suspending the operation of the treaty.

2. Impossibility of performance may not be invoked by a party as a ground for terminating, withdrawing from or suspending the operation of a treaty if the impossibility is the result of a breach by that party either of an obligation under the treaty or of any other international obligation owed to any other party to the treaty.

Article 62 Fundamental changes of circumstances

1. A fundamental change of circumstances which has occurred with regard to those existing at the time of the conclusion of a treaty, and which was not foreseen by the parties, may not be invoked as a ground for terminating or withdrawing from the treaty unless:
   (a) the existence of those circumstances constituted an essential basis of the consent of the parties to be bound by the treaty; and
   (b) the effect of the change is radically to transform the extent of obligations still to be performed under the treaty.

2. A fundamental change of circumstances may not be invoked as a ground for terminating or withdrawing from a treaty:
   (a) if the treaty establishes a boundary; or
   (b) if the fundamental change is the result of a breach by the party invoking it either of an obligation under the treaty or of any other international obligation owed to any other party to the treaty.

3. If, under the foregoing paragraphs, a party may invoke a fundamental change of circumstances as a ground for terminating or withdrawing from a treaty it may also invoke the change as a ground for suspending the operation of the treaty.

Article 70 Consequences of the termination of a treaty

1. Unless the treaty otherwise provides or the parties otherwise agree, the termination of a treaty under its provisions or in accordance with the present Convention:
   (a) releases the parties from any obligation further to perform the treaty;
   (b) does not affect any right, obligation or legal situation of the parties created through the execution of the treaty prior to its termination.

2. If a State denounces or withdraws from a multilateral treaty, paragraph 1 applies in the relations between that State and each of the other parties to the treaty from the date when such denunciation or withdrawal takes effect.

Article 72 Consequences of the suspension of the operation of a treaty

1. Unless the treaty otherwise provides or the parties otherwise agree, the suspension of the operation of a treaty under its provisions or in accordance with the present Convention:
   (a) releases the parties between which the operation of the treaty is suspended from the obligation to perform the treaty in their mutual relations during the period of the suspension;
   (b) does not otherwise affect the legal relations between the parties established by the treaty.

2. During the period of the suspension the parties shall refrain from acts tending to obstruct the resumption of the operation of the treaty.

Article 73 Case of State Succession, State Responsibility and Outbreak of Hostilities

The provisions of the present Convention shall not prejudge any question that may arise in regard to a treaty… from the outbreak of hostilities between States.

Report of the International Law Commission to the General Assembly
Yearbook of the International Law Commission (1966) vol II

(1) The great majority of jurists recognize that a violation of a treaty by one party may give rise to a right in the other party to abrogate the treaty or to suspend the performance of its own obligations under the treaty. A violation of a treaty obligation, as of any other obligation, may give rise to a right in the other party to take non-forcible reprisals, and these reprisals may properly relate to the defaulting party's rights under the treaty. Opinion differs, however, as to the extent of the right to abrogate the treaty and

the conditions under which it may be exercised. Some jurists, in the absence of effective international machinery for securing the observance of treaties, are more impressed with the innocent party's need to have this right as a sanction for the violation of the treaty. They tend to formulate the right in unqualified terms, giving the innocent party a general right to abrogate the treaty in the event of a breach. Other jurists are more impressed with the risk that a State may allege a trivial or even fictitious breach simply to furnish a pretext for denouncing a treaty which it now finds embarrassing. These jurists tend to restrict the right of denunciation to 'material' or 'fundamental' breaches and also to subject the exercise of the right to procedural conditions.

(2) State practice does not give great assistance in determining the true extent of this right or the proper conditions for its exercise. In many cases, the denouncing State has decided for quite other reasons to put an end to the treaty and, having alleged the violation primarily to provide a pretext for its action, has not been prepared to enter into a serious discussion of the legal principles involved. The other party has usually contested the denunciation primarily on the basis of the facts; and, if it has sometimes used language appearing to deny that *unilateral* denunciation is ever justified, this has usually appeared rather to be a protest against the one-sided and arbitrary pronouncements of the denouncing State than a rejection of the right to denounce when serious violations are established.

Fisheries Jurisdiction Case (*United Kingdom* v *Iceland*)
Jurisdiction, ICJ Rep 1973 3, International Court of Justice

The United Kingdom, as part of what was known as 'the Cod War', applied to the Court claiming that the proposed extension of Iceland's exclusive fisheries zone from 12 miles to 50 miles was a breach of an agreement between the two States, evidenced by an Exchange of Notes in 1961. Iceland contended that the Court had no jurisdiction to hear the case and it also submitted that any agreement that it had with the United Kingdom did not extend to its fisheries jurisdiction and was no longer binding due to a fundamental change of circumstances. The Court decided that it did have jurisdiction. It also considered that Article 62 of the Vienna Convention on the Law of Treaties represented customary international law.

37. One of the basic requirements embodied in [Article 62] is that the change of circumstances must have been a fundamental one. In this respect the Government of Iceland has, with regard to developments in fishing techniques, referred…to the increased exploitation of the fishery resources in the seas surrounding Iceland and to the danger of still further exploitation because of an increase in the catching capacity of fishing fleets. The Icelandic statements recall the exceptional dependence of that country on its fishing for its existence and economic development.…

38. The invocation by Iceland of its 'vital interests', which were not made the subject of an express reservation to the acceptance of the jurisdictional obligation under the 1961 Exchange of Notes, must be interpreted, in the context of the assertion of changed circumstances, as an indication by Iceland of the reason why it regards as fundamental the changes which in its view have taken place in previously existing fishing techniques. This interpretation would correspond to the traditional view that the changes of circumstances which must be regarded as fundamental or vital are those which imperil the existence or vital development of one of the parties.

43. Moreover, in order that a change of circumstances may give rise to a ground for invoking the termination of a treaty it is also necessary that it should have resulted in a radical transformation of the extent of the obligations still to be performed. The change must have increased the burden of the obligations to be executed to the extent of rendering the performance something essentially different from that originally undertaken. In respect of the obligation with which the Court is here concerned, this condition is wholly unsatisfied; the change of circumstances alleged by Iceland cannot be said to have transformed radically the extent of the jurisdictional obligation which is imposed in the 1961 Exchange of Notes. The compromissory clause enabled either of the parties to submit to the Court any dispute between them relating to an extension of Icelandic fisheries jurisdiction in the waters above its continental shelf beyond the 12-mile limit. The present dispute is exactly of the character anticipated in the compromissory clause of the Exchange of Notes. Not only has the jurisdictional obligation not been radically transformed in its extent; it has remained precisely what it was in 1961.

Legal Consequences for States of the Continued Presence of South Africa in Namibia (South West Africa) notwithstanding Security Council Resolution 276 (1970)

Advisory Opinion, ICJ Rep 1971 16, International Court of Justice

The Security Council had resolved that South Africa's Mandate over South West Africa (Namibia) was terminated but this had been ignored by South Africa. The Security Council then resolved, by Resolution 276 (1970), that the continued presence of South Africa in Namibia was illegal, as had General Assembly Resolution 2145 (XXI). The Council sought an advisory opinion from the Court, asking what were the legal consequences for States of the continued presence of South Africa in Namibia notwithstanding Resolution 276 (1970). The Court held that South Africa was under an obligation to withdraw its administration in Namibia. It also held that other States were under an obligation not to recognise any acts of South Africa's administration in Namibia (see Chapter 6).

94. In examining this action of the General Assembly [under Resolution 2145 (XXI)] it is appropriate to have regard to the general principles of international law regulating termination of a treaty relationship on account of breach. For even if the mandate is viewed as having the character of an institution, as is maintained, it depends on those international agreements which created the system and regulated its application. As the Court indicated in 1962 'this Mandate, like practically all other similar Mandates' was 'a special type of instrument composite in nature and instituting a novel international régime. It incorporates a definite agreement...' (ICJ Rep 1962, p. 331). The Court stated conclusively in that Judgment that the Mandate '...in fact and in law, is an international agreement having the character of a treaty or convention' (ICJ Rep 1962, p. 330). The rules laid down by the Vienna Convention on the Law of Treaties concerning termination of a treaty relationship on account of breach (adopted without a dissenting vote) may in many respects be considered as a codification of existing customary law on the subject. In the light of these rules, only a material breach of a treaty justifies termination, such breach being defined as:

   (a) a repudiation of the treaty not sanctioned by the present Convention; or

   (b) the violation of a provision essential to the accomplishment of the object or purpose of the treaty (Art. 60, para. 3).

95. General Assembly resolution 2145 (XXI) determines that both forms of material breach had occurred in this case. By stressing that South Africa 'has, in fact, disavowed the Mandate', the General Assembly declared in fact that it had repudiated it. The resolution in question is therefore to be viewed as the exercise of the right to terminate a relationship in case of a deliberate and persistent violation of obligations which destroys the very object and purpose of that relationship.

96. It has been contended that the Covenant of the League of Nations did not confer on the Council of the League power to terminate a mandate for misconduct of the mandatory and that no such power could therefore be exercised by the United Nations, since it could not derive from the League greater powers than the latter itself had. For this objection to prevail it would be necessary to show that the mandates system, as established under the League, excluded the application of the general principle of law that a right of termination on account of breach must be presumed to exist in respect of all treaties, except as regards provisions relating to the protection of the human person contained in treaties of a humanitarian character (as indicated in Art. 60, para. 5, of the Vienna Convention). The silence of a treaty as to the existence of such a right cannot be interpreted as implying the exclusion of a right which has its source outside the treaty, in general international law, and is dependent on the occurrence of circumstances which are not normally envisaged when a treaty is concluded....

101. It has been suggested that, even if the Council of the League had possessed the power of revocation of the Mandate in an extreme case, it could not have been exercised unilaterally but only in co-operation with the mandatory Power. However, revocation could only result from a situation in which the Mandatory had committed a serious breach of the obligations it had undertaken. To contend, on the basis of the principle of unanimity which applied in the League of Nations, that in this case revocation could only take place with the concurrence of the Mandatory, would not only run contrary to the general principle of law governing termination on account of breach, but also postulate an impossibility. For obvious reasons, the consent of the wrongdoer to such a form of termination cannot be required.

Case Concerning the Gabčíkovo-Nagymaros Project Danube Dam Case (*Hungary* v *Slovakia*)

ICJ Rep 1997 7, International Court of Justice

In 1977, Hungary and Czechoslovakia concluded a treaty to facilitate the construction of dams on the Danube River. Hungary later suspended works due to environmental concerns in response to which Czechoslovakia carried out unilateral measures. Slovakia became a party to the 1977 Treaty as successor to Czechoslovakia. Hungary then claimed the right to terminate the treaty, at which point the dispute was submitted to the ICJ. Hungary also submitted that it was entitled to terminate the treaty on the ground that Czechoslovakia/Slovakia had violated Articles of the treaty by undertaking unilateral measures, culminating in the diversion of the Danube. The Court rejected Hungary's claim to terminate the treaty.

100. The 1977 Treaty does not contain any provision regarding its termination...

101. The Court will now turn to the first ground advanced by Hungary, that of the state of necessity. In this respect, the Court will merely observe that, even if a state of necessity is found to exist, it is not a ground for the termination of a treaty. It may only be invoked to exonerate from its responsibility a State which has failed to implement a treaty...

102. Hungary also relied on the principle of the impossibility of performance as reflected in Article 61 ... [I]f the joint exploitation of the investment was no longer possible, this was originally because Hungary did not carry out most of the works for which it was responsible...; Article 61, paragraph 2, of the Vienna Convention expressly provides that impossibility of performance may not be invoked for the termination of a treaty by a party to that treaty when it results from that party's own breach of an obligation flowing from that treaty....

104. Hungary further argued that it was entitled to invoke a number of events which, cumulatively, would have constituted a fundamental change of circumstances [changes of a political nature, the reduced economic viability of the Project, and the progress of environmental knowledge and international environmental law]... The changed circumstances advanced by Hungary are, in the Court's view, not of such a nature...that their effect would radically transform the extent of the obligations still to be performed in order to accomplish the Project. A fundamental change of circumstances must have been unforeseen; the existence of the circumstances must have constituted an essential basis of the consent of the parties to be bound by the treaty...

106.... [I]t is only a material breach of the treaty itself, by a State party to that treaty, which entitles the other party to rely on it as a ground for terminating the treaty. The violation of other treaty rules or of rules of general international law may justify the taking of certain measures, including countermeasures, by the injured State, but it does not constitute a ground for termination under the law of treaties...

108....Czechoslovakia violated the Treaty only when it diverted the waters of the Danube into the bypass canal in October 1992. In constructing the works which would lead to the putting into operation of [the unilateral measure], Czechoslovakia did not act unlawfully.
In the Court's view, therefore, the notification of termination by Hungary on 19 May 1992 was premature.

International Law Commission, *Draft Articles on the Effects of Armed Conflicts on Treaties*

Yearbook of the International Law Commission (2011) Vol II, Part Two

Article 3 General principle

The existence of an armed conflict does not *ipso facto* terminate or suspend the operations of treaties:
(a) As between States parties to the conflict;
(b) As between a State party to the conflict and a State that is not.

Article 5 Application of rules on treaty interpretation

The rules of international law on treaty interpretation shall be applied to establish whether a treaty is susceptible to termination, withdrawal or suspension in the event of an armed conflict.

Article 5 Factors indicating whether a treaty is susceptible to termination, withdrawal or suspension

In order to ascertain whether a treaty is susceptible to termination, withdrawal or suspension in the event of an armed conflict, regard shall be had to all relevant factors, including:

(a) the nature of the treaty, in particular its subject matter, its object and purpose, its content and the number of parties to the treaty; and

(b) the characteristics of the armed conflict, such as its territorial extent, its scale and intensity, its duration and, in the case of non-international armed conflict, also the degree of outside involvement.

Article 7 Continued operation of treaties resulting from their subject matter

An indicative list of treaties the subject matter of which involves an implication that they continue in operation, in whole or in part, during armed conflict, is to be found in the annex of the present draft articles.

Annex: Indicative list of treaties referred to in article 7

(a) Treaties on the law of armed conflict, including treaties on international humanitarian law;

(b) Treaties declaring, creating or regulating a permanent regime or status or related permanent rights, including treaties establishing or modifying land and maritime boundaries;

(c) Multilateral law-making treaties;

(d) Treaties on international criminal justice;

(e) Treaties of friendship, commerce and navigation and agreements concerning private rights;

(f) Treaties for the international protection of human rights;

(g) Treaties relating to the international protection of the environment;

(h) Treaties relating to international watercourses and related installations and facilities;

(i) Treaties relating to aquifers and related installations and facilities;

(j) Treaties which are constituent instruments of international organizations;

(k) Treaties relating to the international settlement of disputes by peaceful means, including resort to conciliation, mediation, arbitration and judicial settlement;

(l) Treaties relating to diplomatic and consular relations.

NOTES

1. A treaty can be terminated by the consent of the parties (Article 54). The main grounds for contested termination in the Vienna Convention are material breach (Article 60) and fundamental change of circumstances (Article 62). In both cases, the Vienna Convention represents customary international law (see Section 2B). However, as can be seen in the above extracts from the *Fisheries Jurisdiction Case*, the *Namibia Opinion* and the *Danube Dam Case*, it can be difficult for a State to prove that there has been a breach of a treaty that entitles a State to terminate the treaty. It seems that the ICJ also implicitly requires that responses to alleged material breaches must be proved to be actually in response to the initial conduct; considerations of temporal proximity seem relevant in this regard—see *Application of the Interim Accord of 13 September 1995 (FYROM v Greece)* ICJ Rep 2011 644, [163].

2. A State cannot invoke its internal law as a justification for a failure to comply with a treaty unless it was objectively manifestly obvious to any State that the first State's consent to be bound by a treaty was contrary to an internal law of fundamental importance to that first State (Articles 27 and 46 Vienna Convention, and the extract from *Nicaragua v Colombia* in Section 6B). As clarified by the ICJ, this rule also applies to the invocation of domestic court judgments as a purported justification for non-compliance—see *Questions relating to the Obligation to Prosecute or Extradite (Belgium v Senegal)* (Merits) ICJ Rep 2012 422, [113].

3. It is possible to suspend the operation of a treaty for a period of time, as an alternative to complete termination (Article 57), including when there is a state of emergency under a human rights treaty (see Chapter 6). In certain instances, a treaty provision may be severed from the rest of the treaty (Article 44). There is no general right of unilateral denunciation of a treaty unless this is provided for by the treaty itself.

4. The process to be followed in cases of termination is set out in Articles 65 to 68. These include procedural safeguards designed to give the State in breach an opportunity to rectify the situation before termination occurs.

4

International Law and Domestic Law

INTRODUCTORY NOTE

The interaction between international law and national (or 'municipal' or 'domestic') law demonstrates the struggle between State sovereignty and the international legal order. While the international legal order seeks to organise international society in accordance with the general interests of the international community, State sovereignty can be used to protect a State against the intervention of international law into its national legal system. However, as international law expands into areas such as human rights and the environment (see Chapters 6 and 12), there has been a reduction in the areas of law which can be considered to be governed solely by the national law of a State.

While the tension between these two systems is often explained by reference to monistic or dualistic theories (see Section 1), the resolution of this struggle is usually determined by the constitution of each State—the constitution having been created by political acts—and by the interpretation of the constitution and national laws by the national courts of each State. As a consequence, the application of international law within a national legal system will vary from State to State. Further, the lack of significant enforcement measures in international law has meant that it is often through national courts that international law is enforced, and therefore national law can often determine the effectiveness of international legal decisions and the lawfulness of international actions.

SECTION 1: THEORIES

H. Lauterpacht, *Oppenheim's International Law*
vol I (8th edn, 1955)

According to what may be called the dualistic view, the Law of Nations and the Municipal Law of the several States are essentially different from each other. They differ, first, as regards their sources. The sources of Municipal Law are custom grown up within the boundaries of the State concerned and statutes enacted by the law-giving authority. The sources of International Law are custom grown up among States and law-making treaties concluded by them.

The Law of Nations and Municipal Law differ, secondly, regarding the relations they regulate. Municipal Law regulates relations between the individuals under the sway of a State and the relations between the State and the individual. International Law, on the other hand, regulates relations between States.

The Law of Nations and Municipal Law differ, thirdly, with regard to the substance of their law: whereas Municipal Law is a law of a sovereign over individuals subjected to his sway, the Law of Nations is a law not above, but between, sovereign States, and is therefore a weaker law.

If the Law of Nations and Municipal Law differ as demonstrated, the Law of Nations can neither as a body nor in parts be *per se* a part of Municipal Law. Just as Municipal Law lacks the power of altering or creating rules of International Law, so the latter lacks absolutely the power of altering or creating rules of Municipal Law. If, according to the Municipal Law of an individual State, the Law of Nations as a body or in parts is considered to be part of the law of the land, this can only be so either by municipal custom or by statute, and then the respective rules of the Law of Nations have by adoption become at the same time rules of Municipal Law. Wherever and whenever such total or partial adoption has not taken place, municipal courts cannot be considered to be bound by International Law, because it has, *per se*, no power over municipal courts. And if it happens that a rule of Municipal Law is in indubitable conflict with a rule of the Law of Nations, municipal courts must apply the former....

The above dualistic view is opposed by what may conveniently be called the monistic doctrine. The latter rejects all three premises of the dualists. It denies, in the first instance, that the subjects of the two systems of law are essentially different and maintains that in both it is ultimately the conduct of the individuals which is regulated by law, the only difference being that in the international sphere the consequences of such conduct are attributed to the State. Secondly, it asserts that in both spheres law is essentially a command binding upon the subjects of the law independently of their will. Thirdly, it maintains that International Law and Municipal Law, far from being essentially different, must be regarded as manifestations of a single conception of law. This is so not only for the terminological reason that it would be improper to give the same designation of law to two fundamentally different sets of rules governing the same conduct. The main reason for the essential identity of the two spheres of law is, it is maintained, that some of the fundamental notions of International Law cannot be comprehended without the assumption of a superior legal order from which the various systems of Municipal Law are, in a sense, derived by way of delegation. It is International Law which determines the jurisdictional limits of the personal and territorial competence of States. Similarly, it is only by reference to a higher legal rule in relation to which they are all equal, that the equality and independence of a number of sovereign States can be conceived. Failing that superior legal order, the science of law would be confronted with the spectacle of some sixty sovereign States [as at 1955] each claiming to be the absolutely highest and underived authority. It is admitted that municipal courts may be bound by the law of their States to enforce statutes which are contrary to International Law. But this, it may be said, merely shows that, in view of the weakness of International Law and organisation, States admit and tolerate what is actually a conflict of duties within the same legal system—a phenomenon not altogether unknown in other spheres of Municipal Law. In any case, from the point of view of International Law the validity of a pronouncement of a municipal court is in such case purely provisional. It still leaves intact the international responsibility of the State. It is a well recognised rule that a State is internationally responsible for the decisions of its courts, even if given in conformity with the law of the State concerned, whenever that law happens to be contrary to International Law.

G. Fitzmaurice, 'The General Principles of International Law Considered from the Standpoint of the Rule of Law'
92 RC 5 (1957-II)

First of all..., a radical view of the whole subject may be propounded to the effect that the entire monist-dualist controversy is unreal, artificial and strictly beside the point, because it assumes something that has to exist for there to be any controversy at all—and which in fact does not exist—namely a *common field* in which the two legal orders under discussion both simultaneously have their spheres of activity. It is proposed here to state the case for this view. In order that there can be controversy about whether the relations between two orders are relations of *co-ordination* between self-existent independent orders, or relations of *subordination* of the one to the other, or of the other to the one—or again whether they are part of the same order, but both subordinate to a superior order—it is necessary that they should both be purporting to be, and in fact be, applicable in the same field—that is, to the same set of relations and transactions....

International and domestic law having no common field, there is no need, nor would there be any point in discussing whether their relationship is one of co-ordination, or of subordination one to another, or of mutual subordination to a common superior order. There is no more point in discussing the abstract question of supremacy in regard to these two legal orders than, as has been seen, there would be in discussing whether abstract supremacy lay with English or French law. Such a question is necessarily meaningless. Each is supreme in its own field, and all that matters for this purpose is that international law is supreme in the international field. The very question of supremacy as between the two orders, national and international, is irrelevant, as is also that of the existence of some superior norm or order conferring supremacy. National law is not and cannot be a rival to international law in the international field, or it would cease to be national and become international, which, *ex hypothesi*, it is not. National law, *by definition*, cannot govern the action of, or relations with, other States. It may govern or fetter the action of its own State in such a way that the latter cannot fulfil its international obligations, but again, by definition only at the national level and without legal effect or operation beyond it. Formally, therefore, international and domestic law as *systems* can never come into conflict. What may occur is something strictly different, namely a conflict of *obligations*, or an inability for the State *on the domestic plane* to act in the manner required by international law. The supremacy of international law in the international field does not in these circumstances entail that the judge in the municipal courts of the State must override local law and apply international law. Whether he does or can do this depends on the local law itself, and on what legislative or administrative steps can be or are taken to deal with the matter. The supremacy of international law in the international field simply means that if nothing can be or is done, the State will, on the international plane, have committed a breach of its international law obligations, for which it will be internationally responsible, and in respect of which it cannot plead the condition of its domestic law by way of absolution. International law does not therefore in any way purport to govern the content of national law in the national field—nor does it need to. It simply says—and this is all it needs to say—that certain things are not valid according to international law, and that if a State in the application of its domestic law acts contrary to international law in these respects, it will commit a breach of its international obligations.

NOTES
1. Lauterpacht indicates the two main theories dealing with the interaction between international law and national law: dualism and monism. Fitzmaurice tries to take a median line by declaring that the systems of international law and national law have no common field, but his position is essentially dualist and is only descriptive not interpretative. Also, contrary to Fitzmaurice's view, the two systems do interact, for example, in human rights law and in economic law (Chapters 6 and 13).
2. While these theories are helpful in attempting to explain why international law and national law interact, rarely do courts or other judicial bodies reach conclusions on the issues before them by applying monism, dualism or any other theory (although see the reference to the 'dualistic' UK in *Ex parte Pinochet* [1999] 2 All ER 97). Instead, usually courts decide cases in the context of the particular constitutional rules and principles of the relevant State and in accordance with that State's laws. As seen below, when courts do make use of theoretical approaches the terminology they use is often different from the international law terminology.

SECTION 2: NATIONAL LAW ON THE INTERNATIONAL PLANE

As was shown in Chapter 2, national law can be of value when determining the sources of international law, particularly as it can be evidence of State practice as part of customary international law.

Brazilian Loans Case (France v Brazil)
PCIJ Ser A (1929) No 21, p. 124, Permanent Court of International Justice

In the context of a case concerning loans made by the Brazilian government, the Court had to consider the meaning and effect of French national law in a dispute between the two States.

Though bound to apply municipal law when circumstances so require, the Court, which is a tribunal of international law, and which, in this capacity, is deemed itself to know what this law is, is not obliged also to know the municipal law of the various countries. All that can be said in this respect is that the Court may possibly be obliged to obtain knowledge regarding the municipal law which has to be applied. And this it must do, either by means of evidence furnished it by the Parties or by means of any researches which the Court may think fit to undertake or to cause to be undertaken.

Once the Court has arrived at the conclusion that it is necessary to apply the municipal law of a particular country, there seems no doubt that it must seek to apply it as it would be applied in that country. It would not be applying the municipal law of a country if it were to apply it in a manner different from that in which that law would be applied in the country in which it is in force.

It follows that the Court must pay the utmost regard to the decisions of the municipal courts of a country, for it is with the aid of their jurisprudence that it will be enabled to decide what are the rules which, in actual fact, are applied in the country the law of which is recognized as applicable in a given case. If the Court were obliged to disregard the decisions of municipal courts, the result would be that it might in certain circumstances apply rules other than those actually applied; this would seem to be contrary to the whole theory on which the application of municipal law is based.

Of course the Court will endeavour to make a just appreciation of the jurisprudence of municipal courts. If this is uncertain or divided, it will rest with the Court to select the interpretation which it considers most in conformity with the law. But to compel the Court to disregard that jurisprudence would not be in conformity with its function when applying municipal law.

Barcelona Traction, Light and Power Company Limited Case (*Belgium* v *Spain*) (*Second Phase*)

ICJ Rep 1970 3, International Court of Justice

The issue arose in this case as to whether the national law concept of 'the company' was applicable in international law. As to the law regarding the nationality of the companies see the extract in Chapter 11.

37. In seeking to determine the law applicable to this case, the Court has to bear in mind the continuous evolution of international law.…These…changes have given birth to municipal institutions, which have transcended frontiers and have begun to exercise considerable influence on international relations. One of these phenomena which has a particular bearing on the present case is the corporate entity.

38. In this field international law is called upon to recognize institutions of municipal law that have an important and extensive role in the international field. This does not necessarily imply drawing any analogy between its own institutions and those of municipal law, nor does it amount to making rules of international law dependent upon categories of municipal law. All it means is that international law has had to recognize the corporate entity as an institution created by States in a domain essentially within their domestic jurisdiction. This in turn requires that, whenever legal issues arise concerning the rights of States with regard to the treatment of companies and shareholders, as to which rights international law has not established its own rules, it has to refer to the relevant rules of municipal law. Consequently, in view of the relevance to the present case of the rights of the corporate entity and its shareholders under municipal law, the Court must devote attention to the nature and interrelation of those rights.…

50. In turning now to the international legal aspects of the case, the Court must, as already indicated, start from the fact that the present case essentially involves factors derived from municipal law—the distinction and the community between the company and the shareholder—which the Parties, however widely their interpretations may differ, each take as the point of departure of their reasoning. If the Court were to decide the case in disregard of the relevant institutions of municipal law it would, without justification, invite serious legal difficulties. It would lose touch with reality, for there are no corresponding institutions of international law to which the Court could resort. Thus the Court has, as indicated, not only to take cognizance of municipal law but also to refer to it. It is to rules generally accepted by municipal legal systems which recognize the limited company whose capital is represented by shares, and not to the municipal law of a particular State, that international law refers. In referring to such rules, the Court cannot modify, still less deform them.

Vienna Convention on the Law of Treaties 1969

1155 UNTS 331

Article 27 Internal law and observance of treaties

A party may not invoke the provisions of its internal law as justification for its failure to perform a treaty. This rule is without prejudice to Article 46.

Article 46 Provisions of internal law regarding competence to conclude treaties

1. A State may not invoke the fact that its consent to be bound by a treaty has been expressed in violation of a provision of its internal law regarding competence to conclude treaties as invalidating its consent unless that violation was manifest and concerned a rule of its internal law of fundamental importance.

2. A violation is manifest if it would be objectively evident to any State conducting itself in the matter in accordance with normal practice and in good faith.

NOTES

1. As national courts are a part of the State—the State often being defined as comprising the executive, the legislature and the judiciary—the decisions of those courts, as well as the national law itself, can help to clarify the content of international law. As such, national law forms a part of the sources of international law (see Chapter 2).
2. Articles 27 and 46 of the Vienna Convention reflect customary international law in providing that a State cannot rely on its national law as a justification for a breach of its international obligations (see *Polish Nationals in Danzig Case*, PCIJ Ser A/B (1932) No 44, 24). If a change in national law is required in order to enable a State to fulfil its international obligations, then the State must make that change or else mitigate its international responsibility by taking action under international law. International tribunals do award damages for injury arising out of decisions of national courts which have breached international law.

SECTION 3: INTERNATIONAL LAW ON THE NATIONAL PLANE

A. Cassese, *International Law*
(2nd edn, 2005)

Generally speaking, in the second half of the twentieth century domestic systems gradually opened the door to international values and States became increasingly willing to bow to international law. Although each State is free to choose its own mechanisms for implementing international rules, even a cursory survey of national legal systems shows that two basic modalities prevail.

The first is *automatic standing incorporation* of international rules. Such incorporation occurs whenever the national constitution, or a law (or, in the case of judge-made law, judicial decisions) enjoin that all State officials as well as all nationals and other individuals living on the territory of the State are bound to apply certain present or future rules of international law. In other words, an internal norm provides in a permanent way for the automatic incorporation into national law of any relevant rule of international (customary or treaty) law, without there being any need for the passing of an ad hoc national statute (subject to the exception of non-self-executing international rules)....

The second mechanism is *legislative ad hoc incorporation* of international rules. Under this system international rules become applicable within the State legal system only if and when the relevant parliamentary authorities pass *specific* implementing legislation. This legislation may take one of two principal forms. First, it may consist of an act of parliament translating the various treaty provisions into national legislation, setting out in detail the various obligations, powers, and rights stemming from those international provisions (*statutory ad hoc incorporation of international rules*). Second, the act of parliament may confine itself to enjoining the automatic applicability of the international rule within the national legal system, without reformulating that rule ad hoc (*automatic ad hoc incorporation of international law*). Under this second modality *in substance* the mechanism works in a similar way to the one that we have termed above 'automatic standing incorporation' (the only difference being that now the incorporation is effected on a case-by-case basis). Now as well, State officials, and all the individuals concerned, become duty-bound to abide by the international provisions to which the act of parliament makes reference....

A survey of national legislation and case law shows that some States tend to put the international rules incorporated into the national legal system (whether automatically or through ad hoc legislative enactment) on the same footing as national legislation of domestic origin. As a consequence, the general principles governing relationships between rules having the same rank apply: a subsequent law repeals or modifies or at any rate supersedes a previous law; a special law prevails over a general law; a subsequent general law does not derogate from a prior special law. It follows that the national legislature may at any time pass a law amending or repealing a rule of international origin. True, in this case the State, if it applies the national law in lieu of the international rule, incurs international responsibility for a breach of international law. The fact remains, however, that the international rule is set aside by a simple act of parliament.

In contrast, other States tend to accord international rules a status and rank higher than that of national legislation. Such an approach is normally linked to the nature of their national constitution. Where the constitution is 'flexible' (that is, it can be amended by simple act of parliament), or in any case the principle of legislative supremacy obtains, the only way of giving international rules overriding importance would be to entrench them, so that it is not possible for legislation passed by simple majority to modify them. Such a course of action, however, does not seem to have occurred so far in those States which have a 'flexible' constitution.

Things are different where the constitution is 'rigid', in particular where it is 'functionally rigid' (that is, the constitution lays down special requirements for constitutional amendments and in addition sets up a court authorized to undertake judicial review of legislation so as to establish whether the legislature exceeds its powers and infringes the constitution). In these constitutional systems, if the constitution provides for the incorporation of international rules, normally those rules enjoy constitutional or quasi-constitutional status and therefore rank higher than normal law. It follows that the legislature is precluded from passing a law contrary to an international rule, unless of course this law is enacted through the special procedure required for constitutional legislation. The logic behind this approach is that international legal standards should always be regarded as having overriding importance. Therefore, in addition to binding the executive branch and all citizens, they cannot be set aside by simple parliamentary majority. Only under special circumstances, when compelling national interests prevail and a special majority (say, a two-thirds majority) is mustered in parliament, may those rules be overridden…

States tend to regulate national incorporation of international rules on the basis of two different requirements. First, they may have to choose between a *statist* (or nationalist) and an *internationalist* approach. Second, they may have to take into account the question of the *relationship between the executive and legislative branch* of government, and shape the mechanism for implementing international law accordingly.

States choosing a statist or nationalist approach incline (i) to adopt legislative ad hoc incorporation and (ii) to put international rules on the same footing as national legislation of domestic origin. In contrast, States taking an international outlook tend (i) to opt for the automatic incorporation (whether standing or ad hoc) of international rules and (ii) to accord international rules a status and rank higher than that of national legislation.…

In sum, most States do not accord primacy to international rules in their national legal systems. Thus, it may be concluded that most members of the world community tend to play down the possible role of international legal standards in their domestic legal setting. It does not follow, however, that they normally and systematically disregard international norms. The contrary is rather the rule. The failure of States to accord to international law pride of place at home only means that they do not intend to tie their hands formally, at the constitutional or legislative level. In other words, subject to the few exceptions already referred to States ultimately prefer not to enshrine in their constitutions or in their laws a firm and irrevocable commitment to unqualified observance of all international rules.

To limit, at least in part, the markedly statist outlook taken by many States, courts may play a crucial role by stepping in to ensure compliance with international legal standards. Whenever their national legislation does not provide them with the legal means for making international values prevail, they have at least two interpretative principles available: that concerning the presumption in favour of international treaties, and the principle of speciality.… By judiciously resorting to either of these principles courts may make international law advance in a significant way.

M. Kirby, 'Transnational Judicial Dialogue, Internationalisation of Law and Australian Judges'

9 *Melbourne Journal of International Law* 171 (2008)

A distinctive feature of the present age has been the increase in dialogue between judges and other lawyers across national boundaries. This dialogue has concerned both the substance of the law and its doctrines and procedures for conducting trials, appeals and the work of the courts generally.

To some extent the dialogue has been comparatively uncontroversial, as in cases where national judges are called upon to interpret international treaties incorporated into municipal law. The growth of treaty law, especially since 1945, has meant that increasing numbers of cases have involved national courts in construing treaty provisions. There are strong reasons why such tasks of interpretation should be carried out, as far as possible, in a consistent way. Recognition of this principle has taken Australian courts to a study of the international law governing the interpretation of treaties; the *travaux préparatoires* that preceded the adoption of the treaty; and the decisions of courts and tribunals of high authority in other countries struggling with the same or similar problems.

More controversial, at least in Australia, has been the extent to which it is legitimate for judges in national courts in non-treaty cases to invoke decisions of courts of other countries, or principles of international law, in discharging their responsibilities of finding and declaring national law. Most controversial of all has been the invocation of the international law of human rights, especially in matters of constitutional adjudication.…[There is] a background of many professional gatherings in which judges and practising lawyers from many countries now participate, share ideas and experience, and receive information and the stimulus of fresh insights from colleagues in other jurisdictions.…

Undoubtedly, the most sensitive question in this regard has been the extent to which international law may be utilised in expressing the requirements of a national constitution. That question has been vigorously contested in countries, like Australia, that observe the dualist theory of international law. According to the strict appreciation of this theory, international law and municipal law comprise 'two essentially different legal systems, existing side by side within different spheres of action—the international plane and the domestic plane'.

It is clear from available literature that the issue of comparative constitutionalism, and specifically of the use of international human rights law in the interpretation of national constitutions, is a lively subject of debate in national courts, academic institutions and other bodies.…

It is in that sense that judges today, in Australia as elsewhere, live in a world in which international law plays an increasing role and impinges on the judicial perceptions of reality and justice. Inevitably, these perceptions spill over into reasoning addressed to the solutions of contemporary problems of municipal law.

It would not be proper for a municipal judge, unilaterally, to attempt to introduce an entire body of international law into domestic jurisdiction—where the executive government and parliament have held back from doing so—by 'the back door', as it were. No one doubts that this is so. But to say this is, in effect, no more than to recognise the interstitial role of the judiciary in expounding the common law and declaring new rules and obligations that bind particular individuals and render them liable to legal sanctions.

Between the use of international texts and jurisprudence as tools in reasoning (which is legitimate) and 'back door' incorporation of entire treaty obligations (which is not), there is obviously a great deal of room for debate and difference amongst particular municipal judges. This is not only true of Australia. There is an equally lively debate upon this topic in other countries, most notably the US.…

For most countries these arguments will be perceived as presenting immaterial concerns because the judges have their own constitutional or statutory charters of fundamental human rights bearing some analogy to the equivalent statements of rights in international human rights law. For judges in such countries, the notion of rejecting the jurisprudence of international or regional courts and treaty bodies would be unthinkable, even where those judges are not bound to follow them as a matter of legal duty. For a country, such as Australia, at an earlier stage of legal development on this issue, the legal culture is partly indifferent and partly hostile. In regard to the field of international human rights law, in particular, the hostility is sometimes acute.…The likelihood is that the transnational judicial dialogue evidenced by the developments described in this article, will continue to gather pace. Thus, the provision of information to judges on international legal developments seems a useful starting point. Some judges would find such materials helpful although not binding. Those who do not want such information are at liberty to ignore it. Those who feel a need to use it in various ways must obviously do so in a manner that conforms to their own municipal law.

NOTES

1. Cassese notes the variety of methods that national law takes in relation to international law. He shows that the particular constitutional rules and principles of the relevant State, and its over-all response to international law, determine how national law interacts with international law. He also indicates how the growing interdependence of States, globalisation and the increasing amount of international law all have an impact on national law.

2. Even where the Constitution of a State appears to provide clear direct application of inter-national law, in many cases, as in Germany and the United States (the latter discussed at Section 4B), this is still subject to interpretation by a Constitutional Court (or its equivalent) to ensure that the resulting national law (created by international law) is consistent with the

constitution. Constitutional provisions incorporating treaties and international customary law are often restrictively applied by national courts, and can be overridden by contrary national legislation and by inconsistent provisions of the constitution. In addition, evidence of customary law must be proved to the satisfaction of the national court and it is often the case that if a treaty is to be fully effective in national law then it will have to be incorporated in legislation generally.

3. While, as shown below, the United Kingdom applies a different approach to the incorporation of international treaties than to the incorporation of international customary law, this distinction is not made in many other European States. While most Commonwealth States inherited versions of the common law developed in the United Kingdom, they usually also have a documentary constitution. However, the majority have no constitutional provision dealing with the impact of international law on national legal systems. As a result, national courts in Commonwealth States have generally adopted a similar approach to that employed in the United Kingdom.

4. There appears to be a definite development by national courts in all States to apply international law into national law with increasing frequency. In most cases, the national courts use international law (including treaties and decisions by international bodies), sometimes through comparisons with the law from other States, to assist in the interpretation of national law and to buttress the court's decisions. This is particularly the situation where the relevant international law concerns human rights or otherwise grants rights to individuals, as shown by the extract from Kirby (a former judge of the highest court in Australia). Despite the reluctance by judges in some national systems to apply international law, this extract shows that there has been increased dialogue between judges across national boundaries on the substance and application of international law by national courts as they approach the resolution of 'local' legal problems.

5. As discussed in Section 4A in relation to the United Kingdom, most States amend their national laws and practices to comply with international legally binding decisions of international bodies, such as the United Nations Security Council. This will include decisions about non-recognition of States, economic sanctions and the establishment of international bodies, such as the International Criminal Tribunal for the Former Yugoslavia (see Chapters 5, 14, 15 and 16). Many States will also change their laws, sometimes through decisions by national courts, as a result of international non-legally binding decisions by international bodies, such as human rights supervisory bodies (see Chapter 6).

SECTION 4: EXAMPLES OF INTERNATIONAL LAW ON THE NATIONAL PLANE

The following examples of national law applications of international law have been chosen as they demonstrate the diversity of the mechanisms for implementing international law described by Cassese above.

A: United Kingdom

The United Kingdom does not have a single document constitution. Instead its constitution is ascertained by an examination of such material as legislation, judicial decisions and political or Parliamentary conventions and practices. One of the fundamental principles of its unwritten constitution is that of 'Parliamentary Sovereignty'. This has been defined as meaning that Parliament 'has, under the English constitution, the right to make or unmake any law whatever; and, further, that no person or body is recognised by the law of England as having a right to override or set aside the legislation of Parliament' (A. Dicey, *Introduction to the Study of the Law of the Constitution*, 5th edn, 1897, p. 38). The relationship between the law of the United Kingdom and international law is said to vary as between customary international law and treaty obligations.

(a) Treaties

International Tin Council Case (J. H. Rayner (Mincing Lane) Ltd v Department of Trade and Industry)

[1990] 2 AC 418, United Kingdom House of Lords

This case was one of a number of actions brought by creditors against the International Tin Council (ITC) after it was unable to meet its debts. The ITC was founded by a treaty (the Sixth International Tin Agreement or ITA 6) which operated in the United Kingdom pursuant to a Headquarters Agreement (another treaty), although neither treaty was incorporated in the national law of the United Kingdom. The claimants argued that the treaty provided them with a right of action against the States parties directly, rather than against the ITC. The House of Lords unanimously rejected the claimants' arguments.

LORD OLIVER: It is axiomatic that municipal courts have not and cannot have the competence to adjudicate upon or to enforce the rights arising out of transactions entered into by independent sovereign states between themselves on the plane of international law.... That is the first of the underlying principles. The second is that, as a matter of the constitutional law of the United Kingdom, the Royal Prerogative, whilst it embraces the making of treaties, does not extend to altering the law or conferring rights upon individuals or depriving individuals of rights which they enjoy in domestic law without the intervention of Parliament. Treaties, as it is sometimes expressed, are not self-executing. Quite simply, a treaty is not part of English law unless and until it has been incorporated into the law by legislation. So far as individuals are concerned, it is *res inter alios acta* from which they cannot derive rights and by which they cannot be deprived of rights or subjected to obligations; and it is outside the purview of the court not only because it is made in the conduct of foreign relations, which are a prerogative of the Crown, but also because, as a source of rights and obligations, it is irrelevant.

These propositions do not, however, involve as a corollary that the court must never look at or construe a treaty. Where, for instance, a treaty is directly incorporated into English law by Act of the legislature, its terms become subject to the interpretative jurisdiction of the court in the same way as any other Act of the legislature. *Fothergill v Monarch Airlines Ltd* [1981] AC 251 is a recent example. Again, it is well established that where a statute is enacted in order to give effect to the United Kingdom's obligations under a treaty, the terms of the treaty may have to be considered and, if necessary, construed in order to resolve any ambiguity or obscurity as to the meaning or scope of the statute. Clearly, also, where parties have entered into a domestic contract in which they have chosen to incorporate the terms of the treaty, the court may be called upon to interpret the treaty for the purposes of ascertaining the rights and obligations of the parties under their contract: see, for instance, *Philippson v Imperial Airways Ltd* [1939] AC 332.

Further cases in which the court may not only be empowered but required to adjudicate upon the meaning or scope of the terms of an international treaty arise where domestic legislation, although not incorporating the treaty, nevertheless requires, either expressly or by necessary implication, resort to be had to its terms for the purpose of construing the legislation (as in *Zoernsch v Waldock* [1964] 1 WLR 675) or the very rare case in which the exercise of the Royal Prerogative directly effects an extension or contraction of the jurisdiction without the constitutional need for internal legislation, as in *Post Office v Estuary Radio Ltd* [1968] 2 QB 740.

It must be borne in mind, furthermore, that the conclusion of an international treaty and its terms are as much matters of fact as any other fact. That a treaty may be referred to where it is necessary to do so as part of the factual background against which a particular issue arises may seem a statement of the obvious. But it is, I think, necessary to stress that the purpose for which such reference can legitimately be made is purely an evidential one. Which states have become parties to a treaty and when and what the terms of the treaty are questions of fact. The legal results which flow from it in international law, whether between the parties inter se or between the parties or any of them and outsiders are not and they are not justiciable by municipal courts....

The creation and regulation by a number of sovereign states of an international organisation for their common political and economic purposes was an act *jure imperii* and an adjudication of the rights and obligations between themselves and that organisation or, inter se, can be undertaken only on the plane of international law. The transactions here concerned—the participation and concurrence in the proceedings of the council authorising or countenancing the acts of the buffer stock manager—were transactions of sovereign states with and within the international organisation which they have created and are not to be subjected to the processes of our courts in order to determine what liabilities arising out of them attached to the members in favour of the ITC.

C. Warbrick, 'The Governance of Britain'

57 International and Comparative Law Quarterly 209 (2008)

The prerogative power to negotiate and conclude treaties puts the Government in a powerful position. It does not need to seek a negotiating mandate from Parliament and can keep its positions confidential until the conclusion of negotiations. There are significant, indirect limitations on the power (and, exceptionally, there may be legislative conditions attached). Where the implementation of a treaty requires action in domestic law, implementing legislation is required in order to do this. The Government's control in Parliament and the likelihood that a treaty would have to be accepted in its totality by Parliament as legislator diminishes the actual bite of this constraint but, nonetheless, the practice is not to ratify any treaty which will require implementing legislation until it has been obtained. The Ponsonby Rule which requires that treaties which come into force on ratification must first be laid before both Houses of Parliament has been supplemented by an undertaking that time for a debate would be provided where major political issues would be raised by ratification and by the practice of governments to append explanatory memoranda to treaties so laid before Parliament.

NOTES

1. The power to conclude treaties in the United Kingdom is an exercise of the Royal Prerogative (as Lord Oliver notes in the *International Tin Council Case*), being part of the Crown's powers exercised by the executive. The practice of the United Kingdom is to ensure that any financial or legislative changes required to satisfy its obligations under a treaty are effected before ratification of that treaty. As Parliament is the only national institution of the United Kingdom which can make law, the constitutional practice is that all treaties are laid before Parliament for at least 21 days before they are ratified (the 'Ponsonby Rule') and so are subject to Parliamentary debate and possible review by a Parliamentary Committee. The Constitutional Reform and Governance Act 2010 (UK) codifies the Ponsonby Rule (section 20) and further specifies Parliament's powers in relation to the ratification of treaties. The Act provides that the Secretary of State may ratify a treaty in 'exceptional circumstances' (section 22) and requires that certain types of treaties (including certain European Union treaties) must be ratified by an Act of Parliament (section 23).

2. In the light of Parliament's role in making the necessary legislative changes required to give effect to a treaty, the courts have required treaties to be incorporated, or implemented, by legislation into United Kingdom law before they will give full effect to a treaty (see, e.g. the Torture Convention in *Ex parte Pinochet* [1999] 2 All ER 97).

3. The courts do refer to unincorporated treaties to resolve ambiguities in legislation (e.g. *Salomon v Commissioners of Customs and Excise* [1967] 2 QB 116), or even in common law (e.g. *Derbyshire County Council v Times Newspapers* [1992] QB 770), in order to interpret national law in conformity with international law, so far as is possible. In undertaking this task of interpretation, the national courts interpret the treaty in accordance with the rules of international law, for example, by referring to the *travaux préparatoires* of the treaty (see *Fothergill v Monarch Airlines* [1981] AC 251). This has had some effect on the United Kingdom courts' interpretation of purely national law for example, where Parliamentary statements may now sometimes be taken into account (see *Pepper v Hart* [1993] AC 593). This presumption of compatibility can be displaced where there is clear evidence that Parliament intended to act in a manner contrary to the United Kingdom's international obligations. This presumption of compatibility also applies to the common law, and the international obligations of the United Kingdom can guide the development of the common law. For example, in *R v G* [2004] 1 AC 1034, Lord Steyn justified a reinterpretation of the notion of recklessness to take into account the United Kingdom's obligations under the Convention on the Rights of the Child, which imposes special obligations on a State's justice system to take into account the special position of children.

4. The consequence of the general rule that unincorporated treaties cannot give rights or obligations in the United Kingdom is that claims based on an unincorporated treaty are non-justiciable by the courts, i.e. outside their jurisdiction. In *Arab Monetary Fund v Hashim (No 3)* [1991] 1 All ER 871 (the *AMF* case), the House of Lords avoided this consequence by finding that the relevant international organisation, which was created by a treaty, had been incorporated in the national law of at least one State (in that case the United Arab Emirates) and those laws gave the AMF a legal identity. Because the United Kingdom recognised that State, its national laws, and the effect of its national laws (as it does with nearly all States—see Chapter 5), the United Kingdom courts

would recognise the legal identity of the AMF. In *Westland Helicopters Ltd* v *Arab Organisation for Industrialisation* [1995] 2 All ER 387, the Queen's Bench Division held that the law which the United Kingdom courts would apply in regard to the existence, constitution and representation of the international organisation was international law and not the national law of the State where the organisation was incorporated. It is at least arguable that this circumvents the non-justiciable rule. The perceived harshness that this rule has created has led some commentators to suggest that the rule should be reconsidered, at least in relation to human rights treaties and fundamental rights. For example, in *Re McKerr*, Lord Steyn commented: 'The rationale of the dualist theory, which underpins the *International Tin Council* case, is that any inroad on it would risk abuses by the executive to the detriment of citizens. It is, however, difficult to see what relevance this has to international human rights treaties which create fundamental rights for individuals against the state and its agencies. A critical re-examination of this branch of the law may become necessary in the future': [2004] UKHL 12, para. 52.

5. Treaties may be incorporated indirectly into United Kingdom law, including by reference to treaty provisions in primary legislation. For example, section 2 of the Asylum and Immigration Appeals Act 1993 provides 'Nothing in the immigration rules...shall lay down any practice which would be contrary to the [Refugee] Convention'. In *R (European Roma Rights Centre and others* v *Immigration Officers at Prague Airport and another (United Nations High Commissioner for Refugees Intervening)*, Lord Steyn held that the reference to the Refugee Convention in the 1993 Act had 'indirectly' or for 'practical purposes' incorporated the Refugee Convention into United Kingdom law: [2004] UKHL 55, paras 41–42. However, it is necessary in such circumstances to consider the extent and manner of any such incorporation.

6. A more controversial manner in which a court may have regard to an unincorporated treaty is reliance upon the concept of legitimate expectation. As is discussed in Section 4B, the High Court of Australia suggested that the act of ratifying an unincorporated treaty gives rise to a legitimate expectation that the executive will in future act compatibly with the obligations under the unincorporated treaty. While there is inconsistent authority on this point in the United Kingdom, decisions have expressed doubt that this notion could be relied upon in the United Kingdom. For example, in *R (European Roma Rights Centre and others)* v *Immigration Officer at Prague Airport and another (United Nations High Commissioner for Refugees Intervening)*, Lord Justice Laws in the Court of Appeal noted that: 'The proposition that the act of ratifying a treaty could *without more* give rise to enforceable legitimate expectations seems to me to amount, pragmatically, to a means of incorporating the substance of obligations undertaken on the international plane into our domestic law without the authority of Parliament': [2004] QB 811 (para. 100).

(b) Customary international law

The United Kingdom has adopted the principle of 'incorporation' in regard to customary international law, by which that law automatically becomes part of the national law without need for legislative or judicial pronouncement. However, the case of *R* v *Jones* (extracted below) indicates that this is not always the case, particularly in relation to crimes under customary international law.

West Rand Central Gold Mining Co. v *The King*

[1905] 2 KB 391, Kings Bench Division

LORD ALVERSTONE CJ: [The proposition] that international law forms part of the law of England, requires a word of explanation and comment. It is quite true that whatever has received the common consent of civilized nations must have received the assent of our country, and that to which we have assented along with other nations in general may properly be called international law, and as such will be acknowledged and applied by our municipal tribunals when legitimate occasion arises for those tribunals to decide questions to which doctrines of international law may be relevant. But any doctrine so invoked must be one really accepted as binding between nations, and the international law sought to be applied must, like anything else, be proved by satisfactory evidence, which must shew either that the particular proposition put forward has been recognised and acted upon by our own country, or that it is of such a nature, and has been so widely and generally accepted, that it can hardly be supposed that any civilized State would repudiate it. The mere opinions of jurists, however eminent or learned, that it ought to be so recognised, are not in themselves sufficient. They must have received the express sanction of international agreement, or gradually have grown to be part of international law by their frequent practical recognition in dealings between various nations.

Trendtex Trading Corporation v *Central Bank of Nigeria*

[1977] QB 529, United Kingdom Court of Appeal

The issue arose in this case as to whether the common law principle of precedent applied to the integration of customary international law into the common law of the United Kingdom in circumstances where the rule of customary international law has been changed or superseded. A majority (Lord Denning MR, Shaw LJ, Stephenson LJ dissenting) concluded that changes to customary international law can effect changes to the common law.

LORD DENNING MR: ... It is certain that international law does change. I would use of international law the words which Galileo used of the earth: 'But it does move.' International law does change: and the courts have applied the changes without the aid of any Act of Parliament. Thus, when the rules of international law were changed (by the force of public opinion) so as to condemn slavery, the English courts were justified in applying the modern rules of international law ...

Seeing that the rules of international law have changed—and do change—and that the courts have given effect to the changes without any Act of Parliament, it follows to my mind inexorably that the rules of international law, as existing from time to time, do form part of our English law. It follows, too, that a decision of this court—as to what was the ruling of international law 50 or 60 years ago—is not binding on this court today. International law knows no rule of *stare decisis*. If this court today is satisfied that the rule of international law on a subject has changed from what it was 50 or 60 years ago, it can give effect to that change—and apply the change in our English law—without waiting for the House of Lords to do it.

SHAW LJ: May it not be that the true principle as to the application of international law is that the English courts must at any given time discover what the prevailing international rule is and apply that rule? ...

What *is* immutable is the principle of English law that the law of nations (not what *was* the law of nations) must be applied in the courts of England. The rule of *stare decisis* operates to preclude a court from overriding a decision which binds it in regard to a particular rule of (international) law; it does not prevent a court from applying a rule which did not exist when the earlier decision was made if the new rule has had the effect in international law of extinguishing the old rule.

R v *Jones*

45 *International Legal Materials* 992 (2006), United Kingdom House of Lords

This case concerned an unsuccessful appeal by several individuals who had been charged under English criminal law with criminal damage, attempted arson and aggravated trespass. These offences were allegedly committed on various United Kingdom and United States military installations in the United Kingdom. In their defence, the individuals argued that they were not responsible, as they had been acting to prevent the commission of a crime, being the crime of aggression under international law, by interfering with the acts of preparation for the 2003 Iraq war (see Chapter 15). The House of Lords was called upon to consider whether aggression was a crime under United Kingdom law.

LORD BINGHAM

2.... [T]he common feature of all the appeals, and the feature which makes the cases important, is that they all raise the question whether the crime of aggression, if established in customary international law, is a crime recognised by or forming part of the domestic criminal law of England and Wales.

...

Customary international law is (without the need for any domestic statute or judicial decision) part of the domestic law of England and Wales.

11. The appellants contended that the law of nations in its full extent is part of the law of England and Wales. The Crown did not challenge the general truth of this proposition, for which there is indeed old and high authority… There was, however, no issue between the parties on this matter, and I am content to accept the general truth of the proposition for present purposes since the only relevant qualification is the subject of consideration below.…

Crimes recognised in customary international law are (without the need for any domestic statute or judicial decision) recognised and enforced by the domestic law of England and Wales.

In supporting this proposition the appellants were able to rely on the great authority of Blackstone who (in Book IV, chap 5, p 68, of his *Commentaries*) listed the 'principal offences against the law of nations, animadverted on as such by the municipal laws of England' as violation of safe conducts, infringement of the rights of ambassadors and piracy.…

22. While the appellants acknowledged the paucity of authority on the assimilation of customary international law crimes into municipal law other than those listed by Blackstone, they contended that war crimes earned inclusion in any modern list. It is true that certain practices have, since mediaeval times, been regarded as contrary to the laws and usages of war. After the Second World War some countries provided for the trial of those accused of this crime by statute (as in Australia), or Order in Council under statutory authority (Canada), and the United States appointed military commissions, a practice which predated the Constitution and was recognised but not established by statute: see Rogers, 'War Crimes Trials under the Royal Warrant: British Practice 1945–1949' (1990) 39 ICLQ 780, 787. In this country, an enabling statute was discussed (Rogers, *op. cit.*, pp 788–789) but in the event a Royal Warrant was issued under the royal prerogative on 18 June 1945 to provide for the trial in military courts of persons charged with 'violations of the laws and usages of war', which were treated as synonymous with war crimes. Such courts were to take judicial notice of the laws and usages of war. Pursuant to this instrument some 500 trials were held during the years 1945–1949 (Rogers, *op. cit.*, p 795). *Re Sandrock and Others* (1945) 13 ILR 297, which concerned the summary execution of a prisoner of war, is one reported example. Since, by 1945, the creation of new offences lay outwith the royal prerogative, the underlying premise of the Royal Warrant must, I think, have been that war crimes, recognised as such in customary international law, had been assimilated into our domestic law. It was, however, contemplated that an Act of Indemnity should be passed to give retrospective validity to the proceedings (Rogers, *op. cit.*, pp 788–799), which may betray some uncertainty on the point. But history has moved on. In 1950 the International Law Commission, summarising the Principles of International Law Recognized in the Charter of the Nürnberg Tribunal and in the Judgment of the Tribunal, listed war crimes ('Violations of the laws or customs of war') as crimes under international law. In section 1(1) of the War Crimes Act 1991, jurisdiction was conferred on British courts to try charges of murder, manslaughter or culpable homicide against a person in this country irrespective of his nationality at the time of the alleged offence if that offence was committed between 1 September 1939 and 5 June 1945 in a place which at the time was part of Germany or under German occupation and 'constituted a violation of the laws and customs of war', an expression which it was not thought necessary to define. It would seem to me at least arguable that war crimes, recognised as such in customary international law, would now be triable and punishable under the domestic criminal law of this country irrespective of any domestic statute. But it is not necessary to decide that question, since war crimes are something quite distinct from the crime of aggression.

23. I would accordingly accept that a crime recognised in customary international law may be assimilated into the domestic criminal law of this country. The appellants, however, go further and contend that that result follows automatically. The authorities, as I read them, do not support that proposition.…

In *R v Bow Street Metropolitan Stipendiary Magistrate, Ex p Pinochet Ugarte (No 3)* [2000] 1 AC 147 the issue was whether British courts had jurisdiction, before section 134 of the Criminal Justice Act 1988 came into force, to try those accused of torture abroad. But I agree with the observation of Buxton LJ in *Hutchinson v Newbury Magistrates' Court* (2000) 122 ILR 499, 506, where a contention similar to the appellants' was advanced:

'It is also in my view impossible to reconcile that contention with the debate in *Pinochet (No 3)* which concluded, illuminatingly subject to the specific dissent on this point of Lord Millett, that although State torture had long been an international crime in the highest sense (to adopt the formulation of Lord Browne-Wilkinson [2000] 1 AC page 198F) and therefore a crime universally in whatsoever territory it occurred, it was only with the passing of Section 134 of the Criminal Justice Act 1998 that the English criminal courts acquired jurisdiction over 'international', that is to say extra territorial, torture.'

In the context of genocide, an argument based on automatic assimilation was rejected by a majority of the Federal Court of Australia in *Nulyarimma v Thompson* (1999) 120 ILR 353. In the context of abduction it was rejected by the Supreme Court of the United States in *Sosa* v *Alvarez-Machain et al* 542 US 692 (2004). It is, I think, true that 'customary international law is applicable in the English courts only where the constitution permits': O'Keefe, 'Customary International Crimes in English Courts' (2001) BYIL 293, 335. I respectfully agree with the observations of Sir Franklin Berman (*Asserting Jurisdiction: International and European Legal Perspectives*, ed M Evans and S Konstantinidis, 2003, p 11) answering the question whether customary international law is capable of creating a crime directly triable in a national court:

> 'The first question is open to a myriad of answers, depending on the characteristic features of the particular national legal system in view. Looking at it simply from the point of view of English law, the answer would seem to be no; international law could not create a crime triable directly, without the intervention of Parliament, in an English court. What international law could, however, do is to perform its well-understood validating function, by establishing the legal basis (legal justification) for Parliament to legislate, so far as it purports to exercise control over the conduct of non-nationals abroad. This answer is inevitably tied up with the attitude taken towards the possibility of the creation of new offences under common law. Inasmuch as the reception of customary international law into English law takes place under common law, and inasmuch as the development of new customary international law remains very much the consequence of international behaviour by the Executive, in which neither the Legislature nor the Courts, nor any other branch of the constitution, need have played any part, it would be odd if the Executive could, by means of that kind, acting in concert with other States, amend or modify specifically the *criminal* law, with all the consequences that flow for the liberty of the individual and rights of personal property. There are, besides, powerful reasons of political accountability, regularity and legal certainty for saying that the power to create crimes should now be regarded as reserved exclusively to Parliament, by Statute.'

28. The lack of any statutory incorporation is not, however, a neutral factor, for two main reasons. The first is that there now exists no power in the courts to create new criminal offences, as decided by a unanimous House in *Knuller (Publishing, Printing and Promotions) Ltd* v *Director of Public Prosecutions* [1973] AC 435. While old common law offences survive until abolished or superseded by statute, new ones are not created. Statute is now the sole source of new criminal offences. The second reason is that when it is sought to give domestic effect to crimes established in customary international law, the practice is to legislate. Examples may be found in the Geneva Conventions Act 1957 and the Geneva Conventions (Amendment) Act 1995, dealing with breaches of the Geneva Conventions of 1949 and the Additional Protocols of 1977; the Genocide Act 1969, giving effect to the Genocide Convention of 1948; the Criminal Justice Act 1988, s 134, giving effect to the Torture Convention of 1984; the War Crimes Act 1991, giving jurisdiction to try war crimes committed abroad by foreign nationals; the Merchant Shipping and Maritime Security Act 1997, s 26, giving effect to provisions of the United Nations Convention on the Law of the Sea 1982 relating to piracy; and sections 51 and 52 of the International Criminal Court Act 2001, giving effect to the Rome Statute by providing for the trial here of persons accused of genocide, crimes against humanity and war crimes, but not, significantly, the crime of aggression. It would be anomalous if the crime of aggression, excluded (obviously deliberately) from the 2001 Act, were to be treated as a domestic crime, since it would not be subject to the constraints (as to the need for the Attorney General's consent, the mode of trial, the requisite *mens rea*, the liability of secondary parties and maximum penalties) applicable to the crimes which were included.

NOTES

1. Customary international law is applied by the United Kingdom courts as part of the common law. These courts may, however, feel unable to apply customary international law in the case before them because they have been unable to discover the relevant customary international law with sufficient certainty. As shown in the extract from the *West Rand*, the courts require clear evidence that a rule of customary international law exists before they will apply it. In seeking this evidence, the courts adopt the international law rules on the ascertainment of customary international law, i.e. evidence of general State practice and *opinio juris* (see Chapter 2).

2. The decision in *R* v *Jones* confirms that crimes under customary international law, including the crime of aggression, will not be considered by United Kingdom courts to have been incorporated as part of the common law. Instead, the creation of these offences as a matter of United Kingdom law requires an Act of Parliament. This reflects the principle that the common law cannot create new criminal offences. However, as Lord Bingham notes, many crimes under customary international law are already criminalised by statute in the United Kingdom. For a discussion of how customary international law and treaty-based rules might be used to interpret

criminal law provisions under UK law, see *R* v *Gul*, [2013] UKSC 64, UK Supreme Court. In that case, the Court had to determine whether the broad definition of 'terrorism' under UK terrorism legislation should be interpreted restrictively so as to reflect international law, which may not classify attacks in the context of an armed conflict as 'terrorist'.

3. As customary international law is part of the common law it can be overridden by unambiguous legislation. As seen in the *Trendtex* case, however, customary international law is not subject to the principle of *stare decisis* (being binding precedent).

4. As with treaties, some matters of customary international law are non-justiciable by national courts (see *Buttes Gas & Oil Co* v *Hammer (Nos 2 and 3)* [1982] AC 88). Similarly, in *R* v *Jones*, Lord Hoffmann held that the non-justiciability of the crime of aggression was a further reason for holding that the crime was not recognised by the common law (paras 63–67). Other matters are affected by decisions of the executive—usually indicated by an executive certificate—and this certificate is often used in relation to the recognition of States (Chapter 5) and immunity from jurisdiction (Chapter 9).

5. It is difficult to justify the different rules for the application of treaties and of customary international law in the United Kingdom. The distinction is based on the principle of Parliamentary sovereignty, as only Parliament can change the laws of the United Kingdom. Thus, it is argued, because the conclusion of treaties is an act of the executive, treaties cannot be applied directly into United Kingdom law, while customary international law is common law and can be overridden by legislation and so does not infringe Parliamentary sovereignty. However, the signing of treaties is a public act of the executive for which questions can be raised in Parliament, and parliamentary scrutiny has been increased following the enactment of the Constitutional Reform and Governance Act (2010). In contrast, customary international law is created by the practices of many States, including their treaty practice, for which actions by Parliament are rarely relevant. Therefore, Parliament has less influence on customary international law than on treaties. In addition, both types of international law can be overridden by contrary, unambiguous national legislation. As such, both treaties and customary international law should be treated in the same way by the United Kingdom courts and applied directly into national law unless national law is expressly contrary. In addition, the United Kingdom courts are now dealing frequently with matters of international law and beginning to show a real skill and some agility in considering international law in matters before them.

(c) The impact of Europe on the United Kingdom

The United Kingdom has ratified two treaties that have had significant effect on its national law. By the Treaty of Accession of the United Kingdom to the European Communities 1972, the United Kingdom became a party to the treaties, in particular to the Treaty of Rome 1957, which established the European Communities. By the European Communities Act 1972, the United Kingdom has incorporated the European Communities (now the European Union) treaties into its national law. Second, the European Convention on Human Rights and Fundamental Freedoms 1950 (ECHR) was ratified by the United Kingdom in 1951 (see further Chapter 6). The ECHR was largely incorporated by the Human Rights Act 1998, which entered into force on 2 October 2000. Both treaties confer rights and obligations on the United Kingdom under international law, but the impact of each on the national law of the United Kingdom has been different.

(i) European Union

European Communities Act 1972 (United Kingdom)

2(1) All such rights, powers, liabilities, obligations and restrictions from time to time created or arising by or under the Treaties, and all such remedies and procedures from time to time provided for by or under the Treaties, as in accordance with the Treaties are without further enactment to be given legal effect or used in the United Kingdom shall be recognised and available in law, and be enforced, allowed and followed accordingly; and the expression "enforceable Community right" and similar expressions shall be read as referring to one to which this subsection applies.

Factortame Ltd v *Secretary of State for Transport (No 2)*

[1991] 1 AC 603, United Kingdom House of Lords

By the United Kingdom's Merchant Fishing Act 1988, 95 deep-sea fishing vessels could not be registered as British fishing vessels as they were substantially managed and controlled by Spanish nationals and not by British nationals as required by the Act. The Act, and regulations under it, were challenged as infringing basic European Community rights, such as non-discrimination against a national of a member state of the European Communities. These latter rights became enforceable as British law in 1972 by virtue of the European Communities Act. The Divisional Court sought a ruling from the Court of Justice of the European Communities (European Court of Justice). Due to the likely delay before that Court had time to consider the matter in its entirety, the applicants sought an order from the House of Lords that the Merchant Fishing Act 1988 be not applied until a final ruling was given by the European Court of Justice.

LORD BRIDGE: My Lords, when this appeal first came before the House last year [[1990] 2 AC 85] your Lordships held that, as a matter of English law, the courts had no jurisdiction to grant interim relief in terms which would involve either overturning an English statute in advance of any decision by the European Court of Justice that the statute infringed Community law or granting an injunction against the Crown. It then became necessary to seek a preliminary ruling from the European Court of Justice as to whether Community law itself invested us with such jurisdiction. In the speech I delivered on that occasion, with which your Lordships agreed, I explained the reasons which led us to those conclusions. It will be remembered that, on that occasion, the House never directed its attention to the question how, if there were jurisdiction to grant the relief sought, discretion ought to be exercised in deciding whether or not relief should be granted.

In June of this year we received the judgment of the European Court of Justice (Case C213/89) ante, p. 852B *et seq.*, replying to the questions we had posed and affirming that we had jurisdiction, in the circumstances postulated, to grant interim relief for the protection of directly enforceable rights under Community law and that no limitation on our jurisdiction imposed by any rule of national law could stand as the sole obstacle to preclude the grant of such relief. In the light of this judgment we were able to conclude the hearing of the appeal in July and unanimously decided that relief should be granted in terms of the orders which the House then made, indicating that we would give our reasons for the decision later....

Some public comments on the decision of the European Court of Justice, affirming the jurisdiction of the courts of member states to override national legislation if necessary to enable interim relief to be granted in protection of rights under Community law, have suggested that this was a novel and dangerous invasion by a Community institution of the sovereignty of the United Kingdom Parliament. But such comments are based on a misconception. If the supremacy within the European Community of Community law over the national law of member states was not always inherent in the EEC Treaty (Cmnd. 5179–II) it was certainly well established in the jurisprudence of the European Court of Justice long before the United Kingdom joined the Community. Thus, whatever limitation of its sovereignty Parliament accepted when it enacted the European Communities Act 1972 was entirely voluntary. Under the terms of the Act of 1972 it has always been clear that it was the duty of a United Kingdom court, when delivering final judgment, to override any rule of national law found to be in conflict with any directly enforceable rule of Community law. Similarly, when decisions of the European Court of Justice have exposed areas of United Kingdom statute law which failed to implement Council directives, Parliament has always loyally accepted the obligation to make appropriate and prompt amendments. Thus there is nothing in any way novel in according supremacy to rules of Community law in those areas to which they apply and to insist that, in the protection of rights under Community law, national courts must not be inhibited by rules of national law from granting interim relief in appropriate cases is no more than a logical recognition of that supremacy.

Although affirming our jurisdiction, the judgment of the European Court of Justice does not fetter our discretion to determine whether an appropriate case for the grant of interim relief has been made out....Unlike the ordinary case in which the court must decide whether or not to grant interlocutory relief at a time when disputed issues of fact remain unresolved, here the relevant facts are all ascertained and the only unresolved issues are issues of law, albeit of Community law. Now, although the final decision of such issues is the exclusive prerogative of the European Court of Justice, that does not mean that an English court may not reach an informed opinion as to how such issues are likely to be resolved.

Thoburn v Sunderland City Council

[2003] QB 151, Divisional Court of the Queen's Bench Division

Thoburn was a greengrocer who had been convicted for using a weighing apparatus that did not comply with the Weights and Measures Act 1985, which required imperial measures to be given alongside metric measures. The Act implemented Community Directive 80/181/EEC, which aimed to harmonise weights and measures within the European Community. He challenged his conviction.

LORD JUSTICE LAWS:

59. Whatever may be the position elsewhere, the law of England disallows any such assumption. Parliament cannot bind its successors by stipulating against repeal, wholly or partly, of the ECA [European Communities Act 1972]. It cannot stipulate as to the manner and form of any subsequent legislation. It cannot stipulate against implied repeal any more than it can stipulate against express repeal. Thus there is nothing in the ECA which allows the Court of Justice, or any other institutions of the EU, to touch or qualify the conditions of Parliament's legislative supremacy in the United Kingdom. Not because the legislature chose not to allow it; because by our law it could not allow it. That being so, the legislative and judicial institutions of the EU cannot intrude upon those conditions. The British Parliament has not the authority to authorise any such thing. Being sovereign, it cannot abandon its sovereignty. Accordingly there are no circumstances in which the jurisprudence of the Court of Justice can elevate Community law to a status within the corpus of English domestic law to which it could not aspire by any route of English law itself. This is, of course, the traditional doctrine of sovereignty. If is to be modified, it certainly cannot be done by the incorporation of external texts. The conditions of Parliament's legislative supremacy in the United Kingdom necessarily remain in the United Kingdom's hands. But the traditional doctrine has in my judgment been modified. It has been done by the common law, wholly consistently with constitutional principle....

60. The common law has in recent years allowed, or rather created, exceptions to the doctrine of implied repeal: a doctrine which was always the common law's own creature. There are now classes or types of legislative provision which cannot be repealed by mere implication. These instances are given, and can only be given, by our own courts, to which the scope and nature of Parliamentary sovereignty are ultimately confided. The courts may say—have said—that there are certain circumstances in which the legislature may only enact what it desires to enact if it does so by express, or at any rate specific, provision. The courts have in effect so held in the field of European law itself.... The present state of our domestic law is such that substantive Community rights prevail over the express terms of any domestic law, including primary legislation, made or passed after the coming into force of the ECA, even in the face of plain inconsistency between the two.... It seems to me that there is no doubt but that in *Factortame (No 1)* the House of Lords effectively accepted that s.2(4) [of the European Communities Act] could not be impliedly repealed, albeit the point was not argued.

62.... In the present state of its maturity the common law has come to recognise that there exist rights which should properly be classified as constitutional or fundamental: see for example such cases as *Simms* [2000] 2 AC 115 *per* Lord Hoffmann at 131, *Pierson v Secretary of State* [1998] AC 539, *Leech* [1994] QB 198, *Derbyshire County Council v Times Newspapers Ltd.* [1993] AC 534, and *Witham* [1998] QB 575. And from this a further insight follows. We should recognise a hierarchy of Acts of Parliament: as it were 'ordinary' statutes and 'constitutional' statutes. The two categories must be distinguished on a principled basis. In my opinion a constitutional statute is one which (a) conditions the legal relationship between citizen and State in some general, overarching manner, or (b) enlarges or diminishes the scope of what we would now regard as fundamental constitutional rights. (a) and (b) are of necessity closely related: it is difficult to think of an instance of (a) that is not also an instance of (b). The special status of constitutional statutes follows the special status of constitutional rights. Examples are the Magna Carta, the Bill of Rights 1689, the Act of Union, the Reform Acts which distributed and enlarged the franchise, the HRA, the Scotland Act 1998 and the Government of Wales Act 1998. The ECA clearly belongs in this family. It incorporated the whole corpus of substantive Community rights and obligations, and gave overriding domestic effect to the judicial and administrative machinery of Community law. It may be there has never been a statute having such profound effects on so many dimensions of our daily lives. The ECA is, by force of the common law, a constitutional statute.

63. Ordinary statutes may be impliedly repealed. Constitutional statutes may not. For the repeal of a constitutional Act or the abrogation of a fundamental right to be effected by statute, the court would apply this test: is it shown that the legislature's *actual*—not imputed, constructive or presumed—intention was to effect the repeal or abrogation? I think the test could only be met by express words in the later statute, or by

words so specific that the inference of an actual determination to effect the result contended for was irresistible. The ordinary rule of implied repeal does not satisfy this test. Accordingly, it has no application to constitutional statutes. I should add that in my judgment general words could not be supplemented, so as to effect a repeal or significant amendment to a constitutional statute, by reference to what was said in Parliament by the minister promoting the Bill pursuant to *Pepper v Hart* [1993] AC 593. A constitutional statute can only be repealed, or amended in a way which significantly affects its provisions touching fundamental rights or otherwise the relation between citizen and State, by unambiguous words on the face of the later statute.

64. This development of the common law regarding constitutional rights, and as I would say constitutional statutes, is highly beneficial. It gives us most of the benefits of a written constitution, in which fundamental rights are accorded special respect. But it preserves the sovereignty of the legislature and the flexibility of our uncodified constitution. It accepts the relation between legislative supremacy and fundamental rights is not fixed or brittle: rather the courts (in interpreting statutes, and now, applying the HRA) will pay more or less deference to the legislature, or other public decision-maker, according to the subject in hand. Nothing is plainer than that this benign development involves, as I have said, the recognition of the ECA as a constitutional statute.

NOTES

1. Some jurists consider that European Union law is not international law but is a form of 'supra-national' law. They note the degree of integration of political, economic and social matters that has occurred between the member States of the European Union. As at March 2016, there are 28 member States, including the United Kingdom. The main institutions include the European Commission (the executive arm), the European Parliament, the Council of Ministers, the European Central Bank and the European Court of Justice (see note 4). The powers accorded to the European Union include the power to pass legislation which can directly affect all member States. The principle of supremacy requires national courts to give effect to the treaties that their member State has ratified and associated laws, even where they conflict with national law, including constitutional provisions. Despite the unusual character of the European Union, it is clear that the determination of European Union laws, and their binding nature, is able to be made by the member States because of the treaties which they have ratified and the rights and obligations contained in those treaties. In the same way that other European treaties, such as the European Convention on Human Rights, are regional international law, European Union law is a part of international law and can be treated as such.

2. On 13 December 2007, the member States signed the Treaty of Lisbon, which entered into force on 1 December 2009. The Treaty amends the main constitutive treaties of the European Union, making changes to the institutions and procedures. It also introduced a President of the European Council and a High Representative of the Union for Foreign Affairs and Security Policy. The Treaty also reaffirms the supremacy of national law.

3. The European Communities Act 1972 is amended, if necessary, subsequent to the signature of each new European Union treaty, including the Single European Act, the Maastricht Treaty and the Treaties of Amsterdam, Nice and Lisbon. The dualist nature of United Kingdom law in respect to treaties is acknowledged by sections 1 and 2 of the European Communities Act, allowing for all European Communities law to be incorporated into United Kingdom law by means of delegated legislation (Orders in Council and statutory instruments) where necessary. The decision in the *Factortame* case (extracted above) confirms that all United Kingdom law (even constitutional principles) must be read subject to directly enforceable rights under European Union law and emphasises the supremacy of European Union law. The significant impact of the European Communities Act on the parliamentary sovereignty of the United Kingdom was confirmed in *Thoburn*. United Kingdom courts do attempt to interpret United Kingdom laws in the light of Community laws.

4. The Court of Justice of the European Union is the final interpreter of European Union law (by the power given in Article 177 of the Treaty of Rome 1957). This is confirmed by section 3(1) of the European Communities Act. However, the national implementation of European Union law and determination of any inconsistency between national law and European Union law are matters for the national legislatures and courts of the member States. Section 2(1) and (4) of the European Communities Act 1972 provide that all European law created and to be created has direct effect in the United Kingdom as if it were United Kingdom law. However, this position applies only to European regulations and some directives and not to all European law.

5. The Court of Justice of the European Union has used the European Convention on Human Rights as an aid to interpretation of European Union law. The Charter of Fundamental Rights of the European Union (initially adopted in 2000, but not made binding), has been incorporated by reference in the Treaty of Lisbon and will now have binding effect with the same legal status as the other European treaties. The European Union may accede to the ECHR in due course. The United Kingdom, Ireland, Poland and Denmark have partially opted out of the Charter in relation to certain policy areas. In relation to the UK, this means that the Court of Justice of the European Union or national courts cannot find that the laws, regulations or administrative provisions, practices or actions of the United Kingdom are inconsistent with the fundamental rights, freedoms and principles of the Charter. In particular, the Charter does not create enforceable rights in the United Kingdom, though UK courts have used it in their reasoning.

6. In June 2016, a referendum was held in the United Kingdom as to whether the United Kingdom remains a member State or should leave the European Union. By a narrow majority, the vote was to leave the European Union. Negotiations will occur to determine the on-going relationship, though it will take at least two years before the United Kingdom could formally leave the European Union.

(ii) *European Convention on Human Rights*

D. Feldman, 'Monism, Dualism and Constitutional Legitimacy'
20 *Australian Yearbook of International Law* (1999)

The new scheme introduced by the *Human Rights Act* 1998…makes 'Convention rights' part of municipal law in the United Kingdom. 'Convention rights' are those rights arising under the European Convention on Human Rights that are identified in section 1 of the Act and set out in Schedule I, subject to various other provisions. Under section 2, the rights are to be interpreted taking into account the case-law of the Convention organs. By section 3, all legislation is to be interpreted so far as possible in a way that is compatible with Convention rights. Under section 6, a public authority (which includes courts and tribunals but excludes Parliament) acts unlawfully to the extent that it does anything which is incompatible with a Convention right, unless its action is required by primary legislation which cannot be interpreted so as to be compatible with Convention rights. Where primary legislation is incompatible with a Convention right, it is not thereby made invalid, but a superior court may make a declaration of incompatibility, which should lead to an amendment of the law. To assist parliamentary scrutiny, section 19 requires a Minister introducing a government Bill to Parliament to make a statement in writing (which is printed on the front cover of the Bill) that in his or her opinion the Bill either does or does not comply with Convention rights. Parliament is to establish a Joint Select Committee of its two Houses to monitor and report on matters relating to human rights in the United Kingdom and report to each House.

This structure preserves the doctrine of parliamentary sovereignty while providing a system for remedying violations of Convention rights in municipal courts and tribunals, whereas previously it would have been necessary for victims of violations to go to Strasbourg [where the European Court of Human Rights is based] for a remedy (after exhausting any domestic remedy which might have been available in municipal law). The 1998 Act, not the Convention, is the source of the authority for municipal tribunals to apply the rights. Even the meaning of the rights in municipal law is not necessarily the same as in international law, as the interpretation of the European Court of Human Rights provisions by Strasbourg organs is persuasive but not binding on municipal tribunals.

However, in practice the separation between municipal and international law is weakened. The Act recognises that the meaning of the Convention rights is dynamic rather than fixed, and acknowledges that the Strasbourg organs have a part to play in driving forward the interpretation of the rights. The Act also makes the Strasbourg case law dispositive of some questions of municipal law, particularly standing to assert Convention rights in proceedings under the Act. Furthermore, the obligation on courts and tribunals under section 2 of the Act to have regard to relevant case-law of the Strasbourg organs will inevitably bring other treaties into play, since the European Court of Human Rights regularly refers to instruments such as the International Covenant on Civil and Political Rights and the Convention on the Rights of the Child, as well as some 'soft law', norms or standards which are intended to guide decisions or actions but which are not intended to be legally enforceable, when interpreting provisions in the European Court of Human Rights.

These steps towards a more outward-looking approach to the development of municipal law in the United Kingdom, tentative though they may seem, represent a fundamental shift. Having been taken by Act of Parliament, the steps are procedurally legitimate, and the objective of protecting human rights should ensure that they are also morally legitimate. On the other hand, the change was not necessitated by any major constitutional upheaval. Nor was it the result of widespread public demands for improved protection for human rights. The *Human Rights Act* 1998 came about through long-term pressure from an influential minority of lawyers, parliamentarians, political scientists and journalists, building on concern about the United Kingdom's reputation abroad in the light of repeatedly having been held in violation of the European [Convention] of Human Rights in cases reaching the European Court of Human Rights. Had there been a sense that a Bill of Rights was historically, socially or constitutionally necessary (rather than just desirable), it would probably have been a more far-reaching instrument than the 1998 Act, giving greater weight to the international instruments and imposing stronger checks on parliamentary sovereignty. There would also probably have been a more intensive and far-reaching campaign of public consultation to ensure that the rights and methods of enforcement commanded maximum support among the population. Public support is important to make constitutional change in a democracy politically legitimate, and would help to maintain its legitimacy in the face of the possible unpopularity of some consequences of applying the rights and of some of the causes espoused by those who may assert them. Instead, the debate was mainly conducted by an informed élite within a charmed circle....

One effect of these constitutional arrangements is to blur the distinction between international and municipal law. As in the United Kingdom under the *Human Rights Act* 1998, it is impossible to say what municipal law is in relation to human rights issues without reference to international law, and, in the case of South African courts, the case law of other jurisdictions, even where international law does not form part of municipal law. This presents a difficulty for dualist positivists. It is hard to accept that municipal law can be a closed system of rules when the system itself makes norms from other systems, over which it exercises no control, decisive of, or persuasive in, the determination of issues. Although these outside influences are likely to be limited in their application by the Constitution, they are not controlled by it. A mixed system like that now operating in the United Kingdom, and *a fortiori* that which has been adopted in South Africa, draws its operating rules from a range of sources, not all of which can be said to be legally validated by reference to criteria contained in the national constitution. This closely resembles Kelsen's model of a monist system in which the application of international law is subject to constitutional constraints.

NOTES

1. Prior to the Human Rights Act 1998 (HRA), individuals who alleged that the United Kingdom had breached their rights guaranteed by the ECHR could only bring a case at the international level before the European Court of Human Rights. The HRA sought to change this position by directly incorporating the ECHR into national law and creating enforceable rights before domestic courts. Section 7 of the HRA provides that where a public authority of the United Kingdom has acted, or proposes to act, in a way which is incompatible with a Convention right, an individual may bring proceedings against that authority before a national court. As discussed in Chapter 8, actions may also be brought before national courts of England and Wales where a public authority of the United Kingdom is alleged to have breached a Convention right in an extra-territorial jurisdiction (see *Al-Skeini*, European Court of Human Rights,). In instances when a national court finds that a public authority has breached a Convention right, section 8 of the HRA provides that it may grant a judicial remedy which it considers just and appropriate.

2. Despite the ECHR being incorporated into national law, it is worth noting that individuals may still bring cases at the international level before the European Court of Human Rights once they have exhausted all of their domestic remedies. For example, following the House of Lords decisions in *Jones* v *Saudi Arabia* [2006] UKHL 26 (discussed in Chapter 9), the applicants petitioned the European Court of Human Rights alleging that the United Kingdom breached their procedural right of access to a court guaranteed by Article 6(1) ECHR when its national courts granted State immunity in civil proceedings for torture.

3. Section 2 of the HRA provides that national courts must take into account any judgment of the European Court of Human Rights. National courts are not required to follow strictly European human rights rulings in the same manner that they are bound to follow those of the European Court of Justice, or as lower courts are bound to follow the decisions of higher national courts under the system of precedent. However, it has been held that national courts should nonetheless follow the decisions of the European Court of Human Rights given that the ECHR is an international instrument whose correct interpretation can only be expounded by that court (see *R (on the application of Ullah)* v *Special Adjudicator* [2004] UKHL 26). In *Kay* v *Lambeth London Borough Council* [2006] UKHL 10, the House of Lords had to consider whether the system of precedent was applicable where a decision of a national court appeared to be inconsistent with a later ruling of

the European Court of Human Rights. The House of Lords held that in situations where there are two contrary findings of law at the national and international level, courts remain bound by the system of precedent and should follow the decision of the higher court. One narrow exception to this principle recognised by the House of Lords was where the domestic decision predated the HRA and would no longer survive following the introduction of the HRA.

4. As at March 2015, there have been 29 declarations of incompatibility under section 4 of the HRA, of which 20 have become final. However, only three declarations of incompatibility have been made in the period 2010–2015, with one remaining under appeal, which suggests a downwards trend in the number of declarations. A declaration of incompatibility does not affect the continuing application of the provision in respect of which it is made, nor does it bind the parties to the proceedings in which it is made. Unlike judgments of the European Court of Human Rights, there is no legal obligation on the government to take remedial action following a declaration of incompatibility. However, of the 20 declarations that had become final (that is not subject to appeal) the United Kingdom government has remedied or taken steps to remedy the associated legislation in all cases. Declarations of incompatibility have been described as an empty remedy, and applications have been brought before the European Court of Human Rights following a declaration being issued by a national court. In *A* v *Secretary of State for the Home Department* [2004] UKHL 56, the House of Lords issued a declaration of incompatibility in respect of the indefinite detention without trial regime of non-nationals contained in the Anti-Terrorism Crime and Security Act 2001. As this decision did not lead to the immediate and automatic release of the detainees, or payment of compensation for their unlawful detention, an application was made to the European Court of Human Rights. The Government shortly repealed the legislation after the application was made, and the Court, accordingly, only awarded damages for the unlawful detention (*A* v *The United Kingdom*, Application No. 3455/05 (19 February 2009)).

5. In 2015 there was some discussion as to whether the UK might withdraw from the European Convention, triggered in part by the extension of the UK's jurisdiction under the Convention to situations in Iraq and Afghanistan (see further Chapter 8). There may be moves to amend the HRA in some way to reduce the impact of the decisions of the European Court of Human Rights on the UK.

(d) The UK and UN Security Council Resolutions

The United Kingdom is a member State of the United Nations. As such, it is required by Article 25 of the United Nations Charter to comply with binding decisions of the Security Council, made pursuant to its powers for international peace and security in Chapter VII of the Charter (see further Chapter 15). Measures not involving the use of force by the United Kingdom may be given effect in United Kingdom law by primary legislation or by a statutory instrument issued under the United Nations Act 1946.

United Nations Act 1946

1 Measures under Article 41

(1) If, under Article forty-one of the Charter of the United Nations…the Security Council of the United Nations call upon His Majesty's Government in the United Kingdom to apply any measures to give effect to any decision of that Council, His Majesty may by Order in Council make such provision as appears to Him necessary or expedient for enabling those measures to be effectively applied, including (without prejudice to the generality of the preceding words) provision for the apprehension, trial and punishment of persons offending against the Order.…

HM Treasury **v** *Mohammed Jabar Ahmed and Others*
[2010] UKSC 2, UK Supreme Court

This case concerned the legality of measures taken by HM Treasury against the applicant under two Orders in Council, the Terrorism (United Nations Measures) Order 2006 and the Al-Qaida and Taliban (United Nations Measures) Order 2006. Both orders were issued under the United Nations Act 1946 so as to allow the United Kingdom to give effect to resolutions of the Security Council requiring member States to impose a freezing order against the financial and other assets of suspected terrorists listed by the Security Council's sanctions committee.

LORD HOPE:

42.… The question is what limits, if any, there are on the power conferred by this Subsection [subsection 1(1) of the United Nations Act 1946]. According to its own terms, it extends to 'any' measures mandated by the Security Council. The word 'any' gives full weight to the obligation to accept and carry out the decisions of the Security Council that article 25 of the Charter lays down. But the provisions that may be imposed by this means in domestic law must be either 'necessary' or 'expedient' to enable those measures to be 'applied' effectively…

44. The section leaves the question whether any given measure is 'necessary' or 'expedient' to the judgment of the executive without subjecting it, or any of the terms and conditions which apply to it, to the scrutiny of Parliament. In the context of what was envisaged when the Bill was debated in 1946, which was the use of non-military, diplomatic and economic sanctions as a means of deterring aggression between states, the surrender of power to the executive to ensure the taking of immediate and effective action in the international sphere is unsurprising. The use of the power as a means of imposing restraints or the taking of coercive measures targeted against individuals in domestic law is an entirely different matter. A distinction must be drawn in this respect between provisions made 'for the apprehension, trial and punishment of persons offending against the Order' (see the concluding words of section 1(1)) and those against whom the Order is primarily directed. So long as the primary purpose of the Order is within the powers conferred by the section, ancillary measures which are carefully designed to ensure their efficacy will be also. The crucial question is whether the section confers power on the executive, without any Parliamentary scrutiny, to give effect in this country to decisions of the Security Council which are targeted against individuals.

45. It cannot be suggested, in view of the word 'any', that the power is available only for use where the Security Council has called for non-military, diplomatic and economic sanctions to deter aggression between states. But the phrase 'necessary or expedient for enabling those measures to be effectively applied' does require further examination. The closer those measures come to affecting what, in *R v Secretary of State for the Home Department, Ex p Simms* [2000] 2 AC 115, 131, Lord Hoffmann described as the basic rights of the individual, the more exacting this scrutiny must become. If the rule of law is to mean anything, decisions as to what is necessary or expedient in this context cannot be left to the uncontrolled judgment of the executive.… The undoubted fact that section 1 of the 1946 Act was designed to enable the United Kingdom to fulfil its obligations under the Charter to implement Security Council resolutions does not diminish this essential principle.… the full honouring of these obligations is an imperative. But these resolutions are the product of a body of which the executive is a member as the United Kingdom's representative. Conferring an unlimited discretion on the executive as to how those resolutions, which it has a hand in making, are to be implemented seems to me to be wholly unacceptable. It conflicts with the basic rules that lie at the heart of our democracy.

76. I would accept…that, as fundamental rights may not be overridden by general words, section 1 of the 1946 Act does not give authority for overriding the fundamental rights of the individual. It does not do so either expressly or by necessary implication. The question is whether the effect of G's designation under the AQO [Al-Qaida and Taliban (United Nations Measures) Order 2006] has that effect. To some extent this must be a question of degree. Some interference with the right to peaceful enjoyment of one's property may have been foreseen by the framers of section 1, as it authorises the making of provision for the apprehension, trial and punishment of persons offending against the Order. To that extent coercive steps to enable the measures to be applied effectively can be regarded as within its scope. But there must come a point when the intrusion upon the right to enjoyment of one's property is so great, so overwhelming and so timeless that the absence of any effective means of challenging it means that this can only be brought about under the express authority of Parliament.

R (On the Application of Al-Jedda) v *Secretary of State for Defence*
47 *International Legal Materials* 611 (2008), UK House of Lords

This case concerned an individual detained by British forces in Iraq on the grounds that his detention was necessary for the imperative security of Iraq. The appellant had been held indefinitely and had not been charged with an offence. One of the questions to be considered by the House of Lords was the relationship between the United Kingdom's obligations under various Security Council resolutions authorising security detention, its obligations under the ECHR, in particular Article 5(1), which prohibits arbitrary detention, and Article 103 of the United Nations Charter, which provides that the obligations of member States under the UN Charter prevail over obligations created by other international agreements.

LORD BINGHAM:

37. The appellant is, however, entitled to submit, as he does, that while maintenance of international peace and security is a fundamental purpose of the UN, so too is the promotion of respect for human rights. On repeated occasions in recent years the UN and other international bodies have stressed the need for effective action against the scourge of terrorism but have, in the same breath, stressed the imperative need for such action to be consistent with international human rights standards such as those which the Convention exists to protect. ... The problem in a case such as the present is acute, since it is difficult to see how any exercise of the power to detain, however necessary for imperative reasons of security, and however strong the safeguards afforded to the detainee, could do otherwise than breach the detainee's rights under article 5(1) ...

39. Thus there is a clash between on the one hand a power or duty to detain exercisable on the express authority of the Security Council and, on the other, a fundamental human right which the UK has undertaken to secure to those (like the appellant) within its jurisdiction. How are these to be reconciled? There is in my opinion only one way in which they can be reconciled: by ruling that the UK may lawfully, where it is necessary for imperative reasons of security, exercise the power to detain authorised by UNSCR 1546 and successive resolutions, but must ensure that the detainee's rights under article 5 are not infringed to any greater extent than is inherent in such detention.

NOTES
1. Section 4 of the United Nations Act provides that Orders in Council made pursuant to section 1(1) need only be laid before Parliament. Orders made pursuant to the Act are thus excluded from the normal process of Parliamentary supervision. The second extract shows, however, that the power of the Executive to give effect to resolutions of the Security Council without reference to Parliament is not unlimited. In addition to meeting the criteria of necessary and expedient set out in section 1(1) of the United Nations Act 1946, the measures taken must not unduly affect the fundamental rights of individuals.
2. The decision of the House of Lords in *Al-Jedda* confirmed that actions taken pursuant to binding resolutions of the Security Council can override the United Kingdom's human rights obligations. However, most members of the House of Lords stressed that the effect of Article 103 of the United Nations Charter was not to dispense with the right altogether; rather the effect was to limit the application of the right to the extent necessary to comply with the requirements of the Security Council resolution. When the European Court of Human Rights considered the case in 2011, it held that, as there was no *obligation* on the UK to place individuals in detention, there was no conflict with Article 5 of the ECHR and Article 103 of the United Nations Charter was not engaged. The Grand Chamber indicated that 'in interpreting its resolutions, there must be a presumption that the Security Council does not intend to impose any obligation on member States to breach fundamental principles of human rights' and that 'clear and explicit language would be used were the Security Council to intend States to take particular measures which would conflict with their obligations under international human rights law' (*Al-Jedda* v *the UK*, 7 July 2011, para. 102). Thus the UK must consider its human rights obligations when giving effect to resolutions of the Security Council.

B: Australia

Mabo v *Queensland (No 2)*
175 CLR 1 (1992), High Court of Australia

This case concerned the claimed legal rights of indigenous communities to islands in the Torres Strait, which had been annexed to the State of Queensland in 1879. The plaintiffs sought a declaration that the Meriam people were entitled to the islands based on a possessory title arising from their long occupation of the islands.

BRENNAN J: If the international law notion that inhabited land may be classified as terra nullius no longer commands general support [see *Western Sahara Opinion*], the doctrines of the common law which depend on the notion that native peoples may be 'so low in the scale of social organization' that it is 'idle to impute to such people some shadow of the rights known to our law' (*In re Southern Rhodesia* (1919) AC, at pp 233–234) can hardly be retained. If it were permissible in past centuries to keep the common law in step with international law, it is imperative in today's world that the common law should neither be nor be seen to be frozen in an age of racial discrimination.

Whatever the justification advanced in earlier days for refusing to recognize the rights and interests in land of the indigenous inhabitants of settled colonies, an unjust and discriminatory doctrine of that kind can no longer be accepted. The expectations of the international community accord in this respect with the contemporary values of the Australian people. The opening up of international remedies to individuals pursuant to Australia's accession to the Optional Protocol to the International Covenant on Civil and Political Rights…brings to bear on the common law the powerful influence of the Covenant and the international standards it imports. The common law does not necessarily conform with international law, but international law is a legitimate and important influence on the development of the common law, especially when international law declares the existence of universal human rights. A common law doctrine founded on unjust discrimination in the enjoyment of civil and political rights demands reconsideration. It is contrary both to international standards and to the fundamental values of our common law to entrench a discriminatory rule which, because of the supposed position on the scale of social organization of the indigenous inhabitants of a settled colony, denies them a right to occupy their traditional lands.

Minister of State for Immigration and Ethnic Affairs v *Teoh*
(1995) 183 CLR 273, High Court of Australia

This case concerned the deportation of Mr Teoh (a Malaysian citizen) from Australia. The issue for the Court was whether, in making the deportation order, the authorities had failed to take into account the interests of Mr Teoh's wife and children (who were Australian citizens and would remain in Australia) under the Convention on the Rights of the Child, which Australia had ratified but not incorporated into national law.

MASON CJ and DEANE J: It is well established that the provisions of an international treaty to which Australia is a party do not form part of Australian law unless those provisions have been validly incorporated into our municipal law by statute. This principle has its foundation in the proposition that in our constitutional system the making and ratification of treaties fall within the province of the Executive in the exercise of its prerogative power whereas the making and the alteration of the law fall within the province of Parliament, not the Executive. So, a treaty which has not been incorporated into our municipal law cannot operate as a direct source of individual rights and obligations under that law. In this case, it is common ground that the provisions of the Convention have not been incorporated in this way. It is not suggested that the declaration made pursuant to s 47(1) of the Human Rights and Equal Opportunity Commission Act has this effect.

But the fact that the Convention has not been incorporated into Australian law does not mean that its ratification holds no significance for Australian law. Where a statute or subordinate legislation is ambiguous, the courts should favour that construction which accords with Australia's obligations under a treaty or international convention to which Australia is a party, at least in those cases in which the legislation is enacted after, or in contemplation of, entry into, or ratification of, the relevant international instrument. That is because Parliament, prima facie, intends to give effect to Australia's obligations under international law.

Apart from influencing the construction of a statute or subordinate legislation, an international convention may play a part in the development by the courts of the common law. The provisions of an international convention to which Australia is a party, especially one which declares universal fundamental rights, may be used by the courts as a legitimate guide in developing the common law. But the courts should act in this fashion with due circumspection when the Parliament itself has not seen fit to incorporate the provisions of a convention into our domestic law. Judicial development of the common law must not be seen as a backdoor means of importing an unincorporated convention into Australian law. A cautious approach to the development of the common law by reference to international conventions would be consistent with the approach which the courts have hitherto adopted to the development of the common law by reference to statutory policy and statutory materials. Much will depend upon the nature of the relevant provision, the extent to which it has been accepted by the international community, the purpose which it is intended to serve and its relationship to the existing principles of our domestic law.

In the present case, however, we are not concerned with the resolution of an ambiguity in a statue. Nor are we concerned with the development of some existing principle of the common law. The critical questions to be resolved are whether the provisions of the Convention are relevant to the exercise of the statutory discretion and, if so, whether Australia's ratification of the Convention can give rise to a legitimate expectation that the decision-maker will exercise that discretion in conformity with the terms of the Convention. The foregoing discussion of the status of the Convention in Australian law reveals no intrinsic reason for excluding its provisions from consideration by the decision-maker simply because it has not been incorporated into our municipal law.

[R]atification of a convention is a positive statement by the executive government of this country to the world and to the Australian people that the executive government and its agencies will act in accordance with the Convention. That positive statement is an adequate foundation for a legitimate expectation, absent statutory or executive indications to the contrary, that administrative decision-makers will act in conformity with the Convention… It is not necessary that a person seeking to set up such a legitimate expectation should be aware of the Convention or should personally entertain the expectation; it is enough that the expectation is reasonable in the sense that there are adequate materials to support it.

Habib v Commonwealth of Australia

(2010) 183 *Federal Court Reports* 62, Federal Court of Australia (Full Court)

Mr Habib, an Australian citizen, had been detained by Pakistani authorities and ultimately transferred to Guantanamo Bay. During his detention, he alleged he had been subjected to inhumane treatment. His lawyers brought a civil law action arguing that Australian officials had aided and abetted his torture overseas. The Australian government argued that consideration of the claim was precluded by the application of the common law act of state doctrine, which provides that the courts of one State will not sit in judgement on the acts of the government of another State done within its own territory.

BLACK CJ:

7. [T]he common law has evolved such that the authorities do not support the application of the act of state doctrine in the present case. If, however, the choice were finely balanced, the same conclusion should be reached. When the common law, in its development, confronts a choice properly open to it, the path chosen should not be in disconformity with moral choices made on behalf of the people by the Parliament reflecting and seeking to enforce universally accepted aspirations about the behaviour of people one to another.

8. Torture offends the ideal of a common humanity and the Parliament has declared it to be a crime wherever outside Australia it is committed. Moreover, and critically in this matter, the Crimes (Torture) Act is directed to the conduct of public officials and persons acting in an official capacity irrespective of their citizenship and irrespective of the identity of their government….

9. The Crimes (Torture) Act reflects the status of the prohibition against torture as a peremptory norm of international law from which no derogation is permitted and the consensus of the international community that torture can never be justified by official acts or policy.

10. As well, and again consistently with Australia's obligations under the Torture Convention, the Parliament has spoken with clarity about the moral issues that may confront officials of governments, whether foreign or our own, and persons acting in an official capacity. It has proscribed torture in all circumstances, answering in the negative the moral and legal questions whether superior orders can absolve the torturer of individual criminal responsibility and whether, in extreme circumstances, torture may be permissible to prevent what may be apprehended as a larger wrong: see the Crimes (Torture) Act, s 11; the Torture Convention, Art 2.

11. In these circumstances, if…the question were finely balanced and the common law were faced with a choice, congruence with the policy revealed by the Crimes (Torture) Act and its intended reach to the officials of foreign governments, even when acting within their own territory and under superior orders, points against the application of the act of state doctrine in the circumstances alleged by Mr Habib in the present proceeding.

12. Consideration of the relevant sections of the Criminal Code, the Geneva Conventions Act and the Third and Fourth Geneva Conventions also, in my view, support these observations.

13. It is not to the point that Mr Habib's proceeding is a civil claim for damages and not a criminal proceeding under the Crimes (Torture) Act, the Geneva Conventions Act or the Criminal Code. The point is that, if a choice were indeed open, in determining whether or not the act of state doctrine operates to deny a civil remedy contingent upon breach of those Acts, the common law should develop congruently with emphatically expressed ideals of public policy, reflective of universal norms.

NOTES

1. While treaties are not directly incorporated into the national law of Australia, the *Mabo* and *Teoh* cases both recognise the important influence of international law on the development of common law principles, and its role in the interpretation of ambiguous legislation that seeks to implement international obligations. The decision in *Teoh* takes this point a step further by examining the effect of international law on administrative decision-making. In *Newcrest Mining* v *Commonwealth* (1997) 147 ALR 42 before the High Court of Australia, Kirby J held (at p. 148) that 'To the full extent that its text permits, Australia's Constitution, as the fundamental law of government in this country, accommodates itself to international law, including insofar as that law expresses basic rights'. See also Kirby's extra-judicial comments above. Other justices of the High Court have been more cautious. For example, in *Al-Kateb* v *Goodwin* [2004] HCA 37, (2004) 219 CLR 562, Justice McHugh commented that 'this Court has never accepted that the Constitution contains an implication to the effect that it should be construed to conform with the rules of international law. The rationale for the rule and its operation is inapplicable to a Constitution—which is a source of, not an exercise of, legislative power…No doubt from time to time the making or existence of (say) a Convention or its consequences may constitute a general political, social or economic development that helps to elucidate the meaning of a constitutional head of power. But that is different from using the *rules* in that Convention to control the meaning of a constitutional head of power' (paras 66 and 71).
2. Successive governments have sought to restrict the application of the decision in *Teoh* by passing legislation contrary to the decision. However, none of this legislation was passed by Parliament. In *Minister for Immigration and Multicultural Affairs, ex parte Lam* (2003) 214 CLR 1, the High Court of Australia was highly critical of its own decision in *Teoh*. Several justices indicated their reservations as to the continued application of the principle of legitimate expectation in Australian administrative law, and confirmed that, even if the principle did apply, it gives rise to procedural, rather than substantive, rights. While the Court did not overrule the decision in *Teoh*, the status of the doctrine now looks weak.
3. In *Nulyarimma* v *Thompson* (1999) 165 ALR 621, the Federal Court of Australia was called upon to consider whether certain members of the Australian government had committed acts of genocide against the indigenous peoples of Australia. There was no relevant Australian legislation incorporating the Genocide Convention (see Chapter 3) and so the issue turned on whether genocide was a crime under customary international law and so was automatically part of Australian common law. While all judges accepted that the crime of genocide was a matter of customary international law, they differed as to the effect the creating of such a common law crime had on Australian law. The Court unanimously held, on the basis of the particular facts of the case, that the claim was not successful. Justice Wilcox, adopting similar public policy arguments to those discussed by the House of Lords in *R* v *Jones* (extracted in Section 4A), found that crimes under customary international law did not form crimes in Australian law in the absence of statute.
4. The extract from *Habib* demonstrates the importance that common law national judges place on developing the common law in a manner consistent with the clear international prohibition against torture, with Black CJ holding that the act of state doctrine could not apply where serious international human rights law violations are alleged. One other judge in the case, Perram J, while reaching the same decision, focused on the role of the judiciary, finding that a common law

doctrine could not preclude the judiciary from scrutinising the limits of government power and that the act of state doctrine did not apply where the Court was asked to review conduct of government officials that was allegedly outside their scope of authority.

C: South Africa

Constitution of the Republic of South Africa 1996

International agreements

231. (1) The negotiating and signing of all international agreements is the responsibility of the national executive.

(2) An international agreement binds the Republic only after it has been approved by resolution in both the National Assembly and the National Council of Provinces, unless it is an agreement referred to in subsection (3).

(3) An international agreement of a technical, administrative or executive nature, or an agreement which does not require either ratification or accession, entered into by the national executive, binds the Republic without approval by the National Assembly and the National Council of Provinces, but must be tabled in the Assembly and the Council within a reasonable time.

(4) Any international agreement becomes law in the Republic when it is enacted into law by national legislation; but a self-executing provision of an agreement that has been approved by Parliament is law in the Republic unless it is inconsistent with the Constitution or an Act of Parliament.

(5) The Republic is bound by international agreements which were binding on the Republic when this Constitution took effect.

Customary international law

232. Customary international law is law in the Republic unless it is inconsistent with the Constitution or an Act of Parliament.

Application of international law

233. When interpreting any legislation, every court must prefer any reasonable interpretation of the legislation that is consistent with international law over any alternative interpretation that is inconsistent with international law.

S v Makwanyane and Mchunu

1995 (3) SA (CC), Constitutional Court of South Africa

The key issue in this case was whether the death penalty was lawful under the South African Constitution. The Constitution was silent on this point. The Court considered the transitional Constitution (1993) but its terms, for these purposes, were similar to those of the 1996 Constitution. The Court held that the death penalty was unlawful.

CHASKALSON P:

34.... In interpreting the provisions of this [Constitution] a court of law shall promote the values which underlie an open and democratic society based on freedom and equality and shall, where applicable, have regard to public international law applicable to the protection of the rights entrenched in this [Constitution], and may have regard to comparable foreign case law.

35. Customary international law and the ratification and accession to international agreements is dealt with in *section* 231 [and 232–233] of the Constitution which sets the requirements for such law to be binding within South Africa.... [P]ublic international law would include non-binding as well as binding law. They may both be used ... as tools of interpretation. International agreements and customary international law accordingly provide

a framework within which the [Constitution] can be evaluated and understood, and for that purpose, decisions of tribunals dealing with comparable instruments, such as the United Nations Committee on Human Rights, the Inter-American Commission on Human Rights, the Inter-American Court of Human Rights, the European Commission on Human Rights, and the European Court of Human Rights, and in appropriate cases, reports of specialised agencies such as the International Labour Organisation may provide guidance as to the correct interpretation of [the Constitution].

National Commissioner of the South African Police Service v *Southern African Human Rights Litigation Centre and Another*

[2014] ZACC 30, Constitutional Court of South Africa

The case concerned the implementation of South Africa's treaty obligations under the Rome Statute of the International Criminal Court, as enacted in national legislation (see Chapter 14). The issue before the Court concerned the extent to which the National Commissioner of Police of South Africa was legally obliged to investigate allegations of crimes against humanity of torture allegedly committed in Zimbabwe by and against Zimbabwean nationals.

23. The Constitution enjoins South African courts, tribunals and other fora to consider international law when interpreting the Bill of Rights and provides that legislation must be interpreted purposively in accordance with international law. Section 231(4) provides for the domestication of international law through national legislation …

24. The Constitution provides that: (a) customary international law is part of our domestic law insofar as it is not inconsistent with the Constitution or an Act of Parliament; (b) international treaty law only becomes law in the Republic once enacted into domestic legislation; and (c) national legislation should, in turn, be interpreted in the light of international law that has not been domesticated into South African law by national legislation but that is nonetheless binding upon it …

31. The preamble to the Rome Statute affirms that states parties are determined 'to put an end to impunity for the perpetrators of [grave] crimes and thus to contribute to the prevention of such crimes' and it recalls 'that it is the *duty* of every State to exercise its criminal jurisdiction over those responsible for international crimes'.

32. The need for states parties to comply with their international obligation to investigate international crimes is most pressing in instances where those crimes are committed by citizens of and within the territory of countries that are not parties to the Rome Statute, because to do otherwise would permit impunity. If an investigation is not instituted by non-signatory countries in which the crimes have been committed, the perpetrators can only be brought to justice through the application of universal jurisdiction, namely the investigation and prosecution of these alleged crimes by states parties under the Rome Statute.

33. South Africa was the first African state to domesticate the Rome Statute into national legislation. This was done in terms of section 231(4) of the Constitution through the enactment of the ICC Act. The international crimes over which the ICC exercises jurisdiction, including the crimes against humanity of torture, are listed in schedule 1 to the ICC Act and have thus become statutory crimes in our national law.

34. It is clear that a primary purpose of the Act is to enable the prosecution, in South African courts or the ICC, of persons accused of having committed atrocities, such as torture, beyond the borders of South Africa.

35. Torture, even if not committed on the scale of crimes against humanity, is regarded as a crime which threatens 'the good order not only of particular states but of the international community as a whole'. Coupled with treaty obligations, the ban on torture has the customary international law status of a peremptory norm from which no derogation is permitted.…

40. Because of the international nature of the crime of torture, South Africa, in terms of sections 231(4), 232 and 233 of the Constitution and various international, regional and sub-regional instruments, is required, where appropriate, to exercise universal jurisdiction in relation to these crimes as they offend against the human conscience and our international and domestic law obligations.…

50. Our international law commitments to investigate crimes against humanity, including torture, must be discharged through our law-enforcement agencies.…

55. The Supreme Court of Appeal held that the SAPS [South African Police Service] has the requisite power to investigate the allegations of torture. I would go further. There is not just a power, but also a duty. While the finding that the SAPS does have the power to investigate is unassailable, the point of departure is that the SAPS has a duty to investigate the alleged crimes against humanity of torture. That duty arises from the Constitution read with the ICC Act, which we must interpret in relation to international law.

56. The Constitution and the ICC Act make it clear that, whilst empowered to investigate crime, the SAPS also bears a duty to do so. This emerges from the interpretation of section 205(3) of the Constitution in *Glenister II*, read with the relevant provisions outlined above. By way of contrast, section 179(2) of the Constitution affords the prosecuting authority a 'power' and thus a discretion to institute criminal proceedings. The word 'power' does not appear in section 205(3) of the Constitution in relation to investigating crime.

57. The statutory designation of international crimes under the SAPS Act domesticated into our law by the ICC Act requires the SAPS to prioritise these types of crimes and indeed imposes a duty on it to do so. For present purposes we must focus on the investigation of one type of domesticated international crime, the crime of torture.

NOTES

1. The South African Constitution was adopted after the end of the apartheid era and after a large number of other constitutions and treaties, particularly human rights treaties, were reviewed. A great deal of national consultation and international input occurred before its adoption (see Feldman (in Section 4A(ii)) in relation to the legitimacy this brings to the Constitution). The Constitution recognises the importance of international law on national law. It also provides that international law must be considered when interpreting the Bill of Rights set out in Chapter 2 of the Constitution (s. 39).

2. The Constitutional Court of South Africa has had to consider a significant number of key issues that have international law aspects. These have included cases concerning the right of access to health care and the right to housing (*Soobramoney* v *Minister of Health* 1998 (1) SA 765 and *Grootboom* v *Government of the Republic of South Africa* 2000 10 BHRC 84), diplomatic protection (*Kaunda* v *President of the Republic of South Africa*, 44 ILM 173 (2005)) and cases concerning same-sex marriages (*Minister of Home Affairs* v *Fourie* Case CCT 10/05). However, the latter case suggests that international law may only be used to expand and not to restrict the scope of a right under the Constitution.

3. International obligations have also been relied upon to impose responsibilities on national actors. In the extract above concerning the South African Police Service (SAPS), the Court, in a unanimous judgment, held that SAPS had a duty to investigate the crimes against humanity of torture allegedly committed in Zimbabwe under the ICC Act and South Africa's international law obligations (incorporated in the Constitution), as there was no evidence that Zimbabwean authorities were willing or able to pursue an investigation. Similarly, the Supreme Court of Appeal relied upon South Africa's obligations to cooperate with the ICC under the Rome Statute, as implemented into domestic law, in holding that the relevant legislation on head of state immunity, which would otherwise preclude the arrest of Sudanese President Al-Bashir by South African authorities (pursuant to ICC arrest warrants), did not apply: *Minister of Justice and Constitutional Development et al* v *Southern Africa Litigation Centre*, Case no: 867/15, 15 March 2016.

D: United States

The Constitution of the United States 1787

Article VI, section 2

This Constitution, and the Laws of the United States which shall be made in Pursuance thereof; and all Treaties made, or which shall be made, under the Authority of the United States, shall be the supreme Law of the Land; and the Judges in every State shall be bound thereby, any Thing in the Constitution or Laws of any State to the Contrary notwithstanding.

Sei Fujii v *State of California*
19 ILR 312 (1952), Supreme Court of California

A Japanese man who was ineligible for American citizenship claimed that a Californian law which prevented him owning land was unenforceable as contrary to the United States Constitution and the United Nations Charter.

It is not disputed that the charter is a treaty, and our federal Constitution provides that treaties made under the authority of the United States are part of the supreme law of the land and that the judges in every state are bound thereby. US Const, Article VI. A treaty, however, does not automatically supersede local laws which are inconsistent with it unless the treaty provisions are self-executing. In the words of Chief Justice Marshall: A treaty is:

> to be regarded in courts of justice as equivalent to an act of the Legislature, whenever it operates of itself, without the aid of any legislative provision. But when the terms of the stipulation import a contract— when either of the parties engages to perform a particular act, the treaty addresses itself to the political, not the judicial department; and the Legislature must execute the contract before it can become a rule for the court. *Foster* v *Neilson*, 1829, 2 Pet 253, 324, 7 LEd 415

In determining whether a treaty is self-executing courts look to the intent of the signatory parties as manifested by the language of the instrument, and, if the instrument is uncertain, recourse may be had to the circumstances surrounding its execution.…In order for a treaty provision to be operative without the aid of implementing legislation and to have the force and effect of a stature, it must appear that the framers of the treaty intended to prescribe a rule that, standing alone, would be enforceable in the courts.…

It is clear that the provisions of the preamble and of Article I of the charter which are claimed to be in conflict with the alien land law are not self-executing. They state general purposes and objectives of the United Nations Organization and do not purport to impose legal obligations on the individual member nations or to create rights in private persons. It is equally clear that none of the other provisions relied on by plaintiff is self-executing. Article 55 declares that the United Nations 'shall promote:…universal respect for, and observance of, human rights and fundamental freedoms for all without distinction as to race, sex, language, or religion,' and in Article 56, the member nations 'pledge themselves to take joint and separate action in co-operation with the Organization for the achievement of the purposes set forth in Article 55.' Although the member nations have obligated themselves to co-operate with the international organization in promoting respect for, and observance of, human rights, it is plain that it was contemplated that future legislative action by the several nations would be required to accomplish the declared objectives, and there is nothing to indicate that these provisions were intended to become rules of law for the courts of this country upon the ratification of the charter.…

The humane and enlightened objectives of the United Nations Charter are, of course, entitled to respectful consideration by the courts and Legislatures of every member nation, since that document expresses the universal desire of thinking men for peace and for equality of rights and opportunities. The charter represents a moral commitment of foremost importance, and we must not permit the spirit of our pledge to be compromised or disparaged in either our domestic or foreign affairs. We are satisfied, however, that the charter provisions relied on by plaintiff were not intended to supersede existing domestic legislation, and we cannot hold that they operate to invalidate the alien land law.

A. Bianchi, 'International Law and US Courts: The Myth of Lohengrin Revisited'
15 *European Journal of International Law* 751 (2004)

The Uncertain Status of Customary International Law and its Practical Consequences
It might seem ill advised to venture into the technicalities of the status of customary international law within the US legal system as a starting point. Yet the subject is quite revealing of the attitude of a legal system to international law as a whole. Since customary rules are binding on states regardless of their express consent, the status of such rules within the domestic legal order provides some evidence of the relevance attributed to 'external' law-making sources. There is hardly any mention in the US Constitution of customary international law. Except for the 'define and punish clause' of Article I, Section 8, the Constitution remains silent on customary law in both Article III and VI. Some commentators have argued that this is not decisive as the drafters may have intended that such an expression as 'Laws of the United States', as it appears in Article III, may well encompass customary international law. Be that as it may, the framers of the Constitution and the early jurisprudence of the Supreme

Court showed a certain sensitivity to the way in which international law was incorporated into the US legal system and applied by courts. This attitude is epitomized in the well-known and much-quoted passage from *The Paquete Habana,* in which Justice Gray, echoing language he had used a few years earlier, held that 'international law is part of our law and must be ascertained and administered by the courts of justice of appropriate jurisdiction, as often as questions of right depending upon it are duly presented for their determination'.

The idea that federal courts may resort to customary international law, in the absence of controlling federal statutory provisions, remains the prevailing view and was adopted in the latest version of the *Restatement* [The *Restatement* is a treatise on US legal issues prepared by the American Law Institute, which aims to set out the relevant law emerging from US statutes and common law]. According to the *Restatement,* customary international law enjoys the status of federal common law and cases arising under it are to be considered as cases 'arising under' the Laws of the United States, 'for purposes of both the "judicial Power" of the United States (Article III) and the jurisdiction of the federal district courts (28 U.S.C. §1331)'. The supremacy of customary international law over state law can be grounded on an expansive interpretation of the Supremacy Clause of Article VI or on considerations that the United States enjoys exclusive authority in international relations. The practical consequences of this supremacy are somewhat limited by the fact that rarely would customary law rules be construed as conferring rights directly on individuals and companies which could be enforceable by courts. However, recognition of customary law as part of the law of the United States, which can be administered by courts of appropriate jurisdiction, gives international law rules not strictly based on consent an internal legitimacy that they would not have otherwise.

The proposition that international customary law amounts to federal common law has been called into question by some strands of US scholarship. Although not fully unprecedented, these attacks have recently challenged with renewed vigour the constitutional foundations of the doctrine of customary law as federal common law as well as its desirability in terms of normative and judicial policy. At the heart of what have been termed 'revisionist theories' lies a different reading of *Erie R.R. v Tompkins,* [304 U.S. 64 (1938)] in which the Supreme Court denied the existence of a federal common law. While to many the considerations made by Justice Brandeis would not apply to customary international law, some commentators, also relying on subsequent case law by lower courts, have taken *Erie* to mean that the development of principles by federal courts could only occur if there were 'definite authority' behind it. Narrowly interpreted, this process would only be valid for constitutional or legislative grants of authority. Interestingly enough, the Supreme Court in *Banco Nacional de Cuba v Sabbatino* [376 U.S. 398 (1964)], indirectly confirmed that the interpretation of customary international law was a matter for the federal courts. Emphasizing that the question of attribution of powers between the judiciary and the executive branch of government in matters bearing on the foreign relations of the United States could only be treated as 'an aspect of federal law', Justice Harlan concluded that 'rules of international law should not be left to divergent and perhaps parochial state interpretations'.

'Revisionists' base their criticism of the 'modern view'—as codified in the *Restatement*—on a number of considerations, among which separation of power and federalism concerns on the one hand and democratic legitimacy on the other, stand out. In particular, the flexibility that the President needs to have in representing the United States internationally could be hampered by judicial enforcement of customary international law. The objection raises issues of deference of the judicial power to the executive branch of government, which will be dealt with later in this article. It suffices here to note that the clearer and more solidly established the rules of customary international law are, the fewer the risks of a conflict between the judiciary and the executive. This point, clearly made by the Supreme Court in *Sabbatino* could well dispose of much of the expressed concerns. Moreover, the administration of customary international law rules by federal courts would allegedly imply an illegitimate transfer of powers to the judicial power and the international community. The argument seems to entail the existence and relevance of state powers in the field of foreign relations, which, however, the Supreme Court has long denied or downplayed. Finally, the fact that *'unelected federal judges* apply customary law made by the *world community* at the expense of state prerogatives' would be conducive to disregarding the internal requirements of the political process and to neglecting states' interests in law-making. The latter contention is quite revealing of the uneasiness with which the US currently relates to general international law. The 'shift away from consensualism to majoritarianism', or in other words from a strictly consent-based notion of general international law to multilateral law-making processes of a varying nature, which, incidentally, the international legal system seems to require more and more, departs from the fundamental tenets of the nationalist constitutional jurisprudence typified by some of the justices currently sitting in the Supreme Court.

Overall, the role played by customary international law remains negligible and, arguably, with the exception of the Alien Tort Claims Act (ATCA), its impact on judicial decisions not particularly relevant. The recent doctrinal shift towards relegating customary international law into the margins of the legal system by denying its status as federal common law attests to the inward-looking attitude of the US legal system at this time and to its diffidence *vis-à-vis* external sources of law-making. Should courts sanction this scholarly attitude, the US legal system may become almost impermeable to that 'law of nations' which the framers and the early Justices considered as part of the law of the land and looked up to as the common legacy of civilization.

Medellin v *Texas*

47 *International Legal Materials* 305 (2008), United States Supreme Court

This case concerned the decision of the International Court of Justice in the *Avena* judgment [*Case Concerning Avena and Other Mexican Nationals (Mexico* v *United States), 2004* ICJ Rep 12], which held that by failing to allow consular access to Mexican nationals sentenced to the death penalty in the United States, the United States had violated its obligations under the Vienna Convention on Consular Relations. The decision for the Supreme Court was whether the ICJ decision, an international binding obligation, was enforceable in the United States as a matter of national law.

Dissenting Opinion of Justice Beyer

The Constitution's Supremacy Clause provides that 'all Treaties…which shall be made…under the Authority of the United States, shall be the supreme Law of the Land; and the Judges in every State shall be bound thereby.' Art. VI, cl. 2. The Clause means that the 'courts' must regard 'a treaty…as equivalent to an act of the legislature, whenever it operates of itself without the aid of any legislative provision.' *Foster* v. *Neilson*, 2 Pet. 253, 314 (1829) (majority opinion of Marshall, C. J.).

The United States has signed and ratified a series of treaties obliging it to comply with ICJ judgments in cases in which it has given its consent to the exercise of the ICJ's adjudicatory authority. Specifically, the United States has agreed to submit, in this kind of case, to the ICJ's 'compulsory jurisdiction' for purposes of 'compulsory settlement.' Optional Protocol Concerning the Compulsory Settlement of Disputes (Optional Protocol or Protocol),…And it agreed that the ICJ's judgments would have 'binding force…between the parties and in respect of [a] particular case. 'United Nations Charter, Art. 59.…President Bush has determined that domestic courts should enforce this particular ICJ judgment. Memorandum to the Attorney General (Feb. 28, 2005), App. to Pet. for Cert. 187a (hereinafter President's Memorandum). And Congress has done nothing to suggest the contrary. Under these circumstances, I believe the treaty obligations, and hence the judgment, resting as it does upon the consent of the United States to the ICJ's jurisdiction, bind the courts no less than would 'an act of the [federal] legislature.' *Foster, supra*, at 314.…

The critical question here is whether the Supremacy Clause requires Texas to follow, *i.e.*, to enforce, this ICJ judgment. The Court says 'no.' And it reaches its negative answer by interpreting the labyrinth of treaty provisions as creating a legal obligation that binds the United States internationally, but which, for Supremacy Clause purposes, is not automatically enforceable as domestic law. In the majority's view, the Optional Protocol simply sends the dispute to the ICJ; the ICJ statute says that the ICJ will subsequently reach a judgment; and the U. N. Charter contains no more than a promise to 'undertak[e]to comply' with that judgment.…Such a promise, the majority says, does not as a domestic law matter (in Chief Justice Marshall's words) 'operat[e] of itself without the aid of any legislative provision.' *Foster*, 2 Pet., at 314. Rather, here (and presumably in any other ICJ judgment rendered pursuant to any of the approximately 70 U. S. treaties in force that contain similar provisions for submitting treaty-based disputes to the ICJ for decisions that bind the parties) Congress must enact specific legislation before ICJ judgments entered pursuant to our consent to compulsory ICJ jurisdiction can become domestic law.…

In my view, the President has correctly determined that Congress need not enact additional legislation. The majority places too much weight upon treaty language that says little about the matter. The words 'undertak[e] to comply,' for example, do not tell us whether an ICJ judgment rendered pursuant to the parties' consent to compulsory ICJ jurisdiction does, or does not, automatically become part of our domestic law. To answer that question we must look instead to our own domestic law, in particular, to the many treaty-related cases interpreting the Supremacy Clause.…

Applying the approach just described, I would find there relevant treaty provisions self-executing as applied to the ICJ judgment before us (giving that judgment domestic legal effect) for the following reasons, taken together. *First*, the language of the relevant treaties strongly supports direct judicial enforceability, at least of judgments of the kind at issue here. The Optional Protocol bears the title 'Compulsory Settlement of Disputes,' thereby emphasizing the mandatory and binding nature of the procedures it sets forth.…The body of the

Protocol says specifically that 'any party' that has consented to the ICJ's 'compulsory jurisdiction' may bring a 'dispute' before the court against any other such party, Art. I. And the Protocol contrasts proceedings of the compulsory kind with an alternative 'conciliation procedure,' the recommendations of which a party may decide 'not' to 'accep[t].' Art. III....Thus, the Optional Protocol's basic objective is not just to provide a forum for *settlement* but to provide a forum for *compulsory* settlement. Moreover, in accepting Article 94(1) of the Charter, '[e]ach Member...undertakes to comply with the decision' of the ICJ 'in any case to which it is a party.' [see Chapter 16]. And the ICJ Statute...makes clear that, a decision of the ICJ between parties that have consented to the ICJ's compulsory jurisdiction has '*binding force*... between the parties and in respect of that particular case.' Art. 59, *id.*, at 1062 (emphasis added). Enforcement of a court's judgment that has 'binding force' involves quintessential judicial activity. True, neither the Protocol nor the Charter explicitly states that the obligation to comply with an ICJ judgment automatically binds a party *as a matter of domestic law* without further domestic legislation. *But how could the language of those documents do otherwise?* The treaties are multilateral....Why, given national differences, would drafters, seeking as strong a legal obligation as is practically attainable, use treaty language that *requires* all signatories to adopt uniform domestic-law treatment in this respect? The absence of that likely unobtainable language can make no difference. We are considering the language for purposes of applying the Supremacy Clause. And for that purpose, this Court has found to be self-executing multilateral treaty language that is far less direct or forceful (on the relevant point) than the language set forth in the present treaties.

NOTES

1. The United States Supreme Court has not been active in applying international law. It has required treaties to be 'self-executing' (see *Fujii*), or incorporated by national law, before they will be applied, despite the words of Article VI(2) of the Constitution (though see *The Paquete Habana* in Chapter 2). It has also ignored international law to protect its government's self-interest, as seen in *United States* v *Alvarez-Machain* 31 ILM (1992) 902, where the forcible abduction of a Mexican national from Mexico by United States government agents was allowed, in apparent contravention of a bilateral treaty and of the customary international law of human rights (see further in Chapter 8).

2. It is apparent from a number of cases that United States courts (like most national courts) require proof of the existence of customary international law before they will apply it—as federal common law—in the United States. See *Filartiga* v *Pena-Irala* 630 F 2nd 876 (1980) (Court of Appeals, Second Circuit), *Tel-Oren* v *Libyan Arab Republic* 726 F 2nd 774 (1984) (Court of Appeal, District of Columbia Circuit) and *Trajano* v *Marcos* 978 F 2nd 493 (1992) (Court of Appeal, Ninth Circuit). The extract by Bianchi discusses the uncertain status of customary international law in United States law, particularly in recent years.

3. The reluctance of the United States judiciary to refer to international law was also reflected in the decision of the United States Supreme Court in *Medellin* v *Texas*. A majority of the US Supreme Court held that, although the United States is obliged to give effect to the decision of the ICJ in the *Avena* case, an obligation flowing from the treaty obligations of the United States, this obligation is not one that has binding effect in US law, i.e. it is not of a self-executing nature. The Supreme Court's opinion, and the separate and dissenting opinions, reveal important differences of opinion on issues such as international law, self-executing treaties and the need for implementing legislation. The decision has created difficulties for the United States government, as it also held that the President does not have the constitutional power to require the individual states within the federal US to comply with the decisions of the ICJ.

5

Personality and Recognition

International law is unlike the law of national legal systems in that the persons or entities to which it applies are not always immediately apparent. National law applies, most obviously (though not exclusively), to natural or legal persons within the territorial borders and to 'nationals' of the home State. In a general way, the 'subjects' of national law, being the persons to whom the legal system is addressed, are reasonably well defined geographically and legally. International law has no territorial boundaries in the same sense and no comparable concept of 'nationals'. Consequently, its 'subjects' are harder to define and even to identify. Of course, the question of 'who' may be subject to international rights and duties is of considerable importance. If a 'State', group of persons, territorial entity (e.g. Northern Ireland, Quebec) or multinational corporation can be said to be a 'subject' of international law and have 'international personality' then have rights and duties in the international legal system. This will include procedural rights and obligations, such as the ability to bring international claims before judicial tribunals and arbitration panels, and the obligation to defend such claims.

In addition to having consequences on the international plane (such as the ability to make treaties, bring claims, participate in multinational events, be held accountable, etc.), international personality (or the absence thereof) may have consequences within the national legal systems of States. These consequences may indeed differ from to State to State. Thus 'recognition' of the statehood of an entity by a State may be critical in determining the rights and duties of that entity in national law of that State.

It is clear that there are many different types of international legal person. It is also clear that 'international personality' is not an absolute concept. It is relative in the sense that different types of international legal person may have different types or layers of international personality. Generally (and not exhaustively), the most extensive international personality entails the ability to bring claims before international tribunals exercising an international legal jurisdiction, to enjoy rights and be subject to international legal obligations, to participate in international law creation (including through customary international law and the conclusion of treaties), to enjoy the immunities attaching to international legal persons within national legal systems and to participate in international organisations. However, not all international persons have the full measure of personality for all purposes. The approach to the issue of international legal personality may depend on the extent to which it is accepted that the international legal system is a solely State-based system. Most commentators today acknowledge that there are other entities that participate in the international legal system, such as international organisations, individuals, corporations, non-State armed groups and non-governmental organisations.

A: Statehood

States are the most important subjects of international law. By definition, if an entity amounts to a 'State' it has the potential or 'capacity' to avail itself of all of the rights and to be subject to all of the duties known to the international system. Of course, individual States may have deliberately limited their capacity in respect of particular rights or duties, often by treaty (e.g. by accepting the Vienna Convention on Diplomatic Relations 1961 States limit their jurisdictional rights), but this does not detract from their paramount claim to those rights and duties. In effect, the rights and duties of States set the benchmark for the other 'subjects' of international law.

Montevideo Convention on the Rights and Duties of States 1933

135 LNTS 19 (1936)

Article 1

The State as a person of international law should possess the following qualifications: (a) a permanent population; (b) a defined territory; (c) government; and (d) capacity to enter into relations with other states.

Customs Regime between Germany and Austria Case

PCIJ Ser A/B (1931) No. 41, Permanent Court of International Justice

In a Protocol (i.e. treaty) signed at Geneva in October 1922, Austria undertook not to give up its independence in economic matters contrary to Article 88 of the Treaty of St-Germain. In a Protocol signed at Vienna in March 1931, Austria agreed to negotiate a customs union with Germany. The Council of the League of Nations requested an Advisory Opinion on whether this proposed union would violate the terms of the 1922 Protocol and Article 88 of the Treaty of St-Germain. A majority of the Court held that it would, and in his Separate Opinion, Judge Anzilotti discussed the nature of 'independence' in international law.

JUDGE ANZILOTTI: With regard [to the meaning of 'independence'] I think the foregoing observations show that the independence of Austria within the meaning of Article 88 is nothing else but the existence of Austria, within the frontiers laid down by the Treaty of Saint-Germain, as a separate State and not subject to the authority of any other State or group of States. Independence as thus understood is really no more than the normal condition of States according to international law; it may also be described as *sovereignty (suprema potestas)*, or *external sovereignty*, by which is meant that the State has over it no other authority than that of international law.

The conception of independence, regarded as the normal characteristic of States as subjects of international law, cannot be better defined than by comparing it with the exceptional and, to some extent, abnormal class of States known as 'dependent States.' These are States subject to the authority of one or more other States. The idea of dependence therefore necessarily implies a relation between a superior State (suzerain, protector, etc.) and an inferior or subject State (vassal, *protégé*, etc.); the relation between the State which can legally impose its will and the State which is legally compelled to submit to that will. Where there is no such relation of superiority and subordination, it is impossible to speak of dependence within the meaning of international law.

It follows that the legal conception of independence has nothing to do with a State's subordination to international law or with the numerous and constantly increasing states of *de facto* dependence which characterize the relation of one country to other countries.

It also follows that the restrictions upon a State's liberty, whether arising out of ordinary international law or contractual engagements, do not as such in the least affect its independence. As long as these restrictions do not place the State under the legal authority of another State, the former remains an independent State however extensive and burdensome those obligations may be.

United Nations Charter 1945

Article 2

1.…The Organization is based on the principle of the sovereign equality of all its Members.…

Article 4

1. Membership in the United Nations is open to all other peace-loving States which accept the obligations contained in the present Charter and, in the judgment of the Organization, are able and willing to carry out these obligations.

2. The admission of any such State to membership in the United Nations will be effected by a decision of the General Assembly upon the recommendation of the Security Council.

J. Crawford, *The Creation of States in International Law*
(2nd edn, 2006)

If the effect of positivist doctrine in international law was to place the emphasis, in matters of statehood, on the question of recognition, then the effect of modern doctrine and practice has been to return the attention to issues of statehood and status, independent of recognition. Nevertheless there has long been no generally accepted and satisfactory legal definition of statehood.…It may be asked how a concept as central as statehood could have gone without a definition, or at least a satisfactory one, for so long. This may be because the question normally arises only in the borderline cases, where a new entity has emerged bearing some but not all of the characteristics of statehood. The resulting problems of characterization cannot be resolved except in relation to the particular issues and circumstances. But, it may be asked, are there any legal consequences that attach to statehood as such, which are not legal incidents of other forms of international personality? To put it another way, is there a legal concept of statehood, or does the meaning of the term vary indefinitely depending on the context?…[S]tatehood is…a central concept of international law, even if it is one of open texture. The following exclusive and general legal characteristics of States may be instanced.

1. In principle, States have plenary competence to perform acts, make treaties and so on, in the international sphere: this is one meaning of the term 'sovereign' as applied to States.

2. In principle States are exclusively competent with respect to their internal affairs, a principle reflected by Article 2, paragraph 7 of the United Nations Charter. This does not of course mean that international law imposes no constraints: it does mean that their jurisdiction is prima facie both plenary and not subject to the control of other States.

3. In principle States are not subject to compulsory international process, jurisdiction or settlement without their consent, given either generally or in the specific case.

4. In international law States are regarded as 'equal', a principle also recognized by the Charter (Article 2(1)). This is in part a restatement of the foregoing principles, but it has other corollaries. It is a formal, not a moral principle. It does not mean, for example, that all States are entitled to an equal vote in international organizations: States may consent to unequal voting (the United Nations, the World Bank…). Still less does it mean that they are entitled to an equal voice or influence. But it does mean that at a basic level, States have equal status and standing: 'A dwarf is as much a man as a giant; a small republic is no less a sovereign state than the most powerful kingdom.'

5. Derogations from these principles will not be presumed: in case of doubt an international court or tribunal will tend to decide in favour of the freedom of action of States, whether with respect to external or internal affairs, or as not having consented to a specific exercise of international jurisdiction, or to a particular derogation from equality. This presumption—rebuttable in any case—has declined in importance, but is still invoked from time to time and is still part of the hidden grammar of international legal language. It will be referred to as the *Lotus* presumption—its classic formulation being the judgment of the Permanent Court in *The Lotus*…

If there is then a legal concept of statehood, there must be means of determining which entities are 'States' with these attributes; in other words, of establishing the criteria for statehood. Two preliminary points should, however, be made. First, it will be noted that the exclusive attributes of States do not prescribe specific rights, powers or capacities that all States must, to be States, possess: they are presumptions as to the existence of such rights, powers or capacities, rules that these exist unless otherwise stipulated. This must be so, since the actual powers, rights and obligations of particular States vary considerably. The legal consequences of statehood are thus seen to be—paradoxically—matters of evidence, or rather of presumption. Predicated on a basic or 'structural' independence, statehood does not involve any inherent substantive rights. Further, the law recognizes no general duty on a State to maintain its independence: independence is protected while it exists, but there is no prohibition on its partial or permanent alienation. The legal concept of statehood provides a measure for determining whether in a given case rights have been acquired or lost.

Second, the criteria for statehood are of a rather special character, in that their application conditions the application of most other international law rules. As a result, existing States have tended to retain for themselves as much freedom of action with regard to new States as possible. This may explain the reluctance of the International Law Commission to frame comprehensive definitions of statehood when engaged on other work—albeit work which assumed that the category 'States' is ascertainable. It follows that, at the empirical level, the question must again be asked whether, given the existence of international law rules determining what are 'States', those rules are sufficiently certain to be applied in specific cases, or have been kept so uncertain or open to manipulation as not to provide any standards at all. And this question is independent of the point that States may on occasions treat as a State an entity which does not come within the accepted definition of the term. The question is rather—can States effectively refuse, under cover of the 'open texture' of rules, to treat entities as States which do in truth qualify as such? To avoid that is the point of having—if we do have—'objective' criteria for statehood.

H. Charlesworth and C. Chinkin, *The Boundaries of International Law*

(2000)

Statehood confers the capacity to claim rights and duties under international law. Other entities, such as individuals and international inter-governmental and NGOs, can assert some degree of international personhood for particular purposes, but the state is considered the most complete expression of international legal personality. The state is of course an artificial entity, a means of allocating political control over territory. Its decisions, policies and strategies are those of the individuals and groups comprising its decision-making elites. International law regards states as independent and autonomous members of the international community. It tends to obliterate the differences between states by considering all states as formally equal, whatever their size, population, geography or wealth. In practice, however, disparities in size, population and wealth create great differences in power between states which are sometimes acknowledged in weighted voting systems in international organisations or differential treaty obligations. The fiction of equality is preserved through such arrangements being presented as dependent on the consent of all states parties.

The monolithic view of statehood upon which traditional international law doctrine depends significantly limits the scope of international law. One consequence is that it establishes a model for full international personality that other claimants for international status cannot replicate. Moreover, the idea of statehood constructed by international law creates a barrier between the entity of the state and those within it. This is exemplified externally by the principles of non-intervention and non-interference in the domestic affairs of states and internally by doctrines of immunity and non-justifiability. International legal theory has little to say about national decision-making processes, providing limited constraints on national action mainly through human rights principles. It is therefore not surprising that there has been little investigation by international lawyers of statehood's differential significance for women and men.

International legal doctrine on the state focuses on the criteria for, and the incidents of, statehood.…

A permanent population

International legal doctrine does not require a minimum number of inhabitants for an entity to qualify as a state. Indeed, the Montevideo definition gives no content to the notion of population, apart from the need for it to be permanent. The constitution of a population appears in many respects as a broad prerogative of statehood. The fact that the Vatican City is recognised as a state in international law suggests that there is no problem if an entity restricts its population almost entirely to adult men and that the population is reproduced asexually, through recruitment.

The concept of permanent population as a criterion of statehood assumes that populations are static. This is inaccurate in a number of ways. In the 1990s there were significant movements of peoples within and between states. For example, the UNHCR estimated that in 1997 there were 50 million forcibly displaced people around the world....

Certain restraints on population have, however, been accepted as undermining a claim to statehood. For example, the 'homelands' or 'Bantustans' created by South Africa were never accepted as states by the international community. The UN General Assembly strongly condemned their establishment 'as designed to consolidate the inhuman policies of apartheid, to destroy the territorial integrity of the country, to perpetuate white minority domination and to dispossess the African people of South Africa of their inalienable rights'.... International practice, therefore, suggests that a certain form of racial policy may be significant but that other forms of population change are insignificant in the assessment of whether a particular group of people constitutes a permanent population....

Defined territory

The territory of a state can vary greatly in size. The fact that the borders, or indeed existence, of a territorial entity are contested is considered no barrier to statehood. What is considered critical is that there be 'a certain coherent territory effectively governed'. A related international legal principle is the right of states to 'territorial integrity'. Article 2(4) of the UN Charter commits all member states to 'refrain in their international relations from the threat or use of force against the territorial integrity or political independence of any state'.

This concern with the coherence and integrity of territory presents the state as a bounded, unified entity. The notions of boundaries, borders, circumferences and peripheries have considerable power in legal rhetoric. Thus minority peoples do not qualify as full subjects of international law.

In the twentieth century territorial claims have expanded to include maritime areas and air space. Delimitation of such areas creates new problems to which traditional international law rules of acquisition of territory are inapplicable. New prescriptive regimes have been developed for these areas which emphasise the durability of the concern with boundary drawing. Innovative schemes for equitable sharing of resources in the post-colonial era such as the concept of 'the common heritage of mankind' have been controversial and resisted by a number of developed countries. In the context of the deep seabed and subsoil, the area beyond national jurisdiction and hence within the common heritage area, was greatly reduced by the extensive definition of the continental shelf. The envisaged operation of mining that area for the common benefit has been subsequently modified because of pressure from developed states, notably the United States and some member states of the EU in ways that effectively undermine the spirit of common heritage in favour of 'market-oriented approaches'.

Government

International law requires that an entity have an organised and effective government before it can be considered a state. Traditionally, there has been little concern with the *form* of the government, only its effectiveness. State practice indicates some outer limits on methods of achieving governmental stability, particularly at the time of the formation of a new entity. For example, the UN's refusal to recognise the declaration of independence of Ian Smith's government in Southern Rhodesia in 1965 was based on its purpose of enabling continued minority white rule, as well as its unilateral assertion. The notion of governmental power assumed in the definition of statehood, however, does not question women's exclusion from systems of power worldwide; indeed it can be seen to depend for its smooth functioning on particular versions of masculinity and femininity, which, like the Athenian *polis*, connect men with public political life and women with the private, domestic infrastructure that is necessary to sustain public life.

The criterion of an organised and effective government, like all the traditional international legal criteria of statehood, depends on a notion of state autonomy built on isolation and separation. It enables the state to be seen as a complete, coherent, bounded entity that speaks with one voice, obliterating the diversity of voices within the state. In this way, government can be seen as the head of the body of the state, which is made up of its population and territory....

Capacity to enter into relations with other states

This criterion of statehood is generally understood to signify independence from the authority of other states, so that agreements with other states can be freely entered into. Independence, or its synonym in international law, sovereignty, is considered the principal criterion of statehood.... Sovereignty means both full competence to act in the international arena, for example by entering into treaties or by acting to preserve state security, and exclusive jurisdiction over internal matters, for example exercise of legislative, executive and judicial competence. Thus sovereignty is a doubled-sided principle: externally, it signifies equality of power, and internally, it signifies pre-eminence of power. The standard view of international law as an essentially consensual regime is a concomitant of sovereignty—a fully sovereign entity can only voluntarily accept restraints on its activities. This capacity distinguishes states from other non-state entities such as indigenous peoples. Consent to the regime of international law thus becomes the vehicle by which the sovereign independence of states is reconciled with the practical imperatives of co-existence with other states.

There are strong connections between the requirement of a defined territory, and the notions of independence and sovereignty. One aspect of the definition of territory and the creation of boundaries is precisely to foster independence and autonomy from other entities....

That capacity to enter into international relations depends upon the willingness of other states to allow particular interests an international voice is illustrated by the somewhat anomalous position of the Holy See. The territorial state of the Vatican City is governed by the Holy See, which is a non-member state maintaining a permanent observer mission to the UN. The Holy See is regarded as the 'juridical personification' of the Roman Catholic Church. It is a full member of some UN specialised agencies and some European intergovernmental organisations. The Holy See receives and sends diplomatic representatives to other states. It can enter into treaties, address the UN General Assembly and participate as an associate member of the UN on the same basis as state delegations in UN conferences and meetings. It has exercised considerable influence within both the specialised agencies and at global conferences.

Decision of the Office of the Prosecutor of the International Criminal Court, addressed to legal representatives of the Palestinian Authority

3 April 2012

The question of Statehood arose before the International Criminal Court (ICC) (see Chapter 14) in connection with Palestine following a declaration of the Palestinian Authority accepting the ICC's jurisdiction to investigate and prosecute alleged crimes committed in Gaza between 2008 and 2009. The declaration was made under Article 12(3) of the ICC Rome Statute, which permits a State which is not a party to the Statute to lodge a declaration accepting the exercise of jurisdiction by the Court on an ad hoc basis, with respect to a core international crime.

4. The jurisdiction of the Court is not based on the principle of universal jurisdiction: it requires that the United Nations Security Council (article 13(b)) or a 'State' (article 12) provide jurisdiction. Article 12 establishes that a 'State' can confer jurisdiction to the Court by becoming a Party to the Rome Statute (article 12(1)) or by making an ad hoc declaration accepting the Court's jurisdiction (article 12(3)).

5. The issue that arises, therefore, is who defines what is a 'State' for the purpose of article 12 of the Statute? In accordance with article 125, the Rome Statute is open to accession by 'all States', and any State seeking to become a Party to the Statute must deposit an instrument of accession with the Secretary-General of the United Nations. In instances where it is controversial or unclear whether an applicant constitutes a 'State', it is the practice of the Secretary-General to follow or seek the General Assembly's directives on the matter. This is reflected in General Assembly resolutions which provide indications of whether an applicant is a 'State'. Thus, competence for determining the term 'State' within the meaning of article 12 rests, in the first instance, with the United Nations Secretary-General who, in case of doubt, will defer to the guidance of General Assembly. The Assembly of States Parties of the Rome Statute could also in due course decide to address the matter in accordance with article 112(2)(g) of the Statute.

6. In interpreting and applying article 12 of the Rome Statute, the Office has assessed that it is for the relevant bodies at the United Nations or the Assembly of States Parties to make the legal determination whether Palestine qualifies as a State for the purpose of acceding to the Rome Statute and thereby enabling the exercise of jurisdiction by the Court under article 12(1). The Rome Statute provides no authority for the Office of the Prosecutor to adopt a method to define the term "State" under article 12(3) which would be at variance with that established for the purpose of article 12(1).

7. The Office has been informed that Palestine has been recognised as a State in bilateral relations by more than 130 governments and by certain international organisations, including United Nations bodies. However, the current status granted to Palestine by the United Nations General Assembly is that of 'observer', not as a 'Non-member State'. The Office understands that on 23 September 2011, Palestine submitted an application for admission to the United Nations as a Member State in accordance with article 4(2) of the United Nations Charter, but the Security Council has not yet made a recommendation in this regard. While this process has no direct link with the declaration lodged by Palestine, it informs the current legal status of Palestine for the interpretation and application of article 12.

8. The Office could in the future consider allegations of crimes committed in Palestine, should competent organs of the United Nations or eventually the Assembly of States Parties resolve the legal issue relevant to an assessment of article 12 or should the Security Council, in accordance with article 13(b), make a referral providing jurisdiction.

D. Akande, 'Can the Pope Be Arrested in Connection with the Sexual Abuse Scandal?'
EJIL Talk, 14 April 2010

The reason the Pope cannot be arrested and prosecuted in the UK is because he is entitled to Head of State immunity.…The Vatican has a tiny territory and a tiny population but it does fulfil the criteria for Statehood.… The size of population or territory are irrelevant for the purposes of Statehood. What is important is that the entity possesses those criteria as well as the two other criteria for Statehood—which are: a government in effective control of the territory and independence (or what is called 'capacity to enter into legal relations' in the words of the Montevideo Convention on the Rights and Duties of States 1935). The Vatican as a territorial entity does have a government: the Holy See which is headed by the Pope.…the Holy See has its own independent legal personality (about which more later on) and that personality predates the Statehood of the Vatican. However, the Holy See is also the government of the Vatican City State. More importantly, the Vatican is independent of any other State. Its independence from Italy which is the State that could have had claims to control that territory is recognised in the Lateran Treaty of 1929. The preamble to the treaty speaks of:

> 'assuring to the Holy See in a permanent manner a position in fact and in law which guarantees it absolute independence for the fulfilment of its exalted mission in the world,'

and states that:

> 'in order to assure the absolute and visible independence of the Holy See, it is required that it be guaranteed an indisputable sovereignty even in the international realm, it has been found necessary to create under special conditions Vatican City, recognizing the full ownership and the exclusive and absolute power and sovereign jurisdiction of the Holy See over the same'

Geoffrey Robertson [The Case of the Pope: Vatican Accountability for Human Rights Abuse, 2010] argues that

> 'The notion that statehood can be created by another country's unilateral declaration is risible: Iran could make Qom a state overnight, or the UK could launch Canterbury on to the international stage.'

But this misunderstands how States are created. Many States are indeed created by the unilateral declaration of one State. This is how colonialism in Africa and Asia ended. This is how the States in the Commonwealth achieved statehood. They were all granted independence by unilateral declaration—in many cases, by national Statutes—of the colonial powers. Independence means the right to control a portion of a globe without being subject to the legal authority of another entity. The way this is achieved in the case of territories previously under the control of another State, is by that other State renouncing the claims that it has to that territory.

But the independence and Statehood of the Vatican are not created solely by unilateral declaration but are also recognised by other States, indeed by most States of the world. The Vatican is a member of a number of international organizations, including the Universal Postal Union [UPU], the International Telecommunications Union and the World Intellectual Property Organization. Although the UPU is open to territorial entities which are not States (see commentary to Art. 1 of the UPU's constitution), the only territorial entities that may be Members of the ITU and WIPO are States. In addition, the Vatican is party to many multilateral treaties including, the Convention on the Rights of the Child (yes that one) and the 1949 Geneva Conventions on the protection of victims of armed conflict.

So, since the Vatican is a State then the head of that State, the Pope, is entitled to head of State immunity under international law…

NOTES

1. It is clear that the criteria of the Montevideo Convention have been accepted as the indicia of Statehood and have now passed into customary international law. However, the question remains whether these criteria are sufficient for Statehood, as well as being necessary. Crawford goes on to consider other possible conditions such as 'permanence', 'willingness and ability to observe international law', 'a certain degree of civilisation', 'recognition', the existence of a 'legal order' within the State, and 'legality'. This indicates that 'Statehood' is a rather more complex legal relationship than the Montevideo Convention suggests. Likewise, the European Union and Member State's Guidelines on Recognition of New States in Eastern Europe and the Soviet Union, and their Declaration on Yugoslavia (see Section 1B) appear to lay down additional criteria for Statehood, or at least for recognition of Statehood. However, as illustrated in the extract from Murphy (Section 2A) it is unwise to stress some 'Western' notions of Statehood (e.g. democracy) as if they were accepted universally. It is noteworthy that several civil law States will normally limit evaluation of Statehood based on the 'doctrine of the three elements'. According to this doctrine, a State requires a territory, a permanent population and 'public authority' or 'public power', but not the capacity to enter into relations with other States.

2. Another problem is who is competent to decide whether an entity has achieved the conditions laid down in the Montevideo Convention and any additional Statehood criteria. In this regard, membership of an international organisation may be strong evidence, as seen in the extract concerning Palestine. Yet, the Saharan Arab Republic (Western Sahara) is a member of the OAU, although not the United Nations. Likewise, Switzerland, which undoubtedly was a State before-hand, only joined the United Nations in 2002. As at March 2016 there are 193 members of the United Nations (see Appendix) but this excludes Taiwan, Kosovo (see Section 1B) and the Turkish Republic of Northern Cyprus. The most recent member States to be admitted were Montenegro (2006) and South Sudan (2011). Membership of the United Nations is a prize for aspirant States, a good example being the admittance of Eritrea on its secession from Ethiopia.

3. Chinkin and Charlesworth point out in their extract that Statehood implies sovereignty. Territorial sovereignty is one of the main principles of international law, and a core feature of Statehood (for an explanation and materials on the concept of sovereignty see Chapter 7). Normally, the State exercises its monopoly of force throughout its territory. However, situations exist in which the State is unable to perform the functions that characterise sovereignty, especially in situations where internal conflict has paralysed government action. While the presence of a functioning government has been a criterion for statehood at least since the Montevideo Convention, the temporary or even long-term absence of a functioning government does not lead to a deprivation of Statehood. A prime example is Somalia. Somalia has been affected by internal conflict for the past 20 years and, since 1991, there has not been a government recognised by all parts of the Somali territory. While there are provinces within Somalia that are practically autonomous, Somalia has never been considered to have 'lost' its Statehood.

4. The two non-member States of the United Nations are Palestine and the Holy See, which enjoy a standing invitation to participate as permanent observers in the session and work of the UN General Assembly. Both have faced controversy concerning their statehood in recent years, as the two extracts above demonstrate. On 31 October 2011, Palestine was admitted as a State member of UNESCO (the UN cultural heritage organisation) by 107 votes in favour of admission, with 14 against and 52 abstentions. However, while the UNESCO vote went some way to advancing Palestine's case for Statehood, it did not settle the question. In the view of the ICC Prosecutor (see extract), the UNESCO vote had granted Palestine 'observer' status only and was insufficient evidence that Palestine constituted a State. However, the issue was settled by a UN General Assembly vote, taken on 29 November 2012, to accord Palestine non-member observer State status in the UN, supported by more than 130 States (see P. Eden, 'Palestinian Statehood: Trapped Between Rhetoric and Realpolitik' (2013) 62 *International and Comparative Law Quarterly* 225). In January 2015, the Palestinian Authority submitted a further declaration under Article 12(3) of the Rome Statute and deposited an instrument of accession to the Rome Statute of the ICC. This was despite the rejection of a draft resolution by the Security Council on December 2014 that aimed at 'upgrading' Palestine's status to a full member State of the United Nations. The Palestine Authority is now apparently considered to be a State party to the ICC.

5. The status of Holy See as a State was raised by the question as to whether the Vatican can be held accountable for the alleged systematic sexual abuse of children by members of the Catholic church and whether state immunity (see Chapter 9) would apply to the Pope, as the head of the Vatican. As seen in the extract from Akande, this depends on the status of the Holy See.

B: Other territorial entities

Clearly there exist many other territorial entities that are not States but which also cannot accurately be described as 'merely' part of the metropolis of an existing State. Taiwan provides a good example, being neither desirous itself of the status of 'Statehood' (because it formally still adheres to a 'one China' policy) but in essence operating as an independent entity. Other, more difficult, examples exist, such as the Saharan Arab Republic, Chechnya, Abkhazia, South Ossetia and Crimea. The latter three have been recognised by only a few States, including Russia. In regard to the the right of self-determination of regions within a State which have a large degree of autonomy see Chapter 6. A related question that has long been discussed is the status of territories under international administration (see also Chapter 7). This question first arose with the United Nations Trusteeship system during the decolonisation process.

C. Stahn, *The Law and Practice of International Territorial Administration*
(2005)

Internationalised entities may be further divided into different sub-categories. One may distinguish at least three forms of territorial arrangements: frameworks of administration, under which domestic sovereignty and territorial jurisdiction coincide; arrangements under which the holders of territorial sovereignty and territorial jurisdiction diverge; and situations in which international administrations assume territorial jurisdiction over a territory independent of the control of any other state entity.

These three scenarios are different in substance. They deserve a further terminological differentiation. A tripartite distinction may be made between 'internationalised states', 'internationalised territories' and 'international territories'.

Territories which fall into the first category remain associated with traditional statehood and do not require a distinct status level. The state entities themselves bear traces of internationalisation. They may be referred to as 'internationalised states'. The notion of international(ised) territories, on the other hand, may be further subdivided in order to distinguish territories of the second and third category.

Territories which enjoy separate legal personality and in which one or several functions of domestic jurisdiction are exercised by an international institution that administers or governs the territory on behalf of the international community, or by a collectivity of states, may be qualified as internationalised territories *stricto sensu*—a label which highlights the dissociation of jurisdiction and sovereignty.

Lastly, territorial entities which are under the jurisdiction of an international authority and are disconnected from any territorial sovereign enjoy an independent international status. They may be directly qualified as international territories.

Internationalised states

Internationalised states may be defined as state entities which are subject to international control and institutionalised power-sharing arrangements within their internal domestic system, while domestic authorities maintain territorial sovereignty and jurisdiction. These requirements are, in particular, met by co-governance missions, which assume governing functions alongside local institutions within the legal system of the administered territory, without replacing or superseding the responsibilities of domestic authorities as the principal territorial ruler.

The typical examples of internationalised statehood are Cambodia and Bosnia and Herzegovina. Both entities were partially internationalised by way of a peace agreement, but preserved their status as sovereign states and holders of territorial jurisdiction.

Internationalised territories

'Internationalised territories' form a separate category of territories. They encompass territorial entities which enjoy some attributes of legal personality as a territory, while remaining attached to the territorial sovereignty of a specific state.

The trademark of 'internationalised territories' is the dissociation of sovereignty and jurisdiction. 'Internationalised territories' are placed under two layers of public power: the jurisdiction of an international(ised) administration and the sovereignty of the territorial state. The actual governing powers (jurisdiction) lie with ruling authorities of the territorial entity, whereas the territorial sovereign retains the formal title over the latter.

This disjunction of jurisdiction and sovereignty typically arises in cases where the public authority of a territorial state is replaced and superseded by the functional authority of an international institution that administers or governs the territory, either exclusively or in cooperation with domestic authorities of the territory…

International territories

Finally, international organisations have exercised jurisdiction over territory in respect of which no state held territorial sovereignty. This category of international administration is the most unusual type of governance in terms of legal status. The respective territories are neither *terra nullis*, nor attached to any territorial sovereign. They are truly 'international territories'. The control over these entities lies with an administering entity which exercises its powers on the basis of an international arrangement related to the territory…

[T]he UN exercised independent administering authority in two other situations: Namibia and East Timor. Namibia came under the direct responsibility of the UN after the termination of the Mandate of South West Africa by Resolution 2145 (XXI). South Africa no longer held territorial rights over Namibia, neither by virtue of military conquest, nor on the basis of Chapter XI of the Charter. The territory was therefore under the sole and exclusive authority of the UN during the period of administration by the Council for Namibia.

C. Warbrick, 'Kosovo: The Declaration of Independence'

(2008) 57 *International and Comparative Law Quarterly* 675

Kosovo was a largely autonomous region of Serbia (then known as the Federal Republic of Yugoslavia) until the early 1990s. Its autonomy was gradually revoked, and its population increasingly discriminated against by pro-Serbian elements. This discrimination and violence escalated in late 1998, leading to an armed intervention by the North Atlantic Treaty Organization (NATO) (see Chapter 15). Security Council Resolution 1244, which authorised the establishment of an international civil administration and NATO presence in Kosovo (known as KFOR), did not address the substance of the long-term legal status of Kosovo, although it did reaffirm the territorial sovereignty of the Federal Republic of Yugoslavia. The following extract examines the legal issues raised by the declaration of independence by the Republic of Kosovo in March 2008.

From 1999 to 2008, no part of the political process went smoothly, though Kosovan institutions were eventually established.…Each side became more committed to incompatible fundamentals—on the one side, that Kosovo must remain a part of Serbia; on the other, that the return of the Kosovars to Serbian authority was impossible.

No scheme of autonomy, however sophisticated, could bridge that gap. The UN negotiators did lay down the principles upon which future Kosovan government was to be based and it was proposed that these 'standards' be implemented before any decisions on Kosovo's final status—'standards before status'. In the end, the intransigence defeated the negotiators. The Secretary General's special representative, Martti Ahtisaari, eventually proposed in February 2007 'supervised independence' for Kosovo as the least bad alternative. He wrote: '…I have come to the conclusion that the only viable option for Kosovo is independence, to be supervised for an initial period by the international community'. Although further attempts were made to bring the parties together, by the end of 2007 all the bodies concerned decided that there was no prospect of reaching agreement, however long negotiations were continued. Some States, notably Russia, and, of course, Serbia rejected both the premise—that negotiations were exhausted—and the conclusion—'supervised independence'. If there were no prospect of the parties agreeing, nor was there any chance of a Security Council resolution to replace Resolution 1244 and provide a basis for supervised independence. At a meeting of the Security Council on 16 January 2008, this proposal was roundly condemned by Serbia.

B. The Declaration of Independence

Doubtless encouraged by indications that it would have the support of the United States and major EU States, the government of Kosovo took the initiative. On 17 February 2008, the Assembly of Kosovo issued its 'Declaration of Independence', in which it declared that the Republic of Kosovo was an 'independent and sovereign State'.

It accepted the principles of the Ahtisaari Plan and welcomed the continued support of the international community on the basis of Resolution 1244....In its final clause, the Declaration says:

> We hereby affirm, clearly, specifically and irrevocably, that Kosovo shall be legally bound to comply with the provisions contained in this Declaration, including especially the obligations for it under the Ahtisaari Plan. In all of these matters, we shall act consistently with the principles of international law and resolutions of the Security Council, including resolution 1244. We declare publicly that all States are entitled to rely upon this Declaration, and appeal to them to extend us their support and friendship.

A remarkable document, then—a unilateral declaration, *erga omnes*. Kosovo's claim to Statehood was recognised by a number of States, not always in the same terms; it was rejected by a smaller number, including Serbia, again, not always in the same terms, some of the reactions referring to the claim to Statehood as being illegal in international law.

C. Assessment

A common, though not universal, feature of the acts of recognition of the Republic of Kosovo was to say that Kosovo was 'unique' or '*sui generis*', that its attainment of Statehood was not to be taken as a precedent which could be relied upon by any other ethnic group in a discrete territory which wished to secede from the State under the sovereignty of which it currently was and to have its own State. If it were to be a precedent (whatever that means) then the Statehood of the Republic of Kosovo could have a destabilising effect on many States. That it might be called in aid in support of other secessionist projects has undoubtedly weighed with some States as they consider whether or not to recognise the Republic of Kosovo. No one factor makes Kosovo unique but a case might be made that certain of its features taken together do make it special. What these factors are depends again upon where we start. The repression of the Kosovars up to 1999 was pretty exceptional but by no means unique....More unusually, it was the unilateral use of force against Yugoslavia in response to the repression which was essential to causing Serbia to withdraw and allowing the unopposed interposition of the international presences in Kosovo. Although there are other examples of international elements in the administration of territory in the Charter period, they have been part of decolonization/self-determination projects or for the consolidation of Statehood obtained as a result of the exercise of self-determination. The two events together—the bombing and the administration—may create a political responsibility to produce a solution in which the position of the victims—the Kosovars—is at least no worse than when the action started. The concern of the States most involved in Kosovo seems to have been that they were not prepared to go on with this commitment forever, indeed the longer that they did so with Kosovo's status unresolved, the greater the danger of instability in the whole area. The belief was that the international administration had started a process which would be effective in providing Kosovo with viable institutions, which would conduct themselves in accordance with the Ahtisaari principles, in particular, that the Serb minority in the Republic of Kosovo could remain confident that they would suffer none of the deprivations of the kind previously inflicted on the Kosovars. Such progress and such potential guarantees of entrenchment would not normally be available in cases of unilateral secession. In essence then, this is the claim of uniqueness about Kosovo—that an identified set of domestic arrangements for the new entity have been established and will be made effective by international participation in the governance of the Republic of Kosovo. Establishing these conditions has followed upon patterns of grievous human rights violations and unilateral military intervention but these events were not the cause of the present situation, they are not of themselves the features of Kosovo's uniqueness.

The other aspect of Kosovo's specialness has been the willingness of some States to reach the conclusion that the territory's link with its State (Serbia) ought to be broken and that Kosovo should be regarded as (some kind of) a State....

D. The Status of (the Republic of) Kosovo

To recap, there are three separate (but possibly related questions) which need to be addressed (and not necessarily in this order):

(1) Whatever the status of the Republic of Kosovo, does it have some international element to it?
(2) Whatever the status of the Republic of Kosovo, does it have some element of Statehood to it?
(3) What part do individual State decisions have in establishing the status of the Republic of Kosovo?

The Republic of Kosovo may continue to have, as Kosovo has had since 1999, some internationalized aspects to its status, elements which may (or may not) be compatible with Serbia's continued claim of sovereignty over Kosovo. If the Republic of Kosovo's status is some kind of Statehood, though, then we must be able to account for how Serbia's previous sovereign claim has been severed, given its continued assertion by Serbia. If the Republic of Kosovo's status is different after the Declaration of Independence from what it was before, it is necessary to establish the legal basis for this (and where necessary, that the legal conditions have been satisfied), in particular, to make an assessment of the significance of individual State acts expressed by recognition/ not recognizing decisions. It is necessary to avoid avoiding the question of how Serbia lost its title simply by postulating a new status for Kosovo which requires (but does not explain) the termination of Serbia's rights, which, it will be suggested, has been a frequent deficiency in the recognition statements.

Accordance with International Law of the Unilateral Declaration of Independence in Respect of Kosovo

Advisory Opinion, 22 July 2010, International Court of Justice

The facts leading to this Advisory Opinion are set out in the extract from Warbrick above. In 2008, the General Assembly requested an advisory opinion from the International Court of Justice (see Chapter 16) on the question of whether the unilateral declaration of the independence of Kosovo was in accordance with international law.

Judge Koroma (Dissenting Opinion):

20.…[T]he Court, in considering the question put before it by the General Assembly, had to apply the rules and principles of general international law. In this regard, it must first be emphasized that it is a misconception to say, as the majority opinion does, that international law does not authorize or prohibit the unilateral declaration of independence. That statement only makes sense when made in the abstract about declarations of independence in general…not with regard to a specific unilateral declaration of independence which took place in a specific factual and legal context against which its accordance with international law can be judged. The question put before the Court is specific and well defined. It is not a hypothetical question. It is a legal question requiring a legal response. Since the Court, according to its Statute, is under an obligation to apply the rules and principles of international law even when rendering advisory opinions, it should have applied them in this case. Had it done so—instead of avoiding the question by reference to a general statement that international law does not authorize or prohibit declarations of independence, which does not answer the question posed by the General Assembly—it would have had to conclude, as discussed below, that the unilateral declaration of independence by the Provisional Institutions of Self-Government of Kosovo amounted to secession and was not in accordance with international law. A unilateral secession of a territory from an existing State without its consent, as in this case under consideration, is a matter of international law.

21. The truth is that international law upholds the territorial integrity of a State. One of the fundamental principles of contemporary international law is that of respect for the sovereignty and territorial integrity of States. This principle entails an obligation to respect the definition, delineation and territorial integrity of an existing State. According to the principle, a State exercises sovereignty within and over its territorial domain.…The unilateral declaration of independence involves a claim to a territory which is part of the Federal Republic of Yugoslavia (Serbia). Attempting to dismember or amputate part of the territory of a State, in this case the Federal Republic of Yugoslavia (Serbia), by dint of the unilateral declaration of independence of 17 February 2008, is neither in conformity with international law nor with the principles of the Charter of the United Nations, nor with resolution 1244 (1999).

General Assembly Resolution on the Territorial Integrity of Ukraine

27 March 2014, A/RES/68/262, Sixty-eighth session, 1 April 2014

This resolution was passed in response to the military occupation of Crimea, a territory forming part of the Ukraine, and its forcible annexation by Russia.

The General Assembly,
    Reaffirming the paramount importance of the Charter of the United Nations in the promotion of the rule of law among nations,
    Recalling the obligations of all States under Article 2 of the Charter to refrain in their international relations from the threat or use of force against the territorial integrity or political independence of any State, and to settle their international disputes by peaceful means,

Recalling also its resolution 2625 (XXV) of 24 October 1970, in which it approved the Declaration on Principles of International Law concerning Friendly Relations and Cooperation among States in accordance with the Charter of the United Nations, and reaffirming the principles contained therein that the territory of a State shall not be the object of acquisition by another State resulting from the threat or use of force, and that any attempt aimed at the partial or total disruption of the national unity and territorial integrity of a State or country or at its political independence is incompatible with the purposes and principles of the Charter,...

1. *Affirms* its commitment to the sovereignty, political independence, unity and territorial integrity of Ukraine within its internationally recognized borders;

2. *Calls upon* all States to desist and refrain from actions aimed at the partial or total disruption of the national unity and territorial integrity of Ukraine, including any attempts to modify Ukraine's borders through the threat or use of force or other unlawful means;

3. *Urges* all parties to pursue immediately the peaceful resolution of the situation with respect to Ukraine through direct political dialogue, to exercise restraint, to refrain from unilateral actions and inflammatory rhetoric that may increase tensions and to engage fully with international mediation efforts;

4. *Welcomes* the efforts of the United Nations, the Organization for Security and Cooperation in Europe and other international and regional organizations to assist Ukraine in protecting the rights of all persons in Ukraine, including the rights of persons belonging to minorities;

5. *Underscores* that the referendum held in the Autonomous Republic of Crimea and the city of Sevastopol on 16 March 2014, having no validity, cannot form the basis for any alteration of the status of the Autonomous Republic of Crimea or of the city of Sevastopol;

6. *Calls upon* all States, international organizations and specialized agencies not to recognize any alteration of the status of the Autonomous Republic of Crimea and the city of Sevastopol on the basis of the above-mentioned referendum and to refrain from any action or dealing that might be interpreted as recognizing any such altered status.

NOTES

1. Provinces/States within federations do not have a distinct international legal personality from the federation. The federation exercises sovereignty over its territory, can be held responsible by other States for breaches of international law and enjoys all other rights and duties connected to legal personality. Provinces/States within federations are simply entities within a federation, and are not bestowed with international personality. However, they are sometimes able to conclude treaties under international law. The German Constitution provides, for example, that the internal German states may enter into treaties with States if the treaty concerns one of the exclusive legislative competencies of the federal State, and after approval by the central (federal) government. Other arrangements between federations and provinces/states within federations exist, conferring treaty-making power to the federal State. This does not transmit international legal personality: the federal State will only be able to exercise treaty-making power (or any other power with implications in the international arena) to the extent provided for in its Constitution.

2. A clear example of entities tied to a territory and being classified as subjects of international law without being States *per se* were the peoples of the UN Trust Territories. Similar to League of Nation's Mandates, such territories were placed under the Trusteeship of a protecting State whose paramount duty was to promote the peoples' right of self-determination. On 1 October 1994, the last remaining Trusteeship territory (Palau) exercised its right of self-determination by becoming an independent State. The Republic of Palau, the Federated States of Micronesia and the Republic of the Marshall Islands were formerly part of the Pacific Trust Territory and all have become independent sovereign States. All three have entered into Compacts with the United States, which, while not compromising their sovereignty, is a loose form of protectorate or free association. The Commonwealth of the Northern Mariana Islands, also part of the former Pacific Trust Territory, has exercised its right of self-determination by becoming a self-governing Commonwealth under the sovereignty of the United States.

3. Stahn argues that one needs to distinguish between internationalised entities (States where the governmental function is exercised jointly with an international institution), internationalised territories (territories where the administration is run by an international institution, but territorial sovereignty remains otherwise intact) and international territories (territories over which

no State holds sovereignty but where an international institution holds full sovereignty). While it is not clear yet whether a distinct category of international legal personality exists under international law, Stahn's approach takes into account the reality of international organisations discharging functions normally attributed to States (on international territorial administration see also Chapter 7).

4. As the extract by Warbrick notes, the case of Kosovo displays some unique features that deserve special attention. It seems to be clear that Kosovo, while in the process of establishing governing authorities, was at the time of the Declaration of Independence not a State, at least not if one applies the traditional criteria. The strong presence of the international community discharging many of the traditional State functions, such as civil administration or security, stands against this. In view of the efforts of the United Nations and other international and regional organisations in terms of 'peace-building' strategies with a civil administration component, one might ask whether Kosovo could be considered a precedent for a form of Statehood 'under international supervision'.

5. In its Advisory Opinion on *Accordance with International Law of the Unilateral Declaration of Independence in Respect of Kosovo* (22 July 2010), the majority of the ICJ did not address the legal consequences of the Declaration and the reactions of States. Instead, the majority found that, as there was no general prohibition against the making of unilateral declarations in international law, and that the authors of the Declaration were acting outside the framework of the transitional administration, the Declaration in this case was in accordance with international law. This Opinion has been rightly criticised and Judge Koroma did consider the Declaration to be invalid, as seen in the above extract, and Judge Simma thought that the majority's opinion reflected an out-of-date view of international law.

6. While the Opinion focused on the 'neutrality' of international law towards declarations of independence, it did indicate that a declaration of independence could be unlawful in some circumstances. In particular, illegality could attach to a declaration of independence 'from the fact that they were, or would have been, connected with the unlawful use of force or other egregious violations of norms of general international law, in particular those of a peremptory character (*jus cogens*)' (para. 81). This was the concern surrounding the referendum and declaration of independence held in Crimea in 2014, with States and commentators agreeing that the declaration was only held and rendered effective due to the unlawful military intervention of Russian forces (see further Chapter 15). As seen in the General Assembly resolution extracted above, member States of the Security Council considered the declaration and subsequent integration with Russia to be a violation of international law and called on member States not to recognize its validity. Russia had earlier vetoed a similarly worded draft resolution in the Security Council.

7. A contrasting example of a referendum potentially leading to a separate state is the 2014 referendum in Scotland where the question of independence from the UK arose. The referendum raised a series of important questions including: the status of Scotland upon gaining independence; its classification as a case of secession or as a dissolution of the UK; and how Scotland would transition to a State or achieve membership in international organisations such as the UN and EU. Ultimately, these issues were not addressed as the referendum generated a negative result, with Scottish nationals choosing to remain part of the United Kingdom (see S. Tierney, 'Legal Issues Surrounding the Referendum on Independence for Scotland' (2013) 9 *European Constitutional Law Review* 359).

C: International organisations

The major international multilateral organisations include the United Nations, African Union (AU; successor organisation of the Organization of African Unity), the European Union (EU) and the Organization of American States (OAS). There are also general organisations (such as the UN), organisations within organisations (e.g. UNESCO within the UN), regional organisations (e.g. the EU, AU, and OAS), single-issue organisations (e.g. International Maritime Organization), economic organisations (e.g. World Trade Organization), military organisations (e.g. NATO) and even two-party organisations (e.g. UK-Ireland Decommissioning Body). All of these may well have international personality to some degree or another, and much will depend on the manner of their creation and the role they are designed to fulfil within the international legal order.

United Nations Charter 1945

Article 104

The Organization shall enjoy in the territory of each of its Members such legal capacity as may be necessary for the exercise of its functions and the fulfilment of its purposes.

Article 105

1. The Organization shall enjoy in the territory of each of its Members such privileges and immunities as are necessary for the fulfilment of its purposes.

2. Representatives of the Members of the United Nations and officials of the Organization shall similarly enjoy such privileges and immunities as are necessary for the independent exercise of their functions in connection with the Organization....

Reparations for Injuries Suffered in the Service of the United Nations Opinion
ICJ Rep 1949 174, International Court of Justice

Following the assassination of Count Bernadotte, a UN official, in Jerusalem in 1948, the General Assembly requested the ICJ to give an Advisory Opinion on whether the United Nations had 'as an Organisation, the capacity to bring an international claim against the responsible *de jure* or *de facto* government with a view to obtaining the reparation due in respect of the damage caused (a) to the United Nations, (b) to the victim or the persons entitled through him?'. The Court held unanimously, in respect of (a) that the UN had such capacity *vis à vis* Members of the Organisation and non-members; and similarly by 11 votes to 4 in respect of question (b).

Competence to bring an international claim is, for those possessing it, the capacity to resort to the customary methods recognized by international law for the establishment, the presentation and the settlement of claims. Among these methods may be mentioned protest, request for an enquiry, negotiation, and request for submission to an arbitral tribunal or to the Court in so far as this may be authorized by the Statute.

This capacity certainly belongs to the State; a State can bring an international claim against another State. Such a claim takes the form of a claim between two political entities, equal in law, similar in form, and both the direct subjects of international law. It is dealt with by means of negotiation, and cannot, in the present state of the law as to international jurisdiction, be submitted to a tribunal, except with the consent of the States concerned.

When the Organization brings a claim against one of its Members, this claim will be presented in the same manner, and regulated by the same procedure. It may, when necessary, be supported by the political means at the disposal of the Organization. In these ways the Organization would find a method for securing the observance of its rights by the Member against which it has a claim.

But, in the international sphere, has the Organization such a nature as involves the capacity to bring an international claim? In order to answer this question, the Court must first enquire whether the Charter has given the Organization such a position that it possesses, in regard to its Members, rights which it is entitled to ask them to respect. In other words, does the Organization possess international personality? This is no doubt a doctrinal expression, which has sometimes given rise to controversy. But it will be used here to mean that if the Organization is recognized as having that personality, it is an entity capable of availing itself of obligations incumbent upon its Members....

To answer this question, which is not settled by the actual terms of the Charter, we must consider what characteristics it was intended thereby to give to the Organization.

The subjects of law in any legal system are not necessarily identical in their nature or in the extent of their rights, and their nature depends upon the needs of the community. Throughout its history, the development of international law has been influenced by the requirements of international life, and the progressive increase in the collective activities of States has already given rise to instances of action upon the international plane by certain entities which are not States. This development culminated in the establishment in June 1945 of an International organization whose purposes and principles are specified in the Charter of the United Nations. But to achieve these ends the attribution of international personality is indispensable....

The Charter has not been content to make the Organization created by it merely a centre 'for harmonizing the actions of nations in the attainment of these common ends' (Article 1, para. 4). It has equipped that centre with organs, and has given it special tasks. It has defined the position of the Members in relation to the Organization by requiring them to give it every assistance in any action undertaken by it (Article 2, para. 5), and to accept and carry out the decisions of the Security Council; by authorizing the General Assembly to make recommendations to the Members; by giving the Organization legal capacity and privileges and immunities in the territory of each of its Members; and by providing for the conclusion of agreements between the Organization and its Members. Practice—in particular the conclusion of conventions to which the Organization is a party—has confirmed this character of the Organization, which occupies a position in certain respects in detachment from its Members, and which is under a duty to remind them, if need be, of certain obligations. It must be added that the Organization is a political body, charged with political tasks of an important character, and covering a wide field namely, the maintenance of international peace and security, the development of friendly relations among nations, and the achievement of international co-operation in the solution of problems of an economic, social, cultural or humanitarian character (Article 1); and in dealing with its Members it employs political means. The 'Convention on the Privileges and Immunities of the United Nations' of 1946 creates rights and duties between each of the signatories and the Organization.…It is difficult to see how such a convention could operate except upon the international plane and as between parties possessing international personality.

In the opinion of the Court, the Organization was intended to exercise and enjoy, and is in fact exercising and enjoying, functions and rights which can only be explained on the basis of the possession of a large measure of international personality and the capacity to operate upon an international plane. It is at present the supreme type of international organization, and it could not carry out the intentions of its founders if it was devoid of international personality. It must be acknowledged that its Members, by entrusting certain functions to it, with the attendant duties and responsibilities, have clothed it with the competence required to enable those functions to be effectively discharged.

Accordingly, the Court has come to the conclusion that the Organization is an international person. That is not the same thing as saying that it is a State, which it certainly is not, or that its legal personality and rights and duties are the same as those of a State. Still less is it the same thing as saying that it is 'a super-State', whatever that expression may mean. It does not even imply that all its rights and duties must be upon the international plane, any more than all the rights and duties of a State must be upon that plane. What it does mean is that it is a subject of international law and capable of possessing international rights and duties, and that it has capacity to maintain its rights by bringing international claims.…

The next question is whether the sum of the international rights of the Organization comprises the right to bring the kind of international claim described in the Request for this Opinion. That is a claim against a State to obtain reparation in respect of the damage caused by the injury of an agent of the Organization in the course of the performance of his duties. Whereas a State possesses the totality of international rights and duties recognized by international law, the rights and duties of an entity such as the Organization must depend upon its purposes and functions as specified or implied in its constituent documents and developed in practice. The functions of the Organization are of such a character that they could not be effectively discharged if they involved the concurrent action, on the international plane, of fifty-eight or more Foreign Offices, and the Court concludes that the Members have endowed the Organization with capacity to bring international claims when necessitated by the discharge of its functions.…

[On Question 1 (a)] the question is concerned solely with the reparation of damage caused to the Organization when one of its agents suffers injury at the same time. It cannot be doubted that the Organization has the capacity to bring an international claim against one of its Members which has caused injury to it by a breach of its international obligations towards it. The damage specified in Question 1 (a) means exclusively damage caused to the interests of the Organization itself, to its administrative machine, to its property and assets, and to the interests of which it is the guardian. It is clear that the Organization has the capacity to bring a claim for this damage. As the claim is based on the breach of an international obligation on the part of the Member held responsible by the Organization, the Member cannot contend that this obligation is governed by municipal law, and the Organization is justified in giving its claim the character of an international claim.

When the Organization has sustained damage resulting from a breach by a Member of its international obligations, it is impossible to see how it can obtain reparation unless it possesses capacity to bring an international claim. It cannot be supposed that in such an event all the Members of the Organization save the defendant State must combine to bring a claim against the defendant for the damage suffered by the Organization.…

The question remains whether the Organization has 'the capacity to bring an international claim against the responsible *de jure* or *de facto* government with a view to obtaining the reparation due in respect of the damage caused (a) to the United Nations, (b) to the victim or to persons entitled through him' when the defendant State is not a member of the Organization.

In considering this aspect of Question 1 (a) and (b), it is necessary to keep in mind the reasons which have led the Court to given an affirmative answer to it when the defendant State is a Member of the Organization. It has now been established that the Organization has capacity to bring claims on the international plane, and that it possesses a right of functional protection in respect of its agents. Here again the Court is authorized to assume that the damage suffered involves the responsibility of a State, and it is not called upon to express an opinion upon the various ways in which that responsibility might be engaged. Accordingly the question is whether the Organization has capacity to bring a claim against the defendant State to recover reparation in respect of that damage or whether, on the contrary, the defendant State, not being a member, is justified in raising the objection that the Organization lacks the capacity to bring an international claim. On this point, the Court's opinion is that fifty States, representing the vast majority of the members of the international community, had the power, in conformity with international law, to bring into being an entity possessing objective international personality, and not merely personality recognized by them alone, together with capacity to bring international claims.

Accordingly, the Court arrives at the conclusion that an affirmative answer should be given to Question 1 (a) and (b) whether or not the defendant State is a Member of the United Nations.

United Nations General Assembly: Report of the Secretary-General, Administrative and Budgetary Aspects of the Financing of United Nations Peacekeeping Operations

37 *International Legal Materials* 700 (1998)

6. The international responsibility of the United Nations for the activities of United Nations forces is an attribute of its international legal personality and its capacity to bear international rights and obligations. It is also a reflection of the principle of State responsibility—widely accepted to be applicable to international organizations—that damage caused in breach of an international obligation and which is attributable to the State (or to the Organization), entails the international responsibility of the State (or of the Organization) and its liability in compensation.

7. In recognition of its international responsibility for the activities of its forces, the United Nations has since the inception of peacekeeping operations assumed its liability for damage caused by members of its forces in the performance of their duties. In conformity with section 29 of the Convention on the Privileges and Immunities of the United Nations, it has undertaken in paragraph 51 of the model status-of-forces agreement (see A/451594) to settle by means of a standing claims commission claims resulting from damage caused by members of the force in the performance of their of official duties and which for reasons of immunity of the Organization and its Members could not have been submitted to local courts.

8. The undertaking to settle disputes of a private law nature submitted against it and the practice of actual settlement of such third-party claims—although not necessarily according to the procedure provided for under the status-of-forces agreement—evidence the recognition on the part of the United Nations that liability for damage caused by members of United Nations forces is attributable to the Organization.

Legality of the Threat or Use of Nuclear Weapons Opinion (WHO Advisory Opinion)

ICJ Rep 1996 66, International Court of Justice

The World Health Organization (WHO) requested an advisory opinion on whether 'the use of nuclear weapons by a State in war or other armed conflict [would] be a breach of its obligations under international law including the WHO Convention'. At the same time, the General Assembly requested an advisory opinion in relation to the threat or use of nuclear weapons (see Chapter 15). In deciding that the Court did not have jurisdiction to decide on this request by WHO, the Court considered the personality of international organisations.

25. The Court need hardly point out that international organizations are subjects of international law which do not, unlike States, possess a general competence. International organizations are governed by the 'principle of speciality', that is to say, they are invested by the States which create them with powers, the limits of which are a function of the common interests whose promotion those States entrusts to them. The Permanent Court of International Justice referred to this basic principle in the following terms:

> As the European Commission is not a State, but an international institution with a special purpose, it only has the functions bestowed upon it by the Definitive Statute with a view to the fulfilment of that purpose,

but it has power to exercise those functions to their full extent, in so far as the Statute does not impose restrictions on it. (*Jurisdiction of the European Commission of the Danube*, Advisory Opinion, PCIJ, Series B, No. 14, p. 64.)

The powers conferred on international organizations are normally the subject of an express statement in their constituent instruments. Nevertheless, the necessities of international life may point to the need for organizations, in order to achieve their objectives, to possess subsidiary powers which are not expressly provided for in the basic instruments which govern their activities. It is generally accepted that international organizations can exercise such powers, known as 'implied' powers....

In the opinion of the Court, to ascribe to the WHO the competence to address the legality of the use of nuclear weapons—even in view of their health and environmental effects—would be tantamount to disregarding the principle of speciality; for such competence could not be deemed a necessary implication of the Constitution of the Organization in the light of the purposes assigned to it by its member States.

United Nations International Law Commission: *Draft Articles on Responsibility of International Organisations adopted by the Commission at its Sixty-Third Session*

UN Document number A/66/10 (2011), Chapter VII Responsibility of International Organisations

Article 1: Scope of the present draft articles

1. The present draft articles apply to the international responsibility of an international organization for an internationally wrongful act.

2. The present draft articles also apply to the international responsibility of a State for an internationally wrongful act in connection with the conduct of an international organization.

Article 2: Use of terms

For the purposes of the present draft articles,

(a) 'international organization' means an organization established by a treaty or other instrument governed by international law and possessing its own international legal personality. International organizations may include as members, in addition to States, other entities; ...

Article 3: General principles

Responsibility of an international organization for its internationally wrongful acts

Every internationally wrongful act of an international organization entails the international responsibility of that organization.

Commentary to Article 2

(1) The definition of 'international organization' given in article 2, subparagraph (a), is considered as appropriate for the purposes of the present draft articles and is not intended as a definition for all purposes. It outlines certain common characteristics of the international organizations to which the following articles apply. The same characteristics may be relevant for purposes other than the international responsibility of international organizations.

(2) The fact that an international organization does not possess one or more of the characteristics set forth in article 2, subparagraph (a), and thus is not within the definition for the purposes of the present articles, does not imply that certain principles and rules stated in the following articles do not apply also to that organization.

(3) Starting with the Vienna Convention on the Law of Treaties of 23 May 1969, several codification conventions have succinctly defined the term 'international organization' as 'intergovernmental organization'. In each case the definition was given only for the purposes of the relevant convention and not for all purposes. The text of some of these codification conventions added some further elements to the definition: for instance, the Vienna Convention on the Law of Treaties between States and International Organizations or between International Organizations of 21 March 1986 only applies to those intergovernmental organizations which have the capacity

to conclude treaties. No additional element would be required in the case of international responsibility apart from possessing an obligation under international law. However, the adoption of a different definition is preferable for several reasons. First, it is questionable whether by defining an international organization as an intergovernmental organization one provides much information: it is not even clear whether the term 'intergovernmental organization' refers to the constituent instrument or to actual membership. Second, the term 'intergovernmental' is in any case inappropriate to a certain extent, because several important international organizations have been established with the participation also of State organs other than governments. Third, an increasing number of international organizations include among their members entities other than States as well as States; the term 'intergovernmental organization' might be thought to exclude these organizations, although with regard to international responsibility it is difficult to see why one should reach solutions that differ from those applying to organizations of which only States are members.

(4) Most international organizations are established by treaties. Thus, a reference in the definition to treaties as constituent instruments reflects prevailing practice. However, forms of international cooperation are sometimes established without a treaty. In certain cases, for instance with regard to the Nordic Council, a treaty was subsequently concluded. In order to cover organizations established by States on the international plane without a treaty, article 2 refers, as an alternative to treaties, to any 'other instrument governed by international law'. This wording is intended to include instruments, such as resolutions adopted by an international organization or by a conference of States. Examples of international organizations that have been so established include the Pan American Institute of Geography and History (PAIGH), and the Organization of the Petroleum Exporting Countries (OPEC).

(5) The reference to 'a treaty or other instrument governed by international law' is not intended to exclude entities other than States from being regarded as members of an international organization. This is unproblematic with regard to international organizations which, so long as they have a treaty-making capacity, may well be a party to a constituent treaty. The situation is likely to be different with regard to entities other than States and international organizations. However, even if the entity other than a State does not possess treaty-making capacity or cannot take part in the adoption of the constituent instrument, it may be accepted as a member of the organization if the rules of that organization so provide.

(6) The definition in article 2 does not cover organizations that are established through instruments governed by municipal law, unless a treaty or other instrument governed by international law has been subsequently adopted and has entered into force. Thus the definition does not include organizations such as the World Conservation Union (IUCN), although over 70 States are among its members, or the Institut du Monde Arabe, which was established as a foundation under French law by 20 States.

(7) Article 2 also requires the international organization to possess 'international legal personality'. The acquisition of legal personality under international law does not depend on the inclusion in the constituent instrument of a provision such as Article 104 of the United Nations Charter, which reads as follows:

> 'The Organization shall enjoy in the territory of each of its Members such legal capacity as may be necessary for the exercise of its functions and the fulfilment of its purposes.'

The purpose of this type of provision in the constituent instrument is to impose on the member States an obligation to recognize the organization's legal personality under their internal laws. A similar obligation is imposed on the host State when a similar text is included in the headquarters agreement.

(8) The acquisition by an international organization of legal personality under international law is appraised in different ways. According to one view, the mere existence for an organization of an obligation under international law implies that the organization possesses legal personality. According to another view, further elements are required. While the International Court of Justice has not identified particular prerequisites, its dicta on the legal personality of international organizations do not appear to set stringent requirements for this purpose. In its advisory opinion on the *Interpretation of the Agreement of 25 March 1951 between the WHO and Egypt* the Court stated:

> 'International organizations are subjects of international law and, as such, are bound by any obligations incumbent upon them under general rules of international law, under their constitutions or under international agreements to which they are parties.'

In its advisory opinion on the *Legality of the Use by a State of Nuclear Weapons in Armed Conflict*, the Court noted:

> 'The Court need hardly point out that international organizations are subjects of international law which do not, unlike States, possess a general competence.'

While it may be held that, when making both these statements, the Court had an international organization of the type of the World Health Organization (WHO) in mind, the wording is quite general and appears to take a liberal view of the acquisition by international organizations of legal personality under international law.

(9) In the passages quoted in the previous paragraph, and more explicitly in its advisory opinion on *Reparation for Injuries Suffered in the Service of the United Nations*, the Court appeared to favour the view that when legal personality of an organization exists, it is an 'objective' personality. Thus, it would not be necessary to enquire whether the legal personality of an organization has been recognized by an injured State before considering whether the organization may be held internationally responsible according to the present articles.

(10) The legal personality of an organization which is a precondition of the international responsibility of that organization needs to be 'distinct from that of its member States'. This element is reflected in the requirement in article 2, subparagraph (a), that the international legal personality should be the organization's 'own', a term that the Commission considers as synonymous with the phrase 'distinct from that of its member States'. The existence for the organization of a distinct legal personality does not exclude the possibility of a certain conduct being attributed both to the organization and to one or more of its members or to all its members.

(11) The second sentence of article 2, subparagraph (a), seeks first of all to emphasize the role that States play in practice with regard to all the international organizations which are covered by the present articles. This key role was expressed by the International Court of Justice, albeit incidentally, in its advisory opinion on the *Legality of the Use by a State of Nuclear Weapons in Armed Conflict*, in the following sentence:

'International organizations are governed by the "principle of speciality", that is to say, they are invested by the States which create them with powers, the limits of which are a function of the common interests whose promotion those States entrust to them.' 58

Many international organizations have only States as members. In other organizations, which have a different membership, the presence of States among the members is essential for the organization to be considered in the present articles. This requirement is intended to be conveyed by the words 'in addition to States'.

(12) The fact that paragraph (a) considers that an international organization 'may include as members, in addition to States, other members' does not imply that a plurality of States as members is required. Thus an international organization may be established by a State and another international organization. Examples may be provided by the Special Court for Sierra Leone and the Special Tribunal for Lebanon.

(13) The presence of States as members may take the form of participation as members by individual State organs or agencies. Thus, for instance, the Arab States Broadcasting Union, which was established by a treaty, lists 'broadcasting organizations' as its full members.

(14) The reference in the second sentence of article 2, subparagraph (a), to entities other than States—such as international organizations, territories or private entities—as additional members of an organization points to a significant trend in practice, in which international organizations increasingly tend to have a mixed membership in order to make cooperation more effective in certain areas.

(15) International organizations within the scope of the present articles are significantly varied in their functions, type and size of membership and resources. However, since the principles and rules set forth in the articles are of a general character, they are intended to apply to all these international organizations, subject to special rules of international law that may relate to one or more international organizations. In the application of these principles and rules, the specific, factual or legal circumstances pertaining to the international organization concerned should be taken into account, where appropriate. It is clear, for example, that most technical organizations are unlikely to be ever in the position of coercing a State, or that the impact of a certain countermeasure is likely to vary greatly according to the specific character of the targeted organization.

NOTES

1. The legal personality of the UN in international law and the national law of UN members are also guaranteed by Article 1 of the Convention on the Privileges and Immunities of the United Nations 1946. State parties to this Convention commonly give effect to the legal personality of the UN in their national legal systems through legislation. See, for example, in the UK the International Organisations Acts 1968 and 1981. In the *Reparations Opinion* (above), the Opinion indicates that the UN has 'objective' legal personality. It is not clear, however, whether this personality is opposable to (that is, enforceable against) non-members through recognition, or

generally whether any State or group of States has the power to create an entity endowed with international personality where such personality *must* then be recognised by the international community at large.

2. In terms of functions, the UN can behave very much like a State. In the past it has had legal (if not factual) control over territory (see Chapter 7). Moreover, the UN has the ability both to bring claims and to be subject to liabilities under international law, although the fora in which such claims may be brought are often limited.

3. The Court in the *Reparations Opinion* was prepared to imply powers for the UN if these were necessary for the fulfilment of the general functions of the organisation. This was taken up by the *WHO Advisory Opinion* referring to so-called 'implied' powers of international organisations. The latter Opinion makes it clear though that the extent of an organisation's personality will depend on its constituent treaty. Ultimately, of course, an organisation's personality can be ended by its dissolution in accordance with international law, as was the fate of the League of Nations.

4. The Vienna Convention on the Law of Treaties between International Organisations, or between States and International Organisations 1986, is significant not only because it establishes a comprehensive code of treaty law for international organisations, but also because its existence testifies to the importance of organisations as international legal persons. The fact that the rules of this Convention follow broadly the rules of the Vienna Convention on Treaties between States 1969 (see Chapter 3) is further evidence of this trend.

5. The question of attribution of responsibility for actions of peacekeeping forces involving the UN has arisen in a number of recent cases, in which the courts have show some willingness to attribute actions to a State even when the State is acting within an international peacekeeping force (see *Jaloud* v *The Netherlands* (2014) European Court of Human Rights). The International Law Commission in 2011 finalised a set of draft principles on the responsibility of international organisations, together with detailed commentary, reflecting in part its previous work on State responsibility (see further Chapter 11).

6. It appears that, as the number and sphere of operation of international organisations swells, as shown by the commentary to Article 2 of the Draft Articles above, the concept of international personality as it applies to international organisations is becoming more sophisticated. However, whether the same rules and principles should apply to international organisations as to States is an issue of debate.

D: Individuals

The place of individuals within the system of international law has been a cause of controversy for some considerable time. Traditionally, international law was a system of rules governing the relations between sovereign States, and many of the rules of the system still reflect this. However, in recent years, the emergence of a substantial body of human rights law (see Chapter 6) and the development of personal criminal responsibility (see Chapter 14) have gone a considerable way to extend the scope of international law beyond its traditional areas and to bestow individuals with both rights and duties under international law.

Optional Protocol to the International Covenant on Civil and Political Rights 1966
Annex to General Assembly Resolution 2200 A, (1966) 21 UNGAOR Supp (No 16) 59

Under the International Covenant on Civil and Political Rights 1966, States undertake to guarantee a number of rights to all persons within their territory and subject to their jurisdiction. This is fortified by a reporting system and an optional system of inter-State complaints to a Human Rights Committee (see further Chapter 6). The Optional Protocol to this Covenant allows for individual complaints to be brought against the State.

Article 1
A State Party to the Covenant that becomes a party to the present Protocol recognises the competence of the Committee to receive and consider communications from individuals subject to its jurisdiction who claim to be

the victims of a violation by that State Party of any of the rights set forth in the Covenant. No communication shall be received by the Committee if it concerns a State Party to the Covenant which is not a party to the present Protocol.

Article 2

Subject to the provisions of Article 1, individuals who claim that any of their rights enumerated in the covenant have been violated and who have exhausted all available domestic remedies may submit a written communication to the Committee for consideration.

R v Bow Street Metropolitan Stipendiary Magistrate and others, ex parte Pinochet Ugarte (No 3)

[2000] 1 AC 147, United Kingdom House of Lords

Senator Pinochet, the ex-Head of State of Chile, was accused of various violations of the human rights of both Chilean and foreign nationals. A Spanish court had issued an arrest warrant in respect of alleged acts against Spanish nationals. While visiting London, Senator Pinochet was arrested on an extradition warrant pending extradition to Spain. One crucial issue was whether Senator Pinochet, as an ex-Head of State, enjoyed immunity from UK courts in respect of acts done while in office (see Chapter 9). If he was immune, he could not be extradited. One alleged offence was the crime of torture which, it was accepted by the Court, was a crime involving personal criminal responsibility and one triggering universal jurisdiction. As a result, Senator Pinochet was held not to have immunity in respect of some of the charges against him. However, although the courts decided that he was amenable to extradition, he was not eventually extradited to Spain due to his poor health.

LORD BROWNE-WILKINSON: Apart from the law of piracy, the concept of personal liability under international law for international crimes is of comparatively modern growth. The traditional subjects of international law are states not human beings. But consequent upon the war crime trials after the 1939–45 War, the international community came to recognise that there could be criminal liability under international law for a class of crimes such as war crimes and crimes against humanity. Although there may be legitimate doubts as to the legality of the Charter of the International Military Tribunal appended to the Agreement for the Prosecution and Punishment of the Major War Criminals of the European Axis (the Nuremberg Charter) (London, 8 August 1945; TS 27 (1946); Cmd 6903), in my judgment those doubts were stilled by the Affirmation of the Principles of International Law recognised by the Charter of Nuremberg Tribunal adopted by the United Nations General Assembly on 11 December 1946 (see UN GA Resolution 95(I) (1946)). That affirmation affirmed the principles of international law recognised by the Nuremberg Charter and the judgment of the tribunal and directed the committee on the codification of international law to treat as a matter of primary importance plans for the formulation of the principles recognised in the Nuremberg Charter. At least from that date onwards the concept of personal liability for a crime in international law must have been part of international law. In the early years State torture was one of the elements of a war crime. In consequence torture, and various other crimes against humanity, were linked to war or at least to hostilities of some kind. But in the course of time this linkage with war fell away and torture, divorced from war or hostilities, became an international crime on its own: see *Oppenheim's International Law* (9th edn, 1992) Vol 1, p 996; note 6 to Art. 18 of the ILC Draft Code of Crimes against the Peace and Security of Mankind; *Prosecutor v Anto Furundzija* (10 December 1998, unreported). Ever since 1945, torture on a large scale has featured as one of the crimes against humanity: see, for example, UN General Assembly Resolutions 3059 (1973), 3452 and 3453 (1975); Statutes of the International Criminal Tribunals for the Former Yugoslavia (Art. 5) (see the Statute of the International Tribunal for the Prosecution of Persons Responsible for Serious Violations of International Humanitarian Law Committed in the Territory of the Former Yugoslavia since 1991 (the Statute of the Tribunal for the Former Yugoslavia) (UN Security Council Resolution 827 (1993)) and Rwanda (Art. 3) (see the Statute of the International Tribunal for the Prosecution of Persons Responsible for Genocide and Other Serious Violations of International Humanitarian Law Committed in the Territory of Rwanda and Rwandan Citizens Responsible for Genocide and other such Violations committed in the territory of neighbouring states between 1 January 1994 and 31 December 1994 (the Statute of the Tribunal for Rwanda) (UN SC Resolution 955 (1994)).

Moreover, the Republic of Chile accepted before your Lordships that the international law prohibiting torture has the character of *jus cogens* or a peremptory norm, i.e. one of those rules of international law which have a particular status. In *Furundzija*'s case at para 153, the Tribunal said:

> Because of the importance of the values it protects, [the prohibition of torture] has evolved into a peremptory norm or jus cogens, that is, a norm that enjoys a higher rank in the international hierarchy than treaty law and even 'ordinary' customary rules. The most conspicuous consequence of this higher rank is that the principle at issue cannot be derogated from by states through international treaties or local or special customs or even general customary rules not endowed with the same normative force…Clearly, the *jus cogens* nature of the prohibition against torture articulates the notion that the prohibition has now become one of the most fundamental standards of the international community. Furthermore, this prohibition is designed to produce a deterrent effect, in that it signals to all members of the international community and the individuals over whom they wield authority that the prohibition of torture is an absolute value from which nobody must deviate.…

The *jus cogens* nature of the international crime of torture justifies states in taking universal jurisdiction over torture wherever committed. International law provides that offences *jus cogens* may be punished by any state because the offenders are 'common enemies of all mankind and all nations have an equal interest in their apprehension and prosecution': *Demjanjuk* v *Petrovsky* (1985) 603 F Supp 1468, 776 F 2d 571.

It was suggested by Miss Montgomery QC, for Senator Pinochet that although torture was contrary to international law it was not strictly an international crime in the highest sense. In the light of the authorities to which I have referred (and there are many others) I have no doubt that long before the Torture Convention, State torture was an international crime in the highest sense.

But there was no tribunal or court to punish international crimes of torture. Local courts could take jurisdiction: see *Demjanjuk*'s case and *A–G of Israel* v *Eichmann* (1961) 36 ILR 5. But the objective was to ensure a general jurisdiction so that the torturer was not safe wherever he went. For example, in this case it is alleged that during the Pinochet regime torture was an official, although unacknowledged, weapon of government and that, when the regime was about to end, it passed legislation designed to afford an amnesty to those who had engaged in institutionalised torture. If these allegations are true, the fact that the local court had jurisdiction to deal with the international crime of torture was nothing to the point so long as the totalitarian regime remained in power: a totalitarian regime will not permit adjudication by its own courts on its own shortcomings. Hence the demand for some international machinery to repress state torture which is not dependent upon the local courts where the torture was committed. In the event, over 110 states (including Chile, Spain and the United Kingdom) became state parties to the Torture Convention. But it is far from clear that none of them practised state torture. What was needed therefore was an international system which could punish those who were guilty of torture and which did not permit the evasion of punishment by the torturer moving from one state to another. The Torture Convention was agreed not in order to create an international crime which had not previously existed but to provide an international system under which the international criminal—the torturer—could find no safe haven. Burgers and Danelius (respectively the chairman of the United Nations Working Group on the Torture Convention and the draftsmen of its first draft) say in their *Handbook on the Convention against Torture and Other Cruel, Inhuman or Degrading Treatment or Punishment* (1984) p 131 that it was 'an essential purpose [of the Convention] to ensure that a torturer does not escape the consequences of his acts by going to another country'.

M. Bothe, 'Security Council's Targeted Sanctions against Presumed Terrorists'

6 *Journal of International Criminal Justice* 541 (2008)

International organizations developed as elements of the interstate system of international law, as tools to regulate the relations between states and to organize their cooperation. Therefore, conceptually, they were not held to address individuals, at least not directly. As a consequence, procedural rules for the relationship between international organizations and individuals, including legal remedies for individuals against acts of international organizations, could be considered as being a non-issue.

There was an early recognition of an obvious exception to this assumption: this was and is the relationship between the organization and its employees. Since the creation of international organizations after the First World War, administrative tribunals or at least independent commissions or appeal boards have been established by these organizations to deal with formal complaints of the employees against the organizations. Apart from this exception, international organizations are sealed off from legal challenges put forward by individuals: no remedy is provided by the organizations, and they are immune from legal process in the courts of states. This, it is submitted, has for a long time constituted a major flaw in the law of international organizations, a serious lacuna in the guaranty of the rule of law in international relations…

In other situations where operations of international organizations directly affect individuals the solution has rather been one of muddling through.…The problem of legal remedies for individuals affected by acts or omissions of international organizations has often been seen as a matter of expediency, of political advisability. But it is more than that. The right to a remedy is a fundamental human right.…In relation to universal organizations, that recognition has been even slower. This may also be due to the fact that it is only recently that the UN has been in a practical situation to violate individual human rights.…

Traditional non-military enforcement measures pursuant to Article 41 of the Charter are value deprivations imposed upon states as collectivities. The measures expressly mentioned are the interruption of economic relations, i.e. embargoes, and of other communications (of which the interruption of air traffic has had a major significance in recent times). This type of measure has rightly been criticized as both ineffective and unjust. It is unjust because it mainly hits the innocent population. It is ineffective because it does not or only rarely reaches those who are personally responsible for a threat to the peace or a breach of the peace. In the light of this experience, a system of 'targeted' sanctions has been developed which is directed specifically against these persons. There are in particular three types of restrictions or deprivations on such persons:

(i)   travel restrictions;
(ii) financial restrictions;
(iii) criminal responsibility.

These targeted sanctions have been used in a number of situations characterized by the Security Council as constituting a threat to the peace: Liberia, Sierra Leone, the Taliban in Afghanistan. They are now used in particular as measures imposed by the Security Council in the fight against terrorism and against the proliferation of weapons of mass destruction.

The implementation of these resolutions requires a two or even three level system: The basic decisions are taken by the Security Council, but they must be implemented on the level of the various states. It is states which freeze assets, deny entry, etc. In the case of the European Union, the Union is a level between the Security Council and the states which has become a major point of legal controversy.

This multilevel system works in two different ways. In some cases, the Sanctions Committee, i.e. the Security Council itself places the individual or entity concerned on a list (listing decision). It is then the function and duty of the lower levels (states, European Community/Union) to make sure that the measures in question are indeed implemented in relation to all individuals or entities so listed. This can be called automatic listing at the lower level(s). The other option is that the Security Council defines the group of persons or entities which are subject to sanctions in a general way. It is then the function and duty of the lower level(s) to make sure that all persons falling into that definition are indeed so listed and the corresponding measures are taken against them. This can be called autonomous listing at the lower level. In the latter case, there are reporting duties and a monitoring mechanism. As far as the need for a remedy is concerned, in the former case, all essential decisions concerning the individual are taken by the Security Council. If the binding character of Security Council resolutions is to be taken seriously, the lower level(s) have no choice but to take the measures against the listed individual.

This is why the Security Council directly affects the legal position of the individual. The Security Council decision constitutes an exercise of public authority vis-à-vis the individual. Therefore, according to customary human rights standards, there must be a remedy against the Security Council's decisions.

In the case of autonomous listing decisions, no individual is named by the Security Council. The names on the list are determined by states or by the European Community/Union. The human rights standards applying to these listing decisions are those binding the state in question or the EC. Those standards may, however, be affected, and the human rights protection limited, by the fact that there is, according to Article 25 of the UN Charter, an international legal duty of the state in question and/or the EC to adopt certain measures. Both types of targeted sanctions have encountered serious criticism. Allegations were made that there were persons on the lists who, according to the applicable standards, should not be there because those persons or entities did not fulfil the criteria for being listed. At both levels, the listing decisions have not been transparent. The individuals in question practically had no way of finding out why they were listed. While in the case of autonomous listing decisions, there is a possibility of judicial review which cannot be excluded, the situation of individuals listed by the Security Council was rather desperate.

Theoretically, states could sponsor an individual's claim and request a delisting. That proved to be difficult. The individual in question had no access to the decision making process of the Sanctions Committee.

NOTES

1. The first extract above concerns the ability of individuals to enforce directly such rights as they are given by international law. It is important to realise that in such cases individuals are in fact being accorded two distinct capacities as international legal persons. First, they are being accorded substantive rights in international law; second, they may also be accorded the procedural capacity to begin proceedings to enforce those rights without having to rely on States to do it for them. An example of the latter is the jurisdiction of the Inter-American Court of Human Rights under which States wishing to join the system must accept the possibility of complaints by individuals but have the option of whether to accept the Court's jurisdiction in cases of complaint by other States. By virtue of Protocol 11 to the European Convention for the Protection of Human Rights and Fundamental Freedoms (ECHR), all European States party to the ECHR must allow any individual in their jurisdiction the right to bring a claim against a State to the European Court of Human Rights (see Article 34 of the Convention). The Convention against Torture, the Convention on the Elimination of Racial Discrimination, the Optional Protocol to the Convention on the Elimination of All Forms of Discrimination against Women and the Optional Protocol to the Convention on the Rights of Persons with Disabilities have similar provisions allowing individuals to bring forward complaints regarding the respective treaty obligations (see Chapter 6).

2. It is sometimes said that when individuals are granted rights by treaty (or indeed where they are under direct criminal obligations—see Chapter 14), such persons are merely 'objects' of the law, not its subjects, because it is States that have both created this personality and who will vindicate it by either acting to enforce human rights obligations, or acting to enforce personal criminal responsibility. However, if international personality means having rights, duties or capacities in international law, this is not a valid distinction.

3. Individuals employed by the United Nations and Specialised Agencies usually have both substantive and procedural rights in relation to the terms and conditions of their employment. The substantive rights and enforcement provisions are not governed by the national law of any one State, but rather by an amorphous set of principles loosely referred to as the law of the international civil service. For example, employees of the United Nations Secretariat with claims arising out of their employment contracts have the possibility to resort to the United Nations Administrative Tribunal. Similar procedures exist within other international organisations. In exceptional cases, matters may be brought to the ICJ.

4. Reference needs to be made to the personal criminal responsibility of individuals (see Chapter 14), now well established in international law. Individuals can be held liable for their acts before international tribunals and subject to rules of international law. Individuals are thus entitled to human (and other) rights on the one hand; on the other hand, they can incur responsibility towards the international community. It seems thus to be evident that they possess some form of international legal personality.

5. Security Council resolutions have traditionally been considered to have an impact upon States only, as, while the acts stipulated may affect individuals within the member States, they do so by way of actions taken by the member States. The practice of targeted sanctions against individuals, discussed by Bothe, constitutes another way in which actions at the international level may directly impact individuals. Various fora, including the General Assembly and the Security Council itself, have considered the serious legal issues raised by the practice of listing individuals and efforts have been made to ensure clear and fair procedures for listing, delisting and humanitarian exceptions. For example, UN Security Council Resolution 1904 (2009) established the Office of the Ombudsperson to review de-listing requests specifically relating to members or associates of Al-Qaida, Usama bin Laden and the Taliban in an independent and impartial manner.

E: Other international persons

There are a number of miscellaneous groups or bodies that have an increasingly high impact in the international arena. Such groups include non-governmental organisations (NGOs) and transnational corporations, and also movements such as the International Red Cross and Red Crescent Movement. These groups, or at least parts of such groups, have some measure of international personality. The precise ambit of this personality will usually depend on the acquiescence of, or recognition by, States.

Texaco Overseas Petroleum Company v *The Libyan Arab Republic*

53 ILR (1977) 389, Dupuy, Sole Arbitrator

This dispute arose out of the nationalisation by Libya of foreign-owned oil interests in 1973–74. One question was whether the contract between the company and the State gave the company any rights enforceable at international law. After finding that the contract was an 'internationalised contract' (on which, see Chapter 13), Professor Dupuy, the arbitrator, commented on the status of Texaco.

DUPUY: The Tribunal must specify the meaning and the exact scope of internationalization of a contractual relationship so as to avoid any misunderstanding: indeed to say that international law governs contractual relations between a State and a foreign private party neither means that the latter is assimilated to a State nor that the contract entered into with it is assimilated to a treaty.

This distinction is worth making, because the situation of individuals, and more generally private persons, in respect of international law, has recently been the subject matter of important doctrinal debates on the occasion of which excessive positions sometimes may have been stated....

This Tribunal will abstain from going that far: it shall only consider as established today the concept that legal international capacity is not solely attributable to a State and that international law encompasses subjects of a diversified nature. If States, the original subjects of the international legal order, enjoy all the capacities offered by the latter, other subjects enjoy only limited capacities which are assigned to specific purposes. The proposition which has just been stated is in conformity with the statement by the International Court of Justice in its *Advisory Opinion on Reparations of 11 April 1949* under which 'the subjects of law, in any legal system, are not necessarily identical in their nature or in the extent of their rights and their nature depends on the needs of the community' ([1949] ICJ 174, at 178). In other words, stating that a contract between a State and a private person falls within the international legal order means that for the purposes of interpretation and performance of the contract, it should be recognized that a private contracting party has specific international capacities. But, unlike a State, the private person has only a limited capacity and his quality as a subject of international law does enable him only to invoke, in the field of international law, the rights which he derives from the contract....

Thus, the internationalization of certain contracts entered into between a State and a private person does not tend to confer upon a private person competences comparable to those of a State but only certain capacities which enable him to act internationally in order to invoke the rights which result to him from an internationalized contract.

Prosecutor v *Kallon and Kamara (Decision on Challenge to Jurisdiction: Lomé Accord Amnesty)*

Appeals Chamber, Special Court for Sierra Leone, 13 March 2004

The Court was called upon to consider the validity of an amnesty provision contained in the Lomé Accord, signed by the Government of Sierra Leone and the Revolutionary United Front (RUF), a main rebel group engaged in an armed conflict with the Government of Sierra Leone, and witnessed by several states and international organisations, including the United Nations. In order to do so, it had to consider the status of the agreement as an international agreement, or an instrument creating an obligation under domestic law only.

45. Notwithstanding the absence of unanimity among international lawyers as to the basis of the obligation of insurgents to observe the provisions of Common Article 3 to the Geneva Conventions, there is now no doubt that this article is binding on States and insurgents alike and that insurgents are subject to international humanitarian law. That fact, however, does not by itself invest the RUF with international personality under international law.

46. Common Article 3 of the Geneva Conventions recognises the existence of 'Parties to the conflict'. The penultimate sentence of Common Article 3 provides that: 'The parties to the conflict should further endeavour to bring into force, by means of special agreements, all or part of the other provisions of the present Convention'. But the final clause of Common Article 3 also provides that '[t]he application of the preceding provisions shall not affect the legal status of the Parties to the conflict.' It has been explained that the penultimate sentence 'underlines the fact that parties to an internal conflict are bound only to observe Article 3, remaining free to disregard the entirety of the remaining provisions in each of the Convention' and that the final clause indicates that the insurgents may still be made subject to the State's municipal criminal jurisdiction. In an authoritative book on international law the view was expressed that:

> a range of factors needs to be carefully examined before it can be determined whether an entity has international personality and, if so, what right, duties and competences apply in the particular case. Personality is a relative phenomenon varying with the circumstances. [M. Shaw, *International Law* (2003)]

47. It suffices to say, for the purpose of the present case, that no one has suggested that insurgents are bound because they have been vested with personality in international law of such a nature as to make it possible for them to be a party to the Geneva Conventions. Rather, a convincing theory is that they are bound as a matter of international customary law to observe the obligations declared by Common Article 3 which is aimed at the protection of humanity. No doubt, the Sierra Leone Government regarded the RUF as an entity with which it could enter into an agreement. However, there is nothing to show that any other State had granted the RUF recognition as an entity with which it could enter into legal relations or that the Government of Sierra Leone regarded it as an entity other than a faction within Sierra Leone.

Although a degree of organisation of the insurgents may be a factor in determining whether the factual situation of internal armed conflict existed, the distinction must be borne in mind between the factual question whether the insurgents are sufficiently organised and the question of law, with which the issue in these proceedings is concerned, whether as between them and the legitimate government international law regarded them as having treaty-making capacity. International law does not seem to have vested them with such capacity. The RUF had no treaty-making capacity so as to make the Lomé Agreement an international agreement. The conclusion seems to follow clearly that the Lomé Agreement is neither a treaty nor an agreement in the nature of a treaty. However, it does not need to have that character for it to be capable of creating binding obligations and rights between the parties to the agreement in municipal law. The consequence of its not being a treaty or an agreement in the nature of a treaty is that it does not create an obligation in international law.

NOTES

1. The question whether any other entity may have international personality, even for a single purpose, may depend on whether a State has granted or recognised that personality. In *Scarfo v Sovereign Order of Malta* 24 ILR 1 (1957), Tribunal of Rome, Italy, the Tribunal seemed to indicate that the sovereignty of the Order is opposable to Italy because of the latter's recognition of the fact. This may mean that other States would not be bound to accept or give effect to that sovereignty without such recognition. Likewise, the International Committee of the Red Cross (ICRC) has been recognised by a vast majority of States to be a subject of international law. The ICRC's legal personality is further evidenced by the 1949 Geneva Conventions and 1977 Additional Protocols, which provide for certain rights and responsibilities of the ICRC in times of armed conflict.

2. Disputes between companies and States on the international plane depend very much on the specific agreement between the parties (see: *Texaco v Libya* and *BP v Libya*, 53 ILR (1974) 329). In many instances, a company has more economic power than the State and so can force a State to accept the international personality of companies. A number of formal systems for the settlement of certain disputes between States and foreign companies, which necessarily involve some measure of personality for the latter, have been established, e.g. by the International Convention on the Settlement of Investment Disputes between States and Nationals of Other States 1965 and the Iran/US Claims Tribunal (see further in Chapter 13). The Optional Rules for Arbitrating Disputes Between Two Parties of Which Only One is a State of the Permanent Court of Arbitration allow non-State entities the possibility of participating in international arbitration in certain cases (see further in Chapter 16). For example, a

panel has adjudicated a dispute between the Government of Sudan and the Sudan People's Liberation Movement/Army in relation to the delimitation of the boundary of the Abyei area (Final Award, (2009) 48 ILM 1254).

3. Non-State actors are also subject to certain duties and responsibilities within the international arena. The UN Secretary-General's Special Representative on Business and Human Rights, John Ruggie, has produced the Guiding Principles on Business and Human Rights, which provide an authoritative global standard for addressing adverse impacts on human rights linked to business activity (see Chapter 6). As corporations have both substantive and procedural possibilities under international law, one may argue that they possess some form of international legal personality. It cannot be denied that their role in the international arena is of tremendous importance. The Special Tribunal for Lebanon has controversially held that the Tribunal's personal jurisdiction, at least in respect of contempt proceedings, can include both natural persons and legal entities such as corporations. This is based on a broad interpretation of the term 'legal person' as encompassing criminal liability for corporations (*In the Case against New TV S.A.L Karma Mohamed Tahsin Al Khayat*, Decision on Interlocutory Appeal Concerning Personal Jurisdiction in Contempt Proceedings, Appeals Panel, 2 October 2014). However, it is unclear whether, at this stage, international efforts to address corporate accountability in the form of State practice in fact supports the criminalisation of corporate conduct as the Tribunal's decision indicates.

4. Rebel groups and insurrectionist movements may also be subject to obligations, particularly those arising under international humanitarian law (see the extract from the decision of the Special Court for Sierra Leone). Such movements may be party to peace agreements with their own government, with other governments and with 'sponsoring' States. In the decision extracted above, the Special Court considered such agreements not to be international in nature, though there are strong contrary views and practices.

5. Likewise, non-governmental organisations (NGOs) now play an increasing role in the international legal order, especially in areas such as environmental protection and human rights (see also Chapters 2, 6 and 12) where States (and organisations created and controlled by States) cannot be relied upon to promote universally beneficial policies. NGOs interact with States at several levels. First, they play a role in the development of international norms, through participation in international fora, including the United Nations. To date, there are more than 3,000 NGOs with consultative status at the United Nations. This allows them to participate in most sessions and to express their point of view. While NGOs do not have voting rights in international fora, they can still exercise a substantial influence on discussion within a given organisation. For example, NGOs participated extensively in the drafting of the Rome Statute of the International Criminal Court and in the UN Declaration on the Rights of Indigenous Peoples. Second, NGOs are increasingly important in the implementation of international law at the national level, lobbying State governments for participation in a treaty system or in how obligations are effected within national law. NGOs are often engaged in monitoring mechanisms at the national level.

SECTION 2: RECOGNITION IN INTERNATIONAL LAW

The role of 'recognition' in both international and national legal systems has traditionally aroused considerable debate. As a matter of international law, recognition is often described as 'declaratory' (being 'merely' a political act recognising a pre-existing state of affairs) or 'constitutive' (being a necessary act before the recognised entity can enjoy international personality). In national law, the 'home' State may choose variously to 'recognise' a foreign State and/or its government, and such recognition may be *'de jure'* (accepting that the entity exists as of right) or simply *'de facto'* (recognising the existence of the entity but with concerns about its legitimacy). In any of these senses, the act of recognition may then have consequences within the national legal system.

A: General considerations

I. Brownlie, 'Recognition in Theory and Practice'

53 *British Yearbook of International Law* 197 (1982)

With rare exceptions the theories on recognition have not only failed to improve the quality of thought but have deflected lawyers from the application of ordinary methods of legal analysis. The confusion which reigns is such that contemporary thinking does not even provide elementary methods of defining what the issues are in a given episode, much less the basis for solutions of the problems presented.

III 'Recognition': a Term of Art?

The standard works fail to warn the student of international law of the important fact that 'recognition' is not a term of art. Indeed, by implication, by dint of repetition and the constant introduction of the word into headings, the standard treatments give the firm impression that 'recognition' and its congener, 'non-recognition', are terms of art with a consistent content and legal significance. Nothing could be further from the truth.

The following proposition may be put by way of example:

> The Government of State A does not recognize [the Government of] State B (*or* the 'entity' calling itself [the Government of] State B).

This statement represents fairly normal usage (although there is no standard form applicable in these matters). In fact and as a matter of necessary interpretation, the proposition could bear two radically different meanings. It could mean that, in the opinion of State A, State B did not exist as such, that is to say that the entity or political organization concerned did not *qualify* in legal terms to be recognized because it did not satisfy the criteria of statehood. Examples of this type of non-recognition are rare. In the alternative, the proposition could signify that although State B was regarded as a State in law, and thus qualifying for recognition, State A was not willing to accord such recognition on political grounds. In this context 'non-recognition' is simply a code for a policy of hostility short of armed conflict and usually accompanied by a range of political and economic sanctions (the last word is not intended to indicate the legality of such measures)....

No assumption is made concerning the legal significance of the State A-State B (above) proposition in either of its possible meanings: the object is, first of all, to discover *what* State A purports to be doing or intends. The *legal appreciation* of what State A says or does is a further question, but it cannot be pursued unless the first enquiry is competently made.

The ultimate question at the first stage is, what is the intention of the government concerned? This may be derived from all the available evidence: diplomatic correspondence, statements in international organizations, official views expressed in national assemblies and so forth. Charges of breaches of international law carry the very strong implication that the entity concerned is a State capable of bearing State responsibility. The terminology used is by no means a dominant feature. Moreover, the word 'recognition' need not be employed, provided the intention of the government concerned is clear. Thus the most common form of the recognition of new States involves the sending of a letter or telegram of felicitations by a Head of State to the Head of State or other appropriate organ of the new State: no formal words are called for and the intention of the recognizing State is unambiguous.

The strange aspect of all this is that the correct approach—seeking the intention of the government concerned on the basis of the documents and other evidence—involves nothing more than ordinary legal technique: what did the government intend on the given occasion? No theory is called for to assist in this process....

The writer's conviction that in the field of 'recognition' the role of theory has not been a happy one has already been made patent. In the literature the theories have tended to stand in front of the issues and to have assumed a 'theological' role as a body of thought with its own validity which tends to distract the student, and to play the role of master rather than servant. In spite of this it is useful (if not at all necessary) to confront the leading theories on their own terms.

By way of preface the complaint is to be made that the very approach in terms of the selection of *the* correct or preferred theory of recognition involves an immediate encouragement to the simplified approach and a diversion from the deployment of ordinary legal analysis.

The most fashionable theory in twentieth-century doctrine has been the 'declaratory' theory. Brierly has expressed its essence in the following passage:

> The better view is that the granting of recognition to a new state is not a 'constitutive' but a 'declaratory' act; it does not bring into legal existence a state which did not exist before. A state may exist without

being recognized, and if it does exist in fact, then, whether or not it has been formally recognized by other states, it has a right to be treated by them *as* a state. The primary function of recognition is to acknowledge as a fact something which has hitherto been uncertain, namely the independence of the body claiming to be a state, and to declare the recognizing state's readiness to accept the normal consequences of that fact, namely the usual courtesies of international intercourse.

The 'declaratory' view has much to commend it as a *general* approach, since it militates in favour of a legal and objective method of analysing situations. None the less the idea that an issue of statehood or of government (the criterion of effectiveness) involves the mere acknowledgement of a fact is really too simple. Certainly, questions of fact are foremost: but the legal criteria have to be *applied* and this may call for some rather nice assessments.... Such an assessment involves elements of appreciation and the choice of a point in a crescent process: in other words the choice is, to a degree and unavoidably, arbitrary.

In general the 'declaratory' theory does not prepare the student of the problems of 'recognition' for the task of evaluating the declarations of governments and the conduct of States in general. As in the *Tinoco* arbitration, a political non-recognition may be compatible with the view—perhaps expressed by the conduct of the same State—that a State (or government) objectively qualifies in law for recognition. Finally, the theory does not help in the case where the facts are clear but there is some feature of illegality, as in the case of Manchukuo (1932–45) or Rhodesia (1965–80).

In opposition to the 'declaratory' theory is the 'constitutive' theory, according to which the political act of recognition on the part of other States is a precondition of the existence of legal rights. In the more extreme version this amounts to saying that the very existence of a State may depend on the political decision of other States. In fact constitutivist doctrine takes various forms and in many cases its partisans give a mitigated version which allows that certain fundamental rights and duties arise prior to recognition. Such essays in coping with the position of the 'unrecognized State' involve an advance toward the 'declaratory' position.

In any event the core of the constitutivist theory is unacceptable. States cannot, by the device of withholding recognition, determine—and in effect thus repudiate—the content of their legal obligations toward other States. Indeed, in practice such conduct is difficult to find, since on examination policies of non-recognition turn out to be examples of political non-recognition of the kind Arbitrator Taft had to deal with in the *Tinoco Concessions* case.

All this having been said, it is necessary to recognize certain elements of truth in the constitutivist approach. As it has been suggested already, in many situations the facts which have to be subjected to legal evaluation involve a process and the court or foreign ministry official or other decision maker has to make a more or less arbitrary appreciation of the question of statehood or effective government. To this extent recognition involves an element of authoritative choice or 'certification'. There is a second element of truth which appears in those cases in which the entity concerned does not prima facie fit into the orthodox categories. Thus it can be argued that polities such as Andorra or the Holy See, which may not clearly qualify as States, but which none the less are generally accepted as having legal personality in international relations, may depend on the role of recognition in overcoming the apparent anomaly of status.

S. Murphy, 'Democratic Legitimacy and the Recognition of States and Governments'

48 *International Comparative Law Quarterly* 545 (1999)

The traditional criteria for recognising States and governments have often been mixed with other factors. One of those factors is that democratic States, driven by deep-seated beliefs within their populace, tend to want to promote democracy in other States. With the considerable increase in the number of democratic States worldwide, there is little doubt that the trend is toward greater use of democratic legitimacy as a factor in recognition practice, and leads to certain tentative conclusions:

(1) There is no international norm obligating States not to recognise an emerging State simply because its political community is not democratic in nature. Were there such a norm, it might be accompanied by a norm permitting intervention so as to establish a democratic government.

(2) When a political community seeks recognition as a State, the existence of a democratic referendum whereby the people of the community proclaim themselves in favour of independence will be one important, but not decisive, element in the international community's decision to recognise it as a State. However, other elements will be equally important, including the international community's adherence to the modern version of the principle of *uti possidetis* and other means for maintaining peace and stability.

(3) When a non-democratic regime usurps a democratically elected government, the international community may react by refusing to recognise the new *de facto* government and imposing comprehensive economic sanctions, in an effort to cajole the new government into a transition back to democratic rule.

(4) However, while the international community is increasingly interested in democratic legitimacy as a factor in its recognition practice, there is an enduring desire to promote economic development, international peace and stability as well. These values—legitimacy, development and stability—do not always go hand in hand. Depending on the situation, one or the other value may dominate the decision within the international community regarding whether to recognise the State or government.

Regarding the role of democratic legitimacy as just another policy element in the practice of recognising States and governments may be regarded as an unattractive conclusion. Rather than resorting to a ready-made legal framework on recognition, policy-makers are left weighing various amorphous policy elements that provide little concrete guidance. Yet, finding the right solutions through the application of differing policies to different cases is what diplomacy is all about. Democratic legitimacy is an important concept and tool, but it should not serve as a straitjacket for governments and others as they seek to find solutions, on a case-by-case basis, that promote the welfare of peoples worldwide. Whether nurturing new democracies, restoring overthrown democracies, promoting the gradual transition from non-democracy to democracy, or pursuing values that do not necessarily entail 'democratic' means (such as promoting regional stability, economic development), the international community has an array of diplomatic and economic tools at its disposal, of which recognition practice is merely one.

Tinoco Arbitration (*United Kingdom* v *Costa Rica*)

1 RIAA 369 (1923), Taft, Sole Arbitrator

In January 1917, Frederico Tinoco came to power in Costa Rica after a *coup d'état*. His government concluded certain contracts with British corporations. After Tinoco's retirement in 1919, the old constitution was restored, and a Law of Nullities was passed annulling the contracts and other matters concluded during the Tinoco regime. The UK made claims in respect of the injuries to its nationals caused by these annulments. Two preliminary issues were the status of the Tinoco regime in international law, and whether the UK was estopped from pursuing the claim because of lack of recognition, either *de jure* or *de facto*, of the Tinoco government.

But it is urged that many leading Powers refused to recognize the Tinoco government, and that recognition by other nations is the chief and best evidence of the birth, existence and continuity of succession of a government. Undoubtedly recognition by other Powers is an important evidential factor in establishing proof of the existence of a government in the society of nations....

Probably because of the leadership of the United States in respect to a matter of this kind, her then Allies in the war, Great Britain, France and Italy, declined to recognize the Tinoco government. Costa Rica was, therefore, not permitted to sign the Treaty of Peace at Versailles, although the Tinoco government had declared war against Germany....

The non-recognition by other nations of a government claiming to be a national personality, is usually appropriate evidence that it has not attained the independence and control entitling it by international law to be classed as such. But when recognition *vel non* of a government is by such nations determined by inquiry, not into its *de facto* sovereignty and complete governmental control, but into its illegitimacy or irregularity of origin, their non-recognition loses something of evidential weight on the issue with which those applying the rules of international law are alone concerned. What is true of the non-recognition of the United States in its bearing upon the existence of a *de facto* government under Tinoco for thirty months is probably in a measure true of the non-recognition by her Allies in the European War. Such non-recognition for any reason, however, cannot outweigh the evidence disclosed by this record before me as to the *de facto* character of Tinoco's government, according to the standard set by international law.

Second. It is ably and earnestly argued on behalf of Costa Rica that the Tinoco government cannot be considered a *de facto* government, because it was not established and maintained in accord with the constitution of Costa Rica of 1871. To hold that a government which establishes itself and maintains a peaceful administration, with the acquiescence of the people for a substantial period of time, does not become a *de facto* government unless it conforms to a previous constitution would be to hold that within the rules of international law a revolution contrary to the fundamental law of the existing government cannot establish a new government. This cannot be, and is not, true. The change by revolution upsets the rule of the authorities in power under the then existing fundamental law, and sets aside the fundamental law in so far as the change of rule makes it necessary. To speak of a revolution creating a *de facto* government, which conforms to the limitations of the old constitution is to use a contradiction in terms. The same government continues internationally, but not the internal law of its being. The issue is not whether the new government assumes power or conducts its administration under constitutional limitations established by the people during the incumbency of the government it has overthrown. The question is, has it really established itself in such a way that all within its influence recognize its control, and that there is no opposing force assuming to be a government in its place? Is it discharging its functions as a government usually does, respected within its own jurisdiction? ...

It is further objected by Costa Rica that Great Britain by her failure to recognize the Tinoco government is estopped now to urge claims of her subjects dependent upon the acts and contracts of the Tinoco government. The evidential weight of such non-recognition against the claim of its *de facto* character I have already considered and admitted. The contention here goes further and precludes a government which did not recognize a *de facto* government from appearing in an international tribunal in behalf of its nationals to claim any rights based on the acts of such government.

To sustain this view a great number of decisions in English and American courts are cited to the point that a municipal court cannot, in litigation before it, recognize or assume the *de facto* character of a foreign government which the executive department of foreign affairs of the government of which the court is a branch has not recognized. This is clearly true. It is for the executive to decide questions of foreign policy and not courts. It would be most unseemly to have a conflict of opinion in respect to foreign relations of a nation between its department charged with the conduct of its foreign affairs and its judicial branch. But such cases have no bearing on the point before us. Here the executive of Great Britain takes the position that the Tinoco government which it did not recognize, was nevertheless a *de facto* government that could create rights in British subjects which it now seeks to protect. Of course, as already emphasized, its failure to recognize the *de facto* government can be used against it as evidence to disprove the character it now attributes to that government, but this does not bar it from changing its position.

EC Declaration on the Guidelines on Recognition of New States in Eastern Europe and the Soviet Union, December 1991

4 European Journal of International Law 72 (1993)

In compliance with the European Council's request, Ministers have assessed developments in Eastern Europe and in the Soviet Union with a view to elaborating an approach regarding relations with new states.

In this connection they have adopted the following guidelines on the formal recognition of new states in Eastern Europe and in the Soviet Union:

> The Community and its Member States confirm their attachment to the principles of the Helsinki Final Act and the Charter of Paris, in particular the principle of self-determination. They affirm their readiness to recognise, subject to the normal standards of international practice and the political realities in each case, those new states which, following the historic changes in the region, have constituted themselves on a democratic basis, have accepted the appropriate international obligations and have committed themselves in good faith to a peaceful process and to negotiations.
>
> Therefore, they adopt a common position on the process of recognition of these new states, which requires:
>
> — respect for the provisions of the Charter of the United Nations and the commitments subscribed to in the Final Act of Helsinki and in the Charter of Paris, especially with regard to the rule of law, democracy and human rights;
>
> — guarantees for the rights of ethnic and national groups and minorities in accordance with the commitments subscribed to in the framework of the CSCE;
>
> — respect for the inviolability of all frontiers which can only be changed by peaceful means and by common agreement'
>
> — acceptance of all relevant commitments with regard to disarmament and nuclear non-proliferation as well as to security and regional stability;
>
> — commitment to settle by agreement, including where appropriate by recourse to arbitration, all questions concerning state succession and regional disputes.

The Community and its Member States will not recognise entities which are the result of aggression. They would take account of the effects of recognition on neighbouring states.

   The commitments to these principles opens the way to recognition by the Community and its Member States and to the establishment of diplomatic relations. It could be laid down in agreements.

EC Declaration on Yugoslavia, 16 December 1991
4 *European Journal of International Law* 72 (1993)

In addition to the above Declaration, the EC also adopted a specific Declaration on Yugoslavia, inviting the former Republics to apply for recognition by 23 December 1991. Such recognition was to be conditional on fulfilment of the above Guidelines and also:

   The Community and its member States also require a Yugoslav Republic to commit itself, prior to recognition, to adopt constitutional and political guarantees ensuring that it has no territorial claims towards a neighbouring Community State and that it will conduct no hostile propaganda activities versus a neighbouring Community State, including the use of a denomination which implies territorial claims.

NOTES
1. The debate between proponents of the so-called 'declaratory' and 'constitutive' theories of recognition (see Brownlie above) should be read in conjunction with the materials on Statehood discussed earlier. Many international lawyers believe that the debate is fruitless because it does not assist in the resolution of 'real life' problems. Moreover, it may well be that the declaratory and constitutive theories are not dealing with the same question. There may be a difference between the circumstances in which a body may acquire the abstract right to exercise the capacities of Statehood on the international plane (declaratory) and the actual exercise of those capacities in a concrete case (constitutive).
2. The *Tinoco Arbitration* has often been cited as the classic illustration of the declaratory theory. One should point out however that it deals with the recognition of a government within an area already recognised as a State. But even for States, the declaratory theory seemed long to be predominant in State practice and legal opinion. In the *Deutsche Continental Gas Gesellschaft*-Arbitration, the Tribunal stated that 'the recognition of a state is not constitutive but merely declaratory. The state exists by itself and the recognition is nothing else than the declaration of its existence recognised by the state from which it emanates' (5 ILR 11, 13 (1929)).
3. The European Communities' guidelines were issued in response to the break-up of the former federal States of Eastern Europe. Crucially, these guidelines go beyond simply requiring the attainment of the traditional criteria of Statehood found in Article 33 of the Montevideo Convention. They appear to require 'candidates' for recognition to meet conditions of a subjective and peculiarly Eurocentric nature including issues of governance (as described by Murphy). This has led some commentators to argue that the constitutive theory of recognition is gaining ground. However, an alternative view is that these guidelines represent the EU's minimum standards for the opening of inter-State relations, and that they are not intended to qualify the right of these entities to Statehood. Again, this may illustrate the difference between the achievement of international personality (e.g. Statehood) and its effective exercise in the international community. Note that some non-European States have adopted these guidelines in determining recognition of the former Yugoslavia States—see (1993) 14 *Australian Year Book of International Law* 413. The guidelines are also evidence of a practice of cooperation between EU member States in the recognition of States. A further example of this cooperation is the Conclusions on Montenegro adopted by the EU Council on 12 June 2006, by which member States agreed a common timetable on recognition of Montenegro. A common position was not adopted with respect to Kosovo in 2008 (see Section 1B), with the General Affairs and External Relations Council determining that the recognition of Kosovo was a matter for individual EU member States.
4. The European Communities' Conference on Yugoslavia also established an Arbitration Commission (the Badinter Commission) to resolve certain questions of law submitted to it arising out of the dissolution of the former federal State of Yugoslavia (see Chapter 6). Among the issues referred to this Commission were the questions whether Bosnia-Herzegovina (Opinion

No 4), Croatia (Opinion No 5), Macedonia (Opinion No 6) and Slovenia (Opinion No 7) had fulfilled the criteria for recognition laid down in the guidelines and the EC Declaration on Yugoslavia. Eventually, and in apparent disregard of the Commission's various findings, all four former members of the federation were recognised as States by the EC. These cases are fine examples of how recognition can be a powerful political tool, even though the recognition issue may be dressed up as purely a matter of law. The recognition of Kosovo by certain EU member States coupled with the strong refusal to acknowledge Kosovo's independence by other States is a more recent example of the political implications of recognition (see Warbrick above).

5. The absence of international recognition of Statehood does not leave an entity powerless or unprotected in international law. As has been shown, international personality is relative.

B: Mandatory non-recognition in international law

Following the Unilateral Declaration of Independence by the Smith apartheid regime in Southern Rhodesia (now Zimbabwe) in 1965, the Security Council passed numerous resolutions condemning the action and eventually imposed economic sanctions. The resolution below clearly imposed a legal duty on States not to recognise the 'illegal regime'. It had been preceded by other resolutions (notably SC Res 216 (1965), 12 November 1965), which had called for non-recognition and thereby set the standard for future action.

Security Council Resolution 277 (1965) March 1970

The Security Council....
  Acting under Chapter VII of the Charter

  1. Condemns the illegal proclamation of republican status of the Territory by the illegal regime in Southern Rhodesia;

  2. Decides that Member States shall refrain from recognising this illegal regime or from rendering any assistance to it;

  3. Calls upon Member States to take appropriate measures, at the national level, to ensure that any act performed by officials and institutions of the illegal regime in Southern Rhodesia shall not be accorded any recognition, official or otherwise, including judicial notice, by the competent organs of their State;....

  9. Decides, in accordance with Article 41 of the Charter and in furthering the objective of ending the rebellion, that Member States shall:
     (a) Immediately sever all diplomatic, consular, trade, military and other relations that they may have with the illegal regime in Southern Rhodesia, and terminate any representation that they may maintain in the territory;
     (b) Immediately interrupt any existing means of transportation to and from Southern Rhodesia.

NOTE: In the *Namibia Case*, ICJ Rep 1971 16, on the consequences of South Africa's continued illegal occupation of the territory after the termination of the Mandate (see Chapter 3), the ICJ imposed a duty not to recognise the continuation of the Mandate. Likewise, in SC Res 541 of 18 November 1983, the Security Council called on all States not to recognise the Turkish Republic of Northern Cyprus as it had been created by the unlawful use of force by Turkey against Cyprus. More recently, the General Assembly has called on UN member States not to recognise any change in Crimea's status due to the military occupation of Crimea, a territory forming part of Ukraine, and its forcible annexation by Russia, and to refrain from taking actions or dealings that might be interpreted as such (see Section 1B).

A: Recognition in UK law

(a) States

It is not only on the international plane that the question of international personality is important. On the national level it may well be crucial to know whether an entity has international personality as a sovereign 'State' or 'government'. In the law of the United Kingdom, for example, the status of a foreign entity can determine whether it has immunity from suit (see Chapter 9), whether it may bring proceedings, and whether the laws emanating from that entity may be recognised in national courts. Whether an entity has this sovereign status (or any existence in international law) may well depend on whether it has been 'recognised' by the authorities of the State in which it is acting, although, as is made clear below, this is not the only way by which an entity may acquire the privileges associated with such status.

Luther v *Sagor*
[1921] 1 KB 456, UK King's Bench Division

The defendants imported wood into the UK that had been confiscated by the Soviet government in 1919 and sold to them in 1920. The plaintiffs claimed to be owners of the wood. The issue was whether the UK recognised the Soviet government. If so, a UK court would accept the validity of the confiscation.

ROCHE J: Whether the decree in question is a valid legislative act which can be recognized as such by the Courts of this country must, in my judgment, depend upon whether the power from which it purports to emanate is what it apparently claims to be, a sovereign power, in this case the sovereign power of the Russian Federative Republic. The proper source of information as to a foreign power, its status and sovereignty, is the Sovereign of this country through the Government...At all events, even if I were entitled to look elsewhere for information I am certainly not bound to do so, and in this case I know of no other sources of information available to which I can safely or properly resort.

I therefore propose to deal with the case upon the information furnished by His Majesty's Secretary of State for Foreign Affairs. The attitude proper to be adopted by a Court of this country with regard to foreign governments or powers I understand to be as follows: (1) If a foreign government is recognized by the Government of this country the Courts of this country may and must recognize the sovereignty of that foreign government and the validity of its acts...(2) If a foreign government, or its sovereignty, is not recognized by the Government of this country the Courts of this country either cannot, or at least need not, or ought not, to take notice of, or recognize such foreign government or its sovereignty....

On these materials I am not satisfied that His Majesty's Government has recognized the Soviet Government as the Government of a Russian Federative Republic or of any sovereign state or power. I therefore am unable to recognize it, or to hold it has sovereignty, or is able by decree to deprive the plaintiff company of its property.

Carl Zeiss Stiftung v *Rayner & Keeler*
[1967] 1 AC 853, United Kingdom House of Lords

The defendants were trading under the name Carl Zeiss Stiftung and the plaintiffs were solicitors acting on behalf of an East German corporation of the same name, seeking an injunction against the defendants. The defendants contended that since the East German corporation was incorporated and administered under the laws of East Germany, the Court could not act to protect it, because the courts of the UK would not give effect to the laws of a foreign 'State' or 'government' that had not been recognised formally by the UK.

LORD WILBERFORCE: It is as well, before considering the legal consequences of non-recognition, to appreciate what the respondents' contention involves. The Stiftung is a corporate body established for industrial and trading purposes under the law of Germany; one of whose constitutional organs—the special board—is an administrative authority exercising power at the place of the body's operations. As a fact, there is not doubt that at the relevant date this authority was there, that it was exercising its functions, that it was operating as the special board, that (this is proved by the evidence) it would be recognised by the local courts as so doing. Yet, so it is said, because the law and the order which set it up are derived from a body not recognised as a lawful government, this authority, *qua* organ of the Stiftung, has no legal existence; all its transactions in private law are void, as are presumably all other transactions carried out under its authority or by persons who derive their authority from it. By logical extension it seems to follow, and counsel for the respondents accepted, that there is, for many years has been and, until the attitude of Her Majesty's Government changes, will be, in East Germany a legal vacuum; subject only, it may be, to the qualification that pre-existing German law, so far as it can continue to be operated or have effect, may continue in force. Whether in fact it can continue to be operated to any great extent if its operation depends upon administrative or judicial authorities set up by the non-existent 'government' must be doubtful. But the respondents, so far from shrinking from these consequences, insist up on them as the necessary and, as they say, intended consequences of non-recognition. And correspondingly, they argue that if recognition were to be given by the courts to legislative acts of the non-recognised 'government' that would be tantamount to recognition of that government, and so in conflict with the policy of the executive.

My Lords, if the consequences of non-recognition of the East German 'government' were to bring in question the validity of its legislative acts, I should wish seriously to consider whether the invalidity so brought about is total, or whether some mitigation of the severity of this result can be found. As Locke said: 'A government without laws is, I suppose, a mystery in politics, inconceivable to human capacity and inconsistent with human society,' and this must be true of a society—at least a civilised and organised society—such as we know to exist in East Germany. In the United States some glimmerings can be found of the idea that non-recognition cannot be pressed to its ultimate logical limit, and that where private rights, or acts of everyday occurrence, or perfunctory acts of administration are concerned (the scope of these exceptions has never been precisely defined) the courts may, in the interests of justice and common sense, where no consideration of public policy to the contrary has to prevail, give recognition to the actual facts or realities found to exist in the territory in question....No trace of any such doctrine is yet to be found in English law, but equally, in my opinion, there is nothing in those English decisions, in which recognition has been refused to particular acts of non-recognised governments, which would prevent its acceptance or which prescribes the absolute and total invalidity of all laws and acts flowing from unrecognised governments. In view of the conclusion I have reached on the effect to be attributed to non-recognition in this case, it is not necessary here to resort to this doctrine but, for my part, I should wish to regard it as an open question, in English law, in any future case whether and to what extent it can be invoked....

Her Majesty's Government have not granted any recognition *de jure* or *de facto* to the 'German Democratic Republic' or its 'Government'—the inverted commas are as in the certificate itself....There are only two questions which might arise in relation to the Eastern Zone. The first is whether it is admissible in the courts of this country to take account of the fact (if such be the case, as to which I shall make some observation later) that the USSR itself considers that there is in existence in the Eastern Zone a government independent of the USSR, *viz.*, the 'government' of the 'German Democratic Republic.' In my opinion, the answer to this must be negative: to make any such assertion would be in direct contradiction to the certificate which states without qualification that the USSR and its Government is entitled *de jure* to exercise governing authority there and that nobody else is, either *de jure* or *de facto*. What view another state may take as to the legal or factual situation in any territory is irrelevant to the recognising (or non-recognising) state and, after the latter has defined its own attitude, is inadmissible in its courts....The second question is whether consistently with the certificate it is possible to assert that the USSR is not *de facto* exercising governing authority or control in the Eastern Zone.

In stating that the USSR is exercising *de jure* governing authority and that no other body is exercising *de facto* authority, the two certificates to my mind say all that need or can be said. *De jure* recognition in all cases but one is the fullest recognition which can be given: the one exception is the case where there is concurrently some other body *de facto* exercising a rival authority to that of the *'de jure'* sovereign....But any such possibility as this is...excluded by the terms of the certificates....The certificates therefore in my opinion establish the USSR as *de jure* entitled to exercise governing authority and in full control of the area of the Eastern Zone.

Kibris Türk Hava Yollari CTA Holidays v Secretary of State for Transport

[2009] EWHC 1918 (Admin), UK Queen's Bench Division Administrative Court

The claimant was a Turkish air operator who carried out flights between the UK and Turkey, with Turkey as an intermediate stop for flights to the Turkish Republic of Northern Cyprus (TRNC). The claimant applied to obtain a permit so it could offer direct flights from the UK to Northern Cyprus. The Secretary of State for Transport denied the permit, arguing that it was obliged to do so as a matter of UK law, since granting the permit would give validity to the acts of the government of the TRNC, which had not been recognised by the UK government.

WILLIAMS J:

26. It is not the policy of the Government of the United Kingdom to recognise governments.... The government of the United Kingdom does recognise states....

74. The Government of the United Kingdom has made it clear, consistently, that it does not recognise the area of Cyprus over which the Government of the TRNC exercises effective control as a state.... In these circumstances, why should it be that the grant of the permits sought in this case should be treated as acts which are consistent only with the recognition on the part of the United Kingdom Government of either the TRNC or the Government?

75. Recognition can be express or implicit....

77. ...[I]mplied recognition has taken on a greater significance than hitherto since several states, including the United Kingdom, have adopted a policy of no longer expressly recognising a new Government, but instead leaving the answer to the question whether it qualifies to be treated as a Government to be inferred from the nature of their dealings with it....

79. ...I have reached the clear conclusion that the grant of permits would amount to implied recognition that the Government in control of the TRNC was sovereign over the territory which it effectively controls. The grant of permits would, in my judgment, completely undermine the express statements from the United Kingdom Government to the effect that it does not recognise the TRNC.

80. I reach that conclusion for the following principal reason. The Government of the TRNC is, obviously, in effective control of the northern part of Cyprus. It has created the organs of a State. In relation to international aviation, in particular,...the TRNC is purporting to exercise the rights of the Interested Party [the Republic of Cyprus] under a Treaty, i.e. the Chicago Convention [on International Civil Aviation]....

84. ...the Defendant was obliged as a matter of domestic law to refuse the permits since the grant of such permits would necessarily attribute validity to the acts of the Government and of the TRNC...For this Court to rule to the contrary, would be to ignore the long line of domestic authority which is to the effect that the court cannot take cognizance of a foreign juridical person if to do so would involve the court acting inconsistently with the foreign policy or diplomatic stance of the Government of the Country in relation to that person....

90. In summary, I have reached the conclusion that a legal duty exists whereby the Government of the United Kingdom is obliged not to recognise TRNC or its Government.... This court is obliged to refuse to give effect to the validity of acts carried out in a territory which is unrecognised unless the acts in question can properly be regarded as regulating the day to day affairs of the people within the territory in question and can properly be regarded as essentially private in character.

NOTES

1. The materials on recognition should be read with the change in UK practice clearly in mind (see Section 3A(b)), remembering that the UK has not changed its position in respect of the recognition of *States*, where a UK Foreign Office certificate will still be issued. A certificate confirming the recognition of the Statehood of the United Arab Emirates was issued in *BCCI (Overseas) Ltd v Price Waterhouse* [1997] 4 All ER 108, where it was also confirmed that the UK does not accord recognition to constituent territories of federal entities (see also (1996) 67 BYIL, pp. 710–712).
2. *Kibris Türk Hava Yollari CTA Holidays v Secretary of State for Transport* makes clear that while a certificate from the UK Foreign and Commonwealth Office will give certainty as to whether or

not an entity has been recognised as a State, recognition can also take place implicitly. Implicit recognition, as illustrated in the case, is given if governmental authorities acknowledge and validate acts of another entity whose Statehood is disputed, if such acts normally require the exercise of State sovereignty.

3. Under the UK State Immunity Act 1978, States are granted certain immunities from the jurisdiction of UK courts (see Chapter 9). Whether a body is a 'State' for these purposes is to be determined in accordance with section 21, which specifies that a certificate issued by the Secretary of State for Foreign and Commonwealth Affairs shall be conclusive for the purposes of the Act, as in *BCCI v Price Waterhouse*. The fact that an unrecognised State may have no privileges or immunities in the UK has often been said to support the constitutive theory of recognition. If, however, the effects of non-recognition of a 'State' in the UK are dictated by a rule of UK national law, the status of such bodies in the UK says nothing of their status in international law.

4. The live issue at the heart of the *Carl Zeiss* case is now irrelevant—Germany is a united and sovereign State. However, the case illustrates both the power of the non-recognition doctrine and the extent to which UK courts would go to side-step it.

(b) Governments

UK Practice Statement on the Recognition of Governments, House of Lords (Parliament)
H.L. Deb. Vol. 48, cols 1121–1122, April 1980

Previously, the United Kingdom had recognised foreign governments formally, either *de jure* or *de facto*. Although this was said to be based on the effectiveness of that government within a particular territory, it was often taken to be a sign of approval.

LORD CARRINGTON (Foreign Secretary): [W]e have conducted a re-examination of British policy and practice concerning the recognition of Governments. This has included a comparison with the practice of our partners and allies. On the basis of this review we have decided that we shall no longer accord recognition to Governments. The British Government recognises States in accordance with common international doctrine.

Where an unconstitutional change of régime takes place in a recognised State, Governments of other States must necessarily consider what dealings, if any, they should have with the new régime, and whether and to what extent it qualifies to be treated as the Government of the State concerned. Many of our partners and allies take the position that they do not recognise Governments and that therefore no question of recognition arises in such cases. By contrast, the policy of successive British Governments has been that we should make and announce a decision formally 'recognising' the new Government.

This practice has sometimes been misunderstood, and, despite explanations to the contrary, our 'recognition' interpreted as implying approval. For example, in circumstances where there might be legitimate public concern about the violation of human rights by the new régime, or the manner in which it achieved power, it has not sufficed to say that an announcement of 'recognition' is simply a neutral formality.

We have therefore concluded that there are practical advantages in following the policy of many other countries in not according recognition to Governments. Like them, we shall continue to decide the nature of our dealings with régimes which come to power unconstitutionally in the light of our assessment of whether they are able of themselves to exercise effective control of the territory of the State concerned, and seem likely to continue to do so.

House of Commons
H.C. Deb. Vol. 985, Written Answers, col. 385, 23 May 1980

This was the government's reply to a written question asking how UK Courts were now to assess a foreign entity claiming to be a sovereign government.

In future cases where a new régime comes to power unconstitutionally our attitude on the question whether it qualifies to be treated as a Government, will be left to be inferred from the nature of the dealings, if any, which we may have with it, and in particular on whether we are dealing with it on a normal Government to Government basis.

Somalia (A Republic) v *Woodhouse Drake & Carey (Suisse) SA*

[1993] 1 All ER 371, UK High Court

Somalia was suffering a civil war and it appeared that no faction was in effective control of the State. The plaintiffs claimed to be the 'Government of Somalia' and sought control over certain funds belonging to the Republic of Somalia. The issue was whether the plaintiffs were the 'Government of Somalia' and hence entitled to the funds. Following the UK practice (set out above), there was no Foreign Office certificate concerning the status of the plaintiffs.

HOBHOUSE J: The policy of the United Kingdom is now not to confer recognition upon governments as opposed to upon states. The new policy of Her Majesty's government was stated in two parliamentary answers in April and May 1980.…The position in English law before 1980 is conveniently set out in 18 *Halsbury's Laws* (4th edn) para 1431:

> A foreign government which has not been recognised by the United Kingdom government as either de jure or de facto government has no locus standi in the English courts. Thus it cannot institute an action in the courts…The English courts will not give effect to the acts of an unrecognised government.…

Thus, recognition by Her Majesty's government was the decisive matter and the courts had no role save to inquire of the executive whether or not it had recognised the government in question.

Some writers appear still to feel that the criterion remains one of recognition by the government of this country, the difference being that, whereas before 1980 the government would say expressly whether it recognised the foreign government, now it is to be left to be ascertained as a matter of inference:…The impracticality of the 'inferred recognition' theory as a legal concept for forensic use is obvious and it cannot be though that that was the intention of Her Majesty's government in giving the Parliamentary answers. The use of the phrase 'left to be inferred' is designed to fulfil a need for information in an international or political, not a judicial, context.

If recognition by Her Majesty's government is no longer the criterion of the locus standi of a foreign 'government' in the English courts and the possession of a legal persona in English law, what criteria is the court to apply? The answers do confirm one applicable criterion, namely whether the relevant regime is able of itself to 'exercise effective control of the territory of the State concerned' and is 'likely to continue to do so'; and the statement as to what is to be the evidence of the attitude of Her Majesty's government provides another—to be inferred from the nature of the dealings, if any, that Her Majesty's government has with it and whether they are on a normal government to government basis. The non-existence of such dealings cannot however be conclusive because their absence may be explained by some extraneous consideration—for example lack of occasion, the attitude of the regime to human rights, its relationship to another state. As the answers themselves acknowledge, the conduct of governments' in their relations with each other may be affected by considerations of policy as well as by considerations of legal characterisation. The courts of this country are now only concerned with the latter consideration. How much weight in this connection the courts should give to the attitude of Her Majesty's government was one of the issues before me…

It is clear from this letter [received by the plaintiffs' solicitors from the Foreign Office] that Her Majesty's government does not consider that there is at present any effective government in Somalia. It refers to 'factions' and treats the interim government as merely one among a number of factions.

Accordingly, if the question before the court is to be decided upon the basis of the attitude adopted by Her Majesty's government, an order cannot be made in favour of the interim government or Crossman Block. The basis for its attitude is clearly not any disapproval of an established regime but rather that there is no regime which has control, let alone any administrative control which has the requisite element of stable continuity.

Mr Richards submitted that particular weight should be given to these communications. I have difficulty in accepting that submission without some qualification. Once the question for the court becomes one of making its own assessment of the evidence, making findings of fact on all the relevant evidence placed before it and drawing the appropriate legal conclusion, and is no longer a question of simply reflecting government policy, letters from the Foreign and Commonwealth Office become merely part of the evidence in the case. In the present case no problem of admissibility of evidence arises. In so far as the letters make statements about what is happening in the territory of some foreign state, such letters may not be the best evidence; but as regards the question whether Her Majesty's government has dealings with the foreign government it will almost certainly be the best and only conclusive evidence of that fact.

Where Her Majesty's government is dealing with the foreign government on a normal government to government basis as the government of the relevant foreign state, it is unlikely in the extreme that the inference that the foreign government is the government of that state will be capable of being rebutted and questions of public policy and considerations of the interrelationship of the judicial and executive arms of Government may be paramount....But now that the question has ceased to be one of recognition, the theoretical possibility of rebuttal must exist.

There is no decided English authority upon the effect of the 1980 answers. *GUR Corp* v *Trust Bank of Africa Ltd* was concerned with a question of the recognition of a state and the competence of a subordinate body within the recognised territory of that state under the laws of that state. The 1980 answers were referred to but were not the basis of the decision. Here no question of the recognition of a state is involved. Nor does this case involve any accredited representative of a foreign state in this country. Different considerations would arise if it did, since it would be contrary to public policy for the court not to recognise as a qualified representative of the head of state of the foreign state the diplomatic representative recognised by Her Majesty's government. There is no recognised diplomatic representative of the Republic of Somalia to the United Kingdom.

The statements of fact in the letters from the Foreign and Commonwealth Office are confirmed by the other evidence that is before the court concerning the actual situation in Somalia. The interim government is not governing that country and does not exercise administrative or any control over its territory and population....The criteria of effective control referred to in the Parliamentary answers are clearly not satisfied....The interim government clearly does not satisfy these criteria; the republic currently has no government.

However there are two other aspects upon which counsel for the interim government has relied. These are the recognition of the interim government by some other states and international bodies, and the fact that the interim government was set up by the Djibouti Agreement, which resulted from an international conference attended by many international states and bodies.

In evaluating these arguments it is relevant to distinguish between regimes that have been the constitutional and established government of a state and a regime which is seeking to achieve that position either displacing a former government or to fill a vacuum. Since the question is now whether a government *exists*, there is no room for more than one government at a time nor for separate de jure and de facto governments in respect of the same state. But a loss of control by a constitutional government may not immediately deprive it of its status, whereas an insurgent regime will require to establish control before it can exist as a government.

The argument based on the Djibouti Agreement does not assist the interim government. The Djibouti Agreement was not constitutional. It did not create a de jure status for the interim government in Somalia. The interim government was not and did not become the constitutional successor of the government of President Siad Barre. Accordingly, if the interim government is to be treated as the government of Somalia, it must be able to show that it is exercising administrative control over the territory of the republic. That it is not able to do. Accordingly that argument must fail.

As regards the argument of international recognition and recognition by the United Nations, although this does not as such involve control of territory or a population, it does correspond to one aspect of statehood. A classic definition of a state is that contained in art 1 of the Inter-American Convention on the Rights and Duties of States (Montevideo, 26 December 1933; 137 BFSP 282) as having—'(a) a permanent population; (b) a defined territory; (c) Government; and (d) capacity to enter into relations with other States.' Whilst illustrating that it is difficult to separate the recognition of a state from the recognition of a government of that state, this definition also shows that part of the function of a government of a state is to have relations with other states. This is also implicit in the reference in the 1980 parliamentary answers to dealings on a government to government basis.

Accordingly I consider that the degree of international recognition of an alleged government is a relevant factor in assessing whether it exists as the government of a state. But where, as here, the regime exercises virtually no administrative control at all in the territory of the state, international recognition of an unconstitutional regime should not suffice and would, indeed, have to be accounted for by policy considerations rather than legal characterisation; and it is, of course, possible for states to have relations with bodies which are not states or governments of states.

There is evidence from which it appears that the United Nations Organisation considers that there are persons whom it may treat as the representatives of the Republic of Somalia. Resolution 733 started with the words: 'Considering the request by Somalia for the Security Council to consider the situation in Somalia'....This evidence is not wholly satisfactory. The attitude of the United Nations to interim government could be established in a more direct fashion and more authoritatively....In any event, membership of an international organisation does not amount to recognition nor does a vote on credentials and representation issues: see Warbrick 'The new British policy on recognition of governments' (1981) 30 ICLQ 568 at 583, citing the Secretary General's memorandum 1950 UN Doc S/1466. But any apparent acceptance of the interim government by the United Nations and other international organisations and states does not suffice in the present case to demonstrate that the interim government is the government of the Republic of Somalia. The evidence the other way is too strong.

Accordingly, the factors to be taken into account in deciding whether a government exists as the government of a state are: (a) whether it is the constitutional government of the state; (b) the degree, nature and stability of administrative control, if any, that it of itself exercises over the territory of the state; (c) whether Her Majesty's government has any dealings with it and if so what is the nature of those dealings; and (d) in marginal cases, the extent of international recognition that it has the government of the state.

On the evidence before the court the interim government certainly does not qualify having regard to any of the three important factors.

C. Warbrick, 'British Policy and the National Transitional Council of Libya'

(2012) 61 *International and Comparative Law Quarterly* 247

Before the uprising began, the Gaddafi Government was the sole authority in Libya with which the British Government had inter-governmental relations and President Gaddafi was regarded as the Head of State of Libya, whatever peculiarities attended his position in Libyan domestic law. There was a Libyan embassy in London, with an ambassador and staff appointed by the Gaddafi Government, and Libyan Government property and activity in the UK. There was a UK embassy in Tripoli, with an ambassador and staff from the British diplomatic service. Although there had been no direct statement by the British Government that it 'recognized' the Gaddafi authorities as 'the government of Libya', the nature of its dealings with them (and the absence of any dealings with anyone else) left no doubt about the status of the Libyan Government as a matter of UK law, if the question had arisen. Although there were differences between the two Governments, even friction in the odd case, UK-Libyan relations appeared to fall within the broad notion of normality which prevails in diplomatic life. For instance, one issue (which will be referred to later) was that there was in the UK a substantial amount of Libyan currency, printed for the Libyan Government by a British company, the sort of mundane matter which indicates a certain degree of confidence between the two administrations. Arms sales between the two countries appear to have proceeded in normal ways. The British Government did not endorse every activity of the Libyan Government, especially in the field of human rights, but these differences were nowhere near serious enough to cast any doubts upon its view of the legitimacy, still less the legality, of the regime in Tripoli....

The policy [of recognition] seems to address a single (and, it should be said, largely uncomplicated) situation, where a rebel movement completely supersedes an existing effective authority within a recognized State. It does not in its terms purport to decide what the Government should do in the period prior to the success of a revolution, and in circumstances such as this, even recourse to de facto recognition of the rebels in the east might have been unlikely given the limited territorial scope of their authority and the resistance of the Government. The [1980] policy allowed for procrastination and ambiguity up to and beyond the time when, under the previous policy, a recognition decision would have been required. The 1980 policy has been very largely adhered to. It has been reiterated almost as a matter of course whenever a British Government has been asked for its stance on the recognition of this or that foreign Government. After 1980 until the Libyan case, there were no examples of the Government making a statement recognizing a government in even the most intractable civil war, though forms of words were often found to indicate clearly where the Government stood. The same policy was followed in those few occasions when the question of the status of a foreign authority arose in judicial proceedings in the UK....

The dramatic change in UK policy was announced on 28 July 2011. Speaking after a meeting of the Libya Contact Group, the Foreign Secretary said:

> At the latest Libya Contact Group in Istanbul the international community sent an unequivocal message to Qadhafi: that he had no legitimacy and there was no future for Libya with him in power. As part of this it decided 'to deal with the National Transitional Council (NTC) as the legitimate governing authority in Libya'. This was a significant development, and today I will outline the action that the UK will now take in response.

The point to note here is that the decision of the Contact Group did not constitute recognition of the NTC by each of the participant States, nor did the UK individually act on the assumption that its participation in the decision amounted to recognition of the NTC. Instead, discrete UK action was required. The Foreign Secretary continued:

> The Prime Minister and I have decided that the United Kingdom recognises and will deal with the National Transitional Council as the sole governmental authority in Libya. This decision reflects the NTC's increasing legitimacy, competence and success in reaching out to Libyans across the country. Through

its actions the NTC has shown its commitment to a more open and democratic Libya—something that it is working to achieve through an inclusive political process. This is in stark contrast to Qadhafi, whose brutality against the Libyan people has stripped him of all legitimacy. The NTC is a focal point for people throughout Libya who want a better future for their country. Our decision also reflects the responsibilities that the NTC has taken on in the areas under its control. It means we will deal with the NTC on the same basis as other governments around the world.

These words constitute the revival of the pre-1980 policy of making decisions on the recognition of governments, although the circumstances which would prompt such a decision in this case appear to have been quite out of line with those which would have had to have prevailed before 1980. It is to be emphasized that the motivation for the decision to recognize the NTC as the Government of Libya is explained as its success 'in reaching out to Libyans across the country' and 'its commitment to a more open and democratic Libya'. The recognition is said to reflect 'the responsibilities that the NTC has taken on in the areas under its control'. This is much less demanding than a requirement that the authority has demonstrated effective governmental control over the State territory with a prospect that its authority will be permanent.... This is quite at odds with the insistence that recognition 'should not depend on whether the character of the regime is such as to command His Majesty's Government's approval'....

At the time of the British recognition decision, the Libyan Government declared that it was illegal and that the government would seek redress in whichever court it could find with jurisdiction over the matter, international or domestic. It is hard to imagine that there could have been an international jurisdiction in which the question could have been raised. However, it was only the failure to obtain instructions which pre-empted the representation of Libya in the *British Arab Commercial Bank* case [see following extract]. What might it have argued if it had been able to communicate with its lawyer?

The first argument might have been that the recognition was unlawful under international law as an interference in the internal affairs of Libya—the Libyan Government was fighting to preserve its authority against an unlawful uprising and other States had a duty to keep out of the conflict. Once upon a time, this claim would have been good in international law and it might still be.... Given the frequency and vehemence with which the British Government had reiterated its 'not recognizing foreign governments' policy (even in the present situation), might any applicant not have had a legitimate expectation that the policy would have been adhered to? If the Government wanted to revert to the old recognition policy, then notice ought to have been given. This would have been particularly pertinent to any events occurring before the recognition decision, when anyone dealing with the Libyan authorities might well have reached the conclusion that the Gaddafi regime remained the 'government' of Libya. Such persons ought not to have been disadvantaged by any application of the retrospective effects of recognition. More importantly and central to an orthodox legitimate expectations claim, the procedure for determining who was the government of Libya under the declared prevalent policy would have been the courts; under the revived 'recognition of governments' policy, it was the executive.

British Arab Commercial Bank PLC v National Transitional Council of the State of Libya
[2011] EWHC 2274 (Comm), UK High Court

Libyan students studying in the UK were dependent on financial support by way of payments from accounts of the Libyan Embassy in London, also known as the Libyan People's Bureau, which were held with the British Arab Commercial Bank. Following disturbances in Libya in February 2011, and a change of government, the Bank received conflicting instructions. The Court had to address the question of whether the National Transitional Council (NTC) constituted the Government of Libya, and could give instructions to operate the accounts. A final declaration was granted by the Court to allow disbursement of the student grants.

BLAIR J:

(1) Is the court satisfied that the NTC is, and the Qadhafi regime is not, the Government of Libya?

25. There can only be an affirmative answer to this question. In so far as it goes, the Foreign Secretary's certificate of 24 August 2011 is conclusive, because in the field of foreign relations, the Crown in its executive and judicial

functions speak with one voice (see e.g. *Gur Corporation v Trust Bank of Africa Ltd* [1987] 1 QB 599 at 604H, Steyn J, on appeal at 625G, Nourse LJ). As Lord Atkin put it in a well known passage in *The Arantzazu Mendi* [1939] AC 256 (at page 264), 'Our State cannot speak with two voices on such a matter, the judiciary saying one thing, the executive another. Our Sovereign has to decide whom he will recognise as a fellow sovereign in the family of States …'.

(2) Does the Libyan embassy and its Chargé d'Affaires Mr Mahmud Nacua constitute the accredited diplomatic mission of Libya to the United Kingdom?

26. This is not a question which is directly addressed in the certificate. It is however directly and unambiguously addressed in the letters from the Foreign & Commonwealth Office to the Bank which I have quoted above, and in much other evidence before the court. See for example the letters of 8 and 12 August 2011: 'The UK recognises and is now dealing with the National Transitional Council (NTC) as the sole governmental authority in Libya. We therefore no longer have diplomatic relations with the Qadhafi regime, nor do we accept that they have the authority to accredit diplomatic representatives of Libya to the UK. On 4 August 2011 the Government accepted the nomination of Mr Mahmud Nacua as the Libyan Chargé d'Affaires ad interim, and will accredit him accordingly'. In his oral submissions for the Foreign & Commonwealth Office, Mr David Perry QC said (correctly in my view) that the position is entirely clear, and (importantly) confirmed the factual accuracy of the material before the court. In *Khurts Bat v The Investigating Judge of the German Federal Court* [2011] EWHC 2029 Moses LJ (with whom Foskett J agreed on this point) said at [33] that, 'The acceptance of accreditation to a permanent diplomatic mission is a matter within the discretion of the Executive, or, more accurately, the Royal Prerogative'. This is a so-called fact of state, being 'facts which the court accepts, not so much because they are within the exclusive knowledge of the UK Government, but because they represent matters which are exclusively for decision by the Government and not for the courts' ([34]). There was a certificate in *Khurts Bat*, but in the circumstances of the present case in which the decision is manifest on the evidence and confirmed by counsel for the Foreign & Commonwealth Office at the hearing, it appears to me that the absence of a certificate expressly dealing with the point is not material. In the *Somalia* case [see extract in Section 3A(b)] at p.66C, it was said that '…it would be contrary to public policy for the court not to recognise as a qualified representative of the head of state of the foreign state the diplomatic representative recognised by Her Majesty's Government'. The second question must therefore also be answered affirmatively.

NOTES
1. The change in the UK practice concerning recognition (or rather non-recognition) of governments required a shift in the relationship between the UK government and UK courts. The burden of assessing the status of an entity claiming to be a foreign sovereign government was passed from the former to the latter. Indeed, although the cases decided soon after the change in practice (e.g. *Gur Corporation* v *Trust Bank of Africa* [1986] 3 WLR 583) suggest a deference to the executive despite the change in practice, the *Somalia* case has made it clear that the role of the courts is now central. In this respect, the *Somalia* case is a decision of considerable importance. It is the clearest indication that the change in UK practice concerning recognition of governments has brought about a substantive change in the law of recognition. This was confirmed by the decision in *Sierra Leone Telecommunications* v *Barclays Bank plc* [1998] 2 All ER 821.
2. The change in practice could simply have meant that UK courts would ask 'what course of dealings' does the UK have with the disputed entity, and then determine the status of that entity in line with the Foreign Office answer to this question. This would be a doctrine of recognition in all but name. In *Somalia* and *Sierra Leone*, it is made clear that the court may determine the status of an alleged foreign sovereign government by reference to its own criteria, only part of which is the 'course of dealings' that the UK has with the entity. Furthermore, the case opens up the possibility that a UK court will accept the sovereignty of a foreign government even if the UK government would, as a matter of policy, be opposed to such a move. In an action in the High Court of Hong Kong in 1991 (that is, while Hong Kong was under UK sovereignty), a Foreign Office reply indicated that the UK does not recognise Taiwan as a State and has no *official* dealings with any authority there ((1996) 67 BYIL, pp. 716–717). However, given that the reply makes it clear that the UK has *unofficial* dealings with the authorities in Taiwan, it would be possible for a UK court to conclude that Taiwan had a 'government' for the purposes of UK law.
3. As has been mentioned before, the shift of UK practice concerning recognition of governments does not affect recognition of States. This has been confirmed by *Kibris Türk Hava Yollari CTA Holidays* v *Secretary of State for Transport* (see Section 3A(a)) where Williams J reiterated that the

case of *Republic of Somalia* v *Woodhouse Drake & Carey (Suisse)* was concerned with 'whether or not a particular regime was exercising effective administrative control in Somalia...[and] no question of recognition of a state was concerned.'

4. The express recognition of the Libyan NTC by the UK government in July 2011 and the issue of a Foreign Office certificate to that effect in legal proceedings (see extracts above) reverted to the previous policy of recognising governments, although as Warbrick argues, applying different criteria to the former policy. This shifted responsibility for making the decision as to whether an entity was recognised from the courts back to the executive. It is not yet clear whether this marks a formal shift in recognition policy for states such as the UK that do not formally recognise governments or was a one-off reaction.

5. There is also a distinction between recognising governments and opposition movements. During 2012 and 2013, the UK along with other governments (including the US), recognised the Syrian Opposition Coalition as 'the sole legitimate representative' of the Syrian people in opposition to the Assad regime but has so far stopped short of recognising the Coalition as the legitimate government (for discussion of the US position, see: 'United States Recognizes Syrian Opposition as "Legitimate Representative of the Syrian People", Will Provide Small Arms and Ammunition to Opposition Forces' 107 *American Journal of International Law* 650 (2013)). As is discussed further in Chapter 15, recognition of the 'legitimate' government of a territory can have implications for the use of force, in particular in identifying which entity is lawfully able to invite and consent to military assistance from other States.

(c) International organisations

Arab Monetary Fund v *Hashim (No 3)*
[1990] 2 All ER 769, United Kingdom Court of Appeal

The Arab Monetary Fund (AMF) was an international organisation created by treaty. The UK was not a party to this treaty, and the AMF had not been given the status of a company in English law. The AMF sued Hashim for misappropriated funds. The defendant contended that the AMF had no status in English law and, therefore, could not maintain an action. It was not disputed that the AMF was a 'person' in international law. The question was, therefore, whether English law would 'recognise' the status of an international legal person, although that body had no separate English personality. The judgment of the Court of Appeal is noted below. On appeal to the House of Lords ([1991] 1 All ER 871), their lordships allowed the AMF to sue, but only because it had been incorporated in Abu Dhabi law and could be regarded as an Abu Dhabian corporation to be recognised under the 'conflict of laws' rules.

LORD DONALDSON MR: The decision of the House of Lords in the *International Tin Council* case [see Chapter 4] ... confirms that our courts have no competence to adjudicate on or to enforce rights arising out of transactions entered into by independent sovereign states between themselves on the plane of international law. It also confirms that treaties to which the United Kingdom government is a party, and a *fortiori* those to which it is not, are not self-executing. They do not therefore create rights and obligations.... Hence the need for the International Organisations Act 1968, which enables Her Majesty by Order in Council to 'confer on the organisation the legal capacities of a body corporate' if it is an organisation of which the United Kingdom government is a member or if it maintains or proposes to maintain an establishment in the United Kingdom and, in the former case, may also provide that it shall enjoy certain privileges and immunities (see ss 1(2) and 4(a)). The fund is not, of course, such an organisation, since the United Kingdom government is not a member and it does not propose to maintain an establishment in this country. The *International Tin Council* case itself was concerned with the extent to which such an Order in Council invested the organisation with a separate personality distinct from its constituent members and, if so, to what extent (if at all) liability, whether primary or secondary, for its obligations attached to its constituent members. The House of Lords answered the first question 'Yes' and the second question 'Not at all'. Neither question arises directly on this appeal, but the discussion of the nature of an international organisation on which the legal capacities of a body corporate have been conferred casts some light on how English law would or should regard an international organisation on which an Abu Dhabi or United Arab Emirates decree has conferred similar capacities....

As I see it, absent an Order in Council, an international organisation is something which, in the eyes of English law, is as much a fact as a tree, a road or a hill. But it is not a person and the law can only deal in the rights and liabilities of persons. Once it is touched by the magic wand of the Order in Council it becomes a person, but one which is quite unlike other persons. Self-evidently it is not a natural person. But equally it is not a United Kingdom juridical person; nor is it a foreign juridical person. It is a person *sui generis*, which has all the capacities of a United Kingdom juridical person, but is not subject to the controls to which such a person is subject under United Kingdom law. It is not a native, but nor is it a visitor from abroad. It comes from the invisible depths of outer space.

Westland Helicopters Ltd v *Arab Organisation for Industrialisation*
[1995] 2 All ER 387, Queen's Bench Division

The Arab Organisation for Industrialisation (AOI) was an international organisation incorporated as a legal person in the national law of many States, but not the UK. In consequence, one question was whether the Bank had legal personality in the UK.

An international organisation would be recognised by English law as having legal personality if it had been accorded the legal capacity of a corporation under the law of one of its member states or the state where it had its seat (if that state was not a member state) and the fact that it had been accorded such capacity by more than one state did not mean that there was more than one international organisation for the English courts to recognise, but merely that there was more than one factual basis on which recognition could be accorded to the same organisation. Once it was accepted that an international organisation had been recognised by the English courts, questions as to the meaning, effect and operation of its constitution in so far as they arose between parties to the founding treaty were matters which could only be determined by reference to the treaty and to the principles of public international law, indeed, it would be contrary to the comity of nations for the English courts to impose the domestic law of one of the member states of the international organisation as its governing law, particularly where the terms of the treaty included a provision expressly insulating the international organisation from the domestic law of any participating state. It followed that the proper law governing the existence, constitution and representation of the AOI was public international law and not Egyptian domestic law.

NOTE: If an international organisation is 'personalised' in UK law then its status as a UK legal person is beyond doubt. This may arise through incorporation in the UK, or by statutory instrument under the International Organisations Acts. According to *Hashim*, an international organisation incorporated in the law of a State recognised by the UK has the personality of that State and so also has legal status in the UK. In the *Westland* case, a further step is taken by noting that, provided the organisation is incorporated in a recognised State, its 'true' legal attributes are to be determined by the treaty which established it—even if this treaty is unenacted in the UK. This case suggests that all international organisations now have personality in the UK—as defined by their constituent treaty. This is a long way from the non-recognition theory of the *International Tin Council* cases.

B: Recognition practice of other states

The recognition practice of other common law States is very similar to that of the UK.

Australia's New Recognition Policy
Department of Foreign Affairs and Trade: *Backgrounder* No 611, 16 March 1988

Previously Australia recognised (or did not recognise) both States and governments in existing States. We now recognise States only [as of 19 January 1988]. Recognition of a State essentially means acceptance of it as a fully independent and sovereign member of the community of nations....

Under our old policy the recognition of a new [government] which had come to power in an existing State as the government of that State was technically a formal acknowledgment that the government was in effective control of that State and in a position to represent that State internationally. However, recognition of a new government inevitably led to public assumptions of approval or disapproval of the government concerned, and could thereby create domestic or other problems for the recognising government. On the other hand 'non-recognition' limited the non-recognising government's capacity to deal with the new regime.

Considerations such as these have led a number of western governments to change to a policy of recognising States only. Australia now follows this policy…In future, Australia will no longer announce that it recognises, or does not recognise, a new regime in an existing State. Australia's attitude to a new regime will be ascertained by the nature of our policies towards and relations with the new regime. Important indicators of Australia's attitude to a new regime will be: public statements; establishment of and/or the conduct of diplomatic relations with it; ministerial contact; and other contacts, such as entering into aid, economic or defence arrangements, technical and cultural exchanges.

Abandoning the device of recognition of governments will enable us to react more flexibly and quickly to developments and to avoid giving rise to speculation about recognition and, consequently, assumptions of approval.

First National City Bank v *Banco Para El Comercio Exterior De Cuba*

462 US 611 (1983), United States Court of Appeals

The Cuban government established the Banco Para El Comercio Exterior De Cuba (Bancec) to serve as an official autonomous credit institution for foreign trade with full legal capacity. After a dispute over a contract with the applicant bank, the Cuban government seized the First National City Bank's assets in Cuba. The issue was whether the Bancec's separate juridical status shielded it from liability for the acts of the Cuban government.

Increasingly during this century, governments throughout the world have established separately constituted legal entities to perform a variety of tasks.…Freely ignoring the separate status of government instrumentalities would result in substantial uncertainty over whether an instrumentality's assets would be diverted to satisfy a claim against the sovereign, and might thereby cause third parties to hesitate before extending credit to a government instrumentality without the government's guarantee. As a result, the efforts of sovereign nations to structure their governmental activities in a manner deemed necessary to promote economic development and efficient administration would surely be frustrated. Due respect for the actions taken by foreign sovereigns and for principles of comity between nations, see *Hilton* v *Guyot*, 159 U.S. 113, 163–164 (1895), leads us to conclude—as the courts of Great Britain have concluded in other circumstances [*I Congreso del Partido*] that government instrumentalities established as juridical entities distinct and independent from their sovereign should normally be treated as such.

We find support for this conclusion in the legislative history of the Foreign Sovereign Immunities Act [US] (FSIA). During its deliberations, Congress clearly expressed its intention that duly created instrumentalities of a foreign State are to be accorded a presumption of independent status.…In discussing the legal status of private corporations, courts in the United States and abroad, have recognized that an incorporated entity—described by Chief Justice Marshall as 'an artificial being, invisible intangible, and existing only in contemplation of law' [*Trustees of Dartmouth College* v *Woodward*, 4 Wheat 518, 636 (1819)]—is not to be regarded as legally separate from its owners in all circumstances. Thus, where a corporate entity is so extensively controlled by its owner that a relationship of principal and agent is created, we have held that one may be held liable for the actions of the other. In addition, our cases have long recognized 'the broader equitable principle that the doctrine of corporate entity, recognized generally and for most purposes, will not be regarded when to do so would work fraud or injustice.' *Taylor* v *Standard Gas Co.*, 306 U.S. 307, 322 (1939). In particular, the Court has consistently refused to give effect to the corporate form where it is interposed to defeat legislative policies…

Giving effect to Bancec's separate juridical status in these circumstances, even though it has long been dissolved, would permit the real beneficiary of such an action, the Government of the Republic of Cuba, to obtain relief in our courts that it could not obtain in its own right without waiving its sovereign immunity and answering for the seizure of Citibank's assets—a seizure previously held by the Court of Appeals to have violated international law. We decline to adhere blindly to the corporate form where doing so would cause such an injustice…Having dissolved Bancec and transferred its assets to entities that may be held liable on Citibank's counterclaim, Cuba cannot escape liability for acts in violation of international law simply by retransferring the assets to separate juridical entities. To hold otherwise would permit governments to avoid the requirements of international law simply by creating juridical entities whenever the need arises…Our decision today announces no mechanical formula for determining the circumstances under which the normally separate juridical status of a government instrumentality is to be disregarded. Instead, it is the product of the application of internationally recognized equitable principles to avoid the injustice that would result from permitting a foreign state to reap the benefits of our courts while avoiding the obligations of international law.

NOTES

1. Most States have now adopted a policy of not formally recognising governments. Part of the reason for this is, as the extract on Australia's policy shows, due to the assumptions of approval or non-approval that it can create. However, one notable exception to this has been the express recognition of the Libyan NTC by several States including the US and Australia, which has been discussed in relation to the UK.

2. In civil law States, notably in Germany, the recognition of States by the government will have binding force on national courts. This means that national courts will not be able to assess the lawfulness of the recognition, unless there is evidence that the recognition was overtly unlawful. However, it has been clearly stated that this question is independent from the question of Statehood.

3. The courts of all States tend to seek to minimise the effect of non-recognition on the ordinary activities of individuals and groups (and corporations) as well as to avoid fraud and injustice (see *First National City Bank* above). However, the courts differ in the extent to which they will go beyond official government statements and executive certificates in order to acknowledge the realities of the situation—see *Attorney-General for Fiji* v *Robert Jones House* (New Zealand High Court) 80 ILR (1988) 1.

6

International Human Rights Law

INTRODUCTORY NOTE

The United Nations Charter begins with these words: 'We the Peoples of the United Nations determined...to reaffirm faith in fundamental human rights, in the dignity and worth of the human person, in the equal rights of men and women'. This acknowledgement of the importance of human rights by all States has done much to stimulate the large amount of international law protecting human rights now in place. While there was considerable academic acceptance of international human rights law from an early date, some national constitutions specifically provided for the protection of the human rights of their nationals, development of the protection of human rights in international law has generally been subsequent to the United Nations Charter.

The impact of international human rights on the international community is profound. For example, it has developed the role of the individual as a subject of international law, (as discussed in Chapters 5 and 14); claims of title to territory cannot be made without some consideration of the rights of the inhabitants of that territory (see Chapter 7); and it has meant that a State's sovereignty has been limited, as the treatment of an individual by a State is a matter of international concern and not a matter purely for national jurisdiction (see Chapter 11). It has also changed many perceptions of the nature of international law, as seen in Chapter 1.

Human rights are a matter of international law, as the rights of humans do not depend on an individual's nationality and so the protection of these rights cannot be limited to the jurisdiction of any one State. Of course, national protection of human rights is vital, and many States do specifically provide for such protection. Also, both the protection and the enforcement of international human rights, as with all international law, can depend on national courts (as seen in Chapter 4). However, as most breaches of human rights are caused by a State acting against its own nationals or against those persons in its jurisdiction, much of international human rights law operates beyond the national legal system in order to afford redress to those whose human rights are infringed and to provide an international standard by which States can be judged. This chapter aims to introduce the principal ideas, issues and framework of international human rights law.

Ultimately, if human rights mean anything in international law, then the traditional international law of State-based jurisdictional exclusivity must give way to a realisation that the rights of humans matter more than the interests of States.

SECTION 1: HUMAN RIGHTS THEORIES

The crux of international human rights law is to afford legal protection of human rights. To do this it is first necessary to decide what are human rights. Virtually all major legal theorists have considered the nature of human rights.

R. Wasserstrom, 'Rights, Human Rights and Racial Discrimination'

in J. Rachels (ed), *Moral Problems* (3rd edn, 1979)

First, [a human right] must be possessed by all human beings, as well as only by human beings. Second, because it is the same right that all human beings possess, it must be possessed equally by all human beings. Third, because human rights are possessed by all human beings, we can rule out as possible candidates any of those rights which one might have in virtue of occupying any particular status or relationship, such as that of parent, president or promisee. And fourth, if there are human rights, they have the additional characteristic of being assertable, in a manner of speaking, 'against the whole world'.

P. Williams, *The Alchemy of Race and Rights*

(1991)

[F]or the historically disempowered, the conferring of rights is symbolic of all the denied aspects of their humanity: rights imply a respect that places one in referential range of self and others, that elevates one's status from human body to social being.... 'Rights' feels new in the mouths of most black people. It is still deliciously empowering to say. It is the magic wand of inclusion and exclusion, of power and no power. The concept of rights, both positive and negative, is the maker of citizenship, our relation to others.

J. Shestack, 'The Jurisprudence of Human Rights'

in T. Meron (ed), *Human Rights in International Law: Legal and Policy Issues* (1984)

One of the initial questions is what is meant by human rights.... How we understand the meaning of human rights will influence our judgments on such issues as which rights are regarded as absolute, which are universal, which should be given priority, which can be overruled by other interests, which call for international pressures, which can demand programs for implementation, and which will be fought for.

The definitional process is not easy. Consider first the term 'rights', a chameleon hued word as Professor Hohefeld ['Fundamental Legal Conceptions as Applied in Judicial Reasoning' (1913) 23 Yale LJ 16] has taught us.... [W]e will observe that 'rights' is an ambiguous term used to describe a variety of legal relationships. According to Hohefeldian analysis, 'right' sometimes is used in its strict sense of the right-holder being *entitled* to something with a correlative duty in another. Sometimes, 'right' is used to indicate an *immunity* from having a legal status altered. Sometimes it indicates a *privilege* to do something. Sometimes it refers to a *power* to create a legal relationship.... [I]n the case of international human rights one is always faced with the question of what are rights worth where the type of enforcement procedures we find in a domestic system do not exist. It has often been said that there cannot be a right without a remedy. But is that so where there are various alternative forms of redress achieved through non-legal processes such as quiet diplomacy, threats of linkage, public opinion pressures, and other measures? ...

Natural law: the autonomous individual

Natural law theory has underpinnings in Sophocles and Aristotle, but it was first elaborated by the stoics of the Hellenistic period and later of the Roman period. Natural law, they believed, embodied those elementary principles of justice which were right reason, i.e., in accordance with nature, unalterable and eternal....

Natural law theory led to natural rights theory—the theory most closely associated with modern human rights. The chief exponent of this theory was John Locke, who developed his philosophy within the framework of seventeenth-century humanism and political activity. Locke imagined the existence of human beings in a state of nature. In that state men and women were in a state of freedom, able to determine their actions, and also in a state of equality in the sense that no one was subjected to the will or authority of another. To end the certain hazards and inconveniences of the state of nature, men and women entered into a contract by which they mutually agreed to form a community and set up a body politic. However, in setting up that political authority they retained the natural rights of life, liberty, and property which were their own. Government was obliged to protect the natural rights of its subjects and if government neglected this obligation it would forfeit its validity and office....

Positivism: the authority of the state

Another approach to human rights study is that of legal positivism.... Under [classical] positivist theory, the source of human rights is to be found only in the enactments of a system of law with sanctions attached to it. Views on what the law *ought* to be have no place in law and are cognitively worthless. The need to distinguish with maximum clarity law as it *is* from what it *ought to be* is the theme that haunts positivist philosophers, and they condemned natural law thinkers because they had blurred this vital distinction....

An influential moral philosopher, Professor H.L.A. Hart, [*The Concept of Law* (1961)]...finds the authority for the rules of law in the background of legal standards against which the government acts, standards that have been recognized and accepted by the community for that government. This legitimizes the decisions of the government and gives them the warp and woof of obligation that the naked commands of classical positivism lacked....In short, he continues to argue for a concept of law which allows the invalidity of law to be distinguished from its morality. And this remains a basic difference between natural rights philosophy and positivist philosophy...

Marxism: man as a specie being

[Marx] regarded the notion of individual rights as a bourgeois illusion. Concepts such as law, justice, morality, democracy, freedom, etc., are considered historical categories, whose content is determined by the material conditions of the life of a people and by their social circumstances. As the conditions of life change, so the content of notions and ideas may change....

Marxist recognition of rights stems from its view of persons as indivisible from the social whole; only by meeting the will of the whole can the higher freedom of individuals be achieved. Under this view, even satisfaction of basic needs can become contingent on realization of societal goals such as industrialization or the building of communism....

Theories based on justice

The monumental thesis of modern moral philosophy is John Rawls' *A Theory of Justice* [1971]. 'Justice is the first virtue of social institutions', says Rawls. Human rights, of course, are an end of justice; consequently, the role of justice is crucial to understanding human rights. No theory of human rights can be advanced today without considering Rawls' thesis.

Principles of justice, according to Rawls, provide a way of assigning rights and duties in the basic institutions of society. Those principles define the appropriate distribution of the benefits and burdens of social cooperation...The First Principle is that each person is to have an equal right to the most extensive total system of equal basic liberties compatible with a similar system of liberty for others. The Second Principle is that social and economic inequalities are to be arranged so they are both (a) to the greatest benefit of the least advantaged, and (b) attached to positions and offices open to all (equal opportunity).

The general conception of justice behind these principles is one of fairness and provides that all social primary goods—liberty and opportunity, income and wealth, and the bases of self-respect—are to be distributed equally unless an unequal distribution of any or all of these goods is to the advantage of the least favored. (This latter aspect is important in Rawls' theory and is known as the Difference Principle.)...

Theories based on dignity

McDougal, Lasswell, and Chen [*Human Rights and World Public Order: The Basic Policies of an International Law of Human Dignity* (1980)] follow what they call a value-policy oriented approach based on the protection of human dignity on the premise that demands for human rights are [widely-shared] in all the values upon which human rights depend on and for effective participation in all community value processes. The interdependent values they specify are the demands relating to (1) respect, (2) power, (3) enlightenment, (4) well-being, (5) health, (6) skill, (7) affection, and (8) rectitude. They assemble a huge catalogue of the demands which satisfy those eight values, as well as all of the ways in which they are denigrated....

The ultimate goal, as they see it, is a world community in which a democratic distribution of values is encouraged and promoted; all available resources are utilized to the maximum; and the protection of human dignity is regarded as a paramount objective of social policy....

Theory based on equality of respect and concern

Dworkin [*Taking Rights Seriously* (1977)] proceeds from the postulate of political morality, i.e., that governments must treat all their citizens with equal concern and respect....Dworkin next endorses the egalitarian character of the utilitarian principle that 'everybody can count for one, nobody for more than one

'.... Under this principle he believes that the state may exercise wide interventionist functions in order to advance social welfare.

Dworkin believes that a right to liberty in general is too vague to be meaningful. However, certain specific liberties, such as freedom of speech, freedom of worship, rights of association and personal and sexual relations, do require special protection against government interference. This is so not because these preferred liberties have some special substantive or inherent value...but because of a kind of procedural impediment that these preferred liberties might face. The impediment is that if those liberties were left to a utilitarian calculation, that is, an unrestricted calculation of the general interest, the balance would be tipped in favor of restrictions....

H. Lauterpacht, *International Law and Human Rights*
(1950)

The claim of the State to unqualified exclusiveness in the field of international relations was tolerable at a time when the actuality and the interdependence of the interests of the individual cutting across national frontiers were less obvious than they are today. It is this latter fact which explains why the constant expansion of the periphery of individual rights—an enduring feature of legal development—cannot stop short of the limits of the State. What is much more important, the recognition of the individual, by dint of the acknowledgment of his fundamental rights and freedoms, as the ultimate subject of international law, is a challenge to the doctrine which in reserving that quality exclusively to the State tends to a personification of the State as a being distinct from the individuals who compose it, with all that such personification implies. That recognition brings to mind the fact that, in the international as in the municipal sphere, the collective good is conditioned by the good of the individual human beings who comprise the collectivity. It denies, by cogent implication, that the corporate entity of the State is of a higher order than its component parts. It challenges the absolute moral superiority of groups, and in particular of the collective agency of the State which when thus artificially personified is prone to and certainly capable of disregard of all moral restraints....

International law, which has excelled in punctilious insistence on the respect owed by one sovereign State to another, henceforth acknowledges the sovereignty of man. For fundamental human rights are rights superior to the law of the sovereign State. The hope, expressed by Emerson, that 'man shall treat with man as a sovereign state with a sovereign state' may be brought nearer to fruition by sovereign States recognising the duty to treat man with the respect which traditional law exacted from them in relation to other States. To that vital extent the recognition of inalienable human rights and the recognition of the individual as a subject of international law are synonymous. To that vital extent they both signify the recognition of a higher, fundamental law not only on the part of States but also, through international law, on the part of the organised international community itself. That fundamental law, as expressed in the acknowledgment of the ultimate reality and the independent status of the individual, constitutes both the moral limit and the justification of the international legal order. Through them, it implies the promise that the organised international society will not, in turn, degenerate into a tyrannical accumulation of power. It is that danger which has been for many the reason of the determined opposition to the idea of an organised commonwealth of nations embracing all humanity. In that perspective the acknowledgment of human rights and fundamental freedom on the part of the Members of the United Nations assumes an added significance of its own. The consequent recognition of the individual human being as a subject of international law lends to the law obtaining between sovereign States the beneficent complexion of a law of nations conceived as the universal law of mankind.

P. Gabel and D. Kennedy, 'Roll Over Beethoven'
36 *Stanford Law Review* 1 (1984)

This is the essence of the problem with rights discourse. People don't realise that what they are doing is recasting the real existential feelings that led them to become political people into an ideological framework that coopts them into adopting the very consciousness they want to transform. Without even knowing it, they start talking as if 'we' were rights-bearing citizens who are 'allowed' to do this or that by something called 'the state,' which is a passivising illusion—actually an hallucination which establishes the presumptive political legitimacy of the status quo....

Exactly what people don't need is their *rights*. What they need are the actual forms of social life that have to be created through the building of movements that can overcome illusions about the nature of what is political, like the illusion that there is an entity called the state, that people possess rights. It may be necessary to use the rights argument in the course of political struggle, in order to make gains. But the thing to be understood is the extent to which it is enervating to use it. It's a diversion from true political language, political modes of communication about the nature of reality and what it is that people are trying to achieve.... [it is] an hallucination that as long as people believe in it, they will disempower themselves.... [A right] can be, in some circumstances, a marginal gain in power. It can force officials to obey their own rules. There are things about it that can lead to protective spaces that there's no reason for us to criticise. But it is critical for people not to 'return' this power to the state, to remember that the state is an illusion and that there are no rights.

H. Charlesworth, 'What are "Women's International Human Rights"?'

in R. Cook (ed), *Human Rights of Women: National and International Perspectives* (1994)

[T]he development of international human rights law generally has been partial and androcentric, privileging a masculine worldview. Non-governmental organizations have recently begun to document abuse of women that falls within the traditional scope of human rights law. But the very structure of this law has been built on silence of women. The fundamental problem women face worldwide is not discriminatory treatment compared with men, although this is a manifestation of the larger problem. Women are in an inferior position because they have no real power in either the public or the private worlds, and international human rights law, like most economic, social, cultural and legal constructs, reinforces this powerlessness. Noreen Burrows writes ['International Law and Human Rights: The Case of Women's Rights' in T. Campbell et al. (eds), *Human Rights: From Rhetoric to Reality*]: 'For most women, what it is to be human is to work long hours in agriculture or the home, to receive little or no remuneration, and to be faced with political and legal processes which ignore their contribution to society and accord no recognition of their particular needs.' A more fundamental treatment of the skewed nature of the international human rights system would redefine the boundaries of the traditional human rights canon, rather than tinkering with the limited existing model of non discrimination....

It is worth noting...that, with the exception of the Convention on the Rights of the Child, all 'general' human rights instruments refer only to men. The importance of language in constructing and reinforcing the subordination of women has been much analyzed by feminist scholars, and the consistently masculine vocabulary of human rights law operates at both a direct and subtle level to exclude women. More basically, all international human rights law rests on and reinforces a distinction between public and private worlds, and this distinction operates to muffle, and often completely silence, the voices of women....

How can international human rights law tackle the oppressed position of women worldwide? Women's international human rights must be developed on a number of fronts. Certainly the relevance of the traditional canon of human rights to women is important to document. The instruments and institutions of the 'first wave' of international law with respect to women must also be supported and strengthened. The potential of an individual complaints procedure under the Women's Convention, for example, should be seriously explored. At the same time, rights that focus on harms sustained by women in particular need to be identified and developed, challenging the public/private distinction by bringing rights discourse into the private sphere. But, most fundamental and important, we must work to ensure that women's voices find a public audience, to reorient the boundaries of mainstream human rights law so that it incorporates an understanding of the world from the perspective of the socially subjugated. One way forward in international human rights law is to challenge the gendered dichotomy of public and private worlds.

R. Falk, J. Stevens and B. Rajagopal, *International Law and the Third World: Reshaping Justice*

(2008)

The idea that human rights can be hegemonic can strike its core believers as nothing less than sacrilege. The self-image of human rights discourse is that of a post-imperial discourse, unsullied by the ugly colonial politics of pre-1948, when the Universal Declaration of Human Rights (UDHR) initiated the modern human rights movement. In this self-image the new international law of human rights effectively superseded the old international law of colonialism. To the contrary, one could argue that a true historical reading of the role played by the international human rights corpus in anti-imperial struggles (a task to be performed thoroughly) may reveal several uncomfortable facts. These include the following: 1) the UDHR did not apply directly to the colonial areas and was subjected to intense manoeuvring by Britain at the drafting stage to prevent its application to its colonies despite Soviet pressure; 2) anti-colonial struggles were hardly ever taken up for scrutiny at the UN Commission on Human Rights before many Third World states came on board in 1967, when membership was enlarged, and even then remained tangential on the agenda formally; 3) anti-colonial nationalist revolts in places such as Kenya and Malaya were successfully characterized by the British as 'emergencies' to be dealt with as law and order issues, thereby avoiding the application of either human rights or humanitarian law to these violent encounters; 4) the main anti-imperial strand of the human rights discourse—the critique of apartheid in South Africa and of Israeli policies in Palestinian territories using human rights terms by the Third World during the 1960s to 1980s—remained tangential to the mainstream human rights discourse coming from the West; and 5) very little of the mainstream human rights scholarship acknowledges that human rights discourse influenced or was influenced in any significant way by anti-colonial struggles after World War I.

M. Koskenniemi, 'Human Rights Mainstreaming as a Project of Power'
1 *Humanity* 47 (2010)

[T]here are no authoritative lists of prelegislative rights. This is why political actors are always able to dress their claims in rights-language. As every significant rights-claim involves the imposition of a burden on some other person, then the latter may likewise invoke his or her preference to be free from such burden in rights-terms. An ownership right for example, may conflict with many kinds of collective or economic rights but also [other rights such as] the right of freedom of speech. May protesters against genetically manipulated foodstuffs enter the localities in which such foodstuffs are being sold? One highly publicised rights-conflict was decided by the South African Constitutional Court in 2002 in connection with the country's HIV/AIDS crisis as the Court held that South Africa must either require pharmaceutical companies to sell products at determined prices or to issue licences for domestic production. In this case, the 'right of pregnant women and their new-born children' trumped over what were expressed in terms of the human rights of the persons who benefit from the medicines produced through the research activities that were financed [by drug companies]....As is well-known, this lead eventually to a negotiated settlement on the basis of the Doha Declaration of November 2001 and the Cancun TRIPS Council decisions in August 2003. Each right was thoroughly negotiable, and negotiated in a thoroughly political process. Perhaps more familiar is the conflict over freedom-rights and security-rights that is played out before the whole world under the banner of 'fight against terrorism'. Traditionally, rights of security and right to personal freedom were both recognised and submitted to a 'balancing test'. Has there been a rights-violation when a person loses his or her job owing to secret information received by the employer from public authorities? According to the European Court of Human Rights [ECHR, *Leander v Sweden*, A.116 (1987) (para. 59)], the matter needs (again) to be assessed taking all relevant circumstances into account.

> The Court recognizes that the national authorities enjoy a margin of appreciation, the scope of which will depend not only on the nature of the legitimate aim pursued but also on the particular nature of the interference involved. In the instant case, the interest of the respondent State in protecting its national security must be balanced against the seriousness of the interference with the applicant's right to respect for his private life.

...Human rights arose from revolution, not from a call for mainstreaming. The ethos of revolution not only happens to be opposite to the ethos of mainstream, its identity is dependent on that opposition. If human rights cannot—as I have suggested here—be identified with any distinct projects of social policy or economic distribution, they can be identified with a professional sensibility, a set of biases and preferences. One cannot be a revolutionary and participate in the regular management of things and human beings without some cost to both of these projects. The more revolutionary one tries to be, the more difficult it is to occupy those administrative [places] in which the main lines of policy are being set. The more influential one is as an administrative or regulatory agent, the less 'revolutionary' one's policies can be. I do not think there is any easy way out of this predicament. To deal with it involves some capacity for critical reflection, engagement and distance, passion and coolness. This, I think, [is] what legal training ought to produce.

NOTES

1. Understanding the different theories of human rights provides an insight into the content and interpretation of rights throughout this chapter. For example, decisions as to whether any limitations can be allowed to be placed on human rights, questions of the allocation of priorities between human rights (see Koskenniemi above), the extent to which human rights are universal and concerns over the recognition of 'new' human rights, among many other issues, require some consideration of the concept of what is a human right. Wasserstrom's definition (above) is one of many definitions of human rights, with other theorists placing emphasis on human dignity, others on their role in developing every person's capacities and others on capabilities.

2. The theories summarised in the extracts above are only a selection of the major theories and are, necessarily, briefly described. For example, Gabel and Kennedy are part of the Critical Legal Studies school of legal thought and Charlesworth offers an example of the feminist perspective on human rights, whilst Falk, Stevens and Rajagopal raise some of the concerns of international lawyers in the developing world. A number of the theories were formed within the context of national constitutional law, so there is some limitation on their relevance to international human

rights law. However, they are important in that they illustrate some of the developments in the theoretical debates about human rights.

3. The first part of the extract from Shestack shows, by reference to Hohfeld's categories, that the use of the term 'rights' does not imply that if they are infringed then an individual is necessarily able to bring a claim against a State before a judicial body and directly enforce any decision made. However, by describing them as 'rights', it elevates these concepts from what could be considered to be purely moral standards to those having legal characteristics, as well as giving them moral and social power (as shown in Williams' extract). International human rights law constructs human rights as being only activated in relation to a State, however, the concept of human rights is not restricted to relationships only with a State (see Section 8A).

4. There are different types of rights, being civil and political rights (e.g. freedom from torture, right to a fair trial); economic, social and cultural rights (e.g. right to education, right to access to health care); and group or 'peoples' rights (e.g. freedom from genocide, right of self-determination). These rights are interdependent and of equal status. There is no hierarchy of rights because, as has often been said, 'rights begin with breakfast'. Therefore to categorise rights in terms of 'generations' is a mistake as it implies that some rights can only be respected, protected and fulfilled subsequent to other rights. In addition, no one type of right requires one type of action or inaction by a State. For example, to ensure the right to a fair trial a State must finance a legal system with courts, judges, etc., and all rights are to some extent justiciable.

SECTION 2: HUMAN RIGHTS AND THE INTERNATIONAL COMMUNITY

A: Universal obligations

The first major statement after the United Nations Charter on the international legal protection of human rights was the Universal Declaration of Human Rights. It was adopted by the General Assembly on 10 December 1948 in Resolution 217A(III) by a vote of 48 in favour, none against and 8 abstentions (being Byelorussian SSR, Czechoslovakia, Poland, Saudi Arabia, South Africa, Ukrainian SSR, USSR and Yugoslavia). The rights it declares are not set out here but are readily available. It is considered to set out some of the customary international law obligations on States with respect to the protection of human rights (see further Section 3C). All subsequent treaties and other international documents tend to refer to the Universal Declaration of Human Rights.

Vienna Declaration and Programme of Action 1993
32 *International Legal Materials* 1661 (1993)

In June 1993, a World Conference on Human Rights was organised by the United Nations. All States participated and there was input from many non-governmental organisations and individuals. At the end of the conference, the Vienna Declaration was agreed by consensus.

Preamble

Recognising and affirming that all human rights derive from the dignity and worth inherent in the human person, and that the human person is the central subject of human rights and fundamental freedoms, and consequently should be the principal beneficiary and should participate actively in the realization of these rights and freedoms...

Emphasising that the Universal Declaration of Human Rights, which constitutes a common standard of achievement for all peoples and all nations, is the source of inspiration and has been the basis for the United Nations in making advances in standard setting as contained in the existing international human rights instruments, in particular the International Covenant on Civil and Political Rights and the International Covenant on Economic, Social and Cultural Rights, …

1. The World Conference on Human Rights reaffirms the solemn commitment of all States to fulfil their obligations to promote universal respect for, and observance and protection of, all human rights and fundamental freedoms for all in accordance with the Charter of the United Nations, other instruments relating to human rights, and international law. The universal nature of these rights and freedoms is beyond question.

In this framework, enhancement of international cooperation in the field of human rights is essential for the full achievement of the purposes of the United Nations.

Human rights and fundamental freedoms are the birthright of all human beings; their protection and promotion is the first responsibility of Governments. …

4. The promotion and protection of all human rights and fundamental freedoms must be considered as a priority objective of the United Nations in accordance with its purposes and principles, in particular the purpose of international cooperation. In the framework of these purposes and principles, the promotion and protection of all human rights is a legitimate concern of the international community. The organs and specialized agencies related to human rights should therefore further enhance the coordination of their activities based on the consistent and objective application of international human rights instruments.

5. All human rights are universal, indivisible and interdependent and interrelated. The international community must treat human rights globally in a fair and equal manner, on the same footing, and with the same emphasis. While the significance of national and regional particularities and various historical, cultural and religious background must be borne in mind, it is the duty of States, regardless of their political, economic and cultural systems, to promote and protect all human rights and fundamental freedoms.

6. The efforts of the United Nations system towards the universal respect for, and observance of, human rights and fundamental freedoms for all, contribute to the stability and well-being necessary for peaceful and friendly relations among nations, and to improved conditions for peace and security as well as economic and social development, in conformity with the Charter of the United Nations. …

8. Democracy, development and respect for human rights and fundamental freedoms are interdependent and mutually reinforcing. Democracy is based on the freely expressed will of the people to determine their own political, economic, social and cultural systems and their full participation in all aspects of their lives. …

10. The World Conference on Human Rights reaffirms the right to development, as established in the Declaration on the Right to Development, as a universal and inalienable right and an integral part of fundamental human rights.

NOTES
1. Most human rights treaties explicitly assume that the rights enumerated in them pre-exist their legal formulation. They tend to adopt the theory that human rights derive from the inherent dignity of the human person.
2. Every State in the world has ratified at least one treaty that protects human rights. This extraordinary fact indicates the extent to which international human rights law is now a part of the international legal system. Of course, the ratification by States of a human rights treaty does not necessarily mean that they comply with their obligations under it, or that they accept all the terms of the treaty (see reservations in Section 5B and in Chapter 3).
3. Human rights have made a significant impact on international law. It has particularly affected the sovereignty of States and takes away the assumption that international law is solely a State-based system. There is now general agreement that human rights are a matter of legitimate international concern and they are appropriately a part of the international legal system (see paragraph 4 of the Vienna Declaration). The vast amount of international and regional instruments concerning both human rights in general and specific human rights—being evidence of State practice—testify to this. Therefore, a State can no longer claim that human rights is a matter within its exclusive 'domestic jurisdiction' within Article 2(7) of the United Nations Charter (see Chapter 15) and so claim that the international community is not able to be concerned about human rights within that State. Instead, how a State treats all persons on its territory is not a matter for the State alone but is a matter of international law. International human rights law provides a standard whereby the conduct of each State in regard to human rights can be judged.

4. While there are many breaches of human rights by States, very rarely will a State claim that it is allowed to breach a human right. It will either deny the facts concerning the breach, or will try and justify its action by reference to some exception to, derogation on, or limitation of, those rights. In so doing, the State affirms the legal obligation to protect human rights, as was acknowledged by the International Court of Justice in *Military and Paramilitary Activities in and against Nicaragua* ICJ Rep 1986 14 (para. 185), when it held that if a State 'defends its conduct by appealing to exceptions or justifications contained within the [recognised international law] rule itself, then whether or not the State's conduct is in fact justifiable on that basis, the significance of that attitude is to confirm rather than to weaken the rule'.

B: Cultural relativism

If human rights are universal then they apply to all persons no matter where, or within which cultures, they live. However, if human rights are relative to each society or culture (hence the term 'cultural relativism') then any international system of protecting human rights could be seen as inappropriate.

M.-B. Dembour, 'Critiques'
in D. Moeckli, S. Shah and S. Sivakumaran (eds), *International Human Rights* (2nd edn, 2014)

[W]hat do we mean by 'cultural relativism'? The theory is founded on the double observation that moral systems are embedded in culture and that different cultures produce different moralities. However, to become an 'ism', ethical inferences must be derived from these (assuredly sound) empirical observations. What are these inferences? According to its detractors, cultural relativism would dictate tolerance of any culturally embedded moral system on earth, perhaps even any morality. However, whether self-declared cultural relativists hold this position is doubtful.

Recognizing that different societies hold different values need not logically lead to the conclusion that all these different values and practices must be tolerated. The observation that cultures produce different moral norms does not say anything about the respective value of these norms. Despite this, and no doubt also due to excessive formulations by its proponents, cultural relativism came to be denigrated for demanding that the intolerable be tolerated. The doctrine is even said to have been an embarrassment to anthropologists, because of the difference and/or inaction which it advocated. It has also been criticized for lending itself for abuse, allowing those in power to make spurious or disingenuous cultural arguments in pursuit of their own political ends. Undoubtedly, cultural relativism, like other theories, has been abused, and the last point must indeed be conceded. This, however, should not detract from appreciating what the doctrine offers....

The universality of human rights is *not* a fact. At best, human rights universal*ism* is a theory. It is a worthwhile project, directed at discussing, agreeing upon, and practising principles of governance which should benefit all individuals equally, but which also has a dark side which it would be either disingenuous or naïve not to recognize. This dark side includes the inherent danger not to respect the ways of others, if not an active collusion in their destruction. Universalists too often assume that they are on firm ground in making judgments about others. They can easily end up imposing their ways on others for no other reason than sheer dominant position, without even realizing it, so full are they of their good intentions. By contrast, instead of saying 'we know best' or 'we know', relativism poses the question, 'What do we know?'.

Universalism has a good side—the elaboration of minimal common standards—but it has also a bad side—arrogance. Similarly, relativism has a good side—respect for different ways—but it also has a bad side—inaction or indifference....

Universalism cannot exist independently of its opposite, most aptly named 'particularism'. (Etymologically, what is not universal is special, specific, or particular; what is not relative is absolute. Using the word 'particularism' presents the further advantage of avoiding both the possibly reifying tone of the reference to 'culture' and the embarrassment of the faint moral position commonly associated with 'cultural relativism'.) It is in opposition to practices that appear abhorrent that universal norms are being set, and it is by reference to local particularities that these universal norms are implemented. The reverse is true. Particularism does not exist independently of universalism. As moral beings concerned with ethics, we are not just beings of culture but respond to what could be termed the call of universalism. This is to say that we are always somewhere between the ideal represented by universalism (which should be recognized as an ideal) and the reality of our being embedded in culture (which is inescapable). We are bound to oscillate between two positions in a pendulum-like motion.

I. Shivji, *The Concept of Human Rights in Africa*
(1989)

Human rights talk constitutes one of the main elements in the ideological armoury of imperialism. Yet from the point of view of the African people, human rights struggles constitute the stuff of their daily lives....[T]he first important building-block of the new perspective on human rights in Africa [is that it] must be thoroughly anti-imperialist, thoroughly democratic and unreservedly in the interest of the 'people'.

Secondly, human rights, as we have seen, is an ideology. It ideologises certain social interests in the course of class struggles. And it plays either a legitimising role or a mobilising one. For the new perspective, the human rights ideology has to be appropriated in the interest of the people to play a mobilising role in their struggle against imperialism and compradorial classes and their state. Therefore the new perspective must distance itself openly from imperialist ideology of human rights at the international level and cultural-chauvinist/developmentalist ideology of the compradorial classes, at the national level. This is the second...building block....

Thirdly,...the new conceptualisation must clearly break from both the metaphysics of natural law as well as the logical formalism and legalism of positive law. It must be rooted in the perspective of class struggle. This means, first, that counter-posed to the individualist/liberal paradigm must be the collectivist/revolutionary conception. The right-holder, if you like, is not exclusively an autonomous individual but a collective: a people, a nation, a nationality, a national group, an interest/social group, a cultural/oppressed minority, etc. But this notion of 'collective' must be clearly distinguished from a fascist concept where the 'collective' is expressed in the oppressor state or a revisionist-'Marxist' concept where both the 'collective' and the state cease to bear any class character. Secondly, here right is not theorised simply as a legal right, which implies both a static and an absolutist paradigm, in the sense of an entitlement or a claim, but a means of struggle. In that sense it is akin to righteousness rather than right. Seen as a means of struggle, 'right' is therefore not a standard granted as charity from above but a standard-bearer around which people rally for struggle from below. By the same token, the correlate of 'right' is not duty (in the Hohfeldian sense) where duty-holders are identified and held legally or morally responsible but rather the correlate is power/privilege where those who enjoy such power/privilege are the subject of being exposed and struggled against....

Therefore, the human rights vocabulary too undergoes transformation. In the new perspective one does not simply sympathise with the 'victims' of human rights violations and beg the 'violators' to mend their ways in numerous catalogued episodes of violations; rather one joins the oppressed/exploited/dominated or ruled against the oppressors/exploiters/dominant and ruling to expose and resist, with a view ultimately to overcome, the situation which generates human rights violations.

Finally, the new perspective lends a totally different meaning to the prioritization debate as well as a new content and form to human rights activity and community.

M. Baderin, International Human Rights and Islamic Law
(2003)

Traditionally, a number of difficulties confront the discourse of human rights from an Islamic legal perspective....On one hand is the domineering influence of the 'Western' perspective of human rights, which creates a tendency of always using 'Western' values as a yardstick in every human rights discourse. While it is true that the impetus for the formulation of international human rights standards originated from the West, the same cannot be said of the whole concept of human rights, which is perceivable within different human civilizations. Related to that, is the negative image of Islam in the West. Often, some of the criminal punishments under Islamic law and the political cum human rights situation in many parts of the Muslim world today are, inter alia, cited by some Western analysts as evidence of lack of provision for respect for human rights in Islamic law. This is part of what has been termed 'Islamophobia' in the West, which adversely affects the view about human rights in Islam generally. In the academic realm there is also what Strawson has called the 'orientalist problematique' by which 'Islamic law is represented within Anglo-American scholarship as an essentially defective legal system', especially with regards to international law.

On the other hand is the obstacle of static hardline interpretations of the Shari'ah and non-relative application of traditional Islamic jurisprudence on some aspects of inter-human relations. Islamic law or Shari'ah are both sometimes vaguely advanced by some Muslim countries as an excuse for their poor human rights records without exhaustive elaboration of the position of Islamic law on the matter.

Due to the above difficulties, the concept of human rights under Islamic law has often been discussed from either a reproachful or a defensive angle, depending on the leanings of the discussant. Piscatori has frowned at the defensive approach of most Muslim writers in the international human rights discourse. We need to determine however, whether the defensiveness is merely an apology in the face of genuine challenges posed by international human rights to Islamic law, or reasonable defence against criticisms of Islamic law for human rights situations in Muslim countries not necessarily justifiable even under the Shari'ah. On one hand, it is undeniable that Western initiatives and modern challenges, which include the international human rights regime, have forced contemporary Muslim thinkers and intellectuals to propose strongly a review of some traditional Islamic jurisprudential views, especially in the area of international law and relations. On the other hand, there have also been general erroneous reproaches of Islamic law for the sometimes appalling attitudes or actions of some governments in Muslim countries that are not justifiable even under the Shari'ah. At the end of a Seminar on Human Rights in Islam held in Kuwait in 1980, jointly organized by the International Commission of Jurists, the University of Kuwait and the Union of Arab Lawyers, the conclusion, inter alia, was that:

It is unfair to judge Islamic law (Shari'a) by the political systems which prevailed in various periods of Islamic history. It ought to be judged by the general principles which are derived from its sources....Regrettably enough, contemporary Islamic practices cannot be said to conform in many aspects with the true principles of Islam. Further, it is wrong to abuse Islam by seeking to justify certain political systems in the face of obvious contradictions between those systems and Islamic law.

While the theoretic arguments concerning the conceptual foundations of human rights may be difficult to settle, the indisputable fact is that international human rights are today not a prerogative of a single nation. They are a universal affair that concern the dignity and well-being of every human being. However, there is yet to emerge what we may call a 'universal universalism' in international human rights. What exists now has been described as 'provincialism masquerading as universalism'. While the flagrant abuse of human rights in Muslim States under the pretext of cultural differences is unacceptable, the role and influence of the Muslim world in achieving a peaceful coexistence within the international community does permit Muslim States to question a universalism 'within which Islamic law (generally) has no normative value and enjoys little prestige'. Since human rights are best achieved through the domestic law of States, recognition of relevant Islamic law principles in that regard will enhance the realization of international human rights objectives in Muslim States that apply Islamic law fully or partly as State law Conversely, there is a need for the Muslim world also to acknowledge change as a necessary ingredient in law. The adaptability of the Shari'ah must be positively utilized to enhance human rights in the Muslim world. While Muslims must be true to their heritage, the noble ideals of international human rights can shed new light on their interpretation of the Shari'ah, their international relations and self-awareness within the legal limits of Islamic law.

Y. Ghai, 'Human Rights and Governance: The Asia Debate'
15 Australian Yearbook of International Law 1 (1994)

It is easy to believe that there is a distinct Asian approach to human rights because some government leaders speak as if they represent the whole continent when they make their pronouncements on human rights. This view is reinforced because they claim that their views are based on perspectives which emerge from the Asian culture or religion or Asian realities. The gist of their position is that human rights as propounded in the West are founded on individualism and therefore have no relevance to Asia which is based on the primacy of the community. It is also sometimes argued that economic underdevelopment renders most of the political and civil rights (emphasised in the West) irrelevant in Asia. Indeed, it is sometimes alleged that such rights are dangerous in view of fragmented nationalism and fragile Statehood.

It would be surprising if there were indeed one Asian perspective, since neither Asian culture nor Asian realities are homogenous throughout the continent. All the world's major religions are represented in Asia, and are in one place or another State religions (or enjoy a comparable status: Christianity in the Philippines, Islam in Malaysia, Hinduism in Nepal and Buddhism in Sri Lanka and Thailand). To this list we may add political ideologies like socialism, democracy or feudalism which animate peoples and governments of the region. Even apart from religious differences, there are other factors which have produced a rich diversity of cultures. A culture, moreover, is not static and many accounts given of Asian culture are probably true of an age long ago. Nor are the economic circumstances of all the Asian countries similar. Japan, Singapore and Hong Kong are among the world's most prosperous countries, while there is grinding poverty in Bangladesh, India and the Philippines. The economic and political systems in Asia likewise show a remarkable diversity, ranging from semi-feudal kingdoms in Kuwait and Saudi Arabia, through military dictatorships in Burma and formerly Cambodia, effectively one party regimes in Singapore and Indonesia, communist regimes in China and Vietnam, ambiguous democracies in Malaysia and Sri Lanka, to well established democracies like India. There are similarly differences in their economic systems, ranging from tribal subsistence economies in parts of Indonesia through highly developed market economies of Singapore, Hong Kong and Taiwan and the mixed economy model of India to the planned economies of China and Vietnam. Perceptions of human rights are undoubtedly reflective of these conditions, and suggest that they would vary from country to country.

Perceptions of human rights are reflective of social and class positions in society. What conveys an apparent picture of a uniform Asian perspective on human rights is that it is the perspective of a particular group, that of the ruling elites, which gets international attention. What unites these elites is their notion of governance and the expediency of their rule. For the most part, the political systems they represent are not open or democratic, and their publicly expressed views on human rights are an emanation of these systems, of the need to justify authoritarianism and occasional repression. It is their views which are given wide publicity domestically and internationally....

[S]ome Asian governments claim that their societies place a higher value on the community than in the West, that individuals find fulfilment in their participation in communal life and community tasks, and that this factor constitutes a primary distinction in the approach to human rights.... This argument is advanced as an instance of the general proposition that rights are culture specific.

The 'communitarian' argument is Janus-faced. It is used against the claim of universal human rights to distinguish the allegedly Western, individual-oriented approaches to rights from the community centred values of the East. Yet it is also used to deny the claims and assertions of communities in the name of national unity and stability. It suffers from at least two further weaknesses. First, it overstates the 'individualism' of Western society and traditions of thought...

Secondly, Asian governments...fall into the easy but wrong assumption that they or the State are the 'community'....Nothing can be more destructive of the community than this conflation. The community and State are different institutions and to some extent in a contrary juxtaposition. The community, for the most part, depends on popular norms developed through forms of consensus and enforced through mediation and persuasion. The State is an imposition on society, and unless humanised and democratised (as it has not been in most of Asia), it relies on edicts, the military, coercion and sanctions. It is the tension between them which has elsewhere underpinned human rights. In the name of the community, most Asian governments have stifled social and political initiatives of private groups....Governments have destroyed many communities in the name of development or State stability....

Another attack on the community comes from the economic, market oriented policies of the governments. Although Asian capitalism appears to rely on the family and clan associations, there is little doubt that it weakens the community and its cohesion. The organising matrix of the market is not the same as that of the community. Nor are its values or methods particularly 'communitarian'. The moving frontier of the market, seeking new resources, has been particularly disruptive of communities which have managed to preserve intact a great deal of their culture and organisation during the colonial and post-colonial periods. The emphasis on the market, and with it individual rights of property are also at odds with communal organisation and enjoyment of property....

A final point is the contradiction between claims of a consensus and harmonious society, and the extensive arming of the State apparatus. The pervasive use of draconian legislation like administrative detention, disestablishment of societies, press censorship, and sedition, belies claims to respect alternative views, promote a dialogue, and seek consensus. The contemporary State intolerance of opposition is inconsistent with traditional communal values and processes.

NOTES

1. It is clear that developed/industrialised (Western) States promoted the international legal protection of human rights. It is also clear that some developed States pressed for the protection of certain rights (civil and political rights, such as freedom of expression) to the apparent exclusion of other rights. This does not mean that the concepts of human rights are solely Western concepts or that the rhetoric by some States equates to the legal position. Indeed, many of the rights protected by international law were promoted by developing/non-industrialised States and theorists from those States. These include some of the economic, social and cultural rights, as well as group rights, such as the right of self-determination (see Section 6). It should be recalled that all human rights are 'universal, indivisible and interdependent and interrelated' (see paragraph 5 of the Vienna Declaration, Section 2A).

2. While many societies, religions and cultures have not used the terminology of 'human rights', contemporary scholars have discerned the existence of concepts of human rights across the world, as is evident in the extracts from Shivji, Baderin and Ghai above. This is consistent with

the position that all humans have rights. The universal acceptance of the concepts of human rights can also be seen in the fact that all States have ratified at least one treaty protecting human rights.

3. Nevertheless, there is a need to recognise that, while the concepts of human rights are universal, the application of these rights within each society and culture will vary. This position was acknowledged in paragraph 5 of the Vienna Declaration (Section 2A), where the significance of different cultural backgrounds is to be 'borne in mind'. Those backgrounds are borne in mind by the international human rights supervisory bodies when they apply the relevant treaty (see the 'margin of appreciation' in Section 4). At the same time, as Ghai indicates, caution is needed so that too much weight is not given to the arguments of States seeking to assert their own authoritarian rule and to avoid their obligations to protect human rights. It is therefore important to listen to the voices of those whose rights are being violated.

4. There is a great difficulty in defining 'culture', with there being many disputes over the definition in anthropology. Human rights law does not resolve this and can confuse 'culture' with 'society' (see Dembour above), and it does not deal well with religion and culture (see Section 5)

SECTION 3: INTERNATIONAL PROTECTION OF HUMAN RIGHTS

A: International documents

This section introduces some of the key documents and themes on the international protection of human rights. The detailed provisions of the major international instruments protecting human rights can be found in books of documents on international human rights or on accessible websites and so are not extracted here.

United Nations Charter 1945

Article 1

The Purposes of the United Nations are:....

3. To achieve international co-operation in solving international problems of an economic, social, cultural, or humanitarian character, and in promoting and encouraging respect for human rights and for fundamental freedoms for all without distinction as to race, sex, language, or religion.

Article 55

With a view to the reaction of conditions of stability and well-being which are necessary for peaceful and friendly relations among nations based on respect for the principle of equal rights and self-determination of peoples, the United Nations shall promote:
  (a) higher standards of living, full employment, and conditions of economic and social progress and development;
  (b) solutions of international economic, social, health, and related problems; and international cultural and educational co-operation; and
  (c) universal respect for, and observance of, human rights and fundamental freedoms for all without distinction as to race, sex, language, or religion.

Article 56

All Members pledge themselves to take joint and separate action in co-operation with the Organization for the achievement of the purposes set forth in Article 55.

Article 68

The Economic and Social Council shall set up commissions in economic and social fields and for the promotion of human rights, and such other commissions as may be required for the performance of its functions.

Article 76

The basic objectives of the trusteeship system, in accordance with the Purposes of the United Nations laid down in Article I of the present Charter, shall be:...

    (c) to encourage respect for human rights and for fundamental freedoms for all without distinction as to race, sex, language, or religion, and to encourage recognition of the interdependence of the peoples of the world.

M. Baderin and R. McCorquodale, *Economic, Social and Cultural Rights in Action*

(2007)

Barely had the excitement died down about the adoption on 10 December 1948 of the Universal Declaration of Human Rights (UDHR), before the drafting of a legally binding treaty on human rights was commenced. Indeed, it had been decided in 1947, at only the second session of the UN Commission on Human Rights (the HR Commission), that the HR Commission should draft a Declaration, a human rights treaty (to be called a 'Covenant') and a document setting out measures of implementation. The drafting process for the Covenant ended up taking nearly twenty years and was so difficult to do that, barely half-way through the process, it was declared to be a 'probable failure'. The drafting process involved a range of UN bodies, principally the [Human Rights] Commission (comprised of members voted on by governments and chaired for the first five years by Eleanor Roosevelt), the Economic and Social Council (ECOSOC), which had responsibility for the HR Commission), the Third Committee (being the Committee on Social, Humanitarian and Cultural Questions), and the General Assembly (GA)....

    A participant at the time considered that there were four main reasons underpinning this decision to have separate Covenants: it would enable states to ratify one or other Covenant; CP [Civil and Political Rights] rights were 'rights' to be given effect to promptly, while ESC [Economic, Social and Cultural Rights] rights were 'goals' to be achieved progressively; CP rights would be implemented primarily by legislation, whilst ESC rights would be implemented by a variety of methods, both public and private, would be costly and would not be immediate; and ESC rights could not be defined precisely and were not justiciable by a legal body, in contrast to CP rights....These reasons have proved to be mistaken or overstated, though they were decisive at this point in the drafting process. From this time onwards, two separate Covenants were drafted: one to deal with CP rights and one to deal with ESC rights. Yet, it should not be overlooked that the GA resolution that decided that there were to be two Covenants also affirmed the position that 'the enjoyment of civil and political freedoms and of economic, social and cultural rights are interconnected and interdependent'.

International Covenant on Economic, Social and Cultural Rights 1966

993 UNTS 3

This treaty entered into force on 3 January 1976. As at March 2016, 164 States have ratified the Covenant.

Articles 2–5 set out the general obligations of States under this treaty. Articles 6 to 15 of this Covenant set out the economic, social and cultural rights protected by the Covenant. These are: the right to work (Article 6); right to just and favourable conditions of work (Article 7); right to form and join trade unions (Article 8); right to social security (Article 9); protection of the family (Article 10); right to adequate standard of living (Article 11); right to highest attainable standard of physical and mental health (Article 12); right to education (Article 13); adoption of compulsory, free, primary education (Article 14); right to take part in cultural life, benefit from scientific progress and protection of copyright (Article 15). A few of these Articles are extracted here. Article 1 (right of self-determination) is discussed further in Section 6.

The First Optional Protocol to the Covenant, which entered into force on 5 May 2013, allows individual communications to the Committee on Economic, Social and Cultural Rights. As at March 2016, 21 States have ratified the Optional Protocol.

Article 2

1. Each State Party to the present Covenant undertakes to take steps, individually and through international assistance and cooperation, especially economic and technical, to the maximum of its available resources, with a view to achieving progressively the full realization of the rights recognized in the present Covenant by all appropriate means, including particularly the adoption of legislative measures.

2. The States Parties to the present Covenant undertake to guarantee that the rights enunciated in the present Covenant will be exercised without discrimination of any kind as to race, colour, sex, language, religion, political or other opinion, national or social origin, property, birth or other status.

3. Developing countries, with due regard to human rights and their national economy, may determine to what extent they would guarantee the economic rights recognized in the present Covenant to non-nationals.

Article 3

The States Parties to the present Covenant undertake to ensure the equal right of men and women to the enjoyment of all economic, social and cultural rights set forth in the present Covenant.

Article 4

The States Parties to the present Covenant recognize that, in the enjoyment of those rights provided by the State in conformity with the present Covenant, the State may subject such rights only to such limitations as are determined by law only in so far as this may be compatible with the nature of these rights and solely for the purpose of promoting the general welfare in a democratic society....

Article 5

1. Nothing in the present Covenant may be interpreted as implying for any State, group or person any right to engage in any activity or to perform any act aimed at the destruction of any of the rights or freedoms recognized herein, or at their limitation to a greater extent than is provided for in the present Covenant.

2. No restriction upon or derogation from any of the fundamental human rights recognized or existing in any country in virtue of law, conventions, regulations or custom shall be admitted on the pretext that the present Covenant does not recognize such rights or that it recognizes them to a lesser extent.

Article 7

The States Parties to the present Covenant recognize the right of everyone to the enjoyment of just and favourable conditions of work which ensure, in particular:
  (a) Remuneration which provides all workers, as a minimum, with:
    (i) Fair wages and equal remuneration for work of equal value without distinction of any kind, in particular women being guaranteed conditions of work not inferior to those enjoyed by men, with equal pay for equal work;
    (ii) A decent living for themselves and their families in accordance with the provisions of the present Covenant;
  (b) Safe and healthy working conditions;
  (c) Equal opportunity for everyone to be promoted in his employment to an appropriate higher level, subject to no considerations other than those of seniority and competence;
  (d) Rest, leisure and reasonable limitation of working hours and periodic holidays with pay, as well as remuneration for public holidays....

Article 13

1. The States Parties to the present Covenant recognize the right of everyone to education. They agree that education shall be directed to the full development of the human personality and the sense of its dignity, and shall strengthen the respect for human rights and fundamental freedoms. They further agree that education shall enable all persons to participate effectively in a free society, promote understanding, tolerance and friendship among all nations and all racial, ethnic or religious groups, and further the activities of the United Nations for the maintenance of peace.

2. The States Parties to the present Covenant recognize that, with a view to achieving the full realization of this right:
  (a) Primary education shall be compulsory and available free to all;

(b) Secondary education in its different forms, including technical and vocational secondary education, shall be made generally available and accessible to all by every appropriate means, and in particular by the progressive introduction of free education;

(c) Higher education shall be made equally accessible to all, on the basis of capacity, by every appropriate means, and in particular by the progressive introduction of free education;

(d) Fundamental education shall be encouraged or intensified as far as possible for those persons who have not received or completed the whole period of their primary education;

(e) The development of a system of schools at all levels shall be actively pursued, an adequate fellowship system shall be established, and the material conditions of teaching staff shall be continuously improved.

3. The States Parties to the present Covenant undertake to have respect for the liberty of parents and, when applicable, legal guardians to choose for their children schools, other than those established by the public authorities, which conform to such minimum educational standards as may be laid down or approved by the State and to ensure the religious and moral education of their children in conformity with their own convictions....

International Covenant on Civil and Political Rights 1966
999 UNTS 171

This treaty entered into force on 23 March 1976. As at March 2016, 168 States have ratified this Covenant.

Articles 2–5 set out the general obligations of States under this treaty (with Article 5 being in essentially the same terms as Article 5 of the International Covenant on Economic, Social and Cultural Rights. Articles 6 to 27 set out the civil and political rights protected by the Covenant. These are: the right to life (Article 6); freedom from torture (Article 7); freedom from slavery (Article 8); right to liberty (Articles 9 and 10); freedom from imprisonment for failure to fulfil a contractual obligation (Article 11); freedom of movement (Article 12); freedom from expulsion of an alien (Article 13); right to a fair trial (Article 14); freedom from retroactive criminal laws (Article 15); right to recognition as a person (Article 16); right to privacy (Article 17); freedom of thought, conscience and religion (Article 18); freedom of expression (Article 19); prohibition against war propaganda and national, racial or religious hatred (Article 20); freedom of assembly (Article 21); freedom of association (Article 22); right to marry and found a family (Article 23); rights of a child (Article 24); right to vote and right of participation in political and public life (Article 25); freedom from discrimination (Article 26); rights of ethnic, religious and linguistic minorities (Article 27). Article 1 concerns the right of self-determination (see further Section 6). A few of these Articles are extracted here.

The (First) Optional Protocol to the Covenant, which entered into force on 23 March 1976 and has 115 State parties as at March 2016, enables individual communications to the Human Rights Committee (see further Section 3B). The Second Optional Protocol to the Covenant, which entered into force on 11 July 1991 and has 81 State parties as at March 2016, deals with the abolition of the death penalty.

Article 2

1. Each State Party to the present Covenant undertakes to respect and to ensure to all individuals within its territory and subject to its jurisdiction the rights recognized in the present Covenant, without distinction of any kind, such as race, colour, sex, language, religion, political or other opinion, national or social origin, property, birth or other status.

2. Where not already provided for by existing legislative or other measures, each State Party to the present Covenant undertakes to take the necessary steps, in accordance with its constitutional processes and with the provisions of the present Covenant, to adopt such legislative or other measures as may be necessary to give effect to the rights recognized in the present Covenant.

3. Each State Party to the present Covenant undertakes:

(a) To ensure that any person whose rights or freedoms as herein recognized are violated shall have an effective remedy, notwithstanding that the violation has been committed by persons acting in an official capacity;

(b) To ensure that any person claiming such a remedy shall have his right thereto determined by competent judicial, administrative or legislative authorities, or by any other competent authority provided for by the legal system of the State, and to develop the possibilities of judicial remedy;

(c) To ensure that the competent authorities shall enforce such remedies when granted.

Article 3

The States Parties to the present Covenant undertake to ensure the equal right of men and women to the enjoyment of all civil and political rights set forth in the present Covenant.

Article 4

1. In time of public emergency which threatens the life of the nation and the existence of which is officially proclaimed, the State Parties to the present Covenant may take measure derogating from their obligations under the present Covenant to the extent strictly required by the exigencies of the situation, provided that such measures are not inconsistent with their other obligations under international law and do not involve discrimination solely on the ground of race, colour sex, language, religion or social origin.

2. No derogation from Articles 6, 7, 8 (paragraphs 1 and 2), 11, 15, 16 and 18 may be made under this provision.

3. Any State Party to the present Covenant availing itself of the right of derogation shall immediately inform the other States Parties to the present Covenant, through the intermediary of the Secretary-General of the United Nations of the provisions from which it has derogated and of the reasons by which it was actuated. A further communication shall be made, through the same intermediary on the date on which it terminates such derogation.

Article 5

1. Nothing in the present Covenant may be interpreted as implying for any State, group or person any right to engage in any activity or perform any act aimed at the destruction of any of the rights and freedoms recognized herein or at their limitation to a greater extent than is provided for in the present Covenant.

2. There shall be no restriction upon or derogation from any of the fundamental human rights recognized or existing in any State Party to the present Covenant pursuant to law, conventions, regulations or custom on the pretext that the present Covenant does not recognize such rights or that it recognizes them to a lesser extent.

Article 6

1. Every human being has the inherent right to life. This right shall be protected by law. No one shall be arbitrarily deprived of his life.

2. In countries which have not abolished the death penalty, sentence of death may be imposed only for the most serious crimes in accordance with the law in force at the time of the commission of the crime and not contrary to the provisions of the present Covenant and to the Convention on the Prevention and Punishment of the Crime of Genocide. This penalty can only be carried out pursuant to a final judgment rendered by a competent court....

Article 7

No one shall be subjected to torture or to cruel, inhuman or degrading treatment or punishment. In particular, no one shall be subjected without his free consent to medical or scientific experimentation....

Article 9

1. Everyone has the right to liberty and security of person. No one shall be subjected to arbitrary arrest or detention. No one shall be deprived of his liberty except on such grounds and in accordance with such procedure as are established by law.

2. Anyone who is arrested shall be informed, at the time of arrest, of the reasons for his arrest and shall be promptly informed of any charges against him.

3. Anyone arrested or detained on a criminal charge shall be brought promptly before a judge or other officer authorized by law to exercise judicial power and shall be entitled to trial within a reasonable time or to release. It shall not be the general rule that persons awaiting trial shall be detained in custody, but release may be subject

to guarantees to appear for trial, at any other stage of the judicial proceedings, and, should occasion arise, for execution of the judgement.

4. Anyone who is deprived of his liberty by arrest or detention shall be entitled to take proceedings before a court, in order that that court may decide without delay on the lawfulness of his detention and order his release if the detention is not lawful.

5. Anyone who has been the victim of unlawful arrest or detention shall have an enforceable right to compensation.

Article 19

1. Everyone shall have the right to hold opinions without interference,

2. Everyone shall have the right to freedom of expression; this right shall include freedom to seek, receive and impart information and ideas of all kinds, regardless of frontiers, either orally, in writing or in print, in the form of art, or through any other media of his choice.

3. The exercise of the rights provided for in paragraph 2 of this article carries with it special duties and responsibilities. It may therefore be subject to certain restrictions, but these shall only be such as are provided by law and are necessary:
  (a) For respect of the rights or reputations of others;
  (b) For the protection of national security or of public order (*ordre public*), or of public health or morals....

Article 26

All persons are equal before the law and are entitled without any discrimination to the equal protection of the law. In this respect, the law shall prohibit any discrimination and guarantee to all persons equal and effective protection against discrimination on any ground such as race, colour, sex, language, religion, political or other opinion, national or social origin, property, birth or other status.

Article 27

In those States in which ethnic, religious or linguistic minorities exist, persons belonging to such minorities shall not be denied the right, in community with the other members of their group, to enjoy their own culture, to profess and practice their own religion, or to use their own language.

P. Alston and R. Goodman, *International Human Rights*
(2012)

Differences Between the ICESCR and the ICCPR
The two Covenants use different terminology in relation to each right. Thus where the ICCPR contains terms such as 'everyone has the right to…' or 'no one shall be…', the ICESCR usually employs the formula 'States Parties recognize the right of everyone to…'. There are no major differences in terms of the general obligations clause. Article 2(1) provides that these are subject to the availability of resources ('to the maximum of its available resources'), and that the obligation is one progressive realization ('with a view to achieving progressively').

This language has been subject to conflicting critiques. On the one hand, it is often suggested that the nature of the obligation under the ICESCR is so onerous that virtually no government will be able to comply. Developing countries, in particular, are seen to be confronting an impossible challenge. On the other hand, it is argued that the relative open-endedness of the concept of progressive realization, particularly in light of the qualification about availability of resources, renders the obligation devoid of meaningful content. Governments can present themselves as defenders of ESR [economic and social rights] without international imposition of any precise constraints on their policies and behaviour. A related criticism is that the Covenant imposes only 'programmatic' obligations upon governments—that is, obligations to be fulfilled incrementally through the ongoing execution of a programme. It therefore becomes difficult if not impossible to determine when those obligations ought to be met or indeed have been met.

Interdependence of the Two Covenants
The interdependence of the two categories of rights has always been part of UN doctrine. The UDHR of 1948 included both categories without any sense of separateness or priority. The Preamble to the ICESCR,

in terms mirroring those use in the ICCPR, states that 'in accordance with the Universal Declaration..., the ideal of free human beings enjoying freedom from fear and want can only be achieved if conditions are created whereby everyone may enjoy his economic, social and cultural rights, as well as his civil and political rights'.

The interdependence principle, apart from its use as a political compromise between advocates of one or two covenants, reflects the fact that the two sets of rights can neither logically nor practically be separated in watertight compartments. Civil and political rights may constitute the condition for and thus be implicit in ESR.

Similarly, a given right might fit equally well within either covenant, depending on the purpose for which it is declared. Some illustrations follow:

(1) The right to form trade unions is contained in the ICESCR, while the right to freedom of association is recognized in the ICCPR.

(2) The ICESCR recognizes various 'liberties' and 'freedoms' in relation to scientific research and creative activity.

(3) While the right to education and the parental liberty to choose a child's school are dealt with the ICESCR (Art. 13), the liberty of parents to choose their child's religious and moral education is recognized in the ICCPR (Art. 18).

(4) The prohibition of discrimination in relation to the provision of, and access to, educational facilities and opportunities can be derived from both Article 2 of the ICESCR and Article 26 of the ICCPR.

(5) Even the European Convention on Human Rights, which is generally considered to cover only civil and political rights issues, states (in Art. 2 of Protocol 1) that 'no person shall be denied the right to education'.

NOTES

1. There are a vast array of international human rights treaties and other instruments sponsored by the United Nations which protect a specific right, or which protect a series of rights relating to a specific matter. The major ones include the ones referred to above and, for example, the following: the International Convention on the Elimination of All Forms of Racial Discrimination 1966; the Convention on the Elimination of All Forms of Discrimination against Women 1979; The Convention Against Torture and Other Cruel, Inhumane or Degrading Treatment or Punishment 1984, the Convention on the Rights of the Child 1989; International Convention on the Protection of the Rights of All Migrant Workers and Members of their Families 1990; Convention on the Rights of Persons with Disabilities 2006; Declaration on the Right to Development 1986; Declaration on the Rights of Persons belonging to National or Ethnic, Religious and Linguistic Minorities 1992; and Declaration on the Rights of Indigenous Peoples 2007 (see Section 6A).

2. The proliferation of international instruments protecting specific human rights can be seen as an indication of the growing awareness that broad instruments protecting a wide variety of rights may not be sufficient to protect some rights that do not easily fit within that scheme. Many treaties enable States, and others, to focus on the need to protect a specific right or rights. This proliferation is also an example of the constant evolution of the international community as its members begin to understand about those who are oppressed within societies and who require the protection of human rights instruments. At the same time, there is the criticism that the increasing volume of rights protected can dilute the power and coherence of international human rights law.

3. Most human rights treaties refer to the obligation on a State to protect human rights within its territory and jurisdiction (see, for example, Article 2(1) of the ICCPR). It is generally considered to apply to all human rights treaties unless expressly excluded. This means that a State's obligations extend to actions outside its territory but within its jurisdiction (e.g. the US in relation to Guantanamo Bay—see Chapter 8) and where it has some form of control over another territory or person (e.g. in the decisions of the European Court of Human Rights in *Ilaşcu v Moldova and Russia*, App no 48787/99, ECHR 2004-VII and *Jaloud v The Netherlands*, App no 47708/08, Judgment 2015).

B: Procedure for protecting human rights

The United Nations has created a number of procedures for protecting and promoting human rights and ascertaining where human rights violations occur. Primarily these procedures are through independent bodies established by either general or specific human rights treaties, as well as some inter-governmental bodies operating directly within the United Nations system. The Office of the High Commissioner for Human Rights provides operational and coordination support for both the human rights treaty monitoring bodies and the United Nations Charter-based bodies.

(a) Charter-based bodies

On 19 June 2006 the institutional structure of the UN Charter-based human rights system changed. A Human Rights Council replaced the UN Human Rights Commission, as the latter had become discredited. The Special Procedures of the Human Rights Council—supported by the Office of the High Commissioner for Human Rights—are independent human rights experts with mandates to report and advise on human rights from a thematic or country-specific perspective.

Human Rights Council
General Assembly Resolution 60/251, 15 March 2006

1. Decides to establish the Human Rights Council, based in Geneva, in replacement of the Commission on Human Rights, as a subsidiary organ of the General Assembly; the Assembly shall review the status of the Council within five years;

2. Decides that the Council shall be responsible for promoting universal respect for the protection of all human rights and fundamental freedoms for all, without distinction of any kind and in a fair and equal manner;

3. Decides also that the Council should address situations of violations of human rights, including gross and systematic violations, and make recommendations thereon. It should also promote the effective coordination and the mainstreaming of human rights within the United Nations system.

5. (e) Undertake a universal periodic review, based on objective and reliable information of the fulfilment by each State of its human rights obligations and commitments in a manner which ensures universality of coverage and equal treatment with respect to all States; the review shall be cooperative mechanism based on an interactive dialogue with the full involvement of the country concerned and with consideration given to its capacity-building needs; such a mechanism shall complement and not duplicate the work of treaty-bodies;…

7. Decides further that the Council shall consist of forty-seven Member States, which shall be elected directly and individually by secret ballot by the majority of the members of the General Assembly; the membership shall be based on equitable geographical distribution, and seats shall be distributed as follows among regional groups: Group of African States, thirteen: Group of Asian States, thirteen; Group of Eastern European States, six; Group of Latin American and Caribbean States, eight; and Group of Western European and other States, seven; the members of the Council shall serve for a period of three years and shall not be eligible for re-election after two consecutive terms;

8. …when electing members of the Council, Member States shall take into account the contribution of candidates to the promotion and protection of human rights and their voluntary pledges and commitments made thereto…;

10. Decides further that the Council shall meet regularly throughout the year and schedule not fewer than three sessions per year, including a main session, for a total duration of no less than ten weeks, and shall be able to hold special sessions, when needed, at the request of a member of the Council with the support of one third of the membership of the Council.

Office of the High Commissioner for Human Rights, Procedures

http://www.ohchr.org/EN/HRBodies/SP/Pages/Introduction.aspx

As at March 2016 there are 41 thematic and 14 country mandates.

The system of Special Procedures is a central element of the United Nations human rights machinery and covers all human rights: civil, cultural, economic, political and social. In the context of the 2011 review of its work and functioning, the Human Rights Council reaffirmed the obligation of States to cooperate with the Special Procedures, and the integrity and independence of Special Procedures. It also reaffirmed the principles of cooperation, transparency, and accountability and the role of the system of Special Procedures in enhancing the capacity of the Human Rights Council to address human rights situations. Member States confirmed their strong opposition to reprisals against persons cooperating with the United Nations and its human rights mechanism and representatives....

Special Procedures are either an individual (called 'Special Rapporteur' or 'Independent Expert') or a working group composed of five members, one from each of the five United Nations regional groupings: Africa, Asia, Latin America and the Caribbean, Eastern Europe and the Western group. The Special Rapporteurs, Independent Experts and members of the Working Groups are appointed by the Human Rights Council and serve in their personal capacities. They undertake to uphold independence, efficiency, competence and integrity through probity, impartiality, honesty and good faith. They are not United Nations staff members and do not receive financial remuneration. The independent status of the mandate-holder is crucial for them to be able to fulfill their functions in all impartiality. A mandate-holder's tenure in a given function, whether it is a thematic or country mandate, is limited to a maximum of six years.

With the support of the Office of the United Nations High Commissioner for Human Rights (OHCHR), Special Procedures undertake country visits; act on individual cases of alleged violations and concerns of a broader, structural nature by sending communications to States; conduct thematic studies and convene expert consultations, contributing to the development of international human rights standards; engage in advocacy and raise public awareness; and provide advice for technical cooperation. Special Procedures report annually to the Human Rights Council and the majority of the mandates also report to the General Assembly.

NOTES

1. The establishment of the Human Rights Council was a significant change for the UN Charter-based human rights system. As seen in the extract above, it reports directly to the General Assembly and the 47 States which are voted on to this Council (using the usual UN geographical distribution of seats) serve for three-year terms and can have no more than two consecutive terms.

2. In June 2007, the Human Rights Council passed resolution 5/1, entitled 'UN Human Rights Council: Institution Building', which created a revised complaints procedure. The procedure creates two working groups—the Working Group on Communications (being 5 independent experts) and the Working Group on Situations (being 5 members of the Council)—which examine communications sent to them by individuals and groups, and who have the responsibility to bring to the attention of the Council consistent patterns of gross and reliably attested violations of human rights. This system is criticised as it is a confidential system, which is disappointing in terms of publicity, there is a strong State involvement in the decision-making, and it cannot deal with the individual or group complaint directly, as the procedure only seeks to discern consistent patterns of gross and reliably attested violations of human rights. However, in contrast to the human rights treaty system, this complaints system applies to every State in the world.

3. The Human Rights Council has an Advisory Committee, which replaces the former Sub-Commission on the Promotion and Protection of Human Rights. This is composed of 18 independent experts and is intended to assist the Council on general human rights matters.

4. The Security Council can make a decision on a matter which concerns human rights, if it considers that a threat to international peace and security is involved (see Chapter 15). Those decisions are binding on all member States of the United Nations, as provided by Article 25 of the United Nations Charter. Thus the Security Council has made decisions in regard to South Africa's apartheid system and its presence in Namibia and in respect of Iraq's actions during the 1990–91 Gulf War, particularly concerning the Kurds. The Security Council can also create new institutions to deal with violations of human rights such as the international criminal tribunals considering matters in Yugoslavia and Rwanda (see further Chapter 14).

5. Many United Nations organisations have some responsibility for issues that concern the protection of specific human rights, such as the United Nations Educational, Scientific and Cultural Organization (UNESCO), the World Health Organization (WHO), and even the World Bank, which should consider human rights breaches and environmental matters when deciding on funding (see Chapter 13). The International Labour Organization (ILO) is particularly active in regard to labour rights, with ILO representatives (who are not limited to States) being able to complain about abuses of these rights, and each State is required to produce an annual report.

(b) Treaty-based bodies

A number of human rights treaty bodies monitor the implementation of international human rights treaties, for example, the Human Rights Committee (CCPR), Committee on Economic, Social and Cultural Rights (CESCR), Committee on the Elimination of Racial Discrimination (CERD), Committee on the Elimination of Discrimination Against Women (CEDAW), Committee Against Torture (CAT), Committee on the Rights of the Child (CRC), Committee on Migrant Workers (CMW), Committee on the Rights of Persons with Disabilities (CRPD) and Committee on Enforced Disappearances (CED). These are all composed of independent experts, ranging from 10 to 25 in number.

A. Boyle and C. Chinkin, *The Making of International Law*
(2007)

The evolution of human rights treaties is in part the responsibility of the parties, through the adoption of protocols that add new substantive provisions or procedures…In these cases negotiation and adoption will take place through the relevant intergovernmental institutions.…But human rights treaties also make use of independent, expert bodies to receive reports on and monitor treaty compliance, and in some cases to make recommendations and give opinions on the interpretation of a treaty as a 'living instrument'. The UN human rights institutions provide a good example of how these independent specialist bodies can interact with states in evolving law-making.

Members of the Human Rights Committee, established by the ICCPR, are not state delegates but are elected for their individual expertise. Similar committees have been established under other human rights treaties. Through a range of activities, including the adoption of General Comments and Recommendations, asking questions of states' representatives at periodic reporting sessions, adopting Concluding Comments to the reporting procedure, and issuing opinions in response to individual complaints, these human rights treaty bodies have articulated their understanding of the requirements of their respective treaties. Their statements may either be viewed as interpretive of the treaty provisions, or as going beyond the treaty and as such developing the law.

For example, there is no specific provision on violence against women in the Convention on the Elimination of All Forms of Discrimination against Women, an obvious omission. In 1992, the Committee on the Elimination of Discrimination against Women adopted General Recommendation No. 19 on Violence against Women. It rooted this Recommendation firmly in the Convention by emphasizing that violence against women is a form of discrimination that prevents women's enjoyment of their Convention rights on a basis of equality with men. The General Recommendation shows how specific articles of CEDAW are violated by violence against women. While the Recommendation contains innovative provisions (for example the definition of gender-based violence), it is drafted so as to derive its legal authority from the Convention itself. States parties are accordingly expected to report on the measures taken to comply with the Recommendation and are questioned upon them by the Committee. On this basis it is now clear that violence against women may violate human rights treaty obligations.

Human Rights Committee, General Comment 31, 'Nature of the General Legal Obligations on States Parties to the Covenant'
UN Doc CCPR/C/21/Rev 1/Add 13 (2004)

Article 40(4) of the International Covenant on Civil and Political Rights (ICCPR) allows the Human Rights Committee to issue 'general comments' to States concerning compliance with the ICCPR. These general comments clarify the obligations of States under the ICCPR.

3. Article 2 defines the scope of the legal obligations undertaken by States Parties to the Covenant. A general obligation is imposed on States Parties to respect the Covenant rights and to ensure them to all individuals in their territory and subject to their jurisdiction.

4. ... Although article 2, paragraph 2, allows States Parties to give effect to Covenant rights in accordance with domestic constitutional processes, the same principle operates so as to prevent States parties from invoking provisions of the constitutional law or other aspects of domestic law to justify a failure to perform or give effect to obligations under the treaty. In this respect, the Committee reminds States Parties with a federal structure of the terms of article 50, according to which the Covenant's provisions 'shall extend to all parts of federal states without any limitations or exceptions'.

5. The article 2, paragraph 1, obligation to respect and ensure the rights recognized by in the Covenant has immediate effect for all States parties. Article 2, paragraph 2, provides the overarching framework within which the rights specified in the Covenant are to be promoted and protected. The Committee has as a consequence previously indicated in its General Comment 24 that reservations to article 2 would be incompatible with the Covenant when considered in the light of its objects and purposes.

6. The legal obligation under article 2, paragraph 1, is both negative and positive in nature. States Parties must refrain from violation of the rights recognized by the Covenant, and any restrictions on any of those rights must be permissible under the relevant provisions of the Covenant. Where such restrictions are made, States must demonstrate their necessity and only take such measures as are proportionate to the pursuance of legitimate aims in order to ensure continuous and effective protection of Covenant rights. In no case may the restrictions be applied or invoked in a manner that would impair the essence of a Covenant right.

8. The article 2, paragraph 1, obligations are binding on States [Parties] and do not, as such, have direct horizontal effect as a matter of international law. The Covenant cannot be viewed as a substitute for domestic criminal or civil law. However the positive obligations on States Parties to ensure Covenant rights will only be fully discharged if individuals are protected by the State, not just against violations of Covenant rights by its agents, but also against acts committed by private persons or entities that would impair the enjoyment of Covenant rights in so far as they are amenable to application between private persons or entities. There may be circumstances in which a failure to ensure Covenant rights as required by article 2 would give rise to violations by States Parties of those rights, as a result of States Parties permitting or failing to take appropriate measures or to exercise due diligence to prevent, punish, investigate or redress the harm caused by such acts by private persons or entities. States are reminded of the interrelationship between the positive obligations imposed under article 2 and the need to provide effective remedies in the event of breach under article 2, paragraph 3. The Covenant itself envisages in some articles certain areas where there are positive obligations on States Parties to address the activities of private persons or entities. For example, [it is] implicit in article 7 that States Parties have to take positive measures to ensure that private persons or entities do not inflict torture or cruel, inhuman or degrading treatment or punishment on others within their power.

10. States Parties are required by article 2, paragraph 1, to respect and to ensure the Covenant rights to all persons who may be within their territory and to all persons subject to their jurisdiction. This means that a State party must respect and ensure the rights laid down in the Covenant to anyone within the power or effective control of that State Party, even if not situated within the territory of the State Party.

12. Moreover, the article 2 obligation requiring that States Parties respect and ensure the Covenant rights for all persons in their territory and all persons under their control entails an obligation not to extradite, deport, expel or otherwise remove a person from their territory, where there are substantial grounds for believing that there is a real risk of irreparable harm, such as that contemplated by articles 6 and 7 of the Covenant, either in the country to which removal is to be effected or in any country to which the person may subsequently be removed.

14. The requirement under article 2, paragraph 2, to take steps to give effect to the Covenant rights is unqualified and of immediate effect. A failure to comply with this obligation cannot be justified by reference to political, social, cultural or economic considerations within the State.

16. Article 2, paragraph 3, requires that States Parties make reparation to individuals whose Covenant rights have been violated. Without reparation to individuals whose Covenant rights have been violated, the obligation to provide an effective remedy, which is central to the efficacy of article 2, paragraph 3, is not discharged.

Committee on Economic, Social and Cultural Rights, General Comment 3: 'The Nature of States Parties Obligations'

UN Doc E/1991/23 (1994) 6

No supervisory body was provided for in the International Covenant on Economic, Social and Cultural Rights (ICESCR) to consider compliance by State parties with that Covenant. Only in 1986 was the Committee on Economic, Social and Cultural Rights (CESCR) set up as a supervisory body to review the annual reports of States on compliance with the ICESCR.

1. Article 2 is of particular importance to a full understanding of the Covenant and must be seen as having a dynamic relationship with all the other provisions of the Covenant. It describes the nature of the general legal obligations undertaken by States parties to the Covenant. These obligations include both what may be termed (following the work of the International Law Commission) obligations of conduct and obligations of result. While great emphasis has sometimes been placed on the difference between the formulations used in this provision and that contained in the equivalent article 2 of the [ICCPR], it is not always recognized that there are also significant similarities. In particular, while the Covenant provides for progressive realization and acknowledges the constraints due to the limits of available resources, it also imposes various obligations which are of immediate effect....

2. ...Thus while the full realization of the relevant rights may be achieved progressively, steps towards that goal must be taken within a reasonably short time after the Covenant's entry into force for the States concerned. Such steps should be deliberate, concrete and targeted as clearly as possible to meeting the obligations recognized in the Covenant.

3. ...In fields such as health, the protection of children and mothers, and education, as well as in respect of the matters dealt with in articles 6 to 9, legislation may also be an indispensable element for many purposes.

4. ...However, the ultimate determination as to whether all appropriate measures have been taken [by a State] remains one for the Committee to take.

5. Among the measures which might be considered appropriate, in addition to legislation, is the provision of judicial remedies with respect to rights which may, in accordance with the national legal system, be considered justiciable. The Committee notes, for example that the enjoyment of the rights recognized, without discrimination, will often be appropriately promoted, in part, through the provision of judicial or other effective remedies. Indeed, those States parties which are also parties to the [ICCPR] are already obligated (by virtue of arts. 2 (paragraphs 1 and 3), 3 and 26) of that Covenant to ensure that any person whose rights or freedoms (including the right to equality and non-discrimination) recognized in that Covenant are violated, 'shall have an effective remedy' (Article 2(3)(a)). In addition, there are a number of other provisions in the [ICESCR], including articles 3, 7(a)(i), 8, 10(3), 13(2)(a), (3) and (4) and 15(3) which would seem to be capable of immediate application by judicial and other organs in many national legal systems. Any suggestion that the provisions indicated are inherently non-self-executing would seem to be difficult to sustain.

8. The Committee notes that the undertaking 'to take steps...by all appropriate means including particularly the adoption of legislative measures' neither requires nor precludes any particular form of government or economic system being used as the vehicle for the steps in question, provided only that it is democratic and that all human rights are thereby respected. Thus, in terms of political and economic systems the Covenant is neutral.

9. ...The concept of progressive realization constitutes a recognition of the fact that full realization of all economic, social and cultural rights will generally not be able to be achieved in a short period of time. In this sense the obligation differs significantly from that contained in article 2 of the [ICCPR] which embodies an immediate obligation to respect and ensure all of the relevant rights. Nevertheless, the fact that realization over time, or in other words progressively, is foreseen under the Covenant should not be misinterpreted as depriving the obligation of all meaningful content. It is on the one hand a necessary flexibility device, reflecting the realities of the real world and the difficulties involved for any country in ensuring full realization of economic, social and cultural rights. On the other hand, the phrase must be read in the light of the overall objective, indeed the *raison d'être*, of the Covenant which is to establish clear obligations for States parties in respect of the full realization of the rights in question. It thus imposes an obligation to move as expeditiously and effectively as possible towards that goal. Moreover, any deliberately retrogressive measures in that regard would require the most careful

consideration and would need to be fully justified by reference to the totality of the rights provided for in the Covenant and in the context of the full use of the maximum available resources.

10. On the basis of the extensive experience gained by the Committee, as well as the body that preceded it, over a period of more than a decade of examining States parties' reports, the Committee is of the view that a minimum core obligation to ensure the satisfaction of, at the very least, minimum essential levels of each of the rights in incumbent upon every State party. Thus, for example, a State party in which any significant number of individuals is deprived of essential foodstuffs, of essential primary health care, of basic shelter and housing, or of the most basic forms of education is, prima facie, failing to discharge its obligations under the Covenant. If the Covenant were to be read in such a way as not to establish such a minimum core obligation, it would be largely deprived of its *raison d'être*. By the same token, it must be noted that any assessment as to whether a State has discharged its minimum core obligation must also take account of resource constraints applying within the country concerned....In order for a State party to be able to attribute its failure to meet at least its minimum core obligations to a lack of available resources it must demonstrate that every effort has been made to use all resources that are at its disposition in an effort to satisfy, as a matter of priority, those minimum obligations.

11. The Committee wishes to emphasize, however, that even where the available resources are demonstrably inadequate, the obligation remains for a State party to strive to ensure the widest possible enjoyment of the relevant rights under the prevailing circumstances. Moreover, the obligations to monitor the extent of the realization, or more especially of the non-realization, of economic, social and cultural rights, and to devise strategies and programmes for their promotion, are not in any way eliminated as a result of resource constraints....

12. Similarly, the Committee underlines the fact that even in times of severe resources constraints, whether caused by a process of adjustment, of economic recession, or by other factors, the vulnerable members of society can and indeed must be protected by the adoption of relatively low-cost targeted programmes.

Effect of Reservations on Entry into Force of the American Convention (Articles 74 and 75)

67 *International Legal Materials* 559 (1982), Inter-American Court of Human Rights

The Inter-American Court of Human Rights (see Section 4) was asked to advise on the question: 'From what moment is a State deemed to have become a party to the American Convention on Human Rights when it ratifies or adheres to the Convention with one or more reservations: from the date of the deposit of the instrument of ratification or adherence or upon the termination of the period specified in Article 20 of the Vienna Convention on the Law of Treaties?' (See also Chapter 3, concerning the effects of reservations).

29. The Court must emphasize, however, that modern human rights treaties in general, and the American Convention in particular, are not multilateral treaties of the traditional type concluded to accomplish the reciprocal exchange of rights for the mutual benefit of the contracting States. Their object and purpose is the protection of the basic rights of individual human beings, irrespective of their nationality, both against the State of their nationality and all other contracting States. In concluding these human rights treaties, the States can be deemed to submit themselves to a legal order within which they, for the common good, assume various obligations, not in relation to other States, but towards all individuals within their jurisdiction....

32. It must be emphasized also that the Convention, unlike other international human rights treaties, including the European Convention, confers on private parties the right to file a petition with the Commission against any State as soon as it has ratified the Convention (Convention, Art. 44). By contrast, before one State may institute proceedings against another State, each of them must have accepted the Commission's jurisdiction to deal with inter-State communications. (Convention, Art. 45). This structure indicates the overriding importance the Convention attaches to the commitments of the States Parties *vis-à-vis* individuals, which can be readily implemented without the intervention of any other State.

33. Viewed in this light and considering that the Convention was designed to protect the basic rights of individual human beings irrespective of their nationality, against States of their own nationality or any other

State Party, the Convention must be seen for what in reality it is: a multilateral legal instrument or framework enabling States to make binding unilateral commitments not to violate the human rights of individuals within their jurisdiction.

THE COURT IS OF THE OPINION

By unanimous vote, that the Convention enters into force for a State which ratifies or adheres to it with or without a reservation on the date of the deposit of its instrument of ratification or adherence.

NOTES

1. Each treaty body has slightly different powers and functions from each other body, though there are many similarities between them. There is some overlapping of functions, for example, in areas of non-discrimination; there are some differences in protections provided which can cause concerns about compatibility; and they can create substantial material and logistical difficulties for States, particularly developing States, to provide a number of detailed reports. The appointment of a United Nations High Commissioner for Human Rights in 1993 has led to greater co-ordination between these bodies.

2. The effectiveness of these bodies in leading to increased protection of human rights is not always apparent. It is uncertain that a report-based system leads to any real changes, especially where the State is not subject to internal scrutiny by its population, before or after a report is presented, because of deliberate State restrictions on information. It is difficult to determine the extent to which States comply with recommendations by these bodies, even after a determination on an individual complaint, as any recommendation or determination by these bodies is not usually directly legally binding on the State concerned and the State may not publicly refer to the role of the treaty body in its decision-making. However, many States do comply with the recommendations. The public nature of the monitoring by these bodies and the potential for embarrassment of States when they are condemned for violations of human rights, can have some effect on States' behaviour, even if their response is more dictated by fear of losing investment or diplomatic clout. In this regard, the role of non-governmental organisations can be vital (see Section 8).

3. The obligations of States under human rights treaties are not reciprocal between States. Instead, the State has obligations and individuals or groups have rights, and so each State's obligations are unlikely to be closely monitored by other States (*Effect of Reservations Case*). Therefore, there is a requirement for the international human rights supervisory body itself to ensure that States comply with their obligations.

4. As well as clarifying the general legal obligations of States under human rights treaties, the supervisory bodies can elaborate on the substantive rights themselves. This is part of their role of interpreting the treaty, which the States parties to the treaty have allocated to that body.

5. The UN Security Council can also act to protect human rights. For example, in Resolution 2170 (2014) Condemning Gross, Widespread Abuse of Human Rights in Syria, Iraq, paragraph 1 states that it: 'Deplores and condemns in the strongest terms the terrorist acts of ISIL and its violent extremist ideology, and its continued gross, systematic and widespread abuses of human rights and violations of international humanitarian law'. It then demands that ISIL (the so-called Islamic State), Al Nusra Front and others are held accountable for international human rights violations and requires States to take steps to ensure that those groups responsible are stopped from committing further violations and brought to justice.

C: Customary international law

Even if a State has not ratified a human rights treaty, it could be bound by customary international law to protect some human rights. All States would also be bound when the human right is considered part of *jus cogens* (see Chapter 3 and Article 53 of the Vienna Convention on the Law of Treaties).

Namibia Opinion

ICJ Rep 1971 16, International Court of Justice

The facts of this case are set out in Chapter 3.

131. Under the Charter of the United Nations, the former Mandatory [South Africa] had pledged itself to observe and respect, in a territory having an international status, human rights and fundamental freedoms for all without distinction as to race. To establish instead, and to enforce, distinctions, exclusions, restrictions and limitations exclusively based on grounds of race, colour, descent or national or ethnic origin which constitute a denial of fundamental human rights is a flagrant violation of the purposes and principles of the Charter.

JUDGE AMMOUN (Separate Opinion): [While the provisions of the Universal Declaration of Human Rights] are not binding *qua* international convention within the meaning of Article 38, paragraph 1(a), of the Statute of the Court, they can bind States on the basis of custom within the meaning of paragraph 1(b) of the same Article, whether because they constituted a codification of customary law as was said in respect of Article 6 of the Vienna Convention on the Law of Treaties, or because they have acquired the force of custom through a general practice accepted as law, in the words of Article 38, paragraph 1(b), of the Statute. One right which must certainly be considered a pre-existing binding customary norm which the Universal Declaration of Human Rights codified is the right to equality, which by common consent has ever since the remotest times been deemed inherent in human nature.

The equality demanded by the Namibians and by other peoples of every colour, the right to which is the outcome of prolonged struggles to make it a reality, is something of vital interest to us here, on the one hand because it is the foundation of other human rights which are no more than its corollaries and, on the other, because it naturally rules out racial discrimination and *apartheid*, which are the gravest of the facts with which South Africa, as also other States, stands charged.

Filartiga v Pena-Irala

630 F.2nd 876 (1980), United States Court of Appeals, Second Circuit

This case raised the issue of whether torture was in breach of customary international law. This arises due to the Alien Torts Claims Act 1789, a very unusual legislation in the United States of America (USA), which allows torts claims to be brought in the USA for breaches of 'the law of nations' (or a treaty to which the USA is a party), no matter where the tort itself occurred.

12. In light of the universal condemnation of torture in numerous international agreements, and the renunciation of torture as an instrument of official policy by virtually all of the nations of the world (in principle if not in practice), we find that an act of torture committed by a state official against one held in detention violates established norms of the international law of human rights, and hence the law of nations.... The United Nations Charter (a treaty of the United States, see 59 Stat. 1033 (1945)) makes it clear that in this modern age a state's treatment of its own citizens is a matter of international concern....

24. For although there is no universal agreement as to the precise extent of the 'human rights and fundamental freedoms' guaranteed to all by the Charter, there is at present no dissent from the view that the guarantees include, at a bare minimum, the right to be free from torture. This prohibition has become part of customary international law, as evidenced and defined by the Universal Declaration of Human Rights, General Assembly Resolution 217 (III)(A) (Dec. 10, 1948) which states, in the plainest of terms 'no one shall be subjected to torture.' The General Assembly has declared that the Charter precepts embodied in this Universal Declaration 'constitute basic principles of international law.' G.A.Res. 2625 (XXV) (Oct. 24, 1970)....

26. These UN declarations are significant because they specify with great precision the obligations of member nations under the Charter. Since their adoption, '[m]embers can no longer contend that they do not know what human rights they promised in the Charter to promote' [Sohn, *The United Nations and Human Rights* (Commission to Study the Organization of Peace 1968)]. Moreover, a UN Declaration is, according to one authoritative definition, 'a formal and solemn instrument, suitable for rare occasions when principles of great and lasting

importance are being enunciated' [34 U.N. ESCOR, Supp. (No. 8) 15, U.N. Doc. E/cn.4/1/610 (1962) (memorandum of Office of Legal Affairs, UN Secretariat)]. Accordingly, it has been observed that the Universal Declaration of Human Rights 'no longer fits into the dichotomy of "binding treaty" against "non-binding pronouncement," but is rather an authoritative statement of the international community.' [E. Schwelb, *Human Rights and the International Community* 70 (1964)]. Thus, a Declaration creates an expectation of adherence, and 'insofar as the expectation is gradually justified by State practice, a declaration may by custom become recognized as laying down rules binding upon the States.' 34 UN ESCOR, *supra*. Indeed, several commentators have concluded that the Universal Declaration has become *in toto*, a part of binding, customary international law....

27. Turning to the act of torture, we have little difficulty discerning its universal renunciation in the modern usage and practice of nations.

32. Having examined the sources from which customary international law is derived the usage of nations, judicial opinions and the works of jurists we conclude that official torture is now prohibited by the law of nations. The prohibition is clear and unambiguous, and admits of no distinction between treatment of aliens and citizens....The treaties and accords cited above, as well as the express foreign policy of our own government, all make it clear that international law confers fundamental rights upon all people vis-à-vis their own governments. While the ultimate scope of those rights will be a subject for continuing refinement and elaboration, we hold that the right to be free from torture is now among them.

54. In the twentieth century the international community has come to recognize the common danger posed by the flagrant disregard of basic human rights and particularly the right to be free of torture....Indeed, for purposes of civil liability, the torturer has become like the pirate and slave trader before him *hostis humani generis*, an enemy of all mankind. Our holding today, giving effect to a jurisdictional provision enacted by our First Congress, is a small but important step in the fulfillment of the ageless dream to free all people from brutal violence.

Prosecutor v *Furundzija*

Case No. IT-95-17/1-T, Judgment (1998), International Criminal Tribunal for the Former Yugoslavia

This case involved war crimes under the International Criminal Tribunal for the former Yugoslavia, one of the international tribunals established by the United Nations (see Chapter 14).

147. There exists today universal revulsion against torture: as a USA Court put it in *Filartiga v. Pena-Irala*, 'the torturer has become, like the pirate and the slave trader before him, hostis humani generis, an enemy of all mankind'. This revulsion, as well as the importance States attach to the eradication of torture, has led to the cluster of treaty and customary rules on torture acquiring a particularly high status in the international normative system, a status similar to that of principles such as those prohibiting genocide, slavery, racial discrimination, aggression, the acquisition of territory by force and the forcible suppression of the right of peoples to self-determination. The prohibition against torture exhibits three important features, which are probably held in common with the other general principles protecting fundamental human rights.

(a) The Prohibition Even Covers Potential Breaches

148. Firstly, given the importance that the international community attaches to the protection of individuals from torture, the prohibition against torture is particularly stringent and sweeping. States are obliged not only to prohibit and punish torture, but also to forestall its occurrence: it is insufficient merely to intervene after the infliction of torture, when the physical or moral integrity of human beings has already been irremediably harmed. Consequently, States are bound to put in place all those measures that may pre-empt the perpetration of torture. As was authoritatively held by the European Court of Human Rights in [*Soering* v *United Kingdom* II ECHR (ref A) (1989)], international law intends to bar not only actual breaches but also potential breaches of the prohibition against torture (as well as any inhuman and degrading treatment). It follows that international rules prohibit not only torture but also (i) the failure to adopt the national measures necessary for implementing the prohibition and (ii) the maintenance in force or passage of laws which are contrary to the prohibition.

(b) The Prohibition Imposes Obligations *Erga Omnes*

151. Furthermore, the prohibition of torture imposes upon States obligations *erga omnes*, that is, obligations owed towards all the other members of the international community, each of which then has a correlative right. In addition, the violation of such an obligation simultaneously constitutes a breach of the correlative right of all members of the

international community and gives rise to a claim for compliance accruing to each and every member, which then has the right to insist on fulfilment of the obligation or in any case to call for the breach to be discontinued.

152. Where there exist international bodies charged with impartially monitoring compliance with treaty provisions on torture, these bodies enjoy priority over individual States in establishing whether a certain State has taken all the necessary measures to prevent and punish torture and, if they have not, in calling upon that State to fulfil its international obligations. The existence of such international mechanisms makes it possible for compliance with international law to be ensured in a neutral and impartial manner.

(c) The Prohibition Has Acquired the Status of *Jus Cogens*

153. While the *erga omnes* nature just mentioned appertains to the area of international enforcement (*lato sensu*), the other major feature of the principle proscribing torture relates to the hierarchy of rules in the international normative order. Because of the importance of the values it protects, this principle has evolved into a peremptory norm or *jus cogens*, that is, a norm that enjoys a higher rank in the international hierarchy than treaty law and even 'ordinary' customary rules. The most conspicuous consequence of this higher rank is that the principle at issue cannot be derogated from by States through international treaties or local or special customs or even general customary rules not endowed with the same normative force.

154. Clearly, the *jus cogens* nature of the prohibition against torture articulates the notion that the prohibition has now become one of the most fundamental standards of the international community. Furthermore, this prohibition is designed to produce a deterrent effect, in that it signals to all members of the international community and the individuals over whom they wield authority that the prohibition of torture is an absolute value from which nobody must deviate.

155. The fact that torture is prohibited by a peremptory norm of international law has other effects at the inter-state and individual levels....In short, in spite of possible national authorisation by legislative or judicial bodies to violate the principle banning torture, individuals remain bound to comply with that principle. As the International Military Tribunal at Nuremberg put it: 'individuals have international duties which transcend the national obligations of obedience imposed by the individual State'.

156. Furthermore, at the individual level, that is, that of criminal liability, it would seem that one of the consequences of the *jus cogens* character bestowed by the international community upon the prohibition of torture is that every State is entitled to investigate, prosecute and punish or extradite individuals accused of torture, who are present in a territory under its jurisdiction. Indeed, it would be inconsistent on the one hand to prohibit torture to such an extent as to restrict the normally unfettered treaty-making power of sovereign States, and on the other hand bar States from prosecuting and punishing those torturers who have engaged in this odious practice abroad. This legal basis for States' universal jurisdiction over torture bears out and strengthens the legal foundation for such jurisdiction found by other courts in the inherently universal character of the crime.

157. It would seem that other consequences include the fact that torture may not be covered by a statute of limitations, and must not be excluded from extradition under any political offence exemption.

A v *Secretary of State for the Home Department (No 2)*
[2005] UKHL 71, United Kingdom House of Lords

This case concerned the extent to which torture could be used as evidence before a British court. This case should not be confused with *A v Secretary of State for the Home Department* [2004] UKHL 56, regarding the UK government's actions against terrorism (see Derogations in Section 5C).

HELD: It is common ground in these proceedings that the international prohibition of the use of torture enjoys the enhanced status of a *jus cogens* or peremptory norm of general international law....In *R v Bow Street Metropolitan Stipendiary Magistrate, Ex p Pinochet Ugarte (No 3)* [2000] 1 AC 147, 197–199, the *jus cogens* nature of the international crime of torture, the subject of universal jurisdiction, was recognised. The implications of this finding were fully and authoritatively explained by the International Criminal Tribunal for the Former Yugoslavia in *Prosecutor v Furundzija* [1998] ICTY....

There can be few issues on which international legal opinion is more clear than on the condemnation of torture. Offenders have been recognised as the 'common enemies of mankind' (*Demjanjuk v Petrovsky* 612 F Supp

544 (1985), 566), Lord Cooke of Thorndon has described the right not to be subjected to inhuman treatment as a 'right inherent in the concept of civilisation' (*Higgs v Minister of National Security* [2000] 2 AC 228, 260), the Ninth Circuit Court of Appeals has described the right to be free from torture as 'fundamental and universal' (*Siderman de Blake v Argentina* 965 F 2d 699 (1992), 717) and the UN Special Rapporteur on Torture (Mr Peter Koojimans) has said that '[If ever a phenomenon was outlawed unreservedly and unequivocally it is torture' (Report of the Special Rapporteur on Torture, E/CN.4/1986/15, para 3).

H. Thirlway, 'Human Rights in Customary Law: An Attempt to Define some of the Issues'
28 *Leiden Journal of International Law* (2015)

It appears to be still a perfectly tenable view that there is in fact no general international customary law of human rights, all the existing rights and obligations of states in this domain (with some exceptions) being based, mediately or immediately, on treaty commitments, or on general international declarations that have in some manner (but what manner?) a similar degree of binding force. This is not however the universal view; for a number of scholars, there are norms of human rights law that are custom-based, although generally these are seen as somehow deriving from an adaptation of international instruments, rather than as having emerged from the interchange of state relations that normally constitutes the material element of custom. Thus for Buergenthal, some of the provisions of the Universal Declaration of Human Rights are 'deemed to have become customary international law' (but what is the force and nature of that 'deeming' process?).

The view that there is as yet no customary law in this field is supported by (or perhaps derives from) the virtual absence of state practice in the traditional sense. One reason for this is the domination of the field by treaty instruments…, and by tribunals established to oversee their workings, so that there exists a large measure of protection of human rights without any need for custom to play a role. At the risk of stating the obvious, however, one may note that there would seem to be a basic theoretical difficulty with the operation of traditional custom-formation in the field of human rights. International custom has traditionally derived from practice in the form of the effective interrelation of equal sovereign states….In principle, it results from acts (or omissions) with an inter-state aspect. Historically, states have recognized the legality of another state's action, or the validity of a claim made, if the state concerned considers that, in the reverse case, it would expect or desire that its act would be accepted, or its claim be regarded as valid. The basis of such relations may be crudely expressed as 'do as you would be done by'. The rights that emerge in this way, and the obligations that are the counterpart of those rights, are the rights and obligations of states toward one another. Seen in this light, the basis of customary law, it may be suggested, is less consent than potential reciprocity. On that basis, states that have not reacted need not be taken to have consented, but merely to have tacitly recognized the merits of the solution arrived at; and similarly the recognition of individual human rights does not need to be seen as something actively consented to.

A right recognized as (or claimed to be) a 'human right' is however, as its name implies, initially a right belonging to an individual human being, or a group of individuals. The corresponding obligation will (for our present purposes) generally rest on a state, but a state as seen from within and below, as it were, rather than a state seen laterally as an equal. A state may be obliged to respect the human rights of its citizens and the persons or groups within its territory; and an obligation to respect human rights may of course also rest on other individuals or groups, normally also within that territory. In either case, however, this obligation will exist because such is the domestic law of the state whose legislation is applicable, not (or not directly) as a matter of international law….

Taking these difficulties into account, it may be that little has changed since Oscar Schachter noted, as long ago as 1991, that 'whether human rights obligations have become customary law cannot readily be answered on the basis of the usual process of customary law formation', and that none of the items of 'evidence' of custom advanced in support of a finding that human rights are part of customary law 'conform to the traditional criteria'. A tentative conclusion may be that, if there is a customary law of human rights, its processes of formation, while involving both a factual and a conceptual element, are not necessarily identical with those of general international law, and might therefore have to be given special examination by the [International Law Commission] in the present context.

NOTES
1. The cases above make a powerful argument that some human rights are a matter of customary international law and so bind all States. They go further to suggest that there are some human rights that are matters of *jus cogens*, so that there are no circumstances in which a State— or non-State actor—can argue that there are legitimate exceptions to their protection. In

reaching their conclusions, each of these national and international courts and tribunals rely on treaties, UN resolutions and other State practice and *opinio juris*, as well as making extensive cross-references to each other. The latter action makes for good and healthy comparative law, leading to a stronger international legal position, though Thirlway shows the difficulty in finding separate State practice outside the treaty bodies to discern customary international law in this area.

2. These cases are uniform in accepting that the prohibition on torture is a matter of *jus cogens*. Indeed, the International Court of Justice reaffirmed this in *Questions Concerning the Obligation to Prosecute or Extradite (Belgium v Senegal)* Judgment, ICJ Reports 2012, para. 99. Other rights, such as the right to life, freedom from slavery, freedom from racial discrimination, prohibition on genocide (and see other international criminal issues in Chapter 14), and the right of self-determination (see further Section 6), can be considered to be customary international law and so binding on States which have not ratified treaties to protect those rights. Indeed, some of these rights may be *jus cogens* (see Chapter 3).

3. Despite the suggestion in the *Filartiga Case*, it was unclear if the entire Universal Declaration of Human Rights (UDHR) embodies customary international law. While it does not bind States as a treaty obligation, it may reflect ideals held by the international community. Any consideration of it as customary international law can only be made after an article-by-article examination, as was done in *Filartiga v Pena-Irala* in regard to the prohibition on torture. Nevertheless, the UDHR has significantly influenced other international, regional and national human rights agreements.

4. In the Universal Periodic Review undertaken by the Human Rights Committee (see Section 3B(b)), the human rights obligations addressed include those under the UDHR, in addition to human rights treaties to which a State is a party, the UN Charter and applicable international humanitarian law (see Human Rights Council Resolution 5/1, 18 June 2007). As the Universal Periodic Review applies to all States, this is a significant step towards the position that the entire UDHR is assumed to be customary international law.

SECTION 4: REGIONAL HUMAN RIGHTS PROTECTIONS

There are three regions where broad-based, binding human rights treaties have been ratified: Europe; the Americas; and Africa. This section will set out some specific and distinct aspects of each regional human rights system, as well as the rationale for a regional human rights system. The principal treaties are not extracted here, nor are any detailed materials, as these are readily available elsewhere.

Commission to Study the Organization of Peace, *Regional Promotion and Protection of Human Rights*

(1980)

[There are] four grounds [for favouring regional human rights systems]: (1) the existence of geographic, historical, and cultural bonds among States of a particular region; (2) the fact that recommendations of a regional organization may meet with less resistance than those of a global body; (3) the likelihood that publicity about human rights will be wider and more effective; and (4) the fact that there is less possibility of 'general, compromise formulae,' which in global bodies are more likely to be based on 'considerations of a political nature'....

Opposition to the establishment of regional human rights commissions has been expressed on numerous occasions by the Eastern European States and other Members of the United Nations, on several grounds. First, they argue that human rights, being global in nature and belonging to everyone, should be defined in global instruments and implemented by global bodies. 'The African and the Asian should have the same human rights as the European or the American.' Second, regional bodies in the human rights field would, at best, duplicate the work of United Nations bodies and, at worst, develop contradictory policies and procedures.... Third, the Eastern European States in particular object that any cooperation between regional commissions and the United Nations would add to the financial burdens of the latter. Fourth, several Western European States contend that preoccupation with regional arrangements might deflect official and public attention from the two International Covenants and delay their ratification.

It may be argued that the global approach and the regional approach to promotion and protection of human rights are not necessarily incompatible; on the contrary, they are both useful and complementary. The two approaches can be reconciled on a functional basis: the normative content of all international instruments, both global and regional, should be similar in principle, reflecting the Universal Declaration of Human Rights, which was proclaimed 'as a common standard of achievement for all peoples and all nations.' The global instrument would contain the minimum normative standard, whereas the regional instrument might go further, add further rights, refine some rights, and take into account special differences within the region and between one region and another.

Thus what at first glance might seem to be a serious dichotomy—the global approach and the regional approach to human rights—has been resolved satisfactorily on a functional basis....

The further question arises whether if human rights commissions were established in certain regions, they might interpret international standards too narrowly and thus adversely affect the work of global bodies in this field. It might be necessary in such a case to establish the right of global institutions to consider a particular matter *de novo*.

K. Starmer and T. Christou, *Human Rights Manual and Sourcebook for Africa*

(2005)

Africa

- The African Charter on Human and Peoples' Rights (ACHPR) was adopted in 1981 by the Organization of African Unity and entered into force in 1986. It is monitored by the African Commission on Human and Peoples' Rights (ACmHPR).
- The ACmHPR, established by the ACHPR, is charged with ensuring the promotion and protection of human and peoples' rights throughout the African Continent...The Commission is empowered to receive and consider Communications submitted by States, individuals and organizations alleging that a State party to the Charter has violated one or more rights guaranteed therein...The mandate of the Commission is quasi-judicial and as such, its final recommendations are not in themselves legally binding on the States concerned....
- The African Court on Human and Peoples' Rights was created under the Protocol to the ACHPR adopted in 1998 [and entered into force] on 25 January 2004....The Court's *ratione personae* competence comprises two types of jurisdiction: compulsory and optional. The optional jurisdiction relates to cases submitted by individuals or non-governmental organizations with observer status before the African Commission...

America

- The American Declaration on the Rights and Duties of Man (ADRM) was adopted in 1948 by the Ninth Inter-American Conference, which also adopted the Charter of the Organization of American States (OAS).
- The American Convention on Human Rights (ACHR) was adopted in 1969 and came into force in 1978. It provides for the Inter-American Commission on Human Rights and the Inter-American Court of Human Rights to have competence to hear cases and receive reports.
- The Inter-American Commission on Human Rights (IACmHR)...has the principle function of promoting the observance and the defense of human rights. In carrying out its mandate, the Commission can receive individual petitions which allege human rights violations and submit cases to the Inter-American Court and appears before the Court in the litigation of cases. The Commission may only process individual cases where it is alleged that one of the Member States of the OAS is responsible for the human rights violation at issue.
- The Inter-American Court of Human Rights (IACtHR) created by the entry into force of the American Convention on Human Rights in 1978, is an autonomous judicial institution whose purpose is the application and interpretation of the Convention...The Court has adjudicatory and advisory jurisdiction.

Europe

- The European Convention for the Protection of Human Rights and Fundamental Freedoms (ECHR) entered into force in 1953. Ratification of or accession to the ECHR is a condition of joining the Council of Europe. It provides for the European Court of Human Rights (ECtHR) to have competence to hear cases. Before its abolition, the European Commission of Human Rights also had competence to hear cases. Protocol No 11, which came into force on 1 November 1998, [replaced the] part-time Court and Commission with a single, full-time Court...[In 2004, Protocol No 14 came into force, which was to modify the procedures of the ECHR, specifically to restrict admissibility for the increasing number of individual applications.]

- ...Any Contracting State (State application) or individual claiming to be a victim of a violation of the Convention (individual application) may lodge an application directly with the Court in Strasbourg alleging a breach by a Contracting State of one of the Convention rights...Member States have undertaken to respect the final judgment of the Court in any action to which they are a party. However, a final judgment of the Court is not binding on States and will not have the effect of quashing national decisions or striking down legislation.

J. Cavallaro and S. Brewer, 'Re-evaluating Regional Human Rights Litigation in the Twenty-First Century: The Case of the Inter-American Court'

102 *American Journal of International Law* 768 (2008)

Since the creation of the Inter-American Court [of Human Rights], its jurisprudence has evolved and expanded in several ways. First, the Court has recognized an increasing array of situations in which governments incur responsibility for rights violations. For instance, the Court will hold states accountable for a violation of the right to life not only if state agents kill a victim, but also if the state fails to take positive measures to protect victims from imminent harm or to provide known groups of vulnerable victims with basic services needed for life. Overall, the Court has developed increasingly detailed and sometimes quite progressive understandings of the requirements of the system's human rights instruments, often drawing on developments from other systems such as the jurisprudence of the European Court, as well as on a growing universe of international declarations and norms. Finally, the range of the Court's reparations orders has expanded.

The Court's sometimes progressive explications of protected human rights, frequently framed by reference to an overarching global system of human rights norms, enrich the content of inter-American jurisprudence, following (and on occasion leading) international legal understandings. However, while pushing the legal boundaries of human rights at the global level would necessarily translate into better human rights practices if states obeyed Court orders to the letter, here and elsewhere we have argued that this focus is potentially misplaced given the actual relationship between Court jurisprudence and its reception by many Latin American states. Indeed, the Court continues to face passive noncompliance with even basic, established lines of jurisprudence (for instance, that states are obligated to investigate violations of the right to life committed by their own agents), as well as occasional explicit challenges to its authority. In this climate, the Court should be less concerned with expanding understandings of human rights than with maximizing the relevance and implementability of its jurisprudence.

In a positive development, the Court has demonstrated an awareness in recent years of the need for its jurisprudence to be more accessible to human rights activists and the public. In response to feedback from NGOs, governments, and others, it has reduced the length of its judgments. It has also moved away from highly philosophical dissenting opinions (formerly a common feature of its judgments).

J. Sweeney, 'Margins of Appreciation: Cultural Relativity and the European Court of Human Rights in the Post-Cold War Era'

54 *International and Comparative Law Quarterly* 459 (2005)

The [European Court of Human Rights] allows states a certain discretion to 'do things their own way' from time to time. This 'margin of appreciation' can be distinguished from the general discretion left by the [European] Convention [on Human Rights] to states in how to implement detailed human rights protection in their domestic law. The idea of a margin of appreciation is used in the Court's reasoning to measure and police states' discretion to interfere with or otherwise limit human rights in specific instances. In essence it expresses that Contracting Parties have some space in which they can balance for themselves conflicting public goods. The practice of recognizing and respecting states' margin of appreciation is derived from the case law of the Court and [the former European Commission on Human Rights], not from the text of the Convention itself.

Its relevance can be raised by the Court on its own initiative, or by the Contracting Parties themselves, by way of a 'defence' to the allegation that they have violated a Convention right. The margin of appreciation doctrine's implications for universality can be seen as far back as the well-known 1976 case of *Handyside*. The European Court was called upon to discuss to what extent free expression could be limited in order to protect morals. The Court stated that,

> It is not possible to find in the domestic law of the various Contracting States a uniform European conception of morals. The view taken by their respective laws of the requirements of morals *varies from time to time and from place to place* which is characterised by a rapid and far-reaching evolution of opinions on the subject....Consequently, Article 10 para. 2 leaves to the Contracting States a margin of appreciation. (emphasis added)

The Court thus appeared to recognise some form of inter-temporal, European, moral diversity.

Such comments have provoked hostile reactions to the continued recognition of a national margin of appreciation. For example Lord Lester has expressed his deep concern in the following terms:

> The danger of continuing to use the standardless doctrine of the margin of appreciation is that, especially in the enlarged Council of Europe, it will become the source of a pernicious, variable geometry of human rights, eroding the acquis of existing jurisprudence and giving undue deference to local conditions, traditions, and practices. [A. Lester, 1 *European Human Rights Law Review* 73 (1998) 76]

M. wa Mutua, 'The Banjul Charter and the African Cultural Fingerprint: An Evaluation of the Language of Duties'
35 *Virginia Journal of International Law* 339 (1995)

The series of explicit duties spelled out in articles 27 through 29 of the African Charter could be read as intended to recreate the bonds of the pre-colonial era among individuals and between individuals and the State. They represent a rejection of the individual 'who is utterly free and utterly irresponsible and opposed to society' [Organisation of African Unity Draft Charter]. In a proper reflection of the nuanced nature of societal obligations in the pre-colonial era, the African Charter explicitly provides for two types of duties: direct and indirect. A direct duty is contained, for example, in Article 29(4) of the Charter which requires the individual to 'preserve and strengthen social and national solidarity, particularly when the latter is threatened.' There is nothing inherently sinister about this provision; it merely repeats a duty formerly imposed on members of pre-colonial communities. The African Charter provides an example of an indirect duty in Article 27(2), which states that '[t]he rights and freedoms of each individual shall be exercised with due regard to the rights of others, collective security, morality and common interest.' This duty is in fact a limitation on the enjoyment of certain individual rights. It merely recognizes the practical reality that in African societies, as elsewhere in the world, individual rights are not absolute. Individuals are asked to reflect on how the exercise of their rights in certain circumstances might adversely affect other individuals or the community. The duty is based on the presumption that the full development of the individual is only possible where individuals care about how their actions would impact on others. By rejecting the egotistical individual whose only concern is fulfilling self, Article 27(2) raises the level of care owed to neighbors and the community. Duties are also grouped according to whether they are owed to individuals or to larger units such as the family, society, or the state. Parents, for example, are owed a duty of respect and maintenance by their children....

The most damaging criticism of the language of duties in Africa sees them as 'little more than the formulation, entrenchment, and legitimation of state rights and privileges against individuals and peoples' [Okoth-Ogeno in R. Cohen (ed), *Human Rights and Governance in Africa* (1993)]. However, critics who question the value of including duties in the Charter point only to the theoretical danger that states might capitalize on the duty concept to violate other guaranteed rights. The fear is frequently expressed that emphasis on duties may lead to the 'trumping' of individual rights if the two are in opposition. It is argued that: If the state has a collective right and obligation to develop the society, economy, and polity (Article 29), then as an instrument it can be used to defend coercive state actions against both individuals and constituent groups to achieve state policies rationalized as social and economic improvement....

The African Charter distinguishes human rights from peoples' or collective rights, but sees them in cooperation, not competition or conflict. The Charter's preambular paragraph notes this relationship and recognizes 'on the one hand, that fundamental human rights stem from the attributes of human beings, which justifies their national and international protection and on the other hand, that the reality and respect for peoples rights should necessarily guarantee human rights.' This unambiguous statement, notes van Boven [7 *Human Rights Law Journal* 1986], is conclusive proof of the Charter's view: human rights are inalienable and intrinsic to man individuals and are not in conflict with peoples' rights, which they complement. The exercise of sovereignty rights by a 'people' or 'peoples' as contemplated by the Charter is a necessary precondition for the enjoyment of individual rights. This dialectic between individual and peoples' rights is one of the bases for the Charter's imposition of duties on individuals. Solidarity between the individual and the greater society safeguards collective rights, without which individual rights would be unattainable.

NOTES

1. One of the arguments in favour of regional human rights treaties is that they are seen as reflecting the cultures and societies of those within a State better than an international human rights treaty. Hence there should be an increased likelihood of States ratifying at least their region's human rights treaty. Each of the principal regional human rights treaties—the European Convention on Human Rights 1950 (ECHR), the American Convention on Human Rights 1978 (ACHR) and the African Charter of Human and Peoples' Rights 1981 (ACHPR)—has been ratified by nearly all States in their region (with the major exception of the United States of America in regard to the ACHR). Of course, there are a number of regions where there is no human rights treaty, such as Asia (for the ASEAN Declaration on Human Rights, see N. Doyle, 'The ASEAN Human Rights Declaration and the Implications of Recent Southeast Asian Initiatives in Human Rights Institution-Building and Standard-Setting', 63 *ICLQ* (2014)) and the Pacific, as well as Arab States and Islamic States, despite some noble attempts.

2. Each of the principal regional human rights treaties protects primarily civil and political rights, though not in identical terms. The ACHPR also protects some economic, social and cultural rights, and these rights are protected (in slightly different terms) by separate regional treaties in Europe and the Americas (e.g. the European Social Charter 1961 (revised in 1998) and the Protocol on Economic Social and Cultural Rights 1988, respectively). The ACHPR also protects some group rights, such as the right of self-determination (see Section 6), as well as including some provisions about individual's duties (as discussed by wa Mutua above). Within Europe, the Organization on Security and Cooperation in Europe (OSCE) has developed institutional structures for the protection of human rights, including an Office for Democratic Institutions and Human Rights and a High Commissioner on National Minorities.

3. The supervisory mechanisms for each of the principal regional human rights treaties are different. With the changes to the ECHR brought about by a number of Protocols (e.g. Protocols 11, 14, 15 and 16) (and due to the huge number of individual complaints received), there is now an entire judicial system of supervision and a full-time Court under the ECHR, with a right of individual complaint directly to that Court. The ACHR has a two-tier system of a Commission, which checks for admissibility and tries to reach a friendly settlement, and a Court (the Inter-American Court of Human Rights); the ACHPR has a similar system. In each case, though, the final supervision of compliance with a decision or report of the Court or Commission lies with an inter-governmental body of State representatives from that region. Each of the rights protected and the supervisory mechanisms adopted are justified on the basis of being reflective of the particular cultures of the region.

4. The combined impact of these regional systems has been to contribute significantly to the development of international law generally, such as in the increasing role of the individual in international law (see Chapter 5), and to the impact of (regional) international law in the national laws of many States (see Chapter 4).

SECTION 5: LIMITATIONS ON THE HUMAN RIGHTS TREATY OBLIGATIONS OF STATES

Human rights treaties, both international and regional, place legal obligations on States. However, as States themselves draft these treaties, they have allowed States to place limitations on their obligations under the treaties.

A: General limitations

Nearly all human rights have exceptions to, and/or limitations, on them. These limitations are to protect the rights of others and to protect the general interests of society.

Handyside v *United Kingdom*
24 ECHR Ser A (1976), European Court of Human Rights

Handyside intended to publish *The Little Red Schoolbook* in the United Kingdom, and it had been available in other European States. It was seized under the United Kingdom Obscene Publications Act 1959, and he was convicted and fined. The Court held that there was no breach of Article 10 (freedom of expression) as the restriction could be justified within Article 10(2) on the ground of 'protection of morals'.

48. The Court points out that the machinery of protection established by the Convention is subsidiary to the national systems safeguarding human rights (judgment of 23 July 1968 on the merits of the *'Belgian Linguistic'* case, Series A no. 6, p. 35, § 10 *in fine*). The Convention leaves to each Contracting State, in the first place, the task of securing the rights and freedoms it enshrines. The institutions created by it make their own contribution to this task but they become involved only through contentious proceedings and once all domestic remedies have been exhausted (Article 26).

49. …The Court…is responsible for ensuring the observance of those States' engagements (Article 19), is empowered to give the final ruling on whether a 'restriction' or 'penalty' is reconcilable with freedom of expression as protected by Article 10.…Freedom of expression constitutes one of the essential foundations of [a democratic] society, one of the basic conditions for its progress and for the development of every man. Subject to paragraph 2 of Article 10, it is applicable not only to 'information' or 'ideas' that are favourably received or regarded as inoffensive or as a matter of indifference, but also to those that offend, shock or disturb the State or any sector of the population. Such are the demands of that pluralism, tolerance and broadmindedness without which there is no 'democratic society'. This means, amongst other things, that every 'formality', 'condition', 'restriction' or 'penalty' imposed in this sphere must be proportionate to the legitimate aim pursued.

From another standpoint, whoever exercises his freedom of expression undertakes 'duties and responsibilities' the scope of which depends on his situation and the technical means he uses. The Court cannot overlook such a person's 'duties' and 'responsibilities' when it enquires, as in this case, whether 'restrictions' or 'penalties' were conducive to the 'protection of morals' which made them 'necessary' in a 'democratic society'.

50. It follows from this that it is in no way the Court's task to take the place of the competent national courts but rather to review under Article 10 the decisions they delivered in the exercise of their power of appreciation.

However, the Court's supervision would generally prove illusory if it did no more than examine these decisions in isolation; it must view them in the light of the case as a whole, including the publication in question and the arguments and evidence adduced by the applicant in the domestic legal system and then at the international level. The Court must decide, on the basis of the different data available to it, whether the reasons given by the national authorities to justify the actual measures of 'interference' they take are relevant and sufficient under Article 10 § 2.…

In these circumstances, despite the variety and the constant evolution in the United Kingdom of views on ethics and education, the competent English judges were entitled, in the exercise of their discretion, to think at the relevant time that the Schoolbook would have pernicious effects on the morals of many of the children and adolescents who would read it.

Toonen v *Australia*
1 *International Human Rights Reports* 97 (1994), United Nations Human Rights Committee

Toonen claimed that provisions of the Criminal Code of the Australian state of Tasmania (for which the State of Australia is responsible in international law) breached the rights contained in the ICCPR, including Article 17 (right to privacy), as they made criminal 'various forms of sexual conduct between men, including all forms of sexual contact between consenting adult homosexual men in private'. Tasmania was the only Australian state to have such laws, although they were rarely enforced. The HRC found that the existence of these laws breached Article 17. Subsequently, the Australian government complied with the HRC's views and, eventually, the Tasmanian provisions were repealed.

8.2 Inasmuch as article 17 is concerned, it is undisputed that adult consensual sexual activity in private is covered by the concept of 'privacy', and that Mr Toonen is actually and currently affected by the continued existence of the Tasmanian laws. The Committee considers that Sections 122(a), (c) and 123 of the Tasmanian Criminal Code 'interfere' with the author's privacy, even if these provisions have not been enforced for a decade....

8.3 The prohibition against private homosexual behaviour is provided for by law, namely, Sections 122 and 123 of the Tasmanian Criminal Code. As to whether it may be deemed arbitrary, the Committee recalls that pursuant to its General Comment 16 (32) on article 17, the 'introduction of the concept of arbitrariness is intended to guarantee that even interference provided for by the law should be in accordance with the provisions, aims and objectives of the Covenant and should be, in any event, reasonable in the circumstances'. The Committee interprets the requirement of reasonableness to imply that any interference with privacy must be proportional to the end sought and be necessary in the circumstances of any given case.

8.5 As far as the public health argument of the Tasmanian authorities is concerned, the Committee notes that the criminalization of homosexual practices cannot be considered a reasonable means or proportionate measure to achieve the aim of preventing the spread of AIDS/HIV....

8.6 The Committee cannot accept either that for the purposes of article 17 of the Covenant, moral issues are exclusively a matter of domestic concern, as this would open the door to withdrawing from the Committee's scrutiny a potentially large number of statutes interfering with privacy. It further notes that with the exception of Tasmania, all laws criminalizing homosexuality have been repealed throughout Australia and that, even in Tasmania, it is apparent that there is no consensus as to whether Sections 122 and 123 should not also be repealed. Considering further that these provisions are not currently enforced, which implies that they are not deemed essential to the protection of morals in Tasmania, the Committee concludes that the provisions do not meet the 'reasonableness' test in the circumstances of the case, and that they arbitrarily interfere with Mr Toonen's right under article 17, paragraph 1.

8.7 The State party has sought the Committee's guidance as to whether sexual orientation may be considered an 'other status' for the purposes of article 26. The same issue could arise under article 2, paragraph 1, of the Covenant. The Committee confines itself to noting, however, that in its view the reference to 'sex' in articles 2, paragraph 1, and 26 is to be taken as including sexual orientation.

10. Under article 2(3)(a) of the Covenant, the author, victim of a violation of article 17, paragraph 1, *juncto* 2, paragraph 1, of the Covenant, is entitled to a remedy. In the opinion of the Committee, an effective remedy would be the repeal of Sections 122(a), (c) and 123 of the Tasmanian Criminal Code.

S.A.S. v *France*

1 July 2014, European Court of Human Rights Grand Chamber

The applicant challenged the French law no 2010-1192 (11 October 2010) prohibiting the covering of the face in public (colloquially called the 'burqa ban'). In this case, the European Court of Human Rights had to decide whether the ban was contrary to the right to manifest religion under Article 9(2) and the right to private life under Article 8 of the European Convention on Human Rights (ECHR). The Court found no violation of these rights.

139. As regards the question of necessity in relation to public safety, within the meaning of Articles 8 and 9 [of the ECHR]...the Court understands that a State may find it essential to be able to identify individuals in order to prevent danger for the safety of persons and property and to combat identity fraud. It has thus found no violation of Article 9 of the Convention in cases concerning the obligation to remove clothing with a religious connotation in the context of security checks and the obligation to appear bareheaded on identity photos for use on official

documents (see paragraph 133 above). However, in view of its impact on the rights of women who wish to wear the full-face veil for religious reasons, a blanket ban on the wearing in public places of clothing designed to conceal the face can be regarded as proportionate only in a context where there is a general threat to public safety. The Government has not shown that the ban introduced by the Law of 11 October 2010 falls into such a context. As to the women concerned, they are thus obliged to give up completely an element of their identity that they consider important, together with their chosen manner of manifesting their religion or beliefs, whereas the objective alluded to by the Government could be attained by a mere obligation to show their face and to identify themselves where a risk for the safety of persons and property has been established, or where particular circumstances entail a suspicion of identity fraud. It cannot therefore be found that the blanket ban imposed by the Law of 11 October 2010 is necessary, in a democratic society, for public safety, within the meaning of Articles 8 and 9 of the Convention.

140. The Court will now examine the questions raised by the other aim that it has found legitimate: to ensure the observance of the minimum requirements of life in society as part of the 'protection of the rights and freedoms of others'...

141. The Court observes that this is an aim to which the authorities have given much weight. This can be seen, in particular, from the explanatory memorandum accompanying the Bill, which indicates that '[t]he voluntary and systematic concealment of the face is problematic because it is quite simply incompatible with the fundamental requirements of "living together" in French society' and that '[t]he systematic concealment of the face in public places, contrary to the ideal of fraternity,... falls short of the minimum requirement of civility that is necessary for social interaction'.... It indeed falls within the powers of the State to secure the conditions whereby individuals can live together in their diversity. Moreover, the Court is able to accept that a State may find it essential to give particular weight in this connection to the interaction between individuals and may consider this to be adversely affected by the fact that some conceal their faces in public places....

142. Consequently, the Court finds that the impugned ban can be regarded as justified in its principle solely in so far as it seeks to guarantee the conditions of 'living together'.

157. Consequently, having regard in particular to the breadth of the margin of appreciation afforded to the respondent State in the present case, the Court finds that the ban imposed by the Law of 11 October 2010 can be regarded as proportionate to the aim pursued, namely the preservation of the conditions of 'living together' as an element of the 'protection of the rights and freedoms of others'.

158. The impugned limitation can thus be regarded as 'necessary in a democratic society'. This conclusion holds true with respect both to Article 8 of the Convention and to Article 9.

159. Accordingly, there has been no violation either of Article 8 or of Article 9 of the Convention.

NOTES
1. Human rights do not exist in a vacuum and so many human rights have limitations in order to protect the rights of others or the general interests of society. For example, in the extracts from the ICCPR and ICESCR above, it can be seen that Article 19(3) of the ICCPR has general limitations on freedom of expression and Article 13(3) and (4) of the ICESCR has limitations on State actions to allow for parental choice of education. Sometimes rights have exceptions to protect perceived individual or State interests, such as the exception in regard to seniority and competence under Article 7(c) of the ICESCR and the exception for the death penalty in Article 6(2) of the ICCPR, though this is now prohibited by the Second Optional Protocol to that treaty. Article 7 of the ICCPR on the prevention of torture, cruel, inhuman and degrading treatment is an example of an absolute right.
2. The international and regional human rights supervisory bodies correctly see their role as being subsidiary to national protections of human rights, although with the authority to review compliance by the State with its human rights treaty obligations. However, as the decisions in *Handyside* v *UK* and *Toonen* v *Australia* make clear, the body will review the extent to which the limitations placed on the human right by the State is proportional to a legitimate (and not arbitrary) aim pursued by the State to address a pressing social need in the State. Thus, when reviewing compliance with a treaty, these bodies may allow a degree of flexibility to a State, particularly in matters of moral views. This could be seen to be an application of appropriate cultural relativism (see Section 2B). In *S.A.S.* v *France*, the Court afforded

to the French government a certain degree of flexibility (using the concept of margin of appreciation).

3. There are many other limitations on individuals or others being able to bring a claim successfully against a State under a human rights treaty. In the first instance, the State must be a party to the relevant treaty (without a relevant reservation or derogation—see Sections 5B and C) and, second, the person complaining must have standing to bring the claim (i.e. they are a 'victim') and third, they must have exhausted all effective national remedies. The view of the HRC in *Toonen* v *Australia* is unusual in that it was the mere existence of the law that gave rise to the violation of human rights. In addition, generally, the person making the complaint does not need to be a national of the State against which a complaint has been made, as it is territorial jurisdiction, not nationality, which is crucial (see Chapter 8).

B: Reservations

Both the general international law with regard to treaties and the specific application of that law to human rights treaties, which is different due to the nature of human rights obligations, are considered in Chapter 3.

C: Derogations

Most human rights treaties allow States to limit their obligations to protect certain human rights when a 'state of emergency' exists. The conditions necessary for lawful derogations are set out in the treaties.

Human Rights Committee, General Comment 29: 'States of Emergency'
UN Doc CCPR/C/21/Rev.1 Add. 11 (2001)

2. Measures derogating from the provisions of the Covenant must be of an exceptional and temporary nature. Before a State moves to invoke article 4, two fundamental conditions must be met: the situation must amount to a public emergency which threatens the life of the nation, and the State party must have officially proclaimed a state of emergency. The latter requirement is essential for the maintenance of the principles of legality and rule of law at times when they are most needed. When proclaiming a state of emergency with consequences that could entail derogation from any provision of the Covenant, States must act within their constitutional and other provisions of law that govern such proclamation and the exercise of emergency powers; it is the task of the Committee to monitor the laws in question with respect to whether they enable and secure compliance with article 4. In order that the Committee can perform its task, States parties to the Covenant should include in their reports submitted under article 40 sufficient and precise information about their law and practice in the field of emergency powers.

3. Not every disturbance or catastrophe qualifies as a public emergency which threatens the life of the nation, as required by article 4, paragraph 1. During armed conflict, whether international or non-international, rules of international humanitarian law become applicable and help, in addition to the provisions in article 4 and article 5, paragraph 1, of the Covenant, to prevent the abuse of a State's emergency powers. The Covenant requires that even during an armed conflict measures derogating from the Covenant are allowed only if and to the extent that the situation constitutes a threat to the life of the nation. If States parties consider invoking article 4 in other situations than an armed conflict, they should carefully consider the justification and why such a measure is necessary and legitimate in the circumstances. On a number of occasions the Committee has expressed its concern over States parties that appear to have derogated from rights protected by the Covenant, or whose domestic law appears to allow such derogation in situations not covered by article 4.

6. The fact that some of the provisions of the Covenant have been listed in article 4 (paragraph 2), as not being subject to derogation does not mean that other articles in the Covenant may be subjected to derogations at will, even where a threat to the life of the nation exists. The legal obligation to narrow down all derogations to those strictly required by the exigencies of the situation establishes both for States parties and for the Committee a

duty to conduct a careful analysis under each article of the Covenant based on an objective assessment of the actual situation.

9. Furthermore, article 4, paragraph 1, requires that no measure derogating from the provisions of the Covenant may be inconsistent with the State party's other obligations under international law, particularly the rules of international humanitarian law. Article 4 of the Covenant cannot be read as justification for derogation from the Covenant if such derogation would entail a breach of the State's other international obligations, whether based on treaty or general international law. This is reflected also in article 5, paragraph 2, of the Covenant according to which there shall be no restriction upon or derogation from any fundamental rights recognized in other instruments on the pretext that the Covenant does not recognize such rights or that it recognizes them to a lesser extent.

Brannigan and McBride v United Kingdom

ECHR Ser A (1993) No. 258–B, European Court of Human Rights

The two applicants had been detained for over four days by the police in Northern Ireland under the provisions of the United Kingdom Prevention of Terrorism (Temporary Provisions) Act 1984. The United Kingdom government conceded that it had breached Article 5(3) and (5) of the ECHR as the applicants were not brought promptly before a judge after their detention. The issue was whether the derogation to the ECHR by the United Kingdom (explained in the extract below) exonerated it of any breach.

31. On 23 December 1988 the United Kingdom informed the Secretary General of the Council of Europe that the Government had availed itself of the right of derogation conferred by Article 15(1) [to the ECHR] to the extent that the exercise of powers under section 12 of the 1984 Act might be inconsistent with the obligations imposed by Article 5(3) of the Convention....

43. The Court recalls that it falls to each Contracting State, with its responsibility for 'the life of [its] nation', to determine whether that life is threatened by a 'public emergency' and, if so, how far it is necessary to go in attempting to overcome the emergency. By reason of their direct and continuous contact with the pressing needs of the moment, the national authorities are in principle in a better position than the international judge to decide both on the presence of such an emergency and on the nature and scope of derogations necessary to avert it. Accordingly, in this matter a wide margin of appreciation should be left to the national authorities (see the *Ireland* v *the United Kingdom* judgment of 18 January 1978, Series A No. 25, pp. 78–79, para. 207).

Nevertheless, Contracting Parties do not enjoy an unlimited power of appreciation. It is for the Court to rule on whether *inter alia* the States have gone beyond the 'extent strictly required by the exigencies' of the crisis. The domestic margin of appreciation is thus accompanied by a European supervision (ibid.). At the same time, in exercising its supervision the Court must give appropriate weight to such relevant factors as the nature of the rights affected by the derogation, the circumstances leading to, and the duration of, the emergency situation....

47. Recalling its case-law in *Lawless* v *Ireland* (judgment of 1 July 1961, Series A No. 3, p. 56, para. 28) and *Ireland* v *The United Kingdom* (*loc. cit.*, Series A No. 25, p. 78, para. 205) and making its own assessment, in the light of all the material before it as to the extent and impact of terrorist violence in Northern Ireland and elsewhere in the United Kingdom (see paragraph 12 above) the Court considers there can be no doubt that such a public emergency existed at the relevant time.

It does not judge it necessary to compare the situation which obtained in 1989 with that which prevailed in December 1988 since a decision to withdraw a derogation is, in principle, a matter within the discretion of the State and since it is clear that the Government believed that the legislation in question was in fact compatible with the Convention (see paragraphs 49–51 below).

[The Court then considered whether the measures taken were strictly required by the exigencies of the situation. In doing so, it considered four main questions:

(i)   Was the derogation a genuine response to an emergency situation?
(ii) Was the derogation premature?
(iii) Was the absence of judicial control of extended detention justified?
(iv) Were there safeguards against abuse of the detention power?]

59. It is not the Court's role to substitute its view as to what measures were most appropriate or expedient at the relevant time in dealing with an emergency situation for that of the Government which have direct responsibility for establishing the balance between the taking of effective measures to combat terrorism on the one hand, and respecting individual rights on the other (see the above-mentioned *Ireland* v *The United Kingdom* judgment, Series A No. 25, p. 82, para. 214 and the *Klass and Others* v *Germany* judgment of 6 September 1978, Series A No. 28, p. 23, para. 49). In the context of Northern Ireland where the judiciary is small and vulnerable to terrorist attacks, public confidence in the independence of the judiciary is understandably a matter to which the Government attach great importance....

66. Having regard to the nature of the terrorist threat in Northern Ireland, the limited scope of the derogation and the reasons advanced in support of it, as well as the existence of basic safeguards against abuse, the Court takes the view that the Government have not exceeded their margin of appreciation in considering that the derogation was strictly required by the exigencies of the situation....

69. For the Government, it was open to question whether an official proclamation was necessary for purposes of Article 4 of the Covenant, since the emergency existed prior to the ratification of the Covenant by the United Kingdom and has continued to the present day. In any event, the existence of the emergency and the fact of derogation were publicly and formally announced by the Secretary of State for the Home Department to the House of Commons on 22 December 1988. Moreover there had been no suggestion by the United Nations Human Rights Committee that the derogation did not satisfy the formal requirements of Article 4....

73....In the Court's view, the [22 December 1988] statement, which was formal in character and made public the Government's intentions as regards derogation, was well in keeping with the notion of an official proclamation. It therefore considers that there is no basis for the applicant's arguments in this regard.

74. In the light of the above examination, the Court concludes that the derogation lodged by the United Kingdom satisfies the requirements of Article 15 and that therefore the applicants cannot validly complain of a violation under Article 5(3). It follows that there was no obligation under Article 5(5) to provide the applicants with an enforceable right to compensation.

UK Derogation to the International Covenant on Civil and Political Rights

18 December 2001

Notification to the United Nations of the United Kingdom's derogation from article 9 of the International Covenant on Civil and Political Rights

I have the honour to present my compliments, Excellency, and to convey the following information in order to ensure compliance with the obligations of Her Majesty's Government in the United Kingdom under Article 4 (3) of the International Covenant on Civil and Political Rights adopted by the General Assembly on 16 December 1966.

Public emergency in the United Kingdom

The terrorist attacks in New York, Washington, D.C. and Pennsylvania on 11th September 2001 resulted in several thousand deaths, including many British victims and others from 70 different countries. In its resolutions 1368 (2001) and 1373 (2001), the United Nations Security Council recognised the attacks as a threat to international peace and security.

The threat from international terrorism is a continuing one. In its resolution 1373 (2001), the Security Council, acting under Chapter VII of the United Nations Charter, required all States to take measures to prevent the commission of terrorist attacks, including by denying safe haven to those who finance, plan, support or commit terrorist attacks.

There exists a terrorist threat to the United Kingdom from persons suspected of involvement in international terrorism. In particular, there are foreign nationals present in the United Kingdom who are suspected of being concerned in the commission, preparation or instigation of acts of international terrorism, of being members of organisations or groups which are so concerned or of having links with members of such organisations or groups, and who are a threat to the national security of the United Kingdom.

As a result, a public emergency, within the meaning of Article 4(1) of the Covenant, exists in the United Kingdom.

The Anti-terrorism, Crime and Security Act 2001

As a result of the public emergency, provision is made in the Anti-terrorism, Crime and Security Act 2001, inter alia, for an extended power to arrest and detain a foreign national which will apply where it is intended to remove or deport the person from the United Kingdom but where removal or deportation is not for the time being possible, with the consequence that the detention would be unlawful under existing domestic law powers. The extended power to arrest and detain will apply where the Secretary of State issues a certificate indicating his belief that the person's presence in the United Kingdom is a risk to national security and that he suspects the person of being an international terrorist. That certificate will be subject to an appeal to the Special Immigration Appeals Commission ('SIA'), established under the Special Immigration Appeals Commission Act 1997, which will have power to cancel it if it considers that the certificate should not have been issued. There will be an appeal on a point of law from a ruling by SIAC. In addition, the certificate will be reviewed by SIAC at regular intervals. SIAC will also be able to grant bail, where appropriate, subject to conditions. It will be open to a detainee to end his detention at any time by agreeing to leave the United Kingdom.

The extended power of arrest and detention in the Anti-terrorism, Crime and Security Act 2001 is a measure which is strictly required by the exigencies of the situation. It is a temporary provision which comes into force for an initial period of 15 months and then expires unless renewed by Parliament. Thereafter, it is subject to annual renewal by Parliament. If, at any time, in the Government's assessment, the public emergency no longer exists or the extended power is no longer strictly required by the exigencies of the situation, then the Secretary of State will, by Order, repeal the provision.

Domestic law powers of detention (other than under the Anti-terrorism, Crime and Security Act 2001)

The Government has powers under the Immigration Act 1971 ('the 1971 Act') to remove or deport persons on the ground that their presence in the United Kingdom is not conducive to the public good on national security grounds. Persons can also be arrested and detained under Schedules 2 and 3 to the 1971 Act pending their removal or deportation. The courts in the United Kingdom have ruled that this power of detention can only be exercised during the period necessary, in all the circumstances of the particular case, to effect removal and that, if it becomes clear that removal is not going to be possible within a reasonable time, detention will be unlawful (*R v Governor of Durham Prison, ex parte Singh* [1984] All ER 983).

Article 9 of the Covenant

In some cases, where the intention remains to remove or deport a person on national security grounds, continued detention may not be consistent with Article 9 of the Covenant. This may be the case, for example, if the person has established that removal to their own country might result in treatment contrary to Article 7 of the Covenant. In such circumstances, irrespective of the gravity of the threat to national security posed by the person concerned, it is well established that the international obligations of the United Kingdom prevent removal or deportation to a place where there is a real risk that the person will suffer treatment contrary to that article. If no alternative destination is immediately available then removal or deportation may not, for the time being, be possible even though the ultimate intention remains to remove or deport the person once satisfactory arrangements can be made. In addition, it may not be possible to prosecute the person for a criminal offence given the strict rules on the admissibility of evidence in the criminal justice system of the United Kingdom and the high standard of proof required.

Derogation under Article 4 of the Covenant

The Government has considered whether the exercise of the extended power to detain contained in the Anti-terrorism, Crime and Security Act 2001 may be inconsistent with the obligations under Article 9 of the Covenant. To the extent that the exercise of the extended power may be inconsistent with the United Kingdom's obligations under Article 9, the Government has decided to avail itself of the right of derogation conferred by Article 4(1) of the Covenant and will continue to do so until further notice.

Please accept, Excellency, the assurances of my highest consideration.

15 March 2005

The provisions referred to in the 18 December 2001 notification, namely the extended power of arrest and detention in the Anti-terrorism, Crime and Security Act 2001, ceased to operate on 14 March 2005. Accordingly, the notification is withdrawn as from that date, and the Government of the United Kingdom confirm that the relevant provisions of the Covenant will again be executed as from then.

France Derogation to the European Convention on Human Rights

24 November 2015

The Permanent Representation of France informs the Secretary General of the Council of Europe of the following:

On 13 November 2015, large-scale terrorist attacks took place in the Paris region.

The terrorist threat in France is of a lasting nature, having regard to information from the intelligence services and to the international context.

The French Government has decided, by Decree No. 2015-1475 of 14 November 2015, to apply Law No. 55-385 of 3 April 1955 on the state of emergency. Decrees No. 2015-1475, No. 2015-1476 and No. 2015-1478 of 14 November 2015 and No. 2015-1493 and No. 2015-1494 of 18 November 2015 have defined a number of measures that may be taken by the administrative authorities.

The extension of the state of emergency for three months, with effect from 26 November 2015, was authorised by Law No. 2015-1501 of 20 November 2015. This law also amends certain of the measures provided for by the Law of 3 April 1955 in order to adapt its content to the current context. The texts of the decrees and laws mentioned above are attached to this letter.

Such measures appeared necessary to prevent the commission of further terrorist attacks.

Some of them, prescribed by the decrees of 14 November 2015 and 18 November 2015 and by the Law of 20 November 2015, may involve a derogation from the obligations under the Convention for the Protection of Human Rights and Fundamental Freedoms. I would therefore kindly request you to consider that this letter constitutes information for the purposes of Article 15 of the Convention.

NOTES

1. There is always the difficulty in determining whether any derogation from the application of human rights treaties should be allowed. If derogations are allowed, as is generally the case, then they could be used whenever a State simply considers it is expedient. This possibility is increased by the decision of the Court in *Brannigan and McBride* v *United Kingdom*, which suggests that Article 15 may serve as a significant tool for preserving government action. Therefore, the protection of human rights under the Convention is substantially diminished as a result of wide sanctioning of derogations.

2. The derogation by the United Kingdom from Article 9 of the ICCPR was based on the terrorist attacks in the United States on 11 September 2001. It would seem difficult to argue successfully that a situation in another non-bordering State gave rise to a state of emergency in a State. However, a later terrorist attack on 7 July 2005 in the United Kingdom would appear to be a sounder basis for the derogation, and the basis for the French derogation was terrorist attacks on its territory. The United Kingdom withdrew part of its derogation after the decision by its judicial House of Lords, which held that the Anti-Terrorism, Crime and Security Act 2001 was contrary to the United Kingdom's Human Rights Act 1998 (which incorporates the ECHR, see Chapter 4) as it operated in discriminatory way against non-nationals (see *A* v *Secretary of State for the Home Department* [2004] UKHL 56).

3. Each treaty usually sets out which rights are non-derogable. Other rights may be non-derogable as being a necessary part of the protection of rights in a state of emergency, as was held by the Inter-American Court of Human Rights in *Habeas Corpus in Emergency Situations Opinion* (1988) I-ACtHR, para. 42: '[The writ of *habeas corpus* is] among those judicial remedies that are essential for the protection of various rights whose derogation is prohibited by A27(2) and that serve, moreover, to preserve legality in a democratic society'.

4. If a human right is non-derogable it does not mean that it has a priority over other human rights. It is simply to indicate that it should not be limited in a particular situation where there is a state of emergency. A few rights are both non-derogable and have no legal limitations in any situation, such as the prohibition on torture. See also the discussion on international human rights law and international humanitarian law in Section 8B.

SECTION 6: THE RIGHT OF SELF-DETERMINATION

Most human rights protect the right of individual human beings. There are also collective or group rights, such as the prohibition against genocide, that protect the right of a group *as a group*. The right of self-determination is a group (or collective) right. This right requires separate consideration here because of its impact on different aspects of international law. In particular it has a direct effect on issues of sovereignty over territory (see Chapter 7).

A: International documents

United Nations Charter 1945

Article 1
The Purposes of the United Nations are:…

2. To develop friendly relations among nations based on respect for the principle of equal rights and self-determination of peoples, and to take other appropriate measures to strengthen universal peace.

Article 73
Members of the United Nations which have or assume responsibilities for the administration of territories whose peoples have not yet attained a full measure of self-government recognize the principle that the interests of the inhabitants of these territories are paramount, and accept as a sacred trust the obligation to promote to the utmost, within the system of international peace and security established by the present Charter, the well-being of the inhabitants of these territories…

International Covenant on Economic, Social and Cultural Rights 1966 and the International Covenant on Civil and Political Rights 1966

Article 1

1. All peoples have the right of self-determination. By virtue of that right they freely determine their political status and freely pursue their economic, social and cultural development.

2. All peoples may, for their own ends, freely dispose of their natural wealth and resources without prejudice to any obligations arising out of international economic co-operation, based upon the principle of mutual benefit, and international law. In no case may a people be deprived of its own means of subsistence.

3. The States Parties to the present Covenant, including those having responsibility for the administration of Non-Self-Governing and Trust Territories, shall promote the realization of the right of self-determination, and shall respect that right, in conformity with the provisions of the Charter of the United Nations.

Declaration on Principles of International Law concerning Friendly Relations and Cooperation among States in Accordance with the Charter of the United Nations General Assembly Resolution 2625 (XXV) 24 October, 1970
UN Doc A/8028 (1970), 25 UN GAOR Supp (No 28) 121

This Declaration is often seen as providing a clarification of the principles of the United Nations Charter.

The principle of equal rights and self-determination of peoples
By virtue of the principle of equal rights and self-determination of peoples enshrined in the Charter, all peoples have the right freely to determine, without external interference, their political status and to pursue their economic, social and cultural development, and every State has the duty to respect this right in accordance with the provisions of the Charter.

Every State has the duty to promote, through joint and separate action, the realisation of the principle of equal rights and self-determination of peoples, in accordance with the provisions of the Charter, and to render assistance to the United Nations in carrying out the responsibilities entrusted to it by the Charter regarding the implementation of the principle in order:

(a) To promote friendly relations and co-operation among States; and
(b) To bring a speedy end to colonialism, having regard to the freely expressed will of the peoples concerned;

and bearing in mind that subjection of peoples to alien subjugation, domination and exploitation constitutes a violation of the principle, as well as a denial of fundamental human rights, and is contrary to the Charter of the United Nations.

Every State has the duty to promote through joint and separate action universal respect for the observance of human rights and fundamental freedoms in accordance with the Charter.

The establishment of a sovereign and independent State, the free association or integration with an independent State or the emergence into any other political status freely determined by a people constitute modes of implementing the right of self-determination by that people.

Every State has the duty to refrain from any forcible action which deprives peoples referred to above in the elaboration of the present principle of their right to self-determination and freedom and independence. In their actions against and resistance to such forcible action in pursuit of the exercise of their right to self-determination, such peoples are entitled to seek and to receive support in accordance with the purposes and principles of the Charter of the United Nations.

The territory of a colony or other non-governing territory has, under the charter of the United Nations, a status separate and distinct from the territory of the State administering it; and such separate and distinct status under the Charter shall exist until the people of the colony or non-self-governing territory have exercised their right of self-determination in accordance with the Charter and particularly its purposes and principles.

Nothing in the foregoing paragraph shall be construed as authorizing or encouraging any action which would dismember or impair, totally or in part, the territorial integrity or political unity of sovereign and independent States conducting themselves in compliance with the principle of equal rights and self-determination of peoples as described above and thus possessed of a government representing the whole people belonging to the territory without distinction as to race, creed or colour.

Every State shall refrain from any action aimed at the partial or total disruption of the national unity and territorial integrity of any other State or country.

United Nations Declaration on the Rights of Indigenous Peoples

General Assembly Resolution 61/295, A/RES/61/295 (2007)

Acknowledging that the Charter of the United Nations, the International Covenant on Economic, Social and Cultural Rights and the International Covenant on Civil and Political Rights, as well as the Vienna Declaration and Programme of Action, affirm the fundamental importance of the right to self-determination of all peoples, by virtue of which they freely determine their political status and freely pursue their economic, social and cultural development,

Bearing in mind that nothing in this Declaration may be used to deny any peoples their right to self-determination, exercised in conformity with international law,

Article 3

Indigenous peoples have the right to self-determination. By virtue of that right they freely determine their political status and freely pursue their economic, social and cultural development.

Article 4

Indigenous peoples, in exercising their right to self-determination, have the right to autonomy or self-government in matters relating to their internal and local affairs, as well as ways and means for financing their autonomous functions.

NOTES
1. The idea of self-determination has been part of the debate in the international community for nearly a century. In 1918, United States President Wilson warned that 'peoples may now be dominated and governed only by their own consent. "Self-determination" is not a mere phrase. It is an imperative principle of action, which statesmen will henceforth ignore at their peril' (W. Wilson, *War Aims of Germany and Austria* (1918)). In 1917, Lenin had upheld self-determination and applied it to all peoples and so rejected the imperialist distinction between the 'civilised' and 'uncivilised' rationale. A few plebiscites to discern the wishes of the peoples occurred between the two World Wars and the idea continued into the United Nations Charter. The right of self-determination was then applied to colonial territories in the General Assembly Resolutions of 14 and 15 December 1960. The link between a colonial State's obligations under Article 73 of the United Nations Charter and its obligations to protect the right of self-determination became inseparable.

2. The right of self-determination was most clearly defined in common Article 1 of the two International Human Rights Covenants (above) and its limits were clarified by the Declaration on Principles of International Law (above). The right has also been declared in other international and regional instruments, such as Part VIII of the Helsinki Final Act 1975 (part of the Organization on Security and Cooperation in Europe) and Article 20 of the African Charter on Human and Peoples' Rights.

B: Clarification of the right of self-determination

Final Report and Recommendations of an International Meeting of Experts on the Further Study of the Concept of the Right of People for UNESCO
SNS–89/CONF. 602/7, 22 February, 1990

A people for the [purposes of the] rights of people in international law, including the right to self-determination, has the following characteristics:

(a) A group of individual human beings who enjoy some or all of the following common features:
  (i)   A common historical tradition;
  (ii) Racial or ethnic identity;
  (iii) Cultural homogeneity;
  (iv) Linguistic unity;
  (v)   Religious or ideological affinity;
  (vi) Territorial connection;
  (vii) Common economic life.
(b) The group must be of a certain number who need not be large (e.g. the people of micro States) but must be more than a mere association of individuals within a State.
(c) The group as a whole must have the will to be identified as a people or the consciousness of being a people—allowing that groups or some members of such groups, though sharing the foregoing characteristics, may not have the will or consciousness.
(d) Possibly the group must have institutions or other means of expressing its common characteristics and will for identity.

Human Rights Committee, General Comment 12
39 UN GAOR, Supp 40 (A/39/40), pp. 142–3 (1994)

1. The right of self-determination is of particular importance because its realization is an essential condition for the effective guarantee and observance of individual human rights and for the promotion and strengthening of those rights. It is for that reason that States set forth the right of self-determination in a provision of positive law in both Covenants and placed this provision as article 1 apart from and before all of the other rights in the two Covenants.

6. Paragraph 3 [of Article 1], in the Committee's opinion, is particularly important in that it imposes specific obligations on States parties, not only in relation to their own peoples but *vis-à-vis* all peoples which have not been able to exercise or have been deprived of the possibility of exercising their right to self-determination.…The obligations exist irrespective of whether a people entitled to self-determination depends on a State party to the Covenant or not. It follows that all States parties to the Covenant should take positive action to facilitate realization of and respect for the right of peoples to self-determination.

Namibia Opinion
ICJ Rep 1971 16, International Court of Justice

As part of its Advisory Opinion in this case (see Chapter 3), the Court dealt with the responsibility of a State for a colonial (or colonial-type) territory, and so considered the issues of both self-determination and the 'sacred trust' of a League of Nations

Mandate over a territory, this 'sacred trust' now continuing under Article 73 of the United Nations Charter.

THE COURT: [T]he subsequent development of international law in regard to non-self-governing territories, as enshrined in the Charter of the United Nations, made the principle of self-determination applicable to all of them....[T]he ultimate objective of the sacred trust was the self-determination and independence of the peoples concerned....As to the general consequences resulting from the illegal presence of South Africa in Namibia, all States should bear in mind that the injured entity is a people which must look to the international community for assistance in its progress towards the goals for which the sacred trust was instituted.

JUDGE AMMOUN (Separate Opinion): Indeed one is bound to recognize that the right of peoples to self-determination, before being written into charters that were not granted but won in bitter struggle, had first been written painfully, with the blood of the peoples, in the finally awakened conscience of humanity....If any doubts had remained on this matter [of the right of self-determination] in the mind of the States Members of the United Nations, they would not have resolved to proclaim the legitimacy of the struggle of peoples—and more specifically the Namibian people—to make good their right of self-determination. If this right is still not recognized as a juridical norm in the practice of a few rare States or the writings of certain even rarer theoreticians, the attitude of the former is explained by their concern for their traditional interests, and that of the latter by a kind of extreme respect for certain long-entrenched postulates of classic international law. Law is a living deed, not a brilliant honours-list of past writers whose work of course compels respect but who cannot, except for a few great minds, be thought to have had such a vision of the future that they could always see beyond their own times.

NOTES

1. As was made clear in the *Namibia Opinion*, the right of self-determination is now a rule of customary international law, at least in its application to colonial territories. Many jurists consider it a *jus cogens* norm in relation to its colonial application (see Chapter 3 on the concept of *jus cogens*). The application of the right to self-determination beyond colonial situations is examined in the next section.

2. There is a close connection between the protection of the right of self-determination and the protection of other human rights, as is indicated by the Human Rights Committee's General Comment above. There is even a connection with humanitarian law (see Section 8B), in that the Geneva Protocol I 1977 on the law relating to the protection of victims of armed conflict expressly includes situations where peoples are exercising their right of self-determination as being within its scope (Article 1(4)).

3. One of the principal difficulties in clarifying the right of self-determination is to decide the 'self' or 'peoples' who have this right. Many definitions have been considered, both objective and subjective, and the UNESCO Report (above) brings most of these proposed definitions together. While it is certainly to the advantage of the 'people' concerned that they are recognised by States as a peoples having the right of self-determination, recognition is ultimately a political decision by States (see Chapter 5) which may not accord with the legal position. Above all, those entitled to the benefit of the protection of a human right should not be dependent on the whims of States.

C: Application of the right of self-determination

Western Sahara Opinion
ICJ Rep 1975 12, International Court of Justice

The facts are set out in Chapter 7.

THE COURT: [Affirms] the decision in the [*Namibia Opinion*] and emphasises that the application of the right of self-determination requires a free and genuine expression of the will of the peoples concerned....The validity of the principle of self-determination, defined as the need to pay regard to the freely expressed will of peoples, is not affected by the fact that in certain cases the General Assembly has dispensed with the requirement of consulting the inhabitants of a given territory. Those instances were based either on the consideration that a certain population did not constitute a 'people' entitled to self-determination or on the conviction that a consultation was totally unnecessary, in view of special circumstances....

The Court has already concluded that the two questions [for which an Advisory Opinion is sought] must be considered in the whole context of the decolonization process. The right of self-determination leaves the General Assembly a measure of discretion with respect to the forms and procedures by which that right is to be realized.

JUDGE DILLARD (Separate Opinion): The pronouncements of the Court thus indicate, in my view, that a norm of international law has emerged applicable to the decolonization of those non-self-governing territories which are under the aegis of the United Nations....

It seemed hardly necessary to make more explicit the cardinal restraint which the legal right of self-determination imposes. That restraint may be captured in a single sentence. It is for the people to determine the destiny of the territory and not the territory the destiny of the people. Viewed in this perspective it becomes almost self-evident that the existence of ancient 'legal ties' of the kind described in the Opinion, while they may influence some of the projected procedures for decolonization, can have only a tangential effect in the ultimate choices available to the people.... [I]t may be suggested that self-determination is satisfied by a free choice not by a particular consequence of that choice or a particular method of exercising it.

Reference Re Secession of Quebec

[1998] 2 SCR 217, Canadian Supreme Court

The Canadian Supreme Court was asked several questions about whether Quebec could secede from Canada, including the following question [Question 2]: 'Is there a right of self-determination under international law that would give the National Assembly, legislature or government of Quebec the right to effect the secession of Quebec from Canada unilaterally?'

111. It is clear that international law does not specifically grant component parts of sovereign states the legal right to secede unilaterally from their 'parent' state.... [P]roponents...are therefore left to attempt to found their argument...on the implied duty of states to recognize the legitimacy of secession brought about by the exercise of the well-established international law right of a 'people' to self-determination....

114. The existence of the right of a people to self-determination is now so widely recognized in international conventions that the principle has acquired a status beyond 'convention' and is considered a general principle of international law....

124. It is clear that 'a people' may include only a portion of the population of an existing state. The right to self-determination has developed largely as a human right, and is generally used in documents that simultaneously contain references to 'nation' and 'state'. The juxtaposition of these terms is indicative that the reference to 'people' does not necessarily mean the entirety of a state's population....

125. While much of the Quebec population certainly shares many of the characteristics (such as a common language and culture) that would be considered in determining whether a specific group is a 'people', as do other groups within Quebec and/or Canada, it is not necessary to explore this legal characterization to resolve Question 2 appropriately. Similarly, it is not necessary for the Court to determine whether, should a Quebec people exist within the definition of public international law, such a people encompasses the entirety of the provincial population or just a portion thereof. Nor is it necessary to examine the position of the aboriginal population within Quebec.

126. The recognized sources of international law establish that the right to self-determination of a people is normally fulfilled through internal self-determination a people's pursuit of its political, economic, social and cultural development within the framework of an existing state. A right to external self-determination (which in this case potentially takes the form of the assertion of a right to unilateral secession) arises in only the most extreme of cases and, even then, under carefully defined circumstances....

130....There is no necessary incompatibility between the maintenance of the territorial integrity of existing states, including Canada, and the right of a 'people' to achieve a full measure of self-determination. A state whose government represents the whole of the people or peoples resident within its territory, on a basis of equality and without discrimination, and respects the principles of self-determination in its own internal arrangements, is entitled to the protection under international law of its territorial integrity....

133. The other clear case [in addition to colonial domination] where a right to external self-determination accrues is where a people is subject to alien subjugation, domination or exploitation outside a colonial context. This recognition finds its roots in the Declaration on Friendly Relations...

134. A number of commentators have further asserted that the right to self-determination may ground a right to unilateral secession in a third circumstance...when a people is blocked from the meaningful exercise of its right to self-determination internally, it is entitled, as a last resort, to exercise it by secession. The Vienna Declaration requirement that governments represent 'the whole people belonging to the territory without distinction of any kind' adds credence to the assertion that such a complete blockage may potentially give rise to a right of secession.

135....Even assuming that the third circumstance is sufficient to create a right to unilateral secession under international law, the current Quebec context cannot be said to approach such a threshold....

136. The population of Quebec cannot plausibly be said to be denied access to government. Quebecers occupy prominent positions within the government of Canada. Residents of the province freely make political choices and pursue economic, social and cultural development within Quebec, across Canada, and throughout the world. The population of Quebec is equitably represented in legislative, executive and judicial institutions. In short, to reflect the phraseology of the international documents that address the right to self-determination of peoples, Canada is a 'sovereign and independent state conducting itself in compliance with the principle of equal rights and self-determination of peoples and thus possessed of a government representing the whole people belonging to the territory without distinction'....

139. We would not wish to leave this aspect of our answer to Question 2 without acknowledging the importance of the submissions made to us respecting the rights and concerns of aboriginal peoples in the event of a unilateral secession, as well as the appropriate means of defining the boundaries of a seceding Quebec with particular regard to the northern lands occupied largely by aboriginal peoples. However, the concern of aboriginal peoples is precipitated by the asserted right of Quebec to unilateral secession. In light of our finding that there is no such right applicable to the population of Quebec, either under the Constitution of Canada or at international law, but that on the contrary a clear democratic expression of support for secession would lead under the Constitution to negotiations in which aboriginal interests would be taken into account, it becomes unnecessary to explore further the concerns of the aboriginal peoples in this Reference.

142. No one doubts that legal consequences may flow from political facts, and that 'sovereignty is a political fact for which no purely legal authority can be constituted.'...Secession of a province from Canada, if successful in the streets, might well lead to the creation of a new state. Although recognition by other states is not, at least as a matter of theory, necessary to achieve statehood, the viability of a would-be State in the international community depends, as a practical matter, upon recognition by other States. That process of recognition is guided by legal norms. However, international recognition is not alone constitutive of statehood and, critically, does not relate back to the date of secession to serve retroactively as a source of a 'legal' right to secede in the first place. Recognition occurs only after a territorial unit has been successful, as a political fact, in achieving secession.

143....[A]n emergent State that has disregarded legitimate obligations arising out of its previous situation can potentially expect to be hindered by that disregard in achieving international recognition, at least with respect to the timing of that recognition. On the other hand, compliance by the seceding province with such legitimate obligations would weigh in favour of international recognition.

Legal Consequences of the Construction of a Wall in the Occupied Palestinian Territory
Advisory Opinion, ICJ Rep 2004 136, International Court of Justice

The General Assembly asked the International Court of Justice to answer the following question: 'What are the legal consequences arising from the construction of the wall being built by Israel, the occupying Power, in the Occupied Palestinian Territory, including in and around East Jerusalem, as described in the report of the Secretary-General, considering the rules and principles of international law, including the Fourth Geneva Convention of 1949, and relevant Security Council and General Assembly resolutions?'

118. As regards the principle of the right of peoples to self-determination, the Court observes that the existence of a 'Palestinian People' is no longer an issue. Such existence has moreover been recognized by Israel....The Israeli-Palestinian Interim Agreement on the West Bank and the Gaza Strip of 28 September 1995 also refers a number of times to the Palestinian people and its 'legitimate rights'....The Court considers that those rights include the right to self-determination, as the General Assembly has moreover recognized on a number of occasions (see, for example, resolution 98/163 of 22 December 2003).

122. The Court recalls moreover that, according to the report of the Secretary-General, the planned route would incorporate in the area between the Green Line and the wall more than 16 per cent of the territory of the West Bank. Around 80 per cent of the settlers living in the Occupied Palestinian Territory, that is 320,000 individuals, would reside in that area, as well as 237,000 Palestinians. Moreover, as a result of the construction of the wall, around 160,000 other Palestinians would reside in almost completely encircled communities....There is also a risk of further alterations to the demographic composition of the Occupied Palestinian Territory resulting from the construction of the wall inasmuch as it is contributing…to the departure of Palestinian populations from certain areas. That construction, along with measures taken previously, thus severely impedes the exercise by the Palestinian people of its right to self-determination, and is therefore a breach of Israel's obligation to respect that right.

155. The Court would observe that the obligations violated by Israel include certain obligations *erga omnes*. As the Court indicated in the *Barcelona Traction* case, such obligations are by their very nature 'the concern of all States' and, 'in view of the importance of the rights involved, all States can be held to have a legal interest in their protection' *(Barcelona Traction, Light and Power Company, Limited, Second Phase, Judgment, I.C.J. Reports 1970*, p. 32, para. 33). The obligations *erga omnes* violated by Israel are the obligation to respect the right of the Palestinian people to self-determination, and certain of its obligations under international humanitarian law.

156. As regards the first of these, the Court has already observed…that in the *East Timor* case, it described as 'irreproachable' the assertion that 'the right of peoples to self-determination, as it evolved from the Charter and from United Nations practice, has an *erga omnes* character'.

R. McCorquodale, 'Self-Determination: A Human Rights Approach'

43 *International and Comparative Law Quarterly* 857 (1994)

The right of self-determination applies to all situations where peoples are subject to oppression by subjugation, domination and exploitation by others. It is applicable to all territories, colonial or not, and to all peoples. The legal approaches to the right of self-determination which have been used so far have focused on the 'peoples' and on the 'territory' involved. These have been shown to be too rigid to be able to be used in the present variety of applications and exercises of the right, especially to internal self-determination.

The human rights approach to the right of self-determination recognises that the right is a human right but is not an absolute human right. This approach relies on the general legal rules developed within the international human rights law framework to enable the limitations on the right to be discerned and elaborated. By interpreting the right in the context of current State practice and current international standards, full account can be given to the development of the right over time and to its broad range of possible exercises, in contrast to the restrictive 'territorial' approach which limit its exercise to secession or independence. Use can also be made of the broad and flexible rules concerning who is a 'victim' able to bring a claim for violation of a human right to give a flexible definition of 'peoples', which avoids the barrenness and rigidity of the 'peoples' approach.

The approach provides a coherent and consistent body of general legal rules by relying on the framework of international human rights law. By using this framework, the limitations on the right are discerned and considered. The right of self-determination does have limitations, both to protect the rights of others and to protect the general interests of society, especially the need to maintain international peace and security. But those limitations are applicable only in certain circumstances, such as where internal self-determination has already occurred, and where there is a pressing need for the limitations in the society concerned.

This approach is able to deal with the changing of values in international society away from the State-based international law towards a more flexible system. Indeed, many of the claims for self-determination arose because the unjust, State-based, international legal order failed to respond to legitimate aspirations of peoples. The limitations on the right of territorial integrity and *uti possidetis* are both attempts to reassert the exclusivity of the State in international law at the expense of the people of a territory. By reasserting the primacy of the State over the rights of people, these limitations are at odds with the development of international human rights law and so, under the human rights approach, are given priority over the right of self-determination only in restricted circumstances.

While the human rights approach does not make it possible to say in the abstract which peoples have the right of self-determination and the extent of any exercise of this right, it does provide a framework to enable every situation to be considered and all the relevant rights and interests to be taken into account, balanced and analysed. This balance means that the geo-political context of the right being claimed—the particular historical circumstances—and the present constitutional order of the State and of international society, is acknowledged and addressed. Thus a claim for the exercise of the right of self-determination by secession may be considered contrary to the pressing social need in the particular society for territorial integrity, or it may be able to be exercised by different means, such as by internal self-determination. The decision by the State as to the balance between its interests and the rights that need to be protected within its territory against the right of self-determination claimed by peoples within its territory is very important but it is not conclusive, as the State, and the international community, must still comply with obligations under international human rights law. The increasing acceptance by States of these obligations could assist to foster international adjudication on claims concerning the infringement of the right of self-determination.

Thus the human rights approach to the right of self-determination creates a framework to balance competing rights and interests and seeks to provide legal rules to deal with disputes. Once this legal process has been completed then the relevant political and moral forces will be able to act on a clear and coherent legal position.

P. Macklem, 'Indigenous Recognition in International Law'

30 *Michigan Journal of International Law* 177 (2008–09)

Some international legal instruments provide guidance on what constitutes an indigenous population or people, but they are not explicit about what constitutes its international legal status. Others, such as the U.N. Declaration on the Rights of Indigenous Peoples, specify no criteria for determining whether a community constitutes an indigenous people in international law.... That the international legal order continues to exclude indigenous peoples from its distribution of sovereign power is underscored by the role and function of the right of self-determination in international law. Although the right of self-determination extended legal validity to claims of sovereign independence by colonized populations, it only validated such claims made in relation to territories geographically separate from colonizing power.... International law not only excluded indigenous peoples from the international distribution of sovereignty and included them under the sovereign power of States not of their making; it restricted the legal capacity to acquire sovereign independence by right to populations not located in sovereign States....

Although international law excludes indigenous peoples from its distribution of sovereign authority and renders them subject to the sovereign authority and renders them subject to the sovereign power of the States in which they live, international law also purports to protect indigenous peoples from the exercise of sovereign power. Contemporary international legal protection of indigenous populations formally emerged at the first Berlin Conference on Africa, initiated in 1884 by France and Germany in an effort to stem mounting tensions over competing imperial claims of sovereignty to various regions of Africa. At the Berlin Conference, imperial powers divided up Africa for the purposes of establishing and maintaining colonial territories and mutually recognized their claims of sovereign power to large swathes of the continent. Conference participants also undertook to 'watch over the preservation of the native tribes, and to care for the improvement of the conditions of their moral and material well-being....' [General Act of the Conference of Berlin Concerning the Congo, Art. 6, Feb. 26, 1885]. As a result of the Berlin Conference, what was a justification for excluding indigenous peoples from the distribution of sovereign power—their perceived lack of civilization—began also to form the basis of an international legal duty borne by imperial powers to exercise their sovereign authority in ways that improve moral and material conditions in colonies under their control.

NOTES

1. The extent of the application of the right of self-determination is still subject to debate. The right has an economic, social and cultural dimension as well as a political dimension. While it is generally accepted, as discussed above, that it applies to all colonial situations, it is now also clear that it applies outside the colonial context and therefore possibly in every State, as each State has an obligation with respect to it (i.e. there is an *erga omnes* obligation). This is confirmed by the ICJ in the *Wall Opinion* above. For example, the Preamble to the Treaty on the Final Settlement

With Respect to Germany 1990 (see Chapter 7) stated that the 'German people, freely exercising their right of self-determination, have expressed their will to bring about the unity of Germany as a State'.

2. The right of self-determination can be exercised in a variety of ways, with there being a strong presumption against secession or independence in non-colonial situations (see *Reference Re Secession of Quebec* above). Even in colonial situations other options to independence were available, though some writers argue that all peoples retain a possibility of exercising the right by independence/secession. At the same time, the right of self-determination has an 'internal' aspect, which enables peoples within a State to exercise their right of self-determination by choosing their political status, the extent of their political participation and the form of their government. This aspect was proclaimed in the Declaration on Friendly Relations (above), as it provided that only 'a government representing the whole people belonging to the territory without distinction as to race, creed or colour' can be considered as complying with the right. This was relevant for the decision in *Reference Re Secession of Quebec*.

3. In any exercise of the right of self-determination, the rights of others must be taken into account, so that the human rights of all are protected. There are also State limitations on the right of self-determination, including the territorial integrity of a State and the principle of *uti possidetis*, being the respect for the established colonial boundaries. The purpose of the latter is to protect the territorial integrity and stability of newly independent States. This was reiterated by a Chamber of the International Court of Justice in the *Land, Island and Maritime Dispute Case (El Salvador v Honduras) (Merits)* ICJ Rep 1992 351, though it also noted (at p. 388) that '*uti possidetis juris* is essentially a retrospective principle, investing as international boundaries administrative limits intended originally for quite other purposes' (see further in Chapter 7). Thus, as McCorquodale makes clear in the extract above, care must be taken so that these limitations are applied only in appropriate situations and that they do not become another method by which States, and elites in non-States, assert their power in international law at the expense of the people of a territory and so violate the right of self-determination.

4. In October 2008, the General Assembly requested an Advisory Opinion from the International Court of Justice on whether the unilateral declaration of the independence of Kosovo was in accordance with international law (see Chapter 5). The Court gave its Opinion in July 2010, where it stated that it was 'not required by the question it has been asked to take a position on whether international law conferred a positive right on Kosovo unilaterally to declare its independence or, *a fortiori*, on whether international law generally confers an entitlement on entities situated within a State unilaterally to break away from it' (para. 56). In answering this limited question, the Court considered that there was no prohibition in general international law on the making of a declaration of independence. The Court's approach has been understandably criticised, including by several of the judges who issued separate or dissenting Opinions, as the Court could have addressed the legality of the declaration more positively and considered its link to the exercise of the right of self-determination.

5. The impact on international law of the right of self-determination is potentially very broad, with its important impact on sovereignty over territory considered in Chapter 7, as it has an *erga omnes* character (see *East Timor Case* ICJ Rep 1995 90). The right has potential relevance to minorities and indigenous peoples (as indicated by Macklem above), as well as to women. It is also part of the movement away from an exclusively State-based system of international law.

SECTION 7: OTHER HUMAN RIGHTS ISSUES

States are under an obligation to protect everyone under their jurisdiction, including non-citizens and those with specific needs. Refugee law developed largely separately to international human rights law, with its aim to protect individuals from persecution (by States and by non-State actors) having a human rights dimension. Refugee law is usually extended to include the law concerning internally displaced persons.

Persons with disabilities were either assumed to be already protected by the general human rights treaties or considered as part of social concerns and so not included in human rights protections. The creation of a global treaty, being the Convention on the Rights of Persons with Disabilities 2006, to protect those with disabilities (with the appropriate descriptive terminology being debated) was a triumph of civil society in persuading States that there needed to be a specific human rights treaty to protect the rights of these groups. The Convention came into force on 3 May 2008 and, as at March 2016, has 162 State parties, with the European Union also a party.

G. Goodwin-Gill and J. McAdam, *The Refugee in International Law*

(3rd edn, 2007)

The refugee in international law occupies a legal space characterized, on the one hand, by the principle of State sovereignty and the related principles of territorial supremacy and self-preservation; and, on the other hand, by competing humanitarian principles deriving from general international law (including the purposes and principles of the United Nations) and from treaty. Refugee law nevertheless remains an incomplete legal regime of protection, imperfectly covering what ought to be a situation of exception. It goes some way to alleviate the plight of those affected by breaches of human rights standards or by the collapse of an existing social order in the wake of revolution, civil strife, or aggression; but it is incomplete so far as refugees and asylum seekers may still be denied even temporary protection, safe return to their homes, or compensation. The international legal status of the refugee necessarily imports certain legal consequences, the most important of which is the obligation of States to respect the principle of *non-refoulement* [being no return of the person to the place of fear of persecution] through time. In practice, the (legal) obligation to respect this principle, independent and compelling as it is, may be difficult to isolate from the (political) options which govern the availability of solutions. The latter necessarily depend upon political factors, including whether anything can be done about the conditions which gave rise to the refugee's flight. For any solution to be ultimately satisfactory, however, the wishes of the individual cannot be entirely disregarded, for example the connections which he or she may have with one or another State.

The existence of the class of refugees in international law not only entails legal consequences for States, but also the entitlement and the responsibility to exercise protection on behalf of refugees. The Office of the United Nations High Commissioner for Refugees (UNHCR) is the agency presently entrusted with this function, as the representative of the international community, but States also have a protecting role, even though their material interests are not engaged, and notwithstanding their common reluctance to take up the cause. Moreover, the 'interest' of the international community is expanding, and this is raising new legal and institutional questions on issues such as internal displacement, complex humanitarian emergencies, and the 'responsibility to protect'....

Refugee protection is not only about the rules governing the relation between States, but also about how States themselves treat those in search of asylum. The substantial growth and elaboration of refugee determination procedures in the developed world, and the equally substantial body of jurisprudence that has accompanied it at various levels of appeal, have exposed the words of the 1951 Convention [relating to the Status of Refugees] to close scrutiny, often apparently at one or more removes from its protection objectives. Besides questions of evidence and proof, national determination bodies have also considered the questions of attribution and causation—whether a claimant, for example, in fact fears persecution for reasons of or on account of his or her political opinion, given the motives of the persecutor, if any; whether prosecution and punishment under a law of general application can amount to persecution, in the absence of evidence of discriminatory application; whether a single act of an otherwise non-political claimant should be characterized as (sufficiently) political to qualify the resulting treatment or punishment as persecution within the meaning of the Convention; whether the refugee definition implies and requires 'good faith' conduct on the part of the claimant; whether conscientious objection to military service can form a sufficient basis for a refugee claim, and if so, in what circumstances; whether 'political offenders' are refugees; whether the notion of 'particular social group' is flexible enough to encompass any number of groups and categories in search of protection; and whether and to what extent human rights law contributes to or complements protection in refugee and analogous claims. No treaty is self-applying and the meaning of words, such as 'well-founded', 'persecution', 'expel', 'return' or 'refouler', is by no means self-evident. The Vienna Convention on the Law of Treaties confirms that a treaty 'shall be interpreted in good faith in accordance with the ordinary meaning to be given to the terms of the treaty in their context and in the light of its object and purpose'. For the 1951 Convention relating to the Status of Refugees, this means interpretation by reference to the object and purpose of extending the protection of the international community to refugees, and assuring to 'refugees the widest possible exercise of...fundamental rights and freedoms'.

F. Mégret, 'The Disabilities Convention: Towards a Holistic Concept of Rights'

12 *International Journal of Human Rights* 274 (2008)

The Disabilities Convention is about more than simply the status of persons with disabilities. It also speaks, more generally, to the larger project of which it is a part, human rights.... [T]he reason persons with disabilities have had inferior enjoyment of rights has lain, traditionally, in the complex relationship of human rights with disability, the presumptively able-bodied subject, and the very dichotomies that make much of contemporary international human rights what it is. The Convention truly has an approach which...rides roughshod over the many neat divisions, both theoretical and practical, upon which human rights are often implicitly premised. In the process, I would argue that it produces a unique vision of human rights, one which is grounded in a plural, relational concept of the human in society; one which is, in a word, considerably more holistic than that seen in international human rights treaties to this day.

The question, then, is whether this is a development that is mostly relevant to the field of disabilities, or whether it has a larger lesson for human rights generally. I would argue that it produces in favour of the latter. It is not simply the case that disabilities are a 'special issue', requiring special and *sui generis* arrangements. Nor is it the case that human rights concepts are having to 'adapt' their structure to take care of the needs of persons with disabilities, and that this is a further symptom of the fragmentation of human rights. Rather, the Disabilities Convention, in forcing us to think about the rights of *some* provides a unique opportunity to rethink how we conceive of the human rights of *all*, and could, as such, be a very fruitful way of charting the future of human rights. One way of understanding how this is so is by relativising the concept of disability. While the Convention speaks of 'disabled persons' —and there sometimes seems to be a sense that disability is an inherent characteristic of individuals— disability can be a very fluid concept and a very transient state, so that the frontier that separates disability from non-disability is in fact quite porous. Disability has always been a condition one was susceptible of acquiring or losing (not least because of its changing, social definition) and will, for example, probably increasingly in some form be the condition of many of the world's senior population. In understanding that 'we are all disabled', at least potentially, lies one way in which the Disabilities Convention can be seen as being about more than its title.

Disabled or not, however, it remains that all human beings are less in need of being further disaggregated into the mental categories that the human rights techno-structure has produced, than they are of complex and ambitious strategies that reduce, transcend, and play around disciplinary divisions. The Disabilities Convention's most significant contribution, in this respect, is to show a way out of some of the persistent dichotomies that have beset human rights. By emphasizing the dimensions of community, care, sociability, vulnerability, assistance involved in the day-to-day experience of persons with disability, the Convention can be a test-case for studying the sheer paradoxical nature of many human rights. Perhaps because it focuses on a smaller group than the entire human species, finally, the Convention may be in a better position to recapture the sense of unity and interdependence of rights which otherwise seems to elude the human rights project. Human rights lawyers should pay attention.

NOTES
1. Human rights protect everyone in a jurisdiction. This can be difficult for those States that are dealing with the consequences of either conflict in another State or within their own State, which leads to a large number of those claiming refugee status within that State. The vast majority of States that have to deal with these issues are those in the developing world close to the conflict. This raises humanitarian and human rights issues, as is seen in the extract from Goodwin-Gill and McAdam, and includes an important role for both non-governmental organisations and international organisations, such as the United Nations High Commission on Refugees.
2. The need for human rights protections to include all humans is made most evident by the completion of the Convention on the Rights of Persons with Disabilities. As Mégret makes clear, it also challenged the way in which being 'human' is perceived.

SECTION 8: BEYOND THE STATE

The framework of the international human rights legal system is State-based in terms of obligations. However, the protection of human rights is heavily influenced in many ways (positively and negatively) by a range of non-State actors. These non-State actors include individuals, non-governmental organisations, transnational corporations, inter-governmental organisations, armed opposition groups and others. Much of the impact of these bodies is also felt through the process of globalisation, so that activities in one part of the world can affect people in another part of the world. A related issue is the extent to which international human rights law applies during armed conflicts, including armed conflicts with a State or whether that is solely a matter for international humanitarian law.

A: Non-State actors

D. Kennedy, 'The Human Rights Movement: Part of the Problem?'

15 *Harvard Human Rights Journal* 101 (2002)

People have made many different claims about the narrowness of human rights. Here are some: the human rights movement foregrounds harms done explicitly by *governments* to individuals or groups—leaving largely unaddressed and more legitimate by contrast harms brought about by governments indirectly or by private parties. Even when addressing private harms, human rights focuses attention on *public* remedies—explicit rights formalized and implemented by the state. One criticizes the *state* and seeks *public* law remedies, but leaves unattended or enhanced the powers and felt entitlements of private actors. Human rights implicitly legitimates ills and delegitimates remedies in the domain of private law and nonstate action....

There needs to be some caution about assuming that the human rights movement is always a progressive and positive movement for universal human rights protection....The human knowledge about the shape of emancipation and human possibility that can be 'applied' and rights movement proposes itself as a vocabulary of the general good—as 'enforced.' As an emancipatory vocabulary, it offers answers rather than questions, answers that are not only outside political, ideological and cultural differences, but also beyond the human experience of specificity and against the human capacity to hope for more, in denial of the tawdry and uncertain quality of our available dreams about the experience with justice and injustice.

A. Clapham, *Human Rights Obligations of Non-State Actors*

(2006)

[V]arious non-state entities today have enough international legal personality to enjoy directly rights and obligations under general international law as well as under treaties. The burden would now seem to be on those who claim that states are the sole bearers of human rights obligations under international law to explain away the obvious emergence onto the international scene of a variety of actors with sufficient international personality to be the bearers of rights and duties under international law. If *The Sunday Times* has sufficient personality and the capacity to enjoy rights under the European Convention on Human Rights, it might surely have enough personality and capacity to be subject to duties under international human rights law. Similarly, if non-governmental organizations can claim their internationally protected rights in multiple international fora, they might also have the capacity to be the bearers of appropriate international obligations....

[Both humanitarian organizations and] corporations are developing their own guidelines to determine whether they should raise human rights issues when working in countries with serious problems. Again, it makes little sense to present advocacy and denunciation as a human rights obligation under international law. The duties and expectation depend entirely on the involvement and capacity of the non-state actor in question. As an entity becomes more involved with those committing human rights violations, the question of complicity becomes clearer, not only in the sense of placing the humanitarian organization in a moral dilemma, where those who remain silent feel themselves to be complicit in the violations, but also in a strict legal sense where activity or even mere presence assists or encourages the commission of international crimes....

In sum, the development of human rights obligations of non-state actors is complex due to three factors: first is the rather unspecified and evolving nature of the obligations as they are adapted from the traditional realm of state obligations to obligations for non-state actors. Second, although international law binds states and non-state actors, the obligations vary in scope according to the context. Third, the complexity of modern life mans that we have to try to disentangle complex networks and the influence and support that different actors lend each other before we can respond to enforce human rights obligations....The concept of complicity allows human rights groups to invoke familiar international human rights law framework for states, and then to show how corporate activity, which contributes to such state behaviour, amounts to complicity in a state's violations of international law. Complicity is the concept that helps lawyers and human rights organizations to fuse the state/non-state actor divide and apply international human rights law to non-state actor corporations....Complementarity allows us also to see things differently in three contexts. First, an entity can be regarded as public and private at the same time....Second, complementarity allows us to see the multiplicity of actors involved in a human rights infringement...[and] the multiple overlapping layers of responsibility....Third, the act could give rise to multiple breaches of national law, international human rights law, international humanitarian law, and international criminal law...and of non-binding instrument[s].

J. Ruggie, 'Guiding Principles on Business and Human Rights: Implementing the United Nations "Protect, Respect and Remedy" Framework'

Report of the Special Representative of the Secretary-General on the issue of human rights and transnational corporations and other business enterprises, UN Doc A/HRC/17/31(2011)

These Guiding Principles are grounded in recognition of:

(a) States' existing obligation to respect, protect and fulfil human rights and fundamental freedoms;
(b) The role of business enterprises as specialized organs of society performing specialized functions, required to comply with all applicable laws and to respect human rights;
(c) The need for rights and obligations to be matched to appropriate and effective remedies when breached.

These Guiding Principles apply to all States and to all business enterprises, both transnational and others, regardless of their size, sector, location, ownership and structure.

These Guiding Principles should be understood as a coherent whole and should be read, individually and collectively, in terms of their objective of enhancing standards and practices with regard to business and human rights so as to achieve tangible results for affected individuals and communities, and thereby also contributing to a socially sustainable globalization.

Nothing in these Guiding Principles should be read as creating new international law obligations, or as limiting or undermining any legal obligations a State may have undertaken or be subject to under international law with regard to human rights.

These Guiding Principles should be implemented in a non-discriminatory manner, with particular attention to the rights and needs of, as well as the challenges faced by, individuals from groups or populations that may be at heightened risk of becoming vulnerable or marginalized, and with due regard to the different risks that may be faced by women and men.

General Principles

1. States must protect against human rights abuse within their territory and/or jurisdiction by third parties, including business enterprises. This requires taking appropriate steps to prevent, investigate, punish and redress such abuse through effective policies, legislation, regulations and adjudication.

2. States should set out clearly the expectation that all business enterprises domiciled in their territory and/or jurisdiction respect human rights throughout their operations.

4. States should take additional steps to protect against human rights abuses by business enterprises that are owned or controlled by the State, or that receive substantial support and services from State agencies such as export credit agencies and official investment insurance or guarantee agencies, including, where appropriate, by requiring human rights due diligence.

11. Business enterprises should respect human rights. This means that they should avoid infringing on the human rights of others and should address adverse human rights impacts with which they are involved.

12. The responsibility of business enterprises to respect human rights refers to internationally recognized human rights—understood, at a minimum, as those expressed in the International Bill of Human Rights and the principles concerning fundamental rights set out in the International Labour Organization's Declaration on Fundamental Principles and Rights at Work.

13. The responsibility to respect human rights requires that business enterprises:

(a) Avoid causing or contributing to adverse human rights impacts through their own activities, and address such impacts when they occur;

(b) Seek to prevent or mitigate adverse human rights impacts that are directly linked to their operations, products or services by their business relationships, even if they have not contributed to those impacts.

14. The responsibility of business enterprises to respect human rights applies to all enterprises regardless of their size, sector, operational context, ownership and structure. Nevertheless, the scale and complexity of the means through which enterprises meet that responsibility may vary according to these factors and with the severity of the enterprise's adverse human rights impacts.

15. In order to meet their responsibility to respect human rights, business enterprises should have in place policies and processes appropriate to their size and circumstances, including:

(a) A policy commitment to meet their responsibility to respect human rights;

(b) A human rights due-diligence process to identify, prevent, mitigate and account for how they address their impacts on human rights;

(c) Processes to enable the remediation of any adverse human rights impacts they cause or to which they contribute.

17. In order to identify, prevent, mitigate and account for how they address their adverse human rights impacts, business enterprises should carry out human rights due diligence. The process should include assessing actual and potential human rights impacts, integrating and acting upon the findings, tracking responses, and communicating how impacts are addressed. Human rights due diligence:

(a) Should cover adverse human rights impacts that the business enterprise may cause or contribute to through its own activities, or which may be directly link to its operations, products or services by its business relationships;

(b) Will vary in complexity with the size of the business enterprise, the risk of severe human rights impacts, and the nature and context of its operations;

(c) Should be ongoing, recognizing that the human rights risks may change over time as the business enterprise's operations and operating context evolve.

22. Where business enterprises identify that they have caused or contributed to adverse impacts, they should provide for or cooperate in their remediation through legitimate processes.

25. As part of their duty to protect against business-related human rights abuses, States must take appropriate steps to ensure, through judicial, administrative, legislative or other appropriate means, that when such abuses occur within their territory and/or jurisdiction those affected have access to effective remedy.

29. To make possible for grievances to be addressed early and remediated directly, business enterprises should establish or participate in effective operational-level grievance mechanisms for individuals and communities who may be adversely impacted.

R. McCorquodale and P. Simons, 'Responsibility Beyond Borders: State Responsibility for Extraterritorial Violations by Corporations of International Human Rights Law'

70 Modern Law Review 598 (2007)

The growth of transnational corporations (TNCs) operating across more than one state, has raised questions about how international law would deal with these entities. This is partly because the distribution of power and control of TNCs are arranged in ways that defy territorial boundaries, with a 'parent' corporation being a 'national' in one state and its various subsidiaries being 'nationals' in those states where they operate. Despite the wealth of documents, reports and academic literature that have suggested that corporations should have direct international legal liability for such violations, there is—as yet—no international human rights law to this effect. This is due to the fact that international human rights law has developed to protect human rights on states alone, and has not yet developed so as to regulate effectively the activities of corporations, or other non-state actors, which violate human rights in their extraterritorial operations.

There are clear human rights legal obligations on a state to place an effective restraint on activities within its territory that violate human rights. However, the reality is that for many states, particularly non-industrialised states, the economic power of a TNC operating within that state (the 'host state') is such that the host state may be unable or unwilling to control effectively the activities of that corporation, or the host state may be prevented from doing so by other international treaty obligations, such as bilateral investment agreements. This means that, while the host state undoubtedly will be in breach of its human rights obligations if it does not act to prevent these human rights violations occurring, the TNC will remain accountable and unrestrained, and those whose rights are violated will be without an effective remedy. In contrast, the state where the headquarters of the TNC is incorporated or otherwise has its main centre of operations (the 'home state'), is usually an industrialized state, with the resources, power and legal interests to regulate in relation to the extraterritorial activities of the relevant corporation, if it chooses to do so....

Under customary international law a state will incur international responsibility for a breach of an international legal obligation, where the act in question can be attributed to the states. This has been codified by the International Law Commission (ILC) in its Articles on the Responsibility of States for Internationally Wrongful Acts... State obligations under international human rights law are not territorially confined. The major international human rights treaties expressly extend state obligations both to individuals within a state's territory and to those individuals who are subject to a state's jurisdiction....

The jurisprudence of the international human rights supervisory bodies has shown that states have extraterritorial human rights obligations where they exercise power, authority or effective control over individuals, or where they exercise effective control of an area of territory within another state....The activities of a corporate national (and its subsidiaries) acting extraterritorially can be attributed to the home state where the corporation is exercising elements of governmental authority, or where it is acting under the instruction, direction or control of the state. A home state will also be responsible if it knowingly aids and assists in either a host state's international wrongful act relating to the activities of a home state's corporate national (or its foreign subsidiaries) that constitute international crimes. Failure by a home state to exercise due diligence by, inter alia, regulating and monitoring the activities of corporate nationals in conflict zones and in host states with which a home state has ratified a BIT [Bilateral Investment Treaty], may also give rise to international responsibility in cases where corporate nationals violate, or are complicit in violations of, human rights.

J. Oloka-Onyango and D. Udagama, 'The Realization of Economic, Social and Cultural Rights: Globalization and its Impact on the full enjoyment of Human Rights'

Preliminary Report to UN Sub-Commission on Human Rights E/CN.4/Sub.2/2000/13 (2000)

26. It would be absurd to claim that globalization created inequality. Inequality and discrimination unfortunately existed long before globalization was recognized as a distinct phenomenon on the international scene. That globalization has caused global conditions of inequality and discrimination to worsen is clear even by simply examining the statistical data....If we ask a further question, viz. what is the colour, race or sex of those left out? The connection between globalization and the forces of inequality and discrimination become all the more graphic....In a continent like Africa where the vast majority of the populace is based in the rural area eking out a subsistence existence, the fact is that globalization has not improved things. Partaking in the processes of globalization, represented by the opening of free markets, the liberalization of trade barriers and the removal of protectionist barriers, is thus no guarantee that all will benefit.

28. There are clearly also problems concerning whether globalization is even of benefit to those who contribute a considerable amount to its success - workers around the world, legal and otherwise. Thus, while the countries of the developed part of the world clearly rely on migrant labour to sustain and operate their economies, the extent to which they either recognize or reward this category of person is debatable....

41. ...the impact of the adverse consequences of globalization on the enjoyment of human rights is multidimensional; all aspects of human existence, be they political, economic, social or cultural, are affected. The negative impact on one dimension of human rights, e.g. economic rights, necessarily has a domino effect on other rights...

44. The negative impact of globalization—especially on vulnerable sections of the community—results in the violation of a plethora of rights guaranteed by the Covenants. In particular, the enjoyment of fundamental aspects of the right to life, freedom from cruel, inhuman or degrading treatment, freedom from servitude, the right to equality and non-discrimination, the right to an adequate standard of living (including the right to adequate food, clothing and housing), the right to maintain a high standard of physical and mental health, and the right to work accompanied by the right to just and fair conditions of labour, freedom of association and assembly and the right to collective bargaining, have been severely impaired. Developing States are, more often

than not, compelled by the dynamics of globalization to take measures that negatively impact on the enjoyment of those rights. The result is that States cannot fulfill their international human rights obligations, even if they are desirous of improving the human rights situation in their countries. The critical question is the following: Can international economic forces that are engineered by both State and private actors be unleashed on humanity in a manner that ignores international human rights law?

NOTES

1. The primary obligation to protect human rights of everyone in their jurisdiction remains on States, including where those actions that violate human rights are actions by non-State actors. These obligations can be very extensive, as McCorquodale and Simons indicate. There can also be actions in the supposedly private sphere for which a State is traditionally not held to be responsible, such as domestic violence. Feminist legal theory has challenged this division into public/private spheres in the determination of when a State is responsible (see Charlesworth above). It is hoped that international human rights law will develop to protect the victim of a violation of human rights, no matter who is the violator, and no matter what is the cause or the place of the violation.

2. It is impossible to determine the exact correlation between the efforts of non-governmental organisations (NGOs) and the protection of human rights, but clearly their influence on States in promoting and protecting human rights—and preventing violations of human rights—through fact-finding, publicity and action has had some impact. As well, information provided by NGOs is often used by human rights bodies to clarify a particular situation and to counter-balance a State's assertions of facts. Some NGOs have (limited) standing in United Nations organisations, which can enable them to comment on issues before those organisations.

3. Transnational corporations and international organisations are largely outside the international human rights legal system in terms of legal obligations. However, their impact on the daily lives of people around the globe and on the violation of human rights is very significant. To limit their obligations to non-legal 'social expectations' raises the issue as to how the expectations of the oppressed can be met without some ability to bring a legal claim. There is a considerable development in the crafting of laws and practices to ensure that corporations have responsibility for their human rights impacts.

4. Oloka-Onyango and Udagama consider the unequal effect of globalisation on human rights. Globalisation is primarily an economic process, although it is also a political, social and cultural process. It is a process where developments in technology and communications, the creation of intricate international economic and trade arrangements, increasing activity by international organisations and transnational corporations are moving at a rapid pace and beyond the control of any one State. By diminishing the relevance of territorial boundaries, globalisation highlights the extent of interdependence of the international community. As such, the process of globalisation affects all aspects of international law, including territorial sovereignty and jurisdiction (see Chapters 7 and 8). At the same time it requires a reconsideration of the nature of international law so that it can deal effectively with the activities by non-State actors.

B: International humanitarian and international human rights law

Human Rights Committee, General Comment 31, 'Nature of the General Legal Obligations on States Parties to the Covenant'

UN Doc CCPR/C/21/Rev.1/Add.13 (2004)

3....[T]he Covenant applies also in situations of armed conflict to which the rules of international humanitarian law are applicable. While, in respect of certain Covenant rights, more specific rules of international humanitarian law may be specially relevant for the purposes of the interpretation of Covenant rights, both spheres of law are complementary, not mutually exclusive.

Legal Consequences of the Construction of a Wall in the Occupied Palestinian Territory
Advisory Opinion, ICJ Rep 2004 136, International Court of Justice

The facts are set out at Section 6C.

105. In its Advisory Opinion of 8 July 1996 on the *Legality of 'the Threat or Use of' Nuclear Weapons*, the Court had occasion to address [the relationship between international humanitarian law and human rights law] in relation to the International Covenant on Civil and Political Rights. In those proceedings certain States had argued that 'the Covenant was directed to the protection of human rights in peacetime, but that questions relating to unlawful loss of life in hostilities were governed by the law applicable in armed conflict' (I.C.J. Reports 1996 (I), p. 239, para. 24). The Court rejected this argument, stating that 'the protection of the International Covenant of Civil and Political Rights does not cease in times of war, except by operation of Article 4 of the Covenant whereby certain provisions may be derogated from in a time of national emergency. Respect for the right to life is not, however, such a provision. In principle, the right not arbitrarily to be deprived of one's life applies also in hostilities. The test of what is an arbitrary deprivation of life, however, then falls to be determined by the applicable *lex specialis*, namely, the law applicable in armed conflict which is designed to regulate the conduct of hostilities.' (*Ibid*, p. 240, para. 25.)

106. More generally, the Court considers that the protection offered by human rights conventions does not cease in case of armed conflict, save through the effect of provisions for derogation of the kind to be found in Article 4 of the International Covenant on Civil and Political Rights. As regards the relationship between international humanitarian law and human rights law, there are thus three possible situations: some rights may be exclusively matters of international humanitarian law; others may be exclusively matters of human rights law; yet others may be matters of both these branches of international law. In order to answer the question put to it, the Court will have to take into consideration both these branches of international law, namely human rights law and, as *lex specialis*, international humanitarian law.

109. The Court would observe that, while the jurisdiction of States is primarily territorial, it may sometimes be exercised outside the national territory. Considering the object and purpose of the International Covenant on Civil and Political Rights, it would seem natural that, even when such is the case, States parties to the Covenant should be bound to comply with its provisions. The constant practice of the Human Rights Committee is consistent with this. Thus, the Committee has found the Covenant applicable where the State exercises its jurisdiction on foreign territory. It has ruled on the legality of acts by Uruguay in cases of arrests carried out by Uruguayan agents in Brazil or Argentina (case No. 52/79, *Lopez Burgos v. Uruguay*; case No. 56/79, *Lilian Celiberti de Casariego v. Uruguay*). It decided to the same effect in the case of the confiscation of a passport by a Uruguayan consulate in Germany (case No. 106181, *Montero v. Uruguay*). The *travaux preparatoire* of the Covenant confirm the Committee's interpretation of Article 2 of that instrument. These show that, in adopting the wording chosen, the drafters of the Covenant did not intend to allow States to escape from their obligations when they exercise jurisdiction outside their national territory. They only intended to prevent persons residing abroad from asserting, vis-à-vis their State of origin, rights that do not fall within the competence of that State, but of that of the State of residence (see the discussion of the preliminary draft in the Commission on Human Rights, EICN.4ISR.194, para. 46; and United Nations, Official records of the General Assembly, Tenth Session, Annexes, AI2929, Part II, Chap. V, para. 4 (1955)).

111. In conclusion, the Court considers that the International Covenant on Civil and Political Rights is applicable in respect of acts done by a State in the exercise of its jurisdiction outside its own territory.

112. The International Covenant on Economic, Social and Cultural Rights contains no provision on its scope of application. This may be explicable by the fact that this Covenant guarantees rights which are essentially territorial. However, it is not to be excluded that it applies both to territories over which a State party has sovereignty and to those over which that State exercises territorial jurisdiction.

S. Sivakumaran, 'International Humanitarian Law'

in D.Moeckli, S. Shah and S. Sivakumaran (eds) *International Human Rights Law* (2nd edn, 2014)

That international human rights law applies in armed conflict is, today, beyond question. This is clear from the human rights treaties themselves. The ICCPR, for example, provides that a state party to the ICCPR may derogate from certain of its obligations 'in time of public emergency which threatens the life of the nation', a phrase that includes armed conflict. Other, non-derogable, obligations continue to bind the state: armed conflict does not give a free pass to torture, enslave and the like. A number of human rights treaties—the African Charter on Human and Peoples' Rights for one—do no contain derogation clauses. In respect of these treaties, no derogation is permitted; the whole host of obligations remain applicable....Far more difficult—and still unsettled—is the precise relationship between international human rights law and international humanitarian law. The most authoritative, though ultimately inconclusive, statement on the point is the pronouncement of the ICJ in its *Wall* advisory opinion.

5.1 Rights exclusively matters of international humanitarian law

It is only natural that international humanitarian law, that body of law particularly designed to regulate hostilities, contains rights that are not to be found in international human rights law. Take, for example, occupied territory. International humanitarian law contains a detailed body of rules relating to the law of belligerent occupation. The law of belligerent occupation strikes a delicate balance between the rights of the occupied, the occupying power, and the displaced sovereign....These rules reflect the competing interests of the different actors—the occupied, the occupying power, and the displaced sovereign. This tripartite relationship does not map neatly onto classical international human rights law, which regulates the relationship between the state and the individual. Accordingly, many of the features of the law of occupation are not replicated in international human rights law.

5.2 Rights exclusively matters of international human rights law

Equally, there are rights grounded in international human rights law that are nowhere to be found in international humanitarian law. The right not to be imprisoned on the ground of inability to fulfil a contractual obligation and the right to recognition as a person before the law are rights featured in the ICCPR from which there may be derogation. International humanitarian law contains no equivalent provisions....

5.3 Rights matters of both international human rights law and international humanitarian law

In the majority of situations, a particular right will be grounded in both international human rights law and international humanitarian law. In such instance, the principle of *lex specialis* governs, such that the more specific rule will take precedence over the more general. There are two variants of the *lex specialis* principle. The first applies in the event of a conflict between the two norms. In this situation, the specific rule *modifies* the general rule to the extent of the inconsistency between them. The general rule does not fall away. It remains in the background and applicable to the extent that it does not conflict with the specific rule. The second variant applies when one norm is of greater specificity than the other norm, or is more tailored to the circumstances at hand, but there is no inconsistency between them. Here, the more specific rule is but an *application* of the more general rule. Although it may be useful to distinguish between these variants, a firm distinction between modification and application is difficult to draw and somewhat artificial.

Care needs to be taken when importing ideas from one body of law to another, for they may be appropriate in one context but not in another. Some modification may be required in order to render the idea being transferred suitable to the body of law in which it now finds itself. As the International Criminal Tribunal for the former Yugoslavia has had occasion to observe, 'notions developed in the field of human rights can be transposed in international humanitarian law only if they take into consideration the specificities of the latter body of law' [*Prosecutor* v *Kenarac et al*, 22 February 2001, para. 471].

NOTES

1. A further discussion of international criminal law is found in Chapter 14.
2. Only some aspects of international human rights law have been dealt with in this chapter. Other human rights issues will be referred to in later Chapters, for example, human rights and the environment (Chapter 12) and violations of rights in extradition/abduction cases (Chapter 8), or were raised in previous chapters, as with the role of the individual in international law considered in Chapter 5. There are also issues of the protection of human rights in situations where the Security Council has acted in relation to terrorism sanctions (see Chapter 15). Indeed, as noted at the beginning of this chapter, international human rights law continues to have a significant effect on most areas of international law, not least in its challenge to traditional ideas of sovereignty and its extraterritorial applications.

7

Sovereignty over Territory

INTRODUCTORY NOTE

Sovereignty is one of the fundamental concepts in international law. It is an integral part of the principles of equality of States, territorial integrity and political independence that are referred to in Article 2 of the United Nations Charter. Sovereignty is crucial to the exercise of powers by a State over both its territory and the people living in that territory. Accordingly, Chapters 7, 8 and 10 are concerned primarily with issues of sovereignty. Further, as a corollary to a State's own sovereignty, it has responsibilities to respect the sovereignty of other States (see Chapter 9) and not to abuse its sovereignty, for example, by causing environmental damage (see Chapter 12).

SECTION 1: SOVEREIGNTY AND TERRITORY

Island of Palmas Case (*The Netherlands* v *United States*)
2 RIAA 829 (1928), Huber, Sole Arbitrator

The facts of this case are set out in Section 3.

Sovereignty in the relations between States signifies independence. Independence in regard to a portion of the globe is the right to exercise therein, to the exclusion of any other State, the functions of a State. The development of the national organisation of States during the last few centuries and, as a corollary, the development of international law, have established this principle of the exclusive competence of the State in regard to its own territory in such a way as to make it the point of departure in settling most questions that concern international relations. The special cases of the composite State, of collective sovereignty, etc., do not fall to be considered here and do not, for that matter, throw any doubt upon the principle which has just been enunciated. Under this reservation it may be stated that territorial sovereignty belongs always to one, or in exceptional circumstances to several States, to the exclusion of all others. The fact that the functions of a State can be performed by any State within a given zone is, on the other hand, precisely the characteristic feature of the legal situation pertaining in those parts of the globe which, like the high seas or lands without a master, cannot or do not yet form the territory of a State....

Territorial sovereignty, as has already been said, involves the exclusive right to display the activities of a State. This right has as corollary a duty: the obligation to protect within the territory the rights of other States, in particular their right to integrity and inviolability in peace and in war, together with the rights which each State may claim for its nationals in foreign territory. Without manifesting its territorial sovereignty in a manner corresponding to circumstances, the State cannot fulfil this duty. Territorial sovereignty cannot limit itself to its negative side, i.e. to excluding the activities of other States; for it serves to divide between nations the space upon which human activities are employed, in order to assure them at all points the minimum of protection of which international law is the guardian.

V. Lowe, *International Law*

(2007)

Sovereignty is an elusive concept—in philosophical terms, an essentially contexted concept—with a complex genealogy as a topic of debate in political theory. It makes sense to discuss the likely effect of a particular policy or action on the 'sovereignty' of a State; and that normally entails reference to a knot of concepts centering on two inter-related ideas—the formal independence of decision-making of the State, and its freedom to exercise that independence in practice. It is less clear that the concept of sovereignty has much use in international legal reasoning…But the practice is to express the relationship between a State and its 'own' territory in terms of the State's sovereignty of its territory, with the consequence that one State may be sovereign and another may actually occupy the territory, as China was sovereign over the territories that Britain leased from it in Hong Kong, and Cuba is sovereign over the US base at Guantanamo….

International law is not concerned with the mythical histories by which States first gained their territory; but it does speak of the processes by which sovereignty over territory changes hands, and it operates a presumption against disturbing states of affairs that have long existed peacefully—of letting sleeping dogs lie. If we ask what right a State—say the United Kingdom or India—has to its territory, the answer given by international law is pragmatic. It has its territory (or more accurately, the State is recognized as having sovereignty over its territory) because so far as we can tell it has acquired that territory by processes that are recognized as lawful.

R. McCorquodale, 'International Law, Boundaries and Imagination'

in D. Miller and S. Hashmi (eds), *Boundaries and Justice* (2001)

Boundaries are integral to international law. They are a cause of conflict and a reason for peace. They establish order and lead to disorder. They provide a protection and a weapon. They include and exclude. They define and divide. They are real and imagined….

The prevailing concept of the international legal system is that territorial boundaries establish statehood and that territorial boundaries are the basis for state sovereignty (ownership). Accordingly, the distribution of natural resources, concepts of diversity, and the mobility of people are considered within this state-based framework, and the political autonomy of the state and territorial boundaries are completely entwined. The current international legal system recreates and affirms the dispositions by colonial powers, it privileges certain voices and silences others, and it restricts the identities of individuals to those defined by state boundaries. The effect of this is to reinforce the state-based framework of the international legal system and to limit the influence of other factors. This is because this system, as traditionally conceived 'naturalises and legitimises the subjugating and disciplinary effects of European, masculinist, heterosexual and capitalist regimes of power.' [D. Otto, 18 *Australian Yearbook of International Law* (1998)]

While territorial boundaries are artificially created by the international legal system, they tend to arise only from the imagination of these regimes of power. There is little room for the imagination of the developing states, of non-state actors, of women or of alternative concepts of the international legal system. Occasionally, these different imaginations do have some expression, such as in the development of internal self-determination and of the common heritage of mankind, but they are quickly limited by the prevailing international legal system. Law, in determining rules (and hence legal boundaries), is self-limiting because 'law purports to preserve institutional stability and continuity [and] reform must build from existing legal precedents and doctrines,' [K. Bartlett and R. Kennedy (eds), *Feminist Legal Theory* (1991)] and so law allows change incrementally from the status quo position. However, as the 'intrusive, intersubjective, and symbolic qualities of modern law continually interact with social practices and relationships, making legal change is an integral, necessary component of social change.' [K. Powers, *Wisconsin Law Review* (1979)]. It does leave open the possibilities for new imaginations of international law to emerge.

There are new ways to imagine the international legal role of territorial boundaries. Some of these ways are institutional, as seen in the multilevel sovereignties in Europe, and some are structural, such as the diminished importance of territorial boundaries due to the process of globalization. Above all, the new imaginations are conceptual. They have to be able 'to convert those borders from their prevailing postures as ramparts into a new veritable function as bridges' [A. Asiwaju in C. Schofield (ed), *Global Boundaries* (1994)], and to focus on relationships and not on imaginary constructs. This language of international law in relation to territorial boundaries must be in terms of an international society that is inclusive of all, allows all to find and use their voices, is creative of identity opportunities, and recognizes diversity within the universality of international society.

E. Crawford and R. Rayfuse, 'Climate Change and Statehood'

in R. Rayfuse and S. Scott (eds), *International Law in the Era of Climate Change* (2012)

Climate change presents a unique threat to the territorial integrity of states, indeed, to the very concept of statehood itself. As the Intergovernmental Panel on Climate Change (IPCC) has noted, climate change will affect the physical territory of states in a number of ways through, for example, the loss of viable eco-systems due to desertification, increased soil salinity, flooding of coastal and low-lying regions, or loss of reliable access to land due to increased severe weather events such as hurricanes. Coastal states, in particular those with low-lying coastal areas, will also be affected by permanent loss of land through shoreline erosion caused by extreme weather events and sea-level rise.

Moreover, it has been recognised that by rendering some inhabited land incapable of sustaining human habitation, climate change will also result in the forced migration of some or all of a population from their lands. At the extreme end of the scale, climate change induced territorial degradation coupled with climate change induced migration may threaten the very existence of some states. In particular, it has been suggested that by the end of this century a number of low-lying small island states such as Tuvalu, Kiribati, the Marshall Islands and the Maldives, may be rendered totally uninhabitable. This begs the question as to the continued statehood of these 'disappearing states'....

A distinct body of law regarding the parameters of the continuance of states exists. It consists of the complex and unsettled customary law on state succession and the treaty rules on state succession articulated in the Vienna Convention on Succession of States in Respect of Treaties and the Vienna Convention on Succession of States in Respect of State Property, Archives and Debts. However, this law is designed to deal with situations in which a state simply changes its borders, its government, or the extent of its territorial control, and reconstitutes itself in an altered but still recognisable form. Central to this paradigm is that such reconstitution is always essentially within, or at least contiguous with, the territory in which the predecessor state originally existed. International law does not yet apprehend a process of dissolution in the context of the total inhabitability or actual physical disappearance of a state's territory and no rules exist to determine whether, and if so when, a state ceases to exist by virtue of the actual physical disappearance of its population or its territory....

If scientific predictions are to be believed, the total loss of habitable territory is the prospect facing some small low-lying island states. Should climate change result in total population displacement from a small island state, either because of rising sea levels or because of extreme weather events and other climate change associated environmental degradation making habitation unsustainable, these states may be forced to abandon their territory. In the absence of a positive decision to dissolve the state, the question is whether these states can continue to exist as states even in the face of the loss of the fundamental Montevideo criteria of a permanent population living in a defined territory under effective control raises. This 'statehood dilemma' lies at the heart of the challenge to the international law on statehood presented by climate change.

Traditional responses to the resolution of the statehood dilemma include the acquisition of new sovereign territory from a distant state by treaty of cession or merger with another state by way of some form of federation. In the case of cession, like the Alaska purchase, sovereignty over the ceded land would transfer in its entirety to the disappearing state which could then relocate its population to the new territorial location. The continued existence of the state would be secured in accordance with traditional rules of international law. While undoubtedly a neat solution from a legal perspective, from a practical perspective it is difficult to envisage any state now agreeing to cede a part of its territory to another. The political, social and economic ramifications of ceding valued and/or inhabited territory may simply exceed the capacities—and courage—of existing governments. In the case of federation, the disappearing state would cease to exist. Its continued relationship with its territory and population would be governed by the terms of confederation.

A third alternative that has been suggested is the recognition of a new category of state—the 'deterritorialised state' or, as Burkett calls it, the 'nation-ex situ'. Analogous to a 'government in exile' the state would continue to exist as an international legal person despite its physical disappearance through population loss or inundation of territory. Particularly relevant in the context of small island states, the maritime zones of the disappearing state would continue to inure to the deterritorialised state and the resource rents from their exploitation would be used both to ensure the conservation and management of those zones in accordance with international law and to fund the relocation and continued livelihood of the displaced population, whether diasporic or wholly located within one other 'host' state.

The question of whether a state can exist in the absence of territory would, at first blush, appear to be answered in the negative. In his famous dictum in the *Island of Palmas* case Arbitrator Huber stated that '[i]nternational law, the structure of which is not based on any super-State organisation, cannot be presumed to reduce a right such as territorial sovereignty, with which almost all international relations are bound up, to the category of an abstract right, without concrete manifestations'. The concrete manifestations to which he was referring were occupation and the exercise of governmental authority over the population located in the relevant territory. However, a more contemporary analysis suggests that 'territory is not necessary to statehood, at least after statehood has been established.' (Grant, (1999) 37 *Columbia Journal of Transnational Law* 403)

NOTES
1. In the *North Atlantic Coast Fisheries Case* (*United Kingdom* v *United States*) 11 RIAA (1910) 167, the Permanent Court of Arbitration stated (at p. 180) that 'one of the essential elements of sovereignty is that it is to be exercised within territorial limits, and that, failing proof to the contrary, the territory is co-terminous with Sovereignty'. Territory is also one criterion for Statehood (see Chapter 5) and hence is essential for an entity to become a State. More problematic is whether States, particularly island States, faced with the permanent loss of territory due to the threat of climate change can continue to exist in their current form (see Crawford and Rayfuse above).
2. Title to territory is not merely concerned with changes in the occupation of that territory but with changes in the right to territorial sovereignty (see R. Jennings, *The Acquisition of Territory in International Law* (1963), p. 14). Despite the 'imaginary' nature of territorial boundaries and the legal position that successor States are bound by boundary treaties, many disputes occur between States over competing claims to territory.
3. Territorial disputes also occur due to hopes about potential natural resources. For example, the strategic location of the uninhabited Senkaku or Diaoyu Islands near potential gas and oil reserves has been a key feature of the dispute between China and Japan, and with other States in the South China Sea. The International Court of Justice and other international tribunals, such as the Permanent Court of Arbitration, have been generally effective in resolving those territorial boundary disputes or claims which the parties have trusted to them (see Chapter 16).
4. Disputes may also arise due to the violation of a State's territorial integrity. For example, in May 2011, the US sent military forces to locate and kill Osama Bin Laden, who was at the time on Pakistan's territory and within its jurisdiction, leading to tensions between the two States. The US stated that it neither sought nor obtained consent from Pakistan and the Pakistan government viewed the 'invasion' as a violation of its territorial sovereignty.
5. Perspectives on the nature of sovereignty and its relationship to territory are changing over time from the State-centred view seen in the first extract. Alternative sovereignties reflect the changes to the nature of international law (as reflected in the extract from McCorquodale), where States are no longer the only participants in the development of international law (see also Chapter 1). Concepts of sovereignty may also have to change to accommodate the effects of climate change, as discussed by Crawford and Rayfuse.

SECTION 2: TRADITIONAL MEANS OF ACQUISITION OF TERRITORY

Traditionally there have been five means of acquisition of territory. These are occupation, prescription, cession, accretion (being the geographical addition of new territory—not discussed here) and conquest. They are of current value only as a means of exposition.

A: Occupation and prescription

Occupation is the exercise of sovereignty (often initially by discovery) over previously unclaimed territory (*terra nullius*). Prescription is the peaceful exercise of sovereignty for a reasonable period without objection by another State.

Clipperton Island Arbitration (France v Mexico)
2 RIAA 1105 (1932); transl. in 26 *American Journal of International Law* 390, Victor Emmanuel III, Sole Arbitrator

Clipperton Island is situated in the Pacific Ocean, about 1,200 kilometres south west of Mexico. On 17 November 1858, a French lieutenant on board a commercial vessel cruising past the island, declared the island (which was uninhabited) to be French territory. The lieutenant notified the French consulate in Honolulu, which informed the government of Hawaii and published the declaration of French sovereignty in a local Hawaiian journal. Very little was then done in relation to the island by the French authorities. In 1897 a Mexican gun-boat landed and forced the three inhabitants to raise the Mexican flag, claiming that the island had been discovered by Spain, to which Mexico was the successor State from 1836. The Arbitrator held that this discovery by Spain had not been proved, and that France had not abandoned her claim and so had title to the island.

[T]he proof of an historic right of Mexico's is not supported by any manifestation of her sovereignty over the island, a sovereignty never exercised until the expedition of 1897; and the mere conviction that this was territory belonging to Mexico, although general and of long standing, cannot be retained.

Consequently, there is ground to admit that, when in November, 1858, France proclaimed her sovereignty over Clipperton, that island was in the legal situation of *territorium nullius*, and, therefore, susceptible of occupation.

The question remains whether France proceeded to an effective occupation, satisfying the conditions required by international law for the validity of this kind of territorial acquistion. In effect, Mexico maintains, secondarily to her principal contention which has just been examined, that the French occupation was not valid, and consequently her own right to occupy the island which must still be considered as *nullius* in 1897.

In whatever concerns this question, there is, first of all, ground to hold as incontestable, the regularity of the act by which France in 1858 made known in a clear and precise manner, her intention to consider the island as her territory.

On the other hand, it is disputed that France took effective possession of the island, and it is maintained that without such a taking of possession of an effective character, the occupation must be considered as null and void.

It is beyond doubt that by immemorial usage having the force of law, besides the *animus occupandi*, the actual, and not the nominal, taking of possession is a necessary condition of occupation. This taking of possession consists in the act, or series of acts, by which the occupying state reduces to its possession the territory in question and takes steps to exercise exclusive authority there. Strictly speaking, and in ordinary cases, that only takes place when the state establishes in the territory itself an organization capable of making its laws respected. But this step is, properly speaking, but a means of procedure to the taking of possession, and, therefore, is not identical with the latter. There may also be cases where it is unnecessary to have recourse to this method. Thus, if a territory, by virtue of the fact that it was completely uninhabited, is, from the first moment when the occupying state makes its appearance there, at the absolute and undisputed disposition of that state, from that moment the taking of possession must be considered as accomplished, and the occupation is thereby completed....

It follows from these premises that Clipperton Island was legitimately acquired by France on November 17, 1858. There is no reason to suppose that France has subsequently lost her right by *derelictio*, since she never had the *animus* of abandoning the island, and the fact that she has not exercised her authority there in a positive manner does not imply the forfeiture of an acquisition already definitively perfected.

Chamizal Arbitration (Mexico v United States)
11 RIAA 309 (1911), International Boundary Commission

The Rio Grande was established, by treaties dated 1848 and 1853, as being the boundary between Mexico and the United States. The river-bed moved over time. The

Chamizal Tract lies between the old bed of the Rio Grande and the present bed of that river.

In the argument it is contended that the Republic of Mexico is estopped from asserting the national title over the territory known as 'El Chamizal' by reason of the undisturbed, uninterrupted, and unchallenged possession of said territory by the United States of America since the treaty of Guadalupe Hidalgo.

Without thinking it necessary to discuss the very controversial question as to whether the right of prescription invoked by the United States is an accepted principle of the law of nations, in the absence of any convention establishing a term of prescription, the commissioners are unanimous in coming to the conclusion that the possession of the United States in the present case was not of such a character as to found a prescriptive title. Upon the evidence adduced it is impossible to hold that the possession of El Chamizal by the United States was undisturbed, uninterrupted, and unchallenged from the date of the treaty [to] the creation of a competent tribunal to decide the question....On the contrary, it may be said that the physical possession taken by citizens of the United States and the political control exercised by the local and Federal Governments, have been constantly challenged and questioned by the Republic of Mexico, through its accredited diplomatic agents....

The very existence of that convention precludes the United States from acquiring by prescription against the terms of their title, and, as has been pointed out above, the two Republics have ever since the signing of that convention treated it as a source of all their rights in respect of accretion to the territory on one side or the other of the river. Another characteristic of possession serving as a foundation for prescription is that it should be peaceable....

Under these circumstances the commissioners have no difficulty in coming to the conclusion that the plea of prescription should be dismissed.

Western Sahara Opinion
ICJ Rep 1975 12, International Court of Justice

After much dispute over sovereignty to Western Sahara, the General Assembly, by Resolution 3292 (XXIX) adopted on 13 December 1974, sought an advisory opinion from the International Court of Justice on a number of questions, including the following:

    I. Was Western Sahara (Rio de Oro and Sakiet El Hamra) at the time of colonization by Spain a territory belonging to no one (*terra nullius*)?
        If the answer to the first question is in the negative,

    II. What were the legal ties between this territory and the Kingdom of Morocco and the Mauritian entity?

The Court answered the first question in the negative but found legal ties between the territory and each of the two States.

79. Turning to Question I, the Court observes that the request specifically locates the question in the context of 'the time of colonization by Spain', and it therefore seems clear that the words 'Was Western Sahara...a territory belonging to no one (*terra nullius*)?' have to be interpreted by reference to the law in force at that period. The expression '*terra nullius*' was a legal term of art employed in connection with 'occupation' as one of the accepted legal methods of acquiring sovereignty over territory. 'Occupation' being legally an original means of peaceably acquiring sovereignty over territory otherwise than by cession or succession, it was a cardinal condition of a valid 'occupation' that the territory should be *terra nullius*—a territory belonging to no-one—at the time of the act alleged to constitute the 'occupation' (cf. *Legal Status of Eastern Greenland*, PCIJ, Series A/B, No. 53, pp. 44 f. and 63 f.). In the view of the Court, therefore, a determination that Western Sahara was a '*terra nullius*' at the time of colonization by Spain would be possible only if it were established that at that time the territory belonged to no-one in the sense that it was then open to acquisition through the legal process of 'occupation'.

80. Whatever differences of opinion there may have been among jurists, the State practice of the relevant period indicates that territories inhabited by tribes or peoples having a social and political organization were not regarded as *terrae nullius*. It shows that in the case of such territories the acquisition of sovereignty was not generally considered as effected unilaterally through 'occupation' of *terra nullius* by original title but through

agreements concluded with local rulers. On occasion, it is true, the word 'occupation' was used in a non-technical sense denoting simply acquisition of sovereignty; but that did not signify that the acquisition of sovereignty through such agreements with authorities of the country was regarded as an 'occupation' of a '*terra nullius*' in the proper sense of these terms. On the contrary, such agreements with local rulers, whether or not considered as an actual 'cession' of the territory, were regarded as derivative roots of title, and not original titles obtained by occupation of *terrae nullius*.

81. In the present instance, the information furnished to the Court shows that at the time of colonization Western Sahara was inhabited by peoples which, if nomadic, were socially and politically organized in tribes and under chiefs competent to represent them. It also shows that, in colonizing Western Sahara, Spain did not proceed on the basis that it was establishing its sovereignty over *terrae nullius*. In its Royal Order of 26 December 1884, far from treating the case as one of occupation of *terra nullius*, Spain proclaimed that the King was taking the Rio de Oro under his protection on the basis of agreements which had been entered into with the chiefs of the local tribes…

[Question II]…As the Permanent Court stated in the case concerning the *Legal Status of Eastern Greenland*, a claim to sovereignty based upon continued display of authority involves 'two elements each of which must be shown to exist: the intention and will to act as sovereign, and some actual exercise or display of such authority' (*ibid.*, pp. 45 f). True, the Permanent Court recognized that in the case of claims to sovereignty over areas in thinly populated or unsettled countries, 'very little in the way of actual exercise of sovereign rights' (*ibid.*, p. 46) might be sufficient in the absence of a competing claim. But, in the present instance, Western Sahara, if somewhat sparsely populated, was a territory across which socially and politically organized tribes were in constant movement and where armed incidents between these tribes were frequent. In the particular circumstances outlined in paragraphs 87 and 88 above, the paucity of evidence of actual display of authority unambiguously relating to Western Sahara renders it difficult to consider the Moroccan claim as on all fours with that of Denmark in the *Eastern Greenland* case. Nor is the difficulty cured by introducing the argument of geographical unity or contiguity. In fact, the information before the Court shows that the geographical unity of Western Sahara with Morocco is somewhat debatable, which also militates against giving effect to the concept of contiguity. Even if the geographical contiguity of Western Sahara with Morocco could be taken into account in the present connection, it would only make the paucity of evidence of unambiguous display of authority with respect to Western Sahara more difficult to reconcile with Morocco's claim to immemorial possession….

93. In the view of the Court, however, what must be of decisive importance in determining its answer to Question II is not indirect inferences drawn from events in past history but evidence directly relating to effective display of authority in Western Sahara at the time of its colonization by Spain and in the period immediately preceding that time (cf. *Minquiers and Ecrehos, Judgment*, ICJ Reports 1953, p. 57)….

161. As already indicated in paragraph 70 of this Opinion, the General Assembly has made it clear, in resolution 3292 (XXIX), that the right of the population of Western Sahara to self-determination is not prejudiced or affected by the present request for an advisory opinion, nor by any other provision contained in that resolution. It is also clear that, when the General Assembly asks in Question II what were the legal ties between the territory of Western Sahara and the Kingdom of Morocco and the Mauritanian entity, it is addressing an enquiry to the Court as to the nature of these legal ties. This question, as stated in paragraph 85 above, must be understood as referring to such legal ties as may affect the policy to be followed in the decolonization of Western Sahara. In framing its answer, the Court cannot be unmindful of the purpose for which its opinion is sought. Its answer is requested in order to assist the General Assembly to determine its future decolonization policy and in particular to pronounce on the claims of Morocco and Mauritania to have had legal ties with Western Sahara involving the territorial integrity of their respective countries.

162. The materials and information presented to the Court show the existence, at the time of Spanish colonization, of legal ties of allegiance between the Sultan of Morocco and some of the tribes living in the territory of Western Sahara. They equally show the existence of rights, including some rights relating to the land, which constituted legal ties between the Mauritanian entity, as understood by the Court, and the territory of Western Sahara. On the other hand, the Court's conclusion is that the materials and information presented to it do not establish any tie of territorial sovereignty between the territory of Western Sahara and the Kingdom of Morocco or the Mauritanian entity. Thus the Court has not found legal ties of such a nature as might affect the application of resolution 1514 (XV) in the decolonization of Western Sahara and, in particular, of the principle of self-determination through the free and genuine expression of the will of the peoples of the Territory (cf. paragraphs 54–59 above).

Case Concerning Sovereignty Over Pedra Branca/Pulau Batu Puteh, Middle Rocks and South Ledge (Malaysia/Singapore)

ICJ Rep 2008 12, International Court of Justice

This dispute concerned competing territorial claims by Malaysia and Singapore regarding several islets at the eastern entrance to the Singapore Strait, namely Pedra Branca (previously called Pulau Batu Puteh and now Batu Puteh by Malaysia), Middle Rocks and South Ledge. Singapore claimed that Pedra Branca was *terra nullius*, and had never fallen under the sovereignty of Malaysia's predecessor, the Johor Sultanate. In the alternative, Singapore asserted that sovereignty in respect of the island had passed to Singapore, as the actions of its predecessor, the United Kingdom, in the period from 1847 to 1851 constituted a taking of lawful possession of the island, which was maintained by the continuous exercise of authority by the United Kingdom and Singapore ever since.

118. As the Court has shown in the preceding part of this Judgment, Johor had sovereignty over Pedra Branca/Pulau Batu Puteh at the time the planning for the construction of the lighthouse on the island began. Singapore does not contend that anything had happened before then which could provide any basis for an argument that it or its predecessors had acquired sovereignty. But Singapore does of course contend that it has acquired sovereignty over Pedra Branca/Pulau Batu Puteh since 1844. The Singapore argument is based on the construction and operation of Horsburgh lighthouse and the many other actions it took on, and in relation to Pedra Branca/Pulau Batu Puteh, as well as on the conduct of Johor and its successors. By contrast, Malaysia contends that all of those actions of the United Kingdom were simply actions of the operator of the lighthouse, being carried out precisely in terms of the permission which Johor granted in the circumstances which the Court will soon consider.

119. Whether Malaysia has retained sovereignty over Pedra Branca/Pulau Batu Puteh following 1844 or whether sovereignty has since passed to Singapore can be determined only on the basis of the Court's assessment of the relevant facts as they occurred since 1844 by reference to the governing principles and rules of international law. The relevant facts consist mainly of the conduct of the Parties during that period.

120. Any passing of sovereignty might be by way of agreement between the two States in question. Such an agreement might take the form of a treaty,... The agreement might instead be tacit and arise from the conduct of the Parties. International law does not, in this matter, impose any particular form. Rather it places its emphasis on the parties' intentions (cf. e.g. *Temple of Preah Vihear (Cambodia v. Thailand), I.C.J. Reports 1961*, pp. 17, 31).

121. Under certain circumstances, sovereignty over territory might pass as a result of the failure of the State which has sovereignty to respond to conduct *à titre de souverain* of the other State or, as Judge Huber put it in the *Island of Palmas* case, to concrete manifestations of the display of territorial sovereignty by the other State (*Island of Palmas Case (Netherlands/United States of America), Award of 4 April 1928, RIAA*, Vol. II, p. 839). Such manifestations of the display of sovereignty may call for a response if they are not to be opposable to the State in question. The absence of reaction may well amount to acquiescence. The concept of acquiescence 'is equivalent to tacit recognition manifested by unilateral conduct which the other party may interpret as consent...' (*Delimitation of the Maritime Boundary in the Gulf of Maine Area (Canada/United States of America), Judgment, I.C.J. Reports 1984*, p. 305, para. 130). That is to say, silence may also speak, but only if the conduct of the other State calls for a response.

122. Critical for the Court's assessment of the conduct of the Parties is the central importance in international law and relations of State sovereignty over territory and of the stability and certainty of that sovereignty. Because of that, any passing of sovereignty over territory on the basis of the conduct of the Parties, as set out above, must be manifested clearly and without any doubt by that conduct and the relevant facts. That is especially so if what may be involved, in the case of one of the Parties, is in effect the abandonment of sovereignty over part of its territory....

149. The facts about the construction and commissioning of the lighthouse on Pedra Branca/Pulau Batu Puteh and indeed for the most part its operation over the many years since are not themselves the subject of significant dispute between the Parties. They also agree on the law: it 'requires an intention to acquire sovereignty, a permanent intention to do so and overt action to implement the intention and to make the intention to acquire manifest to other States'. There is some disagreement on whether practice also requires elements of formality.

Symbolic acts accompanying the acquisition of territory are very common both generally and in British practice. They are not however always present. The Court does not consider that the practice demonstrates a requirement that there be a symbolic act. Rather the intention to acquire sovereignty may appear from the conduct of the Parties, particularly conduct occurring over a long period....

274. The conduct of the United Kingdom and Singapore was, in many respects, conduct as operator of Horsburgh lighthouse, but that was not the case in all respects. Without being exhaustive, the Court recalls their investigation of marine accidents, their control over visits, Singapore's installation of naval communication equipment and its reclamation plans, all of which include acts *à titre de souverain*, the bulk of them after 1953. Malaysia and its predecessors did not respond in any way to that conduct, or the other conduct with that character identified earlier in this Judgment, of all of which (but for the installation of the naval communication equipment) it had notice.

275. Further, the Johor authorities and their successors took no action at all on Pedra Branca/Pulau Batu Puteh from June 1850 for the whole of the following century or more. And, when official visits (in the 1970s for instance) were made, they were subject to express Singapore permission. Malaysia's official maps of the 1960s and 1970s also indicate an appreciation by it that Singapore had sovereignty. Those maps, like the conduct of both Parties which the Court has briefly recalled, are fully consistent with the final matter the Court recalls. It is the clearly stated position of the Acting Secretary of the State of Johor in 1953 that Johor did not claim ownership of Pedra Branca/Pulau Batu Puteh. That statement has major significance.

276. The Court is of the opinion that the relevant facts, including the conduct of the Parties, previously reviewed and summarized in the two preceding paragraphs, reflect a convergent evolution of the positions of the Parties regarding title to Pedra Branca/Pulau Batu Puteh. The Court concludes, especially by reference to the conduct of Singapore and its predecessors *à titre de souverain*, taken together with the conduct of Malaysia and its predecessors including their failure to respond to the conduct of Singapore and its predecessors, that by 1980 sovereignty over Pedra Branca/Pulau Batu Puteh had passed to Singapore.

277. For the foregoing reasons, the Court concludes that sovereignty over Pedra Branca/Pulau Batu Puteh belongs to Singapore.

NOTES
1. The concept of occupation was based on a notion of European hegemony over the 'uncivilised world'. Even if there were some inhabitants of a territory, it was still assumed that the territory was *terra nullius* if the inhabitants did not have obvious European forms of social or political institutions and so could be occupied. This concept of *terra nullius* was discredited in the *Western Sahara Opinion* (and see *Mabo v Queensland (No 2)* in Section 5C).
2. The doctrine of prescription provides that defects in a title can be cured by the passage of time and the acquiescence of other States. If a State has been in peaceful possession of a territory for a period of time, international law considers that it is a better result to recognise that that State has gained a good title to the territory, unless the other State has objected. Accordingly, with prescription, it is important that the sovereign actions be public and open, so that all interested States are aware of the actions and so, if appropriate, can protest. Though, as seen in the *Clipperton Island Case*, the amount of publicity given to the sovereign actions can be very limited. Statements or acts by States may have the often unintended effect of confirming the newly acquired title. For example, in the *Case Concerning Sovereignty over Pedra Branca*, one piece of conduct appeared particularly influential on the Court's final decision, being a letter in 1953 from the Acting Secretary of State of Johor to the Colonial Secretary of Singapore, which stated that 'the Johore Government does not claim ownership of Pedra Branca'. The Court held that this correspondence established that 'as of 1953 Johor understood that it did not have sovereignty over Pedra Branca' (para. 230). That the State in question acted in mistake, or did not understand the significance of its action, does not prevent its conduct supporting the claim of the other State.
3. The notion of historical consolidation differs from prescription in that it does not require acquiescence. Instead a series of acts by the claiming State, third States and, possibly, international organisations such as the United Nations, constitute the gradual building of a title. However, the ICJ has apparently rejected the notion of historical consolidation as a method of acquiring title, at least in cases where there is a contrary treaty-based title: see *Case Concerning the*

Land and Maritime Boundary Between Cameroon and Nigeria (Cameroon v Nigeria; Equatorial Guinea Intervening) ICJ Rep 2002 303, para. 62.

4. The *Case Concerning Sovereignty over Pedra Branca* also confirms that sovereignty cannot be separately claimed in respect of maritime features other than islands, such as rocks exposed only at low tide. The Court held that sovereignty in respect of South Ledge, a low-tide elevation, belongs to the State in the territorial waters of which it is located (para. 299). See also *Maritime Delimitation and Territorial Questions between Qatar and Bahrain (Qatar v Bahrain)*, ICJ Rep 2001 40.

B: Cession

Cession is the transfer of territory from one sovereign to another, usually by means of a treaty.

M. Davis, *Constitutional Confrontation in Hong Kong*

(1989)

In September of 1982 the British Prime Minister, Margaret Thatcher, reached agreement with Chinese leaders to 'enter into talks through diplomatic channels with the common aim of maintaining the stability and prosperity of Hong Kong'. While parts of the colony of Hong Kong had in the middle of the last century been ceded to Britain in perpetuity the largest section of the colony, the so called New Territories, was held under a lease that was due to expire in 1997. Protracted negotiations followed the 1982 announcement and resulted in the signing of the Sino-British Joint Declaration in 1984. Under the terms of the Joint Declaration China will resume sovereignty over the entire territory of Hong Kong on 1 July 1997. As suggested by the original 1982 announcement, the Joint Declaration seeks to maintain Hong Kong's stability and prosperity under a capitalist common law system and afford a high degree of autonomy. The Joint Declaration calls for the drafting by China of a Basic Law for Hong Kong to provide a framework or constitution for the future Hong Kong Special Administrative Region of the People's Republic of China [SAR], thus implementing China's announced policy of 'one country, two systems'. The final draft of the Basic Law has now been prepared and thus substantial movement towards Hong Kong's promised future has been made....

The basis for this arrangement is thus a binding international agreement that provides for a level of self-government, constitutional democracy and foreign relations competence sufficient to ensure the successful operation of a capitalist region, even in the national context of a dramatically opposed Marxist-Leninist Chinese economic and political system. This is no small task and may demand more from autonomy than has ever been achieved before. Even the main cases for associated state status have not been marked by such contrast. It is in this context that the powers expressly afforded that bear on external support may exceed those often evident even with regard to associated states. It is difficult to imagine how anything less will achieve the policy objective.

In orchestrating the Joint Declaration's formula for Hong Kong, the Chinese government has in practice indicated a willingness to set aside many of the labels to which it is so strongly committed in rhetoric. In light of evolving notions of statehood and autonomy, they have taken the leading edge and contrived a formula designed to maintain adequate central control over foreign political and defence affairs, while otherwise permitting Hong Kong to conduct its own affairs. This formula aims to maintain the SAR in China's national orbit, and demonstrate the little which is demanded of the modern conception of sovereignty, while otherwise permitting Hong Kong to continue doing what it does well....

On the positive side, the PRC is generally considered to have a good record for conformity to its treaty obligations unlike its purely domestic commitments. Nevertheless the rather liberal and inventive autonomy model evident in the Joint Declaration is generally inconsistent with Chinese policy and practice. Historically, the Chinese have rejected the internationalism implied by the Hong Kong formula in the Joint Declaration, a formula which preserves many aspects of Hong Kong's status as an international actor. Even committing this formula to an international treaty seems inconsistent with past practices. Historically, the Chinese have insisted on the inviolability and inalienability of national sovereignty. China has supported a positivist conception of sovereignty as the core of all fundamental principles of international law and as the foundation on which other international institutions and norms are based. Under this view, China would not invite international scrutiny of the Hong Kong formula or any other regional or human rights problem, such as that evident in Tibet. Such would be viewed as meddling in China's internal affairs.

In spite of this, the Joint Declaration at its heart seems to invite such scrutiny of the Hong Kong formula. Dr Roda Mushkat ['*Transition*', 14 *Denver Jnl of International Law and Policy*, p. 178] suggests that historically the Chinese have tacitly accepted a form of divided sovereignty over Hong Kong. Britain has 'effective sovereignty' while China has 'titular' or 'residual' sovereignty. The Joint Declaration and the draft Basic Law, therefore speak of 'resuming the exercise' of sovereignty. Nevertheless in its overall policy and practical content the Joint Declaration seems tacitly to continue this ambiguity. This creative ambiguity reflects a practical side of Chinese policy content.

Treaty on the Final Settlement With Respect to Germany
29 *International Legal Materials* 1186 (1990)

This treaty was entered into by France, the USSR, the United Kingdom and the United States, being the Four Powers which had rights and responsibilities over Berlin and Germany consequent upon the end of the Second World War, and also by the Federal Republic of Germany and the German Democratic Republic.

Article 1

1. The united Germany shall comprise the territory of the Federal Republic of Germany, the German Democratic Republic and the whole of Berlin. Its external borders shall be the borders of the Federal Republic of Germany and the German Democratic Republic and shall be definitive from the date on which the present Treaty comes into force. The confirmation of the definitive nature of the borders of the united Germany is an essential element of the peaceful order in Europe.

2. The united Germany and the Republic of Poland shall confirm the existing border between them in a treaty that is binding under international law.

3. The united Germany has no territorial claims whatsoever against other states and shall not assert any in the future.

4. The Governments of the Federal Republic of Germany and the German Democratic Republic shall ensure that the constitution of the united Germany does not contain any provision incompatible with these principles. This applies accordingly to the provisions laid down in the preamble, the second sentence of Article 23, and Article 146 of the Basic Law for the Federal Republic of Germany.

5. The Governments of the French Republic, the Union of Soviet Socialist Republics, the United Kingdom of Great Britain and Northern Ireland and the United States of America take formal note of the corresponding commitments and declarations by the Governments of the Federal Republic of Germany and the German Democratic Republic and declare that their implementation will confirm the definitive nature of the united Germany's borders.

Article 7

1. The French Republic, the Union of Soviet Socialist Republics, the United Kingdom of Great Britain and Northern Ireland and the United States of America hereby terminate their rights and responsibilities relating to Berlin and to Germany as a whole. As a result, the corresponding, related quadripartite agreements, decisions and practices are terminated and all related Four Power institutions are dissolved.

2. The united Germany shall have accordingly full sovereignty over its internal and external affairs.

Statement, Secretary of State for the Foreign and Commonwealth Office
Hansard, 12 July 2002

There has been a dispute between Britain and Spain over Gibraltar for the last 300 years. As the House will be aware, in 1984 the then Conservative Government decided that the only way in which to make progress to resolve the dispute was to talk to Spain about both the practical issues of concern to Gibraltar and the sovereignty issue which mattered to Spain. The so-called Brussels process was thus born.

This Government decided last year to relaunch those negotiations. We did so because we had reached the same conclusion as our predecessors—that the status quo was damaging to Gibraltar, and also damaging to Britain....

The only way of securing a stable and prosperous future for Gibraltar is through a comprehensive and permanent settlement of the dispute, and that means an agreement with Spain on all issues including—as flagged up by the Brussels communiqué itself in 1984—sovereignty.

By taking the latter approach, we have made significant progress towards a solution. It may be helpful if I remind the House of the phases of the process on which we are embarked. In the first phase, the current one, our objective has been to agree the framework—the principles—of a new permanent settlement for Gibraltar. That is what we have been working on for the past year or so. If and when we were able to reach agreement with Spain on such a framework, we would publish it in a joint declaration—a statement of intent by the two Governments. Thereafter, in the second phase, there would be further detailed negotiations—in which the Government of Gibraltar would again be invited to participate fully—to produce a comprehensive package, including a new draft treaty, based on the principles set out in the joint declaration. The United Kingdom would ratify such a treaty only after securing the consent of the Gibraltarians in a referendum.

After 12 months of negotiation, we and Spain are in broad agreement on many of the principles that should underpin a lasting settlement. They include the principles that Britain and Spain should share sovereignty over Gibraltar, including the disputed territory of the isthmus; that Gibraltar should have more internal self-government; that Gibraltar should retain its British traditions, customs and way of life; that Gibraltarians should retain the right to British nationality, and should gain the right to Spanish nationality as well; that Gibraltar should retain its institutions—its Government, House of Assembly, courts and police service; and that Gibraltar could, if it chose, participate fully in the European Union single market and other EU arrangements....

I profoundly believe that such a future is in the interests of the people of Gibraltar; but, as I have stressed many times, it is not in the end a decision for me or even for the House. The decision rests with the people of Gibraltar. If we and Spain can, after taking stock, reach agreement on the kind of framework that I have outlined, and if thereafter all parties can build on those principles to produce a comprehensive settlement, the whole package will be put to the people of Gibraltar in a referendum and they will decide....

We and Spain have not yet resolved all differences. In respect of the duration of co-sovereignty, we must have a permanent settlement. Co-sovereignty cannot be just a stepping stone to full Spanish sovereignty, however long delayed. I know and understand that Spain has a long-standing historical aspiration to regain full sovereignty one day, but any agreement between us and Spain must be permanent. Gibraltar must have certainty.

NOTES

1. Cession transfers all rights of sovereignty from one State to another. Yet the State transferring sovereignty cannot transfer more rights than it possesses. Due to the right of self-determination (see below and Chapter 6), now there is a requirement to consult the inhabitants of a territory before cession occurs.

2. New States can acquire territory by succession, such as when the former Yugoslavia divided into separate States. This is discussed in Chapter 3.

3. States may also exercise powers in respect of territory they have occupied following an armed conflict. As is seen in the treaty establishing a reunified Germany, the United Kingdom, the United States, France and the USSR continued to exercise powers in respect of occupied Germany following the end of the Second World War.

4. States may exercise rights of control and possession in respect of territory of which the State is not sovereign. International leases are a key example of this. For example, the United States leases the land on which the US naval base stands at Guantanamo Bay from Cuba pursuant to the terms of two lease agreements. As is discussed further in Chapter 8, the United States Supreme Court has held that, while the United States is not the *de jure* sovereign, it acts as the *de facto* sovereign, and, as such certain protections under the US Constitution extend to those individuals detained at the base (*Boumedine* v *Bush*, 47 ILM 650 (2008), extracted in Chapter 8).

5. States may agree to 'share' sovereignty, as was envisaged by the potential agreement between the United Kingdom and Spain concerning Gibraltar, discussed in the extract above. The proposed arrangement did not eventuate, as the people of Gibraltar overwhelmingly rejected the principle of shared sovereignty at a referendum in November 2002. Three-way talks between Gibraltar, the United Kingdom and Spain in 2006 did not discuss sovereignty issues, although they did enable the re-establishment of air travel between Spain and Gibraltar for the first time in 30 years.

C: Conquest

Conquest is the acquisition of territory by the use of force.

United Nations Charter 1945

Article 2

4. All Members shall refrain in their international relations from the threat or use of force against the territorial integrity or political independence of any State, or in any other manner inconsistent with the Purposes of the United Nations.

Declaration on Principles of International Law concerning Friendly Relations and Cooperation among States in Accordance with the Charter of the United Nations, General Assembly

Annex to Resolution 2625 (XXV), 24 October 1970

Every State has the duty to refrain in its international relations from the threat or use of force against the territorial integrity or political independence of any State, or in any other manner inconsistent with the purposes of the United Nations. Such a threat or use of force constitutes a violation of international law and the Charter of the United Nations and shall never be employed as a means of settling international issues....

The territory of a State shall not be the object of military occupation resulting from the use of force in contravention of the provisions of the Charter. The territory of a State shall not be the object of acquisition by another State resulting from the threat or use of force. No territorial acquisition resulting from the threat or use of force shall be recognized as legal. Nothing in the foregoing shall be construed as affecting:

(a) Provisions of the Charter or any international agreement prior to the Charter régime and valid under international law; or

(b) The powers of the Security Council under the Charter.

Security Council Resolution 662 (1990)

Adopted on 9 August 1990

The Security Council,

Recalling its resolutions 660 (1990) and 661 (1990),

Gravely alarmed by the declaration by Iraq of a 'comprehensive and eternal merger' with Kuwait,

Demanding, once again, that Iraq withdraw immediately and unconditionally all its forces to the positions in which they were located on 1 August 1990,

Determined to bring the occupation of Kuwait by Iraq to an end and to restore the sovereignty, independence and territorial integrity of Kuwait,

Determined also to restore the authority of the legitimate Government of Kuwait,

1. *Decides* that annexation of Kuwait by Iraq under any form and whatever pretext has no legal validity, and is considered null and void;

2. *Calls upon* all States, international organizations and specialized agencies not to recognize that annexation, and to refrain from any action or dealing that might be interpreted as an indirect recognition of the annexation;

3. *Further demands* that Iraq rescind its actions purporting to annex Kuwait;

4. *Decides* to keep this item on its agenda and to continue its efforts to put an early end to the occupation.

NOTES

1. At least since the signing of the United Nations Charter, the use of force has been illegal in international law (see Chapter 15). Acquisitions of territory by force since that date are illegal and

usually are condemned by the international community, a recent example of which is the international response to the annexation of Crimea by Russia (see Chapter 5). Acquisitions of territory prior to that date are affected by 'intertemporal law'.

2. The doctrine of intertemporal law requires that sovereignty be considered in the light of the rules of international law that prevailed at the time at which the claim of sovereignty is based and not the rules of international law prevailing at the time the dispute is being adjudicated. While the creation of the entitlement to a territory is dependent on the rules of international law at the earlier time, it seems that the continued existence of that entitlement is dependent on the current rules of international law. This was made clear in the *Island of Palmas Case* (see Section 3) where it was stated that 'a juridical fact must be appreciated in the light of the law contemporary with it, and not of the law in force at the time when a dispute in regard to it arises or falls to be settled.... [However] a distinction must be made between the creation of rights and the existence of rights. The same principle which subjects the act creative of a right to the law in force at the time the right arises, demands that the existence of [a] right, in other words, its continued manifestation, shall follow the conditions required by the evolution of law.'

SECTION 3: EFFECTIVE OCCUPATION

Contemporary approaches to international law consider three primary matters with respect to sovereignty over territory: effective occupation; consent; and the right of self-determination (see Chapter 6 for the latter). The main basis for establishing sovereignty over territory today is by effective occupation, being the continuous and peaceful display of sovereignty.

Island of Palmas Case (The Netherlands v United States)
2 RIAA 829 (1928), Huber, Sole Arbitrator

This dispute related to sovereignty over the Island of Palmas (or Miangas), just south of the Island of Mindanao in (present day) The Philippines. The United States' claim to the island was derived from Spain by way of cession under the Treaty of Paris 1898, and they relied, as successor to Spain, on acts of discovery, recognition by treaty and on contiguity. The Netherlands challenged this by relying on the historical connection between it and neighbouring States, of which the island was a part, since about 1700, and on acts of sovereignty by The Netherlands since that date. The Arbitrator upheld the Netherlands' title to the Island.

Territorial sovereignty is, in general, a situation recognized and delimited in space, either by so-called natural frontiers as recognised by international law or by outward signs of delimitation that are undisputed, or else by legal engagements entered into between interested neighbours, such as frontier conventions, or by acts of recognition of States within fixed boundaries. If a dispute arises as to the sovereignty over a portion of territory, it is customary to examine which of the States claiming sovereignty possesses a title—cession, conquest, occupation, etc.—superior to that which the other State might possibly bring forward against it. However, if the contestation is based on the fact that the other Party has actually displayed sovereignty, it cannot be sufficient to establish the title by which territorial sovereignty was validly acquired at a certain moment; it must also be shown that the territorial sovereignty has continued to exist and did exist at the moment which for the decision of the dispute must be considered as critical. This demonstration consists in the actual display of State activities, such as belongs only to the territorial sovereign....

Titles of acquisition of territorial sovereignty in present-day international law are either based on an act of effective apprehension, such as occupation or conquest, or, like cession, presuppose that the ceding and the cessionary Powers or at least one of them, have the faculty of effectively disposing of the ceded territory. In the same way natural accretion can only be conceived of as an accretion to a portion of territory where there exists an actual sovereignty capable of extending to a spot which falls within its sphere of activity. It seems therefore natural that an element which is essential for the constitution of sovereignty should not be lacking in its continuation. So true is this, that practice, as well as doctrine, recognizes—though under different legal formulae and with certain differences as to the conditions required—that the continuous and peaceful display of territorial sovereignty (peaceful in relation to other States) is as good as a title. The growing insistence with which international law, ever since the middle of the 18th century, has demanded that the occupation shall be effective would be inconceivable, if effectiveness were required only for the act of acquisition and not equally for the maintenance of the right. If the effectiveness has above all been insisted on in regard to occupation, this is because the question rarely arises in connection with territories in which there is already an established order of things. Just as before the rise of international law, boundaries of lands were necessarily determined by the fact that the power of a State was exercised within them, so too, under the reign of international law, the fact of peaceful and continuous display is still one of the most important considerations in establishing boundaries between States....

[O]n the other hand the view is adopted that discovery does not create a definitive title of sovereignty, but only an 'inchoate' title, such a title exists, it is true, without external manifestation. However, according to the view that has prevailed at any rate since the 19th century, an inchoate title of discovery must be completed within a reasonable period by the effective occupation of the region claimed to be discovered. This principle must be applied in the present case, for the reasons given above in regard to the rules determining which of successive legal systems is to be applied (the so-called intertemporal law). Now, no act of occupation nor, except as to a recent period, any exercise of sovereignty at Palmas by Spain has been alleged. But even admitting that the Spanish title still existed as inchoate in 1898 and must be considered as included in the cession under Article III of the Treaty of Paris, an inchoate title could not prevail over the continuous and peaceful display of authority by another State; for such display may prevail even over a prior, definitive title put forward by another State....

Manifestations of territorial sovereignty assume, it is true, different forms, according to conditions of time and place. Although continuous in principle, sovereignty cannot be exercised in fact at every moment on every point of a territory. The intermittence and discontinuity compatible with the maintenance of the right necessarily differ according as inhabited or uninhabited regions are involved, or regions enclosed within territories in which sovereignty is incontestably displayed or again regions accessible from, for instance, the high seas. It is true that neighbouring States may by convention fix limits to their own sovereignty, even in regions such as the interior of scarcely explored continents where such sovereignty is scarcely manifested, and in this way each may prevent the other from any penetration of its territory. The delimitation of Hinterland may also be mentioned in this connection.

The United States base their claim on the titles of discovery, of recognition by treaty and of contiguity, i.e. titles relating to acts or circumstances leading to the acquisition of sovereignty; they have however not established the fact that sovereignty so acquired was effectively displayed at any time. The Netherlands on the contrary found their claim to sovereignty essentially on the title of peaceful and continuous display of State authority over the island. Since this title would in international law prevail over a title of acquisition of sovereignty not followed by actual display of State authority, it is necessary to ascertain in the first place, whether the contention of the Netherlands is sufficiently established by evidence, and, if so, for what period of time....

The acts of the *East India Company* (Generale Geoctroyeerde Nederlandsch Oost-Indische Compagnie), in view of occupying or colonizing the regions at issue in the present affair must, in international law, be entirely assimilated to acts of the Netherlands State itself. From the end of the 16th till the 19th century, companies formed by individuals and engaged in economic pursuits (Chartered Companies), were invested by the State to whom they were subject with public powers for the acquisition and administration of colonies. The Dutch East India Company is one of the best known....

An inchoate title however cannot prevail over a definite title founded on continuous and peaceful display of sovereignty. The title of contiguity, understood as a basis of territorial sovereignty, has no foundation in international law....The Netherlands title of sovereignty, acquired by continuous and peaceful display of State authority during a long period of time going probably back beyond the year 1700, therefore holds good.

Legal Status of Eastern Greenland Case (Norway v Denmark)

PCIJ Rep Ser A/B (1933) No. 53, Permanent Court of International Justice

Norway occupied Eastern Greenland in July 1931, claiming that it was *terra nullius*, while Denmark insisted that Danish sovereignty existed over all Greenland from about 1721, at the time when Denmark and Norway were one State. The Court determined that Denmark had a valid title to Eastern Greenland.

Before proceeding to consider in detail the evidence submitted to the Court, it may be well to state that a claim to sovereignty based not upon some particular act or title such as a treaty of cession but merely upon continued display of authority, involves two elements each of which must be shown to exist: the intention and will to act as sovereign, and some actual exercise or display of such authority.

Another circumstance which must be taken into account by any tribunal which has to adjudicate upon a claim to sovereignty over a particular territory, is the extent to which the sovereignty is also claimed by some other Power. In most of the cases involving claims to territorial sovereignty which have come before an international tribunal, there have been two competing claims to the sovereignty, and the tribunal has had to decide which of the two is the stronger. One of the peculiar features of the present case is that up to 1931 there was no claim by any Power other than Denmark to the sovereignty over Greenland. Indeed, up till 1921, no Power disputed the Danish claim to sovereignty.

It is impossible to read the records of the decisions in cases as to territorial sovereignty without observing that in many cases the tribunal has been satisfied with very little in the way of the actual exercise of sovereign rights, provided that the other State could not make out a superior claim. This is particularly true in the case of claims to sovereignty over areas in thinly populated or unsettled countries....Legislation is one of the most obvious forms of the exercise of sovereign power....

The conclusion to which the Court is led is that, bearing in mind the absence of any claim to sovereignty by another Power, and the Arctic and inaccessible character of the uncolonized parts of the country, the King of Denmark and Norway displayed during the period from the founding of the colonies by Hans Egede in 1721 up to 1814 his authority to an extent sufficient to give his country a valid claim to sovereignty, and that his rights over Greenland were not limited to the colonized area....The result of all the documents connected with the grant of the [trading, hunting and mining] concession is to show that, on the one side, it was granted upon the footing that the King of Denmark was in a position to grant a valid monopoly on the East coast and that his sovereign rights entitled him to do so, and, on the other, that the concessionaires in England regarded the grant of a monopoly as essential to the success of their projects and had no doubt as to the validity of the rights conferred....

The concessions granted for the erection of telegraph lines and the legislation fixing the limits of territorial waters in 1905 are also manifestations of the exercise of sovereign authority.

In view of the above facts, when taken in conjunction with the legislation she had enacted applicable to Greenland generally, the numerous treaties in which Denmark, with the concurrence of the other contracting Party, provided for the non-application of the treaty to Greenland in general, and the absence of all claim to sovereignty over Greenland by any other Power, Denmark must be regarded as having displayed during this period of 1814 to 1915 her authority over the uncolonized part of the country to a degree sufficient to confer a valid title to the sovereignty.

Case Concerning Sovereignty Over Pulau Ligitan and Pulau Sipadan (Indonesia v Malaysia)

ICJ Rep 2002 625, International Court of Justice

This dispute concerned sovereignty in respect of the islands of Ligitan and Sipadan, both located in the Celebes Sea, off the coast of the large island of Borneo, parts of which are under the sovereignty of Indonesia and parts of which are under the sovereignty of Malaysia. Neither island was inhabited on a permanent basis until the 1980s, when Sipadan was developed into a tourist resort. Ligitan remains uninhabited.

132 ...In particular in the case of very small islands which are uninhabited or not permanently inhabited—like Ligitan and Sipadan, which have been of little economic importance (at least until recently)—*effectivités* will indeed generally be scarce.

135. The Court further observes that it cannot take into consideration acts having taken place after the date on which the dispute between the Parties crystallized unless such acts are a normal continuation of prior acts and are not undertaken for the purpose of improving the legal position of the Party which relies on them (see the Arbitral Award in the *Palena* case, 38 *International Law Reports (ILR)*, pp. 79–80). The Court will, therefore, primarily, analyse the *effectivités* which date from the period before 1969, the year in which the Parties asserted conflicting claims to Ligitan and Sipadan.

136. The Court finally observes that it can only consider those acts as constituting a relevant display of authority which leave no doubt as to their specific reference to the islands in dispute as such. Regulations or administrative acts of a general nature can therefore be taken as *effectivités* with regard to Ligitan and Sipadan only if it is clear from their terms or their effects that they pertained to these two islands.

137. Turning now to the *effectivités* relied on by Indonesia, the Court will begin by pointing out that none of them is of a legislative or regulatory character…

141. The Court concludes that the activities relied upon by Indonesia do not constitute acts *a titre de souverain* reflecting the intention and will to act in that capacity…

148. The Court notes that the activities relied upon by Malaysia, both in its own name and as successor State of Great Britain, are modest in number but that they are diverse in character and include legislative, administrative and quasi-judicial acts. They cover a considerable period of time and show a pattern revealing an intention to exercise State functions in respect of the two islands in the context of the administration of a wider range of islands. The Court moreover cannot disregard the fact that at the time when these activities were carried out, neither Indonesia nor its predecessor, the Netherlands, ever expressed its disagreement or protest. In this regard, the Court notes that in 1962 and 1963 the Indonesian authorities did not even remind the authorities of the colony of North Borneo, or Malaysia after its independence, that the construction of the lighthouses at those times had taken place on territory which they considered Indonesian; even if they regarded these lighthouses as merely destined for safe navigation in an area which was of particular importance for navigation in the waters off North Borneo, such behaviour is unusual.

149. Given the circumstances of the case, and in particular in view of the evidence furnished by the Parties, the Court concludes that Malaysia has title to Ligitan and Sipadan on the basis of the *effectivités* referred to above.

NOTES

1. It is clear that effective occupation or 'the continuous and peaceful display of territorial sovereignty…is as good as title' (see *Island of Palmas*). However, what number of sovereign acts is needed will depend on the nature of the territory, with thinly populated, inhospitable or uninhabited territory, such as in the *Eastern Greenland Case*, requiring very few acts. In addition to the lighthouses mentioned in the extract above, in the *Case Concerning Palau Ligitan and Palau Sipadan*, Malaysia also relied upon measures taken to regulate and control the collecting of turtle eggs on the islands and the inclusion of Sipadan in a proclaimed nature reserve. The Court noted that the construction and operation of lighthouses and navigational aids are not normally an exercise of sovereign power (para. 147).

2. The Court followed the approach it adopted in the *Case Concerning Palau Ligitan and Palau Sipadan* in the *Case Concerning Territorial and Maritime Disputes Between Nicaragua and Honduras in the Caribbean Sea* (*Nicaragua v Honduras*) (ICJ Rep 2007 659, para 175). Taking into account that the four islands in question were not of economic or strategic importance, the Court required Honduras to establish *effectivités* 'that constitute a modest but real display of authority over the four islands' (para. 208).

3. The amount of evidence of effective occupation that is necessary for a State to show also depends, like all claims to territory, on the existence and nature of rival claims. Title to territory is, after all, relative and not absolute. The failure of one State to object to an exercise of authority by another State in respect of disputed territory can be fatal to the first State's claim. A failure to protest may be particularly significant where the nature of the territory claimed means that there will be few exercises of authority.

4. The extract from the *Case Concerning Palau Ligitan and Palau Sipadan* emphasises the importance of the 'critical date'. This date is the date upon which the dispute between the parties crystallised. The Court will generally accord greater consideration to acts taken before this date, as acts taken after the dispute has crystallised may be taken with the sole objective of bolstering the territorial claim.

5. The evidence of sovereign acts to show effective occupation must be acts by States or attributable to States. This would usually include acts by a State's military forces, legislation, administrative actions, treaties and the conduct of legal proceedings. For example, in the *Case Concerning Palau Ligitan and Palau Sipadan*, the Court disregarded the use of the waters surrounding the islands in question by Indonesian fishermen, as 'activities by private persons

cannot be seen as *effectivités* if they do not take place on the basis of official regulations or under governmental authority' (para. 140). Occasionally acts by private individuals or corporations can be attributable to a State, as happened in the *Island of Palmas Case* and in *Nicaragua v Honduras* (para. 195), where the Court found that Honduran licensing of fishing was an act of governmental authority. The key issue is whether their actions are attributable to a State and there is an intention to act as a sovereign over that territory: see *Ethiopia/Eritrea Boundary Commission*, 41 ILM 1057 (2002).

SECTION 4: CONSENT BY OTHER STATES

As sovereignty over territory is determined on the basis of relative title, the acts of the other party, as well as the acts of the international community in respect of the disputed territory, must be relevant.

A: Consent by the other party to the dispute

Temple of Preah Vihear Case (*Cambodia v Thailand*)
Merits, ICJ Rep 1962 6, International Court of Justice

Cambodia claimed, as successor to France, sovereignty over an area of land which included the Temple of Preah Vihear. One of the key pieces of evidence upon which Cambodia relied was a map made in 1907 that showed the temple to be in French territory, and that map was sent to the authorities of Siam (now Thailand) (see also Chapter 3). The Court found that the Temple was situated in Cambodian territory.

It has been contended on behalf of Thailand that this communication of the maps by the French authorities was, so to speak, *ex parte*, and that no formal acknowledgment of it was either requested of, or given by, Thailand. In fact, as will be seen presently, an acknowledgment by conduct was undoubtedly made in a very definite way; but even if it were otherwise, it is clear that the circumstances were such as called for some reaction, within a reasonable period, on the part of the Siamese authorities, if they wished to disagree with the map or had any serious question to raise in regard to it. They did not do so, either then or for many years, and thereby must be held to have acquiesced....

The Court moreover considers that there is no legal foundation for the consequence it is attempted to deduce from the fact that no one in Thailand at that time may have known of the importance of the Temple or have been troubling about it. Frontier rectifications cannot in law be claimed on the ground that a frontier area has turned out to have an importance not known or suspected when the frontier was established.

It follows from the preceding findings that the Siamese authorities in due course received the Annex I map and that they accepted it. Now, however, it is contended on behalf of Thailand, so far as the disputed area of Preah Vihear is concerned, that an error was committed, an error of which the Siamese authorities were unaware at the time when they accepted the map.

It is an established rule of law that the plea of error cannot be allowed as an element vitiating consent if the party advancing it contributed by its own conduct to the error, or could have avoided it, or if the circumstances were such as to put that party on notice of a possible error. The Court considers that the character and qualifications of the persons who saw the Annex I map on the Siamese side would alone make it difficult for Thailand to plead error in law. These persons included the members of the very Commission of Delimitation within whose competence this sector of the frontier had lain. But even apart from this, the Court thinks that there were other circumstances relating to the Annex I map which make the plea of error difficult to receive.

An inspection indicates that the map itself drew such pointed attention to the Preah Vihear region that no interested person, nor anyone charged with the duty of scrutinizing it, could have failed to see what the map was purporting to do in respect of that region....much the most significant episode consisted of the visit paid to the Temple in 1930 by Prince Damrong, formerly Minister of the Interior, and at this time President of the Royal Institute of Siam, charged with duties in connection with the National Library and with archaeological monuments. The visit was part of an archaeological tour made by the Prince with the permission of the King of Siam, and it clearly had a quasi-official character. When the Prince arrived at Preah Vihear, he was officially received there by the French Resident for the adjoining Cambodian province, on behalf of the Resident Superior, with the French flag flying. The Prince could not possibly have failed to see the implications of a reception of this character. A clearer affirmation of title on the French Indo-Chinese side can scarcely be imagined. It demanded a reaction. Thailand did nothing. Furthermore, when Prince Damrong on his return to Bangkok sent the French Resident some photographs of the occasion, he used language which seems to admit that France, through her Resident, had acted as the host country.

The explanations regarding Prince Damrong's visit given on behalf of Thailand have not been found convincing by the Court. Looking at the incident as a whole, it appears to have amounted to a tacit recognition by Siam of the sovereignty of Cambodia (under French Protectorate) over Preah Vihear, through a failure to react in any way, on an occasion that called for a reaction in order to affirm or preserve title in the face of an obvious rival claim. What seems clear is that either Siam did not in fact believe she had any title—and this would be wholly consistent with her attitude all along, and thereafter, to the Annex I map and line—or else she decided not to assert it, which again means that she accepted the French claim, or accepted the frontier at Preah Vihear as it was drawn on the map.

NOTE: In 2013, the ICJ was requested to interpret the operative parts of its 1962 Judgment, and in particular the territorial scope of the area or 'vicinity' of the temple on Cambodian territory to which it had referred. It found that the temple area encompassed the whole territory of the promontory of Preah Vihear, which was found to be under the territorial sovereignty of Cambodia. However, it clarified that this did not include the hill of Phnom Trap, which was shown as a separate area on the map to which the Court had referred in its 1962 Judgment: *Temple of Preah Vihear Case, Request for the Interpretation of the Judgment of 15 June 1962 (Cambodia v Thailand)*, 11 November 2013.

B: Consent by other States

Legal Status of Eastern Greenland Case (Norway v Denmark)
PCIJ Rep Ser A/B (1933) No 53, Permanent Court of International Justice

The facts are set out in Section 3.

In order to establish the Danish contention that Denmark has exercised in fact sovereignty over all Greenland for a long time, Counsel for Denmark have laid stress on the long series of conventions—mostly commercial in character—which have been concluded by Denmark and in which, with the concurrence of the other contracting Party, a stipulation has been inserted to the effect that the convention shall not apply to Greenland. In the case of multilateral treaties, the stipulation usually takes the form of a Danish reserve at the time of signature. In date, these conventions cover the period from 1782 onwards. As pointed out in the earlier part of the judgment, the exclusion of Greenland is, with one exception, made without qualification. In that case alone it is 'the Danish colonies in Greenland' to which the treaty is not to apply. In many of these cases, the wording is quite specific; for instance, Article 6 of the Treaty of 1826 with the United States of America: 'The present Convention shall not apply to the Northern possessions of His Majesty the King of Denmark, that is to say Iceland, the Faerö Islands and Greenland....'

The importance of these treaties is that they show a willingness on the part of the States with which Denmark has contracted to admit her right to exclude Greenland. To some of these treaties, Norway has herself been a Party, and these must be dealt with later because they are relied on by Denmark as constituting binding admissions by Norway that Greenland is subject to Danish sovereignty. For the purpose of the present argument, the importance of these conventions, with whatever States they have been concluded, is due to the support which they lend to the Danish argument that Denmark possesses sovereignty over Greenland as a whole....

If the Parties were agreed that the treaty was not to apply in a particular area and the area is only designated by name, the natural conclusion is that no difference existed between them as to the extent of the area which that name covered....

To the extent that these treaties constitute evidence of recognition of her sovereignty over Greenla
general, Denmark is entitled to rely upon them. These treaties may also be regarded as demonstrating suffic
Denmark's will and intention to exercise sovereignty over Greenland.

C: Consent by the international community

Q. Wright, 'The Goa Incident'

56 *American Journal of International Law* 617 (1962)

This incident concerned the actions by India in December 1961 in occupying the Portuguese colonies of Goa, Damao and Diu on the western coast of the Indian sub-continent. A Security Resolution condemning India's use of force was vetoed by the USSR, with three other members of the Security Council voting against it.

The significant feature, however, of the Goa situation was that many of the new states, and also the Soviet Union, felt that colonialism was such an evil that the use of force to eliminate it should be tolerated. The argument was, in fact, political and moral rather than legal....

Throughout Asia and Africa it is argued that ex-colonial peoples cannot be expected to accept the validity of the claims of colonial Powers to overseas territories acquired and maintained by force, on the theory, prevalent in the age of discoveries, that territories not in the possession of a Christian prince were *'territorium nullius'* subject to acquisition by Papal grant or by discovery and occupation without regard to the wishes of the native inhabitants. These peoples, it is argued, submitted because of military weakness, but never accepted the justifying theories of European jurists....

The argument is, therefore, supported by the principle that positive international law rests on the express or tacit consent of the states bound by it. While European Powers may have recognized a customary rule permitting the acquisition of non-Christian territory by discovery and occupation, the rulers and peoples of such territories never recognized such a rule.... The conclusion seems to be that no action is likely to be taken by the United Nations, in which case the states of the world will, doubtless, recognize or acquiesce in the Indian annexation of Goa.

It should be noted that while individual recognition of the fruits of aggression is forbidden by Charter principles, as it was by the Stimson Doctrine of 1932, the United Nations itself may recognize a situation which it regards as, on the whole, beneficial, even if this situation originated in illegality.

NOTES
1. Other States can consent to sovereignty by a claimant State either by positive actions, such as by recognition or by ratification of a treaty (as in the *Eastern Greenland Case*), or by acquiescence, where there is a failure to protest in a situation where some kind of reaction signifying objection is called for (as in the *Temple Case*). In the situation of Goa, the international community acknowledged Indian sovereignty, even though illegally obtained, over time, with Portugal itself recognising Indian sovereignty in 1974.
2. Consent by other States affects a State's claim to title to a territory in two main ways: it can mean that the other claimant State is precluded from denying the opposing State's title; or it can provide strong external evidence to support a State's claim, including a claim that title has been acquired by prescription. The role of consent by a State is also important in understanding the nature of international law (see Chapter 1).

SECTION 5: LIMITATIONS ON SOVEREIGNTY OVER TERRITORY

A: The right of self-determination

The right of self-determination has a major impact on sovereignty over territory. The extent and application of the right are explained in Chapter 6 and *must* be considered in any issue of sovereignty over territory.

B: *Uti possidetis juris*

Uti possidetis juris, being the principle that colonial boundaries are maintained on independence, was also explained in Chapter 6 in the context of the right of self-determination (see especially the *Frontier Dispute Case* ICJ Rep 1986 554). This principle has an impact on the determination of territorial disputes.

Case Concerning the Land, Island and Maritime Frontier Dispute
(*El Salvador* v *Honduras; Nicaragua intervening*)
ICJ Rep 1992 351, Chamber of the International Court of Justice

The dispute between El Salvador and Honduras (for which Nicaragua was allowed to intervene—see Chapter 16) concerned the Gulf of Fonseca: the land around it; the islands in it; and the waters of and beyond it. The aspect which is extracted here concerns the general issues of the land boundary dispute.

42. Thus the principle of *uti possidetis juris* is concerned as much with title to territory as with the location of boundaries; certainly a key aspect of the principle is the denial of the possibility of *terra nullius*.

43. To apply this principle is not so easy when, as in Spanish Central America, there were administrative boundaries of different kinds or degrees....Besides, in addition to the various civil territorial jurisdictions, general or special, there were the ecclesiastical jurisdictions, which were supposed to be followed in principle, pursuant to general legislation, by the territorial jurisdiction of the main civil administrative units in Spanish America; such adjustment often needed, however, a certain span of time within which to materialize....Moreover it has to be remembered that no question of international boundaries could ever have occurred to the minds of those servants of the Spanish Crown who established administrative boundaries; *uti possidetis juris* is essentially a retrospective principle, investing as international boundaries administrative limits intended originally for quite other purposes....

57. As already mentioned above, El Salvador contends that the *uti possidetis juris* principle is the primary but not the only, legal element to be taken into consideration for the determination of the land boundary. It has put forward in addition in that respect a body of arguments referred to either as 'arguments of a human nature' or as arguments based on '*effectivités*'.

58. The factual considerations which El Salvador has brought to the attention of the Chamber fall into two categories. On the one hand, there are arguments and material relating to demographic pressures in El Salvador creating a need for territory, as compared with the relatively sparsely populated Honduras; and on the other the superior natural resources (e.g., water for agriculture and hydroelectric power) said to be enjoyed by Honduras. On the first point, El Salvador apparently does not claim that a frontier deriving from the principle of the *uti possidetis juris* could be adjusted subsequently (except by agreement) on the grounds of unequal population density, and this is clearly right. It will be recalled that the Chamber in the *Frontier Dispute* case emphasized that even equity *infra legem*, a recognised concept of international law, could not be resorted to in order to modify an established frontier inherited from colonization, whatever its deficiencies (see *ICJ Reports 1986*, p. 633, para. 149). El Salvador claims that such an inequality existed even before independence, and that its ancient possession of the territories in dispute, 'based on historic titles, is also based on reasons of crucial human necessity'. The Chamber will not lose sight of this dimension of the matter; but it is one without direct legal incidence. For the *uti possidetis juris*, the question is not whether the colonial province needed wide boundaries to accommodate its population, but where those boundaries actually were; and post-independence *effectivités*, where relevant, have to be assessed in terms of actual events, not their social origins. As to the argument of inequality of natural resources, the Court, in the case concerning the *Continental Shelf* (*Tunisia/Libyan Arab Jamahiriya*), took the view that economic considerations of this kind could not be taken into account for the delimitation of the continental shelf areas appertaining to two States (*ICJ Reports 1982*, p. 77, para. 107); still less can they be relevant for the determination of a land frontier which came into existence on independence....

61. Both parties have invoked, in relation to this claim of El Salvador, the analysis in the Judgment of the Chamber of the Court in the *Frontier Dispute* case of the relationship between 'titles' and '*effectivités*' (*I.C.J. Reports 1986*, pp. 586–587, para. 63). The passage in question reads as follows:

The role played in this case by such *effectivités* is complex, and the Chamber will have to weigh carefully the legal force of these in each particular instance. It must however state forthwith, in general terms, what legal relationship exists between such acts and the titles on which the implementation of the principle of *uti possidetis* is grounded. For this purpose, a distinction must be drawn among several eventualities. Where the act corresponds exactly to law, where effective administration is additional to the *uti possidetis juris*, the only role of *effectivité* is to confirm the exercise of the right derived from a legal title. Where the act does not correspond to the law, where the territory which is the subject of the dispute is effectively administered by a State other than the one possessing the legal title, preference should be given to the holder of the title. In the event that the *effectivité* does not co-exist with any legal title, it must invariably be taken into consideration. Finally, there are cases where the legal title is not capable of showing exactly the territorial expanse to which it relates. The *effectivités* can then play an essential role in showing how the title is interpreted in practice. (*ICJ Reports 1986*, pp. 586–587, para. 63.)

62. With regard to the interrelation of title and *effectivité*, it should however be borne in mind that the *titulos* submitted to the Chamber by both Parties, including the 'formal title-deeds to commons' are not what are here referred to as 'the titles on which the implementation of the principle of *uti possidetis* is grounded'; as already explained, they can be compared to 'colonial *effectivités*', to the extent that they are acts of effective administration by the colonial authorities, not acts of private individuals. What the Chamber has to do in respect of the land frontier is to arrive at a conclusion as to the position of the 1821 *uti possidetis juris* boundary; to this end it cannot but take into account, for reasons already explained, the colonial *effectivités* as reflected in the documentary evidence of the colonial period submitted by the Parties. The Chamber may have regard also, in certain instances, to documentary evidence of post-independence *effectivités* when it considers that they afford indications in respect of the 1821 *uti possidetis juris* boundary, providing a relationship exists between the *effectivités* concerned and the determination of that boundary....

67. ...[T]he *uti possidetis juris* position can be qualified in other ways, for example, by acquiescence or recognition. There seems to be no reason in principle why these factors should not operate, where there is sufficient evidence to show that the parties have in effect clearly accepted a variation, or at least an interpretation, of the *uti possidetis juris* position.

NOTES

1. The Chamber of the International Court of Justice in the *Land, Island and Maritime Dispute Case* was aware of the problem in using the principle of *uti possidetis* to form international boundaries from divisions of territory based on administrative convenience. But this principle, combined with issues of a general historical nature, can place limitations on determinations of sovereignty over territory.

2. There are many issues of evidence which a court is required to weigh up in any territory boundary dispute: see A. Riddell and B. Plant, *Evidence before the International Court of Justice* (2009). The Court followed this approach to *effectivités* that are inconsistent with the legal title. In the *Case Concerning the Land and Maritime Boundary Between Cameroon and Nigeria (Cameroon v Nigeria; Equatorial Guinea intervening)*, the Court found that administrative activity by Nigeria in respect of Nigerian villages on the Cameroon side of Lake Chad did not constitute acquiescence by Cameroon. As the situation was one where the *effectivités* submitted by Nigeria did not correspond with the law, preference should be given to the holder of the title (ICJ Rep 2002 303, para. 70).

3. In the *Case Concerning the Territorial Dispute (Libya v Chad)* ICJ Rep 1994 6 the Court stressed that there was a 'fundamental principle of the stability of boundaries' (para. 72) and, accordingly, the terms of a treaty agreeing a boundary will be upheld as far as possible.

4. The Court has confirmed that the principle of *uti possidetis juris* may, in principle, apply to offshore possessions and maritime spaces, including islands. However, in the *Case Concerning Territorial and Maritime Disputes between Nicaragua and Honduras in the Caribbean Sea (Nicaragua v Honduras)* ICJ Rep 2007 659, the Court held that the invocation of the principle would not of itself provide a clear answer to sovereignty. In that case there was no evidence that the colonial power, Spain, had allocated the islands to a particular State, and the islands were located too great a distance from the coastline to assume they should be allocated on the basis of adjacency and there was no evidence of colonial *effectivités* regarding the island. Accordingly, the Court had to decide sovereignty on the basis of post-colonial acts.

C: Indigenous people

The International Court of Justice in the *Western Sahara Opinion* (see Section 2A) noted that 'territories inhabited by tribes or peoples having a social and political organisation were not regarded as *terra nullius*' (at para. 80). This decision and other matters have had an impact on the claims of many indigenous peoples, particularly those where no treaty (or similar agreement) was entered into by a colonial power.

Mabo v *Queensland (No 2)*
175 CLR 1 (1992), High Court of Australia

This case raised many issues of the continuing existence of native title and associated rights to land in Australia. No acts of cession or conquest had occurred on the particular islands in dispute (being the Murray Islands in the Torres Strait between Australia and Papua New Guinea) as they had been annexed by the application of common law and statute by the State of Queensland in the federation of Australia. The High Court decided, by 6:1, that native title did continue to exist in these circumstances.

BRENNAN J [with whom Mason CJ and McHugh J agreed]: Although the question whether a territory has been acquired by the Crown is not justiciable before municipal courts, those courts have jurisdiction to determine the consequences of an acquisition under municipal law. Accordingly, the municipal courts must determine the body of law which is in force in the new territory. By the common law, the law in force in a newly-acquired territory depends on the manner of its acquisition by the Crown. Although the manner in which a sovereign state might acquire new territory is a matter for international law, the common law has had to march in step with international law in order to provide the body of law to apply in a territory newly acquired by the Crown.

International law recognized conquest, cession, and occupation of territory that was terra nullius as three of the effective ways of acquiring sovereignty. No other way is presently relevant. The great voyages of European discovery opened to European nations the prospect of occupying new and valuable territories that were already inhabited. As among themselves, the European nations parcelled out the territories newly discovered to the sovereigns of the respective discoverers, provided the discovery was confirmed by occupation and provided the indigenous inhabitants were not organized in a society that was united permanently for political action. To these territories the European colonial nations applied the doctrines relating to acquisition of territory that was terra nullius. They recognized the sovereignty of the respective European nations over the territory of 'backward peoples' and, by State practice, permitted the acquisition of sovereignty of such territory by occupation rather than by conquest....The enlarging of the concept of terra nullius by international law to justify the acquisition of inhabited territory by occupation on behalf of the acquiring sovereign raised some difficulties in the expounding of the common law doctrines as to the law to be applied when inhabited territories were acquired by occupation (or 'settlement', to use the term of the common law)....

It is one thing for our contemporary law to accept that the laws of England, so far as applicable, became the laws of New South Wales and of the other Australian colonies. It is another thing for our contemporary law to accept that, when the common law of England became the common law of the several colonies, the theory which was advanced to support the introduction of the common law of England accords with our present knowledge and appreciation of the facts. When it was sought to apply Lord Watson's assumption in *Cooper* v *Stuart* that the colony of New South Wales was 'without settled inhabitants or settled law' to Aboriginal society in the Northern Territory, the assumption proved false. In *Milirrpum* v *Nabalco Pty Ltd* Blackburn J said ((1971) 17 FLR 141 at 267)

> The evidence shows a subtle and elaborate system highly adapted to the country in which the people led their lives, which provided a stable order of society and was remarkably free from the vagaries of personal whim or influence. If ever a system could be called 'a government of laws, and not of men' it is that shown in the evidence before me....

The theory of terra nullius has been critically examined in recent times by the International Court of Justice in its *Advisory Opinion on Western Sahara*...If the international law notion that inhabited land may be classified as terra nullius no longer commands general support, the doctrines of the common law which depend on the notion that native peoples may be 'so low in the scale of social organization' that it is 'idle to impute to such people some shadow of the rights known to our law' [In *re Southern Rhodesia* [1919] AC 211 at pp. 233–234] can hardly be retained. If it were permissible in past centuries to keep the common law in step with international law, it is imperative in today's world that the common law should neither be nor be seen to be frozen in an age of racial discrimination.

The fiction by which the rights and interests of indigenous inhabitants in land were treated as non-existent was justified by a policy which has no place in the contemporary law of this country....Whatever the justification advanced in earlier days for refusing to recognize the rights and interests in land of the indigenous inhabitants of settled colonies, and unjust and discriminatory doctrine of that kind can no longer be accepted. The expectations of the international community accord in this respect with the contemporary values of the Australian people. The opening up of international remedies to individuals pursuant to Australia's accession to the Optional Protocol to the International Covenant on Civil and Political Rights brings to bear on the common law the powerful influence of the Covenant and the international standards it imports. The common law does not necessarily conform with international law, but international law is a legitimate and important influence on the development of the common law, especially when international law declares the existence of universal human rights. A common law doctrine founded on unjust discrimination in the enjoyment of civil and political rights demands reconsideration. It is contrary both to international standards and to the fundamental values of our common law to entrench a discriminatory rule which, because of the supposed position on the scale of social organization of the indigenous inhabitants of a settled colony, denies them a right to occupy their traditional lands.

United Nations Declaration on the Rights of Indigenous Peoples 2007
Adopted by General Assembly Resolution 61/295 on 13 September 2007

This Declaration was adopted by the General Assembly, following more than twenty years of discussion within the United Nations system. Work towards the Declaration was carried out under the auspices of the United Nations Commission on Human Rights by representatives of both indigenous peoples and States. The Declaration was adopted with an overwhelming majority of 143 votes in favour, only 4 negative votes cast (Canada, Australia, New Zealand, United States) and 11 abstentions.

Article 25
Indigenous peoples have the right to maintain and strengthen their distinctive spiritual relationship with their traditionally owned or otherwise occupied and used lands, territories, waters and coastal seas and other resources and to uphold their responsibilities to future generations in this regard.

Article 26
1. Indigenous peoples have the right to the lands, territories and resources which they have traditionally owned, occupied or otherwise used or acquired.

2. Indigenous peoples have the right to own, use, develop and control the lands, territories and resources that they possess by reason of traditional ownership or other traditional occupation or use, as well as those which they have otherwise acquired.

3. States shall give legal recognition and protection to these lands, territories and resources. Such recognition shall be conducted with due respect to the customs, traditions and land tenure systems of the indigenous peoples concerned.

Article 27
States shall establish and implement, in conjunction with indigenous peoples concerned, a fair, independent, impartial, open and transparent process, giving due recognition to indigenous peoples' laws, traditions, customs and land tenure systems, to recognize and adjudicate the rights of indigenous peoples pertaining to their lands, territories and resources, including those which were traditionally owned or otherwise occupied or used. Indigenous peoples shall have the right to participate in this process.

Article 28

1. Indigenous peoples have the right to redress, by means that can include restitution or, when this is not possible, just, fair and equitable compensation, for the lands, territories and resources which they have traditionally owned or otherwise occupied or used, and which have been confiscated, taken, occupied, used or damaged without their free, prior and informed consent.

2. Unless otherwise freely agreed upon by the peoples concerned, compensation shall take the form of lands, territories and resources equal in quality, size and legal status or of monetary compensation or other appropriate redress.

Article 29

1. Indigenous peoples have the right to the conservation and protection of the environment and the productive capacity of their lands or territories and resources. States shall establish and implement assistance programmes for indigenous peoples for such conservation and protection, without discrimination.

2. States shall take effective measures to ensure that no storage or disposal of hazardous materials shall take place in the lands or territories of indigenous peoples without their free, prior and informed consent....

Article 32

1. Indigenous peoples have the right to determine and develop priorities and strategies for the development or use of their lands or territories and other resources.

2. States shall consult and cooperate in good faith with the indigenous peoples concerned through their own representative institutions in order to obtain their free and informed consent prior to the approval of any project affecting their lands or territories and other resources, particularly in connection with the development, utilization or exploitation of mineral, water or other resources.

3. States shall provide effective mechanisms for just and fair redress for any such activities, and appropriate measures shall be taken to mitigate adverse environmental, economic, social, cultural or spiritual impact.

NOTES

1. International law, like most law, responds to changes in society—political, ideological and moral—as seen in the way conquest has become an illegal mode of acquisition (see intertemporal law in Section 2C). By denigrating the indigenous peoples' way of life, colonial powers (and even independent States) could claim that certain territory was *terra nullius* and so able to be occupied with minimal acts of sovereignty being necessary. As understanding and concern for indigenous peoples have increased, so have the challenges to the laws imposed on those peoples by the colonial powers. These challenges have been primarily before national courts.

2. The decision in *Mabo* v *Queensland (No 2)* led to significant changes in the Australian legislation dealing with land (and other) rights of indigenous peoples. Similar case law—with resulting changes to legislation—has occurred elsewhere, particularly in New Zealand, Canada and the United States. In each State, the national courts have referred to international law developments in the protection of indigenous peoples. Some of these developments are discussed in Chapter 6.

3. Some protection for the inhabitants of a territory was intended by the League of Nations Mandate system, which was carried forward by the Trusteeship system of the United Nations. The International Court of Justice had to consider the Trusteeship system in the *Case Concerning Certain Phosphate Lands in Nauru (Australia* v *Nauru)* ICJ Rep 1992 240. It is clear (from para. 30 of the preliminary objections judgment) that the termination of a Trust by the General Assembly does not necessarily discharge all responsibilities of the State administering the Trust towards the inhabitants of the Trust territory.

4. The UN Declaration extracted above is another important step in this (slow) process. It is concerning, however, that the four abstentions in the vote adopting the Declaration were made by States with significant indigenous populations (though each State—under successor governments—appears to have now accepted the Declaration).

SECTION 6: **OTHER TERRITORY**

A: The polar regions

The Antarctic Treaty 1959
UNTS 402 (1961) 71

The original parties to this Treaty were Argentina, Australia, Chile, France, New Zealand, Norway and the United Kingdom, each of whom asserted a claim of sovereignty to part or parts (including some overlapping claims) of Antarctica, together with Belgium, Japan, South Africa, the USSR and the United States. The Treaty entered into force on 23 June 1961. As at March 2016, there are 53 State parties to this Treaty, with some having only 'observer' status. Regular meetings occur between the parties to the Treaty.

Article I

1. Antarctica shall be used for peaceful purposes only. There shall be prohibited, *inter alia*, any measures of a military nature, such as the establishment of military bases and fortifications, the carrying out of military manoeuvres as well as the testing of any type of weapons.

2. The present Treaty shall not prevent the use of military personnel or equipment for scientific research or for any other peaceful purpose.

Article IV

1. Nothing contained in the present Treaty shall be interpreted as:
   (a) a renunciation by any Contracting Party of previously asserted rights of or claims to territorial sovereignty in Antarctica;
   (b) a renunciation or diminution by any Contracting Party of any basis of claim to territorial sovereignty in Antarctica which it may have whether as a result of its activities or those of its nationals in Antarctica, or otherwise;
   (c) prejudicing the position of any Contracting party as regards its recognition or non-recognition of any other State's right of or claim or basis of claim to territorial sovereignty in Antarctica.

2. No acts or activities taking place while the present Treaty is in force shall constitute a basis for asserting, supporting or denying a claim to territorial sovereignty in Antarctica or create any rights of sovereignty in Antarctica. No new claim, or enlargement of an existing claim, to territorial sovereignty in Antarctica shall be asserted while the present Treaty is in force.

Article XII

1. (a) The present Treaty may be modified or amended at any time by unanimous agreement of the Contracting Parties...

2. (a) If after the expiration of thirty years from the date of entry into force of the present Treaty, any of the Contracting Parties whose representatives are entitled to participate in the meetings provided for under Article IX so request by a communication addressed to the depositary Government, a Conference of all the Contracting Parties shall be held as soon as practicable to review the operation of the Treaty.

Antarctic Treaty Consultative Meeting XXXII Washington Ministerial Declaration on the Fiftieth Anniversary of the Antarctic Treaty
Bureau of Oceans and International Environmental and Scientific Affairs Washington, DC, 6 April 2009

In the year of the fiftieth anniversary of the signing of the Antarctic Treaty (the 'Treaty') in Washington on December 1, 1959, the Consultative Parties to the Antarctic Treaty,

Recognizing the historic achievements of the Treaty in promoting peace and international cooperation in the Antarctic region over the past half century,

Recognizing that it is in the interest of all humankind that Antarctica continue to be used exclusively for peaceful purposes and shall not become the scene or object of international discord,...

Hereby:

1. *Reaffirm* their continued commitment to the objectives and purposes of the Antarctic Treaty and the other elements of the Antarctic Treaty system;

2. *Reaffirm* the importance of the Treaty's provisions guaranteeing freedom of scientific investigation and reserving Antarctica exclusively for peaceful purposes, free from measures of a military nature;

3. *Reaffirm* the importance they attach to the contribution made by the Treaty, and by Article IV in particular, to ensuring the continuance of international harmony in Antarctica;...

12. *Decide* to continue and extend for the benefit of all humankind their cooperation established in the Treaty and in the Treaty system over the last fifty years.

United States Mission to the United Nations New York
Diplomatic Note, 3 December 2004

The Deputy Representative of the United States of America to the United Nations presents her compliments to the Secretary-General of the United Nations and refers to the recent Australian submission to the Commission on the Limits of the Continental Shelf (the Commission). The United States recalls the principles and objectives shared by the Antarctic Treaty and the United Nations Convention on the Law of the Sea (the Convention), and the importance of the Antarctic system and the Convention working in harmony and thereby ensuring the continuing peaceful cooperation, security and stability in the Antarctic area. The United States wishes to inform you that, recalling Article IV of the Antarctic Treaty, the United States does not recognize any State's claim to territory in Antarctica and consequently does not recognize any State's rights over the seabed and subsoil of the submarine areas beyond and adjacent to the continent of Antarctica. The United States acknowledges with appreciation Australia's request to the Commission that it not take any action on that portion of its submission relating to areas of the seabed and subsoil adjacent to Antarctica.

D. Rothwell, 'The Arctic in International Affairs: Time for a New Regime?'
XV *Brown Journal of World Affairs* 241 (2008)

The management of Arctic affairs has traditionally fallen under the purview of those coastal states whose territories abut the Arctic Ocean or whose lands extend north of the Arctic Circle. However, because by and large the status of the territorial claims made by those states has not been in dispute, there has often been little incentive for the Arctic states to work together at a bilateral or regional level to address common issues. Accordingly, with the exception of a groundbreaking 1973 agreement with respect to the conservation of polar bears, there has not been any longstanding history of cooperation amongst Arctic states.

The status quo in the Arctic was challenged with the development of the new law of the sea first with the 1958 Geneva Conventions on the Law of the Sea, and then with the 1982 United Nations Convention on the Law of the Sea (LOSC). The significance of these developments in international law was that they gave legitimacy to a variety of maritime zones which extended offshore both continental and island land masses. Most relevantly for the Arctic, the ability of coastal states to proclaim either a 200 nautical mile exclusive economic zone (EEZ) or a continental shelf which extended in some instances as far as 350 nautical miles meant that parts of the Arctic Ocean could increasingly come under national sovereignty. Initially, not all of the Arctic states gave much attention to their capacity to assert these various maritime claims, and given that much of the Arctic Ocean was either permanently ice-covered or ice-free for only very short summer seasons, there was not a great deal to be immediately gained from these new maritime claims. Nevertheless, these developments did provide something of an indicator of how Arctic issues were developing as some of the Arctic states began a process of negotiating adjacent maritime boundaries, and claims were staked to parts of the Arctic Ocean and its related seas....

The other factor which is at play is the melting of the Arctic sea ice. In recent years the effect of the melt has been dramatic, with significant tracts of open water appearing in parts of the Arctic Ocean and a shifting ice pattern becoming discernable. The impact of retreating ice in the Arctic is potentially very significant. First, the implications for Arctic fauna and flora are considerable, especially for iconic species such as the polar bear....In turn, there is the potential for impact upon the life-styles and culture of the indigenous peoples of the north who can be found spread across all of the adjoining continents. Melting of the sea ice and permafrost will have significant impacts upon access to wildlife, for which hunting and townships across the Arctic will possibly need to be resettled.

A melting of the ice also has resource access implications. Previously inaccessible areas of the Arctic Ocean will potentially become accessible for various forms of resource exploitation ranging from the non-living resources of the seabed to fish stocks and other living resources of the water column....With increased resource exploitation, there is clearly the potential for enhanced risk of environmental impact, but also demands for greater foreign access by states which may not traditionally have had an interest in the region. This may especially be the case with respect to Arctic fisheries and that area of Arctic high seas beyond the limits of coastal state jurisdiction. It follows that this will in turn raise issues of increased navigational interest in Arctic waters not only with respect to navigation within the Arctic, but also by the members of the international community eager to gain access to new shipping routes between the North Pacific and North Atlantic....

The first comprehensive effort to implement an Arctic-wide regime dealing with the protection of the Arctic environment began with the 1991 Arctic Environmental Protection Strategy (AEPS). The AEPS, which had eight Arctic states as parties, was an ambitious document which sought to identify Arctic environmental problems and develop action plans for their management....However, the AEPS process was never intended to create legally binding obligations. Rather, it sought to assist in collective policy development with ultimate implementation channels being individual state environmental laws and policies. There was also an emphasis on the need to engage Arctic indigenous peoples in this process in recognition of the impact these environmental issues would have upon their culture.

Building on the success of this initiative, the Arctic states moved to form an Arctic Council in the 1990s which was designed to provide a high-level ministerial forum for discussion of issues of common interest amongst the Arctic States. The Arctic Council has over the past decade evolved so as to have much greater oversight for the ongoing monitoring and implementation of the AEPS, with the result that a permanent Secretariat has now been established in Tromsø, Norway. However, a problem with the Arctic Council is that it has always been a soft law regime, and there has never been any intention to create legally binding obligations for the Arctic states. When this constraint is combined with the fact that the United States acts more like a 'minor power' in Arctic affairs, 'refusing to take its Arctic responsibilities seriously,' the Arctic Council has never been able to realise some of its potential to fully manage Arctic affairs.

The future of the Arctic Council and its ability to represent with one voice the views of Arctic States has now been cast into doubt by the May 2009 independent gathering of only five of the eight Council members to discuss Arctic Ocean issues. While the Ilulissat Declaration stressed the 'sovereignty, sovereign rights and jurisdiction in large areas of the Arctic Ocean' of the five participating Arctic States, it seems difficult to reconcile how these select states believed they had a singular capacity to reach certain agreements on the future of the Arctic in the absence of the other Arctic Council members, let alone the indigenous peoples of the region. While the declaration does refer to the contributions of the Arctic Council and other international fora to a range of Arctic issues, given the legal, political, and strategic importance of the matters addressed during the May 2008 Greenland Conference and the centrality of the ocean to the region, the Ilulissat Declaration participants seem to now very much see themselves as the only major players capable of providing solutions to Arctic issues....

When the above issues are considered, it becomes clear that the Arctic is beginning to face some considerable challenges with respect to its management, which the Arctic states individually do not want to address. To date the collective response has primarily been through reliance upon 'soft law' mechanisms and arrangements with an avoidance of hard law treaty frameworks. Yet, the Ilulissat Declaration endorsed the law of the sea as being a framework for the resolution of Arctic Ocean issues, while rejecting the need for a comprehensive international legal regime to govern the Arctic Ocean. Is the law of the sea, however, particularly the LOSC, the appropriate legal framework for the resolution of Arctic Ocean issues?...

Could the Antarctic model be a useful way forward for the Arctic? There is in principle nothing to stop the Arctic states from looking towards an Antarctic Treaty-type model for the Arctic region. Such a treaty would need to be based upon respect for the existing international legal frameworks which apply within the region such as the LOSC and would also inevitably need to respect existing sovereign rights. Within that framework, however, there is potential to develop some innovative responses to some of the region's challenges. What form could an Arctic treaty take? A relatively short framework treaty addressing some fundamental sovereignty and dispute resolution mechanisms which included a set of overarching regional management principles would provide a sound foundation for the regime.

The treaty would need to address the following. First, given the sensitivities which currently exist over some sovereignty issues, it would be necessary to include a clear and unambiguous statement respecting pre-existing Arctic sovereign rights. On the other hand, where territory—both land and maritime—is in dispute, the treaty could make clear that nothing would in any way diminish or enhance existing or potential claims. Such an approach would mirror the Antarctic bi-focal approach. This would assist in setting aside some of the sovereignty tensions which have emerged in the Arctic over claims to territory, such as Hans Island in Davis Strait, and to the seabed that sits beneath the North Pole. Second, in order to facilitate resource management, there could be clear mechanisms built into the treaty which would allow for the negotiation of settlements where overlapping claims to the seabed were stalling resource development. Third, a set of fundamental guiding principles could be included dealing with matters such as respect for the environment, conservation and sustainable management of natural resources, freedom of scientific research, and respect for the rights of indigenous peoples. Fourth, in terms of its geographic reach, the treaty would need to extend to all of the Arctic Ocean and seek to establish a comprehensive environmental management regime for the whole region, including the high seas. This regime would then provide the Arctic states with a much greater capacity to regulate the activities of non-Arctic states who will inevitably begin to express an interest in the Arctic's high seas. Finally, in terms of membership, it is possible to envisage a regime which would include the eight Arctic states as core members, with associate membership for non-Arctic states which had significant interests in the region. This would permit many of the existing frameworks and initiatives developed under the Arctic Council to be rolled over into the new regime.

Such a treaty would, however, only be a starting point. There would inevitably be a need for additional protocols to address specific issues such as navigation and shipping, seabed resource management, marine environmental protection, and the rights and interests of indigenous peoples.

NOTES

1. In 1991, the parties to the Antarctic Treaty adopted a Protocol to the Treaty (30 ILM 1455 (1991)). This Protocol concerns environmental protection of the Antarctic and designates it a natural reserve devoted to peace and science (see Chapter 12). It includes six technical Annexes (five of which have entered into force), which establish a comprehensive set of basic principles and detailed mandatory rules applicable to human activities in Antarctica. All activities relating to mineral resources are prohibited, other than for scientific research. The Environmental Protocol does not constitute a change in the legal position under the Antarctic Treaty. This was made clear by the words of the Final Act of the Eleventh Antarctic Treaty Special Consultative Meeting (which adopted the Environmental Protocol), which state that: 'The Meeting agreed that the contents of this Final Act are without prejudice to the legal position of any Party under Article IV of the Antarctic Treaty.'

2. The parties to the Antarctic Treaty have also had to consider the impact of the United Nations Convention on the Law of the Sea (see Chapter 10) on the treaty regime. In particular, several claimant States, such as Australia, have included claims to the extended continental shelf generated by claimed Antarctic territory in their submissions to the United Nations Commission on the Limits of the Continental Shelf. Such claims have generated responses from other States, such as that of the United States. Other claimant States, including the United Kingdom, have not made submissions in respect of claimed Antarctic territories, adopting a second option, that of making a partial submission in respect of such territory at a later stage. The Commission has not considered the substance of any claims to continental shelf arising in respect of Antarctic territory and is unlikely to do so in the foreseeable future.

3. In 2011, the Consultative Parties developed a set of general guidelines for visitors to protect Antarctic wildlife and areas that have particular ecological, scientific and historic value. In addition, the guidelines require visitors to keep Antarctica pristine by not disposing litter on land or polluting lakes or streams. The Consultative Parties have also agreed to adopt a multi-year strategic work plan, which is subject to ongoing discussions, to focus on matters of priority and improve environmental protection. This includes scientific cooperation and electronic information exchange relating to tourism activities.

4. It is interesting to compare the Antarctic Treaty regime with the legal framework found in the other polar region, the Arctic. As the extract from Rothwell points out, there is not a comparable regime for the Arctic. Recent events, including claims by States of areas of continental shelf in the Arctic, the melting of polar ice creating more viable shipping routes through the region, and environmental threats, have led to increased calls for an 'Arctic Treaty'.

B: Deep seabed

The UN Convention on the Law of the Sea 1982 is intended to lay down a comprehensive framework governing all uses of the world's oceans and the management of its resources (see Chapter 10). The Convention controls all human uses of the seas and, in particular, the right of States to explore and exploit the deep seabed for mining purposes. The deep seabed or 'the Area' as it is defined in the Convention refers to 'the seabed and ocean floor and subsoil thereof, beyond the limits of national jurisdiction'. It is designated as the 'common heritage of mankind' in recognition of its importance as a source of life for all humankind. This fundamental principle, which governs the deep seabed, prohibits States from claiming or exercising sovereign rights over any part of the deep seabed or its resources. Moreover, it requires that activities in the seabed be carried out for the benefit of all humankind. The deep seabed regime is considered in more detail in Chapter 10.

C: Airspace

Chicago Convention on International Civil Aviation 1944
15 UNTS (1944) 295

As at March 2016 there are 190 parties to this treaty, which came into force on 4 April 1947.

Article 1 Sovereignty

The contracting States recognize that every State has complete and exclusive sovereignty over the airspace above its territory.

Article 2 Territory

For the purposes of this Convention the territory of a State shall be deemed to be the land areas and territorial waters adjacent thereto under the sovereignty, suzerainty, protection or mandate of such State.

Article 3 Civil and state aircraft

(a) This Convention shall be applicable only to civil aircraft, and shall not be applicable to state aircraft.
(b) Aircraft used in military, customs and police services shall be deemed to be state aircraft.
(c) No state aircraft of a contracting State shall fly over the territory of another State or land thereon without authorization by special agreement or otherwise, and in accordance with the terms thereof.
(d) The contracting States undertake, when issuing regulations for their state aircraft, that they will have due regard for the safety of navigation of civil aircraft.

Article 5 Right of non-scheduled flight

Each contracting State agrees that all aircraft of the other contraction States, being aircraft not engaged in scheduled international air services shall have the right, subject to the observance of the terms of this Convention, to make flights into or in transit non-stop across its territory and to make stops for non-traffic purposes without the necessity of obtaining prior permission and subject to the right of the State flown over to require landing. Each contracting State nevertheless reserves the right, for reasons of safety of flight, to require aircraft desiring to proceed over regions which are inaccessible or without adequate air navigation facilities to follow prescribed routes, or to obtain special permission for such flights.

Such aircraft, if engaged in the carriage of passengers, cargo, or mail for remuneration or hire on other than scheduled international air services, shall also, subject to the provisions of Article 7, have the privilege of taking on or discharging passengers, cargo, mail, subject to the right of any State where such embarkation or discharge takes place to impose such regulations, conditions or limitations as it may consider desirable.

Article 6 Scheduled air services

No scheduled international air service may be operated over or into the territory of a contracting State, except with the special permission or other authorization of that State, and in accordance with the terms of such permission or authorization.

Article 17 Nationality of aircraft

Aircraft have the nationality of the State in which they are registered.

Article 89 War and emergency conditions

In case of war, the provisions of this Convention shall not affect the freedom of action of any of the contracting States affected, whether as belligerents or as neutrals. The same principle shall apply in the case of any contracting State which declares a state of national emergency and notifies the fact to the Council.

Military and Paramilitary Activities in and against Nicaragua Case (*Nicaragua* v *United States*)

Merits, ICJ Rep 1986 14, 111, International Court of Justice

The facts are set out in Chapter 2.

The basic legal concept of State sovereignty in customary international law, expressed in, *inter alia*, Article 2, paragraph 1, of the United Nations Charter, extends to the internal waters and territorial sea of every State and to the air space above its territory. As to superjacent air space, the 1994 Chicago convention on Civil Aviation (Art. 1) reproduces the established principle of the complete and exclusive sovereignty of a State over the air space above its territory. That convention, in conjunction with the 1958 Geneva Convention on the Territorial Sea, further specifies that the sovereignty of the coastal State extends to the territorial sea and to the air space above it, as does the United Nations Convention on the Law of the Sea adopted on 10 December 1982. The Court has no doubt that these prescriptions of treaty-law merely respond to firmly established and longstanding tenets of customary international law.

Opinion on the International Legal Obligations of Council of Europe member States in respect of Secret Detention Facilities and Inter-State Transport of Prisoners

Adopted by the Venice Commission at its 66th Plenary Session, 17–18 March 2006

In late 2005, evidence emerged of secret US (CIA) detention centres and the practice of 'extraordinary rendition', whereby suspected terrorists were captured in the territory of one State, placed in the custody of US officials and transferred for interrogations in another State, outside the normal legal framework and where the captive faced torture or inhuman and degrading treatment during transfer and interrogation. It was suggested that several rendition flights had landed or travelled through the airspace of member States of the Council of Europe. The President of the Parliamentary Assembly of the Council of Europe asked the Committee on Legal Affairs and Human Rights to consider the matter. As part of that investigation, the Rapporteur requested a legal opinion from the Venice Commission (European Commission for Democracy, through Law) examining, among other issues, the legal obligations of member States, under human rights and international law, regarding the transport of detainees by other States through their territory, including their airspace.

86. International air law has a codified framework in the Convention on International Civil Aviation (commonly referred to as the 'Chicago Convention'), signed in Chicago on 7 December 1944.

87. The Chicago Convention sets out in Article 1 the principle that every State has complete and exclusive sovereignty over the airspace above its territory, that is to say above the land areas and territorial waters adjacent thereto....

88. Article 4 of the Chicago Convention provides that: 'Each contracting State agrees not to use civil aviation for any purpose inconsistent with the aims of this Convention'.

89. The Chicago Convention sets out the regime for civil aircraft and civil aviation. According to Article 3 (a), such regime does not apply to State aircraft.

90. Under the Convention, aircraft 'used in military, customs and police services' are deemed to be state aircraft (Article 3(b)). This presumption, however, is not irrebuttable. Moreover, aircraft engaged in other state activities such as coast guard and search and rescue could also be either state aircraft or civil aircraft in the sense of the Convention.

91. It has generally been admitted that, in case of doubt, the status of an airplane as 'civil aircraft' or 'state aircraft' will be determined by the function it actually performs at a given time. As a general rule, 'aircraft are recognised as state aircraft when they are under the control of the State and used exclusively by the State for state intended purposes' [Diederiks-Verschoor, *Introduction to Air Law*, Kluwer, pp. 30 § 12]. Accordingly, the same airplane can be considered to be 'civil aircraft' and 'state aircraft' on different occasions.

92. Civil aircraft that are not engaged in scheduled international air services of a State party to the Chicago Convention are entitled to make flights into or in transit non-stop across the territory of another State party and to make stops for non-traffic purposes without the necessity of obtaining prior permission and subject to the right of the State flown over to require landing. The authorities of each State party have the right, without unreasonable delay, to search aircraft of the other State party on landing or departure, and to inspect the certificates and other documents prescribed by the Chicago Convention (Article 16)....

144. The situation may arise that a Council of Europe member State has serious reasons to believe that the mission of an airplane crossing its airspace is to carry prisoners with the intention of transferring them to countries where they would face ill-treatment.

145. If such an airplane does not require landing, as long as the plane is in the air, all persons on board are subject to the jurisdiction of both the flag State and the territorial State. In the Commission's view, Council of Europe member States' responsibility under the European Convention on Human Rights is engaged if they do not take the preventive measures which are within their powers. In addition, their responsibility for aiding another State to commit an unlawful act would be at issue. It follows, in the Commission's view, that the territorial State is entitled to, and must take all possible measures in order to prevent the commission of human rights violations in its territory, including in its air space.

146. There are obviously practical difficulties involved in securing the effective enjoyment of Convention rights in aircraft transiting a Council of Europe member State's airspace or military base for foreign forces on its territory. Without prejudice to the wider question of how such difficulties can affect the scope of a State's obligations to secure generally the rights under the Convention, the case-law of the European Court of Human Rights makes it clear that the State's duty to secure the most elementary rights at issue in the present case (right to security of person; freedom from torture and right to life) continues to apply, regardless of acquiescence or connivance.

148. If the state airplane in question has presented itself as if it were a civil plane, that is to say it has not duly sought prior authorisation pursuant to Article 3 c) of the Chicago Convention, it is in breach of the Chicago Convention: the territorial State may therefore require landing. The airplane having failed to declare its State functions, it will not be entitled to claim State aircraft status and subsequently not be entitled to immunity: the territorial State will therefore be entitled to search the plane pursuant to Article 16 of the Chicago Convention and take all necessary measures to secure human rights. In addition, it will be entitled to protest through appropriate diplomatic channels.

149. If the plane has presented itself as a State plane and has obtained overflight permission without however disclosing its mission, the territorial State can contend that the flag State has violated its international obligations. The flag State could thus face international responsibility. The airplane however will, in principle, be entitled to immunity according to general international law and to the applicable treaties: the territorial State will therefore be unable to search the plane, unless the captain consents.

150. However, the territorial State may refuse further overflight clearances in favour of the flag State or impose, as a condition therefore, a duty to submit to searches. If the overflight permission derives from a bilateral treaty or a SOFA [status of forces agreement] or a military base agreement, the terms of such treaty might be questioned if and to the extent that they do not allow for any control in order to ensure respect for human rights, or their abuse might be advanced....

151. While mutual trust and economic and military co-operation amongst friendly States need to be encouraged, in granting foreign state aircraft authorisation for overflight, Council of Europe member States must secure respect for their human rights obligations. This means that they may have to consider whether it is necessary to insert new clauses, including the right to search, as a condition for diplomatic clearances in favour of State planes carrying prisoners. If there are reasonable grounds to believe that, in certain categories of cases, the

human rights of certain passengers risk being violated, States must indeed make overflight permission conditional upon respect of express human rights clauses. Compliance with the procedures for obtaining diplomatic clearance must be strictly monitored; requests for overflight authorisation should provide sufficient information as to allow effective monitoring (for example, the identity and status (voluntary or involuntary passenger) of all persons on board and the destination of the flight as well as the final destination of each passenger). Whenever necessary, the right to search civil planes must be exercised.

152. With a view to discouraging repetition of abuse, any violations of civil aviation principles in relation to irregular transport of prisoners should be denounced, and brought to the attention of the competent authorities and eventually of the public. Council of Europe member States could bring possible breaches of the Chicago Convention before the Council of the International Civil Aviation Organisation pursuant to Article 54 of the Chicago Convention.

Security Council Resolution 2166
(2014) 21 July 2014

On 17 July 2014, a civilian aircraft, Malaysian Airlines Flight MH17, was brought down while flying through Ukrainian airspace, allegedly by a missile fired by a separatist movement in effective control of part of Ukrainian territory (including the crash site). The Security Council adopted the following Resolution.

1. *Condemns* in the strongest terms the downing of Malaysia Airlines flight MH17 on 17 July in Donetsk Oblast, Ukraine resulting in the tragic loss of 298 lives;

2. *Reiterates* its deepest sympathies and condolences to the families of the victims of this incident and to the people and governments of the victims' countries of origin;

3. *Supports* efforts to establish a full, thorough and independent international investigation into the incident in accordance with international civil aviation guidelines;

4. *Recognizes* the efforts under way by Ukraine, working in coordination with ICAO and other international experts and organizations, including representatives of States of Occurrence, Registry, Operator, Design and Manufacture, as well as States who have lost nationals on MH17, to institute an international investigation of the incident, and *calls on* all States to provide any requested assistance to civil and criminal investigations related to this incident;

5. *Expresses grave concern* at reports of insufficient and limited access to the crash site;

6. *Demands* that the armed groups in control of the crash site and the surrounding area refrain from any actions that may compromise the integrity of the crash site, including by refraining from destroying, moving, or disturbing wreckage, equipment, debris, personal belongings, or remains, and immediately provide safe, secure, full and unrestricted access to the site and surrounding area for the appropriate investigating authorities, the OSCE Special Monitoring Mission and representatives of other relevant international organizations according to ICAO and other established procedures;

7. *Demands* that all military activities, including by armed groups, be immediately ceased in the immediate area surrounding the crash site to allow for security and safety of the international investigation;

8. *Insists* on the dignified, respectful and professional treatment and recovery of the bodies of the victims, and *calls upon* all parties to ensure that this happens with immediate effect;

9. *Calls on* all States and actors in the region to cooperate fully in relation to the international investigation of the incident, including with respect to immediate and unrestricted access to the crash site as referred to in paragraph 6;...

11. *Demands* that those responsible for this incident be held to account and that all States cooperate fully with efforts to establish accountability;

12. *Urges* all parties to the Convention on International Civil Aviation to observe to the fullest extent applicable, the international rules, standards and practices concerning the safety of civil aviation, in order to prevent the recurrence of such incidents, and *demands* that all States and other actors refrain from acts of violence directed against civilian aircraft

NOTES
1. The Chicago Convention attempts to provide international agreement as to the regulation and protection of civilian aircraft. However, the requirement in Article 6 that scheduled air flights must operate with the consent of the territorial State has resulted in a parallel system of bilateral and regional agreements. In *R (Yollari and Anor)* v *Secretary of State for Transport* (2009] EWHC 1918 (Admin)), Mr Justice Wyn Williams of the UK High Court confirmed that the meaning of sovereignty in Article 1 of the Convention was to be given its normal meaning in public international law, and was not to be restricted to territory that was under the effective control of the State in question. Moreover, it was held that for the United Kingdom to grant rights for flights to and from airports in Northern Cyprus, without the consent of the Republic of Cyprus, would constitute a violation of Articles 5, 6, 10 and 68 of the Chicago Convention.
2. As a consequence of the destruction by Soviet military planes of Korean Airlines Flight 007 in September 1983, the United States said in the Security Council (22 ILM 1121 (1983)) that 'sovereignty neither requires nor permits the shooting down of airlines in peacetime'. However, the USSR replied that there was a 'sovereign right of every State to protect its borders including its airspace'. The issue remains contentious even for surveillance (spy) aircraft.
3. The extract from the legal opinion of the Venice Commission demonstrates the interplay between sovereignty, airspace law and the protection of human rights. The evidence of rendition flights through the airspace of European States led to calls for greater inspection and regulation of flights. The opinion emphasises the duty of the territorial State to ensure that its territory, including its airspace, is not used to facilitate violations of its human rights obligations. The rendition flights also raised issues of State complicity in facilitating human rights abuses (see Chapter 11).
4. The shooting down of Flight MH17 highlighted the vulnerability of civilian aircraft to attacks from the ground. It also demonstrated the difficulties in extending the civil aviation regime to non-State actors, both in terms of ensuring that a State's territory is not used to launch attacks against aircraft in its airspace and in enabling appropriate access and cooperation for rescue and recovery operations and crash investigation. In its Final Report on the incident, the Dutch Safety Board emphasised that States have obligations to protect civilian aircraft from attack. This included obligations on the territorial State to close its airspace either partially (i.e. limit the height at which aircraft can fly) or fully when a threat to civilian aircraft from ongoing hostilities is evident, but also on other States to preclude airlines registered within their jurisdiction or their nationals from flying through conflict-affected airspace: see *Investigation crash MH17, 17 July 2014, Donetsk*, October 2015. A joint criminal investigation into those responsible for MH17, led by the Dutch authorities, is ongoing. The Prosecutor of the ICC is also monitoring the outcome of that investigation, to determine whether she will investigate the incident as part of the investigation into the situation concerning the Ukraine.
5. The US practice of targeting suspected terrorists through armed attacks using fighter aircraft and unmanned drones raises serious issues of international human rights and humanitarian law, as they are arguably extrajudicial executions and may involve civilian casualties. In addition, such attacks represent a violation of the sovereignty and territorial airspace of the State in which the attack occurs. While some attacks appear to have been conducted with at least tacit approval and, in some situations, the consent and active cooperation of the territorial State, some States have protested against such attacks.

D: Outer space

Treaty on Principles Governing the Activities of States in the Exploration and Use of Outer Space, including the Moon and other Celestial Bodies 1967
610 UNTS (1967) 205

As at March 2016, 103 States have ratified this Treaty, which entered into force in October 1967.

Article I
The exploration and use of outer space, including the moon and other celestial bodies, shall be carried out for the benefit and in the interests of all countries, irrespective of their degree of economic or scientific development, and shall be the province of all mankind.

Outer space, including the moon and other celestial bodies, shall be free for exploration and use by all States without discrimination of any kind, on a basis of equality and in accordance with international law, and there shall be free access to all areas of celestial bodies.

There shall be freedom of scientific investigation in outer space, including the moon and other celestial bodies, and States shall facilitate and encourage international co-operation in such investigation.

Article II

Outer space, including the moon and other celestial bodies, is not subject to national appropriation by claim of sovereignty, by means of use or occupation, or by any other means.

Article IV

States Parties to the treaty undertake not to place in orbit around the earth any objects carrying nuclear weapons or any other kinds of weapons of mass destruction, install such weapons on celestial bodies, or station such weapons in outer space in any other manner.

The moon and other celestial bodies shall be used by all States Parties to the Treaty exclusively for peaceful purposes. The establishment of military bases, installations and fortifications, the testing of any type of weapons and the conduct of military manoeuvres on celestial bodies shall be forbidden. the use of military personnel for scientific research or for any other peaceful purposes shall not be prohibited. The use of any equipment or facility necessary for peaceful exploration of the moon and other celestial bodies shall also not be prohibited.

Article VIII

A State Party to the Treaty on whose registry an object launched into outer space is carried shall retain jurisdiction and control over such object, and over any personnel thereof, while in outer space or on a celestial body. Ownership of objects launched into outer space, including objects landed or constructed on a celestial body, and of their component parts, is not affected by their presence in outer space or on a celestial body or by their return to the Earth. Such objects or component parts found beyond the limits of the state Party to the treaty on whose registry they are carried shall be returned to that State Party, which shall, upon request, furnish identifying data prior to their return.

Cosmos 954 Claim (Canada v USSR)

18 *International Legal Materials* 899 (1979), Claim Nos 15, 20–23

In January 1978, a Soviet satellite, which had a nuclear reactor, disintegrated through Canadian airspace on to Canadian territory. Canada issued a Statement of Claim to the USSR seeking compensation of six million dollars for cleaning up the affected area. The matter was settled by a payment of three million dollars without admission of liability. This is an extract from Canada's claim.

On behalf of CANADA:...

(a) *International agreements*

15. Under Article II of the Convention on International Liability for Damage caused by Space Objects, hereinafter also referred to as the Convention, 'A launching State shall be absolutely liable to pay compensation for damage caused by its space object on the surface of the earth....' The Union of Soviet Socialist Republics, as the launching State of the cosmos 954 satellite, has an absolute liability to pay compensation to Canada for the damage caused by this satellite. The deposit of hazardous radioactive debris from the satellite throughout a large area of Canadian territory, and the presence of that debris in the environment rendering part of Canada's territory unfit for use, constituted 'damage to property' within the meaning of the Convention....

20. The liability of the Union of Soviet Socialist Republics for damage caused by the satellite is also founded in Article VII of the Treaty on Principles Government the Activities of States in the Exploration and Use of Outer Space, including the Moon and Other Celestial Bodies, done in 1967, and to which both Canada and the Union of Soviet Socialist Republics are parties. This liability places an obligation on the Union of Soviet Socialist Republics to compensate Canada in accordance with international law for the consequences of the intrusion of the satellite into Canadian air space and the deposit on Canadian territory of hazardous radioactive debris from the satellite.

(b) *General principles of international law*

21. The intrusion of the Cosmos 954 satellite into Canada's air space and the deposit on Canadian territory of hazardous radioactive debris from the satellite constitutes a violation of Canada's sovereignty. This violation is established by the mere face of the trespass of the satellite, the harmful consequences of this intrusion, being the damage caused to Canada by the presence of hazardous radioactive debris and the interference with the sovereign right of Canada to determine the acts that will be performed on its territory. International precedents recognize that a violation of sovereignty gives rise to an obligation to pay compensation.

22. The standard of absolute liability for space activities, in particular activities involving the use of nuclear energy, is considered to have become a general principle of international law. A large number of states, including Canada and the Union of Soviet Socialist Republics, have adhered to this principle as contained in the 1972 Convention on International Liability for Damage caused by Space Objects. The principle of absolute liability applies to fields of activities having in common a high degree of risk. It is repeated in numerous international agreements and is one of 'the general principles of law recognized by civilized nations' (Article 38 of the Statute of The International Court of Justice). Accordingly this principle has been accepted as a general principles of international law.

23. In calculating the compensation claimed, Canada has applied the relevant criteria established by general principles of international law according to which fair compensation is to be paid, by including in its claim only those costs that are reasonable, proximately caused by the intrusion of the satellite and deposit of debris and capable of being calculated with a reasonable degree of certainty.

NOTE: The 1979 Agreement Governing the Activities of States on the Moon and other Celestial Bodies was meant to supplement the Outer Space Treaty (see extract). Although there are only 16 State parties to it (as at March 2016) and none of the Permanent Members of the Security Council are party, it seeks to make the Moon and its resources part of the 'common heritage of mankind'. This is part of an attempt to make areas of the Earth and its surrounds beyond the sovereignty of any one State. This concept is also seen in developments in the law of the sea over the high seas (see Chapter 10) and over the environment (see Chapter 12), as well as placing pressure on the parties to the Antarctic Treaty (see Section 6A) to make the Antarctic part of the common heritage of humankind.

E: International territorial administration

States are not the only entities that can control territory. Territory can be controlled by non-State actors, such as armed opposition groups and national liberation movements, as well as by international organisations, the latter of which has a form of sovereignty over the territory (see Chapter 5).

R. Wilde, 'From Danzig to East Timor and Beyond: The Role of International Territorial Administration'
95 American Journal of international Law 583 (2001)

To understand the official purposes of granting administrative control over territory to international organizations, one must appreciate how such control operates. In certain circumstances, states hand over responsibility for running camps, housing refugees and/ or internally displaced persons (refugee camps) to UNHCR [United Nations High Commissioner for Refugees].... These camps resemble small cities where education, medical services, and basic infrastructure are provided by a network of international agencies under the control of UNHCR. More generally, UN agencies, notably the World Food Programme, implement programs of material assistance in a variety of places.... In Bosnia and Herzegovina, the OHR [Office of the High Representative of the International Community], created by the 1995 Dayton Agreement [Agreement on Peace in Bosnia and Herzegovina], has interpreted its vague powers in that Agreement to encompass various governmental acts, including the passing of laws and the dismissal of elected officials.... In June 1999, the United Nations Mission in Kosovo (UNMIK) was created to provide an 'interim administration' in that territory. In the same year, the United Nations Mission in

East Timor (UNAMET) conducted a popular consultation on East Timor's future status, and the United Nations Transitional Authority in East Timor (UNTAET) was later created to administer the territory until independence.

Each project involves a claim made by an international organization relating to territorial administration. Here, 'territorial administration' refers to a formally constituted, locally based management structure operating with respect to a particular territorial unit; it can be limited (e.g., a territorial program concerned with certain matters) or plenary (e.g., a territorial government) in scope. The international organization asserts the right either to supervise and control the operation of this structure by local actors, or to operate the structure directly. The right is exercised from within the territory, and can pertain to the structure as a whole, or certain parts of it (e.g., the legislature). This activity should be contrasted with merely monitoring and/or assisting local actors in operating such a structure, although the distinction is sometimes difficult to make in practice, particularly in the case of conduct and assistance. The spatial identity of the international organization and its officials—as 'international'—is distinct from and opposed to the 'local' identity of the territorial unit and population affected, even if the organization's activities are limited to that territory and some of the 'internationals' are actually local nationals. This divergence between the two spatial identities marks the projects off from the European Communities [EC]. There, the EC institutions share the same spatial identity as the legal order in respect of which they perform administrative functions (even if this legal order cuts across the distinct legal orders of member states). Similarly, although the enjoyment of privileges and immunities in state territory gives international organizations near-exclusive administrative competence by default, such competence usually covers only the property and personnel of the organization (the provision of consular protection is similarly limited)....

ITA [International Territorial Administration] ... is seen as a substitute for territorial administration as it is 'normally' practiced: by actors whose spatial identity, as local, corresponds to that of the territorial unit and its population. ITA has been and is being used as a device to replace local actors in the activity of administration either partially or fully, because of two perceived problems with the 'normal' model. In the first place, ITA is used to respond to a perceived sovereignty problem with the presence of local actors exercising control over the territory. In the second place, ITA is used to respond to a perceived governance problem with the conduct of governance by local actors. The first problem concerns the identity of the local actors being excluded from administration; the second problem concerns the quality of governance being exercised in the territory.

NOTE: The degree of sovereignty over territory of international organisations is a reflection of both their international legal personality and the changes to the notion of sovereignty away from an absolute and State-based concept of sovereignty.

8

Jurisdictional Sovereignty

INTRODUCTORY NOTE

As noted in Chapter 7, 'sovereignty' is one of the most fundamental concepts known to international law. However, the 'sovereignty' of a State is a nebulous concept, comprising many facets, and its implications may be felt both in the national and international spheres. A State's administrative, judicial, executive and legislative activity is part of the exercise of its sovereignty, sometimes known as its jurisdictional sovereignty. The principal concern of this chapter is to examine the objects of a State's jurisdictional sovereignty (both natural and legal persons) and the circumstances in which it may be exercised.

The exercise of jurisdiction over persons and property by a State necessarily comprises action in the national sphere through its legislature, police force and courts. This action may also have international consequences, such as where jurisdiction is exercised over a foreign national, or the assets of a foreign State or in respect of acts occurring outside the State's territory. Jurisdiction is usually described as being either 'prescriptive' or 'enforcement' in nature. Prescriptive jurisdiction describes a State's ability to define its own laws in respect of any matters it chooses. Enforcement jurisdiction describes a State's ability to enforce those laws and is necessarily dependent on the existence of prescriptive jurisdiction. As a general rule, a State's prescriptive jurisdiction is unlimited and a State may legislate for any matter irrespective of where the event occurs (even if in the territory of another State) or the nationality of the persons involved. However, the sovereign equality of States means that one State may not exercise its enforcement jurisdiction in a concrete sense (for example, by arresting suspects, or by establishing its own courts) in another State's territory irrespective of the reach of its prescriptive jurisdiction, at least not without the latter State's consent. As a corollary to these principles, a State's enforcement jurisdiction within its own territory is normally absolute over all matters and persons situated therein. There are exceptions to this absolute territorial jurisdiction, as where persons are immune from the jurisdiction of local courts (see Chapter 9), but this occurs only by reason of a specific rule of international or national law to that effect.

The principles of jurisdiction are rules of international law that represent an attempt to regulate the extent to which one State's enforcement jurisdiction impinges or conflicts with another State's jurisdiction. These principles attempt to resolve disputed questions of jurisdiction by determining which of two or more States competing to exercise an enforcement jurisdiction may properly do so. The jurisdiction exercised by international criminal courts and tribunals, in particular the International Criminal Court, is considered in Chapters 14 and 16.

SECTION 1: GENERAL PRINCIPLES OF JURISDICTION

United Nations Charter 1945

Article 2

The Organization and its Members, in pursuit of the Purposes stated in Article 1, shall act in accordance with the following Principles:…

7. Nothing contained in the present Charter shall authorize the United Nations to intervene in matters which are essentially within the domestic jurisdiction of any State or shall require the Members to submit such matters to settlement under the present Charter; but this principle shall not prejudice the application of enforcement measures under Chapter VII.

SS Lotus Case (*France* v *Turkey*)

PCIJ Ser A (1927) No 9, Permanent Court of International Justice

A collision occurred on the high seas in the Mediterranean between a French steamer, the *Lotus*, and a Turkish steamer, *Boz-Kourt*, in which the latter was sunk with the loss of eight Turkish sailors. Upon the arrival of the *Lotus* at a Turkish port, its French officer on watch, Lieutenant Demons, was arrested on the criminal charge of involuntary manslaughter. By special agreement, the parties brought the matter before the Court, asking whether Turkey, by exercising its criminal jurisdiction in prosecuting the French citizen, was acting contrary to international law, in particular Article 15 of the Convention of Lausanne 1923. The Court held, by the casting vote of the President, that Turkey had not acted contrary to international law.

International law governs relations between independent States. The rules of law binding upon States therefore emanate from their own free will as expressed in conventions or by usages generally accepted as expressing principles of law and established in order to regulate the relations between these co-existing independent communities or with a view to the achievement of common aims. Restrictions upon the independence of States cannot therefore be presumed.

Now the first and foremost restriction imposed by international law upon a State is that—failing the existence of a permissive rule to the contrary—it may not exercise its power in any form in the territory of another State. In this sense jurisdiction is certainly territorial; it cannot be exercised by a State outside its territory except by virtue of a permissive rule derived from international custom or from a convention.

It does not, however, follow that international law prohibits a State from exercising jurisdiction in its own territory, in respect of any case which relates to acts which have taken place abroad, and in which it cannot rely on some permissive rule of international law. Such a view would only be tenable if international law contained a general prohibition to States to extend the application of their laws and the jurisdiction of their courts to persons, property and acts outside their territory, and if, as an exception to this general prohibition, it allowed States to do so in certain specific cases. But this is certainly not the case under international law as it stands at present. Far from laying down a general prohibition to the effect that States may not extend the application of their laws and the jurisdiction of their courts to persons, property and acts outside their territory, it leaves them in this respect a wide measure of discretion which is only limited in certain cases by prohibitive rules; as regards other cases, every State remains free to adopt the principles which it regards as best and most suitable…

In these circumstances, all that can be required of a State is that it should not overstep the limits which international law places upon its jurisdiction; within these limits, its title to exercise jurisdiction rests in its sovereignty.

Though it is true that in all systems of law the principle of the territorial character of criminal law is fundamental, it is equally true that all or nearly all these systems of law extend their action to offences committed outside the territory of the State which adopts them, and they do so in ways which vary from State to State. The territoriality of criminal law, therefore, is not an absolute principle of international law and by no means coincides with territorial sovereignty…

Consequently, once it is admitted that the effects of the offence were produced on the Turkish vessel, it becomes impossible to hold that there is a rule of international law which prohibits Turkey from prosecuting

Lieutenant Demons because of the fact that the author of the offence was on board the French ship.…[T]here is no reason preventing the Court from confining itself to observing that, in this case, a prosecution may also be justified from the point of view of the so-called territorial principle…

It is certainly true that—apart from certain special cases which are defined by international law—vessels on the high seas are subject to no authority except that of the State whose flag they fly. In virtue of the principle of the freedom of the seas, that is to say, the absence of any territorial sovereignty upon the high seas, no State may exercise any kind of jurisdiction over foreign vessels upon them…

This conclusion could only be overcome if it were shown that there was a rule of customary international law which, going further than the principle stated above, established the exclusive jurisdiction of the State whose flag was flown.…In the Court's opinion, the existence of such a rule has not been conclusively proved…

The conclusion at which the Court has therefore arrived is that there is no rule of international law in regard to collision cases to the effect that criminal proceedings are exclusively within the jurisdiction of the State whose flag is flown. This conclusion moreover is easily explained if the manner in which the collision brings the jurisdiction of two different countries into play be considered.…

Neither the exclusive jurisdiction of either State, nor the limitations of the jurisdiction of each to the occurrences which took place on the respective ships would appear calculated to satisfy the requirements of justice and effectively to protect the interests of the two States. It is only natural that each should be able to exercise jurisdiction and to do so in respect of the incident as a whole. It is therefore a case of concurrent jurisdiction.

American Law Institute, *Restatement (Third) Foreign Relations Law of the United States*
(1987)

The rules given in this Restatement are said to reflect the law as given effect by Courts in the United States. In general, those Courts construe US national law so as not to conflict with international law (although see the case of *United States* v *Alvarez-Machain* in Section 3). Moreover, the so-called 'principles of jurisdiction to prescribe'—being the applicable rules when two or more States are claiming jurisdiction over the same events—are not accepted by all scholars as reflecting customary international law.

§401. Categories of Jurisdiction
Under international law, a state is subject to limitations on

(a) jurisdiction to prescribe, i.e., to make its law applicable to the activities, relations, or status of persons, or the interests of persons in things, whether by legislation, by executive act or order, by administrative rule or regulation, or by determination of a court;

(b) jurisdiction to adjudicate, i.e., to subject persons or things to the process of its courts or administrative tribunals, whether in civil or in criminal proceedings, whether or not the state is a party to the proceedings;

(c) jurisdiction to enforce, i.e., to induce or compel compliance or to punish noncompliance with its laws or regulations, whether through the courts or by use of executive, administrative, police, or other nonjudicial action.

International law has long recognized limitations on the authority of states to exercise jurisdiction to prescribe in circumstances affecting the interests of other states. In the past, the jurisdiction of a state to make its law applicable in a translational context was determined by formal criteria supposedly derived from concepts of state sovereignty and power. In principle, it was accepted that a state had jurisdiction to exercise its authority within its territory and with respect to its nationals abroad. Ambiguous cases were seen as raising issues in the definition and application of those principles.…If the regulation of two (or more) states conflicted, that was unfortunate for the actor caught between two masters, but international law, it was thought, offered neither resolution nor remedy.

Increasingly, the practice of states has reflected conceptions better adapted to the complexities of contemporary international intercourse. State sovereignty was to be controlled by law, and its power tempered by reason and reasonableness. States have not in fact regulated all the foreign activities of their nationals (or affiliates of their nationals), nor every activity that could be said to have some effect in their territory. Attempts by some states—notably the United States—to apply their law on the basis of very broad conceptions of territoriality or nationality bred resentment and brought forth conflicting assertions of the rules of international law. Relations with Canada, and also with several states in Western Europe, have at times been strained by efforts of the United States to implement economic sanctions—against China, the Soviet Union, Cuba, and other states—through restraints on foreign subsidiaries of corporations based in the United States....The application of antitrust and securities laws, on both governmental and private initiative, has reached beyond the territorial frontiers of the United States, and from time to time has been perceived by other states as intrusion into their rightful domain....Partly in response to the reactions of other states, the United States has modified its assertions of jurisdiction in some areas...

Territoriality and nationality remain the principal bases of jurisdiction to prescribe, but in determining their meaning rigid concepts have been replaced by broader criteria embracing principles of reasonableness and fairness to accommodate overlapping or conflicting interests of states, and affected private interests. Courts and other decision makers, learning from the approach to comparable problems in private international law, are increasingly inclined to consider various interests, examine contacts and links, give effect to justified expectations, search for the 'center of gravity' of a given situation, and develop priorities. This Restatement follows this approach in adopting the principle of reasonableness.

NOTES

1. The limits of the 'domestic' or 'national' jurisdiction of a State have been altered over time by the development of international law. For example, national jurisdiction has generally been expanded by the changes in the extent of a State's maritime jurisdiction under the Law of the Sea (see Chapter 10), and it has been limited by international human rights law (see Chapter 6).

2. The Court in the *Lotus Case* (above) adopted a positivist view that prevents any limitations being placed on the sovereignty of States unless there is a clear rule to the contrary. This decision does not reflect contemporary customary international law, as now a State asserting jurisdiction over any given issue must show a positive basis of jurisdiction if challenged by a State having or alleging a greater jurisdictional right. Thus national courts must now seek a ground for the assertion of their jurisdiction, i.e. a reason why the local adjudication and enforcement process should proceed, at least in cases where another State may also have a claim to exercise enforcement jurisdiction.

SECTION 2: GROUNDS FOR THE ASSERTION OF JURISDICTION BY NATIONAL COURTS

The following section discusses the principles that national courts have used to explain why they should, or should not, exercise enforcement jurisdiction in any given case. The issue usually arises in cases where another State is claiming jurisdiction (perhaps through an application to extradite an offender), or where the defendant herself denies the national court's jurisdiction. In many cases, the subject matter of the case involves non-nationals or events wholly or partly performed abroad and often concerns criminal law. The principal grounds for the assertion of jurisdiction are where there is either a territorial or nationality link between the case and the court, as where the events take place in the State or are committed by a national of that State. An extension of these is the 'protective' and 'passive personality' principles, both of which are now being invoked more frequently. The 'effects doctrine' is a contentious ground for invoking national jurisdiction as it often has an extraterritorial reach and affects non-nationals. Its principal proponent is the United States.

A: Territorial

Al-Skeini and others v United Kingdom
Judgment 7 July 2011, European Court of Human Rights

This case concerned an application by the relatives of six individuals who had been killed by British armed forces operating in Iraq. The applicants claimed violations of various rights under the European Convention on Human Rights (see Chapter 6) which are given effect in the United Kingdom by the Human Rights Act 1998 (see Chapter 4). It was necessary for the European Court of Human Rights to consider whether the Convention had extraterritorial effect.

132. To date, the Court in its case-law has recognised a number of exceptional circumstances capable of giving rise to the exercise of jurisdiction by a Contracting State outside its own territorial boundaries. In each case, the question whether exceptional circumstances exist which require and justify a finding by the Court that the State was exercising jurisdiction extraterritorially must be determined with reference to the particular facts.

(a) State agent authority and control

133. The Court has recognised in its case-law that, as an exception to the principle of territoriality, a Contracting State's jurisdiction under Article 1 may extend to acts of its authorities which produce effects outside its own territory…The statement of principle…is very broad: the Court states merely that the Contracting Party's responsibility 'can be involved' in these circumstances. It is necessary to examine the Court's case-law to identify the defining principles.

134. Firstly, it is clear that the acts of diplomatic and consular agents, who are present on foreign territory in accordance with provisions of international law, may amount to an exercise of jurisdiction when these agents exert authority and control over others….

135. Secondly, the Court has recognised the exercise of extraterritorial jurisdiction by a Contracting State when, through the consent, invitation or acquiescence of the Government of that territory, it exercises all or some of the public powers normally to be exercised by that Government (see *Banković and Others* § 71[41 *International Legal Matters* 517 (2002), European Court of Human Rights]). Thus, where, in accordance with custom, treaty or other agreement, authorities of the Contracting State carry out executive or judicial functions on the territory of another State, the Contracting State may be responsible for breaches of the Convention thereby incurred, as long as the acts in question are attributable to it rather than to the territorial State…

136. In addition, the Court's case-law demonstrates that, in certain circumstances, the use of force by a State's agents operating outside its territory may bring the individual thereby brought under the control of the State's authorities into the State's Article 1 jurisdiction. This principle has been applied where an individual is taken into the custody of State agents abroad….The Court does not consider that jurisdiction in the above cases arose solely from the control exercised by the Contracting State over the buildings, aircraft or ship in which the individuals were held. What is decisive in such cases is the exercise of physical power and control over the person in question.

137. It is clear that, whenever the State, through its agents, exercises control and authority over an individual, and thus jurisdiction, the State is under an obligation under Article 1 to secure to that individual the rights and freedoms under Section I of the Convention that are relevant to the situation of that individual. In this sense, therefore, the Convention rights can be 'divided and tailored' (compare *Banković and Others* § 75).

(b) Effective control over an area

138. Another exception to the principle that jurisdiction under Article 1 is limited to a State's own territory occurs when, as a consequence of lawful or unlawful military action, a Contracting State exercises effective control of an area outside that national territory. The obligation to secure, in such an area, the rights and freedoms set out in the Convention, derives from the fact of such control, whether it be exercised directly, through the Contracting State's own armed forces, or through a subordinate local administration…Where the fact of such domination over the territory is established, it is not necessary to determine whether the Contracting State exercises detailed control over the policies and actions of the subordinate local administration. The fact that the local administration survives as a result of the Contracting State's military and other support entails that State's responsibility for its policies and actions. The controlling State has the responsibility under Article 1 to secure, within the area under its control, the entire range of substantive rights set out in the Convention and those additional Protocols which it has ratified. It will be liable for any violations of those rights…

139. It is a question of fact whether a Contracting State exercises effective control over an area outside its own territory. In determining whether effective control exists, the Court will primarily have reference to the strength of the State's military presence in the area…Other indicators may also be relevant, such as the extent to which its military, economic and political support for the local subordinate administration provides it with influence and control over the region…

140. The 'effective control' principle of jurisdiction set out above does not replace the system of declarations under Article 56 of the Convention (formerly Article 63) which the States decided, when drafting the Convention, to apply to territories overseas for whose international relations they were responsible. Article 56 § 1 provides a mechanism whereby any State may decide to extend the application of the Convention, 'with due regard…to local requirements', to all or any of the territories for whose international relations it is responsible. The existence of this mechanism, which was included in the Convention for historical reasons, cannot be interpreted in present conditions as limiting the scope of the term 'jurisdiction' in Article 1. The situations covered by the 'effective control' principle are clearly separate and distinct from circumstances where a Contracting State has not, through a declaration under Article 56, extended the Convention or any of its Protocols to an overseas territory for whose international relations it is responsible…

(c) The legal space ('*espace juridique*') of the Convention

141. The Convention is a constitutional instrument of European public order…It does not govern the actions of States not Parties to it, nor does it purport to be a means of requiring the Contracting States to impose Convention standards on other States…

142. The Court has emphasised that, where the territory of one Convention State is occupied by the armed forces of another, the occupying State should in principle be held accountable under the Convention for breaches of human rights within the occupied territory, because to hold otherwise would be to deprive the population of that territory of the rights and freedoms hitherto enjoyed and would result in a 'vacuum' of protection within the 'legal space of the Convention'…However, the importance of establishing the occupying State's jurisdiction in such cases does not imply, *a contrario*, that jurisdiction under Article 1 of the Convention can never exist outside the territory covered by the Council of Europe member States. The Court has not in its case-law applied any such restriction…

149. It can be seen, therefore, that following the removal from power of the Ba'ath regime and until the accession of the interim Iraqi government, the United Kingdom (together with the United States of America) assumed in Iraq the exercise of some of the public powers normally to be exercised by a sovereign government. In particular, the United Kingdom assumed authority and responsibility for the maintenance of security in south-east Iraq. In these exceptional circumstances, the Court considers that the United Kingdom, through its soldiers engaged in security operations in Basra during the period in question, exercised authority and control over individuals killed in the course of such security operations, so as to establish a jurisdictional link between the deceased and the United Kingdom for the purposes of Article 1 of the Convention.

150. Against this background, the Court recalls that the deaths at issue in the present case occurred during the relevant period…It is not disputed that the deaths of the first, second, fourth, fifth and sixth applicants' relatives were caused by the acts of British soldiers during the course of or contiguous to security operations carried out by British forces in various parts of Basra City. It follows that in all these cases there was a jurisdictional link for the purposes of Article 1 of the Convention between the United Kingdom and the deceased. The third applicant's wife was killed during an exchange of fire between a patrol of British soldiers and unidentified gunmen and it is not known which side fired the fatal bullet. The Court considers that, since the death occurred in the course of a United Kingdom security operation, when British soldiers carried out a patrol in the vicinity of the applicant's home and joined in the fatal exchange of fire, there was a jurisdictional link between the United Kingdom and this deceased also.

Boumediene **v** *Bush*

47 *International Legal Materials* 650 (2008), United States Supreme Court

An application for *habeas corpus* was lodged on behalf of an individual detained in Guantanamo Bay, Cuba, pursuant to an order issued by President Bush. The military base at Guantanamo Bay was held by the United States on a long-term lease agreement with Cuba. The Supreme Court had to consider whether the right of *habeas corpus* and the Constitutional protection for the right (the so-called suspension clause) extended to persons detained at Guantanamo Bay.

Kennedy J (with Stevens, Souter, Ginsburg, and Breyer, JJ): Drawing from its position that at common law the writ ran only to territories over which the Crown was sovereign, the Government says the Suspension Clause affords petitioners no rights because the United States does not claim sovereignty over the place of detention.

Guantanamo Bay is not formally part of the United States....And under the terms of the lease between the United States and Cuba, Cuba retains 'ultimate sovereignty' over the territory while the United States exercises 'complete jurisdiction and control.' See Lease of Lands for Coaling and Naval Stations, Feb. 23, 1903, U. S.-Cuba, Art. III, T. S. No. 418 (hereinafter 1903 Lease Agreement)....Under the terms of the 1934 Treaty, however, Cuba effectively has no rights as a sovereign until the parties agree to modification of the 1903 Lease Agreement or the United States abandons the base....

The United States contends, nevertheless, that Guantanamo is not within its sovereign control. This was the Government's position well before the events of September 11, 2001....And in other contexts the Court has held that questions of sovereignty are for the political branches to decide....Even if this were a treaty interpretation case that did not involve a political question, the President's construction of the lease agreement would be entitled to great respect....

We therefore do not question the Government's position that Cuba, not the United States, maintains sovereignty, in the legal and technical sense of the term, over Guantanamo Bay. But this does not end the analysis. Our cases do not hold it is improper for us to inquire into the objective degree of control the Nation asserts over foreign territory. As commentators have noted, ' "[s]overeignty" is a term used in many senses and is much abused.' See 1 Restatement (Third) of Foreign Relations Law of the United States §206, Comment *b,* p. 94 (1986). When we have stated that sovereignty is a political question, we have referred not to sovereignty in the general, colloquial sense, meaning the exercise of dominion or power,...but sovereignty in the narrow, legal sense of the term, meaning a claim of right...Indeed, it is not altogether uncommon for a territory to be under the *de jure* sovereignty of one nation, while under the plenary control, or practical sovereignty, of another. This condition can occur when the territory is seized during war, as Guantanamo was during the Spanish-American War....Accordingly, for purposes of our analysis, we accept the Government's position that Cuba, and not the United States, retains *de jure* sovereignty over Guantanamo Bay. As we did in *Rasul*, however, we take notice of the obvious and uncontested fact that the United States, by virtue of its complete jurisdiction and control over the base, maintains *de facto* sovereignty over this territory....

The Court has discussed the issue of the Constitution's extraterritorial application on many occasions. These decisions undermine the Government's argument that, at least as applied to noncitizens, the Constitution necessarily stops where *de jure* sovereignty ends....The Government's formal sovereignty-based test raises troubling separation-of-powers concerns as well. The political history of Guantanamo illustrates the deficiencies of this approach. The United States has maintained complete and uninterrupted control of the bay for over 100 years. At the close of the Spanish-American War, Spain ceded control over the entire island of Cuba to the United States and specifically 'relinquishe[d] all claim[s] of sovereignty... and title.'...From the date the treaty with Spain was signed until the Cuban Republic was established on May 20, 1902, the United States governed the territory 'in trust' for the benefit of the Cuban people.... And although it recognized, by entering into the 1903 Lease Agreement, that Cuba retained 'ultimate sovereignty' over Guantanamo, the United States continued to maintain the same plenary control it had enjoyed since 1898. Yet the Government's view is that the Constitution had no effect there, at least as to noncitizens, because the United States disclaimed sovereignty in the formal sense of the term. The necessary implication of the argument is that by surrendering formal sovereignty over any unincorporated territory to a third party, while at the same time entering into a lease that grants total control over the territory back to the United States, it would be possible for the political branches to govern without legal constraint.

Our basic charter cannot be contracted away like this. The Constitution grants Congress and the President the power to acquire, dispose of, and govern territory, not the power to decide when and where its terms apply. Even when the United States acts outside its borders, its powers are not 'absolute and unlimited' but are subject 'to such restrictions as are expressed in the Constitution.' *Murphy* v. *Ramsey*, 114 U. S. 15, 44 (1885). Abstaining from questions involving formal sovereignty and territorial governance is one thing. To hold the political branches have the power to switch the Constitution on or off at will is quite another. The former position reflects this Court's recognition that certain matters requiring political judgments are best left to the political branches. The latter would permit a striking anomaly in our tripartite system of government, leading to a regime in which Congress and the President, not this Court, say 'what the law is.' *Marbury* v. *Madison*, 1 Cranch 137, 177 (1803).

These concerns have particular bearing upon the Suspension Clause question in the cases now before us, for the writ of habeas corpus is itself an indispensable mechanism for monitoring the separation of powers. The test for determining the scope of this provision must not be subject to manipulation by those whose power it is designed to restrain...

There is no indication, furthermore, that adjudicating a habeas corpus petition would cause friction with the host government. No Cuban court has jurisdiction over American military personnel at Guantanamo or the enemy combatants detained there. While obligated to abide by the terms of the lease, the United States is, for all practical purposes, answerable to no other sovereign for its acts on the base. Were that not the case, or if the detention facility were located in an active theater of war, arguments that issuing the writ would be 'impracticable or anomalous' would have more weight....Under the facts presented here, however, there are few practical barriers to the running of the writ. To the extent barriers arise, *habeas corpus* procedures likely can be modified to address them....It is true that before today the Court has never held that noncitizens detained by our Government in territory over which another country maintains *de jure* sovereignty have any rights under our Constitution. But the cases before us lack any precise historical parallel. They involve individuals detained by executive order for the duration of a conflict that, if measured from September 11, 2001, to the present, is already among the longest wars in American history....The detainees, moreover, are held in a territory that, while technically not part of the United States, is under the complete and total control of our Government. Under these circumstances the lack of a precedent on point is no barrier to our holding.

We hold that Art. I, §9, cl. 2, of the Constitution has full effect at Guantanamo Bay. If the privilege of habeas corpus is to be denied to the detainees now before us, Congress must act in accordance with the requirements of the Suspension Clause.

NOTES

1. A State's 'territory' for jurisdictional purposes extends to its land and dependent territories, airspace, aircraft, ships, territorial sea and, for limited purposes, to its contiguous zone, continental shelf and exclusive economic zone (see Chapter 10).

2. As is evident from the *Lotus Case* discussed in the preceding section, the principle of territorial jurisdiction is the preeminent ground for the assertion of jurisdiction. It ensures that all persons within a State's territory are subject to national law, save only for those granted immunity under international law.

3. Most States assert jurisdiction over persons or events where any element of an event takes place within their territory: see Lord Diplock in *Treacy* v *Director of Public Prosecutions* [1971] AC 537. The 'objective' territorial principle permits a State to exercise its jurisdiction over all activities that are completed within its territory, even though some element constituting the crime or civil wrong took place elsewhere: see, e.g. the *Lotus Case*, *R* v *Sansom* [1991] 2 All ER 145 and *United States* v *Neil* (extracted in Section 2D). The 'subjective' territorial principle permits a State to assert jurisdiction over matters commencing in its territory, even though the final element may have occurred abroad. In cases where two or more States may claim jurisdiction based on the territorial principle, the issue is often settled by negotiation, extradition to the most affected State or simply by an exercise of jurisdiction by the State having custody of the individual.

4. In recent years, as seen in the above extracts, several courts have had cause to consider whether constitutional or human rights protections extend to individuals affected by actions outside their territory. In particular, the European Court of Human Rights has developed a growing body of jurisprudence on this issue and, as the extract from *Al-Skeini* shows, has attempted to clarify the legal position regarding extraterritorial jurisdiction under the European Convention on Human Rights (see also *Jaloud* v *the Netherlands*, App no 47708/08, Judgment 2014). Following the decision in *Al-Skeini*, the UK Supreme Court considered itself obliged to recognise that the UK's armed forces were within the jurisdiction of the UK, even when extraterritorially in combat zones: *Smith and others* v *The Ministry of Defence*, [2013] UKSC 41.

5. The exercise of jurisdiction in relation to cyber operations potentially creates new challenges, particularly whether 'cyber space' is viewed as a distinct legal space, separate from territory. The Tallinn Manual on the International Law Applicable to Cyber Warfare (see further Chapter 15), recognises that existing legal principles on jurisdiction apply, confirming that a State may exercise jurisdiction '(a) over persons engaged in cyber activities on its territory; (b) over cyber infrastructure located on its territory; and extraterritorially, in accordance with international law' (Rule 2).

B: Nationality

Hague Convention on Certain Questions Relating to the Conflict of Nationality Laws, Articles 1–4
179 *League of Nations Treaty Series* 89 (1930)

Article 1

It is for each State to determine under its own law who are its nationals. This law shall be recognised by other States in so far as it is consistent with international conventions, international custom, and the principles of law generally recognised with regard to nationality.

Article 2

Any question as to whether a person possesses the nationality of a particular State shall be determined in accordance with the law of that State.

Article 3

Subject to the provisions of the present Convention, a person having two or more nationalities may be regarded as its national by each of the States whose nationality he possesses.

P. Arnell, 'The Case for Nationality Based Jurisdiction'
50 *International and Comparative Law Quarterly* 955 (2001)

There are both negative and positive arguments that support the adoption of a general nationality based jurisdiction. Central to the negative arguments is the fact that territorial jurisdiction is increasingly excepted and stretched. Law and society have evolved to reduce the rationality and efficacy of territorial criminal law. One of the original rationales of territorial jurisdiction was that it was desirable that accused persons' guilt or innocence be decided by those aware of his or her character and reputation and thus be able to judge more accurately. Relatedly, territorial jurisdiction 'promoted the common law ideal of confrontation in criminal cases by ensuring that suspects would face trial near the scene of the crime, where witnesses and evidence were more readily available'. The weight of the former of these factors (that jurors are aware of the accused) has been greatly reduced if not completely negated by the great mobility and transience of persons. Indeed the role of jurors as 'know-ers' of fact is now obsolete and could well possibly give rise to a challenge under Article 6 of the European Convention on Human Rights. The latter factor (the procedural and evidential benefits), whilst undoubtedly significant, has to some extent at least been overcome by the growth in international (and national) co-operation in criminal matters. It is now possible to convict (fairly) persons accused of crimes committed some distance in space as well as time from the trial venue.

The decline in the importance of territory for the purposes of jurisdiction has been accompanied by a lessened significance of borders. This factor is particularly pertinent within the European Union, where borders have come to assume a lesser and lesser importance....

There are several strong positive arguments in favour of a move to nationality based jurisdiction. The incorporation of the European Convention on Human Rights into United Kingdom domestic law by the Human Rights Act 1998 [see Chapter 4] provides the basis of one of them. One result of incorporation is that all criminal trials are now tested against the Convention in United Kingdom courts. The right to a fair trial, the right to liberty and security of the person, and the right to be free from retrospective criminal legislation are all now part of municipal United Kingdom law. Exercising jurisdiction on the basis of nationality would be a method whereby these rights could be applied to those who are accused of crimes abroad and may not otherwise be afforded this protection. That concern over the propriety of criminal proceedings against United Kingdom nationals in various foreign States has been historically and presently raised strengthens this point.....

A second central argument in favour of nationality based jurisdiction arises from a realignment in the relationship between the citizen and the State. Here it can be argued that the original rationale for nationality based jurisdiction has been revived. It has been said to trace 'its roots to ancient times, when territorial boundaries were often vague, and communities were defined by the religion, race or nationality of the people rather [by] the territory' [Watson, (1992) 17 *Yale Journal of International Law* 41, at 46]. As noted above, with the evolution of the

European Union and international mobility generally territorial boundaries are again, although in a new sense, 'vague'. In this new situation it is arguable that the relationship between the State and its citizens is being and should be strengthened....A further factor is a seemingly new extraterritorial dimension to the purposes of the criminal law. It appears that the law has evolved from its relatively narrow self-interested territorial purposes....

Final arguments in favour of a general nationality based jurisdiction emanate from the increasing internationalisation of criminal law and crime. The United Kingdom is bound to provide for the assumption of extraterritorial jurisdiction by international convention with reference to the nationality of the offender with increasing frequency....

Statement of the Prosecutor of the International Criminal Court, Fatou Bensouda, on the Alleged Crimes Committed by ISIS

8 April 2015

Since the summer of 2014, my Office has been receiving and reviewing disturbing allegations of widespread atrocities committed in Syria and Iraq by the so-called Islamic State of Iraq and al-Sham/Greater Syria ('ISIS' *aka* 'ISIL', 'Daesh' or 'IS'). Crimes of unspeakable cruelty have been reported, such as mass executions, sexual slavery, rape and other forms of sexual and gender-based violence, torture, mutilation, enlistment and forced recruitment of children and the persecution of ethnic and religious minorities, not to mention the wanton destruction of cultural property. The commission of the crime of genocide has also been alleged. In response to numerous inquiries about my Office's activities in relation to these allegations, I have decided to provide the following clarification.

The atrocities allegedly committed by ISIS undoubtedly constitute serious crimes of concern to the international community and threaten the peace, security and well-being of the region, and the world. They also occur in the context of other crimes allegedly committed by other warring factions in Syria and Iraq. However, Syria and Iraq are not Parties to the Rome Statute, the founding treaty of the International Criminal Court ('Court' or 'ICC'). Therefore, the Court has no territorial jurisdiction over crimes committed on their soil.

Under the Rome Statute, the ICC may nevertheless exercise *personal jurisdiction* over alleged perpetrators who are nationals of a State Party, even where territorial jurisdiction is absent. On this basis, my Office has reviewed communications received alleging crimes committed by ISIS, with a view to assessing the prospect of exercising personal jurisdiction over States Parties nationals within the ranks of this organisation. In doing so, my Office took into account the scope of its policy, which is to focus on those most responsible for mass crimes.

The information gathered indicates that several thousand foreign fighters have joined the ranks of ISIS in the past months alone, including significant numbers of State Party nationals from, *inter alia*, Tunisia, Jordan, France, the United Kingdom, Germany, Belgium, the Netherlands and Australia. Some of these individuals may have been involved in the commission of crimes against humanity and war crimes. A few have publicised their heinous acts through social media. The information available to the Office also indicates that ISIS is a military and political organisation primarily led by nationals of Iraq and Syria. Thus, at this stage, the prospects of my Office investigating and prosecuting those most responsible, within the leadership of ISIS, appear limited.

NOTES
1. States have an inherent right to exercise jurisdiction over their own nationals irrespective of the place where the relevant acts occurred, even if all elements of the offence took place abroad. In fact, States tend to exercise this jurisdiction extraterritorially (i.e. in respect of acts committed abroad) only where the offence or civil wrong is particularly serious. The extent to which a national court will go to establish jurisdiction based on nationality in serious cases is illustrated by *Joyce* v *Director of Public Prosecutions* ([1946] AC 347), where the defendant was said to owe allegiance to the English Crown even though his UK passport had been obtained unlawfully and had been surrendered in 1940.
2. Common law States generally do not exercise jurisdiction based on nationality alone (that is, where there is no territorial connection at all) unless the offence is particularly serious (e.g. murder, certain sexual offences), the jurisdiction is required because of international agreements and/or the offence is also a crime under international law (e.g. War Crimes Act 1991 (UK)). For example, Australia relies on the nationality principle for its Crimes (Child Sex Tourism) Act 1994. Similarly, as discussed in the extract by Arnell, the United Kingdom has extended its jurisdiction

to nationals and residents accused of committing serious crimes overseas (for example, section 72 of the Sexual Offences Act 2003 and section 51 International Criminal Court Act 2001). The Bribery Act 2010 also extends to acts of corruption committed by United Kingdom nationals (including corporations domiciled in the UK) outside the United Kingdom.

3. As a counterpart, non-nationals found in the jurisdiction who are alleged to have committed an offence elsewhere may be extradited to the territory where the offence was actually committed: see, e.g., *R v Bow Street Metropolitan Stipendiary Magistrate, ex parte Pinochet (No 3)* [1999] 2 All ER 97. This is without prejudice to the right of a State to take action against persons found on its territory who are non-nationals and where the offence occurred abroad if the alleged offence is a crime under international law triggering universal jurisdiction (though see Section 2F).

4. The issue of how the nationality of an individual is to be determined is discussed in the *Nottebohm Case* (ICJ Rep 1955 4, see Chapter 11). In principle, that case affirmed the Hague Convention and supposed that it was for each State to determine the criteria for awarding nationality, although the Court did suggest that in cases where two States were alleging that an individual was their national (as in that case), a 'genuine link' with a State had to be established before that nationality could be recognised. In this regard, the identification of the nationality of a company has given rise to much debate. See *Barcelona Traction Case*, ICJ Rep 1970 3 (see Chapter 11). The International Law Commission has also addressed questions of nationality of individuals and legal persons in the context of diplomatic protection (see Chapter 11).

5. As seen in the extract from the ICC Prosecutor's statement, nationality may also form the basis for the exercise of jurisdiction by an international court, including the ICC (see further Chapter 14). In September 2014, the Security Council highlighted the 'the acute and growing threat posed by foreign terrorist fighters, namely individuals who travel to a State other than their States of residence or nationality for the purpose of the perpetration, planning, or preparation of, or participation in, terrorist acts or the providing or receiving of terrorist training, including in connection with armed conflict' (SCR 2178 (2014), Preamble). Although that Resolution does not mention citizenship, the denial of nationality has emerged as one mechanism to deter and punish those seeking to support ISIL in Syria and Iraq, with several States, including Australia, adopting legislation to remove citizenship from foreign fighters. However, withdrawal of the link of nationality may also break the jurisdictional link that is created by such nationality and may preclude the State, and international courts such as the ICC, from exercising jurisdiction.

C: Protective principle

Harvard Research Convention on Jurisdiction with respect to Crime
29 *American Journal of International Law* (Special Supplement) 435 (1935)

> A State has jurisdiction with respect to any crime committed outside its territory by an alien against the security, territorial integrity or political independence of that State, provided that the act or omission which constitutes the crime was not committed in exercise of a liberty guaranteed the alien by the law of the place where it was committed.

Attorney-General of the Government of Israel v *Eichmann*
36 ILR (1961) 5, District Court of Jerusalem

Eichmann, former head of the Jewish Office in Germany during the Second World War, was abducted by Israeli agents from Argentina in 1960 and brought to Israel to face charges of war crimes, crimes against humanity and crimes against the Jewish people. In Israel, he was prosecuted under the Nazi and Nazi Collaborators (Punishment) Law 1951. Defence counsel submitted, *inter alia*, that since Eichmann was a German national, he could not be subject to Israeli criminal jurisdiction. The Israeli Supreme Court held that Israel did have jurisdiction to try Eichmann.

30. We have discussed at length the international character of the crimes in question because this offers the broadest possible, though not the only, basis for Israel's jurisdiction according to the law of nations. No less important from the point of view of international law is the special connection which the State of Israel has with such crimes, since the people of Israel (*Am Israel*), the Jewish people (*Ha'Am Ha'Yehudi*, to use the term in the Israel legislation), constituted the target and the victim of most of the said crimes. The State of Israel's 'right to punish' the accused derives, in our view, from two cumulative sources: a universal source (pertaining to the whole of mankind), which vests the right to prosecute and punish crimes of this order in every State within the family of nations; and a specific or national source, which gives the victim nation the right to try any who assault its existence.

This second foundation of criminal jurisdiction conforms, according to accepted terminology, to the protective principle (*compétence réelle*) …

Learned counsel for the defence has summed up his argument against the jurisdiction of the Israel legislator by stressing…that under international law there must be a connection between the State and the person who committed the crime and that in the absence of a 'recognized linking point' the State has no authority to inflict punishment for foreign offences.

33. When the question is presented in its widest form, as above, it seems to us that the answer cannot be in doubt. The 'linking point' between Israel and the accused (and for that matter any person accused of a crime against the Jewish people under this Law) is striking in the case of 'crime against the Jewish people', a crime that postulates an intention to exterminate the Jewish people in whole or in part…

34. The connection between the State of Israel and the Jewish people needs no explanation. The State of Israel was established and recognized as the State of the Jews…: this is the sovereign State of the Jewish people…

Indeed, this crime very deeply concerns the 'vital interests' of the State of Israel, and under the 'protective principle' this State has the right to punish the criminals. In terms of Dahm's thesis, the acts referred to in this Law of the State of Israel 'concern it more than they concern other States', and therefore according also to this author there exists a 'linking point'. The punishment of Nazi criminals does not derive from the arbitrariness of a country 'abusing' its sovereignty but is a legitimate and reasonable exercise of a right of penal jurisdiction.

36. Defence counsel contended that the protective principle cannot apply to this Law because that principle is designed to protect only an existing State, its security and its interests, whereas the State of Israel did not exist at the time of the commission of the said crimes…The right of the injured group to punish offenders derives directly, as Grotius explained…from the crime committed against them by the offender, and it is only want of sovereignty that denies it the power to try and punish the offender. If the injured group or people thereafter achieves political sovereignty in any territory, it may exercise such sovereignty for the enforcement of its natural right to punish the offender who injured it.

All this applies to the crime of genocide (including the 'crime against the Jewish people') which, although committed by the killing of individuals, was intended to exterminate the nation as a group.

NOTE: The protective principle tends to be relied upon by a State only when its national security, or a matter of significant public interest, is in issue. This should be contrasted with the 'effects' doctrine considered in Section 2E.

D: Passive personality

SS Lotus Case (*France v Turkey*)
PCIJ Ser A (1927) No 9, Permanent Court of International Justice

MOORE J (Dissenting Opinion): The substance of the jurisdictional claim is that Turkey has a right to try and punish foreigners for acts committed in foreign countries not only against Turkey herself, but also against Turks, should such foreigners afterwards be found in Turkish territory…I cannot escape the conclusion that it is contrary to well-settled principles of international law.…

This claim is defended by its advocates, and has accordingly been defended before the Court, on what is called the 'protective' principle [now known as the 'passive personality principle']; and the countries by which the claim has been espoused are said to have adopted the 'system of protection'.

> What, we may ask, is this system? In substance, it means that the citizen of one country, when he visits another country, takes with him for his 'protection' the law of his own country and subjects those with whom he comes into contact to the operation of that law. In this way an inhabitant of a great commercial city, in which foreigners congregate, may in the course of an hour unconsciously fall under the operation of a number of foreign criminal codes. This is by no means a fanciful supposition; it is merely an illustration of what is daily occurring, if the 'protective' principle is admissible. It is evident that this claim is at variance not only with the principle of the exclusive jurisdiction of a State over its own territory, but also with the equally well-settled principle that a person visiting a foreign country, far from radiating for his protection the jurisdiction of his own country, falls under the dominion of the local law and, except so far as his government may diplomatically intervene in case of a denial of justice, must look to that law for his protection.

United States v *Yunis*

681 F. Supp 896 (1988), United States District Court, District of Columbia

Yunis, a Lebanese citizen, was lured by a US agent from Cyprus into a fishing boat that was in international waters. He was then arrested and transported to the US, where he was charged with hostage taking and piracy in connection with the hijacking in 1985 of an aircraft belonging to Royal Jordanian Airlines. No part of the offences occurred in the US, although two of the passengers were US citizens. The Court considered that it had jurisdiction over the prosecution of Yunis on the basis of both the passive personality and the universality principles (see Section 2F). The Court of Appeal, District of Columbia upheld the decision (30 ILM 463 (1991)).

> This [passive personality] principle authorizes states to assert jurisdiction over offenses committed against their citizens abroad. It recognizes that each state has a legitimate interest in protecting the safety of its citizens when they journey outside national boundaries. Because American nationals were on board the Jordanian aircraft, the government contends that the Court may exercise jurisdiction over Yunis under this principle. Defendant argues that this theory of jurisdiction is neither recognized by the international community nor the United States and is an insufficient basis for sustaining jurisdiction over Yunis.
>
> Although many international legal scholars agree that the principle is the most controversial of the five sources of jurisdiction, they also agree that the international community recognizes its legitimacy. Most accept that 'the extraterritorial reach of a law premised upon the...principle would not be in doubt as a matter of international law.' Paust, *Jurisdiction and Nonimmunity*, 23 Va.J. of Int'l Law, 191, 203 (1983). More importantly, the international community explicitly approved of the principle as a basis for asserting jurisdiction over hostage takers. As noted above,...the Hostage Taking Convention set forth certain mandatory sources of jurisdiction. But it also gave each signatory country discretion to exercise extraterritorial jurisdiction when the offense was committed 'with respect to a hostage who is a national of that state if that state considers it appropriate.' Art. 5(a)(d). Therefore, even if there are doubts regarding the international community's acceptance, there can be no doubt concerning the application of this principle to the offense of hostage taking, an offense for which Yunis is charged...
>
> Defendant's counsel correctly notes that the Passive Personality principle traditionally has been an anathema to United States lawmakers. But his reliance on the Restatement (Revised) of Foreign Relations Laws for the claim that the United States can never invoke the principle is misplaced. In the past, the United States has protested any assertion of such jurisdiction for fear that it could lead to indefinite criminal liability for its own citizens. This objection was based on the belief that foreigners visiting the United States should comply with our laws and should not be permitted to carry their laws with them. Otherwise Americans would face criminal prosecutions for actions unknown to them as illegal. However, in the most recent draft of the Restatement, the authors noted that the theory 'has been increasingly accepted when applied to terrorist and other organized attacks on a state's nationals by reason of their nationality, or to assassinations of a state's ambassadors, or government officials.' Restatement (Revised) § 402, comment g...The authors retreated from their wholesale rejection of the principle, recognizing that perpetrators of crimes unanimously condemned by members of the international community, should be aware of the illegality of their actions. Therefore, qualified application of the doctrine to serious and universally condemned crimes will not raise the specter of unlimited and unexpected criminal liability.

United States v *Neil*

312 F.3d 419 (2002), United States Court of Appeals, Ninth Circuit

Neil was a citizen of St. Vincent and the Grenadines who was employed on a cruise ship departing from and returning to an American port. He was accused of sexual conduct with a minor. The victim, a 12-year-old girl, was a United States citizen, and the crime took place in Mexican territorial waters. Neil contended that the United States did not have extraterritorial jurisdiction over the crime.

13. Congress has defined the 'special maritime and territorial jurisdiction of the United States' as including, '[t]o the extent permitted by international law, any foreign vessel during a voyage having a scheduled departure from or arrival in the United States with respect to an offense committed by or against a national of the United States.' 18 U.S.C. § 7(8). The criminal sexual contact between Neil and the victim occurred on a foreign vessel that departed from and arrived in the United States, and the victim was a United States national. This conduct thus falls squarely into the definition of special maritime and territorial jurisdiction set out in § 7(8).

14. It remains to examine whether the exercise of jurisdiction by the United States in this case would violate international law....

15. International law supports extraterritorial jurisdiction in this case. Two principles of international law permitting extraterritorial jurisdiction are potentially relevant: the territorial principle and the passive personality principle. Under the territorial principle, the United States may assert jurisdiction when acts performed outside of its borders have detrimental effects within the United States....The sexual contact occurred during a cruise that originated and terminated in California. Neil's conduct prompted an investigation by the FBI, and an agent arrested Neil in the United States. The victim was an American citizen who lives and goes to school in the United States, and who sought counseling in this country after the attack. These facts are enough to support jurisdiction under the territorial principle.....

16. Extraterritorial jurisdiction is also appropriate under the passive personality principle. Under this principle, a state may, under certain circumstances, assert jurisdiction over crimes committed against its nationals. We have previously sustained jurisdiction based on the passive personality principle....

17. Neil contends that the passive personality principle is inappropriate in this case...

18. Neil overreads our statements in *Vasquez-Velasco*. The defendants in that case were charged with committing violent crimes in aid of a racketeering enterprise under 18 U.S.C. § 1959. Unlike § 2244, that statute does not explicitly state that it applies extraterritorially, and we were obliged to infer an intent to exercise extraterritorial jurisdiction. We therefore construed the statute somewhat narrowly, stating that we did not believe that Congress intended to invoke the passive personality principle in § 1959, and thereby to criminalize extraterritorial crimes against all Americans under that statute. By contrast, § 2244(a)(3) relies on § 7(8), which invokes the passive personality principle by explicitly stating its intent to authorize extraterritorial jurisdiction, to the extent permitted by international law, when a foreign vessel departs from or arrives in an American port and an American national is a victim. We conclude that the passive personality principle is appropriately invoked to justify the exercise of extraterritorial jurisdiction in the circumstances specified in the statute.

NOTES

1. The passive personality principle extends the nationality principle to apply to any crime committed against a national of a State, wherever that national may be. The practice of States suggests that this ground for the assertion of jurisdiction is rarely advanced and generally only in relation to serious crimes, in particular terrorism. However, States have increasingly incorporated this basis of jurisdiction into their national legislation and it has formed the basis of legal proceedings in France, Spain and Belgium. For example, Belgium relied on passive personality to support the exercise of jurisdiction in relation to the crimes alleged to have been committed by former Chadian President, Hissène Habré, based on a complaint by a Belgian national of Chadian origin: see *Questions Relating to the Obligation to Prosecute or Extradite* (*Belgium* v *Senegal*), International Court of Justice, 2012.

2. Since around the turn of this century the United States has altered its practice concerning passive personality as a basis for jurisdiction. Previously it had always protested to any State that sought

to exercise passive personality jurisdiction over a national of the United States while at the same time asserting the jurisdiction itself. The conclusions in *US* v *Neil* also suggest a rather more flexible interpretation of the territorial principle.

E: The 'effects' doctrine

J. Scott, 'Extraterritoriality and Territorial Extension in EU Law'
(2014) 62 *American Journal of Comparative Law* 87

Scholars in both law and political science have been joined by media commentators in charting the rise of the EU as a global regulatory power. The EU has succeeded in using market access as a tool to leverage the 'migration' of its frequently demanding norms abroad. The EU is said to be engaging in 'unilateral regulatory globalization' known more colloquially as 'The Brussels Effect.' The picture that is beginning to emerge is of an EU that is unilateralist, hegemonic and where the direction of regulatory travel is all one way, namely from the EU to the rest of the world.

This focus on the EU as a global regulatory power has been accompanied by a shift in perspective on extraterritoriality in EU law. Whereas the enactment of extraterritorial legislation was once viewed as the preserve of the United States and as provoking the wrath of the EU; today—so the argument goes—extraterritoriality is a phenomenon that is both tolerated by the EU and that is increasingly practiced in its name. This shift in the EU's perspective on extraterritoriality is said to have occurred across different policy domains. While this is attributed to a variety of factors, the growth of the EU as an international economic actor is said to have mitigated EU fears of being 'overwhelmed' by the United States and to have augmented the EU's interest in regulating foreign behavior that generates EU market effects...

There is uncertainty and disagreement about what counts, and what should count, as a territorial connection for the purpose of distinguishing between the exercise of territorial and extraterritorial jurisdiction....a measure will be regarded as extraterritorial when it imposes obligations on persons who do not enjoy a relevant territorial connection with the regulating state. By contrast, a measure will be regarded as giving rise to territorial extension when its application depends upon the existence of a relevant territorial connection, but where the relevant regulatory determination will be shaped as a matter of law, by conduct or circumstances abroad....

While the line between conduct and presence will not always be easy to draw, where the application of EU law rests upon a requirement that the person in question is, or wishes to be, resident, established or domiciled in the EU, this will be treated as a territorially-grounded, presence-based, test. When EU law applies to those who are authorized or recognized by the EU to offer specified services within its territory, these natural or legal persons may either be regarded as being present within the EU or as engaging in EU conduct on the basis that they are offering the services concerned.

Leaving presence aside, there is also pronounced disagreement about the jurisdictional salience of effects, and about whether a measure whose application is triggered by a finding that foreign conduct is capable of generating domestic effects should be regarded as extra-territorial or not. While most U.S. courts and commentators treat effects-based jurisdiction as extra-territorial, there are commentators and courts who disagree.

Thus, the Third Restatement of the Foreign Relations Law of the United States treats as territorial the exercise of prescriptive jurisdiction over foreign conduct that has or is intended to have substantial effects within the territory of the United States. Also, in one recent judgment, the D.C. Circuit laid aside the presumption against extraterritoriality on the basis that the regulation of foreign conduct is *not* extraterritorial when the application of the law rests upon there being evidence that substantial effects are felt within the territory of the United States.

The EU's attitude toward the jurisdictional status of effects is also equivocal. It considers effects-based jurisdiction to be controversial as a matter of international law, but acknowledges that the territoriality principle has been expanded in some jurisdictions to include extraterritorial conduct that has or is intended to have substantial effects....

The topic of extraterritoriality has been examined very frequently by U.S. commentators and by U.S. courts. While U.S. courts have been willing to accommodate extraterritoriality in the exercise of prescriptive jurisdiction, including recourse to effects-based jurisdiction, they have done so within the framework of a presumption that operates against it and have developed a number of comity-driven constraints.

Extraterritoriality has not formed a topic for detailed analysis in the EU in the same way. The discussion has tended to focus on extraterritoriality in EU competition law, and on the lawfulness of extraterritorial legislation enacted by the United States. Outside of the field of competition law, there has been virtually no careful analysis of the territorial reach of EU law by either academic commentators or, at least until recently, by the European Court of Justice....

While it is relatively common for the EU to exercise jurisdiction over the foreign conduct of its own nationals, it is virtually unknown for the EU to exercise jurisdiction over the foreign conduct of non-EU nationals, except where the persons in question may be considered present—for example, resident, domiciled or established—within the territory of the EU. In short, with the exception of nationality-based jurisdiction, instances of extraterritoriality are exceptionally rare....

It is notable that while the EU has not condemned the extraterritoriality inherent in the most recent U.S. sanctions against Iran, the EU has resisted adopting non-nationality based extraterritorial measures of its own even in the area of common foreign and security policy. The EU's Iran sanctions regime applies only within the territory of the EU and to natural and legal persons who enjoy the nationality of an EU Member State....

The EU's aversion to extraterritoriality is not countered by a strong reliance on effects-based jurisdiction. Effects has reared its head quite recently, though as yet tentatively, in EU financial services regulation. The EU Derivatives Regulation will impose obligations on contracting parties' contracts concluded between two entities in third countries where the contract in question has a direct, substantial and foreseeable effect within the EU. Nonetheless, it is virtually unprecedented for the EU to found its jurisdiction *exclusively* on a finding of EU-felt effects.

In competition law more generally, outside of the area of merger control, the European Court of Justice has favored an 'implementation' test which enables the EU to exercise jurisdiction when an anti-competitive agreement, decision, or concerned practice has been implemented within the EU. In the famous Woodpulp I case it was clear that this was the case as the quarterly price announcements in question made reference to products sold within the EU. The European Court of Justice has not yet clarified what position it would take where there is no clear evidence of EU-based implementation, but merely evidence of (direct, substantial and foreseeable) EU-felt effects. The European Court of Justice's current preference for implementation over effects is consistent with the EU's widespread practice of territorial extension....

We have seen that while the EU only rarely engages in extraterritoriality and that, while EU reliance on effects is not widespread, the practice of territorial extension is pervasive.... territorial extension in EU law is imbued with a strong international orientation.... While the EU has sometimes criticized extraterritoriality and even territorial extension in U.S. law, the real focus of its concerns has been the absence of a comparable international orientation in the relevant U.S. laws.

An international orientation is inherent in the EU's very preference for territorial extension. This preference reflects the EU's often repeated conviction that prescriptive jurisdiction must be exercised in a manner that is consistent with public international law, and its belief that territorial extension complies with this standard. While the EU sometimes does exercise extraterritorial jurisdiction, it does so—with very few exceptions—only when a clear, internationally recognized, alternative to territory provides the jurisdictional basis. While the EU accepts that four alternative bases exist, in practice, extraterritoriality in EU law is almost invariably nationality-based. In keeping with this, the EU desists from frequent reliance on effects-based jurisdiction because it considers that such jurisdiction remains controversial as a matter of international law.

While the compatibility of territorial extension with the territoriality principle in international law has not been definitively proclaimed, it is clear that the European Court considers territorial extension to be consistent with customary international law.... An international orientation is also reflected in the EU practice of territorial extension in that it is oriented towards the enforcement of international standards and/or towards contributing to the attainment of objectives that have been internationally agreed....

In keeping with the EU's insistence that jurisdiction must be exercised in a manner that is consistent with international law, it has criticized the United States for adopting measures that do not appear to be predicated upon an internationally recognized jurisdictional base. We see this, for example, in the EU's condemnation of U.S. legislation that purported to regulate the foreign conduct of foreign firms in order to prevent these firms from trading with the Soviet Union in U.S. technology or goods. The EU argued that the legislation was unacceptable as a matter of international law because it infringed the territoriality principle, could not be justified under the nationality principle, because the protective principle had not been invoked and because it considered the effects doctrine inapplicable....

There are additional factors that seem to exacerbate U.S. extra-territorial jurisdiction in the EU's eyes. The EU has expressed particular concern about the extraterritorial application of U.S. legislation which seeks 'to force' persons or companies outside of the United States to follow U.S. laws or policies, 'to the extent that [this] serves only to protect US trade or political interests.' Here, the absence of an internationally agreed objective underpinning U.S. extraterritoriality would seem to be central to the EU's concerns.

NOTES

1. The 'effects' doctrine could be seen as an extension of the territorial principle where some part of an act might be said to occur on a State's territory, even if the only 'effect' is economic harm indirectly caused by that act. It can also be considered as an extension of the protective principle to situations other than national security, where issues considered of importance to a State are affected. The effects doctrine mixes both these grounds of jurisdiction and has proved highly controversial. Accordingly, it is considered separately in this chapter.

2. The core element of the 'effects' doctrine is that it is an extraterritorial application of national laws where an action by a person with no territorial or national connection with a State has an effect on that State. It is the exercise of jurisdiction over non-nationals in respect of acts that occur abroad. Consequently, it may cause great offence to the State of nationality of the defendant or the State where the actions did occur. This is compounded if the act is actually legal in the place where it was performed. The result has been blocking legislation by other States (mainly against US exercise of this jurisdiction). This type of legislation seeks to protect the activities of persons or companies behaving lawfully in the State where they are situated, even if the acts are unlawful under the 'effects' jurisdiction of another State.

3. The 'effects' doctrine is essentially an American one and originally applied in 'anti-trust' situations, i.e. where there are restrictive trade or anti-competitive agreements between corporations, even where there was no intent to cause any harm in the US.

4. The impact of US extraterritorial anti-trust laws on the trading interests of the European Union caused friction between these two powerful trading blocs. Tensions have again arisen in relation to the implementation of US sanctions regimes against States including Iran, Sudan and Cuba, which have extraterritorial effect, by fining European financial institutions (including Credit Suisse and BNP Paribas) for violating US law, even though the transactions in question were reportedly conducted through European subsidiaries and in compliance with European and national law and only 'transited' through the US banking system.

5. The European Union is not averse to utilising an 'effects' jurisdiction to protect its interests. However, the abstract by Scott suggests that it does so rarely and prefers to use 'territorial extension' rather than rely solely on the effects doctrine. A recent example of territorial extension (as opposed to the effects doctrine) is the Court of Justice of the European Union ruling that an EU regulation on the protection of animals in transport would apply outside EU borders to transport taking place in third States, if that transport began on EU territory: see *Zuchtvieh-Export Gmb* v *Stadt Kempten*, Case C-424/13, Judgment, 23 April 2015.

6. The US Supreme Court has adopted a more restrictive approach to the exercise of extraterritorial jurisdiction by US courts, at least in relation to the protection of human rights pursuant to the Alien Torts Statute (ATS). It held that the ATS is subject to the presumption against extraterritoriality and that nothing in the Statute or its history and context rebuts that presumption. This finding precluded the claims on behalf of Nigerian nationals (resident in the US) against three foreign corporations in respect of violations committed in Nigeria during protests concerning the economic activities (mining) of the corporations in the region, which the claimants alleged the corporations also facilitated. The Court highlighted the dangers of 'unwarranted judicial interference in the conduct of foreign policy' and 'the need for judicial caution in considering which claims could be brought under the ATS, in light of foreign policy concerns': *Kiobel et al* v *Royal Dutch Petroleum Company et al*, 133 S.Ct. 1659 (2013), p. 5.

F: Universality

The Princeton Principles on Universal Jurisdiction (2001)

These principles were drafted by the Princeton Project on Universal Jurisdiction, a joint venture of Princeton University's Program in Law and Public Affairs, the Woodrow Wilson School of Public and International Affairs, the International Commission of Jurists, the American Association for the ICJ, the Urban Morgan Institute for Human Rights and the Netherlands Institute of Human Rights. The Project convened a two-stage colloquium of leading scholars, jurists and legal experts from around the world. The principles are not legally binding, but are intended to provide guidance to States in the exercise of universal jurisdiction.

Principle 1—Fundamentals of Universal Jurisdiction

1. For purposes of these Principles, universal jurisdiction is criminal jurisdiction based solely on the nature of the crime, without regard to where the crime was committed, the nationality of the alleged or convicted perpetrator, the nationality of the victim, or any other connection to the state exercising such jurisdiction.

5. A state shall exercise universal jurisdiction in good faith and in accordance with its rights and obligations under international law.

Case Concerning the Arrest Warrant of 11 April 2000 (Democratic Republic of the Congo v Belgium)

ICJ Rep 2002 p.3, International Court of Justice

The facts are set out in Chapter 9.

JUDGES HIGGINS, KOOIJMANS, AND BUERGENTHAL (SEPARATE OPINION)

19. We therefore turn to the question whether States are entitled to exercise jurisdiction over persons having no connection with the forum State when the accused is not present in the State's territory....

45. That there is no established practice in which States exercise universal jurisdiction, properly so called, is undeniable. As we have seen, virtually all national legislation envisages links of some sort to the forum State; and no case law exists in which pure universal jurisdiction has formed the basis of jurisdiction. This does not necessarily indicate, however, that such an exercise would be unlawful. In the first place, national legislation reflects the circumstances in which a State provides in its own law the ability to exercise jurisdiction. But a State is not required to legislate up to the full scope of the jurisdiction allowed by international law. The war crimes legislation of Australia and the United Kingdom afford examples of countries making more confined choices for the exercise of jurisdiction. Further, many countries have no national legislation for the exercise of well recognized forms of extraterritorial jurisdiction, sometimes notwithstanding treaty obligations to enable themselves so to act. National legislation may be illuminating as to the issue of universal jurisdiction, but not conclusive as to its legality. Moreover, while none of the national case law to which we have referred happens to be based on the exercise of a universal jurisdiction properly so called, there is equally nothing in this case law which evidences an *opinio juris* on the illegality of such a jurisdiction. In short, national legislation and case law—that is, State practice—is neutral as to exercise of universal jurisdiction.

46. There are, moreover, certain indications that a universal criminal jurisdiction for certain international crimes is clearly not regarded as unlawful. The duty to prosecute under those treaties which contain the *aut dedere aut prosequi* provisions opens the door to a jurisdiction based on the heinous nature of the crime rather than on links of territoriality or nationality (whether as perpetrator or victim). The 1949 Geneva Conventions lend support to this possibility, and are widely regarded as today reflecting customary international law....

49. Belgium—and also many writers on this subject—find support for the exercise of a universal criminal jurisdiction *in absentia* in the *'Lotus'* case. Although the case was clearly decided on the basis of jurisdiction over damage to a vessel of the Turkish navy and to Turkish nationals, it is the famous dictum of the Permanent Court which has attracted particular attention. [here the Court cited the *Lotus* case, see the extract above] The Permanent Court acknowledged that consideration had to be given as to whether these principles would apply equally in the field of criminal jurisdiction, or whether closer connections might there be required. The Court noted the importance of the territorial character of criminal law but also the fact that all or nearly all systems of law extend their action to offences committed outside the territory of the State which adopts them, and they do so in ways which vary from State to State. After examining the issue the Court finally concluded that for an exercise of extraterritorial criminal jurisdiction (other than within the territory of another State) it was equally necessary to 'prove the existence of a principle of international law restricting the discretion of States as regards criminal legislation'.

50. The application of this celebrated dictum would have clear attendant dangers in some fields of international law....Nevertheless, it represents a continuing potential in the context of jurisdiction over international crimes.

51. That being said, the dictum represents the high water mark of laissez-faire in international relations, and an era that has been significantly overtaken by other tendencies. The underlying idea of universal jurisdiction properly so-called (as in the case of piracy. and possibly in the Geneva Conventions of 1949), as well as the *aut dedere aut prosequi* variation, is a common endeavour in the face of atrocities. The series of multilateral treaties with their special jurisdictional provisions reflect a determination by the international community that those engaged in war crimes, hijacking, hostage taking, torture should not go unpunished. Although crimes against humanity are not yet the object of a distinct convention, a comparable international indignation at such acts is not to be doubted. And those States and academic writers who claim the right to act unilaterally to assert a universal criminal jurisdiction over persons committing such acts, invoke the concept of acting as 'agents for the international community'. This vertical notion of the authority of action is significantly different from the horizontal system of international law envisaged in the '*Lotus*' case. At the same time, the international consensus that the perpetrators of international crimes should not go unpunished is being advanced by a flexible strategy, in which newly established international criminal tribunals, treaty obligations and national courts all have their part to play. We reject the suggestion that the battle against impunity is 'made over' to international treaties and tribunals, with national courts having no competence in such matters. Great care has been taken when formulating the relevant treaty provisions not to exclude other grounds of jurisdiction that may be exercised on a voluntary basis...

52. We may thus agree with the authors of *Oppenheim's International Law* (9th ed., p. 998), that:

'While no general rule of positive international law can as yet be asserted which gives to states the right to punish foreign nationals for crimes against humanity in the same way as they are, for instance, entitled to punish acts of piracy, there are clear indications pointing to the gradual evolution of a significant principle of international law to that effect.'

53. This brings us once more to the particular point that divides the Parties in this case: is it a precondition of the assertion of universal jurisdiction that the accused be within the territory?

54. Considerable confusion surrounds this topic, not helped by the fact that legislators, courts and writers alike frequently fail to specify the precise temporal moment at which any such requirement is said to be in play. Is the presence of the accused within the jurisdiction said to be required at the time the offence was committed? At the time the arrest warrant is issued? Or at the time of the trial itself? An examination of national legislation, cases and writings reveals a wide variety of temporal linkages to the assertion of jurisdiction. This incoherent practice cannot be said to evidence a precondition to any exercise of universal criminal jurisdiction. The fact that in the past the only clear example of an agreed exercise of universal jurisdiction was in respect of piracy, *outside of any territorial jurisdiction*, is not determinative. The only prohibitive rule (repeated by the Permanent Court in the '*Lotus*' case) is that criminal jurisdiction should not be exercised, without permission, within the territory of another State. The Belgian arrest warrant envisaged the arrest of Mr. Yerodia in Belgium, or the possibility of his arrest in third States at the discretion of the States concerned. This would in principle seem to violate no existing prohibiting rule of international law....

56. Some jurisdictions provide for trial *in absentia* others do not. If it is said that a person must be within the jurisdiction at the time of the trial itself, that may be a prudent guarantee for the right of fair trial but has little to do with bases of jurisdiction recognized under international law.

59. If, as we believe to be the case, a State may choose to exercise a universal criminal jurisdiction *in absentia*, it must also ensure that certain safeguards are in place. They are absolutely essential to prevent abuse and to ensure that the rejection of impunity does not jeopardize stable relations between States....

60. It is equally necessary that universal criminal jurisdiction be exercised only over those crimes regarded as the most heinous by the international community.

61. Piracy is the classical example. This jurisdiction was, of course, exercised on the high seas and not as an enforcement jurisdiction within the territory of a non-agreeing State. But this historical fact does not mean that universal jurisdiction only exists with regard to crimes committed on the high seas or in other places outside national territorial jurisdiction. Of decisive importance is that this jurisdiction was regarded as lawful because the international community regarded piracy as damaging to the interests of all. War crimes and crimes against humanity are no less harmful to the interests of all because they do not usually occur on the high seas. War crimes (already since 1949 perhaps a treaty-based provision for universal jurisdiction) may be added to the list.

United States v *Yunis*

681 F. Supp 896 (1988), United States District Court, District of Columbia

The facts are set out in Section 2D.

PARKER J: The Universal principle recognizes that certain offenses are so heinous and so widely condemned that 'any state if it captures the offender may prosecute and punish that person on behalf of the world community regardless of the nationality of the offender or victim or where the crime was committed.' M. Bassiouini, II International Criminal Law, Ch. 6 at 298 (ed. 1986). The crucial question for purposes of defendant's motion is how crimes are classified as 'heinous' and whether aircraft piracy and hostage taking fit into this category.

Those crimes that are condemned by the world community and subject to prosecution under the Universal principle are often a matter of international conventions or treaties. *See Demjanjuk* v *Petrovsky*, 776 F.2d 571, 582 (6th Cir. 1985) (Treaty against genocide signed by a significant number of states made that crime heinous; therefore, Israel had proper jurisdiction over Nazi war criminals under the Universal principle).

Both offenses [hijacking and hostage taking] are the subject of international agreements. A majority of states in the world community including Lebanon, have signed three treaties condemning aircraft piracy...These... demonstrate the international community's strong commitment to punish aircraft hijackers irrespective of where the hijacking occurred.

The global community has also joined together and adopted the International Convention for the Taking of Hostages an agreement which condemns and criminalizes the offense of hostage taking. Like the conventions denouncing aircraft piracy, this treaty requires signatory states to prosecute any alleged offenders 'present in its territory.'

In light of the global efforts to punish aircraft piracy and hostage taking, international legal scholars unanimously agree that these crimes fit within the category of heinous crimes for purposes of asserting universal jurisdiction....In The Restatement (Revised) of Foreign Relations Law of the United States, a source heavily relied upon by the defendant, aircraft hijacking is specifically identified as a universal crime over which all states should exercise jurisdiction.

Our Circuit has cited the Restatement with approval and determined that the Universal principle, standing alone, provides sufficient basis for asserting jurisdiction over an alleged offender. *See Tel-Oren* v *Libyan Arab Republic*, 726 F.2d at 781, n. 7. Therefore, under recognized principles of international law, and the law of this Circuit, there is clear authority to assert jurisdiction over Yunis for the offenses of aircraft piracy and hostage taking....

United States v *Yousef*

327 F.3d 56; 61 Fed. R. Evid. Serv. 251 (2003), United States Court of Appeals, Second Circuit

Yousef was charged relating to a conspiracy to bomb several United States commercial airliners in southeast Asia. He was also separately charged in regard to the 1993 bombing of the World Trade Center (WTC) in New York City.

Count Nineteen, the bombing of Philippine Airlines Flight 434, appears to present a less straight-forward jurisdictional issue because the airplane that was bombed was not a United States-flag aircraft, it was flying between two destinations outside of the United States, and there is no evidence that any United States citizens were aboard the flight or were targets of the bombing....

We hold that the District Court erred as a matter of law in relying upon the universality principle as a basis for jurisdiction over the acts charged in Count Nineteen and further hold that customary international law currently does not provide for the prosecution of 'terrorist' acts under the universality principle, in part due to the failure of States to achieve anything like consensus on the definition of terrorism....

The District Court erred in holding that the universality principle provides a basis for jurisdiction over Yousef for the acts charged in Count Nineteen because the universality principle permits jurisdiction over only a limited set of crimes that cannot be expanded judicially, as discussed in full below. The District Court's reliance on the qualified language in *Yunis* that aircraft-related crime '*may well be*' one of the few crimes supporting universal jurisdiction,...is facially at odds with this requirement because such language reflects that these crimes are not unequivocally condemned by all States...

The universality principle permits a State to prosecute an offender of any nationality for an offense committed outside of that State and without contacts to that State, but only for the few, near-unique offenses uniformly recognized by the 'civilized nations' as an offense against the 'Law of Nations.' The strictly limited set of crimes subject to universal jurisdiction cannot be expanded by drawing an analogy between some new crime such as placing a bomb on board an airplane and universal jurisdiction's traditional subjects. Nor, as discussed above in our consideration of the use of sources in international law, can universal jurisdiction be created by reliance on treatises or other scholarly works consisting of aspirational propositions that are not themselves good evidence of customary international law, much less primary sources of customary international law.

The historical restriction of universal jurisdiction to piracy, war crimes, and crimes against humanity demonstrates that universal jurisdiction arises under customary international law only where crimes (1) are universally condemned by the community of nations, and (2) by their nature occur either outside of a State or where there is no State capable of punishing, or competent to punish, the crime (as in a time of war).

Unlike those offenses supporting universal jurisdiction under customary international law—that is, piracy, war crimes, and crimes against humanity—that now have fairly precise definitions and that have achieved universal condemnation, 'terrorism' is a term as loosely deployed as it is powerfully charged…

We regrettably are no closer now than eighteen years ago to an international consensus on the definition of terrorism or even its proscription; the mere existence of the phrase 'state-sponsored terrorism' proves the absence of agreement on basic terms among a large number of States that terrorism violates public international law. Moreover, there continues to be strenuous disagreement among States about what actions do or do not constitute terrorism, nor have we shaken ourselves free of the cliché that 'one man's terrorist is another man's freedom fighter.' We thus conclude that the statements of Judges Edwards, Bork, and Robb remain true today, and that terrorism—unlike piracy, war crimes, and crimes against humanity—does not provide a basis for universal jurisdiction.

S. Ratner, 'Belgium's War Crimes Statute: A Postmortem'

97 *American Journal of International Law* 888 (2003)

The Belgian [War crimes] statute dates to 1993, when the government, in response to a proposal by military judges and various legal academics, amended the penal code to include certain violations of the 1949 Geneva Conventions and 1977 Additional Protocols, regardless of where such crimes were committed. This new law was meant to help implement Belgium's obligations under these treaties regarding grave breaches. In 1999, at the behest of various human rights nongovernmental organizations (NGOs), the law was amended to add genocide, as defined in the 1948 Genocide Convention, and crimes against humanity, as defined in the Statute of the International Criminal Court…

In 2001, the government tried two Rwandan nuns and two Rwandan men for participation in the genocide; all four were convicted and sentenced to prison terms ranging from twelve to twenty years. In June 2001, twenty-three survivors of the 1982 massacre of Palestinian refugees by Lebanese militiamen at the Sabra and Shatila camps filed a criminal complaint against Ariel Sharon, who was the Israeli defense minister in 1982 and since 2001 has been the prime minister of Israel, and Amos Yaron, who had been the Israeli general in charge of the Beirut sector in 1982.…

As the investigating judge was undertaking his inquiry and hearing arguments from the public prosecutor and lawyers for Sharon, thirty-three Israelis and Belgians initiated proceedings against Yasir Arafat under the law. The court also faced criminal complaints against Cuban President Fidel Castro, Iraqi President Saddam Hussein, former DRC foreign minister Abuldaye Yerodia, former Iranian President Hashemi Rafsanjani, and others.…In February 2002, the ICJ found the arrest warrant against Yerodia inconsistent with his immunity as the minister of foreign affairs at the time of the warrant, although the judges' vast disagreements over the scope of universal jurisdiction prevented any judgment on that issue. As for Sharon's case, a Belgian appeals court ruled in June 2002 that he and Yaron could not be tried because such cases were inadmissible when the defendant was not in Belgium.…On February 12, 2003, the Belgian Cour de Cassation overruled the court of appeal, finding that the presence of the accused was not necessary under Belgian law for the case to proceed. Nonetheless, it found the immunity of sitting heads of state and government to be a principle of customary international law. It thus dismissed the case against Sharon but allowed the investigation against Yaron to proceed. The tribunal left open the possibility that Sharon could be tried after he left office. Israel vehemently protested the action and withdrew its ambassador to Belgium.

Then, in March 2003, seven Iraqi families requested an investigation of former U.S. President George H. W. Bush, Vice President (and former Secretary of Defense) Dick Cheney, Secretary of State (and former chairman of the joint chiefs of staff) Colin Powell, and retired general Norman Schwarzkopf for allegedly committing war crimes during the 1991 Gulf war. In response, Secretary Powell warned the Belgian government that Belgium was risking its status as a diplomatic capital and the host state for the North Atlantic Treaty Organization (NATO) by allowing investigations of those who might visit Belgium. Almost immediately, Verhofstadt [the Belgian Prime Minister] proposed amendments to the statute to limit its scope.

In April 2003, parliament amended the law (effective May 7) such that only the [Belgian] federal prosecutor could initiate cases if the violation was overseas, the offender was not Belgian or located in Belgium, and the victim was not Belgian or had not lived in Belgium for three years. Furthermore, the prosecutor could refuse to proceed if the complaint was 'manifestly unfounded,' or

> in the interest of administration of justice and in respect of Belgium's international obligations, this matter should be brought either before international tribunals, or before a tribunal in the place where the acts were committed, or before the tribunals of a State in which the offender is a national or where he may be found, and as long as this tribunal is competent, independent, impartial and fair.

After passage of the amendments, Israel sent its ambassador back to Belgium. But the amendment did not prove enough for U.S. officials. On June 12, 2003, Secretary of Defense Donald Rumsfeld announced that the United States would refuse to fund a new headquarters building for NATO in Belgium and consider barring its officials from travelling to meetings there unless Belgium rescinded its law. Rumsfeld stated, 'Belgium appears not to respect the sovereignty of other countries.' Verhofstadt agreed within days to submit further amendments to limit the law's reach to cases with a direct link to Belgium....Under the law that entered into force in early August 2003, Belgian courts can hear cases regarding the three sets of crimes when committed outside Belgium only if the defendant or victim is a citizen or resident of Belgium. For defendants, nationality or residence is determined on the date proceedings commence; for victims, it is the date of the crime. If only the victim has the requisite ties to Belgium, the role for the public prosecutor is extensive: only he can move a case forward (without further recourse for plaintiff-prosecutors), and he is not required to pass the case on to an investigating judge if it fails the criteria that were inserted in the April amendments noted above....Pending cases are to be dismissed unless the plaintiff was a Belgian national or the accused had his principal residence in Belgium at the date of the law's entry into force and the case meets the special criteria noted above.

At the same time, the law does not close the Belgian courts to all victims of human rights abuses outside Belgium. Cases for the three specified crimes may proceed if (1) the requisite tie to Belgium is present; (2) the other states with a link to the crime do not have an independent system of justice; and (3) the accused is not one of the immunized governmental officials specified in the law, but is another sort of governmental official or former official, or has always been a private citizen. Moreover, the new law still does not require the accused to be present in Belgium for an investigation. Finally, Belgian courts are open for prosecution of other crimes if Belgium has an obligation under treaty or customary law to submit cases to its authorities for proceedings.

Criminal Complaint against Donald Rumsfeld et al, Decision not to investigate
3 ARP 156/06-2, 5 April 2007, The Prosecutor General at the Federal Supreme Court of Germany

This case concerned a criminal complaint lodged by a public interest group and four Iraqi citizens against Donald Rumsfeld, former US Secretary of Defense, and ten named and additional unnamed persons accused of participating in crimes under the Code of Crimes Against International Law (CCIL) of Germany. The complaint concerned incidents that had been committed by members of the US armed forces, civilian employees, and possibly also members of intelligence services, especially the CIA, in the prison complex at Abu Ghraib, in Iraq.

1. Sec. 153f(1)(1) of the Criminal Procedure Code establishes the authority not to prosecute...Prosecution can be refused in the case of acts committed abroad...if a perpetrator is neither present in the country nor can be expected to be present. This is the case here...

2. The balancing test to be undertaken under Sec. 153f(1)(1) of the Code of Criminal Procedure yields no area in which German investigative authorities can become active.

a) The purpose of Sec. 153f StPO is to take account of the consequences for the German justice system arising from the applicability of universal jurisdiction. The view that the most consistent possible worldwide prosecution of violations of international criminal law should be ensured militates in favor of carrying out investigations. On the other hand, it is necessary to counteract the danger that complainants will seek out certain states as sites of prosecution—like Germany in this case—that have no direct connection with the acts complained of, simply because their criminal law is favorable to international law (so-called forum shopping...), and in this way force investigative authorities into complicated, but ultimately unsuccessful investigations. Since, under Sec. 1 CCIL, every crime under the Code of Crimes Against International Law is (also) subject to German substantive criminal authority, Sec. 153f StPO establishes a corrective on the procedural level to combat overburdening through inexpedient investigations....In accordance with this, Sec. 153f (1)(1) StPO allows us to decline to prosecute purely foreign acts in certain cases, regardless of whether another justice system is prepared to prosecute... This is especially so if there is no chance that the accused could actually be brought to court in Germany... The exercise of discretion is to be oriented towards this purpose. The view of the complainant that the Federal Republic of Germany must act as a representative of the 'international community' and therefore at least take up investigations is thus mistaken.

b) No circumstances are present that could justify beginning an investigation despite the presence of the conditions of Sec. 153f (1)(1) StPO. They would only exist if significant success in resolving the situation could be achieved by investigations by German prosecution authorities, in order to prepare for future prosecution (either in Germany or abroad). But this is not the case.

To resolve possible accusations, investigation on the scene and in the United States of America would be unavoidable. Because the German investigative authorities have no executive powers abroad, this could only occur through legal assistance. But such requests are obviously futile—especially if we consider the legal and security situation in Iraq. A loss of evidence if German prosecution authorities do not act is not to be feared.... Dealing with possible violations of the prohibition on torture at Guantanamo Bay/Cuba or connected with the Iraq war through criminal law thus remains the task of the justice system of the United States of America, which has been assigned this task and is responsible for it....To justify German jurisdiction to prosecute crimes committed by foreigners against foreigners outside the country, however, a legitimizing domestic linkage is necessary...That is lacking here.

National Commissioner of the South African Police Service v Southern African Human Rights Litigation Centre et al
Judgment, Case CCT 02/14, 30 October 2014 South African Constitutional Court

This case concerned the exercise of universal jurisdiction under South African legislation to investigate acts of torture alleged to have been committed in Zimbabwe by Zimbabwean officials.

[47] ...It would appear that the predominant international position is that presence of a suspect is required at a more advanced stage of criminal proceedings, when a prosecution can be said to have started. This position accords with the section 4(3) requirement of presence for the purposes of prosecution. In regard to presence for purposes of investigation, customary international law is less clear. Scholars point out, however, that presence is generally not required for an investigation and there is no international law rule that imposes that requirement. This reasoning conforms to our Constitution which requires an accused 'to be present when being tried'. Accordingly, the exercise of universal jurisdiction, for purposes of the investigation of an international crime committed outside our territory, may occur in the absence of a suspect without offending our Constitution or international law.

[48] This approach is to be followed for several valid reasons. Requiring presence for an investigation would render nugatory the object of combating crimes against humanity. If a suspect were to enter and remain briefly in the territory of a state party, without a certain level of prior investigation, it would not be practicable to initiate charges and prosecution. An anticipatory investigation does not violate fair trial rights of the suspect or accused person. A determination of presence or anticipated presence requires an investigation in the first instance. Ascertaining a current or anticipated location of a suspect could not occur otherwise. Furthermore, any possible next step that could arise as a result of an investigation, such as a prosecution or an extradition request, requires an assessment of information which can only be attained through an investigation. By way of example, it is only once a docket has been completed and handed to a prosecutor that there can be an assessment as to whether or not to prosecute.

[49] The alleged acts of torture were perpetrated in Zimbabwe, by and against Zimbabwean nationals. None of the perpetrators is present in South Africa. However, the duty to combat torture travels beyond the borders of Zimbabwe. Torture, as a crime against humanity, is listed in schedule 1 to the ICC Act and forms part of the category of crimes in which all states have an interest under customary international law. South Africa may, through universal jurisdiction, assert prescriptive and, to some degree, adjudicative jurisdiction by investigating the allegations of torture as a precursor to taking a possible next step against the alleged perpetrators such as a prosecution or an extradition request.

Decision on the Report of the Commission on the Abuse of the Principle of Universal Jurisdiction
Doc. Assembly/AU/14 (XI), African Union Assembly

The Assembly:

5. Resolve as follows:

(i) The abuse of the Principle of Universal Jurisdiction is a development that could endanger International law, order and security;

(ii) The political nature and abuse of the principle of universal jurisdiction by judges from some non-African States against African leaders, particularly Rwanda, is a clear violation of the sovereignty and territorial integrity of these States;

(iii) The abuse and misuse of indictments against African leaders have a destabilizing effect that will negatively impact on the political, social and economic development of States and their ability to conduct international relations;

(iv) Those warrants shall not be executed in African Union Member States;

(v) There is need for establishment of an international regulatory body with competence to review and/or handle complaints or appeals arising out of abuse of the principle of universal jurisdiction by individual States.

NOTES

1. Universal jurisdiction is available irrespective of who committed the act and where it occurred. It depends solely on the nature of the offence committed. The exercise of this jurisdiction can be supported as being a means of upholding the international legal order by enabling any State to exercise jurisdiction in respect of offences that are destructive of that order. The definition suggested by the Princeton Principles attempts to capture the fundamental elements of the concept. See also the Resolution of the Institute of International Law on *Universal criminal jurisdiction with regard to the crime of genocide, crimes against humanity and war crimes* (26 August 2005).

2. The *Arrest Warrant Case* was the first occasion since the *Lotus Case* upon which the ICJ has been required to consider the issue of jurisdiction in international law. However, the majority determined that it was not necessary to consider issues of jurisdiction, and instead based its decision on the application of State immunity (see Chapter 9). As a result, the Separate Opinions are an interesting and important source of discussion concerning the principle of universal jurisdiction.

3. The question of whether a State can exercise universal jurisdiction is regulated by both treaty-based and customary international law. Several offences give rise to universal jurisdiction derived from treaty provisions, which allow States parties to exercise extraterritorial jurisdiction for those offences. However, while treaty-based universal jurisdiction may satisfy the definitions extracted above, such jurisdiction is not truly universal, as the regime established by the treaty extends to States parties only. For other offences, universal jurisdiction is found in customary international law and, consequently, applies to all States. Universal jurisdiction under customary international law has been referred to as 'true' universal jurisdiction.

4. There is no accepted list as to which crimes are uniformly acknowledged as giving rise to universal jurisdiction under customary international law. For example, in the extract from the *Arrest Warrant Case* above, President Guillaume, in his Separate Opinion, challenged the view that universal jurisdiction existed for a wide range of international crimes. He conceded only one category of crime, that of piracy, as he considered that other examples of universal jurisdiction were actually treaty-based crimes (para. 12). There now appears to be growing support amongst States and academic commentary for the principle that a core group of crimes allow for universal jurisdiction as a matter of customary international law. In addition to piracy, crimes potentially allowing for the exercise of universal jurisdiction include genocide, crimes against humanity, certain war crimes, slavery, torture, and, to a lesser extent, drug-trafficking. The decision in *Yousef*, extracted above, suggests that customary international law as yet does not recognise universal jurisdiction in respect of acts of terrorism.

5. The experience of Belgium in relation to its universal jurisdiction legislation, detailed in the extract by Ratner, demonstrates the political nature of the exercise of universal jurisdiction and the possible consequences for a State in not restricting its judicial authorities to investigate and try such offences. Spain also embarked on several investigations of foreign officials and figures

for international crimes, based on an assertion of universal jurisdiction provided for in Article 23 of the Organic Law 6/1985 of 1 July 1985. Prosecutions have been initiated in cases in respect of high-ranking officials and other individuals from Israel, China, Argentina, Guatemala, Peru, Rwanda and the United States. Spain too has encountered significant pressure to amend its laws and, in 2009, Spain amended its jurisdiction so that, before the Spanish authorities can exercise universal jurisdiction, one of the victims must be Spanish or the offender must be present in Spain.

6. The extracts from the *Arrest Warrant Case* raise the possibilities of limits upon the power of States to exercise universal jurisdiction. Such limits may be required to avoid the political repercussions and accusations of the unlawful exercise of jurisdiction seen in the Belgium context. Limits may also be introduced to prevent the State concerned becoming the focus of such claims by victims and other interest groups, as seen in the balancing exercise undertaken by German prosecutors. Such limits may also address the possible procedural implications for the accused. One such limit is the need for the presence of the accused in the State asserting jurisdiction, the so-called 'presence requirement'. This is linked to, but not the same as, a prohibition against trials *in absentia* (a trial in the absence of the accused). The South African Constitutional Court concluded in the case above that while presence *may* be a requirement for the exercise of universal jurisdiction to prosecute, it was not required to open an investigation.

7. Another restriction on the exercise of universal jurisdiction is the subsidiarity principle, which effectively operates as a rule regulating competing jurisdictions. This principle would bar the exercise of universal jurisdiction by a third State in circumstances where a State with a closer connection to the offence is willing to or is exercising—genuinely—its jurisdiction. This State need not be the territorial State, but may include the State of nationality and claims based on other principles of jurisdiction. This principle would require that universal jurisdiction would be used only as a last resort and that other bases of jurisdiction should be used wherever possible. There is perhaps as yet insufficient evidence to consider this principle as reflecting a requirement for the exercise of universal jurisdiction under customary international law. It has, however, been included in the legislation and jurisprudence of some States, for example, Germany, although it is a matter of discretion for the federal prosecutor (see discussion of section 153 of the Code of Criminal Procedure in the extract of *Criminal Complaint against Donald Rumsfeld et al*). In Spain, the subsidiarity principle was not reflected in statute, but has been relied upon by courts and prosecutors since 1998. While the Spanish Constitutional Court rejected the subsidiarity principle as a legal requirement in 2005 (*Guatemala Genocide Case* judgment, No. STC 237/2005), subsequent practice suggests that courts and prosecutors still apply the principle as a matter of practice. The amended Belgian legislation also incorporates a requirement for the Belgian authorities to defer to a State with a closer jurisdictional nexus. The principle also features in the 2005 resolution of the Institute of International Law on universal jurisdiction and in the African Union (AU) Model Law (see note 9).

8. One form of limitation on the exercise of universal jurisdiction is the requirement that prosecution relying on universal jurisdiction must be initiated or authorised by the Attorney-General, Federal Prosecutor or other senior official. For example, in the United Kingdom, no prosecution may be brought under section 134 of the Criminal Justice Act 1988 or the Geneva Conventions Act 1957 without the consent of the Attorney-General. Similarly, States may impose restrictions on the ability of private actors (victims, non-governmental organisations and others) to initiate criminal proceedings or may allow for the State authorities to intervene in such prosecutions.

9. As has been seen in the extracts in this section and the notes above, the assertion of universal jurisdiction is often controversial. The issue of arrest warrants in respect of African nationals by mainly European States created considerable tension between the AU and the European Union and led to the AU adopting a series of resolutions, for one of which see the extract of the Decision of the AU Assembly above. The AU and the EU agreed to commission a technical expert group to compile a report on the principle of universal jurisdiction and the understanding of the principle in both Africa and Europe. The resultant report (AU-EU Expert Report on the Principle of Universal Jurisdiction, 16 April 2009) reaffirmed universal jurisdiction as a principle of international law, but urged caution in its implementation. The report noted that while several EU member States had initiated proceedings on the basis of universal jurisdiction, no African State was known to have done so. The AU adopted its own Model National Law on Universal Jurisdiction over International Crimes in 2012, with international crimes also including trafficking of narcotics, piracy and terrorism. The Model Law incorporates the requirement of presence

and reflects the principle of subsidiarity (see Article 4). The AU also supported the establishment of an internationalised tribunal, the Extraordinary African Chambers, under Senegalese law, to try former Chadian President Hissenè Habré on the basis of universal jurisdiction. While the majority of States supported the model of universal jurisdiction, underlining its importance to avoid impunity for serious crimes, several States continue to argue for regulation of this concept to limit abuse and potential 'forum shopping'.

SECTION 3: STATE JURISDICTION AND PERSONS APPREHENDED IN VIOLATION OF INTERNATIONAL LAW

Unless a State is prepared to try a person in their absence from that territory, the exercise of enforcement jurisdiction over individuals depends on their physical presence in the territory of the acting State. There have been several cases where an individual has been removed forcibly from the territory of one State to be tried in another, either without the former State's consent or in violation of the procedures laid down in an extradition treaty between the former State and the State seeking to exercise jurisdiction. In such cases, the question arises whether the courts of the State seeking to exercise jurisdiction will object to the violation of the territorial sovereignty of the other State or will take cognisance of the fact that a treaty of extradition has not been complied with.

State v Ebrahim

31 *International Legal Materials* 888 (1991), Supreme Court of South Africa (Appellate Division)

The appellant, a South African citizen, was charged with treason. He had been abducted from Swaziland and transported to South Africa, most likely by agents of the South African government. This was a violation of international law, being a violation of the territorial sovereignty of Swaziland, although Swaziland had not made an official protest. The appellant appealed against his conviction on the ground that the South African courts lacked jurisdiction because his appearance before them was brought about by a violation of international law. The appeal was allowed and the conviction set aside.

> The first question to be decided in the present case is not what the relevant rules of international law are, but what those of our own law are. To answer this question it is necessary to examine our common law on this subject....
>
> Several fundamental legal principles are contained in these rules, namely the protection and promotion of human rights, good inter-state relations and a healthy administration of justice. The individual must be protected against illegal detention and abduction, the bounds of jurisdiction must not be exceeded, sovereignty must be respected, the legal process must be fair to those affected and abuse of law must be avoided in order to protect and promote the integrity of the administration of justice. This applies equally to the state. When the state is a party to a dispute, as for example in criminal cases, it must come to court with 'clean hands'. When the state itself is involved in an abduction across international borders, as in the present case, its hands are not clean.
>
> Principles of this kind testify to a healthy legal system of high standard. Signs of this development appear increasingly in the municipal law of other countries....
>
> It follows that, according to our common law, the trial court had no jurisdiction to hear the case against the appellant. Consequently his conviction and sentence cannot stand.

United States v Alvarez-Machain

31 *International Legal Materials* 902 (1992), United States Supreme Court

The appellant was a Mexican citizen. He was abducted from Mexico and transported to the US where he was charged with the kidnapping and murder of a US Drug Enforcement

Agency agent. The case was dismissed in the lower courts on the ground that the abduction violated the US–Mexican extradition treaty. The Supreme Court held that the abduction did not violate the treaty and, further, that although the abduction may have been a violation of international law (the territorial integrity of Mexico), a US court could still exercise jurisdiction. In the Court's view, alleged violations of international law by the US were for the Executive alone. Dr Alvarez-Machain was eventually acquitted by a US Court and returned to Mexico.

[T]he language of the [US–Mexican extradition] Treaty, in the context of its history, does not support the proposition that the Treaty prohibits abductions outside of its terms. The remaining question, therefore, is whether the Treaty should be interpreted so as to include an implied term prohibiting prosecution where the defendant's presence is obtained by means other than those established by the Treaty....

Respondent contends that the Treaty must be interpreted against the backdrop of customary international law, and that international abductions are 'so clearly prohibited in international law' that there was no reason to include such a clause in the Treaty itself....The international censure of international abductions is further evidence, according to respondent, by the United Nations Charter and the Charter of the Organization of American States....

More fundamentally, the difficulty with the support respondent garners from international law is that none of it relates to the practice of nations in relation to extradition treaties. In *Rauscher*, we implied a term in the Webster-Ashburton Treaty because of the practice of nations with regard to extradition treaties. In the instant case, respondent would imply terms in the extradition treaty from the practice of nations with regard to international law more generally. Respondent would have us find that the Treaty acts as a prohibition against a violation of the general principle of international law that one government may not 'exercise its police power in the territory of another state'....There are many actions which could be taken by a nation that would violate this principle, including waging war, but it cannot seriously be contended an invasion of the United States by Mexico would violate the terms of the extradition treaty between the two nations.

In sum, to infer from this Treaty and its terms that it prohibits all means of gaining the presence of an individual outside of its terms goes beyond established precedent and practice....The general principles cited by respondent simply fail to persuade us that we should imply in the United States-Mexico Extradition Treaty a term prohibiting international abductions.

Respondent and his *amici* may be correct that respondent's abduction was 'shocking',...and that it may be a violation of general international law principles. Mexico has protested the abduction of respondent through diplomatic notes...and the decision of whether respondent should be returned to Mexico, as a matter outside of the Treaty, is a matter for the Executive Branch. We conclude, however, that respondent's abduction was not in violation of the Extradition Treaty between the United States and Mexico...The fact of respondent's forcible abduction does not therefore prohibit his trial in a court in the United States for violations of the criminal laws of the United States.

R v Horseferry Road Magistrates' Court, ex parte Bennett

[1993] 3 All ER 138, United Kingdom House of Lords

Bennett, a New Zealand citizen, was wanted in the UK in respect of allegations of fraud. Bennett was located in South Africa and the UK police asked the South African police to send him forcibly to the UK. This was done. There was no extradition treaty between the UK and South Africa, although special extradition arrangements could have been made under the UK Extradition Act 1989. The House of Lords held that, if Bennett could prove his allegations, there would have been an abuse of the process because the manner by which he came before UK courts would have been a violation of international law and the rule of law.

LORD GRIFFITHS: The respondents have relied upon the United States authorities in which the Supreme Court has consistently refused to regard forcible abduction from a foreign country as a violation of the right by due process of law guaranteed by the Fourteenth Amendment to the Constitution: see in particular the majority opinion in *US* v *Alvarez-Machain* (1992) 112 S Ct 2188 reasserting the *Ker-Frisbie* rule (see *Ker* v *Illinois* (1886) 119 US 436 and *Frisbie* v *Collins* (1952) 342 US 519). I do not, however, find these decisions particularly helpful because they deal with the issue of whether or not an accused acquires a constitutional defence to the *jurisdiction* of the United States courts and not to the question whether, assuming the court has jurisdiction, it has a discretion to refuse to try the accused....

Your Lordships are now invited to extend the concept of abuse of process a stage further. In the present case there is no suggestion that the appellant cannot have a fair trial, nor could it be suggested that it would have been unfair to try him if he had been returned to this country through extradition procedures. If the court is to have the power to interfere with the prosecution in the present circumstances it must be because the judiciary accept a responsibility for the maintenance of the rule of law that embraces a willingness to oversee executive action and to refuse to countenance behaviour that threatens either basic human rights or the rule of law.

My Lords, I have no doubt that the judiciary should accept this responsibility in the field of criminal law. The great growth of administrative law during the latter half of this century has occurred because of the recognition by the judiciary and Parliament alike that it is the function of the High Court to ensure that executive action is exercised responsibly and as Parliament intended. So also should it be in the field of criminal law and if it comes to the attention of the court that there has been a serious abuse of power it should, in my view, express its disapproval by refusing to act upon it.

Let us consider the position in the context of extradition. Extradition procedures are designed not only to ensure that criminals are returned from one country to another but also to protect the rights of those who are accused of crimes by the requesting country. Thus sufficient evidence has to be produced to show a prima facie case against the accused and the rule of speciality protects the accused from being tried for any crime other than that for which he was extradited. If a practice developed in which the police or prosecuting authorities of this country ignored extradition procedures and secured the return of an accused by a mere request to police colleagues in another country they would be flouting the extradition procedures and depriving the accused of the safeguards built into the extradition process for his benefit. It is to my mind unthinkable that in such circumstances the court should declare itself to be powerless and stand idly by; I echo the words of Lord Devlin in *Connelly* v *DPP* [1964] 2 All ER 401 at 442, [1964] AC 1254 at 1354:

> The courts cannot contemplate for a moment the transference to the executive of the responsibility for seeing that the process of law is not abused.

The courts, of course, have no power to apply direct discipline to the police or the prosecuting authorities, but they can refuse to allow them to take advantage of abuse of power by regarding their behaviour as an abuse of process and thus preventing a prosecution.

In my view your Lordships should now declare that where process of law is available to return an accused to this country through extradition procedures our courts will refuse to try him if he has been forcibly brought within our jurisdiction in disregard of those procedures by a process to which our own police, prosecuting or other executive authorities have been a knowing party.

LORD BRIDGE: Whatever differences there may be between the legal systems of South Africa, the United States, New Zealand and this country, many of the basic principles to which they seek to give effect stem from common roots. There is, I think, no principle more basic to any proper system of law than the maintenance of the rule of law itself. When it is shown that the law enforcement agency responsible for bringing a prosecution has only been enabled to do so by participating in violations of international law and of the laws of another state in order to secure the presence of the accused within the territorial jurisdiction of the court, I think that respect for the rule of law demands that the court take cognisance of that circumstance. To hold that the court may turn a blind eye to executive lawlessness beyond the frontiers of its own jurisdiction is, to my mind, an insular and unacceptable view. Having then taken cognisance of the lawlessness it would again appear to me to be a wholly inadequate response for the court to hold that the only remedy lies in civil proceedings at the suit of the defendant or in disciplinary or criminal proceedings against the individual officers of the law enforcement agency who were concerned in the illegal action taken. Since the prosecution could never have been brought if the defendant had not been illegally abducted, the whole proceeding is tainted. If a resident in another country is properly extradited here, the time when the prosecution commences is the time when the authorities here set the extradition process in motion. By parity of reasoning, if the authorities, instead of proceeding by way of extradition, have resorted to abduction, that is the effective commencement of the prosecution process and is the illegal foundation on which it rests. It is apt, in my view, to describe these circumstances, in the language used by Woodhouse J in *Moevao* v *Dept of Labour* [1980] 1 NZLR 464 at 476, as an 'abuse of the criminal jurisdiction in general' or indeed, in the language of Mansfield J in *US* v *Toscanino* (1974) 500 F 2d 267 at 276, as a 'degradation' of the court's criminal process. To hold that in these circumstances the court may decline to exercise its jurisdiction on the ground that its process has been abused may be an extension of the doctrine of abuse of process but is, in my view, a wholly proper and necessary one.

Prosecutor v *Dragan Nikolić,* Decision on Interlocutory Appeal concerning Legality of Arrest

Case No. IT-94-2-AR73, ICTY Appeals Chamber, 5 June 2003

Nikolić was arrested and detained in 2000 by a United Nations peacekeeping force operating in Bosnia and Herzegovina, and was then surrendered to the International Criminal Tribunal for the former Yugoslavia. He claimed to have been abducted in Serbia by unknown individuals and handed to members of the peacekeeping force.

18. ... Thus, the first issue to be addressed is in what circumstances, if any, the International Tribunal should decline to exercise its jurisdiction because an accused brought conduct violating State sovereignty or human rights.

20. The impact of a breach of a State's sovereignty on the exercise of jurisdiction is a novel issue for this Tribunal. There is no case law directly on the point, and the Statute and the Rules provide little guidance. Article 29 of the Statute, inter alia, places upon all States the duty to cooperate with the international Tribunal in the investigation and prosecution of persons accuse of committing serious violations of international humanitarian law. It also requires States to comply without undue delay with requests for assistance or orders issued by Trial Chambers, including the arrest or detention of persons. The Statute, however, does not provide a remedy for breaches of these obligations. In the absence of clarity in the Statute, Rules, and jurisprudence of the international Tribunal, the Appeals Chamber will seek guidance from national case law, where the issue at hand has often arisen, in order to determine State practice on the matter....

24. Although it is difficult to identify a clear pattern in this case law, and caution is needed when generalising, two principles seem to have support in State practice as evidenced by the practice of their courts. First, in cases of crimes such as genocide, crimes against humanity and war crimes which are universally recognised and condemned as such ('Universally Condemned Offences'), courts seem to find in the special character of these offences and, arguably, in their seriousness, a good reason for not setting aside jurisdiction. Second, absent a complaint by the State whose sovereignty has been breached or in the event of a diplomatic resolution of the breach, it is easier for courts to assert their jurisdiction. The initial *iniuria* has in a way been cured and the risk of having to return the accused to the country of origin is no longer present. Drawing on these indications from national practice, the Appeals Chamber adds the following observations...

25. Universally Condemned Offences are a matter of concern to the international community as a whole. There is a legitimate expectation that those accused of these crimes will be brought to justice swiftly. Accountability for these crimes is a necessary condition for the achievement of international justice, which plays a critical role in the reconciliation and rebuilding bases on the rule of law of countries and societies torn apart by international and internecine conflicts.

26. This legitimate expectation needs to be weighed against the principle of State sovereignty and the fundamental human rights of the accused... In the opinion of the Appeals Chamber, the damage caused to international justice by not apprehending fugitives accused of serious violations of international humanitarian law is comparatively higher than the injury, if any, caused to the sovereignty of a State by a limited intrusion in its territory, particularly when the intrusion occurs in default of the State's cooperation. Therefore, the Appeals Chamber does not consider that in the cases of universally condemned offences, jurisdiction should be set aside on the ground that there was a violation of the sovereignty of a State, when the violation is brought about by the apprehension of fugitives from international justice, whatever the consequences for the international responsibility of the State or organisation involved. This is all the more so in cases such as this one, in which the State whose sovereignty has allegedly been breached has not lodged any complaint and thus has acquiesced in the International Tribunal's exercise of jurisdiction. *A fortiori* and leaving aside for the moment human rights considerations, the exercise of jurisdiction should not be declined in cases of abductions carried out by private individuals whose actions, unless instigated, acknowledged or condoned by a State, or an international organisation, or other entity, do not necessarily in themselves violate State sovereignty.

30. ... Although the assessment of the seriousness of the human rights violations depends on the circumstances of each case and cannot be made *in abstracto*, certain human rights violations are of such a serious nature that they require that the exercise of jurisdiction be declined. It would be inappropriate for a court of law to try the victims of the abuses. Apart from such exceptional cases, however, the remedy of setting aside jurisdiction will,

in the Appeals Chamber's view, usually be disproportionate. The correct balance must therefore be maintained between the fundamental rights of the accused and the essential interests of the international community in the prosecution of persons charged with serious violations of international humanitarian law.

31. In the present case, the Trial Chamber examined the facts agreed by the parties. It established that the treatment of the Appellant was not of such an egregious nature as to impede the exercise of jurisdiction...

NOTES
1. The South African and UK cases illustrate that there are circumstances in which national courts will refuse to exercise a jurisdiction that they undoubtedly possess because of the circumstances in which an exercise of that jurisdiction has become possible. A violation of international law in securing the defendant prevents the exercise of jurisdiction. In *Ebrahim*, the Court refused to exercise jurisdiction even though the defendant was a national of the State and irrespective of whether the offended State had actually protested. Note, however, that the UK decision in *R v Staines Magistrates' Court, ex parte Westfallen* [1998] 4 All ER 210, appears to limit the *Bennett* principle. According to the Divisional Court, the national court should decline jurisdiction where the defendant was procured in violation of international law *only* if the UK had themselves acted illegally or procured or connived in the illegality of others. So, an unlawful deportation from another country would not prevent an exercise of jurisdiction by a UK court if the UK authorities simply stood by and let it occur rather than taking part in it. This is a fine line indeed, and does not support the principle behind declining jurisdiction as put forward in *Ebrahim*. In contrast, the decision in *Alvarez-Machain* seems arrogant and unprincipled and says more about the US attitude to the sovereign equality of States and the rule of international law than a thousand pronouncements by US ambassadors in the General Assembly.
2. This issue was also raised in *Attorney-General of the Government of Israel v Eichmann* (see Section 2C) where Eichmann was abducted from Argentina by the Israeli Secret Service. Argentina protested, Israel expressed its regret, but the national court exercised jurisdiction. This case may perhaps be distinguished from the three national court cases extracted above because the crimes with which Eichmann was charged were crimes giving rise to universal jurisdiction, as opposed to crimes under the national laws of the abducting States.
3. The extract from *Nikolić* suggests that international criminal courts may adopt a more nuanced view. In serious crimes (i.e. those for which universal jurisdiction exists) abduction should not automatically defeat the exercise of jurisdiction unless the affected State complains. There does need to be consideration of the human rights of the accused, but this will only defeat jurisdiction where the violation is serious (e.g. torture).
4. Following the attacks against the New York World Trade Center in September 2001, evidence has emerged of a practice known as 'extraordinary rendition', whereby individuals are captured in one State and then transferred to a third State to undergo interrogation. The process is considered extraordinary as it is conducted outside the accepted mechanisms whereby a State can transfer a prisoner to another State (i.e. deportation, extradition, transit and transfer to another country to serve sentence). The process is also extraordinary in that it is outside the normal judicial procedures (which are designed to protect the individual from torture and other forms of mistreatment) and may be inconsistent with relevant national laws. However, as the purpose of such extraordinary renditions is not to render the individual to another State for trial (as opposed to interrogation), it is not considered further in this chapter.

9

Immunities from National Jurisdiction

INTRODUCTORY NOTE

In Chapter 5 on personality and recognition, it was suggested that an entity with international legal personality enjoys certain privileges or rights, both in international and national law. One of the most important of these is the immunity from legal process enjoyed by States and international organisations and their representatives in the courts of other States. This immunity can be split conveniently into State (or sovereign) immunity, and diplomatic and consular immunities. The first concerns foreign States *per se* (including the Head of State), while the second concerns the personal immunities enjoyed by representatives of those States. These immunities may be either because the particular individual or entity enjoys a certain status under their national law or international law (sometimes called immunity *ratione personae*) and sometimes because of the substance of the matter in which the individual has become involved (sometimes called immunity *ratione materiae*). Generally speaking, immunity *ratione personae*—that is, simply because the entity or individual has a certain status (e.g. a Head of State or Ambassador) irrespective of the nature of the matter in which they have become involved—is more limited in scope and endures only while the status endures. Immunity *ratione materiae*, on the other hand, attaches because of the inherently sovereign nature of the incident in which the entity or individual has become embroiled and in consequence finds more favour with national courts and commentators. However, these are descriptive labels, rather than analytical categories, and each claim of immunity must be judged within the factual matrix in which it occurs, including the relevant international rules and the particular approach of the relevant national court. By way of contrast, the immunities enjoyed by international organisations and their staff are purely functional in that they exist only to ensure that the organisation may operate effectively within States. Such immunities are granted by treaty and there are no difficult issues about 'dignity', 'international comity' and 'equality of nations' as there are with States.

In this chapter, both the sections on State and diplomatic immunity deal with the position in international law generally and then the position in national law in particular. As far as most national legal systems are concerned, it should also be noted that a State (and hence its representatives) will not be able to benefit from immunity unless that State has been recognised as a 'Sovereign State' in accordance with the criteria discussed in Chapter 5.

The principle of internationally protected immunity for States and their representatives is a principle of international law. This has the immediate consequence that should a State fail to apply the principle of immunity in an appropriate case, it will be responsible under international law. For example, in the *Arrest Warrant of 11 April 2000 Case (Democratic Republic of Congo v Belgium)* (see Section 3), Belgium's international responsibility was engaged for issuing an arrest warrant against the Congolese Minister of Foreign Affairs in violation of the latter's immunity. However, the actual circumstances in which immunity is to be granted are usually settled by the national law of each State in an attempt to comply with that State's international obligations. For this reason, the situation in one State—the UK—is dealt with at some length.

SECTION 1: GENERAL PRINCIPLES OF STATE IMMUNITY IN INTERNATIONAL LAW

In the past there has been considerable debate over whether a State's immunity before the courts of another State was 'absolute' or 'restrictive'. If absolute, a State was immune for all purposes and in all proceedings. If restrictive, a State was immune only in respect of its 'sovereign' acts, otherwise known as acts *juri imperii*, and not immune in respect of its private law or commercial acts, otherwise known as acts *jure gestionis*. It is now largely settled in the courts of many civil and common law States that States may grant only restrictive immunity to other States without incurring responsibility under international law. Necessarily, however, this means that national courts must be able to draw the distinction between acts *juri imperii* and *jure gestionis*. The extracts below consider these matters as well as the distinction between the principles of State immunity and other similar doctrines such as 'act of State' and non-justiciability. Note that some developing States and those States transitioning from socialist to market economies may continue to apply the absolute approach to immunity.

The Schooner Exchange v McFaddon
7 Cranch 116 (1812), US Supreme Court

MARSHALL CJ: The jurisdiction of the nation within its own territory is necessarily exclusive and absolute. It is susceptible of no limitation not imposed by itself. Any restriction upon it, deriving validity from an external source, would imply a diminution of its sovereignty to the extent of the restriction, and an investment of that sovereignty to the same extent in that power which could impose such restriction.

All exceptions, therefore, to the full and complete power of a nation within its own territories, must be traced up to the consent of the nation itself. They can flow from no other legitimate source.

This consent may be either express or implied....

This full and absolute territorial jurisdiction being alike the attribute of every sovereign, and being incapable of conferring extraterritorial power, would not seem to contemplate foreign sovereigns nor their sovereign rights as its objects. One sovereign being in no respect amenable to another; and being bound by obligations of the highest character not to degrade the dignity of his nation, by placing himself or its sovereign rights within the jurisdiction of another, can be supposed to enter a foreign territory only under an express license, or in the confidence that the immunities belonging to his independent sovereign station, though not expressly stipulated, are reserved by implication, and will be extended to him.

This perfect equality and absolute independence of sovereigns, and this common interest impelling them to mutual intercourse, and an interchange of good offices with each other, have given rise to a class of cases in which every sovereign is understood to waive the exercise of a part of that complete exclusive territorial jurisdiction, which has been stated to be the attribute of every nation.

1st. One of these is admitted to be the exemption of the person of the sovereign from arrest or detention within a foreign territory.

If he enters that territory with the knowledge and license of its sovereign, that license, although containing no stipulation exempting his person from arrest, is universally understood to imply such stipulation.

2d. A second case, standing on the same principles with the first, is the immunity which all civilized nations allow to foreign ministers.

3d. A third case in which a sovereign is understood to cede a portion of his territorial jurisdiction is, where he allows the troops of a foreign prince to pass through his dominions....

The preceding reasoning has maintained the propositions that all exemptions from territorial jurisdiction must be derived from the consent of the sovereign of the territory; that this consent may be implied or expressed; and that when implied, its extent must be regulated by the nature of the case, and the views under which the parties requiring and conceding it must be supposed to act.

United Nations Convention on Jurisdictional Immunities of States and their Property

General Assembly Resolution 53/86, 16 December 2004

The Convention is based on the work of the International Law Commission, which was charged with the task of codifying the international legal principles on State immunity. It was adopted by the General Assembly and opened for signature on 2 December 2004. As at March 2016, the Convention has 21 parties, 14 signatories and requires 30 parties for entry into force.

Article 1 Scope of the present articles

The present articles apply to the immunity of a State and its property from the jurisdiction of the courts of another State.

Article 2 Use of terms

1. For the purposes of the present articles:
    (a) 'court' means any organ of a State, however named, entitled to exercise judicial functions;
    (b) 'State' means:
        (i) the State and its various organs of government;
        (ii) constituent units of a federal State or political subdivisions of the State, which are entitled to perform acts in the exercise of sovereign authority, and are acting in that capacity;
        (iii) agencies or instrumentalities of the State or other entities, to the extent that they are entitled to perform and are actually performing acts in the exercise of sovereign authority of the State;
        (iv) representatives of the State acting in that capacity;
    (c) 'commercial transaction' means:
        (i) any commercial contract or transaction for the sale of goods or supply of services;
        (ii) any contract for a loan or other transaction of a financial nature, including any obligation of guarantee or of indemnity in respect of any such loan or transaction;
        (iii) any other contract or transaction of a commercial, industrial, trading or professional nature, but not including a contract of employment of persons.

2. In determining whether a contract or transaction is a 'commercial transaction' under paragraph 1(c), reference should be made primarily to the nature of the contract or transaction, but its purpose should also be taken into account if the parties to the contract or transaction have so agreed, or if, in the practice of the State of the forum, that purpose is relevant to determining the non-commercial character of the contract or transaction.

3. The provisions of paragraphs 1 and 2 regarding the use of terms in the present Convention are without prejudice to the use of those terms or to the meanings which may be given to them in other international instruments or in the internal law of any State.

Article 3 Privileges and immunities not affected by the present Convention

1. The present Convention is without prejudice to the privileges and immunities enjoyed by a State under international law in relation to the exercise of the functions of:
    (a) its diplomatic missions, consular posts, special missions, missions to international organizations or delegations to organs of international organizations or to international conferences; and
    (b) persons connected with them.

2. The present Convention is without prejudice to privileges and immunities accorded under international law to heads of State *ratione personae*.

3. The present Convention is without prejudice to the immunities enjoyed by a State under international law with respect to aircraft or space objects owned or operated by a State.

Article 5 State immunity

A state enjoys immunity, in respect of itself and its property, from the jurisdiction of the courts of another State subject to the provisions of the present Convention.

Article 10 Commercial transactions

1. If a State engages in a commercial transaction with a foreign natural or juridical person and, by virtue of the applicable rules of private international law, differences relating to the commercial transaction fall within the

jurisdiction of a court of another State, the State cannot invoke immunity from that jurisdiction in a proceeding arising out of that commercial transaction.

2. Paragraph 1 does not apply:
   (a) in the case of a commercial transaction between States; or
   (b) if the parties to the commercial transaction have expressly agreed otherwise.

3. Where a State enterprise or other entity established by a State which has an independent legal personality and is capable of:
   (a) suing or being sued; and
   (b) acquiring, owning or possessing and disposing of property, including property which that State has authorized it to operate or manage,

is involved in a proceeding which relates to a commercial transaction in which that entity is engaged, the immunity from jurisdiction enjoyed by that State shall not be affected.

H. Fox, 'In Defence of State Immunity: Why the UN Convention on State Immunity is Important'

55 *International Comparative Law Quarterly* 399 (2006)

From the point of view of some developed States, the Convention may be judged as little more than a holding position, an endeavour 'to keep immunity within bounds', and to bring it up to date; that is to dismantle immunity to the extent recognized by their own national legislation and courts. But for other States the attractions of the convention are greater. Current State practice relating to immunity is complicated, diverse and, somewhat surprisingly, case law-dependent in many civil law countries in Europe and Latin America. Especially for States such as China and many of the States making up the former USSR, which until recently adhered to an absolute doctrine of State immunity, and whose public authorities are undergoing to varying degrees privatization of their economic activities, the State Immunity Convention provides a source of certainty and detailed international rules for their national courts. . . .

By providing a general rule of immunity for the State 'in respect of itself and its property from the jurisdiction of the courts of another State' (Article 5) the convention may be read as confirming the classical position in which States continue as the principal actors in 'the law of nations'. But the words 'subject to the provisions of the present Convention', the eight exceptions to immunity set out in Articles 10–17, and the authorization in certain circumstances to enforce judgments against State property 'in use or intended use for other than government or non-commercial purposes', immediately swing the balance against this privileged position of the State and subject it to the rule of law in regard to private persons and corporations, at least in respect of contracts and commercial dealings. A particular plus here is the codification for proceedings brought against States in national courts of the rules of procedure dealing with service of process, time limits, default judgment and security for costs; although there is no compulsory production of evidence and fines and penalties are barred, the national court is not prevented from drawing adverse conclusions against a State which fails to produce the requested evidence.

The lack of any restriction on reservations is to be regretted. In the absence of any monitoring body to ensure compliance, States need to be sparing in their reservations, if they value the harmonization of State practice on immunity which the convention offers. The provision for compulsory settlement of disputes by arbitration or reference to the International Court of Justice (Article 27) may go some way to ensure uniformity.

II. An assessment of the Major Criticisms

Three main criticisms may be directed at the convention with regard to its contribution to the development of general international law: the deferment to the forum State of the definition of commercial transaction, and hence of the scope of the main area for which the convention removes immunity; its relationship to other rules of international law including other conventions; and its treatment of jurisdiction.

The definition of 'commercial transaction', for which immunity is removed in Article 10, is to be found in Article 2 paragraphs 2 and 3. Undoubtedly the final limb of this definition, Article 2 (2), represents a compromise of the widely divergent views held by the negotiating States. By permitting the purpose of the transaction to be taken into account 'if in the practice of the State of the forum, the purpose is relevant to determining the non-commercial character of the contract or transaction' it might be contended that no harmonization of State practice can be achieved, and that the demarcation line between public and private activity will continue to vary according to the forum. But this overlooks the preceding sub-paragraph which defines commercial transactions as including the sale of goods, supply of services, a loan, guarantee, indemnity or other transaction of a financial nature, and transactions of a commercial, industrial, trading or professional nature. These are wide categories, which have generally enabled UK courts applying the State Immunity Act to decide whether a transaction is non-immune without having to seek assistance from State practice in the manner envisaged by Article 2(2)....

III. The Convention's contribution to the structure of general International Law

There is currently a school of thought which maintains the discretionary nature of sovereign immunity, a position which finds support in the United States largely by reason of the federal courts, even after the enactment of the FSIA [Foreign Sovereign Immunities Act—US], continuing to defer to the executive's directions on matters of foreign relations....

Any idea that such a reductionist view of immunity prevails solely in academic circles has been dispelled by the US Supreme Court's recent decision in *Republic of Austria v Altmann*....

The practice of civil law courts and common law jurisdictions other than the United States has been totally opposed to such a reduction of immunity as 'a gesture of comity'....

The UN State Immunity Convention would arrest this trend and provide strong authority to support immunity as a rule of international law, not a mere privilege granted for reasons of comity by the territorial State. The preamble to the convention refers to the jurisdictional immunities of States and their property as 'generally accepted as a principle of customary international law' and affirms that 'the rules of customary international law continue to govern matters not regulated' by the convention. When ratified, the treaty will give conventional force to the rules and as such many constitutions will accord it primacy over national law. Even unratified, the convention is likely to consolidate the customary status of its rules on immunity.

State immunity is a necessary principle at the present stage of development of international law. It serves as a neutral way of denying jurisdiction to States over the internal administration of another State and diverting claims to settlement in the courts of that State, or by diplomatic or other international means to which that State has consented.

European Convention on State Immunity 1972

11 *International Legal Materials* 470 (1972)

The 41 Articles of the European Convention on State Immunity cover all aspects of State immunity, and the optional Additional Protocol of 14 Articles establishes a European Tribunal to settle disputes arising out of the Convention that cannot be settled by a State's national law. As at March 2016, the Convention was in force with eight parties and the Additional Protocol with six parties. Apart from its general provisions, the main impact of this Convention was to introduce a mechanism for the enforcement of judgments against States. Previously, many States still allowed absolute immunity against enforcement, even though there was only restrictive immunity for adjudication of the dispute.

Article 20

1. A Contracting State shall give effect to a judgment given against it by a court of another Contracting State:
   (a) if, in accordance with the provisions of Articles 1 to 13, the State could not claim immunity from jurisdiction; and
   (b) if the judgment cannot or can no longer be set aside if obtained by default, or if it is not or is no longer subject to appeal or any other form of ordinary review or to annulment.

2. Nevertheless, a Contracting State is not obliged to give effect to such a judgment in any case:
   (a) where it would be manifestly contrary to public policy in that State to do so, or where, in the circumstances, either party had no adequate opportunity fairly to present his case;
   (b) where proceedings between the same parties, based on the same facts and having the same purpose:
      (i) are pending before a court of that State and were the first to be instituted;
      (ii) are pending before a court of another Contracting State, were the first to be instituted and may result in a judgment to which the State party to the proceedings must give effect under the terms of this Convention;

(c) where the result of the judgment is inconsistent with the result of another judgment given between the same parties:
   (i) by a court of the Contracting State, if the proceedings before that court were the first to be instituted or if the other judgment has been given before the judgment satisfied the conditions specified in paragraph 1 (b); or
   (ii) by a court of another Contracting State where the other judgment is the first to satisfy the requirements laid down in the present Convention;
(d) where the provisions of Article 16 have not been observed and the State has not entered an appearance or has not appealed against a judgment by default.

3. In addition, in the cases provided for in Article 10, a Contracting State is not obliged to give effect to the judgment:
   (a) if the courts of the State of the forum would not have been entitled to assume jurisdiction had they applied, *mutatis mutandis*, the rules of jurisdiction (other than those mentioned in the Annex to the present Convention) which operate in the State against which judgment is given; or
   (b) if the court, by applying a law other than that which would have been applied in accordance with the rules of private international law of that State, has reached a result different from that which would have been reached by applying the law determined by those rules.

However, a Contracting State may not rely upon the grounds of refusal specified in sub-paragraphs (a) and (b) above if it is bound by an agreement with the State of the forum on the recognition and enforcement of judgments and the judgment fulfils the requirement of that agreement as regards jurisdiction and, where appropriate, the law applied.

Article 23

No measures of execution or preventive measures against the property of a Contracting State may be taken in the territory of another Contracting State except where and to the extent that the State has expressly consented thereto in writing in any particular case.

Holland v *Lampen-Wolfe*
[2001] 1 WLR 1573, United Kingdom House of Lords

The claimant was employed at a US military base in the UK in an educational capacity. The defendant, also an employee of the US, made disparaging remarks about the claimant's teaching. The claimant sued for libel and the US raised the defence of State immunity. The House of Lords held that the matter fell outside the UK State Immunity Act 1978 (on which see Section 2A) because it was related to a function of the armed forces of a State (see section 16 of the State Immunity Act 1978) and so was to be treated under the common law. Their Lordships thus had cause to consider the nature of State immunity.

LORD MILLET: It is an established rule of customary international law that one state cannot be sued in the courts of another for acts performed *jure imperii*. The immunity does not derive from the authority or dignity of sovereign States or the need to protect the integrity of their governmental functions. It derives from the sovereign nature of the exercise of the State's adjudicative powers and the basic principle of international law that all States are equal. The rule is *'par in parem non habet imperium'*: see *I Congreso del Partido* [1983] 1 AC 244, 262, *per* Lord Wilberforce. As I explained in *Reg* v *Bow Street Metropolitan Stipendiary Magistrate, ex parte Pinochet Ugarte (No 3)* [2000] 1 AC 147, 269, it is a subject-matter immunity. It operates to prevent the official and governmental acts of one state from being called into question in proceedings before the courts of another. The existence of the doctrine is confirmed by the European Convention on State Immunity (1972) (Cmnd 5081), the relevant provisions of which are generally regarded as reflecting customary international law. In according immunity from suit before the English courts to foreign States the State Immunity Act 1978 and the common law give effect to the international obligations of the United Kingdom.

Where the immunity applies, it covers an official of the state in respect of acts performed by him in an official capacity. In the present case, it is common ground that at all material times the defendant acted in his capacity as an official of the United States Department of Defense, being the department responsible for the armed forces of the United States present in the United Kingdom. The United States has asserted immunity on behalf of the defendant. Dr. Holland has not challenged the proposition that, if the United States is entitled to the immunity it claims, that immunity bars the present proceedings.

H. Fox, 'International Law and the Restraints on the Exercise of Jurisdiction by National Courts of States'

in M. Evans (ed), *International Law* (4th edn, 2014)

A. Act of State

...The principle enunciated in *Underhill v Hernandez* [168 US 250 (1897)] that the courts of one State will not sit in judgment on the acts of the government of another done within its territory provides a further ground for imposing restraint on the English court. Thus in the leading case of *Luthor v Sagor* the English court upheld the validity of an expropriatory decree relating to timber situated in Russia of the newly established Soviet government. The governmental nature of the act performed by a foreign sovereign State was clearly a factor deterring the court from inquiry into the validity of the expropriation, with Scrutton LJ considering it would be 'a serious breach of international comity' to postulate that its legislation is 'contrary to essential principles of justice and morality' [[1921] 3 KB 532]. Later cases held the rule of recognition of foreign decrees applied to aliens as well as to nationals of foreign State. The act of State defence is subject to exceptions, which are comprehensively covered by the general statement that the English court will not enforce a foreign government act if it is contrary to public policy....At this point questions of non-justiciability impinge; whether an exception to the act of State rule is permitted depends not merely on the issue being contrary to public policy but also a justiciable issue....

B. Non-Justiciability

Non-justiciability remains today a doctrine of uncertain scope. It may be raised as a plea in proceedings whether or not a foreign State is itself made a party to them, and may be dealt with as a preliminary issue, but being highly fact specific it may not be possible to decide such issues until after disclosure or even until trial. In origin it operated in a manner similar to a plea of immunity barring further inquiry into matters falling within another State's jurisdiction or for international settlement. In the *Buttes Gas* case Lord Wilberforce sought to formulate nonjusticiability into a distinct doctrine [[1982] AC 888, at 938]. The *Buttes Gas* case concerned a defamation action between companies in which, if it were to proceed, in the House of Lords' view, the English court would have to make a determination on a disputed maritime boundary between foreign States, involving a series of inter-State transactions from 1969 to 1973, of States' motives and the lawfulness of actions taken by Sharjah, and possibly Iran and the UK. The House of Lords held, there were 'no judicial or manageable standards by which to judge these issues, or to adopt another phrase, the court would be in judicial no man's land; the court would be asked to review transactions in which four foreign States were involved, which they had brought to a precarious settlement, after diplomacy, and the use of force'. Lord Wilberforce, who gave the single judgment of the House, after a review of particular rules, and reference to proceedings in US federal courts on the same international incident, declared there to be a general principle, 'not one of discretion but inherent in the very nature of process' that 'There exists in English law a more general principle that the courts will not adjudicate on the transactions of foreign sovereign States' [[1982] AC 888, at 931–932, 938]....

Lord Wilberforce's ruling that courts must declare certain matters non-justiciable continues to apply to matters of international relations which depend on diplomacy, countermeasures, sanctions and the use of force for their resolution. However, in situations where State practice has been reduced to a generally accepted and certain rule, even though it be a rule of international rather municipal law, English courts may find sufficient judicial and manageable standards to determine the issues. In the words of Lord Nicholls in *Kuwait Airways No 2*, the principle of non-justiciability does not 'mean that the judiciary must shut their eyes to a breach of an established principle of international law committed by one State against another when the breach is plain and indeed acknowledged.' As Lord Hope in the same case stated 'restraint is what is needed, not abstention' [[2002] UKHL 19, paras 26 and 141]....

Recently, however, there have been now two further developments which may narrow the distinction between issues subject to international law and those subject to municipal law: the first is where 'a foothold in domestic law' is established so as to permit an English court to make a ruling on international law; and the second is where State immunity barring the exercise of jurisdiction of a national court conflicts with the procedural right of access to court which is now enacted in international and regional human rights conventions to which the UK is a party. Where the facts support one or other of these two developments- that is, where there exists 'a foothold in domestic law', or where the denial of jurisdiction amounts to a disproportionate disregard of right of access to court of the private claimant, there will be no dismissal of a claim on the basis of either act of State or non-justiciability....

The second area of development relating to situations in which a claim may not be dismissed on the basis of either act of State or non-justiciability concerns the procedural right of access to justice granted by Article 14 of the 1966 International Convention on Civil and Political Rights 1966 and by Article 6 of the European Convention on Human Rights. State immunity has been challenged on the grounds that it infringes the right of access to a court in a number of different situations, including alleged torture committed abroad in a prison on the foreign state in *Al-Adsani v UK;* assault by a soldier of the foreign State while within the territory of the forum State in *McElhinney v Ireland* [[GC] no 31253/96, ECHR 2001-XI, 34 *EHRR* 13]; and discrimination on the basis of sex in connection with an appointment to a post in a foreign embassy in *Fogarty v UK* [[GC] no 37112/97, ECHR 2001-XI, 34 *EHRR* 12]. In all three cases it was contended that the national courts had wrongly applied immunity to bar access to a national court and its exercise of jurisdiction. Relying on Article 6(1) of the European Convention of Human Rights, the Court in all three cases confirmed its previous ruling that 'a State could not, without restraint or control by the convention enforcement bodies, remove from the jurisdiction of the courts a whole range of civil claims or confer immunities from civil liability on large groups or categories of persons'. But it distinguished State immunity from immunities imposed by a single municipal law: in *Al-Adsani v UK* it held that State immunity was a party of the body of relevant rules of international law which the Convention as a human rights treaty must take into account; the Convention 'cannot be interpreted in a vacuum' and must 'so far as possible be construed in harmony with other rules of international law of which it forms part including those relating to the grant of State immunity'....

However, while holding that State immunity could not be struck down as contrary to the right of access to a court, the European Court held it to be always necessary to ensure that the barring of a civil right was not disproportionate to the legitimate aim which State immunity pursues....

Account must now be taken of a thorough and authoritative analysis by the unanimous Court of Appeal in 2013 in *Yukos Capital*. Rix LJ has now stated that Lord Wilberforce's principle of non-justiciability has to subsume the act of State doctrine as the 'paradigm principle' preventing adjudication on the validity, legality, lawfulness, acceptability, or motives of State actors. However, the Court in formulating the revised plea of act of State/non-justiciability has declared it subject to five qualifications. The Court concludes that the act of State doctrine does not prevent adjudication of 'the judicial acts of a foreign State', which 'are judged by judicial standards, including international standards regarding jurisdiction...' [*Yukos Capital v OJSC Rosneft Oil* [2013] 3 WLR 1329, at 40–104]....

IV. Comparison and evaluation of the three avoidance techniques

From the account given it will be clear that the pleas are related one to the other. Respect for the independence and equality of a foreign State when it is a party to proceedings is achieved by a plea of State immunity which brings the case to a halt. Where the proceeding is between private parties such an immediate halt will only take place if by reason of the non-justiciability of the issues to be determined the court decides that it had no competence to decide them. In cases where the proceedings between private parties progresses to examination of the substantive law, the court may also conclude that it has no judicial or manageable standards by which to decide the issues and declare them non-justiciable; alternatively it may accept a plea of act of State and decide that the recognition of the validity of a foreign State's governmental act deprives the claim of any basis for its assertion. Thus by accepting a plea of act of State the English court goes some way to endorsing the validity of the act of the foreign State whereas in immunity the court remains neutral, merely deciding that it is not the appropriate forum.

As regards fundamental human rights violations, the choice of an applicable municipal law may be less acute in that for States which have ratified them international human rights conventions provide a set of rules for the consequences of such violations and, in some instances, international or regional tribunal to which complaints may be referred. But in direct proceedings against a foreign State problems still remain as to the jurisdiction of, and cause of action exercisable by, a national court in respect of such violations committed within the territory of another State...

NOTES
1. There are various theories put forward to explain the basis of State immunity, although the view put forward by Marshall CJ in *The Schooner Exchange* (above) is generally regarded as the most apposite. It is echoed in the speech of Lord Millet in *Lampen-Wolfe* extracted above. Note, however, that when we come to consider the immunity of individuals derived from their status (e.g. immunity *ratione personae* such as with Heads of State, Ambassadors etc.), it seems that its justification is purely functional, in that it ensures that the individual may carry out their functions as an officer of the State. As noted in the *Arrest Warrant Case* (see Section 3),

para. 53, 'the immunities accorded to Ministers of Foreign Affairs are not granted for their personal benefit, but to ensure the effective performance of their functions on behalf of their respective states.' In reality, of course, it is not generally the theory behind immunity that is important. The important issue is whether the national court adopts absolute or restrictive immunity in its approach to States and how that distinction is to be drawn. The European Convention on State Immunity clearly favours a restrictive approach and this is the effect of the UN Convention on Jurisdictional Immunities of States and their Property, even if its provisions are less explicit.

2. There are two main views as to the status of immunity. First, that immunity is a rule of international law for the most part recognised by States. Second, that immunity is discretionary, essentially a matter for the executive branch of the State concerned, arising only as a matter of comity and not as a matter of legal obligation, at least until immunity is made a matter of national law by the introduction of national legislation. The practice of most States—both civil and common law—suggests that the former theory is now widely accepted, and it has been endorsed by the ICJ in the *Arrest Warrant Case* (see Section 3). The increasing concern with the rights of individuals and the concern with accountability for international crimes and serious violations of international human rights (see Section 4) will make it harder to defend a discretionary approach to immunity. The main exception to this is the United States, as seen in the decision of the United States Supreme Court in *Republic of Austria* v *Altmann* (2004) 43 ILM 1421. Note that this decision has been strongly criticised (see C. Brower, 'Case note' (2005) 99 AJIL 236 and C. Vazquez, '*Altmann v Austria* and the Retroactivity of the FSIA' (2005) 3 *Journal of International Criminal Justice* 207).

3. The UN Convention on Jurisdictional Immunities of States and their Property (see extract) is the first universal instrument concerning State immunity. It adopts a principle of absolute immunity (Article 5) and then detracts from that in Part III, Articles 10 to 17. The result is a set of Articles establishing restrictive immunity turning on the distinction between acts *juri imperii* and acts *jure gestionis*. Certain activities are presumptively not immune: employment contracts (Article 11), acts causing personal injury or damage to property (Article 12), acts relating to immovable property (Article 13), to intellectual property (Article 14), to State ships (Article 16), matters concerning companies (Article 15), and certain arbitration proceedings (Article 17). Importantly, Article 10 attempts a definition of a 'commercial transaction' in which the purpose of the disputed activity may be relevant in making the decision. The Convention expressly precludes criminal proceedings from its scope and the personal immunity of Heads of State (see Section 3). Certain commentators have queried whether the Convention excludes civil claims in respect of violations of international human rights law and humanitarian law, and have argued for the adoption of a protocol to the Convention on human rights claims (see C. Hall, 'The UN Convention on State Immunity: The Need for a Human Rights Protocol' (2006) 55 *ICLQ* 437).

4. The second extract by Fox distinguishes State immunity from other restraints on jurisdiction, in particular the act of State doctrine and the principle of non-justiciability. UK courts have in recent years considered many claims that have called for discussion of these restraints, sometimes in conjunction with a plea of State immunity. As Fox notes, the extent and application of these restraints has been modified in recent years, and it appears that UK courts are now more willing to engage with politically sensitive issues or questions connected to international affairs, as illustrated by the case of *Belhaj* (see Section 2A). The Court of Appeal in that case held that a public policy limitation was applicable in cases concerning grave violations of human rights, having identified a fundamental change within public international law to include the regulation of human rights and an increased willingness on the part of UK courts to address and investigate the conduct of foreign States, in particular where grave violations of human rights in the form of torture and unlawful rendition is concerned. Importantly, it went on to find that this was not a case in which there was a lack of judicial or manageable standards—the applicable principles of international law and English law were clearly established. However, while UK courts may be more willing to assess issues connected to international law, they may still extend a wide margin of appreciation to the UK government in determining whether and how rights should be protected, having regard to relevant foreign policy decisions.

A: General principles

The law in the UK is governed substantially by the State Immunity Act 1978. For matters falling outside this statute or issues arising before its enactment, the common law prevails.

State Immunity Act 1978

This Act was designed primarily to meet the UK's obligations under the European Convention on State Immunity (see Section 1) and the earlier Brussels Convention for the Unification of Certain Rules relating to the Immunity of State Owned Vessels 1920.

1. General immunity from jurisdiction

(1) A State is immune from the jurisdiction of the courts of the United Kingdom except as provided in the following provisions of this Part of this Act.

(2) A court shall give effect to the immunity conferred by this section even though the State does not appear in the proceedings in question.

2. Submission to jurisdiction

(1) A State is not immune as respects proceedings in respect of which it has submitted to the jurisdiction of the courts of the United Kingdom.

(2) A State may submit after the dispute giving rise to the proceedings has arisen or by a prior written agreement; but a provision in any agreement that it is to governed by the law of the United Kingdom is not to be regarded as a submission.

(3) A State is deemed to have submitted—
  (a) if it has instituted the proceedings; or
  (b) subject to subsections (4) and (5) below, if it has intervened or taken any step in the proceedings.

(4) Subsection (3)(b) above does not apply to intervention or any step taken for the purpose only of—
  (a) claiming immunity; or
  (b) asserting an interest in property in circumstances such that the State would have been entitled to immunity if the proceedings had been brought against it.

3. Commercial transactions and contracts to be performed in United Kingdom

(1) A State is not immune as respects proceedings relating to—
  (a) a commercial transaction, entered into by the State; or
  (b) an obligation of the State which by virtue of a contract (whether a commercial transaction or not) falls to be performed wholly or partly in the United Kingdom.

(2) This section does not apply if the parties to the dispute are States or have otherwise agreed in writing; and subsection (1)(b) above does not apply if the contract (not being a commercial transaction) was made in the territory of the State concerned and the obligation in question is governed by its administrative law.

(3) In this section 'commercial transaction' means—
  (a) any contract for the supply of goods or services;
  (b) any loan or other transaction for the provision of finance and any guarantee or indemnity in respect of any such transaction or of any other financial obligation; and
  (c) any other transaction or activity (whether of a commercial, industrial, financial, professional or other similar character) into which a State enters or in which it engages otherwise than in the exercise of sovereign authority;

But neither paragraph of subsection (1) above applies to a contract of employment between a State and an individual.

4. Contracts of employment

(1) A State is not immune as respects proceedings relating to a contract of employment between the State and an individual where the contract was made in the United Kingdom or the work is to be wholly or partly performed there.

(2) Subject to subsections (3) and (4) below, this section does not apply if—
  (a) at the time when the proceedings are brought the individual is a national of the State concerned; or
  (b) at the time when the contract was made the individual was neither a national of the United Kingdom nor habitually resident there; or
  (c) the parties to the contract have otherwise agreed in writing....

5. Personal injuries and damage to property

A State is not immune as respects proceedings in respect of—
  (a) death or personal injury; or
  (b) damage or loss of tangible property,

caused by an act or omission in the United Kingdom.

6. Ownership, possession and use of property

(1) A State is not immune as respects proceedings relating to—
  (a) any interest of the State in, or its possession or use of, immovable property in the United Kingdom; or
  (b) any obligation of the State arising out of its interest in, or its possession or use of, any such property.

(2) A State is not immune as respects proceedings relating to any interest of the State in movable or immovable property, being an interest arising by way of succession, gift or *bona vacantia.*

(3) The fact that a State has or claims an interest in any property shall not preclude any court from exercising in respect of it any jurisdiction relating to the estates of deceased persons or persons of unsound mind or to insolvency, the winding up of companies or the administration of trusts.

(4) A court may entertain proceedings against a person other than a State notwithstanding that the proceedings relate to property—
  (a) which is in the possession or control of a State; or
  (b) in which a State claims an interest,

if the State would not have been immune had the proceedings been brought against it or, in a case within paragraph (b) above, if the claim is neither admitted nor supported by prima facie evidence.

10. Ships used for commercial purposes

(1) This section applies to—
  (a) Admiralty proceedings; and
  (b) proceedings on any claim which could be made the subject of Admiralty proceedings.

(2) A State is not immune as respects—
  (a) an action *in rem* against a ship belonging to that State; or
  (b) an action *in personam* for enforcing a claim in connection with such a ship,

if, at the time when the cause of action arose, the ship was in use or intended for use for commercial purposes.

(3) Where an action *in rem* is brought against a ship belonging to a State for enforcing a claim in connection with another ship belonging to that State, subsection (2)(a) above does not apply as respects the first-mentioned ship unless, at the time when the cause of action relating to the other ship arose, both ships were in use or intended for use for commercial purposes.

(4) A State is not immune as respects—
  (a) an action *in rem* against a cargo belonging to that State if both the cargo and the ship carrying it were, at the time when the cause of action arose, in use or intended for use for commercial purposes; or
  (b) an action *in personam* for enforcing a claim in connection with such a cargo if the ship carrying it was in use or intended for use as aforesaid. [/LEXTL]

(6) Sections 3 to 5 above do not apply to proceedings of the kind described in subsection (1) above if the State in question is a party to the Brussels Convention and the claim relates to the operation of a ship owned or

operated by that State, the carriage of cargo or passengers on any such ship or the carriage of cargo owned by that State on any other ship.

11. Value added tax, customs duties etc

A State is not immune as respects proceedings relating to its liability for—

(a) value added tax, and duty of customs or excise or any agricultural levy; or

(b) rates in respect of premises occupied by it for commercial purposes.

13. Other procedural privileges

(1) No penalty by way of committal or fine shall be imposed in respect of any failure or refusal by or on behalf of a State to disclose or produce any document or other information for the purposes of proceedings to which it is a party.

(2) Subject to subsection (3) and (4) below—

(a) relief shall not be given against a State by way of injunction or order for specific performance or for the recovery of land or other property; and

(b) the property of a State shall not be subject to any process for the enforcement of a judgment or arbitration award or, in an action *in rem*, for its arrest, detention or sale.

(3) Subsection (2) above does not prevent the giving of any relief or the issue of any process with the written consent of the State concerned; and any such consent (which may be contained in a prior agreement) may be expressed so as to apply to a limited extent or generally; but a provision merely submitting to the jurisdiction of the courts is not to be regarded as a consent for the purposes of this subsection.

(4) Subsection (2)(b) above does not prevent the issue of any process in respect of property which is for the time being in use or intended for use for commercial purposes; but, in a case not falling within section 10 above, this subsection applies to property of a State party to the European Convention on State Immunity only if—

(a) the process is for enforcing a judgment which is final within the meaning of section 18(1)(b) below and the State has made a declaration under Article 24 of the Convention; or

(b) the process is for enforcing an arbitration award.

(5) The head of a State's diplomatic mission in the United Kingdom, or the person for the time being performing his functions, shall be deemed to have authority to give on behalf of the State any such consent as is mentioned in subsection (3) above and, for the purposes of subsection (4) above, his certificate to the effect that any property is not in use or intended for use by or on behalf of the State for commercial purposes shall be accepted as sufficient evidence of that fact unless the contrary is proved.

14. States entitled to immunities and privileges

(1) The immunities and privileges conferred by this Part of this Act apply to any foreign or commonwealth State other than the United Kingdom; and references to a State include reference to—

(a) the sovereign or other head of that State in his public capacity;

(b) the government of that State; and

(c) any department of that government,

but not to any entity (hereafter referred to as a 'separate entity') which is distinct from the executive organs of the government of the State and capable of suing or being sued.

(2) A separate entity is immune from the jurisdiction of the courts of the United Kingdom if, and only if—

(a) the proceedings relate to anything done by it in the exercise of sovereign authority; and

(b) the circumstances are such that a State (or, in the case of proceedings to which section 10 above applies, a State which is not a party to the Brussels Convention) would have been so immune.

(3) If a separate entity (not being a State's central bank or other monetary authority) submits to the jurisdiction in respect of proceedings in the case of which it is entitled to immunity by virtue of subsection (2) above, subsections (1) to (4) of section 13 above shall apply to it in respect of those proceedings as if references to a State were references to that entity.

(4) Property of a State's central bank or other monetary authority shall not be regarded for the purposes of subsection (4) of section 13 above as in use or intended for use for commercial purposes; and where any such bank or authority is a separate entity subsections (1) to (3) of that section shall apply to it as if references to a State were references to the bank or authority.

(5) Section 12 above applies to proceedings against the constituent territories of a federal State; and Her Majesty may by Order in Council provide for the other provisions of this Part of this Act to apply to any such constituent territory specified in the Order as they apply to a State.

(6) Where the provisions of this Part of this Act do not apply to a constituent territory by virtue of any such Order subsections (2) and (3) above shall apply to it as if it were a separate entity.

16. Excluded matters

(1) This Part of this Act does not affect any immunity or privilege conferred by the Diplomatic Privileges Act 1964 or the Consular Relations Act 1968; and—

(a) section 4 above does not apply to proceedings concerning the employment of the members of a mission within the meaning of the Convention scheduled to the said Act of 1964 or of the members of a consular post within the meaning of the Convention scheduled to the said Act of 1968;

(b) section 6(1) above does not apply to proceedings concerning a State's title to or its possession of property used for the purposes of a diplomatic mission.

(2) This Part of this Act does not apply to proceedings relating to anything done by or in relation to the armed forces of a State while present in the United Kingdom and, in particular, has effect subject to the Visiting Forces Act 1952.

(3) This Part of this Act does not apply to proceedings to which section 17(6) of the Nuclear Installations Act 1965 applies.

(4) This Part of this Act does not apply to criminal proceedings.

(5) This Part of this Act does not apply to any proceedings relating to taxation other than those mentioned in section 11 above.

20. Heads of State

(1) Subject to the provisions of this section and to any necessary modifications, the Diplomatic Privileges Act 1964 shall apply to—

(a) a sovereign or other head of State;

(b) members of his family forming part of his household; and

(c) his private servants,

as it applies to the head of a diplomatic mission, to members of his family forming part of his household and to his private servants.

(2) The immunities and privileges conferred by virtue of subsection (1)(a) and (b) above shall not be subject to the restrictions by reference to nationality or residence mentioned in Article 37(1) or 38 in Schedule 1 to the said Act of 1964.

(3) Subject to any direction to the contrary by the Secretary of State, a person on whom immunities and privileges are conferred by virtue of subsection (1) above shall be entitled to the exemption conferred by section 8(3) of the Immigration Act 1971.

(4) Except as respects value added tax and duties of customs or excise, this section does not affect any question whether a person is exempt from, or immune as respects proceedings relating to, taxation.

(5) This section applies to the sovereign or other head of any State on which immunities and privileges are conferred by Part I of this Act and is without prejudice to the application of that Part to any such sovereign or head of State in his public capacity.

Belhaj and Boudchar v Straw et al

[2014] EWCA Civ 1394, United Kingdom Court of Appeal

Mr Belhaj and his wife brought a civil claim for declarations of illegality and damages in relation to their alleged unlawful rendition to Libya in 2004. They claimed they were unlawfully abducted in Thailand while en route to the United Kingdom from Malaysia and rendered illegally into the custody of the Libyan authorities. The question before the Court was whether certain claims were non-justiciable by reason of the act of state doctrine. This was on the basis that the claims called into question the activities of foreign states. Having found that State immunity did not operate as a bar to the proceedings, the Court went on to find that although the act of State doctrine was engaged in these proceedings, the claims fell within a limitation to the doctrine on grounds of public policy. The case is the subject of appeal.

114. The central issue for determination is whether this court should go beyond *Oppenheimer* and *Kuwait Airways* and apply the public policy limitation in a case where the court, if it exercised jurisdiction, would be required to conduct a legal and factual investigation into the validity of the conduct of a foreign state. The *ratio decidendi* of *Kuwait Airways* does not confine the limitation to cases where such an investigation is unnecessary. Furthermore, we consider that there are compelling reasons for concluding that the present case does fall within this limitation on the act of state doctrine. In coming to this conclusion we have been influenced in particular by the following considerations, the force of some of which was recognised by Simon J. in his careful judgment.

115. First, a fundamental change has occurred within public international law. The traditional view of public international law as a system of law merely regulating the conduct of states among themselves on the international plane has long been discarded. In its place has emerged a system which includes the regulation of human rights by international law, a system of which individuals are rightly considered to be subjects. A corresponding shift in international public policy has also taken place. (See the observations of Lord Steyn in *Kuwait Airways* at [115].) These changes have been reflected in a growing willingness on the part of courts in this jurisdiction to address and investigate the conduct of foreign states and issues of public international law when appropriate.

116. Secondly, the allegations in this case—although they are only allegations—are of particularly grave violations of human rights. The abhorrent nature of torture and its condemnation by the community of nations is apparent from the participation of states in the UN Convention against Torture (to which all of the States concerned with the exception of Malaysia are parties) and the International Covenant on Civil and Political Rights (to which Libya, Thailand, the United States and the United Kingdom are parties) and from the recognition in customary international law of its prohibition as a rule of *jus cogens*, a peremptory norm from which no derogation is permitted. While it is impermissible to draw consequences as to the jurisdictional competence of national courts from the *jus cogens* status of the prohibition on torture (see, for example, *Jones v. Saudi Arabia* per Lord Bingham at [22] and following, per Lord Hoffmann at [42] and following; *Arrest Warrant of 11 April 2000 (Democratic Republic of Congo v. Belgium)* ICJ Rep. (2006) 6 at [58], [60], [78]), it is appropriate to take account of the strength of this condemnation when considering the application of a rule of public policy. Moreover, the decision of the House of Lords in *A v. Home Secretary (No. 2)* [2006] 2 AC 221 leaves no doubt as to the attitude of the public policy of the forum towards torture. So far as unlawful rendition is concerned, this too must occupy a position high in the scale of grave violations of human rights and international law, involving as it does arbitrary deprivation of liberty and enforced disappearance.

117. Thirdly, the respondents in these proceedings are either current or former officers or officials of state in the United Kingdom or government departments or agencies. They are not entitled to any immunity before the courts in this jurisdiction, whether *ratione personae* or *ratione materiae*. Furthermore, their conduct, considered in isolation, would not normally be exempt from investigation by the courts. On the contrary there is a compelling public interest in the investigation by the English courts of these very grave allegations. The only ground on which it could be contended that there is any exemption from the exercise of jurisdiction in the present case is because of the alleged involvement of other states and their officials in the conduct alleged. Notwithstanding our view that the present proceedings would entail an investigation of the legality of the conduct of those foreign officials, the fortuitous benefit the act of state doctrine might confer on the respondents is a further factor supporting the application of this public policy limitation.

118. Fourthly, this is not a case in which there is a lack of judicial or manageable standards. On the contrary, the applicable principles of international law and English law are clearly established. The court would not be in a judicial no man's land.

119. Fifthly, the stark reality is that unless the English courts are able to exercise jurisdiction in this case, these very grave allegations against the executive will never be subjected to judicial investigation. The subject matter of these allegations is such that, these respondents, if sued in the courts of another state, are likely to be entitled to plead state immunity. Furthermore, there is, so far as we are aware, no alternative international forum with jurisdiction over these issues. As a result, these very grave allegations would go uninvestigated and the appellants would be left without any legal recourse or remedy.

120. Sixthly, notwithstanding the evidence of Dr. Bristow that there is a risk that damage will be done to the foreign relations and national security interests of the United Kingdom, we do not consider that in the particular

circumstances of this case these considerations can outweigh the need for our courts to exercise jurisdiction. For the reasons set out above, we consider that there is a compelling case in favour of these proceedings being heard in this jurisdiction. In this particular context, the risk of displeasing our allies or offending other states, and even the risk of the consequences of varying severity which it is said are likely to follow, cannot justify our declining jurisdiction on grounds of act of state over what is a properly justiciable claim.

121. For these reasons, considered cumulatively, we consider that the present case falls within the established limitation on the act of state doctrine imposed by considerations of public policy on grounds of violations of human rights and international law and that there are compelling reasons requiring the exercise of jurisdiction.

NOTES

1. In *I Congreso del Partido* [1981] 3 WLR 328 (see Section 2B), the House of Lords confirmed that the restrictive doctrine of immunity applied as a matter of UK common law. Cases that mark the progression from absolute to restrictive immunity in the UK have been omitted as they are now largely of historical interest.

2. The approach of the State Immunity Act is that there is a general principle of absolute immunity (section 1(1)), subject to a number of wide-ranging exceptions (sections 2 to 17). The Act distinguishes between adjudicative jurisdiction (sections 2 to 11), procedural jurisdiction (sections 12 to 14) and enforcement jurisdiction (sections 13(2) to (6) and 14(3) and (4)). The effect of section 1(2) is to require the court itself to consider issues of immunity even in the absence of a claim of immunity by the affected State; that is, the judge must determine immunity *proprio motu*. This is particularly important as the foreign State may not appear before the Court at all stages of the proceedings.

3. A State or other entity entitled to immunity may submit to the jurisdiction by waiver. However, in UK law at least, that waiver must be express, by words or conduct intended to operate as a waiver. So, in *London Branch of the Nigerian Universities Commission v Bastians* [1995] ICR 358, an uncompleted form returned to an Industrial Tribunal (via the UK Foreign Office) by the Commission was not a waiver, and in *Malaysian Industrial Development Authority v Jeyasingham* [1998] ICR 307, the employer's notice of appearance was not a waiver and, in any event, it had not been offered by the High Commissioner, the only person who could waive Malaysian immunity according to section 2(7) of the State Immunity Act 1978. Similarly, in *Aziz v Yemen* [2005] EWCA Civ 745, the Court held that solicitors for the Embassy had not submitted to the jurisdiction (and so had not waived immunity), as this step was required to be taken by a person with knowledge of the right and also the authority to waive it (in this case the head of mission or a member of the mission or agent acting with his or her authority).

4. State immunity must be raised directly in the proceedings in the UK. In the case of *Belhaj* (see extract), the Court rejected the submission by the respondent that the doctrine of State immunity applied to bar the appellants' claims, on the basis that the claims indirectly concerned China, Malaysia, Thailand, the United States and their servants or agents and would necessarily require the Court to consider the legality of their actions when deciding the claim. The Court stated that this would involve an unprecedented extension of State immunity. While it was common ground that the States concerned would be entitled to plead State immunity if they were parties to the proceedings (they were not parties to the proceedings and there was no claim against them), the Court held that proceedings would not be barred on grounds of State immunity simply because it required the Court to rule on the legality of the conduct of a foreign State.

5. The State Immunity Act reverses the pre-existing common law rule so that consent to submit a dispute to litigation or arbitration given in a prior contract may now constitute a waiver of sovereign immunity. This will depend on the terms of the agreement and its construction: see *Svenska Petroleum Exploration AB v Lithuania and Another* [2006] EWCA Civ 1529.

B: Commercial and other excluded transactions

The State Immunity Act, and the common law where it is applicable, require national courts to determine whether a particular act is covered by sovereign immunity. As the following extracts illustrate, this is not always a simple exercise.

I Congreso del Partido

[1981] 3 WLR 328, United Kingdom House of Lords

In 1973, two ships, *The Marble Islands* and *The Playa Larga*, were carrying sugar to Chile on behalf of Cubazucar, a Cuban State enterprise. After a coup in Chile, *The Playa Larga* (essentially owned by Cuba) was ordered to return to Cuba with most of her sugar unloaded, and *The Marble Islands* (essentially chartered to Cuba) was ordered to Vietnam where the sugar was sold. The plaintiffs, who were owners of the sugar, brought an action *in rem* (i.e. to hold the ship) against *I Congreso*, a ship also owned by Cuba. Cuba claimed State immunity. The case was decided at common law, the issue arising before the 1978 Act. The House of Lords rejected the plea of immunity in respect of both ships: in regard to *The Playa Larga* because at all times the actions of Cuba were as owners and not by virtue of sovereign authority, and in regard to *The Marble Islands* (Lords Wilberforce and Edmund Davies dissenting) because the sale of the sugar to Vietnam was made under Cuban law, being analogous to conversion in the law of torts, and not by virtue of the sovereign authority of Cuba.

LORD WILBERFORCE: When therefore a claim is brought against a state…and state immunity is claimed, it is necessary to consider what is the relevant act which forms the basis of the claim: is this, under the old terminology, an act 'jure gestions' or is it an act 'jure imperii': is it…a 'private act' or is it a 'sovereign or public act,' a private act meaning in this context an act of a private law character such as a private citizen might have entered into. It is upon this point that the arguments in these appeals is focussed.…

The activities of states cannot always be compartmentalised into trading or governmental activities; and what is one to make of a case where a state has, and in the relevant circumstances, clearly displayed, both a commercial interest and a sovereign or governmental interest? To which is the critical action to be attributed? Such questions are the more difficult since they arise at an initial stage in the proceedings and, in all probability, upon affidavit evidence. This difficulty is inherent in the nature of the 'restrictive' doctrine, introducing as it does an exception, based upon a certain state of facts, to a plain rule. But as was said in the *Empire of Iran* case…

> The fact that it is difficult to draw the line between sovereign and non-sovereign state activities is no reason for abandoning the distinction. International law knows of other similar difficulties…The distinction between sovereign and non-sovereign state activities cannot be drawn according to the purpose of the state transaction and whether it stands in a recognizable relation to the sovereign duties of the state. For, ultimately, activities of state, if not wholly then to the widest degree, serve sovereign purposes and duties, and stand in a still recognizable relationship to them. Neither should the distinction depend on whether the state has acted commercially. Commercial activities of states are not different in their nature from other non-sovereign state activities.…

Under the 'restrictive' theory the court has first to characterise the activity into which the defendant state has entered. Having done this, and (assumedly) found it to be of a commercial, or private law, character, it may take the view that contractual breaches, or torts, prima facie fall within the same sphere of activity. It should then be for the defendant state to make a case…that the act complained of is outside that sphere, and within that of sovereign action.…

The conclusion which emerges is that in considering, under the 'restrictive' theory whether state immunity should be granted or not, the court must consider the whole context in which the claim against the state is made, with a view to deciding whether the relevant act(s) upon which the claim is based, should, in that context, be considered as fairly within an area of activity, trading or commercial, or otherwise of a private law character, in which the state has chosen to engage, or whether the relevant act(s) should be considered as having been done outside that area, and within the sphere of governmental or sovereign activity.

Holland v *Lampen-Wolfe*

[2000] 1 WLR 1573, United Kingdom House of Lords

The primary facts are stated in Section 1. Under section 16(2) of the State Immunity Act 1978, the Act 'does not apply to proceedings relating to anything done by or in relation to the armed forces of a State while present in the United Kingdom'. The House of Lords decided that this section should be given a wide meaning and thus the employment of a person in an educational capacity on a US military base was 'in relation to' the armed forces of a State and so was not covered by the Act. The matter thus fell to be considered under the common law.

LORD MILLET: Accordingly the question is whether, in accordance with the law laid down in *I Congreso del Partido* [1983] 1 AC 244, 262, the act complained of was *jure imperii* or *jure gestionis*. This must be judged against the background of the whole context in which the claim is made. The question is not an altogether easy one, but I have come to the conclusion that the Court of Appeal was correct to designate the act complained of as being *jure imperii*.

In *Littrell* v *United States of America (No 2)* [1995] 1 WLR 82 the plaintiff claimed damages for personal injuries arising from medical treatment which he had received at a United States military hospital in the United Kingdom while a serving member of the United States Air Force. It was conceded that section 16(2) applied, so that the case fell to be decided at common law. The Court of Appeal held that the proceedings were barred by state immunity. Hoffmann LJ said, at pp. 94–95:

> The context in which the act took place was the maintenance by the United States of a unit of the United States Air Force in the United Kingdom. This looks about as imperial an activity as could be imagined. But it would be facile to regard this context as determinative of the question. Acts done within that context could range from arrangements concerning the flights of the bombers—plainly *jure imperii*—to ordering milk for the base from a local dairy or careless driving by off-duty airmen on the roads of Suffolk. Both of the latter would seem to me to be *jure gestionis*, fairly within an area of private law activity. I do not think that there is a single test or "bright line" by which cases on either side can be distinguished. Rather, there are a number of factors which may characterise the act as nearer to or further from the central military activity…Some acts are wholly military in character, some almost entirely private or commercial and some in between….

The Court of Appeal could find no material distinction between the medical treatment provided in that case and the educational services provided in the present one. I agree with them that the provision of education for members of the armed forces and their families is, in modern conditions, as much a normal and necessary part of the overall activity of maintaining those forces as is the provision of medical treatment.

It is, of course, true that the action is an action for defamation, not for the negligent provision of professional services. The *Littrell* case is clearly distinguishable on this ground. But I do not regard the distinction as material. The defendant was responsible for supervising the provision of educational services to members of the United States armed forces in the United Kingdom and their families. He published the material alleged to be defamatory in the course of his duties. If the provision of the services in question was an official or governmental act of the United States, then so was its supervision by the defendant. I would hold that he was acting as an official of the United States in the course of the performance of its sovereign function of maintaining its armed forces in this country.

Alcom Ltd v *Republic of Colombia*

[1984] AC 580, United Kingdom House of Lords

The plaintiffs had secured judgment in default against Colombia, and now sought to enforce that judgment against monies held in the Colombian Embassy's London bank account. The Colombian Ambassador had certified that the monies in the account were used for the running of the Embassy. The issue was whether the monies were 'property' used for 'commercial purposes' within s. 13 of the State Immunity Act 1978.

LORD DIPLOCK: The crucial question of construction for your Lordships is whether a debt…falls within the description contained in section 13(4) of 'property which is for the time being in use or intended for use for commercial purposes.'…What is clear beyond all question is that if the expression 'commercial purposes' in section 13(4) bore what would be its ordinary and natural meaning in the context in which it there appears, a debt representing the balance standing to the credit of a diplomatic mission in a current bank account used for meeting the day-to-day expenses of running the mission would fall outside the subsection.

'Commercial purposes,' however, is given by section 17(1) the extended meaning which takes one back to the comprehensive definition of 'commercial transaction' in section 3(3). Paragraph (a) of this tripartite definition refers to *any* contract for the supply of goods or services, without making any exception for contracts in either of these two classes that are entered into for purposes of enabling a foreign state to do things in the exercise of its sovereign authority either in the United Kingdom or elsewhere. This is to be contrasted with the other paragraph of the definition that is relevant to the instant case, paragraph (c), which on the face of it would be comprehensive enough to include all transactions into which a state might enter, were it not that it does specifically preserve immunity from adjudicative jurisdiction for transactions or activities into which a state enters or in which it engages in the exercise of sovereign authority, other than those transactions that are specifically referred to either in paragraph (a) or in paragraph (b), with the latter of which the instant appeal is not concerned....

My Lords, the decisive question for your Lordships is whether in the context of the other provisions of the Act to which I have referred, and against the background of its subject matter, public international law, the words 'property which is for the time being in use or intended for use for commercial purposes,' appearing as an exception to a general immunity to the enforcement jurisdiction of United Kingdom courts accorded by section 13(2) to the property of a foreign state, are apt to describe the debt represented by the balance standing to the credit of a current account kept with a commercial banker for the purpose of meeting the expenditure incurred in the day-to-day running of the diplomatic mission of a foreign state.

Such expenditure will, no doubt, include *some* moneys due under contracts for the supply of goods or services to the mission, to meet which the mission will draw upon its current bank account; but the account will also be drawn upon to meet many other items of expenditure which fall outside even the extended definition of 'commercial purposes' for which section 17(1) and section 3(3) provide. The debt owed by the bank to the foreign sovereign state and represented by the credit balance in the current account kept by the diplomatic mission of that state as a possible subject matter of the enforcement jurisdiction of the court is however one and indivisible; it is not susceptible of anticipatory dissection into the various uses to which moneys drawn upon it might have been put in the future if it had not been subjected to attachment by garnishee proceedings. Unless it can be shown by the judgment creditor who is seeking to attach the credit balance by garnishee proceedings that the bank account was earmarked by the foreign state solely (save for *de minimis* exceptions) for being drawn upon to settle liabilities incurred in commercial transactions, as for example by issuing documentary credits in payment of the price of goods sold to the state, it cannot, in my view, be sensibly brought within the crucial words of the exception for which section 13(4) provides.

NOTES

1. In *Littrell* v *United States of America (No 2)* [1994] 4 All ER 203, the UK Court of Appeal held that the alleged negligent medical treatment of a US serviceman by US medical personnel, on a US military base in the UK, was an act *jure imperii* because of the whole context in which it occurred. Normally, medical treatment would be regarded as an act *jure gestionis*, but see also *Arab Republic of Egypt* v *Gamal-Eldin* [1996] 2 All ER 237, where medical offices maintained by the Egyptian Embassy were found not to have a commercial purpose. This case demonstrates why neither a 'purpose' nor 'nature' test can be applied without reference to the background context. In *Kuwait Airways Corp.* v *Iraqi Airways* (see Section 2C), the House of Lords adopted Lord Wilberforce's test in *I Congreso* without dissent, finding that the retention and use of aircraft by the Iraqi Airways Corporation was not an exercise of sovereign authority but should be characterised as acts *jure gestionis*.

2. The State Immunity Act excludes from immunity two types of commercial transactions. First, a commercial transaction entered into by a foreign State and, second, an obligation of the foreign State which by virtue of a contract is to be performed wholly or partly in the UK.

C: Who may claim immunity?

As well as regulating the circumstances in which immunity may be claimed, the State Immunity Act also identifies those persons or entities who may claim such immunity as being 'the State'.

Trendtex Trading Corp v Central Bank of Nigeria
[1977] 2 WLR 356, United Kingdom Court of Appeal

The Central Bank of Nigeria was modelled on the Bank of England. It had issued a letter of credit in favour of the plaintiff, to pay for cement that was to be used to build army barracks in Nigeria. The Central Bank refused to pay for the cement or for charges incurred by delay at the port of delivery (demurrage). The Bank claimed State immunity. As well as accepting unequivocally that immunity was restrictive, Lord Denning considered whether the Bank was an organ of the State of Nigeria so as to be entitled to immunity at all.

LORD DENNING: If we are still bound to apply the doctrine of absolute immunity, there is, even so, an important question arising upon it. The doctrine grants immunity to a foreign government or its department of state, or any body which can be regarded as an 'alter ego or organ' of the government. But how are we to discover whether a body is an 'alter ego or organ' of the government?

The cases on this subject are difficult to follow, even in this country: let alone those in other countries. And yet, we have to find what is the rule of international law for all of them. It is particularly difficult because different countries have different ways of arranging internal affairs. In some countries the government departments conduct all their business through their own offices—even ordinary commercial dealings—without setting up separate corporations or legal entities. In other countries they set up separate corporations or legal entities which are under the complete control of the department, but which enter into commercial transactions, buying and selling goods, owning and chartering ships, just like any ordinary trading concern. This difference in internal arrangements ought not to affect the availability of immunity in international law. A foreign department of state ought not to lose its immunity simply because it conducts some of its activities by means of a separate legal entity....

Another problem arises because of the internal laws of many countries which grant immunities and privileges to its own organisations. Some organisations can sue, or be sued, in their courts. Others cannot. In England we have had for centuries special immunities and privileges for 'the Crown'—a phrase which has been held to cover many governmental departments and many emanations of government departments—but not nationalised commercial undertakings....It includes even the Forestry Commission....It cannot be right that international law should grant or refuse absolute immunity according to the immunities granted internally. I would put on one side, therefore, our cases about the privileges, prerogatives and exceptions of the 'Crown'.

It is often said that a certificate by the ambassador, saying whether or not an organisation is a department of state, is of much weight, though not decisive: see *Krajina* v *Tass Agency* [1949] 2 All ER 274. But even this is not to my mind satisfactory....

I confess that I can think of no satisfactory test except that of looking to the functions and control of the organisation. I do not think that it should depend on the foreign law alone. I would look to all the evidence to see whether the organisation was under government control and exercised governmental functions.

Wilhelm Finance Inc v *Ente Administrator Del Astillero Rio Santiago*

[2009] EWHC 1074 (Comm) United Kingdom High Court

The defendant applied to the Court to set aside an order permitting substituted service on the defendant. The grounds of the application were that the defendant was a State-owned entity within the definition of a State for the purposes of the State Immunity Act 1978 and service on a State was only permitted via the method prescribed in section 12 of the Act and accordingly the Court had no jurisdiction either to make the order or hear the proceedings unless and until validly served.

19. The characteristics of the Defendant as revealed by the 1993 decree which created the Defendant may be summarised as follows. It is a state owned entity responsible to the Ministry of Production (article 1). Whilst it has a board of directors the board is proposed by the Ministry of Production and nominated by the Executive Power, which appears to be a reference to the government either of Argentina or of the Province of Buenos Aires (article 4). The Ministry of Production also carries out audit and management control tasks (article 7) and the Executive Power has power to modify the Defendant's budget (article 10). The objects or purposes of the Defendant include the objects of the Transfer Agreement (managing the shipyard pending privatisation and preserving its capacity for building and repairing war ships) and the development, exploitation and marketing of the shipyard's business (article 3). It has power to act in both the public and private sectors (article 2) and to determine and carry out the commercial policy of the shipyard (article 5(a)). It has power to sign agreements with public or private entities, including international companies, and to purchase assets or services (article 5(b) and (c)) The expenses required to fulfil its objectives come from the Provincial Fund of Astillero Rio Santiago which is funded by the income earned from managing the shipyard (article 9(a)) and by contributions from the state (article 9(c)).

20. Thus, whilst the Defendant is owned and to a significant extent controlled and financed by the state, its functions and activities appear to be those of a commercial shipyard which builds and repairs ships for both the Argentine Navy (and other governmental or public bodies) and private shipowners.

21. If the 1993 Decree were the only evidence as to the nature of the Defendant one would conclude that although it is a state owned shipyard controlled and financed to a significant extent by the state it appears to be an entity which is distinct from the executive organs of the government of the state in that it carries on the business or activity of a shipyard. That business or activity is such as a privately owned company might conduct and is not typically recognised as governmental or sovereign activity. That business or activity, together with the fact that the Defendant has power to sign agreements with public and private entities, indicates that it has the capacity to sue and be sued. The 1993 Decree is thus cogent evidence that the Defendant is, within the meaning of s. 14(1) of the State of Immunity Act 1978, a separate entity and not a department of government.

22. However, the 1993 Decree is not the only evidence as to the nature of the Defendant. In 2006 an Argentine court was called upon to decide whether, in circumstances where Milantic Trans SA (a purchaser of a vessel built by the Defendant) had obtained a London arbitration award against the Defendant, that award could be enforced against the Province of Buenos Aires. It was held that it could be, notwithstanding that Counsel for the Province had argued that, having regard to the terms of the 1993 decree, the Defendant was 'an entity separate from the provincial state, that the Yard has legal capacity and its own assets (Article 9), and accordingly cannot be equated with the province'. The court held that although the Defendant was 'formally conferred with economic independence until privatisation could be effected (decree No.4583/93)….the legal reality shows that in fact the said 'independence' of [the Defendant] never materialised.'

41. I consider, on the balance of probabilities, that the Defendant has the capacity to sue and be sued:
    i) It has been sued in two cases in Argentina in recent years.
    ii) It enters into shipbuilding contracts in its own name which suggests that it is capable of being sued and being sued.
    iii) The Defendant's constitution, function, powers and activities as revealed by the 1993 decree (but omitting the quality of autarchy or economic independence which it has been held to lack notwithstanding the terms of article 1) make it probable that the Defendant has the capacity to sue and be sued;…
    iv) It is improbable that an entity which, by the 1993 decree which created it, has a domicile (article 2) and is given power to sign agreements (article 5) lacks capacity to sue and be sued.
    v) It is improbable that an entity which, in addition to contracting with government bodies such as the Argentine Navy, contracts with foreign shipowners such as the Claimant in this action and Milantic Trans SA does not have a capacity to sue and be sued.

44. The second essential quality of a separate entity mentioned in s.14 of the State Immunity Act is that it must be 'distinct from the executive organs of the government.'

45. Professor Citara refers to the Defendant as 'a governmental organ or department of the Republic of Argentina'. However, the Defendant is not described as such in the 1993 decree which created it. On the contrary it is described as a state-owned economically independent entity….

47. As I have said earlier in this judgment the functions of the Defendant do not appear to me to fall within Lord Wilberforce's description of sovereign or public acts….

48. Whilst the Defendant does work pursuant to contracts with the Argentine government which is of benefit to the Argentine government and which the government requires as a sovereign, for example, the building or repair of warships, it does not follow that the construction or repair work which the Defendant does pursuant to contract with the government is sovereign in nature or not 'distinct from the executive organs of the government of the state'. On the contrary the work of the Defendant both for the Argentine Navy and for commercial shipowners appears to me to be that which a private shipyard does.

49. It was submitted on behalf of the Defendant that the commercial nature of the specific transaction between the parties was 'completely irrelevant' because states and state entities engage in commercial activities without altering their status as sovereign entities. However, the nature of the Defendant's functions have to be examined in order to decide whether the Defendant is, within the meaning of s.14 of the State Immunity Act 1978 as explained by the English authorities to which I have referred, a department of government or an entity distinct from the executive organs of the government of the state.

50. I consider, on the balance of probabilities, that it is not a department of government and is an entity distinct from the executive organs of the government of the State, for these reasons:

   i)   The Defendant was created with the object of managing the shipyard (or more accurately the assets transferred by the national to the provincial state) until the time when the shipyard was privatised.
   ii) It determines and carries out the commercial policy of the shipyard (see article 5 of the 1993 decree).
   iii) It has power 'to act either in the public or private areas' (see article 2 of the 1993 decree) and does so.
   iv) The Defendant is, as Professor Citara accepts (see paragraph 57 of his first statement), 'an organisation aimed at the production of goods and services'.
   v)   The work the Defendant does is not work of a type associated with the executive organs of government. It is on the contrary work such as a private company might do.

51. I have not overlooked the facts that the Defendant is owned by the state, that the government nominates the board of directors, that the Chief of Cabinet of the Province of Buenos Aires was assigned the responsibilities of the President of the board, that the Defendant is responsible to the government through the Ministry of Production or that financial support is provided by the government. These factors show that the entity is 'of the state' but the English authorities to which I have referred make clear that such characteristics are insufficient to make the Defendant a department of government or an entity which is not distinct from the executive organs of government of the state in circumstances where its functions or activities are those which a private company might have in trade or commerce.

Kuwait Airways Corporation v Iraqi Airways Co.

[1995] 1 WLR 1147, United Kingdom House of Lords

Following the invasion of Kuwait by Iraq in August 1990, the Iraqi government ordered the defendants to transport the plaintiff's aircraft to Iraq. Subsequently, the ownership of the aircraft was purportedly transferred to the defendants. A key issue was whether the defendants were entitled to immunity under section 14(2) of the State Immunity Act 1978 as a 'separate entity' exercising sovereign authority in circumstances where the State itself would have been immune. A majority of the Court (3:2) held that the defendants were not immune in respect of all actions occurring after the purported transfer of ownership as such actions were not done in the exercise of sovereign authority but as 'owner'.

LORD GOFF: I turn next to the question whether I.A.C. [Iraqi Airways Co.] is entitled to claim immunity from jurisdiction on the principles embodied in section 14(2) of the State Immunity Act 1978, as a separate entity distinct from the organs of government of the State of Iraq and capable of suing and being sued....

It follows that both conditions have to be satisfied if I.A.C. is to be entitled to immunity. However, as I see it, the central question in the present case is whether the acts performed by I.A.C. to which the proceedings relate were performed in the exercise of sovereign authority, which here means acta jure imperii (in the sense in which that expression has been adopted by English law from public international law).

Section 14 of the Act, however so far as it relates to separate entities, plainly has its origin in article 27 of the [European] Convention [on State Immunity], which provides:

1. For the purposes of the present Convention, the expression 'Contracting State' shall not include any legal entity of a Contracting State which is distinct therefrom and is capable of suing or being sued, even if that entity has been entrusted with public functions.

2. Proceedings may be instituted against any entity referred to in paragraph 1 before the courts of another Contracting State in the same manner as against a private person; however, the courts may not entertain proceedings in respect of acts performed by the entity in the exercise of sovereign authority (acta jure imperii).

3. Proceedings may in any event be instituted against any such entity before those courts if, in corresponding circumstances, the courts would have had jurisdiction if the proceedings had been instituted against a Contracting State.

I interpolate that it seems probable that the expressions 'any entity' and 'separate entity' in section 14 of the Act are intended to refer to an entity or separate entity of a state, a construction which is reinforced by the description in section 14(1) of such an entity as being 'distinct from the executive organs of the government of the State,' and by the fact that section 14(1) finds it necessary to provide expressly that references to a state do not include references to such an entity. However, although the point was touched upon in argument, it does not arise directly for decision in the present case, there being no doubt that I.A.C. is a separate entity of the State of Iraq....

The two conditions imposed by section 14(2) (viz. that the proceedings must relate to something done by the separate entity in the exercise of sovereign authority, and that the circumstances must be such that a state would have been so immune) derive from paragraphs 2 and 3 of article 27 of the Convention. The question however arises whether immunity is excluded in the case of *acta jure gestionis* under the first or the second of these conditions. The puzzle arises from the fact that commercial transactions within section 3 appear to be excluded both as something not done in the exercise of sovereign authority under the first condition (i.e. not acta *jure imperii* as stated in article 27(2) of the Convention), and as a case in which (by virtue of section 3) a state would not be immune under the second condition. This tautology appears to be the effect of the introduction into section 3 of the Act of an exception relating to commercial transactions, while at the same time enacting section 14(2) in a form reflecting article 27 of a Convention which did not recognise any such exception. The logical answer would appear to be first to apply the condition in section 14(2)(*a*), which would have the effect of excluding *acta jure gestionis,* with the practical effect that questions relating to commercial transactions should not arise under section 14(2)(*b*). The latter subsection would of course still apply in other cases in which a state would not have been immune, as for example where there had been a submission to the jurisdiction within section 2. At all events, in considering whether acts done by a separate entity are or are not acts done by it in the exercise of sovereign authority under section 14(2)(*a*), it would, in my opinion, be appropriate to have regard to the English authorities relating to the distinction between *acta jure imperii* and *acta jure gestionis* as adopted from public international law, including the statement of principle by Lord Wilberforce in the *I Congreso del Partido* [1983] 1 AC 244, to which I have already referred. Such an approach is consistent with the opinion expressed by Lord Diplock in *Alcom Ltd* v *Republic of Columbia* [1984] AC 580, 600, that section 14(2) comes close to adopting the straightforward dichotomy between *acta jure imperii* and *acta jure gestionis* which had become familiar doctrine in public international law....

It is apparent from Lord Wilberforce's statement of principle that the ultimate test of what constitutes an act *jure imperii* is whether the act in question is of its own character a governmental act, as opposed to an act which any private citizen can perform. It follows that, in the case of acts done by a separate entity, it is not enough that the entity should have acted on the directions of the state, because such an act need not possess the character of a governmental act. To attract immunity under section 14(2), therefore, what is done by the separate entity must be something which possesses that character....

But where an act done by a separate entity of the state on the directions of the state does not possess the character of a governmental act, the entity will not be entitled to state immunity, though it may be able to invoke a substantive defence such as force majeure despite the fact that it is an entity of the state: see, e.g., *C. Czarnikow Ltd* v *Centrela Handlu Zagranicznego Rolimpex* [1979] AC 351. Likewise, in the absence of such character, the mere fact that the purpose or motive of the act was to serve the purposes of the state will not be sufficient to enable the separate entity to claim immunity under section 14(2) of the Act.

Jones v Ministry of Interior (the Kingdom of Saudi Arabia)
45 *International Legal Materials* 1108 (2006), United Kingdom House of Lords

This case concerned two claims. The first was brought by Mr Jones against two respondents: the Ministry of the Interior of the Kingdom of Saudi Arabia and a military officer. The second concerned four respondents: two Saudi police officers; a colonel in the Ministry of the Interior and a deputy-governor of a prison; and the Head of the Ministry of the Interior. All claimants alleged severe and systematic torture. Saudi Arabia claimed state immunity in respect of the claim against the Ministry and the military officer. The Court refused to serve the claim against the four respondents on the basis of immunity under the State Immunity Act 1978.

10. While the 1978 Act explains what is comprised within the expression 'State', and both it and the 1972 European Convention govern the immunity of separate entities exercising sovereign powers, neither expressly provides for the case where suit is brought against the servants or agents, officials or functionaries of a foreign state ('servants or agents') in respect of acts done by them as such in the foreign state. There is, however, a wealth of authority to show that in such case the foreign state is entitled to claim immunity for its servants as it could if sued itself. The foreign state's right to immunity cannot be circumvented by suing its servants or agents....

11. In some borderline cases there could be doubt whether the conduct of an individual, although a servant or agent of the state, had a sufficient connection with the state to entitle it to claim immunity for his conduct. But these are not borderline cases. Colonel Abdul Aziz is sued as a servant or agent of the Kingdom and there is no suggestion that his conduct complained of was not in discharge or purported discharge of his duties as such. The four defendants in the second action were public officials. The conduct complained of took place in police or prison premises and occurred during a prolonged process of interrogation concerning accusations of terrorism (in two cases) and spying (in the third). There is again no suggestion that the defendants' conduct was not in discharge or purported discharge of their public duties.

12. International law does not require, as a condition of a state's entitlement to claim immunity for the conduct of its servant or agent, that the latter should have been acting in accordance with his instructions or authority. A state may claim immunity for any act for which it is, in international law, responsible, save where an established exception applies.... The fact that conduct is unlawful or objectionable is not, of itself, a ground for refusing immunity.

Jones and Others v *United Kingdom*
Judgment (2014) No. 34356/06 and 40528/06, European Court of Human Rights

The facts of this case are set out above. Following the decision of the House of Lords (extracted above) that the respondents were entitled to immunity, the applicant brought proceedings against the United Kingdom in the European Court of Human Rights. The Fourth Section of the Court was called upon to consider whether the immunity granted to the state officials of Saudi Arabia for alleged acts of torture violated the applicants' right of access to a court under Article 6 of the European Convention.

202. The first question is whether the grant of immunity *ratione materiae* to State officials reflects generally recognised rules of public international law. The Court has previously accepted that the grant of immunity to the State reflects such rules. Since an act cannot be carried out by a State itself but only by individuals acting on the State's behalf, where immunity can be invoked by the State then the starting point must be that immunity *ratione materiae* applies to the acts of State officials. If it were otherwise, State immunity could always be circumvented by suing named officials. This pragmatic understanding is reflected by the definition of 'State' in the 2004 UN Convention..., which provides that the term includes representatives of the State acting in that capacity. The ILC Special Rapporteur, in his second report, said that it was 'fairly widely recognised' that immunity of State officials was 'the norm', and that the absence of immunity in a particular case would depend on establishing the existence either of a special rule or of practice and *opinio juris* indicating that exceptions to the general rule had emerged...

203. There is also extensive case-law at national and international level which concludes that acts performed by State officials in the course of their service are to be attributed, for the purposes of State immunity, to the State on whose behalf they act. Thus in *Propend*, the English Court of Appeal held that immunities conferred on the State pursuant to the 1978 Act must be read as affording to individual State officials 'protection under the same cloak as protects the State itself'...In Canada, the Court of Appeal in *Jaffe* concluded that the notion of 'State' in the SIA covered employees of the State acting in the course of their duties...In *Fang*, the High Court in New Zealand held that State immunity incidentally conferred immunity *ratione materiae* in claims against individuals whose conduct in the exercise of the authority of the State was called into question...In *Zhang*, an Australian Court of Appeal held that individual officers were covered by the Immunities Act since they were entitled to immunity at common law and this had not been changed by the Act...Although the United States Supreme Court in *Samantar* held that officials did not fall under the notion of 'State' within the meaning of the FSIA, it clarified that their immunities were governed by common law, as the statute was deemed to be only a partial codification of immunity rules in the United States...The Court of Appeal (Fourth Circuit) subsequently accepted that, in principle, State officials could enjoy immunity for acts performed in the course of their employment by the State...In *Blaškić*, the ICTY described State officials acting in their official capacity as 'mere instruments of a State' and explained that they enjoyed 'functional immunity'... In *Djibouti v. France*, the ICJ referred to the possibility open to the Djibouti government to claim that the acts of two State officials were its own acts, and that the officials were its organs, agencies or instrumentalities in carrying them out...

204. The weight of authority at international and national level therefore appears to support the proposition that State immunity in principle offers individual employees or officers of a foreign State protection in respect of acts undertaken on behalf of the State under the same cloak as protects the State itself.

NOTES

1. As well as difficult questions about exactly what organ is 'the State' for the purposes of claiming immunity, the above cases demonstrate that even 'separate entities' may be entitled to immunity if (a) they exercise sovereign authority and (b) the State would have been immune in the circumstances of the case. Technically, the question of whether the entity claiming immunity is 'separate' is logically prior to whether it was exercising sovereign authority: that is, the exercise or non-exercise of sovereign authority should not determine whether it is 'separate' or not. In this sense, 'sovereign authority' appears to be used to describe the purpose/nature of the particular action undertaken by an entity that the court has already decided is 'separate'. However, as the *Kuwait Case* shows, it is easy to conflate the issues.

2. The State Immunity Act does not accord immunity as a State to constitutional units within a federal State. Such units may be considered separate entities under section 14(2) of the State Immunity Act. However, as was seen in *Pocket Kings Ltd* v *Safenames Ltd* ([2009] EWHC 2529 (Ch)), it may be difficult for the constituent entity to demonstrate that it is exercising the authority of the sovereign State. The fact that the entity exercises public functions is not, of itself, sufficient to attract immunity. This requirement for the entity to be acting in the exercise of sovereign authority is also reflected in Article 2 of the UN Convention on Jurisdictional Immunities of States and their Property.

3. Central banks of a State are given special consideration under the State Immunity Act. A central bank may be a government department or a separate entity. If it is a separate entity, it will only be immune in relation to proceedings arising from the exercise by the bank of sovereign authority and in circumstances where the State itself would be immune. As is shown in the extract from *Alcom*, the Act also gives special protection to the central banks regarding enforcement procedures: see also *AIG Capital Partners Inc* v *Kazakhstan* [2005] EWHC 2239 (Comm), where the Court held that the property of a central bank is not subject to attachment, regardless as to the purpose for which the property was used or intended to be used.

4. The two extracts from *Jones* above suggest that State officials are entitled to plead State immunity, even when not acting directly on instructions. The issue is then whether there is an exception from such immunity where the conduct of the official is an international crime or otherwise contrary to international law (see Sections 3 and 4). However, note that the US Supreme Court has found that the US Foreign State Immunity Act, which provides that a 'foreign state shall be immune from the jurisdiction', does not extend to individual State officials: *Samartar* v *Yousef et al*, 130 S. Ct. 2278 (2010). In contrast, the Canadian Court of Canada held (by majority), that the Canadian State Immunity Act extends to public officials, but only in respect of official acts, which included the torture of the applicant's mother: *Kazemi* v *Islamic Republic Iran* [2014] 3 S.C.R. 176.

SECTION 3: HEADS OF STATE AND OTHER HOLDERS OF HIGH-RANKING OFFICE

R v *Bow Street Metropolitan Stipendiary Magistrate and others, ex parte Pinochet Ugarte (Amnesty International and others intervening) (No 3)*

[1999] 2 All ER 97, United Kingdom House of Lords

Senator Pinochet, the ex-Head of State of Chile, had been detained in London pending an extradition request from Spain. It was alleged that he had authorised acts of torture while in office against, *inter alia*, Spanish nationals. Senator Pinochet claimed immunity as an ex-Head of State. One issue was whether he could be immune in respect of acts that might be regarded as crimes of universal jurisdiction under customary international law and that, in any event, attracted universal jurisdiction under the Torture Convention (see Chapter 8). The House of Lords held (Lord Goff dissenting) that there could be no immunity.

LORD BROWNE-WILKINSON: This is the point around which most of the argument turned. It is of considerable general importance internationally since, if Senator Pinochet is not entitled to immunity in relation to the acts of torture alleged to have occurred after 29 September 1988 it will be the first time, so far as counsel have discovered, when a local domestic court has refused to afford immunity to a Head of State or former Head of State on the grounds that there can be no immunity against prosecution for certain international crimes.

Given the importance of the point, it is surprising how narrow is the area of dispute. There is general agreement between the parties as to the rules of statutory immunity and the rationale which underlies them. The issue is whether international law grants State immunity in relation to the international crime of torture and, if so, whether the Republic of Chile is entitled to claim such immunity even though Chile, Spain and the United Kingdom are all parties to the Torture Convention and therefore 'contractually' bound to give effect to its provisions from 8 December 1988 at the latest.

It is a basic principle of international law that one sovereign State (the forum state) does not adjudicate on the conduct of a foreign State. The foreign state is entitled to procedural immunity from the processes of the forum State. This immunity extends to both criminal and civil liability. State immunity probably grew from the historical immunity of the person of the monarch. In any event, such personal immunity of the Head of State persists to the present day: the Head of State is entitled to the same immunity as the State itself. The diplomatic representative of the foreign State in the forum State is also afforded the same immunity in recognition of the dignity of the State which he represents. This immunity enjoyed by a Head of State in power and an ambassador in post is a complete immunity attaching to the person of the Head of State or ambassador and rendering him immune from all actions or prosecutions whether or not they relate to matters done for the benefit of the State. Such immunity is said to be granted *ratione personae*.

What then when the ambassador leaves his post or the Head of State is deposed?…The continuing partial immunity of the ambassador after leaving post is of a different kind from that enjoyed *ratione personae* while he was in post. Since he is no longer the representative of the foreign State he merits no particular privileges or immunities as a person. However in order to preserve the integrity of the activities of the foreign State during the period when he was ambassador, it is necessary to provide that immunity is afforded to his *official* acts during his tenure in post. If this were not done the sovereign immunity of the state could be evaded by calling in question acts done during the previous ambassador's time. Accordingly under Art. 39(2) the ambassador, like any other official of the state, enjoys immunity in relation to his official acts done while he was an official. This limited immunity, *ratione materiae*, is to be contrasted with the former immunity *ratione personae* which gave complete immunity to all activities whether public or private.

In my judgment at common law a former Head of State enjoys similar immunities, *ratione materiae*, once he ceases to be Head of State. He too loses immunity *ratione personae* on ceasing to be Head of State…As ex-Head of State he cannot be sued in respect of acts performed whilst Head of State in his public capacity: *Hatch v Baez* (1876) 7 Hun 596. Thus, at common law, the position of the former ambassador and the former Head of State appears to be much the same: both enjoy immunity for acts done in performance of their respective functions whilst in office.

The question then which has to be answered is whether the alleged organisation of State torture by Senator Pinochet (if proved) would constitute an act committed by Senator Pinochet as part of his official functions as Head of State. It is not enough to say that it cannot be part of the functions of the head of state to commit a crime. Actions which are criminal under the local law can still have been done officially and therefore give rise to immunity *ratione materiae*. The case needs to be analysed more closely.

Can it be said that the commission of a crime which is an international crime against humanity and *jus cogens* is an act done in an official capacity on behalf of the State? I believe there to be strong ground for saying that the implementation of torture as defined by the Torture Convention cannot be a State function.…

I have doubts whether, before the coming into force of the Torture Convention, the existence of the international crime of torture as *jus cogens* was enough to justify the conclusion that the organisation of state torture could not rank for immunity purposes as performance of an official function. At that stage there was no international tribunal to punish torture and no general jurisdiction to permit or require its punishment in domestic courts. Not until there was some form of universal jurisdiction for the punishment of the crime of torture could it really be talked about as a fully constituted international crime. But in my judgment the Torture Convention did provide what was missing: a worldwide universal jurisdiction. Further, it required all member states to ban and outlaw torture: Art 2. How can it be for international law purposes an official function to do something which international law itself prohibits and criminalises? Thirdly, an essential feature of the international crime of torture is that it must be committed 'by or with the acquiescence of a public official or other person acting in an official capacity.' As a result all defendants in torture cases will be state officials. Yet, if the former Head of State has immunity, the man most responsible will escape liability while his inferiors (the chiefs of police, junior army officers) who carried out his orders will be liable. I find it impossible to accept that this was the intention.

Finally, and to my mind decisively, if the implementation of a torture regime is a public function giving rise to immunity *ratione materiae*, this produces bizarre results. Immunity *ratione materiae* applies not only to ex-Heads of State and ex-ambassadors but to all State officials who have been involved in carrying out the functions of the State. Such immunity is necessary in order to prevent State immunity being circumvented by prosecuting or suing the official who, for example, actually carried out the torture when a claim against the Head of State would be precluded by the doctrine of immunity. If that applied to the present case, and if the implementation of the torture regime is to be treated as official business sufficient to found an immunity for the former Head of State, it must also be official business sufficient to justify immunity for his inferiors who actually did the torturing. Under the Convention the international crime of torture can only be committed by an official or someone in an official capacity. They would all be entitled to immunity. It would follow that there can be no case outside Chile in which a successful prosecution for torture can be brought unless the state of Chile is prepared to waive its right to its officials' immunity. Therefore the whole elaborate structure of universal jurisdiction over torture committed by officials is rendered abortive and one of the main objectives of the Torture Convention—to provide a system under which there is no safe haven for torturers—will have been frustrated. In my judgment all these factors together demonstrate that the notion of continued immunity for ex-Heads of State is inconsistent with the provisions of the Torture Convention.

For these reasons in my judgment if, as alleged, Senator Pinochet organised and authorised torture after 8 December 1988 he was not acting in any capacity which gives rise to immunity *ratione materiae* because such actions were contrary to international law, Chile had agreed to outlaw such conduct and Chile had agreed with the other parties to the Torture Convention that all signatory states should have jurisdiction to try official torture (as defined in the Convention) even if such torture were committed in Chile.

LORD MILLET: Two overlapping immunities are recognised by international law: immunity *ratione personae* and immunity *ratione materiae*. They are quite different and have different rationales.

Immunity *ratione personae* is a status immunity. An individual who enjoys its protection does so because of his official status. It ensures for his benefit only so long as he holds office. While he does so he enjoys absolute immunity from the civil and criminal jurisdiction of the national courts of foreign states. But it is only narrowly available. It is confined to serving Heads of State and heads of diplomatic missions, their families and servants. It is not available to serving heads of government who are not also Heads of State, military commanders and those in charge of the security forces, or their subordinates. It would have been available to Hitler but not to Mussolini or Tojo.

The immunity of a serving Head of State is enjoyed by reason of his special status as the holder of his State's highest office. He is regarded as the personal embodiment of the State itself. It would be an affront to the dignity and sovereignty of the State which he personifies and a denial of the equality of sovereign States to subject him to the jurisdiction of the municipal courts of another State, whether in respect of his public acts or private affairs. His person is inviolable; he is not liable to be arrested or detained on any ground whatever. The head of a diplomatic mission represents his Head of State and thus embodies the sending state in the territory of the receiving state. While he remains in office he is entitled to the same absolute immunity as his Head of State, in relation both to his public and private acts.

This immunity is not in issue in the present case. Senator Pinochet is not a serving Head of State. If he were, he could not be extradited. It would be an intolerable affront to the Republic of Chile to arrest him or detain him.

Immunity *ratione materiae* is very different. This is a subject matter immunity. It operates to prevent the official and governmental acts of one state from being called into question in proceedings before the courts of another, and only incidentally confers immunity on the individual. It is therefore a narrower immunity but it is more widely available. It is available to former Heads of State and heads of diplomatic missions, and any one whose conduct in the exercise of the authority of the State is afterwards called into question, whether he acted as head of government, government minister, military commander or chief of police, or subordinate public official. The immunity is the same whatever the rank of the office holder. This too is common ground. It is an immunity from the civil and criminal jurisdiction of foreign national courts, but only in respect of governmental or official acts. The exercise of authority by the military and security forces of the State is the paradigm example of such conduct. The immunity finds its rationale in the equality of sovereign States and the doctrine of non-interference in the internal affairs of other States…The immunity is sometimes also justified by the need to prevent the serving Head of State, or diplomat, from being inhibited in the performance of his official duties by fear of the consequences after he has ceased to hold office. This last basis can hardly be prayed in aid to support the availability of the immunity in respect of criminal activities prohibited by international law.

Case Concerning the Arrest Warrant of 11 April 2000 (Democratic Republic of the Congo v Belgium)

ICJ Rep 2002 3, International Court of Justice

A Belgian investigating judge had issued an international arrest warrant against the serving Congolese Minister of Foreign Affairs. The warrant was in respect of alleged serious violations of international humanitarian law, including crimes against humanity. The government of the Democratic Republic of the Congo (DRC) claimed that this constituted a violation of its sovereignty and a contravention of the sovereign equality of States. An essential issue was whether the Minister was entitled to immunity from the Belgian criminal process while a serving Minister, even though the alleged crimes would, if proven, amount to serious breaches of international law. The Court found in favour of the DRC.

53. In customary international law, the immunities accorded to Ministers for Foreign Affairs are not granted for their personal benefit, but to ensure the effective performance of their functions on behalf of their respective States. In order to determine the extent of these immunities, the Court must therefore first consider the nature of the functions exercised by a Minister for Foreign Affairs. The Court further observes that a Minister for Foreign Affairs, responsible for the conduct of his or her State's relations with all other States, occupies a position such that, like the Head of State or the Head of Government, he or she is recognized under international law as representative of the State solely by virtue of his or her office....

54. The Court accordingly concludes that the functions of a Minister for Foreign Affairs are such that, throughout the duration of his or her office, he or she when abroad enjoys full immunity from criminal jurisdiction and inviolability. That immunity and that inviolability protect the individual concerned against any act of authority of another State which would hinder him or her in the performance of his or her duties.

55. In this respect, no distinction can be drawn between acts performed by a Minister for Foreign Affairs in an 'official' capacity, and those claimed to have been performed in a 'private capacity', or, for that matter, between acts performed before the person concerned assumed office as Minister for Foreign Affairs and acts committed during the period of office. Thus, if a Minister for Foreign Affairs is arrested in another State on a criminal charge, he or she is clearly thereby prevented from exercising the functions of his or her office. The consequences of such impediment to the exercise of those official functions are equally serious, regardless of whether the Minister for Foreign Affairs was, at the time of arrest, present in the territory of the arresting State on an 'official' visit or a 'private' visit, regardless of whether the arrest relates to acts allegedly performed before the person became the Minister for Foreign Affairs or to acts performed while in office, and regardless of whether the arrest relates to alleged acts performed in an 'official' capacity or a 'private' capacity. Furthermore, even the mere risk that, by travelling to or transiting another State a Minister for Foreign Affairs might be exposing himself or herself to legal proceedings could deter the Minister from travelling internationally when required to do so for the purposes of the performance of his or her official functions.

56. The Court will now address Belgium's argument that immunities accorded to incumbent Ministers for Foreign Affairs can in no case protect them where they are suspected of having committed war crimes or crimes against humanity....

58. The Court has carefully examined State practice, including national legislation and those few decisions of national higher courts, such as the House of Lords or the French Court of Cassation. It has been unable to deduce from this practice that there exists under customary international law any form of exception to the rule according immunity from criminal jurisdiction and inviolability to incumbent Ministers for Foreign Affairs, where they are suspected of having committed war crimes or crimes against humanity.

The Court has also examined the rules concerning the immunity or criminal responsibility of persons having an official capacity contained in the legal instruments creating international criminal tribunals. It finds that these rules likewise do not enable it to conclude that any such an exception exists in customary international law in regard to national courts.

In view of the foregoing, the Court accordingly cannot accept Belgium's argument in this regard.

59. It should further be noted that the rules governing the jurisdiction of national courts must be carefully distinguished from those governing jurisdictional immunities: jurisdiction does not imply absence of immunity,

while absence of immunity does not imply jurisdiction. Thus, although various international conventions on the prevention and punishment of certain serious crimes impose on States obligations of prosecution or extradition, thereby requiring them to extend their criminal jurisdiction, such extension of jurisdiction in no way affects immunities under customary international law, including those of Ministers for Foreign Affairs. These remain opposable before the courts of a foreign State, even where those courts exercise such a jurisdiction under these conventions.

60. The Court emphasizes, however, that the *immunity* from jurisdiction enjoyed by incumbent Ministers for Foreign Affairs does not mean that they enjoy *impunity* in respect of any crimes they might have committed, irrespective of their gravity. Immunity from criminal jurisdiction and individual criminal responsibility are quite separate concepts. While jurisdictional immunity is procedural in nature, criminal responsibility is a question of substantive law. Jurisdictional immunity may well bar prosecution for a certain period or for certain offences; it cannot exonerate the person to whom it applies from all criminal responsibility

61. Accordingly, the immunities enjoyed under international law by an incumbent or former Minister for Foreign Affairs do not represent a bar to criminal prosecution in certain circumstances.

First, such persons enjoy no criminal immunity under international law in their own countries, and may thus be tried by those countries' courts in accordance with the relevant rules of domestic law.

Secondly, they will cease to enjoy immunity from foreign jurisdiction if the State which they represent or have represented decides to waive that immunity.

Thirdly, after a person ceases to hold the office of Minister for Foreign Affairs, he or she will no longer enjoy all of the immunities accorded by international law in other States. Provided that it has jurisdiction under international law, a court of one State may try a former Minister for Foreign Affairs of another State in respect of acts committed prior or subsequent to his or her period of office, as well as in respect of acts committed during that period of office in a private capacity. Fourthly, an incumbent or former Minister for Foreign Affairs may be subject to criminal proceedings before certain international criminal courts, where they have jurisdiction.

NOTES

1. The *Pinochet Case* (above) held that the immunity of a former Head of State exists in respect of acts done while he or she was in office if those acts were 'official', a view endorsed in a similar context in the *Arrest Warrant Case* (*Congo* v *Belgium*) (above). Lord Goff dissented on the ground that there is no rule of international law denying immunity in cases of torture (see further Section 4).

2. The *Arrest Warrant Case* concerned a foreign minister. While clearly immunity *ratione personae* extends to Heads of State and Heads of Government, the ICJ did not specify which other senior officials would be entitled to such immunity. It is the functions of the official in each case that will determine whether immunity should be accorded. A UK court has held that a defence minister is also entitled to immunity, as States may maintain troops overseas and defence ministers may be called on to attend meetings at which military issues will play a role (see Warbrick, 'Immunity and International Crimes in UK Law' (2004) 53 *ICLQ* 769).

3. In the UK, a Head of State either amounts to 'the State' itself for the purpose of attracting immunity when he or she is acting in a public capacity (section 14(1)(a) of the State Immunity Act 1978) or enjoys immunity equivalent to a Head of Diplomatic Mission (section 20(1) of the State Immunity Act 1978) (see also cases below). Necessarily, there is some overlap. Thus, a serving Head of State has, virtually, absolute immunity while in office.

4. In *Case Concerning Certain Questions of Mutual Criminal Assistance in Criminal Matters (Djibouti* v *France)*, 4 June 2008, the ICJ confirmed that immunity also extends to immunity from process. However, the Court suggested that not all legal process concerning a Head of State will violate the immunity accorded either under customary international law or Article 29 of the Vienna Convention on Diplomatic Relations (see Section 6), particularly where there is no obligation on the Head of State to comply with the request. In that case, a French investigating judge had issued a summons to the President of Djibouti, inviting the President to give evidence in connection with a murder investigation.

5. As the immunity accords to the State, and not the individual, the State concerned may waive the immunity, as noted by the ICJ in the *Arrest Warrant Case*.

By its very nature, a successful plea of immunity removes the State or an individual from the jurisdiction of a national court. While this may generate outrage in that State, it is a generally accepted consequence of the need to preserve the sovereign equality of States on a practical as well as a theoretical level. However, what is the position where the State or individual claiming immunity is alleged to have committed an act that is itself contrary to international law, such as a gross violation of human rights? In such cases, there is a tension between those rules of international law requiring immunity to be given and those rules of international law generally regarded as of central importance to the international legal order and for violation of which an individual may be held personally responsible in addition to engaging the responsibility of the State. For example, can a Head of State or an Ambassador claim immunity from the jurisdiction of another State's courts in respect of alleged war crimes, or torture, or crimes against humanity or genocide?

Jones v Ministry of Interior (the Kingdom of Saudi Arabia)

(2006) UKHL 26, United Kingdom House of Lords

The facts are set out above.

14....The claimants must show that the restriction is not directed to a legitimate objective and is disproportionate. They seek to do so by submitting that the grant of immunity to the Kingdom on behalf of itself or its servants would be inconsistent with a peremptory norm of international law, a *jus cogens* applicable *erga omnes* and superior in effect to other rules of international law, which requires that the practice of torture should be suppressed and the victims of torture compensated....

17. The claimants' key submission is that the proscription of torture by international law, having the authority it does, precludes the grant of immunity to states or individuals sued for committing acts of torture, since such cannot be governmental acts or exercises of state authority entitled to the protection of state immunity *ratione materiae*. In support of this submission the claimants rely on a wide range of materials including: the reasoning of the minority of the Grand Chamber in *Al-Adsani v United Kingdom* (2001) 34 EHRR 273; observations by members of the House in *R v Bow Street Metropolitan Stipendiary Magistrate, Ex p Pinochet Ugarte (No 1)* [2000] 1 AC 61 and *(No 3)* [2000] 1 AC 147 (hereinafter *Pinochet (No 1)* and *Pinochet (No 3)*); a body of United States authority; the decision of the International Criminal Tribunal for the former Yugoslavia in *Prosecutor v Furundzija* (1998) 38 ILM 317; the decision of the Italian Court of Cassation in *Ferrini v Federal Republic of Germany* (2004) Cass sez un 5044/04; 87 Rivista di diritto internazionale 539; and a recommendation made by the Committee against Torture to Canada on 7 July 2005. These are interesting and valuable materials, but on examination they give the claimants less support than at first appears.

18. The Grand Chamber's decision in *Al-Adsani* is very much in point, since it concerned the grant of immunity to Kuwait under the 1978 Act, which had the effect of defeating the applicant's claim in England for damages for torture allegedly inflicted upon him in Kuwait. The claimants are entitled to point out that a powerful minority of the court found a violation of the applicant's right of access to a court under article 6 of the European Convention. The majority, however, held that the grant of sovereign immunity to a state in civil proceedings pursued the legitimate aim of complying with international law to promote comity and good relations between states through the respect of another state's sovereignty (para 54); that the European Convention on Human Rights should so far as possible be interpreted in harmony with other rules of international law of which it formed part, including those relating to the grant of state immunity (para 55); and that some restrictions on the right of access to a court must be regarded as inherent, including those limitations generally accepted by the community of nations as part of the doctrine of state immunity (para 56). The majority were unable to discern in the international instruments, judicial authorities or other materials before the court any firm basis for concluding that, as a matter

of international law, a state no longer enjoyed immunity from civil suit in the courts of another state where acts of torture were alleged (para 61). While noting the growing recognition of the overriding importance of the prohibition of torture, the majority did not find it established that there was yet acceptance in international law of the proposition that states were not entitled to immunity in respect of civil claims for damages for alleged torture committed outside the forum state (para 66). It is of course true, as the claimants contend, that under section 2 of the 1998 Act this decision of the Strasbourg court is not binding on the English court. But it was affirmed in *Kalogeropoulou v Greece and Germany* (App No 50021/00) (unreported) 12 December 2002, when the applicant's complaint against Greece was held to be inadmissible, and the House would ordinarily follow such a decision unless it found the court's reasoning to be unclear or unsound, or the law had changed significantly since the date of the decision. None of these conditions, in my opinion, obtains here.

19. It is certainly true that in *Pinochet (No 1)* and *Pinochet (No 3)* certain members of the House held that acts of torture could not be functions of a head of state or governmental or official acts. I have some doubt about the value of the judgments in *Pinochet (No 1)* as precedent, save to the extent that they were adopted in *Pinochet (No 3)*, since the earlier judgment was set aside, but references may readily be found in *Pinochet (No 3)*: see, for example, p 205 (Lord Browne-Wilkinson, pp 261–262 (Lord Hutton). I would not question the correctness of the decision reached by the majority in *Pinochet (No 3)*. But the case was categorically different from the present, since it concerned criminal proceedings falling squarely within the universal criminal jurisdiction mandated by the Torture Convention and did not fall within Part 1 of the 1978 Act....

24. In countering the claimants' argument the Kingdom, supported by the Secretary of State, is able to advance four arguments which in my opinion are cumulatively irresistible. First, the claimants are obliged to accept, in the light of the *Arrest Warrant* decision of the International Court of Justice [2002] ICJ Rep 3 that state immunity *ratione personae* can be claimed for a serving foreign minister accused of crimes against humanity. Thus, even in such a context, the international law prohibition of such crimes, having the same standing as the prohibition of torture, does not prevail. It follows that such a prohibition does not automatically override all other rules of international law. The International Court of Justice has made plain that breach of a *jus cogens* norm of international law does not suffice to confer jurisdiction (*Democratic Republic of the Congo v Rwanda* (unreported) 3 February 2006, para 64). As Hazel Fox QC put it (*The Law of State Immunity* (2004), p 525),

'State immunity is a procedural rule going to the jurisdiction of a national court. It does not go to substantive law; it does not contradict a prohibition contained in a *jus cogens* norm but merely diverts any breach of it to a different method of settlement. Arguably, then, there is no substantive content in the procedural plea of State immunity upon which a *jus cogens* mandate can bite.'

Where state immunity is applicable, the national court has no jurisdiction to exercise.

25. Secondly, article 14 of the Torture Convention does not provide for universal civil jurisdiction. It appears that at one stage of the negotiating process the draft contained words, which mysteriously disappeared from the text, making this clear. But the natural reading of the article as it stands in my view conforms with the US understanding noted above, that it requires a private right of action for damages only for acts of torture committed in territory under the jurisdiction of the forum state. This is an interpretation shared by Canada, as its exchanges with the Torture Committee make clear. The correctness of this reading is confirmed when comparison is made between the spare terms of article 14 and the much more detailed provisions governing the assumption and exercise of criminal jurisdiction.

26. Thirdly, the UN Immunity Convention of 2004 provides no exception from immunity where civil claims are made based on acts of torture. The Working Group in its 1999 Report makes plain that such an exception was considered, but no such exception was agreed. Despite its embryonic status, this Convention is the most authoritative statement available on the current international understanding of the limits of state immunity in civil cases, and the absence of a torture or jus cogens exception is wholly inimical to the claimants' contention.... Other commentators have criticised the Convention, and opposed ratification, precisely because (in the absence of an additional protocol, which they favour) the Convention does not deny state immunity in cases where jus cogens norms of international are said to have been violated outside the forum state... But these commentators accept that this area of international law is 'in a state of flux', and they do not suggest that there is an international consensus in favour of the exception they would seek. It may very well be that the claimants' contention will come to represent the law of nations, but it cannot be said to do so now.

27. Fourthly, there is no evidence that states have recognised or given effect to an international law obligation to exercise universal jurisdiction over claims arising from alleged breaches of peremptory norms of international law, nor is there any consensus of judicial and learned opinion that they should. This is significant, since these are

sources of international law. But this lack of evidence is not neutral: since the rule on immunity is well-understood and established, and no relevant exception is generally accepted, the rule prevails.

28. It follows, in my opinion, that Part 1 of the 1978 Act is not shown to be disproportionate as inconsistent with a peremptory norm of international law, and its application does not infringe the claimants' Convention right under article 6 (assuming it to apply). It is unnecessary to consider any question of remedies.

Jones and Others v *United Kingdom*
Judgment (2014) No. 34356/06 and 40528/06, European Court of Human Rights

The facts are set out in Section 2C.

213. Having regard to the foregoing, while there is in the Court's view some emerging support in favour of a special rule or exception in public international law in cases concerning civil claims for torture lodged against foreign state officials, the bulk of authority is, as Lord Bingham put it in the House of Lords in the present case, to the effect that the State's right to immunity may not be circumvented by suing its servants or agents instead. Taking the applicants' arguments at their strongest, there is evidence of recent debate surrounding the understanding of the definition of torture in the Convention against Torture; the interaction between State immunity and the rules on attribution in the Draft Articles on State Responsibility; and the scope of Article 14 of the Convention against Torture…However, State practice on the question is in a state of flux, with evidence of both the grant and the refusal of immunity *ratione materiae* in such cases. At least two cases on the question are pending before national Supreme Courts: one in the United States and the other in Canada…International opinion on the question may be said to be beginning to evolve, as demonstrated recently by the discussions around the word of the International Law Commission in the criminal sphere. This work is ongoing and further developments can be expected.

Jurisdictional Immunities of the State (Germany v Italy; Greece intervening)
ICJ Rep (2012) International Court of Justice

Germany brought proceedings against Italy for allowing civil claims to be brought against the State of Germany before Italian courts. The claims concerned reparations relating to injuries caused by violations of international humanitarian law by the German State and its armed forces during World War Two. Germany alleged that Italy had failed to respect its immunity from jurisdiction. A key question for the Court was whether or not the nature of the actions of the German armed forces and other organs of the German State during World War Two operated to deprive Germany of its entitlement to immunity.

83. [T]he Court must nevertheless inquire whether customary international law has developed to the point where a State is not entitled to immunity in the case of serious violations of human rights law or the law of armed conflict. Apart from the decisions of the Italian courts which are the subject of the present proceedings, there is almost no State practice which might be considered to support the proposition that a State is deprived of its entitlement to immunity in such a case. Although the Hellenic Supreme Court in the *Distomo* case adopted a form of that proposition, the Special Supreme Court in *Margellos* repudiated that approach two years later. As the Court has noted in paragraph 76 above, under Greek law it is the stance adopted in *Margellos* which must be followed in later cases unless the Greek courts find that there has been a change in customary international law since 2002, which they have not done. As with the territorial tort principle, the Court considers that Greek practice, taken as a whole, tends to deny that the proposition advanced by Italy has become part of customary international law.

84. In addition, there is a substantial body of State practice from other countries which demonstrates that customary international law does not treat a State's entitlement to immunity as dependent upon the gravity of the act of which it is accused or the peremptory nature of the rule which it is alleged to have violated.

85. That practice is particularly evident in the judgments of national courts. Arguments to the effect that international law no longer required State immunity in cases of allegations of serious violations of international

human rights law, war crimes or crimes against humanity have been rejected by the courts in Canada (*Bouzari v. Islamic Republic of Iran*, Court of Appeal of Ontario, [2004] Dominion Law Reports (DLR) , 4th Series, Vol. 243, p. 406; ILR , Vol. 128, p. 586; allegations of torture), France (judgment of the Court of Appeal of Paris, 9 September 2002, and Cour de cassation, No. 02-45961, 16 December 2003, Bulletin civil de la Cour de cassation (Bull. civ.), 2003, I, No. 258, p. 206 (the Bucheron case); Cour de cassation, No. 03-41851, 2 June 2004, Bull. civ., 2004, I, No. 158, p. 132 (the X case) and Cour de cassation, No. 04-47504, 3 January 2006 (the Grosz case); allegations of crimes against humanity), Slovenia (case No. Up-13/99, Constitutional Court of Slovenia; allegations of war crimes and crimes against humanity), New Zealand (Fang v. Jiang , High Court, [2007] New Zealand Administrative Reports (NZAR) , p. 420; ILR , Vol. 141, p. 702; allegations of torture), Poland (Natoniewski , Supreme Court, 2010, Polish Yearbook of International Law , Vol. XXX, 2010, p. 299; allegations of war crimes and crimes against humanity) and the United Kingdom (Jones v. Saudi Arabia , House of Lords, [2007]1 Appeal Cases (AC) 270 ; ILR , Vol. 129, p. 629; allegations of torture).

86. The Court notes that, in its response to a question posed by a Member of the Court, Italy itself appeared to demonstrate uncertainty about this aspect of its case. Italy commented, 'Italy is aware of the view according to which war crimes and crimes against humanity could not be considered to be sovereign acts for which the State is entitled to invoke the defence of sovereign immunity…While Italy acknowledges that in this area the law of State immunity is undergoing a process of change, it also recognizes that it is not clear at this stage whether this process will result in a new general exception to immunity—namely a rule denying immunity with respect to every claim for compensation arising out [of] international crimes'. A similar uncertainty is evident in the orders of the Italian Court of Cassation in *Mantelli* and *Maietta* (orders of 29 May 2008).

87. The Court does not consider that the United Kingdom judgment in *Pinochet (No. 3)* ([2000] 1 AC 147; ILR , Vol. 119, p. 136) is relevant, notwithstanding the reliance placed on that judgment by the Italian Court of Cassation in *Ferrini*. *Pinochet* concerned the immunity of a former Head of State from the criminal jurisdiction of another State, not the immunity of the State itself in proceedings designed to establish its liability to damages. The distinction between the immunity of the official in the former type of case and that of the State in the latter case was emphasized by several of the judges in *Pinochet* (Lord Hutton at pp. 254 and 264, Lord Millett at p. 278 and Lord Phillips at pp. 280–281). In its later judgment in *Jones v. Saudi Arabia* ([2007] 1 AC 270; ILR, Vol. 129, p. 629), the House of Lords further clarified this distinction, Lord Bingham describing the distinction between criminal and civil proceedings as 'fundamental to the decision' in *Pinochet* (para. 32). Moreover, the rationale or the judgment in *Pinochet* was based upon the specific language of the 1984 United Nations Convention against Torture, which has no bearing on the present case.

88. With reference to national legislation, Italy referred to an amendment to the United States Foreign Sovereign Immunities Act, first adopted in 1996. That amendment withdraws immunity for certain specified acts (for example, torture and extra-judicial killings) if allegedly performed by a State which the United States Government has 'designated as a State sponsor of terrorism' (28 USC 1605A). The Court notes that this amendment has no counterpart in the legislation of other States. None of the States which has enacted legislation on the subject of State immunity has made provision for the limitation of immunity on the grounds of the gravity of the acts alleged.

89. It is also noticeable that there is no limitation of State immunity by reference to the gravity of the violation or the peremptory character of the rule breached in the European Convention, the United Nations Convention or the draft Inter-American Convention. The absence of any such provision from the United Nations Convention is particularly significant, because the question whether such a provision was necessary was raised at the time that the text of what became the Convention was under consideration. In 1999 the International Law Commission established a Working Group which considered certain developments in practice regarding some issues of State immunity which had been identified by the Sixth Committee of the General Assembly. In an appendix to its report, the Working Group referred, as an additional matter, to developments regarding claims 'in the case of death or personal injury resulting from acts of a State in violation of human rights norms having the character of jus cogens' and stated that this issue was one which should not be ignored, although it did not recommend any amendment to the text of the International Law Commission Articles (Yearbook of the International Law Commission, 1999, Vol. II (2), pp. 171–172). The matter was then considered by the Working Group established by the Sixth Committee of the General Assembly, which reported later in 1999 that it had decided not to take up the matter as 'it did not seem to be ripe enough for the Working Group to engage in a codification exercise over it' and commented that it was for the Sixth Committee to decide what course of action, if any, should be taken (United Nations doc. A/C.6/54/L.12, p. 7, para. 13). During the subsequent debates in the Sixth Committee no State suggested that a *jus cogens* limitation to immunity should be included in the Convention. The Court considers

that this history indicates that, at the time of adoption of the United Nations Convention in 2004, States did not consider that customary international law limited immunity in the manner now suggested by Italy.

90. The European Court of Human Rights has not accepted the proposition that States are no longer entitled to immunity in cases regarding serious violations of international humanitarian law or human rights law. In 2001, the Grand Chamber of that Court, by the admittedly narrow majority of nine to eight, concluded that,

'Notwithstanding the special character of the prohibition of torture in international law, the Court is unable to discern in the international instruments, judicial authorities or other materials before it any firm basis for concluding that, as a matter of international law, a State no longer enjoys immunity from civil suit in the courts of another State where acts of torture are alleged'. (*Al-Adsani v. United Kingdom* [GC], application No. 35763/97, judgment of 21 November 2001, ECHR Reports 2001-XI, p. 101, para. 61; ILR, Vol. 123, p. 24).

The following year, in *Kalogeropoulou and Others v. Greece and Germany*, the European Court of Human Rights rejected an application relating to the refusal of the Greek Government to permit enforcement of the *Distomo* judgment and said that, 'The Court does not find it established, however, that there is yet acceptance in international law of the proposition that States are not entitled to immunity in respect of civil claims for damages brought against them in another State for crimes against humanity'. (Application No. 59021/00, decision of 12 December 2002, ECHR Reports 2002-X, p. 417; ILR, Vol. 129, p. 537.)

91. The Court concludes that, under customary international law as it presently stands, a State is not deprived of immunity by reason of the fact that it is accused of serious violations of international human rights law or the international law of armed conflict. In reaching that conclusion, the Court must emphasize that it is addressing only the immunity of the State itself from the jurisdiction of the courts of other States; the question of whether, and if so to what extent, immunity might apply in criminal proceedings against an official of the State is not in issue in the present case.

NOTES

1. As noted earlier, for many years the immunity of a Head of State was absolute. However, there have been suggestions in recent years that there is now an exception to the principle of absolute immunity for criminal proceedings against current and former Heads of State where the acts in question constitute international crimes. There are currently two views in international law. The first, shown by the majority in *Pinochet* (extracted in Section 3), holds that there is an exception to immunity for international crimes; that is the official capacity of the individual is not a defence to the commission of an international crime. The second, as shown in the *Arrest Warrant Case* (also extracted in Section 3), is that there is no such exception. The conflict remains unresolved and, as noted in the various extracts above, the law in this area is in a state of 'flux'.

2. Factors that have been considered in the case law and by the International Law Commission as being relevant to immunity in relation to human rights violations are: whether sovereign equality of States should be surrendered in the face of human rights violations; whether the individual was acting in an official capacity; whether the individual had caused a breach of a rule of *jus cogens*; whether the individual could be held personally responsible under international law for the alleged acts; and whether the individual was at the time of trial in the local court still holding the official position that appears to attract the immunity. In addition to the cases referred to in this section, reference should also be made to the extracts from *Pinochet* and the *Arrest Warrant Cases*.

3. Proponents of an exception do not agree as to the scope of, and basis for, the exception. This is apparent from the various judgments in *Pinochet*, where it appears that there were two connected grounds for denying immunity. The first is that an ex-Head of State only enjoyed immunity in respect of acts done while he was a Head of State if these were in exercise of his official functions and torture could not be an official function. This is the essence of Lord Browne-Wilkinson's analysis. Alternatively, immunity could not attach to acts that were themselves in violation of fundamental rules of international law and the prevention of torture was such a rule of *jus cogens*. This is the essence of Lord Millet's analysis and he linked denial of immunity with international crimes attracting universal jurisdiction. Lord Millet's view has a certain logic about it, as immunity is available in respect of violation of national laws but can never be available in respect of violations of international law. However, this has not been followed in subsequent cases. For his part, Lord Goff (dissenting) could find nothing in customary law or the Torture Convention suggesting that immunity *ratione materiae* was removed for an ex-Head of State.

4. The issue in the *Arrest Warrant Case* concerned a current serving State representative and it is no surprise that the ICJ (following a classical State-based approach to international law) determined that such a person's immunity covered all matters, including alleged violations of international human rights law. It was immunity *ratione personae*. Indeed, the ICJ was clear that such immunity extended even to non-official acts while the individual was still serving. The ICJ was quick to point out that immunity from jurisdiction does not imply immunity from responsibility. Hence, the ICJ identifies ways (e.g. in para. 61) in which a person who is immune from one type of jurisdiction may nevertheless be made to bear their criminal responsibility.

5. In contrast to the decision of the House of Lords in *Jones*, the Italian Court of Cassation in the *Ferrini* decision (*Ferrini* v *Federal Republic of Germany* (2004) Casssez un 5044/04), recognised an exception to immunity in civil proceedings for conduct constituting an international crime. The Court declared that Italy could exercise jurisdiction with respect to a civil claim by a person who had been deported to Germany from Italy during World War Two to perform forced labour in the armaments industry. The ICJ held that, under customary international law, a State is not deprived of immunity simply because it is accused of serious violations of international law (see extract). Yet the issue does not appear to be resolved. While the Italian government adopted legislation reflecting the ICJ's determination, in October 2014 the Italian Constitutional Court quashed the legislation as violating constitutional provisions.

6. In general terms, the immunity of the State and at least senior State officials has not been overcome by the application of international human rights law and *jus cogens*. The Supreme Court of Appeal of South Africa has confirmed that, in the absence of the national implementing legislation, such immunity would preclude South African authorities from arresting Sudanese President Bashir even when requested to do so by the ICC, pursuant to an ICC arrest warrant (South Africa being a state party): see *Minister of Justice and Constitutional Development et al* v *Southern Africa Litigation Centre*, Case No: 867/15, 15 March 2016. The 2014 amendments to the AU protocol to confer jurisdiction in respect of international crimes on the African Court of Justice and Human Rights extends absolute immunity to senior officials (see Article 46A).

7. The position of State officials is perhaps less certain. While the ICJ was careful to limit its findings in *Germany* v *Italy* to the immunity of the *State,* the European Court of Human Rights extended that finding to State officials in *Jones*. This is arguably inconsistent with a trend towards greater accountability for State officials for unlawful acts. The International Law Commission continues to gather State practice concerning immunity of State officials for the purpose of its proposed draft articles, which will hopefully provide greater clarity in this contentious area.

8. The discussion in this chapter has been restricted to immunities before national courts. There is also the possibility, as noted by the ICJ in the *Arrest Warrant Case*, of bringing criminal proceedings before international criminal courts. The availability of immunity before such tribunals is considered in Chapter 14.

SECTION 5: THE IMMUNITIES OF INTERNATIONAL ORGANISATIONS AND THEIR STAFF

As was seen in Chapter 5, international organisations may well have international legal personality. Furthermore, the functions of some international organisations may be so important that they and their staff are granted privileges and immunities in order both to protect them from the vagaries of each State's domestic legal system and in order to facilitate their functions. The most obvious candidate for such immunities is the UN and its subsidiary and related organisations.

Stichting Mothers of Srebrenica and others v *the Netherlands*
Application No. 65542/12, 11 June 2013, European Court of Human Rights

These proceedings arose from a complaint by relatives of victims of the 1995 Srebrenica massacre, following a decision by the Netherlands courts to declare their case against the United Nations inadmissible on the ground that the UN enjoyed immunity from national courts' jurisdiction. The applicants alleged in particular that their right of access to court had been violated by that decision.

152. …At its root is a dispute between the applicants and the United Nations based on the use by the Security Council of its powers under Chapter VII of the United Nations Charter.

153. Like resolutions of the Security Council, the United Nations Charter and other instruments governing the functioning of the United Nations will be interpreted by the Court as far as possible in harmony with States' obligations under international human rights law.

154. The Court finds that since operations established by United Nations Security Council resolutions under Chapter VII of the United Nations Charter are fundamental to the mission of the United Nations to secure international peace and security, the Convention cannot be interpreted in a manner which would subject the acts and omissions of the Security Council to domestic jurisdiction without the accord of the United Nations. To bring such operations within the scope of domestic jurisdiction would be to allow individual States, through their courts, to interfere with the fulfilment of the key mission of the United Nations in this field, including with the effective conduct of its operations (see, mutatis mutandis, *Behrami and Behrami v. France* and *Saramati v. France, Germany and Norway*, cited above, § 149).

155. Moreover, the Court cannot but have regard to the Advisory Opinion of the ICJ concerning the Difference Relating to Immunity from Legal Process of a Special Rapporteur of the Commission on Human Rights, Advisory Opinion, I.C.J. Reports 1999, p. 62 and following (delivered on 29 April 1999), at § 66, where the ICJ holds as follows:
'Finally, the Court wishes to point out that the question of immunity from legal process is distinct from the issue of compensation for any damages incurred as a result of acts performed by the United Nations or by its agents acting in their official capacity.
The United Nations may be required to bear responsibility for the damage arising from such acts. However, as is clear from Article VIII, Section 29, of the General Convention [on Privileges and Immunities of the United Nations], any such claims against the United Nations shall not be dealt with by national courts but shall be settled in accordance with the appropriate modes of settlement that "[t]he United Nations shall make provisions for" pursuant to Section 29.…'

β. The nature of the applicants' claim

157. The Court recognised the prohibition of genocide as a rule of *ius cogens* in *Jorgić v. Germany* (no. 74613/01, § 68, ECHR 2007-III). In that case it found, based on the Genocide Convention, that Germany could claim jurisdiction to put the applicant on trial (loc. cit., §§ 68–70).

158. However, unlike *Jorgić*, the present case does not concern criminal liability but immunity from domestic civil jurisdiction. International law does not support the position that a civil claim should override immunity from suit for the sole reason that it is based on an allegation of a particularly grave violation of a norm of international law, even a norm of ius cogens. In respect of the sovereign immunity of foreign States this has been clearly stated by the ICJ in *Jurisdictional Immunities of the State (Germany v. Italy: Greece intervening)*, judgment of 3 February 2012, §§ 81-97. In the Court's opinion this also holds true as regards the immunity enjoyed by the United Nations.

159. Notwithstanding the possibility of weighing the immunity of an official of the United Nations in the balance, suggested in paragraph 61 of the ICJ's Advisory Opinion concerning the Difference Relating to Immunity from Legal Process of a Special Rapporteur of the Commission on Human Rights, the Court sees no reason to reach a different finding as regards the immunity enjoyed by the United Nations in the present case, especially since— unlike the acts impugned in the Jurisdictional Immunities case—the matters imputed to the United Nations in the present case, however they may have to be judged, ultimately derived from resolutions of the Security Council acting under Chapter VII of the United Nations Charter and therefore had a basis in international law.

160. Nor can the statements of the current Secretary-General of the United Nations (Highlights of the noon briefing by Marie Okabe, Deputy Spokesperson for Secretary-General Ban Ki-Moon, U.N. Headquarters, New York, Friday, June 8, 2007) and the former President of the ICTY (Address of the President of the ICTY to the General Assembly of the United Nations, 8 October 2009), cited by the applicants, lead the Court to find otherwise. Although both purport to encourage States to secure 'justice' to surviving relatives of the Srebrenica massacre, neither calls for the United Nations to submit to Netherlands domestic jurisdiction: the former calls for the perpetrators to be put on trial and for the recovery of Srebrenica itself to be assisted; the latter, for the setting up of a claims commission or a compensation fund.

NOTES:
1. The Convention on the Privileges and Immunities of the United Nations 1946 (which as at March 2016 has 162 parties) and the Convention on the Privileges and Immunities of the Specialized Agencies 1947 (which as at March 2016 has 127 parties) establish and codify the immunities that the UN and its staff enjoy. These are quite extensive, ranging from the immunity from legal process (as with State immunity) to the immunity of UN staff members from income tax, and civil and criminal procedures in similar fashion to diplomats. Such privileges and immunities will be effective against all States which have signed the Conventions and have given effect to their provisions in their national law. They are protected vigorously: see ICJ Advisory Opinion on the *Difference Relating to Immunity from Legal Process of a Special Rapporteur of the Commission on Human Rights*, 38 ILM 873 (1999).
2. As shown in the extract above, the immunity extended to the United Nations itself will apply even where the acts concerned relate to international crimes or violations of *jus cogens* norms. The Court found the role of the United Nations in securing international peace and security to be relevant to the question of immunity. Proceedings in The Netherlands concerning Srebrenica were also initiated against the Dutch government, on the basis of State responsibility and are considered in Chapter 11.
3. There is no reason why other international organisations should not have certain privileges and immunities, although this will stem from specific treaties establishing those agreements and specific provisions of national law.
4. In national law whether an international organisation (and its staff) has immunity from legal process and other obligations depends on the particular legislation and practices of the State.
5. In *Entico Corp Ltd* v *United Nations Educational Scientific and Cultural Association* [2008] EWHC 531 (Comm), the UK High Court held that there was nothing in the 1947 Convention on the Privileges and Immunities of the Specialized Agencies that made the immunity of an international organisation dependent on the organisation establishing another process for dispute settlement. Moreover, as is the case with State immunity, the Convention must be interpreted in accordance with international law, and should not be read narrowly, so as to take account of the European Convention on Human Rights (ECHR). Even if the ECHR was engaged, if the UK International Organisations Act (and the 1974 Order) reflected recognised rules of public international law, the conferral of immunity could not be considered a disproportionate restriction on the rights of the claimant to a fair trial. This is consistent with the views of the European Court of Human Rights, as seen in the extract above.

SECTION 6: DIPLOMATIC AND CONSULAR IMMUNITIES

The law of diplomatic privileges and immunities is as old as the system of international law itself. They exist in the main because of the identity of a particular person, being the diplomat or consular representative of a foreign sovereign State, and as such they are essentially immunities *ratione personae*. It is clear that these immunities from the jurisdiction of the 'host' State, being the State where the representatives are stationed, exist in order that the representative may carry out his or her functions effectively and without interference. Thus, although diplomatic privileges and immunities may seem to benefit an individual personally, that is not their *raison d'être*. As a matter of international law, the relevant principles are to be found in the multilateral treaty extracted below, supplemented by customary international law.

Vienna Convention on Diplomatic Relations 1961
UNTS 500 (1965) 95

The Convention was adopted by a UN Conference on Diplomatic Intercourse and Immunities in April 1961, and entered into force in April 1964. As at March 2016, there were 190 parties to the Convention. As well as being one of the most widely ratified multilateral treaties, much of the Convention also reflects existing customary international law.

Article 9

1. The receiving state may at any time and without having to explain its decision, notify the sending state that the head of the mission or any member of the diplomatic staff of the mission is *persona non grata* or that any other member of the staff of the mission is not acceptable. In any such case, the sending state shall, as appropriate, either recall the person concerned or terminate his functions with the mission. A person may be declared *non grata* or not acceptable before arriving in the territory of the receiving state.

2. If the sending state refuses or fails within a reasonable period to carry out its obligations under paragraph 1 of this article, the receiving state may refuse to recognize the person concerned as a member of the mission.

Article 22

1. The premises of the mission shall be inviolable. The agents of the receiving state may not enter them, except with the consent of the head of the mission.

2. The receiving state is under a special duty to take all appropriate steps to protect the premises of the mission against any intrusion or damage and to prevent any disturbance of the peace of the mission or impairment of its dignity.

3. The premises of the mission, their furnishings and other property thereon and the means of transport of the mission shall be immune from search, requisition, attachment or execution.

Article 24

The archives and documents of the mission shall be inviolable at any time and wherever they may be.

Article 27

1. The receiving state shall permit and protect free communication of the part of the mission for all official purposes. In communicating with the government and the other missions and consulates of the sending state, wherever situated, the mission may employ all appropriate means, including diplomatic couriers and messages in code or cipher. However, the mission may install and use a wireless transmitter only with the consent of the receiving state.

2. The official correspondence of the mission shall be inviolable. Official correspondence means all correspondence relating to the mission and its functions.

3. The diplomatic bag shall not be opened or detained.

4. The packages constituting the diplomatic bag must bear visible external marks of their character and may contain only diplomatic documents or articles intended for official use.

5. The diplomatic courier, who shall be provided with an official document indicating his status and the number of packages constituting the diplomatic bag, shall be protected by the receiving state in the performance of his functions. He shall enjoy personal inviolability and shall not be liable to any form of arrest or detention.

Article 29

The person of a diplomatic agent shall be inviolable. He shall not be liable to any form of arrest or detention. The receiving state shall treat him with due respect and shall take all appropriate steps to prevent any attack on his person, freedom or dignity.

Article 30

1. The private residence of a diplomatic agent shall enjoy the same inviolability and protection as the premises of the mission.

2. His papers, correspondence and, except as provided in paragraph 3 of Article 31, his property, shall likewise enjoy inviolability.

Article 31

1. A diplomatic agent shall enjoy immunity from the criminal jurisdiction of the receiving state. He shall also enjoy immunity from its civil and administrative jurisdiction, except in the case of:
    (a) a real action relating to private immovable property situated in the territory of the receiving state, unless he holds it on behalf of the sending state for the purposes of the mission;

(b) an action relating to succession in which the diplomatic agent is involved as executor, administrator, heir or legatee as a private person and not on behalf of the sending state;

(c) an action relating to any professional or commercial activity exercised by the diplomatic agent in the receiving state outside his official functions.

2. A diplomatic agent is not obliged to give evidence as a witness.

3. No measures of execution may be taken in respect of a diplomatic agent except in the cases coming under sub-paragraphs (a), (b) and (c) of paragraph 1 of this article, and provided that the measures concerned can be taken without infringing the inviolability of his person or of his residence.

4. The immunity of a diplomatic agent from the jurisdiction of the receiving state does not exempt him from the jurisdiction of the sending state.

Article 32

1. The immunity from jurisdiction of diplomatic agents and of persons enjoying immunity under Article 37 may be waived by the sending state.

2. Waiver must always be express.

3. The initiation of proceedings by a diplomatic agent or by a person enjoying immunity from jurisdiction under Article 37 shall preclude him from invoking immunity from jurisdiction in respect of any counter-claim directly connected with the principal claim.

4. Waiver of immunity from jurisdiction in respect of civil or administrative proceedings shall not be held to imply waiver of immunity in respect of the execution of the judgment, for which a separate waiver shall be necessary.

Article 39

1. Every person entitled to privileges and immunities shall enjoy them from the moment he enters the territory of the receiving state on proceeding to take up his post or, if already in its territory, from the moment when his appointment is notified to the Ministry for Foreign Affairs or such other ministry as may be agreed.

Article 41

1. Without prejudice to their privileges and immunities, it is the duty of all person enjoying such privileges and immunities to respect the laws and regulations of the receiving state. They also have a duty not to interfere in the internal affairs of that state.

2. All official business with the receiving state entrusted to the mission by the sending state shall be conducted with or through the Ministry for Foreign Affairs of the receiving state or such other ministry as may be agreed.

3. The premises of the mission must not be used in any manner incompatible with the functions of the mission as laid down in the present Convention or by other rules of general international law or by any special agreements in force between the sending and the receiving state.

Article 42

A diplomatic agent shall not in the receiving state practise for personal profit any professional or commercial activity.

US Diplomatic and Consular Staff in Iran Case (*United States* v *Tehran*)
ICJ Rep 1980 3, International Court of Justice

On 4 November 1979, Iranian students seized the US Embassy in Tehran and a number of consulates in outlying cities. The Iranian authorities failed to protect the Embassy and later appeared to adopt the students' actions (see Chapter 11). Over 50 US nationals (mostly diplomatic and consular staff) were held for 444 days. The US sought a declaration, *inter alia*, that Iran had violated the two Vienna Conventions, and calling for the release of the hostages and the vacation of the Embassy and consulates. The Court considered whether the initial attack by the students could be attributed to the Iranian Government, the conduct of Iran at that time and subsequently, and whether Iran was therefore in violation of its international obligations.

68. The Court is therefore led inevitably to conclude, in regard to the first phase of the events which has so far been considered, that on 4 November 1979 the Iranian authorities:

(a) were fully aware of their obligations under the conventions in force to take appropriate steps to protect the premises of the United States Embassy and its diplomatic and consular staff from any attack and from any infringement of their inviolability, and to ensure the security of such other persons as might be present on the said premises;

(b) were fully aware, as a result of the appeals for help made by the United States Embassy, of the urgent need for action on their part;

(c) had the means at their disposal to perform their obligations;

(d) completely failed to comply with these obligations.

Similarly, the Court is led to conclude that the Iranian authorities were equally aware of their obligations to protect the United States Consulates at Tabriz and Shiraz, and of the need for action on their part, and similarly failed to use the means which were at their disposal to comply with their obligations.

69. The second phase of the events which are the subject of the United States' claims comprises the whole series of facts which occurred following the completion of the occupation of the United States Embassy by the militants, and the seizure of the Consulates at Tabriz and Shiraz. The occupation having taken place and the diplomatic and consular personnel of the United States' mission having been taken hostage, the action required of the Iranian Government by the Vienna Conventions and by general international law was manifest. Its plain duty was at once to make every effort, and to take every appropriate step, to bring these flagrant infringements of the inviolability of the premises, archives and diplomatic and consular staff of the United States Embassy to a speedy end, to restore the Consulates at Tabriz and Shiraz to United States control, and in general to re-establish the status quo and to offer reparation for the damage.

76. The Iranian authorities' decision to continue the subjection of the premises of the United States Embassy to occupation by militants and of the Embassy staff to detention as hostages, clearly gave rise to repeated and multiple breaches of the applicable provisions of the Vienna Conventions even more serious than those which arose from their failure to take any steps to prevent the attacks on the inviolability of these premises and staff.

84. The Vienna Conventions of 1961 and 1963 contain express provisions to meet the case when members of an embassy staff, under the cover of diplomatic privileges and immunities, engage in such abuses of their functions as espionage or interference in the internal affairs of the receiving State. It is precisely with the possibility of such abuses in contemplation that Article 41, paragraph 1, of the Vienna Convention on Diplomatic Relations, and Article 55, paragraph 1, of the Vienna Convention on Consular Relations, provide

Without prejudice to their privileges and immunities, it is the duty of all persons enjoying such privileges and immunities to respect the laws and regulations of the receiving State. They also have a duty not to interfere in the internal affairs of that State.

Paragraph 3 of Article 41 of the 1961 Convention further states: 'The premises of the mission must not be used in any manner incompatible with the functions of the missions…': an analogous provision, with respect to consular premises is to be found in Article 55, paragraph 2, of the 1963 Convention.

85. Thus, it is for the very purpose of providing a remedy for such possible abuses of diplomatic functions that Article 9 of the 1961 Convention on Diplomatic Relations stipulates:

1. The receiving State may at any time and without having to explain its decision, notify the sending State that the head of the mission or any member of the diplomatic staff of the mission is *persona non grata* or that any other member of the staff of the mission is not acceptable.…

Beyond that remedy for dealing with abuses of the diplomatic function by individual members of a mission, a receiving State has in its hands a more radical remedy if abuses of their functions by members of a mission reach serious proportions. This is the power which every receiving State has, at its own discretion, to break off diplomatic relations with a sending State and to call for the immediate closure of the offending mission.

86. The rules of diplomatic law, in short, constitute a self-contained regime which, on the one hand, lays down the receiving State's obligations regarding the facilities, privileges and immunities to be accorded to diplomatic missions and, on the other, foresees their possible abuse by members of the mission and specifies the means at the disposal of the receiving State to counter any such abuse. These means are, by their nature, entirely efficacious, for unless the sending State recalls the member of the mission objected to forthwith, the prospect of the almost immediate loss of his privileges and immunities, because of the withdrawal by the receiving State of his recognition as a member of the mission, will in practice compel that person, in his own interest, to

depart at once. But the principle of the inviolability of the persons of diplomatic agents and the premises of diplomatic missions is one of the very foundations of this long-established regime, to the evolution of which the traditions of Islam made a substantial contribution.... Even in the case of armed conflict or in the case of a breach in diplomatic relations those provisions require that both the inviolability of the members of a diplomatic mission and of the premises, property and archives of the mission must be respected by the receiving State. Naturally, the observance of this principle does not mean—and this the Applicant Government expressly acknowledges—that a diplomatic agent caught in the act of committing an assault or other offence may not, on occasion, be briefly arrested by the police of the receiving State in order to prevent the commission of the particular crime. But such eventualities bear no relation at all to what occurred in the present case.

92. It is a matter of deep regret that the situation which occasioned those observations has not been rectified since they were made. Having regard to their importance the Court considers it essential to reiterate them in the present Judgment. The frequency with which at the present time the principles of international law governing diplomatic and consular relations are set at naught by individuals or groups of individuals is already deplorable. But this case is unique and of very particular gravity because here it is not only private individuals or groups of individuals that have disregarded and set at naught the inviolability of a foreign embassy, but the government of the receiving State itself. Therefore in recalling yet again the extreme importance of the principles of law which it is called upon to apply in the present case, the Court considers it to be its duty to draw the attention of the entire international community, of which Iran itself has been a member since time immemorial, to the irreparable harm that may be caused by events of the kind now before the Court. Such events cannot fail to undermine the edifice of law carefully constructed by mankind over a period of centuries, the maintenance of which is vital for the security and well-being of the complex international community of the present day, to which it is more essential than ever that the rules developed to ensure the ordered progress of relations between its members should be constantly and scrupulously respected.

Diplomatic Claim, Ethiopia's Claim 8

45 *International Legal Materials* 621 (2006), Eritrea/Ethiopia Claims Commission

The claim was brought to the specially constituted Commission by Ethiopia pursuant to a bilateral Agreement between it and Eritrea. Ethiopia asked the Commission to find Eritrea liable for loss, damage and injury suffered by Ethiopia from the injuries sustained by the Ethiopian diplomatic mission and consular post and personnel in Eritrea as a result of Eritrea's alleged violations of the international law of diplomatic and consular relations.

25. While unilateral derogations from key obligations are not authorized, the foundational principle of diplomatic reciprocity provides some guidance to the Commission in assessing the Parties' application of the Vienna Convention on Diplomatic Relations during an armed conflict. Accepting that a receiving State must have somewhat greater latitude in wartime to monitor and even to limit activities of the diplomatic mission of an enemy, the Commission has taken particular note of the specific manner in which both Parties performed their diplomatic obligations during the conflict. The Commission, not surprisingly, has found broadly corresponding compliance and noncompliance in certain areas. As cautioned above, this is not to say that matching violations of fundamental obligations under the Vienna Convention on Diplomatic Relations can cancel each other out. It is to say that, in dealing with the uncertainties generated by the Parties' reciprocal (and laudable) decisions to maintain diplomatic relations despite war, reciprocity can provide a helpful indicator in applying the flexibility provided in the Convention, for example, in assessing the reasonableness of the deadlines set for the departure of diplomats and the level of monitoring of each other's diplomats.

26. A critical standard for the Commission in applying international diplomatic law must be the impact of the events complained about on the functioning of the diplomatic mission. Particularly in light of the limited resources and time allocated to this Commission and the serious claims of international humanitarian law violations presented by the Parties, and remaining attentive to the principle of reciprocity, the Commission again is constrained to look for serious violations impeding the effective functioning of the diplomatic mission....

33. The Claimant contends that Eritrean guards twice arrested and then briefly (for less than one hour) detained and interrogated the Chargé at local police stations after he visited Ethiopian nationals in Aba Shawl in September 1998 and Medebere in October 1999. Ethiopia presented clear and convincing evidence of these events in the

form of declarations from the Chargé and the Embassy driver and contemporaneous notes from the Ethiopian Embassy to the Eritrean Ministry of Foreign Affairs objecting to the Chargé's mistreatment. Eritrea bases its defense primarily on the lack of corroborating descriptions in press accounts by foreign reporters who accompanied the Chargé on the relevant consular visits, which the Commission does not find sufficient to overcome Ethiopia's prima facie case. The Commission finds Eritrea liable for violating Article 29 of the Vienna Convention on Diplomatic Relations by arresting and briefly detaining the Chargé in September 1998 and October 1999 without regard to his diplomatic immunity.

34. The Commission does not consider that these circumstances also gave rise to violations of Article 26 or Article 31 of the Convention. The Commission is not convinced that Eritrean officials questioning the Chargé for less than one hour constituted interrogation in the context of compulsion of evidence. Nor is the Commission convinced that the arrests and detentions of the Chargé inhibited his freedom to travel in Eritrea to perform his consular functions for Ethiopian nationals. Indeed, the events complained of occurred while the Chargé was traveling in Asmara in the performance of his official duties. These claims are dismissed.

35. Similarly, the Commission dismisses the related claim that the Respondent violated Article 29 of the Vienna Convention on Consular Relations by failing to protect the Chargé from students allegedly throwing rocks at his car when he was leaving Medebere in October 1999. The Claimant failed to prove that this relatively minor incident chilled the Chargé's performance of his functions.

Aziz v Aziz

[2007] EWCA Civ 712, United Kingdom Court of Appeal

The Sultan of Brunei intervened in the proceedings seeking an order to prevent publication of his name or any material that might identify him in connection with the proceedings. The claimant was the Sultan's former wife.

5. The Sultan, relying on his status as a foreign head of state, sought directions preventing the publication of his name, or the publication of any matters which could lead to him being identified, in connection with the proceedings.

6. He relied on the application to a head of state by section 20 of the State Immunity Act 1978 ('the 1978 Act') of Article 29 of the Vienna Convention on Diplomatic Relations (1961) ('the Vienna Convention'), which is given the force of law by the Diplomatic Privileges Act 1964 ('the 1964 Act') and which, it is said, requires the United Kingdom (including its courts) to 'treat him with due respect and…take all appropriate steps to prevent any attack on his…dignity.'…

86. What this practice indicates is that in the context of diplomatic immunity mere speech (except perhaps of an extreme kind), as distinct from conduct which impedes the conduct of the activities of a mission, is not conduct which the receiving State is obliged to take steps to prevent, or which it is constitutionally entitled to prevent.

87. This is consistent with the fact that the obligations in Articles 22 and 29 are mainly concerned with protection against physical attack or obstruction. Thus according to Denza, *Diplomatic Law*, 2nd ed., 1998 (a noted authority), at p. 212 the third sentence of Article 29 provides for 'the positive duty to treat the diplomatic agent with due respect and to protect him from physical interference by others with his person, freedom or dignity.' This is because the requirement of the physical protection of diplomats and diplomatic premises is a fundamental requisite for the conduct of diplomatic relations: see *United States Diplomatic and Consular Staff in Tehran (United States of America v Iran)* 1980 ICJ Rep 3, at 38; and also *Armed Activities on the Territory of the Congo (Democratic Republic of the Congo v Uganda)*, judgment of 19 December 2005 (physical attacks on Ugandan diplomatic staff by Democratic Republic of the Congo army personnel); *Federal Democratic Republic of Ethiopia v State of Eritrea*, Eritrea Ethiopia Claims Commission, Partial Award, Claim 8, December 19, 2005 (detention and mistreatment of diplomats).

88. What then is the present state of international law on the right to dignity of a head of state? There is no doubt that a State is obliged to take steps to prevent physical attacks on, or physical interference with, a foreign head of state who is in this country. This would be so equally under customary international law, and the combination of section 20 of the 1978 Act and Article 29. Nor would I doubt that the duty would apply to acts in

this country preparatory to, or directed at, some form of physical attack against a head of state who is in his or her own country or in a third country.

89. But, outside physical attack or interference, the material in relation to the prevention of offensive conduct supports the view that to the extent there is any uniform practice (which is doubtful) it amounts to no more than courtesy or comity.... Sir Arthur draws a distinction between offensive conduct by an official representative of the State, and conduct by a private party. As regards the latter, Sir Arthur says that it is uncertain to what extent international law imposes a positive obligation on States to prevent offensive conduct by private individuals directed against foreign heads of state, or requires them to punish such conduct if it occurs. His view is that it is not clear in State practice whether it is a matter of diplomatic courtesy rather than a recognition of legal responsibility....

91. The establishment of a rule of customary international law requires settled state practice on the basis that the practice is rendered obligatory by the existence of a rule of law requiring it:...I am far from convinced by the material before us that there is a rule of customary international law which imposes an obligation on a State to take appropriate steps to prevent conduct by individuals which is simply offensive or insulting to a foreign head of state abroad.

R (Bancoult) v Secretary of State for Foreign and Commonwealth Affairs
[2013] EWHC 1502 (Admin), United Kingdom Court of Appeal

This case concerned a challenge by Mr Bancoult of the decision taken by the Secretary of State to create a Marine Protected Area (MPA) in the British Indian Ocean Territory (BIOT), a colony of the UK. Bancoult argued that the declaration of the MPA was for an improper motive, which was to preclude the native population from the Chagos Archipelago from resettling islands within BIOT, in particular the island of Diego Garcia, which was used by the US government pursuant to an agreement with the UK government. Of significance in these proceedings was whether a purported copy of a communication sent from the US Embassy in London to departments of the US government in Washington outlining the details of a meeting held between UK and US officials (which indicated that the purpose of the MPA was in fact to exclude the Chagossians from resettlement) was admissible in legal proceedings in the UK. The communication had been obtained unlawfully and published by Wikileaks.

51. ...Inviolability involves the placing of a protective ring around the ambassador, the embassy and its archives and documents which neither the receiving state nor the courts of the receiving state may lawfully penetrate. If, however, a relevant document has found its way into the hands of a third party, even in consequence of a breach of inviolability, it is prima facie admissible in evidence. The concept of inviolability has no relevance where no attempt is being made to exercise *compulsion* against the embassy. Inviolability, like other diplomatic immunities, is a defence against an attempt to exercise state power and nothing more....

61. In short, the universal definition of 'inviolability' is freedom from any act of interference on the part of the receiving state. None of the definitions contains any reference to inadmissibility. Dr Mann says (*Inviolability and Other Problems of the Vienna Convention on Diplomatic Relations* (1990) p 330) that a state which, without the use of force or without exercising executive authority has obtained possession of the diplomat's documents and uses them without his objection cannot be said to 'violate' them within the meaning of article 24. He acknowledges that the position would be different if the state was responsible for the removal of the documents from the mission. In that event, the act of removal would itself amount to a violation of the documents and the unlawfulness of the removal would make it unlawful to benefit from the fruits of the unlawful activity....

63. For the purpose of resolving the issue that arises in this appeal, however, it is not necessary to explore the circumstances in which documents removed from a mission without the consent of the sending state may be admitted in evidence. On the assumed facts of the present case, the documents were sent from the US mission in London to Washington with the consent of the sending state and were communicated to the world by a third party. Mr Bancoult was not implicated in the removal of the documents from the mission or their publication to the world. There is nothing in the case-law or the writings of the commentators (apart from those of Professor Denza [*Diplomatic Law, Commentary on the Vienna Convention on Diplomatic Relations* (2008)]) which says that the

use of documents disclosed in such circumstances in legal proceedings would be contrary to articles 24 and 27.2 of the 1961 Convention. Professor Denza gives no reasons for her opinion that it would be.

64. Quite apart from the fact that the weight of opinion is against the professor's view, it seems to us that it does not sit well with the object and purpose of the 1961 Convention. The purpose of the immunity conferred by articles 24 and 27.2 is to 'ensure the efficient performance of the functions of the diplomatic missions'....Even if inviolability can in principle extend to inadmissibility of documents in some circumstances, it should not do so where the inadmissibility cannot promote or contribute to the efficient performance of the functions of a mission. The protection against the disclosure and use of the archives and documents of a mission can unquestionably promote and contribute to the efficient performance of a mission's functions in some cases. But it cannot do so where any damage that is done to a mission by the disclosure of an archive or document has already been done by their disclosure by a third party for which the party who wishes to adduce the evidence has no responsibility. In our judgment, it makes no sense for the concept of inviolability of the mission to be extended to prevent a document that is in the worldwide public domain from being admitted in proceedings in England and Wales, simply because it emanated from a diplomatic mission in the UK. Had the document emanated from the US embassy in Paris, we doubt whether the argument would have got off the ground. There is the further relevant point, derived from *Rose v The King*, that the US Government has not objected to the use of the cable in these proceedings.

65. To summarise, we would allow the appeal on the admissibility issue on the narrow basis that admitting the cable in evidence in the instant case did not violate the archive and documents of the US mission, since it had already been disclosed to the world by a third party.

NOTES
1. The above extracts deal with the substantive principles of international law that require a State to grant diplomatic privileges and immunities. Parties to the Vienna Convention on Diplomatic Relations must ensure that their national courts meet the standards of those treaties, while non-parties will be governed by a similar standard under customary international law. Failure to meet the obligation involves international responsibility (see Chapter 11).
2. The Vienna Convention on Diplomatic Relations continues to apply notwithstanding a state of armed conflict or where diplomatic relations are broken off between States. This principle was confirmed in the *Case Concerning Armed Activities on the Territory of the Congo* (*Democratic Republic of the Congo* v *Uganda*) ICJ Rep 2005.
3. The Eritrea/Ethiopia Claims Commission decision adopts a functional approach to diplomatic immunity, such that acts would constitute a violation of diplomatic immunity if they interfered with the ability of the diplomatic mission and its staff to fulfil its functions (see extract). The Court of Appeal endorsed a similar functional approach in *Bancoult* (extracted above) in respect of when protection should be extended to diplomatic documents.
4. As the ICJ observed in the *US Diplomatic and Consular Staff in Iran Case*, the law of diplomatic immunities is one of the most important areas of international law. The immunities contained in these Conventions are far-reaching, and many commentators have questioned whether they go too far. Indeed, they appear to offer protection to the diplomat but seem to deny the host State the opportunity of defending itself from hostile actions by that diplomat, especially if diplomatic agents are seen (or believed) to be engaged in criminal activities (see the decision of the Australian High Court in *Minister for Foreign Affairs and Trade* v *Magno* (1992) 112 ALR 529. The UK was embroiled in a dispute concerning the treatment of its diplomats in Iran, with Iran accusing UK diplomats of unduly interfering in the national affairs of Iran following the elections in Iran in 2009. The British Prime Minister informed Parliament that Iran:

> took the unjustified step of expelling two British diplomats, over allegations of support for the Iranian opposition which are absolutely without foundation. In response to this action, we informed the Iranian ambassador earlier today that we would expel two Iranian diplomats from their embassy in London. I am disappointed that Iran placed us in this position. But we will continue to seek good relations with Iran and to call for the regime to respect the human rights and democratic freedoms of the Iranian people [statement to House of Commons 23 June 2009]

5. The Vienna Convention on Consular Relations 1963 has 177 parties as at March 2016. It concerns the activities of consuls, whose role is to protect the interests of the State and its nationals in the receiving State (Article 5). As a general rule, the functions of consuls are more administrative in

nature, for example, the issue of passports and visas and arranging legal and other assistance for nationals within the receiving State. This is reflected in the more limited immunities granted to consuls and consular staff. For example, consular officers are only immune in respect of acts performed in the course of their consular functions (Article 43). The functions of consular officers, and the importance of the receiving State enabling the consul to fulfil its functions, was discussed in the *Avena* and *LaGrand* decisions before the ICJ (see Chapters 4 and 16 respectively).

6. Increasingly, States may dispatch so-called special missions to conduct government affairs in other States. The nature and functions of these missions vary, as do views of their legal status. The Convention on Special Missions 1969 attempts to address the privileges and immunities attaching to such missions. However, while this Convention entered into force in 1985, only 38 States are party to the treaty (as at March 2016) and its provisions may not reflect customary international law.

7. The UK is a party to the Vienna Convention on Diplomatic Relations. In order to ensure compliance with its international obligations, it was necessary to pass national legislation that gave diplomats immunity from legal process in the UK, being the Diplomatic Privileges Act 1964 and the Diplomatic and Consular Premises Act 1987. The Convention on Consular Relations is given effect by the Consular Relations Act 1968, which enables the UK to give effect to other international agreements under which the privileges and immunities may differ. The UK signed the Convention on Special Missions in 1970, but has not become a party. UK courts have recognised that special missions do enjoy immunity as a matter of customary international law and the Foreign and Commonwealth has certified that individuals visiting the UK are participating in special missions and subject to immunity. For example, the UK government has twice certified that Tzipi Livni, Israel's Justice Minister, enjoys immunity as part of a special mission, which has effectively precluded UK courts from issuing an arrest warrant in respect of alleged crimes against humanity committed by Israel.

10

Law of the Sea

The law of the sea is of great importance to the world community. This is reflected in the wealth of treaty law, customary law and judicial decisions concerning this subject. The most important of all is the United Nations Law of the Sea Convention 1982, which entered into force on 16 November 1994. This is a multilateral treaty of considerable significance, and the conclusion in July 1994 of an Agreement Relating to the Implementation of Part XI of the Convention in regard to deep sea mining meant that many States once reluctant to ratify the Convention have become parties, including the United Kingdom and other members of the European Union. Moreover, even if there are some States that have chosen not to ratify the 1982 Convention and the 1994 Agreement (such as the United States), many of the Convention's principles are now accepted as being part of customary international law.

In addition, there are four other Conventions concerning the law of the sea stemming from the First UN Conference on the Law of the Sea in 1958. Although still in force to some extent for the parties to them, these 1958 Conventions are largely superseded by the 1982 Convention and customary law. As at March 2016, there were 167 parties to the 1982 Convention (including the European Union) and 147 parties to the 1994 Agreement, (including the European Union), 63 parties to the Convention on the High Seas 1958, 39 parties to the Convention on Fishing and Conservation of the Living Resources of the High Seas 1958, 58 parties to the Convention on the Continental Shelf 1958 and 52 parties to the Convention on the Territorial Sea and Contiguous Zone 1958.

SECTION 1: LAW OF THE SEA CONVENTION 1982

The 1982 Convention was the result of nine years' work by the Third United Nations Conference on the Law of the Sea. It is a comprehensive multilateral treaty covering all aspects of the use of the sea and seabed. The Convention should be viewed as an integrated whole, for the development of the text was the result of compromise and bargain between the various fluctuating interest groups (and so no reservations were permitted). Nevertheless, it soon became clear that some developed States were not prepared to accept Part XI of the Convention as it was originally drafted. This led to concern for the overall efficacy of the Convention, a matter resolved by the 1994 Agreement. Consequently an overall view of the Convention requires an understanding of the changes made by the 1994 Agreement (which is addressed more fully below).

D. Anderson, 'Legal Implications of the Entry into Force of the UN Convention on the Law of the Sea'

44 International and Comparative Law Quarterly 313 (1995)

On 16 November 1993, Guyana became the 60th State to ratify the 1982 Convention. Consequently, in accordance with Article 308, the Convention came into force on 16 November 1994, as modified provisionally by the 1994 Agreement relating to Part XI (Deep Sea Bed). The Agreement relating to Part XI came into force on 28 July 1996—thus modifying the Convention permanently....

III. Legal implications of entry into force of the Convention and the provisional application of the Agreement

A. For States Parties

The entry into force of the Convention carries with it the normal implications under the Vienna Convention of the Law of Treaties. That is to say, as between the States parties to the Convention, the basic rule of *pacta sunt servanda* applies. Their relations in many maritime matters are governed by the Convention. More widely, the relevant practice of the States parties must be based on the Convention. States are repealing legislation based on the terms of the Geneva Conventions and enacting new laws in line with the Convention. Entry into force will result in an addition to State practice by States which are parties....

Article 311(1) provides that the Convention is to prevail, as between the States parties, over the Geneva Conventions on the Law of the Sea of 1958. As the number of parties grows, the Convention will prevail to an increasing extent. This provision signals rather clearly a formal stage in the process of evolution in the law of the sea. The law as it stood in the 1960s, following the First and Second UN Conferences on the Law of the Sea, is giving way more and more. The process of evolution began many years ago, at least by the 1970s when the 200-mile limit was accepted; but it has accelerated since 1982. Entry into force marks and formalises the change.

The Convention of 1982 breaks much new ground: new concepts abound. Entry into force of all Parts of the Convention (subject to the qualifications mentioned above) means that States parties can take advantage of possibilities set out in the different Parts and Annexes. Equally, each State party has to accept claims by other States parties based on the Convention. A party to the Convention must therefore accept new concepts articulated in its terms, for example the archipelagic State under Part IV, the fishing rights of landlocked States under Article 69 and extended pollution jurisdiction under Part XII.

...It is very likely that the provisions of the Convention of 1982 will be the primary influence on State practice worldwide. Entry into force will lead to legitimisation *ex post facto* of some past practice, e.g. archipelagic claims.

B. For Non-Parties

As regards States which have not yet become parties to the Convention, as a matter of strict law its provisions are not binding upon them: Vienna Convention, Article 34. However, many of these States have already been applying much of the Convention, day by day, since 1982, or even earlier in some respects. Many provisions are expressive of rules of customary law. States have been following the Convention in matters such as the 12-mile territorial sea and the 200-mile economic zone, as well as rights of passage. They have ceased to protest about a wide range of claims by other States in line with, or explicitly based on, the Convention. Many of these non-parties are industrialised States with major maritime interests: in many cases they are applying provisionally the Agreement adopted on 28 July 1994 and enjoying membership on a provisional basis of the Authority. They are also helping to pay for the Authority from the UN budget, on a temporary basis. They are preparing to ratify or accede in many cases....

IV. The nature of the Convention

Apart from Part XI, there is little room in the Convention for our old friends the 'persistent dissenters' or 'objectors': they were all represented at the Conference and afforded ample opportunity to argue their cases. Some unique problems faced by single States met with sympathetic responses: for example, Bangladesh and Norway both benefited from special provisions. But the Conference did not accept all such special pleas: the element of a negotiation, leading to the adoption of an overall negotiated text, has now to be taken into account in assessing the strength of what may have become lost causes....

The Convention balances the differing interests of States. The typical balance is between the rights and interests of the coastal State and those of the distant water State or flag State. But there are other balances: between States interested in mining manganese nodules and the generality of States (a balance which has been adjusted by the Agreement of 28 July 1994); between the landlocked State and the transit State; and between the broad-margin

State and the international community as a whole. The Convention has been described as a 'package deal' by some commentators; but the expression is not entirely apt in that it has too strong a contractual flavour. The process of balancing was done on individual issues, as well as on clusters of issues (e.g. 12-mile limit/straits passage/200-mile limit), in the Second Committee. In many instances the process was one of finding middle ground or the equitable solution more than of contractual dealing.

The text which emerged at the end of the Conference was a negotiated text. It is a text of high intrinsic quality. It is coherent, internally balanced and forward-looking (especially on environmental issues). At the same time, it takes into account the historical development of the law of the sea through customary law, decisions by international tribunals and the Geneva Conventions, much of which it incorporates or 're-enacts' (often with updating). The Convention represents codification, consolidation, progressive development and the conscious revision or reform of the law of the sea....

NOTES

1. The above extract indicates the position following the entry into force of the 1982 Convention and 1994 Agreement. See also the Agreement for the Implementation of the Provisions of the United Nations Convention on the Law of the Sea of 10 December 1982 relating to the Conservation and Management of Straddling Fish Stocks and Highly Migratory Fish Stocks 1995, which entered into force on 11 December 2001 and, as at March 2016, has 83 parties.

2. The impact of the Convention on customary international law was considerable even before it entered into force. The decisions of the ICJ given before 16 November 1994 confirm this. Many of its provisions have passed into customary law, although for State parties the Convention will prevail in the event of any inconsistencies. The 1982 Convention will also prevail for parties over any inconsistent obligations they may have *inter se* under the 1958 Geneva Conventions on the Law of the Sea (see Article 311).

3. In the *Case Concerning Maritime Delimitation and Territorial Questions Between Qatar and Bahrain* (*Qatar* v *Bahrain*), Merits, ICJ Rep, 16 March 2001, the 1982 Convention was not in force between the two States because it had been ratified only by Bahrain. However, both parties agreed that the provisions of the Convention that would have been applicable did indeed represent customary international law. This approach was adopted readily by the ICJ. In the main, these were uncontroversial matters dealing with applicable rules of maritime delimitation (e.g. the 'equidistance/ special circumstance' rule), although one contested issue was the status of 'low-tide elevations' in customary law, being small areas of land mass that were visible only at low tide. A majority of the Court took the view that the 1982 Convention provision (Article 13) reflected customary international law.

4. In *Eritrea/Yemen Arbitration, Second Stage, Maritime Delimitation*, (2001) 40 ILM 983, the parties had submitted a dispute to the Permanent Court of Arbitration under an Arbitration Agreement. The Award in the Second Stage notes at para. 130 that 'the requirement to take into account the United Nations Convention on the Law of the Sea of 1982 is important because Eritrea has not become a party to that Convention but has in the Arbitration Agreement thus accepted the application of provisions of the Convention that are found to be relevant to the present stage. There is no reference in the Arbitration Agreement to the customary law of the sea, but many of the relevant elements of customary law are incorporated in the provisions of the Convention'.

5. As was predicted in the above extract, the 1982 Convention has now become the dominant international legal instrument in this area, particularly as the number of States parties has increased. After lengthy negotiations, in January 2015, a UN working group adopted a formal recommendation to develop a legally binding agreement, which was adopted by the UN General Assembly in June 2015 (UNGA, UN Doc A/RES/69/292 (19 June 2015)). This new agreement may take the form of a further implementing agreement for the 1982 Convention. The need for a new agreement arises from the weakness in the current marine governance system which, with its fragmented and sectoral approach, does not adequately ensure the conservation of marine biodiversity in areas beyond national jurisdiction. A preparatory commission will consider the issues during 2016–17, following which a decision will be taken as to whether a new agreement is required (or wanted). It is expected that any new agreement would cover four issues: marine genetic resources, including questions on the sharing of benefits; measures such as area-based management tools, including marine protected areas; environmental impact assessments; and capacity building and the transfer of marine technology.

SECTION 2: THE TERRITORIAL SEA AND THE CONTIGUOUS ZONE

A: Territorial sea

The territorial sea is a belt of water immediately lying off the coast. It is an area over which the coastal State has full sovereignty and in this sense it is legally equivalent to land territory. All coastal States may enjoy a territorial sea for this is inherent in sovereignty. Historically, the seaward limit of the territorial sea extended so far as the coastal State could effectively exercise sovereignty from the coast: usually a limit of three miles, being the range of a canon-ball! This hardened in to a rule that three miles was the acceptable seaward extent of territorial sea. In the late twentieth century, it became clear that many States favoured an extension of the limit of the territorial sea, not least to preserve coastal states' rights and security. The 1982 Convention provides for a limit of 12 miles (Article 3) and this is generally accepted to reflect customary international law. According to the most recent published survey of the UK Hydrographic Office (2016), only six States claimed a territorial sea greater than 12 miles.

Necessarily, it becomes important to know from which point the territorial sea can be measured. Twelve nautical miles from where? Various methods exist but it is particularly problematic where the 'base point' is an island or low-tide elevation located some way off the coast. Such areas may have a significant impact on the reach of coastal State sovereignty and sometimes a disproportionate affect, as was seen in the *Qatar* v *Bahrain* Case (see Section 4B) where the existence of low-tide elevations was discounted in delimiting the territorial sea precisely because of their disproportionate effect on the maritime boundary between the two States.

Anglo-Norwegian Fisheries Case (UK v Norway)
ICJ Rep 1951 116, International Court of Justice

The UK objected to the method of delimitation employed by Norway to define its territorial sea. Essentially, the Norwegian method was to draw straight lines (baselines) from selected points on the coast from which the breadth of the territorial sea could be measured. Norway alleged that this was necessary because of the fragmented nature of her coastline (the *skjaergaard*), and it meant that the baselines assumed a geometrical and regular pattern. One consequence was that a greater proportion of water on the landward side of the baseline became 'internal waters'. The ICJ confirmed the legality of the straight baseline system, and its judgment was incorporated substantially in the 1958, and subsequently, the 1982 Conventions.

The Court has no difficulty in finding that, for the purpose of measuring the breadth of the territorial sea, it is the low-water mark as opposed to the high-water mark, or the mean between the two tides, which has generally been adopted in the practice of States. This criterion is the most favourable to the coastal State and clearly shows the character of territorial waters as appurtenant to the land territory. The Court notes that the Parties agree as to this criterion, but that they differ as to its application....

Three methods have been contemplated to effect the application of the low-water mark rule. The simplest would appear to be the method of the *tracé parallèle*, which consists of drawing the outer limit of the belt of territorial waters by following the coast in all its sinuosities. This method may be applied without difficulty to an ordinary coast, which is not too broken. Where a coast is deeply indented and cut into, as is that of Eastern Finnmark, or where it is bordered by an archipelago such as the 'skjægaard' along the western sector of the coast here in question, the base-line becomes independent of the low-water mark, and can only be determined by means of a geometric construction. In such circumstances the line of the low-water mark can no longer be put forward as a rule requiring the coast line to be followed in all its sinuosities; nor can one speak of exceptions when contemplating so rugged a coast in detail. Such a coast, viewed as a whole, calls for the application of a different method. Nor can one characterize as exceptions to the rule the very many derogations which would be necessitated by such a rugged coast. The rule would disappear under the exceptions.

The arcs of circles method, which is constantly used for determining the position of a point or object at sea, is a new technique in so far as it is a method for delimiting the territorial sea.... Its purpose is to secure the application of the principle that the belt of territorial waters must follow the line of the coast. It is not obligatory by law, as was admitted by Counsel for the United Kingdom Government in his oral reply....

The principle that the belt of territorial waters must follow the general direction of the coast makes it possible to fix certain criteria valid for any delimitation of the territorial sea; these criteria will be elucidated later. The Court will confine itself at this stage to noting that, in order to apply this principle, several States have deemed it necessary to follow the straight base-lines method and that they have not encountered objections of principle by other States. This method consists of selecting appropriate points on the low-water mark and drawing straight lines between them. This has been done, not only in the case of well-defined bays, but also in cases of minor curvatures of the coast line where it was solely a question of giving a simpler form to the belt of territorial waters....

[On the validity of the specific straight baseline system preferred by Norway] It does not at all follow that, in the absence of rules having the technically precise character alleged by the United Kingdom Government, the delimitation undertaken by the Norwegian Government in 1935 is not subject to certain principles which make it possible to judge as to its validity under international law. The delimitation of sea areas has always an international aspect; it cannot be dependent merely upon the will of the coastal State as expressed in its municipal law. Although it is true that the act of delimitation is necessarily a unilateral act, because only the coastal State is competent to undertake it, the validity of the delimitation with regard to other States depends upon international law.

In this connection, certain basic considerations inherent in the nature of the territorial sea, bring to light certain criteria which, though not entirely precise, can provide courts with an adequate basis for their decisions, which can be adapted to the diverse facts in question.

Among these considerations, some reference must be made to the close dependence of the territorial sea upon the land domain. It is the land which confers upon the coastal State a right to the waters off its coasts. It follows that while such a State must be allowed the latitude necessary in order to be able to adapt its delimitation to practical needs and local requirements, the drawing of base-lines must not depart to any appreciable extent from the general direction of the coast.

Another fundamental consideration, of particular importance in this case, is the more or less close relationship existing between certain sea areas and the land formations which divide or surround them. The real question raised in the choice of base-lines is in effect whether certain sea areas lying within these lines are sufficiently closely linked to the land domain to be subject to the regime of internal waters. This idea, which is at the basis of the determination of the rules relating to bays, should be liberally applied in the case of a coast, the geographical configuration of which is as unusual as that of Norway.

Finally, there is one consideration not to be overlooked, the scope of which extends beyond purely geographical factors: that of certain economic interests peculiar to a region, the reality and importance of which are clearly evidenced by a long usage.

Law of the Sea Convention 1982

The 1982 Convention repeats with only minor modifications the Articles of the 1958 Geneva Convention on the Territorial Sea and the Contiguous Zone.

Article 2 Legal status of the territorial sea, of the air space over the territorial sea and of its bed and subsoil

1. The sovereignty of a coastal State extends beyond its land territory and internal waters and, in the case of an archipelagic State, its archipelagic waters, to an adjacent belt of sea, described as the territorial sea.

2. This sovereignty extends to the air space over the territorial sea as well as to its bed and subsoil.

3. The sovereignty over the territorial sea is exercised subject to this Convention and to other rules of international law.

Article 3 Breadth of the territorial sea

Every State has the right to establish the breadth of its territorial sea up to a limit not exceeding 12 nautical miles, measured from baselines determined in accordance with this Convention.

Article 4 Outer limit of the territorial sea

The outer limit of the territorial sea is the line every point of which is at a distance from the nearest point of the baseline equal to the breadth of the territorial sea.

Article 5 Normal baseline

Except where otherwise provided in this Convention, the normal baseline for measuring the breadth of the territorial sea is the low-water line along the coast as marked on large-scale charts officially recognized by the coastal State....

Article 7 Straight baselines

1. In localities where the coastline is deeply indented and cut into, or if there is a fringe of islands along the coast in its immediate vicinity, the method of straight baselines joining appropriate points may be employed in drawing the baseline from which the breadth of the territorial sea is measured.

2. Where because of the presence of a delta and other natural conditions the coastline is highly unstable, the appropriate points may be selected along the furthest seaward extent of the low-water line and, notwithstanding subsequent regression of the low-water line, the straight baselines shall remain effective until changed by the coastal State in accordance with this Convention.

3. The drawing of straight baselines must not depart to any appreciable extent from the general direction of the coast, and the sea areas lying within the lines must be sufficiently closely linked to the land domain to be subject to the régime of internal waters.

4. Straight baselines shall not be drawn to and from low-tide elevations, unless lighthouses or similar installations which are permanently above sea level have been built on them or except in instances where the drawing of baselines to and from such elevations has received general international recognition.

5. Where the method of straight baselines is applicable under paragraph 1, account may be taken, in determining particular baselines, of economic interests peculiar to the region concerned, the reality and the importance of which are clearly evidenced by long usage.

6. The system of straight baselines may not be applied by a State in such a manner as to cut off the territorial sea of another State from the high seas or an exclusive economic zone....

Article 17 Right of innocent passage

Subject to this Convention, ships of all States, whether coastal or land-locked, enjoy the right of innocent passage through the territorial sea…

Article 19 Meaning of innocent passage

1. Passage is innocent so long as it is not prejudicial to the peace, good order or security of the coastal State. Such passage shall take place in conformity with this Convention and with other rules of international law.

2. Passage of a foreign ship shall be considered to be prejudicial to the peace, good order or security of the coastal State if in the territorial sea it engages in any of the following activities:
    (a) any threat or use of force against the sovereignty, territorial integrity or political independence of the coastal State, or in any other manner in violation of the principles of international law embodied in the Charter of the United Nations;
    (b) any exercise or practice with weapons of any kind;
    (c) any act aimed at collecting information to the prejudice of the defence or security of the coastal State;
    (d) any act of propaganda aimed at affecting the defence or security of the coastal State;
    (e) the launching, landing or taking on board of any aircraft;
    (f) the launching, landing or taking on board of any military device;
    (g) the loading or unloading of any commodity, currency or person contrary to the customs, fiscal, immigration or sanitary laws and regulations of the coastal State;
    (h) any act of wilful and serious pollution contrary to this Convention;
    (i) any fishing activities;
    (j) the carrying out of research or survey activities;
    (k) any act aimed at interfering with any system of communication or any other facilities or installations of the coastal State;
    (l) any other activity not having a direct bearing on passage.

Corfu Channel Case (*UK* v *Albania*)

Merits, ICJ Rep 1949 4, International Court of Justice

In October 1946, British warships sought to pass through the North Corfu Strait. Two were badly damaged by mines, allegedly laid by Albania. After deciding that this strait was a strait used for international navigation, one issue was whether the passage of British warships was 'innocent', so as to be permissible under customary international law.

It is, in the opinion of the Court, generally recognized and in accordance with international custom that States in time of peace have a right to send their warships through straits used for international navigation between two parts of the high seas without the previous authorization of a coastal State, provided that the passage is *innocent*. Unless otherwise prescribed in an international convention, there is no right for a coastal State to prohibit such passage through straits in time of peace....

The Albanian Government has further contended that the sovereignty of Albania was violated because the passage of the British warships on October 22nd, 1946, was not an *innocent passage*. The reasons advanced in support of this contention may be summed up as follows: The passage was not an ordinary passage, but a political mission; the ships were manœuvring and sailing in diamond combat formation with soldiers on board; the position of the guns was not consistent with innocent passage; the vessels passed with crews at action stations; the number of the ships and their armament surpassed what was necessary in order to attain their object, and showed an intention to intimidate and not merely to pass; the ships had received orders to observe and report upon the coastal defences and this order was carried out.

It is shown by the Admiralty telegram of September 21st, cited above, and admitted by the United Kingdom Agent, that the object of sending the warships through the Strait was not only to carry out a passage for purposes of navigation, but also to test Albania's attitude.... The legality of this measure taken by the Government of the United Kingdom cannot be disputed, provided that it was carried out in a manner consistent with the requirements of international law. The 'mission' was designed to affirm a right which had been unjustly denied. The Government of the United Kingdom was not bound to abstain from exercising its right of passage which the Albanian Government had illegally denied.

It remains, therefore, to consider whether the *manner* in which the passage was carried out was consistent with the principle of innocent passage, and to examine the various contentions of the Albanian Government in so far as they appear to be relevant....

It is shown by the evidence that the ships were not proceeding in combat formation, but in line, one after the other, and that they were not manœuvring until after the first explosion.... It is known...that ships, when using the North Corfu Strait, must pass with armament in fore and aft position. That this order was carried out during the passage on October 22nd is stated by the Commander-in-Chief, Mediterranean, in a telegram of October 26th to the Admiralty.... In the light of this evidence, the Court cannot accept the Albanian contention that the position of the guns was inconsistent with the rules of innocent passage.

In the above-mentioned telegram of October 26th, the Commander-in-Chief reported that the passage 'was made with ships at action stations in order that they might be able to retaliate quickly if fired upon again'. In view of the firing from the Albanian battery on May 15th, this measure of precaution cannot, in itself, be regarded as unreasonable. But four warships—two cruisers and two destroyers—passed in this manner, with crews at action stations, ready to retaliate quickly if fired upon. They passed one after another through this narrow channel, close to the Albanian coast, at a time of political tension in this region. The intention must have been, not only to test Albania's attitude, but at the same time to demonstrate such force that she would abstain from firing again on passing ships. Having regard, however, to all the circumstances of the case, as described above, the Court is unable to characterize these measures taken by the United Kingdom authorities as a violation of Albania's sovereignty.

USA/USSR Joint Statement on Uniform Interpretation of Rules of International Law Governing Innocent Passage, 23 September 1989

28 *International Legal Materials* 1444 (1989)

For maritime States, the right of innocent passage is of special importance. This joint statement is significant for it confirms (at least for these two States) that the Articles in the 1982 Convention reflect customary international law.

1. The relevant rules of international law governing innocent passage of ships in the territorial sea are stated in the 1982 United Nations Convention on the Law of the Sea (Convention of 1982), particularly in Part II, Section 3.

2. All ships, including warships, regardless of cargo, armament or means of propulsion, enjoy the right of innocent passage through the territorial sea in accordance with international law, for which neither prior notification nor authorization is required.

3. Article 19 of the Convention of 1982 sets out in paragraph 2 an exhaustive list of activities that would render passage not innocent. A ship passing through the territorial sea that does not engage in any of those activities is in innocent passage....

5. Ships exercising the right of innocent passage shall comply with all laws and regulations of the coastal State adopted in conformity with relevant rules of international law as reflected in Articles 21, 22, 23 and 25 of the Convention of 1982....

7. If a warship engages in conduct which violates such laws or regulations or renders its passage not innocent and does not take corrective action upon request, the coastal State may require it to leave the territorial sea, as set forth in Article 30 of the Convention of 1982. In such case the warship shall do so immediately.

NOTES

1. While there was early agreement over the nature of the territorial sea as a belt of water adjacent to the coast over which the coastal State exercised sovereignty, there was considerable disagreement over the permissible breadth of the territorial sea. The 1958 Convention on the Territorial Sea and Contiguous Zone contains no relevant provision, and a Second United Nations Conference on the Law of the Sea in 1962 failed by one vote to adopt a compromise solution. The provision adopted in the 1982 Convention reflects customary international law and is in any event binding on the parties. To some extent, however, the issue has become less pressing given the extension of State jurisdiction seawards under the Continental Shelf and Exclusive Economic Zone (EEZ) regimes (see Sections 3 and 4).

2. A problem related to that of the width of the territorial sea has been the method of its delimitation. The matter was brought to a head by the *Anglo-Norwegian Fisheries Case*, above, where the Court accepted the use of the 'straight baseline' system by Norway, at least in its dealings with the United Kingdom. The straight baseline system now seems to be valid *erga omnes*, irrespective of the opposition or agreement of other States, provided that the shape of the coastline merits its application. However, there are very many examples of the use of straight, geometric baselines in circumstances not falling within Article 7 of the 1982 Convention. It could be that customary international law is going beyond the Convention so as to permit straight baselines in all cases. The UK has made it clear that it opposes such baselines where they are not justified by the terms of Article 7 of the 1982 Convention.

3. Under Article 25(3) of the 1982 Convention, a State may suspend temporarily innocent passage in areas of its territorial sea for reasons of security, including weapons exercises. Such suspension must be publicised (see the list maintained at http://www.un.org/depts/los/convention_agreements/innocent_passages_suspension.htm). For example, in 2015, Mexico suspended the right of innocent passage temporarily in order to conduct naval exercises.

4. The ICJ has emphasised that the sovereignty enjoyed in relation to the territorial sea differs from the rights enjoyed by coastal States in respect of the EEZ and the continental shelf. For this reason, claims in respect of the territorial sea cannot be restricted due to competing claims by other States in respect of the EEZ or continental shelf: see, for example, *Territorial and Maritime Dispute (Nicaragua v Colombia)*, ICJ Reports II 624 (2012), paras 177–178.

B: The contiguous zone

Law of the Sea Convention 1982

Article 33

1. In a zone contiguous to its territorial sea, described as the contiguous zone, the coastal State may exercise the control necessary to:
   (a) prevent infringement of its customs, fiscal, immigration or sanitary laws and regulations within its territory or territorial sea;

(b) punish infringement of the above laws and regulations committed within its territory or territorial sea.

2. The contiguous zone may not extend beyond 24 nautical miles from the baselines from which the breadth of the territorial sea is measured.

Sorensen and Jensen, Case No. 3134
89 ILR 78 (1991), Supreme Court of Chile

The two defendants were foreign nationals charged with various crimes arising out of a collision 41 miles off the Chilean coast. They submitted that the Chilean courts lacked territorial jurisdiction. Chile had a 12-mile territorial sea, 12-mile contiguous zone, and a 200-mile EEZ.

3. Article 593 of the Chilean Civil Code provides that the maritime area contiguous to the territorial sea covers a further twelve miles beyond the territorial sea, which itself extends for twelve miles from the coast. Chile is therefore entitled to exercise jurisdiction over an area of twenty-four miles from the coast, with regard to the prevention and punishment of offences against the Chilean laws and regulations concerning customs, fiscal, immigration and sanitary matters. Article 596 of the Civil Code establishes that Chile enjoys exclusive sovereignty over the area beyond twenty-four miles and up to two hundred miles from its coast, with respect solely to economic matters.

4. In the light of the above considerations…it must be concluded that, since the events at issue occurred forty-one miles from the coast, they took place outside national territory, so that the Chilean courts are unable to exercise jurisdiction…Chilean criminal jurisdiction is limited to facts occurring within the national territory.

SECTION 3: THE CONTINENTAL SHELF

A: General principles

The continental shelf is rich in natural resources and highly prized by coastal States fortunate enough to possess a continental margin. It is not surprising, therefore, that this is one area of the law of the sea where reasonably detailed rules have emerged governing the rights to explore and exploit the resources of this region. These customary rules are mirrored and developed in the 1982 Convention. Many of the principles of continental shelf delimitation have developed through the jurisprudence of the ICJ. Of particular interest is the question of the seaward limit of the continental shelf. The 1958 Convention adopts a criterion of exploitability, while the 1982 Convention favours an automatic right to a shelf within 200 miles, with an extension if geomorphology permits. Clearly, for State parties to the 1982 Convention the matter is now settled. For other States, it may be that customary international law has developed to such an extent that the 1958 Convention is redundant.

Geneva Convention on the Continental Shelf 1958
499 UNTS 311

Article 1

For the purpose of these articles, the term 'continental shelf' is used as referring (a) to the seabed and subsoil of the submarine areas adjacent to the coast but outside the area of the territorial sea, to a depth of 200 metres or, beyond that limit, to where the depth of the superjacent waters admits of the exploitation of the natural resources of the said areas; (b) to the seabed and subsoil of similar submarine areas adjacent to the coasts of islands.

Article 6

1. Where the same continental shelf is adjacent to the territories of two or more states whose coasts are opposite each other, the boundary of the continental shelf appertaining to such states shall be determined by

agreement between them. In the absence of agreement, and unless another boundary line is justified by special circumstances, the boundary is the median line, every point of which is equidistant from the nearest points of the baselines from which the breadth of the territorial sea of each state is measured.

2. Where the same continental shelf is adjacent to the territories of two adjacent states, the boundary of the continental shelf shall be determined by agreement between them. In the absence of agreement, and unless another boundary line is justified by special circumstances, the boundary shall be determined by application of the principle of equidistance from the nearest points of the baselines from which the breadth of the territorial sea of each state is measured.

3. In delimiting the boundaries of the continental shelf, any lines which are drawn in accordance with the principles set out in paragraphs 1 and 2 of this article should be defined with reference to charts and geographical features as they exist at a particular date, and reference should be made to fixed permanent identifiable points on the land.

Law of the Sea Convention 1982

Article 76 Definition of the continental shelf

1. The continental shelf of a coastal State comprises the sea-bed and subsoil of the submarine areas that extend beyond its territorial sea throughout the natural prolongation of its land territory to the outer edge of the continental margin, or to a distance of 200 nautical miles from the baselines from which the breadth of the territorial sea is measured where the outer edge of the continental margin does not extend up to that distance.

2. The continental shelf of a coastal State shall not extend beyond the limits provided for in paragraphs 4 to 6.

3. The continental margin comprises the submerged prolongation of the land mass of the coastal State, and consists of the sea-bed and subsoil of the shelf, the slope and the rise. It does not include the deep ocean floor with its oceanic ridges or the subsoil thereof.

4. (a) For the purposes of this Convention, the coastal State shall establish the outer edge of the continental margin wherever the margin extends beyond 200 nautical miles from the baselines from which the breadth of the territorial sea is measured, by either:
    (i) a line delineated in accordance with paragraph 7 by reference to the outermost fixed points at each of which the thickness of sedimentary rocks is at least 1 per cent of the shortest distance from such point to the foot of the continental slope; or
    (ii) a line delineated in accordance with paragraph 7 by reference to fixed points not more than 60 nautical miles from the foot of the continental slope.
   (b) In the absence of evidence to the contrary, the foot of the continental slope shall be determined as the point of maximum change in the gradient at its base.

5. The fixed points comprising the line of the outer limits of the continental shelf on the sea-bed, drawn in accordance with paragraph 4(a) (i) and (ii), either shall not exceed 350 nautical miles from the baselines from which the breadth of the territorial sea is measured or shall not exceed 100 nautical miles from the 2,500 metre isobath, which is a line connecting the depth of 2,500 metres.

6. Notwithstanding the provisions of paragraph 5, on submarine ridges, the outer limit of the continental shelf shall not exceed 350 nautical miles from the baselines from which the breadth of the territorial sea is measured. This paragraph does not apply to submarine elevations that are natural components of the continental margin, such as its plateaux, rises, caps, banks and spurs.

7. The coastal State shall delineate the outer limits of its continental shelf, where that shelf extends beyond 200 nautical miles from the baselines from which the breadth of the territorial sea is measured, by straight lines not exceeding 60 nautical miles in length, connecting fixed points, defined by co-ordinates of latitude and longitude.

10. The provisions of this article are without prejudice to the question of delimitation of the continental shelf between States with opposite or adjacent coasts.

Article 77 Rights of the coastal State over the continental shelf

1. The coastal State exercises over the continental shelf sovereign rights for the purpose of exploring it and exploiting its natural resources.

2. The rights referred to in paragraph 1 are exclusive in the sense that if the coastal State does not explore the continental shelf or exploits its natural resources, no one may undertake these activities without the express consent of the coastal State.

3. The rights of the coastal State over the continental shelf do not depend on occupation, effective or notional, or on any express proclamation.

4. The natural resources referred to in this Part consist of the mineral and other non-living resources of the sea-bed and subsoil together with living organisms belonging to sedentary species, that is to say, organisms which, at the harvestable stage, either are immobile on or under the sea-bed or are unable to move except in constant physical contact with the sea-bed or the subsoil.

Article 78 Legal status of the superjacent waters and air space and the rights and freedoms of other states

1. The rights of the coastal State over the continental shelf do not affect the legal status of the superjacent waters or of the air space above those waters.

2. The exercise of the rights of the coastal State over the continental shelf must not infringe or result in any unjustifiable interference with navigation and other rights and freedoms of other States as provided for in this Convention.

Article 79 Submarine cables and pipelines on the continental shelf

1. All States are entitled to lay submarine cables and pipelines on the continental shelf, in accordance with the provisions of this article.

2. Subject to its right to take reasonable measures for the exploration of the continental shelf, the exploitation of its natural resources and the prevention, reduction and control of pollution from pipelines, the coastal State may not impede the laying or maintenance of such cables or pipelines.

3. The delineation of the course for the laying of such pipelines on the continental shelf is subject to the consent of the coastal State.

Article 82 Payments and contributions with respect to the exploitation of the continental shelf beyond 200 nautical miles

1. The coastal State shall make payments or contributions in kind in respect of the exploitation of the non-living resources of the continental shelf beyond 200 nautical miles from the baselines from which the breadth of the territorial sea is measured.

3. A developing State which is a net importer of a mineral resource produced from its continental shelf is exempt from making such payments or contributions in respect of that mineral resource.

4. The payments or contributions shall be made through the Authority, which shall distribute them to States Parties to this Convention, on the basis of equitable sharing criteria, taking into account the interests and needs of developing States, particularly the least developed and the land-locked among them.

Article 83 Delimitation of the continental shelf between states with opposite or adjacent coasts

1. The delimitation of the continental shelf between States with opposite or adjacent coasts shall be effected by agreement on the basis of international law, as referred to in Article 38 of the Statute of the International Court of Justice, in order to achieve an equitable solution.

2. If no agreement can be reached within a reasonable period of time, the States concerned shall resort to the procedures provided for in Part XV.

3. Pending agreement as provided for in paragraph 1, the States concerned, in a spirit of understanding and co-operation, shall make every effort to enter into provisional arrangements of a practical nature and, during this transitional period, not to jeopardize or hamper the reaching of the final agreement. Such arrangements shall be without prejudice to the final delimitation.

4. Where there is an agreement in force between the States concerned, questions relating to the delimitation of the continental shelf shall be determined in accordance with the provisions of that agreement.

NOTES
1. As Article 76 makes clear, the outer edge of the legal institution of the shelf may extend beyond 200 miles if the physical feature continues. The ICJ has confirmed that the definition of the continental shelf set out in Article 76(1) reflects customary international law, although it did not need to determine if other aspects of the Article were also customary: see *Territorial and Maritime Dispute (Nicaragua v Colombia)*, Judgment ICJ Reports II 624 (2012), para. 118.
2. In order to establish with clarity where such shelf rights end, the 1982 Convention (Article 76(8)) established the Commission on the Limits of the Continental Shelf (CLCS) whose purpose it is to consider data submitted by coastal States concerning the outer edge of the shelf beyond 200 miles (the extended continental shelf), to provide technical and scientific advice, and to make recommendations (see Annex II to the 1982 Convention). The Commission comprises scientific and technical, but not legal, experts. For more on the role and composition of the Commission, see the extract from *Bangladesh v Myanmar*, in Section 3B.
3. The 1982 Convention initially provided for a ten-year deadline for the submission of claims to the CLSC. However, this deadline proved problematic for developing countries (due to the resources and expertise required to prepare the detailed technical submissions for the CLCS) and was subsequently extended. In 2008, the requirement for submission was varied to provide that the submission of preliminary material by the deadline would suffice and a trust fund was established to support States to prepare submissions. As at December 2015, some 73 submissions had been made and recommendations have been made in relation to 22 of them. The submissions include submissions by Australia and the Russian Federation and a joint submission by France, Ireland, Spain and the United Kingdom in respect of the Bay of Biscay (see H. Llewellyn, 'The Commission on the Limits of the Continental Shelf: Joint Commission by France, Ireland, Spain, and the United Kingdom' (2007) 56 *International and Comparative Law Quarterly* 677). States disagreeing with recommendations made by the Commission may make revised submissions, as occurred in relation to claims submitted by the Russian Federation, Brazil and Barbados.
4. The CLCS has adopted procedures for instances where a submission relates to an area in which there is a maritime or territorial dispute (See Annex I to the Rules of Procedure). Where a dispute exists, the CLCS will not consider the submission without the prior consent of all parties to the dispute, and any recommendations made shall not affect the position of parties to the dispute. This need not be a dispute between coastal States—as discussed in Chapter 7, disputes as to sovereignty in respect of Antarctic territory led to the CLCS not considering claims in relation to the extended continental shelf generated from Antarctic territory.

B: Delimitation of the shelf

Delimitation of a shared continental shelf between opposite or adjacent States has provided the ICJ with considerable work. The relevant legal provisions are found in Article 6 of the 1958 Convention, Article 83 of the 1982 Convention and customary international law. As is evident from the extracts in this section there has been disagreement as to how these legal principles can be given practical effect in concrete cases. In addition, reference must also be made to the principles applicable to delimitation of the EEZ and so-called single maritime boundaries, that is, a delimitation of the continental shelf, EEZ, territorial sea and contiguous zone (or any combination thereof) between opposite or adjacent States by means of a single boundary rather than a boundary for each jurisdictional zone.

North Sea Continental Shelf Cases (Federal Republic of Germany v Denmark; FRG v The Netherlands)
ICJ Rep 1969 3, International Court of Justice

The Federal Republic of Germany (FRG) and Denmark, and the FRG and The Netherlands, had failed to agree on the division of their common continental shelf. The FRG was not a party to the 1958 Convention and thus Article 6 was not binding on it as a matter of treaty law. Denmark and The Netherlands argued that the 'equidistance-special circumstance' rule in that Article was now part of customary international law.

The FRG objected, especially since the equidistance principle would operate unjustly where there was a concave coast such as here. The Court decided that Article 6 did not then reflect customary international law and thus went on to discuss what principles of customary international law were applicable to continental shelf delimitation.

83. The legal situation therefore is that the Parties are under no obligation to apply either the 1958 Convention, which is not opposable to the Federal Republic, or the equidistance method as a mandatory rule of customary law, which it is not. But as between States faced with an issue concerning the lateral delimitation of adjacent continental shelves, there are still rules and principles of law to be applied....

85. It emerges from the history of the development of the legal régime of the continental shelf, which has been reviewed earlier, that the essential reason why the equidistance method is not to be regarded as a rule of law is that, if it were to be compulsorily applied in all situations, this would not be consonant with certain basic legal notions which...have from the beginning reflected the *opinio juris* in the matter of delimitation; those principles being that delimitation must be the object of agreement between the States concerned, and that such agreement must be arrived at in accordance with equitable principles. On a foundation of very general precepts of justice and good faith, actual rules of law are here involved which govern the delimitation of adjacent continental shelves—that is to say, rules binding upon States for all delimitations;—in short, it is not a question of applying equity simply as a matter of abstract justice, but of applying a rule of law which itself requires the application of equitable principles, in accordance with the ideas which have always underlain the development of the legal régime of the continental shelf in this field, namely:

   (a) the parties are under an obligation to enter into negotiations with a view to arriving at an agreement, and not merely to go through a formal process of negotiation as a sort of prior condition for the automatic application of a certain method of delimitation in the absence of agreement; they are under an obligation so to conduct themselves that the negotiations are meaningful, which will not be the case when either of them insists upon its own position without contemplating any modification of it;
   (b) the parties are under an obligation to act in such a way that, in the particular case, and taking all the circumstances into account, equitable principles are applied,—for this purpose the equidistance method can be used, but other methods exist and may be employed, alone or in combination, according to the areas involved;
   (c) ...the continental shelf of any State must be the natural prolongation of its land territory and must not encroach upon what is the natural prolongation of the territory of another State.

89. It must next be observed that, in certain geographical circumstances which are quite frequently met with, the equidistance method, despite its known advantages, leads unquestionably to inequity, in the following sense:

   (a) The slightest irregularity in a coastline is automatically magnified by the equidistance line as regards the consequences for the delimitation of the continental shelf. Thus it has been seen in the case of concave or convex coastlines that if the equidistance method is employed, then the greater the irregularity and the further from the coastline the area to be delimited, the more unreasonable are the results produced. So great an exaggeration of the consequences of a natural geographical feature must be remedied or compensated for as far as possible, being of itself creative of inequity.
   (b) In the case of the North Sea in particular, where there is no outer boundary to the continental shelf, it happens that the claims of several States converge, meet and intercross in localities where, despite their distance from the coast, the bed of the sea still unquestionably consists of continental shelf. A study of these convergences, as revealed by the maps, shows how inequitable would be the apparent simplification brought about by a delimitation which, ignoring such geographical circumstances, was based solely on the equidistance method.

91. Equity does not necessarily imply equality. There can never be any question of completely refashioning nature, and equity does not require that a State without access to the sea should be allotted an area of continental shelf, any more than there could be a question of rendering the situation of a State with an extensive coastline similar to that of a State with restricted coastline. Equality is to be reckoned within the same plane, and it is not such natural inequalities as these that equity could remedy....

95. The institution of the continental shelf has arisen out of the recognition of a physical fact; and the link between this fact and the law, without which that institution would never have existed, remains an important element for the application of its legal régime. The continental shelf is, by definition, an area physically extending the territory of most coastal States into a species of platform which has attracted the attention first of geographers and hydrographers and then of jurists.... The appurtenance of the shelf to the countries in front

of whose coastlines it lies, is therefore a fact, and it can be useful to consider the geology of that shelf in order to find out whether the direction taken by certain configurational features should influence delimitation because, in certain localities, they point-up the whole notion of the appurtenance of the continental shelf to the State whose territory it does in fact prolong.

97. Another factor to be taken into consideration in the delimitation of areas of continental shelf as between adjacent States is the unity of any deposits. The natural resources of the subsoil of the sea in those parts which consist of continental shelf are the very object of the legal régime established subsequent to the Truman Proclamation....

98. A final factor to be taken account of is the element of a reasonable degree of proportionality which a delimitation effected according to equitable principles ought to bring about between the extent of the continental shelf appertaining to the States concerned and the lengths of their respective coastlines,—these being measured according to their general direction in order to establish the necessary balance between States with straight, and those with markedly concave or convex coasts, or to reduce very irregular coastlines to their truer proportions....

Continental Shelf Case (*Libya* v *Malta*)
ICJ Rep 1985 13, International Court of Justice

By special agreement the States requested the Court to indicate the principles and rules applicable to the delimitation of their shared continental shelf, and also how such principles could be applied in practice. The two States were, 'opposite' rather than 'adjacent'. The 1958 Convention did not apply. The Court considered the 'distance' principle and the extent to which regard must be paid to the EEZ when delimiting the shelf.

33. In the view of the Court, even though the present case relates only to the delimitation of the continental shelf and not to that of the exclusive economic zone, the principles and rules underlying the latter concept cannot be left out of consideration. As the 1982 Convention demonstrates, the two institutions—continental shelf and exclusive economic zone—are linked together in modern law. Since the rights enjoyed by a State over its continental shelf would also be possessed by it over the sea-bed and subsoil of any exclusive economic zone which it might proclaim, one of the relevant circumstances to be taken into account for the delimitation of the continental shelf of a State is the legally permissible extent of the exclusive economic zone appertaining to that same State. This does not mean that the concept of the continental shelf has been absorbed by that of the exclusive economic zone; it does however signify that greater importance must be attributed to elements, such as distance from the coast, which are common to both concepts.

34. For Malta, the reference to distance in Article 76 of the 1982 Convention represents a consecration of the 'distance principle'; for Libya, only the reference to natural prolongation corresponds to customary international law. It is in the Court's view incontestable that, apart from those provisions, the institution of the exclusive economic zone, with its rule on entitlement by reason of distance, is shown by the practice of States to have become a part of customary law.... Although the institutions of the continental shelf and the exclusive economic zone are different and distinct, the rights which the exclusive economic zone entails over the sea-bed of the zone are defined by reference to the régime laid down for the continental shelf. Although there can be a continental shelf where there is no exclusive economic zone, there cannot be an exclusive economic zone without a corresponding continental shelf. It follows that, for juridical and practical reasons, the distance criterion must now apply to the continental shelf as well as to the exclusive economic zone; and this quite apart from the provision as to distance in paragraph 1 of Article 76. This is not to suggest that the idea of natural prolongation is now superseded by that of distance. What it does mean is that where the continental margin does not extend as far as 200 miles from the shore, natural prolongation, which in spite of its physical origins has throughout its history become more and more a complex and juridical concept, is in part defined by distance from the shore, irrespective of the physical nature of the intervening sea-bed and subsoil. The concepts of natural prolongation and distance are therefore not opposed but complementary; and both remain essential elements in the juridical concept of the continental shelf....

46. The normative character of equitable principles applied as a part of general international law is important because these principles govern not only delimitation by adjudication or arbitration, but also, and indeed primarily, the duty of Parties to seek first a delimitation by agreement, which is also to seek an equitable result....

49. It was argued by Libya that the relevant geographical considerations include the landmass behind the coast, in the sense that that landmass provides in Libya's view the factual basis and legal justification for the State's entitlement to continental shelf rights, a State with a greater landmass having a more intense natural prolongation. The Court is unable to accept this as a relevant consideration. Landmass has never been regarded as a basis of entitlement to continental shelf rights, and such a proposition finds no support in the practice of States, in the jurisprudence, in doctrine, or indeed in the work of the Third United Nations Conference on the Law of the Sea....

50. It was argued by Malta, on the other hand, that the considerations that may be taken account of include economic factors and security.... The Court does not however consider that a delimitation should be influenced by the relative economic position of the two States in question, in such a way that the area of continental shelf regarded as appertaining to the less rich of the two States would be somewhat increased in order to compensate for its inferiority in economic resources. Such considerations are totally unrelated to the underlying intention of the applicable rules of international law....

51. Malta contends that the 'equitable consideration' of security and defence interests confirms the equidistance method of delimitation, which gives each party a comparable lateral control from its coasts. Security considerations are of course not unrelated to the concept of the continental shelf. They were referred to when this legal concept first emerged, particularly in the Truman Proclamation. However, in the present case neither Party has raised the question whether the law at present attributes to the coastal State particular competences in the military field over its continental shelf, including competence over the placing of military devices. In any event, the delimitation which will result from the application of the present Judgment is, as will be seen below, not so near to the coast of either Party as to make questions of security a particular consideration in the present case.

58. [T]o use the ratio of coastal lengths as of itself determinative of the seaward reach and area of continental shelf proper to each Party, is to go far beyond the use of proportionality as a test of equity, and as a corrective of the unjustifiable difference of treatment resulting from some method of drawing the boundary line.... Its weakness as a basis of argument, however, is that the use of proportionality as a method in its own right is wanting of support in the practice of States, in the public expression of their views at (in particular) the Third United Nations Conference on the Law of the Sea, or in the jurisprudence.... That does not however mean that the 'significant difference in lengths of the respective coastlines' is not an element which may be taken into account at a certain stage in the delimitation process; this aspect of the matter will be returned to at the appropriate stage in the further reasoning of the Court.

Dispute Concerning Delimitation of the Maritime Boundary Between Bangladesh and Myanmar in the Bay of Bengal (Bangladesh v Myanmar)

Judgment, 14 March 2012, International Tribunal for the Law of the Sea

The facts are set out in Section 4B. One issue was whether the International Tribunal for the Law of the Sea (ITLOS) had jurisdiction to delimit the extended continental shelf.

369. The Tribunal will now examine the issue of whether it should refrain in the present case from exercising its jurisdiction to delimit the continental shelf beyond 200 nm [nautical miles] until such time as the outer limits of the continental shelf have been established by each Party pursuant to article 76, paragraph 8, of the Convention or at least until such time as the Commission has made recommendations to each Party on its submission and each Party has had the opportunity to consider its reaction to the recommendations.

370. The Tribunal wishes to point out that the absence of established outer limits of a maritime zone does not preclude delimitation of that zone. Lack of agreement on baselines has not been considered an impediment to the delimitation of the territorial sea or the exclusive economic zone notwithstanding the fact that disputes regarding baselines affect the precise seaward limits of these maritime areas. However, in such cases the question of the entitlement to maritime areas of the parties concerned did not arise.

371. The Tribunal must therefore consider whether it is appropriate to proceed with the delimitation of the continental shelf beyond 200 nm given the role of the Commission as provided for in article 76, paragraph 8, of the Convention and article 3, paragraph 1, of Annex II to the Convention....

374. The right of the coastal State under article 76, paragraph 8, of the Convention to establish final and binding limits of its continental shelf is a key element in the structure set out in that article. In order to realize this right, the

coastal State, pursuant to article 76, paragraph 8, is required to submit information on the limits of its continental shelf beyond 200 nm to the Commission, whose mandate is to make recommendations to the coastal State on matters related to the establishment of the outer limits of its continental shelf. The Convention stipulates in article 76, paragraph 8, that the 'limits of the shelf established by a coastal State on the basis of these recommendations shall be final and binding'.

375. Thus, the Commission plays an important role under the Convention and has a special expertise which is reflected in its composition. Article 2 of Annex II to the Convention provides that the Commission shall be composed of experts in the field of geology, geophysics or hydrography. Article 3 of Annex II to the Convention stipulates that the functions of the Commission are, *inter alia*, to consider the data and other material submitted by coastal States concerning the outer limits of the continental shelf in areas where those limits extend beyond 200 nm and to make recommendations in accordance with article 76 of the Convention.

376. There is a clear distinction between the delimitation of the continental shelf under article 83 and the delineation of its outer limits under article 76. Under the latter article, the Commission is assigned the function of making recommendations to coastal States on matters relating to the establishment of the outer limits of the continental shelf, but it does so without prejudice to delimitation of maritime boundaries. The function of settling disputes with respect to delimitation of maritime boundaries is entrusted to dispute settlement procedures under article 83 and Part XV of the Convention, which include international courts and tribunals.

377. There is nothing in the Convention or in the Rules of Procedure of the Commission or in its practice to indicate that delimitation of the continental shelf constitutes an impediment to the performance by the Commission of its functions.

378. Article 76, paragraph 10, of the Convention states that '[t]he provisions of this article are without prejudice to the question of delimitation of the continental shelf between States with opposite or adjacent coasts'. This is further confirmed by article 9 of Annex II, to the Convention, which states that the 'actions of the Commission shall not prejudice matters relating to delimitation of boundaries between States with opposite or adjacent coasts'.

379. Just as the functions of the Commission are without prejudice to the question of delimitation of the continental shelf between States with opposite or adjacent coasts, so the exercise by international courts and tribunals of their jurisdiction regarding the delimitation of maritime boundaries, including that of the continental shelf, is without prejudice to the exercise by the Commission of its functions on matters related to the delineation of the outer limits of the continental shelf....

409. A coastal State's entitlement to the continental shelf exists by the sole fact that the basis of entitlement, namely, sovereignty over the land territory, is present. It does not require the establishment of outer limits. Article 77, paragraph 3, of the Convention confirms that the existence of entitlement does not depend on the establishment of the outer limits of the continental shelf by the coastal State.

410. Therefore, the fact that the outer limits of the continental shelf beyond 200 nm have not been established does not imply that the Tribunal must refrain from determining the existence of entitlement to the continental shelf and delimiting the continental shelf between the parties concerned.

411. The Tribunal's consideration of whether it is appropriate to interpret article 76 of the Convention requires careful examination of the nature of the questions posed in this case and the functions of the Commission established by that article. It takes note in this regard that, as this article contains elements of law and science, its proper interpretation and application requires both legal and scientific expertise. While the Commission is a scientific and technical body with recommendatory functions entrusted by the Convention to consider scientific and technical issues arising in the implementation of article 76 on the basis of submissions by coastal States, the Tribunal can interpret and apply the provisions of the Convention, including article 76. This may include dealing with uncontested scientific materials or require recourse to experts.

NOTES

1. As regards delimitation of the shelf between opposite and adjacent States, the ICJ has attempted to develop a set of criteria to enable a delimitation to be made that is objectively valid and based on legal principles. The move from the formalistic approach of the *North Sea Cases* to the flexible, result-orientated approach of *Libya* v *Malta* and *Denmark* v *Norway* (see Section 4B) has been welcomed by some and rejected by others. Essentially, customary international law, the 1958 Convention and the 1982 Convention are all said to require the same result: an equitable

solution. However, it is questionable whether the principles and rules identified by the Court enable States to delimit their shelf *themselves* with any degree of certainty. Delimitation of the continental shelf is discussed further in Section 4B, in the context of the delimitation of common maritime boundaries for both the EEZ and the continental shelf.

2. ITLOS has become the first tribunal to delimit claims to the extended continental shelf. In *Bangladesh* v *Myanmar* (extracted above), both States were parties to the 1982 Convention and had made submissions to the CLCS. Distinguishing between the role of the CLCS in determining the outer limit of the continental shelf, and its own role in delimiting between two competing claims, the Court found it could proceed to delimit the boundary. However, the Court said it should only do so where there would be overlapping claims to the extended continental shelf, which was established by the data already provided to the CLCS. In contrast, the ICJ declined to delimit a boundary between Nicaragua and Colombia, as Nicaragua (having only filed preliminary, inconclusive data with the CLCS), had not yet established its claim to an extended continental shelf: see *Territorial and Maritime Dispute (Nicaragua* v *Colombia)*, ICJ Reports II 624 (2012), para. 129. Note that in September 2013, Nicaragua filed a subsequent application, specifically requesting delimitation of the extended continental shelf.

3. ITLOS confirmed that the same principles apply to delimitation of the extended continental shelf as to the continental shelf within 200 nautical miles, namely the equidistance/relevant circumstances approach: para. 455.

SECTION 4: THE EXCLUSIVE ECONOMIC ZONE

A: General principles

The EEZ is a post-1958 development, largely brought about because of the pressure to extend coastal States' rights beyond the territorial sea. The EEZ is particularly important for those States that have little or no geological continental shelf, such as many States in South America. Although the principle of the EEZ is firmly established in customary international law, it is important to consider the relationship between this maritime zone, and that of the territorial sea and continental shelf. All three represent different aspects of the seaward extension of coastal State jurisdiction developed in the second half of the twentieth century. In this regard, the extracts considered earlier in relation to shelf delimitation provide considerable evidence as to how EEZ delimitation should be conducted. The entry into force of the 1982 Convention also brings with it detailed provisions regulating use of the EEZ that were absent from customary international law.

Law of the Sea Convention 1982

Article 55 Specific legal régime of the exclusive economic zone

The exclusive economic zone is an area beyond and adjacent to the territorial sea, subject to the specific legal régime established in this Part, under which the rights and jurisdiction of the coastal State and the rights and freedoms of other States are governed by the relevant provisions of this Convention.

Article 56 Rights, jurisdiction and duties of the coastal state in the exclusive economic zone

1. In the exclusive economic zone, the coastal State has:
    (a) sovereign rights for the purpose of exploring and exploiting, conserving and managing the natural resources, whether living or non-living, of the waters superjacent to the sea-bed and of the sea-bed and its subsoil, and with regard to other activities for the economic exploitation and exploration of the zone, such as the production of energy from the water, currents and winds;
    (b) jurisdiction as provided for in the relevant provisions of this Convention with regard to:
        (i) the establishment and use of artificial islands, installations and structures;

     (ii) marine scientific research;
     (iii) the protection and preservation of the marine environment;
  (c) other rights and duties provided for in this Convention.

2. In exercising its rights and performing its duties under this Convention in the exclusive economic zone, the coastal State shall have due regard to the rights and duties of other States and shall act in a manner compatible with the provisions of this Convention.

3. The rights set out in this article with respect to the sea-bed and subsoil shall be exercised in accordance with Part VI.

Article 57 Breadth of the exclusive economic zone

The exclusive economic zone shall not extend beyond 200 nautical miles from the baselines from which the breadth of the territorial sea is measured.

Article 58 Rights and duties of other states in the exclusive economic zone

1. In the exclusive economic zone, all States, whether coastal or land-locked, enjoy, subject to the relevant provisions of this Convention, the freedoms referred to in article 87 of navigation and overflight and of the laying of submarine cables and pipelines, and other internationally lawful uses of the sea related to these freedoms, such as those associated with the operation of ships, aircraft and submarine cables and pipelines, and compatible with the other provisions of this Convention.

2. Articles 88 to 115 and other pertinent rules of international law apply to the exclusive economic zone in so far as they are not incompatible with this Part.

3. In exercising their rights and performing their duties under this Convention in the exclusive economic zone, States shall have due regard to the rights and duties of the coastal State and shall comply with the laws and regulations, adopted by the coastal State in accordance with the provisions of this Convention and other rules of international law in so far as they are not incompatible with this Part.

Article 61 Conservation of the living resources

1. The coastal State shall determine the allowable catch of the living resources in its exclusive economic zone.

2. The coastal State, taking into account the best scientific evidence available to it, shall ensure through proper conservation and management measures that the maintenance of the living resources in the exclusive economic zone is not endangered by over-exploitation. As appropriate, the coastal State and competent international organizations, whether subregional, regional or global, shall co-operate to this end.

Article 70 Right of geographically disadvantaged states

1. Geographically disadvantaged States shall have the right to participate, on an equitable basis, in the exploitation of an appropriate part of the surplus of the living resources of the exclusive economic zones of coastal States of the same subregion or region, taking into account the relevant economic and geographical circumstances of all the States concerned and in conformity with the provisions of this article and of articles 61 and 62....

Article 74 Delimitation of the exclusive economic zone between states with opposite or adjacent coasts

1. The delimitation of the exclusive economic zone between States with opposite or adjacent coasts shall be effected by agreement on the basis of international law as referred to in Article 38 of the Statute of the International Court of Justice, in order to achieve an equitable solution.

2. If no agreement can be reached within a reasonable period of time, the States concerned shall resort to the procedures provided for in Part XV.

3. Pending agreement as provided for in paragraph 1, the States concerned, in a spirit of understanding and co-operation, shall make every effort to enter into provisional arrangements of a practical nature and, during this transitional period, not to jeopardize or hamper the reaching of the final agreement. Such arrangements shall be without prejudice to the final delimitation.

4. Where there is an agreement in force between the States concerned, questions relating to the delimitation of the exclusive economic zone shall be determined in accordance with the provisions of that agreement.

Request for an Advisory Opinion Submitted by the Sub-Regional Fisheries Commission

Advisory Opinion, 2 April 2015, International Tribunal for the Law of the Sea

In March 2013, the Sub-Regional Fisheries Commission (SFRC) requested an Advisory Opinion from ITLOS in respect of four questions concerning the obligations and liability of States in respect of fishing and other activities, in particular illegal, unreported and unregulated (IUU) fishing. The following extract relates to the first question: What are the obligations of the flag State in cases where IUU fishing activities are conducted within the EEZ of third party States?

101. The Tribunal will now address the issue of conservation and management of living resources within the exclusive economic zone in view of the negative impact of IUU fishing thereon.

102. One of the goals of the Convention, as stated in its preamble, is to establish 'a legal order for the seas and oceans which…will promote' *inter alia* 'the equitable and efficient utilization of their resources, the conservation of their living resources, and the study, protection and preservation of the marine environment'. Consequently, laws and regulations adopted by the coastal State in conformity with the provisions of the Convention for the purpose of conserving the living resources and protecting and preserving the marine environment within its exclusive economic zone, consitute part of the legal order for the seas and oceans established by the Convention and therefore must be complied with by other States Parties whose ships are engaged in fishing activities within that zone.

103. The Convention provides in article 55 that the exclusive economic zone is an area beyond and adjacent to the territorial sea which is subject to the specific legal regime established in Part V of the Convention, 'under which the rights and jurisdiction of the coastal State and the rights and freedoms of other States are governed by the relevant provisions of [the] Convention.'

104. Under the Convention, responsibility for the conservation and management of living resources in the exclusive economic zone rests with the coastal State, which, pursuant to article 56, paragraph 1, of the Convention, has in that zone sovereign rights for the purpose of exploring and exploiting, conserving and managing the natural resources, whether living or non-living. In this regard, in accordance with article 61, paragraphs 1 and 2, of the Convention, the coastal State is entrusted with the responsibility to determine the allowable catch of the living resources in its exclusive economic zone and to 'ensure through proper conservation and management measures that the maintenance of the living resources in the exclusive economic zone is not endangered by over-exploitation.' Pursuant to article 62, paragraph 2, of the Convention, the coastal State is required through agreements or other arrangements to give other States access to the surplus of the allowable catch if it does not have the capacity to harvest the entire allowable catch. To meet its responsibilities, in accordance with article 62, paragraph 4, of the Convention, the coastal State is required to adopt the necessary laws and regulations, including enforcement procedures, which must be consistent with the Convention.

105. To ensure compliance with its laws and regulations concerning the conservation and management measures for living resources pursuant to article 73, paragraph 1, of the Convention, the coastal State may take such measures, including boarding, inspection, arrest and judicial proceedings, as may be necessary to ensure compliance with the laws and regulations adopted by it in conformity with the Convention.

106. Thus, in light of the special rights and responsibilities given to the coastal State in the exclusive economic zone under the Convention, the primary responsibility for taking the necessary measures to prevent, deter and eliminate IUU fishing rests with the coastal State.

107. This responsibility of the coastal State is also acknowledged in the MCA Convention [Convention on the Determination of the Minimal Conditions for Access and Exploitation of Marine Resources within the Maritime Areas Under Jurisdiction of the Member States of the SRFC], which states in article 25 that the SRFC Member States commit themselves to take such measures, and, to this end, to strengthen cooperation to fight against IUU fishing, in accordance with international law.

108. The Tribunal wishes to emphasize that the primary responsibility of the coastal State in cases of IUU fishing conducted within its exclusive economic zone does not release other States from their obligations in this regard.

109. The Tribunal will now turn to the examination of the obligations of flag States in the exclusive economic zones of the SRFC Member States in relation to the living resources in these zones. These will be considered from

two perspectives: that of general obligations of States under the Convention with regard to the conservation and management of marine living resources and that of specific obligations of flag States in the exclusive economic zone of the coastal State.

110. The Tribunal observes that the issue of flag State responsibility for IUU fishing activities is not directly addressed in the Convention. Therefore, this issue is examined by the Tribunal in light of general and specific obligations of flag States under the Convention for the conservation and management of marine living resources.

111. The Convention contains provisions concerning general obligations which are to be met by the flag State in all maritime areas regulated by the Convention, including the exclusive economic zone of the coastal State. These general obligations are set out in articles 91, 92 and 94 as well as articles 192 and 193 of the Convention. At the same time, the Convention imposes specific obligations on the flag State in article 58, paragraph 3, and article 62, paragraph 4, of the Convention with regard to its activities within the exclusive economic zone of the coastal State, in particular in respect of fishing activities conducted by nationals of the flag State.

112. The Tribunal wishes to observe that general and specific obligations of flag States for the conservation and management of marine living resources set out in the Convention are further specified in fisheries access agreements concluded between coastal States and flag States concerned. The Tribunal also observes, in this regard, that the MCA Convention contains specific provisions on the minimum conditions for access and exploitation of marine resources within the maritime zones under the jurisdiction of the SRFC Member States.

113. The Tribunal notes that the provisions of the MCA Convention require, *inter alia*, that fishing vessels belonging to a non-Member State obtain a fishing licence issued by the SRFC Member State concerned and land all their catches in the ports of the SRFC Member State that issued the fishing licence. Such provisions also require fishing vessels to carry out any transhipment in harbours designated by the SRFC Member State, provide declarations of catches in their logbook, and refrain from employing prohibited gear or equipment. In addition, the provisions of the MCA Convention require fishing vessels to give notice of their entry into and exit from maritime zones under the jurisdiction of an SRFC Member State and to take on board observers or inspectors from the SRFC Member State.

114. The Tribunal further notes that bilateral fisheries access agreements concluded by the SRFC Member States contain provisions setting out obligations for the flag State and vessels flying its flag. Such obligations require the flag State, *inter alia*, to: ensure compliance by its vessels with the laws and regulations of the SRFC Member State governing fisheries in the maritime zone under the jurisdiction of the SRFC Member State as well as with the relevant fisheries access agreements; ensure that its vessels undertake responsible fishing on the basis of the principle of sustainable exploitation of fishery resources; and, with regard to highly migratory species, ensure compliance with measures and recommendations of the International Commission for the Conservation of Atlantic Tunas (hereinafter 'ICCAT'). Vessels of the flag State are required, *inter alia*, to: possess a valid fishing authorization issued by the SRFC Member State; forward to the SRFC Member State statements of their catches; report to the SRFC Member State the date and time of their entry into and exit from the maritime zones; allow on board officials from the SRFC Member State for the inspection and control of fishing activities; take on board observers appointed by the SRFC Member State; be equipped with a satellite monitoring system. In addition, such vessels are required to send the position messages to the SRFC Member State when they are in the maritime zones under its jurisdiction.

115. Article 92 of the Convention stipulates that, save in exceptional cases expressly provided for in international treaties or in the Convention, ships are subject to the exclusive jurisdiction of the flag State on the high seas; by virtue of article 58, this also applies to the exclusive economic zone in so far as it is not incompatible with Part V of the Convention.

116. Article 94, paragraph 1, of the Convention requires the flag State to effectively exercise its jurisdiction and control over ships flying its flag in 'administrative, technical and social matters'. To achieve this purpose, the flag State is required by article 94, paragraph 2, subparagraph (b), to 'assume jurisdiction under its internal law over each ship flying its flag and its master, officers and crew in respect of administrative, technical and social matters concerning the ship.' Article 94 specifies in paragraphs 2, subparagraph (a), 3 and 4, that such exercise of jurisdiction and control by the flag State must include, in particular, maintaining a register of ships containing the names and particulars of the ships flying its flag, and taking necessary measures: to ensure safety of navigation and periodical surveying by a qualified surveyor of ships; to ensure that each ship flying its flag is in the charge

of a master and officers who possess appropriate qualifications; and to ensure that the crew is appropriate in qualification and numbers for the type, size, machinery and equipment of the ship.

117. The Tribunal holds the view that, since article 94, paragraph 2, of the Convention starts with the words '[i]n particular', the list of measures that are to be taken by the flag State to ensure effective exercise of its jurisdiction and control over ships flying its flag in administrative, technical and social matters is only indicative, not exhaustive.

118. Further, under article 94, paragraph 6, of the Convention, if a State has clear grounds to believe that proper jurisdiction and control with respect to a ship have not been exercised, it may report the facts to the flag State and the latter is obliged to investigate the matter upon receiving such a report and, if appropriate, take any action necessary to remedy the situation. The Tribunal is of the view that the flag State is under the obligation to inform the reporting State about the action taken.

119. It follows from the provisions of article 94 of the Convention that as far as fishing activities are concerned, the flag State, in fulfilment of its responsibility to exercise effective jurisdiction and control in administrative matters, must adopt the necessary administrative measures to ensure that fishing vessels flying its flag are not involved in activities which will undermine the flag State's responsibilities under the Convention in respect of the conservation and management of marine living resources. If such violations nevertheless occur and are reported by other States, the flag State is obliged to investigate and, if appropriate, take any action necessary to remedy the situation.

120. Article 192 of the Convention imposes on all States Parties an obligation to protect and preserve the marine environment. Article 193 of the Convention provides that 'States have the sovereign right to exploit their natural resources pursuant to their environmental policies and in accordance with their duty to protect and preserve the marine environment.' In the *Southern Bluefin Tuna Cases*, the Tribunal observed that 'the conservation of the living resources of the sea is an element in the protection and preservation of the marine environment' (*Southern Bluefin Tuna (New Zealand v. Japan; Australia v. Japan), Provisional Measures, Order of 27 August 1999, ITLOS Reports 1999*, p. 280, at p. 295, para. 70). As article 192 applies to all maritime areas, including those encompassed by exclusive economic zones, the flag State is under an obligation to ensure compliance by vessels flying its flag with the relevant conservation measures concerning living resources enacted by the coastal State for its exclusive economic zone because, as concluded by the Tribunal, they constitute an integral element in the protection and preservation of the marine environment.

121. As to the specific obligations of flag States in the exclusive economic zone of the coastal State, article 58, paragraph 3, of the Convention provides that:

> In exercising their rights and performing their duties…in the exclusive economic zone, States shall have due regard to the rights and duties of the coastal State and shall comply with the laws and regulations adopted by the coastal State in accordance with the provisions of this Convention and other rules of international law in so far as they are not incompatible with this Part.

122. The Convention further stipulates, in article 62, paragraph 4, that '[n]ationals of other States fishing in the exclusive economic zone shall comply with the conservation measures and with the other terms and conditions established in the laws and regulations of the coastal State.'

123. The Tribunal is of the view that article 62, paragraph 4, of the Convention imposes an obligation on States to ensure that their nationals engaged in fishing activities within the exclusive economic zone of a coastal State comply with the conservation measures and with the other terms and conditions established in its laws and regulations.

124. It follows from article 58, paragraph 3, and article 62, paragraph 4, as well as from article 192, of the Convention that flag States are obliged to take the necessary measures to ensure that their nationals and vessels flying their flag are not engaged in IUU fishing activities. In accordance with the MCA Convention and the national legislation of the SRFC Member States, such activities also constitute an infringement of the conservation and management measures adopted by these States within their exclusive economic zones. In other words, while under the Convention the primary responsibility for the conservation and management of living resources in the exclusive economic zone, including the adoption of such measures as may be necessary to ensure compliance with the laws and regulations enacted by the coastal State in this regard, rests with the coastal State, flag States also have the responsibility to ensure that vessels flying their flag do not conduct IUU fishing activities within the exclusive economic zones of the SRFC Member States.

NOTES
1. As with the continental shelf, the coastal State has 'sovereign rights' over the EEZ. However, the 1982 Convention also imposes obligations on coastal States as the counterpart of the benefits that coastal States gained from the EEZ. The obligations of the coastal State in relation to the protection of the maritime environment and regulation of fishing in the EEZ are outlined in the extract from the ITLOS Advisory Opinion. The detention by coastal States of vessels unlawfully fishing in the EEZ is a key feature of the law of the sea regime. ITLOS has mandatory jurisdiction in relation to these 'prompt release' cases under Article 292 of the 1982 Convention: see for example, the Tribunal's first case, *The M/V 'SAIGA' Case (Saint Vincent and the Grenadines v Guinea), Prompt Release*, 4 December 1997.
2. The EEZ regime is legally distinct from that of the continental shelf, although they may well overlap physically. In this respect it is important to consider the differences between the two legal regimes as they are set out in the 1982 Convention. However, should a case arise where opposite or adjacent States request a delimitation of only their respective EEZs, Article 74 of the 1982 Convention is so similar in content to Article 83 on shelf delimitation that the same principles would be relevant (though possibly with different emphasis).
3. As observed in the ITLOS Advisory Opinion extracted above, flag States also have obligations under the 1982 Convention with respect to the marine environment and activities in the EEZ of coastal States, such as fishing. In *The M/V 'Virginia G' Case (Panama/Guinea-Bissau)*, Judgment, 14 April 2014, ITLOS confirmed that there is a requirement for a genuine link between a vessel and the flag State. However, it defined the genuine link as the ability to 'exercise effective jurisdiction and control over that ship in order to ensure that it operates in accordance with generally accepted international regulations, procedures and practices' (para. 113) (See also *M/V 'SAIGA' (No. 2) (Saint Vincent and the Grenadines v Guinea)*, Judgment, ITLOS Reports 1999, p. 10, para. 83). The case of *M/V 'Virginia G'* concerned the practice of 'bunkering', the selling of fuel from specialised vessels, such as oil tankers, to other vessels while at sea. The Tribunal held that 'the regulation by a coastal State of bunkering of foreign vessels fishing in its exclusive economic zone is among those measures which the coastal State may take in its exclusive economic zone to conserve and manage its living resources' (para. 217).

B: A common maritime boundary

The extent to which the continental shelf and the EEZ should share the same delimitation solution between opposite or adjacent States has been the source of much academic and judicial comment. A key issue is whether it will always be 'equitable' for the continental shelf and the EEZ (or other zones) to share a common maritime boundary. More recent cases suggest a clear preference for a common maritime boundary, and a clear methodology for ensuring the boundary is equitable.

Gulf of Maine Case (Canada v USA)
ICJ Rep 1984 246, Chamber of the International Court of Justice

The parties asked a five-judge Chamber of the ICJ to determine a single boundary dividing their fisheries zones and shared continental shelf in the Gulf of Maine area. The 1958 Convention was in force between the parties.

116. [T]he question therefore arises whether the fact (already noted by the Chamber) that the 1958 Convention on the Continental Shelf is in force between the Parties does or does not make it obligatory to use, for the delimitation requested in the present case, the method specified in Article 6 of that Convention and, by implication, the application of the criterion on which it is based....

118. The Chamber therefore takes the view that if a question as to the delimitation of the continental shelf only had arisen between the two States, there would be no doubt as to the mandatory application of the method prescribed in Article 6 of the Convention, always subject, of course, to the condition that recourse is to be had to another method or combination of methods where special circumstances so require.

119. The purpose of the present proceedings is not, however, to obtain a delimitation of the continental shelf alone, as it might have been if they had taken place prior to the adoption by the two Parties of an exclusive fishery zone and the consequent emergence of the idea of delimitation by a single line. Their purpose is—and both Parties have abundantly emphasized the fact—to draw a single delimitation line for both the continental shelf and the superjacent fishery zone. It is doubtful whether a treaty obligation which is in terms confined to the delimitation of the continental shelf can be extended, in a manner that would manifestly go beyond the limits imposed by the strict criteria governing the interpretation of treaty instruments, to a field which is evidently much greater, unquestionably heterogeneous, and accordingly fundamentally different. Apart from this formal, but important, consideration, there is the more substantive point that such an interpretation would, in the final analysis, make the maritime water mass overlying the continental shelf a mere accessory of that shelf. Such a result would be just as unacceptable as the converse result produced by simply extending to the continental shelf the application of a method of delimitation adopted for the 'water column' only and its fish resources....

125. The Chamber must therefore conclude in this respect that the provisions of Article 6 of the 1958 Convention on the Continental Shelf, although in force between the Parties, do not entail either for them or for the Chamber any legal obligation to apply them to the single maritime delimitation which is the subject of the present case.

Maritime Delimitation in the Area between Greenland and Jan Mayen (Denmark v Norway)
ICJ Rep 1993 38, International Court of Justice

Denmark made an application to the Court requesting delimitation of its maritime boundary with Norway in the area surrounding Jan Mayen Island, a Norwegian island off the coast of Greenland, part of Denmark. Denmark claimed a single delimitation line corresponding to a 200-mile zone, while Norway relied on equidistance. This was the first case in which delimitation was based on the compulsory jurisdiction of the Court and not by special agreement of the parties.

41. The Parties also differ on the question whether what is required is one delimitation line or two lines, Denmark asking for 'a single line of delimitation of the fishery zone and continental shelf area', and Norway contending that the median line constitutes the boundary for delimitation of the continental shelf, and constitutes also the boundary for the delimitation of the fishery zone, i.e., that the two lines would coincide, but the two boundaries would remain conceptually distinct....

42. At first sight it might be thought that asking for the drawing of a single line and asking for the drawing of two coincident lines amounts in practical terms to the same thing. There is, however, in Norway's view, this important difference, that the two lines, even if coincident in location, stem from different strands of the applicable law, the location of the one being derived from the 1958 Convention, and the location of the other being derived from customary law....

44. It is sufficient for it to note, as do the Parties, that the 1958 Convention is binding upon them, that it governs the continental shelf delimitation to be effected, and that it is certainly a source of applicable law, different from that governing the delimitation of fishery zones. The Court will therefore examine separately the two strands of the applicable law; the effect of Article 6 of the 1958 Convention applicable to the delimitation of the continental shelf boundary, and then the effect of the customary law which governs the fishery zone.

45. It may be observed that the Court has never had occasion to apply the 1958 Convention.... In the present case, both States are parties to the 1958 Convention and, there being no joint request for a single maritime boundary as in the *Gulf of Maine* case, the 1958 Convention is applicable to the delimitation of the continental shelf between Greenland and Jan Mayen.

47. Regarding the law applicable to the delimitation of the fishery zone, there appears to be no decision of an international tribunal that has been concerned only with a fishery zone; but there are cases involving a single dual-purpose boundary asked for by the parties in a special agreement, for example the *Gulf of Maine* case, already referred to, which involved delimitation of 'the continental shelf and fishery zones' of the parties. The question was raised during the hearings of the relationship of such zones to the concept of the exclusive economic zone as proclaimed by many States and defined in Article 55 of the 1982 United Nations Convention on the Law of the Sea. Whatever that relationship may be, the Court takes note that the Parties

adopt in this respect the same position, in that they see no objection, for the settlement of the present dispute, to the boundary of the fishery zones being determined by the law governing the boundary of the exclusive economic zones, which is customary law; however the Parties disagree as to the interpretation of the norms of such customary law....

49. Turning first to the delimitation of the continental shelf, since it is governed by Article 6 of the 1958 Convention, and the delimitation is between coasts that are opposite, it is appropriate to begin by taking provisionally the median line between the territorial sea baselines, and then enquiring whether 'special circumstances' require 'another boundary line'. Such a procedure is consistent with the words in Article 6, 'In the absence of agreement, and unless another boundary line is justified by special circumstances, the boundary is the median line.'

Thus, in respect of the continental shelf boundary in the present case, even if it were appropriate to apply, not Article 6 of the 1958 Convention, but customary law concerning the continental shelf as developed in the decided cases, it is in accord with precedents to begin with the median line as a provisional line and then to ask whether 'special circumstances' require any adjustment or shifting of that line.

52. Turning now to the delimitation of the fishery zones, the Court must consider, on the basis of the sources listed in Article 38 of the Statute of the Court, the law applicable to the fishery zone, in the light also of what has been said above (paragraph 47) as to the exclusive economic zone. Of the international decisions concerned with dual-purpose boundaries, that in the *Gulf of Maine* case—in which the Chamber rejected the application of the 1958 Convention, and relied upon the customary law—is here material. After noting that a particular segment of the delimitation was one between opposite coasts, the Chamber went on to question the adoption of the median line 'as final without more ado', and drew attention to the 'difference in length between the respective coastlines of the two neighbouring States which border on the delimitation area' and on that basis affirmed 'the necessity of applying to the median line as initially drawn a correction which, though limited, will pay due heed to the actual situation' (*ICJ Reports 1984*, pp. 334–335, paras. 217, 218).

54. The Court is now called upon to examine every particular factor of the case which might suggest an adjustment or shifting of the median line provisionally drawn. The aim in each and every situation must be to achieve 'an equitable result'. From this standpoint, the 1958 Convention requires the investigation of any 'special circumstances'; the customary law based upon equitable principles on the other hand requires the investigation of 'relevant circumstances'....

56. Although it is a matter of categories which are different in origin and in name, there is inevitably a tendency towards assimilation between the special circumstances of Article 6 of the 1958 Convention and the relevant circumstances under customary law, and this if only because they both are intended to enable the achievement of an equitable result. This must be especially true in the case of opposite coasts where, as has been seen, the tendency of customary law, like the terms of Article 6, has been to postulate the median line as leading prima facie to an equitable result. It cannot be surprising if an equidistance-special circumstances rule produces much the same result as an equitable principles-relevant circumstances rule in the case of opposite coasts, whether in the case of a delimitation of continental shelf, of fishery zone, or of an all-purpose delimitation of continental shelf, of fishery zone, or of an all-purpose single boundary....

60. Both Parties have brought to the Court's attention various circumstances which they each regard as appropriate to be taken into account for the purposes of the delimitation. Neither Party has however presented these specifically in the context of the possible adjustment or shifting of a median line provisionally drawn: Norway, because it argues that the median line itself is the correct and equitable solution, and Denmark, because it contends that the median line should not be used, even as a provisional solution. Denmark does however, assert that, on the basis of the 1958 Convention, it could contend,

> that the island of Jan Mayen, *par excellence*, falls within the concept of 'special circumstances' and should be given no effect on Greenland's 200-mile continental shelf area....

87. Having thus completed its examination of the geophysical and other circumstances brought to its attention as appropriate to be taken into account for the purposes of the delimitation of the continental shelf and the fishery zones, the Court has come to the conclusion that the median line adopted provisionally for both, as first stage in the delimitation, should be adjusted or shifted to become a line such as to attribute a larger area of maritime space to Denmark than would the median line. The line drawn by Denmark 200 nautical miles from the baselines of eastern Greenland would however be excessive as an adjustment, and would be inequitable in its effects. The delimitation line must therefore be drawn within the area of overlapping claims, between the lines proposed by each Party.

Case Concerning Maritime Delimitation and Territorial Questions between Qatar and Bahrain (Qatar v Bahrain)

Merits, ICJ Rep 2001 40, International Court of Justice

The parties asked the ICJ to draw a single maritime boundary consequent upon the resolution of certain territorial questions relating to islands in the area.

167. The Parties are in agreement that the Court should render its decision on the maritime delimitation in accordance with international law. Neither Bahrain nor Qatar is party to the Geneva Conventions on the Law of the Sea of 29 April 1958; Bahrain has ratified the United Nations Convention on the Law of the Sea of 10 December 1982 but Qatar is only a signatory to it. Customary international law, therefore, is the applicable law. Both Parties, however, agree that most of the provisions of the 1982 Convention which are relevant for the present case reflect customary law....

169. It should be kept in mind that the concept of 'single maritime boundary' may encompass a number of functions. In the present case the single maritime boundary will be the result of the delimitation of various jurisdictions. In the southern part of the delimitation area, which is situated where the coasts of the Parties are opposite to each other, the distance between these coasts is nowhere more than 24 nautical miles. The boundary the Court is expected to draw will, therefore, delimit exclusively their territorial seas and, consequently, an area over which they enjoy territorial sovereignty.

170. More to the north, however, where the coasts of the two States are no longer opposite to each other but are rather comparable to adjacent coasts, the delimitation to be carried out will be one between the continental shelf and exclusive economic zone belonging to each of the Parties, areas in which States have only sovereign rights and functional jurisdiction. Thus both Parties have differentiated between a southern and a northern sector....

173. The Court observes that the concept of a single maritime boundary does not stem from multilateral treaty law but from State practice, and that it finds its explanation in the wish of States to establish one uninterrupted boundary line delimiting the various—partially coincident—zones of maritime jurisdiction appertaining to them. In the case of coincident jurisdictional zones, the determination of a single boundary for the different objects of delimitation:

> can only be carried out by the application of a criterion, or combination of criteria, which does not give preferential treatment to one of these...objects to the detriment of the other, and at the same time is such as to be equally suitable to the division of either of them,

as was stated by the Chamber of the Court in the *Gulf of Maine* case (*ICJ Reports 1984*, p. 327, para. 194). In that case, the Chamber was asked to draw a single line which would delimit both the continental shelf and the superjacent water column.

174. Delimitation of territorial seas does not present comparable problems, since the rights of the coastal State in the area concerned are not functional but territorial, and entail sovereignty over the sea-bed and the superjacent waters and air column. Therefore, when carrying out that part of its task, the Court has to apply first and foremost the principles and rules of international customary law which refer to the delimitation of the territorial sea, while taking into account that its ultimate task is to draw a single maritime boundary that serves other purposes as well....

212. The Court observes that the method of straight baselines, which is an exception to the normal rules for the determination of baselines, may only be applied if a number of conditions are met. This method must be applied restrictively. Such conditions are primarily that either the coastline is deeply indented and cut into, or that there is a fringe of islands along the coast in its immediate vicinity.

213. The fact that a State considers itself a multiple-island State or a *de facto* archipelagic State does not allow it to deviate from the normal rules for the determination of baselines unless the relevant conditions are met. The coasts of Bahrain's main islands do not form a deeply indented coast, nor does Bahrain claim this. It contends, however, that the maritime features off the coast of the main islands may be assimilated to a fringe of islands which constitute a whole with the mainland.

214. The Court does not deny that the maritime features east of Bahrain's main islands are part of the overall geographical configuration; it would be going too far, however, to qualify them as a fringe of islands along the coast. The islands concerned are relatively small in number. Moreover, in the present case it is only possible to

speak of a 'cluster of islands' or an 'island system' if Bahrain's main islands are included in that concept. In such a situation, the method of straight baselines is applicable only if the State has declared itself to be an archipelagic State under Part IV of the 1982 Convention on the Law of the Sea, which is not true of Bahrain in this case.

215. The Court, therefore, concludes that Bahrain is not entitled to apply the method of straight baselines. Thus each maritime feature has its own effect for the determination of the baselines, on the understanding that, on the grounds set out before, the low-tide elevations situated in the overlapping zone of territorial seas will be disregarded. It is on this basis that the equidistance line must be drawn.

Case Concerning Maritime Delimitation in the Black Sea (Romania v Ukraine)

ICJ Rep 2009 61, International Court of Justice

Romania asked the ICJ to establish a single maritime boundary between the two States in the Black Sea, thereby delimiting the continental shelf and the EEZ. Jurisdiction was not disputed but Ukraine did not consider that the single delimitation would also effectively delimit areas of territorial sea.

26. The Court observes that Ukraine is not contending that under international law, as a matter of principle, there cannot be a delimitation line separating the territorial sea of one State from the exclusive economic zone and the continental shelf of another State. In fact, such a line was determined by the Court in its latest judgment on maritime delimitation (see *Territorial and Maritime Dispute between Nicaragua and Honduras in the Caribbean Sea*, Judgment of 8 October 2007). Ukraine rather relies on the terms of paragraph 4(h) of the Additional Agreement, which in its view, 'suggest[s] that the Parties did not anticipate that the Court would be called upon to delimit an all-purpose maritime boundary along the outer limit of Ukraine's territorial sea' around Serpents' Island.

30. In discharging its task, the Court will duly take into account the agreements in force between the Parties relating to the delimitation of their respective territorial seas. The Court has no jurisdiction to delimit the territorial seas of the Parties. Its jurisdiction covers the delimitation of their continental shelf and the exclusive economic zones. However, contrary to what has been suggested by Ukraine, nothing hinders that jurisdiction from being exercised so that a segment of the line may result in a delimitation between, on the one hand, the exclusive economic zone and the continental shelf of one State, and, on the other hand, the territorial sea of the other State at its seaward limit.

110. The Court observes that the legal concept of the 'relevant area' has to be taken into account as part of the methodology of maritime delimitation. In the first place, depending on the configuration of the relevant coasts in the general geographical context and the methods for the construction of their seaward projections, the relevant area may include certain maritime spaces and exclude others which are not germane to the case in hand. Secondly, the relevant area is pertinent to checking disproportionality. This will be done as the final phase of the methodology. The purpose of delimitation is not to apportion equal shares of the area, nor indeed proportional shares. The test of disproportionality is not in itself a method of delimitation. It is rather a means of checking whether the delimitation line arrived at by other means needs adjustment because of a significant disproportionality in the ratios between the maritime areas which would fall to one party or other by virtue of the delimitation line arrived at by other means, and the lengths of their respective coasts.

111. The Court further observes that for the purposes of this final exercise in the delimitation process the calculation of the relevant area does not purport to be precise and is approximate. The object of delimitation is to achieve a delimitation that is equitable, not an equal apportionment of maritime areas ....

112. The Court notes that the delimitation will occur within the enclosed Black Sea, with Romania being both adjacent to, and opposite Ukraine, and with Bulgaria and Turkey lying to the south. It will stay north of any area where third party interests could become involved....

115. When called upon to delimit the continental shelf or exclusive economic zones, or to draw a single delimitation line, the Court proceeds in defined stages.

116. These separate stages, broadly explained in the case concerning *Continental Shelf (Libyan Arab Jamahiriya/Malta) (Judgment, I.C.J. Reports 1985*, p. 46, para. 60), have in recent decades been specified with precision. First, the Court will establish a provisional delimitation line, using methods that are geometrically objective and also appropriate for the geography of the area in which the delimitation is to take place. So far as delimitation

between adjacent coasts is concerned, an equidistance line will be drawn unless there are compelling reasons that make this unfeasible in the particular case (see *Territorial and Maritime Dispute between Nicaragua and Honduras in the Caribbean Sea (Nicaragua v. Honduras)*, Judgment of 8 October 2007, para. 281). So far as opposite coasts are concerned, the provisional delimitation line will consist of a median line between the two coasts. No legal consequences flow from the use of the terms 'median line' and 'equidistance line' since the method of delimitation is the same for both.

117. Equidistance and median lines are to be constructed from the most appropriate points on the coasts of the two States concerned, with particular attention being paid to those protuberant coastal points situated nearest to the area to be delimited. The Court considers elsewhere (see paragraphs 135–137 below) the extent to which the Court may, when constructing a single-purpose delimitation line, deviate from the base points selected by the parties for their territorial seas. When construction of a provisional equidistance line between adjacent States is called for, the Court will have in mind considerations relating to both parties' coastlines when choosing its own base points for this purpose. The line thus adopted is heavily dependent on the physical geography and the most seaward points of the two coasts.

118. In keeping with its settled jurisprudence on maritime delimitation, the first stage of the Court's approach is to establish the provisional equidistance line. At this initial stage of the construction of the provisional equidistance line the Court is not yet concerned with any relevant circumstances that may obtain and the line is plotted on strictly geometrical criteria on the basis of objective data.

119. In the present case the Court will thus begin by drawing a provisional equidistance line between the adjacent coasts of Romania and Ukraine, which will then continue as a median line between their opposite coasts.

120. The course of the final line should result in an equitable solution (Articles 74 and 83 of UNCLOS). Therefore, the Court will at the next, second stage, consider whether there are factors calling for the adjustment or shifting of the provisional equidistance line in order to achieve an equitable result (*Land and Maritime Boundary between Cameroon and Nigeria (Cameroon v. Nigeria: Equatorial Guinea intervening), Judgment, I.C.J. Reports 2002*, p. 441, para. 288). The Court has also made clear that when the line to be drawn covers several zones of coincident jurisdictions, 'the so-called equitable principles/relevant circumstances method may usefully be applied, as in these maritime zones this method is also suited to achieving an equitable result' (*Territorial and Maritime Dispute between Nicaragua and Honduras in the Caribbean Sea (Nicaragua v. Honduras)*, Judgment of 8 October 2007, para. 271).

121. This is the second part of the delimitation exercise to which the Court will turn, having first established the provisional equidistance line.

122. Finally, and at a third stage, the Court will verify that the line (a provisional equidistance line which may or may not have been adjusted by taking into account the relevant circumstances) does not, as it stands, lead to an inequitable result by reason of any marked disproportion between the ratio of the respective coastal lengths and the ratio between the relevant maritime area of each State by reference to the delimitation line (see paragraphs 214–215). A final check for an equitable outcome entails a confirmation that no great disproportionality of maritime areas is evident by comparison to the ratio of coastal lengths.

This is not to suggest that these respective areas should be proportionate to coastal lengths as the Court has said 'the sharing out of the area is therefore the consequence of the delimitation, not vice versa' (*Maritime Delimitation in the Area between Greenland and Jan Mayen (Denmark v. Norway), Judgment, I.C.J. Reports 1993*, p. 67, para. 64).

Dispute Concerning Delimitation of the Maritime Boundary Between Bangladesh and Myanmar in the Bay of Bengal (Bangladesh v Myanmar)

Judgment, 14 March 2012, ITLOS

Bangladesh and Myanmar requested ITLOS to delimit the maritime boundary in respect of the territorial sea, EEZ and continental shelf.

227. Beginning with the *North Sea Continental Shelf* cases, it was emphasized in the early cases that no method of delimitation is mandatory, and that the configuration of the coasts of the parties in relation to each other may render an equidistance line inequitable in certain situations. This position was first articulated with respect to the continental shelf, and was thereafter maintained with respect to the exclusive economic zone as well.

228. Over time, the absence of a settled method of delimitation prompted increased interest in enhancing the objectivity and predictability of the process. The varied geographic situations addressed in the early cases nevertheless confirmed that, even if the pendulum had swung too far away from the objective precision of equidistance, the use of equidistance alone could not ensure an equitable solution in each and every case. A method of delimitation suitable for general use would need to combine its constraints on subjectivity with the flexibility necessary to accommodate circumstances in a particular case that are relevant to maritime delimitation.

229. In the case concerning *Maritime Delimitation in the Area between Greenland and Jan Mayen*, the ICJ expressly articulated the approach of dividing the delimitation process into two stages, namely 'to begin with the median line as a provisional line and then to ask whether "special circumstances" require any adjustment or shifting of that line' (*Judgment, I.C.J. Reports 1993*, p. 38, at p. 61, para. 51). This general approach has proven to be suitable for use in most of the subsequent judicial and arbitral delimitations. As developed in those cases, it has come to be known as the equidistance/relevant circumstances method.

230. In the case concerning *Maritime Delimitation and Territorial Questions between Qatar and Bahrain*, the ICJ adopted the same approach (*Merits, Judgment, I.C.J. Reports 2001*, p. 40, at p. 111, para. 230). In 2002, in the case concerning the *Land and Maritime Boundary between Cameroon and Nigeria (Cameroon v. Nigeria: Equatorial Guinea intervening)*, the ICJ confirmed its previous two-stage approach to the delimitation (*Judgment, I.C.J. Reports 2002*, p. 303, at p. 441, para. 288).

231. The Arbitral Tribunal in the *Arbitration between Barbados and the Republic of Trinidad and Tobago*, affirmed that '[t]he determination of the line of delimitation [...] normally follows a two-step approach', involving the positing of a provisional line of equidistance and then examining it in the light of the relevant circumstances. The Arbitral Tribunal further pointed out that 'while no method of delimitation can be considered of and by itself compulsory, and no court or tribunal has so held, the need to avoid subjective determinations requires that the method used start with a measure of certainty that equidistance positively ensures, subject to its subsequent correction if justified' (*Decision of 11 April 2006, RIAA, Vol. XXVII*, p. 147, at p.214, para. 242, and at p. 230, para. 306).

232. Similarly, the Arbitral Tribunal in the case between Guyana and Suriname noted:

> The case law of the International Court of Justice and arbitral jurisprudence as well as State practice are at one in holding that the delimitation process should, in appropriate cases, begin by positing a provisional equidistance line which may be adjusted in the light of relevant circumstances in order to achieve an equitable solution (*Arbitration between Guyana and Suriname, Award of 17 September 2007, ILM, Vol. 47 (2008)*, p. 116, at p. 213, para. 342).

233. In the *Black Sea* case, the ICJ built on the evolution of the jurisprudence on maritime delimitation. In that case, the ICJ gave a description of the three-stage methodology which it applied. At the first stage, it established a provisional equidistance line, using methods that are geometrically objective and also appropriate for the geography of the area to be delimited. 'So far as delimitation between adjacent coasts is concerned, an equidistance line will be drawn unless there are compelling reasons that make this unfeasible in the particular case' (*Maritime Delimitation in the Black Sea (Romania v. Ukraine), Judgment, I.C.J. Reports 2009*, p. 61, at p. 101, para. 116). At the second stage, the ICJ ascertained whether 'there are factors calling for the adjustment or shifting of the provisional equidistance line in order to achieve an equitable result' (*ibid.*, at pp. 101, para. 120). At the third stage, it verified that the delimitation line did not lead to 'an inequitable result by reason of any marked disproportion between the ratio of the respective coastal lengths and the ratio between the relevant maritime area of each State by reference to the delimitation line' (*ibid.*, at p. 103, para. 122).

234. The Tribunal notes that, as an alternative to the equidistance/relevant circumstances method, where recourse to it has not been possible or appropriate, international courts and tribunals have applied the angle-bisector method, which is in effect an approximation of the equidistance method. The angle-bisector method was applied in cases preceding the *Libyan Arab Jamahiriya/Malta* judgment, namely, *Continental Shelf (Tunisia/Libyan Arab Jamahiriya) (Judgment, I.C.J. Reports 1982*, p. 18, at p. 94, para. 133 (C) (3)), *Delimitation of the Maritime Boundary in the Gulf of Maine Area (Judgment, I.C.J. Reports 1984*, p. 246, at p. 333, para. 213), and *Delimitation of the Maritime Boundary between Guinea and Guinea-Bissau (Decision of 14 February 1985, ILR, Vol. 77*, p. 635, at pp. 683–685, paras. 108–111). It was more recently applied in the case concerning *Territorial and Maritime Dispute between Nicaragua and Honduras in the Caribbean Sea (Nicaragua v. Honduras) (Judgment, I.C.J. Reports 2007*, p. 659, at p. 741, para. 272 and at p. 746, para. 287).

235. The Tribunal observes that the issue of which method should be followed in drawing the maritime delimitation line should be considered in light of the circumstances of each case. The goal of achieving an

equitable result must be the paramount consideration guiding the action of the Tribunal in this connection. Therefore the method to be followed should be one that, under the prevailing geographic realities and the particular circumstances of each case, can lead to an equitable result.

NOTES

1. The above cases, together with those in Section 3 on the continental shelf, illustrate the debate between various scholars and judges as to the proper approach to maritime delimitation. There is an essential difference between those who favour relatively fixed criteria such as 'equidistance' or 'natural prolongation' and those who believe that relatively open-ended general equitable principles possibly combined with a presumptive distance criterion (i.e. 200 miles from the coast) are required to meet the unique nature of each maritime zone. It seems from the case of *Romania* v *Ukraine* and subsequent decisions that the more flexible criteria are to be adopted.

2. There is clear preference for the delimitation of single maritime boundaries between opposite and adjacent states: one boundary for all the overlapping zones. Whatever the legal difficulties with such an approach under the strict terms of the 1982 Convention, it seems that most States (and the ICJ) regard this as a pragmatic and workable solution. There are enough jurisdictional conflicts within the law of the sea without adding to them by preferring different boundary lines for different types of maritime zone.

3 The Court in *Romania* v *Ukraine* lays out with some clarity the three-stage approach that should be adopted: provisional equidistance line; special circumstances; and then a check for an equitable outcome through the application of a 'disproportionality test'. This approach has been followed in subsequent cases: see *Territorial and Maritime Dispute (Nicaragua* v *Colombia)* ICJ Reports II 624 (2012) and *Dispute Concerning Delimitation of the Maritime Boundary Between Bangladesh and Myanmar in the Bay of Bengal (Bangladesh* v *Myanmar)* ITLOS, 14 March 2012.

4. The sovereignty of islands and low tide elevations in maritime delimitation is often critical, as islands can generate their own territorial sea and maritime zones. However, the impact of the use of islands and low tide elevations as a baseline for maritime boundaries is considered one of the special circumstances that may lead to a disproportionate (and hence inequitable) outcome and may lead to the provisional equidistance line being varied. See, for example, the treatment of several islands by the ICJ in the *Territorial and Maritime Dispute (Nicaragua* v *Colombia)* decision. Other factors identified as potentially relevant circumstances in that case include: where there is a substantial difference in the length of the relevant coastlines; the geographical context (which includes reliance on islands); the conduct of the parties; security and law enforcement concerns; equitable access; and existing delimitations.

5. In *Maritime Dispute (Peru* v *Chile)* (Judgment of 27 January 2014), the ICJ held that the parties had already agreed a maritime boundary, at least partially, on the basis of previous agreements, conduct and acknowledgements. The Court relied on this existing maritime boundary, and then applied the three-stage approach identified in *Romania* v *Ukraine* to delimit the remaining portion of the boundary.

SECTION 5: THE HIGH SEAS

The area of sea beyond national jurisdiction is known as the 'high seas'. For all practical purposes this means that the high seas commence from the outer edge of the territorial sea or the outer edge of the EEZ, should one exist. Waters that are not part of an EEZ but that are super-adjacent to a continental shelf that extends beyond 200 miles from the coast are also high seas, as are those beyond the territorial sea if no EEZ has been claimed. The 'freedom of the seas' has legal as well as political connotations, and it has been one of the cornerstones of maritime law ever since the rejection of the doctrine of 'closed seas' in the seventeenth century. Many jurists would argue that the 'freedom of the seas' has attained the status of *jus cogens*.

Law of the Sea Convention 1982

Article 86 Application of the provisions of this part

The provisions of this Part apply to all parts of the sea that are not included in the exclusive economic zone, in the territorial sea or in the internal waters of a State, or in the archipelagic waters of an archipelagic State. This article does not entail any abridgement of the freedoms enjoyed by all States in the exclusive economic zone in accordance with article 58.

Article 87 Freedom of the high seas

1. The high seas are open to all States, whether coastal or land-locked. Freedom of the high seas is exercised under the conditions laid down by this Convention and by other rules of international law. It comprises, *inter alia*, both for coastal and land-locked States:
    (a) freedom of navigation;
    (b) freedom of overflight;
    (c) freedom to lay submarine cables and pipelines, subject to Part VI;
    (d) freedom to construct artificial islands and other installations permitted under international law, subject to Part VI;
    (e) freedom of fishing, subject to the conditions laid down in section 2;
    (f) freedom of scientific research, subject to Parts VI and XIII.

2. These freedoms shall be exercised by all States with due regard for the interests of other States in their exercise of the freedom of the high seas, and also with due regard for the rights under this Convention with respect to activities in the Area.

Article 88 Reservation of the high seas for peaceful purposes

The high seas shall be reserved for peaceful purposes.

Article 89 Invalidity of claims of sovereignty over the high seas

No State may validly purport to subject any part of the high seas to its sovereignty.

Article 90 Right of navigation

Every State, whether coastal or land-locked, has the right to sail ships flying its flag on the high seas.

Article 99 Prohibition of the transport of slaves

Every State shall take effective measures to prevent and punish the transport of slaves in ships authorized to fly its flag and to prevent the unlawful use of its flag for that purpose. Any slave taking refuge on board any ship, whatever its flag, shall *ipso facto* be free.

Article 100 Duty to co-operate in the repression of piracy

All States shall co-operate to the fullest possible extent in the repression of piracy on the high seas or in any other place outside the jurisdiction of any State.

Article 101 Definition of piracy

Piracy consists of any of the following acts:
    (a) any illegal acts of violence or detention, or any act of depredation, committed for private ends by the crew or the passengers of a private ship or a private aircraft, and directed:
        (i) on the high seas, against another ship or aircraft, or against persons or property on board such ship or aircraft;
        (ii) against a ship, aircraft, persons or property in a place outside the jurisdiction of any State;
    (b) any act of voluntary participation in the operation of a ship or of an aircraft with knowledge of facts making it a pirate ship or aircraft;
    (c) any act of inciting or of intentionally facilitating an act described in subparagraph (a) or (b).

Article 108 Illicit traffic in narcotic drugs or psychotropic substances

1. All States shall co-operate in the suppression of illicit traffic in narcotic drugs and psychotropic substances engaged in by ships on the high seas contrary to international conventions.

Article 110 Right of visit

1. Except where acts of interference derive from powers conferred by treaty, a warship which encounters on the high seas a foreign ship, other than a ship entitled to complete immunity in accordance with articles 95 and 96, is not justified in boarding it unless there is reasonable ground for suspecting that:

    (a) the ship is engaged in piracy;

    (b) the ship is engaged in the slave trade;

    (c) the ship is engaged in authorized broadcasting and the flag State of the warship has jurisdiction under article 109;

    (d) the ship is without nationality; or

    (e) though flying a foreign flag or refusing to show its flag, the ship is, in reality, of the same nationality as the warship.

Article 111 Right of hot pursuit

1. The hot pursuit of a foreign ship may be undertaken when the competent authorities of the coastal State have good reason to believe that the ship has violated the laws and regulations of that State. Such pursuit must be commenced when the foreign ship or one of its boats is within the internal waters, the archipelagic waters, the territorial sea or the contiguous zone of the pursuing State, and may only be continued outside the territorial sea or the contiguous zone if the pursuit has not been interrupted. It is not necessary that, at the time when the foreign ship within the territorial sea or the contiguous zone receives the order to stop, the ship giving the order should likewise be within the territorial sea or the contiguous zone. If the foreign ship is within a contiguous zone, as defined in article 33, the pursuit may only be undertaken if there has been a violation of the rights for the protection of which the zone was established.

2. The right of hot pursuit shall apply *mutatis mutandis* to violations in the exclusive economic zone or on the continental shelf, including safety zones around continental shelf installations, of the laws and regulations of the coastal State applicable in accordance with this Convention to the exclusive economic zone or the continental shelf, including such safety zones.

3. The right of hot pursuit ceases as soon as the ship pursued enters the territorial sea of its own State or of a third State.

4. Hot pursuit is not deemed to have begun unless the pursuing ship has satisfied itself by such practicable means as may be available that the ship pursued or one of its boats or other craft working as a team and using the ship pursued as a mother ship is within the limits of the territorial sea, or, as the case may be, within the contiguous zone or the exclusive economic zone or above the continental shelf. The pursuit may only be commenced after a visual or auditory signal to stop has been given at a distance which enables it to be seen or heard by the foreign ship.

5. The right of hot pursuit may be exercised only by warships or military aircraft, or other ships or aircraft clearly marked and identifiable as being on government service and authorized to that effect.

6. Where hot pursuit is effected by an aircraft:

    (a) the provisions of paragraphs 1 to 4 shall apply *mutatis mutandis*;

    (b) the aircraft giving the order to stop must itself actively pursue the ship until a ship or another aircraft of the coastal State, summoned by the aircraft, arrives to take over the pursuit, unless the aircraft is itself able to arrest the ship. It does not suffice to justify an arrest outside the territorial sea that the ship was merely sighted by the aircraft as an offender or suspected offender, if it was not both ordered to stop and pursued by the aircraft itself or other aircraft or ships which continue the pursuit without interruption.

Article 112 Right to lay submarine cables and pipelines

1. All States are entitled to lay submarine cables and pipelines on the bed of the high seas beyond the continental shelf.

Article 116 Right to fish on the high seas

All States have the right for their nationals to engage in fishing on the high seas subject to:

    (a) their treaty obligations;

    (b) the rights and duties as well as the interests of coastal States provided for, *inter alia*, in article 63, paragraph 2, and articles 64 to 67; and

    (c) the provisions of this section.

Article 117 Duty of states to adopt with respect to their nationals measures for the conservation of the living resources of the high seas

All States have the duty to take, or to co-operate with other States in taking, such measures for their respective nationals as may be necessary for the conservation of the living resources of the high seas.

Article 121 Régime of Islands

1. An island is a naturally formed area of land, surrounded by water, which is above water at high tide.

2. Except as provided for in paragraph 3, the territorial sea, the contiguous zone, the exclusive economic zone and the continental shelf of an island are determined in accordance with the provisions of this Convention applicable to other land territory.

3. Rocks which cannot sustain human habitation or economic life of their own shall have no exclusive economic zone or continental shelf.

D. Guilfoyle 'Piracy off Somalia: UN Security Council Resolution 1816 and IMO Regional Counter-Piracy Efforts'

57 International and Comparative Law Quarterly 690 (2008)

In recent years the high seas off Somalia have become a dangerous place: cruise-liners have been shot at, aid deliveries jeopardized and the crews of fishing, recreational and aid vessels have been taken hostage for ransom. In 2005 and 2007 attacks or attempted attacks against shipping in international waters off East Africa exceeded reported incidents for the traditional piracy hotspots of the Malacca Straits and the South China Seas combined. This lawlessness at sea clearly follows from the chaos on the Somalian shore. Somalia has lacked a government controlling its entire territory since 1991. The Transitional Federal Government (TFG), internationally recognized since 2000, has only limited control over Somalian territory ...

The High Seas Convention and the United Nations Convention on the Law of the Sea (UNCLOS) define piracy as:

(1) an act of violence, detention or depredation;
(2) committed for private ends;
(3 on the high seas or in a place outside the jurisdiction of any State; and
(4) committed by the crew or passengers of a private craft, against another vessel or persons or property aboard.

This definition is generally, though not universally, accepted as having codified pre-existing customary international law. In international waters any State warship or government vessel may board a ship suspected of piracy as an exception to the otherwise exclusive jurisdiction of the flag State. Further:

> every State may seize a pirate ship…and arrest the persons and seize the property on board. The courts of the State which carried out the seizure may decide upon the penalties to be imposed…[Article 105, 1982 Convention]

Customary international law also permits any State subsequently finding a pirate within its territory to prosecute him or her as an exercise of universal jurisdiction. The fact that every State *may* prosecute piracy does not mean they will be eager to or will have appropriate national laws....

The definition of piracy and the enforcement powers granted to suppress it contain several limitations. The least important is the requirement that piracy be for 'private ends'. It is commonly and mistakenly presumed that these words must exclude all politically motivated violence. In fact, the words 'for private ends' simply denote that the violence involved is not *public* and were originally included to acknowledge the historic exception for civil-war insurgencies who attacked only the vessels of the government they sought to overthrow. All acts of violence lacking State sanction are acts undertaken 'for private ends'. Pirates are criminals not because of their subjective motives but because their acts impinge upon States' monopoly on legitimate violence and their interests in freedom of navigation. The words 'for private ends' must thus be understood broadly. At least one national court decision has sensibly applied this approach and found that violence in international waters committed by one private vessel against another in pursuit of political protest still constituted piracy. [*Castle John* v *NV Mabeco*, Belgium, Court of Cassation (1986) 77 ILR 537].

The more significant restriction is the geographical limitation of both the offence and enforcement action to the high seas. 'The high seas' or 'international waters' refers to all waters beyond the territorial sea, including the EEZ. This has two consequences. The first is that attacks against vessels in territorial waters or port are not piracy. Such attacks within territorial jurisdiction are commonly referred to as 'armed robbery against ships' by the International Maritime Oganisation (IMO) and other bodies, a term including hijacking. Further, the enforcement jurisdiction granted to all States in international waters does not extend to pursuing pirate vessels into the territorial sea of any State. As with conventional cases of hot pursuit, pursuit must cease 'as soon as the ship pursued enters the territorial sea of its own [flag] State or of a third State' [Article 11, 1982 Convention]. The ability of pirates to evade pursuit by crossing into territorial waters remains a real problem, particularly in the waters off Somalia.

Security Council Resolution 1816

2 June 2008, UN Security Council

Determining that the incidents of piracy and armed robbery against vessels in the territorial waters of Somalia and the high seas off the coast of Somalia exacerbate the situation in Somalia which continues to constitute a threat to international peace and security in the region,

 Acting under Chapter VII of the Charter of the United Nations,

 1. *Condemns and deplores* all acts of piracy and armed robbery against vessels in territorial waters and the high seas off the coast of Somalia;

 2. *Urges* States whose naval vessels and military aircraft operate on the high seas and airspace off the coast of Somalia to be vigilant to acts of piracy and armed robbery and, in this context, *encourages*, in particular, States interested in the use of commercial maritime routes off the coast of Somalia, to increase and coordinate their efforts to deter acts of piracy and armed robbery at sea in cooperation with the TFG [Transitional Federal Government];

 3. *Urges* all States to cooperate with each other, with the IMO and, as appropriate, with the relevant regional organizations in connection with, and share information about, acts of piracy and armed robbery in the territorial waters and on the high seas off the coast of Somalia, and to render assistance to vessels threatened by or under attack by pirates or armed robbers, in accordance with relevant international law; ...

 7. *Decides* that for a period of six months from the date of this resolution, States cooperating with the TFG in the fight against piracy and armed robbery at sea off the coast of Somalia, for which advance notification has been provided by the TFG to the Secretary-General, may:
   (a) Enter the territorial waters of Somalia for the purpose of repressing acts of piracy and armed robbery at sea, in a manner consistent with such action permitted on the high seas with respect to piracy under relevant international law; and
   (b) Use, within the territorial waters of Somalia, in a manner consistent with action permitted on the high seas with respect to piracy under relevant international law, all necessary means to repress acts of piracy and armed robbery;

 8. *Requests* that cooperating states take appropriate steps to ensure that the activities they undertake pursuant to the authorization in paragraph 7 do not have the practical effect of denying or impairing the right of innocent passage to the ships of any third State;

 9. *Affirms* that the authorization provided in this resolution applies only with respect to the situation in Somalia and shall not affect the rights or obligations or responsibilities of member states under international law, including any rights or obligations under the [1982] Convention, with respect to any other situation, and underscores in particular that it shall not be considered as establishing customary international law, and affirms further that this authorization has been provided only following receipt of the letter from the Permanent Representative of the Somalia Republic to the United Nations to the President of the Security Council dated 27 February 2008 conveying the consent of the TFG; ...

 11. *Calls upon* all States, and in particular flag, port and coastal States, States of the nationality of victims and perpetrators or piracy and armed robbery, and other States with relevant jurisdiction under international law and national legislation, to cooperate in determining jurisdiction, and in the investigation and prosecution of persons responsible for acts of piracy and armed robbery off the coast of Somalia, consistent with applicable international law including international human rights law, and to render assistance by, among other actions, providing disposition and logistics assistance with respect to persons under their jurisdiction and control, such victims and witnesses and persons detained as a result of operations conducted under this resolution.

T. Treves, 'Piracy, Law of the Sea, and Use of Force: Developments off the Coast of Somalia'

20 *European Journal of International Law* 399 (2009)

[I]nternational law accords universal jurisdiction to the courts of the seizing state. This jurisdiction, applicable under Article 105 of UNCLOS for the seizure and arrest of pirates on the high seas, applies also to seizures and arrests in the territorial sea of Somalia under the Security Council resolutions....

The seizing states—in other words, the states fighting pirates and armed robbers in the waters off Somalia and having arrested them—are, however, reluctant to exercise such broad powers by prosecuting and submitting to criminal proceedings in their courts the pirates and armed robbers arrested. They seem concerned by the expense involved, by legal complexities, relating for instance to evidence, inherent in criminal proceedings to be held far away from the place where the alleged crime was committed, and, perhaps especially, by the human rights implications of exercising jurisdiction.

A recent case highlights these difficulties. The Danish Navy ship *Absalon* on 17 September 2008 captured 10 pirates in the waters off Somalia. After six days' detention and the confiscation of their weapons, ladders, and other implements used to board ships, the Danish government decided to free the pirates by putting them ashore on a Somali beach. The Danish authorities had come to the conclusion that the pirates risked torture and the death penalty if surrendered to (whatever) Somali authorities. This was unacceptable, as Danish law prohibits the extradition of criminals when they may face the death penalty. Moreover, they were not ready to try them in Denmark as it would be difficult (in light of the possible abuses they would risk) to deport them back to Somalia after their sentences were served. It is clear that human rights considerations, or perhaps reasons of expediency presented as human rights concerns, prevailed over considerations concerning the fight against piracy. In the same vein, the British Foreign Office reportedly warned the Royal Navy against detaining pirates since this might violate their human rights and could lead to claims to asylum in Britain.

The capture and detention at sea of criminals later brought to trial in far away courts of the state of the arresting vessel have been referred by those captured to the judgment of the European Court of Human Rights (ECtHR). This happened in the *Rigopoulos* and *Medveyev* cases decided on 12 January 1999 and 10 July 2008 respectively. [Requests 37388/97 and 3394/03] In these cases the applicants were arrested on the high seas on a ship boarded, with the authorization of the flag state, under suspicion, later proved to be well founded, of being engaged in smuggling narcotic drugs. The question submitted to the Court was whether detention on the arresting naval vessel for about two weeks was compatible with Article 5(3) of the European Convention on Human Rights according to which, *inter alia*, arrested or detained persons 'shall be brought promptly before a judge or other officer authorized by law to exercise judicial power'. The Court, even though in both cases it decided that the circumstances were exceptional enough to justify an affirmative answer, stated clearly that the principle was that such a long period of detention was not compatible with the provision in question. Consequently, states parties to the European Convention may, in different circumstances, be confronted by a decision finding a violation of the human rights of the detained criminal (be it a drug trafficker or a pirate). Moreover, in the 2008 *Medveyev* case the ECtHR found a violation of Article 5(1) of the European Convention, according to which *inter alia*, '[n]o one shall be deprived of his liberty save in the following cases and in accordance with a procedure prescribed by law' on the basis of a strict interpretation of the agreement authorizing the boarding and arrest, but allegedly not sufficiently clear as to the right to submit the arrested person to trial. The possibility of a similar decision seems highly unlikely in the case of piracy, in light of the broad powers recognized by general international law and the Security Council resolutions. It shows, nevertheless, that a court like the ECtHR will tend to interpret the law of the sea and international law rules in such a way as to offer maximum protection to the individuals involved.

NOTES

1. Although the 'high seas' are not open to acquisition by any State, the Geneva Convention on the High Seas 1958, the Geneva Convention on the Fishing and Conservation of Living Resources of the High Seas 1958 and the 1982 Convention contain fairly detailed rules about activities on, in or under the high seas. They also deal with matters such as the question of jurisdiction over vessels and structures (e.g. oil platforms), broadly speaking granting such jurisdiction to the 'flag State', except in cases of crimes against international law (such as piracy and slavery) where jurisdiction is universal.

2. The development of maritime zones extending 200 miles seaward from the coast has necessarily led to a shrinking of waters legally classed as 'high seas'. The 1982 Convention contains certain

compensatory provisions for maritime States, including the right of 'transit passage' through straits used for international navigation and the right of passage through archipelagic waters. The advent of mining in the deep seabed (see Section 6) and claims to a continental shelf beyond the 200-mile limit will not affect the legal status of the super-adjacent waters, although there will of necessity be some reduction in the scope of the freedoms of the seas contained in Article 87 of the Convention.

3. As seen in the *Qatar* case, the question of sovereignty over islands is intimately connected with the reach of a State's maritime jurisdiction. Not only can islands have their own territorial sea, contiguous zone, shelf regime and EEZ, they are important in the delimitation of general maritime boundaries between opposite and adjacent States, especially where islands lie close to the coast of more than one State. In the *Sovereignty over Pedra Branca/Pulau Batu Puteh, Middle Rocks and South Ledge (Malaysia/Singapore) Case*, ICJ Rep 2008 12, the Court determined sovereignty over various islands and low tide elevations in the Strait of Singapore (see Chapter 7).

4. Piracy has assumed an increasing importance in recent years. As is seen in Resolution 1816 and subsequent resolutions, the Security Council has considered piracy to constitute a threat to international peace and security, and has authorised States to use force to repress acts of piracy or armed robbery, even within the territorial seas of Somalia. This mandate is, however, subject to strict limits on its exercise, including a requirement for the consent of the Somali authorities. States have shown various degrees of willingness to apprehend and try those accused of committing acts of piracy, and have either tried such individuals before national courts, or have 'outsourced' trials to courts of States in the region (see the agreement between the UK and Kenya for enabling trials of individuals apprehended by UK naval forces to occur in Kenyan courts). As shown in the extract from Treves, what to do with captured pirates raises serious legal and human rights concerns.

SECTION 6: THE DEEP SEABED

Part XI of the 1982 Convention proved to be the most controversial aspect of this wide-ranging treaty. It soon became clear that a majority of developed States would not ratify the Convention because they disagreed with the regime established to regulate mining in the deep seabed area. Although the non-participation of these States would not prevent the Convention from entering into force, clearly the Convention as a whole would have had a limited impact with so many maritime (developed) States refusing to ratify it. Furthermore, the prospect of any deep sea mining from which the international community would benefit remained remote while the only States financially and technologically able to undertake it were preparing to act independently of the Convention. This led eventually to the Agreement Relating to Part XI of the Convention 1994. This has been generally accepted by developed States and has now led to widespread ratification of the Convention itself. In essence, this Agreement modifies the deep seabed regime found in Part XI and is to be regarded as an integral part of the Convention. No State can become bound by the Agreement unless it first becomes bound by the Convention.

There is no doubt that the deep seabed area—the area 'beyond the limits of national jurisdiction'—is not open to the sovereignty of any State. More importantly, the area is now accepted as 'the common heritage of mankind', meaning that the benefits of any mining activity must be shared in some measure with all members of the international community, not just among those willing and able to undertake deep sea mining (see Chapter 7). The original Part XI of the Convention was an attempt to give effect to the principle of common heritage. The dissenting developed States did not object to the principle of common heritage but rather to the manner in which the unmodified Convention proposed to carry it out in practice.

Law of the Sea Convention 1982

Article 1 Use of terms and scope

1. For the purposes of this Convention:

(1) 'Area' means the sea-bed and ocean floor and subsoil thereof, beyond the limits of national jurisdiction;

(2) 'Authority' means the International Sea-Bed Authority;

(3) 'activities in the Area' means all activities of exploration for, and exploitation of, the resources of the Area....

Part XI: Deep Sea Bed

Article 136 Common heritage of mankind

The Area and its resources are the common heritage of mankind.

Article 137 Legal status of the area and its resources

1. No State shall claim or exercise sovereignty or sovereign rights over any part of the Area or its resources, nor shall any State or natural or juridical person appropriate any part thereof. No such claim or exercise of sovereignty or sovereign rights, nor such appropriation shall be recognized.

2. All rights in the resources of the Area are vested in mankind as a whole, on whose behalf the Authority shall act. These resources are not subject to alienation. The minerals recovered from the Area, however, may only be alienated in accordance with this Part and the rules, regulations and procedures of the Authority.

3. No State or natural or juridical person shall claim, acquire or exercise rights with respect to the minerals recovered from the Area except in accordance with this Part. Otherwise, no such claim, acquisition or exercise of such rights shall be recognized.

Article 140 Benefit of mankind

1. Activities in the Area shall, as specifically provided for in this Part, be carried out for the benefit of mankind as a whole, irrespective of the geographical location of States, whether coastal or land-locked, and taking into particular consideration the interests and needs of developing States and of peoples who have not attained full independence or other self-governing status recognized by the United Nations in accordance with General Assembly resolution 1514 (XV) and other relevant General Assembly resolutions.

2. The Authority shall provide for the equitable sharing of financial and other economic benefits derived from activities in the Area through any appropriate mechanism, on a non-discriminatory basis, in accordance with article 160, paragraph 2(f)(i).

Article 141 Use of the area exclusively for peaceful purposes

The Area shall be open to use exclusively for peaceful purposes by all States, whether coastal or land-locked, without discrimination and without prejudice to the other provisions of this Part.

Article 144 Transfer of technology

1. The Authority shall take measures in accordance with this Convention:

(a)   to acquire technology and scientific knowledge relating to activities in the Area; and

(b)   to promote and encourage the transfer to developing States of such technology and scientific knowledge so that all States Parties benefit therefrom …

D. Anderson, 'Further Efforts to Ensure Universal Participation in the United Nations Convention on The Law of the Sea'

43 International and Comparative Law Quarterly 886 (1994)

At the outset of the consultations in July 1990 some nine specific topics (later reduced to eight, with the deferment of the environment) had been identified as obstacles to ratification of the Convention by the industrialised States. They were: (1) costs to State parties; (2) the Enterprise; (3) decision-making; (4) the review conference; (5) transfer of technology; (6) production limitation; (7) compensation fund; (8) financial terms of contracts.

D. The terms for entry into force of the new agreement

In order to meet the concerns of States which had already ratified the Convention, the provisions in the proposed agreement about its entry into force provided a special option for such States. They could establish their consent to be bound by the agreement by means of a system of tacit consent. At a later stage in the consultations, the arrangement required a prior signature of the agreement in the case of States which had ratified the Convention. Signature was perceived to give added certainty to the process of establishing consent. These arrangements were set out in Article 5 of the agreement.

In order to meet the concerns of developing countries, both ratifiers and non-ratifiers alike, that their concessions might still fail to attract ratifications from major countries which had shown interest in deep seabed mining, a special requirement was included in Article 6 about entry into force. Entry into force of the agreement requires 40 ratifications, etc., of which at least seven must be States to which paragraph 1(a) of Resolution II of the Third UN Conference on the Law of the Sea applies (namely Belgium, Canada, France, Germany, Italy, Japan, the Netherlands, Russia, the United Kingdom and the United States, plus India and China: South Korea joined this group in August 1994). Five of the seven must be developed States. Such States would contribute a significant amount to the cost of the ISA, especially if they included the United States, Japan, Germany, France and the United Kingdom....

F. Legal Status of the Agreement

The agreement provides that the annex thereto is an integral part of the agreement. The fundamental obligation on States parties is to implement Part XI in accordance with the terms of the agreement. In the event of any inconsistency between its terms and those of Part XI, the provisions of the agreement are to prevail and the two are to be interpreted and applied together as a single instrument. Provision is made for States to express their consent to be bound by the agreement by the usual methods of signature not subject to ratification, or signature subject to ratification followed by ratification, or signature and recourse to the tacit procedure described above, as well as by means of accession....

The agreement is clearly a treaty, governed by the Vienna Convention on the Law of Treaties. Although it does not expressly amend any provisions of Part XI, there is no doubt that the agreement will result in the terms of Part XI being implemented, interpreted and applied in a new way, as described in the annex....

G. The Adoption of the Resolution and Signature of the Agreement

On July 27 [1994], the resumed 48th session of the General Assembly took up again Agenda item 36, Law of the Sea.... The Resolution [incorporating the Agreement] was adopted without change by a vote of 121 to 0, with 7 abstentions, on 28 July (G.A. Res. 48/263). On 29 July, the Agreement was opened for signature for one year at UN Headquarters in New York. The Agreement was signed by 41 States at a ceremony in the General Assembly Hall. In the following days 8 further signatures were affixed....

H. Concluding Remarks

The origins of the Secretary-General's consultations can be traced back to the statement made by the Chairman of the Group of 77 at the end of the meeting of the Preparatory Commission in the summer of 1989. This led directly to the opening of the consultations during 1990, amid some trepidation from all sides. The consultations started out with a specific agenda of eight problems perceived by developed countries and although other suggestions about the best approach were made from several sources, in the end it was this approach based on following the specific agenda and finding solutions to the eight problems which found expression in the draft agreement and its annex. Implicit in this approach was acceptance of both the principle of the common heritage of mankind, as it would be articulated, and a UN-administered system of mining. Gradually, the industrialised countries were able to demonstrate their wish to negotiate seriously, especially following the election of the Clinton administration. The member States of the European Union, together with the Union itself, were staunch supporters of the process. The deposit of the 60th ratification in November 1993 was greeted with different reactions from ratifiers and non-ratifiers, but in the event it turned out to be helpful in that it provided all concerned with a target date, November 1994, for finishing the consultations and drawing up the necessary new arrangements. Although hard bargaining continued until the very end of the consultations, they took place in a constructive, non-confrontational atmosphere between the different groups, notably between the Group of 77 and the industrialised countries. The new Agreement takes account of the political and economic changes, including a growing reliance on market principles and similar market-orientated approaches to economic issues, which have taken place since 1982. As a result, there now exist much improved prospects for universal participation in the UN Convention on the Law of the Sea, together with the Agreement on the Implementation of Part XI: 1994 could be a milestone towards the attainment of that goal.

Agreement Relating to the Implementation of Part XI of the United Nations Convention on the Law of the Sea General Assembly Resolution and Annex, 17 August 1994

33 *International Legal Materials* 1099 (1994)

Article 1 Implementation of Part XI

1. The States Parties to this Agreement undertake to implement Part XI in accordance with this Agreement.

2. The Annex forms an integral part of this Agreement.

Article 2 Relationship between this Agreement and Part XI

1. The provisions of this Agreement and Part XI shall be interpreted and applied together as a single instrument. In the event of any inconsistency between this Agreement and Part XI, the provisions of this Agreement shall prevail.

2. Articles 309 to 319 of the Convention shall apply to this Agreement as they apply to the Convention.

Article 4 Consent to be bound

1. After the adoption of this Agreement, any instrument of ratification or formal confirmation of or accession to the Convention shall also represent consent to be bound by this Agreement.

2. No state or entity may establish its consent to be bound by this Agreement unless it has previously established or establishes at the same time its consent to be bound by the Convention....

Article 5 Simplified procedure

1. A state or entity which has deposited before the date of the adoption of this Agreement an instrument of ratification or formal confirmation of or accession to the Convention and which has signed this Agreement in accordance with article 4, paragraph 3(c), shall be considered to have established its consent to be bound by this Agreement 12 months after the date of its adoption, unless that State or entity notifies the depositary in writing before that date that it is not availing itself of the simplified procedure set out in this article.

Annex

SECTION 1. COSTS TO STATES PARTIES AND INSTITUTIONAL ARRANGEMENTS

1. The powers and functions of the Authority shall be those expressly conferred upon it by the Convention. The Authority shall have such incidental powers, consistent with the Convention, as are implicit in, and necessary for, the exercise of those powers and function with respect to activities in the Area.

SECTION 2. THE ENTERPRISE

1. The Secretariat of the Authority shall perform the functions of the Enterprise until it begins to operate independently of the Secretariat....

2. The Enterprise shall conduct its initial deep seabed mining operations through joint ventures. Upon the approval of a plan of work for exploitation for an entity other than the Enterprise, or upon receipt by the Council of an application for joint-venture operation with the Enterprise, the Council shall take up the issue of the functioning of the Enterprise independently of the Secretariat of the Authority. If joint-venture operations with the Enterprise accord with sound commercial principles, the Council shall issue a directive pursuant to article 170, paragraph 2, of the Convention providing for such independent functioning.

3. The obligation of States Parties to fund one mine site of the Enterprise as provided for in Annex IV, article 11, paragraph 3, of the Convention shall not apply and States Parties shall be under no obligation to finance any of the operations in any mine site of the Enterprise or under its joint-venture arrangements.

6. Article 170, paragraph 4, Annex IV and other provisions of the Convention relating to the Enterprise shall be interpreted and applied in accordance with this section.

SECTION 3. DECISION-MAKING

1. The general policies of the Authority shall be established by the Assembly in collaboration with the Council.

2. As a general rule, decision-making in the organs of the Authority should be by consensus.

3. If all efforts to reach a decision by consensus have been exhausted, decision by voting in the Assembly on questions of procedure shall be taken by a majority of members present and voting, and decisions on questions

of substance shall be taken by a two-thirds majority of members present and voting, as provided for in article 159, paragraph 8, of the Convention.

SECTION 5. TRANSFER OF TECHNOLOGY

1. In addition to the provisions of article 144 of the Convention, transfer of technology for the purpose of Part XI shall be governed by the following principles:

    (a) The Enterprise, and developing States wishing to obtain deep seabed mining technology, shall seek to obtain such technology in fair and reasonable commercial terms and conditions on the open market, or through joint-venture arrangements;

    (b) If the Enterprise or developing States are unable to obtain deep seabed mining technology, the Authority may request all or any of the contractors and their respective sponsoring State or States to cooperate with it in facilitating the acquisition of deep seabed mining technology by the Enterprise or its joint venture, or by a developing State or States seeking to acquire such technology on fair and reasonable commercial terms and conditions, consistent with the effective protection of intellectual property rights....

2. The provisions of Annex III, article 5, of the Convention shall not apply.

Responsibilities and Obligations of States Sponsoring Persons and Entities with Respect to Activities in the Area

Advisory Opinion, 1 February 2011, Seabed Disputes Chamber, International Tribunal for the Law of the Sea

In May 2010, the Council of the International Seabed Authority (ISA) set out three questions on which it sought an advisory opinion from the Seabed Disputes Chamber. These questions concerned: (1) the legal responsibilities and obligations of States Parties to the Convention with respect to the sponsorship of activities in the Area; (2) the extent of liability of a State Party for any failure to comply with the provisions of the Convention by an entity whom it has sponsored; and (3) the necessary and appropriate measures that a sponsoring State must take in order to fulfil its responsibility under the Convention. The following extract relates to the first question.

73. This question concerns the obligations of sponsoring States. Before examining the provisions of the Convention, the 1994 Agreement as well as the Nodules Regulations and the Sulphides Regulations (hereinafter 'the Convention and related instruments'), the Chamber must determine the meaning of two of the terms used in the Question, namely: 'sponsorship' and 'activities in the Area'.

74. The notion of 'sponsorship' is a key element in the system for the exploration and exploitation of the resources of the Area set out in the Convention. Article 153, paragraph 2, of the Convention describes the 'parallel system' of exploration and exploitation activities indicating that such activities shall be carried out by the enterprise, and, in association with the Authority, by States Parties or state enterprises or natural or juridical persons. It further states that, in order to be eligible to carry out such activities, natural and juridical persons must satisfy two requirements. First, they must be either nationals of a State Party or effectively controlled by it or its nationals. Second, they must be 'sponsored by such States'. Article 153, paragraph 2(b), of the Convention makes the requirement of sponsorship applicable also to state enterprises.

75. The purpose of requiring the sponsorship of applicants for contracts for the exploration and exploitation of the resources of the Area is to achieve the result that the obligations set out in the Convention, a treaty under international law which binds only States Parties thereto, are complied with by entities that are subjects of domestic legal systems. This result is obtained through the provisions of the Authority's Regulations that apply to such entities and through the implementation by the sponsoring States of their obligations under the Convention and related instruments.

76. The role of the sponsoring State, as set out in the Convention, contributes to the realization of the common interest of all States in the proper application of the principle of the common heritage of mankind which requires faithful compliance with the obligations set out in Part XI. The common interest role of the sponsoring State is further confirmed by its obligation, set out in article 153, paragraph 4, of the Convention, to 'assist' the Authority, which, as stated in article 137, paragraph 2, of the Convention, acts on behalf of mankind.

77. The connection between States Parties and domestic law entities required by the Convention is twofold, namely, that of nationality and that of effective control. All contractors and applicants for contracts must secure and maintain the sponsorship of the State or States of which they are nationals. If another State or its nationals exercises effective control, the sponsorship of that State is also necessary. This is provided for in Annex III, article 4, paragraph 3, of the Convention and confirmed in regulation 11, paragraph 2, of the Nodules Regulations and of the Sulphides Regulations.

78. No provision of the Convention imposes an obligation on a State Party to sponsor an entity that holds its nationality or is controlled by it or by its nationals. As the Convention does not consider the links of nationality and effective control sufficient to obtain the result that the contractor conforms with the Convention and related instruments, it requires a specific act emanating from the will of the State or States of nationality and of effective control. Such act consists in the decision to sponsor.

79. As subjects of international law, States Parties engaged in deep seabed mining under the Convention are directly bound by the obligations set out therein. Consequently, there is no reason to apply to them the requirement of sponsorship. Article 153, paragraph 2(b), of the Convention as well as the identical regulation 11, paragraph 1, of the Nodules Regulations and the Sulphides Regulations confirm that the requirement of sponsorship does not apply to States. This point is further supported by Annex III, article 4, paragraph 5, of the Convention which reads as follows: 'The procedures for assessing the qualifications of States Parties which are applicants shall take into account their character as States'.

99. The key provisions concerning the obligations of the sponsoring States are: article 139, paragraph 1; article 153, paragraph 4 (especially the last sentence); and Annex III, article 4, paragraph 4, of the Convention (especially the first sentence).

103. The three provisions mentioned in paragraph 100 specify that the obligation (responsibility) of the sponsoring State is 'to ensure' that the 'activities in the Area' conducted by the sponsored contractor are 'in conformity' or in 'compliance' with the rules to which they refer....

107. The central issue in relation to Question 1 concerns the meaning of the expression 'responsibility to ensure' in article 139, paragraph 1, and Annex III, article 4, paragraph 4, of the Convention.

108. 'Responsibility to ensure' points to an obligation of the sponsoring State under international law. It establishes a mechanism through which the rules of the Convention concerning activities in the Area, although being treaty law and thus binding only on the subjects of international law that have accepted them, become effective for sponsored contractors which find their legal basis in domestic law. This mechanism consists in the creation of obligations which States Parties must fulfil by exercising their power over entities of their nationality and under their control.

109. As will be seen in greater detail in the reply to Question 2, a violation of this obligation entails 'liability'. However, not every violation of an obligation by a sponsored contractor automatically gives rise to the liability of the sponsoring State. Such liability is limited to the State's failure to meet its obligation to 'ensure' compliance by the sponsored contractor.

110. The sponsoring State's obligation 'to ensure' is not an obligation to achieve, in each and every case, the result that the sponsored contractor complies with the aforementioned obligations. Rather, it is an obligation to deploy adequate means, to exercise best possible efforts, to do the utmost, to obtain this result. To utilize the terminology current in international law, this obligation may be characterized as an obligation 'of conduct' and not 'of result', and as an obligation of 'due diligence'.

111. The notions of obligations 'of due diligence' and obligations 'of conduct' are connected. This emerges clearly from the Judgment of the ICJ in the *Pulp Mills on the River Uruguay*: 'An obligation to adopt regulatory or administrative measures ... and to enforce them is an obligation of conduct. Both parties are therefore called upon, under article 36 [of the Statute of the River Uruguay], to exercise due diligence in acting through the [Uruguay River] Commission for the necessary measures to preserve the ecological balance of the river' (paragraph 187 of the Judgment).

112. The expression 'to ensure' is often used in international legal instruments to refer to obligations in respect of which, while it is not considered reasonable to make a State liable for each and every violation committed by persons under its jurisdiction, it is equally not considered satisfactory to rely on mere application of the principle

that the conduct of private persons or entities is not attributable to the State under international law (see ILC Articles on State Responsibility, Commentary to article 8, paragraph 1).

117. The content of 'due diligence' obligations may not easily be described in precise terms. Among the factors that make such a description difficult is the fact that 'due diligence' is a variable concept. It may change over time as measures considered sufficiently diligent at a certain moment may become not diligent enough in light, for instance, of new scientific or technological knowledge. It may also change in relation to the risks involved in the activity. As regards activities in the Area, it seems reasonable to state that prospecting is, generally speaking, less risky than exploration activities which, in turn, entail less risk than exploitation. Moreover, activities in the Area concerning different kinds of minerals, for example, polymetallic nodules on the one hand and polymetallic sulphides or cobalt rich ferromanganese crusts on the other, may require different standards of diligence. The standard of due diligence has to be more severe for the riskier activities.

118. Article 153, paragraph 4, last sentence, of the Convention states that the obligation of the sponsoring State in accordance with article 139 of the Convention entails 'taking all measures necessary to ensure' compliance by the sponsored contractor. Annex III, article 4, paragraph 4, of the Convention makes it clear that sponsoring States' 'responsibility to ensure' applies 'within their legal systems'. With these indications the Convention provides some elements concerning the content of the 'due diligence' obligation to ensure. Necessary measures are required and these must be adopted within the legal system of the sponsoring State.

NOTES

1. The Articles of the 1982 Convention extracted above give the general scheme of the deep seabed regime. The detailed matters to which developed States objected are generally found in the original Annexes to the Convention and it is largely these that have been modified by the 1994 Agreement. The precise details of the modifications are quite complicated, although a general idea can be obtained from the above extracts. There is no doubt that the conclusion of the Agreement and the subsequent widespread participation in the Convention is a major achievement of the United Nations.

2. Although the United States signed the 1994 Agreement, it is still not a party to the 1982 Convention or the Agreement, although it considers many of its provisions to reflect customary international law. It is thus not legally bound by either treaty and had to vacate its provisional membership of the ISA on 16 November 1998. Despite the Bush, Clinton and Obama administrations and significant business lobbies (for example, US Chamber of Commerce) supporting ratification, the Senate Committee on Foreign Relations voted against ratification in 2012, reflecting the concerns of several senators that becoming a party to the 1982 Convention would threaten US sovereignty and economic interests.

3. The ISA has adopted several key instruments, in particular the Mining Code, which refers to the 'whole of the comprehensive set of rules, regulations and procedures issued by the International Seabed Authority to regulate prospecting, exploration and exploitation of marine minerals in the international seabed Area'. To date, the ISA has issued Regulations on Prospecting and Exploration for Polymetallic Nodules in the Area (adopted 13 July 2000), which were later updated and adopted in 25 July 2013; the Regulations on Prospecting and Exploration for Polymetallic Sulphides in the Area (adopted 7 May 2010); and the Regulations on Prospecting and Exploration for Cobalt-Rich Crusts (adopted 27 July 2012). The ISA has also issued several recommendations to contractors.

4. As shown in the extract from the Advisory Opinion of the Seabed Chamber, the deep seabed regime is unusual in that contractors will perform most of the activities in the Area, yet States are the subject of the obligations under the relevant international framework. One of the main issues for consideration in the Advisory Opinion was the nature and extent of States' obligations in relation to contractors. Given the high-risk nature of many deep seabed activities for the environment, and the obligations on the ISA and States to preserve the marine environment, how contactors can be held accountable is a key issue. This is achieved through clarifying that it is a duty of sponsoring States to ensure that contractors comply with obligations through the application of national law to those contractors. As at March 2016, the ISA has entered into 15-year contracts for exploration for polymetallic nodules, polymetallic sulphides and cobalt-rich ferromanganese crusts in the deep seabed with 23 contractors.

SECTION 7: PEACEFUL SETTLEMENT OF DISPUTES

Part XV of the 1982 Convention requires States to settle compulsorily peacefully any disputes concerning the Convention. Failing a bilateral settlement, Article 286 provides that any dispute be submitted for compulsory settlement to one of the tribunals having jurisdiction. These include ITLOS, established by the Convention itself, the ICJ, and an arbitral or special arbitral tribunal constituted under the Convention. Peaceful settlement is thus compulsory.

UN Division for Ocean Affairs and the Law of the Sea
Briefing Note, 17 February 1999

International Tribunal for the Law of the Sea

The International Tribunal for the Law of the Sea is the central forum established by the *United Nations Convention on the Law of the Sea* for the peaceful settlement of disputes. Its seat is at the Free and Hanseatic City of Hamburg, Germany. The Tribunal may sit and exercise its functions elsewhere whenever it considers this desirable.

Jurisdiction

The jurisdiction of the Tribunal comprises all disputes and all applications submitted to it in accordance with the *United Nations Convention on the Law of the Sea* and all matters specifically provided for in any other agreement which confers jurisdiction on the Tribunal.

The Tribunal has exclusive jurisdiction, through its Seabed Disputes Chamber, with respect to disputes relating to activities in the international seabed Area. These matters include disputes between States Parties concerning the interpretation or application of the provisions of the Convention, along with those of the *Agreement relating to the Implementation of the Part XI of the Convention*, concerning the deep seabed Area; and disputes between States Parties or a contractor and the International Seabed Authority.

The Tribunal, through its Seabed Disputes Chamber, has jurisdiction to provide advisory opinions at the request of the Assembly or the Council of the International Seabed Authority on legal questions arising within the scope of their activities.

The Tribunal has special jurisdiction in matters calling for provisional measures. Failing agreement between parties to a dispute within two weeks of the request by either party for provisional measures, the Tribunal, or with respect to activities in the Area, the Seabed Disputes Chamber, may prescribe, modify or revoke provisional measures.

Where the authorities of a States Party have detained a vessel flying the flag of another State Party and it is alleged that the detaining State has not complied with the provisions of the Convention for the prompt release of the vessel or its crew upon the posting of a reasonable bond or other financial security, the question of release from detention may be submitted to the Tribunal, failing agreement between the Parties within ten days from the time of detention.

Composition

The Tribunal is composed of 21 independent members elected by States Parties to the Convention on the Law of the Sea from among persons with recognized competence in the field of the law of the sea and representing the principal legal systems of the world. The first election was held in August 1996....

In hearing a dispute, all available members of the Tribunal may sit, although a quorum of 11 members is required to constitute the Tribunal. All disputes and applications submitted to the Tribunal shall be heard and determined by it, unless the dispute is to be submitted to the Seabed Disputes Chamber or the parties request that it be submitted to a special chamber.

The Seabed Disputes Chamber is to be composed of 11 members selected by a majority of the members of the Tribunal from among them.... A quorum of seven members is required to constitute the Chamber.

In addition to the Seabed Disputes Chamber, the Tribunal will form annually a chamber composed of five of its members which may hear and determine disputes by summary procedure. The Tribunal will also form special chambers for dealing with a particular dispute submitted to it if the parties so request. The composition of those chambers will be determined by the Tribunal with the approval of the parties. Finally, the Tribunal may form such other chambers, composed of three or more its members, as it considers necessary for dealing with particular categories of disputes....

Applicable Law

The Tribunal will apply the provisions of the *United Nations Convention on the Law of the Sea* and other rules of international law not incompatible with the Convention in deciding disputes submitted to it. It does, however, have to the power to decide a case *ex aequo et bono*, if the parties so agree.

Procedure

Disputes are to be submitted to the Tribunal, depending on the case, either by notification of a special agreement, or by written application, addressed to the Registrar.

The Tribunal and its Seabed Disputes Chamber have the power to prescribe provisional measures. If the Tribunal is not in session or a sufficient number of its members is not available to constitute a quorum, the provisional measures can be prescribed by the chamber of summary procedure. Such measures are subject to review and revision by the Tribunal....

States Parties not party to a dispute but which consider that they have an interest of a legal nature which may be affected by the decision in any dispute may submit a request to the Tribunal to be permitted to intervene. Whenever the interpretation or application of the Convention or any other agreement is in question, the Registrar will notify all States Parties to the Convention or to such agreements. Those parties have the right to intervene in the proceedings.

Decisions of the Tribunal are final and shall be complied with by all the parties to the dispute. However, decisions will not have a binding force except between the parties in respect of the particular dispute.

Judge Shunji Yanai, President of ITLOS, Statement on Agenda item 75(a), 'Oceans and the law of the sea' at the Plenary of the Sixty-seventh Session of the United Nations General Assembly

11 December 2012, www.itlos.org

3. The International Tribunal for the Law of the Sea is one of the key dispute settlement mechanisms established by the Convention. It has been set up as a specialized court, universal in nature, to be called upon to deal with disputes of any kind concerning the sea or activity carried out at sea.

4. A dispute between States Parties to the Convention may be submitted to the Tribunal by means of unilateral application if the parties have made declarations under article 287 of the Convention in which they have chosen the Tribunal as a forum for the settlement of disputes. As at 1 December 2012, declarations had been made by 47 States, 34 of which have chosen the Tribunal as a means for settlement.

5. The choice of procedure is of paramount importance. For example, if the disputing States Parties are not bound by declarations, the mandatory procedure is arbitration under Annex VII of the Convention, which can prove costly for those States. To be noted is that, where States have not made declarations under article 287 of the Convention, they may nevertheless agree to submit the dispute to the Tribunal by means of a special agreement concluded for the purpose. A special agreement may even be entered into after the dispute has been submitted to arbitration under Annex VII. To date, this has been done in four cases brought before the Tribunal.

6. The Tribunal has jurisdiction over any dispute concerning the interpretation or application of an international agreement related to the purposes of the Convention which is submitted to it in accordance with that agreement (Statute of the Tribunal, article 21; Convention, article 288). In this connection, I note with satisfaction that the Tribunal is named as a forum for the settlement of disputes in a number of multilateral or bilateral conventions on such subjects as fisheries, protection and preservation of the marine environment, conservation of marine resources, underwater cultural heritage and removal of wrecks, among others.

7. In addition, the Tribunal enjoys advisory jurisdiction separate from that of the Seabed Disputes Chamber. Advisory proceedings are provided for in article 138 of the Rules of the Tribunal and can be an attractive option for States wishing to obtain an opinion on a point of law dividing them.

8. Turning now from this overview of the main aspects of the Tribunal's jurisdiction, I would like to speak about its judicial work, and more specifically about the most recent cases to have come before it.

9. Twenty cases have been submitted to the International Tribunal for the Law of the Sea since its entry into operation in 1996. They have concerned a number of questions, such as the lawfulness of enforcement measures taken against foreign vessels in the exclusive economic zone, use of force at sea, prompt release of detained

vessels and crews, protection of fishery resources and of the marine environment, delimitation of maritime areas, and the lawfulness of the boarding of vessels. Of these cases, 15 were settled by way of litigation, two were discontinued further to agreement between the parties and three are in progress.... Under article 290, paragraph 5, of the Convention, the Tribunal may prescribe provisional measures if it considers that *prima facie* the arbitral tribunal to be constituted in accordance with Annex VII has jurisdiction and that the urgency of the situation so requires....

20. The Tribunal's role in settling disputes relating to the law of the sea is not confined to its judicial function. Under Annex VII, article 3, of the Convention, if the parties to a dispute are unable to agree on the appointment of one or more arbitral tribunal members to be appointed by agreement, or on the appointment of the president of the arbitral tribunal, the President of the International Tribunal for the Law of the Sea makes the appointment at the request of a party to the dispute and in consultation with the parties. Support of this kind has been given through the appointment of arbitrators in two recent cases: the arbitral proceedings under Annex VII of the Convention for the settlement of the dispute over the delimitation of the maritime boundary between Bangladesh and India in the Bay of Bengal; and the arbitral proceedings under Annex VII of the Convention in the dispute between Mauritius and the United Kingdom concerning the marine protected area around the Chagos Archipelago.

NOTES

1. The International Tribunal for the Law of the Sea (ITLOS) heard its first case in 1997, being an application by St Vincent and the Grenadines for the 'prompt release' of a vessel seized by Guinea for alleged violations of Guinean customs law: see M.D. Evans and V. Lowe, '*The M/V Saiga*: The First Case in the International Tribunal for the Law of the Sea' (1999) 49 *International and Comparative Law Quarterly* 187. As at March 2016, 25 cases have been submitted to ITLOS, including the first Advisory Opinion from the Seabed Disputes Chamber, which was requested in May 2010 and is extracted above.

2. In April 2015, the Tribunal itself delivered its first Advisory Opinion, which was requested by the Sub-Regional Fisheries Commission in March 2013 (see extract). The Tribunal determined that it had jurisdiction to issue advisory opinions, although (unlike the Seabed Disputes Chamber—see Article 191, 1982 Convention), jurisdiction for advisory opinions is not expressly or impliedly conferred on the full Tribunal. The Tribunal found that Article 21 of its Statute envisages jurisdiction for advisory opinions, but only where an international agreement related to the purposes of the Convention specifically provides for the submission to the Tribunal of a request for an advisory opinion: *Request for an Advisory Opinion Submitted by the Sub-regional Fisheries Commission (SRFC), Advisory Opinion*, 2 April 2015, paras 60–61.

11

State Responsibility

The international legal system offers considerable benefits to a State, from conferring recognition of its sovereignty to protecting its territorial integrity. Accordingly, as part of a State's consent to the operation of that system, it must accept corresponding legal obligations. Primarily, it must accept responsibility for its actions that have an effect on other international legal persons and the international community. As stated by Judge Huber in the *Spanish Zone of Morocco Claims Case* (1925) 2 RIAA 615: 'responsibility is the necessary corollary of a right. All rights of an international character involve international responsibility.'

State responsibility arises from the violation by a State (or other international legal person) of an international obligation. That obligation can be one of customary international law or arising from a treaty. The violation must be due to conduct attributable to a State. The enforcement of this responsibility is generally undertaken by a State either on its own behalf or on behalf of its injured nationals. However, as each State (or other international legal person) may decide for itself whether to enforce an apparent violation of an international obligation by another State, it is possible that no legal action will be taken against a State that has violated international law. Additionally, as States themselves largely determine the scope of customary international law and of treaty obligations, they can allow certain exceptions to international obligations, and so determine for themselves when State responsibility exists.

The law of State responsibility can be divided conveniently into two parts, although it must be emphasised that this is for the purposes of exposition only. First, issues of general concern, which comprise the nature of State responsibility, attribution (imputability) of internationally unlawful acts to the State, the mechanics of enforcement (including nationality of claims and the exhaustion of local remedies), and defences to responsibility. Such matters are relevant irrespective of the type of international obligation said to have been violated and apply as much to an alleged violation of a treaty as to alleged mistreatment of a national abroad contrary to customary international law. Second, there is a subset of substantive rules concerning international responsibility for the mistreatment of aliens (i.e. non-nationals). These rules indicate both when a State will be responsible for such mistreatment and the consequences of such responsibility.

Factory at Chorzów (Claim for Indemnity) Case (Germany v Poland)
Merits, PCIJ Ser A (1928) No. 17, Permanent Court of International Justice

The facts are set out in Section 5A.

[T]he Court observes that it is a principle of international law, and even a general conception of law, that any breach of an engagement involves an obligation to make reparation...reparation is the indispensble complement of a failure to apply a convention, and there is no necessity for this to be stated in the convention itself.

International Law Commission, Articles on Responsibility of States for Internationally Wrongful Acts (2001)

The International Law Commission (ILC) had been considering the general topic of State responsibility for a number of years. The ILC adopted in 2001 a set of Articles and they stand as a code of the general principles of State responsibility. The Articles have been commented on extensively by States and they command widespread, though not universal, support. The content of some Articles (especially the initial ones) reflect customary international law, though some parts of them remain controversial (e.g. Articles 40 and 41).

Article 1 Responsibility of a state for its internationally wrongful acts

Every internationally wrongful act of a State entails the international responsibility of that State.

Article 2 Elements of an internationally wrongful act of a State

There is an internationally wrongful act of a State when conduct consisting of an action or omission:
    (a) Is attributable to the State under international law; and
    (b) Constitutes a breach of an international obligation of the State.

Article 3 Characterization of an act of a State as internationally wrongful

The characterization of an act of a State as internationally wrongful is governed by international law. Such characterization is not affected by the characterization of the same act as lawful by internal law.

P. Allott, 'State Responsibility and the Unmaking of International Law'
29 Harvard International Law Journal 1 (1988)

To international lawyers from the United States and other countries with similar interests and backgrounds, state responsibility was essentially a matter of codifying the obligations of states in the treatment of aliens.... In contrast, international lawyers from Latin America and other countries with similar interests viewed state responsibility as essentially a matter of confining the diplomatic protection of aliens within limits which respected the sovereignty of all states. The particular history and culture of Latin America had led writers from that region to take significantly different views not only of diplomatic protection and state responsibility but also of the fundamental nature and principles of international law ...

The aspect of the draft articles on state responsibility [being an earlier draft than the 2001 Articles but this issue is still relevant] that demands our particular attention is their fundamental structural feature—the postulation of a concept of 'responsibility-arising-from-wrongfulness' distinct from the wrongful act and from the consequences of a wrongful act. This middle category is a dangerous fiction, an unnecessary intrusion into the systematic structure of a legal system. But it is not merely analytically unnecessary. In the particular case of international law, it entails consequences of the most serious and undesirable kind.

The draft articles are based on the initial premise that state responsibility results from the 'internationally wrongful act of a State.' [The English text of the draft articles uses the unexpected word 'wrongful', with its interesting moral overtone, rather than the word 'unlawful'.] The internationally wrongful act of a state involves conduct 'attributable to the State under international law' that 'constitutes a breach of an international obligation of the State.' The act of a state is to be characterized as internationally wrongful only 'by international law.' Putting these ideas together, 'every internationally wrongful act of a State entails the international responsibility of that State.'

In short, the draft articles postulate that all the different kinds of obligation and different kinds of breach give rise to a single kind of consequence called 'responsibility.' Responsibility in this sense has two characteristics: (a) it has a particular substantive content of its own; and (b) it gives rise to certain further consequences in terms of liabilities, rights, and, eventually, remedies.

In the normal course of events, a wrongful act entails painful consequences: a judgment and possibly a penalty. The Benthamite price of lawbreaking is the risk of pain, not the possibility of an idea. The wages of sin are death, not responsibility for sin. In the terms of legal analysis, wrongdoing gives rise to a liability in the offender owed to others who have rights which may be enforced by legal processes. Liability is not a consequence of some intervening concept of responsibility. It is a direct consequence flowing from the nature of the wrong (the content of the rights of the offended party and the duties of the offender) and from the nature of the actual wrongful act in the given case (in particular, the content of the specific rights and duties which have been affected by the breach in question). The remedies available are a function of integrating the nature of the liability in the given case with the nature of the particular wrongful act ...

Two especially vicious consequences result from using responsibility as a general and independent category in international law. First, it consecrates the idea that wrongdoing is the behavior of a general category known as 'states' and is not the behavior of morally responsible human beings. It therefore obscures the fact that breaches of international law are attributable formally to the legal persons known as states but morally to the human beings who determine the behaviour of states.

Second, if responsibility exists as a legal category, it must be given legal substance. In particular, general conditions of responsibility have to be created which are then applicable to all rights and duties. The net result is that the deterrent effect of the imposition of responsibility is seriously compromised, not only by notionalizing it (the first vicious consequence) but also by leaving room for argument in every conceivable case of potential responsibility (the second vicious consequence). When lawyers leave room for argument there is much room for injustice.

J. Crawford and S. Olleson, 'The Continuing Debate on a UN Convention on State Responsibility'

54 *International and Comparative Law Quarterly* 4 (2005)

At its 56th session in 2001, the Sixth Committee [of the UN] had considered what action to take in relation to the final Articles contained (together with the accompanying Commentaries) in the Report of the ILC on its 53rd session.

The question was a controversial one even before the Articles were finally adopted on second reading in August 2001. Significant divisions existed within the ILC as to what course of action should be recommended to the General Assembly. Some members strongly supported the immediate convening of a diplomatic conference in order to conclude a convention based on the Articles. Others, including the Special Rapporteur, were of the view that the General Assembly should simply take note of the Articles, and that any decision as to the preparation of an international convention on the subject should be deferred for a period of years in order to allow States to become familiar with the Articles in practice. A compromise was reached: the ILC recommended to the General Assembly that it take note of the Articles and annex them to a resolution, deferring to a later stage the question whether an international conference should be convened with a view to concluding a convention on the topic....

[On] the ultimate form of the Articles there was a clear division of views: some governments thought that there was no prospect that the Articles could be transformed into a convention along the lines of the Vienna Convention on the Law of Treaties; the best course was not to adopt the Articles in any formal manner but to allow them to exert an influence on the crystallization of the law of State responsibility through application by international courts and tribunals and State practice. Others thought that a convention on State responsibility was both desirable and achievable. A few governments thought the matter should be immediately referred to a working group or even a diplomatic conference. The views of the majority of delegations who spoke, however, were against any immediate move to a convention, and the Sixth Committee's draft resolution reflected this position. Adopted by the General Assembly by consensus, Resolution 56/83 of 12 December 2001 took note of the Articles, the text of which was annexed to the resolution, and commend[ed] them to the attention of Governments without prejudice to the question of their future adoption or other appropriate action. By operative paragraph 4, the General Assembly decided to include the topic. Responsibility of States for Internationally Wrongful Acts in the provisional agenda for its 59th session in the autumn of 2004....

Given the previous divergence of views in 2001, it was to be expected that a number of States would press for the convening of a diplomatic conference when the subject returned to the Sixth Committee ... On the one hand, a number of speakers suggested that the only appropriate means by which to reflect the importance of the Articles was for them to be transformed into a convention. Some seem to have taken this position in order to provide a chance to reopen certain controversial issues, in particular the triad of countermeasures (Articles 49–54), invocation by States other than the injured State (Article 48), and the question of the aggravated régime of responsibility for serious breaches of obligations arising under peremptory norms of general international law (Articles 40–1)....

On the other hand, a group of States expressed the view that the action of the General Assembly in 2001 in commending the Articles to the attention of governments was sufficient and that no further action was necessary or desirable. Notably this was the position taken by the United Kingdom and the United States of America. The United Kingdom emphasized the fragility of the compromises reached in the final text of the Articles, and warned against the reopening of old and fruitless debates which could lead to the unravelling of the text and a convention which would receive few ratifications....

As a matter of impression the number of delegations supporting the eventual elaboration of a convention or at least prepared to keep that option open has increased between 2001 and 2004, although it is difficult to be certain given that not all States which made statements in 2001 did so in 2004 (and vice versa).

NOTES
1. The International Law Commission (ILC) was established in 1947 by the General Assembly for the purpose of codifying and progressively developing international law (see Chapter 2). In some areas the draft conventions or 'articles' issued by the ILC are considered to be, at least in part, representative of customary international law, and may become the basis for a multilateral treaty.
2. The ILC acknowledge that the 2001 ILC Articles express secondary rules that 'indicate the consequences of a breach of an applicable primary obligation'. The ILC Articles are a mixture of progressive development of the law and codification of customary international law. Necessarily, the Articles will help to promote the development of new customary international law on similar lines to the content of the Articles. Indeed, the *Nicaragua Case* and the *Danube Dam Case* (see Sections 2B and 4 respectively) make it clear that earlier versions of the Articles have already had this effect. The compilation of cases prepared by the Secretary-General in 2007 (at the request of the General Assembly and with the assistance of States) demonstrates that the Articles continue to be relied upon in a variety of contexts, including investment law, trade law and human rights.

SECTION 2: ATTRIBUTION

International Law Commission, Articles on Responsibility of States for Internationally Wrongful Acts (2001)

Article 4 Conduct of organs of a State

1. The conduct of any State organ shall be considered an act of that State under international law, whether the organ exercises legislative, executive, judicial or any other functions, whatever position it holds in the organization of the State, and whatever its character as an organ of the central government or of a territorial unit of the State.

2. An organ includes any person or entity which has that status in accordance with the internal law of the State.

Article 5 Conduct of persons or entities exercising elements of governmental authority

The conduct of a person or entity which is not an organ of the State under Article 4 but which is empowered by the law of that State to exercise elements of the governmental authority shall be considered an act of the State under international law, provided the person or entity is acting in that capacity in the particular instance.

Article 6 Conduct of organs placed at the disposal of a State by another State

The conduct of an organ placed at the disposal of a State by another State shall be considered an act of the former State under international law if the organ is acting in the exercise of elements of the governmental authority of the State at whose disposal it is placed.

Article 7 Excess of authority or contravention of instructions

The conduct of an organ of a State or of a person or entity empowered to exercise elements of the governmental authority shall be considered an act of the State under international law if the organ, person or entity acts in that capacity, even if it exceeds its authority or contravenes instructions.

Article 8 Conduct directed or controlled by a State

The conduct of a person or group of persons shall be considered an act of a State under international law if the person or group of persons is in fact acting on the instructions of, or under the direction or control of, that State in carrying out the conduct.

Article 9 Conduct carried out in the absence or default of the official authorities

The conduct of a person or group of persons shall be considered an act of a State under international law if the person or group of persons is in fact exercising elements of the governmental authority in the absence or default of the official authorities and in circumstances such as to call for the exercise of those elements of authority.

Article 10 Conduct of an insurrectional or other movement

1. The conduct of an insurrectional movement which becomes the new government of a State shall be considered an act of that State under international law.

2. The conduct of a movement, insurrectional or other, which succeeds in establishing a new State in part of the territory of a pre-existing State or in a territory under its administration shall be considered an act of the new State under international law.

3. This article is without prejudice to the attribution to a State of any conduct, however related to that of the movement concerned, which is to be considered an act of that State by virtue of articles 4 to 9.

Article 11 Conduct acknowledged and adopted by a State as its own

Conduct which is not attributable to a State under the preceding articles shall nevertheless be considered an act of that State under international law if and to the extent that the State acknowledges and adopts the conduct in question as its own.

A: Officials

Application of the Convention on the Prevention and Punishment of the Crime of Genocide, (Bosnia and Herzegovina v Serbia and Montenegro)

Merits, ICJ Rep 2007, International Court of Justice

The Court was faced with the question of whether the conduct of members of the Bosnian Serb troops under the command of General Mladić forming the army of the Republika Srpska (the VRS), as well as the actions of various paramilitary Serb groups, in relation to the massacre at Srebrenica and other atrocities committed within the territory of Bosnia and Herzegovina, were attributable to the Federal Republic of Yugoslavia (FRY, later Serbia and Montenegro).

384. This question has in fact two aspects, which the Court must consider separately. First, it should be ascertained whether the acts committed at Srebrenica were perpetrated by organs of the Respondent, i.e., by persons or entities whose conduct is necessarily attributable to it, because they are in fact the instruments of its action. Next, if the preceding question is answered in the negative, it should be ascertained whether the acts in question were committed by persons who, while not organs of the Respondent, did nevertheless act on the instructions of, or under the direction or control of, the Respondent ...

385. The first of these two questions relates to the well-established rule, one of the cornerstones of the law of State responsibility, that the conduct of any State organ is to be considered an act of the State under international law, and therefore gives rise to the responsibility of the State if it constitutes a breach of an international obligation of the State....

386. When applied to the present case, this rule first calls for a determination whether the acts of genocide committed in Srebrenica were perpetrated by 'persons or entities' having the status of organs of the Federal Republic of Yugoslavia (as the Respondent was known at the time) under its internal law, as then in force. It must be said that there is nothing which could justify an affirmative response to this question. It has not been shown that the FRY army took part in the massacres, nor that the political leaders of the FRY had a hand in preparing, planning or in any way carrying out the massacres. It is true that there is much evidence of direct or indirect

participation by the official army of the FRY, along with the Bosnian Serb armed forces, in military operations in Bosnia and Herzegovina in the years prior to the events at Srebrenica. That participation was repeatedly condemned by the political organs of the United Nations, which demanded that the FRY put an end to it.... It has however not been shown that there was any such participation in relation to the massacres committed at Srebrenica.... Further, neither the Republika Srpska, nor the VRS were *de jure* organs of the FRY, since none of them had the status of organ of that State under its internal law …

388. The Court notes first that no evidence has been presented that either General Mladic´ or any of the other officers whose affairs were handled by the 30th Personnel Centre were, according to the internal law of the Respondent, officers of the army of the Respondent a *de jure* organ of the Respondent. Nor has it been conclusively established that General Mladic´ was one of those officers; and even on the basis that he might have been, the Court does not consider that he would, for that reason alone, have to be treated as an organ of the FRY for the purposes of the application of the rules of State responsibility. There is no doubt that the FRY was providing substantial support, *inter alia*, financial support, to the Republika Srpska…, and that one of the forms that support took was payment of salaries and other benefits to some officers of the VRS, but this did not automatically make them organs of the FRY. Those officers were appointed to their commands by the President of the Republika Srpska, and were subordinated to the political leadership of the Republika Srpska. In the absence of evidence to the contrary, those officers must be taken to have received their orders from the Republika Srpska or the VRS, not from the FRY. The expression 'State organ', as used in customary international law and in Article 4 of the ILC Articles, applies to one or other of the individual or collective entities which make up the organization of the State and act on its behalf…The functions of the VRS officers, including General Mladic´, were however to act on behalf of the Bosnian Serb authorities, in particular the Republika Srpska, not on behalf of the FRY; they exercised elements of the public authority of the Republika Srpska. The particular situation of General Mladic´, or of any other VRS officer present at Srebrenica who may have been being 'administered' from Belgrade, is not therefore such as to lead the Court to modify the conclusion reached in the previous paragraph.

Caire Claim (*France* v *Mexico*)
5 RIAA 516 (1929) (transl. for the authors by Mr M. Nasta) French-Mexican Claims Commission

Caire, who was French, was killed in Mexico during a revolution by Mexican soldiers after refusing to give them money. The relevant question for the Commission was what was 'the responsibility of Mexico for actions of individual military personnel, acting without orders or against the wishes of their commanding officers and independently of the needs and aims of the revolution'.

PRESIDING COMMISSIONER VERZIJL: [The] solution [to the question asked] is to be found by having regard to the general principles governing the conditions of the international responsibility of States for acts committed by their public officials. However, this statement requires the following remarks:

  (a) the special features distinguishing military from civil officials influence the conditions and the extent of the responsibility caused by their acts....

  (c) Mexico, having assumed the responsibility for damages caused by non-governmental, i.e. revolutionary, forces, is also responsible for their acts, as if they were committed by military forces under the control of the lawful government …

I should like to make clear first of all that I am interpreting the said principles in accordance with the doctrine of the 'objective responsibility' of the State, that is, the responsibility for the acts of the officials or organs of a State,…even in the absence of any 'fault' of its own. It is widely known that theoretical conceptions in this sphere have advanced a great deal in recent times…I can say that I regard them as perfectly correct in that they tend to impute to the State, on an international plane, the responsibility for all the acts committed by its officials or organs which constitute criminal acts from the point of view of the law of nations, no matter if the official or organ in question has acted within or exceeded the limits of his competence. 'It is generally agreed,' as M. Bourquin has rightly said, 'that acts committed by the officials and agents of a State entail the international responsibility of that State, even if the perpetrator did not have specific authorisation. This responsibility does not find its justification in general principles—I mean those principles regulating the judicial organisation of the State. The act of an official is only judicially established as an act of State if such an act lies within the official's sphere of competence. The act of an official operating beyond his competence is not an act of State. It should not in principle, therefore, affect the responsibility of the State. If it is accepted in international law that the position is different, it is for reasons peculiar to the mechanism of international life; it is because it is felt that international relations would become too difficult, too complicated and too insecure if foreign States were obliged to take into account the often complex judicial arrangements that regulate competence in the internal affairs of a State. From this it is immediately clear that in the hypothesis under consideration the international responsibility of the State is purely *objective* in character, and that it rests on an idea of *guarantee*, in which the subjective notion of fault plays no part.'

But in order to be able to admit this so-called objective responsibility of the State for acts committed by its officials or organs outside their competence, they must have acted at least to all appearances as competent officials or organs, or they must have used powers or methods appropriate to their official capacity....

If the principles stated above are applied to the present case, and if it is taken into account that the perpetrators of the murder of M.J.-B. Caire were military personnel occupying the ranks of 'major' and 'capitan primero' aided by a few privates, it is found that the conditions of responsibility formulated above are completely fulfilled.... Under these circumstances, there remains no doubt that, even if they are to be regarded as having acted outside their competence, which is by no means certain, and even if their superior officers issued a counter-order, these two officers have involved the responsibility of the State, in view of the fact that they acted in their capacity of officers and used the means placed at their disposition by virtue of that capacity.

Southern Pacific Properties (Middle East) Ltd v Arab Republic of Egypt
32 *International Legal Materials* 933 (1993), International Centre for the Settlement of Investment Disputes

Southern Pacific entered into a contract with Egypt to develop land for tourism around the sites of the Pyramids at Giza. There was considerable opposition in Egypt, especially because of the possibility of disturbance of undiscovered antiquities. Egyptian authorities withdrew Southern Pacific's permission to develop the site. Southern Pacific claimed compensation and damages. The dispute to be decided fell according to international legal principles because the contract provided for arbitration by the International Centre for the Settlement of Investment Disputes. Egypt claimed, *inter alia*, that certain acts of Egyptian officials were null and void under Egyptian law and could not therefore be attributable to the State itself.

81. The Respondent has contended that certain acts of Egyptian officials upon which the Claimants rely are under Egyptian law, legally non-existent or absolutely null and void.... The Respondent argues further that certain decisions of high-ranking government officials are invalid because they were not taken pursuant to the procedures prescribed by Egyptian law.

82. It is possible that under Egyptian law certain acts of Egyptian officials, including even Presidential Decree No. 475, may be considered legally nonexistent or null and void or susceptible to invalidation. However, these acts were cloaked with the mantle of Governmental authority and communicated as such to foreign investors who relied on them in making their investments.

83. Whether legal under Egyptian law or not, the acts in question were the acts of Egyptian authorities, including the highest executive authority of the Government. These acts, which are now alleged to have been in violation of the Egyptian municipal legal system, created expectations protected by established principles of international law. A determination that these acts are null and void under municipal law would not resolve the ultimate question of liability for damages suffered by the victim who rallied on the acts. If the municipal law does not provide a remedy, the denial of any remedy whatsoever cannot be the final answer....

85. The principle of international law which the Tribunal is bound to apply is that which establishes the international responsibility of States when unauthorised or *ultra vires* acts of officials have been performed by State agents under cover of their official character. If such unauthorised or *ultra vires* acts could not be ascribed to the State, all State responsibility would be rendered illusory. For this reason.

> ...the practice of states has conclusively established the international responsibility for unlawful acts of state organs, even if accomplished outside the limits of their competence and contrary to domestic law. (Sorensen (ed.), *Manual of Public International Law*, New York 1968, at p. 548.)

Al-Jedda v United Kingdom
(2011) European Court of Human Rights, Grand Chamber, 27021/08

The applicant was a British national from Iraq. While visiting Iraq in 2004 he was detained and held in a detention centre run by British forces until December 2007. He challenged the lawfulness of his detention before the UK Courts, but was unsuccessful. Before the European Court of Human Rights he claimed that his detention by British forces deprived him of his right to liberty and security of person under Article 5 of the Convention. An issue that was raised before Court was whether the applicant's detention was attributable to the United Nations or the United Kingdom.

76. When examining whether the applicant's detention was attributable to the United Kingdom or, as the Government submit, the United Nations it is necessary to examine the particular facts of the case. These include the terms of the United Nations Security Council resolutions which formed the framework for the security regime in Iraq during the period in question....

77. The Court takes as its starting point that, on 20 March 2003, the United Kingdom together with the United States of America and their Coalition partners, through their armed forces, entered Iraq with the aim of displacing the Ba'ath regime then in power. At the time of the invasion, there was no United Nations Security Council resolution providing for the allocation of roles in Iraq in the event that the existing regime was displaced. Major combat operations were declared to be complete by 1 May 2003 and the United States of America and the United Kingdom became Occupying Powers within the meaning of Article 42 of the Hague Regulations (see paragraph 42 above). As explained in the letter dated 8 May 2003 sent jointly by the Permanent Representatives of the United Kingdom and the United States of America to the President of the United Nations Security Council (see paragraph 27 above), the United States of America and the United Kingdom, having displaced the previous regime, created the CPA 'to exercise powers of government temporarily'. One of the powers of government specifically referred to in the letter of 8 May 2003 to be exercised by the United States of America and the United Kingdom through the CPA was the provision of security in Iraq. The letter further stated that '[t]he United States, the United Kingdom and Coalition partners, working through the Coalition Provisional Authority, shall, *inter alia*, provide for security in and for the provisional administration of Iraq, including by…assuming immediate control of Iraqi institutions responsible for military and security matters'. The letter acknowledged that the United Nations had 'a vital role to play in providing humanitarian relief, in supporting the reconstruction of Iraq, and in helping in the formation of an Iraqi interim authority' and stated that the United States of America, the United Kingdom and Coalition partners were ready to work closely with representatives of the United Nations and its specialised agencies and would also welcome the support and contributions of member States, international and regional organisations, and other entities, 'under appropriate coordination arrangements with the Coalition Provisional Authority'. In its first legislative act, CPA Regulation No. 1 of 16 May 2003, the CPA declared that it would 'exercise powers of government temporarily in order to provide for the effective administration of Iraq during the period of transitional administration, to restore conditions of security and stability' (see paragraph 28 above).

78. The first United Nations Security Council resolution after the invasion was Resolution 1483, adopted on 22 May 2003 (see paragraph 29 above). In the Preamble, the Security Council noted the letter of 8 May 2003 from the Permanent Representatives of the United States of America and the United Kingdom and recognised that the United States of America and the United Kingdom were Occupying Powers in Iraq, under unified command (the CPA), and that specific authorities, responsibilities, and obligations applied to them under international humanitarian law. The Security Council noted further that other States that were not Occupying Powers were working or might in the future work under the CPA, and welcomed the willingness of member States to contribute to stability and security in Iraq by contributing personnel, equipment and other resources 'under the Authority'. Acting under Chapter VII of the Charter of the United Nations, the Security Council called upon the Occupying Powers, through the CPA, 'to promote the welfare of the Iraqi people through the effective administration of the territory, including in particular working towards the restoration of conditions of security and stability'. The United Kingdom and the United States of America were encouraged 'to inform the Council at regular intervals of their efforts under this Resolution'. The Preamble to Resolution 1483 recognised that the United Nations were to 'play a vital role in humanitarian relief, the reconstruction of Iraq and the restoration and establishment of national and local institutions for representative governance'. The Secretary-General of the United Nations was requested to appoint a Special Representative for Iraq, whose independent responsibilities were to include, *inter alia*, reporting regularly to the Security Council on his activities under this Resolution, coordinating activities of

the United Nations in post-conflict processes in Iraq and coordinating among United Nations and international agencies engaged in humanitarian assistance and reconstruction activities in Iraq. Resolution 1483 did not assign any security role to the United Nations. The Government does not contend that, at this stage in the invasion and occupation, the acts of its armed forces were in any way attributable to the United Nations.

79. In Resolution 1511, adopted on 16 October 2003, the United Nations Security Council, again acting under Chapter VII of the Charter, underscored the temporary nature of the exercise by the CPA of the authorities and responsibilities set out in Resolution 1483, which would cease as soon as an internationally recognised, representative Iraqi government could be sworn in. In paragraphs 13 and 14, the Security Council authorised 'a Multinational Force under unified command to take all necessary measures to contribute to the maintenance of security and stability in Iraq' and urged member States 'to contribute assistance under this United Nations mandate, including military forces, to the Multinational Force referred to in paragraph 13' (see paragraph 31 above). The United States of America, on behalf of the Multinational Force, was requested periodically to report on the efforts and progress of the Force. The Security Council also resolved that the United Nations, acting through the Secretary-General, his Special Representative, and the United Nations Assistance Mission for Iraq, should strengthen its role in Iraq, including by providing humanitarian relief, promoting the economic reconstruction of and conditions for sustainable development in Iraq, and advancing efforts to restore and establish national and local institutions for representative government.

80. The Court does not consider that, as a result of the authorisation contained in Resolution 1511, the acts of soldiers within the Multinational Force became attributable to the United Nations or—more importantly, for the purposes of this case—ceased to be attributable to the troop-contributing nations. The Multinational Force had been present in Iraq since the invasion and had been recognised already in Resolution 1483, which welcomed the willingness of member States to contribute personnel. The unified command structure over the Force, established from the start of the invasion by the United States of America and the United Kingdom, was not changed as a result of Resolution 1511. Moreover, the United States of America and the United Kingdom, through the CPA which they had established at the start of the occupation, continued to exercise the powers of government in Iraq. Although the United States of America was requested to report periodically to the Security Council about the activities of the Multinational Force, the United Nations did not, thereby, assume any degree of control over either the Force or any other of the executive functions of the CPA.

81. The final resolution of relevance to the present issue was Resolution 1546 (see paragraph 35 above). It was adopted on 8 June 2004, twenty days before the transfer of power from the CPA to the Iraqi interim government and some four months before the applicant was taken into detention. Annexed to the Resolution was a letter from the Prime Minister of the interim government of Iraq, seeking from the Security Council a new resolution on the Multinational Force mandate. There was also annexed a letter from the US Secretary of State to the President of the United Nations Security Council, confirming that 'the Multinational Force [under unified command] [wa]s prepared to continue to contribute to the maintenance of security in Iraq' and informing the President of the Security Council of the goals of the Multinational Force and the steps which its Commander intended to take to achieve those goals. It does not appear from the terms of this letter that the US Secretary of State considered that the United Nations controlled the deployment or conduct of the Multinational Force. In Resolution 1546 the Security Council, acting under Chapter VII of the Charter of the United Nations, reaffirmed the authorisation for the Multinational Force established under Resolution 1511. There is no indication in Resolution 1546 that the Security Council intended to assume any greater degree of control or command over the Multinational Force than it had exercised previously.

82. In Resolution 1546 the Security Council also decided that, in implementing their mandates in Iraq, the Special Representative of the Secretary-General and the United Nations Assistance Mission for Iraq (UNAMI) should play leading roles in assisting in the establishment of democratic institutions, economic development and humanitarian assistance. The Court notes that the Secretary-General and UNAMI, both clearly organs of the United Nations, in their quarterly and bi-monthly reports to the Security Council for the period during which the applicant was detained, repeatedly protested about the extent to which security internment was being used by the Multinational Force. It is difficult to conceive that the applicant's detention was attributable to the United Nations and not to the United Kingdom when United Nations organs, operating under the mandate of Resolution 1546, did not appear to approve of the practice of indefinite internment without trial and, in the case of UNAMI, entered into correspondence with the United States embassy in an attempt to persuade the Multinational Force under American command to modify the internment procedure.

83. In the light of the foregoing, the Court agrees with the majority of the House of Lords that the United Nations' role as regards security in Iraq in 2004 was quite different from its role as regards security in Kosovo

in 1999. The comparison is relevant, since in its decision in *Behrami and Saramati* (cited above) the Court concluded, *inter alia*, that Mr Saramati's detention was attributable to the United Nations and not to any of the respondent States. It is to be recalled that the international security presence in Kosovo was established by United Nations Security Council Resolution 1244, adopted on 10 June 1999, in which, 'determined to resolve the grave humanitarian situation in Kosovo', the Security Council 'decide[d] on the deployment in Kosovo, under United Nations auspices, of international civil and security presences'. The Security Council therefore authorised 'member States and relevant international organisations to establish the international security presence in Kosovo' and directed that there should be 'substantial North Atlantic Treaty Organization participation' in the Force, which 'must be deployed under unified command and control'. In addition, Resolution 1244 authorised the Secretary-General of the United Nations to establish an international civil presence in Kosovo in order to provide an interim administration for Kosovo. The United Nations, through a Special Representative appointed by the Secretary-General in consultation with the Security Council, was to control the implementation of the international civil presence and coordinate closely with the international security presence (see *Behrami and Saramati*, cited above, §§ 3, 4 and 41). On 12 June 1999, two days after the Resolution was adopted, the first elements of the NATO-led Kosovo Force (KFOR) entered Kosovo.

Mothers of Srebrenica v *The Netherlands*

C/09/295247, 17 July 2014, The Hague District Court,

In July 1995, a UN safe haven was established in the Bosnian enclave of Srebrenica. Members of the Dutch battalion (Dutchbat), acting as a UN peacekeeping force, were stationed in the area and were entrusted with safeguarding the enclave. When the Bosnian Serbian army took over Srebrenica, the Dutch battalion retreated to a nearby compound where some refugees from Srebrenica were admitted, but not others. Those who remained outside the compound were subsequently killed by the Bosnian Serb army. The key question before the Court was whether the actions of the Dutch battalion were attributable to the Dutch State. To answer this question, the Court had to assess whether and to what extent the State exercised effective control over Dutchbat's actions.

4.46. First and foremost the District Court hereby pronounces that in order to accept *effective control* there would be no requirement for the State in giving instructions to Dutchbat to have broken the structure of the chain of command at the UN or exercised independent operational authority to give orders. It comes down to the actual say over specific actions whereby all of the actual circumstances and the particular context of the case must be examined. In the *Nuhanović* and *Mustafić* cases the Appeals Court considered that there not only is the question significant as to whether the actions constituted implementation of a specific instruction the State had given but also whether in the absence of any such specific instruction the State had it in its powers to prevent the actions concerned. These considerations remained undisputed on cassation.

4.47. Referring to a quotation from the Claimants, [they] argue that the Dutch Government itself found that it did exercise effective control over Dutchbat despite transferring *command and control* and that for that reason alone there is room for attributing all of Dutchbat's actions to the State. The quotation concerned is as follows:

'The Minister of Defence, Voorhoeve, adopted the following position vis-à-vis NIOD namely that the regulation surrounding Command and Control in The Netherlands and the question as to where everyone's responsibility lay was more or less clear but that in practice it did not appear to be possible to separate these kinds of matters meaning they got mixed up together. According to him in a strict international law sense it was possible to argue that once The Netherlands had put units at the disposal of the UN the only right it still had was to withdraw its units but that everything else was up to the UN. The Hague would say about this: these military personnel are now UN blue helmets so this is no longer our problem. In practice however things were not like that, argued Voorhoeve.' (NIOD, p. 2283).

4.48. The substance of this quotation provides insufficient grounds for [the] Claimants' conclusion. It fits into the previously sketched framework for attribution in which transfer of *command and control* over the operational implementation of the mandate to the UN is not decisive and leaves open the possibility that the State exercises *effective control* over Dutchbat's actions.

4.49. As summarised above in 2.18 there were within UNPROFOR Dutch officers appointed to various high levels of command. Claimants argue that this 'Dutch line' within UNPROFOR maintained close links with 'The Hague' (read: the Dutch Government hereinafter also referred to as: The Hague) crossing the UN's *command and control* meaning. The Hague exercised continuous influence by passing formal lines and responsibilities.

4.50. The State correctly points out that the mere fact that Dutch military personnel were appointed to UNPROFOR does not mean *per se* that the State exercised *effective control*. Dutch officers worked in the UN chain of command whence operational implementation of the mandate was directed. It is usual for military personnel from countries that supply troops form part of the UN chain of command for UN peacekeeping operations.

4.51. Even the fact that Dutch UNPROFOR officers as and when necessary had direct contact with Dutchbat and in doing so missed a link or two in the UN chain of command is not *per se* accompanied by *effective control* of the State…

4.52. Nor does the fact that Dutch officers in the UN chain of command maintained contact with The Hague constitute grounds for assuming *effective control*. Claimants argue that the influence of The Hague expressed itself *inter alia* in frequent requests for information. The State correctly points out that requests for information by the Dutch Government do not constitute exercise of *effective control*…

4.53. A further general point is that communications between Dutch UNPROFOR officers and the Dutch Government is not accompanied by *effective control* unless in that regard we can talk of there having been orders or instructions to said Dutch officers or some other form of operational guidance by the State.

4.54. The fact has become established that in the period leading up to the fall of Srebrenica contact between The Hague on the one hand and the Dutch UNPROFOR officers and Dutchbat on the other hand was intensified, though on its own this would not constitute *effective control*. Claimants argue with reference to page 2276 of the NIOD Report that the DCBC in this period concerned itself more with operational matters. On this page under the heading '*verhoudingen tussen DCBC en KL Crisisstaf*' ['relations between DCBC and KL Crisis Staff'] the relations between these two units are described *inter alia* as follows:

'As matters in Srebrenica became more and more tense under the political pressure of the moment DCBC began to get more and more involved with implementation of the operation and the dividing line between DCBC's tasks and those of KL Crisis Staff became vague.'

That DCBC in relation to KL Crisis Staff 'concerned' itself more with operational matters again does not result in *effective control*; even leaving aside the fact that this concern can consist of heightened interest and need for information here above all as the State has sufficiently explained we are dealing with the relationship and division of tasks between two organisational units within The Netherlands.

4.55. Claimants further argue that in conflict with express orders of the UN there was 'an invariable line of conduct' at Dutchbat to allow its own interest to prevail. This is why according to them it has become established that Dutchbat's actions are the result of *effective control* being exercised by the State 'since military personnel hardly ever act on their own initiative'. Quite apart from the question whether the latter remark is true or is true in all circumstances these generalisations on the part of Claimants provide insufficient basis to be able to conclude that such actions were always preceded by instructions from the State.

4.56. With their arguments about Dutchbat's actions being in conflict with the orders the UN gave and their argument that the State may not appeal to *inter alia* inadequate training and preparation of Dutchbat in order to excuse itself for the accusations made against it Claimants do indeed lay a basis for attributing Dutchbat's actions to the State namely Dutchbat acting *ultra vires* over and against UN instructions. As to this the District Court deliberates as follows.

4.57. If a military force's *command and control* over operational implementation of the mandate is transferred to the UN and said military force then goes on to act beyond the authority given it by the UN or on its own initiative acts against the instructions of the UN as Claimants point out said military force acts *ultra vires* [beyond its legal power or authority]. Such action is attributable to the State supplying the troops because the State has a say over the mechanisms underlying said *ultra vires* actions, selection, training and the preparations for the mission of the troops placed at the disposal of the UN. Moreover the State supplying the troops has it in its powers to take measures to counter *ultra vires* actions on the part of its troops given the fact that it has a say about personal matters and disciplinary punishments.

4.58. In order to attribute *ultra vires* actions to the State supplying the troops there is no requirement for said state to give any instruction or order relating to *ultra vires* action or that this specifically influences the case in some other way. What is decisive is that the State delivering the troops retains the powers it has after transfer of *command and control* to the UN as well as the relevant say in respect of and with it *effective control* over self-willed powers acting beyond the powers the UN has granted or against the instructions of the UN concerning the actions of troops put at the UN's disposal…

NOTES

1. In one sense, no real entity exists which is 'the State', it being a construct of international law (see Chapter 5). However, individuals act in the name of 'the State' and may use 'the State' as a shield against direct personal responsibility. Acts done in the name of 'the State' include the normal daily functions of the State's police force, judiciary, armed forces and government ministers. Note, however, Chapter 14 in regard to individual responsibility for international crimes, which is not affected or dominated by State responsibility: see ILC Article 58 and note the Commentary to Article 10 (Section 2C). It is also clear that when such individuals act for the State, there is no restriction on the types of obligation for which the State itself may be responsible should the official occasion a breach. So, in the *Genocide Case* (see Section 2B), the Court accepted that a State could be held directly responsible for genocide even though the actual events were ordered or carried out by individuals and the individuals were also directly responsible under international law.

2. International law attempts to regulate the conduct of States but rarely can it regulate directly the conduct of individuals. Therefore, it is necessary that a State be held responsible for all cases of acts or omissions by any person actually or apparently acting as an official of the State, even when they are acting outside their official activity, except where it would not be reasonable for any injured non-national to have expected that the person was acting in the capacity of an official of the State. Otherwise the injured non-national has recourse only against the official personally and within the national law of the State of that official: see the the extract of *Southern Pacific Case*.

3. As a general rule, any act or omission of an organ of the State, which has that status in national law, is attributable to the State provided that the organ was acting in that capacity at the time of performing the unlawful act. The fact that the acts were unlawful or *ultra vires* under national law does not prevent the State from incurring responsibility at the international level, even if the unlawful or *ultra vires* nature of the action was manifest or undiscoverable. Responsibility is to be determined by international law and not by national laws.

4. Similarly, the State is responsible for the acts of its armed forces, even when those forces are acting contrary to orders. In the *Youmans Claim (US v Mexico)* (1926) 4 RIAA 110, the Commission commented that 'Soldiers inflicting personal injuries or committing wanton destruction or looting always act in disobedience of some rules laid down by superior authority. There could be no liability whatever for such misdeeds if the view were taken that any acts committed by soldiers in contravention of instructions must always be considered as personal acts'.

5. In *Al-Jedda*, the European Court of Human Rights found, on the facts, that British soldiers had been operating under UK command and control from the start of the invasion and occupation of Iraq. Thus it held that the UK, rather than the UN, was responsible for the actions of British soldiers in Iraq—the UN having assumed control of humanitarian assistance rather than security. The attribution of conduct to the contributing State is usually linked to the command structure, as well as to the retention of the State's powers over its national contingent in respect of the conduct in question. The test for deciding whether conduct is attributable to the UN or a member state is based on 'effective control', which is set forth in the ILC Draft Articles on Responsibility of International Organisations (see Article 7 and Chapter 5 for discussion of the Draft Articles). Under this rule, the conduct of troop contingents placed at the UN's disposal, for example, in peacekeeping missions, will be attributable to the UN only when the UN itself exercises effective control. The UK Court of Appeal considered that detention of individuals in Afghanistan by UK forces pursuant to a separate UK policy, could not be attributed to the multinational force, in particular as the detentions fell within a UK command and control structure: see *Serdar Mohammed and others* v *Secretary of State for Defence*, [2015] EWCA Civ 843. However, this does not necessarily rule out the possibility that attribution may be dual or even multiple, meaning that

the same action or inaction can be attributable both to the UN and one or more member States (see *Jaloud v The Netherlands* (2014) European Court of Human Rights). In the *Mothers of Srebrenica* case extracted above, effective control by the Dutch State was established over certain actions of Dutchbat as a result of the State's interference with an operational matter. It was decisive that the Dutch government gave instructions that interfered with the operational implementation of the mandate by Dutch troops that it had transferred to the UN mission. However, both the State and the UN may escape liability, as in *Azemi v Serbia* (2013), where the European Court of Human Rights found that the level of control exercised by the UN in Kosovo was so extensive that it displaced any positive obligations under the Convention in respect of Serbia. Consequently, the Court could not consider the acts of the UN (as they were outside its jurisdiction); nor could it attribute those acts to Serbia.

6. A more recent issue to emerge concerns State responsibility for armed forces personnel embedded within the military of third States, in the context of the armed conflict in Syria (see Chapter 15). UK and Australian pilots and military personnel have been embedded with US and Canadian forces and have reportedly participated in airstrikes against ISIS targets in Syria. Are the actions of those personnel attributable to the sending States (i.e., UK and Australia) or the receiving States (i.e., US and Canada)? The key issue is whether the threshold in Article 6 of the Articles is satisfied and if so are the UK and Australian personnel acting in the exercise of elements of the governmental authority of the State at whose disposal it is placed (i.e., US or Canada), or do they remain under the authority and control of their sending States?

7. The question of State responsibility for the actions of security and intelligence forces has also been raised in the light of allegations of torture and extraordinary rendition of detainees held in Guantanamo Bay and secret US 'black sites', following the 9/11 attacks. In December 2014, a report produced by the US Senate Intelligence Committee found that the US intelligence service (the CIA) had conducted interrogations of detainees with excessive force far beyond the measures permitted by national and international law. The report also included evidence that suggested that UK intelligence and security officials—although not directly involved in torture—may have been complicit in, or benefited from, acts of torture and unlawful rendition.

B: Private persons, corporations and other entities

United States Diplomatic and Consular Staff in Tehran Case (*United States v Iran*)

Merits, ICJ Rep 1980 3, International Court of Justice

This case arose from the occupation by a group of Iranian citizens of the United States Embassy in Tehran and the taking of the Embassy staff as hostages (see further in Chapter 9).

56. The events which are the subject of the United States' claims fall into two phases which it will be convenient to examine separately.

57. The first of these phases covers the armed attack on the United States Embassy by militants on 4 November 1979, the overrunning of its premises, the seizure of its inmates as hostages, the appropriation of its property and archives and the conduct of the Iranian authorities in the face of those occurrences. The attack and the subsequent overrunning, bit by bit, of the whole Embassy premises, was an operation which continued over a period of some three hours without any body of police, any military unit or any Iranian official intervening to try to stop or impede it from being carried through to its completion. The result of the attack was considerable damage to the Embassy premises and property, the forcible opening and seizure of its archives, the confiscation of the archives and other documents found in the Embassy and, most grave of all, the seizure by force of its diplomatic and consular personnel as hostages, together with two United States nationals.

58. No suggestion has been made that the militants, when they executed their attack on the Embassy, had any form of official status as recognized 'agents' or organs of the Iranian State. Their conduct in mounting the attack, overrunning the Embassy and seizing its inmates as hostages cannot, therefore, be regarded as imputable to that State on that basis. Their conduct might be considered as itself directly imputable to the Iranian State only if it were established that, in fact, on the occasion in question the militants acted on behalf of the State, having been

charged by some competent organ of the Iranian State to carry out a specific operation. The information before the Court does not, however, suffice to establish with the requisite certainty the existence at that time of such a link between the militants and any competent organ of the State.

59. Previously, it is true, the religious leader of the country, the Ayatollah Khomeini, had made several public declarations inveighing against the United States as responsible for all his country's problems. In so doing, it would appear, the Ayatollah Khomeini was giving utterance to the general resentment felt by supporters of the revolution at the admission of the former Shah to the United States. The information before the Court also indicates that a spokesman for the militants, in explaining their action afterwards, did expressly refer to a message issued by the Ayatollah Khomeini, on 1 November 1979.... In the view of the Court, however, it would be going too far to interpret such general declarations of the Ayatollah Khomeini to the people or students of Iran as amounting to an authorization from the State to undertake the specific operation of invading and seizing the United States Embassy....

69. The second phase of the events which are the subject of the United States' claims comprises the whole series of facts which occurred following the completion of the occupation of the United States Embassy by the militants, and the seizure of the Consulates at Tabriz and Shiraz. The occupation having taken place and the diplomatic and consular personnel of the United States' mission having been taken hostage, the action required of the Iranian Government by the Vienna Conventions and by general international law was manifest. Its plain duty was at once to make every effort, and to take every appropriate step, to bring these flagrant infringements of the inviolability of the premises, archives and diplomatic and consular staff of the United States Embassy to a speedy end, to restore the Consulates at Tabriz and Shiraz to United States control, and in general to re-establish the status quo and to offer reparation for the damage.

70. No such step was, however, taken by the Iranian authorities....

71. In any event expressions of approval of the take-over of the Embassy, and indeed also of the Consulates at Tabriz and Shiraz, by militants came immediately from numerous Iranian authorities, including religious, judicial, executive, police and broadcasting authorities. Above all, the Ayatollah Khomeini himself made crystal clear the endorsement by the State...The result of that policy was fundamentally to transform the legal nature of the situation created by the occupation of the Embassy and the detention of its diplomatic and consular staff as hostages. The approval given to these facts by the Ayatollah Khomeini and other organs of the Iranian State, and the decision to perpetuate them, translated continuing occupation of the Embassy and detention of the hostages into acts of that State. The militants, authors of the invasion and jailers of the hostages, had now become agents of the Iranian State for whose acts the State itself was internationally responsible.

Military and Paramilitary Activities in and against Nicaragua (*Nicaragua* v *US*)

Merits, ICJ Rep 1986 14, International Court of Justice

The aspect of the dispute relevant here was whether the military activities of a significant insurrection movement, the *contras*, against the Nicaraguan government were imputable to the United States (see further Chapters 2 and 15).

114. The Court notes that according to Nicaragua, the *contras* are no more than bands of mercenaries which have been recruited, organized, paid and commanded by the Government of the United States. This would mean that they have no real autonomy in relation to that Government. Consequently, any offences which they have committed would be imputable to the Government of the United States, like those of any other forces placed under the latter's command. In the view of Nicaragua, '*stricto sensu*, the military and paramilitary attacks launched by the United States against Nicaragua do not constitute a case of civil strife. They are essentially the acts of the United States.' If such a finding of the imputability of the acts of the *contras* to the United States were to be made, no question would arise of mere complicity in those acts, or of incitement of the *contrast* to commit them.

115. The Court has taken the view...that United States participation, even if preponderant or decisive, in the financing, organizing, training, supplying and equipping of the *contras*, the selection of its military or paramilitary targets, and the planning of the whole of its operation, is still insufficient in itself, on the basis of the evidence in the possession of the Court, for the purpose of attributing to the United States the acts committed by the *contras* in the course of their military or paramilitary operations in Nicaragua. All the forms of United States participation mentioned above, and even the general control by the respondent State over a force with a high degree of

dependency on it, would not in themselves mean, without further evidence, that the United States directed or enforced the perpetration of the acts contrary to human rights and humanitarian law alleged by the applicant State. Such acts could well be committed by members of the *contras* without the control of the United States. For this conduct to give rise to legal responsibility of the United States, it would in principle have to be proved that that State had effective control of the military or paramilitary operations in the course of which the alleged violations were committed.

116. The Court does not consider that the assistance given by the United States to the *contras* warrants the conclusion that these forces are subject to the United States to such an extent that any acts they have committed are imputable to that State. It takes the view that the *contras* remain responsible for their acts, and that the United States is not responsible for the acts of the *contras*, but for its own conduct vis-à-vis Nicaragua, including conduct related to the acts of the *contras*. What the Court has to investigate is not the complaints relating to alleged violations of humanitarian law by the *contras*, regarded by Nicaragua as imputable to the United States, but rather unlawful acts for which the United States may be responsible directly in connection with the activities of the *contras*.

Application of the Convention on the Prevention and Punishment of the Crime of Genocide (Bosnia and Herzegovina v Serbia and Montenegro)
Merits, ICJ Rep 2007, International Court of Justice

The key facts are set out in Section 2A.

391. The…issue…is whether it is possible in principle to attribute to a State conduct of persons or groups of persons who, while they do not have the legal status of State organs, in fact act under such strict control by the State that they must be treated as its organs for purposes of the necessary attribution leading to the State's responsibility for an internationally wrongful act. The Court has in fact already addressed this question, and given an answer to it in principle, in its Judgment of 27 June 1986 in the case concerning *Military and Paramilitary Activities in and against Nicaragua (Nicaragua* v. *United States of America) (Merits, Judgment, I.C.J. Reports 1986*, pp. 62–64).…

392. The passages quoted show that, according to the Court's jurisprudence, persons, groups of persons or entities may, for purposes of international responsibility, be equated with State organs even if that status does not follow from internal law, provided that in fact the persons, groups or entities act in 'complete dependence' on the State, of which they are ultimately merely the instrument. In such a case, it is appropriate to look beyond legal status alone, in order to grasp the reality of the relationship between the person taking action, and the State to which he is so closely attached as to appear to be nothing more than its agent: any other solution would allow States to escape their international responsibility by choosing to act through persons or entities whose supposed independence would be purely fictitious.

393. However, so to equate persons or entities with State organs when they do not have that status under internal law must be exceptional, for it requires proof of a particularly great degree of State control over them, a relationship which the Court's Judgment quoted above expressly described as 'complete dependence'. It remains to be determined in the present case whether, at the time in question, the persons or entities that committed the acts of genocide at Srebrenica had such ties with the FRY that they can be deemed to have been completely dependent on it; it is only if this condition is met that they can be equated with organs of the Respondent for the purposes of its international responsibility.

394. The Court can only answer this question in the negative. At the relevant time, July 1995, neither the Republika Srpska nor the VRS could be regarded as mere instruments through which the FRY was acting, and as lacking any real autonomy. While the political, military and logistical relations between the federal authorities in Belgrade and the authorities in Pale, between the Yugoslav army and the VRS, had been strong and close in previous years…, and these ties undoubtedly remained powerful, they were, at least at the relevant time, not such that the Bosnian Serbs' political and military organizations should be equated with organs of the FRY. It is even true that differences over strategic options emerged at the time between Yugoslav authorities and Bosnian Serb leaders; at the very least, these are evidence that the latter had some qualified, but real, margin of independence. Nor, notwithstanding the very important support given by the Respondent to the Republika Srpska, without which it could not have 'conduct[ed] its crucial or most significant military and paramilitary activities' (*I.C.J. Reports 1986*, p. 63, para. 111), did this signify a total dependence of the Republika Srpska upon the Respondent.

396. As noted above (paragraph 384), the Court must now determine whether the massacres at Srebrenica were committed by persons who, though not having the status of organs of the Respondent, nevertheless acted on its instructions or under its direction or control, as the Applicant argues in the alternative; the Respondent denies that such was the case ....

397. The Court must emphasize, at this stage in its reasoning, that the question just stated is not the same as those dealt with thus far. It is obvious that it is different from the question whether the persons who committed the acts of genocide had the status of organs of the Respondent under its internal law; nor however, and despite some appearance to the contrary, is it the same as the question whether those persons should be equated with State organs *de facto*, even though not enjoying that status under internal law. The answer to the latter question depends, as previously explained, on whether those persons were in a relationship of such complete dependence on the State that they cannot be considered otherwise than as organs of the State, so that all their actions performed in such capacity would be attributable to the State for purposes of international responsibility. Having answered that question in the negative, the Court now addresses a completely separate issue: whether, in the specific circumstances surrounding the events at Srebrenica the perpetrators of genocide were acting on the Respondent's instructions, or under its direction or control ....

398. On this subject the applicable rule, which is one of customary law of international responsibility, is laid down in Article 8 of the ILC Articles on State Responsibility ...

400.... it has to be proved that they acted in accordance with that State's instructions or under its 'effective control'. It must however be shown that this 'effective control' was exercised, or that the State's instructions were given, in respect of each operation in which the alleged violations occurred, not generally in respect of the overall actions taken by the persons or groups of persons having committed the violations.

R. McCorquodale and P. Simons, 'Responsibility Beyond Borders: State Responsibility for Extraterritorial Violations by Corporations of International Human Rights Law'
70 Modern Law Review 599 (2007)

The general law of state responsibility provides for the possibility of attribution to a state for the acts committed by its corporate nationals in violation of international law giving rise to international responsibility in two situations. First, where a state empowers a corporation to exercise elements of public authority [ILC Article 5]; second, where a corporation acts on the 'instructions of, or under the direction or control of', a state [ILC Article 8]. In addition, where the state through aiding and assisting corporate activity is complicit in the commission of an internationally wrongful act committed by another state or by the corporation itself, then the state will be internationally responsible [ILA Article 16]. In all of these cases, such acts will be attributable to the state even where they are committed outside the territory of that state ....

[In the first category for] there to be attribution to the state, the conduct by the corporation must relate to 'governmental activity and not other private or commercial activity'. This is consistent with the developments in the law of state immunity. Governmental authority would seem to include a wide variety of public functions, from running prisons, health and education facilities, to private airline corporations having delegated immigration or quarantine power and a corporation having a role in the identification of property to be expropriated by the state. The key factor for attribution is the empowerment to exercise governmental authority and not the degree of ownership of the corporation by the state.

The extraterritorial activities of AWB Ltd, an Australian corporation, provide an example of this type of situation. AWB was a government agency—the Australian Wheat Board—with, *inter alia*, the sole responsibility for the marketing and export of Australian wheat around the world and, on being privatised, it retained this power. AWB was active in the Iraqi Oil for Food programme managed by the UN, being the largest supplier of food to that programme. The investigation into that programme led to, *inter alia*, allegations that AWB was involved in the bribing of Iraqi officials in order to sell Australian wheat, contrary to United Nations resolutions and with clear impacts on the human rights of Iraqis, such as the right to food. These allegations were found to be substantiated both by a Royal Commission and by an Australian court but without expressly deciding whether some of the actions of AWB were attributable to the Australian government. The situation of possible attribution to a state could be the same for many other privatised government entities ...

[In the second category, where] a corporation acts on the instructions of the home state, there is no requirement for such acts to constitute governmental activity. This issue has become more prominent since the beginning of the (illegal) action by the occupying forces in Iraq, where it became clear how many private corporations were contracted by the states involved to provide a wide variety of services, from providing intelligence to re-creating state infrastructure to support such military action. Indeed, the investigations after the discovery of prisoner abuse in Abu Ghraib (and elsewhere) have shown that some of these abuses were committed by employees of private contractors....Yet there is a possibility that cases brought before international human rights treaty bodies may have some possibility of success if those bodies attribute the actions of the corporations to the state, on the basis that they are acting on the instructions of the state (which is highly probable in such a tightly controlled area). Where such acts are found to be attributable to the state, the treaty bodies will then need to determine the extent of power, effective control or authority exercised by the state or its agents over the area or over the victims, and whether it is sufficient to bring the victims 'within the jurisdiction' of the state. In the case of Iraq, it may be possible to prove sufficient power, effective control or authority, on the basis of the ICJ's decision in *Democratic Republic of Congo v Uganda* 'that human rights treaties may apply to a state's conduct even where that state's level of control falls short of that of an [O]ccupying Power'. Indeed, a UK court, in applying a much narrower definition of jurisdiction than that reflected in the case law of international human rights tribunals, found that an Iraqi who was killed in the custody of UK forces on a military base in Iraq was within the jurisdiction of the UK for the purposes of the ECHR (and the UK's Human Rights Act 1998) [*Al-Skeini v Secretary of State for Defence*]

[In regard to complicity, according] to the ILC, examples of situations where a state would be responsible for aiding and assisting, include 'knowingly providing an essential facility or financing the activity in question...facilitating the abduction of persons on foreign soil, or assisting in the destruction of property belonging to nationals of a third country'. In each case the assisting state must be aware that it is aiding or assisting in the commission of an internationally unlawful act, it must provide such aid or assistance in order to facilitate the act in question, and the act must constitute an internationally wrongful act if committed by the assisting state. States have argued, for example, that providing military aid to the opposing state during an armed conflict, where that aid included chemical weapons, gives rise to state responsibility, and the ICJ hinted at the possibility of state responsibility arising by complicity in *Nicaragua v US*....

[W]here a home state aids or assists a corporation in the commission of, or in the latter's complicity in, acts that, if committed by that home state would constitute internationally wrongful acts, that state will incur international responsibility, at least where the aid or assistance 'contributed significantly to that act'. So, where a home state aids or assists a corporation, for example, by supporting it in seeking 'regime change' or through its [Export Credit Agency (ECA)] by providing loans, political risk insurance or investment guarantees and the corporation then violates human rights that constitute international crimes, then that state can be considered responsible under international human rights law.

In order for the state to be held responsible for complicity in the above situations, it must be shown that the state knew that it was aiding or assisting in the commission of the wrongful act. Yet, where the assistance is provided by ECAs, constructive knowledge can be assumed where the agency maintains that it takes the human rights or social impact of a project into account in its decision-making or it is normally required to undertake assessments of, or investigations into, the human rights impacts of a particular project ....

Yet, because corporations generally conduct extraterritorial operations through a subsidiary incorporated in a state other than the home state (i.e. the host state) the question arises whether, apart from the situations of complicity, a home state may be found to be internationally responsible for the acts of a corporate national's foreign subsidiary that violate human rights in another state.... [There are now] developments in the understanding of corporate groups, including [transnational corporations (TNCs)], away from the traditional concept of separate legal entities.... There is a long-standing practice of some courts to look at the whole operation of a TNC, and not just its notionally separate parts, in order to bring a foreign *parent* corporation within the jurisdiction of a state. For example, the US 'has developed very broad theories of the unity or integration of the enterprise, of acting as 'alter ego' or whatever other phrases may have been employed to establish that the foreign parent is in fact present, resident or 'found' in the United States'. Likewise, the approach of the European Court of Justice in competition cases has been to 'investigate the parameters of the [corporate] group structure and the reality of the interrelationships within the group'.

Moreover, states have extensive authority and capacity under international law to exercise prescriptive and adjudicative jurisdiction over the extraterritorial activity of corporate nationals. In addition, where such corporation is a parent corporation, the home state is entitled under international law to regulate *indirectly* any wholly owned or controlled foreign subsidiaries by requiring the parent to impose on such subsidiaries a particular course of action or to include in any contract particular terms. There is now substantial state practice of extending national law to regulate the conduct of corporate nationals operating extraterritorially through foreign subsidiaries, such as in areas of competition law, shareholder and consumer protection, anti-bribery and corruption, and tax law. In relation to bribery and corruption, states have concluded treaties imposing obligations on them to regulate extraterritorial conduct of corporate nationals and their subsidiaries.

More recently, national courts of a number of states have begun to 'pierce the corporate veil', or to examine the entire corporate group, to impose liability on the parent company (which is a corporate national) for the acts of foreign subsidiaries that constitute violations of international human rights norms. This would seem to apply where there is effective central managerial control over a subsidiary by a parent within the same TNC entity....

[It] is arguable that, although the acts of a foreign subsidiary of a corporate national cannot be directly attributed to the home state, the latter exercises sufficient control over the parent company and has constructive knowledge of the potential for the subsidiary to violate human rights law to justify the imposition of an obligation to exercise due diligence in relation to the human rights impacts of such activity. The obligation requires a state to take reasonable steps to ensure that such entities do not operate in violation of international human rights law even where such operations are conducted through a foreign subsidiary. This obligation would include, but not be limited to, a requirement that the home state enact domestic regulation, requiring human rights impact assessments, the subsequent mitigation of any such impacts, and the provision of a remedy in the home state's courts.

NOTES

1. The *Tehran Hostages* case demonstrates that conduct of private persons may be attributable to the State where it has subsequently endorsed the action. It also shows that the State may be held responsible for a failure to prevent or to bring to an end the conduct in question.

2. In the *Tadić Case* (1999 ILM 1518), the Appeals Chamber of the International Criminal Tribunal for the Former Yugoslavia did not follow the jurisprudence of the ICJ in the *Military and Paramilitary Activities Case*. It held that the appropriate criterion was that of the 'overall control' exercised over Bosnian Serbs by the FRY, which went 'beyond the mere financing and equipping of such forces and involving also participation in the planning and supervision of military operations' (para. 145). The Appeals Chamber did not require the Prosecution to prove that each operation during which acts were committed in breach of international law was carried out on the FRY's instruction, or under its effective control. However, the question in *Tadić* was not one of State responsibility, but instead whether the conflict in Bosnia was of an international character, which would determine the applicable rules of international humanitarian law. In the *Genocide Case* the ICJ reaffirmed its jurisprudence on the 'effective control' test stating that the application of the 'overall control test' to other entities as (*de jure* or *de facto*) organs goes beyond the principles governing the law on State responsibility as recognised under customary international law.

3. The European Court of Human Rights in *Ilascu v Moldova and Russia* (App No 48787/99) ECHR 8 July 2004), considered that the necessary degree of control in relation to the attribution of conduct of a Moldovian separatist regime (the MRT) to Russia was shown where Russia had provided political and military support to the MRT and the latter remained 'under the effective authority, or *at the very least the decisive influence*, of the Russian Federation' (para. 392). This was the position even though the Court did not decide that Russia was in effective control of the Transdniestrian region. Similarly, the Court found that Armenia exercised control in respect of the Nagorno-Karabakh territories, which Armenia had argued formed a separate, independent region. The Court found that 'it is hardly conceivable that Nagorno-Karabakh—an entity with a population of less than 150,000 ethnic Armenians—was able, without the substantial military support of Armenia, to set up a defence force in early 1992 that, against the country of Azerbaijan with approximately seven million people, not only established control of the former NKAO but also, before the end of 1993, conquered the whole or major parts of seven surrounding Azerbaijani districts': *Chiragov v Armenia*, 13216/05, Judgment (Merits), 16 June 2015, para. 174. This seems to indicate that the Court is not requiring a high degree of effective control (and certainly not territorial control) under the European Convention of Human Rights (ECHR) for it to find that the actions of non-State actors in another territory can be attributed to a State in such a way that a State is considered to have jurisdiction over such actors and, hence, has extraterritorial obligations under the ECHR. It may be that there is a different threshold for effective control in specific areas such as international human rights law and international criminal law compared with general international law.

4. The international responsibility of States for the actions of their corporations is undergoing significant changes. With the economic power of corporations, with their impact on the daily lives of people across the world, and with the increasing use of corporations by States in their

extraterritorial military activities, as well as in trade and other areas, there are clearly situations where the State will be internationally responsible for the activities of these corporations, as McCorquodale and Simons show. There is also the issue of the extent to which these corporations have some international legal personality for which they have international responsibility (see Chapter 5) and may be subject to human rights obligations (see Chapter 6).

5. Cyber attacks also raise issues concerning attribution of attacks to States. The Tallinn Manual on the International Law Applicable to Cyber Warfare (see further Chapter 15) emphasises that a State will only be held responsible for a cyber operation where that operation is attributable to it through applying ordinary principles of attribution under the law of state responsibility (Rule 6). Moreover, the manual indicates that a cyber operation should not be attributable to a State merely because the operation has 'been launched or otherwise originates from governmental cyber infrastructure' (Rule 7) or has been routed via the cyber infrastructure located in the territory of a State (Rule 8).

C: Armed non-State actors

Commentary on the ILC Articles on Responsibility of States for Internationally Wrongful Acts (2001)

Official Records of the General Assembly, Fifty-sixth session, Supplement No. 10

(1) Article 10 deals with the special case of attribution to a State of conduct of an insurrectional or other movement which subsequently becomes the new government of the State or succeeds in establishing a new State.

(2) At the outset, the conduct of the members of the movement presents itself purely as the conduct of private individuals. It can be placed on the same footing as that of persons or groups who participate in a riot or mass demonstration and it is likewise not attributable to the State. Once an organized movement comes into existence as a matter of fact, it will be even less possible to attribute its conduct to the State, which will not be in a position to exert effective control over its activities. The general principle in respect of the conduct of such movements, committed during the continuing struggle with the constituted authority, is that it is not attributable to the State under international law. In other words, the acts of unsuccessful insurrectional movements are not attributable to the State, unless under some other article of chapter II, for example in the special circumstances envisaged by article 9 …

(4) The general principle that the conduct of an insurrectional or other movement is not attributable to the State is premised on the assumption that the structures and organization of the movement are and remain independent of those of the State. This will be the case where the State successfully puts down the revolt. In contrast, where the movement achieves its aims and either installs itself as the new government of the State or forms a new State in part of the territory of the pre-existing State or in a territory under its administration, it would be anomalous if the new regime or new State could avoid responsibility for conduct earlier committed by it. In these exceptional circumstances, article 10 provides for the attribution of the conduct of the successful insurrectional or other movement to the State. The basis for the attribution of conduct of a successful insurrectional or other movement to the State under international law lies in the continuity between the movement and the eventual government …

(15) Exceptional cases may occur where the State was in a position to adopt measures of vigilance, prevention or punishment in respect of the movement's conduct but improperly failed to do so. This possibility is preserved by paragraph 3 of article 10, which provides that the attribution rules of paragraphs 1 and 2 are without prejudice to the attribution to a State of any conduct, however related to that of the movement concerned, which is to be considered an act of that State by virtue of other provisions in Chapter II. The term however related to that of the movement concerned is intended to have a broad meaning. Thus the failure by a State to take available steps to protect the premises of diplomatic missions, threatened from attack by an insurrectional movement, is clearly conduct attributable to the State and is preserved by paragraph 3.

(16) A further possibility is that the insurrectional movement may itself be held responsible for its own conduct under international law, for example for a breach of international humanitarian law committed by its forces. The topic of the international responsibility of unsuccessful insurrectional or other movements, however, falls outside the scope of the present Articles, which are concerned only with the responsibility of States.

Short v Iran

(1987–III) 16 Iran-US CTR 76, Iran-United States Claims Tribunal

This claim was based on the loss of employment benefits and personal property caused by the alleged forceful expulsion of the claimant from Iran following the Islamic Revolution in Iran in 1978–79.

31. In examining whether the Claimant's departure from Iran was due to acts or circumstances attributable to the Respondent, the Tribunal has to take into account the existence of a revolutionary situation in Iran during the period under consideration....

33. Where a revolution leads to the establishment of a new government the State is held responsible for the acts of the overthrown government insofar as the latter maintained control of the situation. The successor government is also held responsible for the acts imputable to the revolutionary movement which established it, even if those acts occurred prior to its establishment, as a consequence of the continuity existing between the new organization of the State and the organization of the revolutionary movement. *See* Draft Articles on State Responsibility, *supra*, Commentary on Article 15, paras. 3 and 4, 1975 Y.B. Int'l L. Comm'n, Vol. 2 at 100. These rules are of decisive importance in the present Case, since the Claimant departed from Iran on 8 February 1979, a few days before the proclamation on 11 February of the Islamic Revolutionary Government. At that time, the revolutionary movement had not yet been able to establish control over any part of Iranian territory, and the Government had demonstrated its loss of control.

34. The Claimant relies on acts committed by revolutionaries and seeks to attribute responsibility for their acts to the government that was established following the success of the Revolution. He is unable, however, to identify any agent of the revolutionary movement, the actions of which compelled him to leave Iran. The acts of supporters of a revolution cannot be attributed to the government following the success of the revolution just as the acts of supporters of an existing government are not attributable to the government. This was clearly recalled by the International Court of Justice in *United States Diplomatic and Consular Staff in Tehran* (*United States* v *Iran*), 1980 ICJ 3, 29, para. 58 (Judgment of 24 May 1980).... In these circumstances, the Tribunal is of the view that the Claimant has failed to prove that his departure from Iran can be imputed to the wrongful conduct of Iran. The claim is therefore dismissed.

Asian Agricultural Products Ltd (AAPL) v Republic of Sri Lanka

30 *International Legal Materials* 577 (1991), International Centre for the Settlement of Investment Disputes

Sri Lankan security forces destroyed an installation belonging to a company partly owned by AAPL. The Sri Lankan security forces claimed that the installation was being used by the 'Tamil Tigers', a secessionist movement in Sri Lanka. The Tribunal concluded that although Sri Lanka was not responsible for the acts of the Tamil Tigers, it was responsible in its own right for failure to exercise due diligence in protecting AAPL's property.

72. It is generally accepted rule of International Law, clearly stated in international arbitral awards and in the writings of the doctrinal authorities, that:
   (i) A State on whose territory an insurrection occurs is not responsible for loss or damage sustained by foreign investors unless it can be shown that the Government of that state failed to provide the standard of protection required, either by treaty, or under general customary law, as the case may be; and
   (ii) Failure to provide the standard of protection required entails the state's international responsibility for losses suffered, regardless of whether the damages occurred during an insurgents' offensive act [or] resulting from governmental counter-insurgency activities.

73. The long established arbitral case-law was adequately expressed by Max Huber, the *Rapporteur* in the *Spanish Zone of Morocco* claims (1923), in the following terms:

The principle of non-responsibility in no way excludes the duty to exercise a certain degree of vigilance. If a state is not responsible for the revolutionary events themselves, it may nevertheless be responsible, for what its authorities do or not do to ward the consequence, within the limits of possibility....

76. In the light of all the above-mentioned arbitral precedents, it would be appropriate to consider that adequate protection afforded by the host State authorities constitutes a primary obligation, the failure to comply with which creates international responsibility. Furthermore, 'there is an extensive and consistent state practice supporting the duty to exercise due diligence' (Brownlie, *System of the Law of Nations, State Responsibility—Part 1*, Oxford, 1986, p. 162).

As a doctrinal authority, relied upon by both Parties during the various stages of their respective pleadings in the present case, Professor Brownlie stated categorically that:

> There is general agreement among writers that the rule of non-responsibility cannot apply where the government concerned has failed to show due diligence (*Principles of Public International Law*, Third Edition, Oxford, 1979, p. 453).

After reviewing all categories of precedents, including more recent international judicial case-law, the learned Oxford University Professor arrived, not only to confirm that international responsibility arises from the mere 'failure to exercise due diligence' in providing the required protection, but also to note 'a sliding scale of liability related to the standard of due diligence' (*State Responsibility. op. cit.* p. 162 and p. 168).

NOTES

1. The two main theories on the responsibility of States are 'objective responsibility', where a State is strictly liable for all acts of its officials, and 'subjective responsibility', where it is necessary to show some fault or negligence by the State in its control of the official concerned. The former is preferred, and is the approach taken in ILC Article 10 and, to a slightly lesser extent, in the *Caire Claim*. However, as both the *Short* and the *AAPL* cases illustrate, some element of fault, negligence or lack of due diligence may be required where the State is said to be 'responsible' for the acts of insurrectionists. Nevertheless, in the case of unsuccessful rebellions, the better view is that the existing government is responsible for failure to fulfil *its* own obligations (albeit only if acting negligently) rather than being responsible for the acts of persons dedicated to its overthrow.

2. The ICJ has indicated that Article 10(2) only concerns attribution of acts to a new state; it does not create new obligations for that State: *Application of the Convention on the Prevention and Punishment of Genocide (Croatia v Serbia)* 3 February 2015, para. 104. The Court found that Article 10(2) could not create obligations for the FRY under the Genocide Convention in respect of acts taken before the FRY became a party to the Genocide Convention. However, it noted that it may be possible to attribute responsibility for the acts of the predecessor State (the SFRY, which *was* a party to the Genocide Convention at the relevant time) to the FRY under the law of State succession; however, as the Court found genocide had not been committed, it did not need to consider that issue.

SECTION 3: BREACH OF AN INTERNATIONAL OBLIGATION OF THE STATE

A: International obligations

International Law Commission, Articles on Responsibility of States for Internationally Wrongful Acts (2001)

Article 12 Existence of a breach of an international obligation

There is a breach of an international obligation by a State when an act of that State is not in conformity with what is required of it by that obligation, regardless of its origin or character.

Article 13 International obligation in force for a State

An act of a State does not constitute a breach of an international obligation unless the State is bound by the obligation in question at the time the act occurs.

Questions Relating to the Obligation to Prosecute or Extradite (Belgium v Senegal)
ICJ Rep 2012, International Court of Justice

The case arose from Senegal's alleged failure to prosecute or extradite Hissène Habré for alleged acts of torture committed during his term in office as President of Chad. Based on its standing as a State Party to the Convention against Torture, Belgium issued several extradition requests for Mr Habré to be extradited to Belgium where he could be prosecuted. However, this did not eventuate and Belgium subsequently invoked Senegal's responsibility under the Convention. In its decision, the Court confirmed the obligation of States Parties to the Convention to either prosecute alleged perpetrators or extradite them to another country with jurisdiction for prosecution (also known as 'aut dedere aut judicare'). It further held that the failure to do so constituted a wrongful act engaging the responsibility of the State.

92. According to Belgium, the State is required to prosecute the suspect as soon as the latter is present in its territory, whether or not he has been the subject of a request for extradition to one of the countries referred to in Article 5, paragraph 1—that is, if the offence was committed within the territory of the latter State, or if one of its nationals is either the alleged perpetrator or the victim—or in Article 5, paragraph 3, that is, another State with criminal jurisdiction exercised in accordance with its internal law. In the cases provided for in Article 5, the State can consent to extradition. This is a possibility afforded by the Convention, and, according to Belgium, that is the meaning of the maxim *aut dedere aut judicare* under the Convention. Thus, if the State does not opt for extradition, its obligation to prosecute remains unaffected. In Belgium's view, it is only if for one reason or another the State concerned does not prosecute, and a request for extradition is received, that that State has to extradite if it is to avoid being in breach of this central obligation under the Convention.

93. For its part, Senegal takes the view that the Convention certainly requires it to prosecute Mr. Habré, which it claims it has endeavoured to do by following the legal procedure provided for in that instrument, but that it has no obligation to Belgium under the Convention to extradite him.

94. The Court considers that Article 7, paragraph 1, requires the State concerned to submit the case to its competent authorities for the purpose of prosecution, irrespective of the existence of a prior request for the extradition of the suspect. That is why Article 6, paragraph 2, obliges the State to make a preliminary inquiry immediately from the time that the suspect is present in its territory. The obligation to submit the case to the competent authorities, under Article 7, paragraph 1, may or may not result in the institution of proceedings, in the light of the evidence before them, relating to the charges against the suspect.

95. However, if the State in whose territory the suspect is present has received a request for extradition in any of the cases envisaged in the provisions of the Convention, it can relieve itself of its obligation to prosecute by acceding to that request. It follows that the choice between extradition or submission for prosecution, pursuant to the Convention, does not mean that the two alternatives are to be given the same weight. Extradition is an option offered to the State by the Convention, whereas prosecution is an international obligation under the Convention, the violation of which is a wrongful act engaging the responsibility of the State.

NOTES
1. The second requirement for the international responsibility of a State is breach of an international obligation of the State. Obligations may arise under both treaty and customary international law. Breach of these obligations may constitute acts or omissions (or both). The extract from *Belgium* v *Senegal* above is an example of 'an internationally wrongful act', in that case the failure to comply with a treaty obligation to extradite or prosecute.
2. Jurisprudence and academic debate have been divided as to whether international law requires a finding of fault before responsibility will arise, or whether the system of international responsibility is an objective one. Some cases, including the *Caire Case* (Section 2A) support the objective approach. Others, such as the *Corfu Channel Case*, have required fault. The ILC Articles adopt an intermediate approach; the Articles do not generally require evidence of fault on the part of the State, but fault may be an essential element of the primary obligation that is breached. Similarly, the ILC Articles do not as a general rule require harm or damage to have occurred before responsibility can be established. However, as with fault, this may form an element of the primary rule in question.

3. Article 13 reflects the basic rule that a State may only be held responsible for obligations that are in force for that State at the time of the alleged breach. It is thus necessary to consider carefully when an obligation arose. For example, in the *Mondev* Case, the tribunal rejected the applicant's claim, as the actions complained of had occurred before the North American Free Trade Agreement (NAFTA) had entered into force and its provisions could not be applied retroactively (*Mondev International Ltd* v *United States of America*, Award of 11 October 2002, 42 ILM 85 (2003)). Determining when an obligation has arisen may be more problematic in relation to customary international law, when it is not necessarily clear when a rule has emerged, or when a new rule has replaced the previous rule.

4. It is also necessary to determine when the alleged breach has occurred. In many situations, this may be very clear. ILC Articles 14 and 15 address the more difficult situations of a continuous or ongoing breach and where a breach is constituted by a series of acts or omissions.

B: Responsibility of a State in connection with an act of another State

International Law Commission, Articles on Responsibility of States for Internationally Wrongful Acts (2001)

Article 16 Aid or assistance in the commission of an internationally wrongful act

A State which aids or assists another State in the commission of an internationally wrongful act by the latter is internationally responsible for doing so if:

(a) That State does so with knowledge of the circumstances of the internationally wrongful act; and

(b) The act would be internationally wrongful if committed by that State.

Article 17 Direction and control exercised over the commission of an internationally wrongful act

A State which directs and controls another State in the commission of an internationally wrongful act by the latter is internationally responsible for that act if:

(a) That State does so with knowledge of the circumstances of the internationally wrongful act; and

(b) The act would be internationally wrongful if committed by that State.

Article 18 Coercion of another State

A State which coerces another State to commit an act is internationally responsible for that act if:

(a) The act would, but for the coercion, be an internationally wrongful act of the coerced State; and

(b) The coercing State does so with knowledge of the circumstances of the act.

NOTES

1. The extent of complicity by one State in the breach of an international obligation by another State does arise in practice. Instances include the responsibility of third States in support of the US-led invasion of Iraq in 2003, Serbian complicity in genocide in Bosnia and Herzegovina (see Section 2), responsibility of European States for assisting or condoning the US practice of extraordinary rendition (see Chapter 7), and alleged complicity in torture and violations of the prohibition against the use of force. In 2014, there were allegations that the UK government and its security (M15) and intelligence (MI6) agencies were complicit in and aware of the torture and rendition of British detainees held by other States in counter-terrorism operations overseas. In addition, a series of cases has been brought before national and regional courts by those detained by the CIA, alleging complicity by national authorities in their alleged torture and ill-treatment by foreign officials (see, for example *Belhaj* v *Straw*, extracted in Chapter 9); *Khadr* v *The Prime Minister of Canada*, 2010 SCR 3, Supreme Court of Canada; *Habib* v *Commonwealth of Australia* (extracted in Chapter 4); and the European Court of Human Rights (*El Nashri* v *Poland* (2014) 28761/11, Judgment of 24 July 2014)).

2. The ICJ in the *Genocide Case* (see Section 2), confirmed that Article 16 reflects a rule of customary international law (para. 420). It held that the test of 'aid or assistance' in Article 16 did not differ substantially from the test of complicity under Article III(e) of the Genocide Convention.

SECTION 4: CIRCUMSTANCES PRECLUDING WRONGFULNESS (DEFENCES)

International Law Commission, Articles on Responsibility of States for Internationally Wrongful Acts (2001)

Article 20 Consent

Valid consent by a State to the commission of a given act by another State precludes the wrongfulness of that act in relation to the former State to the extent that the act remains within the limits of that consent.

Article 21 Self-defence

The wrongfulness of an act of a State is precluded if the act constitutes a lawful measure of self-defence taken in conformity with the Charter of the United Nations.

Article 22 Countermeasures in respect of an internationally wrongful act

The wrongfulness of an act of a State not in conformity with an international obligation towards another State is precluded if and to the extent that the act constitutes a countermeasure taken against the latter State in accordance with Chapter II of Part Three.

Article 23 Force majeure

1. The wrongfulness of an act of a State not in conformity with an international obligation of that State is precluded if the act is due to *force majeure*, that is the occurrence of an irresistible force or of an unforeseen event, beyond the control of the State, making it materially impossible in the circumstances to perform the obligation.

2. Paragraph 1 does not apply if:
   (a) the situation of *force majeure* is due, either alone or in combination with other factors, to the conduct of the State invoking it; or
   (b) the State has assumed the risk of that situation occurring.

Article 24 Distress

1. The wrongfulness of an act of a State not in conformity with an international obligation of that State is precluded if the author of the act in question has no other reasonable way, in a situation of distress, of saving the author's life or the lives of other persons entrusted to the author's care.

2. Paragraph 1 does not apply if:
   (a) the situation of distress is due, either alone or in combination with other factors, to the conduct of the State invoking it; or
   (b) the act in question is likely to create a comparable or greater peril.

Article 25 Necessity

1. Necessity may not be invoked by a State as a ground for precluding the wrongfulness of an act not in conformity with an international obligation of that State unless the act:
   (a) is the only way for the State to safeguard an essential interest against a grave and imminent peril; and
   (b) does not seriously impair an essential interest of the State or States towards which the obligation exists, or of the international community as a whole.

2. In any case, necessity may not be invoked by a State as a ground for precluding wrongfulness if:
   (a) the international obligation in question excludes the possibility of invoking necessity; or
   (b) the State has contributed to the situation of necessity.

Article 26 Compliance with peremptory norms

Nothing in this chapter precludes the wrongfulness of any act of a State which is not in conformity with an obligation arising under a peremptory norm of general international law.

Article 27 Consequences of invoking a circumstance precluding wrongfulness

The invocation of a circumstance precluding wrongfulness in accordance with this chapter is without prejudice to:
   (a) compliance with the obligation in question, if and to the extent that the circumstance precluding wrongfulness no longer exists;
   (b) the question of compensation for any material loss caused by the act in question.

Commentary on the ILC Articles
Official Records of the General Assembly, Fifty-sixth session, Supplement No. 10

(1) Chapter V sets out six circumstances precluding the wrongfulness of conduct that would otherwise not be in conformity with the international obligations of the State concerned. The existence in a given case of a circumstance precluding wrongfulness in accordance with this chapter provides a shield against an otherwise well-founded claim for the breach of an international obligation. The six circumstances are: consent (article 20), self-defence (article 21), countermeasures (article 22), *force majeure* (article 23), distress (article 24) and necessity (article 25). Article 26 makes it clear that none of these circumstances can be relied on if to do so would conflict with a peremptory norm of general international law. Article 27 deals with certain consequences of the invocation of one of these circumstances.

(2) Consistently with the approach of the present articles, the circumstances precluding wrongfulness set out in Chapter V are of general application. Unless otherwise provided, they apply to any internationally wrongful act whether it involves the breach by a State of an obligation arising under a rule of general international law, a treaty, a unilateral act or from any other source. They do not annual or terminate the obligation; rather they provide a justification or excuse for non-performance while the circumstance in question subsists. This was emphasized by the International Court in the *Gabčíkovo-Nagymaros Project* case.... Thus a distinction must be drawn between the effect of circumstances precluding wrongfulness and the termination of the obligation itself. The circumstances in Chapter V operate as a shield rather than a sword. As Fitzmaurice noted, where one of the circumstances precluding wrongfulness applies, the non-performance is not only justified, but looks towards a resumption of performance as soon as the factors causing and justifying the non-performance are no longer present.

Rainbow Warrior Arbitration (*New Zealand v France*)
82 *International Law Reports* (1990) 499, France-New Zealand Arbitration Tribunal

Among many submissions, France claimed that the health of its nationals gave rise to the defences of *force majeure* and distress and, further, that these were available defences to a claim of State responsibility based on breach of a treaty even though such defences were not regarded as reasons for non-performance of a treaty obligation in the law of treaties.

(1) According to Article 2 of the Supplementary Agreement, the Tribunal was required to reach its decision on the basis of...the Agreements concluded between the Government of New Zealand and the Government of the French Republic by Exchange of Letters of 9 July 1986, this Agreement and the applicable rules and principles of customary international law. Both the customary international law of treaties and the law of State responsibility were thus relevant. From the law of treaties, codified in the Vienna Convention on the Law of Treaties, 1969, the principle *pacta sunt servanda* and the provisions relating to the consequences of material breach and the expiry of agreements were particularly relevant. However, international law made no distinction between contractual and tortious liability. It followed that the violation by a State of a treaty obligation gave rise to State responsibility and had therefore to be evaluated in the light of the principles of the law of State responsibility, including the determination of the circumstances which might exclude wrongfulness....

(2) Of the principles which the International Law Commission, in its Draft Articles on State Responsibility, had recognized as grounds for excluding wrongfulness three—*force majeure* (Article 31), distress (Article 32) and necessity (Article 33)—might be relevant to the present case.
   (a) *Force majeure* was cast in absolute terms and applied only where circumstances rendered compliance by a State with an international obligation impossible. It did not apply where, as here, circumstances merely made compliance more difficult or burdensome....
   (b) Distress had to be distinguished from the more controversial notion of necessity. What was involved in distress was a choice between departure from an international obligation and a serious threat to the life or physical integrity of a State organ or of persons entrusted to its care. Necessity, on the other hand, was concerned with departure from international obligations on the ground of vital interests of State. For distress to be applicable in the cases of Major Mafart and Captain Prieur, three conditions were requested:
      (i) the existence of exceptional medical or other circumstances of an elementary nature of extreme urgency, provided that a prompt recognition of the existence of those circumstances was subsequently obtained from, or demonstrated by, the other Party;

> (ii) the re-establishment of the original situation of compliance in Hao as soon as the circumstances of emergency had disappeared; and
>
> (iii) a good faith attempt to obtain the consent of New Zealand under the terms of the First Agreement....

The Case Concerning the Gabčíkovo-Nagymaros Project (Hungary/Slovakia)
ICJ Rep 1997 7, International Court of Justice

Czechoslovakia and Hungary agreed by Treaty in 1977 to construct a series of dams along the Danube. In 1989 Hungary abandoned work on its part of the project. In 1991, Czechoslovakia began work on a unilateral modification to the original scheme ('Variant C') and put this into effect in October 1992. In the intervening period (May 1992), Hungary purported to terminate the Treaty. Having failed to negotiate a solution, the parties (now Slovakia, following the division of the Czech-Slovak State) submitted various questions to the Court. One major issue concerned the parties' alleged responsibility for breach of treaty. The ICJ confirmed the *Rainbow Warrior* view that a State could rely on general 'circumstances precluding wrongfulness' when denying a breach of treaty and were not limited to 'treaty-specific' defences. The Court also confirmed that the then ILC Draft Article on 'necessity' (now Art. 25) represented customary international law.

47. Nor does the Court need to dwell upon the question of the relationship between the law of treaties and the law of State responsibility, to which the Parties devoted lengthy arguments, as those two branches of international law obviously have a scope that is distinct. A determination of whether a convention is or is not in force, and whether it has or has not been properly suspended or denounced, is to be made pursuant to the law of treaties. On the other hand, an evaluation of the extent to which the suspension or denunciation of a convention, seen as incompatible with the law of treaties, involves the responsibility of the State which proceeded to it, is to be made under the law of State responsibility.

Thus the Vienna Convention of 1969 on the Law of Treaties confines itself to defining—in a limitative manner—the conditions in which a treaty may lawfully be denounced or suspended; while the effects of a denunciation or suspension seen as not meeting those conditions are, on the contrary, expressly excluded from the scope of the Convention by operation of Article 73. It is moreover well established that, when a State has committed an internationally wrongful act, its international responsibility is likely to be involved whatever the nature of the obligation it has failed to respect (cf. *Interpretation of Peace Treaties with Bulgaria, Hungary and Romania Second Phase, Advisory Opinion, ICJ Reports 1950*, p. 228, and see Article 17 of the Draft Articles on State Responsibility provisionally adopted by the International Law Commission on first reading, *Yearbook of the International Law Commission*, 1980, Vol. II, Part 2, p. 32).

Legal Consequences of the Construction of a Wall in the Occupied Palestinian Territories
Advisory Opinion, ICJ Rep 2004 136, International Court of Justice

The Advisory Opinion is based on a request from the UN General Assembly on 'the legal consequences arising from the construction of the wall being built by Israel, the occupying Power, in the Occupied Palestinian Territory, including in and around East Jerusalem'.

140. The Court has...considered whether Israel could rely on a state of necessity which would preclude the wrongfulness of the construction of the wall. In this regard the Court is bound to note that some of the conventions at issue in the present instance [i.e. conventions on international humanitarian law and human rights law] include qualifying clauses of the rights guaranteed or provisions for derogation...Since those treaties already address considerations of this kind within their own provisions, it might be asked whether a state of necessity as recognized in customary international law could be invoked with regard to those treaties as a ground for precluding the wrongfulness of the measures or decisions being challenged. However, the Court will not

need to consider that question. As the Court observed in the case concerning the *Gabčíkovo-Nagymaros Project (Hungary/Slovakia)*, 'the state of necessity is a ground recognized by customary international law' that 'can only be accepted on an exceptional basis'; it 'can only be invoked under certain strictly defined conditions which must be cumulatively satisfied; and the State concerned is not the sole judge of whether those conditions have been met' (*I.C.J. Reports 1997*, p. 40, para. 51). One of those conditions was stated by the Court in terms used by the International Law Commission, in a text which in its present form requires that the act being challenged be 'the only way for the State to safeguard an essential interest against a grave and imminent peril' (article 25 of the International Law Commission's articles on responsibility of States for internationally wrongful acts; see also former article 33 of the draft articles on the international responsibility of States, with slightly different wording in the English text). In the light of the material before it, the Court is not convinced that the construction of the wall along the route chosen was the only means to safeguard the interests of Israel against the peril which it has invoked as justification for that construction.

NOTES

1. The defences to State responsibility or, as the ILC Articles entitle them, 'circumstances precluding wrongfulness, indicate the extent to which States have control over their own responsibility through the development of exceptions to the imposition of liability. Moreover, as the *Rainbow Warrior* and *Danube Dam* cases illustrate, most defences to State responsibility are generally applicable and are not limited to breaches of certain kinds of obligation. Thus, the Vienna Convention on the Law of Treaties is arguably not exhaustive as to the circumstances in which a State can be excused non-performance of a treaty obligation (see Chapter 3).

2. The *Rainbow Warrior* case also illustrates how the interpretation of the extent of an international legal obligation can be crucial to determining the existence of State responsibility or the appropriate remedy. France was under an obligation to detain the French agents in the Pacific 'for a period not less than three years'. At first sight, this might be thought to mean that the total period of detention should be three years, and this was the view of Kenneth Keith (dissenting). The majority, however, determined that France's obligation was to detain the agents for an absolute period of three years from the date of their first incarceration. Consequently, once three years had passed in absolute terms, France was no longer under an obligation and the agents could not be returned to the island, irrespective of how long they had actually been there. France might be responsible for their unlawful removal within the three-year period but France's obligation ended once three years had passed.

3. In the extract from *Danube Dam* the Court touches on the relationship between the law of treaties and the law of State responsibility. Its conclusion—that there is almost a two-stage test, with treaty law determining validity and State responsibility determining liability—might be considered to be artificial and unnecessarily complicated, especially as it is difficult to see how State relations can be forensically dissected in the way the Court suggests.

SECTION 5: CONSEQUENCES OF A BREACH

A: General

International Law Commission, Articles on Responsibility of States for Internationally Wrongful Acts (2001)

Article 28 Legal consequences of an internationally wrongful act

The international responsibility of a State which is entailed by an internationally wrongful act in accordance with the provisions of Part One involves legal consequences as set out in this Part.

Article 29 Continued duty of performance

The legal consequences of an internationally wrongful act under this Part do not affect the continued duty of the responsible State to perform the obligation breached.

Article 30 Cessation and non-repetition

The State responsible for the internationally wrongful act is under an obligation:

    (a) To cease that act, if it is continuing;

    (b) To offer appropriate assurances and guarantees of non-repetition, if circumstances so require.

Article 31 Reparation

1. The responsible State is under an obligation to make full reparation for the injury caused by the internationally wrongful act.

2. Injury includes any damage, whether material or moral, caused by the internationally wrongful act of a State.

Article 34 Forms of reparation

Full reparation for the injury caused by the internationally wrongful act shall take the form of restitution, compensation and satisfaction, either singly or in combination, in accordance with the provisions of this chapter.

Factory at Chorzów (Claim for Indemnity) Case (Germany v Poland)

Merits, PCIJ Ser A (1928) No 17, Permanent Court of International Justice

The case arose after the end of World War I, when Upper Silesia, which had previously been German territory, became part of Poland. A German corporation had established a nitrate factory at Chorzów in Upper Silesia pursuant to a contract with the German government. However, the new Polish government took possession of the factory. Germany sought reparation.

The Court…regarded reparation as the corollary of the violation of the obligations resulting from an engagement between States.…

It is a principle of international law that the reparation of a wrong may consist in an indemnity corresponding to the damage which the nationals of the injured State have suffered as a result of the act which is contrary to international law.… The reparation due by one State to another does not however change its character by reason of the fact that it takes the form of an indemnity for the calculation of which the damage suffered by a private person is taken as the measure. The rules of law governing the reparation are the rules of international law in force between the two States concerned, and not the law governing relations between the State which has committed a wrongful act and the individual who has suffered damage.…

On approaching this question, it should first be observed that, in estimating the damage caused by an unlawful act, only the value of property, rights and interests which have been affected and the owner of which is the person on whose behalf compensation is claimed, or the damage done to whom is to serve as a means of gauging the reparation claimed, must be taken into account. This principle, which is accepted in the jurisprudence of arbitral tribunals, has the effect, on the one hand, of excluding from the damage to be estimated, injury resulting for third parties from the unlawful act and, on the other hand, of not excluding from the damage the amount of debts and other obligations for which the injured party is responsible.…

The essential principle contained in the actual notion of an illegal act—a principle which seems to be established by international practice and in particular by the decisions of arbitral tribunals—is that reparation must, as far as possible, wipe out all the consequences of the illegal act and reestablish the situation which would, in all probability, have existed if that act had not been committed. Restitution in kind, or, if this is not possible, payment of a sum corresponding to the value which a restitution in kind would bear; the award, if need be, of damages for loss sustained which would not be covered by restitution in kind or payment in place of it—such are the principles which should serve to determine the amount of compensation due for an act contrary to international law.

Eritrea v Ethiopia: Final Award (Ethiopia's Damages Claims)

17 August 2009, Eritrea-Ethiopia Claims Commission

18. In assessing both Parties' damages claims, the Commission has been mindful of the harsh fact that these countries are among the poorest on earth. In both rounds of damages proceedings, both Parties sought amounts that were huge, both absolutely and in relation to the economic capacity of the country against which they were

directed. Ethiopia calculated its Group Number One damages claims against Eritrea to equal nearly 7.4 billion U.S. dollars and its Group Number Two damages claims to equal approximately 6.9 billion U.S. dollars. These amounts are more than three times Eritrea's estimated total national product in 2005, measured on a purchasing power parity basis. Eritrea's claims against Ethiopia, while less dramatic in relation to Ethiopia's larger size and economy, approached 6 billion U.S. dollars.

19. The size of the Parties' claims raised potentially serious questions involving the intersection of the law of State responsibility with fundamental human rights norms. Both Ethiopia and Eritrea are parties to the International Covenant on Economic, Social and Cultural Rights ('ICESCR') and the International Covenant on Civil and Political Rights. Both Covenants provide in Article I(2) that '[i]n no case may a people be deprived of its own means of subsistence.' During the hearings, it was noted that early drafts of the International Law Commission's ('ILC') Draft Articles on State Responsibility included this qualification, but that it was not retained in the Articles as adopted. That does not alter the fundamental human rights law rule of common Article I(2) in the Covenants, which unquestionably applies to the Parties.

20. Similarly, Article 2(1) of the ICESCR obliges both Parties to take steps to achieve the 'full realization' of rights recognized by that instrument. The Commission is mindful that in its General Comments, the Committee on Economic, Social and Cultural Rights has identified a range of steps to be taken by States where necessary, *inter alia*, to improve access to health care, education (particularly for girls) and resources to improve the conditions of subsistence. These General Comments have been endorsed and taken as guides to action by many interested observers and the United Nations' development agencies. Such measures are particularly relevant to the needs of the rural poor in countries like Eritrea and Ethiopia. These matters are considered further in the Commission's Decision Number 7, and in its discussion below of compensation owed to Ethiopia for Eritrea's violation of the *jus ad bellum*.

21. Awards of compensation of the magnitude sought by each Party would impose crippling burdens upon the economies and populations of the other, notwithstanding the obligations both have accepted under the Covenants. Ethiopia urged the Commission not to be concerned with the impact of very large adverse awards on the affected country's population, because the obligation to pay would fall on the government, not the people. The Commission does not agree. Huge awards of compensation by their nature would require large diversions of national resources from the paying country—and its citizens needing health care, education and other public services—to the recipient country. In this regard, the prevailing practice of States in the years since the Treaty of Versailles has been to give very significant weight to the needs of the affected population in determining amounts sought as post-war reparations.

22. Article 5(13) of the December 2000 Agreement directs that, '[i]n considering claims, the Commission shall apply relevant rules of international law,' which include rules of human rights law applicable as between the Parties. Accordingly, the Commission could not disregard the possibility that large damages awards might exceed the capacity of the responsible State to pay or result in serious injury to its population if such damages were paid. It thus considered whether it was necessary to limit its compensation awards in some manner to ensure that the ultimate financial burden imposed on a Party would not be so excessive, given its economic condition and its capacity to pay, as to compromise its ability to meet its people's basic needs.

23. In the circumstances, the Commission concluded that it need not decide the question of possible capping of the award in light of the Parties' obligations under human rights law.

24. The Parties' overall economic positions are relevant to determining compensation in another manner as well. In considering both Parties' claims for violation of the *jus in bello*, the Commission has been mindful of the principle, set out by the Permanent Court of International Justice in *Chorzów Factory*, that the purpose of compensation payable by a responsible State is 'to seek to wipe out all the consequences of the illegal act and reestablish the situation which would, in all probability, have existed if that act had not been committed.' This notion underlies Article 31 of the ILC's Articles on State Responsibility, that '[t]he responsible State is under an obligation to make full reparation for the injury caused by the internationally wrongful act.'

25. *Chorzów Factory* offers an important reference point for assessing both Parties' compensation claims. For reasons that are readily understandable, given limits of time and resources, both Parties filed their claims as inter-State claims. Although Eritrea filed claims on behalf of six individuals, neither Party utilized the option, available under Article 5(8) of the Agreement and the Commission's Rules of Procedure, of presenting claims directly on behalf of large numbers of individuals. Nevertheless, some of both States' claims are made in the exercise of diplomatic protection, in that they are predicated upon injuries allegedly suffered by numbers of the Claimant State's nationals. While the injury in such cases is injury to the State, the extent of injury to affected

individuals—insofar as it can be quantified—can play a significant role in assessing the State's injury. In this regard, in its Decision Number 8 and elsewhere in this Final Award, the Commission has encouraged the Parties to consider how, in the exercise of their discretion, compensation can best be used to accomplish the humanitarian objectives of Article 5(1) of the Agreement.

26. *Chorzów Factory* teaches that compensation has a limited function. Its role is to restore an injured party, in so far as possible, to the position it would have occupied but for the injury. This function is remedial, not punitive. Accordingly, in situations involving diplomatic protection, compensation must be assessed in light of the actual social and economic circumstances of the injured individuals in respect of whom the State is claiming. The difficult economic conditions found in the affected areas of Ethiopia and Eritrea must be taken into account in assessing compensation there. Compensation determined in accordance with international law cannot remedy the world's economic disparities.

27. Both Parties recognized this, and generally framed their claims in ways that, in the first instance at least, took account of the low incomes and limited property of most of those affected by the war.

NOTE: The decision of the Eritrea-Ethiopia Claims Commission is the first occasion on which an international tribunal has directly considered the ability of the States concerned to pay compensation awarded, and the associated impact upon the affected population, as a relevant factor when assessing reparations.

B: Serious breach of a peremptory norm

International Law Commission, Articles on Responsibility of States for Internationally Wrongful Acts (2001)

Article 40 Application of this chapter

1. This chapter applies to the international responsibility which is entailed by a serious breach by a State of an obligation arising under a peremptory norm of general international law.

2. A breach of such an obligation is serious if it involves a gross or systematic failure by the responsible State to fulfil the obligation.

Article 41 Particular consequences of a serious breach of an obligation under this chapter

1. States shall cooperate to bring to an end through lawful means any serious breach within the meaning of article 40.

2. No State shall recognize as lawful a situation created by a serious breach within the meaning of article 40, nor render aid or assistance in maintaining that situation.

3. This article is without prejudice to the other consequences referred to in this Part and to such further consequences that a breach to which this chapter applies may entail under international law.

Commentary on the ILC Articles

Official Records of the General Assembly, Fifty-sixth session, Supplement No. 10

[T]he present Articles [40–41] do not recognize the existence of any distinction between State crimes and delicts for the purposes of Part One. On the other hand, it is necessary for the Articles to reflect that there are certain *consequences* flowing from the basic concepts of peremptory norms of general international law and obligations to the international community as a whole within the field of State responsibility. Whether or not peremptory norms of general international law and obligations to the international community as a whole are aspects of a single basic idea, there is at the very least substantial overlap between them. The examples which the International Court has given of obligations towards the international community as a whole all concern obligations which, it is generally accepted, arise under peremptory norms of general international law. Likewise the examples of peremptory norms given by the Commission in its commentary to what became Article 53 of the Vienna Convention involve obligations to the international community as a whole. But there is at least a difference in emphasis. While peremptory norms of general international law focus on the scope and priority to be given to a certain number of fundamental obligations, the focus of obligations to the international community as a whole is essentially on the legal interest of all States in compliance—i.e., in terms of the present Articles, in being entitled to invoke the responsibility of any State in breach. Consistently with the difference in their focus, it is appropriate to reflect the consequences of the two concepts in two distinct ways. First, serious breaches of obligations arising under peremptory norms of general international law can attract additional consequences, not only for the responsible State but for all other States. Secondly, all States are entitled to invoke responsibility for breaches of obligations to the international community as a whole. The first of these propositions is the concern of the present chapter; the second is dealt with in Article 48 [see Section 6].

(1) Article 40 serves to define the scope of the breaches covered by the chapter. It establishes two criteria in order to distinguish serious breaches of obligations under peremptory norms of general international law from other types of breaches. The first relates to the character of the obligation breached, which must derive from a peremptory norm of general international law. The second qualifies the intensity of the breach, which must have been serious in nature. Chapter III only applies to those violations of international law that fulfil both criteria.

(2)…In accordance with Article 53 of the Vienna Convention on the Law of Treaties, a peremptory norm of general international law is one which is accepted and recognized by the international community of States as a whole as a norm from which no derogation is permitted and which can be modified only by a subsequent norm of general international law having the same character. The concept of peremptory norms of general international law is recognized in international practice, in the jurisprudence of international and national courts and tribunals and in legal doctrine.

(3) It is not appropriate to set out examples of the peremptory norms referred to in the text of Article 40 itself, any more than it was in the text of Article 53 of the Vienna Convention. The obligations referred to in Article 40 arise from those substantive rules of conduct that prohibit what has come to be seen as intolerable because of the threat it presents to the survival of States and their peoples and the most basic human values.

(4) Among these prohibitions, it is generally agreed that the prohibition of aggression is to be regarded as peremptory…There also seems to be widespread agreement with other examples listed in the Commission's commentary to Article 53: viz., the prohibitions against slavery and the slave trade, genocide, and racial discrimination and apartheid.

(5) Although not specifically listed in the Commission's commentary to Article 53 of the Vienna Convention, the peremptory character of certain other norms seems also to be generally accepted. This applies to the prohibition against torture as defined in article 1 of the Convention against Torture and Other Cruel, Inhuman or Degrading Treatment or Punishment of 10 December 1984. In the light of the International Court's description of the basic rules of international humanitarian law applicable in armed conflict as intransgressible in character, it would also seem justified to treat these as peremptory. Finally, the obligation to respect the right of self-determination deserves to be mentioned. As the International Court noted in the *East Timor* case,…[t]he principle of self-determination…is one of the essential principles of contemporary international law, which gives rise to an obligation to the international community as a whole to permit and respect its exercise.…

(7) Apart from its limited scope in terms of the comparatively small number of norms which qualify as peremptory, Article 40 applies a further limitation for the purposes of the chapter, viz. that the breach should itself have been serious. A serious breach is defined in paragraph 2 as one which involves a gross or systematic failure by the responsible State to fulfil the obligation in question. The word serious signifies that a certain order of magnitude of violation is necessary in order not to trivialize the breach and it is not intended to suggest that any violation of these obligations is not serious or is somehow excusable.

(8) To be regarded as systematic, a violation would have to be carried out in an organized and deliberate way. In contrast, the term gross refers to the intensity of the violation or its effects; it denotes violations of a flagrant nature, amounting to a direct and outright assault on the values protected by the rule. The terms are not of course mutually exclusive; serious breaches will usually be both systematic and gross. Factors which may establish the seriousness of a violation would include the intent to violate the norm; the scope and number of individual violations, and the gravity of their consequences for the victims. It must also be borne in mind that some of the peremptory norms in question, most notably the prohibitions of aggression and genocide, by their very nature require an intentional violation on a large scale.

Legal Consequences of the Construction of a Wall in the Occupied Palestinian Territories
Advisory Opinion, ICJ Rep 2004 136, International Court of Justice

The facts are set out above. In its Opinion, the ICJ took the position that the obligations it found to have been violated by Israel, being the right to self-determination and certain principles of international humanitarian law, were essentially of an *erga omnes* character.

154. The Court will now consider the legal consequences of the internationally wrongful acts flowing from Israel's construction of the wall as regards other States.

159. Given the character and the importance of the rights and obligations involved, the Court is of the view that all States are under an obligation not to recognize the illegal situation resulting from the construction of the wall in the Occupied Palestinian Territory, including in and around East Jerusalem. They are also under an obligation not to render aid or assistance in maintaining the situation created by such construction. It is also for all States, while respecting the United Nations Charter and international law, to see to it that any impediment, resulting from the construction of the wall, to the exercise by the Palestinian people of its right to self-determination is brought to an end. In addition, all the States parties to the Geneva Convention relative to the Protection of Civilian Persons in Time of War of 12 August 1949 are under an obligation, while respecting the United Nations Charter and international law, to ensure compliance by Israel with international humanitarian law as embodied in that Convention.

160. Finally, the Court is of the view that the United Nations, and especially the General Assembly and the Security Council, should consider what further action is required to bring to an end the illegal situation resulting from the construction of the wall and the associated régime, taking due account of the present Advisory Opinion.

NOTE: Articles 40 and 41 are, in effect, a compromise between those States wanting a full concept of international crimes (see the much criticised Draft Article 19 of the 1980 Draft ILC Articles, which was not replicated in the 2001 ILC Articles) and those States unconvinced that any special consequences should flow from certain 'important' or fundamental rules of international law. As the Special Rapporteur made clear in his Fourth Report (UN Doc. A/CN 4/517, August 2000) the reason for these Articles is to identify rules of international law that create obligations towards the international community as a whole (*erga omnes* rules) rather than obligations owed only to particular States with whom the violator might be bound in law. He sees these Articles as a framework for the progressive development, within a narrow compass, of a concept which is, or ought to be, broadly acceptable, as it does not call into question established understandings of the conditions for State responsibility, but it recognises that there can be egregious breaches of obligations owed to the community as a whole; breaches which warrant some response by the community and by its members'.

SECTION 6: ENFORCEMENT OF A CLAIM

A: Ability to bring a claim

International Law Commission, Articles on Responsibility of States for Internationally Wrongful Acts (2001)

Article 42 Invocation of responsibility by an injured State

A State is entitled as an injured State to invoke the responsibility of another State if the obligation breached is owed to:

    (a) That State individually; or

    (b) A group of States including that State, or the international community as a whole, and the breach of the obligation:

        (i) Specially affects that State; or

(ii) Is of such a character as radically to change the position of all the other States to which the obligation is owed with respect to the further performance of the obligation.

Article 48 Invocation of responsibility by a State other than an injured state

1. Any State other than an injured State is entitled to invoke the responsibility of another State in accordance with paragraph 2 if:
   (a) The obligation breached is owed to a group of States including that State, and is established for the protection of a collective interest of the group; or
   (b) The obligation breached is owed to the international community as a whole.

2. Any State entitled to invoke responsibility under paragraph 1 may claim from the responsible State:
   (a) Cessation of the internationally wrongful act, and assurances and guarantees of non-repetition in accordance with article 30; and
   (b) Performance of the obligation of reparation in accordance with the preceding articles, in the interest of the injured State or of the beneficiaries of the obligation breached.

3. The requirements for the invocation of responsibility by an injured State under articles 43, 44 and 45 apply to an invocation of responsibility by a State entitled to do so under paragraph 1.

NOTES
1. International responsibility is deemed to arise automatically once a breach has occurred. However, it is generally necessary for another State or entity to invoke such responsibility. International law, like many national systems, insists on standing rules requiring that a State (or other entity) has a recognisable legal claim or interest before an action may be brought. For example, in the *South West Africa* cases (*South West Africa (Libya* v *South Africa)*; *South West Africa (Ethiopia* v *South Africa)*), the ICJ dismissed the applicants' claim, finding that the States concerned did not have a sufficient interest in the subject matter of the claim, being the administration by South Africa of a mandate territory. Article 42 of the ILC Articles reflects this general rule and defines the concept of the 'injured' State.
2. Article 48 of the ILC Articles incorporates the exception to this general requirement for a legal interest, through the idea of collective interests or obligations *erga omnes*. The Article enables States other than the injured State to invoke responsibility if the obligation in question was owed to the international community as a whole. Although it does not use the term *erga omnes*, the provision follows the statement of the ICJ in the *Barcelona Traction Case*, where the Court drew an essential distinction between obligations owed to particular States and those owed towards the international community as a whole. With regard to the latter, the Court went on to state that '[i]n view of the importance of the rights involved, all States can be held to have a legal interest in their protection; they are obligations *erga omnes*.' (*Barcelona Traction, Light and Power Company, Limited*, Judgment, ICJ Rep 1970, p. 3 at para. 33). Each State is entitled, as a member of the international community, to invoke the responsibility of another State for breaches of such obligations.

B: Diplomatic protection: the nature of a state's claim

Articles on Diplomatic Protection International Law Commission (2006)

2006 International Law Commission Official Records of the General Assembly, Sixty-first Session, Supplement No 10 (A/61/10)

The ILC worked for a number of years on a project on the law surrounding diplomatic protection. It culminated in these Articles being adopted by the ILC in 2006 and referred to the Sixth Committee of the General Assembly, with the recommendation that the articles form the basis of a convention. The General Assembly deferred consideration of the future of the articles (as it has with the Articles on State Responsibility).

Article 1 Definition and scope

For the purposes of the present draft articles, diplomatic protection consists of the invocation by a State, through diplomatic action or other means of peaceful settlement, of the responsibility of another State for an injury caused by an internationally wrongful act of that State to a natural or legal person that is a national of the former State with a view to the implementation of such responsibility.

Article 19 Recommended practice

A State entitled to exercise diplomatic protection according to the present draft articles, should:

- (a) Give due consideration to the possibility of exercising diplomatic protection, especially when a significant injury has occurred;
- (b) Take into account, wherever feasible, the views of injured persons with regard to resort to diplomatic protection and the reparation to be sought; and
- (c) Transfer to the injured person any compensation obtained for the injury from the responsible State subject to any reasonable deductions.

Panevezys-Saldutiskis Railway Case (Estonia v Lithuania) (Preliminary Objections)

PCIJ Ser A/B (1939) No. 76, Permanent Court of International Justice

In the opinion of the Court, the rule of international law on which the first Lithuanian objection is based is that in taking up the case of one of its nationals, by resorting to diplomatic action or international judicial proceedings on his behalf, a State is in reality asserting its own right, the right to ensure in the person of its nationals respect for the rules of international law. This right is necessarily limited to intervention on behalf of its own nationals because, in the absence of a special agreement, it is the bond of nationality between the State and the individual which alone confers upon the State the right of diplomatic protection, and it is as a part of the function of diplomatic protection that the right to take up a claim and to ensure respect for the rules of international law must be envisaged. Where the injury was done to the national of some other State, no claim to which such injury may give rise falls within the scope of the diplomatic protection which a State is entitled to afford nor can it give rise to a claim which that State is entitled to espouse.

R (Al Rawi and Others) v Secretary of State for Foreign and Commonwealth Affairs and Secretary of State for the Home Department

[2006] EWHC 972 (Admin), United Kingdom Court of Appeal

This case concerned the continued detention in Guantanamo Bay of the three claimants by the US authorities. None of them was a British national but each had been a long-term resident of the UK. They claimed that their connection with the UK was such that they have a legitimate expectation that the British government will make a formal and unequivocal request for their return to the UK, in the same way as it did in relation to British nationals, who were returned after such requests in 2004 and 2005.

41. [A] central plank of the first defendant's case is the fact that because the first three claimants are not British nationals, the United Kingdom cannot provide them with consular protection or support. The basis of this, and its consequences, are set out in more detail in the witness statement in the following terms:

'23. I turn now to the UK Government's relationship with the US Government specifically as regards to the detainee claimants held at Guantanamo (obviously, their interests are also included within the general issues which the UK is pressing with the US Authorities, to which I have just referred). Those individuals were formerly resident in the UK. However, they are not British citizens. It is the long-standing policy of the UK Government not to offer consular or similar assistance to non-British Nationals, except in cases where a specific agreement to do so exists with another State. It should also be noted that the UK does not have the right to exercise diplomatic protection (in the form of a State to State claim arising from a wrong done to a national of the State asserting the claim); such diplomatic protection is governed by rules of international law, which are reflected in the UK's rules on international claims……Under those rules, the UK can exercise diplomatic protection only in respect of British nationals and even then the decision whether or not to do so is a matter of discretion. Any representations on behalf of non British nationals would have to be made on a humanitarian basis rather than as consular assistance or diplomatic protection.

24. The FCO recognises that it would be possible as a matter of international law for the UK Government to take up with a third State a breach by the latter of its international human right obligations, even if the breach was

manifested by actions against persons who are not nationals of the UK. However, normally any such action by the UK Government would be directed towards encouraging the third State to bring its actions into conformity with international law: it would not be directed towards the sort of action which the claimants are seeking in this case, namely a formal request for their return to the UK.

25. It is important to emphasise that this is the relief sought by the claimants. However, a formal request for their return on humanitarian grounds is a request which a State would normally make in the exercise of consular functions in relation to its own nationals for whom it has a clear legal locus. Such a request is not one which a State would have any legal right to make in relation to non-nationals. Accordingly, to assert as a matter of humanitarian concern a formal request that would ordinarily be regarded by States as a matter of consular concern would be likely to be regarded as diminishing its legitimacy in the eyes of the State to whom it is addressed. Further, a state making such a request may risk losing credibility with the State to whom it is made, such that it will not be taken seriously when it seeks to influence the behaviour of that State in relation to other matters of legitimate concern. Thus it is only in exceptional cases that the FCO seeks to intervene and make humanitarian representations; and even then, the representations made are not of the type which the Claimants demand in this case.

26. Any decision on making humanitarian representations is regarded by the FCO as a matter of discretion for the Foreign Secretary, taking into account a wide range of factors relating to the particular circumstances of the case and wider international relations considerations. Where a request for assistance is made to the FCO, FCO Ministers have to make an informed and considered judgment on the merits of intervening and on the most appropriate way in which the interests of the individual may be protected, including the nature, manner and timing of any diplomatic representation to the country concerned. Such assessments of whether, when and how to press another State require fine judgments to be made by Ministers, drawing on the FCO's experience and expertise.

27. In deciding whether to make humanitarian representations in any case, the UK Government would have to take into account the extent to which it would have to expend significant political credit, and would have to risk losing a measure of credibility, with the State to whom the representations are made. This is so, irrespective of the context. It is particularly true in relation to such highly controversial and (especially from the US Government's point of view) sensitive matters as Guantanamo and the circumstances and conditions of persons detained there.'

NOTES

1. Because a State brings an international claim for its own injury, it is neither under an obligation to exercise diplomatic protection nor to pay any reparation (including compensation) received by it to the national actually injured (on the latter see *Lonhro* v *ECGD* [1996] 4 All ER 673). The ILC Special Rapporteur's proposal to establish 'a legal duty to exercise diplomatic protection on behalf of the injured person upon request, if the injury results from a grave breach of a *jus cogens* norm attributable to another State' did not find the support of the ILC. Article 19 of the ILC Articles (above) is a recommendation only and does not create a binding legal obligation for States. Thus, it is generally considered that diplomatic protection remains the prerogative of the State to be exercised at its discretion.

2. The UK courts have considered this issue in at least two cases connected with representations concerning detainees at Guantanamo Bay. In both cases, the Court of Appeal accepted submissions by the government that, as a general rule, diplomatic protection may be exercised in relation to British nationals only, and is a matter of discretion and not obligation. Moreover, human rights considerations (including under the European Convention on Human Rights) do not create an obligation to make representations: *R (Abbasi)* v *Secretary of State for Foreign and Commonwealth Affairs and Secretary of State for the Home Department* [2003] UKHRR 76; *R (Al Rawi and Others)* v *Secretary of State for Foreign and Commonwealth Affairs* (extracted above).

3. National law may require governments to act in particular ways in regard to diplomatic protection. For example, in *Samuel Kaunda and Others* v *The President of the Republic of South Africa*, Case CCT 23/04 (2004), Justice O'Regan of the Constitutional Court of South Africa held that the citizenship provision in the Constitution gave rise to an obligation on the government to exercise diplomatic protection. Similarly, the German Constitutional Court has confirmed that the basic rights provision of the Constitution imposes a duty on the State to protect its nationals and their legal rights and interests, including against foreign States. However, the Court has held that the government has a wide discretion in how it chooses to do so: *Rudolph Hess* (Case No. 2 BVR 4 19/80) 90 ILR 386 (1992)). In contrast, in *The Prime Minister of Canada* v *Khadr* (2010 SCC 3), the Supreme Court of Canada found that the trial judge had erred in ordering the Canadian

government to request the immediate repatriation by the US of Omar Khadr, a Canadian citizen captured by US forces in Afghanistan at the age of 15 and held at Guantanamo Bay and allegedly abused, with the complicity of Canadian officials. In the Court's reasoning, it is the constitutional responsibility of the executive to make decisions on matters of foreign affairs. Although the Supreme Court found that Canadian officials contributed to Khadr's continued deprivation of liberty, it held that the appropriate remedy was to declare that Khadr's rights under section 7 of the Canadian Charter of Fundamental Rights and Freedoms were violated, leaving it to the government to decide how best to respond.

C: Diplomatic protection of natural persons: nationality of claims

International Law Commission, Articles on Diplomatic Protection (2006)

Article 4 State of nationality of a natural person

For the purposes of the diplomatic protection of a natural person, a State of nationality means a State whose nationality that person has acquired, in accordance with the law of that State, by birth, descent, naturalization, succession of States or in any other manner, not inconsistent with international law.

Article 5 Continuous nationality of a natural person

1. A State is entitled to exercise diplomatic protection in respect of a person who was a national of that State continuously from the date of injury to the date of the official presentation of the claim. Continuity is presumed if that nationality existed at both these dates.

2. Notwithstanding paragraph 1, a State may exercise diplomatic protection in respect of a person who is its national at the date of the official presentation of the claim but was not a national at the date of injury, provided that the person had the nationality of a predecessor State or lost his or her previous nationality and acquired, for a reason unrelated to the bringing of the claim, the nationality of the former State in a manner not inconsistent with international law.

3. Diplomatic protection shall not be exercised by the present State of nationality in respect of a person against a former State of nationality of that person for an injury caused when that person was a national of the former State of nationality and not of the present State of nationality.

4. A State is no longer entitled to exercise diplomatic protection in respect of a person who acquires the nationality of the State against which the claim is brought after the date of the official presentation of the claim.

Article 6 Multiple nationality and claim against a third State

1. Any State of which a dual or multiple national is a national may exercise diplomatic protection in respect of that national against a State of which that person is not a national.

2. Two or more States of nationality may jointly exercise diplomatic protection in respect of a dual or multiple national.

Article 7 Multiple nationality and claim against a State of nationality

A State of nationality may not exercise diplomatic protection in respect of a person against a State of which that person is also a national unless the nationality of the former State is predominant, both at the date of injury and at the date of the official presentation of the claim.

Article 8 Stateless persons and refugees

1. A State may exercise diplomatic protection in respect of a stateless person who, at the date of injury and at the date of the official presentation of the claim, is lawfully and habitually resident in that State.

2. A State may exercise diplomatic protection in respect of a person who is recognized as a refugee by that State, in accordance with internationally accepted standards, when that person, at the date of injury and at the date of the official presentation of the claim, is lawfully and habitually resident in that State.

3. Paragraph 2 does not apply in respect of an injury caused by an internationally wrongful act of the State of nationality of the refugee.

Nottebohm Case (*Liechtenstein v Guatemala*)

ICJ Rep 1955 4, International Court of Justice

Liechtenstein instituted proceedings against Guatemala, seeking a declaration by the Court that in 1943 Guatemala had unlawfully expelled, and seized the property of, Mr Nottebohm, who had been naturalised under the laws of Liechtenstein. Nottebohm was born in Germany in 1881 and had German nationality until his naturalisation by Liechtenstein. In 1905 he went to Guatemala, where he resided and conducted his business activities until 1943, although he occasionally went to Germany, and a few times to Liechtenstein, on holiday. He visited Liechtenstein in October 1939, one month after the outbreak of the Second World War, and applied there for naturalisation. Guatemala's main objection was that Liechtenstein's claim was inadmissible, as Liechtenstein could not extend diplomatic protection to Nottebohm in a claim against Guatemala. The Court upheld Guatemala's objection.

> In order to decide upon the admissibility of the Application, the Court must ascertain whether the nationality conferred on Nottebohm by Liechtenstein by means of a naturalization which took place in the circumstances which have been described, can be validly invoked as against Guatemala, whether it bestows upon Liechtenstein a sufficient title to the exercise of protection in respect of Nottebohm as against Guatemala and therefore entitles it to seise the Court of a claim relating to him …
>
> The naturalization of Nottebohm was an act performed by Liechtenstein in the exercise of its domestic jurisdiction. The question to be decided is whether that act has the international effect here under consideration….
>
> [A] State cannot claim that the rules it has thus laid down are entitled to recognition by another State unless it has acted in conformity with this general aim of making the legal bond of nationality accord with the individual's genuine connection with the State which assumes the defence of its citizens by means of protection as against other States.
>
> According to the practice of States, to arbitral and judicial decisions and to the opinions of writers, nationality is a legal bond having as its basis a social fact of attachment, a genuine connection of existence, interests and sentiments, together with the existence of reciprocal rights and duties. It may be said to constitute the juridical expression of the fact that the individual upon whom it is conferred, either directly by the law or as the result of an act of the authorities, is in fact more closely connected with the population of the State conferring nationality than with that of any other State. Conferred by a State, it only entitles that State to exercise protection vis-à-vis another State, if it constitutes a translation into juridical terms of the individual's connection with the State which has made him its national.
>
> These facts clearly establish, on the one hand, the absence of any bond of attachment between Nottebohm and Liechtenstein and, on the other hand, the existence of a long-standing and close connection between him and Guatemala, a link which his naturalization in no way weakened. That naturalization was not based on any real prior connection with Liechtenstein, nor did it in any way alter the manner of life of the person upon whom it was conferred in exceptional circumstances of speed and accommodation. In both respects, it was lacking in the genuineness requisite to an act of such importance, if it is to be entitled to be respected by a State in the position of Guatemala. It was granted without regard to the concept of nationality adopted in international relations.
>
> Guatemala is under no obligation to recognize a nationality granted in such circumstances. Liechtenstein consequently is not entitled to extend its protection to Nottebohm vis-à-vis Guatemala and its claim must, for this reason, be held to be inadmissible.

Iran-United States Case No. A/18

(1984–1) 5 Iran-USCTR 251, Iran-United States Claims Tribunal

The issue was whether the Tribunal had jurisdiction over claims against Iran by persons who were, under US law, citizens of the US and who were, under Iranian law, citizens of the Islamic Republic of Iran.

> On 12 April 1930, a Convention was concluded at The Hague 'Concerning Certain Questions relating to the Conflict of Nationality Laws' (the 'Hague Convention'). As Article 1 of that Convention makes plain, a determination by one State as to who are its nationals will be respected by another State 'in so far as it is consistent' with international

law governing nationality. International law, then, does not determine who is a national, but rather sets forth the conditions under which that determination must be recognized by other States …

While *Nottebohm* itself did not involve a claim against a State of which Nottebohm was a national, it demonstrated the acceptance and approval by the International Court of Justice of the search for the real and effective nationality based on the facts of a case, instead of an approach relying on more formalistic criteria. The effects of the *Nottebohm* decision have radiated throughout the international law of nationality …

This trend toward modification of the Hague Convention rule of non-responsibility by search for the dominant and effective nationality is scarcely surprising as it is consistent with the contemporaneous development of international law to accord legal protections to individuals, even against the State of which they are nationals. Moreover…, many of the relevant decisions, even in the 19th century, reflected similar concerns by giving weight to domicile.

Thus, the relevant rule of international law which the Tribunal may take into account for purposes of interpretation, as directed by Article 31, paragraph 3(c), of the Vienna Convention, is the rule that flows from the *dictum* of *Nottebohm*, the rule of real and effective nationality, and the search for 'stronger factual ties between the person concerned and one of the States whose nationality is involved'. In view of the pervasive effect of this rule since the *Nottebohm* decision, the Tribunal concludes that the references to 'national' and 'nationals' in the Algiers Declarations must be understood as consistent with that rule unless an exception is clearly stated. As stated above, the Tribunal does not find that the text of the Algiers Declarations provides such a clear exception.

For the reasons stated above, the Tribunal holds that it has jurisdiction over claims against Iran by dual Iran-United States nationals when the dominant and effective nationality of the claimant during the relevant period from the date the claim arose until 19 January 1981 was that of the United States. [The question of interpretation posed in this case by the Government of Iran relates only to claims against Iran; however, it follows that the reasoning in this Decision is equally applicable to any claims against the United States.] In determining the dominant and effective nationality, the Tribunal will consider all relevant factors, including habitual residence, center of interests, family ties, participation in public life and other evidence of attachment.

To this conclusion the Tribunal adds an important caveat. In cases where the Tribunal finds jurisdiction based upon a dominant and effective nationality of the claimant, the other nationality may remain relevant to the merits of the claim.…

NOTES
1. The UK has consistently held that it will only exercise diplomatic protection in respect of British nationals, although it may choose to make representations in respect of non-nationals on humanitarian grounds. This is reflected in its submissions in *Al Rawi* (extracted in Section 6B) and in Article 1 of its Claims Rules (extracted in Section 6D).
2. There has always been some confusion regarding the Court's decision in the *Nottebohm Case*, and whether the ICJ had intended to lay down a general rule, or whether its decision—and the requirement for a genuine link—was restricted to the circumstances of that case, i.e. where the person was a dual national or where nationality had been obtained fraudulently. In the *Case Concerning Ahmadou Sadio Diallo* (see facts and extracts in Sections 6D and E), the DRC did not challenge the right of Guinea to bring the claim on behalf of Mr Diallo as an individual, despite the fact that Mr Diallo had lived for the 32 years preceding his expulsion in the DRC and that most, if not all, of his links were to the DRC during that period. The Court noted that Mr Diallo was a national of Guinea and had held that nationality continuously. The DRC's reluctance to challenge admissibility of the claim on this basis may suggest that the rule is not one of general application. It is also consistent with the approach adopted by the ILC, which requires evidence of the 'predominant' nationality only where a claim is sought to be brought by a dual national against one of the States of nationality (see Article 7 above).
3. Article 8 of the ILC Articles on Diplomatic Protection is considered *lex ferenda*, or aspirational. It does not, as yet, reflect a rule of customary international law. For example, in *R (Al Rawi)* (see Section 6B), the Court of Appeal, referring to Article 8, stated: 'It is clear from the material with which we have been provided that those proposals are considered to be *lex ferenda*, that is that they are indeed proposals and not statements as to the present position in International Law. It follows that whatever the merits of these proposals may be, they are not yet part of international law' (para. 63). The Court did not, however, preclude the Article from becoming part of customary international law in the future.

D: Diplomatic protection of legal persons: nationality of claims

International Law Commission, Articles on Diplomatic Protection (2006)

Article 9 State of nationality of a corporation

For the purposes of the diplomatic protection of a corporation, the State of nationality means the State under whose law the corporation was incorporated. However, when the corporation is controlled by nationals of another State or States and has no substantial business activities in the State of incorporation, and the seat of management and the financial control of the corporation are both located in another State, that State shall be regarded as the State of nationality.

Article 10 Continuous nationality of a corporation

1. A State is entitled to exercise diplomatic protection in respect of a corporation that was a national of that State, or its predecessor State, continuously from the date of injury to the date of the official presentation of the claim. Continuity is presumed if that nationality existed at both these dates.

2. A State is no longer entitled to exercise diplomatic protection in respect of a corporation that acquires the nationality of the State against which the claim is brought after the presentation of the claim.

3. Notwithstanding paragraph 1, a State continues to be entitled to exercise diplomatic protection in respect of a corporation which was its national at the date of injury and which, as the result of the injury, has ceased to exist according to the law of the State of incorporation.

Article 11 Protection of shareholders

A State of nationality of shareholders in a corporation shall not be entitled to exercise diplomatic protection in respect of such shareholders in the case of an injury to the corporation unless:
  (a) The corporation has ceased to exist according to the law of the State of incorporation for a reason unrelated to the injury; or
  (b) The corporation had, at the date of injury, the nationality of the State alleged to be responsible for causing the injury, and incorporation in that State was required by it as a precondition for doing business there.

Article 12 Direct injury to shareholders

To the extent that an internationally wrongful act of a State causes direct injury to the rights of shareholders as such, as distinct from those of the corporation itself, the State of nationality of any such shareholders is entitled to exercise diplomatic protection in respect of its nationals.

Article 13 Other legal persons

The principles contained in this chapter shall be applicable, as appropriate, to the diplomatic protection of legal persons other than corporations.

Barcelona Traction, Light and Power Company Limited Case (Belgium v Spain) (Second Phase)
ICJ Rep 1970 3, International Court of Justice

Belgium brought a claim on behalf of its nationals, who comprised the vast majority of shareholders in the Barcelona Traction, Light and Power Company Limited, a company incorporated in Canada. This company had been affected by acts of the Spanish authorities. The Court upheld the Spanish objections to Belgium's ability to bring the claim.

35. In the present case it is therefore essential to establish whether the losses allegedly suffered by Belgian shareholders in Barcelona Traction were the consequence of the violation of obligations of which they were the beneficiaries. In other words: has a right of Belgium been violated on account of its nationals having suffered infringement of their rights as shareholders in a company not of Belgian nationality?

36. Thus it is the existence or absence of a right, belonging to Belgium and recognized as such by international law, which is decisive for the problem of Belgium's capacity.... It follows that the same question is determinant

in respect of Spain's responsibility towards Belgium. Responsibility is the necessary corollary of a right. In the absence of any treaty on the subject between the Parties, this essential issue has to be decided in the light of the general rules of diplomatic protection.

37. In seeking to determine the law applicable to this case, the Court has to bear in mind the continuous evolution of international law. Diplomatic protection deals with a very sensitive area of international relations, since the interest of a foreign State in the protection of its nationals confronts the rights of the territorial sovereign, a fact of which the general law on the subject has had to take cognizance in order to prevent abuses and friction. From its origins closely linked with international commerce, diplomatic protection has sustained a particular impact from the growth of international economic relations, and at the same time from the profound transformations which have taken place in the economic life of nations. These latter changes have given birth to municipal institutions, which have transcended frontiers and have begun to exercise considerable influence on international relations. One of these phenomena which has a particular bearing on the present case is the corporate entity.

44. Notwithstanding the separate corporate personality, a wrong done to the company frequently causes prejudice to its shareholders. But the mere fact that damage is sustained by both company and shareholder does not imply that both are entitled to claim compensation. Thus no legal conclusion can be drawn from the fact that the same event caused damage simultaneously affecting several natural or juristic persons.

47. The situation is different if the act complained of is aimed at the direct rights of the shareholder as such. It is well known that there are rights which municipal law confers upon the latter distinct from those of the company, including the right to any declared dividend, the right to attend and vote at general meetings, the right to share in the residual assets of the company on liquidation. Whenever one of his direct rights is infringed, the shareholder has an independent right of action. On this there is no disagreement between the Parties. But a distinction must be drawn between a direct infringement of the shareholder's rights, and difficulties or financial losses to which he may be exposed as the result of the situation of the company.... Only in the event of the legal demise of the company are the shareholders deprived of the possibility of a remedy available through the company; it is only if they became deprived of all such possibility that an independent right of action for them and their government could arise.

67. In the present case, Barcelona Traction is in receivership in the country of incorporation. Far from implying the demise of the entity or of its rights, this much rather denotes that those rights are preserved for so long as no liquidation has ensued. Though in receivership, the company continues to exist. Moreover, it is a matter of public record that the company's shares were quoted on the stock-market at a recent date.

69. The Court will now turn to the second possibility, that of the lack of capacity of the company's national State to act on its behalf. The first question which must be asked here is whether Canada—the third apex of the triangular relationship—is, in law, the national State of Barcelona Traction.

70. In allocating corporate entities to States for purposes of diplomatic protection, international law is based, but only to a limited extent, on an analogy with the rules governing the nationality of individuals. The traditional rule attributes the right of diplomatic protection of a corporate entity to the State under the laws of which it is incorporated and in whose territory it has its registered office. These two criteria have been confirmed by long practice and by numerous international instruments. This notwithstanding, further or different links are at times said to be required in order that a right of diplomatic protection should exist. Indeed, it has been the practice of some States to give a company incorporated under their law diplomatic protection solely when it has its seat (*siège social*) or management or centre of control in their territory, or when a majority or a substantial proportion of the shares has been owned by nationals of the State concerned. Only then, it has been held, does there exist between the corporation and the State in question a genuine connection of the kind familiar from other branches of international law. However, in the particular field of the diplomatic protection of corporate entities, no absolute test of the 'genuine connection' has found general acceptance. Such tests as have been applied are of a relative nature, and sometimes links with one State have had to be weighed against those with another. In this connection reference has been made to the *Nottebohm* case. In fact the Parties made frequent reference to it in the course of the proceedings. However, given both the legal and factual aspects of protection in the present case the Court is of the opinion that there can be no analogy with the issues raised or the decision given in that case.

71. In the present case, it is not disputed that the company was incorporated in Canada and has its registered office in that country …

78. The Court would here observe that, within the limits prescribed by international law, a State may exercise diplomatic protection by whatever means and to whatever extent it thinks fit, for it is its own right that the State is asserting. Should the natural or legal persons on whose behalf it is acting consider that their rights are not adequately protected, they have no remedy in international law. All they can do is to resort to municipal law, if means are available, with a view to furthering their cause or obtaining redress. The municipal legislator may lay upon the State an obligation to protect its citizens abroad, and may also confer upon the national a right to demand the performance of that obligation, and clothe the right with corresponding sanctions. However, all these questions remain within the province of municipal law and do not affect the position internationally.

79. The State must be viewed as the sole judge to decide whether its protection will be granted, to what extent it is granted, and when it will cease. It retains in this respect a discretionary power the exercise of which may be determined by considerations of a political or other nature, unrelated to the particular case. Since the claim of the State is not identical with that of the individual or corporate person whose cause is espoused, the State enjoys complete freedom of action. Whatever the reasons for any change of attitude, the fact cannot in itself constitute a justification for the exercise of diplomatic protection by another government, unless there is some independent and otherwise valid ground for that.

80. This cannot be regarded as amounting to a situation where a violation of law remains without remedy: in short, a legal vacuum. There is no obligation upon the possessors of rights to exercise them. Sometimes no remedy is sought, though rights are infringed. To equate this with the creation of a vacuum would be to equate a right with an obligation.

81. The cessation by the Canadian Government of the diplomatic protection of Barcelona Traction cannot, then, be interpreted to mean that there is no remedy against the Spanish Government for the damage done by the allegedly unlawful acts of the Spanish authorities. It is not a hypothetical right which was vested in Canada, for there is no legal impediment preventing the Canadian Government from protecting Barcelona Traction. Therefore there is no substance in the argument that for the Belgian Government to bring a claim before the Court represented the only possibility of obtaining redress for the damage suffered by Barcelona Traction and, through it, by its shareholders.

92. Since the general rule on the subject does not entitle the Belgian Government to put forward a claim in this case, the question remains to be considered whether nonetheless, as the Belgian Government has contended during the proceedings, considerations of equity do not require that it be held to possess a right of protection. It is quite true that it has been maintained that, for reasons of equity, a State should be able, in certain cases, to take up the protection of its nationals, shareholders in a company which has been the victim of a violation of international law. Thus a theory has been developed to the effect that the State of the shareholders has a right of diplomatic protection when the State whose responsibility is invoked is the national State of the company. Whatever the validity of this theory may be, it is certainly not applicable to the present case, since Spain is not the national State of Barcelona Traction.

93. On the other hand, the Court considers that, in the field of diplomatic protection as in all other fields of international law, it is necessary that the law be applied reasonably. It has been suggested that if in a given case it is not possible to apply the general rule that the right of diplomatic protection of a company belongs to its national State, considerations of equity might cal1 for the possibility of protection of the shareholders in question by their own national State. This hypothesis does not correspond to the circumstances of the present case.

94. In view, however, of the discretionary nature of diplomatic protection, considerations of equity cannot require more than the possibility for some protector State to intervene, whether it be the national State of the company, by virtue of the general rule mentioned above, or, in a secondary capacity, the national State of the shareholders who claim protection. In this connection, account should also be taken of the practical effects of deducing from considerations of equity any broader right of protection for the national State of the shareholders. It must first of all be observed that it would be difficult on an equitable basis to make distinctions according to any quantitative test: it would seem that the owner of 1 per cent and the owner of 90 per cent of the share-capital should have the same possibility of enjoying the benefit of diplomatic protection. The protector State may, of course, be disinclined to take up the case of the single small shareholder, but it could scarcely be denied the right to do so in the name of equitable considerations. In that field, protection by the national State of the shareholders can hardly be graduated according to the absolute or relative size of the shareholding involved.

96. The Court considers that the adoption of the theory of diplomatic protection of shareholders as such, by opening the door to competing diplomatic claims, could create an atmosphere of confusion and insecurity

in international economic relations. The danger would be all the greater inasmuch as the shares of companies whose activity is international are widely scattered and frequently change hands. It might perhaps be claimed that, if the right of protection belonging to the national States of the shareholders were considered as only secondary to that of the national State of the company, there would be less danger of difficulties of the kind contemplated. However, the Court must state that the essence of a secondary right is that it only comes into existence at the time when the original right ceases to exist. As the right of protection vested in the national State of the company cannot be regarded as extinguished because it is not exercised, it is not possible to accept the proposition that in case of its non-exercise the national States of the shareholders have a right of protection secondary to that of the national State of the company.

100. In the present case, it is clear from what has been said above that Barcelona Traction was never reduced to a position of impotence such that it could not have approached its national State, Canada, to ask for its diplomatic protection, and that, as far as appeared to the Court, there was nothing to prevent Canada from continuing to grant its diplomatic protection to Barcelona Traction if it had considered that it should do so.

101. For the above reasons, the Court is not of the opinion that, in the particular circumstances of the present case, *jus standi* is conferred on the Belgian Government by considerations of equity.

Case Concerning Ahmadou Sadio Diallo (Republic of Guinea v Democratic Republic of the Congo)

Preliminary Objections, ICJ Rep 2007, International Court of Justice

Guinea instituted proceedings against the DRC by way of diplomatic protection on behalf of Mr Diallo, a national of Guinea who had been resident in DRC for 32 years. Mr Diallo had established two companies, which had accumulated large debts owed to them by the government of the DRC. The DRC blocked attempts by Mr Diallo and his companies to recover these amounts and, ultimately, expelled Mr Diallo from the DRC. In addition to claims of direct injury to the rights of Mr Diallo as an individual, Guinea made two other claims. First, on the basis of his rights as a shareholder (*associé*) in the two companies and, second, on the basis of an entitlement to exercise diplomatic protection of shareholders by way of 'substitution' for the corporation, where the State whose responsibility is at issue is also the state of nationality of the corporation. The DRC raised preliminary objections based on a lack of standing on the part of Guinea to bring the complaint on behalf of Mr Diallo.

82. For its part, Guinea observes that it is not asking the Court to resort to equity *contra legem* to decide the present case when invoking Mr. Diallo's protection by substitution for Africom-Zaire and Africontainers-Zaire. Rather, Guinea contends that, in the *Barcelona Traction* case, the Court referred, in a dictum, to the possibility of an exception, founded on reasons of equity, to the general rule of the protection of a company by its national State, 'when the State whose responsibility is invoked is the national State of the company'. In this connection, it quotes the following passage from the Judgment, which it considers apposite: [Court quotes paragraph 93, see extract above] …

According to Guinea, the equity concerned in this case is equity *infra legem*. The alleged purpose of such recourse is to permit 'a reasonable application'…of the rules relating to diplomatic protection', in order 'not to deprive foreign shareholders in a company having the nationality of the State responsible for the internationally wrongful act of all possibility of protection'. Guinea recognizes that the Court did not definitively settle the question of the existence of diplomatic protection by substitution in the *Barcelona Traction* case. It nevertheless considers that the text of the Judgment, read in the light of the opinions of the Members of the Court appended to it, leads one 'to believe that a majority of the Judges regarded the exception as established in law'.

83. Guinea contends that the existence of the rule of protection by substitution and its customary nature are confirmed by numerous arbitral awards establishing 'that the shareholders of a company can enjoy the diplomatic protection of their own national State as regards the national State of the company when that State is responsible for an internationally wrongful act against it'. Further, according to Guinea, '[s]ubsequent practice [following *Barcelona Traction*], conventional or jurisprudential…has dispelled any uncertainty…on the positive nature of the "exception"'. Guinea thus refers to certain decisions of the European Commission of Human Rights,

to the Washington Convention establishing the ICSID, to the latter's jurisprudence and to the jurisprudence of the Iran/United States Claims Tribunal.

84. In Guinea's view, the application of protection by substitution is particularly appropriate in this case. Guinea again emphasizes that Africom-Zaire and Africontainers-Zaire are SPRLs, which have a marked *intuitu personae* character and which, moreover, are statutorily controlled and managed by one and the same person. Further, it especially points out that Mr. Diallo was bound, under Zairean legislation, and in particular Article 1 of the Legislative Order of 7 June 1966 concerning the registered office and the administrative seat of companies 'whose main centre of operations is situated in the Congo', to incorporate the companies in Zaire. In this regard, Guinea refers to Article 11, paragraph *(b)*, of the draft Articles on Diplomatic Protection adopted in 2006 by the ILC [see extract], providing that the rule of protection by substitution applies specifically in situations where the shareholders in a company have been required to form the company in the State having committed the alleged violation of international law....

87. Since its dictum in the *Barcelona Traction* case (*ibid.*, p. 48, para. 93) (see paragraph 82 above), the Court has not had occasion to rule on whether, in international law, there is indeed an exception to the general rule 'that the right of diplomatic protection of a company belongs to its national State' (*ibid.*, p. 48, para. 93), which allows for protection of the shareholders by their own national State 'by substitution', and on the reach of any such exception. It is true that in the case concerning *Electronica Sicula S.p.A. (ELSI) (United States of America* v. *Italy)*, [see Section 6E] the Chamber of the Court allowed a claim by the United States of America on behalf of two United States corporations (who held 100 per cent of the shares in an Italian company), in relation to alleged acts by the Italian authorities injuring the rights of the latter company. However, in doing so, the Chamber based itself not on customary international law but on a Treaty of Friendship, Commerce and Navigation between the two countries directly granting to their nationals, corporations and associations certain rights in relation to their participation in corporations and associations having the nationality of the other State. The Court will now examine whether the exception invoked by Guinea is part of customary international law, as claimed by the latter.

88. The Court is bound to note that, in contemporary international law, the protection of the rights of companies and the rights of their shareholders, and the settlement of the associated disputes, are essentially governed by bilateral or multilateral agreements for the protection of foreign investments, such as the treaties for the promotion and protection of foreign investments, and the Washington Convention of 18 March 1965 on the Settlement of Investment Disputes between States and Nationals of Other States, which created an International Centre for Settlement of Investment Disputes (ICSID), and also by contracts between States and foreign investors. In that context, the role of diplomatic protection somewhat faded, as in practice recourse is only made to it in rare cases where treaty régimes do not exist or have proved inoperative. It is in this particular and relatively limited context that the question of protection by substitution might be raised. The theory of protection by substitution seeks indeed to offer protection to the foreign shareholders of a company who could not rely on the benefit of an international treaty and to whom no other remedy is available, the allegedly unlawful acts having been committed against the company by the State of its nationality. Protection by 'substitution' would therefore appear to constitute the very last resort for the protection of foreign investments.

89. The Court, having carefully examined State practice and decisions of international courts and tribunals in respect of diplomatic protection of *associés* and shareholders, is of the opinion that these do not reveal—at least at the present time—an exception in customary international law allowing for protection by substitution, such as is relied on by Guinea.

United Kingdom Rules regarding the Taking Up of International Claims by Her Majesty's Government, July 1983

54 British Yearbook of International Law 520 (1983)

Rule I

HMG [Her Majesty's Government] will not take up the claim unless the claimant is a United Kingdom national and was so at the date of the injury.

Rule II

Where the claimant has become or ceases to be a UK national after the date of the injury, HMG may in an appropriate case take up his claim in concert with the government of the country of his former or subsequent nationality.

Rule III

Where the claimant is a dual national, HMG may take up his claim, (although in certain circumstances it may be appropriate for HMG to do so jointly with the other government entitled to do so). HMG will not normally take up his claim as a UK national if the respondent State is the State of his second nationality, but may do so if the respondent State has, in the circumstances which gave rise to the injury, treated the claimant as a UK national.

Rule IV

HMG may take up the claim of a corporation or other juridical person which is created and regulated by the law of the United Kingdom or of any territory for which HMG are internationally responsible.

Rule V

Where a UK national has an interest, as a shareholder or otherwise, in a company incorporated in another State, and that company is injured by the acts of a third State, HMG may normally take up his claim only in concert with the government of the State in which the company is incorporated. Exceptionally, as where the company is defunct, there may be independent intervention.

Rule VI

Where a UK national has an interest, as a shareholder or otherwise, in a company incorporated in another State and of which it is therefore a national, and that State injures the company, HMG may intervene to protect the interests of that UK national.

Comment

In some cases the State of incorporation of a company does not possess the primary national interest in the company. A company may be created for reasons of legal or economic advantage under the law of one State though nearly all the capital is owned by nationals of another. In such circumstances, the State in which the company is incorporated may have little interest in protecting it, while the State to which the nationals who own the capital belong has considerable interest in so doing. In the Barcelona Traction Case, the International Court of Justice denied the existence under customary international law of an inherent right for the national State of shareholders in a foreign company to exercise diplomatic protection. However, the majority of the Court accepted the existence of a right to protect shareholders in the two cases described in Rules V and VI (when the company is defunct, and where the State in which the company is incorporated, although theoretically the legal protector of the company, itself causes injury to the company).

Where the capital in a foreign company is owned in various proportions by nationals of several States, including the United Kingdom, it is unusual for HMG to make representations unless the States whose nationals hold the bulk of the capital will support them in making representations.

NOTES

1. The *Barcelona Traction Case* has been criticised for drawing an unnecessary distinction between when diplomatic protection can be exercised for natural and legal persons. The corporation may have little 'genuine link' with its State of incorporation, and that State may have little interest in that corporation or any connection with that corporation's activities, particularly where it is a 'tax haven' State. By acknowledging that there could be an exception to the general principle where the State of incorporation is the State which has acted against the corporation, the Court in the *Barcelona Traction Case* and the provision of Rule VI above, give special international protection to those shareholders who, by good fortune, own shares in a corporation where the majority of shareholders do not reside in the State of incorporation. However, the Court, in its decision in *Guinea* v *DRC* extracted above denied that the argued exception allowing diplomatic representation by substitution exists as a matter of customary international law. It therefore upheld the DRC's preliminary objection as to the admissibility of this part of the claim. This decision seems to accord with the finding of the majority in the *Barcelona Traction Case* that, although a wrong to a company may affect the shareholders, it is the company only that is entitled to those rights as a matter of law. Article 11 of the Articles on Diplomatic Protection allows a more limited exception to that considered here, allowing protection of shareholders only where a company's incorporation in the allegedly responsible State was a precondition of doing business there. The Court found that this was not the case in the circumstances of Mr Diallo, and it thus expressed no view as to the customary international law status of Article 11(b). It did, however, reject the objection of the DRC that Guinea did not have standing to pursue Mr Diallo's claim as

a shareholder for the direct injury suffered to him, leaving the scope and nature of his rights to be determined at the merits stage (para. 67). This is consistent with Article 12 of the ILC Articles on Diplomatic Protection.

2. To require a corporation to be defunct and so lacking any legal personality—and not merely to be without any assets—before the State of the shareholders can bring a claim, is to ignore the situation that shareholders are the 'economic reality' behind the 'corporate fiction' of a corporation. Consequently, some specialist settlement regimes—such as the US-Iran Claims Tribunal—define the nationality of a claim of a company by reference to the nationality of its shareholders.

3. Attempts have been made to limit the situations where a State can intervene, by diplomatic protection of its nationals, in a contractual dispute between a State and non-national. The 'Calvo clause' is the main example of this. It is a clause of a contract, usually in terms to the effect that 'under no conditions shall the intervention of foreign diplomatic agents be permitted, in any matter related to this contract'. In the *North American Dredging Company Claim* 4 RIAA (1926) 26, the Mexico-United States General Claims Commission said that the clause meant that the terms of the contract were binding on the non-national but did not prevent an application by him to his State for protection against violations of international law arising from his contract or otherwise. It also did not, and could not, prevent a State bringing diplomatic protection itself, as that was a right of a sovereign State. Some limitations also can be placed on the right of diplomatic protection by specific agreement between States, as seen in the Convention on the Settlement of Investment Disputes between States and Nationals of Other States 1966 (ICSID Convention) (see further below and in Chapter 13). Article 27(1) of that Convention provides that no Contracting State shall give diplomatic protection, or bring an international claim, in respect of a dispute which one of its nationals and another Contracting State shall have consented to submit or shall have submitted to arbitration under this Convention, unless such other Contracting State shall have failed to abide by and comply with the award rendered in such dispute.

E: Exhaustion of local remedies

International Law Commission, Articles on Responsibility of States for Internationally Wrongful Acts (2001)

Article 44 Admissibility of claims

The responsibility of a State may not be invoked if:
    (a) The claim is not brought in accordance with any applicable rule relating to the nationality of claims;
    (b) The claim is one to which the rule of exhaustion of local remedies applies and any available and effective local remedy has not been exhausted.

International Law Commission, Articles on Diplomatic Protection (2006)

Article 14 Exhaustion of local remedies

1. A State may not present an international claim in respect of an injury to a national or other person referred to in draft article 8 before the injured person has, subject to draft article 15, exhausted all local remedies.

2. 'Local remedies' means legal remedies which are open to an injured person before the judicial or administrative courts or bodies, whether ordinary or special, of the State alleged to be responsible for causing the injury.

3. Local remedies shall be exhausted where an international claim, or request for a declaratory judgement related to the claim, is brought preponderantly on the basis of an injury to a national or other person referred to in draft article 8.

Article 15 Exceptions to the local remedies rule

Local remedies do not need to be exhausted where:
    (a) There are no reasonably available local remedies to provide effective redress, or the local remedies provide no reasonable possibility of such redress;
    (b) There is undue delay in the remedial process which is attributable to the State alleged to be responsible;

    (c) There was no relevant connection between the injured person and the State alleged to be responsible at the date of injury;

    (d) The injured person is manifestly precluded from pursuing local remedies; or

    (e) The State alleged to be responsible has waived the requirement that local remedies be exhausted.

Norwegian Loans Case (*France* v *Norway*)

ICJ Rep 1957 9, International Court of Justice

France brought a claim on behalf of its nationals who were holders of Norwegian bonds. Norway objected to the action on the ground, *inter alia*, that remedies in the Norwegian courts had not been exhausted.

JUDGE LAUTERPACHT (Separate Opinion): [T]he requirement of exhaustion of local remedies is not a purely technical or rigid rule. It is a rule which international tribunals have applied with a considerable degree of elasticity. In particular, they have refused to act upon it in cases in which there are, in fact, no effective remedies available owing to the law of the State concerned or the conditions prevailing in it....

    The Norwegian Government has contended that the burden of proving the inefficacy of local remedies rests upon France. There is, in general, a degree of unhelpfulness in the argument concerning the burden of proof. However, some *prima facie* distribution of the burden of proof there must be. This being so, the following seems to be the accurate principle on the subject: (1) As a rule, it is for the plaintiff State to prove that there are no effective remedies to which recourse can be had; (2) no such proof is required if there exists legislation which on the face of it deprives the private claimants of a remedy; (3) in that case it is for the defendant State to show that, notwithstanding the apparent absence of a remedy, its existence can nevertheless reasonably be assumed; (4) the degree of burden of proof thus to be adduced ought not to be so stringent as to render the proof unduly exacting.

Finnish Shipowners Arbitration (*Finland* v *United Kingdom*)

3 RIAA (1934) 1479, Bagge, Single Arbitrator

During the First World War, 13 ships belonging to Finnish shipowners were used by the UK government, of which four were lost. After fruitless negotiation, the Finnish shipowners submitted the case to the Admiralty Transport Arbitration Board in the UK. This Board decided in January 1926 that the ships were not requisitioned by the UK but by Russia, and so no compensation was payable. No appeal was taken from this decision. The matter was later brought by Finland before an international arbitration tribunal. The UK objected on the ground that the Finnish shipowners had not exhausted local remedies in the UK. The Arbitrator rejected this objection.

The remedy of appeal relied on by the British Government may be said always to be open to a claimant in that sense that there is a right to file a notice of appeal and to have the contentions of the appellant as to his formal right of appeal dealt with by the Court of Appeal. It is, however, common ground that this is not sufficient to bring in the local remedies rule; the remedy must be effective and adequate.

    A remedy of appeal is effective only if the Court of Appeal may enter into the merits of the case. But even this does not exhaust the condition of effectiveness under international law.... The rule as to local remedies is not a rule devised for the purpose of preventing international claims from being made because they are, or are thought to be ill founded, but it is based upon quite different conceptions: in cases of the present character the basis of the rule is that the foreign State should, first of all, be given the opportunity of redressing the wrong alleged. Whether a wrong has really been committed is a different question altogether, with which the international rule under discussion is not concerned; the only point under that rule is: Does the municipal means of redress exist? ...

    [T]he respondent State is entitled, first of all to discharge its responsibility by doing justice in its own way, but also to the investigation and adjudication of its own tribunals upon the questions of law and fact which the claim involves and then on the basis of this adjudication to appreciate its international responsibility and to meet or reject the claim accordingly.

    According to the principles approved by the Arbitrator every relevant contention, whether it is well founded or not, brought forward by the claimant Government in the international procedure, must under the local remedies rule have been investigated and adjudicated upon by the highest competent municipal court.

The parties in the present case, however, agree—and rightly—that the local remedies rule does not apply where there is no effective remedy. And the British Government, as previously mentioned, submit that this is the case where a recourse is obviously futile. It is evident that the British Government there include not only cases where recourse is futile because on formal grounds there is no remedy or no further remedy, e.g. where there is no appealable point of law in the judgment, but also cases where on the merits of the claim recourse is obviously futile, e.g. where there may be appealable points of law but they are obviously insufficient to reverse the decision of the Court of first instance. The British Government, however, contend that in this latter case the merits must be considered upon the hypothesis that every allegation of fact in the claim is true and every legal proposition upon which it is based is correct.

The Arbitrator is of the same opinion, with the reservation only that, of course, where it is, as here, a question of remedy on appeal, and contentions of fact maintained by the claimant Government but rejected by the Arbitration Board, are not appealable, such contentions may not be taken as well founded.... [T]he Arbitrator comes to the conclusion that the appealable points of law, whether directly referring to British requisition or not, obviously would have been insufficient to reverse the decision of the Arbitration Board as to there not being a British requisition and that, in consequence, there was no effective remedy against this decision.

Elettronica Sicula SpA (ELSI) Case (United States v Italy)

ICJ Rep 1989 15, International Court of Justice

The dispute arose out of the requisition by Italy of the plant and other assets of ELSI, an Italian corporation wholly owned by two US corporations, Raytheon and Machlett. Prior to this requisition, due to financial difficulties, the US corporations had begun to plan for the liquidation of ELSI. The US claimed compensation for the two US corporate shareholders of ELSI pursuant to a treaty (the 'FCN Treaty') with Italy, as the planned liquidation was intended to pay the creditors in full, while the requisition meant that creditors received less than 1 per cent of their claims and the shareholders received nothing. Italy had objected to the admissibility of the claim on the ground that the US corporations had failed to exhaust the remedies available to them in Italy. This objection was unanimously rejected by the Chamber.

50. The Chamber has no doubt that the parties to a treaty can therein either agree that the local remedies rule shall not apply to claims based on alleged breaches of that treaty; or confirm that it shall apply. Yet the Chamber finds itself unable to accept that an important principle of customary international law should be held to have been tacitly dispensed with, in the absence of any words making clear an intention to do so....

51. The United States further argued that the local remedies rule would not apply in any event to the part of the United States claim which requested a declaratory judgment finding that the FCN Treaty had been violated. The argument of the United States is that such a judgment would declare that the United States own rights under the FCN Treaty had been infringed; and that to such a direct injury the local remedies rule, which is a rule of customary international law developed in the context of the espousal by a State of the claim of one of its nationals, would not apply. The Chamber, however, has not found it possible in the present case to find a dispute over alleged violation of the FCN Treaty resulting in direct injury to the United States, that is both distinct from, and independent of, the dispute over the alleged violation in respect of Raytheon and Machlett....

52. Moreover, when the Court was, in the *Interhandel* case, faced with a not dissimilar argument by Switzerland that in that case its 'principal submission' was in respect of a 'direct breach of international law' and therefore not subject to the local remedies rule, the Court, having analysed that 'principal submission', found that it was bound up with the diplomatic protection claim, and that the Applicant's arguments 'do not deprive the dispute...of the character of a dispute in which the Swiss Government appears as having adopted the cause of its national...' (*Interhandel, Judgment, ICJ Reports 1959*, p. 28). In the present case, likewise, the Chamber has no doubt that the matter which colours and pervades the United States claim as a whole, is the alleged damage to Raytheon and Machlett, said to have resulted from the actions of the Respondent. Accordingly, the Chamber rejects the argument that in the present case there is a part of the Applicant's claim which can be severed so as to render the local remedies rule inapplicable to that part....

[T]he local remedies rule does not, indeed cannot, require that a claim be presented to the municipal courts in a form, and with arguments, suited to an international tribunal, applying different law to different parties: for an international claim to be admissible, it is sufficient if the essence of the claim has been brought before the competent tribunals and pursued as far as permitted by local law and procedures, and without success.... It thus appears to the Chamber to be impossible to deduce, from the recent jurisprudence cited, what the attitude of the Italian courts would have been had Raytheon and Machlett brought an action, some 20 years ago, in reliance on Article 2043 of the Civil Code in conjunction with the provisions of the FCN Treaty and the Supplementary Agreement. Where the determination of a question of municipal law is essential to the Court's decision in a case, the Court will have to weight the jurisprudence of the municipal courts, and 'If this is uncertain or divided, it will rest with the Court to select the interpretation which it considers most in conformity with the law' (*Brazilian Loans, PCIJ, Series A, Nos. 20/21*, p. 124). In the present case, however, it was for Italy to show, as a matter of fact, the existence of a remedy which was open to the United States stockholders and which they failed to employ. The Chamber does not consider that Italy has discharged that burden.

63. It is never easy to decide, in a case where there has in fact been much resort to the municipal courts, whether local remedies have truly been 'exhausted'. But in this case Italy has not been able to satisfy the Chamber that there clearly remained some remedy which Raytheon and Machlett, independently of ELSI, and of ELSI's trustee in bankruptcy, ought to have pursued and exhausted. Accordingly, the Chamber will now proceed to consider the merits of the case.

Case Concerning Ahmadou Sadio Diallo (Republic of Guinea v Democratic Republic of the Congo)
Preliminary Objections, ICJ Rep 2007, International Court of Justice

The facts are set out in Section 6D. In addition to raising objections as to the standing of Guinea to bring proceedings on behalf of Mr Diallo, the DRC also objected that he had failed to exhaust domestic remedies in the DRC.

46. The Court notes that the expulsion was characterized as a 'refusal of entry' when it was carried out, as both Parties have acknowledged and as is confirmed by the notice drawn up on 31 January 1996 by the national immigration service of Zaire. It is apparent that refusals of entry are not appealable under Congolese law. Article 13 of Legislative Order No. 83-033 of 12 September 1983, concerning immigration control, expressly states that the 'measure [refusing entry] shall not be subject to appeal'. The Court considers that the DRC cannot now rely on an error allegedly made by its administrative agencies at the time Mr. Diallo was 'refused entry' to claim that he should have treated the measure as an expulsion. Mr. Diallo, as the subject of the refusal of entry, was justified in relying on the consequences of the legal characterization thus given by the Zairean authorities, including for purposes of the local remedies rule.

47. The Court further observes that, even if this was a case of expulsion and not refusal of entry, as the DRC maintains, the DRC has also failed to show that means of redress against expulsion decisions are available under its domestic law. The DRC did, it is true, cite the possibility of requesting reconsideration by the competent administrative authority.... The Court nevertheless recalls that, while the local remedies that must be exhausted include all remedies of a legal nature, judicial redress as well as redress before administrative bodies, administrative remedies can only be taken into consideration for purposes of the local remedies rule if they are aimed at vindicating a right and not at obtaining a favour, unless they constitute an essential prerequisite for the admissibility of subsequent contentious proceedings. Thus, the possibility open to Mr. Diallo of submitting a request for reconsideration of the expulsion decision to the administrative authority having taken it—that is to say the Prime Minister—in the hope that he would retract his decision as a matter of grace cannot be deemed a local remedy to be exhausted.

48. Having established that the DRC has not proved the existence in its domestic legal system of available and effective remedies allowing Mr. Diallo to challenge his expulsion, the Court concludes that the DRC's objection to admissibility based on the failure to exhaust local remedies cannot be upheld in respect of that expulsion.

NOTES

1. The principle of the equality of States requires that the State responsible for an international wrong must first be given an opportunity to redress the wrong in its own legal system. However, the principle applies only where a diplomatic protection claim is made (i.e. a claim on 'behalf' of

an injured national), and not where there is direct injury to a State, as then a submission to a national court would be inappropriate. A State can by specific agreement waive the local remedies rule, as was done by the US and Iran when establishing the Iran-United States Claims Tribunal.

2. In the *Ambatielos Arbitration* (*Greece* v *United Kingdom*) 12 RIAA (1956) 83, the Commission of Arbitration decided that if an appeal was futile because of the neglect of the national to call relevant evidence, then the rule of exhaustion of local remedies was not satisfied and so the international arbitration tribunal was prevented from deciding the claim. The various international and regional human rights tribunals have also upheld the principle of the exhaustion of local remedies (see Chapter 6).

3. In its judgment in the case concerning *Armed Activities on the Territory of the Congo* (*DRC* v *Uganda*), the ICJ confirmed its own case law and the commentary to Article 45 in relation to the argument, made by the DRC, that Uganda had waived its claim against the DRC. The Court observed that 'waivers or renunciations of claims or rights must either be express or unequivocally implied from the conduct of the State alleged to have waived or renounced its right' (ICJ Rep 2005 p. 168, para. 293). The decision in *Guinea* v *DRC* also confirms the Court's previous jurisprudence that the requirement to exhaust local remedies is a mandatory prerequisite to bringing a claim at the international level. However, it also provided that this obligation only applies to legal remedies, and not to discretionary procedures.

F: Special enforcement regimes

It is in the nature of international relations that two or more States may be embroiled in an international controversy that affects the lives and well-being of many of their nationals. These events—such as the Islamic Revolution in Iran 1978/9 or the Iraq/Kuwait Gulf War 1990/91—may give rise to international responsibility because of injury to the nationals of the disputants or because of injury directly to the States themselves. These claims could be settled on an *ad hoc* basis, with each individual claim being heard by a tribunal specially composed for the task, or adjudicated by means of a generic claims procedure specifically established for that purpose. The latter will save time and money, will promote consistency of legal reasoning and allows the disputing States to choose the procedural and substantive legal rules they find most suitable (see Chapter 16). Good examples are: the US-Iran Claims Tribunal, established by the parties to deal with claims by nationals against either State after the Islamic Revolution; the United Nations Compensation Commission established by the UN Security Council in 1991 (SC Res 687) to provide compensation to natural and legal persons suffering loss because of Iraq's unlawful invasion of Kuwait; and the Eritrea-Ethiopia Claims Commission, established by the parties to decide all claims for loss, damage or injury by one State against the other, and by nationals of one party against the government of the other party or entities owned or controlled by the other party. The US-Iran Claims Tribunal and the Eritrea-Ethiopia Claims Commission are essentially judicial, while the UN Commission is rather more administrative in scope, although it decides which claimants may share in the compensation fund established from Iraq's oil revenues.

States may sometimes enter into what are known as 'lump sum' settlements with other States that are alleged to be internationally responsible for some violation of international law. However, a lump sum settlement does not necessarily involve the assignment or admission of responsibility under international law. Under such settlements, the alleged delinquent State will pay a sum in full and final settlement of all claims. The final sum usually will *not* have been calculated by reference to the actual loss of the nationals of the claimant State. Examples include the US-Cambodia (1994) and US-Vietnam (1995) Claims Settlement Agreements, whereby both Cambodia and Vietnam agreed to pay a lump sum in full and final settlement of US claims and those of its nationals. The US has also reached agreement with Libya concerning the payment of compensation to victims of the Lockerbie bombing.

SECTION 7: TREATMENT OF ALIENS

One important aspect of State responsibility concerns the obligations that a State owes to another State with regard to the treatment of that other State's nationals within the first State's territory. Mistreatment of these nationals by organs or officers of the State may give rise to responsibility on the international plane. This will not arise out of every incident in which a non-national is harmed (either physically or economically) but applies when the 'host' State has fallen below the standard of treatment that international law requires it to show to 'aliens'. Importantly, this responsibility can arise either directly through an act or omission attributable to the State that causes physical or economic harm to the non-national, or indirectly where the territorial sovereign is guilty of a 'denial of justice', being cases where the non-nationals are prejudiced in their attempts to obtain a national law remedy in a dispute against any other party (e.g. another private individual). If there is a failure to treat a non-national according to the standard required by international law, it is then the State of nationality of the non-national that may pursue, at its option, an action on the international plane against the territorial sovereign.

G. Hackworth, *Digest of International Law*

(1943), vol. 5

The admission of aliens into a State immediately calls into existence certain correlative rights and duties. The alien has a right to the protection of the local law. He owes a duty to observe that law and assumes a relationship toward the State of his residence sometimes referred to as 'temporary allegiance.'

The State has the right to expect that the alien shall observe its laws and that his conduct shall not be incompatible with the good order of the State and of the community in which he resides or sojourns. It has the obligation to give him that degree of protection for his person and property which he and his State have the right to expect under local law, under international law, and under treaties and conventions between his State and the State of residence. Failure of the alien or of the State to observe these requirements may give rise to responsibility in varying degrees, the alien being amenable to the local law or subject to expulsion from the State, or both, and the State being responsible to the alien or to the State of which he is a national.

We are here concerned primarily with responsibility of the State. State responsibility may arise directly or indirectly. It does not arise merely because an alien has been injured or has suffered loss within the State's territory. If the alien has suffered an injury at the hands of a private person his remedy usually is against that person, and State responsibility does not arise in the absence of a dereliction of duty on the part of the State itself in connection with the injury, as for example by failure to afford a remedy, or to apply an existing remedy. When local remedies are available the alien is ordinarily not entitled to the interposition of his government until he has exhausted those remedies and has been denied justice. This presupposes the existence in the State of orderly judicial and administrative processes. In theory an unredressed injury to an alien constitutes an injury to his State, giving rise to international responsibility.

Neer Claim (United States v Mexico)

4 RIAA 60 (1926), Mexico-United States General Claims Commission

Mr Neer, a national of the United States, was working in Mexico when he was stopped by armed men and shot. It was claimed that the Mexican authorities were not diligent in their investigations into the murder and that they should pay damages to Neer's family. This was rejected by the Commission.

Without attempting to announce a precise formula, it is in the opinion of the Commission possible...to hold (first) that the propriety of governmental acts should be put to the test of international standards, and (second) that the treatment of an alien, in order to constitute an international delinquency, should amount to an outrage, to bad faith, to wilful neglect of duty, or to an insufficiency of governmental action so far short of international standards that every reasonable and impartial man would readily recognize its insufficiency. Whether the insufficiency proceeds from deficient execution of an intelligent law or from the fact that the laws of the country do not empower the authorities to measure up to international standards is immaterial.... In the light of the entire record in this case the Commission is not prepared to hold that the Mexican authorities have shown such lack of diligence or such lack of intelligent investigation in apprehending and punishing the culprits as would render Mexico liable before this Commission.

The Loewen Group, Inc. and Raymond L. Loewen v United States of America
128 ILR (2006), NAFTA Arbitration Tribunal

The claim grew out of a dispute between O'Keefe, a US national and the Loewen Group, Inc., a Canadian company. O'Keefe was successful in a US court in regard to various contract, tort and anti-trust claims against Loewen. Loewen then brought claims against the US under the NAFTA Chapter 11, arguing that the trial court violated the minimum standard of treatment by allowing prejudicial comments, racial attitudes, and economic class arguments.

133. In the words of the NAFTA Tribunal in *Mondev International Ltd v United States of America* ICSID Case No. ARB (AF)/99/2, Award dated October 11, 2002, 'the question is whether, at an international level and having regard to generally accepted standards of the administration of justice, a tribunal can conclude in the light of all the facts that the impugned decision was clearly improper and discreditable, with the result that the investment has been subjected to "unfair and inequitable treatment"'.

135. International law does...attach special importance to discriminatory violations of municipal law (Harvard Draft Convention on the Law of Responsibility of States for Damage done in their Territory to the Person or Property of Foreigners 1929: 'a judgment [which] is manifestly unjust, especially if it has been inspired by ill-will towards foreigners as such or as citizens of a particular states')...A decision which is in breach of municipal law and is discriminatory against the foreign litigant amounts to manifest injustice according to international law.

136. In the present case, the trial court permitted the jury to be influenced by persistent appeals to local favouritism as against a foreign litigant.

137.... the whole trial and its resultant verdict were clearly improper and discreditable and cannot be squared with minimum standards of international law and fair and equitable treatment.

NOTES
1. Responsibility arising through a denial of justice may occur even though the initial act against the non-national (even if it was committed by the State) did not itself give rise to State responsibility, and even if the non-national is pursuing an ordinary action against another party in the national courts.
2. Many issues relating to the treatment of non-nationals (and nationals) are now within international human rights law (see Chapter 6).
3. There is now a considerable amount of international law that deals with issues where a corporation of one State (its 'home State') is affected by the actions of a State in which it has invested (the 'host State'). In most instances, the corporation will have a contract with the host State (or with an entity that is part of the host State), and that contract will be made under the umbrella of a bilateral investment treaty (BIT) between the two States. This BIT will normally have a range of restrictions on the actions that the host State can take, which include that it cannot act to the economic disadvantage of the home State's corporations and that all disputes are subject to international arbitration and are not subject to the host State's own national courts. This area of international law, known as international investment law, is considered in Chapter 13, though aspects of expropriation and compensation are not covered in this book (though see S. Ripinsky, *Damages in International Investment Law* (BIICL, 2008)). Chapter 13 also considers situations of nationalisation or expropriation of non-nationals' property.

12

International Environmental Law

International environmental law challenges many fundamental concepts of traditional international law. It puts new limits on State sovereignty, it intrudes into the domestic jurisdiction and territorial integrity of States, it creates greater responsibilities for States, and it involves many non-State entities in the process of international law. The global nature of environmental issues means that national action by itself, while important, may be insufficient, and that significant international cooperation is required.

'The environment' is a description of physical matter that encompasses the air, the sea, the land, natural resources, flora and fauna, and cultural heritage (being items of archaeological, historical, artistic and scientific interest). It can also be a description of a non-physical sense of surroundings and perceptions. Protection of the environment includes the control, reduction and elimination of existing causes of damage to the environment, the prevention and prohibition of additional kinds of damage, and the preservation and rational use of the environment. While the term 'the environment' has been criticised, and terms such as 'ecosystems' and 'biological diversity' have been proposed as alternatives, 'the environment' is a generally understood term and will be used here.

In the last few decades concern and awareness about the need for long-term environmental protection has increased dramatically, both nationally and internationally. One way of putting this concern into action is the law, being a means to structure and regulate behaviour. Sources of international environmental law include many treaties, declarations and a body of State practice, as well as soft law.

There are many competing interests to be taken into account when seeking to protect the environment, including population growth and poverty. In particular, the paramountcy of economic development, including the right of States to determine their own development goals and how they are to be achieved, continues to force compromises in the law protecting the environment. These tensions between economic development, environment and sovereignty necessarily challenge the ability of international law to protect the environment, and so require recourse to non-legal processes. In addition, it is clear that international organisations, non-governmental organisations and individuals are having a significant input in this area.

A: Environmental context

The World Commission on Environment and Development, *Our Common Future*
(1987)

This Commission was established in response to a request from the General Assembly in Resolution 38/161 in December 1983. It was chaired by Gro Harlem Brundtland, former Prime Minister of Norway.

Over the course of this century, the relationship between the human world and the planet that sustains it has undergone a profound change. When the century began neither human numbers nor technology had the power radically to alter planetary system. As the century closes, not only do vastly increased human numbers and their activities have that power, but major, unintended changes are occurring in the atmosphere, in soils, in waters, among plants and animals, and in the relationships among all of these. The rate of change is outstripping the ability of scientific disciplines and our current capabilities to assess and advise. It is frustrating the attempts of political and economic institutions, which evolved in a different, more fragmented world, to adapt and cope. It deeply worries many people who are seeking ways to place those concerns on the political agendas.

The onus lies with no one group of nations. Developing countries face the obvious life-threatening challenges of desertification, deforestation, and pollution, and endure most of the poverty associated with environmental degradation. The entire human family of nations would suffer from the disappearance of rain forests in the tropics, the loss of plant and animal species, and changes in rainfall patterns. Industrial nations face the life-threatening challenges of toxic chemicals, toxic wastes, and acidification. All nations may suffer from the releases by industrialized countries of carbon dioxide and of gases that react with the ozone layer, and from any future war fought with the nuclear arsenals controlled by those nations. All nations will have a role to play in changing trends, and in righting an international economic system that increases rather than decreases inequality, that increases rather than decreases numbers of poor and hungry....

The changes in human attitudes that we call for depend on a vast campaign of education, debate, and public participation. This campaign must start now if sustainable human progress is to be achieved....We are unanimous in our conviction that the security, well-being, and very survival of the planet depend on such changes, now.

NOTE: Concerns about the increasing degradation and destruction of the environment, as well as the awareness that environmental issues are not contained within State borders, have been major factors behind the development of international environmental law.

B: Legal context

Stockholm Declaration on the Human Environment 1972
11 *International Legal Materials* 1416 (1972), Report of the UN Conference on the Human Environment

Principle 1
Man has the fundamental right to freedom, equality and adequate conditions of life, in an environment of a quality that permits a life of dignity and well-being, and he bears a solemn responsibility to protect and improve the environment for present and future generations. In this respect, policies promoting or perpetuating apartheid, racial segregation, discrimination, colonial and other forms of oppression and foreign domination stand condemned and must be eliminated.

Principle 2
The natural resources of the earth including the air, water, land, flora and fauna and especially representative samples of natural ecosystems must be safeguarded for the benefit of present and future generations through careful planning or management, as appropriate.

Principle 3
The capacity of the earth to produce vital renewable resources must be maintained and, wherever practicable, restored or improved.

Principle 4
Man has a special responsibility to safeguard and wisely manage the heritage of wildlife and its habitat which are now gravely imperiled by a combination of adverse factors. Nature conservation including wildlife must therefore receive importance in planning for economic development.

Principle 5
The non-renewable resources of the earth must be employed in such a way as to guard against the danger of their future exhaustion and to ensure that benefits from such employment are shared by all mankind.

Principle 6

The discharge of toxic substances or of other substances and the release of heat, in such quantities or concentrations as to exceed the capacity of the environment to render them harmless, must be halted in order to ensure that serious or irreversible damage is not inflicted upon ecosystems. The just struggle of the peoples of all countries against pollution should be supported.

Principle 7

States shall take all possible steps to prevent pollution of the seas by substances that are liable to create hazards to human health, to harm living resources and marine life, to damage amenities or to interfere with other legitimate uses of the sea.

Principle 8

Economic and social development is essential for ensuring a favourable living and working environment for man and for creating conditions on earth that are necessary for the improvement of the quality of life....

Principle 21

States have, in accordance with the Charter of the United Nations and the principle of international law, the sovereign right to exploit their own resources pursuant to their own environmental policies, and the responsibility to ensure that activities within their jurisdiction or control do not cause damage to the environment of other States or of areas beyond the limits of national jurisdiction....

Principle 23

Without prejudice to such criteria as may be agreed upon by the international community, or to standards which will have to be determined nationally, it will be essential in all cases to consider the systems of values prevailing in each country and the extent of the applicability of standards which are valid for the most advanced countries but which may be inappropriate and of unwarranted social cost for the developing countries.

Rio Declaration on Environment and Development

31 *International Legal Materials* 876 (1992), United Nations Conference on Environment and Development

Principle 1

Human beings are at the centre of concerns for sustainable development. They are entitled to a healthy and productive life in harmony with nature.

Principle 2

States have, in accordance with the Charter of the United Nations and the principles of international law, the sovereign right to exploit their own resources pursuant to their own environmental and developmental policies, and the responsibility to ensure that activities within their jurisdiction or control do not cause damage to the environment of other States or of areas beyond the limits of national jurisdiction.

Principle 3

The right to development must be fulfilled so as to equitably meet developmental and environmental needs of present and future generations.

Principle 4

In order to achieve sustainable development, environmental protection shall constitute an integral part of the development process and cannot be considered in isolation from it.

Principle 5

All States and all people shall cooperate in the essential task of eradicating poverty as an indispensable requirement for sustainable development, in order to decrease the disparities in standards of living and better meet the needs of the majority of the people of the world.

Principle 6

The special situation and needs of developing countries, particularly the least developed and those most environmentally vulnerable, shall be given special priority. International actions in the field of environment and development should also address the interests and needs of all countries.

Principle 7

States shall cooperate in a spirit of global partnership to conserve, protect and restore the health and integrity of the Earth's ecosystem. In view of the different contributions to global environmental degradation, States have common but differentiated responsibilities. The developed countries acknowledge the responsibility that they bear in the international pursuit of sustainable development in view of the pressures their societies place on the global environment and of the technologies and financial resources they command.

Principle 8

To achieve sustainable development and a higher quality of life for all people, States should reduce and eliminate unsustainable patterns of production and consumption and promote appropriate demographic policies.

Principle 9

States should cooperate to strengthen endogenous capacity-building for sustainable development by improving scientific understanding through exchanges of scientific and technological knowledge, and by enhancing the development, adaptation, diffusion and transfer of technologies, including new and innovative technologies.

Principle 10

Environmental issues are best handled with the participation of all concerned citizens, at the relevant level. At the national level, each individual shall have appropriate access to information concerning the environment that is held by public authorities, including information on hazardous materials and activities in their communities, and the opportunity to participate in decision-making processes. States shall facilitate and encourage public awareness and participation by making information widely available. Effective access to judicial and administrative proceedings, including redress and remedy, shall be provided.

Principle 11

States shall enact effective environmental legislation. Environmental standards, management objectives and priorities should reflect the environmental and developmental context to which they apply. Standards applied by some countries may be inappropriate and of unwarranted economic and social cost to other countries, in particular developing countries.

Principle 12

States should cooperate to promote a supportive and open international economic system that would lead to economic growth and sustainable development in all countries, to better address the problems of environmental degradation. Trade policy measures for environmental purposes should not constitute a means of arbitrary or unjustifiable discrimination or a disguised restriction on international trade. Unilateral actions to deal with environmental challenges outside the jurisdiction of the importing country should be avoided. Environmental measures addressing transboundary or global environmental problems should, as far as possible, be based on an international consensus.

Principle 13

States shall develop national law regarding liability and compensation for the victims of pollution and other environmental damage. States shall also cooperate in an expeditious and more determined manner to develop further international law regarding liability and compensation for adverse effects of environmental damage caused by activities within their jurisdiction or control to areas beyond their jurisdiction.

Principle 14

States should effectively cooperate to discourage or prevent the relocation and transfer to other States of any activities and substances that cause severe environmental degradation or are found to be harmful to human health.

Principle 15

In order to protect the environment, the precautionary approach shall be widely applied by States according to their capabilities. Where there are threats of serious or irreversible damage, lack of full scientific certainty shall not be used as a reason for postponing cost-effective measures to prevent environmental degradation.

Principle 16

National authorities should endeavour to promote the internalization of environmental costs and the use of economic instruments, taking into account the approach that the polluter should, in principle, bear the cost of pollution, with due regard to the public interest and without distorting international trade and investment....

Principle 22

Indigenous people and their communities, and other local communities, have a vital role in environmental management and development because of their knowledge and traditional practices. States should recognize and duly support their identity, culture and interests and enable their effective participation in the achievement of sustainable development.

Principle 23

In the environment and natural resources of people under oppression, domination and occupation shall be protected.

Principle 24

Warfare is inherently destructive of sustainable development. States shall therefore respect international law providing protection for the environment in times of armed conflict and cooperate in its further development, as necessary.

NOTES
1. The international obligations to protect the environment were largely initiated by the Stockholm Declaration. As a result of the Stockholm Declaration (made by 113 States) and Conference, the United Nations Environment Programme (UNEP) was established and is now based in Nairobi, Kenya. The World Charter for Nature 1982 (UN General Assembly Resolution 37/7, 28 October 1982) followed ten years after the Stockholm Declaration and other major conferences on the environment have included one in Rio in 1992 (see extract), where more than 170 states participated, one held in Johannesburg in 2002, one held in Copenhagen in 2009, and another in Rio in 2012, where more than 190 States participated.
2. The principles of the Rio Declaration and the provisions of Agenda 21, an 800-page document setting out actions which need to be taken, are generally considered to be a turning point in increasing the commitment of States to take action to protect the environment. Undoubtedly one of the achievements of the Rio Conference was to place environmental issues high on the agenda of the international community. The Rio Conference was also a further step from the Stockholm Declaration towards more definite international legal obligations on States to protect the environment, with a number of key treaties agreed there: the United Nations Framework Convention on Climate Change (UNFCCC) and the Convention on Biological Diversity (CBD) (see Section 4A).
3. All these documents reaffirm that protection of the environment requires international cooperation. They also show an awareness of the needs of developing States, so that 'environmental imperialism' by developed States does not occur; as well as the need to continue to undertake scientific, economic and social research into the environment.

SECTION 2: ENVIRONMENTAL THEORIES

The development of international environmental law has been influenced by different philosophical approaches, particularly in regard to the rights and obligations conferred on States and individual actors.

C. Stone, 'Should Trees have Standing?—Toward Legal Rights for Natural Objects'
45 Southern Californian Law Review 450 (1972)

Now, to say that the natural environment should have rights is not to say anything as silly as that no one should be allowed to cut down a tree. We say human beings have rights, but—at least as of the time of this writing—they can be executed.... Thus, to say that the environment should have rights is not to say that it should have every right we can imagine, or even the same body of rights as human beings have. Nor is it to say that everything in the environment should have the same rights as every other thing in the environment.

What the granting of rights does involve has two sides to it. The first involves what might be called the legal-operational aspects; the second, the psychic and sociopsychic aspects.... First and most obviously, if the term ['legal rights'] is to have any content at all, an entity cannot be said to hold a legal right unless and until *some public authoritative body* is prepared to give *some amount of review* to actions that are colorably inconsistent with that 'right.' ...But for a thing to be a *holder of legal rights*, something more is needed than that some authoritative body will review the actions and processes of those who threaten it.... They are, first, that the thing can institute legal actions *at its behest*; second, that in determining the granting of legal relief, the court must take *injury to it* into account; and, third, that relief must run to the *benefit of it*....

It is not inevitable, nor is it wise, that natural objects should have no rights to seek redress on their own behalf. It is no answer to say that streams and forests cannot have standing because streams and forests cannot speak. Corporations cannot speak either; nor can states, estates, infants, incompetents, municipalities or universities. Lawyers speak for them, as they customarily do for the ordinary citizen with legal problems. One ought, I think, to handle the legal problems of natural objects as one does the problems of legal incompetents—human beings who have become vegetable....

On a parity of reasoning, we should have a system in which, when a friend of a natural object perceives it to be endangered, he can apply to a court for the creation of a guardianship. Natural objects would have standing in their own right, through a guardian; damage to and through them would be ascertained and considered as an independent factor; and they would be the beneficiaries of legal awards. But these considerations only give us the skeleton of what a meaningful rights-holding would involve. To flesh out the 'rights' of the environment demands that we provide it with a significant body of rights for it to invoke when it gets to court....

Witness the School Desegregation Cases [in the US] which, more importantly than to integrate the schools (assuming they did), awakened us to moral needs which, when made visible, could not be denied. And so here, too, in the case of the environment, the Supreme Court may find itself in a position to award 'rights' in a way that will contribute to a change in popular consciousness. It would be a modest move, to be sure, but one in furtherance of a large goal: the future of the planet as we know it.

A. Springer, *The International Law of Pollution—Protecting the Global Environment in a World of Sovereign States*

(1983)

Scholars have questioned whether the present international legal system is sufficiently developed to resolve the disputes that arise over environmental issues and, more generally, to provide a constructive, forward-looking framework for environmental protection. Reflecting the decentralized nature of the international political context, international law accords to the state a degree of control over human activity within its boundaries that often appears incompatible with effective protection of the biosphere.... In critiques perhaps less sweeping, other scholars have attacked the limitations of both the existing norms of environmental protection and the mechanisms available to implement them.

On the normative level, international law traditionally relies on state practice and treaties for the creation of rules restricting state freedom. [Particularly in environmental matters], which have only recently become of significant international concern, rules often must be deduced from general state practice in the form of principles such as the 'reasonable use' of shared resources. What constitutes a 'reasonable use' as derived from past practice may be the very activity that has given rise to the present environmental threat, and even in a contemporary setting, military and other interests may have inherent priority in the minds of national leaders. When the immediate political fate of a nation is weighed against the future of the human species, uses concomitant with political survival, even though they threaten the long-term existence of mankind, may win acceptance as reasonable....

A treaty approach, while offering the potential of greater specificity in normative standards, is also viewed as having significant limitations. Most basic is the necessity of arriving at a consensus among all states with a significant impact in an area of environmental concern. Differing state perceptions of their national self-interest and a general reluctance to commit themselves to overly restrictive rules can make this an extremely difficult and time-consuming process. Common environmental standards may be seen as imposing unfair economic burdens on developing countries, and the net result of negotiations may be weak obligations reflecting the lowest common denominator among participating states. Where prodded by major environmental accidents, such as the *Torrey Canyon* oil spill, what Goldie ['Development of International Environmental Law: An Appraisal' in Hargrove, *Law, Institutions and the Global Environment* (1976)] has termed a 'fire-brigade mentality' on the part of negotiators may produce reactive ad hoc agreements with limited general application. Furthermore, nonparticipation of states with a potential environmental impact can limit the effectiveness of whatever obligations are eventually agreed upon. In the case of the oceans, the use of 'flags of convenience could greatly stultify, if not render completely ineffective, an international regime for controlling pollution from tankers, pipelines, deep-sea mining and high seas mineral extraction from seawater.'

Finally, the consequence of violating the 'pollution limits' is often simply to impose legal liability and require payment of compensation, a penalty that may do little either to satisfy the injured party or to prevent future pollution. Thus, from a critical perspective, the standards of international environmental law are perceived as insufficiently restrictive and creating, at best, a patchwork system of normative restraints on environmental degradation....

Under traditional international law, a state must meet relatively restrictive standards to attempt to invoke the responsibility of another state for polluting activity. Injury must be shown to an interest that the claimant state is legally entitled to protect.... Both state-to-state correspondence and third-party dispute-settlement mechanisms can be criticized: the former, for its tendency to produce 'compromise' solutions designed primarily to resolve divisive international disputes rather than to promote environmental protection; and the latter, for their limited jurisdiction and inaccessibility to nonstate claimants.... Politically, environmental issues may not be seen as sufficiently significant to risk jeopardizing the government's interest in promoting cooperative relations in other areas. From a legal perspective rules of reciprocity may discourage a state from criticizing a neighbor for transboundary pollution with moderate impact if it wishes to retain the right to 'protect' similar pollution that may be generated within its borders.

International organizations have also been the target of criticism for the limited role that states have been willing to give them in the creation and implementation of binding environmental standards. With power to do little more than recommend measures for national adoption, and lacking even the ability to receive and comment on complaints of member states, the United Nations Environment program (UNEP) has been cited as an example of the 'relative primitiveness of environmental protection.' The need for a UNEP is evidenced by the previously fragmented approach to international organization in environmental matters in which a plethora of specialized agencies carved out particular areas of competence, a development hardly conductive to the holistic perspective that many feel is so urgently needed. Where international organizations do offer the potential to perform at least a catalytic function, there is still the problem of creating within the organization a sufficiently unified and environmentally conscious consensus to permit effective policy action. The Intergovernmental Maritime Consultative Organization (IMCO), for example, has been accused of being unduly influenced by the shipping interests its marine-pollution programs are designed to regulate, and the International Whaling Commission has had great difficulty in persuading its membership to adopt catch limits that recognize the endangered status of several important species.

M. Anderson, 'Human Rights Approaches to Environmental Protection'

in A. Boyle and M. Anderson (eds), *Human Rights Approaches to Environmental Protection* (1996)

What are the advantages and disadvantages of using a human rights approach rather than an approach based in regulation, criminal law, or the law of tort? Looking to the advantages, several are apparent. First, a human rights approach is a strong claim, a claim to an absolute entitlement theoretically immune to the lobbying and trade-offs which characterize bureaucratic decision-making. Its power lies in its ability to trump individual greed and short-term thinking. A second advantage is that the procedural dimensions of an environmental right can provide access to justice in a way that bureaucratic regulation, or tort law, simply cannot. A robust environmental right can mobilize redress where other remedies have failed. This is particularly important in cases like the Asian Rare Earth litigation in Malaysia, where proof of causation and other technical barriers make tort law ineffective. It was also important in the Indian context, where procedural simplicity has made environmental rights highly attractive to aggrieved parties. An environmental right may serve as the ultimate 'safety net' to catch legitimate claims which have fallen through the procedural cracks of public and private law. Thirdly, a human rights approach may stimulate concomitant political activism on environmental issues. Concerned citizens and NGOs are more likely to rally around a general statement of right than a highly technical, bureaucratic regulation expressed in legalese. Fourthly, a human rights approach can provide the conceptual link to bring local, national, and international issues within the same frame of legal judgment. At present, environmental damage is unequally distributed at both the national and international level; a non-discriminatory human rights standard could facilitate comparison, and foster political mobilization linking local concerns with more global issues. For example,...the operations of the World Bank could be made subject to a human rights standard which would apply equally to its international transactions, its national programmes, and its local projects. Fifthly, a general expression of right can be interpreted creatively as issues and contexts change. This is evident in the Indian jurisprudence, where the right to a healthy environment held to be implicit in the right to life has been given more precise definition on a case-by-case basis as specific disputes have come before the courts. Thus, definitions and trade-offs evolve gradually in the light of experience rather than needing to be defined comprehensively and rigidly in a single piece of regulatory legislation.

A number of disadvantages are also apparent.... First of all, it is not clear to what extent a simple right may address the complex and often technical issues of environmental management. Environmental protection, in both decision-making and implementation, requires a legal language capable of incorporating highly technical specifications, distinguishing among industrial processes, evaluating elusive causal relationships, and protecting complicated biological and ecological systems. Not all issues can be resolved in the simple language of rights (although environmental rights may be supplemented with technical expertise and specific standards)...[and] disputes which essentially require the balancing of interests may be more difficult to resolve where two rights-holders are involved.... Secondly, a rights approach may not address the relationships of political economy which underlie much environmental damage. The causes of environmental damage—including technology choice, forms of production, and distribution of the social product—will not be addressed by a right directed merely to their symptoms. If environmental rights serve as nothing more than symbolic gestures, as in Hungary, or as mere palliatives which inculcate a sense of environmental responsibility while denigration of the environment continues largely unabated, then those rights may be positively counter-productive, drawing attention away from the structural causes of environmental change. Just as the prescription of anti-diarrhoea drugs in the poorer villages of Bangladesh can only be an expensive and ineffective short-term remedy for people without access to clean drinking water, likewise, the right to object to environmental damage will have little effect unless the social and economic forces causing the damage are confronted directly. Thirdly, rights, especially procedural rights, may be used by affluent groups or 'cosmetic environmentalists' to protect a privileged quality of life, which may impose further environmental costs upon the dispossessed or environmentally vulnerable communities, who are in turn denied access to justice by poverty or lack of institutional skills. Legal recognition of environmental rights will not necessarily change anything unless disadvantaged groups possess economic and political power to mobilize legal institutions. Fourthly, the expansion of rights-based litigation may well displace other forms of legal remedy, such as tort law or negotiated settlements, which are better suited to environmental issues. This danger is identified in the Indian context...[where] writ petitions under the Constitution are now displacing statutory regulation and civil suits as the main means of distributing environmental benefits and burdens. This raises the twin dangers of inconsistent standards and the transfer of essentially bureaucratic functions to the courts. Fifthly...the language of human rights may politicize and draw attention to environmental claims in a way that may attract more overt opposition from polluters, or even exacerbate government repression. Sometimes what may be easily achieved by quiet lobbying and technical regulation may not be possible through public campaigns and prominent litigation. And the explicit incorporation of environmental rights into the Malaysian legal system may invite a series of statutory restrictions and limitations which may leave environmentalists with fewer rights than they held at the outset.

On balance, our deliberations show that human rights approaches to environmental protection offer many attractions, and could play a key role in fostering equitable and sustainable human communities. If very real problems of theory and practice remain, they should stimulate careful analysis and jurisprudential innovation rather than intellectual surrender.

NOTES

1. Theoretical approaches to international environmental law continue to expand (see also the final section of this chapter). In a significant development, the World Commission on Environment and Development adopted the concept of 'sustainable development' to recognise the competing claims made by many States for the preservation of the environment and by developing States for the right to development (see Section 3A). Another approach is to see an international public duty on States to act in the public interest, and that the public interest is to ensure that its citizens are not harmed by actions having effects on the environment.

2. Approaches to international environmental law are generally described in anthropocentric terms, with humans at the centre, with a responsibility to save, protect and preserve the environment. This leads, for example, to the acceptance of a human right to a clean environment (see the extract from Anderson). However, the law could be conceived in terms of an environmentally centred concern, so that the environment would be preserved for its own sake and not only to maintain human life and human interests: see *Sierra Club* v *Morton* 405 US 727 (1972) (United States Supreme Court); and Alexander Gillespie, *International Environmental Law Policy and Ethics* (2014), 1–13.

The general rules and principles of international environmental law are found in the traditional sources of international law, namely treaties and customary international law, as well as reflected in binding acts of international organisations, State practice and in 'soft law' commitments (see Chapter 2). In particular, there is now a vast array of international instruments concerning environmental matters and all States have agreed to some international instrument that contains provisions relating to the protection of the environment. In 2012, the Vienna Convention for the Protection of the Ozone Layer 1985 became the first international environmental treaty to receive universal ratification. Many international environmental law instruments utilise a framework agreement format, setting out broad 'framework' principles, which are subsequently refined and developed by the parties to the treaty at regular meetings or in protocols. International environmental law, which has developed relatively quickly in response to previously unknown threats to the environment and developments in technology, also relies to a considerable extent on a soft law approach. The following section outlines some of the main rules and principles of international environmental law.

A: Sustainable development

P. Sands, *Principles of International Environmental Law*
(3rd edn, 2012)

The term 'sustainable development' is generally considered to have been coined by the 1987 Brundtland Report, which defined it as 'development that meets the needs of the present without compromising the ability of future generations to meet their own needs'. It contains within it two concepts:

1. the concept of 'needs', in particular the essential needs of the world's poor, to which overriding priority should be given; and
2. the idea of limitations imposed, by the state of technology and social organization, on the environment's ability to meet present and future needs....

Four recurring elements appear to comprise the legal elements of the concept of 'sustainable development', as reflected in international agreements:

1. the need to preserve natural resources for the benefit of future generations (the principle of intergenerational equity);
2. the aim of exploiting natural resources in a manner which is 'sustainable', or 'prudent', or 'rational', or 'wise' or 'appropriate' (the principle of sustainable use);
3. the 'equitable' use of natural resources, which implies that use by one state must take account of the needs of other states (the principle of equitable use or intragenerational equity); and
4. the need to ensure that environmental considerations are integrated into economic and other development plans, programmes and projects, and that development needs are taken into account in applying environmental objectives (the principle of integration).

These four elements are closely related and often used in combination (and frequently interchangeably), which suggests that they do not yet have a well-established, or agreed, legal definition or status.

Danube Dam Case (Hungary v Slovakia)
ICJ Rep 1997 7, International Court of Justice

The facts of this case are set out in Chapter 3.

140. It is clear that the Project's impact upon, and its implications for, the environment are of necessity a key issue. The numerous scientific reports which have been presented to the Court by the Parties—even if their

conclusions are often contradictory—provide abundant evidence that this impact and these implications are considerable.

In order to evaluate the environmental risks, current standards must be taken into consideration. This is not only allowed by the wording of Articles 15 and 19 [of the 1977 Treaty between Hungary and Czechoslovakia], but even prescribed, to the extent that these articles impose a continuing—and thus necessarily evolving—obligation on the parties to maintain the quality of the water of the Danube and to protect nature.

The Court is mindful that, in the field of environmental protection, vigilance and prevention are required on account of the often irreversible character of damage to the environment and of the limitations inherent in the very mechanism of reparation of this type of damage.

Throughout the ages, mankind has, for economic and other reasons, constantly interfered with nature. In the past, this was often done without consideration of the effects upon the environment. Owing to new scientific insights and to a growing awareness of the risks for mankind—for present and future generations—of pursuit of such interventions at an unconsidered and unabated pace, new norms and standards have been developed, set forth in a great number of instruments during the last two decades. Such new norms have to be taken into consideration, and such new standards given proper weight, not only when States contemplate new activities but also when continuing with activities begun in the past. This need to reconcile economic development with protection of the environment is aptly expressed in the concept of sustainable development.

For the purposes of the present case, this means that the Parties together should look afresh at the effects on the environment of the operation of the Gabcikovo power plant. In particular they must find a satisfactory solution for the volume of water to be released into the old bed of the Danube and into the side-arms on both sides of the river.

JUDGE WEERAMANTRY (Separate Opinion): The problem of steering a course between the needs of development and the necessity to protect the environment is a problem alike of the law of development and the law of the environment. Both these vital and developing areas of the law require, and indeed assume, the existence of a principle which harmonizes both needs....

The people of both Hungary and Slovakia are entitled to development for the furtherance of their happiness and welfare. They are likewise entitled to the preservation of their human right to the protection of their environment ...

The protection of the environment is...a vital part of contemporary human rights doctrine, for it is a *sine qua non* for numerous human rights such as the right to health and the right to life itself. It is scarcely necessary to elaborate on this, as damage to the environment can impair and undermine all the human rights spoken of in the Universal Declaration and other human rights instruments ...

While, therefore, all peoples have the right to initiate development projects and enjoy their benefits, there is likewise a duty to ensure that those projects do not significantly damage the environment.... The concept of sustainable development is thus a principle accepted not merely by the developing countries, but one which rests on a basis of worldwide acceptance.

When we enter the arena of obligations which operate *erga omnes* rather than *inter partes*, rules based on individual fairness and procedural compliance may be inadequate...International environmental law will need to proceed beyond weighing the rights and obligations of parties within a closed compartment of individual State interest, unrelated to the global concept of humanity as a whole.

Case Concerning Pulp Mills on the River Uruguay (Argentina v Uruguay)

Merits, ICJ Rep 2010, International Court of Justice

This case concerned the authorisation by Uruguay of two pulp mills on the River Uruguay, which forms the international boundary between Uruguay and Argentina. Use of the river by the two States was managed by the 1975 Statute of the River Uruguay, a treaty, which established a bilateral river management agency (CARU) and imposed obligations on both States to cooperate and consult, and to monitor and prevent pollution arising from activities affecting the river.

174. The Court recalls that the Parties concluded the treaty embodying the 1975 Statute...requiring the Parties jointly to establish a regime for the use of the river covering, *inter alia*, provisions for preventing pollution and protecting and preserving the aquatic environment. Thus, optimum and rational utilization may be viewed as

the cornerstone of the system of co-operation established in the 1975 Statute and the joint machinery set up to implement this co-operation.

175. The Court considers that the attainment of optimum and rational utilization requires a balance between the Parties' rights and needs to use the river for economic and commercial activities on the one hand, and the obligation to protect it from any damage to the environment that may be caused by such activities, on the other. The need for this balance is reflected in various provisions of the 1975 Statute establishing rights and obligations for the Parties....

177. Regarding Article 27 [of the 1975 Statute], it is the view of the Court that its formulation reflects not only the need to reconcile the varied interests of riparian States in a transboundary context and in particular in the use of a shared natural resource, but also the need to strike a balance between the use of the waters and the protection of the river consistent with the objective of sustainable development.... The Court wishes to add that such utilization could not be considered to be equitable and reasonable if the interests of the other riparian State in the shared resource and the environmental protection of the latter were not taken into account. Consequently, it is the opinion of the Court that Article 27 embodies this interconnectedness between equitable and reasonable utilization of a shared resource and the balance between economic development and environmental protection that is the essence of sustainable development.

UN Resolution 70/1 (2015) Transforming Our World: The 2030 Agenda for Sustainable Development
Adopted by the General Assembly on 25 September 2015

9. We envisage a world in which every country enjoys sustained, inclusive and sustainable economic growth and decent work for all. A world in which consumption and production patterns and use of all natural resources—from air to land, from rivers, lakes and aquifers to oceans and seas—are sustainable. One in which democracy, good governance and the rule of law, as well as an enabling environment at the national and international levels, are essential for sustainable development, including sustained and inclusive economic growth, social development, environmental protection and the eradication of poverty and hunger. One in which development and the application of technology are climate-sensitive, respect biodiversity and are resilient. One in which humanity lives in harmony with nature and in which wildlife and other living species are protected....

16. Almost 15 years ago, the Millennium Development Goals were agreed. These provided an important framework for development and significant progress has been made in a number of areas. But the progress has been uneven, particularly in Africa, least developed countries, landlocked developing countries and small island developing States, and some of the Millennium Development Goals remain off- track, in particular those related to maternal, newborn and child health and to reproductive health. We recommit ourselves to the full realization of all the Millennium Development Goals, including the off-track Millennium Development Goals, in particular by providing focused and scaled-up assistance to least developed countries and other countries in special situations, in line with relevant support programmes. The new Agenda builds on the Millennium Development Goals and seeks to complete what they did not achieve, particularly in reaching the most vulnerable.

17. In its scope, however, the framework we are announcing today goes far beyond the Millennium Development Goals. Alongside continuing development priorities such as poverty eradication, health, education and food security and nutrition, it sets out a wide range of economic, social and environmental objectives. It also promises more peaceful and inclusive societies. It also, crucially, defines means of implementation. Reflecting the integrated approach that we have decided on, there are deep interconnections and many cross-cutting elements across the new Goals and targets.

18. We are announcing today 17 Sustainable Development Goals with 169 associated targets which are integrated and indivisible. Never before have world leaders pledged common action and endeavour across such a broad and universal policy agenda. We are setting out together on the path towards sustainable development, devoting ourselves collectively to the pursuit of global development and of 'win-win' cooperation which can bring huge gains to all countries and all parts of the world. We reaffirm that every State has, and shall freely exercise, full permanent sovereignty over all its wealth, natural resources and economic activity. We will implement the Agenda for the full benefit of all, for today's generation and for future generation.

E. Brown-Weiss, 'Our Rights and Obligations to Future Generations for the Environment'
84 *American Journal of International Law* 198 (1990)

In Fairness to Future Generations [E. Brown-Weiss (1989), I argue] that we, the human species, hold the natural environment of our planet in common with all members of our species: past generations, the present generation, and future generations. As members of the present generation, we hold the earth in trust for future generations. At the same time, we are beneficiaries entitled to use and benefit from it.

There are two relationships that must shape any theory of intergenerational equity in the context of our natural environment: our relationship to other generations of our own species and our relationship to the natural system of which we are a part.... The purpose of human society must be to realize and protect the welfare and well-being of every generation. This requires sustaining the life-support systems of the planet, the ecological processes and the environmental conditions necessary for a healthy and decent human environment....

It is not enough, however, to apply a theory of intergenerational equity only among generations. It also carries an intragenerational dimension. When future generations become living generations, they have certain rights and obligations to use and care for the planet that they can enforce against one another. Were it otherwise, members of one generation could allocate the benefits of the world's resources to some communities and the burdens of caring for it to others and still potentially claim on balance to have satisfied principles of equity among generations...

I have proposed three basic principles of intergenerational equity. First, each generation should be required to conserve the diversity of the natural and cultural resource base, so that it does not unduly restrict the options available to future generations in solving their problems and satisfying their own values, and should also be entitled to diversity comparable to that enjoyed by previous generations. This principle is called 'conservation of options.' Second, each generation should be required to maintain the quality of the planet so that it is passed on in no worse condition than that in which it was received, and should also be entitled to planetary quality comparable to that enjoyed by previous generations. This is the principle of 'conservation of quality.' Third, each generation should provide its members with equitable rights of access to the legacy of past generations and should conserve this access for future generations. This is the principle of 'conservation of access.' These proposed principles constrain the actions of the present generation in developing and using the planet, but within these constraints do not dictate how each generation should manage its resources.

These principles of intergenerational equity form the basis of a set of intergenerational obligations and rights, or planetary rights and obligations, that are held by each generation. These rights and obligations derive from each generation's position as part of the intertemporal entity of human society.... The planetary, or intergenerational, rights proposed in *In Fairness to Future Generations* are not rights possessed by individuals. They are, instead, *generational* rights, which must be conceived of in the temporal context of generation. Generations hold these rights as groups in relation to other generations—past, present and future....

Enforcement of these intergenerational rights is appropriately done by a guardian or representative of future generations as a *group*, not of future individuals, who are of necessity indeterminate. While the holder of the right may lack the capacity to bring grievances forward and hence depends upon the representative's decision to do so, this inability does not affect the existence of the right or the obligation associated with it.

NOTES
1. The principle of sustainable development recognises that the right to development is not absolute. Principles of sustainable development encourage development in a manner and by methods which do not compromise the ability of future generations, and other States, to meet their own needs. While the exact normative status of the principle is unclear, the concept is reflected in a number of different treaties and instruments. The concept was invoked in the *Danube Dams* and *Pulp Mills* cases above. See also Virginie Barral, 'Sustainable Development in International Law: Nature and Operation of an Evolutive Legal Norm' (2012) *European Journal of International Law* 23, 377.
2. The concept of intergenerational equity in relation to international environmental law was developed by Brown-Weiss, though the concept of custodianship on behalf of future generations is much older (e.g. *Pacific Fur Seals Arbitration* (1893) 1 Moore's Int Arb Awards 755). It is found in many of the major environmental law instruments, including the Convention on International Trade in Endangered Species of Wild Fauna and Flora 1963 (see Section 4A(d)) and in the Preamble to the International Whaling Convention 1946. Intergenerational equity essentially comprises two elements: an inter/intra-generational element, where there is a relationship

that is both spatial (between members of the present generation) and temporal (between members of future generations); and an equity, or fairness, element. The precautionary principle (considered in Section 3C) could be considered to be part of intergenerational equity, and technology transfer (being part of the obligation of cooperation) could be considered as part of intragenerational equity. In *Minos Oposa* v *Secretary of the Department of Environment and Natural Resources*, the Supreme Court of the Philippines adopted Brown-Weiss's theory on intergenerational equity when deciding whether a group had standing to sue on environmental issues (33 ILM 173 (1994)).

3. The Sustainable Development Goals are contained in the '2030 Agenda for Sustainable Development', the outcome document of the UN Sustainable Development Summit held in New York in September 2015. They came into force in January 2016, replacing the Millennium Development Goals that expired in 2015. They are intended as a blueprint for international development for the next 15 years and seek to integrate the environmental, social and economic dimensions of sustainable development.

B: Prevention of transboundary pollution or environmental harm

Trail Smelter Arbitration (US v Canada)
3 RIAA 1905 (1941), Arbitral Tribunal

A smelter commenced production in 1896 near Trail, British Columbia, Canada. From 1925 to at least 1937, damage occurred in the state of Washington, United States, due to the sulphur dioxide emitted from the smelter. The two States agreed to submit the dispute to arbitration to determine the amount of compensation payable but, importantly, Canada did not dispute liability. The Tribunal decided that damage had occurred since 1 January 1932, and that the indemnity to be paid was $78,000.

The Tribunal...finds that...under the principles of international law, as well as of the law of the United States, no State has the right to use or permit the use of its territory in such a manner as to cause injury by fumes in or to the territory of another or the properties or persons therein, when the case is of serious consequence and the injury is established by clear and convincing evidence....

Considering the circumstances of the case, the Tribunal holds that the Dominion of Canada is responsible in international law for the conduct of the Trail Smelter.... [I]t is, therefore, the duty of the Government of the Dominion of Canada to see to it that this conduct should be in conformity with the obligation of the Dominion under international law as herein determined.... So long as the present conditions in the Columbia River Valley prevail, the Trail Smelter shall be required to refrain from causing any damage through fumes in the State of Washington; the damaged herein referred to and its extent being such as would be recoverable under the decisions of the courts of the United States in suits between private individuals. The indemnity for such damage should be fixed in such manner as the Governments...should agree upon.

International Law Commission, Commentary on the Articles on the Prevention of Transboundary Harm from Hazardous Activities
Yearbook of the International Law Commission 2001, Vol II, 148

The ILC has been working on the topic of international liability for injurious consequences arising out of acts not prohibited by international law since 1978. This part of the study, on the prevention of transboundary harm from hazardous activities, led to the adoption by the General Assembly in 2008 of a set of articles on prevention.

The concept of prevention has assumed great significance and topicality. The emphasis upon the duty to prevent as opposed to the obligation to repair, remedy or compensate has several important aspects. Prevention should be a preferred policy because compensation in case of harm often cannot restore the situation prevailing prior to the event or accident. Discharge of the duty of prevention or due diligence is all the more required as knowledge regarding the operation of hazardous activities, materials used and the process of managing them and the risks involved is steadily growing. From a legal point of view, the enhanced ability to trace the chain of causation, i.e. the physical link between the cause (activity) and the effect (harm), and even the several intermediate links in such a chain of causation, makes it also imperative for operators of hazardous activities to take all steps necessary to prevent harm. In any event, prevention as a policy is better than cure.

International Law Commission, Articles on Prevention of Transboundary Harm from Hazardous Activities (2001)

UN GA Res 62/68, 6 December 2007

Article 3 Prevention

The State of origin shall take all appropriate measures to prevent significant transboundary harm or at any event to minimize the risk thereof.

Article 4 Cooperation

States concerned shall cooperate in good faith and, as necessary, seek the assistance of one or more competent international organizations in preventing significant transboundary harm or at any event in minimizing the risk thereof.

Case Concerning Pulp Mills on the River Uruguay (Argentina v Uruguay)

Merits, ICJ Rep 2010, International Court of Justice

The facts of this case are set out in Section 3A.

101. The Court points out that the principle of prevention, as a customary rule, has its origins in the due diligence that is required of a State in its territory. It is 'every State's obligation not to allow knowingly its territory to be used for acts contrary to the rights of other States' (*Corfu Channel (United Kingdom* v. *Albania), Merits, Judgment, I.C.J. Reports 1949*, p. 22). A State is thus obliged to use all the means at its disposal in order to avoid activities which take place in its territory, or in any area under its jurisdiction, causing significant damage to the environment of another State. This Court has established that this obligation 'is now part of the corpus of international law relating to the environment' (*Legality of the Threat or Use of Nuclear Weapons, Advisory Opinion, I.C.J. Reports 1996 (I)*, p. 242, para. 29).

102. In the view of the Court, the obligation to inform CARU allows for the initiation of co-operation between the Parties which is necessary in order to fulfil the obligation of prevention …

103. The Court observes that with regard to the River Uruguay, which constitutes a shared resource, 'significant damage to the other party'…may result from impairment of navigation, the régime of the river or the quality of its waters….

105. The Court considers that the State planning activities…is required to inform CARU as soon as it is in possession of a plan which is sufficiently developed to enable CARU to make the preliminary assessment…of whether the proposed works might cause significant damage to the other party. At that stage, the information provided will not necessarily consist of a full assessment of the environmental impact of the project, which will often require further time and resources, although, where more complete information is available, this should, of course, be transmitted to CARU to give it the best possible basis on which to make its preliminary assessment. In any event, the duty to inform CARU will become applicable at the stage when the relevant authority has had the project referred to it with the aim of obtaining initial environmental authorization and before the granting of that authorization….

204. It is the opinion of the Court that in order for the Parties properly to comply with their obligations…they must, for the purposes of protecting and preserving the aquatic environment with respect to activities which may be liable to cause transboundary harm, carry out an environmental impact assessment…. In this sense, the obligation to protect and preserve…has to be interpreted in accordance with a practice, which in recent years has gained so much acceptance among States that it may now be considered a requirement under general international law to undertake an environmental impact assessment where there is a risk that the

proposed industrial activity may have a significant adverse impact in a transboundary context, in particular, on a shared resource. Moreover, due diligence, and the duty of vigilance and prevention which it implies, would not be considered to have been exercised, if a party planning works liable to affect the régime of the river or the quality of its waters did not undertake an environmental impact assessment on the potential effects of such works.

205. The Court observes that neither the 1975 Statute nor general international law specify the scope and content of an environmental impact assessment.... Consequently, it is the view of the Court that it is for each State to determine in its domestic legislation or in the authorization process for the project, the specific content of the environmental impact assessment required in each case, having regard to the nature and magnitude of the proposed development and its likely adverse impact on the environment as well as to the need to exercise due diligence in conducting such an assessment. The Court also considers that an environmental impact assessment must be conducted prior to the implementation of a project. Moreover, once operations have started and, where necessary, throughout the life of the project, continuous monitoring of its effects on the environment shall be undertaken.

NOTES

1. The *Trail Smelter* decision was that there is an obligation on States not to cause transboundary environmental damage. This obligation is often known as the 'preventative principle', 'Principle 21/2' (as it is based on the identical words of Principle 21 of the Stockholm Declaration and Principle 2 of the Rio Declaration (see Section 1B) or the 'good neighbour principle'. The principle provides that States have 'the responsibility to ensure that activities within their jurisdiction or control do not cause damage to the environment of other States or of areas beyond the limits of national jurisdiction'. See also the due diligence obligations on States in relation to mining in the deep seabed, as set out in Chapter 10.

2. This obligation has been repeated in many international instruments and is customary international law, as confirmed by the ICJ in the *Pulp Mills Case* (see Sections 3A and B). The obligation includes the obligation to prevent, reduce and control pollution and the effects of transboundary harm. The rule requires States to adopt a due diligence approach to transboundary harm, introducing laws, regulations, policies and practices which prevent or minimise the risk of environmental harm and to encourage the use of best environmental technology and practices.

3. The preventative principle includes an obligation to provide information on environmental damage and to cooperate in the mitigation and reduction of harm caused. The obligation to cooperate is found in most of the major environmental law instruments, such as in Article 9 of the Rio Declaration (see Section 1B). The obligation to cooperate has many elements, including notification and prior consultation as to possible transboundary risks and emergency notification, response and assistance in the event of an accident or emergency likely to cause environmental harm. It also extends to obtaining an environmental risk assessment. The ICJ has confirmed that the due diligence principle does not apply only to industrial activities, but applies generally applies generally to proposed activities which may have a significant adverse impact in a transboundary context: see *Certain activities carried out by Nicaragua in the Border Area (Costa Rica v Nicaragua)* and *Construction of a Road in Costa Rica along the San Juan River (Nicaragua v Costa Rica)*, Judgment 16 December 2015.

C: Precautionary principle

Framework Convention on Climate Change 1992
31 *International Legal Materials* 849 (1992)

This Convention is discussed in Section 4A.

Article 3: Principles
The Parties should take precautionary measures to anticipate, prevent or minimize the causes of climate change and mitigate its adverse effects. Where there are threats of serious or irreversible damage, lack of full scientific certainty should not be used as a reason for postponing such measures, taking into account that policies and measures to deal with climate change should be cost-effective so as to ensure global benefits at the lowest possible cost. To achieve this, such policies and measures should take into account different socio-economic contexts, be comprehensive, cover all relevant sources, sinks and reservoirs of greenhouse gases and adaptation, and comprise all economic sectors. Efforts to address climate change may be carried out cooperatively by interested Parties.

Southern Bluefin Tuna (Provisional Measures) (Australia and New Zealand v Japan)

38 *International Legal Materials* 1624 (1999), International Tribunal for the Law of the Sea

In 1999, Australia and New Zealand filed a request for provisional measures against Japan. The application alleged that Japan had failed to comply with its obligations under the United Nations Convention on the Law of the Sea 1982 (UNCLOS) (see Section 4 and Chapter 10) to conserve and manage the stock of southern bluefin tuna.

77. *Considering* that, in the view of the Tribunal, the parties should in the circumstances act with prudence and caution to ensure that effective conservation measures are taken to prevent serious harm to the stock of southern bluefin tuna;

78. *Considering* that the parties should intensify their efforts to cooperate with other participants in the fishery for southern bluefin tuna with a view to ensuring conservation and promoting the objective of optimum utilization of the stock;

79. *Considering* that there is scientific uncertainty regarding measures to be taken to conserve the stock of southern bluefin tuna and that there is no agreement among the parties as to whether the conservation measures taken so far have led to the improvement in the stock of southern bluefin tuna;

80. *Considering* that, although the Tribunal cannot conclusively assess the scientific evidence presented by the parties, it finds that measures should be taken as a matter of urgency to preserve the rights of the parties and to avert further deterioration of the southern bluefin tuna stock;

JUDGE LAING (Separate Opinion):

14. The notion of environmental precaution largely stems from diplomatic practice and treaty-making in the spheres, originally, of international marine pollution and, now, of biodiversity, climate change, pollution generally and, broadly, the environment. Its main thesis is that, in the face of serious risk to or grounds (as appropriately qualified) for concern about the environment, scientific uncertainty or the absence of complete proof should not stand in the way of positive action to minimize risks or take actions of a conservatory, preventative or curative nature. In addition to scientific uncertainty, the most frequently articulated conditions or circumstances are concerns of an intergenerational nature and forensic or proof difficulties, generally in the context of rapid change and perceived high risks. The thrust of the notion is vesting a broad dispensation to policy makers, seeking to provide guidance to administrative and other decision-makers and shifting the burden of proof to the State in control of the territory from which the harm might emanate or to the responsible actor. The notion has been rapidly adopted in most recent instruments and policy documents on the protection and preservation of the environment.

15. Even as questioning of the acceptability of the precautionary notion diminishes, challenges increase regarding such specifics as: the wide potential ambit of its coverage; the clarity of operational criteria; the monetary costs of environmental regulation; possible public health risks associated with the very remedies improvised to avoid risk; diversity and vagueness of articulations of the notion; uncertainties about attendant obligations, and the imprecision and subjectivity of such a value-laden notion. Nevertheless, the notion has been 'broadly accepted for international action, even if the consequence of its application in a given situation remains open to interpretation' (A. D'Amato and K. Engel, *International Environmental Law Anthology* (1996), p. 22).

NOTES

1. The precautionary principle is found in most of the major environmental law instruments, at least since 1992, such as in Article 15 of the Rio Declaration (see Section 1B) and Article 6 and Annex II of the Agreement for the Implementation of the Provisions of the United Nations Convention on the Law of the Sea (UNCLOS) relating to the Conservation and Management of Highly Migratory Fish Stocks 1995 (34 ILM 1542 (1995).

2. The precautionary principle is a vital part of the long-term protection of the environment, especially in the usual environmental situation where there is no scientific certainty. The existence of this uncertainty cannot be used, under this principle, as a justification of action or inaction due to the possibility of serious or irreversible damage by such action or inaction.

3. The precautionary principle has been argued by States in a number of international proceedings, including the *Danube Dam* and *Pulp Mills* cases before the ICJ. The concept was applied by the Seabed Disputes Chamber of the International Tribunal on the Law of the Sea (ITLOS) in its Advisory Opinion on *Responsibilities and Obligations of States Sponsoring Persons and Entities with respect to Activities in the Area* (see Chapter 10).

4. Several commentators and governments, as well as the Seabed Disputes Chamber of ITLOS in the above *Advisory Opinion* have asserted that the principle reflects customary international law. Boyle has suggested that the more appropriate way to view the principle is as a general principle, without legal effect, that can influence 'the interpretation, application and development of other rules of law [for example,] existing rules on state responsibility . . . from this perspective, the real importance of the precautionary principle is that it redefines existing rules of international law on control of environmental risks and conservation of natural resources and brings them into play at an earlier stage than before. No longer is it necessary to show that significant or irreversible harm is certain or likely before requiring that appropriate preventative measures be taken' (A. Boyle, 'The Environmental Jurisprudence of the International Tribunal for the Law of the Sea' (2007) 22 *International Journal of Marine and Coastal Law* 369, 375).

5. One issue is which party should bear the burden of proof when applying the precautionary principle. The traditional approach places the burden of proof on those contesting an activity to establish that the activity will cause environmental harm. It is now being suggested that a new approach to this issue should be adopted, such that the person who wishes to carry out an activity must prove that environmental harm will not result. However, in the decision on the merits in the *Pulp Mills Case* (see Sections 3A and B), the ICJ commented that 'while a precautionary approach may be relevant in the interpretation and application of the provisions of the Statute [the 1975 Statute on the River Uruguay], it does not follow that it operates as a reversal of the burden of proof' (para. 164).

D: Common but differentiated responsibility

Framework Convention on Climate Change 1992
31 *International Legal Materials* 849 (1992)

This Convention is discussed in Section 4A.

Article 3 Principles

1. The Parties should protect the climate system for the benefit of present and future generations of humankind, on the basis of equity and in accordance with their common but differentiated responsibilities and respective capabilities. Accordingly, the developed country Parties should take the lead in combating climate change and the adverse effects thereof.

NOTES

1. The principle of common but differentiated responsibility is set out in Principle 7 of the Rio Declaration (see Section 1B). The principle is perhaps more pronounced in the area of climate change than in any other area, with the Framework Convention on Climate Change (UNFCCC) and the Kyoto Protocol both incorporating the principle (see Section 4A). The differing responsibility and obligations of developing and developed States also featured heavily in the negotiations for an agreement to replace or amend the Kyoto Protocol (see Section 4A).

2. The principle incorporates two elements. First, a responsibility to undertake obligations for the preservation of a shared resource, generally where the resource is beyond the jurisdiction of any one State. Second, differentiated environmental standards for developing States. The justification for such different standards is often based on such factors as the special needs of developing States, historical accountability of developed States for existing environmental harm, and the ability of developed States to pay for preventative and restorative measures.

3. It is arguable that the principle enables watered-down or deferred obligations for some States, which undermines the effectiveness of the environmental protection mechanisms included in the treaty regime.

E: Reparation: polluter-pays principle

Framework Convention on Climate Change 1992
31 *International Legal Materials* 849 (1992)

Article 3
3. The Parties should take precautionary measures to anticipate, prevent or minimize the causes of climate change and mitigate its adverse effects. Where there are threats of serious or irreversible damage, lack of full scientific certainty should not be used as a reason for postponing such measures, taking into account that policies and measures to deal with climate change should be cost-effective so as to ensure global benefits at the lowest possible cost. To achieve this, such policies and measures should take into account different socio-economic contexts, be comprehensive, cover all relevant sources, sinks and reservoirs of greenhouse gases and adaptation, and comprise all economic sectors. Efforts to address climate change may be carried out cooperatively by interested Parties.

International Law Commission, Principles on the Allocation of Loss in the Case of Transboundary Harm Arising out of Hazardous Activities
GA Res 61/36, 4 December 2006

Principle 4
Prompt and adequate compensation
1. Each State should take all necessary measures to ensure that prompt and adequate compensation is available for victims of transboundary damage caused by hazardous activities located within its territory or otherwise under its jurisdiction or control.

2. These measures should include the imposition of liability on the operator or, where appropriate, other person or entity. Such liability should not require proof of fault. Any conditions, limitations or exceptions to such liability shall be consistent with draft principle 3.

3. These measures should also include the requirement on the operator or, where appropriate, other person or entity, to establish and maintain financial security such as insurance, bonds or other financial guarantees to cover claims of compensation.

4. In appropriate cases, these measures should include the requirement for the establishment of industry-wide funds at the national level.

5. In the event that the measures under the preceding paragraphs are insufficient to provide adequate compensation, the State of origin should also ensure that additional financial resources are made available.

NOTES
1. The basis of the polluter-pays principle is that the costs of pollution should be borne by the person responsible for causing the harm. It is mainly invoked in the allocation of civil liability and State responsibility for environmental harm. The principle has been incorporated in a number of international environmental treaties.
2. The legal status of the principle is uncertain, as is its application in particular situations. The ILC principles are based on the polluter-pays principle, yet they are non-binding and are considered by some States to be aspirational in nature, rather than reflective of customary international law. The General Assembly commended the principles to States, but has deferred consideration of their final status.

F: State responsibility, compliance and enforcement

C. Redgwell, 'International Environmental Law'
in M. Evans (ed), *International Law* (4th edn, 2014)

A question of over-arching importance is what happens in the event of the breach of an international obligation? Here the traditional rules regarding State responsibility...would apply. Yet these rules are of only limited assistance in the environmental field for a number of reasons. One is that responsibility rules generally operate once damage has already occurred, rather than to prevent damage occurring in the first place. The second difficulty, illustrated particularly well by the climate change example, is that harm may be incremental and difficult to link to the specific actions or omissions of another State. Problems of causation and proof will loom large. The generally non-reciprocal character of international environmental obligations will also render it difficult to meet the requirement of breach of an obligation owed to another State. Both the *Trail Smelter* Arbitration between the United States and Canada and the *Gabčíkovo-Nagymaros Dam* dispute between Hungary and Slovakia saw the application of traditional rules on State responsibility because of the bilateral character of the dispute and the obligations thereunder. Had it proceeded to the merits, the ICJ case brought in 1974 against France by Australia and New Zealand regarding French atmospheric nuclear testing would have likewise largely fit within this bilateral model. But what of the example of a breach by a State of its obligation to conserve biological diversity, expressly acknowledged as 'the common concern of humankind'? A complainant State is required to show that the obligation is owed to it and (usually) that injury has resulted to it in order for standing requirements to be satisfied; there is no such thing (yet) under international law as an *actio popularis* whereby a State may bring an action on behalf of the international community. There are glimmerings of such an approach in Articles 42 and 48 of the 2001 Articles on State Responsibility drafted by the International Law Commission, wherein the possibility exists for a State party to a multilateral treaty to complain of breach of a multilateral obligation by another State party. While there is not yet been international judicial recognition of this possibility in the environmental context, in the 2012 *Obligation to Prosecute or Extradite Case (Belgium v Senegal)*, the ICJ explicitly recognised that the Convention against Torture imposed obligations *erga omnes partes* giving rise to a common interest in compliance and 'the entitlement of each State party to the Convention to make a claim concerning the cessation of an alleged breach by another State party' [para. 69].

There are several consequences of the inadequacies of traditional rules of State responsibility for the development of international environmental law. The first is a relative paucity of cases at the international level in which environmental matters have figured largely. Recourse to the dispute settlement under international environmental treaties is rare…Moreover, few dispute settlement clauses in international environmental treaties provide for compulsory third-party settlement of interstate claims…Sparse examples include the Ozone Layer Convention and the Montreal Protocol, and the Framework Convention on Climate Change (FCCC) and the Kyoto Protocol. A second consequence has been pressure further to develop the rules of State responsibility, including standing. Few environmental treaties address standing; rarer still is to provide for reciprocal standing for non-State actors.…

A third consequence is the development of alternatives to traditional dispute settlement techniques under specific treaty instruments directly to address the issue of non-compliance with treaty obligations from both a facilitative and a coercive point of view. The 1987 Montreal Protocol is pioneering in this regard, establishing the first non-compliance procedure in an environment agreement. A handful of other treaty instruments have established implementation and compliance procedures, including the 1997 Kyoto Protocol to the 1992 Framework Convention on Climate Change, the 1989 Basel Convention on the Transboundary Movement of Hazardous Wastes and their Disposal, the 2000 Cartagena Protocol to the 1992 Convention on the Conservation of Biological Diversity, and the 1998 Aarhus Convention on Access to Information, Public Participation in Decision-Making, and Access to Justice in Environmental Matters. These generally exist alongside traditional dispute settlement clauses and are suspended in the event of the invocation of traditional dispute settlement procedures…Finally, a further consequence of the inadequacies of State responsibility in the environmental field is the development of liability regimes which side-step the necessity to rely on the route of inter-State claims.… the development of specific liability instruments has been particularly marked in the field of hazardous activities with transboundary consequences (eg, nuclear activities, vessel source oil pollution, and hazardous waste movements) and in the protection of common spaces.

NOTES

1. The conditions determining the international responsibility of a State are set out in Chapter 11. While it is questionable that applying certain provisions on State responsibility to environmental claims is appropriate (in particular, the provisions on standing), it is clear that some principles, such as attribution of conduct to the State, do apply. For example, several of the extracts in this chapter demonstrate that responsibility may be incurred where a State corporation causes pollution, or even where a State refuses to take any legislative, judicial or administrative action against perpetrators of environmental damage (who are often non-State actors).

2. Principles of liability and compensation would also presumably apply to environmental harm. The International Law Commission has produced principles, endorsed by the UN General

Assembly, on allocation of loss in the case of transboundary harm arising out of hazardous activities. The principles aim to ensure prompt and adequate compensation to victims of transboundary harm and to protect and preserve the environment in the event of transboundary damage (Principle 3). This is achieved by requiring States to take all necessary measures to achieve these objectives, including by imposing liability on the operator.

3. As Redgwell notes, the ICJ has considered a number of cases which raised environmental questions. The Statute of the ICJ (see Chapter 16) provides for a Chamber for Environmental Disputes, established in 1993. However, this mechanism was never used and in 2006 the ICJ announced that it would no longer elect judges to serve in this Chamber, though cases involving environmental matters continue to be argued before the Court.

4. Several other tribunals and bodies have been involved in dispute settlement concerning environmental issues. The ITLOS has heard several cases concerning directly the protection of the marine environment (see Chapter 10). The World Trade Organization and panels under the NAFTA have considered trade disputes with environmental aspects, and human rights tribunals and commissions have also considered the relationship between human rights and the environment. The European Court of Justice has also become involved in environmental issues, both in its attempts to balance the requirements of market integration with environmental issues (see Section 5C) and in regulating disputes between member States. The Permanent Court of Arbitration has adopted Optional Rules for the arbitration of disputes concerning natural resources or the environment (41 ILM 202 (2002)). There is evidence of a trend of increasing reliance on dispute settlement mechanisms in relation to environmental issues. This evidence also suggests that environmental concerns may give rise to a multiplicity of jurisdictional claims, with several different tribunals potentially able to exercise jurisdiction.

SECTION 4: SELECTED ENVIRONMENTAL TREATIES

There are hundreds of international and regional environmental law treaties and other instruments. The following is a selection of some of the more interesting and broad-based ones.

A: Global treaties

(a) Ozone

Vienna Convention for the Protection of the Ozone Layer 1985
26 *International Legal Materials* 1516 (1987)

As at March 2016, 197 parties have ratified this Convention.

Article 1 Definitions
For the purposes of this Convention:
1.1 'The ozone layer' means the layer of atmospheric ozone above the planetary boundary layer.

Article 2 General obligations
1. The Parties shall take appropriate measures in accordance with the provisions of this Convention and of those protocols in force to which they are party to protect human health and the environment against adverse effects resulting or likely to result from human activities which modify or are likely to modify the ozone layer.

2. To this end the Parties shall, in accordance with the means at their disposal and their capabilities:
  (a) Co-operate by means of systematic observation, research and information exchange in order to better understand and assess the effects of human activities on the ozone layer and the effects on human health and the environment from modification of the ozone layer;

(b) Adopt appropriate legislative or administrative measures and co-operate in harmonising appropriate policies to control, limit, reduce or prevent human activities under their jurisdiction or control should it be found that these activities have or are likely to have adverse effects resulting from modification or likely modification of the ozone layer;

(c) Co-operate in the formulation of agreed measures, procedures and standards for the implementation of this Convention, with a view to the adoption of protocols and annexes;

(d) Co-operate with competent international bodies to implement effectively this Convention and protocols to which they are party.

3. The provisions of this Convention shall in no way affect the right of Parties to adopt, in accordance with international law, domestic measures additional to those referred to in paragraphs 1 and 2 above, nor shall they affect additional domestic measures already taken by a Party, provided that these measures are not incompatible with their obligations under this Convention.

4. The application of this article shall be based on relevant scientific and technical considerations.

NOTES

1. One of the first environmental treaties involving both Western and Eastern European States was the Convention on Long-Range Transboundary Air Pollution (18 ILM 1442 (1979)). The Convention provides a system for the exchange of environmental information, a common method adopted both to advance general knowledge on the pollution of the air and sea and also as a (albeit weak) supervisory means to ensure compliance with the Convention.

2. The preamble to the Vienna Convention for the Protection of the Ozone Layer refers to Principle 21 of the Stockholm Declaration. However, it contained few substantive obligations, with parties required only to assess the causes and effects of ozone depletion, to transmit information and to exchange information and technology. The Convention did not list the substances to be regulated by the Convention; instead, it lists in an Annex substances that may have an effect on the ozone layer. It is therefore largely a framework convention and required further action by the States parties. It also became clear that scientific and technological advances had impacted upon the ability to reduce further, and to reduce more rapidly, pollutants in the ozone layer. The Ozone Convention was subsequently supplemented by a Protocol, adopted in Montreal in 1987 and entering into force in 1989. The Protocol was further amended in 1990 (see 30 ILM 539 (1991)). As at March 2016, there are 197 parties to the Protocol. The Protocol has been amended on four occasions, in 1990 (London Amendment), 1992 (Copenhagen Amendment), 1997 (Montreal Amendment) and 1999 (Beijing Amendment).

3. The Montreal Protocol represents a significant improvement on the Ozone Convention, with several important advances. First, it sets binding targets for reducing and eliminating consumption. Second, it expanded the range of ozone-depleting substances subject to regulation. Third, the Protocol includes a formal non-compliance regime, the first such regime in a multilateral environmental treaty. Fourth, the Protocol specifically provides for the position of developing States, recognising their limited contribution to the depletion of the ozone layer. Article 5 included a 10-year opt out provision for developing States from the compliance regime (and the obligation to phase out commenced in 1999), while the multilateral fund enables the transfer of technology and technical cooperation to such States to encourage compliance. Finally, the Protocol attempts to resolve the issue of non-States parties, by prohibiting trade in controlled substances or products containing controlled substances between parties and non-parties.

4. The regime for protection of the ozone layer appears to have been largely successful, with most developed States phasing out controlled substances by the agreed timetable (1996), and developing States have reduced consumption. Provided the Convention and the Protocol continue to be adhered to, it is estimated ozone losses will have recovered by 2050. The former UN Secretary-General has called the Protocol 'perhaps the single most successful international agreement to date'.

5. Nuclear energy is a source of major risk for every State and the environment, regardless of whether a particular State has chosen to utilise this source of power, as was demonstrated by the Chernobyl reactor accident in 1986. Yet, as the environmental harm caused by other forms of energy become apparent, many States are considering new, or increased, reliance on nuclear power. For such States, it is a matter of assessing the risks of this form of energy, taking into

account mechanisms for management of those risks, against the benefits to be gained from nuclear power, including its impact upon other risks, such as climate change. The International Atomic Energy Agency (IAEA) was established to encourage and spread the use of nuclear power. One of its functions is the regulation of the risks of nuclear power, including setting (non-binding) standards for health and safety and entering into safeguards agreements. The IAEA can (on a non-compulsory basis) act as a safety inspector for nuclear power facilities. In addition to the IAEA, there are several international agreements concerning nuclear safety (e.g. the Convention on Nuclear Safety 1994 and the Joint Convention on the Safety of Spent Fuel and Radioactive Waste Management 1997) and on cooperation and assistance in the event of a nuclear accident.

6. Another long-running issue in international environmental law concerns the impact of nuclear testing on the atmosphere. Despite a variety of treaties, such as the Comprehensive Test Ban Treaty 1996 (35 ILM 1439 (1996) (not yet in force), and cases before the ICJ (see *Nuclear Tests Case* in Chapter 3 and *Legality of the Threat or Use of Nuclear Weapons Opinion* below), certain States continue to test nuclear weapons. While the five permanent members of the Security Council have agreed not to test weapons, other States, such as North Korea, continue to do so. The Nuclear Non-Proliferation Treaty, which recognises the right to use nuclear power for peaceful purposes, ties this right to non-proliferation of nuclear weapons, and is being considered in a case brought by the Marshall Islands to the ICJ in 2016.

(b) Climate change

Framework Convention on Climate Change 1992
31 *International Legal Materials* 849 (1992)

This treaty was signed during the Rio Conference (see Section 1B) and, as at March 2016, 197 parties, including the EU, have ratified this Convention.

Article 2 Objective

The ultimate objective of this Convention and any related legal instruments that the Conference of the Parties may adopt is to achieve, in accordance with the relevant provisions of the Convention, stabilization of greenhouse gas concentrations in the atmosphere at a level that would prevent dangerous anthropogenic interference with the climate system. Such a level should be achieved within a time-frame sufficient to allow ecosystems to adapt naturally to climate change, to ensure that food production is not threatened and to enable economic development to proceed in a sustainable manner....

Article 4 Commitments

1. All Parties, taking into account their common but differentiated responsibilities and their specific national and regional development priorities, objectives and circumstances, shall:

    (a) Develop, periodically update, publish and make available to the Conference of the Parties, in accordance with Article 12, national inventories of anthropogenic emissions by sources and removals by sinks of all greenhouse gases not controlled by the Montreal Protocol, using comparable methodologies to be agreed upon by the Conference of the Parties;

    (b) Formulate, implement, publish and regularly update national and, where appropriate, regional programmes containing measures to mitigate climate change by addressing anthropogenic emissions by sources and removals by sinks of all greenhouse gases not controlled by the Montreal Protocol, and measures to facilitate adequate adaptation to climate change; ...

    (j) Communicate to the Conference of the Parties information related to implementation, in accordance with Article 12.

7. The extent to which developing country Parties will effectively implement their commitments under the Convention will depend on the effective implementation by developed country Parties of their commitments under the Convention related to financial resources and transfer of technology and will take fully into account that economic and social development and poverty eradication are the first and overriding priorities of the developing country Parties.

8. In the implementation of the commitments in this Article, the Parties shall give full consideration to what actions are necessary under the Convention, including actions related to funding, insurance and the transfer of

technology, to meet the specific needs and concerns of developing country Parties arising from the adverse effects of climate change and/or the impact of the implementation of response measures, especially on:

    (a) Small island countries;

    (b) Countries with low-lying coastal areas;

    (c) Countries with arid and semi-arid areas, forested areas and areas liable to forest decay;

    (d) Countries with areas prone to natural disasters;

    (e) Countries with areas liable to drought and desertification;

    (f) Countries with areas of high urban atmospheric pollution;

    (g) Countries with areas with fragile ecosystems, including mountainous ecosystems;

    (h) Countries whose economies are highly dependent on income generated from the production, processing and export, and/or on consumption of fossil fuels and associated energy-intensive products; and

    (i) Land-locked and transit countries.

Further, the Conference of the Parties may take actions, as appropriate, with respect to this paragraph....

Article 7 Conference of the parties

1. A Conference of the Parties is hereby established.

2. The Conference of the Parties, as the supreme body of this Convention, shall keep under regular review the implementation of the Convention and any related legal instruments that the Conference of the Parties may adopt, and shall make, within its mandate, the decisions necessary to promote the effective implementation of the Convention. To this end, it shall:

    (a) Periodically examine the obligations of the Parties and the institutional arrangements under the Convention, in the light of the objective of the Convention, the experience gained in its implementation and the evolution of scientific and technological knowledge;

    (b) Promote and facilitate the exchange of information on measures adopted by the Parties to address climate change and its effects, taking into account the differing circumstances, responsibilities and capabilities of the Parties and their respective commitments under the Convention;

Kyoto Protocol Conference of the Parties to the Framework Convention on Climate Change 1998

37 International Legal Materials 22 (1998)

This Protocol has been ratified by 192 parties, including the European Union, as at March 2016, and is the result of negotiations by the Conference of Parties established under Article 7 of the Framework Convention.

Article 3

1. The Parties included in Annex 1 shall, individually or jointly, ensure that their aggregate anthropogenic carbon dioxide equivalent emissions of the greenhouse gases listed in Appendix A do not exceed their assigned amounts... with a view to reducing their overall emissions of such gases by at least 5 per cent below 1990 levels in the commitment period 2008 to 2012.

2. Each party included in Annex 1 shall, by 2005, have made demonstrable progress in achieving its commitments under this Protocol....

Article 6

1. For the purpose of meeting its requirements under Article 3, any party included in Annex 1 may transfer to, or acquire from, any other such Party emission reduction units resulting from projects aimed at reducing anthropogenic emissions by sources or enhancing anthropogenic removals by sinks of greenhouse gases in any sector of the economy, provided that:

    (a) Any such project has the approval of the Parties involved ...

    (d) The acquisition of emission reduction units shall be supplemental to domestic actions for the purposes of meeting commitments under Article 3 ...

3. A Party included in Annex 1 may authorize legal entities to participate, under its responsibility, in actions leading to the generation, transfer or acquisition under this Article of emission reduction units....

Article 12

1. A clean development mechanism is hereby defined.

2. The purpose of the clean development mechanism shall be to assist the Parties not included in Annex 1 in achieving sustainable development and in contributing to the ultimate objective of the Convention, and to assist Parties included in Annex 1 in achieving compliance with their quantified emission limitation and reduction commitments under Article 3.

3. Under the clean development mechanism
   (a) Parties not included in Annex 1 will benefit from project activities resulting in certified emission reductions; and
   (b) Parties included in Annex 1 may use the certified emissions reductions accruing from such project activities to contribute to compliance with part of their quantified emission limitation and reduction commitments under Article 3....

Article 16 bis

The Conference of Parties shall define the relevant principles, modalities, rules and guidelines, in particular for verification, reporting and accountability for emissions trading. The parties included in Annex B may participate in emissions trading for the purposes of fulfilling their commitments under Article 3 of this Protocol. Any such trading shall be supplemental to domestic actions for the purpose of meeting quantified emission limitation and reduction commitments under that Article.

Paris Agreement under the United Nations Framework Convention on Climate Change 2015

FCCC/CP/2015/L.9/Rev.1

Article 2

1. This Agreement, in enhancing the implementation of the Convention, including its objective, aims to strengthen the global response to the threat of climate change, in the context of sustainable development and efforts to eradicate poverty, including by:
   (a) Holding the increase in the global average temperature to well below 2 °C above pre-industrial levels and pursuing efforts to limit the temperature increase to 1.5 °C above pre-industrial levels, recognizing that this would significantly reduce the risks and impacts of climate change;
   (b) Increasing the ability to adapt to the adverse impacts of climate change and foster climate resilience and low greenhouse gas emissions development, in a manner that does not threaten food production; and
   (c) Making finance flows consistent with a pathway towards low greenhouse gas emissions and climate-resilient development.

2. This Agreement will be implemented to reflect equity and the principle of common but differentiated responsibilities and respective capabilities, in the light of different national circumstances.

Article 4

1. In order to achieve the long-term temperature goal set out in Article 2, Parties aim to reach global peaking of greenhouse gas emissions as soon as possible, recognizing that peaking will take longer for developing country Parties, and to undertake rapid reductions thereafter in accordance with best available science, so as to achieve a balance between anthropogenic emissions by sources and removals by sinks of greenhouse gases in the second half of this century, on the basis of equity, and in the context of sustainable development and efforts to eradicate poverty.

Article 9

1. Developed country Parties shall provide financial resources to assist developing country Parties with respect to both mitigation and adaptation in continuation of their existing obligations under the Convention....

2. Other Parties are encouraged to provide or continue to provide such support voluntarily.

3. As part of a global effort, developed country Parties should continue to take the lead in mobilizing climate finance from a wide variety of sources, instruments and channels, noting the significant role of public funds,

through a variety of actions, including supporting country-driven strategies, and taking into account the needs and priorities of developing country Parties. Such mobilization of climate finance should represent a progression beyond previous efforts.

4. The provision of scaled-up financial resources should aim to achieve a balance between adaptation and mitigation, taking into account country-driven strategies, and the priorities and needs of developing country Parties, especially those that are particularly vulnerable to the adverse effects of climate change and have significant capacity constraints, such as the least developed countries and small island developing States, considering the need for public and grant-based resources for adaptation.

In Larger Freedom: Towards Security, Development and Human Rights for All
Report of the Secretary-General, UN Doc. A/59/2005

60. One of the greatest environmental and development challenges in the twenty-first century will be that of controlling and coping with climate change. The overwhelming majority of scientists now agree that human activity is having a significant impact on the climate. Since the advent of the industrial era in the mid-eighteenth century, atmospheric concentrations of greenhouse gases have increased significantly, and the earth has warmed considerably and sea levels have risen measurably. The 1990s were the warmest decade on record, forcing glaciers and Arctic ice to retreat. With the concentration of greenhouse gases projected to rise still further over the next century, a corresponding increase in the global mean surface temperature is likely to trigger increased climate variability and greater incidence and intensity of extreme weather events, such as hurricanes and droughts. The countries most vulnerable to such changes—small island developing States, coastal nations with large numbers of people living in low-lying areas, and countries in the arid and semi-arid tropics and subtropics—are least able to protect themselves. They also contribute least to the global emissions of greenhouse gases. Without action, they will pay a bitter price for the actions of others.

61. The entry into force in February 2005 of the 1997 Kyoto Protocol to the United Nations Framework Convention on Climate Change is an important step towards dealing with global warming, but it only extends until 2012. The international community must agree on stabilization targets for greenhouse gas concentrations beyond that date. Scientific advances and technological innovation have an important role to play in mitigating climate change and in facilitating adaptation to the new conditions. They must be mobilized now if we are to develop the tools needed in time. In particular, research and development funding for renewable energy sources, carbon management and energy efficiency needs to increase substantially. Policy mechanisms, such as carbon trading markets, should also be expanded. As agreed at Johannesburg, the primary responsibility for mitigating climate change and other unsustainable patterns of production and consumption must lie with the countries that contribute most to the problems. We must develop a more inclusive international framework beyond 2012, with broader participation by all major emitters and both developed and developing countries, to ensure a concerted globally defined action, including through technological innovation, to mitigate climate change, taking into account the principle of common but differentiated responsibilities.

NOTES
1. The Framework Convention on Climate Change (UNFCCC) and subsequent Kyoto Protocol embody the approach that is being taken within many areas of environmental law, which is to take account of each State's level of development, particular geographical characteristics and access to resources. Similar bifurcated procedures are also emerging in international trade law (see Chapter 13).
2. Under the Kyoto Protocol the difference between Annex 1 (which is a list of developed or indus-trialised States) and non-Annex 1 Parties (developing States or States in transition to a market economy) is particularly apparent in the methods provided to States to reduce emissions through 'emission trading'. Emission trading, it is argued, allows polluters flexibility in choosing how to control and reduce air pollution, enabling reductions to be achieved in the most cost-efficient manner. Article 6 enables developed States to undertake 'joint implementation' projects whereby a State can earn emission 'credits' by investing in projects in other States. Article 16 *bis* also ena-bles developed States to participate in emission trading to meet reduction targets (that are set out in Annex B to the Protocol) as long as the trading is supplemental to domestic reduction activi-ties. Article 12, in contrast, enables developed States to initiate environmental projects designed to reduce emissions or create greenhouse 'sinks' (usually reforestation or afforestation projects)

in non-Annex 1 Parties, and to use the 'emission reductions' to count towards their own reduction targets. The United States, which is a signatory to the Kyoto Protocol, indicated in 2001 that it would not ratify this Protocol.

3. The commitments made by States under the Kyoto Protocol ended on 31 December 2012. Since the UNFCCC and the Kyoto Protocol were adopted, scientific understanding has developed significantly, and it has become apparent that the existing emissions reductions are insufficient. The 2007 report of the Intergovernmental Panel on Climate Change recommended more demanding targets and a more stringent regulatory system. Demand for energy, particularly in developing States has increased, and any legal regime must involve the major developing States.

4. The application period of the Kyoto Protocol was extended until 2020 by the Doha Agreement, adopted at the 2012 UN Climate Change Conference, in Doha, Qatar. However, before Doha, at the 2011 Conference, parties to the UNFCCC had agreed on the Durban Platform for Enhanced Action. This recognised the need to draw up a fresh international climate change agreement that would apply beyond 2020. The Paris Agreement, agreed in December 2015 at the 21st Conference of the Parties to the UNFCCC, is the outcome of the Durban Platform for Enhanced Action.

5. The Paris Agreement is an international climate change treaty that provides that signatories should hold the increase in global temperature to 'well below' 2°C above pre-industrial levels (Article 2). It will be open for signature from 22 April 2016 to 21 April 2017 and requires at least 55 States representing 55 per cent of global emissions to ratify it before it comes into effect. Crucially, and to the criticism of some commentators, the Paris Agreement does not include any binding enforcement mechanism.

6. At the 21st Conference of Parties, it was also agreed that developed countries would continue to provide financial support for developing countries seeking to fulfil the obligations of the UNFCCC. It was agreed that $US100 billion would be provided initially and this amount would be a 'floor' which would rise over time, taking into account the needs and priorities of developed countries.

(c) Marine environment

Law of the Sea Convention 1982
21 *International Legal Materials* 1261 (1982)

This Convention is discussed extensively in Chapter 10.

Article 192 General obligation
States have the obligation to protect and preserve the marine environment.

Article 193 Sovereign right of States to exploit their natural resources
States have the sovereign right to exploit their natural resources pursuant to their environmental policies and in accordance with their duty to protect and preserve the marine environment.

Article 194 Measures to prevent, reduce and control pollution of the marine environment
1. States shall take, individually or jointly as appropriate, all measures consistent with this Convention that are necessary to prevent, reduce and control pollution of the marine environment from any source, using for this purpose the best practicable means at their disposal and in accordance with their capabilities, and they shall endeavour to harmonize their policies in this connection.

2. States shall take all measures necessary to ensure that activities under their jurisdiction or control are so conducted as not to cause damage by pollution to other States and their environment, and that pollution arising from incidents or activities under their jurisdiction or control does not spread beyond the areas where they exercise sovereign rights in accordance with this Convention.

3. The measures taken pursuant to this Part shall deal with all sources of pollution of the marine environment. These measures shall include, *inter alia*, those designed to minimize to the fullest possible extent:
   (a) the release of toxic, harmful or noxious substances, especially those which are persistent, from land-based sources, from or through the atmosphere or by dumping;
   (b) pollution from vessels, in particular measures for preventing accidents and dealing with emergencies, ensuring the safety of operations at sea, preventing intentional and unintentional discharges, and regulating the design, construction, equipment, operation and manning of vessels;

(c) pollution from installations and devices used in exploration or exploitation of the natural resources of the sea-bed and subsoil, in particular measures for preventing accidents and dealing with emergencies, ensuring the safety of operations at sea, and regulating the design, construction, equipment, operation and manning of such installations or devices;

(d) pollution from other installations and devices operating in the marine environment, in particular measures for preventing accidents and dealing with emergencies, ensuring the safety of operations at sea, and regulating the design, construction, equipment, operation and manning of such installations or devices.

4. In taking measures to prevent, reduce or control pollution of the marine environment, States shall refrain from unjustifiable interference with activities carried out by other States in the exercise of their rights and in pursuance of their duties in conformity with this Convention.

5. The measures taken in accordance with this Part shall include those necessary to protect and preserve rare or fragile ecosystems as well as the habitat of depleted, threatened or endangered species and other forms of marine life.

NOTES

1. There are many other treaties concerning air and marine pollution, for example, the International Convention for the Prevention of Pollution from Ships (MARPOL) 1973 (12 ILM 1319 (1973)). There are also treaties about preservation of fish and other maritime resources, e.g. Agreement for the Implementation of the Provisions of UNCLOS relating to the Conservation and Management of Highly Migratory Fish Stocks 1995 and the Agreement of Port State Measures to Prevent, Deter and Eliminate Illegal, Unreported and Unregulated Fishing 2009. The application of some of these treaties is discussed in Chapter 10.

2. The Basel Convention on the Control of Transboundary Movements of Hazardous Wastes and their Disposal 1989 seeks to establish the right to prohibit the import of hazardous wastes and limit their export. The Convention is designed to reduce hazardous waste generation by increasing the cost of its exportation, and to prevent what has been called the 'environmental racism' that results from the export of such wastes to developing States. The underlying objectives of the Convention have been affirmed in Principle 14 of the Rio Declaration (see Section 1B).

3. There are also a number of international instruments regulating the use and protection of shared or international watercourses, in particular, the 1997 Convention on the Law of the Non-Navigational Uses of International Watercourses, which provides for the equitable and reasonable utilisation of international watercourses (Articles 5 and 6) and an obligation not to cause significant harm to an international watercourse (Article 7). The 1997 Convention entered into force 17 August 2014, following ratification by 35 States (Article 36). Such instruments are likely to gain significance as water resources become increasingly scarce (see also the work of the ILC on transboundary aquifers).

4. In 2011, the International Maritime Organization's Marine Environmental Protection Committee adopted mandatory measures to the International Convention for the Prevention of Pollution from Ships 1973. This represented the first mandatory global greenhouse gas reduction regime for an international industry sector.

(d) Wildlife and biological diversity

Convention on International Trade in Endangered Species of Wild Fauna and Flora 1973

12 *International Legal Materials* 1085 (1973)

As at March 2016, 181 States have ratified this Convention.

Article II Fundamental principles

1. Appendix I shall include all species threatened with extinction which are or may be affected by trade. Trade in specimens of these species must be subject to particularly strict regulation in order not to endanger further their survival and must only be authorized in exceptional circumstances.

2. Appendix II shall include:
  (a) all species which although not necessarily now threatened with extinction may become so unless trade in specimens of such species is subject to strict regulation in order to avoid utilization incompatible with their survival; and
  (b) other species which must be subject to regulation in order that trade in specimens of certain species referred to in sub-paragraph (a) of this paragraph may be brought under effective control.

3. Appendix III shall include all species which any Party identifies as being subject to regulation within it jurisdiction for the purpose of preventing or restricting exploitation, and as needing the co-operation of other parties in the control of trade.

4. The Parties shall not allow trade in specimens of species included in Appendices I, II and III except in accordance with the provisions of the present Convention....

Article VIII Measures to be Taken by the Parties

1. The Parties shall take appropriate measures to enforce the provisions of the present Convention and to prohibit trade in specimens in violation thereof. These shall include measures:
  (a) to penalize trade in, or possession of, such specimens, or both; and
  (b) to provide for the confiscation or return to the State of export of such specimens.

2. In addition to the measures taken under paragraph 1 of this Article, a Party may, when it deems it necessary, provide for any method of internal reimbursement for expenses incurred as a result of the confiscation of a specimen traded in violation of the measures taken in the application of the provisions of the present Convention.

Convention on Biological Diversity 1992

31 *International Legal Materials* 818 (1992)

This treaty was signed during the Rio Conference and as at March 2016, 196 parties (including the European Union) have ratified this Convention, the United States being the only State not to do so.

Article 1 Objectives

The objectives of this Convention, to be pursued in accordance with its relevant provisions, are the conservation of biological diversity, the sustainable use of its components and the fair and equitable sharing of the benefits arising out of the utilization of genetic resources, including by appropriate access to genetic resources and by appropriate transfer of relevant technologies, taking into account all rights over those resources and to technologies, and by appropriate funding....

Article 8 In-situ Conservation

Each Contracting Party shall, as far as possible and as appropriate:
  (a) Establish a system of protected areas or areas where special measures need to be taken to conserve biological diversity;
  (b) Develop, where necessary, guidelines for the selection, establishment and management of protected are as or areas where special measures need to be taken to conserve biological diversity;
  (c) Regulate or manage biological resources important for the conservation of biological diversity whether within or outside protected areas, with a view to ensuring their conservation and sustainable use;
  (d) Promote the protection of ecosystems, natural habitats and the maintenance of viable populations of species in natural surroundings;
  (e) Promote environmentally sound and sustainable development in areas adjacent to protected areas with a view to furthering protection of these areas;
  (f) Rehabilitate and restore degraded ecosystems and promote the recovery of threatened species, *inter alia*, through the development and implementation of plans or other management strategies;
  (g) Establish or maintain means to regulate, manage or control the risks associated with the use and release of living modified organisms resulting from biotechnology which are likely to have adverse environmental impacts that could affect the conservation and sustainable use of biological diversity, taking also into account the risks to human health;

    (h)   Prevent the introduction of, control or eradicate those alien species which threaten ecosystems, habitats or species;

    (i)   Endeavour to provide the conditions needed for compatibility between present uses and the conservation of biological diversity and the sustainable use of its components;

    (j)   Subject to its national legislation, respect, preserve and maintain knowledge, innovations and practices of indigenous and local communities embodying traditional lifestyles relevant for the conservation and sustainable use of biological diversity and promote their wider application with the approval and involvement of the holders of such knowledge, innovations and practices and encourage the equitable sharing of the benefits arising from the utilization of such knowledge, innovations and practices;

    (k)   Develop or maintain necessary legislation and/or other regulatory provisions for the protection of threatened species and populations;

    (l)   Where a significant adverse effect on biological diversity has been determined pursuant to Article 7, regulate or manage the relevant processes and categories of activities; and

    (m) Cooperate in providing financial and other support for *in-situ* conservation outlined in subparagraphs (a) to (l) above, particularly to developing countries.

Article 9 Ex-situ Conservation

Each Contracting Party shall, as far as possible and as appropriate, and predominantly for the purpose of complementing *in-situ* measures:

    (a)   Adopt measures for the *ex-situ* conservation of components of biological diversity, preferably in the country of origin of such components; …

Article 23 Conference of the Parties

    4. The Conference of the Parties shall keep under review the implementation of this Convention, and, for this purpose, shall:

    (a)   Establish the form and the intervals for transmitting the information to be submitted in accordance with Article 26 and consider such information as well as reports submitted by any subsidiary body;

    (b)   Review scientific, technical and technological advice on biological diversity provided in accordance with Article 25; …

Article 26 Reports

Each Contracting Party shall, at intervals to be determined by the Conference of the Parties, present to the Conference of the Parties, reports on measures which it has taken for the implementation of the provisions of this Convention and their effectiveness in meeting the objective of this Convention.

NOTES

1. The mechanisms for supervising compliance with the Convention on Biological Diversity are similar to the Framework Convention on Climate Change (see Section 4A), with a body of State representatives which reviews periodic reports. There is also some provision for financial assistance to developing States.

2. In 2000, the Cartagena Protocol on Biosafety 2000 was signed as Protocol to the Convention on Biological Diversity. As at March 2016 there were 170 parties to the Protocol (including the European Union). The Protocol 'seeks to protect biological diversity from the potential risks of modern biotechnology, particularly living modified organisms'. It contains advance information procedures with a Biosafety Clearing-House to facilitate information exchange. The Protocol uses a precautionary approach as it reaffirms the precaution language in Principle 15 of the Rio Declaration (see Section 1B). The Protocol provided for the establishment of a compliance regime and for further rules on liability and redress at a later stage. The compliance mechanism has been established but it has not yet considered any instances of non-compliance.

3. States also have an obligation to identify and to preserve the natural and cultural heritage where they have ratified the Convention for the Protection of the World Cultural and Natural Heritage 1972. As at March 2016, there are 191 States parties to this Convention. This heritage includes items of archaeological, historical, artistic and scientific interest, and geological formations. The Convention also establishes the World Heritage Committee, which can place certain property of 'outstanding and universal value' on the World Heritage List. In March 2016, there were 1,031 sites listed, comprising 802 cultural sites, 197 natural sites and 32 mixed sites in 163 States.

B: Protection of particular territory

There have been a number of treaties that have dealt with environmental protection of particular territories that are outside the traditional sovereignty of any one State. This territory includes the moon and other celestial bodies, the deep seabed and the Antarctic. There are also areas of environmental interest that cross State borders rather than being outside the sovereign territory of any one State, such as the Amazon. In contrast with regional treaties that are based on a pre-existing economic association, such territories have been the focus of specific declarations and treaties.

Protocol on Environmental Protection to the Antarctic Treaty 1991

30 *International Legal Materials* 1461 (1991)

This Protocol was adopted by the State parties to the Antarctic Treaty (see Chapter 7). As at March 2016, there were 29 Consultative Parties and 8 Non-Consultative Parties to the Protocol. The Protocol entered into force on 14 January 1998.

Article 2 Objective and designation

The Parties commit themselves to the comprehensive protection of the Antarctic environment and dependent and associated ecosystems and hereby designate Antarctica as a natural reserve, devoted to peace and science.

Article 3 Environmental principles

1. The protection of the Antarctic environment and dependent and associated ecosystems and the intrinsic value of Antarctica, including its wilderness and aesthetic values and its value as an area for the conduct of scientific research, in particular research essential to understanding the global environment, shall be fundamental considerations in the planning and conduct of all activities in the Antarctic Treaty area.

2. To this end:
    (a) activities in the Antarctic Treaty area shall be planned and conducted so as to limit adverse impacts on Antarctic environment and dependent and associated ecosystems;
    (d) regular and effective monitoring shall take place to allow assessment of the impacts of ongoing activities, including the verification of predicted impacts;
    (e) regular and effective monitoring shall take place to facilitate early detection of the possible unforeseen effects of activities carried on both within and outside the Antarctic Treaty area on the Antarctic environment and dependent and associated ecosystems....

Article 7 Prohibition of mineral resource activities

Any activity relating to mineral resources, other than scientific research, shall be prohibited.

Article 8 Environmental impact assessment

1. Proposed activities referred to in paragraph 2 below shall be subject to the procedures set out in Annex I for prior assessment of the impacts of those activities on the Antarctic environment or on dependent or associated ecosystems according to whether those activities are identified as having:
    (a) less than a minor or transitory impact;
    (b) a minor or transitory impact; or
    (c) more than a minor or transitory impact.

2. Each Party shall ensure that the assessment procedures set out in Annex I are applied in the planning processes leading to decisions about any activities undertaken in the Antarctic Treaty area pursuant to scientific research programmes, tourism and all other governmental and non-governmental activities in the Antarctic Treaty area for which advance notice is required under Article VII (5) of the Antarctic Treaty, including associated logistic support activities....

Article 12 Functions of the Committee

1. The functions of the Committee [for Environmental Protection] shall be to provide advice and formulate recommendations to the Parties in connection with the implementation of this Protocol, including the operation

of its Annexes, for consideration at Antarctic Treaty Consultative Meetings, and to perform such other functions as may be referred to it by the Antarctic Treaty Consultative Meetings....

Article 17 Annual report by parties

1. Each Party shall report annually on the steps taken to implement this Protocol. Such reports shall include notifications made in accordance with Article 13(3), contingency plans established in accordance with Article 15 and any other notifications and information called for pursuant to this Protocol for which there is no other provision concerning the circulation and exchange of information.

2. Reports made in accordance with paragraph 1 above shall be circulated to all Parties and to the Committee, considered at the next Antarctic Treaty Consultative Meeting, and made publicly available.

Amazon Declaration 1989

28 International Legal Materials 1303 (1989)

Bolivia, Brazil, Colombia, Ecuador, Guyana, Peru, Suriname and Venezuela are signatories to this Declaration and are the Parties to the Treaty for Amazonian Cooperation (17 ILM 1045 (1978)), which promotes the rational use of natural resources with the objective of maintaining a balance between economic growth and environmental cooperation.

2. Conscious of the importance of protecting the cultural, economic and ecological heritage of our Amazon regions and of the necessity of using this potential to promote the economic and social development of our peoples, we reiterate that our Amazon heritage must be preserved through the rational use of the resources of the region, so that present and future generations may benefit from this legacy of nature....

4. We reaffirm the sovereign right of each country to manage freely its natural resources, bearing in mind the need for promoting the economic and social development of its people and the adequate conservation of the environment. In the exercise of our sovereign responsibility to define the best ways of using and conserving this wealth and in addition to our national efforts and to the co-operation among our countries, we express our willingness to accept co-operation from countries in other regions of the world, as well as from international organizations, which might contribute to the implementation of national and regional projects and programmes that we decide freely to adopt without external impositions, in accordance with the priorities of our Governments.

5. We recognize that the defence of our environment requires the study of measures, both bilateral and regional, to prevent contamination-causing accidents and to deal with their consequences once they have occurred.

6. We stress that the protection and conservation of the environment in the region, one of the essential objectives of the Treaty for Amazonian Co-operation to which each of our nations is firmly committed, cannot be achieved without improvement of the distressing social and economic conditions that oppress our peoples and that are aggravated by an increasingly adverse international context....

8. We emphasize the need for the concerns expressed in the highly developed countries in relation to the conservation of the Amazon environment to be translated into measures of co-operation in the financial and technological fields. We call for the establishment of new resource flows in additional and concessional terms to projects oriented to environmental protection in our countries, including pure and applied scientific research, and we object to attempts to impose conditionalities in the allocation of international resources for development. We expect the establishment of conditions to allow free access to scientific knowledge, to clean technologies and to technologies to be used in environmental protection and we reject any attempts made to use legitimate ecological concerns to realize commercial profits. This approach is based above all on the fact that the principal causes for the deterioration of the environment on a world-wide scale are the patterns of industrialization and consumption as well as waste in the developed countries.

NOTES
1. States have made territorial claims to the Antarctic, though these have been placed on hold under the Antarctic Treaty 1959 (see Chapter 7). The moon has been declared to be part of the common heritage of mankind—see Agreement Governing the Activities of States on the Moon and other Celestial Bodies 1979 (Chapter 7)—as has the deep seabed—see Article 136 of the Law of the Sea Convention 1982 (Chapters 7 and 10). No territorial claim had been made to these areas by any State.

2. The risk to the marine environment created by activities in the deep seabed are discussed in more detail in Chapter 10, as are proposals for a new agreement linked to UNCLOS to protect biodiversity in the marine environment.

3. The Amazon Declaration recognises the difficulties in protecting the environment in those States with low levels of economic development. Some developing States have sought technology transfers from developed States to assist in sustainable development in order to prevent development in a manner that is as environmentally damaging as has been the development by the developed States.

SECTION 5: RELATIONSHIP OF THE ENVIRONMENT WITH OTHER INTERNATIONAL LAW ISSUES

A: Human rights and the environment

Joint Statement of the United Nations Special Procedures—'Climate Change and Human Rights'

This is a statement made in June 2015 by a number of Special Rapporteurs with different mandates appointed by the United Nations Human Rights Council.

As human rights experts of the United Nations system, we take this occasion to draw attention again to the grave harm climate change poses to the worldwide enjoyment of human rights. Last December, on Human Rights Day, all of the UN human rights experts came together to urge States to recognize that climate change threatens human rights, and to urge States to include language in the 2015 climate agreement providing that the Parties shall respect, protect and fulfil human rights, in all of their climate change related actions. Since then, our work has further confirmed the urgent need to take effective action. Many of us recently prepared a report for the Climate Vulnerable Forum, an international partnership of twenty countries highly vulnerable to a warming planet, which explains that an average increase in global temperature of even 2.0° C will adversely affect a wide range of human rights, including the rights to life, health, food, and water, among many others.

Climate change threatens these rights in many ways. Deaths, injuries and displacement of persons from climate-related disasters, such as tropical cyclones, will increase, as will mortality from heat waves, drought, disease and malnutrition. The Fifth Assessment Report of the Intergovernmental Panel on Climate Change (IPCC) states that the foreseeable consequences of even a 2°C rise include an increasing probability of 'declining work productivity, morbidity (e.g., dehydration, heat stroke, and heat exhaustion), and mortality from exposure to heat waves'. Particularly at risk are agricultural and construction workers as well as children, homeless people, the elderly, and women who have to walk long hours to collect water.

Climate change will exacerbate existing stresses on water resources and compound the problem of access to safe drinking water, currently denied to an estimated 1.1 billion people globally and a major cause of morbidity and disease. It is estimated that about 8% of the global population will see a severe reduction in water resources with a 1°C rise in global mean temperature, rising to 14% at 2°C. Climate change is already affecting the ability of some communities to feed themselves, and the number affected will grow as temperatures rise. As the IPCC report states, 'all aspects of food security are potentially affected by climate change, including food access, utilization, and price stability'.

Climate change will affect most severely the lives of those who already struggle to enjoy their human rights, including women, children, the elderly and the poor. In the words of the Fifth Assessment report, 'People who are socially, economically, culturally, politically, institutionally or otherwise marginalized are especially vulnerable to climate change and also to some adaptation and mitigation responses.' The report states that 'future impacts of climate change, extending from the near term to the long term, mostly expecting 2°C scenarios, will slow down economic growth and poverty reduction, further erode food security, and trigger new poverty traps, the latter particularly in urban areas and emerging hotspots of hunger.' Poverty becomes a particular vulnerability factor for children to fall victims of sexual abuse and exploitation. Some people will be forced to migrate. However, because the ability to migrate often depends on mobility and resources, migration opportunities may be least available to those who are most vulnerable to climate change, resulting in people becoming trapped in locations vulnerable to environmental hazards, further exacerbating their suffering. Moreover, where climate-change-induced migration is forced, people may be migrating in an irregular situation and therefore may be more vulnerable to human rights violations through the migration process.

Climate change will also devastate the other forms of life that share this planet with us. As temperatures increase more than 2°C, studies predict increasingly disastrous consequences for biodiversity. For example, one study found that 20-30% of the assessed plant and animal species are likely to be at increasingly high risk of extinction as global mean temperatures exceed a warming of 2 to 3°C. These consequences will be felt by humans as well: with respect to the right to health, the fifth assessment report explains that biodiversity loss 'can lead to an increase in the transmission of infectious diseases such as Lyme, schistosomiasis, and hantavirus in humans'.

A. Boyle 'Human Rights or Environmental Rights? A Reassessment'

18 *Fordham Environmental Law Review* 471 (2007)

Environmental rights do not fit neatly into any single category or 'generation' of human rights. They can be viewed from at least three perspectives, straddling all the various categories or generations of human rights. First, existing civil and political rights can be used to give individuals, groups and non-governmental organizations (NGOs) access to environmental information, judicial remedies and political processes. On this view their role is one of empowerment: facilitating participation in environmental decision-making and compelling governments to meet minimum standards of protection for life, private life and property from environmental harm. A second possibility is to treat a decent, healthy or sound environment as an economic or social right, comparable to those whose progressive attainment is promoted by the 1966 United Nations (UN) Covenant on Economic, Social and Cultural Rights. The main argument for this approach is that it would privilege environmental quality as a value, giving it comparable status to other economic and social rights, such as development, and priority over non rights-based objectives. Like other economic and social rights, it would be programmatic and in most cases enforceable only through relatively weak international supervisory mechanisms. The third option would treat environmental quality as a collective or solidarity right, giving communities ('peoples') rather than individuals a right to determine how their environment and natural resources should be protected and managed.

The first approach is essentially anthropocentric insofar as it focuses on the harmful impact on individual humans rather than on the environment itself: it amounts to a 'greening' of human rights law, rather than a law of environmental rights. The second comes closer to seeing the environment as a good in its own right but, nevertheless one that will always be vulnerable to trade-offs against other similarly privileged but competing objectives, including the right to economic development. The third approach is the most contested. Not all human rights lawyers favor the recognition of third generation rights, arguing that they devalue the concept of human rights, and divert attention from the need to implement existing civil, political, economic and social rights fully. The concept hardly featured in the agenda of the 1993 UN World Conference on Human Rights, and in general it adds little to an understanding of the nature of environmental rights, which are not inherently collective in character. However, there are some significant examples of collective rights that in certain contexts can have environmental implications, such as the protection of minority cultures and indigenous peoples or the right of all peoples to freely dispose of their natural resources, which was recognised in the 1966 U.N. Covenants on Civil and Political Rights and Economic, Social and Cultural Rights, and in the 1981 African Charter on Human and Peoples Rights.

Put simply, the question…is the following: should we continue to think about human rights and the environment within the existing framework of human rights law in which the protection of humans is the central focus—essentially a greening of the rights to life, private life, and property—or has the time come to talk directly about environmental rights—in other words a right to have the environment itself protected? Should we transcend the anthropocentric in favor of the eco-centric?

The Social and Economic Rights Action Center and the Center for Economic and Social Rights v Nigeria

African Commission on Human and Peoples Rights, Communication 155/96, 27 May 2002

The complaint was brought by two NGOs, which alleged that the military government of Nigeria was directly involved in oil production consortium through the State oil company, the Nigerian National Petroleum Company (NNPC), the majority shareholder in a consortium with Shell Petroleum Development Corporation (SPDC), and that these operations caused environmental degradation and health problems resulting from the contamination of the environment among the Ogoni people in Nigeria. The Consortium was alleged to have exploited oil reserves in Ogoniland with no regard for the health or environment of the local communities, disposing toxic wastes into the environment and local waterways in violation of applicable international environmental standards. They argued that the consortium also neglected and/or failed to maintain its facilities, causing numerous avoidable spills in the proximity of villages. The resulting contamination of water, soil and air had serious short- and long-term health impacts, including skin infections, gastrointestinal and respiratory ailments, and increased risk of cancers, and neurological and reproductive problems.

50. The Complainants allege that the Nigerian government violated the right to health and the right to clean environment as recognized under Articles 16 and 24 of the African Charter by failing to fulfil the minimum duties required by these rights. This, the Complainants allege, the government has done by -:

- – Directly participating in the contamination of air, water and soil and thereby harming the health of the Ogoni population,
- – Failing to protect the Ogoni population from the harm caused by the NNPC Shell Consortium but instead using its security forces to facilitate the damage
- – Failing to provide or permit studies of potential or actual environmental and health risks caused by the oil operations ...

51. These rights recognise the importance of a clean and safe environment that is closely linked to economic and social rights in so far as the environment affects the quality of life and safety of the individual. As has been rightly observed by Alexander Kiss, 'an environment degraded by pollution and defaced by the destruction of all beauty and variety is as contrary to satisfactory living conditions and the development as the breakdown of the fundamental ecologic equilibria is harmful to physical and moral health' [A. Kiss, 'Concept and Possible Implications of the Right to Environment' in Mahoney (eds), *Human Rights in the Twenty-first Century: A Global Challenge*, (1993) 553].

52. The right to a general satisfactory environment, as guaranteed under Article 24 of the African Charter or the right to a healthy environment, as it is widely known, therefore imposes clear obligations upon a government.

It requires the State to take reasonable and other measures to prevent pollution and ecological degradation, to promote conservation, and to secure an ecologically sustainable development and use of natural resources. Article 12 of the International Covenant on Economic, Social and Cultural Rights (ICESCR), to which Nigeria is a party, requires governments to take necessary steps for the improvement of all aspects of environmental and industrial hygiene. The right to enjoy the best attainable state of physical and mental health enunciated in Article 16(1) of the African Charter and the right to a general satisfactory environment favourable to development (Article 16(3)) already noted obligate governments to desist from directly threatening the health and environment of their citizens. The State is under an obligation to respect the just noted rights and this entails largely non-interventionist conduct from the State for example, not from carrying out, sponsoring or tolerating any practice, policy or legal measures violating the integrity of the individual.

53. Government compliance with the spirit of Articles 16 and 24 of the African Charter must also include ordering or at least permitting independent scientific monitoring of threatened environments, requiring and publicising environmental and social impact studies prior to any major industrial development, undertaking appropriate monitoring and providing information to those communities exposed to hazardous materials and activities and providing meaningful opportunities for individuals to be heard and to participate in the development decisions affecting their communities.

54. We now examine the conduct of the government of Nigeria in relation to Articles 16 and 24 of the African Charter. Undoubtedly and admittedly, the government of Nigeria, through NNPC has the right to produce oil, the income from which will be used to fulfil the economic and social rights of Nigerians. But the care that should have been taken as outlined in the preceding paragraph and which would have protected the rights of the victims of the violations complained of was not taken. To exacerbate the situation, the security forces of the government engaged in conduct in violation of the rights of the Ogonis by attacking, burning and destroying several Ogoni villages and homes.

UN Declaration on the Rights of Indigenous Peoples
Adopted by General Assembly Resolution 61/295, 13 September 2007

Article 29

1. Indigenous peoples have the right to the conservation and protection of the environment and the productive capacity of their lands or territories and resources. States shall establish and implement assistance programmes for indigenous peoples for such conservation and protection, without discrimination.

2. States shall take effective measures to ensure that no storage or disposal of hazardous materials shall take place in the lands or territories of indigenous peoples without their free, prior and informed consent.

3. States shall also take effective measures to ensure, as needed, that programmes for monitoring, maintaining and restoring the health of indigenous peoples, as developed and implemented by the peoples affected by such materials, are duly implemented.

Article 31

1. Indigenous peoples have the right to maintain, control, protect and develop their cultural heritage, traditional knowledge and traditional cultural expressions, as well as the manifestations of their sciences, technologies and cultures, including human and genetic resources, seeds, medicines, knowledge of the properties of fauna and flora, oral traditions, literatures, designs, sports and traditional games and visual and performing arts. They also have the right to maintain, control, protect and develop their intellectual property over such cultural heritage, traditional knowledge, and traditional cultural expressions.

2. In conjunction with indigenous peoples, States shall take effective measures to recognize and protect the exercise of these rights.

Article 32

1. Indigenous peoples have the right to determine and develop priorities and strategies for the development or use of their lands or territories and other resources.

2. States shall consult and cooperate in good faith with the indigenous peoples concerned through their own representative institutions in order to obtain their free and informed consent prior to the approval of any project affecting their lands or territories and other resources, particularly in connection with the development, utilization or exploitation of mineral, water or other resources.

3. States shall provide effective mechanisms for just and fair redress for any such activities, and appropriate measures shall be taken to mitigate adverse environmental, economic, social, cultural or spiritual impact.

Statement of the CEDAW Committee on Gender and Climate Change
Committee on the Elimination of Discrimination Against Women, 44th Session, 2009

The Committee on the Elimination of Discrimination against Women (CEDAW) expresses its concern about the absence of a gender perspective in the United Nations Framework Convention on Climate Change (UNFCCC) and other global and national policies and initiatives on climate change. From CEDAW's examination of State Parties reports, it is apparent that climate change does not affect women and men in the same way and has a gender-differentiated impact. However, women are not just helpless victims of climate change—they are powerful agents of change and their leadership is critical. All stakeholders should ensure that climate change and disaster risk reduction measures are gender responsive, sensitive to indigenous knowledge systems and respect human rights. Women's right to participate at all levels of decision-making must be guaranteed in climate change policies and programmes.

As the report of the Intergovernmental Panel on Climate Change noted, climate change has differential impacts on societies varying among regions, generations, ages, classes, income groups, occupations and gender lines. Women are the main producers of the world's staple crops, but they face multiple discriminations such as unequal access to land, credit and information. Particularly at risk are poor urban and rural women who live in densely populated coastal and low-lying areas, drylands and high mountainous areas and small islands. Vulnerable groups such as older women and disabled women and minority groups such as indigenous women, pastoralists, nomads and hunters and gatherers are also of concern.

NOTES

1. Human rights and the environment have been linked by theorists (see Section 2) as well as in case law. For a discussion of human rights generally see Chapter 6.

2. The African Charter is unique in that it refers expressly to the environment, advancing and protecting environmental rights (Article 24). The decision of the African Commission (extracted above) is a highly significant decision, extending far beyond previous human rights jurisprudence, and it places substantive obligations on States. The decision is also based on the rights of indigenous peoples to dispose freely of their natural resources under Article 21 of the Charter. Article 37 of the European Charter of Fundamental Rights, with the entry into force of the Treaty of Lisbon, is now binding on member States of the European Union (see Chapter 4). It provides that environmental protection and the improvement of the quality of the environment must be integrated into the policies of the European Union, and ensured in accordance with the principle of sustainable development.

3. The Convention on Access to Information, Public Participation in Decision-making and Access to Justice in Environmental Matters 1998 (the Aarhus Convention) (38 ILM 517) provides for environmental rights, and thus contributes to the protection of associated human rights. Its focus is on procedural issues, in particular the right of public participation in environmental decision-making, access to justice and availability of relevant information. The Convention aims to enhance the role of NGOs in protecting the environment. It entered into force on 30 October 2001 and, as at March 2016, has 47 States parties. It is widely ratified by European States and the European Union, where it has been incorporated under Directive 2003/4. It has influenced the jurisprudence of both the European Court of Human Rights and the Court of Justice of the European Union.

4. Other human rights treaties do not protect environmental rights *per se*. Instead, protection is achieved by the so-called 'greening' of other rights. For example, the European Court of Human Rights (ECtHR) has interpreted the ECHR as a 'living instrument' (see *Tyrer* v *United Kingdom* (1978)), so as to reflect current social values. This has allowed consideration of environmental issues as part of other Convention rights, in particular the right to life (Article 2(1)), the right to respect for private and family life (Article 8), the right to peaceful enjoyment of possessions and property (Article 1 Protocol 1), and the right to a fair hearing (Article 6). The ECtHR has developed extensive jurisprudence on environmental issues, and the Council of Europe has issued a *Manual on Human Rights and the Environment*, which discusses the jurisprudence and sets out guiding principles. However, the ECtHR cannot oblige States directly to protect the environment; instead, the environmental issue must be linked to the violation of a Convention right and the ECtHR can only require States to protect the rights of those that may be substantially affected by environmental factors.

5. The United Nations Human Rights Council (HRC) has also been active in this area, with a series of resolutions concerning human rights and climate change. The HRC adopted Resolution 16/11 in April 2011, which requested the Office of the High Commissioner for Human Rights to conduct a 'detailed analytical study on the relationship between human rights and the environment'. This report was submitted in December 2011. In March 2012, the HRC decided to appoint for three years an independent expert on the issue of human rights obligations relating to the enjoyment of a safe, clean, healthy and sustainable environment. One task of the Special Rapporteur is to produce an annual report on the issue of human rights and the environment; the latest report was issued in December 2015.

6. Various international instruments provide for the right of indigenous peoples to the lands they own or occupy or with which they have traditional and cultural affiliations. In addition to the UN Declaration extracted above, other instruments recognise the important role of indigenous communities in protecting the environment of their tribal areas (for example, the ILO Convention No. 169 on Indigenous and Tribal People 1989) and the need for indigenous peoples to be able to assert their rights in relation to their environment. As shown in the *Nigeria* decision above, several human rights bodies have recognised that environmental harm may have negative impacts for the right of indigenous peoples to their communal property (see also the findings of the Inter-American Commission of Human Rights in *Maya Indigenous Community of the Toledo District* v *Belize* (2004) and the decision of the Inter-American Court of Human Rights in *The Case of the Mayagna (Sumo) Awas Tingni Community* v *Nicaragua*, 31 August 2001).

7. While the UNFCCC does not address gender equality, there are global agreements, such as the International Conference on Population and Development (1994), the Beijing Declaration and

Platform for Action (1995), the World Summit on Sustainable Development (2002) and the 2005 World Summit, which recognise the role of women in relation to sustainable development. The United Nations Secretary-General, in the lead-up to the negotiations in Copenhagen in December 2009, emphasised the need for the global discussions to have regard to the 'special perspective' of women and girls. However, while draft texts considered at the Copenhagen summit included wording that recognised the particular impact of climate change on women and girls, and included several references to gender issues (for example, the need to enhance the role of women in decision-making processes), the Copenhagen Accord is silent on this issue.

8. National legislation to protect the environment is continually growing. However, it is often difficult to enforce international environment standards in national courts, particularly because of procedural issues, such as standing to bring a claim. The 1974 Nordic Convention on the Protection of the Environment (13 ILM 591 (1974)) is an unusual treaty, in that it gives some rights to individuals affected by environmentally harmful activities in another contracting State to bring a claim in their own State. A private right of action is also provided by the North American Agreement on Environmental Cooperation. The Aarhus Convention may also assist in enforcing environmental rights, although its provisions fall short of providing a direct right of enforcement.

B: Armed conflict and the environment

International Law Commission, Preliminary Report on the Protection of the Environment in relation to Armed Conflicts

A/CN.4/674, 30 May 2014

1. It has long been recognized that environmental effects that occur both during and after an armed conflict have the potential to pose a serious threat to the livelihoods and even the existence of individual human beings and communities. Unlike many of the other consequences of armed conflict, environmental harm may be long-term and irreparable and has the potential to prevent an effective rebuilding of the society, destroy pristine areas and disrupt important ecosystems.

2. The protection of the environment in armed conflicts to this point has been viewed primarily through the lens of the law of armed conflict. However, this perspective is too narrow, as modern international law recognizes that the international law applicable during an armed conflict may be wider than the law of armed conflict. This has also been recognized by the International Law Commission, including in its recent work on the effects of armed conflicts on treaties. This work takes, as its starting point, the presumption that the existence of an armed conflict does not ipso facto terminate or suspend the operation of treaties.

3. Since the applicable law in relation to armed conflict clearly extends beyond the realm of the law of armed conflict, it is sometimes not sufficient to refer to international humanitarian law as lex specialis in the hope of finding a solution to a specific legal problem. Other areas of international law may be applicable, such as international human rights and international environmental law. The International Court of Justice has recognized as much—albeit without elaborating on when one set of rules takes precedence over the other:

> More generally, the Court considers that the protection offered by human rights conventions does not cease in case of armed conflict, save through the effect of provisions for derogation of the kind to be found in Article 4 of the International Covenant on Civil and Political Rights. As regards the relationship between international humanitarian law and human rights law, there are thus three possible situations: some rights may be exclusively matters of international humanitarian law; others may be exclusively matters of human rights law; yet others may be matters of both these branches of international law. In order to answer the question put to it, the Court will have to take into consideration both these branches of international law, namely human rights law and, as lex specialis, international humanitarian law.

4. In its advisory opinion on the legality of the threat or use of nuclear weapons, the Court has also recognized that environmental considerations must be taken into account in wartime:

> The Court thus finds that while the existing international law relating to the protection and safeguarding of the environment does not specifically prohibit the use of nuclear weapons, it indicates important environmental factors that are properly to be taken into account in the context of the implementation of the principles and rules of the law applicable in armed conflict.

In arriving at this finding, the Court recalled its conclusion in the order related to the request for an examination of the situation in accordance with paragraph 63 of the Court's judgment of 20 December 1974 in the Nuclear Tests (New Zealand v. France) case, where the Court stated that its conclusion was 'without prejudice to the obligations of States to respect and protect the natural environment'. The Court indicated that '[a]lthough that statement was made in the context of nuclear testing, it naturally also applies to the actual use of nuclear weapons in armed conflict'. It should also be noted that the underlying assumption of the Court's reasoning has also been recognized by the International Law Commission, inter alia, in its work on fragmentation.

5. Even if one were to assume that only the law of armed conflict is applicable during an armed conflict, that law contains rules relating to measures taken before and after an armed conflict. The law of armed conflict is therefore not confined to the situation of an armed conflict as such. Accordingly, applicable rules of the lex specialis (the law of armed conflict) coexist with other rules of international law.

6. It appears as if no State or judicial body questions the parallel application of different branches of international law, such as human rights law, refugee law and environmental law. It also seems as if States and judicial bodies are undecided as to the precise application of those areas of the law. The caution on the part of States and judicial bodies to determine exactly how parallel application may work or when the lex specialis clearly prevails as the only applicable law may be understandable. At the same time, there is a need to analyse and reach conclusions with respect to this uncertainty.

7. The legal and political landscape has changed since specific rules for the purpose of protecting the environment during armed conflict were adopted almost 40 years ago, namely, the 1976 Convention on the Prohibition of Military or Any Other Hostile Use of Environmental Modification Techniques (ENMOD) and Protocol I additional to the 1949 Geneva Conventions. At that time, international environmental law was in its infancy. Moreover, armed conflicts back then were of a different character. That is to say, most conflicts were classified as being of an international character or a liberation war, whereas non-international armed conflicts of a different character are most common today. This new reality may pose a challenge when applying existing law.

Report of the Commission of Inquiry on Lebanon pursuant to Human Rights Council Resolution S-2/1

A/HRC/3/2, 23 November 2006

In August 2006, the UN Human Rights Council mandated a fact-finding commission to investigate alleged violations of international human rights law and international humanitarian law during the conflict between Israel and Lebanon between July and August 2006.

209. Already in the early stages of the conflict, [the Israeli Defence Force (IDF)] attacks on Lebanese infrastructure created large-scale environmental damage. The Commission considered the devastating effect the oil spill from the Jiyyeh power plant has had and will continue to have in the years to come over the flora and fauna on the Lebanese coast. This very serious event took place when the Israeli Air Force bombed the fuel storage tanks of the Jiyyeh electrical power station, situated 30 km south of Beirut. Due to its location by the sea, the attack resulted in an environmental disaster. The plant's damaged storage tanks gave way. According to the Lebanese Ministry of Environment, between 10,000 and 15,000 tons of oil spilled into the eastern Mediterranean Sea. A 10 km-wide oil slick covered 170 km of the Lebanese coastline ....

216. Article 35(3) of Additional Protocol I to the 1949 Geneva Conventions establishes a general prohibition on employing methods or means of warfare which are intended, or may be expected, to cause widespread, long-term and severe damage to the natural environment. Similarly, article 55(1) of the Protocol further indicates that special care shall be taken during armed conflict to protect the natural environment against widespread, long-term and severe damage.

217. Furthermore, as indicated by the International Court of Justice (ICJ) and reiterated in the legal literature, the principle that parties to a conflict shall take all necessary measures to avoid serious damage to the natural environment constitutes a norm of customary international law. In this respect, ICJ has stated the following:

> (...) States must take environmental considerations into account when assessing what is necessary and proportionate in the pursuit of legitimate military objectives. Respect for the environment is one of the elements that go to assessing whether an action is in conformity with the principles of necessity and proportionality. [*Legality of the Threat or Use of Nuclear Weapons*, advisory opinion of 8 July 1996, *I.C.J. Reports 1996 (I)*, p. 226, para. 30.]

218. Moreover, under article 8(2)(b)(iv) of the Rome Statute [establishing the International Criminal Court], the intentional launching of an attack in the knowledge that such attack will cause widespread, long-term and severe damage to the natural environment is considered a war crime.

219. The Commission finds that, while Israel may argue that attacks on these facilities were justified under military necessity, the fact is that it clearly ignored or chose to ignore the potential threats these attacks posed to the well-being of the civilian population. While Israel may have attained its military objective, it did so by putting the health of part of the population at risk. The Commission does not see how this potential threat can be outweighed by considerations of military necessity. It thus finds that Israel violated its international legal obligations to adequately take into consideration environmental and health minimum standards when evaluating the legitimacy of the attacks against the above-mentioned facilities.

220. Furthermore, the Commission holds the view that Israel should have taken into account the possibility that the attacks on the Jiyyeh power plant could lead to a massive oil spill into the sea. Despite the risks, IDF went ahead and attacked the site, with the consequences already explained. Whether the attack was justified or not by military necessity, the fact remains that the consequences went far beyond whatever military objective Israel may have had.

NOTES

1. Principle 24 of the Rio Declaration (see Section 1B) indicates how armed conflicts can harm the environment. The requirements in Articles 35 and 55 of the Additional Protocol I to the Geneva Conventions prohibit damage to the environment that is 'widespread, long-term and severe' and, in practice, this triple cumulative standard is nearly impossible to achieve. These Articles apply only in relation to international armed conflict. As treaty provisions, these Articles will bind only parties to the Additional Protocol I, although several commentators argue that these provisions may now constitute customary international law.

2. The Rome Statute of the International Criminal Court (see further Chapter 14) also criminalises an attack that causes widespread, long-term and severe damage to the natural environment, but only where that damage would be clearly excessive in relation to the concrete and direct overall military advantage anticipated: Article 8(2)(b)(iv). Again, this provision only applies in international armed conflicts and sets a very high threshold.

2. Provisions regulating the means of warfare (i.e. the types of weapons that may be used) may also indirectly protect the environment. Examples include the Biological Weapons Convention and the Convention on Cluster Munitions. However, new technology in the design and delivery of weapons may not yet be regulated. Moreover, the general humanitarian law principles of distinction, necessity and proportionality, while clearly principles of customary international law, may not be sufficient to protect the environment. It is also likely that existing environmental law treaties will continue to apply during an armed conflict.

3. Very few proceedings have been brought in relation to environmental damage caused during armed conflict, although there have been several United Nations-mandated commissions of inquiry that have considered environmental harm as part of their investigations, including the Commission regarding the 2006 conflict in Lebanon and the 2009 Goldstone mission, mandated to investigate allegations arising from Operation Cast Lead in 2008. In addition, the Security Council may decide that a State which has caused environmental damage is a threat to international peace and security (see Chapter 15) and can determine liability for such damage. In particular, Security Council Resolution 687 (see Chapter 15) affirms that Iraq is liable under international law for any direct loss, damage, including environmental damage, and the depletion of natural resources as a result of the invasion and occupation of Kuwait in 1991. The United Nations Compensation Commission, established in 1991 to process claims arising from the invasion, commissioned a panel of commissioners to consider environmental claims (known as F4 claims). The panel recommended the issue of compensation to Kuwait and other affected States for harm suffered to the environment and resources. The Commission is, to date, the only international body to have awarded compensation for environmental damage *per se*.

4. In contrast to the position regarding protection of the environment *per se*, objects of cultural property are protected by a specific convention: the Hague Convention for the Protection of Cultural Property in the Event of Armed Conflict 1954. This is designed to prevent the destruction or removal of items of cultural significance. An example would be the looting of various

museums and libraries in Baghdad during the invasion and occupation of Iraq in 2003 (see Chapter 15). Destruction of cultural property is criminalised under the Rome Statute for the International Criminal Court (see further Chapter 14) and the ICC has commenced proceedings in respect of the destruction of cultural property during the armed conflict in Mali.

C: Trade, finance and the environment

World Trade Organization, Doha Development Agenda
World Trade Organization Ministerial Declaration, 14 November 2001, 41 *International Legal Materials* 746 (2002)

31. With a view to enhancing the mutual supportiveness of trade and environment, we agree to negotiations, without prejudging their outcome, on:
    (i) the relationship between existing WTO rules and specific trade obligations set out in multilateral environmental agreements (MEAs). The negotiations shall be limited in scope to the applicability of such existing WTO rules as among parties to the MEA in question. The negotiations shall not prejudice the WTO rights of any Member that is not a party to the MEA in question;
    (ii) procedures for regular information exchange between MEA Secretariats and the relevant WTO committees, and the criteria for the granting of observer status;
    (iii) the reduction or, as appropriate, elimination of tariff and non-tariff barriers to environmental goods and services.

NOTES
1. The issues arising from the interaction of international economic law, particularly trade, and the environment are significant. The linking of environment and trade through the World Trade Organization (WTO) and the General Agreement on Tariffs and Trade (GATT) framework was a potentially significant development for environmental protection.
2. While multilateral environmental treaties have in many instances used bans on imports and exports of species, goods or technologies to protect the environment, the WTO/GATT system has introduced rules on the use of such trade measures. This system establishes a general prohibition on import and export bans with only limited environmental exceptions (see Chapter 13). The WTO has recognised that member States must, in some circumstances, be able to take measures to protect the environment that would otherwise be unlawful. The jurisprudence does suggest, however, that the exemption allowing for barriers to protect the environment is interpreted strictly, thus leading to environmental concerns being trumped by economic considerations.
3. The Doha Development Agenda commenced in late 2001. The Agenda provides for negotiations on a number of issues, including the linkage between environment and trade (see Article 31, extracted above). The Doha Round is the first time environmental issues have featured explicitly in the context of a multilateral trade negotiation and the overarching objective is to enhance the mutual supportiveness of trade and environment. The significance of the consideration of the environment was reaffirmed by States in Hong Kong in 2005. Other parts of the Doha negotiations are also relevant to the environment, for example aspects of the agriculture negotiations and also negotiations concerning fisheries subsidies. The UN Committee on Trade and Environment also provides a forum for dialogue on trade and the environment.
4. The Global Environment Facility, established in 1991, is a permanent and independent financial mechanism providing funds to developing States and States with economies in transition for activities that protect the environment. After much pressure, the World Bank began to take environmental matters into account in the 1990s. On 17 July 2001, the World Bank Group's Board of Directors endorsed an Environment Strategy titled *Making Sustainable Commitments: An Environment Strategy for the World Bank*. The document outlines how the World Bank would work with its client States to address their environmental challenges and ensure that projects and programmes integrate principles of environmental sustainability. In an independent evaluation of the Bank's performance, conducted in 2008, the assessor noted that the World Bank Group had made progress since 1990 as an advocate for the environment; however, it noted several constraints affecting the treatment of environmental issues in several programmes.

5. Another mechanism for ensuring compliance with social and environmental policies is the Inspection Panel system. This mechanism allows individuals who believe that they will be affected detrimentally by a project in a State that is to be funded by the World Bank to ask the Panel to investigate their claim (Resolution No. 93–6, 1993). The Bank can do this even if the State is opposed to such investigation. As at March 2016, the Inspection Panel had investigated some 105 claims. A similar system operates in the Asian Development Bank and the Inter-American Development Bank. These issues are considered further in Chapter 13.

6. Another way in which environmental concerns may influence financial decisions is through the adoption of industry benchmarks or frameworks. The Equator Principles were drafted by a number of banks, together with the World Bank Group's International Finance Corporation, and launched in 2003. The Principles provide a banking industry framework for addressing environmental and social risks in project financing, whereby participating banks agree not to finance projects unless the borrower can demonstrate compliance with the bank's own social and environmental policies. Adherence to the Principles is voluntary; however, over 83 financial institutions in 36 countries have adopted them. The Principles were updated in 2013.

7. Corporations may be held liable for environmental damage in national courts, including those of their State of incorporation, the State(s) in which they operate and the State in which the harm has been suffered. Accountability is, however, less likely when the State(s) in question has weak or non-existent regulatory frameworks. Various steps are being taken to address this risk, including through the development of standards on business and human rights issues and court actions in some States.

13

International Economic Law

With a flurry of developments over the past two decades, international economic law has become an increasingly vital and distinctive part of the international legal system. While the regulation of inter-State trade has always been an aspect of international law, the formation of international economic institutions together with binding rules governing an extensive range of economic matters and a wide array of dispute settlement methods has lead to a coherent body of law that can be described as international economic law.

International economic law also influences developments in other areas of international law. For example, the involvement in international economic law of entities other than States, in particular transnational corporations, is part of the broader movement of international law away from being a State-only system (see Chapter 5). International economic law also challenges some concepts of State sovereignty and territorial integrity, as well as often being both part of the processes of globalisation and a potential regulator of those processes. Indeed, international economic law issues are now found on the front pages of daily newspapers. Some of the extent of international economic law will be considered in this chapter, though only a representative sample will be given.

SECTION 1: DEFINING INTERNATIONAL ECONOMIC LAW

J. Jackson, 'International Economic Law: Reflections on the "Boiler room" of International Relations'

in C. Ku and P. Diehl (eds), *International Law: Classic and Contemporary Readings* (1998)

At the outset, it is appropriate to ask what we mean by 'international economic law'. This phrase can cover a very broad inventory of subjects: embracing the law of economic transactions; government regulation of economic matters; and related legal relations including litigation and international institutions for economic relations. Indeed, it is plausible to suggest that ninety per cent of international law work is in reality international economic law in some form or another. Much of this, of course, does not have the glamour or visibility of nation-state relations (use of force, human rights, intervention, etc.), but does indeed involve many questions of international law and particularly treaty law. Increasingly, today's international economic law issues are found on the front pages of the daily newspapers....

In trying to describe international economic law, I would like to mention four characteristics about the subject:

(1) International Economic Law (IEL) cannot be separated or compartmentalized from general or 'public' international law. The activities and cases relating to IEL contain much practice which is relevant to general principles of international law, especially concerning treaty law and practice. Conversely general international law has considerable relevance to economic relations and transactions....

(2) The relationship of international economic law to national or 'municipal' law is particularly important. It is an important part of understanding international law generally, but this 'link', and the interconnections between

IEL and municipal law are particularly significant to the operation and effectiveness of IEL rules. For example, an important question is the relationship of treaty norms to municipal law, expressed by such phrases as 'self executing' or 'direct application.'

(3) As the title phrase—international economic law—suggests, there is necessarily a strong component of multi-disciplinary research and thinking required for those who work on IEL projects. Of course, 'economics' is important and useful, especially for understanding the policy motivations of many of the international and national rules on the subject…In addition to economics, of course, other subjects are highly relevant. Political science (and its intersection with economics found generally in the 'public choice' literature) is very important, as are many other disciplines, such as cultural history and anthropology, geography, etc.

(4) As previously noted, work on IEL matters often seems to necessitate more empirical study than some other international law subjects. Empirical research, however, does not necessarily mean statistical research, in the sense used in many policy explorations. For some key issues of international law there are too few 'cases' on which to base statistical conclusions (such as correlations), so we are constrained to use a more 'anecdotal', or case study approach. This type of empiricism, however, is nevertheless very important, and a good check on theory or on sweeping generalizations of any kind.

NOTE: As Jackson notes, international economic law is found within many areas of international law and a significant number of activities that lead to the development of international law are economically generated. Despite its impact on a wide array of issues, Cottier (see Section 7) rightly points out that '[t]he interest of most international economic lawyers centres on international trade regulation and investment, less so on the transactional part of the equation, i.e. contracts, credit and insurance and monetary issues broadly speaking'. In the wake of the global financial crisis that began in 2008, this focus might be shifting. Indeed some have argued that the ineffectiveness of international legal rules on finance regulation was a key contributor to the conditions leading to the outbreak of the crisis.

SECTION 2: MAIN INTERNATIONAL ECONOMIC INSTITUTIONS

Primarily, international economic law is founded on the desire of States and other entities to reduce barriers to cross-border trade and foreign investment as a means to achieve domestic and global efficiency gains. This project was also motivated by the philosophical belief that closer economic integration between States provided a means for ensuring enhanced global security. The institutions that enable this to happen and to supervise compliance have evolved since the inception of modern treaty rules in the aftermath of the Second World War.

Agreement Establishing the World Trade Organization 1994

Article II Scope of the WTO

1. The WTO shall provide the common institutional framework for the conduct of trade relations among its Members in matters related to the agreements and associated legal instruments included in the Annexes to this Agreement.

2. The agreements and associated legal instruments included in Annexes 1, 2 and 3 (hereinafter referred to as 'Multilateral Trade Agreements') are integral parts of this Agreement, binding on all Members.

3. The agreements and associated legal instruments included in Annex 4 (hereinafter referred to as 'Plurilateral Trade Agreements') are also part of this Agreement for those Members that have accepted them, and are binding on those Members. The Plurilateral Trade Agreements do not create either obligations or rights for Members that have not accepted them.

The IMF and the World Bank—Fact Sheet

International Monetary Fund, External Relations Department, September 2015 http://www.imf.org/external/np/exr/facts/imfwb.htm

The IMF and the World Bank are institutions in the United Nations system. They share the same goal of raising living standards in their member countries. Their approaches to this goal are complementary, with the IMF focusing on macroeconomic issues and the World Bank concentrating on long-term economic development and poverty reduction.

The International Monetary Fund and the World Bank were both created at an international conference convened in Bretton Woods, New Hampshire, United States in July 1944. The goal of the conference was to establish a framework for economic cooperation and development that would lead to a more stable and prosperous global economy. While this goal remains central to both institutions, their work is constantly evolving in response to new economic developments and challenges.

The IMF's mandate. The IMF promotes international monetary cooperation and provides policy advice and technical assistance to help countries build and maintain strong economies. The Fund also makes loans and helps countries design policy programs to solve balance of payments problems when sufficient financing on affordable terms cannot be obtained to meet net international payments. IMF loans are short and medium term and funded mainly by the pool of quota contributions that its members provide. IMF staff are primarily economists with wide experience in macroeconomic and financial policies.

The World Bank's mandate. The World Bank promotes long-term economic development and poverty reduction by providing technical and financial support to help countries reform particular sectors or implement specific projects—such as, building schools and health centers, providing water and electricity, fighting disease, and protecting the environment. World Bank assistance is generally long term and is funded both by member country contributions and through bond issuance. World Bank staff are often specialists in particular issues, sectors, or techniques.

Framework for cooperation. The IMF and World Bank collaborate regularly and at many levels to assist member countries and work together on several initiatives. In 1989, the terms for their cooperation were set out in a concordat to ensure effective collaboration in areas of shared responsibility.

High-level coordination. During the Annual Meeting of the Boards of Governors of the IMF and the World Bank, Governors consult and present their countries' views on current issues in international economics and finance. The Boards of Governors decide how to address international economic and financial issues and set priorities for the organizations.

A group of IMF and World Bank Governors also meet as part of the Development Committee, whose meetings coincide with the Spring and Annual Meetings of the IMF and the World Bank. This committee was established in 1974 to advise the two institutions on critical development issues and on the financial resources required to promote economic development in low-income countries.

Management consultation. The Managing Director of the IMF and the President of the World Bank meet regularly to consult on major issues. They also issue joint statements and occasionally write joint articles, and have visited several regions and countries together.

Staff collaboration. The staffs of the IMF and the Bank collaborate closely on country assistance and policy issues that are relevant for both institutions. The two institutions also often conduct country missions participate in each other's missions. IMF assessments of a country's general economic situation and policies provide input to the Bank's assessments of potential development projects or reforms. Similarly, Bank advice on structural and sectoral reforms is taken into account by the IMF in its policy advice. The staffs of the two institutions also cooperate on the conditionality involved in their respective lending programs....

Reducing debt burdens. The IMF and World Bank also work together to reduce the external debt burdens of the most heavily indebted poor countries under the Heavily Indebted Poor Countries (HIPC) Initiative and the Multilateral Debt Relief Initiative (MDRI). The objective is to help low-income countries achieve their development goals without creating future debt problems. IMF and Bank staff jointly prepare country debt sustainability analyses under the Debt Sustainability Framework (DSF) developed by the two institutions.

Reducing poverty. In 1999, the IMF and the World Bank initiated the Poverty Reduction Strategy Paper (PRSP) approach as a key component in the process leading to debt relief under the HIPC Initiative and an important anchor in concessional lending by the Fund and the Bank. While PRSPs continue to underpin the HIPC Initiative, the World Bank has adopted in July 2014 a new consultative approach to country engagement focused on supporting its members' policies to eliminate extreme poverty and promote shared prosperity. The Fund continues to rely on PRSPs to support the link between poverty reduction and Fund engagement under the Extended Credit Facility and the Policy Support Instrument.

Setting the Stage for the 2030 development agenda. Since 2004, the Fund and Bank have worked together on the *Global Monitoring Report* (GMR), which assesses progress needed to achieve the UN Millennium

Development Goals (MDGs). The forthcoming GMR (2015/2016) will discuss the Sustainable Development Goals (SDGs) that have replaced the MDGs as the basis for the 2030 development agenda. The Fund and the Bank have been active participants in the global debate on the 2030 development agenda. Each institution has committed to new initiatives, within their respective remits, to support member countries in reaching their development goals, and are working together on development initiatives to better assist the joint membership.

Assessing financial stability. The IMF and World Bank are also working together to make financial sectors in member countries resilient and well regulated. The Financial Sector Assessment Program (FSAP) was introduced in 1999 to identify the strengths and vulnerabilities of a country's financial system and recommend appropriate policy responses.

NOTES

1. The World Trade Organization (WTO) was created in 1995 as an international organisation (though not a UN entity), as a successor to the treaty system established under the General Agreement on Tariffs and Trade (GATT). As at March 2016, there are 162 State members of the WTO. There are also 22 States that have observer status, which enables them to attend WTO meetings but also requires them to begin accession negotiations within five years of becoming observers.

2. The WTO Agreement provides that all agreements included in Annexes 1, 2 and 3 are integral parts of the Agreement (Article II: 2). In total, there are four annexes to the WTO Agreement. The first annex is by far the most extensive and sets out substantive international trade law standards. It contains a wide range of Multilateral Agreements on Trade in Goods, including the GATT 1994 (which incorporates GATT 1947 with a few minor amendments) as well as several specialised agreements (e.g. on agriculture, sanitary and phytosanitary measures, textiles and clothing, trade-related investment measures, subsidies and countervailing measures, anti-dumping, etc.). The first annex also includes the General Agreement on Trade in Services and the Agreement on Trade-related Aspects of Intellectual Property Rights (TRIPS).

3. Aside from these substantive obligations, the WTO Agreement also covers a range of important procedural mechanisms to ensure member State compliance. In particular, Annex 2 provides for an Understanding on Rules and Procedures Governing the Settlement of Disputes (DSU). The DSU sets out a complex, two-tiered system of dispute settlement that is unique in public international law. Disputes between member States are first heard before an *ad hoc* WTO panel. A losing WTO member State has the right to appeal from a panel's report on issues of law to a standing Appellate Body, which is comprised of 'persons of recognized authority with demonstrated expertise in law, international trade and the subject matter of the covered agreements generally' (DSU, Article 17.3). Aside from formal dispute settlement mechanisms, Annex 3 establishes a Trade Policy Review Mechanism (TPRM) within WTO. Under the TPRM, member States are obliged to report their trade policies to the WTO as a part of a review process designed to achieve greater coherence and compliance with the GATT, GATS and other provisions of the WTO.

4. The WTO Agreement also provides for the creation of bodies responsible for overseeing the functioning of the WTO and the annexed ('covered') agreements set out above. The Ministerial Conference, composed of ministerial representatives of every member State, meets at least every two years and is the main body responsible for the functioning of the WTO as well as for outlining major policy lines of the organisation. The General Council, also a State representative body, is charged with overseeing the WTO between meetings of the Ministerial Conference. The General Council also convenes as the Dispute Settlement Body under the DSU (Article IV) and is responsible in this capacity for overseeing dispute settlement procedures within the WTO, such as monitoring compliance with decisions of dispute settlement bodies. Separate councils also exist for Trade in Goods, Trade in Services and TRIPS to oversee the respective agreements. A number of committees have also been created to examine specific issues of relevance to the WTO, such as the Committee on Trade and the Environment.

5. Article XVI: 1 of the WTO Agreement declares that 'except as otherwise provided under this Agreement or the Multilateral Trade Agreements, the WTO shall be guided by the decisions, procedures and customary practices followed by the Contracting Parties to GATT 1947 and the bodies established in the framework of GATT 1947'. This emphasises the continuing relevance of earlier GATT practice to current international economic law.

6. The World Bank consists of two separate institutions: the International Bank for Reconstruction and Development (IBRD; established at Bretton Woods in 1944), and the International Development Association (IDA; established in 1950). The IBRD provides credits to bolster development in

middle-income countries whilst the IDA lends all its resources to States with the lowest *per capita* income. Three other institutions are closely connected to the World Bank, namely the Multilateral Investment Guarantee Agency, which acts as an insurance agency liaising on World Bank funding projects, the International Centre for the Settlement of Investment Disputes, which provides a dispute settlement regime applying both to agreements between States and agreements between private investors and States (see Section 4A and Chapter 16) and the International Finance Corporation, which provides investments to support the private sector in developing States. Together, these five institutions form the World Bank Group.

7. As shown, the World Bank and the IMF cooperate very closely and on various levels. There is no formal relationship between the World Bank Group and the IMF on the one hand and the WTO on the other hand. Nevertheless, the organisations do operate with some collaboration. For example, Article III of the Agreement Establishing the World Trade Organization provides that: 'With a view to achieving greater coherence in global economic policy-making, the WTO shall cooperate, as appropriate, with the International Monetary Fund and with the International Bank for Reconstruction and Development and its affiliated agencies.'

8. The main purpose and working methods of the IMF have changed considerably over the decades. When it was established in 1944, it worked with fixed exchange rates for currencies in relation to the US dollar, and also foresaw a fixed value for gold. However, the system of fixed exchange rates collapsed in the 1970s following the 1973 oil crisis. Since then, States can adopt any form of exchange agreement regarding their currencies (except for pegging it to gold). The IMF continued supervising the global monetary development and its members' monetary policies. It tries to prevent adverse effects of certain policies through consultations and policy advice.

SECTION 3: KEY PRINCIPLES OF INTERNATIONAL TRADE LAW

There are four key principles that underpin international trade law relating to trade in goods: tariffication; binding of tariffs; most favoured nation treatment; and the national treatment obligation. Tariffication and the binding of tariffs relate solely to trade in goods. However, the most favoured nation treatment and national treatment principles have been incorporated where relevant in other parts of the WTO, such as the General Agreement on Trade in Services (GATS).

All principles are subject to a set of exceptions, foreseen by the GATT or other relevant texts. There are also specific rules designed to enable WTO member States to enter into regional trade arrangements, as well mechanisms to guarantee 'special and differential treatment' for developing States.

A: Tariffication

The principle of tariffication prohibits the use of quantitative restrictions on imports or exports of goods. Most importantly, this principle aims to ensure that there are no barriers to the entry of goods at the border other than tariffs (which are then subject to obligations described in Parts B and C below). As will be seen below, there are a variety of economic and political justifications for this strong prohibition.

General Agreement on Tariffs and Trade 1947

Article XI General Elimination of Quantitative Restrictions

1. No prohibitions or restrictions other than duties, taxes or other charges, whether made effective through quotas, import or export licences or other measures, shall be instituted or maintained by any contracting party on the importation of any product of the territory of any other contracting party or on the exportation or sale for export of any product destined for the territory of any other contracting party.

NOTES
1. The strategic goal of Article XI is to promote the conversion of all national border barriers to trade (especially quantitative restrictions) into tariffs (a tax applied to the entry of foreign goods), which can then be reduced through multilateral negotiation. In general, quantitative restrictions (such as quotas and licences) pose a greater impediment than tariffs to cross-border trade. For example, depending on the level of a given tariff, an efficient exporter may be able to incorporate the cost of a tariff and still compete with domestic producers in the importing State. Quantitative restrictions are also far less transparent and can lead to arbitrary decision-making by State officials. In contrast, because tariffs are a tax they can be measured and reduced incrementally over time through successive rounds of negotiations between WTO member States. This has important implications for many developing States for whom tariffs remain an important source of governmental revenue.
2. An exception to this principle of tariffication is provided in Article XIII of GATT, which permits developing States to impose quantitative restrictions on a temporary basis for balance of payments or infant industry reasons (see Section 3H). Other exceptions allow the use of export prohibitions or restrictions to meet internal shortages (Article XI: 2) and allow a State to safeguard its external financial position and its balance of payments (Articles XII and XIII: B).

B: Binding of tariffs

Binding of tariffs is a principle by which individual States agree to tariff levels for particular products and 'bind' those tariff levels in schedules to the GATT. There is a schedule for each State, which forms the subject of negotiating rounds in the WTO. Under Article II of the GATT, States agree not to raise tariffs above the levels (bounds) contained in their tariff schedules. Where States act contrary to these schedules, the GATT provides for compensatory adjustments and other remedies (Article XXVIII). As an outcome of the Uruguay Round in 1994, tariffs for industrial products were bound; the WTO has subsequently also negotiated disciplines on tariffs for agricultural products.

C: Most favoured nation treatment

General Agreement on Tariffs and Trade 1947

Article I General Most-Favoured-Nation Treatment

With respect to customs duties and charges of any kind imposed on or in connection with importation or exportation or imposed on the international transfer of payments for imports or exports, and with respect to the method of levying such duties and charges, and with respect to all rules and formalities in connection with importation and exportation, and with respect to all matters referred to in paragraphs 2 and 4 of Article III, any advantage, favour, privilege or immunity granted by any contracting party to any product originating in or destined for any other country shall be accorded immediately and unconditionally to the like product originating in or destined for the territories of all other contracting parties.

NOTES
1. The most favoured nation (MFN) clause embodies the norm of non-discrimination, prohibiting discrimination between trading partners (States). The principle provides that any special treatment given to a product from one trading partner must be available to all like products originating in, or destined for, other contracting parties. As a result a contracting party cannot treat imports from one WTO member State more favourably than any other WTO member State.
2. In practice the MFN clause means that a tariff concession made by one State with another is in effect granted to all other parties, without the conceding party being able to demand a *quid pro quo* as a condition for the extension of the concession. This obligation has been blamed for limiting the readiness of contracting parties to make offers and concessions in multilateral negotiations, particularly when larger economies appear unwilling to act reciprocally. However, arguably,

unconditional MFN treatment helps spread trade liberalisation more quickly by reducing the process of tariff negotiations.

3. The principle of most favoured nation treatment in GATT 1947 has been subject to much criticism because, despite the legal obligations found in Article I, there are both departures in trade practice and exceptions within the GATT itself. These exceptions generally relate to preferential trading arrangements, anti-dumping rights, regional trading arrangements or in regard to developing States. Some of these exceptions are discussed below.

D: National treatment obligation

Whereas the MFN principle prevents discrimination between imports from different WTO member States, the national treatment obligation prohibits the use of national taxes and regulations so as to advantage domestic over foreign producers. In effect, national treatment acts as a fail-safe for the project of liberalisation of national border barriers to trade in goods. It prevents a State from circumventing its tariff reduction commitments by substituting national (tax or regulatory) restrictions which discriminate against foreign goods.

General Agreement on Tariffs and Trade 1947

Article III National Treatment on Internal Taxation and Regulation

1. The contracting parties recognize that internal taxes and other internal charges, and laws, regulations and requirements affecting the internal sale, offering for sale, purchase, transportation, distribution or use of products, and internal quantitative regulations requiring the mixture, processing or use of products in specified amounts or proportions, should not be applied to imported or domestic products so as to afford protection to domestic production.

2. The products of the territory of any contracting party imported into the territory of any other contracting party shall not be subject, directly or indirectly, to internal taxes or other internal charges of any kind in excess of those applied, directly or indirectly, to like domestic products. Moreover, no contracting party shall otherwise apply internal taxes or other internal charges to imported or domestic products in a manner contrary to the principles set forth in paragraph 1....

4. The products of the territory of any contracting party imported into the territory of any other contracting party shall be accorded treatment no less favourable than that accorded to like products of national origin in respect of all laws, regulations and requirements affecting their internal sale, offering for sale, purchase, transportation, distribution or use.

Japan—Taxes on Alcoholic Beverages II
WT/DS8/AB/R WT/DS10/AB/R WT/DS11/AB/R, Adopted 11 November 1996, World Trade Organization, Report of the Appellate Body

The broad and fundamental purpose of Article III is to avoid protectionism in the application of internal tax and regulatory measures. More specifically, the purpose of Article III 'is to ensure that internal measures "not be applied to imported or domestic products so as to afford protection to domestic production"'. Toward this end, Article III obliges Members of the WTO to provide equality of competitive conditions for imported products in relation to domestic products. '[T]he intention of the drafters of the Agreement was clearly to treat the imported products in the same way as the like domestic products once they had been cleared through customs. Otherwise indirect protection could be given'. Moreover, it is irrelevant that 'the trade effects' of the tax differential between imported and domestic products, as reflected in the volumes of imports, are insignificant or even non-existent; Article III protects expectations not of any particular trade volume but rather of the equal competitive relationship between imported and domestic products. Members of the WTO are free to pursue their own domestic goals through internal taxation or regulation so long as they do not do so in a way that violates Article III or any of the other commitments they have made in the WTO Agreement....

> [T]he panel is correct in seeing a distinction between Article III:1, which 'contains general principles', and Article III:2, which 'provides for specific obligations regarding internal taxes and internal charges'. Article III:1 articulates a general principle that internal measures should not be applied so as to afford protection to domestic production. This general principle informs the rest of Article III.

NOTES

1. The national treatment obligation explicitly recognises the tariff bindings to which States have committed themselves. Thus, once border duties have been paid in accordance with a State's tariff bindings, the principle of national treatment operates to prohibit any additional burdens being placed discriminately on the foreign producer or products.

2. As the above extract shows, the Appellate Body in the *Japan—Alcoholic Beverages II* case differentiates between Article III:1, which contains general underlying principles, and Article III:2 and 4, which regulates specific obligations regarding internal taxes and charges, and internal laws and regulations respectively. This was confirmed by *European Union—Measures Affecting Asbestos and Asbestos Containing Products* (the *Asbestos Case*) (Report of the Appellate Body, WT/DS135/AB/R, 12 March 2001). Article III:1 plays a critical role in the delineation of the scope of the national treatment obligation as it confirms that the overall purpose of this legal obligation is to constrain protectionism in the use of national taxes and regulations.

3. Article III:2 comprises two distinct principles and Article III:1 informs each sentence in a different manner. The first sentence establishes that if imported products are taxed in excess of like domestic products, then that tax measure is inconsistent with Article III. In order to determine whether there has been a violation of Article III:2, first sentence, the Appellate Body in the *Canada—Periodicals* case (Report of the Appellate Body, WT/DS31/AB/R, 30 July 1997) held (at pp. 23/23) that there were two distinct questions that needed to be examined: First, whether imported and domestic products are 'like' products and second, whether the imported products were taxed in excess of the domestic products. The Appellate Body in *Japan—Alcoholic Beverages II* confirmed the GATT 1947 practice that 'like products' in the sense of Article III:2, first sentence, needs to be construed narrowly and on a case-by-case basis. With regard to the phrase 'in excess of', the Appellate Body held (at p. 23) that '[e]ven the smallest amount of "excess" is too much'.

4. If there is no violation of Article III:2, first sentence, it is still possible that a tax measure is inconsistent with Article III:2, second sentence. The Appellate Body in the *Japan—Alcoholic Beverages II* case established three issues that need to be examined under Article III:2, second sentence: first, an analysis of whether the imported and domestic products are 'directly competitive or substitutable products'; second, whether they are 'not similarly taxed'; and last whether the dissimilar taxation affords protection to domestic production. The Appellate Body further held (pp. 27–36) that 'directly competitive or substitutable products' is a broader category than 'like products'; that 'not similarly taxed' is something more than being a little more in excess; and that to determine whether the tax in question affords protection to domestic production, the effect of the measure on each product must be analysed.

5. The Appellate Body in the *Asbestos Case* confirmed that the 'general principle' contained in Article III:1 and recognised in the *Japanese Beverages Case* (above) also informs Article III:4 such that there must be 'consonance between the objective pursued by Article III, and enunciated in the "general principle" articulated in Article III:1, and the interpretation of the specific expression of this principle in the text of Article III:4' (at para. 98). Article III:4, therefore, is concerned to prevent the application of internal regulations 'in a manner which effects the competitive relationship, in the marketplace, between the domestic and imported products' (at para. 98).

6. While Article III:2 is exclusively concerned with tax measures, Article III:4 deals with discrimination against imported like products by internal laws, regulations and requirements. The Appellate Body in the *Asbestos Case* held that 'the determination of likeness under Article III:4 is, fundamentally, a determination about the nature and extent of a competitive relationship between and among products (at para. 99). The Appellate Body further noted (at para. 99) that the scope of 'like' in Article III:4 is broader than the same term in Article III:2 but that the provision is not broader than 'the combined product scope of the two sentences of Article III:2'. The Appellate Body considered that a difference in the product scope of the two provisions would 'frustrate a consistent application of the "general principle"' in Article III:1 as fiscal and non-fiscal measures covered by the provisions are often used to achieve the same ends (at para. 99).

E: Exceptions to the key principles of international trade law

Despite the commitment by the GATT Contracting Parties to the above principles, the GATT includes many exceptions to its key obligations. If it is determined that a State is in breach of its obligations under the GATT (e.g. if it has imposed a measure contrary to Article III, see Section 3D), it must then be asked whether the State's actions fall within an exception and therefore still comply with GATT rules.

General Agreement on Tariffs and Trade 1947

Article XX General Exceptions

Subject to the requirement that such measures are not applied in a manner which would constitute a means of arbitrary or unjustifiable discrimination between countries where the same conditions prevail, or a disguised restriction on international trade, nothing in this Agreement shall be construed to prevent the adoption or enforcement by any contracting party of measures:

    (a) necessary to protect public morals;

    (b) necessary to protect human, animal or plant life or health;

    (c) relating to the importations or exportations of gold or silver;

    (d) necessary to secure compliance with laws or regulations which are not inconsistent with the provisions of this Agreement, including those relating to customs enforcement, the enforcement of monopolies operated under paragraph 4 of Article II and Article XVII, the protection of patents, trade marks and copyrights, and the prevention of deceptive practices;

    (e) relating to the products of prison labour;

    (f) imposed for the protection of national treasures of artistic, historic or archaeological value;

    (g) relating to the conservation of exhaustible natural resources if such measures are made effective in conjunction with restrictions on domestic production or consumption.

United States—Standards for Reformulated and Conventional Gasoline
WT/DS2/AB/R, 29 April 1996, World Trade Organization, Report of Appellate Body

This case concerned a US measure designed to limit the pollution from the combustion of gasoline. Acceptable levels of pollution were calculated by reference to 1990 levels, referred to as baselines, which could be determined using two methods: one permitted refiners to establish individual baselines and the other was a statutory baseline based on average US levels. Foreign refiners, unlike US domestic refiners, were generally only able to use the statutory baseline, which was claimed to be discriminatory in violation of the national treatment obligation.

In order that the justifying protection of Article XX may be extended to it, the measure at issue must not only come under one or another of the particular exceptions—paragraphs (a) to (j)—listed under Article XX; it must also satisfy the requirements imposed by the opening clauses of Article XX. The analysis is, in other words, two-tiered: first, provisional justification by reason of characterization of the measure under XX(g); second, further appraisal of the same measure under the introductory clauses of Article XX.

The chapeau [the introductory part of an Article] by its express terms addresses, not so much the questioned measure or its specific contents as such, but rather the manner in which that measure is applied. It is, accordingly, important to underscore that the purpose and object of the introductory clauses of Article XX is generally the prevention of 'abuse of the exceptions of [what was later to become] Article [XX]' This insight drawn from the drafting history of Article XX is a valuable one. The chapeau is animated by the principle that while the exceptions of Article XX may be invoked as a matter of legal right, they should not be so applied as to frustrate or defeat the legal obligations of the holder of the right under the substantive rules of the [GATT]. If those exceptions are not to be abused or misused, in other words, the measures falling within the particular exceptions must be applied reasonably, with due regard both to the legal duties of the party claiming the exception and the legal rights of the other parties concerned....

United States—Import Prohibition of Certain Shrimp and Shrimp Products

WT/DS58/AB/R, 12 October 1998, World Trade Organization, Report of the Appellate Body

The US, in an attempt to reduce the death of sea turtles associated with shrimp harvesting, imposed an import ban on any shrimp harvested using fishing technology not in accordance with specific requirements set out in a US law and that could adversely affect certain species of sea turtle listed as endangered under US legislation. The Panel and the Appellate Body found that the US law in question, despite falling within Article XX(g), constituted arbitrary and unjustifiable discrimination and did not therefore satisfy the chapeau of Article XX.

150. In order for a measure to be applied in a manner which would constitute 'arbitrary or unjustifiable discrimination between countries where the same conditions prevail', three elements must exist. First, the application of the measure must result in *discrimination*....[T]he nature and quality of this discrimination is different from the discrimination in the treatment of products which was already found to be inconsistent with one of the substantive obligations of the GATT 1994, such as Articles I, III or XI. Second, the discrimination must be *arbitrary* or *unjustifiable* in character....Third, this discrimination must occur *between countries where the same conditions prevail*. In *United States—Gasoline*, we accepted the assumption of the participants in that appeal that such discrimination could occur not only between different exporting Members, but also between exporting Members and the importing Member concerned.

157. In our view, the language of the chapeau makes clear that each of the exceptions in paragraphs (a) to (j) of Article XX is a *limited and conditional* exception from the substantive obligations contained in the other provisions of the GATT 1994, that is to say, the ultimate availability of the exception is subject to the compliance by the invoking Member with the requirements of the chapeau...

161. Perhaps the most conspicuous flaw in this measure's application relates to its intended and actual coercive effect on the specific policy decisions made by foreign governments, Members of the WTO. [The law in question] is, in effect, an economic embargo which requires *all other exporting Members*, if they wish to exercise their GATT rights, to adopt *essentially the same* policy (together with an approved enforcement program) as that applied to, and enforced on, United States domestic shrimp trawlers.

NOTES

1. The method of interpretation adopted in the *Reformulated Gasoline Case* (Appellate Body Report, WT/DS2/AB/R, adopted 20 May 1996) requires the provisional justification of a measure under one of the substantive grounds in Article XX(a) to (j), and then further appraisal of the measure under the introduction (or 'chapeau') of the Article. A two-tiered test is thus required. The Appellate Body in the *Reformulated Gasoline Case* determined that the heads of exception in Article XX concern the design or character of the measure in question whereas the chapeau is concerned with the application of that measure.

2. In the *Shrimp Turtle Case*, the Appellate Body further indicated that the chapeau contains three distinct elements that need to be examined separately. The different standard for 'discrimination' between Articles XX and e.g. III:4 had already been considered in the *Reformulated Gasoline Case*, where the Appellate Body found that 'The provisions of the chapeau cannot logically refer to the same standard(s) by which a violation of a substantive rule has been determined to have occurred'.

3. Prior to the formation of the WTO in 1994, the GATT Panels in both *Tuna-Dolphins Cases* (30 ILM 1594 (1991), GATT Panel Report; and DS29/R (1994), GATT Panel Report) considered that Article XX(b) and (g) could not be used to justify measures having extra-jurisdictional application, such as an import ban aimed at forcing another State to change its environmental policy. The *Tuna-Dolphins 1* Panel (at para 5.27) considered that this would permit States 'unilaterally [to] determine ... policies from which other parties could not deviate without jeopardising their rights under the General Agreement'. Although the Appellate Body in the *Shrimp Turtle Case* did not consider that the extra-jurisdictional effect of a measure rendered it *prima facie* incapable of justification under the Article XX exceptions, its report suggests that it will be difficult for member States to justify unilateral measures that distinguish without cause between different States under the terms of the chapeau.

4. The interpretation applied in a number of cases concerning environmental measures to the particular environmental exceptions in Article XX(b) and (g) has created the perception amongst environmental groups that the WTO places commercial concerns above environmental protection. Dispute settlement bodies have indicated that there is little possibility of a State justifying a trade-related environmental measure under Article XX unless it relies on a multilateral environmental treaty that is in force between the parties (see Chapter 12) or has attempted to negotiate an agreement with the States concerned (though see *Brazil—Measures Affecting Imports of Retreaded Tyres* (Appellate Body, December 2007). By emphasising the object and purpose of the GATT 1994 and the WTO Agreement these decisions confirm that their central focus is the promotion of economic development through trade and a desire to deter States from resorting to environmental reasons for protectionist measures.

5. Next to the general exceptions contained in Article XX, Article XXI foresees exceptions for security reasons. The basic justification for invoking the security exception is to provide for national defence and security by securing the production of goods essential for defence. Furthermore, Article XXI(c) provides an exception permitting trade sanctions imposed in the performance of State's obligations under the United Nations Charter (see Chapter 15).

F: Anti-dumping and subsidies

Anti-dumping and subsidies, together with countervailing duties, constitute important exceptions to the key principles of most favoured nation treatment and non-discrimination. Both were originally foreseen in the GATT of 1947, but a much more detailed framework was introduced during the WTO Uruguay Round through the Agreement on the Implementation of Article VI GATT ('Anti-dumping agreement') and the Agreement on Subsidies and Countervailing Measures. Both agreements are part of Annex I to the Agreement Establishing the WTO and are thus mandatory for all WTO members (see Section 2). The main issue with subsidies and dumping is whether the original action (dumping or subsidisation) or the response (anti-dumping duty or countervailing duty) is the greater threat to international free trade.

General Agreement on Tariffs and Trade 1994

Article VI Anti-dumping and Countervailing Duties

1. The contracting parties recognize that dumping, by which products of one country are introduced into the commerce of another country at less than the normal value of the products, is to be condemned if it causes or threatens material injury to an established industry in the territory of a contracting party or materially retards the establishment of a domestic industry. For the purposes of this Article, a product is to be considered as being introduced into the commerce of an importing country at less than its normal value, if the price of the product exported from one country to another:

    (a) is less than the comparable price, in the ordinary course of trade, for the like product when destined for consumption in the exporting country, or,

    (b) in the absence of such domestic price, is less than either

        (i) the highest comparable price for the like product for export to any third country in the ordinary course of trade, or

        (ii) the cost of production of the product in the country of origin plus a reasonable addition for selling cost and profit...

Article XVI Subsidies

If any contracting party grants or maintains any subsidy, including any form of income or price support, which operates directly or indirectly to increase exports of any product from, or to reduce imports of any product into, its territory, it shall notify the Contracting Parties in writing of the extent and nature of the subsidization, of the estimated effect of the subsidization on the quantity of the affected product or products imported into or exported from its territory and of the circumstances making the subsidization necessary. In any case in which it is determined that serious prejudice to the interests of any other contracting party is caused or threatened by any such subsidization, the contracting party granting the subsidy shall, upon request, discuss with the other contracting party or parties concerned, or with the Contracting Parties, the possibility of limiting the subsidization.

NOTES
1. Dumping is a practice by which a product is exported by a company at a price that is considerably inferior to the 'normal' value of the product (i.e. the price at which the product is sold by that company in the domestic market). A subsidy is direct or indirect financial contribution by the State that confers a benefit. Because WTO law regulates States' conduct, it includes provisions regulating the imposition of subsidies, but does not regulate dumping (as this practice is widely exercised by private companies which are outside the scope of WTO legal regulation). However, both anti-dumping rights and countervailing duties against subsidies follow the same underlying idea, namely to neutralise what some regard as an 'unfair' trade practice. Fairness is however a contestable concept and when it comes to anti-dumping duties, most economists criticise the logic of such duties given their adverse impacts on consumers in importing States.
2. In early GATT texts there was little regulation of subsidies, though, over time, this was changed. In the Uruguay Round, the Agreement on Subsidies and Countervailing Measures 1994 (SCM) introduced the first definition of subsidies, set out specific conditions under which subsidies could be put into place and placed limitations on the use of countervailing duties. There are two types of subsidies: Prohibited Subsidies and Actionable Subsidies. Prohibited Subsidies directly convey a right to a countervailing duty, whereas Actionable Subsidies are allowed as long as they do not have an adverse effect on the interests of another State. To be able to respond to a subsidy with a countervailing duty, the subsidy must be specific to an enterprise or industry, rather than applying generally.
3. Article VI provides for the imposition of anti-dumping duties on dumped products up to the level of the margin of the dumping, that is, the difference between the export price of the good and its domestic price, provided that the imports are causing material injury to the importing State (Article VI:2). The provisions of GATT do not ban dumping, rather they provide a permitted response that would otherwise be in breach of GATT. The Agreement on the Implementation of Article IV of GATT 1994 adopted a series of tests about how to determine whether a good has been dumped, and made it harder for a State to establish a material injury. The Agreement also established a process for the investigation of dumping charges and the imposition of anti-dumping duties.

G: Regional trading arrangements

The principles of most favoured nation and national treatment are potentially threatened by the development of preferential trading arrangements such as the European Union (EU) and the North American Free Trade Agreement (NAFTA). Regional free-trade areas and customs unions have experienced an unprecedented popularity in the past decade.

General Agreement on Tariffs and Trade 1947

Article XXIV Territorial Application—Frontier Traffic—Customs Unions and Free-trade Areas

4. The contracting parties recognize the desirability of increasing freedom of trade by the development, through voluntary agreements, of closer integration between the economies of the countries parties to such agreements. They also recognize that the purpose of a customs union or of a free-trade area should be to facilitate trade between the constituent territories and not to raise barriers to the trade of other contracting parties with such territories.

5. Accordingly, the provisions of this Agreement shall not prevent, as between the territories of contracting parties, the formation of a customs union or of a free-trade area or the adoption of an interim agreement necessary for the formation of a customs union or of a free-trade area; *Provided* that:
   (a) with respect to a customs union, or an interim agreement leading to a formation of a customs union, the duties and other regulations of commerce imposed at the institution of any such union or interim agreement in respect of trade with contracting parties not parties to such union or agreement shall not on the whole be higher or more restrictive than the general incidence of the duties and regulations of commerce applicable in the constituent territories prior to the formation of such union or the adoption of such interim agreement, as the case may be;

(b) with respect to a free-trade area, or an interim agreement leading to the formation of a free-trade area, the duties and other regulations of commerce maintained in each of the constituent territories and applicable at the formation of such free-trade area or the adoption of such interim agreement to the trade of contracting parties not included in such area or not parties to such agreement shall not be higher or more restrictive than the corresponding duties and other regulations of commerce existing in the same constituent territories prior to the formation of the free-trade area, or interim agreement as the case may be; and

(c) any interim agreement referred to in sub-paragraphs (a) and (b) shall include a plan and schedule for the formation of such a customs union or of such a free-trade area within a reasonable length of time.

Turkey—Restrictions on Imports of Textile and Clothing Products
WT/DS34/AB/R, 22 October 1999, World Trade Organization, Report of the Appellate Body

Pursuant to the Turkey-European Commission customs union, Turkey imposed quantitative import restrictions of a broad range of textile and clothing products from India. India claimed that those measures are inconsistent with Articles XI and XIII of GATT 1994.

58. [W]e are of the view that Article XXIV may justify a measure which is inconsistent with certain other GATT provisions. However, in a case involving the formation of a customs union, this 'defence' is only available when two conditions are fulfilled. First, the party claiming the benefit of this defence must demonstrate that the measure at issue is introduced upon the formation of a customs union that fully meets the requirements of sub-paragraphs 8(a) and 5(a) of Article XXIV. And, second, that party must demonstrate that the formation of that customs union would be prevented if it were not allowed to introduce the measure at issue. Again, *both* these conditions must be met to have the benefit of the defence under Article XXIV.

NOTES
1. The regional trade exception provides for the establishment of three types of regional trading arrangements that can operate as exceptions to the GATT framework: customs unions; free-trade areas; and interim arrangements that lead to the establishment of either a customs union or a free-trade area. Customs unions involve an abolition of import duties between members and the imposition of a common external tariff against all non-members of the customs union. To be permitted under GATT, the duties and restrictions on trade applying to non-members cannot be on the whole more restrictive than before the formation of the customs union (Article XXIV:5(a)). A free-trade area is less integrated than a customs union, with the abolition of import duties between members and the retention of independent tariffs against non-members. To be permitted under GATT, tariffs with non-members cannot be on the whole more restrictive than before the formation of the free-trade area (Article XXIV:5(b)).

2. While regional trading arrangements may appear to be a form of protectionism, it is possible that such an arrangement between similar States can provide faster and deeper economic integration that can lead to later multilateral trade liberalisation. This can occur outside the complex negotiating process of the WTO.

H: Developing states in the WTO

Many WTO Agreements, including the GATT, contain special provisions regarding developing States, including exemption from basic trade principles under certain conditions and so-called 'special and differential treatment'. This is based on the assumption that developing States have specific economic needs in order to advance development that must be taken into consideration. The special and differential treatment provisions have generated much discussion as to whether they genuinely assist developing States in furthering their economic development. In 2001, the Ministerial Conference at Doha, Qatar, adopted the Doha Declaration and Doha Development Agenda. Development has been an increasingly important issue within WTO in the past years. However, the discussion on how to best enhance the economic development of States is far from being concluded, with many conferences failing to reach consensus conclusions.

General Agreement of Tariffs and Trade 1947

Article XVIII Governmental Assistance to Economic Development

1. The contracting parties recognize that the attainment of the objectives of this Agreement will be facilitated by the progressive development of their economies, particularly of those contracting parties the economies of which can only support low standards of living and are in the early stages of development.

2. The contracting parties recognize further that it may be necessary for those contracting parties, in order to implement programmes and policies of economic development designed to raise the general standard of living of their people, to take protective or other measures affecting imports, and that such measures are justified in so far as they facilitate the attainment of the objectives of this Agreement. They agree, therefore, that those contracting parties should enjoy additional facilities to enable them (*a*) to maintain sufficient flexibility in their tariff structure to be able to grant the tariff protection required for the establishment of a particular industry and (*b*) to apply quantitative restrictions for balance of payments purposes in a manner which takes full account of the continued high level of demand for imports likely to be generated by their programmes of economic development.

4. (*a*) Consequently, a contracting party, the economy of which can only support low standards of living and is in the early stages of development, shall be free to deviate temporarily from the provisions of the other Articles of this Agreement…

7. (*a*) If a contracting party coming within the scope of paragraph 4 (*a*) of this Article considers it desirable, in order to promote the establishment of a particular industry with a view to raising the general standard of living of its people, to modify or withdraw a concession…it shall notify the CONTRACTING PARTIES to this effect and enter into negotiations with any contracting party with which such concession was initially negotiated, and with any other contracting party determined by the CONTRACTING PARTIES to have a substantial interest therein. If agreement is reached between such contracting parties concerned, they shall be free to modify or withdraw concessions.

9. In order to safeguard its external financial position and to ensure a level of reserves adequate for the implementation of its programme of economic development, a contracting party coming within the scope of paragraph 4 (*a*) of this Article may…control the general level of its imports by restricting the quantity or value of merchandise permitted to be imported…

Differential and More Favourable Treatment, Reciprocity and Fuller Participation of Developing Countries ('Enabling Clause')

Decision of the Contracting Parties to the GATT of 28 November 1979 (L/4903)

Following negotiations within the framework of the Multilateral Trade Negotiations, the CONTRACTING PARTIES *decide* as follows:

1. Notwithstanding the provisions of Article 1 of the General Agreement, contracting parties may accord differential and more favourable treatment to other contracting parties.

2. The provisions of paragraph 1 apply to the following:
   a) Preferential tariff treatment accorded by developed contracting parties to products originating in developing countries…
   b) Differential and more favourable treatment with respect to the provisions of the General Agreement concerning non-tariff measures in accordance with the Generalized System of Preferences,…
   d) Special treatment on the least developed among the developing countries in the context of any general or specific measures in favour of developing countries…

5. The developed countries do not expect reciprocity for commitments made by them in trade negotiations to reduce or remove tariffs and other barriers to the trade of developing countries, i.e. the developed countries do not

expect the developing countries, in the course of trade negotiations, to make contributions which are inconsistent with their individual development, financial and trade needs.

6. Having regard to the special economic difficulties and the particular development, financial and trade needs of the least-developed countries, the developed countries shall exercise the utmost restraint in seeking any concessions or contributions for commitments made by them to reduce or remove tariffs and other barriers to the trade of such countries, and the least-developed countries shall not be expected to make concessions or contributions that are inconsistent with the recognition of their particular situation and problems.

European Communities—Conditions for the Granting of Tariff Preferences to Developing Countries
WT/DS246/AB/R, 7 April 2004, World Trade Organization, Report of the Appellate Body

India brought a complaint against the European Communities (EC) for granting tariff preferences to certain developing countries based on an EC regulation. The EC regulation contained various tariff preference schemes including one arrangement that foresaw preferential tariffs for States engaged in drug combat (the 'drug arrangement'). This arrangement applied only to 12 predefined developing countries, namely 11 Latin American States and Pakistan. India challenged the consistency of this arrangement with the GATT provisions, especially Article I:1 GATT; whereas the EC argued that the arrangement was consistent with the Enabling Clause. In discussing whether the applicant (India) had to prove not only an inconsistency with the GATT but also that the arrangement did not comply with the Enabling Clause, the Appellate Body addressed the relevance of the Enabling Clause within the WTO system.

106. The Enabling Clause authorizes developed country Members to grant enhanced market access to products from developing countries beyond that granted to products from developed countries. Enhanced market access is intended to provide developing countries with increasing returns from their growing exports, which returns are critical for those countries' economic development. The Enabling Clause thus plays a vital role in promoting trade as a means of stimulating economic growth and development. In this respect, the Enabling Clause is not a typical 'exception' or 'defence', in the style of Article XX of the GATT…

108. In his report at the conclusion of the Tokyo Round negotiations [which led to the adoption of the Enabling Clause], the then-Director General observed: 'The Enabling Clause meets a fundamental concern of developing countries by introducing differential and more favourable treatment as an integral part of the GATT system…

109. We thus understand that, between the entry into force of the GATT and the adoption of the Enabling Clause, the Contracting Parties determined that the Most-Favoured-Nation obligation failed to secure adequate market access for developing countries so as to stimulate their economic development.…

111. [T]he history and objective of the Enabling Clause lead us to agree…that Members are *encouraged* to deviate from Article I in the pursuit of 'differential and more favourable treatment' for developing countries.

World Trade Organization, Doha Declaration
WT/MIN(01)/DEC/1, 20 November 2001

2. International trade can play a major role in the promotion of economic development and the alleviation of poverty. We recognise the need for all our peoples to benefit from the increased opportunities and welfare gains that the multilateral trading system generates. The majority of WTO Members are developing countries. We seek to place their needs and interests at the heart of the Work Program adopted in this Declaration. Recalling the Preamble to the Marrakesh Agreement, we shall continue to make positive efforts designed to ensure that developing countries, especially least developing countries among them, secure a share in the growth of world trade commensurate with the needs of their economic development. In this context, enhanced market access, balanced rules, and well targeted, sustainably financed technical assistance and capacity building programs have important roles to play.

3. We recognise the particular vulnerability of the least-developed countries and the special structural difficulties they face in the global economy. We are committed to addressing the marginalisation of least-developed countries in international trade and to improving their effective participation in the multilateral trading system....

42. ...We recognise that the integration of the LDCs [Least-Developed Countries] into the multilateral trading system requires meaningful market access, support for the diversification of their production and export base, and trade-related technical assistance and capacity building. We agree that the meaningful integration of LDCs into the trading system and the global economy will involve efforts by all WTO Members. We commit ourselves to the objective of duty-free, quota-free market access for products originating from LDCs...We further commit ourselves to consider additional measures for progressive improvements in market access for LDCs.

44. We reaffirm that provisions for special and differential treatment are an integral part of the WTO Agreements We note the concerns expressed regarding their operation in addressing specific constraints faced by developing countries, particularly least-developed countries...We therefore agree that all special and differential treatment provisions shall be reviewed with a view to strengthening them and making them more precise, effective and operational.

S.W. Chang, 'WTO for Trade and Development Post-Doha'
10 *Journal of International Economic Law* 3 (2007)

One of the most contentious and critical issues currently facing the WTO is the debate over whether and to what extent differentiated rights and obligations will be recognized between developed and developing countries. In order to bridge the gap between developed and developing countries, the GATT system introduced the concept of special and differential treatment (SDT), which was further developed and expanded under the WTO system...[I]t is widely agreed that the Uruguay Round approach to SDT—based upon (i) preferences with unilaterally imposed non-economic conditions and exclusion of 'sensitive products', (ii) opt-outs from WTO rules, (iii) uniform and arbitrary transition periods without economic foundation, and (iv) technical assistance without consideration of supply-side constraints—has not been helpful in promoting economic development in most developing countries. Consequently, many developing countries and LDCs [least developed countries] are still unprepared to be fully integrated into the multilateral trading system. From the developing countries' perspective, most SDT provisions are not mandatory, and therefore unenforceable through dispute settlement procedures...While there is a broadly shared agreement amongst WTO members that developing country Members should be accorded some kind of SDT, WTO Members have failed to reach consensus on the forms and contents of such treatment in spite of several years of hot debates.

NOTES
1. There is no definition of 'developing country' in any WTO text. The WTO operates a system of so-called 'self-designation', i.e. States declare themselves as being developing countries or not. Yet there is a distinction between developing countries and least developed countries (LDCs). Since 1971, LDCs are denominated by the UN on a regular basis and according to a number of internationally agreed criteria including population, national income and weak human assets (comprising a composite index of health, nutrition, and educational indicators). The UN list after the latest triennial review in 2015 comprised 48 States. This list is also applied by the WTO under Article XI.2 of the WTO Agreement.
2. The Uruguay Round saw a renewed focus on developing countries' needs. The Preamble of the Marrakesh Agreement establishing the WTO provides that 'there is need for positive efforts designed to ensure that developing countries, and especially the least developed among them, secure a share in the growth in international trade commensurate with the needs of their economic development'. The Enabling Clause also became an integral part of the GATT in 1994. In the *EC—Tariff Preferences Case* (see extract), the Appellate Body stated that the Enabling Clause was among the 'positive efforts' called for in the Preamble of the Agreement establishing the WTO (para. 92). In the same case, the Appellate Body (at para. 145) further explained that preferential treatment of developing countries as provided for in the Enabling Clause had to be generalised and non-discriminatory. However, this does not mean that preferential measures need to benefit all developing countries, as similar situations have to be addressed in the same way but different development needs can justify differentiated treatment of various developing countries.

3. The Doha Declaration (see extract) came after at least two years of sustained concern by developing States and widespread public protests against the WTO. Much of this was based on increasing evidence that the free trade and globalisation processes fostered by the WTO were having an unequal and heavy impact on developing States (see Chapter 6 in relation to globalisation and its impact on human rights). Chang in the extract above points out that there is a general consensus that current special and differential treatment provisions are not sufficient to address development needs.

I: Dispute settlement within the WTO

Under the original GATT procedures, Articles XXII and XXIII provided for bilateral consultations between disputing States. If this method failed to resolve the dispute, States had the option of using good offices, or entering into mediation and conciliation before a request for a GATT Panel was made. While there is no mention of a Panel in the GATT 1947, the practice developed that after the dispute was referred to the Council of Contracting Parties, a panel of experts was established to hear the dispute. The Council would then adopt the panel's report if any Contracting Party did not oppose it. However, these procedures were seen as being insufficiently rules-based and too dependent on consensus between the disputing States, compliance with Panels' decisions was variable, and it was incapable of taking account of broader issues such as environmental and labour standards. Thus the Uruguay Round established a new unified, streamlined and strengthened dispute resolution system.

Understanding on Rules and Procedures Governing the Settlement of Disputes 1994

Article 1 Coverage and Application

1. The rules and procedures of this Understanding shall apply to disputes brought pursuant to the consultation and dispute settlement provisions of the agreements listed in Appendix 1 to this Understanding (referred to in this Understanding as the 'covered agreements'). The rules and procedures of this Understanding shall also apply to consultations and the settlement of disputes between Members concerning their rights and obligations under the provisions of the Agreement Establishing the World Trade Organization (referred to in this Understanding as the 'WTO Agreement') and of this Understanding taken in isolation or in combination with any other covered agreement....

Article 3 General Provisions

1. Members affirm their adherence to the principles for the management of disputes heretofore applied under Articles XXII and XXIII of GATT 1947, and the rules and procedures as further elaborated and modified herein.

2. The dispute settlement system of the WTO is a central element in providing security and predictability to the multilateral trading system. The Members recognize that it serves to preserve the rights and obligations of Members under the covered agreements, and to clarify the existing provisions of those agreements in accordance with customary rules of interpretation of public international law. Recommendations and rulings of the DSB cannot add to or diminish the rights and obligations provided in the covered agreements....

7. Before bringing a case, a Member shall exercise its judgment as to whether action under these procedures would be fruitful. The aim of the dispute settlement mechanism is to secure a positive solution to a dispute. A solution mutually acceptable to the parties to a dispute and consistent with the covered agreements is clearly to be preferred. In the absence of a mutually agreed solution, the first objective of the dispute settlement mechanism is usually to secure the withdrawal of the measures concerned if these are found to be inconsistent with the provisions of any of the covered agreements. The provision of compensation should be resorted to only if the immediate withdrawal of the measure is impracticable and as a temporary measure pending the withdrawal of the measure which is inconsistent with a covered agreement. The last resort which this Understanding provides to the Member invoking the dispute settlement procedures is the possibility of suspending the application of concessions or other obligations under the covered agreements on a discriminatory basis *vis-à-vis* the other Member, subject to authorization by the DSB of such measures.

J. Trachtman, 'The Domain of WTO Dispute Resolution'
40 *Harvard International Law Journal* 333 (1999)

Many trade diplomats, environmentalists and scholars have expressed concern regarding the magnitude of decision-making power allocated to World Trade Organization (WTO) dispute resolution panels and the WTO Appellate Body. While trade diplomats and scholars have expressed pride at the Uruguay Round achievement of more binding and more 'law-oriented' dispute resolution, the same group and a variety of non-governmental organizations (NGOs) and other commentators question the jurisdictional scope of dispute resolution. After all, should these small tribunals, lacking direct democratic legitimacy, determine profound issues such as the relationship between trade and environmental values or trade and labor values? Many voices, including this author's, have called for greater international legislation in these important fields. ...

[W]here decision-making authority is allocated to a dispute resolution body, less specific standards are consistent with a transfer of power to an international organization—the dispute resolution body itself—while more specific rules are more consistent with the reservation of continuing power by member states. From a more critical standpoint, it might be argued that allocation of authority to a transnational dispute resolution body by virtue of standards can be used as a method to integrate *sub rosa*, and outside the visibility of democratic controls.

It will be recalled that article 3(2) of the DSU provides that the vocation of dispute settlement is to preserve and to clarify rights and obligations under the covered agreements 'in accordance with customary rules of public international law.' This phrase has been interpreted by the Appellate Body to refer to the interpretative rules of the Vienna Convention [on Law of Treaties]. ...

To understand the role of dispute resolution, one must recognize that dispute resolution is not simply a mechanism for neutral application of legislated rules but is itself a mechanism of legislation and of governance. We must also recognize that today dispute resolution often works in tandem with legislation in that dispute resolution tribunals function in part as agents of legislatures. Moreover, legislatures, intentionally or unintentionally but often efficiently, delegate wide authority to dispute resolution.

The WTO dispute resolution process begins with a requirement of consultations. If consultations are unsuccessful, the complaining state may request the establishment of a three-person panel to consider the matter. The panel issues a report which may be appealed to the Appellate Body. The panel report, as it may be modified by the Appellate Body, is subject to adoption by the Dispute Settlement Body (DSB) of the WTO. Adoption is automatic unless there is a consensus not to adopt the report. What is the vocation of WTO dispute resolution? There are several answers. Panels determine the facts. They determine those facts that are relevant under the applicable law, so that they must determine the applicable law and relevant facts concurrently and interactively. Interestingly, because of a design flaw in the DSU, the Appellate Body has no right of remand. Therefore, the Appellate Body is constrained where it determines to apply law for which the panel has made no findings of fact. Within the determination of the applicable law are several subfunctions. First, panels (and here the Appellate Body acts as well) determine which law is applicable, by virtue of factors including, but not limited to, the activity, the location, the persons, and the timing. Second, where there is a dispute regarding the meaning of the law, the panel must definitively interpret the law. Third, where the law does not apply by its specific terms but was intended to address the issue, the panel may construe the law. Fourth, the law may have a lacuna and therefore not provide a response. Fifth, where two legal rules overlap, the panel must determine whether both were meant to apply or whether one takes precedence. Sixth, where two legal rules conflict, the panel must determine whether the laws are of unequal or equal stature. If they are of equal stature, the panel must determine how to accommodate both. As shall be discussed in more detail below, one persistent problem of the WTO legal system is the recognition and application of legal rules from outside the system. Penultimately, after the complete determination of the applicable law, the tribunal applies the law to the facts. Finally, the tribunal may fashion a remedy: it may recommend a resolution to be adopted by the DSB. ...

The disparity between the positive law dispute resolution system of the WTO and the more political, natural law style of dispute resolution available in connection with most other forms of international law raises jurisprudential and practical concern. How can a WTO dispute resolution decision ignore other international law? On the other hand, how can the WTO dispute resolution process purport to interpret and apply non-WTO international law? While present WTO law seems clearly to exclude direct application of non-WTO international law, this position seems unsustainable as increasing conflicts between trade values and non-trade values arise. These conflicts may be addressed through standards such as the exceptional provisions of article XX, or by legislated rules regarding the more specific interaction between trade values and non-trade values.

NOTES
1. The WTO Agreement established a Dispute Settlement Body (DSB), consisting of the General Council of the WTO (comprising all State parties), which convenes to discharge the functions of

the DSB under the Understanding on Rules and Procedures Governing the Settlement of Disputes 1994 (DSU).

2. Article 3 of the DSU embodies both the legal and the political aspects of dispute resolution. Article 3.2 emphasises the rule-based nature of the system, providing that the DSB can interpret and apply the rights and obligations only under the covered agreements as they have been negotiated, with no capacity for law-making. This view of the system is augmented by the automatic right of a State to the establishment of a Panel; the adoption of a Panel report within 60 days unless there is an appeal or a consensus in the DSB to reject the report; and an appeals process with a report within 60 days. Article 3.7, however, entrenches the principle that a State must consider the probable success of an action, taking into account interests other than its own in service of the goal of maintaining an effective world trading system. This provision shows an emphasis on mutually satisfactory solutions with the DSB as a forum for the diplomatic discussion and resolution of trade disputes.

3. The DSU established a permanent Appellate Body for appeals from Panel decisions (Article 17). This Body is to be comprised of persons of recognised authority, with demonstrated expertise in law, international trade and the subject matter of the covered agreements generally, who are unaffiliated with any government. The Appellate Body was established to create legal certainty regarding the developing GATT/WTO jurisprudence, with its decisions now being the most authoritative statements of economic law in the GATT/WTO system. Decisions of the Panel and the Appellate Body since 1995 can be found on the WTO website: https://www.wto.org/english/tratop_e/dispu_e/dispu_e.htm.

4. The DSU is also designed to improve compliance by the introduction of surveillance procedures with regard to the compliance with recommendations or rulings of the DSB (Article 21). In addition, the DSB has power to authorise compensation or the suspension of concessions if a State fails to comply with those recommendations or rulings, including same sector or cross-sector retaliation (Article 22).

5. Overall, the dispute settlement procedure is designed to reduce the use of unilateral action. However, while the DSU makes illegal any unilateral interpretations or determinations of violations of the GATT, in practice it may depend on whether an affected State is determined to pursue a matter to a DSB decision. There is also the issue, as Trachtman raises, of the compliance of the WTO DSB with general international law. On international dispute settlement generally, see Chapter 16.

SECTION 4: KEY PRINCIPLES OF INTERNATIONAL INVESTMENT LAW

International investment agreements have seen an unprecedented surge in the past decades. The numbers of Bilateral Investment Treaties (BITs) rose from several hundreds in the 1980s to almost 2,000 by 2000 and to over 3,000 by 2016. This illustrates the importance of foreign investment by corporations, a development that has also brought about the emergence of a specific body of international law on the subject.

A: Foreign direct investment in international law

One of the consequences of globalisation is an increased interdependence of national and international law.

Convention on the Settlement of Disputes between States and Nationals of Other States 1965 (ICSID Convention)

Article 25

(1) The jurisdiction of the Centre [International Centre for the Settlement of Investment Disputes] shall extend to any legal dispute arising directly out of an investment, between a Contracting State (or any constituent subdivision

or agency of a Contracting State designated to the Centre by that State) and a national of another Contracting State, which the parties to the dispute consent in writing to submit to the Centre. When the parties have given their consent, no party may withdraw its consent unilaterally.

(2) 'National of another Contracting State' means:
   (a) any natural person who had the nationality of a Contracting State other than the State party to the dispute…; and
   (b) any juridical person which had the nationality of a Contracting State other than the State party to the dispute on the date on which the parties consented to submit such dispute to conciliation or arbitration and any juridical person which had the nationality of the Contracting State party to the dispute on that date and which, because of foreign control, the parties have agreed should be treated as a national of another Contracting State for the purposes of this Convention.

Article 42

(1) The Tribunal shall decide a dispute in accordance with such rules of law as may be agreed by the parties. In the absence of such agreement, the Tribunal shall apply the law of the Contracting State party to the dispute (including its rules on the conflict of laws) and such rules of international law as may be applicable.

F. Orrego Vicuña, 'Of Contracts and Treaties in the Global Market'
8 Max-Planck-Yearbook of United Nations Law 341 (2004)

What used to be a useful comparison between international law and a separate domestic legal framework—treaties and contracts—has now become a part of a single legal structure which encompasses both contracts and treaties as well as a host of other instruments. This phenomenon is of course noticeable in respect of activities that have become to a greater extent globalized, such as trade and investment…

Following the conflicting relationship between those who favoured submission of all disputes [relating to foreign investment] to domestic courts under some form or other of the 'Calvo Clause' and those who would insist on the role of diplomatic protection, and hence of state intervention to protect their investments and other rights, arbitration gradually emerged as the common ground where the interests of all could be satisfied. This was the key turning point of the 1965 Convention establishing ICSID [the International Centre for the Settlement of Investment Disputes]. No further diplomatic protection, except in unusual situations, no further submission to domestic courts and recourse instead to international arbitration, largely institutionalized under ICSID or UNCITRAL [United Nations Commission on International Trade Law] rules, are the core elements of the new balance…[T]his particular development covers the most important international transactions of the modern world, which take the form of investments…Over 2000 bilateral investment treaties assuring the protection of foreign investments are today in existence, together with a host of multilateral conventions and a number of free trade agreements. They all share the common feature that in spite of being inter-state agreements, individual private investors can avail themselves of the provisions of such instruments both in terms of the standards of treatment and the choice of forum for the settlement of disputes, including most prominently international arbitration.

Most investments, however, are done by means of contracts with the state and it is here where the new connection between contracts and treaties has emerged. Not infrequently, contracts provide for the application of domestic law and for the submission of disputes to domestic courts…[But in the *Lanco International Inc.* v *The Argentine Republic Case*] the investor chose to take the dispute to the ICSID under a bilateral investment treaty even though the concession contract executed with Argentina provided for the submission of disputes to local courts. The Tribunal held that consent to arbitration under the treaty prevailed over any other provision to the contrary and that such consent could not be diminished by the submission of a dispute to local courts under the concession contract…

[E]ven though contracts have been increasingly considered as subject to international law and detached from domestic legal constraints this does not mean that they have been transformed into treaties. Similarly, many of the attributes of treaties can be extended to contracts, including *pacta sunt servanda* and observance in good faith, but this does not mean that treaties are contracts as they govern a different relationship in the international community.

What is interesting to realize is that the closer the interactions between treaties and contracts the greater the nexus between one and the other that will develop. This is noticeable, for example, when states undertake…to treat breaches of a contract as a breach of a treaty protecting the rights of investors. This is also the case of the extraordinary development embodied in the ICSID Convention to the extent that states enter into treaties that provide for the consent of host states to international arbitration in respect of unnamed investors who at any point in time may exercise the option of resorting to such arbitral jurisdiction. Investment contracts are thus linked automatically by the treaty to international arbitration and the standards of treatment laid down by the treaty and international law.

NOTES
1. The practice of foreign investment goes back over a century, when mainly natural resources such as gold were exploited by foreign corporations. For most of the nineteenth century, the relationship between the host State and the foreign investor was considered to be largely a matter of the national law of the host State supplemented by customary international law, which guaranteed a minimum standard of treatment for foreigners (see Chapter 11). After 1945, along with the decolonisation process, a main concern of newly independent States related to obtaining control over their natural resources that had been exploited during the colonial era. Consequently, while the benefits of foreign direct investment were recognised, such investment was normally subject to some form of control or even forced expropriation by the host State. This has changed over the past two decades, as many treaties, agreements and contracts provide extensive protections for the foreign investor, often at the expense of the sovereignty of the host State.
2. The relation between the investor (normally a private corporation) and the host State in which the investment is undertaken may be governed by a contract between the host State and the foreign investor (a State contract). While this relationship was traditionally governed by the national law of the host State, foreign investment is now generally subject to extensive principles of international law. As Vicuña points out, investors do not only have the possibility to raise contract claims before the jurisdiction designed by the State but also claims arising out of a bilateral investment treaty (BIT). Clauses through which States undertake to respect and guarantee commitments entered into *vis-à-vis* the foreign investor are called 'umbrella clauses'. Such a clause in a BIT can under certain circumstances elevate a breach of a contract under national law to a breach of an international treaty. However, the extent to which contracts enjoy protection of the BIT has been subject to much discussion and even disagreement between various international arbitral tribunals.
3. Article 42 of the ICSID Convention mentions various sources of law to be applied by a tribunal: agreement of the parties (i.e. the State contract), the national law of the host State (many States have laws regulating the admission and protection standards for foreign investments) and 'such rules of international law as may be applicable'. Such international legal rules include BITs as well as general international law. International investment law is thus a complex interplay between these different sources of law which are further interpreted by an ever-increasing body of arbitral awards as well as scholars. One of the most important consequences of this development, as discussed by Vicuña, is the blurring of traditional distinctions between national and international law. A related question is the impact of such legal rules on State sovereignty (see Section 6 and Chapter 11) given the expansive protections afforded to foreign investment under those rules. That impact is especially severe because, unlike the WTO, there is no equivalent of a GATT Article XX-type exception in older investment treaties to exempt State laws or regulations passed for environmental, health or other protective purposes.
4. There have been several efforts to negotiate a single multilateral investment agreement, all of which have failed. While there is to date no global agreement dealing with foreign investment, there are select investment areas in the WTO (including in the GATS) and several regional treaties that contain investment rules. The latter include Chapter 11 of NAFTA, two protocols on foreign investment from States within and outside of the 'Mercado Commún del Sur' (Common Market of the South; MERCOSUR) and the 2009 Comprehensive Investment Agreement of the Association of Southeast Asian Nations (ASEAN). Part III of the Energy Charter Treaty sets out investment disciplines and is a prominent example of a sectoral treaty addressing investment issues.

B: Defining international investment

The Energy Charter Treaty
Annex 1 to the Final Act of the European Energy Charter Conference, 1994, 35 *International Legal Materials* 500 (1996)

Article 1 Definitions

(6) 'Investment' means every kind of asset, owned or controlled directly or indirectly by an Investor and includes:

(a) tangible and intangible, and movable and immovable, property, and any property rights such as leases, mortgages, liens, and pledges;

(b) a company or business enterprise, or shares, stock, or other forms of equity participation in a company or business enterprise, and bonds and other debt of a company or business enterprise;

(c) claims to money and claims to performance pursuant to contract having an economic value and associated with an Investment;

(d) Intellectual Property;

(e) Returns;

(f) any right conferred by law or contract or by virtue of any licences and permits granted pursuant to law to undertake any Economic Activity in the Energy Sector.

A change in the form in which assets are invested does not affect their character as investments.

Salini Costruttori S.P.A. and Italstrade S.P.A. v *Kingdom of Morocco*
Decision on Jurisdiction, ICSID Case No. ARB/00/4, 23 July 2001, 42 *International Legal Materials* 609 (2003)

The dispute concerned the construction of a highway that took four months longer than the period provided for in the contract. The companies argued that the Moroccan government should pay them for the extra time worked as a result.

52. The Tribunal notes that there have been almost no cases where the notion of investment within the meaning of Article 25 of the [ICSID] Convention was raised. However, it would be inaccurate to consider that the requirement that a dispute be 'in direct relation to an investment' is diluted by the consent of the Contracting Parties. To the contrary, ICSID case law and legal authors agree that the investment requirement must be respected...

The criteria for characterization are ... derived from cases in which the transaction giving rise to the dispute was considered to be an investment without there ever being a real discussion of the issue in almost all cases.

The doctrine generally considers that investment infers: contributions, a certain duration of performance of the contract and a participation in the risks of the transaction...one may add the contribution to the economic development of the host State of the investment as an additional condition.

In reality, these elements may be interdependent. Thus, the risks of the transaction may depend on the contributions and the duration of performance of the contract. As a result, these various criteria should be assessed globally.

Malaysian Historical Salvors, SDN, BHD v *Malaysia*
Decision on the Application for Annulment, ICSID Case No. ARB/05/10, 29 February 2009

Malaysian Historical Salvors (the applicant) concluded a contract with the Malaysian government to find the wreck of a British vessel and salvage the cargo which contained antique Chinese porcelain. The applicant found the wreck and recovered approximately 24,000 pieces of porcelain. The issue was whether the resources spent to salvage a shipwreck constituted an investment within the meaning of Article 25(1) of the ICSID Convention.

57. The 'ordinary meaning' of the term 'investment' is the commitment of money or other assets for the purpose of providing a return. In its context and in accordance with the object and purpose of the treaty—which is to promote the flow of private investment to contracting countries by provision of a mechanism which, by enabling international settlement of disputes, conduces to the security of such investment—the term 'investment' is

unqualified. The purpose of the ICSID Convention was described in a draft of the Convention conveyed by the Bank's General Counsel to the Executive Directors of the Bank in these terms: '[t]he purpose of this Convention is to promote the resolution of disputes arising between the Contracting States and nationals of other Contracting States by encouraging and facilitating recourse to international conciliation and arbitration.' The meaning of the term 'investment' may however be regarded as 'ambiguous or obscure' under Article 32 of the Vienna Convention and hence justifying resort to the preparatory work of the Convention 'to determine the meaning.' As the pleadings in the instant case illustrate, there certainly have been marked differences among ICSID tribunals and among commentators on the meaning of 'investment' as that term appears in Article 25(1) of the Convention. Thus the provision may be regarded as ambiguous. In any event, courts and tribunals interpreting treaties regularly review the *travaux préparatoires* whenever they are brought to their attention; it is mythological to pretend that they do so only when they first conclude that the term requiring interpretation is ambiguous or obscure.

58. At issue in this case is the measuring of the treaty term 'investment' as that term is used in Article 25(1) of the ICSID Convention—but also in Article 1 of the Agreement between the Government of the United Kingdom of Great Britain and Northern Ireland and the Government of Malaysia for the Promotion and Protection of Investments because that instrument is the medium through which the Contracting States involved have given their consent to the exercise of jurisdiction of ICSID.

59. Article 1 of that Agreement defines 'investment' capaciously.

For the purpose of this Agreement

(1)(a) 'investment' means every kind of asset and in particular, though not exclusively, includes:

   ...

   (ii)   shares, stock and debentures of companies or interests in the property of such companies;

   (iii) claims to money or to any performance under contract having a financial value;

   (iv) intellectual property rights...;

   (v)   business concessions conferred...under contract...

60. The Contract between the Government of Malaysia and Malaysian Historical Salvors is one of a kind of asset, what is precisely at issue between the Government and the Salvor is a claim to money and to performance under a contract having financial value, the contract involves intellectual property rights, and the rights granted to salvage may be treated as a business concession conferred under contract.

61. It follows that, by the terms of the Agreement, and for its purposes, the Contract is an investment. There is no room for another conclusion....Nevertheless the Sole Arbitrator observed that, 'while the Contract did provide some benefit to Malaysia,' there was not 'a sufficient contribution to Malaysia's economic development to qualify as an "investment" for the purposes of Article 25(1)'...

62. Under Article 7 of the Agreement, the sole recourse in the event that a legal dispute between the investor and the host State should arise which is not settled by agreement between them through pursuit of local remedies or otherwise is reference to the International Centre for Settlement of Investment Disputes. Unlike some other BITs, no third party dispute settlement options are provided in the alternative to ICSID. It follows that, if jurisdiction is found to be absent under the ICSID Convention, the investor is left without international recourse altogether....

63. What of the intentions of the Parties in concluding the Washington Convention [another name for the ICSID Convention]? The term 'investment' was deliberately left undefined. But light is shed on the intentions of the Parties in respect of that term by the Convention's *travaux préparatoires* as well as the Convention's interpretation by the Executive Directors of the International Bank for Reconstruction and Development in adopting and opening it for signature....

69. ...[i]t is important to note that the *travaux préparatoires* do not support the imposition of 'outer limits' such as those imposed by the Sole Arbitrator in this case. Little more about the nature of outer limits is indicated in the *travaux* than is contained in Article 25(1), namely that, '[t]he jurisdiction of the Centre shall extend to any legal dispute arising directly out of an investment...' It appears to have been assumed by the Convention's drafters that use of the term 'investment' excluded a simple sale and like transient commercial transactions from the jurisdiction of the Centre. Judicial or arbitral establishment of criteria or hallmarks may or may not be regarded as plausible, but the intentions of the draftsmen of the ICSID Convention, as the *travaux* show them to have been, lend those criteria (and still less, conditions) scant support....

71. The preparatory work of the Convention as well as the Report of the Executive Directors thus shows that: (a) deliberately no definition of 'investment' as that term is found in Article 25(1) was adopted; (b) a floor limit to

the value of an investment was rejected; (c) a requirement of indefinite duration of an investment or of a duration of no less than five years was rejected; (d) the critical criterion adopted was the consent of the parties. By the terms of their consent, they could define jurisdiction under the Convention....

73. While it may not have been foreseen at the time of the adoption of the ICSID Convention, when the number of bilateral investment treaties in force were few, since that date some 2800 bilateral, and three important multilateral, treaties have been concluded, which characteristically define investment in broad, inclusive terms such as those illustrated by the above-quoted Article 1 of the Agreement between Malaysia and the United Kingdom. Some 1700 of those treaties are in force, and the multilateral treaties, particularly the Energy Charter Treaty, which are in force, of themselves endow ICSID with an important jurisdictional reach. It is those bilateral and multilateral treaties which today are the engine of ICSID's effective jurisdiction. To ignore or depreciate the importance of the jurisdiction they bestow upon ICSID, and rather to embroider upon questionable interpretations of the term 'investment' as found in Article 25(1) of the Convention, risks crippling the institution.

75. Nevertheless, the Committee recognises that the Sole Arbitrator acted in the train of several prior ICSID arbitral awards which lend a considerable measure of support to his approach. The seminal award is the Decision on Jurisdiction of a distinguished tribunal in *Salini* v. *Morocco*....

78. While this Committee's majority has every respect for the authors of the *Salini* v. *Morocco* Award and those that have followed it...[i]t gives precedence to awards and analyses that are consistent with its approach, which it finds consonant with the intentions of the Parties to the ICSID Convention.

NOTES
1. Virtually all model BITs contain a vast definition of the term 'investment', which normally provides a non-exhaustive list of examples of assets that constitute an investment. This broad definition confers enormous discretion on adjudicators to decide about what is an investment and what is not. The definitions contained in the Energy Charter Treaty and NAFTA Chapter 11 are good examples of this broad and open-textured approach.
2. Article 25 of the ICSID Convention (see Section 4A) provides ICSID jurisdiction in respect of 'any legal dispute arising directly out of an investment'. It has therefore been necessary for the ICSID to define the term in order to delimit the jurisdiction *ratione materiae* of the Centre. The criteria listed in the *MHS Case* above now seem to be the criteria for determining whether there is investment in the sense of Article 25(1) of the ICSID Convention. However, these criteria are not fixed or mandatory and should not be interpreted strictly (see *Biwater Gauff Ltd* v *Tanzania*, ICSID Award 18 July 2008) and *Postova Banka* v *Greece*, ICSID Award 2015). Indeed, in *Malaysian Historical Salvors* Judge Shahabuddeen disagreed with the majority both on the question of whether an 'ICSID Investment' differed from ordinary investments under BITs and on the question of whether the BIT ought to have been considered by the arbitrator. While the majority consider that it would be undesirable for investments that meet the criteria agreed to by States under their BITs to fall outside ICSID jurisdiction, Judge Shahabuddeen considers this in fact to be highly desirable. In any event, a tribunal will need to examine whether the operation at hand constitutes firstly a dispute in the sense of the BIT, and secondly whether it can also be qualified as an investment under Article 25(1) of the ICSID Convention.
3. Both the tribunals in the *Salini* and the *Malaysian Historical Salvors* cases pointed out that the criteria are interdependent and that the strong presence of one of the criteria can infer the presence of another. This is especially true for the contribution to the economic development. The Tribunal in *L.E.S.I.-Dipenta* v *People's Democratic Republic of Algeria* ICSID Case No. ARB/03/8 10 January 2005, ruled for instance (at para. 13) that 'it is not necessary that the investment contribute more specifically to the host country's economic development, something that is difficult to ascertain and that is implicitly covered by the other three criteria'. Some commentators have questioned the capacity and expertise of investment treaty arbitrators to adjudge on sensitive questions surrounding the causes and effects of development in a host State.

C: Protection standards in international investment law

BITs and regional treaties contain substantive standards of protection pertaining to international investments. Some of the protection standards are similar to what is found in the

WTO agreements, including national and most-favoured-nation treatment (see Sections 3C and D). Other treaty standards however are specific to investment law, such as guarantees of fair and equitable treatment, full protection and security and compensation in the event of expropriation. This section will outline some basic features of these standards.

The Energy Charter Treaty 1994

Annex 1 to the Final Act of the European Energy Charter Conference, 17 December 1994, 35 *International Legal Materials* 509 (1996)

Article 10 Promotion, Protection and Treatment of Investments

(1) Each Contracting Party shall, in accordance with the provisions of this Treaty, encourage and create stable, equitable, favourable and transparent conditions for Investors of other Contracting Parties to make Investments in its Area. Such conditions shall include a commitment to accord at all times to Investments of Investors of other Contracting Parties fair and equitable treatment. Such Investments shall also enjoy the most constant protection and security and no Contracting Party shall in any way impair by unreasonable or discriminatory measures their management, maintenance, use, enjoyment or disposal. In no case shall such Investments be accorded treatment less favourable than that required by international law, including treaty obligations. Each Contracting Party shall observe any obligations it has entered into with an Investor or an Investment of an Investor of any other Contracting Party.

(3) For the purposes of this Article, 'Treatment' means treatment accorded by a Contracting Party which is no less favourable than that which it accords to its own Investors or to Investors of any other Contracting Party or any third state, whichever is the most favourable.

(5) Each Contracting Party shall, as regards the Making of Investments in its Area, endeavour to:
(a) limit to the minimum the exceptions to the Treatment described in paragraph (3);
(b) progressively remove existing restrictions affecting Investors of other Contracting Parties.

(7) Each Contracting Party shall accord to Investments in its Area of Investors of other Contracting Parties, and their related activities including management, maintenance, use, enjoyment or disposal, treatment no less favourable than that which it accords to Investments of its own Investors or of the Investors of any other Contracting Party or any third state and their related activities including management, maintenance, use, enjoyment or disposal, whichever is the most favourable.

(12) Each Contracting Party shall ensure that its domestic law provides effective means for the assertion of claims and the enforcement of rights with respect to Investments, investment agreements, and investment authorizations.

North American Free Trade Agreement 1992

17 December 1992, 32 *International Legal Materials* 289 (1993)

Article 1102 National Treatment

1. Each Party shall accord to investors of another Party treatment no less favorable than that it accords, in like circumstances, to its own investors with respect to the establishment, acquisition, expansion, management, conduct, operation, and sale or other disposition of investments.

2. Each Party shall accord to investments of investors of another Party treatment no less favorable than that it accords, in like circumstances, to investments of its own investors with respect to the establishment, acquisition, expansion, management, conduct, operation, and sale or other disposition of investments.

3. The treatment accorded by a Party under paragraphs 1 and 2 means, with respect to a state or province, treatment no less favorable than the most favorable treatment accorded, in like circumstances, by that state or province to investors, and to investments of investors, of the Party of which it forms a part.

4. For greater certainty, no Party may:
(a) impose on an investor of another Party a requirement that a minimum level of equity in an enterprise in the territory of the Party be held by its nationals, other than nominal qualifying shares for directors or incorporators of corporations; or

    (b) require an investor of another Party, by reason of its nationality, to sell or otherwise dispose of an investment in the territory of the Party.

Article 1103 Most-Favored-Nation Treatment

1. Each Party shall accord to investors of another Party treatment no less favorable than that it accords, in like circumstances, to investors of any other Party or of a non-Party with respect to the establishment, acquisition, expansion, management, conduct, operation, and sale or other disposition of investments.

2. Each Party shall accord to investments of investors of another Party treatment no less favorable than that it accords, in like circumstances, to investments of investors of any other Party or of a non-Party with respect to the establishment, acquisition, expansion, management, conduct, operation, and sale or other disposition of investments.

Article 1104 Standard of Treatment

Each Party shall accord to investors of another Party and to investments of investors of another Party the better of the treatment required by Articles 1102 and 1103.

Article 1105 Minimum Standard of Treatment

1. Each Party shall accord to investments of investors of another Party treatment in accordance with international law, including fair and equitable treatment and full protection and security.

2. Without prejudice to paragraph 1 and notwithstanding Article 1108(7)(b), each Party shall accord to investors of another Party, and to investments of investors of another Party, non-discriminatory treatment with respect to measures it adopts or maintains relating to losses suffered by investments in its territory owing to armed conflict or civil strife.

3. Paragraph 2 does not apply to existing measures relating to subsidies or grants that would be inconsistent with Article 1102 but for Article 1108(7)(b).

Waste Management Inc v Mexico, Award
ICSID Case No: ARB(AF)/00/3, 30 April 2004

Waste Management Inc (the applicant) alleged that Mexico was liable under Articles 1110 and 1105 of NAFTA for the actions of various organs of the State concerning the applicant's investment in an enterprise to provide waste management services to the Mexican City of Acapulco.

89. Article 1105 is entitled 'Minimum Standard of Treatment'. The relevant provision here is paragraph 1, which provides as follows:

    '(1) Each Party shall accord to investments of investors of another Party treatment in accordance with international law, including fair and equitable and full protection and security.'

90. On 31 July 2001, the Free Trade Commission, acting under NAFTA Article 1131, issued the following interpretation of Article 1105(1):

    'B. Minimum Standard of Treatment in Accordance with International Law
      1. Article 1105(1) prescribes the customary international law minimum standard of treatment of aliens as the minimum standard of treatment to be afforded to investments of investors of another Party.
      2. The concept of 'fair and equitable treatment' and 'full protection and security' do not require treatment in addition to or beyond that which is required by the customary international law minimum standard of treatment of aliens....'

99. Evidently the standard is to some extent a flexible one which must be adapted for the circumstances of each case. Accordingly, it is to the facts of the present case that the Tribunal turns.

100. The Claimant asserted that the failure of Acaverde's enterprise arose from a combination of conduct of local, provincial and federal authorities, together with the failure of Mexican courts and tribunals to provide it any relief. In the first place the Tribunal will consider separately the conduct of each of the various Mexican authorities concerned. Subsequently it will deal with the claim that there was collusion or conspiracy between these authorities.

Técnicas Medioambientales Tecmed, S.A. v *United Mexican States, Award*
ICSID Case No. ARB(AF)/00/2, 29 May 2003

The company argued that the refusal by Mexico to renew the landfill's operating permit constituted an expropriation of its investment, without any compensation or justification in violation of the BIT.

152. According to Article 4(1) of the [BIT between Spain and Mexico]: 'Each Contracting Party will guarantee in its territory fair and equitable treatment, according to International Law, for the investments made by investors of the other Contracting Party.'

153. The Arbitral Tribunal finds that the commitment of fair and equitable treatment included in Article 4(1) of the Agreement is an expression and part of the *bona fide* principle recognized in international law, although bad faith from the State is not required for its violation…

154. The Arbitral Tribunal considers that this provision of the Agreement, in light of the good faith principle established by international law, requires the Contracting Parties to provide to international investments treatment that does not affect the basic expectations that were taken into account by the foreign investor to make the investment. The foreign investor expects the host State to act in a consistent manner, free from ambiguity and totally transparently in its relations with the foreign investor, so that it may know beforehand any and all rules and regulations that will govern its investments, as well as the goals of the relevant policies and administrative practices or directives, to be able to plan its investment and comply with such regulations. Any and all State actions conforming to such criteria should relate not only to the guidelines, directives or requirements issued, or the resolutions approved thereunder, but also to the goals underlying such regulations. The foreign investor also expects the host State to act consistently, i.e. without arbitrarily revoking any preexisting decisions or permits issued by the State that were relied upon by the investor to assume its commitments as well as to plan and launch its commercial and business activities. The investor also expects the State to use the legal instruments that govern the actions of the investor or the investment in conformity with the function usually assigned to such instruments, and not to deprive the investor of its investment without the required compensation. In fact, failure by the host State to comply with such pattern of conduct with respect to the foreign investor or its investments affects the investor's ability to measure the treatment and protection awarded by the host State and to determine whether the actions of the host State conform to the fair and equitable treatment principle. Therefore, compliance by the host State with such pattern of conduct is closely related to the above-mentioned principle, to the actual chances of enforcing such principle, and to excluding the possibility that state action be characterized as arbitrary.

Azurix Corp. v *The Argentine Republic, Award*
ICSID Case No. ARB/01/12, 14 July 2006

The company argued that Argentina violated its BIT obligations regarding the company's investment in a utility which distributed drinking water and treated and disposed of sewerage water in Buenos Aires.

406. [T]here are…cases in which tribunals have found that full protection and security has been breached because the investment was subject to unfair and inequitable treatment…or, conversely, they have held that the obligation of fair and equitable treatment was breached because there was a failure to provide full protection and security.… The inter-relationship of the two standards indicates that full protection and security may be breached even if no physical violence or damage occurs…

408. The Tribunal is persuaded of the interrelationship of fair and equitable treatment and the obligation to afford the investor full protection and security.…[F]ull protection and security [is] understood to go beyond protection and security ensured by the police. It is not only a matter of physical security; the stability afforded by a secure investment environment is as important from an investor's point of view. The Tribunal is aware that in recent free trade agreements signed by the United States, for instance, with Uruguay, full protection and security is understood to be limited to the level of police protection required under customary international law. However, when the terms 'protection and security' are qualified by 'full' and no other adjective or explanation, they extend, in their ordinary meaning, the content of this standard beyond physical security. To conclude, the Tribunal, having held that the Respondent failed to provide fair and equitable treatment to the investment, finds that the Respondent also breached the standard of full protection and security under the BIT.

NOTES

1. The host State's obligation to accord fair and equitable treatment to the foreign investor arises from the assumption that the relation between a State and an investor is inherently unequal, with the State having much more power. This imbalance is said to justify why the investor should be accorded special treatment so as to ensure the prosperity of the investment in the host State. Certain treaty formulations of the fair and equitable standard, such as NAFTA Article 1105, are expressly tied to the broader corpus of the public international law including the customary minimum standard of protection for aliens. Some cases have linked fair and equitable treatment with legitimate expectations and proportionality (see *Venezuela Holdings BV v Venezuela* (2014) and *Occidental Petroleum Corporation v Ecuador* (2012)).

2. The United States Model BIT of 2012, Article 5(2)(a) includes the obligation not to deny justice as part of the fair and equitable standard, which requires States to ensure access to justice, no unreasonable delays in administering justice, and no irregularities in the conduct of proceedings. Even in the absence of such express provisions, tribunals have included such an obligation (e.g. *Loewen v United States* (2003) and *Pantechniki v Albania* (2009)).

3. Despite this linkage to public international law, the *Tecmed* tribunal prioritises transparency as the primary legal requirement under the guarantee of fair and equitable treatment. Some have argued that the issue of transparency is closely related to the host State's obligation to protect the investor's legitimate expectations in view of the conditions to which the investment is subjected (e.g. C. Schreuer, 'Fair and Equitable Treatment in Arbitral Practice', *Journal of World Investment & Trade* 6 (2005)). There is still some uncertainty about the difference between the standard of fair and equitable treatment and the customary international law minimal standard of treatment.

4. The standard of full protection and security was originally intended to protect the investment from physical violence (e.g. the destruction of the premises). However, the *Azurix Case* makes clear that a violation of the obligation to provide full protection and security does not necessarily require an act of physical violence and that it is rather closely related to the standard of fair and equitable treatment. This further widens the scope of the fair and equitable treatment standard. As the Tribunal in *ADF v United States of America* (ICSID Case No. ARB(AF)/00/1, 9 January 2003) pointed out: 'any general requirement to accord "fair and equitable treatment" and "full protection and security" must be disciplined by being based upon State practice and judicial or arbitral case law or other sources of customary or general international law' (at para. 184).

5. National treatment clauses are part of the standard clauses in a BIT as well as in regional treaties (see Article 10(3) of the Energy Charter Treaty and Article 1102 NAFTA). By a national treatment clause, as already discussed, the host State guarantees that the treatment of the foreign investor will at least be at the same level as the treatment accorded to its own nationals. However, this treatment only applies if the national corporation and the foreign investor are placed in 'like circumstances'. The Arbitral Tribunal in *SD Myers v Canada* (40 ILM 1408, 2001, Partial Award of 13 November 2000) considered that 'the concept of "like circumstances" invites an examination of whether a non-national investor complaining of less favourable treatment is in the same "sector" as the national investor'. It also added that ' "sector" has a wide connotation that includes the concepts of "economic sector" and "business sector" '. Most tribunals have followed this competition-based approach, which roughly approximates the test used in WTO law (see Section 3). However, unlike the WTO, there is no appellate organ to guarantee consistency and coherence in this area on questions of legal interpretation by tribunals.

6. Most favoured nation (MFN) treatment clauses are now found in virtually all BITs (see also Article 10(3) of the Energy Charter Treaty and Article 1103 of the NAFTA). An MFN clause, as discussed earlier, obliges the host State to accord the same treatment to one investor that it accords to other investors from other States. This means that a foreign investor may, if an MFN clause exists in the BIT between the host State and the investor's State (the 'basic treaty'), invoke the substantial guarantees from other BITs if these provide for a higher level of protection. Again, as Article 1103 of the NAFTA provides, the MFN clause only applies in 'like circumstances'. Consequently, an MFN clause will still allow for different treatment of investors that find themselves in objectively differing circumstances.

7. One question that has occupied several arbitral tribunals is whether an MFN clause also applies to procedural provisions (e.g. access to international arbitration, or the conditions thereof). In

Maffezzini v *Kingdom of Spain* (Decision on Jurisdiction, ICSID Case No ARB/97/7, 25 January 2000), the tribunal stated that 'today dispute settlement arrangements are inextricably related to the protection of foreign investors' (at para. 54) and that consequently, 'if a third party treaty contains provisions for the settlement of disputes that are more favorable to the protection of the investor's rights and interests than those in the basic treaty, such provisions may be extended' and they attached great importance to the original intention of the parties to the BIT containing the MFN clause, concluding that 'an MFN provision in the basic treaty does not incorporate by reference dispute settlement provisions in whole or in part set forth in another treaty, unless the MFN provision leaves no doubt that the Contracting Parties intended to incorporate them' (at para. 223). It is important to note that in *Maffezzini*, the claimant sought to invoke a more favourable dispute settlement clause that provided for faster access to ICSID arbitration (the basic treaty did also foresee ICSID arbitration; however only after the expiration of a certain delay) whereas the claimant in *Plama* (see Section 4E) sought to entirely substitute arbitration for another dispute settlement procedure.

D: Expropriation

Concern about the possible expropriation by a State of the property of a foreign corporation can be the reason why parties subject their dispute to international investment arbitration.

United Nations General Assembly Resolution 1803 (XVII) on Permanent Sovereignty over Natural Resources
14 December 1962

The General Assembly, ...

Considering that it is desirable to promote international co-operation for the economic development of developing countries, and that economic and financial agreements between the developed and the developing countries must be based on the principles of equality and of the right of peoples and nations to self-determination,

Considering that the provision of economic and technical assistance, loans and increased foreign investment must not be subject to conditions which conflict with the interests of the recipient State, ...

Declares that:

1. The right of peoples and nations to permanent sovereignty over their natural wealth and resources must be exercised in the interest of their national development and of the well-being of the people of the State concerned.

2. The exploration, development and disposition of such resources, as well as the import of the foreign capital required for these purposes, should be in conformity with the rules and conditions which the peoples and nations freely consider to be necessary or desirable with regard to the authorization, restriction or prohibition of such activities.

3. In cases where authorization is granted, the capital imported and the earnings on that capital shall be governed by the terms thereof, by the national legislation in force, and by international law. The profits derived must be shared in the proportions freely agreed upon, in each case, between the investors and the recipient State, due care being taken to ensure that there is no impairment, for any reason, of that State's sovereignty over its natural wealth and resources.

4. Nationalization, expropriation or requisitioning shall be based on grounds of public utility, security or the national interest which are recognized as overriding purely individual or private interests, both domestic and foreign. In such cases the owner shall be paid appropriate compensation, in accordance with international law. In any case where the question of compensation gives rise to a controversy, the national jurisdiction of the State taking such measures shall be exhausted. However, upon agreement by sovereign States and other parties concerned, settlement of the dispute should be made through arbitration or international adjudication.

North American Free Trade Agreement 1992

Article 1110 Expropriation and Compensation

1. No Party may directly or indirectly nationalize or expropriate an investment of an investor of another Party in its territory or take a measure tantamount to nationalization or expropriation of such an investment ('expropriation'), except:

    (a) for a public purpose;

    (b) on a non-discriminatory basis;

    (c) in accordance with due process of law and Article 1105(1); and

    (d) on payment of compensation in accordance with paragraphs 2 through 6.

2. Compensation shall be equivalent to the fair market value of the expropriated investment immediately before the expropriation took place ('date of expropriation'), and shall not reflect any change in value occurring because the intended expropriation had become known earlier. Valuation criteria shall include going concern value, asset value including declared tax value of tangible property, and other criteria, as appropriate, to determine fair market value.

3. Compensation shall be paid without delay and be fully realizable.

4. If payment is made in a G7 currency, compensation shall include interest at a commercially reasonable rate for that currency from the date of expropriation until the date of actual payment.

5. If a Party elects to pay in a currency other than a G7 currency, the amount paid on the date of payment, if converted into a G7 currency at the market rate of exchange prevailing on that date, shall be no less than if the amount of compensation owed on the date of expropriation had been converted into that G7 currency at the market rate of exchange prevailing on that date, and interest had accrued at a commercially reasonable rate for that G7 currency from the date of expropriation until the date of payment.

6. On payment, compensation shall be freely transferable as provided in Article 1109....

8. For purposes of this Article and for greater certainty, a non-discriminatory measure of general application shall not be considered a measure tantamount to an expropriation of a debt security or loan covered by this Chapter solely on the ground that the measure imposes costs on the debtor that cause it to default on the debt.

LG&E Energy Corp., LG&E Capital Corp. and LG&E International Inc. v *Argentine Republic, Decision on Liability*

ICSID Case No. ARB/02/1, 3 October 2006

The company alleged that Argentina had violated the BIT as a result of the enactment of the Public Emergency and Currency Exchange Law, which adversely affected the company's investment in Argentina. The investment concerned the transport and distribution of natural gas.

185. In order to establish the sustainability of an indirect expropriation, the Tribunal must define the concept. Generally, bilateral treaties do not define what constitutes an expropriation—they just make an express reference to 'expropriation' and add the language 'any other action that has equivalent effects.'...

186. A State may, at its discretion, under...the Bilateral Treaty and in accordance with general principles of international law, make use of its sovereign power to expropriate private property with the purpose of satisfying a public interest. However, expropriation in any of its modalities requires due process and compensation under international law.

187. Although in scholarly authority two kinds of expropriation are known, we will obviously skip the direct one, understood as the forcible appropriation by the State of the tangible or intangible property of individuals by means of administrative or legislative action. The parties admit that the claim at issue does not involve a direct expropriation...Instead, we shall limit ourselves to the assumption of the indirect expropriation, one qualified by the Bilateral Treaty itself as 'measures tantamount to expropriation.'

188. Generally, the expression 'equivalent to expropriation' or 'tantamount to expropriation' found in most bilateral treaties, may refer both, to the so-called 'creeping expropriation' and to the *de facto* expropriation. Their common point rests in the fact that the host State's actions or conduct do not involve 'overt taking' but the taking occurs when governmental measures have 'effectively neutralize[d] the benefit of property of the foreign owner.' Ownership or enjoyment can be said to be 'neutralized' where a party no longer is in control of the investment, or where it cannot direct the day-to-day operations of the investment. As to the differences, it is usual to say that indirect expropriation may show itself in a gradual or growing form—creeping expropriation—or through a sole and unique action, or through actions being quite close in time or simultaneous—*de facto* expropriation.

189. In order to establish whether State measures constitute expropriation…the Tribunal must balance two competing interests: the degree of the measure's interference with the right of ownership and the power of the State to adopt its policies.

190. In evaluating the degree of the measure's interference with the investor's right of ownership, one must analyze the measure's economic impact—its interference with the investor's reasonable expectations—and the measure's duration.

191. In considering the severity of the economic impact, the analysis focuses on whether the economic impact unleashed by the measure adopted by the host State was sufficiently severe as to generate the need for compensation due to expropriation. In many arbitral decisions, the compensation has been denied when it has not affected all or almost all the investment's economic value. Interference with the investment's ability to carry on its business is not satisfied where the investment continues to operate, even if profits are diminished. The impact must be substantial in order that compensation may be claimed for the expropriation.

192. The tribunal in *Tecmed* required a finding that Claimant had been 'radically deprived of the economical use and enjoyment of its investments, as if the rights related thereto—such as the income or benefits related to the [investment…]—had ceased to exist.' In other words, if due to the actions of the Respondent, the assets involved have lost their value or economic use for the Claimants and the extent of the loss.

193. Similarly, one must consider the duration of the measure as it relates to the degree of interference with the investor's ownership rights. Generally, the expropriation must be permanent, that is to say, it cannot have a temporary nature, unless the investment's successful development depends on the realization of certain activities at specific moments that may not endure variations.

194. There is no doubt that the facts relating to the severity of the changes on the legal status and the practical impact endured by the investors in this case, as well as the possibility of enjoying the right of ownership and use of the investment are decisive in establishing whether an indirect expropriation is said to have occurred. The question remains as to whether one should only take into account the effects produced by the measure or if one should consider also the context within which a measure was adopted and the host State's purpose. It is this Tribunal's opinion that there must be a balance in the analysis both of the causes and the effects of a measure in order that one may qualify a measure as being of an expropriatory nature. It is important not to confound the State's right to adopt policies with its power to take an expropriatory measure. 'This determination is important because it is one of the main elements to distinguish, from the perspective of an international tribunal between a regulatory measure, which is an ordinary expression of the exercise of the state's police power that entails a decrease in assets or rights, and a *de facto* expropriation that deprives those assets and rights of any real substance.'

M. Mendelson and M. Paparinskis, 'Bail-Ins and the International Investment Law of Expropriation: In and beyond Cyprus'
28 *Journal of International Banking and Financial Law* 475 (2013)

Investment protection treaties almost invariably contain rules on expropriation that, while differing at the level of small print, would usually define expropriation (as both direct and indirect); formulate criteria of lawfulness of expropriation (legitimate public purpose, non-discrimination, compensation, and sometimes also due process); and spell out certain elements in more detail (the criteria for calculation of compensation, conditions of transfer of compensation, rights of review under due process, additional assurances of non-discriminatory treatment etc). Determination of whether direct expropriation has occurred should be fairly straightforward: the title to property is taken away from its private owner by a public act (and either vested in the State or another person). Nationalisations of the last century were mostly clear-cut cases of direct expropriation, with the debate mainly focusing on compensation. Indirect expropriation is more challenging to define. One might draw a distinction between cases that focus on the effect of measures on the investments, and those that take the character of the public measures as the starting point; two awards dealing with alleged mistreatment of banks may illustrate the difference. According to the *Deutsche Bank AG v Sri Lanka* Tribunal:

> 'many tribunals in other cases have tested governmental conduct in the context of indirect expropriation claims by reference to the effect of relevant acts [e.g. of major unilateral increases in royalties], rather than the intention behind them. In general terms, a substantial deprivation of rights, for at least a meaningful period of time, is required' (*Deutsche Bank AG v Sri Lanka*, ICSID Case no ARB/09/02, Award, 31 October 2012, para 503).

Conversely, the *Saluka v Czech Republic* Tribunal suggested that:

> 'It is now established in international law that States are not liable to pay compensation to a foreign investor when, in the normal exercise of their regulatory powers, they adopt in a non-discriminatory manner bona fide regulations that are aimed at the general welfare' (*Saluka Investment BV v Czech Republic*, UNCITRAL Arbitration, Partial Award, 17 March 2006, para 255).

Each strand of the law of expropriation would thus formulate the definitional question in different terms. For direct expropriation, one would ask whether the title to the investment has been lost. For the *Deutsche Bank* version of indirect expropriation, one would ask whether, despite the title not being lost, the substantial and temporal effect on property has reached the level of direct expropriation. On the *Saluka* approach, one might ask whether the regulations, whatever their effect might be, have been non-discriminatory, aimed at public welfare, and adopted in a non-arbitrary manner in accordance with due process. Finally, an intermediate position might take into account all considerations by articulating an inquiry in terms of proportionality, considering the effect, purpose, and formal and procedural quality of the measures....

An intermediate method of determining whether there had been indirect expropriation would draw together all the considerations identified and ask whether an ultimate relationship of proportionality has been maintained between the very severe deprivation of rights, very important public interests, and the form and procedure through which the measures have been formulated and implemented. A possible criticism of this approach, however, is that it uses criteria for determination whether indirect expropriation has taken place similar to those applicable in determination whether the expropriation has been lawful.

NOTES

1. States have a right to expropriation and/or nationalisation. This right stems directly from State sovereignty and has been reaffirmed in numerous documents, such as UN General Assembly Resolution 1803 (XVII), which highlights the permanent sovereignty over natural resources. Whilst it was different in the immediate post-colonial era, today States seldom explicitly introduce an official measure to nationalise entire industrial sectors. However, if the investor is deprived of the possibility to use the investment in a meaningful way, this is tantamount to an expropriation. An unlawful expropriation by the host State constitutes an internationally wrongful act (see Chapter 11).

2. As illustrated by the explanations of the tribunal in the *LG&E* v *Argentine Republic* above, such an indirect expropriation can assume various forms. In the first interim award on the merits in *Pope & Talbot Inc.* v *Canada* (Interim Award on Merits—Phase One, 26 June 2000), the tribunal found that there was no indirect expropriation, because 'the Investor remains in control of the Investment, and no officers or employees of the Investment have been detained by virtue of the Regime. Canada does not supervise the work of the officers or employees of the Investment, does not take any of the proceeds of company sales (apart from taxation), does not interfere with management or shareholders' activities, does not prevent the Investment from paying dividends to its shareholders, does not interfere with the appointment of directors or management and does not take any other actions ousting the Investor from full ownership and control of the Investment'. These criteria have also been used by other arbitral tribunals in order to determine whether the investor could still use the investment in a meaningful way.

3. Customary international law submits the legality of an expropriation to the following conditions: (1) The expropriation must serve a public purpose; (2) The measure amounting to an expropriation must not be arbitrary or discriminatory; (3) The host State must pay the former owner a prompt, adequate and effective compensation. Regarding compensation, the underlying principle in the law of State responsibility is *restitutio in integrum*, and compensation will be determined accordingly, which can differ substantially compared to the fair market value approach. This is often a very complex procedure and the question of what constitutes 'adequate' compensation has given rise to many disputes.

4. Under the law of State responsibility, the host State may invoke circumstances precluding wrongfulness. For example, Argentine sought to invoke a state of necessity as a defence in a number of cases, including the *LG&E Case* (above) and *Enron Corp. and Ponderosa Assets, L. P.* v *Argentine Republic,* (ICSID Case ARB/01/3, Award of 22 May 2007). While in all cases the tribunals accepted that Article 25 of the Articles on State Responsibility (see Chapter 11) reflected customary international law and was applicable to the case, the tribunal in *Enron* found that the conditions of a state of necessity had not been fulfilled whereas the tribunal in *LG&E* concluded that there had been a state of necessity between 1 December 2001 and 26 April 2003. This illustrates the difficulty of determining the exact conditions of a state of necessity justifying an otherwise illegal expropriation. As a consequence, some States have introduced exception clauses into their BITs.

E: Dispute settlement in international investment law

North American Free Trade Agreement 1992

Article 1120 Submission of a Claim to Arbitration

1. Except as provided in Annex 1120.1, and provided that six months have elapsed since the events giving rise to a claim, a disputing investor may submit the claim to arbitration under:
   (a) the ICSID Convention, provided that both the disputing Party and the Party of the investor are parties to the Convention;
   (b) the Additional Facility Rules of ICSID, provided that either the disputing Party or the Party of the investor, but not both, is a party to the ICSID Convention; or
   (c) the UNCITRAL Arbitration Rules.

The Energy Charter Treaty 1994

Article 26 Settlement of Disputes Between an Investor and a Contracting Party

(1) Disputes between a Contracting Party and an Investor of another Contracting Party relating to an Investment of the latter in the Area of the former, which concern an alleged breach of an obligation of the former…shall, if possible, be settled amicably.

(2) If such disputes can not be settled according to the provisions of paragraph (1) within a period of three months from the date on which either party to the dispute requested amicable settlement, the Investor party to the dispute may choose to submit it for resolution:
   (a) to the courts or administrative tribunals of the Contracting Party party to the dispute;
   (b) in accordance with any applicable, previously agreed dispute settlement procedure; or
   (c) in accordance with the following paragraphs of this Article.

(3) (a) Subject only to subparagraphs (b) and (c), each Contracting Party hereby gives its unconditional consent to the submission of a dispute to international arbitration or conciliation in accordance with the provisions of this Article…

(4) In the event that an Investor chooses to submit the dispute for resolution under subparagraph (2)(c), the Investor shall further provide its consent in writing for the dispute to be submitted to:
   (a) (i) The International Centre for Settlement of Investment Disputes,…if the Contracting Party of the Investor and the Contracting Party to the dispute are both parties to the ICSID Convention;…
   (b) a sole arbitrator or ad hoc arbitration tribunal established under the Arbitration Rules of the United Nations Commission on International Trade Law (hereinafter referred to as 'UNCITRAL'); or
   (c) an arbitral proceeding under the Arbitration Institute of the Stockholm Chamber of Commerce.…

(8) The awards of arbitration, which may include an award of interest, shall be final and binding upon the parties to the dispute. An award of arbitration concerning a measure of a sub-national government or authority of the disputing Contracting Party shall provide that the Contracting Party may pay monetary damages in lieu of any other remedy granted. Each Contracting Party shall carry out without delay any such award and shall make provision for the effective enforcement in its Area of such awards.

Plama Consortium Limited v *Republic of Bulgaria, Decision on Jurisdiction*
ICSID Case No ARB/03/24, 8 February 2005

The company alleged that the actions and omissions of Bulgarian public authorities caused material damage to the operations of their petrol refinery and had a direct negative impact on the reputation and market value of the Plama group of companies.

138. The Claimant contends that Bulgaria's signature and accession to the ECT [Energy Charter Treaty] constitutes the Respondent's 'consent in writing' to ICSID arbitration, required by Article 25(1) of the ICSID Convention. It submits that Article 26 ECT contains a standing, open written offer of *(inter alia)* ICSID arbitration by Contracting States to Investors of other Contracting States. By filing its Request for Arbitration, as already noted, the Claimant accepted that offer; and having given its own written consent to arbitration under Article 25(1) of the ICSID Convention, the Tribunal's jurisdiction is established under the ICSID Convention and Article 26 ECT.

140. The Tribunal accepts the Claimant's analysis of the ECT and ICSID Convention of investor-state arbitration; but for purposes which will appear later, it wishes to emphasize several characteristics of the parties' arbitration agreement created by these two instruments. First, Article 26(3)(a) ECT provides that the Contracting Parties thereby give their 'unconditional assent' to such state-investor arbitration (subject to specific exceptions which are here immaterial); and accordingly, as a Contracting Party, the Respondent thereby expressed unconditionally its written consent required under the ICSID Convention. Second, Article 46 ECT provides that no reservations may be made to the ECT; none were in fact made in regard to Article 26 by Bulgaria; and accordingly Bulgaria's consent was unreserved. Third, under Article 25(1) of the ICSID Convention, when the parties have given their consent, no party 'may withdraw its consent unilaterally'; and accordingly the Respondent's consent was also irrevocable from the date of the Claimant's Request for Arbitration.

NOTES
1. There has been an unprecedented surge in international investment arbitration over the past two decades. Arbitration, like all international dispute settlement, requires the consent of the State (see also Chapter 16). In international investment law, such consent is increasingly of a general nature and given in advance. Both the NAFTA and the Energy Charter Treaty, as well as virtually all BITs, include a clause that provides for the possibility to submit investors' claims to international arbitration. Such a clause constitutes the standing consent of the host State. The submission of a claim to an international arbitral tribunal is considered to constitute the investor's consent (see *Plama* v *Bulgaria Case* above). This amounts to compulsory international arbitration for host States once they have ratified the respective treaty. For an investor, an international arbitration presents the advantages of an international proceeding, rather than a national court, with a legally binding award that can normally be enforced before national courts.
2. The ICSID is the most popular forum for international investment arbitration, followed by arbitral tribunals in accordance with UNCITRAL. There are also other fora for investor–State disputes.

SECTION 5: THE INTERNATIONAL FINANCIAL ARCHITECTURE

Articles of Agreement of the International Monetary Fund
Adopted at the United Nations Monetary and Financial Conference, Bretton Woods, 22 July 1944; last amended on 11 November 1992

Article I Purposes
The purposes of the International Monetary Fund are:
  (i) To promote international monetary cooperation through a permanent institution which provides the machinery for consultation and collaboration on international monetary problems.

(ii) To facilitate the expansion and balanced growth of international trade, and to contribute thereby to the promotion and maintenance of high levels of employment and real income and to the development of the productive resources of all members as primary objectives of economic policy.

(iii) To promote exchange stability, to maintain orderly exchange arrangements among members, and to avoid competitive exchange depreciation.

(iv) To assist in the establishment of a multilateral system of payments in respect of current transactions between members and in the elimination of foreign exchange restrictions which hamper the growth of world trade.

(v) To give confidence to members by making the general resources of the Fund temporarily available to them under adequate safeguards, thus providing them with opportunity to correct maladjustments in their balance of payments without resorting to measures destructive of national or international prosperity.

(vi) In accordance with the above, to shorten the duration and lessen the degree of disequilibrium in the international balances of payments of members.

The Fund shall be guided in all its policies and decisions by the purposes set forth in this Article.

Article IV Obligations Regarding Exchange Arrangements

Section 1. General obligations of members

Recognizing that the essential purpose of the international monetary system is to provide a framework that facilitates the exchange of goods, services, and capital among countries, and that sustains sound economic growth, and that a principal objective is the continuing development of the orderly underlying conditions that are necessary for financial and economic stability, each member undertakes to collaborate with the Fund and other members to assure orderly exchange arrangements and to promote a stable system of exchange rates. In particular, each member shall:

(i) endeavor to direct its economic and financial policies toward the objective of fostering orderly economic growth with reasonable price stability, with due regard to its circumstances;

(ii) seek to promote stability by fostering orderly underlying economic and financial conditions and a monetary system that does not tend to produce erratic disruptions;

(iii) void manipulating exchange rates or the international monetary system in order to prevent effective balance of payments adjustment or to gain an unfair competitive advantage over other members

Section 3. Surveillance over exchange arrangements

(a) The Fund shall oversee the international monetary system in order to ensure its effective operation, and shall oversee the compliance of each member with its obligations under Section 1 of this Article.

(b) In order to fulfill its functions under (a) above, the Fund shall exercise firm surveillance over the exchange rate policies of members, and shall adopt specific principles for the guidance of all members with respect to those policies. Each member shall provide the Fund with the information necessary for such surveillance, and, when requested by the Fund, shall consult with it on the member's exchange rate policies. The principles adopted by the Fund shall be consistent with cooperative arrangements by which members maintain the value of their currencies in relation to the value of the currency or currencies of other members, as well as with other exchange arrangements of a member's choice consistent with the purposes of the Fund and Section 1 of this Article. These principles shall respect the domestic social and political policies of members, and in applying these principles the Fund shall pay due regard to the circumstances of members.

Declaration of the Summit on Financial Markets and the World Economy

Leaders of the Group of Twenty, 15 November 2008. Available at: http://www.un.org/ga/president/63/commission/declarationG20.pdf

Common Principles for Reform of Financial Markets

8. [W]e will implement reforms that will strengthen financial markets and regulatory regimes so as to avoid future crises. Regulation is first and foremost the responsibility of national regulators who constitute the first line of defense against market instability. However, our financial markets are global in scope, therefore, intensified international cooperation among regulators and strengthening of international standards, where necessary, and their consistent implementations is necessary to protect against adverse cross-border, regional and global

developments affecting international financial stability.... Financial institutions must also bear their responsibility for the turmoil and should do their part to overcome it including by recognizing losses, improving disclosure and strengthening their governance and risk management practices.

9. We commit to implementing policies consistent with the following common principles for reform.

* Strengthening Transparency and Accountability: We will strengthen financial market transparency, including by enhancing required disclosure on complex financial products and ensuring complete and accurate disclosure by firms of their financial conditions. Incentives should be aligned to avoid excessive risk-taking.

* Enhancing Sound Regulation: We pledge to strengthen our regulatory regimes, prudential oversight, and risk management, and ensure that all financial markets, products and participants are regulated or subject to oversight, as appropriate to their circumstances. We will exercise strong oversight over credit rating agencies, consistent with the agreed and strengthened international code of conduct....

* Reforming International Financial Institutions: We are committed to advancing the reform of the Bretton Woods Institutions so that they can more adequately reflect changing economic weights in the world economy in order to increase their legitimacy and effectiveness. In this respect, emerging and developing economies, including the poorest countries, should have greater voice and representation.... The IMF, in collaboration with ... other bodies, should work to better identify vulnerabilities, anticipate potential stresses, and act swiftly to play a key role in crisis response.

K. Alexander, 'Global Financial Standard Setting, the G10 Committees, and International Economic Law'

34 *Brooklyn Journal of International Law* 861 (2008–09)

The global financial and credit crisis of 2007–2009 has highlighted the important role of the G10 committees in setting international standards for the regulation of bank capital adequacy, payment systems, and related issues pertaining to global financial stability. The main three G10 committees—consisting of the Basel Committee on Banking Supervision ('Basel Committee' or 'BCBS'), the Committee on Payment and Settlement Systems ('CPSS'), and the Committee on the Global Financial System—are the most influential international financial standard-setting bodies and exercise either direct or indirect influence over the development of banking and payment system law and regulation for all developed countries and most developing countries. Specifically, the Basel Committee has produced a number of important international agreements that regulate the amount of capital that banks must set aside against their risk-based assets, and the allocation of jurisdictional responsibility for bank regulators in overseeing the international operations of banks.... The CPSS has created important agreements setting forth principles and recommendations for the regulation of bank payment systems and for the regulation of clearing and settlement of securities trading, and recommendations regarding counterparties. The Committee on Global Financial Systems, though it has not yet adopted regulatory principles or recommendations, has produced a number of influential reports that have influenced the debate on the credit crisis and have analyzed other issues that affect financial stability....

International financial law has been defined as covering both the private law relationships of banking and financial services and the public international law of currency and foreign exchange arrangements ... Indeed, ... the purpose of international monetary law is to form 'a complex of relationships among countries on matters ... that are governed by rules and understandings that are more extensive than international monetary law as a branch of public international law'....

Sovereign States ... continue to be the main actors in economic policy and regulation, usually in both formal international economic organizations, such as the International Monetary Fund ('IMF') and the WTO, and international financial standard-setting bodies, such as the G10 committees, which include the Basel Committee. In these international institutions, States typically establish the initial terms of reference and decide on membership for States, interstate organizations, and non-state actors, as well as approve the financing and general operational oversight of these international bodies and organizations. States, though, are finding it increasingly difficult to regulate and manage cross-border trading activities and financial transactions, given the new modes of production, distribution, and consumption, and the rising interconnectedness of governments, societies, and private actors in the world economy. Indeed the forces of globalization are changing the structure of the world economy and are posing major regulatory challenges for States.... For international financial markets, the process of globalization has been no different. Expansion, diversification, and international coordination of banking activities and operations have been transformed with the increase of 'global competition among bank and non-bank financial intermediaries' and have resulted in the rise of global financial service companies and the consolidation and conglomeration of the banking and financial services industry....

In contrast to international economic organizations such as the WTO, or BIS [Bank for International Settlements], international standard-setting bodies [i.e. the Basel Committee, the Committee on Payment and Settlement Systems, and the Committee on the Global Financial System] are not entities with separate legal personality created by States, but rather informal associations of state representatives and/or professionals that meet to address specific problems or to identify issues of concern. In international finance, the globalization of financial services has necessitated that regulators develop cooperative relations to facilitate their oversight and regulation of banking and financial services...

Significantly, these Committees have resolved not to adopt legally binding international standards in a public international law sense, but rather to influence domestic regulatory law, practices and standards by adopting what has become known as 'international soft law'....[T]he overwhelming opinion of experts and policymakers clearly holds that the international standards adopted by these committees are not legally binding in any sense. They are, however, important international norms that influence and shape state behavior and are an effective form of legally non-binding international soft law that has significant public policy relevance in the global financial governance debate.

The Basel Committee's capital adequacy standards and rules on consolidated supervision were intended to apply only to credit institutions based in G10 countries that had cross-border operations. But this changed in 1998 during the Asian financial crisis when, at the urging of the G7 finance ministers and the world's largest financial institutions, which were lobbying for more market sensitive capital standards, the Basel Committee stated its intent to amend the Capital Accord and to begin working on Basel II with a view to making it applicable to all countries where banks operate on a cross-border basis. Many non-G10 countries have incorporated the Basel standards into their regulatory frameworks for a variety of reasons, including strengthening the soundness of their commercial banks, raising their credit rating in international financial markets, and achieving a universally recognized international standard. The IMF and World Bank have also required many countries to demonstrate adherence or a realistic effort to implement the Basel Accord in order to qualify for financial assistance...

[I]nternational [financial] standard-setting bodies have been characterized as 'networks' of international technical experts...[They] lack the requisite attributes of an international organization, namely, they are not subject to international law, and do not have international personality, the capacity to conclude treaties, or international legal immunities. It is precisely because of these non-legal attributes that these international standard-setting bodies—composed of state representatives and international organizations—have been praised for having a more flexible decision-making structure with a powerful normative component that significantly influences the development of national economic law and regulatory practices. Indeed, the type of international financial standard setting engaged in by the Basel Committee has been praised as an alternative form of international lawmaking without the burden of cumbersome treaty formation rules and the imprecise and often politically impractical requirements for the formation of customary international law. The international financial standard-setting bodies have been praised for being more effective in adopting economically beneficial regulatory norms and standards for most countries, while exercising far more influence over state economic and regulatory practice than the influence exerted by many formal international and regional economic organizations. The worldwide credit crisis, however, has called the efficacy of this flexible and unstructured international decision-making process into question....

[In recent years,] the more flexible institutional structure of the Basel Committee with its opaque decision-making processes...led to weaker capital adequacy measurement processes for banks, which resulted in lower bank capital levels that did not cover the social costs (or negative externalities) of bank lending and overall risk-taking...Essentially, Basel II permitted regulators to approve more market-risk sensitive capital models, which led to lower levels of regulatory capital and created an incentive for banks to increase their leverage levels in the structured finance and securitization markets. The failure of the Basel Committee and other international financial standard-setting bodies to anticipate the virulent risks created in the financial system over the last ten years has resulted in tremendous criticism of the bodies and the G10 committees for their failure to oversee adequately the international standard-setting process. The legal implications of the international financial standards produced by these bodies have raised important questions regarding the definition, relevance, and development of international economic law. The growing importance of the international financial standards, such as the Basel Capital Accord, and their acceptance by most countries for their domestic regulatory systems have demonstrated the importance of international financial soft law in influencing state practice. It has also shown that States in the financial regulatory arena have a certain disregard for using traditional public international law to govern state practice and the operations of global financial markets.

NOTES

1. As can be seen from the IMF's Articles of Agreement, the IMF's primary role consists in the supervision of monetary policies by its member States that have an impact on the international exchange market. Originally, the IMF was focused on maintaining a fixed exchange-rate system (see Section 2), and closed national financial systems. Setting financial standards was traditionally left to the domestic realm of each State. However, an increased internationalisation of financial transactions soon necessitated some form of international regulation. The G10 Committees fulfilled that function. As Kern points out, the soft-law character of the standards produced by the G10 Committee has long been considered to ensure sufficient flexibility needed in order to respond to the rapidly changing market conditions.

2. The global financial crisis following the US sub-prime mortgage crisis in 2008 has fundamentally challenged the concept of flexible financial standards. The Declaration of the G20 Leaders, while maintaining the principle of national competency to set financial regulatory standards, emphasises the importance of some underlying international regulatory structures and also highlights the important role of the IMF in crisis response. These issues remain of considerable concern across the world. As Kern points out, one of the main sources of controversy in the current international legal environment is the under-representation of a wide range of States, especially in the poor and emerging economies. The integration of developing States into the international financial standard-setting process remains one of the greatest challenges.

SECTION 6: INTERNATIONAL ECONOMIC LAW AND STATE SOVEREIGNTY

The sovereignty of States could be considered to be under threat by the integration and interdependence of the world economy, and the resulting inability of governments to give force to national policy objectives because of the ratification of international economic agreements.

Military and Paramilitary Activities in and against Nicaragua (Nicaragua v United States of America)

Merits Judgment, ICJ Rep 1986 140, International Court of Justice

The facts of the case are set out in Chapter 2. One of the questions that the Court had to answer was whether the United States had breached the principle of non-intervention. On this occasion, the Court briefly addressed state sovereignty and the resulting principle of non-intervention.

205. As regards the first problem—that of the content of the principle of non-intervention—the Court will define only those aspects of the principle which appear to be relevant to the resolution of the dispute. In this respect it notes that, in view of the generally accepted formulations, the principle forbids all States or groups of States to intervene directly or indirectly in internal or external affairs of other States. A prohibited intervention must accordingly be one bearing on matters in which each State is permitted, by the principle of State sovereignty, to decide freely. One of these is the choice of a political, economic, social and cultural system, and the formulation of foreign policy. Intervention is wrongful when it uses methods of coercion in regard to such choices, which must remain free ones.

A. Orford, 'Locating the International: Military and Monetary Interventions after the Cold War'

38 *Harvard International Law Journal* 443 (1997)

The IMF and the World Bank influence the policies of governments in two ways. First, they directly influence government policy through the imposition of conditions on access to credits and loans. Such conditions may even relate explicitly to issues of 'governance', despite the explicit prohibition in the Articles of Agreement of the Bank against interference in the political affairs of any member state. The IMF and the World Bank are also able to influence the direction of government policies indirectly. First, due to the weight that private banks place on the IMF's approval, such approval determines a country's creditworthiness and thus its ability to access private capital markets. Second, the IMF exercises influence through its role in organising debt rescheduling. Since 1982, the IMF has played a central role in arranging for private banks to take part in concerted or coordinated lending packages. The involvement of the IMF is seen as desirable, not only because it provides extra liquidity, but more importantly because private banks assume that a lending package that includes the imposition of IMF conditionality will guarantee better and more stable economic policies in the debtor country...

Decision-making over ever larger areas of what was once considered to be central to popular sovereignty and substantive democracy is now treated as legitimately within the province of economists in institutions such as the IMF and the World Bank. The supposedly economic and technocratic changes required by those institutions shape the policy choices available to governments, alter existing constitutional and political arrangements, determine the extent to which people in many states can access health care, education, pensions, and social security, and shape labour markets—thus affecting functions that go to the heart of political and constitutional authority. The shifting of decision-making authority from governments to international economic institutions affects both popular sovereignty and substantive democracy. In some cases, IMF and World Bank conditions have also challenged existing constitutional and governmental arrangements.

J. Jackson, 'Sovereignty-Modern: A New Approach to an Outdated Concept'

97 American Journal of International Law 782 (2003)

[A] powerful tension is generated between traditional core 'sovereignty', on the one hand, and the international institution, on the other hand. This tension is constantly apparent, and addressed in numerous situations, some of which are poignantly and elaborately verbalized in the work of international juridical institutions such as the dispute settlement system of the WTO. In fact, the now extraordinarily elaborate jurisprudence of the WTO exemplifies the tension between internationalism and national governments' desires to govern and deliver to their democratic constituencies, a tension that is also manifested in a large number of international law and international relations context.

These considerations suggest the need for further rethinking (or reshaping) of the core concept and roles of sovereignty, and for a new phrase to differentiate these directions from the old and, some argue, outmoded 'Westphalian' model.... [A] key question is *how* to allocate power among different human institutions...

[O]ne of the more intricate and elaborate (and some say controversial) examples of power allocation can be witnessed in relation to the WTO. Globalization and the problems that accompany it are forcing institutions to adapt or the creation of institutions that can cope. Clearly, many of these problems relate to treaty clauses that penetrate deeply into a nation-state's 'sovereignty' decisions about economic regulation. Thus, any international cooperative mechanism will, of necessity, clash with national 'sovereignty', and with special national interests whose own economic well-being will be affected by the international decisions. Not surprisingly, therefore, the WTO not only is a candidate for filling institutional needs to solve current international-level problems, but is also a target currently under attack.

Nevertheless...increasingly often nation-states cannot regulate effectively in the globalized economy, and this inability is particularly relevant to economic factors that are global and mobile (investment, monetary payments, and monetary policy, and even free movement of persons)...[M]arkets will not work unless there are effective human institutions to provide the framework that protects the market function...

The WTO plays two major, and somewhat conflicting, parts with respect to the power allocated on it. On the one hand, it moderately enhances the institutional structure for negotiating and formulating rules, and changing them as needed for the conduct of international trade and certain other economic activities at the international level. On the other hand, the WTO operates an extraordinarily powerful dispute settlement system, which is basically unique in international law history. This system has rare characteristics for an international institution: mandatory jurisdiction and submittal to its procedures, as well as an appellate process that was established to try to achieve a higher degree of coherence and rationality in the rules of the massive treaty clauses applying to the WTO's subject competence. One can immediately see a series of power allocation issues, not only as between nation-states and the WTO, with regard to its two different parts, but also allocation as between those parts.... [T]he power allocation analysis...can...help policymakers weigh and balance the various factors to reach better decisions on questions such as accepting treaty norms, dispute settlement mechanisms and results, necessary interpretive evolution of otherwise rigid treaty norms, and even in some cases new customary norms of international law. Such an analysis recognizes that there are desiderata in sovereignty concepts other than the 'core' power allocation issues, and that even as regards the core issues there are clearly cases that the world must resolve by explicit (or well-recognized implicit) departures from traditional sovereignty concepts. Taken together, these considerations can be labelled 'sovereignty-modern'.

NOTES

1. In the *Nicaragua Case*, the ICJ clearly stated that the choice of an economic system was one that each State could undertake freely as a matter of sovereignty. However, it is clear from Orford's and Jackson's analyses that both the ratification of international economic agreements and the application of these agreements by the international economic institutions have placed significant limits on State sovereignty. This is particularly true for the WTO's dispute settlement system, which is mandatory for all member States of the WTO. While the limits on State sovereignty are part of the increasing interdependence of States, it can have severe consequences on those who operate within the national systems. One consequence is seen in the impact on human rights (see Chapter 6). It is also evidence of the increasing power of corporations, particularly transnational corporations, over States, as it is often these corporations which prompt the action taken by States and the corporations which effectively manage the litigation under the DSB. Under BITs, only corporations may bring a claim, and not States (though States can bring a counter-claim).

2. While States have in the past been reluctant to cede parts of their sovereignty to international institutions, the past decades have experienced a notable shift in this attitude. This is evidenced in all branches of international economic law, be it trade law with the WTO dispute settlement procedure, international investment law where States are brought before international arbitral tribunals by corporations or the efforts of the international community to design international standards to regulate the international financial system, traditionally a prime realm of national legal regulation. Jackson argues that the traditional understanding of sovereignty might be out of date and should be reformulated as a question of allocation of power between different actors in the international economic arena, as a consequence of an increasingly interdependent world.

3. An additional concern is that some aspects of international economic law are leading to the 'levelling down' of labour and environmental standards, creating a 'lowest common denominator' effect on national social policies. Indeed, one of the most significant impacts on international economic law in the past few years has been the combined effect of those who seek to include social values and human rights within this law and the effect of 'anti-globalisation' forces, first seen in a major way at a meeting of the WTO in Seattle in 1999. This is discussed in Section 7.

SECTION 7: FUTURE DIRECTIONS

D. Leebron, 'Linkages'

96 *American Journal of International Law* 5 (2002)

Trade and the environment. Trade and workers' rights. Trade and competition policy. Trade and eighteen million tiny feet. It begins to resemble a question from an IQ test: which of the preceding pairs of issues does not fit? Increasingly, it seems there is no pairing with trade for which some argument cannot be made. The 'trade and ...' industry is booming. The growth of the 'trade and ...' business derives from two converging forces. First, more issues are now regarded as trade related in the narrow sense that the norms governing those issues affect trade, or conversely, that changes in trade flows affect the realization of those norms. Second, an increasing number of substantive areas are the subject of international coordinated action or multilateral agreements. Even if conduct in such areas does not directly affect trade flows, the creation of formalized regimes governing them raises the question how such regimes should be related to the trade regime and whether, for example, trade sanctions should be employed to enforce non-trade policies and agreements. In three important areas—human rights, workers' rights, and environmental protection—claims are based in part on concerns for the welfare of those in other nations. Domestic measures alone cannot address such concerns, and means (short of war) are therefore sought to influence governments abroad.

These issues came to the fore in both official negotiations and street protests at the Third Ministerial Conference of the World Trade Organization held in Seattle in 1999. Many developed nations sought to link issues of environmental protection and labor standards to the trade negotiations, an effort that most developing nations vehemently opposed....

A claim that issues should be linked ultimately rests on the view that the resolution of one issue or group of related issues will or should affect, or be affected by, the resolution of the other issues or group of issues. Such interdependence might result solely from the actions of the claimant, meaning that the claimant's position on the resolution of one of the issues will potentially be affected by how the other issue is resolved. Alternatively, the claimant might not assert that its position on one issue is dependent on the other, but only suggest that for exogenous reasons the two issues ought to be resolved together....[T]he linkage claim might in this sense be strategic or substantive or both....

The general presumption in the multilateral context that strategic linkage across regimes or issue areas that are not substantively related...is unfair or counterproductive. This will not always be the case, but it leads most nations to resist it. Perhaps the fundamental problem boils down to the lack of consensus as to whether the linked issue ought to be the subject of an international agreement, or at least doubt as to whether a strong international regime is appropriate to the governance of that issue. That is, it seems inappropriate to use linkage to create pressure to reach an agreement on a subject on which few believe there should be a multilateral agreement at all. Where linkage is sought, it generally ought to be by weaker means that do not undermine the ability to reach agreements. Substantive linkage, on the other hand, provokes an array of responses for both substantive and strategic reasons. Where it is strongly supported (as for linking labor and environmental issues with trade), such linkage can probably not be resisted altogether. Rather, the goal must be to choose the means of linkage that most effectively advance the policies sought to be linked (e.g., environmental and labor), without undermining the ability to reach agreement and make progress in the other regime. Interpretive linkage holds promise in this respect, and the WTO now seems in effect to have endorsed this approach. With regard to the role of environmental agreements and norms in the interpretation of GATT obligations, for example, the WTO dispute panels have basically done an about-face. They have moved from a wooden, formalistic approach that largely ignored the evolution of international environmental law, to one that tries in a nuanced way to incorporate this evolution into a dynamic interpretation of the GATT rules [see *Shrimp Case* in Section 3E].

Carefully tailoring the modality of linkage to the substantive (or on occasion strategic) claims advanced for linkage will enable us to see that these are not all-or-nothing claims but, rather, steps in the evolution of a complex multilateral regulatory framework across a variety of issue areas. Linkage so pursued should not obstruct agreement; on the contrary, it should further enhance the coherence of that multilateral world and the legitimacy of its institutions. In general, however, linkage ought not to substitute for attempts to formulate and improve the distinct international regimes that govern the linked areas. Regime borrowing and sanction linkage in particular tend to reflect frustration and disappointment with the borrowing regime (or non-regime) governing the issue area to be linked. In most such situations, linkage is a second-best solution. It would be preferable to develop the unsatisfactory regime independently.

T. Cottier, 'Challenges Ahead in International Economic Law'

12 *Journal of International Economic Law* 3 (2009)

The interest of most international economic lawyers centres on international trade regulation and investment, less so on the transactional part of the equation, i.e. contracts, credits and insurance and monetary issues broadly speaking. The many linkages to other fields, in particular, environmental law, human rights, culture and many others, have broadened perspectives and assisted in the process of bringing trade regulation fully into the realm of public international law...

The financial crisis of autumn 2008 and the turmoil of financial markets building up since 2007 call the familiar preoccupation of the trade law community with WTO law and its fascinating intricacies brutally into question. The sub-prime mortgage crisis unravelling in the US market triggered a severe loss of confidence in and within the international banking system...[T]he open trading system today is threatened from an angle for which it is badly prepared, and for which no legal disciplines of comparable importance and effectiveness are in place in international economic law...The institutional architecture of the Bretton Woods system dissociated the planned International Trade Organization and subsequently the GATT both from the United Nations and the financial system...The GATT and the WTO brought about stability based upon the rule of law. The IMF and the World Bank, other than for constitutional structure and facilities, developed upon the basis of informal policy choices and programmes shaped by the Washington consensus aiming at open and liberal market structures as a prime tool of social and economic development. Conditional lending agreements were simply the legal form for implementing economic policies. Substantive international law plays a minor part in this field…

The financial crisis…is also a crisis of social sciences, in particular of law, economics and international relations theory. It epitomizes the failures of a strictly disciplinary tradition of fragmentation and specialization, and the lack of truly interdisciplinary research…We essentially face five challenges:

First, the debate and discussion on the relationship between international economic law and economics need deepening. We have to accept that economic models in financial and monetary affairs are not able to reflect the complexities of the real world…Markets and the exercise of power need roadmaps and regulation. They are essentially constituted by law, often beyond basic institutions of protecting contracts, property and competition. Risks to the system, to consumers or the environment must be addressed and contained by legal means. The proper question relates to the proper form and adequate degree of regulation. Answers vary from field to field and give rise to argument and debate. Yet, clearly, there is more to international economic law than implementing economics. We must recall what lawyers bring to the table: a principled approach to problems combined with case by case assessment, the ability to deal with exceptions and irregularity, the relevance of values and justice, the relevance of human experience and psychology…These qualities also inform the evolution of international economic law, and WTO law perhaps amounts to one of the most prominent examples of this process. They complement economics and induce qualities which abstract and mathematical models lack. The experience of WTO law shows that the traditions of legal thinking and legalization and economic theory are not mutually exclusive but supportive…Interdisciplinary efforts emanating from trade regulation can and should be equally employed in the other challenging fields of international economic law that lie ahead, in particular, financial and monetary regulation and climate change mitigation and adaptation.

Second, the debate on horizontal problems of fragmentation and functionalism of international organizations and different regulatory fields in international economic law needs to be accelerated. Much of public international law, in the end, is economic law…The boundaries are blurred and the fields interact…It is thus important to clarify the interfacing of different fields and institutions, such as the WTO, IMF and the World Bank, as well as other pertinent bodies…The main challenges consist of bringing about procedural devices of discourse and interaction on the level of international organizations. While cooperation on the level of secretariats has made progress in recent years, it has not extended to decision making by Member States…We need to develop a more comprehensive view of regulating the global economic system. We need a broader view of international economic law.

Third, international economic law continues to face the challenge of appropriate vertical allocation of powers… The financial crisis showed that regimes essentially based upon the nation state are no longer able to cope with the challenges. Informal networking was useful in bringing about relief, but was not able to prevent the crisis. It needs completion by more formal and binding roadmaps in the future.

Fourth, we need to debate the proper structures of legal research and teaching. The traditions of functionalism and fragmentation no longer serve us well. Moving from fragmentation to greater coherence will render research more complex. Do we have the structures to address the complexity of these issues? Can they be addressed by single scholars mirroring the virtues of individualist scholarship, or do we need to work much more in research groups bringing specialists in different areas of law, economics and international relations to the table? How do we better integrate scholars in developing countries and emerging economies? How do we bring about true interdisciplinarity not only among different disciplines, but also within the different fields of international economic law?

Finally, we need to rethink our priorities in research and its role in international policy making. The financial crisis caught us by surprise. We need to discuss how this came about…How do we need to be organized in order to perform a critical public function and to have a proper voice of our own in international affairs and a media-driven world?

It is hoped that the challenges identified beyond trade regulation and investment protection will be taken up in depth and that a new impetus emerges out of the present economic crisis.

B. Simma, 'Foreign Investment Arbitration: A Place for Human Rights?'
60 International and Comparative Law Quarterly 573 (2011)

[T]he current system of investment arbitration 'seems to be leaning toward separation of human rights and investor's rights like oil and water'….Oil and water do not mix, at least not readily. Is this also true of human rights and the protection of foreign investment here also in the sense that they ought to be kept apart? Some observers, or rather stakeholders, might think so. There is, of course a way to overcome this separation: science and industry employ some sort of mediators between the water and the oil (so-called 'emulgators') to achieve this. To translate this into the relevant 'experimental' questions for our Grotian purposes is to ask how we can mediate the tension between investment protection and human rights concerns. What legal mechanisms and arguments may we employ to assure a harmonious interface of the two? What are possible, and acceptable, legal avenues for an international investment tribunal to consider international human rights law in investor-state disputes?

Before I turn to answer these questions, let me state the reasons why I think that they are relevant. First, the positive side: the protection of foreign investment by way of treaties is one of the great international legal success stories. While we don't really seem to know whether, and eventually in what measure, it has been responsible for the huge increase in foreign investment in our globalized world (with more than a trillion dollars involved), international investment protection as such has developed into a growth industry, with several multi-or plurilateral systems in place (NAFTA, CAFTA, ASEAN, the European Energy Charter), but even more staggering, with now close to 3,000 bilateral investment treaties in force worldwide, for around 170 countries, Germany alone having concluded about 150 of them. With these treaties there has occurred what can only be called an explosion of international investment arbitration, with ICSID alone registering 331 cases as of December of last year [2010]. What is not such good news is that this awesome edifice has more recently developed some visible cracks. We are confronted with claims of a lack of balance leading to apprehension, disillusionment and disappointment on the part of participants—voiced not just by left-wing regimes in Latin America or the usual suspects among the NGOs but, for instance, also by US presidential candidates in their electoral campaigns. So, do we face something like a legitimacy crisis, particularly in investment protection by international investment agreements (IIAs)? In their practical application, do such IIAs unduly favor the investor, often the mighty transnationals? The statistics of ICSID do not confirm these suspicions; neither does empirical analysis by authors such as Susan Franck, but all this cannot dispel doubts. The criticism has been fuelled, for instance, by the situation of Argentina against which alone more than 50 arbitrations have been brought. To point at a few further crisis symptoms: the stance of Bolivia in the Aguas del Tunari case as well as Bolivia and Ecuador now having left ICSID altogether; Nicaragua is openly advocating doing so; Ecuador has gone as far as rejecting the idea of foreign investment arbitration in its constitution and precluding the possibility of future treaties that would confer jurisdiction over investor-state disputes to arbitral tribunals outside Latin America....

Let me now proceed to answering [these questions] and submit, as a first point, as a matter of policy, that international investment protection and human rights are not 'separate worlds'. They are not as foreign to each other as some make it appear, preferring to see this branch of the law as a cluster of more or less de-politicized 'self-contained regimes', splendidly isolated from the dynamics and tensions of the rest of the legal universe, including human rights. After all, the ultimate concern at the basis of both areas of international law is one and the same: the protection of the individual against the power of the State. But also in economic terms, foreign investment and human rights are not to be seen as separate as it might appear at first glance. One of the more comprehensive empirical studies on the 'bite' of BITs has shown that their success in actually attracting foreign investment depends to a considerable degree upon the political environment in a potential host State; rule of law and respect for human rights in tandem with investor protection can thus form a sort of virtuous circle in improving welfare. Despite such attempts at reconciling the two matters, however, I still sense quite a bit of reticence, *Berührungsangst*, vis-a-vis human rights within the foreign investment protection/arbitration profession. This might be in the investment arbitrators' genes, because what is probably the large majority of them has a private or commercial law rather than a public law or public international law background and might thus tend to see international human rights as a potential, or probable, cause of political disturbances, intruding in their 'purely legal', autonomous field, with its ground rules being determined by neo-liberal thought. In a way, this is not hard to understand, because, after all, protection of foreign investment is to benefit the investor, while human-rights-based claims, if and when they arise in investment disputes, will mainly appear as defenses argued by States that have interfered in such investments. Let me say already at this point that the conclusion I draw from this is to also explore, and put the emphasis on, entry points for human rights which appear much earlier in our legal scenario, before disputes have a chance to arise, namely at the stage of the negotiation of the individual foreign investment contract....

Investment law practitioners might tend to regard the importance of human rights issues in international investment law as overstated. And while it is true that in the last decade or so there has developed a robust scholarly debate on the interface between human rights and international investment law, in practice human rights-based claims have not overrun the dockets of foreign investment arbitral tribunals. To investment practitioners, it might thus appear that international human rights fulfil no more than an ancillary role in the settlement of investor-state disputes, manifested in the few known instances when arbitrators '[have] look[ed] to human rights law for analogies or as an aid in constructing the meaning of the investment treaty obligations'. I would submit, however, that this is a myopic way of looking at our subject. Nowadays, human rights compliance is a priority in any decent host State's public policy agenda and thus it cannot but affect the regulatory spaces of a host State vis-a-vis foreign investors and other States. The current 'thinness' of jurisprudence involving direct clashes between treaty norms on human rights and investment should not deceive us into believing that this is merely a controversy at the fringes of international investment law. That the inherent long-term nature of foreign investment contracts will implicate the host State's international duties stemming from economic and social rights appears to me inevitable....

The tension between investment protection and human rights thus translates into a problem of aiming at two 'moving targets': for the foreign investor, how to accurately estimate the political risks of the investment before, or at the time of, its establishment in the host State so as to enable the investor to 'price' the contract cost correctly according to its projected returns on investment; and for the host State, how to determine the optimal degree of police powers and regulatory authority to be retained during the life of the investment, needed to perform its international human rights obligations. The problem is that the present architecture of international investment dispute settlement cannot adequately respond to this challenge. The remedies provided in the system as it stands essentially only become available *ex post*. What is desirable, indeed necessary, therefore is that host States and foreign investors must mutually consider other strategies available within the framework of the international investment regime to harmonize investment protection with human rights compliance. These objectives need not be incompatible.

C. Henckels, 'Protecting Regulatory Autonomy Through Greater Precision in Investment Treaties: The TTP, CETA and TTIP'

19 *Journal of International Economic Law* (2016)

International investment treaties (bilateral and multilateral investment treaties and investment chapters in preferential trade agreements) typically contain broadly worded, open-textured obligations that do not address the relationship between investment protection and the continuing powers of host states to regulate. These provisions give investment tribunals significant discretion in interpreting states' obligations toward foreign investors and investments. It can be difficult to predict when a state will be held liable to compensate an investor, due to the variety of approaches taken by tribunals to the question of state liability. As a result, a concern—borne out in some of the decided cases—is that these treaty provisions may unduly expose governments to compensate investors for non-discriminatory laws, regulations and administrative decisions adopted to promote public welfare. While in recent years, many investment tribunals have shown greater receptiveness to states' right to regulate when determining regulatory disputes, claims such as the challenges to Australian and Uruguayan tobacco control laws and to Germany's decision to phase out the use of nuclear power, among others, have highlighted the potential impact of tribunals' broad adjudicative discretion on the regulatory autonomy of states. States have adopted various strategies in response to these concerns. These include terminating bilateral investment treaties, denouncing the ICSID Convention, disengaging from negotiations for new investment treaties and failing to comply with awards. Other states have chosen to continue to engage with the system, but to change their approach to treaty making. As the numbers of claims filed against them have increased, states that were historically net exporters of capital have begun to redraft model treaties and conclude new treaties with provisions that seek to permit greater freedom for governments to regulate and take other actions to promote public welfare. They have done so by clarifying the substantive standards of investment protection and related provisions in a way that constrains investment tribunals' adjudicative discretion to a greater extent than older treaties.

Current negotiations underway for the US-EU Transatlantic Trade and Investment Partnership (TTIP) and the recently concluded Trans-Pacific Partnership Agreement (TPP) and Canada-EU Comprehensive Economic and Trade Agreement (CETA) have drawn renewed attention to the potential for states to reframe the substantive provisions of investment treaties in an attempt to exert greater control over the manner in which cases are decided. The EU, in particular, has expressed a desire to ensure as far as possible that the provisions of the TTIP and other new investment treaties will permit governments to adopt non-discriminatory measures to protect legitimate public policy objectives without liability. The coverage of these agreements and the influence of their negotiating parties mean that their provisions are likely to substantially influence future treaty design....

Despite the absence of textual guidance in fair and equitable treatment clauses, investment tribunal decisions have increasingly converged around a number of elements that are said to comprise the normative content of the obligation. Most significantly, many tribunals have embarked upon substantive review of legislative or policy changes and administrative acts under the rubric of fair and equitable treatment. In earlier cases, tribunals emphasised obligations of 'stability' and 'consistency' in the legal environment, but increasingly they have framed their approach as a question of the legitimate expectations of the investor. Undertaking substantive review of this nature creates the potential—borne out in some of the decided cases—for the fair and equitable treatment obligation to effectively restrict governments' ability to act to promote public welfare.

These concerns have animated states' approaches to drafting the fair and equitable treatment clause in recently concluded investment treaties....

[The] relevant features of the fair and equitable treatment clauses in the TPP, CETA and TTIP...set out the normative content of the obligation in more detail or provide more clarity in relation to the applicable threshold for breach. [Article 9.6 of the TTP provides]: 'Parties must accord treatment to investments in accordance with [the customary international law minimum standard of treatment of aliens]'. The concept of fair and equitable treatment: does not require treatment in addition to or beyond that which is required by customary international law; does not create any additional substantive rights; includes the obligation not to deny justice in criminal, civil or administrative adjudicatory proceedings in accordance with the principle of due process. Breach is not established merely because: [a] party takes or fails to take action that may be inconsistent with an investor's expectations; a subsidy or grant has not been issued, renewed or maintained, or has been modified or reduced....

[CETA Chapter 10, Article X:9 and TTIP Chapter II, Section 2, Article 3 provide]: 'A Party breaches the obligation of fair and equitable treatment...where a measure or series of measures constitutes: denial of justice in criminal, civil or administrative proceedings; fundamental breach of due process, including a fundamental breach of transparency [and obstacles to effective access to justice (TTIP)], in judicial and administrative proceedings; manifest arbitrariness; targeted discrimination on manifestly wrongful grounds, such as gender, race or religious belief; abusive treatment of investors, such as coercion, duress and harassment.' A tribunal may take into account whether a Party made a specific representation to an investor to induce a covered investment, that created a legitimate expectation, and upon which the investor relied in deciding to make or maintain the covered investment, but that the Party subsequently frustrated.

S. Luttrell and R. Weeramantry, *Trans-Pacific Partnership Submission to the Australian Parliament's Joint Standing Committee on Treaties*, 2016

The TPP contains a number of other provisions that are designed to rein-in BIT practice and case law. These include:

- Article 9.1, which requires that, before an investment will be covered by the TPP, it must have '*the characteristics of an investment, including such characteristics as the commitment of capital or other resources, the expectation of gain or profit, or the assumption of risk*'. This qualification, which follows the approach adopted in *Salini v Morocco* (a BIT case), is not found in most BITs. Its effect is to limit the class of investments entitled to protection under the TPP, and to give a TPP State a posited basis for objecting to the jurisdiction of an ISDS tribunal over a claim in respect of an asset or interest that lacks the '*characteristics of an investment*';
- Article 9.5, which provides that the Most Favoured Nation (MFN) clause does not apply to international dispute resolution procedures or mechanisms such as the ISDS provision in Section B of Chapter 9. This means that the principle in *Maffezini v Spain* (a BIT case) is excluded. In *Maffezini*, the ISDS tribunal held that the MFN provision in the Spain-Argentina BIT could apply to dispute resolution provisions (a number of ISDS tribunals thereafter either agreed or disagreed with this aspect of *Maffezini*, creating a body of divergent jurisprudence);
- Article 9.15, which contains a 'Denial of Benefits' clause. Provisions of this kind are rarely found in early-generation BITs, but are now a standard feature of the new crop of multilateral treaties. They are a response to the practice of 'treaty shopping', which (under certain conditions) allows investors to incorporate holding companies in a particular State for the sole purpose of taking advantage of that State's treaty program;
- Articles 9.23 and 9.24, which address perceptions that ISDS proceedings are conducted 'behind closed doors' and by 'secret tribunals', even though they may affect the public at large (for example, in cases concerning measures to protect public health or the environment). Subject to certain conditions and exceptions, the TPP requires ISDS pleadings, hearings and decisions to be accessible by the public, much like national court procedures. indeed, the TPP goes further rby permitting *amicus curiae* submission from persons who are not disputing parties.

NOTES

1. It is now widely acknowledged that international trade has implications in almost all areas of international law. Some of the issues identified by Cottier and Leebron include the link between labour issues and trade, trade and the environment, and trade and human rights. The human rights obligations of transnational corporations and the means of integrating human rights obligations within the international economic system have been an issue of high priority, as highlighted by Simma (see also Chapter 6). Trade and its links to environment have also been addressed within

WTO in the past years, and the Doha Declaration of 2001 explicitly states that 'We are convinced that the aims of upholding and safeguarding an open and non-discriminatory multilateral trading system, and acting for the protection of the environment and the promotion of sustainable development can and must be mutually supportive'. However, the substantial cooperation between different parts of the complex system of international organisations, including the UN, WTO and many UN specialised agencies, leaves much room for improvement.

2. There are concerns as to whether international economic institutions are capable of dealing with social issues, such as labour, environmental and human rights matters. For example, there are a series of cases involving the right of access to water (see *Azurix Corp.* v *Argentina* (above), *Vivendi Universal* v *Argentina* (2007) and *Biwater* v *Tanzania* (2008)), where Tribunals determined that the State's obligation to protect this right does not mean that it should not comply with its obligations under a BIT. Yet these institutions must begin to take more account of these issues in their decision-making in order to ensure that they remain relevant and effective for the long-term benefit of all members of the international community. Cottier points out that institutional cooperation at the secretariat level will not be sufficient. Member States need to design more coherent and stringent regulations that govern various aspects of international(ised) economical processes. A truly interdisciplinary approach is needed to enhance the effectiveness of such rules.

3. The creation of new international trade and investment agreements across regions has become a new form of international economic arrangement, as shown by Henckels. The Trans-Pacific Partnership was agreed in October 2015 and has 12 State parties (as at March 2016), being Australia, Brunei, Canada, Chile, Japan, Malaysia, Mexico, Peru, New Zealand, Singapore, the United States and Vietnam. Luttrell and Weeramantry indicate that it includes provisions on trade liberalisation, as well as on services, environmental protection, labour standards and investment provisions. The US–EU Transatlantic Trade and Investment Partnership (TTIP) had not been concluded by March 2016 (and is being resisted by some who see it as undermining democracy, labour and environmental standards). The Canada-EU Comprehensive Economic and Trade Agreement (CETA) was completed in February 2016, and it includes an investment court system, with a permanent roster of arbitrators appointed by Canada and the EU, as well as an appeals mechanism, which will have the power to review the merits of first-instance rulings, going beyond the limited grounds for annulment of awards in the existing ICSID system.

4. The power of transnational corporations will affect the roles of international economic institutions and the development of international economic law. It is vital for the effectiveness of international law that these organisations come within the international legal framework, not only by being able to claim rights, as is the case in international investment law, but also subject to obligations under international law (see Simma and Chapter 5). A first step into this direction is done by addressing the human rights obligations of these corporations.

14

International Criminal Law

INTRODUCTORY NOTE

Chapter 6 discussed international human rights law and various mechanisms for ensuring that such law is implemented and enforced, including addressing accountability for violations through both domestic and international fora. Chapter 8 outlined the various bases of jurisdiction in international law: territorial; nationality (both passive and active); protective; and universal. The sources in that chapter demonstrate that violations of human rights law and international humanitarian law may potentially be prosecuted before the national courts of several States each claiming different bases of jurisdiction. Moreover, in the case of universal jurisdiction, the national court may have very limited connection with the alleged perpetrator or the crimes. In some cases, the presence of an accused on the territory of a State may be sufficient to justify prosecution based on universal jurisdiction.

This chapter addresses prosecution of crimes before international criminal courts according to international—not national—criminal law. International law has long recognised that certain conduct, for example piracy and slavery, are crimes against international law that may be tried by international bodies or by any State. This principle has been expanded to cover other substantive crimes. International mechanisms for criminal accountability may be established where national courts have failed or are unable to try offenders due to a lack of political will (for example, where the offenders are still in power), insufficient resources, deficiencies in national law (the conduct in question may not have been criminalised in national law or a statute of limitation or amnesty may bar prosecution) and/or ongoing conflict. This chapter will consider the establishment and jurisdiction of the existing international criminal tribunals, including the International Criminal Court.

SECTION 1: DEFINING INTERNATIONAL CRIMINAL LAW

B. Broomhall, *International Justice and the International Criminal Court: Between Sovereignty and the Rule of Law*
(2003)

Schematically speaking, the phrase 'international criminal law' encompasses increasingly narrow concentric rings of doctrine. Outermost is the whole area of comparative transnational or inter-State criminal law, that is, of national laws that deal with the international or cross-border aspects of substantive and procedural criminal law. Next is the area of the 'suppression conventions', whereby international treaties define offences (such as drug trafficking or hijacking) and set out procedures (including the characteristic obligation to extradite or prosecute) that States agree to follow in taking action through their national systems. In this case, individual responsibility arises only under national law, while a State's failure to act (whether by passing laws or by commencing procedures under those laws) gives rise to its own international responsibility…A related but *sui generis* phenomenon is that of proposed 'international crimes of State', which would apply criminal responsibility not to individuals but to the abstract collective entity of the State. Finally, at the core of international criminal law are the doctrines by which international law imposes criminal responsibility directly upon individuals, regardless of the national law….Within the 'core crimes', unlike most of the other crimes that might legitimately fall within a broader conception of international criminal law, individual responsibility arises directly under international law, with no need (as a matter of international law) to have domestic legislation in place….The justification for this departure from the requirement of domestic legality—of prohibition at national law as a precondition to imposing criminal responsibility upon individuals—lies in the assumption that these crimes undermine the international community's interest in peace and security and, by their exceptional gravity, 'shock the conscience of humanity'.

A. Cassese, 'Reflections on International Criminal Justice'

61 *Modern Law Review* 1 (1998)

Why is justice better than revenge, in the case of war crimes and crimes against humanity? Revenge is undoubtedly a primitive form of justice—a private system of law enforcement. It has, however, an altogether different foundation from justice—an implacable logic of hatred and retaliation. Revenge can nevertheless be the last resort of persons who are denied due process. As the history of the Armenian genocide illustrates, when there is no justice in response to the extermination of a people, the result is that victims are led to take the law into their own hands, both to exact retribution and to draw attention to the denied historical fact….Many forget that, after the annihilation of the Armenians, on 28 May 1915 Great Britain, Russia and France had called for those responsible for the frightful massacres and deportations to be tried for their crimes. Indeed the Treaty of Sevres even contained a provision to the effect that the Turkish leaders responsible for the genocide would be brought to justice. But as time went by, political compromises were reached, the impetus for such trials dissipated and the Armenian massacres became the 'forgotten genocide' of the twentieth century. This had two lethal results. First, as I have just recalled, the 'Justice Commandos of the Armenian Genocide' eventually took it upon themselves to achieve justice and assassinated several of the Young Turks on the streets of Germany between 1921 and 1922…Acts of revenge were also committed by Armenian volunteers attached to the Caucasian Russian Army, which in 1916 had captured several provinces in eastern Turkey where the Armenian population had been destroyed. The second—unforeseen—result of the impunity of the leaders and organisers of the Armenian genocide is that it gave a nod and a wink to Adolf Hitler and others to pursue the Holocaust some twenty years later. There are many indications that Hitler and his cohorts were fully aware of the Armenian genocide and that they drew from it lessons suitable for emulating the Turkish model of enacting a 'final solution'…

To turn to the second part of the question: why is justice better than forgetting? Justice is preferable to forgetting both on a moral and a practical level…forgetting crimes against humanity and war crimes is, in any event a fiction—in fact, massacres and 'disappearances' are never forgotten. The memory of the exterminations of the American Indians, of the Armenians, of Australian Aborigines, of the South American 'desaparecidos' is never really buried along with the victims. The memory always lingers, and—if nothing is done to remedy the injustice—festers…

Turning now to criminal justice, as opposed to revenge, forgetting and amnesty. I know that many politicians and commentators have advocated the need for pardon, at the end of a war, for crimes committed during the armed conflict, on the ground that criminal trials can prolong or rekindle animosity and prevent return to peace and reconciliation….I have already pointed out why to my mind forgetting appalling crimes is both immoral, counterproductive and practically pointless. Let me now add that bringing culprits to justice has some notable merits that can be briefly enumerated as follows:

- trials establish individual responsibility over collective assignation of guilt, ie, they establish that not all Germans were responsible for the Holocaust, nor all Turks for the Armenian genocide, nor all Serbs, Muslims, Croats or Hutus but individual perpetrators—although, of course, there may be a great number of perpetrators;
- justice dissipates the call for revenge, because when the Court metes out to the perpetrator his just deserts, then the victims' calls for retribution are met;
- by dint of dispensation of justice, victims are prepared to be reconciled with their erstwhile tormentors, because they know that the latter have now paid for their crimes;

- a fully reliable record is established of atrocities so that future generations can remember and be made fully cognisant of what happened.

Prosecutor v *Todorović*

Sentencing Judgment, 31 July 2001, ICTY Trial Chamber

28. At the outset, the Chamber observes that, while the Appeals Chamber of the International Tribunal has held that retribution and deterrence are the main principles in sentencing for international crimes, in the Chamber's opinion these purposive considerations merely form the backdrop against which an individual accused's sentence must be determined.

29. The principle of retribution ... must be understood as reflecting a fair and balanced approach to the exaction of punishment for wrongdoing. This means that the penalty imposed must be proportionate to the wrongdoing; in other words, that the punishment be made to fit the crime. The Chamber is of the view that this principle is reflected in the account, which the Chamber is obliged by the Statute and the Rules to take, of the gravity of the crime.

30. The Appeals Chamber has held that deterrence 'is a consideration that may legitimately be considered in sentencing' [*Tadić*, Appeals Chamber, Judgment on Sentencing Appeals, 26 January 2000, para. 48] and has further recognised the 'general importance of deterrence as a consideration in sentencing for international crimes' [*Aleksovski*, Appeals Chamber Judgment, 24 March 2000, para. 185]. The Chamber understands this to mean that deterrence is one of the principles underlying the determination of sentences, in that the penalties imposed by the International Tribunal must, in general, have sufficient deterrent value to ensure that those who would consider committing similar crimes will be dissuaded from doing so.

Case Concerning the Application of the Convention on the Prevention and Punishment of the Crime of Genocide (Bosnia and Herzegovina v *Serbia and Montenegro)*

Merits, ICJ Rep 2007, International Court of Justice

The facts of this case are set out in Chapter 11.

171. The second argument of the Respondent is that the nature of the [Genocide] Convention is such as to exclude from its scope State responsibility for genocide and the other enumerated acts. The Convention, it is said, is a standard international criminal law convention focused essentially on the criminal prosecution and punishment of individuals and not on the responsibility of States. The emphasis of the Convention on the obligations and responsibility of individuals excludes any possibility of States being liable and responsible in the event of breach of the obligations reflected in Article III. In particular, it is said, that possibility cannot stand in the face of the references, in Article III to punishment (of individuals), and in Article IV to individuals being punished, and the requirement, in Article V for legislation in particular for effective penalties for persons guilty of genocide, the provision in Article VI for the prosecution of persons charged with genocide, and requirement in Article VII for extradition.

172. The Court is mindful of the fact that the famous sentence in the Nuremberg Judgment that '[c]rimes against international law are committed by men, not by abstract entities ...' (Judgment of the International Military Tribunal, Trial of the Major War Criminals, 1947, *Official Documents*, Vol. 1, p. 223) might be invoked in support of the proposition that only individuals can breach the obligations set out in Article III. But the Court notes that that Tribunal was answering the argument that 'international law is concerned with the actions of sovereign States, and provides no punishment for individuals' (*ibid.*, p. 222), and that thus States alone were responsible under international law. The Tribunal rejected that argument in the following terms: '[t]hat international law imposes duties and liabilities upon individuals as well as upon States has long been recognized' (*ibid.*, p. 223; the phrase 'as well as upon States' is missing in the French text of the Judgment).

173. The Court observes that that duality of responsibility continues to be a constant feature of international law. This feature is reflected in Article 25, paragraph 4, of the Rome Statute for the International Criminal Court: 'No

provision in this Statute relating to individual criminal responsibility shall affect the responsibility of States under international law.' The Court notes also that the ILC's Articles on the Responsibility of States for Internationally Wrongful Acts (Annex to General Assembly resolution 56/83, 12 December 2001) … affirm in Article 58 the other side of the coin: 'These articles are without prejudice to any question of the individual responsibility under international law of any person acting on behalf of a State.' In its Commentary on this provision, the Commission said:

> 'Where crimes against international law are committed by State officials, it will often be the case that the State itself is responsible for the acts in question or for failure to prevent or punish them. In certain cases, in particular aggression, the State will by definition be involved. Even so, the question of individual responsibility is in principle distinct from the question of State responsibility. The State is not exempted from its own responsibility for internationally wrongful conduct by the prosecution and punishment of the State officials who carried it out.' (ILC Commentary on the Draft Articles on Responsibility of States for Internationally Wrongful Acts, ILC Report A/56/10, 2001, Commentary on Article 58, para 3.)

The Commission quoted Article 25, paragraph 4, of the Rome Statute, and concluded as follows:

> 'Article 58… [makes] it clear that the Articles do not address the question of the individual responsibility under international law of any person acting on behalf of a State. The term 'individual responsibility' has acquired an accepted meaning in light of the Rome Statute and other instruments; it refers to the responsibility of individual persons, including State officials, under certain rules of international law for conduct such as genocide, war crimes and crimes against humanity.'

174. The Court sees nothing in the wording or the structure of the provisions of the Convention relating to individual criminal liability which would displace the meaning of Article I, read with paragraphs *(a)* to *(e)* of Article III, so far as these provisions impose obligations on States distinct from the obligations which the Convention requires them to place on individuals. Furthermore, the fact that Articles V, VI and VII focus on individuals cannot itself establish that the Contracting Parties may not be subject to obligations not to commit genocide and the other acts enumerated in Article III.

A. Bianchi, 'State Responsibility and Criminal Liability of Individuals'

in A. Cassese (ed), *Oxford Companion to International Criminal Law* (2009)

In fact, state and individual responsibility at international law are distinct regimes which present different features. State responsibility is objective in scope and requires no fault to be established, unless fault forms part of the primary obligation which is breached.…By contrast, intent remains a foundational element of the responsibility of the individual in international law. The intention of the wrongdoer is determinant to establish responsibility, particularly as regards crimes against humanity and genocide. Nevertheless, some degree of overlap may occur. For instance, intent may be relevant to establish the serious character of a breach of a peremptory norm of international law by a state. Intent, as part of the primary rule prohibiting genocide, is also required to establish the crime of genocide at the inter-state level. As a psychological attitude, intent can only be referred to individuals, in this case state agents, to trigger the responsibility of the state. Whenever a primary rule of conduct requires intent to be established, such intent can only be referred to individual agents and not to the state as the abstract entity. As the Nuremberg IMT aptly put it, international law violations are not committed by abstract entities but by individuals acting for the state.

The establishment of the individual criminal responsibility of a state agent, however, does not automatically imply attribution of his conduct to the state for the purpose of state responsibility. In order to do so, the organ needs to have acted within the scope of his functions (even if he has acted ultra vires).…

Further distinctions can be traced to the two regimes of responsibility. For instance, one may note that the standard of proof varies a great deal depending on the nature of the proceedings. When the responsibility of states is considered by the ICJ, the relevant standard of proof often consists of balancing the evidence submitted by the parties. When dealing with charges of exceptional gravity the ICJ requires a 'fully conclusive evidence' standard, appropriate to the seriousness of the allegations. By contrast, before international criminal jurisdictions the burden is that of proving guilt 'beyond a reasonable doubt'. Similarly, available defences differ and may operate differently in the different context in which they are invoked. Moreover, while the primary purpose of state responsibility is to provide reparation when an internationally wrongful act has been committed, international individual responsibility is punitive in character and attaches criminal liability to the commission of particularly heinous crimes. The attempt to attach criminal liability to states has failed and the ILC codification does not contemplate any such hypothesis.

NOTES

1. As seen from these extracts, there are several different views of what constitutes international criminal law. This chapter adopts a narrow view, and will focus only on those crimes that are criminalised and enforced directly by international law as opposed to requiring States to criminalise the conduct as the result of a treaty-based obligation (although they may also be criminalised by national law—see Chapter 4). The so-called 'core crimes' are genocide, crimes against humanity, war crimes and aggression. These crimes are considered below. Other crimes, in particular torture and terrorism, have been argued to be crimes under customary international law. However they are not yet accepted as constituting international crimes in this sense (see Section 3E).

2. The extracts from Cassese and *Todorović* outline some of the justifications for international criminal law, including deterrence and retribution. There are also alternatives to criminal justice, including amnesties, truth and reconciliation commissions, lustration and reparations.

3. Conduct that may amount to a crime under international criminal law gives rise to individual criminal responsibility, that is the individual committing the crime is held accountable for their actions, generally through the imposition of a sentence of imprisonment for a number of years (the death penalty is not normally a sentencing option in international criminal tribunals or tribunals assisted by the United Nations but may be an option in hybrid or internationalised tribunals, for example the Iraqi High Tribunal). However, the same conduct may also constitute a violation of international law for which the State itself may be responsible. Thus, as is seen in the extract from the *Bosnia Genocide Case*, there may be overlap between individual criminal responsibility and the principles of State responsibility discussed in Chapter 11 (see also the ICJ decision in *Application of the Convention on the Prevention and Punishment of Genocide (Croatia v Serbia)* 3 February 2015, para. 129). As yet, the concept of criminal responsibility for a State, as opposed to its leaders, is not generally accepted in international law. However, note the concept of violations of peremptory norms in the ILC's Articles on State Responsibility (Chapter 11).

SECTION 2: SOURCES OF INTERNATIONAL CRIMINAL LAW

Rome Statute of the International Criminal Court
2187 UNTS 3

The Rome Statute is the treaty establishing the International Criminal Court. As at March 2016, there are 124 States parties to the Rome Statute, including States from all regions.

Article 2
1—Applicable law
1. The Court shall apply:
    (a) In the first place, this Statute, Elements of Crimes and its Rules of Procedure and Evidence;
    (b) In the second place, where appropriate, applicable treaties and the principles and rules of international law, including the established principles of the international law of armed conflict;
    (c) Failing that, general principles of law derived by the Court from national laws of legal systems of the world including, as appropriate, the national laws of States that would normally exercise jurisdiction over the crime, provided that those principles are not inconsistent with this Statute and with international law and internationally recognized norms and standards.

2. The Court may apply principles and rules of law as interpreted in its previous decisions.

NOTES

1. Like other areas studied in this book, international criminal law is part of public international law and relies on the same sources (see Chapter 2). It is, however, necessary to check the relevant instruments of the tribunal tasked with enforcing violations of international criminal law. Various international criminal tribunals may apply different sources of law, including the constituent instrument (its treaty; often called a 'Statute') and relevant national laws. International criminal tribunals are also governed by secondary instruments governing the conduct of proceedings, known

as the tribunal's Rules of Procedure and Evidence (RPE). The International Criminal Court must also apply the Elements of Crimes, which provide further guidance as to the mental and physical elements to be established for each of the crimes within the Courts jurisdiction (see Section 3A(c)).

2. Unlike other international tribunals, international criminal tribunals do follow the principle of *stare decisis* (precedent) albeit in a limited form. While an Appeals Chamber may depart from its own decisions, a Trial Chamber is generally bound by decisions of the Appeals Chamber, though not those of another Trial Chamber. Moreover, international criminal tribunals do rely to some extent on the judicial decisions of other courts, including decisions of national courts, although they are not formally bound to apply these decisions.

3. General principles of criminal law that are significant in international criminal law are the principle against non-retroactivity (not imposing criminal sanctions for conduct that was not criminalised at the time it occurred), the principle of legality (*nullum crimen sine lege*—a person may be held criminally liable only where the act was regarded a criminal offence by the relevant legal order at the time it was alleged to have been committed) and *nulla poena sine lege* (no punishment without law). The principle of legality has been interpreted so that conduct is considered to have been criminalised provided it was a crime under the relevant national law or under customary international law at the time it was committed.

4. There are a number of international criminal tribunals that contribute to the development of international criminal law. These include the International Criminal Tribunal for the former Yugoslavia (ICTY), the International Criminal Tribunal for Rwanda (ICTR) and the International Criminal Court (ICC). These institutions are discussed in detail in Section 5.

SECTION 3: SUBSTANTIVE INTERNATIONAL CRIMES

A: Genocide

(a) General

Convention on the Prevention and Punishment of the Crime of Genocide 1948
78 UNTS 277

As at March 2016, there were 147 States parties to this Convention, which entered into force on 12 January 1951.

Article 2

In the present Convention, genocide means any of the following acts committed with intent to destroy, in whole or in part, a national, ethnical, racial or religious group, as such:

(a) Killing members of the group;
(b) Causing serious bodily or mental harm to members of the group;
(c) Deliberately inflicting on the group conditions of life calculated to bring about its physical destruction in whole or in part;
(d) Imposing measures intended to prevent births within the group;
(e) Forcibly transferring children of the group to another group.

Reservations to the Convention on the Prevention and Punishment of the Crimes of Genocide
Advisory Opinion, ICJ Rep 1951, International Court of Justice

The facts leading to this Advisory Opinion are set out in Chapter 3.

The origins of the Convention show that it was the intention of the United Nations to condemn and punish genocide as 'a crime under international law' involving a denial of the right of existence of entire human groups, a denial which shocks the conscience of mankind and results in great losses to humanity, and which is contrary to moral law and to the spirit and aims of the United Nations (Resolution 96 (1) of the General Assembly, December 11th 1946). The first consequence arising from this conception is that the principles underlying the Convention are principles which are recognized by civilized nations as binding on States, even without any conventional obligation. A second consequence is the universal character both of the condemnation of genocide and of the co-operation required 'in order to liberate mankind from such an odious scourge' (Preamble to the Convention). The Genocide Convention was therefore intended by the General Assembly and by the contracting parties to be definitely universal in scope....

The objects of such a convention must also be considered. The Convention was manifestly adopted for a purely humanitarian and civilizing purpose. It is indeed difficult to imagine a convention that might have this dual character to a greater degree, since its object on the one hand is to safeguard the very existence of certain human groups and on the other to confirm and endorse the most elementary principles of morality.

NOTE: The definition of genocide found in Article II of the Genocide Convention is reproduced in the Statutes of the ICTY, the ICTR and the ICC. The prohibition against genocide as set out in Article II of the Genocide Convention is regarded as a rule of customary international law, as seen in the extract from the Advisory Opinion of the ICJ above. In 2006, the ICJ said that the principle was also one of *jus cogens: Case Concerning Armed Activities on the Territory of the Congo (New Application 2002) (Democratic Republic of Congo v Rwanda)*, Jurisdiction and Admissibility, ICJ Rep 2006, para. 64 (see Chapter 3).

(b) The protected group and its members

Prosecutor v Bagilishema

Judgment, 7 June 2001, ICTR Trial Chamber

65. The Chamber notes that the concepts of national, ethnical, racial, and religious groups enjoy no generally or internationally accepted definition. Each of these concepts must be assessed in the light of a particular political, social, historical, and cultural context. Although membership of the targeted group must be an objective feature of the society in question, there is also a subjective dimension. A group may not have precisely defined boundaries and there may be occasions when it is difficult to give a definitive answer as to whether or not a victim was a member of a protected group. Moreover, the perpetrators of genocide may characterize the targeted group in ways that do not fully correspond to conceptions of the group shared generally, or by other segments of society. In such a case, the Chamber is of the opinion that, on the evidence, if a victim was perceived by a perpetrator as belonging to a protected group, the victim could be considered by the Chamber as a member of the protected group, for the purposes of genocide.

Case Concerning the Application of the Convention on the Prevention and Punishment of the Crime of Genocide (Bosnia and Herzegovina v Serbia and Montenegro)

Merits, ICJ Rep 2007, International Court of Justice

The facts of this case are set out in Chapter 11.

191. [I]t is necessary to have in mind the identity of the group against which genocide may be considered to have been committed...

193. The Court recalls first that the essence of the intent is to destroy the protected group, in whole or in part, as such. It is a group which must have particular positive characteristics—national, ethnical, racial or religious—and not the lack of them.

The intent must also relate to the group 'as such'. That means that the crime requires an intent to destroy a collection of people who have a particular group identity. It is a matter of who those people are, not who they are not.

Remarks on Daesh and Genocide, by John Kerry, US Secretary of State

17 March 2016, available at http://www.state.gov/secretary/remarks/2016/03/254782.htm

My purpose in appearing before you today is to assert that, in my judgment, Daesh [also known as ISIS and the Islamic State] is responsible for genocide against groups in areas under its control, including Yezidis, Christians, and Shia Muslims. Daesh is genocidal by self-proclamation, by ideology, and by actions—in what it says, what it believes, and what it does. Daesh is also responsible for crimes against humanity and ethnic cleansing directed at these same groups and in some cases also against Sunni Muslims, Kurds, and other minorities.

I say this even though the ongoing conflict and lack of access to key areas has made it impossible to develop a fully detailed and comprehensive picture of all that Daesh is doing and all that it has done. We have not been able to compile a complete record. I think that's obvious on its face; we don't have access to everywhere. But over the past months, we have conducted a review of the vast amount of information gathered by the State Department, by our intelligence community, by outside groups. And my conclusion is based on that information and on the nature of the acts reported.

We know, for example, that in August of 2014 Daesh killed hundreds of Yezidi men and older women in the town of Kocho and trapped tens of thousands of Yezidis on Mount Sinjar without allowing access to food, water, or medical care. Without our intervention, it was clear those people would have been slaughtered. Rescue efforts aided by coalition airstrikes ultimately saved many, but not before Daesh captured and enslaved thousands of Yezidi women and girls—selling them at auction, raping them at will, and destroying the communities in which they had lived for countless generations.

We know that in Mosul, Qaraqosh, and elsewhere, Daesh has executed Christians solely because of their faith; that it executed 49 Coptic and Ethiopian Christians in Libya; and that it has also forced Christian women and girls into sexual slavery.

We know that Daesh massacred hundreds of Shia Turkmen and Shabaks at Tal Afar and Mosul; besieged and starved the Turkmen town of Amerli; and kidnapped hundreds of Shia Turkmen women, raping many in front of their own families.

We know that in areas under its control, Daesh has made a systematic effort to destroy the cultural heritage of ancient communities—destroying Armenian, Syrian Orthodox, and Roman Catholic churches; blowing up monasteries and the tombs of prophets; desecrating cemeteries; and in Palmyra, even beheading the 83-year-old scholar who had spent a lifetime preserving antiquities there.

We know that Daesh's actions are animated by an extreme and intolerant ideology that castigates Yezidis as, quote, 'pagans' and 'devil-worshippers,' and we know that Daesh has threatened Christians by saying that it will, quote, 'conquer your Rome, break your crosses, and enslave your women.'...

One element of genocide is the intent to destroy an ethnic or religious group, in whole or in part. We know that Daesh has given some of its victims a choice between abandoning their faith or being killed, and that for many is a choice between one kind of death and another.

The fact is that Daesh kills Christians because they are Christians; Yezidis because they are Yezidis; Shia because they are Shia. This is the message it conveys to children under its control. Its entire worldview is based on eliminating those who do not subscribe to its perverse ideology.

NOTES

1. The protection of the Genocide Convention is restricted to the four groups listed in Article II. As a result, acts committed against other groups, including political, economic and social groups, cultural groups, and gender-based groups are excluded.

2. Defining the group affected by the act of genocide can be difficult. There are no accepted definitions of any of the groups referred to in the Convention and the terms may overlap. The best approach has been to accept that the four groups do not have different and distinct meanings. The ICJ has confirmed that the definition of the protected group must be a positive rather than negative definition (see also *Prosecutor* v *Stakić* (Case No. IT-97-24-T), Judgment, 31 July 2003, ICTY Trial Chamber, para. 512).

3. It may be challenging to determine whether an individual is a member of a protected group, as discussed in the extract from *Bagilishema*. The approach adopted has been to blend the objective and subjective elements, such that the group itself must have some objective existence, but the perpetrator's belief as to the victim's association with that group is substantially determinative.

4. The indication by the US Secretary of State that the US considers the actions of Daesh [ISIS] to constitute genocide is significant, as this is the first occasion since the genocide in Rwanda in 1994 that the US has characterised conduct as genocide. However, while the remarks are obviously not

a formal legal opinion, they do show the group(s) targeted by Daesh, as well as the intention to destroy that group, including through destruction of cultural heritage.

(c) Material elements—genocidal acts

Prosecutor v Akayesu
Judgment, 2 September 1998, ICTR Trial Chamber

731. With regard, particularly, to…rape and sexual violence, the Chamber wishes to underscore the fact that in its opinion, they constitute genocide in the same way as any other act as long as they were committed with the specific intent to destroy, in whole or in part, a particular group, targeted as such. Indeed, rape and sexual violence certainly constitute infliction of serious bodily and mental harm on the victims and are even…one of the worst ways of inflict harm on the victim as he or she suffers both bodily and mental harm. In light of all the evidence before it, the Chamber is satisfied that the acts of rape and sexual violence described above, were committed solely against Tutsi women, many of whom were subjected to the worst public humiliation, mutilated, and raped several times, often in public, in the Bureau Communal premises or in other public places, and often by more than one assailant. These rapes resulted in physical and psychological destruction of Tutsi women, their families and their communities. Sexual violence was an integral part of the process of destruction, specifically targeting Tutsi women and specifically contributing to their destruction and to the destruction of the Tutsi group as a whole.

732. The rape of Tutsi women was systematic and was perpetrated against all Tutsi women and solely against them. A Tutsi woman, married to a Hutu, testified before the Chamber that she was not raped because her ethnic background was unknown. As part of the propaganda campaign geared to mobilizing the Hutu against the Tutsi, the Tutsi women were presented as sexual objects.…This sexualized representation of ethnic identity graphically illustrates that Tutsi women were subjected to sexual violence because they were Tutsi. Sexual violence was a step in the process of destruction of the Tutsi group—destruction of the spirit, of the will to live, and of life itself.

733. [T]he Chamber finds that in most cases, the rapes of Tutsi women in Taba, were accompanied with the intent to kill those women.…In this respect, it appears clearly to the Chamber that the acts of rape and sexual violence, as other acts of serious bodily and mental harm committed against the Tutsi, reflected the determination to make Tutsi women suffer and to mutilate them even before killing them, the intent being to destroy the Tutsi group while inflicting acute suffering on its members in the process.

Prosecutor v Krstić
Judgment, 2 April 2001, ICTY Trial Chamber

580.…[D]espite recent developments, customary international law limits the definition of genocide to those acts seeking the physical or biological destruction of all or part of the group. Hence, an enterprise attacking only the cultural or sociological characteristics of a human group in order to annihilate these elements which give to that group its own identity distinct from the rest of the community would not fall under the definition of genocide. The Trial Chamber however points out that where there is physical or biological destruction there are often simultaneous attacks on the cultural and religious property and symbols of the targeted group as well, attacks which may legitimately be considered as evidence of an intent to physically destroy the group. In this case, the Trial Chamber will thus take into account as evidence of intent to destroy the group the deliberate destruction of mosques and houses belonging to members of the group.

Case Concerning the Application of the Convention on the Prevention and Punishment of the Crime of Genocide (Bosnia and Herzegovina v Serbia and Montenegro)
Merits, ICJ Rep 2007, International Court of Justice

190.…It will be convenient at this point to consider what legal significance the expression ['ethnic cleansing'] may have. It is in practice used, by reference to a specific region or area, to mean 'rendering an area ethnically homogeneous by using force or intimidation to remove persons of given groups from the area' (S/35374 (1993), para. 55, Interim Report by the Commission of Experts). It does not appear in the Genocide Convention; indeed, a proposal during the drafting of the Convention to include in the definition 'measures intended to oblige members of a group to abandon their homes in order to escape the threat of subsequent ill-treatment' was not accepted (A/C.6/234). It can only be a form of genocide within the meaning of the Convention, if it corresponds to or falls within one of the categories of acts prohibited by Article II of the Convention. Neither the intent, as a matter of policy, to render an area 'ethnically homogeneous', nor the operations that may be carried out to implement such policy, can *as such* be designated as genocide: the intent that characterizes genocide is 'to destroy, in whole or in part' a particular group, and deportation or displacement of the members of a group, even if effected by force, is not necessarily equivalent to destruction of that group, nor is such destruction an automatic consequence of the displacement. This is not to say that acts described as 'ethnic cleansing' may never constitute genocide, if they are such as to be characterized as, for example, 'deliberately inflicting on the group conditions of life calculated to bring about its physical destruction in whole or in part', contrary to Article II, paragraph *(c)*, of the Convention, provided such action is carried out with the necessary specific intent *(dolus specialis)*, that is to say with a view to the destruction of the group, as distinct from its removal from the region.... In other words, whether a particular operation described as 'ethnic cleansing' amounts to genocide depends on the presence or absence of acts listed in Article II of the Genocide Convention, and of the intent to destroy the group as such. In fact, in the context of the Convention, the term 'ethnic cleansing' has no legal significance of its own. That said, it is clear that acts of 'ethnic cleansing' may occur in parallel to acts prohibited by Article II of the Convention, and may be significant as indicative of the presence of a specific intent *(dolus specialis)* inspiring those acts.

ICC Elements of Crime

The Elements of Crime were developed to assist the ICC in the interpretation and application of the provisions of the Rome Statute setting out the substantive crimes of the Court.

Genocide by killing—Elements

1. The perpetrator killed one or more persons.

2. Such person or persons belonged to a particular national, ethnical, racial or religious group.

3. The perpetrator intended to destroy, in whole or in part, that national, ethnical, racial or religious group, as such.

4. The conduct took place in the context of a manifest pattern of similar conduct directed against that group or was conduct that could itself effect such destruction.

NOTES

1. In order to establish that genocide has been committed, it is necessary to prove that the accused committed one of the acts listed in Article II. Not all criminal acts are necessarily genocidal acts. The most obvious act is that of killing; however, as the extract from *Akayesu* shows, other acts, including rape and other sexual violence can constitute genocide. The recognition by the ICTR that rape can be genocide was a major development, as crimes against women in armed conflict and other contexts had traditionally been ignored, or considered to be moral rather than legal violations.

2. As the extracts from *Krstić* and the *Bosnia Genocide Case* show, ethnic cleansing and attacks targeting a group's cultural identity are not *per se* acts of genocide. However, they may be relevant in establishing the necessary intent for genocide (see Section 3A(d)).

3. The ICC Elements of Crime introduce an additional contextual element, requiring a pattern of similar conduct. It is intended to preclude isolated instances of hate crimes falling within the definition of genocide. This context element was not required by the ICTR or ICTY and was not considered to be part of customary international law (see *Krstić*, Judgment, 19 April 2004, ICTY Appeals Chamber, 43 *International Legal Materials* 1301 (2004), para. 224). The ICC has applied the contextual requirement, noting that it 'does not observe any irreconcilable contradiction' between the definition of genocide and the contextual requirement (see *Prosecutor* v *Al-Bashir*, Decision

on Application for an Arrest Warrant, 4 March 2009, ICC Pre-Trial Chamber, 48 ILM 466 (2009), para. 132).

(d) Intent

Case Concerning the Application of the Convention on the Prevention and Punishment of the Crime of Genocide (Bosnia and Herzegovina v Serbia and Montenegro)
Merits, ICJ Rep 2007, International Court of Justice

186. The Court notes that genocide as defined in Article II of the Convention comprises 'acts' and an 'intent'. It is well established that the acts [listed in Article II] themselves include mental elements. 'Killing' must be intentional, as must 'causing serious bodily or mental harm'. Mental elements are made explicit in paragraphs *(c)* and *(d)* of Article II by the words 'deliberately' and 'intended', quite apart from the implications of the words 'inflicting' and 'imposing'; and forcible transfer too requires deliberate intentional acts. The acts, in the words of the ILC, are by their very nature conscious, intentional or volitional acts (Commentary on Article 17 of the 1996 Draft Code of Crimes against the Peace and Security of Mankind, ILC Report 1996, *Yearbook of the International Law Commission, 1996*, Vol. II, Part Two, p. 44, para. 5).

187. In addition to those mental elements, Article II requires a further mental element. It requires the establishment of the 'intent to destroy, in whole or in part,...[the protected] group, as such'. It is not enough to establish, for instance in terms of paragraph (a), that deliberate unlawful killings of members of the group have occurred. The additional intent must also be established, and is defined very precisely. It is often referred to as a special or specific intent or *dolus specialis*;... It is not enough that the members of the group are targeted because they belong to that group, that is because the perpetrator has a discriminatory intent. Something more is required. The acts listed in Article II must be done with intent to destroy the group as such in whole or in part. The words 'as such' emphasize that intent to destroy the protected group.

188. The specificity of the intent and its particular requirements are highlighted when genocide is placed in the context of other related criminal acts, notably crimes against humanity and persecution, as the Trial Chamber of the [ICTY] did in the *Kupreškić et al.* case:

'the *mens rea* requirement for persecution is higher than for ordinary crimes against humanity, although lower than for genocide. In this context the Trial Chamber wishes to stress that persecution as a crime against humanity is an offence belonging to the same *genus* as genocide. Both persecution and genocide are crimes perpetrated against persons that belong to a particular group and who are targeted because of such belonging. In both categories what matters is the intent to discriminate: to attack persons on account of their ethnic, racial, or religious characteristics (as well as, in the case of persecution, on account of their political affiliation). While in the case of persecution the discriminatory intent can take multifarious inhumane forms and manifest itself in a plurality of actions including murder, in the case of genocide that intent must be accompanied by the intention to destroy, in whole or in part, the group to which the victims of the genocide belong. Thus, it can be said that, from the viewpoint of *mens rea*, genocide is an extreme and most inhuman form of persecution. To put it differently, when persecution escalates to the extreme form of wilful and deliberate acts designed to destroy a group or part of a group, it can be held that such persecution amounts to genocide.' (IT-95-16-T, Judgment, 14 January 2000, para. 636.)

189. The specific intent is also to be distinguished from other reasons or motives the perpetrator may have. Great care must be taken in finding in the facts a sufficiently clear manifestation of that intent....

198. In terms of that question of law, the Court refers to three matters relevant to the determination of 'part' of the 'group' for the purposes of Article II. In the first place, the intent must be to destroy at least a substantial part of the particular group. That is demanded by the very nature of the crime of genocide: since the object and purpose of the Convention as a whole is to prevent the intentional destruction of groups, the part targeted must be significant enough to have an impact on the group as a whole....

199. Second, the Court observes that it is widely accepted that genocide may be found to have been committed where the intent is to destroy the group within a geographically limited area. In the words of the ILC, 'it is not necessary to intend to achieve the complete annihilation of a group from every corner of the globe' (ibid.). The area of the perpetrator's activity and control are to be considered.

Report of the International Commission of Inquiry on Darfur to the United Nations Secretary-General
S/2005/60, 25 January 2005

518. On the basis of the foregoing observations, the Commission concludes that the Government of the Sudan has not pursued a policy of genocide. Arguably, two elements of genocide might be deduced from the gross violations of human rights perpetrated by Government forces and the militias under their control. These two elements are, first, the *actus reus* consisting of killing, causing serious bodily or mental harm or deliberately inflicting conditions of life likely to bring about physical destruction, and second, on the basis of a subjective standard, the existence of a protected group being targeted by the perpetrators of criminal conduct. Recent developments have led to the perception and self-perception of members of African tribes and members of Arab tribes as making up two distinct ethnic groups. However, one crucial element appears to be missing, at least as far as the central Government authorities are concerned: genocidal intent. Generally speaking, the policy of attacking, killing and forcibly displacing members of some tribes does not evince a specific intent to annihilate, in whole or in part, a group distinguished on racial, ethnic, national or religious grounds. Rather, it would seem that those who planned and organized attacks on villages pursued the intent to drive the victims from their homes primarily for purposes of counter-insurgency warfare.

Prosecutor v *Akayesu*
Judgment, 2 September 1998, ICTR Trial Chamber

523. On the issue of determining the offender's specific intent, the Chamber considers that intent is a mental factor which is difficult, even impossible, to determine. This is the reason why, in the absence of a confession from the accused, his intent can be inferred from a certain number of presumptions of fact. The Chamber considers that it is possible to deduce the genocidal intent inherent in a particular act charged from the general context of the perpetration of other culpable acts systematically directed against that same group, whether these acts were committed by the same offender or by others. Other factors, such as the scale of atrocities committed, their general nature, in a region or a country, or furthermore, the fact of deliberately and systematically targeting victims on account of their membership of a particular group, while excluding the members of other groups, can enable the Chamber to infer the genocidal intent of a particular act.

NOTES
1. There are two elements to the *mens rea* required for genocide: the intent to commit the underlying crime (i.e. murder) and the special intent required for genocide—that is, to destroy in whole or part a protected group. As the extract from the *Bosnia Genocide Case* suggests, it is sufficient to intend to destroy a substantial part of a group, or the members of a group within a limited geographical area. In the *Bosnia Genocide Case* and in the decision of the ICTY in *Krstić*, it was held that the murder of 7,000–8,000 Bosnian men at Srebrenica was a substantial part of a group. While the motive for committing a criminal act is normally irrelevant, for genocide a discriminatory intent is required; the victims must have been targeted because they are part of a protected group.
2. It may be difficult to determine a genocidal intent, particularly where other explanations for the conduct may exist, as seen in the extract from the Commission of Inquiry for Darfur. When considering the same situation, the Pre-Trial Chamber of the ICC initially refused to confirm charges of genocide, on the basis that the finding that the suspect had genocidal intent was not the 'only reasonable conclusion' that could be drawn from the evidence (*Al-Bashir*, Decision on Application for Arrest Warrant, 4 March 2009, 48 ILM 466 (2009), para. 205). This finding was overturned on appeal (see Judgment of 3 February 2010, Appeal Chamber). Similarly, the ICTY Appeals Chamber held in *Krstić* that, while the killings in Srebrenica did constitute genocide, General Krstić himself did not have the necessary genocidal intent, as he had argued that his actions were undertaken to remove a military threat, rather than to destroy the protected group: *Krstić*, Judgment, 19 April 2004, 43 ILM 1301 (2004), paras 133–134). The ICTY has also confirmed that 'in order to infer the existence of *dolus specialis* from a pattern of conduct, it is necessary and sufficient that this is the only inference that could reasonably be drawn from the acts in question': *Application of the Convention on the Prevention and Punishment of Genocide (Croatia* v *Serbia)*, 3 February 2015, para. 148 and *Bosnia Genocide Judgment*, para. 373.

3. Where direct evidence of genocidal intent is not available, intent can be inferred from the circumstances. What is more controversial is the suggestion in *Akayesu* that intent can be inferred from the actions of others (see also *Stakić*, Judgment, 22 March 2006, ICTY Appeals Chamber, para. 40). This has led some to suggest a 'knowledge-based' test for intent: see A. Greenawalt, 'Rethinking Genocidal Intent: The Case for a Knowledge-Based Interpretation' (99 *Columbia Law Review* 2265 (1999)).

B: Crimes against humanity

Rome Statute

Article 7

1. For the purpose of this Statute, 'crime against humanity' means any of the following acts when committed as part of a widespread or systematic attack directed against any civilian population, with knowledge of the attack:
   (a) Murder;
   (b) Extermination;
   (c) Enslavement;
   (d) Deportation or forcible transfer of population;
   (e) Imprisonment or other severe deprivation of physical liberty in violation of fundamental rules of international law;
   (f) Torture;
   (g) Rape, sexual slavery, enforced prostitution, forced pregnancy, enforced sterilization, or any other form of sexual violence of comparable gravity;
   (h) Persecution against any identifiable group or collectivity on political, racial, national, ethnic, cultural, religious, gender as defined in paragraph 3, or other grounds that are universally recognized as impermissible under international law, in connection with any act referred to in this paragraph or any crime within the jurisdiction of the Court;
   (i) Enforced disappearance of persons;
   (j) The crime of apartheid;
   (k) Other inhumane acts of a similar character intentionally causing great suffering, or serious injury to body or to mental or physical health.

Situation in the Republic of Kenya, **Decision Pursuant to Article 15 of the Rome Statute on the Authorization of an Investigation into the Situation in the Republic of Kenya**
31 March 2010, ICC Pre-Trial Chamber

JUDGE KAUL (Dissenting Opinion):

8. [T]here are, in law and in the existing systems of criminal justice in this world, essentially two different categories of crimes which are crucial in the present case. There are, on the one side, international crimes of concern to the international community as a whole, in particular genocide, crimes against humanity and war crimes pursuant to articles 6, 7, and 8 of the Statute. There are, on the other side, common crimes, albeit of a serious nature, prosecuted by national criminal justice systems, such as that of the Republic of Kenya.

9. There is…a demarcation line between crimes against humanity pursuant to article 7 of the Statute, and crimes under national law. There is, for example, such a demarcation line between murder as a crime against humanity pursuant to article 7(I)(a) of the Statute and murder under the national law of the Republic of Kenya. It is my considered view that the existing demarcation line between those crimes must not be marginalized or downgraded, even in an incremental way. I also opine that the distinction between those crimes must not be blurred.

10. Furthermore, it is my considered view that this would not be in the interest of criminal justice in general and international criminal justice in particular. It is neither appropriate nor possible to examine and explain in this opinion all the potential negative implications and risks of a gradual downscaling of crimes against humanity towards serious ordinary crimes.…I feel, however, duty-bound to point at least to the following: such an approach

might infringe on State sovereignty and the action of national courts for crimes which should not be within the ambit of the Statute. It would broaden the scope of possible ICC intervention almost indefinitely. This might turn the ICC, which is fully dependent on State cooperation, into a hopelessly overstretched, inefficient international court, with related risks for its standing and credibility. Taken into consideration the limited financial and material means of the institution, it might be unable to tackle all the situations which could fall under its jurisdiction with the consequence that the selection of the situations under actual investigation might be quite arbitrary to the dismay of the numerous victims in the situations disregarded by the Court who would be deprived of any access to justice without any convincing justification.

Prosecution v *Kunarac et al*
Judgment, 12 June 2002, ICTY Appeals Chamber

94. [T]he phrase 'widespread' refers to the large-scale nature of the attack and the number of victims, while the phrase 'systematic' refers to 'the organised nature of the acts of violence and the improbability of their random occurrence'. The Trial Chamber correctly noted that 'patterns of crimes—that is the non-accidental repetition of similar criminal conduct on a regular basis—are a common expression of such systematic occurrence'.

95. [T]he assessment of what constitutes a 'widespread' or 'systematic' attack is essentially a relative exercise in that it depends upon the civilian population which, allegedly, was being attacked. A Trial Chamber must therefore 'first identify the population which is the object of the attack and, in light of the means, methods, resources and result of the attack upon the population, ascertain whether the attack was indeed widespread or systematic'. The consequences of the attack upon the targeted population, the number of victims, the nature of the acts, the possible participation of officials or authorities or any identifiable patterns of crimes, could be taken into account to determine whether the attack satisfies either or both requirements of a 'widespread' or 'systematic' attack vis-à-vis this civilian population.

96. ...'only the attack, not the individual acts of the accused, must be widespread or systematic'. In addition, the acts of the accused need only be a part of this attack and, all other conditions being met, a single or relatively limited number of acts on his or her part would qualify as a crime against humanity, unless those acts may be said to be isolated or random....

98. [N]either the attack nor the acts of the accused needs to be supported by any form of 'policy' or 'plan'. There was nothing in the [ICTY] Statute or in customary international law at the time of the alleged acts which required proof of the existence of a plan or policy to commit these crimes. As indicated above, proof that the attack was directed against a civilian population and that it was widespread or systematic, are legal elements of the crime. But to prove these elements, it is not necessary to show that they were the result of the existence of a policy or plan. It may be useful in establishing that the attack was directed against a civilian population and that it was widespread or systematic (especially the latter) to show that there was in fact a policy or plan, but it may be possible to prove these things by reference to other matters. Thus, the existence of a policy or plan may be evidentially relevant, but it is not a legal element of the crime.

99. The acts of the accused must constitute part of the attack. In effect, as properly identified by the Trial Chamber, the required nexus between the acts of the accused and the attack consists of two elements:
    (i) the commission of an act which, by its nature or consequences, is objectively part of the attack; coupled with
    (ii) knowledge on the part of the accused that there is an attack on the civilian population and that his act is part thereof.

100. The acts of the accused must be part of the 'attack' against the civilian population, but they need not be committed in the midst of that attack. A crime which is committed before or after the main attack against the civilian population or away from it could still, if sufficiently connected, be part of that attack. The crime must not, however, be an isolated act. A crime would be regarded as an 'isolated act' when it is so far removed from that attack that, having considered the context and circumstances in which it was committed, it cannot reasonably be said to have been part of the attack....

102. Concerning the required *mens rea* for crimes against humanity,...the accused must have had the intent to commit the underlying offence or offences with which he is charged, and that he must have known 'that

there is an attack on the civilian population and that his acts comprise part of that attack, or at least [that he took] the risk that his acts were part of the attack.' This requirement…does not entail knowledge of the details of the attack.

103. For criminal liability pursuant to Article 5 of the Statute, 'the motives of the accused for taking part in the attack are irrelevant and a crime against humanity may be committed for purely personal reasons.' Furthermore, the accused need not share the purpose or goal behind the attack. It is also irrelevant whether the accused intended his acts to be directed against the targeted population or merely against his victim. It is the attack, not the acts of the accused, which must be directed against the target population and the accused need only know that his acts are part thereof. At most, evidence that he committed the acts for purely personal reasons could be indicative of a rebuttable assumption that he was not aware that his acts were part of that attack.

NOTES
1. Until the adoption of the Rome Statute, there had been no treaty-based definition of crimes against humanity, unlike genocide and war crimes. Article 7 of the Rome Statute is the most widely accepted listing of crimes against humanity, and builds upon the equivalent provisions in the Statutes of the ICTY and ICTR. Article 7(2) provides greater detail in respect of some of the crimes listed.
2. It is the context requirement that distinguishes crimes against humanity from 'ordinary' crimes, such as murder under national law. This requires that the crimes be committed as part of a widespread or systematic attack against a civilian population. As the extract from Judge Kaul notes, it is important that the line between ordinary crimes and crimes against humanity be maintained.
3. Previous tribunals had required the existence of an armed conflict in order for certain actions to constitute crimes against humanity (see the Statutes of the Nuremberg Tribunal and the Tokyo Tribunal). It is now recognised that this is no longer a substantive element of the offence as a matter of customary international law, although it may still be imposed as a jurisdictional restriction (see Article 5 of the ICTY Statute and *Prosecutor* v *Tadić*, Decision on the Defence Motion for Interlocutory Appeal on Jurisdiction, 35 ILM 32 (1996)).
4. The *mens rea* required for crimes against humanity is that the person had the intention to commit the relevant crime (such as murder or rape) and that they have knowledge of the wider context, i.e. the widespread and systematic attack on the civilian population. Article 3 of the ICTR Statute contained an additional mental element, requiring that crimes against humanity must be committed 'as part of a widespread or systematic attack against any civilian population on national, political, ethnic, racial or religious grounds', that is discriminatory intent is required. Again, this has been held to apply only regarding the ICTR and is not an element of crimes against humanity in customary international law. A discriminatory intent is required, however, to establish the offence of persecution as a crime against humanity.
5. Article 7(2) of the Rome Statute defines an 'attack directed against any civilian population' as 'a course of conduct involving the multiple commission of acts referred to in paragraph 1 against any civilian population, pursuant to or in furtherance of a State or organisational policy to commit such attack'. It thus introduces a requirement for the Prosecutor to establish such a policy. This requirement had been rejected by the ICTY in *Kunarac* (see extract). The ICC has found that a policy may be formally adopted or, where not formally adopted, it may be deduced from a number of factors, including the strategy and method employed in the attack, the weaponry used, the involvement of leaders, the occurrence of meetings and training sessions, and the issuance of instructions: see *Situation in the Republic of Kenya*, paras 117–128. However, the requirement has not proven to be straightforward, with Judge Kaul dissenting from the decision on the basis that the acts of violence committed in Kenya did not constitute crimes against humanity as they were not committed pursuant to an organisational policy.

C: War crimes

War crimes concern the criminalisation of certain violations of international humanitarian law, or the laws regulating the conduct of warfare. These rules are found in numerous international conventions that regulate the protection of various groups and objects during war (such as the civilian population, prisoners of war and civilian objects), how war is to be conducted (including targeting and the choice of weapons) and the types of weapons that can be used. The most significant are the four Geneva Conventions of 1949, which entered into force in 21 October 1950 and have been ratified by every State. Their provisions also reflect customary international law. The Geneva Conventions are supplemented by three Additional Protocols: one on international armed conflict (API 1977); one on non-international armed conflict (APII 1977); and one creating an additional protected emblem (APIII, 2005). The Additional Protocols are not as widely ratified as the Geneva Conventions (as at March 2016, API has 174 parties, APII has 168 parties and APIII 72 parties), and several key States are not parties (for example, the US and Israel). Moreover, some States that have ratified API and APII have made significant reservations (e.g. the UK). Several, but not necessarily all, of the provisions of API and APII are considered to reflect customary international law. There is also the Hague Convention for the Protection of Cultural Property in the Event of an Armed Conflict 1954, which requires States to criminalise unlawful attacks on cultural property (as at March 2016, the Hague Convention had 127 parties). In addition, a range of instruments, known collectively as Hague Law, regulate the use of certain weapons. A recent example is the Convention on Cluster Munitions 2008, which entered into force on 30 August 2010 and prohibits the use of cluster bombs (as at March 2016 this treaty has 98 parties).

(a) Threshold elements

Prosecutor* v *Dusko Tadić

Decision on Defence Motion for Interlocutory Appeal, 35 *International Legal Materials* 32 (1996), ICTY Appeals Chamber

70. On the basis of the foregoing, we find that an armed conflict exists whenever there is a resort to armed force between States or protracted armed violence between governmental authorities and organized armed groups or between such groups within a State. International humanitarian law applies from the initiation of such armed conflicts and extends beyond the cessation of hostilities until a general conclusion of peace is reached; or, in the case of internal conflicts, a peaceful settlement is achieved. Until that moment, international humanitarian law continues to apply in the whole territory of the warring States or, in the case of internal conflicts, the whole territory under the control of a party, whether or not actual combat takes place there.

Prosecutor* v *Kunarac

Judgment, 12 June 2002, ICTR Appeals Chamber

58. What ultimately distinguishes a war crime from a purely domestic offence is that a war crime is shaped by or dependent upon the environment—the armed conflict—in which it is committed. It need not have been planned or supported by some form of policy. The armed conflict need not have been causal to the commission of the crime, but the existence of an armed conflict must, at a minimum, have played a substantial part in the perpetrator's ability to commit it, his decision to commit it, the manner in which it was committed or the purpose for which it was committed. Hence, if it can be established, as in the present case, that the perpetrator acted in furtherance of or under the guise of the armed conflict, it would be sufficient to conclude that his acts were closely related to the armed conflict....

59. In determining whether or not the act in question is sufficiently related to the armed conflict, the Trial Chamber may take into account, *inter alia*, the following factors: the fact that the perpetrator is a combatant; the fact that the victim is a non-combatant; the fact that the victim is a member of the opposing party; the fact that the act may be said to serve the ultimate goal of a military campaign; and the fact that the crime is committed as part of or in the context of the perpetrator's official duties.

Prosecutor v *Kordić*

Judgment, 17 December 2004, ICTY Appeals Chamber

> 311. The *nullum crimen sine lege* principle does not require that an accused knew the specific *legal* definition of each element of a crime he committed. It suffices that he was aware of the *factual* circumstances, *e.g.* that a foreign state was involved in the armed conflict. It is thus not required that Kordić could make a correct legal evaluation as to the international character of the armed conflict.

Rome Statute

Article 8

> 1. The Court shall have jurisdiction in respect of war crimes in particular when committed as part of a plan or policy or as part of a large-scale commission of such crimes.

NOTES

1. The application of international humanitarian law depends on the existence of an armed conflict. In determining whether an armed conflict exists, it is necessary to distinguish an armed conflict from violence short of an armed conflict, such as internal riots or disturbances. If an armed conflict does not exist, the conduct in question cannot be considered a war crime, although it may constitute a crime against humanity or genocide, depending on the context (see Sections 3A and B).
2. Different rules apply depending on whether the conflict is international or non-international in nature. This dichotomy is reflected in the law concerning war crimes (see subsections (b) and (c)).
3. Many random acts of violence occur during the chaos and disorder of an armed conflict. While such conduct may still be a crime under national law, it must have a nexus to the armed conflict to constitute a war crime (see *Kunarac* extract). However, the accused need not have knowledge of the legal characterisation of the armed conflict.
4. War crimes were traditionally considered distinct from crimes against humanity and genocide in that, other than the requirement of an armed conflict, they did not have a context element. Article 8(1) of the Rome Statute introduces a limited form of context to prosecution of war crimes before the ICC. However, this provision is not determinative of whether the ICC can try alleged violations where this context is not met, but is intended to serve as guidance to the Court as to the types of situation on which it should focus attention. For example, in response to alleged violations committed by UK forces in Iraq, and while conceding that isolated instances of war crimes had occurred, the Prosecutor concluded there was not sufficient evidence that this 'specific gravity threshold' had been met.

(b) War crimes in international armed conflicts

Prosecutor v *Tadić*

Judgment, 15 July 1999 38 *International Legal Materials* 1518 (1999), ICTY Appeals Chamber

> 163. Having established that in the circumstances of the case the first of the two requirements set out in Article 2 of the Statute for the grave breaches provisions to be applicable, namely, that the armed conflict be international, was fulfilled, the Appeals Chamber now turns to the second requirement, that is, whether the victims of the alleged offences were 'protected persons'.
>
> 164. Article 4(1) of Geneva Convention IV (protection of civilians)…defines 'protected persons'—hence possible victims of grave breaches—as those 'in the hands of a Party to the conflict or Occupying Power of which they are not nationals'. In other words, subject to the provisions of Article 4(2), the Convention intends to protect civilians (in enemy territory, occupied territory or the combat zone) who do not have the nationality of the belligerent in whose hands they find themselves, or who are stateless persons. In addition, as is apparent from the preparatory work, the Convention also intends to protect those civilians in occupied territory who, while having the nationality of the Party to the conflict in whose hands they find themselves, are refugees and thus no longer owe allegiance to this Party and no longer enjoy its diplomatic protection (consider, for instance, a situation similar to that of

German Jews who had fled to France before 1940, and thereafter found themselves in the hands of German forces occupying French territory).

165. Thus already in 1949 the legal bond of nationality was not regarded as crucial and allowance was made for special cases. In the aforementioned case of refugees, the lack of both allegiance to a State and diplomatic protection by this State was regarded as more important than the formal link of nationality. In the cases provided for in Article 4(2), in addition to nationality, account was taken of the existence or non-existence of diplomatic protection: nationals of a neutral State or a co-belligerent State are not treated as 'protected persons' unless they are deprived of or do not enjoy diplomatic protection. In other words, those nationals are not 'protected persons' as long as they benefit from the normal diplomatic protection of their State; when they lose it or in any event do not enjoy it, the Convention automatically grants them the status of 'protected persons'.

166. This legal approach, hinging on substantial relations more than on formal bonds, becomes all the more important in present-day international armed conflicts. While previously wars were primarily between well-established States, in modern inter-ethnic armed conflicts such as that in the former Yugoslavia, new States are often created during the conflict and ethnicity rather than nationality may become the grounds for allegiance. Or, put another way, ethnicity may become determinative of national allegiance. Under these conditions, the requirement of nationality is even less adequate to define protected persons. In such conflicts, not only the text and the drafting history of the Convention but also, and more importantly, the Convention's object and purpose suggest that allegiance to a Party to the conflict and, correspondingly, control by this Party over persons in a given territory, may be regarded as the crucial test.

Rome Statute

Article 8

2. For the purpose of this Statute, 'war crimes' means:

   (a) Grave breaches of the Geneva Conventions of 12 August 1949, namely, any of the following acts against persons or property protected under the provisions of the relevant Geneva Convention:

   (i)   Wilful killing;
   (ii) Torture or inhuman treatment, including biological experiments;
   (iii) Wilfully causing great suffering, or serious injury to body or health;
   (iv) Extensive destruction and appropriation of property, not justified by military necessity and carried out unlawfully and wantonly;
   (v)   Compelling a prisoner of war or other protected person to serve in the forces of a hostile Power;
   (vi) Wilfully depriving a prisoner of war or other protected person of the rights of fair and regular trial;
   (vii) Unlawful deportation or transfer or unlawful confinement;
   (viii) Taking of hostages.

   (b) Other serious violations of the laws and customs applicable in international armed conflict, within the established framework of international law, namely, any of the following acts:

   (i)   Intentionally directing attacks against the civilian population as such or against individual civilians not taking direct part in hostilities;
   (ii) Intentionally directing attacks against civilian objects, that is, objects which are not military objectives;
   (iii) Intentionally directing attacks against personnel, installations, material, units or vehicles involved in a humanitarian assistance or peacekeeping mission in accordance with the Charter of the United Nations, as long as they are entitled to the protection given to civilians or civilian objects under the international law of armed conflict;
   (iv) Intentionally launching an attack in the knowledge that such attack will cause incidental loss of life or injury to civilians or damage to civilian objects or widespread, long-term and severe damage to the natural environment which would be clearly excessive in relation to the concrete and direct overall military advantage anticipated;
   (v)   Attacking or bombarding, by whatever means, towns, villages, dwellings or buildings which are undefended and which are not military objectives;
   (vi) Killing or wounding a combatant who, having laid down his arms or having no longer means of defence, has surrendered at discretion;
   (vii) Making improper use of a flag of truce, of the flag or of the military insignia and uniform of the enemy or of the United Nations, as well as of the distinctive emblems of the Geneva Conventions, resulting in death or serious personal injury;

(viii)   The transfer, directly or indirectly, by the Occupying Power of parts of its own civilian population into the territory it occupies, or the deportation or transfer of all or parts of the population of the occupied territory within or outside this territory;

(ix)   Intentionally directing attacks against buildings dedicated to religion, education, art, science or charitable purposes, historic monuments, hospitals and places where the sick and wounded are collected, provided they are not military objectives;

(x)   Subjecting persons who are in the power of an adverse party to physical mutilation or to medical or scientific experiments of any kind which are neither justified by the medical, dental or hospital treatment of the person concerned nor carried out in his or her interest, and which cause death to or seriously endanger the health of such person or persons;

(xi)   Killing or wounding treacherously individuals belonging to the hostile nation or army;

(xii)   Declaring that no quarter will be given;

(xiii)   Destroying or seizing the enemy's property unless such destruction or seizure be imperatively demanded by the necessities of war;

(xiv)   Declaring abolished, suspended or inadmissible in a court of law the rights and actions of the nationals of the hostile party;

(xv)   Compelling the nationals of the hostile party to take part in the operations of war directed against their own country, even if they were in the belligerent's service before the commencement of the war;

(xvi)   Pillaging a town or place, even when taken by assault;

(xvii)   Employing poison or poisoned weapons;

(xviii)   Employing asphyxiating, poisonous or other gases, and all analogous liquids, materials or devices;

(xix)   Employing bullets which expand or flatten easily in the human body, such as bullets with a hard envelope which does not entirely cover the core or is pierced with incisions;

(xx)   Employing weapons, projectiles and material and methods of warfare which are of a nature to cause superfluous injury or unnecessary suffering or which are inherently indiscriminate in violation of the international law of armed conflict, provided that such weapons, projectiles and material and methods of warfare are the subject of a comprehensive prohibition and are included in an annex to this Statute, by an amendment in accordance with the relevant provisions set forth in articles 121 and 123;

(xxi)   Committing outrages upon personal dignity, in particular humiliating and degrading treatment;

(xxii)   Committing rape, sexual slavery, enforced prostitution, forced pregnancy, as defined in article 7, paragraph 2 (f), enforced sterilization, or any other form of sexual violence also constituting a grave breach of the Geneva Conventions;

(xxiii)   Utilizing the presence of a civilian or other protected person to render certain points, areas or military forces immune from military operations;

(xxiv)   Intentionally directing attacks against buildings, material, medical units and transport, and personnel using the distinctive emblems of the Geneva Conventions in conformity with international law;

(xxv)   Intentionally using starvation of civilians as a method of warfare by depriving them of objects indispensable to their survival, including wilfully impeding relief supplies as provided for under the Geneva Conventions;

(xxvi)   Conscripting or enlisting children under the age of fifteen years into the national armed forces or using them to participate actively in hostilities.

NOTES

1. Article 8(2)(a) refers to violations of treaty-based rules during international armed conflicts. These are known as grave breaches of the Geneva Conventions. Such violations may also be tried on the basis of universal jurisdiction in national courts (see Chapter 8). API contains an additional list of grave breaches applicable in international armed conflicts.

2. Grave breaches must have been committed against persons or property protected by the Geneva Conventions. This includes the sick and wounded at land and sea (GCI and II), prisoners of war (GCIII), civilians in the hands of the enemy, interned civilians and civilians in occupied territory (GCIV). The ICTY has adopted a flexible approach to the concept of 'protected person', as seen in the extract from *Tadić*.

3. In addition to the grave breaches listed in Article 8(2)(a), the ICC may exercise jurisdiction in respect of 26 other war crimes applicable in international armed conflict on the basis of customary international law and listed in Article 8(2)(b). The list in Article 8(2)(b), a matter of extensive controversy and compromise, is not an exhaustive list of all war crimes that may arise in customary international law. Instead, it reflects the crimes which were generally accepted by the negotiating parties as part of customary international law.

(c) Non-international armed conflicts

Rome Statute

Article 8(2)

(c) In the case of an armed conflict not of an international character, serious violations of article 3 common to the four Geneva Conventions of 12 August 1949, namely, any of the following acts committed against persons taking no active part in the hostilities, including members of armed forces who have laid down their arms and those placed *hors de combat* by sickness, wounds, detention or any other cause:

    (i)   Violence to life and person, in particular murder of all kinds, mutilation, cruel treatment and torture;

    (ii) Committing outrages upon personal dignity, in particular humiliating and degrading treatment;

    (iii) Taking of hostages;

    (iv) The passing of sentences and the carrying out of executions without previous judgement pronounced by a regularly constituted court, affording all judicial guarantees which are generally recognized as indispensable.

(d) Paragraph 2 (c) applies to armed conflicts not of an international character and thus does not apply to situations of internal disturbances and tensions, such as riots, isolated and sporadic acts of violence or other acts of a similar nature.

(e) Other serious violations of the laws and customs applicable in armed conflicts not of an international character, within the established framework of international law, namely, any of the following acts:

    (i)   Intentionally directing attacks against the civilian population as such or against individual civilians not taking direct part in hostilities;

    (ii) Intentionally directing attacks against buildings, material, medical units and transport, and personnel using the distinctive emblems of the Geneva Conventions in conformity with international law;

    (iii) Intentionally directing attacks against personnel, installations, material, units or vehicles involved in a humanitarian assistance or peacekeeping mission in accordance with the Charter of the United Nations, as long as they are entitled to the protection given to civilians or civilian objects under the international law of armed conflict;

    (iv) Intentionally directing attacks against buildings dedicated to religion, education, art, science or charitable purposes, historic monuments, hospitals and places where the sick and wounded are collected, provided they are not military objectives;

    (v) Pillaging a town or place, even when taken by assault;

    (vi) Committing rape, sexual slavery, enforced prostitution, forced pregnancy, as defined in article 7, paragraph 2 (f), enforced sterilization, and any other form of sexual violence also constituting a serious violation of article 3 common to the four Geneva Conventions;

    (vii) Conscripting or enlisting children under the age of fifteen years into armed forces or groups or using them to participate actively in hostilities;

    (viii) Ordering the displacement of the civilian population for reasons related to the conflict, unless the security of the civilians involved or imperative military reasons so demand;

    (ix) Killing or wounding treacherously a combatant adversary;

    (x) Declaring that no quarter will be given;

    (xi) Subjecting persons who are in the power of another party to the conflict to physical mutilation or to medical or scientific experiments of any kind which are neither justified by the medical, dental or hospital treatment of the person concerned nor carried out in his or her interest, and which cause death to or seriously endanger the health of such person or persons;

    (xii) Destroying or seizing the property of an adversary unless such destruction or seizure be imperatively demanded by the necessities of the conflict;

(f) Paragraph 2 (e) applies to armed conflicts not of an international character and thus does not apply to situations of internal disturbances and tensions, such as riots, isolated and sporadic acts of violence or other acts of a similar nature. It applies to armed conflicts that take place in the territory of a State when there is protracted armed conflict between governmental authorities and organized armed groups or between such groups.

NOTES

1. Article 8(2)(c) and (e) relates to war crimes committed in non-international armed conflicts. The traditional view had been that individual criminal responsibility did not extend to violations of international humanitarian law committed during a non-international armed conflict. Thus, the

Statute of the ICTY restricted jurisdiction in respect of war crimes to grave breaches of the Geneva Conventions and to other serious violations of the laws and customs of war, which were assumed to be limited to international armed conflicts. At the time of drafting the ICTY Statute, the Secretary-General of the United Nations was unable to accept that criminal responsibility for war crimes extended to the non-international aspects of the conflict in the former Yugoslavia. However, this position quickly changed. Only a year later, the ICTR was given jurisdiction in respect of violations committed in a non-international armed conflict. In 1995, the Appeals Chamber of the ICTY confirmed that violations of international humanitarian law committed during a non-international armed conflict could also lead to individual criminal responsibility. The view that criminal responsibility could arise in a non-international armed conflict is clearly reflected in the Rome Statute.

2. Article 8(2)(c) reflects the wording of Common Article 3 to the Geneva Conventions, which applies in all conflicts not of an international character. Article 8(2)(e) contains a list of 12 crimes applicable in non-international armed conflict, considered to be found in customary international law. As with the list in Article 8(2)(b), this list does not include all crimes that may exist as a matter of customary international law.

3. The Special Court for Sierra Leone and the ICTR may exercise jurisdiction in respect of violations of Additional Protocol II, which applies in more limited circumstances than Common Article 3. Both Sierra Leone and Rwanda were party to Additional Protocol II at the relevant time.

D: Aggression

ICC Prosecutor Response to Communications on Iraq
9 February 2006, www.icc-cpi.int

Many of the communications received related to concerns about the legality of the armed conflict.

> While the Rome Statute includes the crime of aggression, it indicates that the Court may not exercise jurisdiction over the crime until a provision has been adopted which defines the crime and sets out the conditions under which the Court may exercise jurisdiction with respect to it (Article 5(2)). This arrangement was established because there was strong support for including the crime of aggression but a lack of agreement as to its definition or the conditions under which the Court could act....In other words, the International Criminal Court has a mandate to examine the *conduct during the conflict*, but not whether the *decision to engage* in armed conflict was legal. As the Prosecutor of the International Criminal Court, I do not have the mandate to address the arguments on the legality of the use of force or the crime of aggression.

International Criminal Court, Resolution RC/Res.6
11 June 2010, ICC Assembly of State Parties

The Assembly of State Parties comprises all states party to the Rome Statute, and is the forum for the adoption of amendments to the Rome Statute.

> ### Article 8 bis—Crime of aggression
> For the purpose of this Statute, 'crime of aggression' means the planning, preparation, initiation or execution, by a person in a position effectively to exercise control over or to direct the political or military action of a State, of an act of aggression which, by its character, gravity and scale, constitutes a manifest violation of the Charter of the United Nations.
>
> 2. For the purpose of paragraph 1, 'act of aggression' means the use of armed force by a State against the sovereignty, territorial integrity or political independence of another State, or in any other manner inconsistent with the Charter of the United Nations. Any of the following acts, regardless of a declaration of war, shall, in accordance with United Nations General Assembly resolution 3314 (XXIX) of 14 December 1974, qualify as an act of aggression:
>   a) The invasion or attack by the armed forces of a State of the territory of another State, or any military occupation, however temporary, resulting from such invasion or attack, or any annexation by the use of force of the territory of another State or part thereof;

b) Bombardment by the armed forces of a State against the territory of another State or the use of any weapons by a State against the territory of another State;

c) The blockade of the ports or coasts of a State by the armed forces of another State;

d) An attack by the armed forces of a State on the land, sea or air forces, or marine and air fleets of another State;

e) The use of armed forces of one State which are within the territory of another State with the agreement of the receiving State, in contravention of the conditions provided for in the agreement or any extension of their presence in such territory beyond the termination of the agreement;

f) The action of a State in allowing its territory, which it has placed at the disposal of another State, to be used by that other State for perpetrating an act of aggression against a third State;

g) The sending by or on behalf of a State of armed bands, groups, irregulars or mercenaries, which carry out acts of armed force against another State of such gravity as to amount to the acts listed above, or its substantial involvement therein.

NOTES

1. International humanitarian law concerns the conduct of armed hostilities. It is concerned with *how* the war is fought rather than *why*. Consequently, the laws concerning war crimes are not applicable when determining whether a State—or senior individuals authorising such conduct— have violated international law by resorting to force in the first place (see Chapter 15). Instead, the participation of leaders in aggressive action by States may constitute the crime of aggression, also known as a crime against peace.

2. Although aggression is generally considered a crime under customary international law (see *R v Jones*, extracted in Chapter 4), until recently there has been no agreed definition as to its scope and limits. As with genocide, there is also the potential for overlap with principles of State responsibility and the law on the use of force (see Chapters 11 and 15). Early attempts to define the crime of aggression included the Definition of Aggression adopted by United Nations General Assembly (Resolution 3314 (XXIX) (1974)) and Article 16 of the International Law Commission's Draft Code of Crimes against the Peace and Security of Mankind (1996). However, until the creation of the ICC, no international criminal tribunal had been given jurisdiction in respect of aggression.

3. While the crime of aggression was listed in Article 5 of the Rome Statute as a substantive offence within the jurisdiction of the Court, the drafters of the Statute were unable to reach a definition of aggression that had sufficient certainty to form the basis of a criminal offence. Jurisdiction for aggression was deferred until a definition could be agreed, in accordance with the provisions for amendment included in the Statute. The resolution above was adopted at the first Review Conference of the Rome Statute, held in May and June 2010 in Kampala, Uganda, and attended by States parties to the Rome Statute.

4. The resolution suggests amendments to the Rome Statute. These amendments will not enter into force until they have been accepted or ratified by 30 States. Moreover, the exercise of the Court's jurisdiction in respect of the crime of aggression has been restricted (see Sections 4D and 5C). In particular, the Court will not be able to exercise jurisdiction in respect of aggression until the States parties take a further decision endorsing the exercise of jurisdiction. This decision is not to be taken until after 1 January 2017.

E: Other Crimes: Terrorism and Torture

Interlocutory Decision on the Applicable Law: Terrorism, Conspiracy, Homicide, Perpetration, Cumulative Charging
16 February 2011, Special Tribunal for Lebanon, Appeals Chamber

The Special Tribunal for Lebanon was established by a Resolution of the UN Security Council, based on a treaty negotiated between the United Nations and the Government of Lebanon that was never formally ratified by Lebanon. Unlike the other tribunals detailed in this chapter, it was not given jurisdiction in respect of international crimes; rather, its jurisdiction is based only on terrorism as defined in Lebanese law. However, the Appeals Chamber held that the suggested customary international law definition of terrorism was relevant in interpreting national law.

83. The Defence Office and the Prosecutor both forcefully assert that there is currently no settled definition of terrorism under customary international law. However, although it is held by many scholars and other legal experts that no widely accepted definition of terrorism has evolved in the world society because of the marked difference of views on some issues, closer scrutiny demonstrates that in fact such a definition has gradually emerged.

...

85. As we shall see, a number of treaties, UN resolutions, and the legislative and judicial practice of States evince the formation of a general *opinio juris* in the international community, accompanied by a practice consistent with such *opinio*, to the effect that a customary rule of international law regarding the international crime of terrorism, at least *in time of peace*, has indeed emerged. This customary rule requires the following three key elements: (i) the perpetration of a criminal act (such as murder, kidnapping, hostage-taking, arson, and so on), or threatening such an act; (ii) the intent to spread fear among the population (which would generally entail the creation of public danger) or directly or indirectly coercing a national or international authority to take some action, or to refrain from taking it; (iii) when the act involves a transnational element.

86. As a preliminary matter, there is no doubt that there is a commonly shared agreement on the need to 'fight international terrorism in all its forms and irrespective of its motivation, perpetrators and victims, on the basis of international law'. Furthermore, that there exists a crime of terrorism under customary international law has already been recognised by some national courts, including the Supreme Court of Canada in *Suresh v. Canada (Minister of Citizenship and Immigration)*; the Italian Supreme Court of cassation in *Bouyahia Maher Ben Abdelaziz et al.*, which stated that 'a rule of customary international law [is] embodied in various resolutions by the UNGA and the UNSC, as well as in the 1997 Convention for the Suppression of Terrorist Bombings'; and the First 'Judge of Amparo' on Criminal Matters in the Federal District of Mexico, who noted that 'the multiple conventions to which reference has been made, provide that the crimes of genocide, torture and terrorism are internationally wrongful in nature and impose on member States of the world community the obligation to prevent, prosecute and punish those culpable of their commission'. Reference to customary law regulating terrorism was also made by Judge Antonio Boggiano in his Concurring Opinion in the *Enrique Lautaro Arancibia Clavel* Case decided on 24 August 2004 by the Argentinean Supreme Court (Corte Suprema de Justicia de la Nacion), as well as by a U.S. federal court in *Almog v. Arab Bank*.

87. However significant these judicial pronouncements may be as an expression of the legal view of the courts of different States, to establish beyond any shadow of doubt whether a customary rule of international law has crystallised one must also delve into other elements. In particular, one must look to the behaviour of States, as it takes shape through agreement upon international treaties that have an import going beyond their conventional scope or the adoption of resolutions by important intergovernmental bodies such as the United Nations, as well as the enactment by States of specific domestic laws and decisions by national courts. This examination will be undertaken in the following paragraphs.

88. Let us first consider international and multilateral instruments that include a definition of the crime of international terrorism. Numerous regional treaties have defined terrorism as criminal acts intended to terrorise populations or coerce an authority. By the same token, UN General Assembly resolutions have, since 1994, insisted that 'criminal acts intended or calculated to provoke a state of terror in the general public, a group of persons or particular persons for political purposes are in any circumstance unjustifiable[.]' Likewise, in 2004 the Security Council, by a unanimous decision taken under Chapter VII of the UN Charter, 'recall[ed]' in Resolution 1566 that:

> criminal acts, including against civilians, committed with the intent to cause death or serious bodily injury, or taking of hostages, with the purpose to provoke a state of terror in the general public or in a group of persons or particular person, intimidate a population or compel a government or an international organization to do or to abstain from doing any act, which constitute offences within the scope of and as defined in the international conventions and protocols relating to terrorism, are under no circumstances justifiable[...]

A similar definition has found a large measure of approval in the Ad Hoc Committee tasked to draft a Comprehensive Convention on Terrorism. For now, the 1999 International Convention for the Suppression of the Financing of Terrorism ('Financing Convention') provides the UN's clearest definition of terrorism, which includes the elements of (i) a criminal act (ii) intended to intimidate a population or compel an authority, and is limited to those crimes containing (iii) a transnational aspect.

89. The Financing Convention and most of the regional and multilateral conventions regarding terrorism incorporate into their definition of terrorism the specific offences criminalised in a long line of terrorism-related conventions. Among the terrorist offences so criminalised are the taking of hostages, the hijacking of planes, and the harming of diplomatic representatives. For political expediency at the time of their drafting, the earliest of these conventions focus solely on particular conduct that is universally condemned and do not require a particular intent (e.g., to terrorise or to coerce). Such an intent element, however, has been specified in the most recent conventions. Further, all of these conventions also require—through the definition of the *actus reus* (the material element of a crime) or by additional provision—a transnational element to the crime. Indeed, the three most recent universal conventions share a nearly identical Article 3, which states:

> This Convention shall not apply where the offence is committed within a single State, the alleged offender and the victims are nationals of that State, the alleged offender is found in the territory of that State and no other State has a basis [under subsequent articles of the Convention] to exercise jurisdiction [...]

It is to be emphasised that the requirement of a cross-border element goes not to the definition of terrorism but to its character as international rather than domestic. The two elements of (i) criminal act and (ii) intention to intimidate a population or compel an authority are common to both domestic and international terrorism.

90. Regarding this transnational element, it will typically be a connection of perpetrators, victims, or means used across two or more countries, but it may also be a significant impact that a terrorist act in one country has on another—in other words, when it is foreseeable that a terrorist attack that is planned and executed in one country will threaten international peace and security, at least for neighbouring countries. The requirement of a transnational element serves to exclude from the definition of international terrorism those crimes that are purely domestic, in planning, execution, and direct impact. However, such purely domestic crimes may be equally serious in terms of human loss and social destruction. The exclusion of the transnational element from the domestic crime of terrorism, as defined by most countries' criminal codes, does not detract from the essential communality of the concept of terrorism in international and domestic criminal law. The exclusion allows those countries to apply the heightened investigative powers, deterrence mechanisms, punishment, and public condemnation that attach with the label 'terrorism' to serious crimes that may not have international connections or a direct 'spill over' effect in other countries.

91. Other than the exclusion of this transnational element, however, the national legislation of countries around the world consistently defines terrorism in similar if not identical terms to those used in the international instruments just surveyed. Consistent national legislation can be another important source of law indicative of the emergence of a customary rule. The ICTY, in determining the definition of rape to be applied by the tribunal, concluded that 'it is necessary to look for principles of criminal law common to the major legal systems of the world,' which 'may be derived with all due caution, from national laws.' ...

93. Elements common across national legislation defining terrorism include the use of criminal acts to terrorise or intimidate populations, to coerce government authorities, or to disrupt or destabilise social or political structures....

102. The conclusion is therefore warranted that a customary rule has evolved in the international community concerning terrorism, the elements of which we outlined in paragraph 85. Relying on the notion of international custom as set out by the International Court of Justice in the *Continental Shelf* case, it can be said that there is a settled practice concerning the punishment of acts of terrorism, as commonly defined, at least when committed in time of peace; in addition, this practice is evidence of a belief of States that the punishment of terrorism responds to a social necessity (*opinio necessitatis*) and is hence rendered obligatory by the existence of a rule requiring it (*opinio juris*).

NOTES

1. The extract from the Special Tribunal for Lebanon decision above purports to establish a customary international law crime of transnational terrorism, at least as applicable outside situations of armed conflict. The decision was controversial among international criminal law scholars. Some argue that no distinct customary crime of terrorism exists. The use of various sources of custom to criminalise new conduct has also been criticised, for example Saul argues that the judges 'misinterpreted' and 'exaggerated' those sources and that the sources of custom relied upon by the Appeals Chamber do not support the customary definition of 'terrorism' identified by it (B. Saul, 'Legislating from a Radical Hague: The United Nations Special Tribunal for Lebanon Invents an

International Crime of Transnational Terrorism', 24 *Leiden Journal of International Law*, 677 (2011)). Another problematic feature of this decision lies in the Chamber's identification of a definition of terrorism, as, to date, States have not been able to agree on a comprehensive definition of terrorism for the purpose of a prohibition on terrorist acts under a legally binding international treaty. Despite increased cooperation in global counter-terrorism, the cliché that 'one man's terrorist is another man's freedom fighter' has posed genuine conceptual difficulties in reaching such agreement.

2. Similar questions arise as to the status of torture as a separate crime under customary international law, as distinct from a war crime or crime against humanity. While the prohibition against torture is accepted as one of customary international law (see Chapter 6), it is not yet generally accepted that individual criminal responsibility is directly incurred as a matter of international criminal law, as opposed to national criminal laws, when it does not meet the contextual elements of war crimes or crimes against humanity.

SECTION 4: PROSECUTING INTERNATIONAL CRIMES

A: Modes of liability

Prosecutor v Tadić

Judgment, 15 July 1999, 38 *International Legal Materials* 1518 (1999), ICTY Appeals Chamber

The Appeals Chamber was addressing the question whether Article 7 of the ICTY Statute, which did not expressly provide for the concept of joint criminal responsibility, could extend to those who planned the commission of a crime.

190. …Thus, all those who have engaged in serious violations of international humanitarian law, whatever the manner in which they may have perpetrated, or participated in the perpetration of those violations, must be brought to justice. If this is so, it is fair to conclude that the [ICTY] Statute does not confine itself to providing for jurisdiction over those persons who plan, instigate, order, physically perpetrate a crime or otherwise aid and abet in its planning, preparation or execution. The Statute does not stop there. It does not exclude those modes of participating in the commission of crimes which occur where several persons having a common purpose embark on criminal activity that is then carried out either jointly or by some members of this plurality of persons. Whoever contributes to the commission of crimes by the group of persons or some members of the group, in execution of a common criminal purpose, may be held to be criminally liable, subject to certain conditions, which are specified below.

191. The above interpretation is not only dictated by the object and purpose of the Statute but is also warranted by the very nature of many international crimes which are committed most commonly in wartime situations. Most of the time these crimes do not result from the criminal propensity of single individuals but constitute manifestations of collective criminality: the crimes are often carried out by groups of individuals acting in pursuance of a common criminal design. Although only some members of the group may physically perpetrate the criminal act (murder, extermination, wanton destruction of cities, towns or villages, etc.), the participation and contribution of the other members of the group is often vital in facilitating the commission of the offence in question. It follows that the moral gravity of such participation is often no less—or indeed no different—from that of those actually carrying out the acts in question.

192. Under these circumstances, to hold criminally liable as a perpetrator only the person who materially performs the criminal act would disregard the role as co-perpetrators of all those who in some way made it possible for the perpetrator physically to carry out that criminal act. At the same time, depending upon the circumstances, to hold the latter liable only as aiders and abettors might understate the degree of their criminal responsibility.

193. This interpretation, based on the Statute and the inherent characteristics of many crimes perpetrated in wartime, warrants the conclusion that international criminal responsibility embraces actions perpetrated by a collectivity of persons in furtherance of common criminal design. It may also be noted that—as will be mentioned

below—international criminal rules on common purpose are substantially rooted in, and to a large extent reflect, the position taken by many States of the world in their national legal systems....

227. In sum, the objective elements (*actus reus*) of this mode of participation in one of the crimes provided for in the Statute (with regard to each of the three categories of cases) are as follows:

  i. *A plurality of persons.* They need not be organised in a military, political or administrative structure....
  ii. *The existence of a common plan, design or purpose which amounts to or involves the commission of a crime provided for in the Statute.* There is no necessity for this plan, design or purpose to have been previously arranged or formulated. The common plan or purpose may materialise extemporaneously and be inferred from the fact that a plurality of persons acts in unison to put into effect a joint criminal enterprise.
  iii. *Participation of the accused in the common design* involving the perpetration of one of the crimes provided for in the Statute. This participation need not involve commission of a specific crime under one of those provisions (for example, murder, extermination, torture, rape, etc.), but may take the form of assistance in, or contribution to, the execution of the common plan or purpose.

228. By contrast, the *mens rea* element differs according to the category of common design under consideration. With regard to the first category, what is required is the intent to perpetrate a certain crime (this being the shared intent on the part of all co-perpetrators). With regard to the second category (which, as noted above, is really a variant of the first), personal knowledge of the system of ill-treatment is required (whether proved by express testimony or a matter of reasonable inference from the accused's position of authority), as well as the intent to further this common concerted system of ill-treatment. With regard to the third category, what is required is the *intention* to participate in and further the criminal activity or the criminal purpose of a group and to contribute to the joint criminal enterprise or in any event to the commission of a crime by the group. In addition, responsibility for a crime other than the one agreed upon in the common plan arises only if, under the circumstances of the case, (i) it was *foreseeable* that such a crime might be perpetrated by one or other members of the group and (ii) the accused *willingly took that risk*.

229. In light of the preceding propositions it is now appropriate to distinguish between acting in pursuance of a common purpose or design to commit a crime, and aiding and abetting.

  (i)   The aider and abettor is always an accessory to a crime perpetrated by another person, the principal.
  (ii) In the case of aiding and abetting no proof is required of the existence of a common concerted plan, let alone of the pre-existence of such a plan. No plan or agreement is required: indeed, the principal may not even know about the accomplice's contribution.
  (iii) The aider and abettor carries out acts specifically directed to assist, encourage or lend moral support to the perpetration of a certain specific crime (murder, extermination, rape, torture, wanton destruction of civilian property, etc.), and this support has a substantial effect upon the perpetration of the crime. By contrast, in the case of acting in pursuance of a common purpose or design, it is sufficient for the participant to perform acts that in some way are directed to the furthering of the common plan or purpose.
  (iv) In the case of aiding and abetting, the requisite mental element is knowledge that the acts performed by the aider and abettor assist the commission of a specific crime by the principal. By contrast, in the case of common purpose or design more is required (i.e., either intent to perpetrate the crime or intent to pursue the common criminal design plus foresight that those crimes outside the criminal common purpose were likely to be committed), as stated above.

Rome Statute

Article 25—Individual criminal responsibility

  1. The Court shall have jurisdiction over natural persons pursuant to this Statute.

  2. A person who commits a crime within the jurisdiction of the Court shall be individually responsible and liable for punishment in accordance with this Statute.

  3. In accordance with this Statute, a person shall be criminally responsible and liable for punishment for a crime within the jurisdiction of the Court if that person:
      (a) Commits such a crime, whether as an individual, jointly with another or through another person, regardless of whether that other person is criminally responsible;

(b) Orders, solicits or induces the commission of such a crime which in fact occurs or is attempted;

(c) For the purpose of facilitating the commission of such a crime, aids, abets or otherwise assists in its commission or its attempted commission, including providing the means for its commission;

(d) In any other way contributes to the commission or attempted commission of such a crime by a group of persons acting with a common purpose. Such contribution shall be intentional and shall either:

   (i) Be made with the aim of furthering the criminal activity or criminal purpose of the group, where such activity or purpose involves the commission of a crime within the jurisdiction of the Court; or

   (ii) Be made in the knowledge of the intention of the group to commit the crime;

(e) In respect of the crime of genocide, directly and publicly incites others to commit genocide;

(f) Attempts to commit such a crime by taking action that commences its execution by means of a substantial step, but the crime does not occur because of circumstances independent of the person's intentions. However, a person who abandons the effort to commit the crime or otherwise prevents the completion of the crime shall not be liable for punishment under this Statute for the attempt to commit that crime if that person completely and voluntarily gave up the criminal purpose.

4. No provision in this Statute relating to individual criminal responsibility shall affect the responsibility of States under international law.

Prosecutor v Thomas Lubanga Dyilo

Judgment on the appeal of Mr Thomas Lubanga Dyilo against his conviction, 1 December 2014, Appeals Chamber, International Criminal Court

Lubanga was accused, and convicted of, the war crimes of enlisting and conscripting children under the age of 15 years and using them to participate actively in hostilities in the armed conflict in the DRC as part of a common plan to build an army for the purpose of establishing and maintaining political and military control over Ituri. One of the grounds of appeal was whether the common plan had to be criminal of itself, and whether Lubanga had the required mental element. Another was whether Lubanga could be guilty of a crime he had not perpetrated and from which he was geographically remote.

445. At the outset, the Appeals Chamber considers that, in order to establish that an accused person committed a crime under the jurisdiction of the Court 'jointly with another [...] person', it has to be established that two or more individuals worked together in the commission of the crime. This requires an agreement between these perpetrators, which led to the commission of one or more crimes under the jurisdiction of the Court. It is this very agreement—express or implied, previously arranged or materialising extemporaneously—that ties the co-perpetrators together and that justifies the reciprocal imputation of their respective acts. This agreement may take the form of a 'common plan'.

446. As to the question of whether the common plan must be 'designed to further a criminal purpose', the Appeals Chamber considers that it is not required that the common plan between individuals was specifically directed at the commission of a crime. The Appeals Chamber recalls that the Trial Chamber held that it was sufficient for the common plan to involve 'a critical element of criminality' and that the Trial Chamber sought to define such an element of criminality by reference to article 30 of the Statute. In the view of the Appeals Chamber, it was as such correct to consider article 30 of the Statute because that provision describes the relevant mental element and may therefore also serve as a yardstick for determining whether two or more individuals agreed to commit a crime. Article 30 of the Statute states:

1. Unless otherwise provided, a person shall be criminally responsible and liable for punishment for a crime within the jurisdiction of the Court only if the material elements are committed with intent and knowledge.

2. For the purposes of this article, a person has intent where:

   (a) In relation to conduct, that person means to engage in the conduct;

   (b) In relation to a consequence, that *person means to cause that consequence or is aware that it will occur in the ordinary course of events.*

3. For the purposes of this article, 'knowledge' means *awareness that a circumstance exists or a consequence will occur in the ordinary course of events.* 'Know' and 'knowingly' shall be construed accordingly. [Emphasis added in original.]

447. At issue here is the second alternative of both article 30 (2) (b) and (3) of the Statute. The Appeals Chamber notes that these provisions do not refer to the notion of 'risk', but employ the term of occurrence of a consequence 'in the ordinary course of events'. The Appeals Chamber considers that the words '[a consequence] will occur' refer to future events. The verb 'occur' is used with the modal verb 'will', and not with 'may' or 'could'. Therefore, this phrase conveys, as does the French version, certainty about the future occurrence. However, absolute certainty about a future occurrence can never exist; therefore the Appeals Chamber considers that the standard for the foreseeability of events is *virtual* certainty. That absolute certainty is not required is reinforced by the inclusion in article 30 (2) (b) and (3) of the Statute of the phrase 'in the ordinary course of events'.

449. The Appeals Chamber considers that the term 'risk' is usually used in the context of '*dolus eventualis*' or 'advertent recklessness', as known in some domestic jurisdictions, a concept that the Trial Chamber specifically excluded from application. The Appeals Chamber considers that it does not help in creating more clarity that the Trial Chamber, in the section on the mental element, explains that this 'involves consideration of the concepts of "possibility" and "probability", which are inherent to the notions of "risk" and "danger"'. The Appeals Chamber finds that the use of this phrase is confusing and reference to 'risk' should have been avoided when interpreting article 30 (2) of the Statute....

451. The Appeals Chamber recalls in this context that, according to the Trial Chamber, Mr Lubanga and the co-perpetrators agreed 'to build an effective army in order to ensure the UPC/FPLC's political and military control over Ituri'. The Trial Chamber found that, in the circumstances prevailing in Ituri at the time (of which the co-perpetrators were aware), the implementation of this plan led to the recruitment and use to participate actively in hostilities of individuals who were both above and under the age of fifteen years, the latter being a crime falling within the scope of the Statute. Thus, the implementation of the plan, which itself may have included non- criminal goals, in addition to criminal ones, resulted in the commission of crimes under article 8 (2) (e) (vii) of the Statute. Accordingly, the Trial Chamber's requirement of a 'critical element of criminality' of the common plan means, in the context of the present case and the specific allegations against Mr Lubanga, that it was virtually certain that the implementation of the common plan led to the commission of the crimes at issue....

456. Mr Lubanga argues in essence that the Trial Chamber erred in finding that a co-perpetrator does not need to personally and directly participate in the commission of the crime...Mr Lubanga specifically challenges the finding of the Trial Chamber that the accused can be absent from the scene of the crime, as long as he has the power to decide whether and how the offence will be carried out....

460. In the view of the Appeals Chamber, the issue at hand must be resolved by interpreting the phrase '[c]ommits such a crime [...] jointly with another [...] person', within the limits set by article 22 of the Statute. The Appeals Chamber notes that the text of article 25 (3) (a) of the Statute does not expressly stipulate that a crime is committed jointly with others only if the co-perpetrators directly and personally carry out the incriminated conduct in question...

462. What is, however, of relevance to the proper interpretation of the term '[c]ommits such a crime [...] jointly with another [...] person' is its interplay with other forms of criminal liability set out in article 25 (3) of the Statute. In that regard, the Appeals Chamber observes that, under this provision, an individual can be held criminally responsible for either *committing* a crime (sub-paragraph a)) or for *contributing* to the commission of a crime by another person or persons in one of the ways described in sub-paragraphs b) to d). This indicates that the Statute differentiates between two principal forms of liability, namely liability as a perpetrator and liability as an accessory. In the view of the Appeals Chamber, this distinction is not merely terminological; making this distinction is important because, generally speaking and all other things being equal, a person who is found to commit a crime him or herself bears more blameworthiness than a person who contributes to the crime of another person or persons. Accordingly, it contributes to a proper labelling of the accused person's criminal responsibility.

463. It follows that, in circumstances where a plurality of individuals are involved in the commission of a crime, it becomes necessary to determine on what basis an individual's role is assessed to amount to that of a perpetrator or that of an accessory. In the view of the Appeals Chamber, and as noted above, the starting point for this analysis must be the interaction between the various forms of individual criminal responsibility set out in article 25 (3) of the Statute and their distinctive characteristics.

464. In this regard, the Appeals Chamber notes that article 25 (3) (a) of the Statute provides expressly for three forms of commission liability: a perpetrator may commit a crime 'as an individual', 'jointly with another [...] person', or 'through another person'.

465. The Appeals Chamber finds that the third form of commission liability assists in the interpretation of the second form of liability, which is at issue in the case at hand. The third form of commission liability is based on the notion that a person can commit a crime 'through another person'. The underlying assumption is that the accused makes use of another person, who actually carries out the incriminated conduct, by virtue of the accused's control over that person, and the latter's conduct is therefore imputed on the former. Accordingly, commission of a crime 'through' another person is a form of criminal responsibility that requires a normative assessment of the relationship between the person actually carrying out the incriminated conduct and the person in the background, as well as of the latter person's relationship to the crime. In that regard, it is noteworthy that article 25 (3) (a) of the Statute provides for commission liability 'through another person' not only in circumstances where that person is not him- or herself criminally liable and therefore serves as a will-less tool in the hand of the individual in the background. Rather, a person can *commit* a crime also through individuals who are themselves fully criminally responsible for that crime. In such a scenario, the person in the background is considered to bear the same or even more blameworthiness than the person actually executing the incriminated conduct. This indicates more generally that the Statute assumes that a person who did not him- or herself carry out the incriminated conduct can, depending on the circumstances, nevertheless be a perpetrator....

473. In sum, the Appeals Chamber considers that, in circumstances where a plurality of persons was involved in the commission of crimes under the Statute, the question of whether an accused 'committed' a crime—and therefore not only contributed to the crime committed by someone else—cannot only be answered by reference to how close the accused was to the actual crime and whether he or she directly carried out the incriminated conduct. Rather, what is required is a normative assessment of the role of the accused person in the specific circumstances of the case. The Appeals Chamber considers that the most appropriate tool for conducting such an assessment is an evaluation of whether the accused had control over the crime, by virtue of his or her essential contribution to it and the resulting power to frustrate its commission, even if that essential contribution was not made at the execution stage of the crime. Accordingly, the Appeals Chamber is not convinced by Mr Lubanga's argument that the Trial Chamber erred in its interpretation of article 25 (3) (a) of the Statute and rejects this ground of appeal.

NOTES

1. Ordinary crimes committed under national law tend to be committed by individuals acting alone. This is not the case for the core crimes discussed in this chapter, where there are usually several 'participants' in a crime. Participants can be considered as those who have encouraged the crime (i.e. 'inciting') or those who have lent assistance to the commission of the crime (aiding and abetting). Moreover, a person who has not physically participated in the acts constituting the crime, but has agreed with others that such acts should be committed and has made an essential contribution to their commission, may also be found responsible as part of a joint criminal enterprise (see the extract from *Tadić*).

2. The Rome Statute did not adopt the approach of the ICTY and ICTR to joint criminal enterprise. Instead, Article 25(3)(a) recognises that a crime may be committed with others in two ways: first, where a crime is committed by co-perpetrators with joint control of the commission of the crime; and, second, where the crime is committed through control of another person (whether or not that person is criminally responsible or not) as indirect or direct perpetrator. The Appeals Chamber approved this 'control' approach in *Lubanga*, but emphasised that determining the form of liability (whether a principal or accessory) depends on an assessment of the role of the accused in the context of the case.

3. As seen in the extract from *Lubanga*, the Appeals Chamber has so far refused to import notions of risk or negligence from national systems as being relevant to criminal responsibility under the Rome Statute.

B: Command responsibility

Prosecutor v *Halilović*

Judgment, 16 November 2005, ICTY Trial Chamber

54. The Trial Chamber finds that under Article 7(3) [of the ICTY Statute] command responsibility is responsibility for an omission. The commander is responsible for the failure to perform an act required by international law.

This omission is culpable because international law imposes an affirmative duty on superiors to prevent and punish crimes committed by their subordinates. Thus 'for the acts of his subordinates' as generally referred to in the jurisprudence of the Tribunal does not mean that the commander shares the same responsibility as the subordinates who committed the crimes, but rather that because of the crimes committed by his subordinates, the commander should bear responsibility for his failure to act. The imposition of responsibility upon a commander for breach of his duty is to be weighed against the crimes of his subordinates; a commander is responsible not as though he had committed the crime himself, but his responsibility is considered in proportion to the gravity of the offences committed. The Trial Chamber considers that this is still in keeping with the logic of the weight which international humanitarian law places on protection values.

55. The principle of individual criminal responsibility of commanders for failure to prevent or to punish crimes committed by their subordinates is an established principle of customary international law. Article 7(3) of the Statute is applicable to all acts referred to in Articles 2 to 5 thereof and applies to both international and non-international armed conflicts.

56. To hold a superior responsible under Article 7(3) of the Statute, the jurisprudence of the Tribunal has established that three elements must be satisfied:
  i. The existence of a superior-subordinate relationship;
  ii. the superior knew or had reason to know that the criminal act was about to be or had been committed; and
  iii. the superior failed to take the necessary and reasonable measures to prevent the criminal act or punish the perpetrator thereof.

Rome Statute

Article 28—Responsibility of commanders and other superiors

In addition to other grounds of criminal responsibility under this Statute for crimes within the jurisdiction of the Court:

  (a) A military commander or person effectively acting as a military commander shall be criminally responsible for crimes within the jurisdiction of the Court committed by forces under his or her effective command and control, or effective authority and control as the case may be, as a result of his or her failure to exercise control properly over such forces, where:
    (i) That military commander or person either knew or, owing to the circumstances at the time, should have known that the forces were committing or about to commit such crimes; and
    (ii) That military commander or person failed to take all necessary and reasonable measures within his or her power to prevent or repress their commission or to submit the matter to the competent authorities for investigation and prosecution.
  (b) With respect to superior and subordinate relationships not described in paragraph (a), a superior shall be criminally responsible for crimes within the jurisdiction of the Court committed by subordinates under his or her effective authority and control, as a result of his or her failure to exercise control properly over such subordinates, where:
    (i) The superior either knew, or consciously disregarded information which clearly indicated, that the subordinates were committing or about to commit such crimes;
    (ii) The crimes concerned activities that were within the effective responsibility and control of the superior; and
    (iii) The superior failed to take all necessary and reasonable measures within his or her power to prevent or repress their commission or to submit the matter to the competent authorities for investigation and prosecution.

Prosecutor v *Bemba Gombo*
Judgment, 21 March 2016, ICC Trial Chamber

Jean-Pierre Bemba was the President and Commander-in-Chief of the *Mouvement de Libération du Congo* (MLC), which aligned with government forces in the Central African Republic to confront a rebel movement. Bemba was charged (and convicted) on the basis of command responsibility under Article 28(a) of the Rome Statute, as he knew that MLC troops were committing crimes and he did not take all necessary and reasonable measures within his power to prevent or repress their commission.

170. Article 28(a) codifies the responsibility of military commanders and persons effectively acting as military commanders. The Chamber finds that, for an accused to be found guilty and convicted as a military commander or person effectively acting as a military commander under Article 28(a), the following elements must be fulfilled:
   a. crimes within the jurisdiction of the Court must have been committed by forces;
   b. the accused must have been either a military commander or a person effectively acting as a military commander;
   c. the accused must have had effective command and control, or effective authority and control, over the forces that committed the crimes;
   d. the accused either knew or, owing to the circumstances at the time, should have known that the forces were committing or about to commit such crimes;
   e. the accused must have failed to take all necessary and reasonable measures within his power to prevent or repress the commission of such crimes or to submit the matter to the competent authorities for investigation and prosecution; and
   f. the crimes committed by the forces must have been a result of the failure of the accused to exercise control properly over them.

171. Before analysing each of these elements, the Chamber considers it appropriate to briefly address the nature of liability under Article 28. While there has been considerable debate regarding the precise nature of superior responsibility, the Chamber concurs with the Pre-Trial Chamber that Article 28 provides for a mode of liability, through which superiors may be held criminally responsible for crimes within the jurisdiction of the Court committed by his or her subordinates.

172. The Chamber considers that Article 28 is designed to reflect the responsibility of superiors by virtue of the powers of control they exercise over their subordinates. These responsibilities of control aim, inter alia, at ensuring the effective enforcement of fundamental principles of international humanitarian law, including the protection of protected persons and objects during armed conflict. The fundamental responsibilities which such superiors assume, and the potential for irreparable harm from a failure to properly fulfil those responsibilities, has long been recognised as subject to regulation by criminal law. Historically, this is most clearly seen in the context of military commanders, whose individual criminal responsibility has been recognised in domestic law, in jurisprudence since at least the aftermath of the Second World War, and was subsequently reflected in Article 86 of Additional Protocol I to the Geneva Conventions.

173. The plain text of Article 28—'[i]n addition to other grounds of criminal responsibility'—and its placement in Part 3 of the Statute indicate that Article 28 is intended to provide a distinct mode of liability from those found under Article 25. Further, the language of Article 28 expressly links the responsibility of the commander to the crimes committed by subordinates—'shall be criminally responsible for crimes within the jurisdiction of the Court committed by forces under his or her effective command and control [...]'. In this regard, it is, however, important to recognise that the responsibility of a commander under Article 28 is different from that of a person who 'commits' a crime within the jurisdiction of the Court. This is supported by the language of Article 28 itself: the crimes for which the commander is held responsible are 'committed' by forces, or subordinates, under his or her effective command and control, or effective authority and control, rather than by the commander directly.

174. Consequently, Article 28 must be viewed as a form of *sui generis* liability. The Chamber recognises that, in certain circumstances, a commander's conduct may be capable of satisfying a material element of one or more modes of liability....

176. The term 'military commander' refers to a person who is formally or legally appointed to carry out a military command function. Commonly, military commanders and their forces will be part of the regular armed forces of a state; such commanders will be appointed and operate according to a state's domestic laws, procedures, or practices (de jure commanders). In addition, the term 'military commander' in Article 28(a) also extends to individuals appointed as military commanders in non-governmental irregular forces, in accordance with their internal practices or regulations, whether written or unwritten.

177. Article 28(a) not only provides for the liability of military commanders, but also extends to 'person[s] effectively acting as military commander[s]'—the latter being, in the submission of the Prosecution, the appropriate characterisation of Mr Bemba's position in the case. These individuals are not formally or legally appointed as military commanders, but they will effectively act as commanders over the forces that committed the

crimes. In addition, the phrase 'military commander or person effectively acting as a military commander' includes individuals who do not perform exclusively military functions....

179. Article 28(a) not only covers the immediate commanders of the forces that committed the crimes, but is applicable to superiors at every level, irrespective of their rank, from commanders at the highest level to leaders with only a few men under their command....

180. Article 28(a) requires the accused to have 'effective command and control', or 'effective authority and control' over the forces who committed the crimes. As noted by the Pre-Trial Chamber, the term 'command' is defined as 'authority, especially over armed forces', and the expression 'authority' refers to the 'power or right to give orders and enforce obedience'.

181. The Chamber concurs with the Pre-Trial Chamber that the terms 'command' and 'authority' have 'no substantial effect on the required level or standard of "control"', but rather denote the modalities, manner, or nature in which a military commander or person acting as such exercises control over his or her forces. Regardless of whether an accused is a military commander or a person effectively acting as such, and regardless of whether he exercises 'effective command' or 'effective authority', the required level of control remains the same....

183. For the purpose of Article 28(a), following consistent international criminal jurisprudence, the Chamber finds that 'effective control' requires that the commander have the material ability to prevent or repress the commission of the crimes or to submit the matter to the competent authorities. Any lower degree of control, such as the ability to exercise influence—even substantial influence—over the forces who committed the crimes, would be insufficient to establish command responsibility.

184. The Chamber concurs with the Pre-Trial Chamber's view that 'effective control' is 'generally a manifestation of a superior-subordinate relationship between the [commander] and the forces or subordinates in a de jure or de facto hierarchical relationship (chain of command)'. By virtue of his position, the commander must be senior in some sort of formal or informal hierarchy to those who commit the crimes. Whether or not there are intermediary subordinates between the commander and the forces which committed the crimes is immaterial; the question is simply whether or not the commander had effective control over the relevant forces.

185. ...The Chamber finds, however, that Article 28 contains no requirement that a commander have sole or exclusive authority and control over the forces who committed the crimes. Further, the effective control of one commander does not necessarily exclude effective control being exercised by another commander. A fact-specific analysis is required in each case to determine whether or not the accused commander did in fact have effective control at the relevant time. Similarly, international criminal jurisprudence supports the possibility that multiple superiors can be held concurrently responsible for actions of their subordinates....

188. The Chamber considers that the question of whether a commander had effective control over particular forces is case specific. There are a number of factors that may indicate the existence of 'effective control', which requires the material ability to prevent or repress the commission of crimes or to submit the matter to the competent authorities; these have been properly considered as 'more a matter of evidence than of substantive law'. These factors may include: (i) the official position of the commander within the military structure and the actual tasks that he carried out; (ii) his power to issue orders, including his capacity to order forces or units under his command, whether under his immediate command or at lower levels, to engage in hostilities; (iii) his capacity to ensure compliance with orders including consideration of whether the orders were actually followed; (iv) his capacity to re-subordinate units or make changes to command structure; (v) his power to promote, replace, remove, or discipline any member of the forces, and to initiate investigations; (vi) his authority to send forces to locations where hostilities take place and withdraw them at any given moment; (vii) his independent access to, and control over, the means to wage war, such as communication equipment and weapons; (viii) his control over finances; (ix) the capacity to represent the forces in negotiations or interact with external bodies or individuals on behalf of the group; and (x) whether he represents the ideology of the movement to which the subordinates adhere and has a certain level of profile, manifested through public appearances and statements.

189. The Chamber also notes that a finding that a person was legally or formally appointed to a position of military command or authority over the relevant forces is neither required, nor sufficient in itself, to satisfy the effective control requirement of Article 28(a). However, it may serve as an indicium of effective control.

190. Conversely, some factors may indicate a lack of effective control over forces, such as (i) the existence of a different exclusive authority over the forces in question; (ii) disregard or non-compliance with orders or instructions of the accused; or (iii) a weak or malfunctioning chain of command.

NOTES

1. The notion of the responsibility for military commanders for the actions of their forces has had a long history, and has been applied by the ICTY and the ICTR. It is also found in Article 28 of the Rome Statute, although not all aspects of this provision reflect customary international law. The conviction in *Bemba Gombo* was the first to be based on command responsibility in the ICC.

2. Article 28 requires a causal link between the commission of the crimes and the failure of the commander. This link was not required in the jurisprudence of the ICTY and the ICTR. In *Bemba Gombo*, the ICC limited the scope and application of this requirement, finding that 'A nexus requirement would clearly be satisfied when it is established that the crimes would not have been committed, in the circumstances in which they were, had the commander exercised control properly, or the commander exercising control properly would have prevented the crimes' (para. 213).

3. The mental element required for command responsibility is not clearly established by the jurisprudence. The ICTY considered that the *mens rea* was present where a commander (1) had actual knowledge that subordinates were committing or about to commit a crime or (2) has sufficient information to put him on notice of the risk that such offences could occur and that further investigation was required (*Prosecutor v Delalić et al ('Čelebići' Case)*, Judgment, ICTY Appeal Chamber, 20 February 2001, paras 223 and 241). In *Bemba Gombo*, the ICC Trial Chamber confirmed that knowledge can be inferred, but only where that inference is the only reasonable inference. It held that: 'Relevant factors that may indicate knowledge include any orders to commit crimes, or the fact that the accused was informed personally that his forces were involved in criminal activity. Other indicia include the number, nature, scope, location, and timing of the illegal acts, and other prevailing circumstances; the type and number of forces involved; the means of available communication; the modus operandi of similar acts; the scope and nature of the commander's position and responsibility in the hierarchical structure; the location of the command at the time; and the notoriety of illegal acts, such as whether they were reported in media coverage of which the accused was aware (para. 193).

4. Command responsibility also extends to civilian supervisors who have effective control. Article 28 introduces a different mental element for civilian leaders to that required for military commanders.

C: Defences

Rome Statute

Article 31—Grounds for excluding criminal responsibility

1. In addition to other grounds for excluding criminal responsibility provided for in this Statute, a person shall not be criminally responsible if, at the time of that person's conduct:

   (a) The person suffers from a mental disease or defect that destroys that person's capacity to appreciate the unlawfulness or nature of his or her conduct, or capacity to control his or her conduct to conform to the requirements of law;

   (b) The person is in a state of intoxication that destroys that person's capacity to appreciate the unlawfulness or nature of his or her conduct, or capacity to control his or her conduct to conform to the requirements of law, unless the person has become voluntarily intoxicated under such circumstances that the person knew, or disregarded the risk, that, as a result of the intoxication, he or she was likely to engage in conduct constituting a crime within the jurisdiction of the Court;

   (c) The person acts reasonably to defend himself or herself or another person or, in the case of war crimes, property which is essential for the survival of the person or another person or property which is essential for accomplishing a military mission, against an imminent and unlawful use of force in a manner proportionate to the degree of danger to the person or the other person or property protected. The fact that the person was involved in a defensive operation conducted by forces shall not in itself constitute a ground for excluding criminal responsibility under this subparagraph;

   (d) The conduct which is alleged to constitute a crime within the jurisdiction of the Court has been caused by duress resulting from a threat of imminent death or of continuing or imminent serious bodily harm against that person or another person, and the person acts necessarily and reasonably to avoid this threat, provided that the person does not intend to cause a greater harm than the one sought to be avoided. Such a threat may either be:

   (i) Made by other persons; or

   (ii) Constituted by other circumstances beyond that person's control.

2. The Court shall determine the applicability of the grounds for excluding criminal responsibility provided for in this Statute to the case before it....

Article 33—Superior orders and prescription of law

1. The fact that a crime within the jurisdiction of the Court has been committed by a person pursuant to an order of a Government or of a superior, whether military or civilian, shall not relieve that person of criminal responsibility unless:

    (a) The person was under a legal obligation to obey orders of the Government or the superior in question;

    (b) The person did not know that the order was unlawful; and

    (c) The order was not manifestly unlawful.

2. For the purposes of this article, orders to commit genocide or crimes against humanity are manifestly unlawful.

Prosecutor v *Erdemović*

Appeal on Sentencing Judgment, 7 October 1997, ICTY Appeal Chamber

The defendant pleaded guilty to crimes against humanity committed at Srebrenica. He was sentenced to 10 years' imprisonment. He challenged his sentence, arguing that he should not serve the sentence, as he had committed the crimes under duress. The Separate Opinion was adopted by the majority of the Appeals Chamber.

JUDGE MCDONALD and JUDGE VOHRAH (Separate Opinion):

75....[W]e cannot but stress that we are not, in the International Tribunal, concerned with ordinary domestic crimes. The purview of the International Tribunal relates to war crimes and crimes against humanity committed in armed conflicts of extreme violence with egregious dimensions. We are not concerned with the actions of domestic terrorists, gang-leaders and kidnappers. We are concerned that, in relation to the most heinous crimes known to humankind, the principles of law to which we give credence have the appropriate normative effect upon soldiers bearing weapons of destruction and upon the commanders who control them in armed conflict situations. The facts of this particular case, for example, involved the cold-blooded slaughter of 1200 men and boys by soldiers using automatic weapons. We must bear in mind that we are operating in the realm of international humanitarian law which has, as one of its prime objectives, the protection of the weak and vulnerable in such a situation where their lives and security are endangered. Concerns about the harm which could arise from admitting duress as a defence to murder were sufficient to persuade a majority of the House of Lords and the Privy Council to categorically deny the defence in the national context to prevent the growth of domestic crime and the impunity of miscreants. Are they now insufficient to persuade us to similarly reject duress as a complete defence in our application of laws designed to take account of humanitarian concerns in the arena of brutal war, to punish perpetrators of crimes against humanity and war crimes, and to deter the commission of such crimes in the future? If national law denies recognition of duress as a defence in respect of the killing of innocent persons, international criminal law can do no less than match that policy since it deals with murders often of far greater magnitude. If national law denies duress as a defence even in a case in which a single innocent life is extinguished due to action under duress, international law, in our view, cannot admit duress in cases which involve the slaughter of innocent human beings on a large scale. It must be our concern to facilitate the development and effectiveness of international humanitarian law and to promote its aims and application by recognising the normative effect which criminal law should have upon those subject to them. Indeed, Security Council resolution 827 (1993) establishes the International Tribunal expressly as a measure to 'halt and effectively redress' the widespread and flagrant violations of international humanitarian law occurring in the territory of the former Yugoslavia and to contribute thereby to the restoration and maintenance of peace.

NOTES

1. Domestic criminal law allows defences to crimes, such as self-defence, necessity and insanity. Some of these defences are also available in relation to international crimes, although the availability of defences for such crimes is controversial, given the nature and extent of the acts committed. This

is seen in the extract from *Erdemović*, where the ICTY refused to consider duress to be a complete defence to the commission of crimes against humanity.

2. A particularly controversial defence is that of superior orders, that is a defendant should be absolved from responsibility as he was following the order of a superior. This defence has been excluded from the Statutes of the Nuremberg and Tokyo tribunals, as well as the ICTY and ICTR. It is included, albeit in a limited form, in Article 31 of the Rome Statute. Given the controversy surrounding the availability of this defence to international crimes, it is unlikely that Article 31 reflects customary international law.

D: Immunity

Rome Statute

Article 27—Irrelevance of official capacity

1. This Statute shall apply equally to all persons without any distinction based on official capacity. In particular, official capacity as a Head of State or Government, a member of a Government or parliament, an elected representative or a government official shall in no case exempt a person from criminal responsibility under this Statute, nor shall it, in and of itself, constitute a ground for reduction of sentence.

2. Immunities or special procedural rules which may attach to the official capacity of a person, whether under national or international law, shall not bar the Court from exercising its jurisdiction over such a person.

Article 98—Cooperation with respect to waiver of immunity and consent to surrender

1. The Court may not proceed with a request for surrender or assistance which would require the requested State to act inconsistently with its obligations under international law with respect to the State or diplomatic immunity of a person or property of a third State, unless the Court can first obtain the cooperation of that third State for the waiver of the immunity.

D. Akande, 'International Law Immunities and the International Criminal Court'

98 American Journal of International Law 407 (2004)

Since state and diplomatic immunities are derived from notions of state equality and are designed for horizontal interstate relationships, it may be thought that these immunities may not be pleaded before international tribunals. In the *Arrest Warrant case* [see extract in Chapter 9], the ICJ stated that 'the immunities enjoyed under international law...do not represent a bar to criminal prosecution in certain circumstances....[A]n incumbent or former Minister for Foreign Affairs may be subject to criminal proceedings before certain international criminal courts, where they have jurisdiction.'...However, the view that international law immunities may never be pleaded in proceedings instituted before international courts and tribunals oversimplifies the matter. Whether or not those wanted for prosecution by an international criminal tribunal may rely on international law immunities to exempt themselves from its jurisdiction depends, firstly, on the provisions of the statute establishing that tribunal. While these texts tend to include a general rule to the effect that the official position of a defendant may not be relied on as a bar to prosecution, it is important to pay attention to the manner in which immunity is provided. Secondly, and more important, the possibility of relying on international law immunities (particularly immunity *ratione personae*) to avoid prosecutions by international tribunals depends on the nature of the tribunal: how it was established and whether the state of the official sought to be tried is bound by the instrument establishing the tribunal. In this regard, there is a distinction between those tribunals established by United Nations Security Council resolution [the ICTY and ICTR] and those established by treaty. Because of the universal membership of the United Nations and because decisions of the Council are binding on all UN members, the provisions of the ICTY and ICTR Statutes are capable of removing immunity with respect to practically all states. But this is only because those states are bound by and have indirectly consented (via the UN Charter) to the decision to remove immunity. On the other hand, since only parties to a treaty are bound by its provisions, a treaty establishing an international tribunal cannot remove immunities that international law grants to officials of states that are not party to the treaty. Those immunities are rights belonging to the non-party states and those states may not be deprived of their rights by a treaty to which they are not party.

It is not an adequate response to assert that those immunities are conferred by international law only with respect to interstate relations and in proceedings before national courts. The immunities are conferred to prevent foreign states from unduly interfering in the affairs of other states and from exercising judicial jurisdiction over another state in circumstances where it has not consented. It makes little difference whether the foreign states seek to exercise this judicial jurisdiction unilaterally or through some collective body that the state concerned has not consented to. To suggest that immunity is nonexistent before an international tribunal that has not been consented to by the relevant state is to allow subversion of the policy under-pinning international law immunities…

In sum, the statement by the ICJ that international immunities may not be pleaded before certain international tribunals must be read subject to the condition (1) that the instruments creating those tribunals expressly or implicitly remove the relevant immunity, and (2) that the state of the official concerned is bound by the instrument removing the immunity. Therefore, a senior serving state official entitled to immunity *ratione personae* (for example, a head of state) is entitled to such immunity before an international tribunal that the state concerned has not consented to.…

[T]he determination whether state, diplomatic, or other immunities are available in relation to the ICC must begin by examining the text of the ICC Statute. Two provisions of the ICC Statute bear on questions of immunity: Articles 27 and 98. Article 27 primarily addresses the position of state officials in relation to the ICC itself.…This provision has now become standard in the founding instruments of international criminal tribunals. Similar provisions were inserted into the relevant agreements for the Nuremberg and Tokyo Tribunals after World War II, as well as the Statutes of the ICTY and the ICTR. Article 27(1) primarily addresses the substantive responsibility of state officials for international crimes rather than questions of immunity. Its main effect is to establish that the official capacity of a person does not relieve him of individual criminal responsibility and it eliminates a substantive defense that may be put forward by state officials. It may be argued that Article 27(1) and similar provisions do not deal with immunity at all since a statement that a person may be legally responsible does not address whether that person is subject to the jurisdiction of a particular forum, that is, whether that forum may determine that responsibility. Those jurisdictional issues are addressed, in part, by the law on international immunities, and the possession of immunity does not mean that the person concerned may not be legally responsible for the act in question. However, deeper analysis shows that Article 27(1) does have the effect of removing at least some of the immunities to which state officials would otherwise be entitled. First of all, questions of legal responsibility are not wholly separate from questions of immunity. As has already been argued, one of the reasons for conferring immunity with respect to official acts is that they are generally regarded as acts of states for which the state and not the official ought to be held responsible. To the extent that an international rule establishes that the official himself ought to be held responsible for the act, that reason for immunity disappears. Secondly, by providing that the ICC Statute applies to state officials, Article 27(1) establishes that those officials are subject to prosecution by the ICC even when they acted in their official capacity. Therefore, Article 27(1) is also jurisdictional in nature. Not only does the second sentence implicitly exclude immunities based on the official nature of the act; the first sentence also implicitly establishes that the official status of defendants does not exclude them from the jurisdiction of the ICC.

Perhaps as a result of doubts as to whether Article 27(1) completely removes the possibility of reliance on immunities in proceedings before the ICC, Article 27(2) contains an explicit denial of international and national law immunities. It provides: 'Immunities or special procedural rules which may attach to the official capacity of a person, whether under national or international law, shall not bar the Court from exercising its jurisdiction over such a person.' This provision is new. It has no counterpart in the Nuremberg or Tokyo Tribunal agreements or in the ICTY and ICTR Statutes. Article 27(2) conclusively establishes that state officials are subject to prosecution by the ICC and that provision constitutes a waiver by states parties of any immunity that their officials would otherwise possess vis-a-vis the ICC. However, the removal of immunity vis-a-vis the ICC by Article 27 is not the end of the matter. Because the Court does not have independent powers of arrest and must rely on states to arrest and surrender wanted persons, the immunities of state officials in national jurisdictions become important. To the extent that the Court is seeking arrest and surrender from the state of the official concerned, Article 27 constitutes a waiver of national law immunities by parties to the Statute. States parties are therefore obliged to arrest and surrender their own officials even if those officials would otherwise be entitled to immunity under national law. However, where an official is outside his or her state and is entitled under international law to immunity from arrest and criminal process in the other state, the matter is more complicated. Thus, while Article 27 provides that a state official's possession of international immunity shall not bar the ICC from exercising jurisdiction, Article 98 directs the Court not to take action that would result in the violation by states of their international obligations to accord immunity to foreign officials.

Prosecutor v Omar Hassan Ahmad Al Bashir

Decision on the Cooperation of the Democratic Republic of the Congo Regarding Omar Al Bashir's Arrest and Surrender to the Court, 9 April 2014, ICC Pre-Trial Chamber II

This decision followed a request by the ICC for the arrest and surrender of President Al-Bashir to the Democratic Republic of Congo (a State party to the Rome Statute). Al-Bashir was subject to an arrest warrant issued by the Court. Sudan was not a State party to the Rome Statute, the situation concerning Darfur having been referred to the Court by the Security Council.

25. At the outset, the Chamber wishes to make clear that it is not disputed that under international law a sitting Head of State enjoys personal immunities from criminal jurisdiction and inviolability before national courts of foreign States even when suspected of having committed one or more of the crimes that fall within the jurisdiction of the Court. Such personal immunities are ensured under international law for the purpose of the effective performance of the functions of sitting Heads of States. This view has also been supported by the International Court of Justice (the 'ICJ'). An exception to the personal immunities of Heads of States is explicitly provided in article 27(2) of the Statute for prosecution before an international criminal jurisdiction. According to this provision, the existence of personal immunities under international law which generally attach to the official capacity of the person 'shall not bar the Court from exercising its jurisdiction over such a person'.

26. Still, the question *sub judice* is how far reaching this provision is meant to be, and whether such an exception for lifting personal immunities applies to Heads of all States, including non-States Parties to the Statute (third States), or whether it is only confined to those States which have adhered to the Statute. Given that the Statute is a multilateral treaty governed by the rules set out in the Vienna Convention on the Law of Treaties, the Statute cannot impose obligations on third States without their consent. Thus, the exception to the exercise of the Court's jurisdiction provided in article 27(2) of the Statute should, in principle, be confined to those States Parties who have accepted it.

27. It follows that when the exercise of jurisdiction by the Court entails the prosecution of a Head of State of a non-State Party, the question of personal immunities might validly arise. The solution provided for in the Statute to resolve such a conflict is found in article 98(1) of the Statute. This provision directs the Court to secure the cooperation of the third State for the waiver or lifting the immunity of its Head of State. This course of action envisaged by article 98(1) of the Statute aims at preventing the requested State from acting inconsistently with its international obligations towards the non-State Party with respect to the immunities attached to the latter's Head of State.

28. In the case *sub judice* the DRC claims that by issuing the 26 February 2014 Decision the Court placed the DRC in a situation where it was called upon to act inconsistently with its international obligations arising from the decision of the African Union 'to respect the immunities that come with [Omar Al Bashir's] position of Head of State'.

29. This position stands to be corrected. The Chamber does not consider that such inconsistency arises in the present case. This is so because by issuing Resolution 1593(2005) the SC *decided* that the 'Government of Sudan [...] *shall* cooperate fully with and provide any necessary assistance to the Court and the Prosecutor pursuant to this resolution'. Since immunities attached to Omar Al Bashir are a procedural bar from prosecution before the Court, the cooperation envisaged in said resolution was meant to eliminate any impediment to the proceedings before the Court, including the lifting of immunities. Any other interpretation would render the SC decision requiring that Sudan 'cooperate fully' and 'provide any necessary assistance to the Court' senseless. Accordingly, the '*cooperation* of that third State [Sudan] for the waiver of the immunity', as required under the last sentence of article 98(1) of the Statute, was already ensured by the language used in paragraph 2 of SC Resolution 1593(2005). By virtue of said paragraph, the SC implicitly waived the immunities granted to Omar Al Bashir under international law and attached to his position as a Head of State. Consequently, there also exists no impediment at the horizontal level between the DRC and Sudan as regards the execution of the 2009 and 2010 Requests.

30. As stated in paragraph 19 above, the DRC maintains to be bound by the obligation that 'no serving AU Head of State or Government [...] shall be required to appear before any international court or tribunal during their term of office'. However, it follows from the above that the conflicting obligations which the DRC claims exist are not merely between the African Union and the Court. Rather, the conflict actually lies between the decision of the African Union to retain the immunity of Omar Al Bashir and the SC Resolution 1593(2005) which removed such immunity for the purpose of the proceedings before the Court. In this case, the conflict is resolved by virtue

of articles 25 and 103 of the UN Charter. According to article 25 of the UN Charter '[t]he Members of the United Nations agree to accept and carry out the decisions of the Security Council in accordance with the [...] Charter'. In its advisory opinion on *Namibia* the ICJ stated, 'when the Security Council adopts a decision under article 25 in accordance with the Charter, it is for member States to comply with that decision [...]. To hold otherwise would be to deprive this principal organ of its essential functions and powers under the Charter'.

31. Further, according to article 103 of the UN Charter '[i]n the event of a conflict between the obligations of the Members of the United Nations under the present Charter and their obligations under any other international agreement, their obligations under the [...] Charter shall prevail'...

NOTES

1. As was discussed in Chapter 9, certain State officials have immunity from prosecution before national courts. The extract from Akande outlines the extent to which international immunities apply before international criminal tribunals. Certainly, several former leaders and senior officials have faced trial in international courts, for example President Milosevic of Serbia before the ICTY, President Charles Taylor before the Special Court for Sierra Leone and President Laurent Gbagbo of Cote d'Ivoire before the ICC. This issue is not, however, straightforward, and requires an examination of the relevant legal texts and the legal basis for the tribunal in question.

2. The ICC Prosecutor initiated proceedings against Kenyatta, who subsequently became the Kenyan Head of State in 2013, while charges were pending. As Kenya is a State party to the Rome Statute, immunity was considered not to apply by virtue of Article 27 of the Rome Statute and President Kenyatta appeared voluntarily before the ICC.

3. The issue of the arrest warrants for President Al Bashir of Sudan sparked a debate as to whether the Rome Statute can—and on what grounds—legitimately extinguish immunity in respect of a Head of State of a State that is not a party to the Statute. Different justifications have been given for the non-applicability of immunity regarding Bashir. In the DRC decision extracted above, the basis for the removal of immunity was Resolution 1593 and the overriding authority of the UN Security Council. This justification was also relied upon in a subsequent Pre-Trial Chamber decision concerning South Africa's failure to arrest Bashir: Decision following the Prosecutor's request for an order further clarifying that the Republic of South Africa is under the obligation to immediately arrest and surrender Omar Al Bashir, 13 June 2015 (for discussion of the relevant national litigation concerning Bashir's visit to South Africa, see Chapter 9). In contrast, an earlier, differently constituted Pre-Trial Chamber relied on an exception to immunity before international criminal tribunals: see Decision Pursuant to Article 87(7) of the Rome Statute on the Failure by the Republic of Malawi to Comply with the Cooperation Requests issued by the Court with Respect to the Arrest and Surrender of Omar Hassan Ahmad Al Bashir, 12 December 2011, Pre-Trial Chamber I. The position remains uncertain.

4. The African Union (AU) has reacted to the arrest warrants against Al Bashir and proceedings against Kenyatta by taking a firm decision on immunity in a number of AU resolutions. For example, in October 2013, during an extraordinary session it took the decision that: 'No charges shall be commenced or continued before any international court or tribunal against any serving head of state or Government or anybody acting in such capacity during his/her term of office.' (Ext/Assembly/AU/Dec.1, 12 October 2013). The AU's decisions potentially create a legal conflict for African States that are parties to both the ICC and AU (as seen in the decision on the DRC cooperation request, above). The African Union also resolved to confer jurisdiction in respect of international crimes on the African Court of Justice and Human Rights, which many considered an attempt to block the exercise of jurisdiction by the ICC in an act of 'negative regional complementarity' (see Max du Plessis, *EJIL Talk*, 27 August 2012). In response to AU concerns, the Assembly of State Parties amended the Rules of Procedure and Evidence so that serving Heads of State need not appear before the ICC at certain points during trial, recognising that they have duties in their home State that should not be subject to undue interference. However, these cases have demonstrated the challenges of prosecuting individuals who are effectively the State itself. In late 2014 the Prosecutor indicated that charges in respect of President Kenyatta would be withdrawn due to a lack of State cooperation from Kenya rendering it impossible for the Prosecution to obtain the necessary evidence, while proceedings regarding President Al Bashir were suspended given the failure to secure his arrest. However, despite such steps, in January 2016, the AU voted for its member States to withdraw from the Rome Statute, although, as the vote is not binding, it will be for each member State to make this decision.

SECTION 5: INTERNATIONAL CRIMINAL INSTITUTIONS

A: Nuremberg and Tokyo Tribunals

Charter of the International Military Tribunal

Annex to the Agreement for the prosecution and punishment of the major war criminals of the European Axis ('London Agreement'), 8 August 1945

Article 1

In pursuance of the Agreement signed on the 8th day of August 1945 by the Government of the United States of America, the Provisional Government of the French Republic, the Government of the United Kingdom of Great Britain and Northern Ireland and the Government of the Union of Soviet Socialist Republics, there shall be established an International Military Tribunal (hereinafter called 'the Tribunal') for the just and prompt trial and punishment of the major war criminals of the European Axis.

Article 6

The Tribunal established by the Agreement referred to in Article 1 hereof for the trial and punishment of the major war criminals of the European Axis countries shall have the power to try and punish persons who, acting in the interests of the European Axis countries, whether as individuals or as members of organizations, committed any of the following crimes.

The following acts, or any of them, are crimes coming within the jurisdiction of the Tribunal for which there shall be individual responsibility:

  (a) Crimes Against Peace: namely, planning, preparation, initiation or waging of a war of aggression, or a war in violation of international treaties, agreements or assurances, or participation in a common plan or conspiracy for the accomplishment of any of the foregoing;

  (b) War Crimes: namely, violations of the laws or customs of war. Such violations shall include, but not be limited to, murder, ill-treatment or deportation to slave labor or for any other purpose of civilian population of or in occupied territory, murder or ill-treatment of prisoners of war or persons on the seas, killing of hostages, plunder of public or private property, wanton destruction of cities, towns or villages, or devastation not justified by military necessity;

  (c) Crimes Against Humanity: namely, murder, extermination, enslavement, deportation, and other inhumane acts committed against any civilian population, before or during the war; or persecutions on political, racial or religious grounds in execution of or in connection with any crime within the jurisdiction of the Tribunal, whether or not in violation of the domestic law of the country where perpetrated. Leaders, organizers, instigators and accomplices participating in the formulation or execution of a common plan or conspiracy to commit any of the foregoing crimes are responsible for all acts performed by any persons in execution of such plan.

The Question of International Criminal Jurisdiction

Yearbook of the International Law Commission Vol II (1950)

128. The General Assembly, by resolution 260 B (III), invited the International Law Commission 'to study the desirability and possibility of establishing an international judicial organ for the trial of persons, charged with genocide or other crimes over which jurisdiction will be conferred upon that organ by international conventions', and requested it, in carrying out that task 'to pay attention to the possibility of establishing a Criminal Chamber of the International Court of Justice'. ...

135. ...With regard to the question of desirability, Mr Alfaro [the special rapporteur appointed by the ILC] stated that if 'desirable' meant useful and necessary, the creation of an international criminal jurisdiction vested with power to try and punish persons who disturbed international public order was desirable as an effective contribution to the peace and security of the world. In the community of States, as in national communities, there were aggressors and disturbers of the peace, and mankind had a right to protect itself against international crimes by means of an adequate system of criminal repression. The rule of law in the community of States could only be ensured by the establishment of such a system. ...

136. As to the possibility of establishing the judicial organ envisaged, Mr Alfaro stated that he could not see any legal reason which made it impossible for States to set up by convention a judicial organ for the trial of persons responsible for crimes under international law....

137. Some members of the Commission referred to the many difficulties which the establishment and functioning of an international criminal jurisdiction would encounter, as for instance, that nations would refuse to give up their territorial jurisdiction or to submit to the compulsory jurisdiction of the international organ; that a tribunal would be unable to bring the accused before it and to enforce its judgments; and that the Tribunals of Nuremberg and Tokyo could function effectively only because the States which established these Tribunals were occupying the territory in which the trials took place and had the accused in their power; that punishment of aggressors would depend on their being on the losing side, and that no illusory ideas should be encouraged as to the possibility of setting up the organ in question.

138. Other members of the Commission held the view that while difficulties undeniably existed, they did not constitute an impossibility. If States were free to refuse to submit to an obligatory international criminal tribunal, they also had the power to agree thereto.

NOTES
1. The idea of an international tribunal to try breaches of international law emerged in the mid-nineteenth century, as the field of international humanitarian law developed. The Treaty of Versailles, which marked the end of World War I, provided for the trial of the German Emperor by an international tribunal, but the Emperor was granted asylum in the Netherlands. The Treaty also recognised the right of the Allies to establish military tribunals to try German soldiers. However, this notion was abandoned.
2. Following the end of World War II, the allies announced their intention to try the Nazis for war crimes. The Agreement for the Prosecution and Punishment of Major War Criminals of the European Axis was adopted by the four major powers, and with it the Charter of the International Military Tribunal (IMT)—see extract. The IMT comprised four judges, one from each of the major Allied powers, and four alternate judges. Twenty-four defendants and six criminal organisations faced trial. Nineteen defendants were convicted and three organisations were found criminally responsible. The judgment of the IMT was a remarkable contribution to the development of international law, and its principles were affirmed by the General Assembly in 1946 (resolution 177(II)).
3. In the Pacific, the Allies established the International Military Tribunal for the Far East (the Tokyo Tribunal), to try Japanese war criminals. The Tokyo Tribunal comprised eleven international judges. Twenty-nine accused faced trial, and all those remaining at the end of the trial were convicted. Both tribunals have been criticised as representing 'victor's justice'.
4. Article VI of the Convention on the Prevention and Punishment of the Crime of Genocide (see Section 3A(a)) contemplates a trial before an international penal tribunal that may be established, in addition to trials before the courts of the territorial State. The General Assembly invited the International Law Commission to devise a Statute for the proposed tribunal as well preparing a draft code of offences against the peace and security of mankind (resolution 177 II, 1946). However, the work of the ILC on both topics was stalled during the Cold War period, ostensibly due to disagreement concerning the definition of the crime of aggression (see Section 3D). Work on the draft statute of an international criminal court recommenced in 1989 and was finished in 1994, with the draft code finalised in 1996.

B: International ad hoc criminal tribunals

(a) International Criminal Tribunal for the former Yugoslavia

Resolution 827 (1993)
25 May 1993, UN Security Council

Expressing once again its grave alarm at continuing reports of widespread and flagrant violations of international humanitarian law occurring within the territory of the former Yugoslavia, and especially in the Republic of Bosnia and Herzegovina, including reports of mass killings, massive, organized and systematic detention and rape of women, and the continuance of the practice of 'ethnic cleansing', including for the acquisition and the holding of territory',

Determining that this situation continues to constitute a threat to international peace and security,

Determined to put an end to such crimes and to take effective measures to bring to justice the persons who are responsible for them,

Convinced that in the particular circumstances of the former Yugoslavia the establishment as an ad hoc measure by the Council of an international tribunal and the prosecution of persons responsible for serious violations of international humanitarian law would enable this aim to be achieved and would contribute to the restoration and maintenance of peace,

Believing that the establishment of an international tribunal and the prosecution of persons responsible for the above-mentioned violations of international humanitarian law will contribute to ensuring that such violations are halted and effectively redressed…

Acting under Chapter VII of the Charter of the United Nations,…

2. *Decides* hereby to establish an international tribunal for the sole purpose of prosecuting persons responsible for serious violations of international humanitarian law committed in the territory of the former Yugoslavia between 1 January 1991 and a date to be determined by the Security Council upon the restoration of peace and to this end to adopt the Statute of the International Tribunal annexed to the above-mentioned report;…

4. *Decides* that all States shall cooperate fully with the International Tribunal and its organs in accordance with the present resolution and the Statute of the International Tribunal and consequently all States shall take any measure necessary under their domestic law to implement the provisions of the present resolution and the Statute, including the obligation of States to comply with requests for assistance or orders issued by a Trial Chamber under Article 29 of the Statute.

Statute of the International Criminal Tribunal for the former Yugoslavia

32 International Legal Materials 1192 (1993)

Article 1 Competence of the International Tribunal

The International Tribunal shall have the power to prosecute persons responsible for serious violations of international humanitarian law committed in the territory of the former Yugoslavia since 1991 in accordance with the provisions of the present Statute.

Article 9 Concurrent jurisdiction

1. The International Tribunal and national courts shall have concurrent jurisdiction to prosecute persons for serious violations of international humanitarian law committed in the territory of the former Yugoslavia since 1 January 1991.

2. The International Tribunal shall have primacy over national courts. At any stage of the procedure, the International Tribunal may formally request national courts to defer to the competence of the International Tribunal in accordance with the present Statute and the Rules of Procedure and Evidence of the International Tribunal.

Article 29 Co-operation and judicial assistance

1. States shall co-operate with the International Tribunal in the investigation and prosecution of persons accused of committing serious violations of international humanitarian law.

2. States shall comply without undue delay with any request for assistance or an order issued by a Trial Chamber, including, but not limited to:
    (a) the identification and location of persons;
    (b) the taking of testimony and the production of evidence;
    (c) the service of documents;
    (d) the arrest or detention of persons;
    (e) the surrender or the transfer of the accused to the International Tribunal.

Prosecutor v *Tadić*

Decision on the Defence Motion for Interlocutory Appeal on Jurisdiction, 35 *International Legal Materials* 32 (1996), ICTY Appeal Chamber

26. Many arguments have been put forward…in support of the contention that the establishment of the International Tribunal is invalid under the Charter of the United Nations or that it was not duly established by law.…

27. These arguments raise a series of constitutional issues which all turn on the limits of the power of the Security Council under Chapter VII of the Charter of the United Nations and determining what action or measures can be taken under this Chapter, particularly the establishment of an international criminal tribunal. Put in the interrogative, they can be formulated as follows:

1. Was there really a threat to the peace justifying the invocation of Chapter VII as a legal basis for the establishment of the International Tribunal?
2. Assuming such a threat existed, was the Security Council authorized, with a view to restoring or maintaining peace, to take any measures at its own discretion, or was it bound to choose among those expressly provided for in Articles 41 and 42 (and possibly Article 40 as well)?
3. In the latter case, how can the establishment of an international criminal tribunal be justified, as it does not figure among the ones mentioned in those Articles, and is of a different nature?…

33. The establishment of an international criminal tribunal is not expressly mentioned among the enforcement measures provided for in Chapter VII, and more particularly in Articles 41 and 42. Obviously, the establishment of the International Tribunal is not a measure under Article 42, as these are measures of a military nature, implying the use of armed force. Nor can it be considered a 'provisional measure' under Article 40.…

34. *Prima facie*, the International Tribunal matches perfectly the description in Article 41 of 'measures not involving the use of force'. Appellant, however, has argued before both the Trial Chamber and this Appeals Chamber, that:

> …[I]t is clear that the establishment of a war crimes tribunal was not intended. The examples mentioned in this article focus upon economic and political measures and do not in any way suggest judicial measures.' (Brief to Support the Motion [of the Defence] on the Jurisdiction of the Tribunal before the Trial Chamber of the International Tribunal, 23 June 1995 (Case No. IT-94-1-T), at para. 3.2.1).

35. The first argument does not stand by its own language.…It is evident that the measures set out in Article 41 are merely illustrative examples which obviously do not exclude other measures. All the Article requires is that they do not involve 'the use of force.' It is a negative definition. That the examples do not suggest judicial measures goes some way towards the other argument that the Article does not contemplate institutional measures implemented directly by the United Nations through one of its organs but, as the given examples suggest, only action by Member States, such as economic sanctions (though possibly coordinated through an organ of the Organization). However, as mentioned above, nothing in the Article suggests the limitation of the measures to those implemented by States. The Article only prescribes what these measures cannot be. Beyond that it does not say or suggest what they have to be.

Moreover, even a simple literal analysis of the Article shows that the first phrase of the first sentence carries a very general prescription which can accommodate both institutional and Member State action. The second phrase can be read as referring particularly to one species of this very large category of measures referred to in the first phrase, but not necessarily the only one, namely, measures undertaken directly by States. It is also clear that the second sentence, starting with 'These [measures]' not 'Those [measures]', refers to the species mentioned in the second phrase rather than to the 'genus' referred to in the first phrase of this sentence.

36. Logically, if the Organization can undertake measures which have to be implemented through the intermediary of its Members, it can *a fortiori* undertake measures which it can implement directly via its organs, if it happens to have the resources to do so. It is only for want of such resources that the United Nations has to act through its Members. But it is of the essence of 'collective measures' that they are collectively undertaken. Action by Member States on behalf of the Organization is but a poor substitute *faute de mieux*, or a 'second best' for want of the first. This is also the pattern of Article 42 on measures involving the use of armed force.

In sum, the establishment of the International Tribunal falls squarely within the powers of the Security Council under Article 41.…

37. The argument that the Security Council, not being endowed with judicial powers, cannot establish a subsidiary organ possessed of such powers is untenable: it results from a fundamental misunderstanding of the constitutional set-up of the Charter.

Plainly, the Security Council is not a judicial organ and is not provided with judicial powers (though it may incidentally perform certain quasi-judicial activities such as effecting determinations or findings). The principal function of the Security Council is the maintenance of international peace and security, in the discharge of which the Security Council exercises both decision-making and executive powers.

38. The establishment of the International Tribunal by the Security Council does not signify, however, that the Security Council has delegated to it some of its own functions or the exercise of some of its own powers. Nor does it mean, in reverse, that the Security Council was usurping for itself part of a judicial function which does not belong to it but to other organs of the United Nations according to the Charter. The Security Council has resorted to the establishment of a judicial organ in the form of an international criminal tribunal as an instrument for the exercise of its own principal function of maintenance of peace and security, i.e., as a measure contributing to the restoration and maintenance of peace in the former Yugoslavia.

R. Zacklin, 'The Failings of Ad Hoc International Tribunals'

2 *Journal of International Criminal Justice* 541 (2004)

From the vantage point of late 2003, it is easy to forget the doubts and skepticism that greeted the establishment of the International Criminal Tribunal for the Former Yugoslavia (ICTY). Within one decade, the notion that crimes such as genocide, war crimes, crimes against humanity and grave breaches of the Geneva Conventions can forever remain beyond the reach of international law has been severely challenged. A new culture of human rights and human responsibility, in which there can be no impunity for such crimes, has gradually taken root and the link between an established system of individual accountability and the maintenance of international peace and security has been confirmed....Looking back, the question is, why did it take so long to reach this, as yet, imperfect point? Why did Nuremberg and Tokyo enter the realm of history rather than lend themselves immediately to the progressive development and codification of international criminal law? For generations after World War II, the promotion of an international criminal court remained the province of a handful of academics and human rights activists...The legal and political problems were deemed to be insurmountable. States would not surrender their sovereignty to an international court and, in any event, there was no international criminal code on the basis of which such a court should function.

The relative success in the advancement of the ideal of international justice...should not, however, lure us into a false sense of achievement. The reality is that the ICTY and the...ICTR were established more as acts of political contrition, because of egregious failures to swiftly confront the situations in the former Yugoslavia and Rwanda, than as part of a deliberate policy, promoting international justice...The establishment of the ICTY was an important event because it showed that an international criminal tribunal could, in fact, work. The Statute of the ICTY, which the Security Council adopted unanimously, showed that it was possible to resolve many of the issues that had obstructed the discussion of international justice since Nuremberg, particularly as regards subject-matter jurisdiction. The status of the ICTY as a subsidiary organ of the Security Council, acting under Chapter VII, gave it legitimacy and credibility, while the financing of the Tribunal through assessed contributions provided it with the necessary administrative and financial stability.

The contribution of the ICTY to the development of international criminal law has been significant....There are a number of lessons to be learned from the ICTY experience, which are central to the manner in which the United Nations must meet the challenge of international justice in the future....The ad hoc Tribunals have been too costly, too inefficient and too ineffective. As mechanisms for dealing with justice in post-conflict societies, they exemplify an approach that is no longer politically or financially viable...The bare truth is that it is impossible today to envisage the establishment of an ICTY-type tribunal in new situations, however egregious the violations of international criminal law may be.

NOTES

1. The International Criminal Tribunal for the former Yugoslavia (ICTY) was established in response to the armed conflicts that emerged following the breakdown of the former Yugoslavia in 1991 (see Chapter 5). Substantial evidence emerged that serious violations of international humanitarian and human rights law were occurring, particularly in Bosnia and Herzegovina. While the conflict was ongoing, the Security Council responded to the allegations, first by establishing a commission to investigate allegations of violations, and second by establishing the ICTY pursuant to Resolution 827, adopted under Chapter VII of the UN Charter (see Chapter 15).

2. Several States and academics questioned the legality of the Council's actions, in particular whether the Council was competent to establish a criminal tribunal. The Tribunal itself considered this question in the *Tadić* case, extracted above. The Trial Chamber determined that it did not have the power to consider the legality of its own establishment. In contrast, the Appeals Chamber held that it could review the legality of its own establishment, as part of its inherent power to confirm that it had jurisdiction in a particular case (para. 20). It considered a number of objections to the tribunal's establishment, but ultimately concluded that the ICTY had been lawfully established as a measure for the maintenance or restoration of international peace and security under Article 41 of the UN Charter (see Chapter 15).

3. The ICTY has substantive jurisdiction in respect of grave breaches of the Geneva Conventions (Article 2), other violations of the laws or customs of war (Article 3), genocide (Article 4) and crimes against humanity (Article 5). It has open-ended jurisdiction (i.e. for crimes occurring after 1 January 1991), and it has exercised jurisdiction in respect of later armed conflicts in Kosovo and the Former Yugoslav Republic of Macedonia.

4. The ICTY enjoys a relationship of primacy in relation to national courts and may require a State to defer any national proceedings to it. This can be contrasted with the ICC, which is based on the principle of complementarity (see Section 5C).

5. Having been established by the Council acting under Chapter VII of the Charter, all member States of the United Nations are required to comply with orders and requests issued by the ICTY, as provided for in Resolution 827 and in Article 29 of the ICTY Statute. This obligation to cooperate was reiterated in relation to the parties to the conflict by the Dayton Peace Agreement 1995, which ended the conflict in the Balkans and included an obligation on parties to the agreement to cooperate with the ICTY (see 35 ILM 75 (1996)).

6. The ICTY sits in The Hague in The Netherlands and it had a very slow start. As the Federal Republic of Yugoslavia (FRY) remained largely uncooperative in arresting and transferring suspects to the ICTY, the ICTY initially concentrated its efforts on trying those individuals for which it could secure custody. These were often relatively low-level offenders, such as Tadić. It also faced a number of legal challenges, which took time to resolve. Eventually, however, the pace of its activities accelerated. In 1999, the ICTY indicted the then President of the FRY, Slobodan Milosevic. As a result of increased financial and political pressure, the FRY gradually began to increase cooperation, including the surrender of Milosevic to the ICTY in 2001 (Milosevic ultimately died during trial).

7. Concerned as to estimates as to the length of time the ICTY would take to complete its proceedings, the Council introduced the Completion Strategy under resolutions 1503 (2003) and 1534 (2004). Steps taken to achieve the Completion Strategy include the use of temporary *ad litem* judges, the expansion of the Appeals Chamber, increased referral of intermediate and less serious cases to national jurisdictions, including the War Crimes Chamber in Bosnia and Herzegovina (see Rule 11*bis* of the ICTY Rules of Procedure and Evidence), and a requirement that the Prosecutor concentrate indictments only on the most senior leaders (Resolution 1534). A key step of the Completion Strategy has been the establishment of an ad hoc judicial body known as The International Residual Mechanism for International Criminal Tribunals to carry out, in an efficient manner, a number of essential functions of the ICTY and ICTR (see subsection (b)) following the completion of their respective mandates. Other factors, such as greater cooperation from the affected States, in particular Serbia, more defendants voluntarily surrendering to the ICTY, and an increase in the number of defendants pleading guilty, have also contributed to this objective. However, the ICTY has not met the original deadlines set and is subject to ongoing review.

(b) International Criminal Tribunal for Rwanda

Resolution 955 (1994)
8 November 1994, UN Security Council

Expressing once again its grave concern at the reports indicating that genocide and other systematic, widespread and flagrant violations of international humanitarian law have been committed in Rwanda, *Determining* that this situation continues to constitute a threat to international peace and security, *Determined* to put an end to such crimes and to take effective measures to bring to justice the persons who are responsible for them,

Convinced that in the particular circumstances of Rwanda, the prosecution of persons responsible for serious violations of international humanitarian law would enable this aim to be achieved and would contribute to the process of national reconciliation and to the restoration and maintenance of peace,

Believing that the establishment of an international tribunal for the prosecution of persons responsible for genocide and the other above-mentioned violations of international humanitarian law will contribute to ensuring that such violations are halted and effectively redressed,

Stressing also the need for international cooperation to strengthen the courts and judicial system of Rwanda, having regard in particular to the necessity for those courts to deal with large numbers of suspects,…

Acting under Chapter VII of the Charter of the United Nations,

1. *Decides* hereby, having received the request of the Government of Rwanda (S/1994/1115), to establish an international tribunal for the sole purpose of prosecuting persons responsible for genocide and other serious violations of international humanitarian law committed in the territory of Rwanda and Rwandan citizens responsible for genocide and other such violations committed in the territory of neighbouring States, between 1 January 1994 and 31 December 1994 and to this end to adopt the Statute of the International Criminal Tribunal for Rwanda annexed hereto;

2. *Decides* that all States shall cooperate fully with the International Tribunal and its organs in accordance with the present resolution and the Statute of the International Tribunal and that consequently all States shall take any measures necessary under their domestic law to implement the provisions of the present resolution and the Statute, including the obligation of States to comply with requests for assistance or orders issued by a Trial Chamber under Article 28 of the Statute, and *requests* States to keep the Secretary-General informed of such measures.

Statute of the International Criminal Tribunal for Rwanda

33 *International Legal Materials* 1602 (1994)

Article 1: Competence of the International Tribunal for Rwanda

The International Tribunal for Rwanda shall have the power to prosecute persons responsible for serious violations of international humanitarian law committed in the territory of Rwanda and Rwandan citizens responsible for such violations committed in the territory of neighbouring States between 1 January 1994 and 31 December 1994, in accordance with the provisions of the present Statute.

NOTES

1. The International Criminal Tribunal for Rwanda (ICTR) was established in response to the genocide in Rwanda in 1994. Its establishment also followed the creation of a commission of inquiry. The affected State, Rwanda (at the time a member of the Security Council), initially supported the establishment of the ICTR, but later withdrew its support as the Council had not included the death penalty as a sentencing option, had precluded jurisdiction prior to 1994 and had refused to limit the ICTR's jurisdiction to genocide. Rwanda ultimately voted against the creation of the ICTR.
2. Like the ICTY, the ICTR was established by a resolution of the Council acting under Chapter VII of the UN Charter. It also faced challenges to the legality of its establishment, which were resolved— albeit in a very brief manner—in favour of its legality in *Kanyabashi* (18 June 1997). The ICTR also enjoys a relationship of primacy in respect of national courts (Article 8, ICTR Statute) and member States of the UN are required to cooperate with its requests (Article 28, ICTR Statute).
3. The seat of the ICTR is in Arusha, Tanzania, due to security concerns when it was established. The ICTR has an Office of the Prosecutor, a Registry and three Trial Chambers. The ICTR shares an appeals chamber with the ICTY, which sits in The Hague. Until 2003, the two tribunals also shared a Prosecutor; however, the Council separated this role in 2003 and appointed a separate Prosecutor to serve the ICTR (see Security Council Resolution 1503 (28 August 2003)).
4. The ICTR has jurisdiction in respect of war crimes (Article 2, ICTR Statute), crimes against humanity (Article 3, ICTR Statute) and genocide (Article 4, ICTR Statute). Unlike the ICTY, it has a closed temporal jurisdiction, as it is limited to examining crimes alleged to have been committed between 1 January and 31 December 2004.
5. The ICTR also started slowly and encountered many difficulties, not least a breakdown in the relationship with Rwanda from 1999. Cooperation with Rwanda has gradually improved, and

additional measures designed to speed up the trial process (such as the appointment of *ad litem* judges) have reduced the backlog of cases.

6. Like the ICTY the ICTR was subject to the Completion Strategy (see subsection (a)), which includes The International Residual Mechanism for International Criminal Tribunals. The Mechanism's top priority involves securing the arrest, transfer and prosecution of nine remaining fugitives still wanted for trial by the ICTR. The ICTR has also now authorised the transfer of several 'lesser' cases to the national courts of Rwanda, following reforms to the Rwandan national system and the elimination of the death penalty. On 31 December 2015, the ICTR formally closed its doors and transferred its remaining functions to the Mechanism, after 21 years of operations.

C: The International Criminal Court

Following the completion in 1994 by the ILC of the draft statute of the international criminal court there was greater enthusiasm among States for the creation of international criminal tribunals than had previously existed, although several concerns remained. A Preparatory Committee was established to prepare a text, based on the ILC draft statute, to form the basis of negotiation at an international conference, held in Rome in 1998. The Rome Conference adopted the text of the Statute and established a Preparatory Commission to take the steps necessary for the establishment of the Court, which would only occur following ratification of the Statute by 60 States. This occurred in April 2002, and the Rome Statute entered into force on 1 July 2002.

Rome Statute

Article 1—The Court

An International Criminal Court ('the Court') is hereby established. It shall be a permanent institution and shall have the power to exercise its jurisdiction over persons for the most serious crimes of international concern, as referred to in this Statute, and shall be complementary to national criminal jurisdictions. The jurisdiction and functioning of the Court shall be governed by the provisions of this Statute.

Article 5—Crimes within the jurisdiction of the Court

1. The jurisdiction of the Court shall be limited to the most serious crimes of concern to the international community as a whole. The Court has jurisdiction in accordance with this Statute with respect to the following crimes:
    (a) The crime of genocide;
    (b) Crimes against humanity;
    (c) War crimes;
    (d) The crime of aggression.

Article 11—Jurisdiction ratione temporis

1. The Court has jurisdiction only with respect to crimes committed after the entry into force of this Statute.

2. If a State becomes a Party to this Statute after its entry into force, the Court may exercise its jurisdiction only with respect to crimes committed after the entry into force of this Statute for that State, unless that State has made a declaration under article 12, paragraph 3.

Article 12—Preconditions to the exercise of jurisdiction

1. A State which becomes a Party to this Statute thereby accepts the jurisdiction of the Court with respect to the crimes referred to in article 5.

2. In the case of article 13, paragraph (a) or (c), the Court may exercise its jurisdiction if one or more of the following States are Parties to this Statute or have accepted the jurisdiction of the Court in accordance with paragraph 3:
    (a) The State on the territory of which the conduct in question occurred or, if the crime was committed on board a vessel or aircraft, the State of registration of that vessel or aircraft;
    (b) The State of which the person accused of the crime is a national.

3. If the acceptance of a State which is not a Party to this Statute is required under paragraph 2, that State may, by declaration lodged with the Registrar, accept the exercise of jurisdiction by the Court with respect to the crime in question. The accepting State shall cooperate with the Court without any delay or exception in accordance with Part 9.

Article 13—Exercise of jurisdiction

The Court may exercise its jurisdiction with respect to a crime referred to in article 5 in accordance with the provisions of this Statute if:

(a) A situation in which one or more of such crimes appears to have been committed is referred to the Prosecutor by a State Party in accordance with article 14;

(b) A situation in which one or more of such crimes appears to have been committed is referred to the Prosecutor by the Security Council acting under Chapter VII of the Charter of the United Nations; or

(c) The Prosecutor has initiated an investigation in respect of such a crime in accordance with article 15.

Article 14—Referral of a situation by a State Party

1. A State Party may refer to the Prosecutor a situation in which one or more crimes within the jurisdiction of the Court appear to have been committed requesting the Prosecutor to investigate the situation for the purpose of determining whether one or more specific persons should be charged with the commission of such crimes.

2. As far as possible, a referral shall specify the relevant circumstances and be accompanied by such supporting documentation as is available to the State referring the situation.

Article 15—Prosecutor

1. The Prosecutor may initiate investigations *proprio motu* on the basis of information on crimes within the jurisdiction of the Court.

2. The Prosecutor shall analyse the seriousness of the information received. For this purpose, he or she may seek additional information from States, organs of the United Nations, intergovernmental or non-governmental organizations, or other reliable sources that he or she deems appropriate, and may receive written or oral testimony at the seat of the Court.

3. If the Prosecutor concludes that there is a reasonable basis to proceed with an investigation, he or she shall submit to the Pre-Trial Chamber a request for authorization of an investigation, together with any supporting material collected. Victims may make representations to the Pre-Trial Chamber, in accordance with the Rules of Procedure and Evidence......

Article 16—Deferral of investigation or prosecution

No investigation or prosecution may be commenced or proceeded with under this Statute for a period of 12 months after the Security Council, in a resolution adopted under Chapter VII of the Charter of the United Nations, has requested the Court to that effect; that request may be renewed by the Council under the same conditions.

Article 17—Issues of admissibility

1. Having regard to paragraph 10 of the Preamble and article 1, the Court shall determine that a case is inadmissible where:

(a) The case is being investigated or prosecuted by a State which has jurisdiction over it, unless the State is unwilling or unable genuinely to carry out the investigation or prosecution;

(b) The case has been investigated by a State which has jurisdiction over it and the State has decided not to prosecute the person concerned, unless the decision resulted from the unwillingness or inability of the State genuinely to prosecute;

(c) The person concerned has already been tried for conduct which is the subject of the complaint, and a trial by the Court is not permitted under article 20, paragraph 3;

(d) The case is not of sufficient gravity to justify further action by the Court.

2. In order to determine unwillingness in a particular case, the Court shall consider, having regard to the principles of due process recognized by international law, whether one or more of the following exist, as applicable:

(a) The proceedings were or are being undertaken or the national decision was made for the purpose of shielding the person concerned from criminal responsibility for crimes within the jurisdiction of the Court referred to in article 5;

(b) There has been an unjustified delay in the proceedings which in the circumstances is inconsistent with an intent to bring the person concerned to justice;

(c) The proceedings were not or are not being conducted independently or impartially, and they were or are being conducted in a manner which, in the circumstances, is inconsistent with an intent to bring the person concerned to justice.

3. In order to determine inability in a particular case, the Court shall consider whether, due to a total or substantial collapse or unavailability of its national judicial system, the State is unable to obtain the accused or the necessary evidence and testimony or otherwise unable to carry out its proceedings.

Security Council Resolution 1593 (2005)
31 March 2005, UN Security Council

Recalling article 16 of the Rome Statute under which no investigation or prosecution may be commenced or proceeded with by the International Criminal Court for a period of 12 months after a Security Council request to that effect,…

Determining that the situation in Sudan continues to constitute a threat to international peace and security,

Acting under Chapter VII of the Charter of the United Nations,

1. *Decides* to refer the situation in Darfur since 1 July 2002 to the Prosecutor of the International Criminal Court;

2. *Decides* that the Government of Sudan and all other parties to the conflict in Darfur, shall cooperate fully with and provide any necessary assistance to the Court and the Prosecutor pursuant to this resolution and, while recognizing that States not party to the Rome Statute have no obligation under the Statute, urges all States and concerned regional and other international organizations to cooperate fully;

3. *Invites* the Court and the African Union to discuss practical arrangements that will facilitate the work of the Prosecutor and of the Court, including the possibility of conducting proceedings in the region, which would contribute to regional efforts in the fight against impunity;

4. *Also encourages* the Court, as appropriate and in accordance with the Rome Statute, to support international cooperation with domestic efforts to promote the rule of law, protect human rights and combat impunity in Darfur;…

6. *Decides* that nationals, current or former officials or personnel from a contributing State outside Sudan which is not a party to the Rome Statute of the International Criminal Court shall be subject to the exclusive jurisdiction of that contributing State for all alleged acts or omissions arising out of or related to operations in Sudan established or authorized by the Council or the African Union, unless such exclusive jurisdiction has been expressly waived by that contributing State.

Prosecutor v *Katanga and Ngudjolo Chui*
Judgment on Admissibility of the case, 25 September 2009, 49 *International Legal Materials* 45 (2010), ICC Appeals Chamber

The DRC referred a situation to the ICC, indicated that it did not intend to investigate the accused in the DRC and surrendered the accused to the ICC. The accused challenged the admissibility of the case.

78. [I]n considering whether a case is inadmissible under article 17 (1)(a) and (b) of the Statute, the initial questions to ask are (1) whether there are ongoing investigations or prosecutions, or (2) whether there have been investigations in the past, and the State having jurisdiction has decided not to prosecute the person concerned. It is only when the answers to these questions are in the affirmative that one has to look to the second halves of sub-paragraphs (a) and (b) and to examine the question of unwillingness and inability. To do otherwise would be to put the cart before the horse. It follows that in case of inaction, the question of unwillingness or inability does not arise; inaction on the part of a State having jurisdiction (that is, the fact that a State is not investigating or prosecuting, or has not done so) renders a case admissible before the Court, subject to article 17 (1)(d) of the Statute. This interpretation of article 17 (1) (a) and (b) of the Statute also finds broad support from academic writers who have commented on the provision and on the principle of complementarity.

79. The Appeals Chamber is therefore not persuaded by the interpretation of article 17 (1) of the Statute proposed by the Appellant, according to which unwillingness and inability also have to be considered in case of inaction. Such an interpretation is not only irreconcilable with the wording of the provision, but is also in conflict with a purposive interpretation of the Statute. The aim of the Rome Statute is 'to put an end to impunity' and to ensure

that 'the most serious crimes of concern to the international community as a whole must not go unpunished'. This object and purpose of the Statute would come to naught were the said interpretation of article 17 (1) of the Statute as proposed by the Appellant to prevail. It would result in a situation where, despite the inaction of a State, a case would be inadmissible before the Court, unless that State is unwilling or unable to open investigations. The Court would be unable to exercise its jurisdiction over a case as long as the State is theoretically willing and able to investigate and to prosecute the case, even though that State has no intention of doing so. Thus, a potentially large number of cases would not be prosecuted by domestic jurisdictions or by the International Criminal Court. Impunity would persist unchecked and thousands of victims would be denied justice....

84. The above interpretation and application of article 17 of the Statute is, in the Appeals Chamber's view, in accord with the complementarity principle.

85. The Appeals Chamber is not persuaded by the argument of the Appellant that it would be to negate the obligation of States to prosecute crimes if they were allowed to relinquish domestic jurisdiction in favour of the International Criminal Court. The Appeals Chamber acknowledges that States have a duty to exercise their criminal jurisdiction over international crimes. The Chamber must nevertheless stress that the complementarity principle, as enshrined in the Statute, strikes a balance between safeguarding the primacy of domestic proceedings vis-à-vis the International Criminal Court on the one hand, and the goal of the Rome Statute to 'put an end to impunity' on the other hand. If States do not or cannot investigate and, where necessary, prosecute, the International Criminal Court must be able to step in. Moreover, there may be merit in the argument that the sovereign decision of a State to relinquish its jurisdiction in favour of the Court may well be seen as complying with the 'duty to exercise [its] criminal jurisdiction', as envisaged in the sixth paragraph of the Preamble. Be this as it may, however, the Appeals Chamber is mindful that the Court, acting under the relevant provisions of the Statute and depending on the circumstances of each case, may decide not to act upon a State's relinquishment of jurisdiction in favour of the Court.

86. In the Chamber's view, the general prohibition of a relinquishment of jurisdiction in favour of the Court is not a suitable tool for fostering compliance by States with the duty to exercise criminal jurisdiction. This is so because under the Rome Statute, the Court does not have the power to order States to open investigations or prosecutions domestically. It is purely speculative to assume that a State that has refrained from opening an investigation into a particular case or from prosecuting a suspect would do so, just because the International Criminal Court has ruled that the case is inadmissible. Thus, contrary to the arguments of the Appellant, his interpretation of the complementarity regime would not necessarily lead to an increase in domestic investigations or prosecutions. It would, instead, intensify the risk of serious crimes going unpunished.

Prosecutor v Francis Kirimi Muthaura, Uhuru Muigai Kenyatta and Mohammed Hussein Ali
Judgment on the appeal of the Republic of Kenya against the decision of Pre-Trial Chamber II of 30 May 2011 entitled 'Decision on the Application by the Government of Kenya Challenging the Admissibility of the Case pursuant to Article 19(2)(b) of the Statute', 30 August 2011, ICC Appeals Chamber

As noted in Section 4D, the ICC Prosecutor brought charges against President Kenyatta of Kenya in respect of crimes committed during the 2007–08 post-election violence. The government of Kenya challenged the admissibility of the case.

40. The Admissibility Challenge that gave rise to the present appeal was brought under article 19 (2) (b) of the Statute in relation to a case in which a summons to appear has been issued against specific suspects for specific conduct. Accordingly, as regards the present appeal, the 'case' in terms of article 17 (1) (a) is the case as defined in the summons. This case is only inadmissible before the Court if the same suspects are being investigated by Kenya for substantially the same conduct. The words 'is being investigated', in this context, signify the taking of steps directed at ascertaining whether those suspects are responsible for that conduct, for instance by interviewing witnesses or suspects, collecting documentary evidence, or carrying out forensic analyses. The mere preparedness to take such steps or the investigation of other suspects is not sufficient. This is because unless investigative steps are actually taken in relation to the suspects who are the subject of the proceedings before the Court, it cannot be said that the same case is (currently) under investigation by the Court and by a national jurisdiction, and there is therefore no conflict of jurisdictions. It should be underlined, however, that determining the existence of an investigation must be distinguished from assessing whether the State is 'unwilling or unable genuinely to carry out the investigation or prosecution', which is the second question to consider when determining the admissibility of

a case. For assessing whether the State is indeed investigating, the genuineness of the investigation is not at issue; what is at issue is whether there are investigative steps.

41. Kenya's submission that 'it cannot be right that in all circumstances in every Situation and in every case that may come before the ICC the persons being investigated by the Prosecutor must be exactly the same as those being investigated by the State if the State is to retain jurisdiction' cannot be accepted. It disregards the fact that the proceedings have progressed and that specific suspects have been identified. At this stage of the proceedings, where summonses to appear have been issued, the question is no longer whether suspects at the same hierarchical level are being investigated by Kenya, but whether the same suspects are the subject of investigation by both jurisdictions for substantially the same conduct.

42. Kenya seeks to counter this conclusion by suggesting that a national jurisdiction may not always have the same evidence available as the Prosecutor and therefore may not be investigating the same suspects as the Court. This argument is not persuasive for two reasons. First, if a State does not investigate a given suspect because of lack of evidence, then there simply is no conflict of jurisdictions, and no reason why the case should be inadmissible before the Court. Second, what is relevant for the admissibility of a concrete case under articles 17 (1) (a) and 19 of the Statute is not whether the same evidence in the Prosecutor's possession is available to a State, but whether the State is carrying out steps directed at ascertaining whether these suspects are responsible for substantially the same conduct as is the subject of the proceedings before the Court.

43. Kenya also argues that there should be a 'leaway [sic] in the exercise of discretion in the application of the principle of complementarity' to allow domestic proceedings to progress. This argument has no merit because, as explained above, the purpose of the admissibility proceedings under article 19 of the Statute is to determine whether the case brought by the Prosecutor is inadmissible because of a jurisdictional conflict. Unless there is such a conflict, the case is admissible. The suggestion that there should be a presumption in favour of domestic jurisdictions does not contradict this conclusion. Although article 17 (1) (a) to (c) of the Statute does indeed favour national jurisdictions, it does so only to the extent that there actually are, or have been, investigations and/or prosecutions at the national level. If the suspect or conduct have not been investigated by the national jurisdiction, there is no legal basis for the Court to find the case inadmissible.

44. Furthermore, proceedings to determine the admissibility of a concrete case under article 19 of the Statute are but one aspect of the complementarity principle. The concerns raised by Kenya regarding its exercise of criminal jurisdiction and protection of its sovereignty are taken into consideration in the proceedings under articles 15, 53, 18 and 19 of the Statute. Nevertheless, under article 19, the focus is on a concrete case that is the subject of proceedings before the Court. For that reason, Kenya's reference to the careful preliminary examination by the Prosecutor in relation to other situations is unpersuasive: the proceedings in relation to those situations are simply at a different stage than the proceedings in the case at hand.

45. Similarly, the argument that once the summons to appear was issued, Kenya was constrained, under article 19 (5) of the Statute, to bring the admissibility challenge 'at the earliest opportunity' and therefore it could not be 'expected to have prepared every aspect of its Admissibility Application in detail in advance of this date' is also misconceived. Article 19 (5) of the Statute requires a State to challenge admissibility as soon as possible once it is in a position to actually assert a conflict of jurisdictions. The provision does not require a State to challenge admissibility just because the Court has issued a summons to appear.

46. Accordingly, the Appeals Chamber finds that given the specific stage that the proceedings had reached, the 'same person/same conduct' test applied by the Pre-Trial Chamber was the correct test. The Pre-Trial Chamber thus made no error of law.

Prosecutor v *Saif Al-Islam Gaddafi and Abdullah Al-Senussi*

Judgment on the appeal of Mr Abdullah Al-Senussi against the decision of Pre-Trial Chamber I of 11 October 2013 entitled 'Decision on the admissibility of the case against Abdullah Al-Senussi', 24 July 2014, ICC Appeals Chamber

In 2011, the UN Security Council referred the situation concerning Libya to the ICC. The Prosecutor brought charges in respect of two individuals. Admissibility of both cases was challenged. In relation to Al-Senussi (the former security chief), the Court accepted that the same person/same conduct test was satisfied (see preceding extract). The question of admissibility then turned on whether the domestic proceedings satisfied Article 17(2) and (3).

190. The Appeals Chamber considers that denying a suspect access to a lawyer may, depending on the specific circumstances, be relevant to a finding that domestic proceedings 'are not being conducted independently or impartially, and they […] are being conducted in a manner which […] is inconsistent with an intent to bring the person concerned to justice' (article 17 (2) (c) of the Statute) and result in a finding of unwillingness. The Appeals Chamber notes the Defence's submissions in this regard, and, in particular, the references to human rights jurisprudence suggesting that the right to a fair trial will often include the right to access to a lawyer also in the early stages of the proceedings. The Appeals Chamber also notes the various arguments advanced by the parties and participants as to the requirements of Libyan law regarding access to a lawyer during the investigation and accusation stages of the proceedings. Nevertheless, the Appeals Chamber recalls that, in the context of admissibility proceedings, the Court is not primarily called upon to decide whether in domestic proceedings certain requirements of human rights law or domestic law are being violated. Rather, what is at issue is whether the State is willing genuinely to investigate or prosecute. In the context of article 17 (2) (c) of the Statute, the question is whether the failure to provide a lawyer constitutes a violation of Mr Al-Senussi's rights which is 'so egregious that the proceedings can no longer be regarded as being capable of providing any genuine form of justice to the accused so that they should be deemed […] to be "inconsistent with an intent to bring [Mr Al-Senussi] to justice".

191. In the view of the Appeals Chamber, even if one accepted that the lack of access to a lawyer during the investigation stage of the proceedings violated Mr Al-Senussi's right to a fair trial and provisions of Libyan law (and may therefore give rise to remedies under both international and national law), and without wishing to downplay in any way the importance of the right to counsel during the investigation phase, which is indeed also provided for under the Statute, such violations would not reach the high threshold for finding that Libya is unwilling genuinely to investigate or prosecute Mr Al-Senussi. In this regard, the Appeals Chamber notes that Libya does not dispute that Mr Al-Senussi's trial could not commence unless he is represented by a lawyer—a fact the Pre-Trial Chamber specifically noted. Thus, this is not a case where the suspect would be unrepresented during the trial itself.

213. The Appeals Chamber observes that, at first sight, the text of article 17 (2) (c) and the chapeau of article 17(2) could potentially be read to support the position argued for by the Defence, namely that a State is unwilling genuinely to carry out the investigation or prosecution if it does not respect the fair trial rights of the suspect. Article 17 (2) (c) refers to proceedings not being conducted 'independently or impartially' and to 'justice', and the chapeau contains the requirement of 'having regard to the principles of due process recognized by international law'. The Appeals Chamber is also aware that some commentators have argued that the provision should be interpreted consistently with the position taken by the Defence.

214. However, the Appeals Chamber observes that a closer analysis of the text, context, object and purpose of article 17 (2) (c) demonstrates that the interpretation proposed by the Defence is not sustainable for the reasons set out below.

215. The Appeals Chamber recalls that article 17 is designed to determine the circumstances in which a case shall be inadmissible before the Court by reference to the actions of a State which has jurisdiction over that case. In making that determination, regard is to be had to the fact that the Court is 'complementary to national criminal jurisdictions' and the question to be resolved is whether the Court or the State is the proper forum to exercise jurisdiction over the case.

216. It is recalled that article 17 (2) as a whole defines the circumstances in which a State is unwilling genuinely to carry out the investigation and/or prosecution. It makes an exception to the rule that a case is inadmissible before the Court if, as in the present case, it is being investigated or prosecuted by a State which has jurisdiction over it.

217. The purpose of this exception is to ensure that the principle of complementarity—which enables States to retain jurisdiction over cases and promotes the exercise of criminal jurisdiction domestically—is not abused, so that it would be contrary to the overall purpose of the Statute, which is to put an end to impunity for the perpetrators of the most serious crimes of concern to the international community as a whole.

218. The concept of being 'unwilling' genuinely to investigate or prosecute is therefore primarily concerned with a situation in which proceedings are conducted in a manner which would lead to a suspect evading justice as a result of a State not being willing genuinely to investigate or prosecute. This is provided for most specifically in article 17 (2) (a), which expressly states that, in order to determine unwillingness, the Court shall consider whether, '[t]he proceedings were or are being undertaken or the national decision was made *for the purpose of shielding the person concerned from criminal responsibility*' (emphasis added). The fact that the other two sub-paragraphs of article 17 (2) do not expressly refer to shielding or protecting the person concerned cannot detract from the fact that they are sub-paragraphs of a provision defining unwillingness. The primary reason for their inclusion is therefore likewise not for the purpose of guaranteeing the fair trial rights of the suspect generally.

219. Indeed, the Court was not established to be an international court of human rights, sitting in judgment over domestic legal systems to ensure that they are compliant with international standards of human rights. However, if the interpretation proposed by the Defence were adopted, the Court would come close to becoming an international court of human rights. A case could be admissible merely because domestic proceedings do not fully respect the due process rights of a suspect. This would necessarily involve the Court passing judgment generally on the internal functioning of the domestic legal systems of States in relation to individual guarantees of due process. Had this been the intention behind article 17, the Appeals Chamber would have expected this to have been included expressly in the text of the provision.

Situation on the Registered Vessels of the Union of the Comoros, the Hellenic Republic and the Kingdom of Cambodia, **Decision on the request of the Union of the Comoros to review the Prosecutor's decision not to initiate an investigation**

16 July 2015, Pre-Trial Chamber, International Criminal Court

The Comoros, Greece and Cambodia referred to the ICC Prosecutor the actions by Israeli armed forces against vessels carrying humanitarian assistance to Gaza, which Israel argued breached a lawful naval blockade. Ten people on the vessels were killed and 50 to 55 people injured. The Prosecutor declined to open an investigation and the States applied to the Pre-Trial Chamber for a review of that decision.

11. In the present case, the consideration underlying the Prosecutor's decision not to investigate the situation referred to her by the Comoros is that the potential cases arising from such situation would not be of sufficient gravity. The Comoros challenge precisely the Prosecutor's interpretation and application to the present case of the gravity test envisaged in article 17(1)(d) of the Statute and raise two main grounds of review, namely: (i) the failure to take into account facts that did not occur on the three vessels over which the Court may exercise territorial jurisdiction; and (ii) the failure to properly address the factors relevant to the determination of gravity under article 17(1)(d) of the Statute. The Chamber's determination in the present review is limited to these aspects.

12. Upon review, the Chamber must request the Prosecutor to reconsider her decision not to investigate if it concludes that the validity of the decision is materially affected by an error, whether it is an error of procedure, an error of law, or an error of fact.

13. The question that is asked of the Prosecutor by article 53(1) of the Statute is merely whether or not an investigation should be opened. The Prosecutor's assessment of the criteria listed in this provision does not necessitate any complex or detailed process of analysis. In the presence of several plausible explanations of the available information, the presumption of article 53(1) of the Statute, as reflected by the use of the word 'shall' in the chapeau of that article, and of common sense, is that the Prosecutor investigates in order to be able to properly assess the relevant facts. Indeed, it is precisely the purpose of an investigation to provide clarity. Making the commencement of an investigation contingent on the information available at the pre-investigative stage being already clear, univocal or not contradictory creates a short circuit and deprives the exercise of any purpose. Facts which are difficult to establish, or which are unclear, or the existence of conflicting accounts, are not valid reasons not to start an investigation but rather call for the opening of such an investigation. If the information available to the Prosecutor at the pre-investigative stage allows for reasonable inferences that at least one crime within the jurisdiction of the Court has been committed and that the case would be admissible, the Prosecutor shall open an investigation, as only by investigating could doubts be overcome. This is further demonstrated by the fact that only during the investigation may the Prosecutor use her powers under article 54 of the Statute; conversely, her powers are more limited under article 53(1) of the Statute.

14. The Chamber recognises that the Prosecutor has discretion to open an investigation but, as mandated by article 53(1) of the Statute, that discretion expresses itself only in paragraph (c), i.e. in the Prosecutor's evaluation of whether the opening of an investigation would not serve the interests of justice. Conversely, paragraphs (a) and (b) require the application of exacting legal requirements. This is not contradicted by the low evidentiary standard of article 53(1)(a) of the Statute, or by the fact that an analysis under article 53(1)(b) of the Statute involves potential and not actual cases.

15. Finally, the Chamber considers it necessary to add that there is also no valid argument for the proposition that in order not to encroach on the independence of the Prosecutor, the Chamber should knowingly tolerate and not request reconsideration of decisions under article 53(1) of the Statute which are erroneous, but within some field of deference. The role of the Chamber in the present proceedings is to exercise independent judicial oversight....

21. In this regard, the Chamber is attentive to the Court's previous decisions in relation to the interpretation of the requirement of 'sufficient gravity' within the meaning of article 17(1)(d) of the Statute, in particular with respect to the assessment of the gravity of the 'potential cases' at the pre-investigative stage. More specifically, the Chamber recalls that: (i) a gravity determination involves a generic assessment (general in nature and compatible with the fact that an investigation is yet to be opened) of whether the groups of persons that are likely to form the object of the investigation capture those who may bear the greatest responsibility for the alleged crimes committed; and (ii) gravity must be assessed from both a 'quantitative' and 'qualitative' viewpoint and factors such as nature, scale and manner of commission of the alleged crimes, as well as their impact on victims, are indicators of the gravity of a given case....

26. The Chamber notes that the Prosecutor and the Comoros essentially agree on the numbers of victims of the identified crimes. In the view of the Chamber, ten killings, 50–55 injuries, and possibly hundreds of instances of outrages upon personal dignity, or torture or inhuman treatment, which would be the scale of the crimes prosecuted in the potential case(s) arising from the referred situation, in addition to exceeding the number of casualties in actual cases that were previously not only investigated but even prosecuted by the Prosecutor (e.g. the cases against Bahar Idriss Abu Garda and Abdallah Banda), are a compelling indicator of sufficient, and not of insufficient gravity. The factor of scale should have been taken into account by the Prosecutor as militating in favour of sufficient gravity, rather than the opposite, and in failing to reach this conclusion, the Prosecutor committed a material error.

47. In the view of the Chamber, the conclusion of the Prosecutor is flawed. The Prosecutor failed to consider that, before attempting a determination of the impact of the identified crimes on the lives of the people in Gaza, the significant impact of such crimes on the lives of the victims and their families, which she duly recognised, is, as such, an indicator of sufficient gravity. The physical, psychological or emotional harm suffered by the direct and indirect victims of the identified crimes must not be undervalued and needs not be complemented by a more general impact of these crimes beyond that suffered by the victims. While considerations with respect to the impact of the crimes beyond the suffering of the victims could be relevant in order to support a finding of sufficient gravity, it is not required that any such impact, let alone one equally 'significant', be discernible such that its absence could be taken into account as outweighing the significant impact of the crimes on the victims and ultimately negating sufficient gravity. The Chamber is therefore of the view that the Prosecutor erred in considering that, as a result of the alleged absence of a significant impact of the identified crimes on the civilian population in Gaza and despite their significant impact on the victims, overall the impact of the identified crimes constituted an indicator of insufficient gravity of the potential case(s).

48. In any case, the Chamber is of the view that, in light of the available information, the Prosecutor should have recognised the possibility that the events at issue had an impact going beyond the suffering of the direct and indirect victims. Indeed, as submitted by the Comoros, the commission of the identified crimes on the Mavi Marmara, which were highly publicised, would have sent a clear and strong message to the people in Gaza (and beyond) that the blockade of Gaza was in full force and that even the delivery of humanitarian aid would be controlled and supervised by the Israeli authorities. Also, the international concern caused by the events at issue, which, inter alia, resulted in several fact-finding missions, including by the UN Human Rights Council and the UN Secretary General, is somehow at odds with the Prosecutor's simplistic conclusion that the impact of the identified crimes points towards the insufficient gravity of the potential case(s) on the mere grounds that the supplies carried by the vessels in the flotilla were ultimately later distributed to the population in Gaza.

P. Akhavan, 'The Rise, and Fall, and Rise, of International Criminal Justice'

11 *Journal of International Criminal Justice* 527 (2013)

Is international criminal justice in decline? Or is it simply in the post-romantic phase of its historical evolution? Once upon a time, international jurists envisioned the contemporary tribunals as a utopian aspiration. Punishing war crimes was seen as a vital but unattainable goal in the struggle between civilization and barbarity. The Nuremberg and Tokyo trials were merely historical anomalies. A culture of impunity reigned throughout the United Nations (UN) era. In the 1990s, at the inception of the contemporary international criminal justice system, what is now a permanent institutional fixture—ripe for intellectual scepticism and critical analysis—was a phenomenal revolutionary development…

If today we can speak about the 'setbacks' of international criminal justice, it is because of the remarkable victories that have been achieved thus far. The fact that there are functioning international criminal tribunals that we can critique is itself a phenomenon that was unthinkable 10 to 20 years ago. The rise of international criminal justice in the nascent phase of its existence—and the projection of exaggerated normative fantasies on to this seeming panacea—has invariably given way to its perceived decline. As the romance fades away, we are confronted with the self-evident complexities and constraints of grafting idyllic rule of law conceptions on to the grim reality of societies emerging from mass atrocities. Whether there is a continuing rise or fall very much depends on how we conceive the boundaries and potentialities of reducing the enormity of the challenges that genocide and other such crimes entail to the antiseptic confines of legal procedures and institutions. How is the plethora of ambitious objectives conceived and ranked? These include, but are not limited to, 'establishing a record of past events', 'bringing to justice those responsible', 'preventing the recurrence of violations', 'promoting national reconciliation', 're-establishing the rule of law' and 'securing peace'. If we appreciate that prosecuting a handful of leaders at The Hague, however desirable and valuable, is not a definitive cure for radical evil, or complete attainment of these myriad objectives, then it is easier to halt the perceived fall of international criminal justice. Instead, beyond the unrealistic fantasy of linear progress, we are able to discern a slow, awkward and meandering development. To better appreciate the relative success or failure of global justice, contemporary institutions must be understood in their proper context. Unlike the historical Nuremberg model, the ICTY and ICTR—and the ICC in situations such as the Democratic Republic of the Congo (DRC) and Darfur—has been decoupled from more effective measures to halt ongoing atrocities. This is not to say that the ICC should have a standing army to invade countries committing atrocities. The point is that we have gone from a model of partial so-called 'victor's justice' to the no less problematic model of so-called 'spectator's justice', watching as civilians are slaughtered only to half-heartedly prosecute *genocidaires* afterwards. This is not to suggest that military intervention is necessarily the solution. Rather, at issue is whether we are placing a burden on international criminal justice that it cannot bear, by making it a substitute for, rather than a complement to, preventive action. If we suffer from the delusion that our moral failure to act against ongoing atrocities can be swept under the ICC carpet, then we are bound to witness the decline of international criminal justice. The inability to arrest accused leaders for instance—as in Sudan—is a failure of political will, and not a failure of international criminal justice. Holding ICTR trials in Arusha while the spillover violence of the genocide wipes out millions in eastern DRC, is an abominable contradiction.

The need for international criminal justice itself reflects the failure to prevent mass atrocities. It is often assumed that genocide is somehow an unforeseen natural disaster, like an earthquake or tsunami. Mass murder is exoticized as an explosion of inexorable primordial hatreds in foreign lands. It is more accurately a rationalized instrument of power, a deliberate political construction. As such, it is predictable, and thus preventable, at least in some situations. A notorious example is the 1994 Rwandan genocide. The first warning signs, the incitement to hatred, extreme politicization of ethnicity, the systematic distribution of weapons and training of militia, the preparation of lists of those to be exterminated, these obvious signs were all disregarded, either because of wishful thinking that the problem would simply disappear, or simply because of indifference to the suffering of millions somewhere in Africa where there are no compelling interests for powerful nations. To imagine that the ICTR could simply sweep away the consequences of this cataclysm is an elaborate self-deception. We have to consider how, in a country with an approximately 50% rate of illiteracy, where a single radio station was the primary source of information, simply shutting down the broadcasts that incited genocide could have saved thousands of lives. Never mind reinforcing UN peacekeepers to protect civilians while machete wielding thugs slaughtered them on the streets of Kigali and elsewhere. How different would the outcome have been in 1994 if the steady stream of incendiary hate speech from that radio station was stopped? We must also consider why in view of the spillover of the Rwandan genocide, there was no need for an international criminal tribunal for neighbouring Burundi, with its highly similar ethnic composition and political tensions. It is at least in part because preventive diplomacy—at the initiative of humanitarian entrepreneurs such as former United States diplomat Howard Wolpe—successfully contained genocidal currents at a crucial juncture. International criminal justice must be situated as simply one tool among a broader set of tools to confront mass atrocities, a measure of last resort in the hierarchy of responses. The first priority must always be prevention. Success must be measured by what does not happen. The need for international tribunals is itself a failure. Prevention may not always be possible, but in many cases it is a feasible option. Our ultimate aspiration should be a world in which the ICC remains idle for lack of cases.

NOTES

1. Unlike the ICTR and the ICTY, the ICC was established by a treaty, the Rome Statute. The ICC may only exercise its jurisdiction from the date the Rome Statute entered into force, i.e. to crimes occurring after 1 July 2002. As a treaty, the Rome Statute binds only those States that are party to it (see Chapter 3 and note 4 of this section). The crimes currently within the Court's jurisdiction are war crimes, crimes against humanity and genocide. The Court's jurisdiction in respect of the crime of aggression may commence at a later date, subject to ratification by a minimum of 30 States and an additional decision to be taken after 1 January 2017 by a two-thirds majority of State parties, as required for adoption of an amendment to the Statute. As at March 2016, only 28 State parties have accepted the Court's jurisdiction in relation to the crime of aggression (see Section 3D, and note 4 of this current section).

2. A case may be brought before the ICC in three ways, as set out in Articles 12 and 13. First, a State party may refer a matter to the ICC (known as 'self-referral'). A State that is a not a party to the Statute may also refer a matter on an ad hoc basis by accepting the Court's jurisdiction with respect to the crime in question (see discussion of Palestine's position in Chapter 5; Ukraine also accepted the Court's jurisdiction in two declarations filed in 2014 and 2015). Second, the Security Council, acting under Chapter VII of the UN Charter, may refer a situation. Finally, the Prosecutor may initiate an investigation acting on her own initiative (known as acting *proprio motu*). Of the ten situations currently before the ICC, five (Democratic Republic of the Congo, Uganda, Central African Republic (two situations), and Mali) have been referred by the State in which territory the crimes are alleged to have been committed. The situations in Darfur, Sudan (see Resolution 1593) and Libya (see Resolution 1970) were referred by the Security Council. The final three situations involving Kenya, Côte d'Ivoire and Georgia were initiated by the Prosecutor acting *proprio motu*.

3. Other than in the case of referrals by the Council (where these requirements do not apply), the ICC may only exercise jurisdiction where the alleged crime occurred on the territory of a State party, or was committed by a national of a State party (Article 12). Moreover, the ICC may only act in respect of 'the most serious crimes of international concern', and the Court must satisfy itself that the acts in question are of a sufficient gravity to justify its involvement (Article 17).

4. In relation to the crime of aggression, the amendments to the Rome Statute agreed at the 2010 Review Conference confirm that the Court cannot exercise jurisdiction in respect of non-State parties. States parties are also permitted to opt out of the Court's jurisdiction for aggression. Where the Prosecutor, acting under Article 15, considers that there is a reasonable basis for an investigation, she must notify the Security Council and may only proceed where the Council has made a determination that aggression has occurred. Where it has not made such a finding within six months of notification, the Prosecutor can apply to the Pre-Trial Chamber for an order authorising an investigation, provided that the Council has not acted under Article 16. The Security Council can also refer situations concerning the possible commission of the crime of aggression under Article 13(b) of the Rome Statute.

5. The Rome Statute extends considerable discretion to the Prosecutor as to whether to initiate an investigation, although that discretion may be reviewed by a Pre-Trial Chamber in some situations. Where a State or the Security Council refers a situation to the Prosecutor, a decision not to open an investigation may be referred to a Pre-Trial Chamber for review. This is what happened in relation to the situation arising from the Gaza flotilla (see extract). The majority of the Pre-Trial Chamber directed the Prosecutor to reconsider her decision not to investigate (an appeal by the Prosecutor was declined by the Appeals Chamber). However, there was considerable disagreement between the majority (extracted above) and the dissenting judge as to the nature and scope of the review to be conducted by the Pre-Trial Chamber, with Judge Kovacs arguing that the Pre-Trial Chamber should 'conduct such a review on the merits only if it is convinced that the issues raised in said application reveal clear error(s) on the part of the Prosecutor, which prompt such a review and reconsideration of her decision. It does not mean that because the Chamber may have arrived at a different conclusion on the basis of the facts presented that the Prosecutor's decision was erroneous and should be accordingly reconsidered' (para. 2). Where the Prosecutor decides to open an investigation *proprio motu*, the decision is subject to review by the Pre-Trial Chamber under Article 15 (see extract). A decision by the Prosecutor not to proceed with an investigation on the interests of justice is always subject to review by the Pre-Trial Chamber.

6. The ICC operates in accordance with the principle of complementarity in relation to national courts and not by primacy (as is the case for the ICTY and ICTR). The Rome Statute recognises the importance of encouraging national legal systems to respond to violations of international criminal law wherever possible (and appropriate). Accordingly, the ICC is unable to exercise its

jurisdiction unless the affected State has failed to act, or is acting in a manner which indicates that it is unable or unwilling to investigate or prosecute genuinely (Article 17, see extract). It is for the ICC, and not the national authorities, to determine whether it may exercise its jurisdiction. For an assessment of the admissibility of a case, the Court applies a two-step test (see extract from *Katanga*). The first limb requires an assessment of whether there are ongoing investigations or prosecutions at the national level. If the answer is in the affirmative, the Court examines the second limb and considers whether the state with jurisdiction is willing and able to investigate or prosecute genuinely. In *Gaddafi and Al-Senussi*, the Appeals Chamber confirmed that admissibility is to be assessed in light of the circumstances existing at the time of proceedings in respect of a challenge to the admissibility of a case (see extract from *Prosecutor* v *Saif Al-Islam Gaddafi and Abdullah Al-Senussi*).

7. In earlier decisions on complementarity, the ICC adopted a practical approach to the assessment of admissibility, effectively allowing a referring State to 'defer' prosecution to the ICC and promoting 'burden-sharing' between the ICC and national jurisdictions (see *Katanga*), although it is not clear that this approach was contemplated by the drafters of the Rome Statute. In a later decision, the ICC has adopted a strict approach in assessing the 'same person, same conduct' test. According to this test, for a case to be deemed inadmissible, the national proceeding must be investigating the same person as well as substantially the same conduct as the ICC. Proposals by the Kenyan government for the test to cover 'persons in the same level in the hierarchy' being investigated by the ICC have been rejected by the Appeals Chamber (see *Francis Kirimi Muthaura, Uhuru Muigai Kenyatta and Mohammed Hussein Ali,* above). In contrast to the Court's stringent application of the same person test in the Kenya cases, it allowed greater deference to the state of Libya in assessing its willingness and ability genuinely to investigate and prosecute the case of *Al-Senussi*. This was arguably due to Libya's willingness to cooperate with the Court and evidence submitted by Libya establishing concrete and progressive steps were being taken to investigate the case. The decision marks the first time that the Court has declared a case to be inadmissible.

8. The case of *Al-Senussi* has led to disagreement among practitioners and scholars about the extent to which a failure to guarantee an accused's fair trial rights renders a case admissible under Article 17. The Appeals Chamber held that a denial of fair trial rights, at least during the investigation stage of a proceeding, does not automatically lead to a finding of unwillingness, and therefore inadmissibility. Only in extreme cases involving fair trial violations will a case be deemed admissible. This is based on the reasoning that the ICC was not established as a court of review and the assessment of admissibility does not necessarily involve passing judgment generally on the internal functioning of domestic legal systems.

9. The effectiveness of the cooperation arrangements are vital to the success of the ICC. Parties to the Rome Statute are subject to an obligation to cooperate with the Court's orders and requests, including an obligation to surrender an individual to the ICC when the individual is found on the territory of that State party (Article 89). If a State party fails to comply, the matter can be referred to the Assembly of State Parties. Where the Council has referred a situation to the Court, it may include in the terms of the referral an obligation on member States of the UN, including States that are not party to the Rome Statute to cooperate with the Court in relation to the situation referred (see Resolution 1593 above). In addition to findings on non-cooperation made in respect of Malawi and the DRC for their failure to arrest and surrender President Al Bashir, recent examples of referrals for non-cooperation are referrals in respect of Kenya and Libya in 2014.

10. Article 16 permits the Council to request the Court to defer an investigation or trial. The initial purpose of this provision was to allow the Council to intervene where the interests of justice were outweighed—albeit temporarily—by the prospects of securing peace, for example to allow sufficient time for a peace agreement to be negotiated. The provision has, however, been used to justify a controversial exception from the Court's jurisdiction for peacekeepers from States that are not party to the Statute (particularly US forces). The African Union also sought—unsuccessfully—to invoke this provision concerning the situations in Kenya and Sudan.

11. The reaction of the United States to the adoption of the Rome Statute was potentially a major setback to the ICC. While the US was an active supporter of the proposed Court, and very active during the Rome Conference, it was unable to accept the compromises reached in the final instrument, particularly the possibility that the Court would exercise jurisdiction in relation to a national of a non-State party. While the Clinton Administration signed the Rome Statute, the

treaty was later 'unsigned' by the Bush Administration and the United States remains outside the treaty framework (see Chapter 3). Moreover, the United States' opposition to the ICC instigated a number of attempts to prevent the exercise of jurisdiction by the ICC in respect of US nationals. In later years the US opposition to the Court has been more measured (for example, the US did not veto the referral of the situation in Darfur), and there has been an increase in cooperation with the Court. However, despite the more positive attitude of the Obama Administration towards the Court, serious legal and political concerns remain that preclude the US from becoming a State Party to the Rome Statute.

12. As Akhavan notes, the ICC is a product both of victories and setbacks. The fact it even exists is considered a measure of its success. However, since opening its doors, a number of charges have been levelled at the Court based on allegations of selective prosecutions and limited effectiveness due to the small number of cases that have reached a final determination, as well as the length and cost of the trials held to date. In total, as at March 2016, only four cases have completed the trial process: *Prosecutor* v *Thomas Lubanga Dyilo*, *Prosecutor* v *Germain Katanga*, *Prosecutor* v *Mathieu Ngudjolo Chui* and *Prosecutor* v *Bemba Gombo*.

D: Hybrid and internationalised tribunals

L. Dickinson, 'The Promise of Hybrid Courts'

97 *American Journal of International Law* 295 (2003)

Much of the transitional justice discussion has centred on four types of accountability mechanisms that have proven to be both significant and controversial. First, the promise and pitfalls of international criminal justice bodies—such as the International Criminal Tribunal for the Former Yugoslavia (ICTY) and the International Criminal Tribunal for Rwanda (ICTR)—have taken on increased importance with the establishment of the International Criminal Court (ICC). Second, the growing use of truth commissions, pioneered in Latin America, developed famously in South Africa, and now being used around the globe from East Timor to Nigeria to Peru, has elicited enormous interest within policy, advocacy, and scholarly communities. Third, transnational accountability efforts—such as Spain's attempt to extradite Augusto Pinochet to stand trial for torture and other human rights abuses committed in Chile, or Belgium's application of its relatively recent universal jurisdiction law—have sparked vigorous debate. Finally, the use of the Alien Tort Claims Act in the United States to allow civil tort claims brought by victims of human rights abuses continues to be controversial.

Comparatively little attention has been paid, however, to a fifth, newly emerging, form of accountability and reconciliation: hybrid domestic-international courts. Such courts are 'hybrid' because both the institutional apparatus and the applicable law consist of a blend of the international and the domestic. Foreign judges sit alongside their domestic counterparts to try cases prosecuted and defended by teams of local lawyers working with those from other countries. The judges apply domestic law that has been reformed to accord with international standards. This hybrid model has developed in a range of settings, generally post-conflict situations where no politically viable full-fledged international tribunal exists, as in East Timor or Sierra Leone, or where an international tribunal exists but cannot cope with the sheer number of cases, as in Kosovo. Most recently, an agreement to create a hybrid court in Cambodia has been reached, and there is discussion about establishing such a court in post-war Iraq.

Frequently, such courts have been conceived in an ad hoc way, the product of on the ground innovation rather than grand institutional design.…Interestingly, one reason the hybrid courts have received comparatively little attention so far may be that their very hybridity has left them open to challenge both from those advocating increased use of formal international justice mechanisms and those who resist all reliance on international institutions. For example, many supporters of international justice seem to fear that hybrid tribunals may be used as an alternative to, and possibly as a means to undermine, the use of full-fledged international criminal courts. Indeed, it is striking that two government officials who played key roles in establishing hybrid tribunals in Kosovo and East Timor have resisted the notion that such courts could serve as a model for the future. Many within the human rights advocacy community have been critical of the hybrid courts as well. From the opposite end of the political spectrum, those who generally eschew international justice mechanisms—such as Bush Administration officials who have opposed the ICC—may see hybrid tribunals as carrying *too many* of the trappings of international courts. For example, administration officials have been wary of international involvement in efforts to establish courts to try those suspected of committing mass atrocities in Iraq, instead advocating an Iraqi-led domestic process. In a sense, then, hybrid courts are being squeezed from both sides.

This dual resistance to hybrid courts is unfortunate....such courts hold a good deal of promise and may even offer an approach to questions of accountability that addresses some of the concerns raised in both camps.... A hybrid court is not a panacea, of course....Hybrid courts are merely the most recent step in this endless process of creative adaptation. Responding to significant shortcomings in both purely international and purely domestic approaches, hybrid courts have been devised in at least four settings and are under consideration elsewhere. These courts, though often hampered by underfunding and other logistical difficulties, at least have the potential to address three serious drawbacks of both international and domestic tribunals. First, they may be more likely to be perceived as legitimate by local and international populations because both have representation on the court. Second, the existence of the hybrid court may help to train local judges and funnel money into local infrastructure, thereby increasing the capacity of domestic legal institutions. Third, the functioning of hybrid courts in the local community, along with the necessary interaction—both formal and informal—among local and international legal actors may contribute to the broader dissemination (and adaptation) of the norms and processes of international human rights law.

Moreover, any fears (or hopes) that these hybrid courts will serve as a complete substitute for purely international or purely domestic courts are misplaced because the hybrid courts are best viewed as a complement to both. Indeed, there is no reason to believe that hybrid courts will divest the ICC of jurisdiction. Rather, because the ICC will never be able to try more than a few cases in any given setting, the hybrid courts may continue to be a necessary part of any transitional justice process.

S. Williams. 'Internationalized Tribunals: A Search for Their Legal Bases'

in K. H. Kaikobad and M. Bohlander (eds), *International Law and Power: Perspectives on Legal Order and Justice* (2010)

Although there is currently no accepted definition of an internationalized tribunal, there is some agreement as to their core features. In particular, the tribunal must exercise a criminal judicial function; there must be a mix of international and national elements, operating at many levels; and the tribunal must have been created as an ad hoc and temporary response to a specific situation. However, it has been observed that, while common characteristics may be identified, 'the general 'species' of internationalized tribunals is highly heterogeneous; the circumstances of their creation are extremely different; their degree of 'internationalization' is far from uniform; the scope of their jurisdiction is varied; their modes of functioning are hardly comparable' [A. Pellet, 'Internationalized Courts: Better than Nothing…' in Romano (ed), *Internationalized Criminal Courts: Sierra Leone, East Timor, Kosovo and Cambodia* (2004)]. This degree of 'ad-hocism' makes it difficult to identify any normative framework within which to assess existing and future internationalized tribunals.

Given the growing number of such tribunals, it is now necessary to examine further the features of these tribunals so as to identify more specific categories, or sub-species. To utilise the generic term 'internationalized' or 'hybrid' potentially masks a number of significant differences between such tribunals. For instance, the tribunals may apply, and be governed by, different legal regimes. Some may have the power to compel compliance with court orders by third States and international organisations, including the power to secure the surrender of suspects, while others are restricted to requesting international cooperation utilising existing domestic arrangements as to extradition and mutual legal cooperation. Tribunals may have varying relationships with the domestic legal regime. Certain tribunals may be able to override domestic and international immunities, whilst others may not. It is submitted here that the most relevant criterion upon which to base any categorization of such tribunals is the legal basis for the creation and operation of the tribunal. Examining the legal basis for each tribunal permits an examination of the key powers and competences of each tribunal and the applicable legal regime.

NOTES

1. There are several examples of hybrid or internationalised tribunals operating or having operated in various situations around the world. In addition to Kosovo and East Timor (referred to in the preceding extract), there are the Extraordinary Chambers in the Courts of Cambodia, the Special Court for Sierra Leone, the Special Tribunal for Lebanon, the War Crimes Chamber in Bosnia and Herzegovina, the Extraordinary African Chambers and the Iraqi High Tribunal (although this is not unanimously endorsed as an internationalised tribunal). This model has been considered for Liberia, Burundi and, prior to the Council referral to the ICC, Darfur. In light of the reluctance to establish further ad hoc tribunals, and the ICC's limited jurisdiction and resources, it appears that

this model will continue to be utilised, as seen by the establishment of internationalised tribunals for Kosovo and the DRC in 2015 and suggestions for an internationalised tribunal for Syria and Sri Lanka.

2. As Williams notes, however, it is very difficult to form general principles concerning such models, due to the differences in the context in which they have been established and the variations in their design and, in particular, their legal basis. Some, such as the Special Court for Sierra Leone and the Special Tribunal for Lebanon, are basically international courts. Others are mainly domestic tribunals, albeit operating with significant international assistance.

15

The Use of Force, Collective Security and Peacekeeping

INTRODUCTORY NOTE

All communities, whether international or national, suffer from the use of violence by their members to resolve some of their disputes. One of the tasks of law when faced with this situation is to regulate the use of force by the members of the community. International law seeks to do this in two ways. First, it stipulates that there is a paramount obligation not to use force to settle disputes, with only limited exceptions. Second, it has at its disposal a procedure whereby the international community itself may use force against those using violence. These are known respectively as the rules on the 'unilateral use of force' and the rules of 'collective security'.

SECTION 1: THE UNILATERAL USE OF FORCE

At one stage in the development of international law, States were entitled to resort to war, or to use force short of war, to achieve their aims. The United Nations Charter definitively changed this with its legal obligation not to use force (see Article 2(4) of the Charter below), though this does not mean that outbreaks of international violence will not occur. The use of force by a State is said to be 'unilateral' when it occurs without the authorisation of a competent international organisation, such as the Security Council of the United Nations. It is possible, therefore, for a use of force to be unilateral in this sense even though it involves more than one acting State. One example is the NATO military action against Yugoslavia (Serbia and Montenegro) during the Kosovo crisis of 1998/9, the legitimacy of which is discussed more fully in Section 1F. In addition, a unilateral use of force may become superseded or suspended by, or even run concurrently with, a collective use of force under the mandate of collective security, as where unilateral acts become authorised by such a competent organisation. One example is the initially unilateral use of force by States in defence of Kuwait following Iraq's invasion in 1990, which subsequently became an exercise in collective security.

A: The general scheme

United Nations Charter

Article 1

The Purposes of the United Nations are:

1. To maintain international peace and security, and to that end: to take effective collective measures for the prevention and removal of threats to the peace, and for the suppression of acts of aggression or other

breaches of the peace, and to bring about by peaceful means, and in conformity with the principles of justice and international law, adjustment or settlement of international disputes or situations which might lead to a breach of the peace;…

Article 2

3. All Members shall settle their international disputes by peaceful means in such a manner that international peace and security, and justice, are not endangered.

4. All Members shall refrain in their international relations from the threat or use of force against the territorial integrity or political independence of any state, or in any other manner inconsistent with the Purposes of the United Nations.

Article 51

Nothing in the present Charter shall impair the inherent right of individual or collective self-defence if an armed attack occurs against a Member of the United Nations, until the Security Council has taken measures necessary to maintain international peace and security. Measures taken by members in the exercise of this right of self-defence shall be immediately reported to the Security Council and shall not in any way affect the authority and responsibility of the Security Council under the present Charter to take at any time such action as it deems necessary in order to maintain or restore international peace and security.

T. Franck, 'Who Killed Article 2(4)?'
64 American Journal of International Law 809 (1970)

[T]oday the high-minded resolve of Article 2(4) mocks us from its grave. That the rules against the use of force should have had so short a life appears due to various factors. The rules, admirable in themselves, were seemingly predicated on a false assumption: that the wartime partnership of the Big Five would continue, providing the means for policing the peace under the aegis of the United Nations. They appeared to address themselves to preventing conventional military aggression at the very moment in history when new forms of attack were making obsolete all prior notions of war and peace strategy. And the Charter itself provided enough exceptions and ambiguities to open the rules to deadly erosion…

Unfortunately these ambitious projects were founded on an invalid premise: that the Security Council would be able to discharge its responsibility as the United Nations' principal organ for world peacekeeping.…The Security Council…in all but procedural matters, can only act with the assent of nine members, including the affirmative vote or at least the benevolent abstention of each of the Big Five. Almost from the moment the San Francisco Charter was signed, this essential prerequisite for UN collective enforcement action—the unanimity of the great Powers—was seen to be an illusion.…As Chapter VII was seen to rust, increasing use began to be made of Articles 51, 52, and 53, which set out the rights of states themselves, under certain exceptional circumstances, to resort to various kinds of force outside the United Nations framework, until today, through practice, the exceptions have overwhelmed the rule and transformed the system.

Article 51 of the UN Charter permits the use of armed force by a state responding in self-defense to an armed attack. This right to respond can either be exercised individually by the state attacked or collectively by a group of states going to its rescue. At first glance, such an exception would appear to be both inevitable and modest…

The simplicity of this is, however, misleading. In the first place, the failure of UN enforcement machinery has not been occasional but endemic, and so, concomitantly, has the resort to 'self-defense.' Equally important, since there is usually no way for the international system to establish conclusively which state is the aggressor and which the aggrieved, wars continue to occur, as they have since time immemorial, between parties both of which are using force allegedly in 'self-defense.'

The outright lie about who attacked first is not, however, the only or, probably, the principal problem. The most significant factor in complicating the 'simple' right of self-defense accorded by Article 51, rather, has been the changing nature of warfare itself.…Modern warfare…has inconveniently by-passed Queensberry-like practices. It tends, instead, to proceed along two radically different lines, one too small and the other too large to be encompassed effectively by Article 51. These two categories are, first, wars of agitation, infiltration and subversion carried on by proxy through national liberation movements; and, second, nuclear wars involving the instantaneous use, in a first strike, of weapons of near-paralyzing destructiveness.

Ambiguities and complexities thus lurk behind the misleadingly simple rule in Article 2(4) prohibiting the use of force in international relations and in the carefully delimited exceptions to that rule. Changing circumstances of international relations, of the way nations perceive their self-interest, of strategy and tactics, have combined to take advantage of these latent ambiguities, enlarging the exceptions to the point of virtually repealing the rule itself.

A particularly significant part in this development has been played by regional organizations. Articles 52 and 53 of the Charter have been interpreted to legitimate the use of force by regional organizations in their collective self-interest, and, specifically, the role and primacy of regional organizations in settling disputes between their members. These exceptions to Article 2(4) and their application in practice have played an important, perhaps the most important, role in the growth of international violence over these past twenty-five years…

The prohibition against the use of force in relations between states has been eroded beyond recognition, principally by three factors: 1, the rise of wars of 'national liberation'; 2, the rising threat of wars of total destruction; 3, the increasing authoritarianism of regional systems dominated by a super-Power. These three factors may, however, be traced back to a single circumstance: the lack of congruence between the international legal norm of Article 2(4) and the perceived national interest of states, especially the super-Powers.

L. Henkin, 'The Reports of the Death of Article 2(4) are Greatly Exaggerated'

65 American Journal of International Law 544 (1971)

It is difficult to quarrel with Dr Franck's diagnosis of the ills of the Charter….Distracted and distraught by these ills, one can indeed fall into the conclusion that Article 2(4) is virtually dead, but that, I believe, would mistake the lives and the ways of the law.

My principal difference with Dr Franck's diagnosis is that it judges the vitality of the law by looking only at its failures. The purpose of Article 2(4) was to establish a norm of national behavior and to help deter violation of it. Despite common misimpressions, Article 2(4) has indeed been a norm of behavior and has deterred violations. In inter-state as in individual penology, deterrence often cannot be measured or even proved, but students of politics agree that traditional war between nations has become less frequent and less likely. The sense that war is not done has taken hold, and nations more readily find that their interests do not in fact require the use of force after all….Even where force is used, the fact that it is unlawful cannot be left out of account and limits the scope, the weapons, the duration, the purposes for which force is used….

Many will refuse credit to Article 2(4), attributing the lack of traditional war to other factors—to nuclear weapons and the changing character of war, to greater territorial stability, to other changes in national interests reducing national temptation to use force. If it were so, Article 2(4) would not be the less a norm: law often reflects dispositions to behavior as much as it shapes them….The occasions and the causes of war remain. What has become obsolete is the notion that nations are as free to indulge it as ever, and the death of that notion is accepted in the Charter….

The fissures of the Charter are worrisome but they, too, are not as wide in international life as they loom in academic imagination. Pre-emptive war as 'anticipatory self-defense' has been hypothesized by many professors but asserted by few governments:…A few nations have falsely claimed self-defense against actual attack, but there are effective limits to unwarranted claims, in what nations dare assert and what others will believe…

The regional loophole, too, is not as wide as might seem, dangerous but not fatal. There have been few instances of groups claiming the right to do together what the Charter forbids them singly, and little reason to expect that it will happen frequently in future…

Dr Franck's dramatic title makes its point, and his cry of alarm is warranted and necessary. But one must not allow it to be seized by the 'super-realists' to prove that the effort to control international violence by law has again failed and the Charter is now as irrelevant as the Kellogg-Briand Pact. For me, if Article 2(4) were indeed dead, I should have to conclude that it rules—not mocks—us from the grave. In fact, despite common misimpressions (from which it suffers in common with other international law) Article 2(4) lives and can live. No government, no responsible official of government, has been prepared or has wished to pronounce it dead. Article 2(4) was written by practical men who knew all about national interest. They believed the norms they legislated to be in their nations' interest, and nothing that has happened in the past twenty-five years suggests that it is not. There is reason to pray and strive for the change in individual and national perceptions which Dr Franck invokes, but the need is not to condemn Article 2(4) to death and pray for its resurrection in the end of days when men and nations will not learn war any more. The need is for citizens, policy-makers, national societies, transnational and international bodies to be reminded that this law is indeed in the national interest of all nations; that a decision to initiate force always involves a preference for one national interest over another; that in the cost-accounting of national interest a decision to go to war grossly depreciates the tangible cost to the citizen—in life, in welfare, in aspiration—and usually prefers the immediate and short-sighted to the longer, deeper national interest.

T. Franck, 'What Happens Now? The United Nations after Iraq'

97 *American Journal of International Law* 607 (2003)

I. WHO KILLED ARTICLE 2(4) AGAIN?

Thirty-three years ago I published an article…entitled Who Killed Article 2(4)?…, which examined the phenomenon of increasingly frequent resort to unlawful force by Britain, France, India, North Korea, the Soviet Union, and the United States. The essay concluded with this sad observation: 'The failure of the U.N. Charter's normative system is tantamount to the inability of any rule, such as that set out in Article 2(4), in itself to have much control over the behavior of states. National self-interest, particularly the national self-interest of the super-Powers, has usually won out over treaty obligations. This is particularly characteristic of this age of pragmatic power politics. It is as if international law, always something of a cultural myth, has been demythologized. It seems this is not an age when men act by principles simply because that is what gentlemen ought to do. But living by power alone…is a nerve-wracking and costly business.'

The recent recourse to force in Iraq recalls this observation, which again seems all too apt. All that has changed is that we now have on offer proposed models for interstatal relations that seem even worse than the dilapidated system to which, by 1970, state misbehavior had reduced the postwar world. That once shiny new postwar system, embodied in the United Nations Charter, had been based on the assumption of states' reciprocal respect for law as their sturdy shield against the prospect of mutual assured destruction in an uncharted nuclear era. The 1970 essay regretted the loss of that vision in a miasma of so-called realpolitik. Should international lawyers guard their faith in such circumstances? Or should we cut our coats according to the cloth? *Si non possis quod velis, velis id quod possis*. Perhaps.

But, then, for one dazzling moment in the 1990s, the end of the Cold War seemed to revive faith in the Charter system, almost giving it a rebirth. Now, however, in the new millennium, after a decade's romance with something approximating law-abiding state behavior, the law-based system is once again being dismantled. In its place we are offered a model that makes global security wholly dependent on the supreme power and discretion of the United States and frees the sole superpower from all restraints of international law and the encumbrances of institutionalized multilateral diplomacy.

There is one major difference, however, between then and now. The unlawful recourses to force, during the period surveyed in the 1970 essay, were accompanied by a fig leaf of legal justification, which, at least tacitly, recognized the residual force of the requirement in Charter Article 2(4) that states 'refrain in their international relations from the threat or use of force against the territorial integrity or political independence of any state'. Then, the aggressors habitually defended the legality of their recourse to force by asserting that their actions, taken in response to an alleged prior attack or provocation, were exercises of the right of self-defense under the terms of Charter Article 51. Now, however, in marked contrast, they have all but discarded the fig leaf. While a few government lawyers still go through the motions of asserting that the invasion of Iraq was justified by our inherent right of self-defense, or represented a collective measure authorized by the Security Council under Chapter VII of the Charter, the leaders of America no longer much bother with such legal niceties. Instead, they boldly proclaim a new policy that openly repudiates the Article 2(4) obligation. What is remarkable, this time around, is that once-obligatory efforts by the aggressor to make a serious effort to stretch law to legitimate state action have given way to a drive to repeal law altogether, replacing it with a principle derived from the Athenians at Melos: 'the strong do what they can and the weak suffer what they must'.

Military and Paramilitary Activities in and against Nicaragua Case (Nicaragua v USA)

Merits, ICJ Rep 1986 14, International Court of Justice

Nicaragua alleged that the United States was responsible for certain military operations in Nicaraguan territory that were directed at the legitimate government. These included the mining of Nicaraguan ports and support for the *Contra* rebels. These actions were said to violate Article 2(4) of the Charter and customary international law. The Court determined that it lacked jurisdiction to try issues based on the Charter because the United States had legitimately refused consent to the Court having jurisdiction in cases concerning multilateral treaties (see Chapter 16). However, the Court did have jurisdiction over questions of customary law (see Chapter 2), and so it was crucial to determine whether the prohibition of Article 2(4) had passed in to customary law.

188. The Court thus finds that both Parties take the view that the principles as to the use of force incorporated in the United Nations Charter correspond, in essentials, to those found in customary international law. The Parties thus both take the view that the fundamental principle in this area is expressed in the terms employed in Article 2, paragraph 4, of the United Nations Charter.…The Court has however to be satisfied that there exists in customary international law an *opinio juris* as to the binding character of such abstention. This *opinio juris* may, though with all due caution, be deduced from, *inter alia*, the attitude of the Parties and the attitude of States towards certain General Assembly resolutions, and particularly resolution 2625 (XXV) entitled 'Declaration on Principles of International Law concerning Friendly Relations and Co-operation among States in accordance with the Charter of the United Nations'…

190. A further confirmation of the validity as customary international law of the principle of the prohibition of the use of force expressed in Article 2, paragraph 4, of the Charter of the United Nations may be found in the fact that it is frequently referred to in statements by State representatives as being not only a principle of customary international law but also a fundamental or cardinal principle of such law…

JUDGE SETTE-CAMARA (Separate Opinion): I firmly believe that the non-use of force as well as non-intervention—the latter as a corollary of equality of States and self-determination—are not only cardinal principles of customary international law but could in addition be recognized as peremptory rules of customary international law which impose obligations on all States.

JUDGE JENNINGS (Dissenting Opinion): There is no doubt that there was, prior to the United Nations Charter, a customary law which restricted the lawful use of force, and which correspondingly provided also for a right to use force in self-defence; as indeed the use of the term 'inherent' in Article 51 of the United Nations Charter suggests. The proposition, however, that, after the Charter, there exists alongside those Charter provisions on force and self-defence, an independent customary law that can be applied as alternative to Articles 2, paragraph 4, and 51 of the Charter, raises questions about how and when this correspondence came about, and about what the differences, if any, between customary law and the Charter provisions, may be.…It could hardly be contended that these provisions of the Charter were merely a codification of the existing customary law. The literature is replete with statements that Article 2, paragraph 4,—for example in speaking of 'force' rather than war, and providing that even a 'threat of force' may be unlawful—represented an important innovation in the law.…Even Article 51, though referring to an 'inherent' and therefore supposedly pre-existing, right of self-defence, introduced a novel concept in speaking of 'collective self-defence'…

If, then, the Charter was not a codification of existing custom about force and self-defence, the question must then be asked whether a general customary law, replicating the Charter provisions, has developed as a result of the influence of the Charter provisions, coupled presumably with subsequent and consonant States' practice… But there are obvious difficulties about extracting even a scintilla of relevant 'practice' on these matters from the behaviour of those few States which are not parties to the Charter; and the behaviour of all the rest, and the *opinio juris* which it might otherwise evidence, is surely explained by their being bound by the Charter itself…

That the Court has not wholly succeeded in escaping from the Charter and other multilateral treaties, is evident from even a casual perusal of the Judgment; the Court has in the event found it impossible to avoid what is in effect a consideration of treaty provisions as such. As the Court puts it, the Court 'can and must take them [the multilateral treaties] into account in determining the content of the customary law which the United States is also alleged to have infringed' (para. 183).

This use of treaty provisions as 'evidence' of custom, takes the form of an interpretation of the treaty text. Yet the Court itself acknowledges that treaty-law and customary law can be distinguished precisely because the canons of interpretation are different (para. 178). To indulge the treaty interpretation process, in order to determine the content of a posited customary rule, must raise a suspicion that it is in reality the treaty itself that is being applied under another name. Of course this way of going about things may be justified where the treaty text was, from the beginning, designed to be a codification of custom; or where the treaty is itself the origin of a customary law rule. But, as we have already seen, this could certainly not be said of Article 2, paragraph 4, or even Article 51, of the United Nations Charter; nor indeed of most of the other relevant multilateral treaty provisions.

The reader cannot but put to himself the question whether the Judgment would, in its main substance, have been noticeably different in its content and argument, had the application of the multilateral treaty reservation been rejected.

NOTES

1. The paramount obligation not to resort to force, as found in Article 2(4) and in customary international law, can now be regarded as a rule of *jus cogens* (see Chapters 2 and 3). Its importance is illustrated by the number of times it is recited in resolutions of the General Assembly and Security

Council. This obligation has real legal content, which means that States that resort to force face two barriers. First, they are faced with a legal presumption that their conduct is illegal, so it is up to the State resorting to force to prove the legitimacy of its actions. Second, if a State's conduct can be described as 'unlawful' rather than merely immoral or 'dangerous', it may suffer action by the Security Council or, as is more likely, from the negative response of other States. This can be a powerful sanction in the world of realpolitik, as with the isolation and subsequent subjugation of Iraq after its invasion of Kuwait and the international isolation of Yugoslavia (Serbia and Montenegro) following the Bosnia and Kosovo incidents. The general rejection of the use of force by the international community, even when that is not expressed by formal condemnation or sanctions, can have far-reaching reciprocal consequences.

2. In the *Nicaragua Case* the ICJ had to decide the merits according to customary international law due to a limitation on its jurisdiction (see Chapters 2 and 16). Undoubtedly, this confirms the continuing validity of customary international law principles, although a majority of the Court did not agree that these principles granted wider freedom of action than the UN Charter. In fact, the majority decision is premised on the assumption that the law of the Charter and customary international law have coincided in all material respects.

3. Article 2(4) does not permit the recovery of disputed territory, as all such disputes should be settled by peaceful means (see Article 2(3) of the Charter and Chapters 7 and 16). Where an unlawful use of force has been alleged in relation to disputed territory, which has subsequently been determined to form part of the territory of another State, the aggressor State is under an obligation to withdraw expeditiously and without condition all its forces from the disputed territory: see *Case Concerning the Land and Maritime Boundary between Cameroon and Nigeria* (*Cameroon v Nigeria; Equatorial Guinea intervening*) ICJ Rep 2002 303, para. 314).

4. The classification of a conflict is often significant; international conflicts are subject to international law rules of the use of force, whereas internal conflicts are not. Principles on the use of force should also be distinguished from international humanitarian law, which regulates the conduct of hostilities (see Chapter 14). It is also often necessary to distinguish between the use of force and other lawful enforcement activities. For example, the Permanent Court of Arbitration had to determine whether an intimidating approach by two naval vessels of Suriname to an oil-drilling rig, licensed by Guyana and undertaking exploratory drilling activity on the disputed continental shelf between Suriname and Guyana, was 'a reasonable and proportionate law enforcement' measure or a threat of military action. While the Tribunal recognised that force could be used in law enforcement activities, the action in question was 'more akin to a threat of military action' and 'therefore constituted a threat of the use of force in contravention of the [Law of the Sea] Convention, the UN Charter and general international law: *Guyana v Suriname*, Arbitral Award, 17 September 2007, para. 445.

B: Individual self-defence

The Caroline Case

(1837) 29 Brit & For St Papers

The *Caroline* was an American ship being used by Canadian rebels to harass the British colonial administration in Canada in 1837. While it was moored in an American port close to the border, it was attacked by the British military and destroyed. The legality of the action was raised when Britain sought the release of one of the men involved in the attack. The letter to the British authorities by American Secretary of State Daniel Webster is regarded as the *locus classicus* of customary self-defence.

Washington, April 24, 1841

The Undersigned has now to signify to Mr Fox [the British representative in America] that the Government of The United States has not changed the opinion which it has heretofore expressed to Her Majesty's Government of the character of the act of destroying the *Caroline*.

It does not think that that transaction can be justified by any reasonable application or construction of the right of self-defence, under the laws of nations. It is admitted that a just right of self-defence attaches always to nations as well as to individuals, and is equally necessary for the preservation of both. But the extent of this right is a question to be judged of by the circumstances of each particular case, and when its alleged exercise has led to the commission of hostile acts within the territory of a Power at peace, nothing less than a clear and absolute necessity can afford ground of justification…

Under these circumstances, and under those immediately connected with the transaction itself, it will be for Her Majesty's Government to show upon what state of facts, and what rules of national law, the destruction of the *Caroline* is to be defended. It will be for that Government to show a necessity of self-defence, instant, overwhelming, leaving no choice of means, and no moment for deliberation. It will be for it to show, also, that the local authorities of Canada, even supposing the necessity of the moment authorized them to enter the territories of The United States at all, did nothing unreasonable or excessive; since the act, justified by the necessity of self-defence, must be limited by that necessity, and kept clearly within it.

J. de Arechega, 'General Course in Public International Law'
159 *Receuil des Cours* 9 (1978)

A strict interpretation of Article 51 of the Charter is attacked from two sides: by those who contend that underlying this provision there is a broad right of self-defence resulting from customary law which has not been limited by the Charter and, on the other side, by those who claim that whatever the terms of Article 51 may be, a legitimate exercise of self-defence arises in support of the right of self-determination.

The combined effect of Article 2(4) and Article 51 of the Charter is that the individual use of force by States is prohibited unless a State is exercising 'the inherent right of individual or collective self-defence if an armed attack occurs'. The Charter incorporates in Article 51, as an essential condition for the existence of the inherent right of self-defence, the precise and restrictive notion of 'armed attack', in French 'une agression armée'. The Charter does not refer to 'use or threat of force' as in Article 2(4) nor to 'a threat to the peace, breach of the peace or act of aggression' as in Article 39. The authorization to use force in self-defence is limited by an 'if' clause, by a condition of fact 'which is comparatively clear, objective, easy to prove, difficult to misinterpret or fabricate'…

It has been contended however that Article 51 does not 'cut down the customary right (of self-defence) and make it applicable only to the case of resistance to armed attack by another State'.

The arguments in support of this view are that the right of self-defence does not have its source in the Charter, but is an independent right rooted in general international law, and the purpose of Article 51 was simply to remove possible doubts as to the impact of the Security Council's powers upon the right of States individually and collectively to have recourse to force in self-defence. The *travaux préparatoires* show that Article 51 was introduced for the purpose of harmonising regional organizations for defence with the powers and responsibilities given to the Security Council.

These arguments do not seem convincing nor in accordance with the canons of treaty interpretation agreed at the Vienna Conference on the Law of Treaties. Whatever may have been the reasons which inspired the proposal to include Article 51 in the Charter, the fact remains that this provision was inserted and that the crucial reference to an 'armed attack' is contained in it.…

In support of the idea that the Charter preserved a supposed pre-existing customary law of self-defence, the argument is made that the qualification of self-defence as an inherent right…in Article 51 cannot have any other meaning than referring back to general international law or to a general principle of law.

It does not appear possible, however, to attribute to this adjective the effect of annulling the substantive meaning of the whole text of Article 51.

The so-called customary law of self-defence supposedly pre-existing the Charter, and dependent on this single word, simply did not exist. Before 1945 self-defence was not a legal concept but merely a political excuse for the use of force. For the concept of legitimate defence to come into existence, it is necessary that a corresponding notion of illegitimate use of force already exists.…

It is only with the United Nations Charter that the prohibition of force and consequently the legitimacy of self-defence have become established as symmetrical legal concepts. It follows that to exercise self-defence legitimately, a State must comply with all the requirements established in Article 51 of the Charter and not with some loose conditions mentioned in a diplomatic incident between the United States and the United Kingdom some 140 years ago, as was the case of the *Caroline*.…

The only aspect of general international law which is relevant in the application of Article 51 is the general principle of law that the defensive action must be commensurate with and in proportion to the armed attack which gave rise to the exercise of the right of self-defence. The object of self-defence is precisely to put an end to the armed attack: it would not be permissible for a State, in the course of its defence, to seize and keep the resources and territory of the attacker.

The Charter requirement that a prior armed attack should occur before the right of self-defence arises does not mean that it is necessary to wait for the armed attack to strike in order lawfully to use force in self-defence. It is sufficient that the armed attack has been launched....

Military and Paramilitary Activities in and against Nicaragua Case (*Nicaragua* v *USA*)

Merits, ICJ Rep 1986 14, International Court of Justice

The facts are set out in Section 1A.

193. The general rule prohibiting force allows for certain exceptions. In view of the arguments advanced by the United States to justify the acts of which it is accused by Nicaragua, the Court must express a view on the content of the right of self-defence, and more particularly the right of collective self-defence. First, with regard to the existence of this right, it notes that in the language of Article 51 of the United Nations Charter, the inherent right (or 'droit natural') which any State possesses in the event of an armed attack, covers both collective and individual self-defence. Thus, the Charter itself testifies to the existence of the right of collective self-defence in customary international law...

194. ...In view of the circumstances in which the dispute has arisen, reliance is placed by the Parties only on the right of self-defence in the case of an armed attack which has already occurred, and the issue of the lawfulness of a response to the imminent threat of armed attack has not been raised. Accordingly the Court expresses no view on that issue. The Parties also agree in holding that whether the response to the attack is lawful depends on observance of the criteria of the necessity and the proportionality of the measures taken in self-defence. Since the existence of the right of collective self-defence is established in customary international law, the Court must define the specific conditions which may have to be met for its exercise, in addition to the conditions of necessity and proportionality to which the Parties have referred.

195. In the case of individual self-defence, the exercise of this right is subject to the State concerned having been the victim of an armed attack. Reliance on collective self-defence of course does not remove the need for this. There appears now to be general agreement on the nature of the acts which can be treated as constituting armed attacks. In particular, it may be considered to be agreed that an armed attack must be understood as including not merely action by regular armed forces across an international border, but also 'the sending by or on behalf of a State of armed bands, groups, irregulars or mercenaries, which carry out acts of armed force against another State of such gravity as to amount to' (*inter alia*) an actual armed attack conducted by regular forces, 'or its substantial involvement therein'. This description, contained in Article 3, paragraph (g), of the Definition of Aggression annexed to General Assembly resolution 3314 (XXIX), may be taken to reflect customary international law. The Court sees no reason to deny that, in customary law, the prohibition of armed attacks may apply to the sending by a State of armed bands to the territory of another State, if such an operation, because of its scale and effects, would have been classified as an armed attack rather than as a mere frontier incident had it been carried out by regular armed forces. But the Court does not believe that the concept of 'armed attack' includes not only acts by armed bands where such acts occur on a significant scale but also assistance to rebels in the form of the provision of weapons or logistical or other support. Such assistance may be regarded as a threat or use of force, or amount to intervention in the internal or external affairs of other States.

JUDGE JENNINGS (Dissenting Opinion): The question of what constitutes 'armed attack' for the purposes of Article 51, and its relation to the definition of aggression, are large and controversial questions in which it would be inappropriate to become involved in this opinion. It is of course a fact that collective self-defence is a concept that lends itself to abuse. One must therefore sympathize with the anxiety of the Court to define it in terms of some strictness (though it is a little surprising that the Court does not at all consider the problems of the quite different French text: 'où un Membre... est l'objet d'une agression armée'). There is a question, however, whether the Court has perhaps gone too far in this direction.

The Court (para. 195) allows that, where a State is involved with the organization of 'armed bands' operating in the territory of another State, this, 'because of its scale and effects', could amount to 'armed attack' under Article 51; but that this does not extend to 'assistance to rebels in the form of the provision of weapons or logistical or other support' (*ibid.*). Such conduct, the Court goes on to say, may not amount to an armed attack; but 'may be regarded as a threat or use of force, or amount to intervention in the internal or external affairs of other States' (*ibid.*).

It may readily be agreed that the mere provision of arms cannot be said to amount to an armed attack. But the provision of arms may, nevertheless, be a very important element in what might be thought to amount to armed attack, where it is coupled with other kinds of involvement. Accordingly, it seems to me that to say that the provision of arms, coupled with 'logistical or other support' is not armed attack is going much too far. Logistical support may itself be crucial.…If there is added to all this 'other support', it becomes difficult to understand what it is, short of direct attack by a State's own forces, that may not be done apparently without a lawful response in the form of collective self-defence; nor indeed may be responded to at all by the use of force or threat of force, for, to cite the Court again, 'States do not have a right of "collective" armed response to acts which do not constitute an "armed attack"'…

This looks to me neither realistic nor just in the world where power struggles are in every continent carried on by destabilization, interference in civil strife, comfort, aid and encouragement to rebels, and the like. The original scheme of the United Nations Charter, whereby force would be deployed by the United Nations itself, in accordance with the provisions of Chapter VII of the Charter, has never come into effect. Therefore an essential element in the Charter design is totally missing. In this situation it seems dangerous to define unnecessarily strictly the conditions for lawful self-defence so as to leave a large area where both a forcible response to force is forbidden, and yet the United Nations employment of force, which was intended to fill that gap, is absent.

Oil Platforms (*Islamic Republic of Iran* v *United States of America*)
Merits, ICJ Rep 2003 161, International Court of Justice

Iran instituted proceedings against the United States following the destruction by US naval forces of commercial oil platforms owned by Iran. Iran alleged that the attacks on the platforms were in contravention of both a bilateral treaty between the two States and customary international law, while the US argued it was acting in self-defence in response to an attack against a US-flagged commercial vessel (the *Sea Isle City*) it alleged was attributable to Iran.

[I]n order to establish that it was legally justified in attacking the Iranian platforms in exercise of the right of individual self-defence, the United States has to show that attacks had been made upon it for which Iran was responsible; and that those attacks were of such a nature as to be qualified as "armed attacks" within the meaning of that expression in Article 51 of the United Nations Charter, and as understood in customary law on the use of force.…The United States must also show that its actions were necessary and proportional to the armed attack made on it, and that the platforms were a legitimate military target open to attack in the exercise of self-defence…

57. For present purposes [in regard to the missile strike on the *Sea Isle City*], the Court has simply to determine whether the United States has demonstrated that it was the victim of an 'armed attack' by Iran such as to justify it using armed force in self-defence; and the burden of proof of the facts showing the existence of such an attack rests on the United States. The Court does not have to attribute responsibility for firing the missile that struck the *Sea Isle City*, on the basis of a balance of evidence, either to Iran or to Iraq; if at the end of the day the evidence available is insufficient to establish that the missile was fired by Iran, then the necessary burden of proof has not been discharged by the United States.

61. In short, the Court has examined with great care the evidence and arguments presented on each side, and finds that the evidence indicative of Iranian responsibility for the attack on the *Sea Isle City* is not sufficient to support the contentions of the United States. The conclusion to which the Court has come on this aspect of the case is thus that the burden of proof of the existence of an armed attack by Iran on the United States, in the form of the missile attack on the *Sea Isle City*, has not been discharged.

62. In its notification to the Security Council, and before the Court, the United States has however not relied solely on the *Sea Isle City* incident as constituting the "armed attack" to which the United States claimed to be responding. It asserted that that incident was 'the latest in a series of such missile attacks against United States flag and other nonbelligerent vessels in Kuwaiti waters in pursuit of peaceful commerce' and that 'These actions are, moreover, only the latest in a series of unlawful armed attacks by Iranian forces against the United States, including laying mines in international waters for the purpose of sinking or damaging United States flag ships, and firing on United States aircraft without provocation'.…Before the Court, it has contended that the missile attack on the *Sea Isle City* was itself an armed attack giving rise to the right of self-defence; the alleged pattern of Iranian use of force, it is said, 'added to the gravity of the specific attacks, reinforced the necessity of action in self-defense, and helped to shape the appropriate response'.…

64. On the hypothesis that all the incidents complained of are to be attributed to Iran, and thus setting aside the question, examined above, of attribution to Iran of the specific attack on the *Sea Isle City*, the question is whether that attack, either in itself or in combination with the rest of the 'series of … attacks' cited by the United States can be categorized as an 'armed attack' on the United States justifying self-defence. The Court notes first that the *Sea Isle City* was in Kuwaiti waters at the time of the attack on it, and that a Silkworm missile fired from (it is alleged) more than 100 km away could not have been aimed at the specific vessel, but simply programmed to hit some target in Kuwaiti waters. Secondly, the *Texaco Caribbean*, whatever its ownership, was not flying a United States flag, so that an attack on the vessel is not in itself to be equated with an attack on that State. As regards the alleged firing on United States helicopters from Iranian gunboats and from the Reshadat oil platform, no persuasive evidence has been supplied to support this allegation. There is no evidence that the mine-laying alleged to have been carried out by [the Iranian vessel] the *Iran Ajr*, at a time when Iran was at war with Iraq, was aimed specifically at the United States; and similarly it has not been established that the mine struck by the *Bridgeton* was laid with the specific intention of harming that ship, or other United States vessels. Even taken cumulatively, and reserving, as already noted, the question of Iranian responsibility, these incidents do not seem to the Court to constitute an armed attack on the United States, of the kind that the Court, in the case *concerning Military and Paramilitary Activities in and against Nicaragua*, qualified as a 'most grave' form of the use of force …

68. The Court notes that the attacks on the Salman and Nasr platforms were not an isolated operation, aimed simply at the oil installations, as had been the case with the attacks of 19 October 1987; they formed part of a much more extensive military action, designated 'Operation Praying Mantis', conducted by the United States against what it regarded as 'legitimate military targets'; armed force was used, and damage done to a number of targets, including the destruction of two Iranian frigates and other Iranian naval vessels and aircraft …

72. The Court notes further that, as on the occasion of the earlier attack on oil platforms, the United States in its communication to the Security Council claimed to have been exercising the right of self-defence in response to the 'attack' on the USS *Samuel B. Roberts*, linking it also with 'a series of offensive attacks and provocations Iranian naval forces have taken against neutral shipping in the international waters of the Persian Gulf' (paragraph 67 above). Before the Court, it has contended, as in the case of the missile attack on the *Sea Isle City*, that the mining was itself an armed attack giving rise to the right of self-defence and that the alleged pattern of Iranian use of force 'added to the gravity of the specific attacks, reinforced the necessity of action in self-defense, and helped to shape the appropriate response' (see paragraph 62 above). No attacks on United States-flagged vessels (as distinct from United States-owned vessels), additional to those cited as justification for the earlier attacks on the Reshadat platforms, have been brought to the Court's attention, other than the mining of the USS *Samuel B. Roberts* itself. The question is therefore whether that incident sufficed in itself to justify action in self-defence, as amounting to an 'armed attack'. The Court does not exclude the possibility that the mining of a single military vessel might be sufficient to bring into play the 'inherent right of self-defence'; but in view of all the circumstances, including the inconclusiveness of the evidence of Iran's responsibility for the mining of the USS *Samuel B. Roberts*, the Court is unable to hold that the attacks on the Salman and Nasr platforms have been shown to have been justifiably made in response to an 'armed attack' on the United States by Iran, in the form of the mining of the USS *Samuel B. Roberts*.

76. The Court is not sufficiently convinced that the evidence available supports the contentions of the United States as to the significance of the military presence and activity on the Reshadat oil platforms; and it notes that no such evidence is offered in respect of the Salman and Nasr complexes. However, even accepting those contentions, for the purposes of discussion, the Court is unable to hold that the attacks made on the platforms could have been justified as acts of self-defence. The conditions for the exercise of the right of self-defence are well settled: as the Court observed in its *Advisory Opinion on Legality of the Threat or Use of Nuclear Weapons*, 'the submission of the exercise of the right of self-defence to the conditions of necessity and proportionality is a rule of customary international law' (I.C.J Reports 1996 (1), p. 245, para 41); and in the *case concerning Military and Paramilitary Activities in and against Nicaragua*, the Court referred to a specific rule 'whereby self-defence would warrant only measures which are proportional to the armed attack and necessary to respond to it' as 'a rule well established in customary international law' (I.C.J. Reports 1986, p. 94, para 176). In the case both of the attack on the *Sea Isle City* and the mining of the USS *Samuel B. Roberts*, the Court is not satisfied that the attacks on the platforms were necessary to respond to these incidents. In this connection, the Court notes that there is no evidence that the United States complained to Iran of the military activities of the platforms, in the same way as it complained repeatedly of mine-laying and attacks on neutral shipping, which does not suggest that the targeting of the platforms was seen as a necessary act. …

77. As to the requirement of proportionality, the attack of 19 October 1987 might, had the Court found that it was necessary in response to the *Sea Isle City* incident as an armed attack committed by Iran, have been considered proportionate. In the case of the attacks of 18 April 1988, however, they were conceived and executed as part of

a more extensive operation entitled "Operation Praying Mantis" (see paragraph 68 above). The question of the lawfulness of other aspects of that operation is not before the Court, since it is solely the action against the Salman and Nasr complexes that is presented as a breach of the 1955 Treaty; but the Court cannot assess in isolation the proportionality of that action to the attack to which it was said to be a response; it cannot close its eyes to the scale of the whole operation, which involved, *inter alia*, the destruction of two Iranian frigates and a number of other naval vessels and aircraft. As a response to the mining, by an unidentified agency, of a single United States warship, which was severely damaged but not sunk, and without loss of life, neither 'Operation Praying Mantis' as a whole, nor even that part of it that destroyed the Salman and Nasr platforms, can be regarded, in the circumstances of this case, as a proportionate use of force in self-defence.

78. The Court thus concludes from the foregoing that the actions carried out by United States forces against Iranian oil installations on 19 October 1987 and 18 April 1988 cannot be justified, … since those actions constituted recourse to armed force not qualifying, under international law on the question, as acts of self-defence.

Armed Activities on the Territory of the Congo (Democratic Republic of the Congo v Uganda)
Merits, ICJ Rep 2005 168, International Court of Justice

The Democratic Republic of the Congo (DRC) alleged that Uganda bore international responsibility for acts of armed aggression perpetrated on the territory of the DRC, including by supporting rebel movements or 'irregular forces' operating within the DRC. Uganda contended that its military presence within the DRC ('Operation Safe Haven') was necessary in order to defend itself against transborder attacks emanating from DRC territory.

143. The Court recalls that Uganda has insisted in this case that operation "Safe Haven" was not a use of force against an anticipated attack. As was the case also in the *Military and Paramilitary Activities in and against Nicaragua (Nicaragua v. United States of America)* case, 'reliance is placed by the Parties only on the right of self-defence in the case of an armed attack which has already occurred, and the issue of the lawfulness of a response to the imminent threat of armed attack has not been raised' (*I.C.J. Reports 1986*, p. 103, para 194). The Court there found that '[a]ccordingly [it] expresses no view on that issue'. So it is in the present case. The Court feels constrained, however, to observe that the wording of the Ugandan High Command document on the position regarding the presence of the UPDF in the DRC makes no reference whatever to armed attacks that have already occurred against Uganda at the hands of the DRC (or indeed by persons for whose action the DRC is claimed to be responsible). Rather, the position of the High Command is that it is necessary 'to secure Uganda's legitimate security interests'. The specified security needs are essentially preventative to ensure that the political vacuum does not adversely affect Uganda, to prevent attacks from "genocidal elements", to be in a position to safeguard Uganda from irresponsible threats of invasion, to 'deny the Sudan the opportunity to use the territory of the DRC to destabilize Uganda'. Only one of the five listed objectives refers to a response to acts that had already taken place: the neutralization of 'Uganda dissident groups which have been receiving assistance from the Government of the DRC and the Sudan'.

144. While relying heavily on this document, Uganda nonetheless insisted to the Court that after 11 September 1998 the Ugandan military force [UPDF] was acting in self-defence in response to attacks that had occurred. The Court has already found that the military operations of August in Beni, Bunia and Watsa, and of 1 September at Kisangani, cannot be classified as coming within the consent of the DRC, and their legality, too, must stand or fall by reference to self-defence as stated in Article 51 of the Charter.

145. The Court would first observe that in August and early September 1998 Uganda did not report to the Security Council events that it had regarded as requiring it to act in self-defence.

146. It is further to be noted that, while Uganda claimed to have acted in self-defence, it did not ever claim that it had been subjected to an armed attack by the armed forces of the DRC. The "armed attacks" to which reference was made came rather from the ADF [an insurgent group]. The Court has found above … that there is no satisfactory proof of the involvement in these attacks, direct or indirect, of the Government of the DRC. …

147. For all these reasons, the Court finds that the legal and factual circumstances for the exercise of a right of self-defence by Uganda against the DRC were not present. Accordingly, the Court has no need to respond to the contentions of the Parties as to whether and under what conditions contemporary international law provides for a right of self-defence against large-scale attacks by irregular forces. Equally, since the preconditions for the exercise

of self-defence do not exist in the circumstances of the present case, the Court has no need to enquire whether such an entitlement to self-defence was in fact exercised in circumstances of necessity and in a manner that was proportionate. The Court cannot fail to observe, however, that the taking of airports and towns many hundreds of kilometres from Uganda's border would not seem proportionate to the series of transborder attacks it claimed had given rise to the right of self-defence, nor to be necessary to that end...

163. The Court considers that the obligations arising under the principles of non-use of force and non-intervention were violated by Uganda even if the objectives of Uganda were not to overthrow President Kabila, and were directed to securing towns and airports for reason of its perceived security needs, and in support of the parallel activity of those engaged in civil war. 164. In the case concerning *Military and Paramilitary Activities in and against Nicaragua (Nicaragua v. United States of America)* case, the Court made it clear that the principle of non-intervention prohibits a State 'to intervene, directly or indirectly, with or without armed force, in support of an internal opposition in another State' (*I.C.J. Reports 1986*, p. 108, para 206). The Court notes that in the present case it has been presented with probative evidence as to military intervention. The Court further affirms that acts which breach the principle of non-intervention 'will also, if they directly or indirectly involve the use of force, constitute a breach of the principle of non-use of force in international relations' (*ibid.*, pp. 109–110, para 209).165. In relation to the first of the DRC's final submissions, the Court accordingly concludes that Uganda has violated the sovereignty and also the territorial integrity of the DRC. Uganda's actions equally constituted an interference in the internal affairs of the DRC and in the civil war there raging. The unlawful military intervention by Uganda was of such a magnitude and duration that the Court considers it to be a grave violation of the prohibition on the use of force expressed in Article 2, paragraph 4, of the Charter.

The Federal Democratic Republic of Ethiopia v *The State of Eritrea* Partial Award, Jus Ad Bellum

45 *International Legal Materials* 430 (2006), Eritrea Ethiopia Claims Commission

Following the conflict between Ethiopia and Eritrea, claims were brought before the Permanent Court of Arbitration by both States in respect of violations of international law during the war and the questions of international responsibility which arose as a result. One issue was whether Eritrea had a valid claim to self-defence.

11. ....In general, recourse to the use of armed force by one State against another is unlawful unless it is used in self defense or occurs with the sanction of the Security Council pursuant to Chapter VII of the UN Charter. As the text of Article 51 of the Charter makes clear, the predicate for a valid claim of self-defense under the Charter is that the party resorting to force has been subjected to an armed attack. Localized border encounters between small infantry units, even those involving the loss of life, do not constitute an armed attack for purposes of the Charter. In that connection, the Commission notes that Eritrea did not report its use of armed force against Ethiopia on May 12, 1998 to the Security Council as measures taken in self-defense, as it would be obligated to do by Article 51 of the Charter in case of self-defense against armed attack.

12. With respect to the events in the vicinity of Badme that occurred during the period from May 6–12, 1998, the Commission takes note of the sharply different accounts offered by the Parties as to the precise location of the incidents of May 6 and 7 and of the numbers and types of forces involved. It need not resolve these differences, because it is clear from the evidence that these incidents involved geographically limited clashes between small Eritrean and Ethiopian patrols along a remote, unmarked, and disputed border. The Commission is satisfied that these relatively minor incidents were not of a magnitude to constitute an armed attack by either State against the other within the meaning of Article 51 of the UN Charter.

14. The evidence showed that, at about 5:30 a.m. on May 12, 1998, Eritrean armed forces, comprised of at least two brigades of regular soldiers, supported by tanks and artillery, attacked the town of Badme and several other border areas in Ethiopia's Tahtay Adiabo Wereda, as well as at least two places in its neighboring Laelay Adiabo Wereda. On that day and in the days immediately following, Eritrean armed forces then pushed across the flat Badme plain to higher ground in the east. Although the evidence regarding the nature of Ethiopian armed forces in the area conflicted, the weight of the evidence indicated that the Ethiopian defenders were composed merely of militia and some police, who were quickly forced to retreat by the invading Eritrean forces. Given the absence of an armed attack against Eritrea, the attack that began on May 12 cannot be justified as lawful self-defense under the UN Charter...

16. Consequently, the Commission holds that Eritrea violated Article 2, paragraph 4, of the Charter of the United Nations by resorting to armed force to attack and occupy Badme, then under peaceful administration by Ethiopia, as well as other territory in the Tahtay Adiabo and Laelay Adiabo Weredas of Ethiopia, in an attack that began on May 12, 1998, and is liable to compensate Ethiopia, for the damages caused by that violation of international law.

17. This leaves Eritrea's third line of argument, based on Ethiopia's alleged declaration of war. On May 13, 1998, the Ethiopian Council of Ministers and Parliament passed a resolution that condemned the May 12 invasion and demanded the unconditional and immediate withdrawal of Eritrean forces from Ethiopian territory. This resolution was not, as Eritrea has asserted, a declaration of war. In international law, the essence of a declaration of war is an explicit affirmation of the existence of a state of war between belligerents. Nevertheless, the resolution made clear that Ethiopia would not accept Eritrea's advances as a *fait accompli* and was determined to act in self-defense until the Eritrean forces withdrew or were compelled to leave the areas they had occupied. Ethiopia so notified the United Nations Security Council, pursuant to Article 51 of the UN Charter. Moreover, the Commission notes that the Parties subsequently maintained diplomatic relations and some economic relations, both of which would appear inconsistent with a formal declaration of war.

Tallinn Manual on the International Law Applicable to Cyber Warfare
(2013) CUP

RULE 10 - Prohibition of Threat or Use of Force
A cyber operation that constitutes a threat or use of force against the territorial integrity or political independence of any State, or that is in any other manner inconsistent with the purposes of the United Nations, is unlawful.

RULE 11 - Definition of Use of Force
A cyber operation constitutes a use of force when its scale and effects are comparable to non-cyber operations rising to the level of a use of force.

RULE 12 - Definition of Threat of Force
A cyber operation, or threatened cyber operation, constitutes an unlawful threat of force when the threatened action, if carried out, would be an unlawful use of force.

RULE 13 – Self-Defence Against Armed Attack
A State that is the target of a cyber operation that rises to the level of an armed attack may exercise its inherent right of self-defence. Whether a cyber operation constitutes an armed attack depends on its scale and effects.

RULE 14 - Necessity and Proportionality
A use of force involving cyber operations undertaken by a State in the exercise of its right of self-defence must be necessary and proportionate.

NOTES

1. There are two schools of thought as to the use of force: the 'restrictive' and the 'permissive' schools of interpretation. The critical question is the extent to which the 'permissive' school allows the use of force to settle disputes in the absence of a recognised exception. This debate between the two schools of thought on the law of the use of force is carried over to the dispute about the scope of the right of self-defence. If self-defence is the only exception to the general prohibition on the use of force apart from collective security, its precise ambit is crucial. The permissive doctrine does not consider that self-defence is available only where an 'armed attack' occurs—either because Article 51 was not intended to replace the customary international law (*The Caroline Case*), or because Article 51 preserves by its terms ('inherent') customary international law. The restrictive school sees Article 51 as the only, and narrowly interpreted exception, to a wide-ranging prohibition on the use of force. As can be seen in the extracts above, the International Court of Justice has adopted a quite narrow interpretation of the right of self-defence.

2. While all States agree that an armed attack gives rise to a right of self-defence, State practice and the relevant cases reveal a number of issues. For example, what constitutes an 'armed attack'? The classical situation is the invasion of a State's territory by the regular armed forces of another State, or an attack against emanations of the State, such as embassies and armed forces. However, many scenarios do not fall within this classical model. For example, in which circumstances will a cross-border attack by irregular forces constitute an armed attack? As the ICJ stated in the *Nicaragua Case*, such conduct can constitute an armed attack where the irregular forces are acting on behalf of the State. The

difficult issue is what extent and level of State involvement is required (see Chapter 11). The Court in the *DRC* v *Uganda Case* left unanswered the question whether there can be an armed attack giving rise to self-defence where the attack is perpetrated without the involvement of the State (but see the discussion on terrorism and the extracts from the *Wall Advisory Opinion* in Section 1C(a)).

3. The facts before the Court in the *Oil Platforms Case* raised another aspect of an 'armed attack': what types and number of acts constitute an armed attack? Could an attack on a single US naval vessel, US-owned or US-flagged vessel constitute an armed attack on the United States? The United States also relied on a series of incidents that it argued when viewed together constituted an armed attack, the so-called 'accumulation' approach to the definition of armed attack. While the Court did not have to decide directly on the validity of this approach (because it found that the acts in question were not attributable to Iran), the Court's discussion on this issue suggests that the Court may be willing to accept the accumulation of incidents in future cases. This may have implications for the approach to be adopted in relation to terrorist attacks (see Section 1C). Another issue is whether a non-forcible threat (for example, economic pressure or a cyber-attack on a State's IT infrastructure) might constitute an armed attack.

4. The ICJ in the *Nicaragua Case* confirmed that not all attacks will constitute an armed attack for the purpose of Article 51 of the UN Charter; only the most grave forms of attack would qualify. This gravity requirement was confirmed in the *Oil Platforms Case*, and it was a deciding factor in the decision of the Eritrea/Ethiopia Claims Commission, extracted above.

5. The use by States and non-State actors of cyber attacks in recent years has led to discussion as to the extent to which international law adequately governs this emerging area of practice. The *Tallinn Manual*, part of which is extracted above, was drafted by an independent international group of experts. While it is not a binding source of law, it reflects the views of some leading publicists and practitioners in this area. The experts concluded that existing international law frameworks do apply to cyber attacks, although it raises questions as to how to apply that law in practice. For example, when is a cyber attack a use of force? When does a cyber attack rise to the level of an armed attack? Can a series of attacks constitute an armed attack? The *Tallinn Manual* and its commentary provide considerable guidance on these issues. Cyber attacks also raise questions as to attribution of attacks to States and State responsibility (see further, Chapter 11).

6. Another issue raised is the timing of the use of force relative to the armed attack. Is it permissible to use force in response to a past armed attack or to an anticipated attack? Certain States (mainly the United States, United Kingdom and Israel) have asserted a broader right of anticipatory self-defence, such that the intended victim may anticipate the attack and take pre-emptive action. Such claims are generally justified by reference to the *Caroline Case* (see extract) and the notion of self-defence in response to an imminent attack. However, claims based on anticipatory self-defence have tended to be controversial, and were rarely made. This appears to be changing following the attacks against the World Trade Center in 2001, and the subsequent developments to address the threat of terrorism (see Section 1C).

7. Where an action is taken in self-defence, customary international law requires that the use of force be both necessary and proportional to the armed attack. This requirement is confirmed in the above extracts (and see *Legality of the Threat or Use of Nuclear Weapons*, Advisory Opinion, ICJ Rep 1996, paras 41–42). Several States raised concerns as to the proportionality of the use of force by Israel in response to attacks by terrorist groups in Lebanon in 2006 (see Section 1C(a)).

8. Article 51 obligates States to report any use of force in exercise of the right of self-defence to the Security Council. Will a failure to report render the action unlawful? In the *Nicaragua Case*, the Court held that the failure to report the use of force to the Security Council may be indicative that the State concerned did not consider itself to be acting in self-defence (para. 200, see Section 1D). The Court in the *DRC* v *Uganda Case* and the Eritrea/Ethiopia Claims Commission both noted the failure of Uganda and Eritrea respectively to report the action to the Council. As a general rule, though there are some exceptions, States should and do tend to report action taken in the exercise of the right of self-defence to the Council.

C: Self-defence and terrorist attacks

The law on self-defence—whatever its precise content—is designed principally to deal with State-on-State attacks. This was the experience of States at the time the Charter was drafted. Today States are subject to attack by non-State entities that may, or may not, have links with established States. This reality was highlighted by the attacks against the World Trade Center and other targets on 11 September 2001. This incident, and subsequent terrorist attacks and threats, have led to a re-evaluation of the principles governing the use of force in the terrorism context. Two areas in particular are significant. First, under what circumstances (if any) is the use of force against non-State actors lawful as an exercise of the right of self-defence? Second, to what extent (if any) can a State use force preventatively, that is in the absence of an actual or imminent armed attack, so as to pre-empt expected attacks in the future? These issues are considered in the following extracts.

(a) Self-defence and non-State actors

S. Murphy (ed), 'Contemporary Practice of the United States Relating to International Law'
96 *American Journal of International Law* 236 (2002)

The United States regarded the September 11 incidents as comparable to a military attack. In the week following the attacks, President Bush declared a national emergency and called to active duty the reserves of the US armed forces. He also signed into law a joint resolution of Congress that, after noting that 'the President has authority under the Constitution to take action to deter and prevent acts of international terrorism against the United States', provided in Section 2:

> (a) IN GENERAL. That the President is authorized to use all necessary and appropriate force against those nations, organizations, or persons he determines planned, authorized, committed, or aided the terrorist attacks that occurred on September 11, 2001, or harbored such organizations or persons, in order to prevent any future acts of international terrorism against the United States by such nations, organizations or persons.

Further, in a speech to the Congress on September 20, President Bush declared: 'On September 11th, enemies of freedom committed an act of war against our country.' The President created an Office of Homeland Security, as well as a Homeland Security Council, charged with developing and coordinating the implementation of a comprehensive national strategy to secure the United States from terrorist threats of attacks. The potential for further attacks was confirmed when, in late September, European law enforcement authorities uncovered a fully developed plan to blow up the U.S. Embassy in Paris. Intelligence reports of possible further attacks deemed credible by U.S. authorities led the Federal Bureau of Investigation (FBI) on October 11 and 29 to issue global alerts that more terrorist attacks might be carried out against U.S. targets in the United States or abroad...

The reaction of the global community was largely supportive. At the United Nations, the Security Council unanimously adopted on September 12 a resolution condemning 'the horrifying terrorist attacks', which the Council regarded, 'like any act of international terrorism, as a threat to international peace and security.' Further, on September 28, the Security Council unanimously adopted, under Chapter VII of the UN Charter, a U.S.-sponsored resolution that obligates all member states to deny financing, support, and safe haven to terrorists, that calls for expanded information-sharing among member states, and that establishes a Security Council committee for monitoring implementation of these measures on a continuous basis. While the two resolutions did not expressly authorize the use of force by the United States, they both affirmed—in the context of such incidents—the inherent right of individual and collective self-defense, as well as the need 'to combat by all means' the 'threats to international peace and security caused by terrorist acts.' By contrast, the General Assembly condemned the 'heinous acts of terrorism' but did not characterize those acts as 'attacks' or recognize a right to respond in self-defense. Instead, that body called for 'international cooperation to bring to justice the perpetrators, organizers and sponsors' of the incidents. The form of cooperation was not specified, but a variety of conventions are already in place that address cooperation among states in dealing with violent or terrorist offenses.

The North Atlantic Council of the North Atlantic Treaty Organization (NATO) decided on September 12 that, if it was determined that the incidents were directed from abroad against the United States, 'it shall be regarded as an action covered by Article 5 of the Washington Treaty, which states that an armed attack against one or more of the Allies in Europe or North America shall be considered an attack against them all.' On October 2, after being briefed on the known facts by the United States, the council determined that the facts were 'clear and compelling' and that 'the attack against the United States on 11 September was directed from abroad and shall therefore be regarded as an action covered by Article 5 of the Washington Treaty.'

Similarly, the Organization of American States meeting of ministers of foreign affairs resolved:

> That these terrorist attacks against the United States of America are attacks against all American states and that in accordance with all the relevant provisions of the Inter-American Treaty of Reciprocal Assistance (Rio Treaty) and the principal of continental solidarity, all States Parties to the Rio Treaty shall provide effective reciprocal assistance to address such attacks and the threat of any similar attacks against any American state, and to maintain the peace and security of the continent.

On October 7, the United States informed the UN Security Council that it had been the victim of 'massive and brutal attacks' and that it was exercising its right of self-defense in taking actions in Afghanistan against Al Qaeda terrorist-training camps and Taliban military installations.

> In accordance with Article 51 of the Charter of the United Nations. I wish, on behalf of my Government, to report that the United States of America, together with other States, has initiated actions in the exercise of its inherent right of individual and collective self-defence following the armed attacks that were carried out against the United States on 11 September 2001.
> The attacks on 11 September 2001 and the ongoing threat to the United States and its nationals posed by the Al-Qaeda organization have been made possible by the decision of the Taliban regime to allow the parts of Afghanistan that it controls to be used by this organization as a base of operation. Despite every effort by the United States and the international community, the Taliban regime has refused to change its policy. From the territory of Afghanistan, the Al-Qaeda organization continues to train and support agents of terror who attack innocent people throughout the world and target United States nationals and interests in the United States and abroad.
> In response to these attacks, and in accordance with the inherent right of individual and collective self-defence, United States armed forces have initiated actions designed to prevent and deter further attacks on the United States. These actions include measures against Al-Qaeda terrorist training camps and military installations of the Taliban regime in Afghanistan. In carrying out these actions, the United States is committed to minimizing civilian casualties and damage to civilian property. In addition, the United States will continue its humanitarian efforts to alleviate the suffering of the people of Afghanistan. We are providing them with food, medicine and supplies.

After the Security Council met for two hours to hear the U.S. and UK justifications for acting in self-defense, the President of the Security Council (Ireland's UN ambassador, John Ryan) stated that the unanimity of support expressed in the Security Council's two prior resolutions 'is absolutely maintained.'

On the same day as the above proceedings in the Security Council, the United States and the United Kingdom launched attacks against Al Qaeda and Taliban targets in Afghanistan (twenty-six days after the September 11 incidents).

Legal Consequences of the Construction of a Wall on Occupied Palestine Territory
Advisory Opinion, ICJ Rep 2004 136, International Court of Justice

By its resolution A/RES/ES-10/14 (2003), the United Nations General Assembly made a request to the ICJ for an urgent Advisory Opinion on the following question:

> What are the legal consequences arising from the construction of the wall being built by Israel, the occupying Power, in the Occupied Palestinian Territory, including in and around East Jerusalem, as described in the report of the Secretary-General, considering the rules and principles of international law, including the fourth Geneva Convention of 1949, and relevant Security Council and General Assembly resolutions?

138. The Court has thus concluded that the construction of the wall constitutes action not in conformity with various international legal obligations incumbent upon Israel. However, Annex 1 to the report of the Secretary-General states that, according to Israel: 'the construction of the Barrier is consistent with Article 51 of the Charter of the United Nations, its inherent right to self-defence and Security Council resolutions 1368 (2001) and 1373 (2001)'. More specifically, Israel's Permanent Representative to the United Nations asserted in the General Assembly on 20 October 2003 that 'the fence is a measure wholly consistent with the right of States to self-defence enshrined in Article 51 of the Charter'; the Security Council resolutions referred to, he continued, 'have clearly recognized the right of States to use force in self-defence against terrorist attacks', and therefore surely recognize the right to use non-forcible measures to that end (A/ES-10/PV.21, p. 6).

139. …Article 51 of the Charter thus recognizes the existence of an inherent right of self-defence in the case of armed attack by one State against another State. However, Israel does not claim that the attacks against it are imputable to a foreign State. The Court also notes that Israel exercises control in the Occupied Palestinian Territory and that, as Israel itself states, the threat which it regards as justifying the construction of the wall originates within, and not outside, that territory. The situation is thus different from that contemplated by Security Council resolutions 1368 (2001) and 1373 (200l), and therefore Israel could not in any event invoke those resolutions in support of its claim to be exercising a right of self-defence. Consequently, the Court concludes that Article 51 of the Charter has no relevance in this case.

JUDGE HIGGINS (Separate Opinion)

33. I do not agree with all that the Court has to say on the question of the law of self-defence.…There is, with respect, nothing in the text of Article 51 that *thus* stipulates that self-defence is available only when an armed attack is made by a State. *That* qualification is rather a result of the Court so determining in *Military and Paramilitary Activities in and against Nicaragua (Nicaragua* v. *United States of America)* (Merits, Judgment, I. C.J. Reports 1986, p. 14). It there held that military action by irregulars could constitute an armed attack if these were sent by or on behalf of the State and if the activity 'because of its scale and effects, would have been classified as an armed attack…had it been carried out by regular armed forces' *(ibid.,* p. 103, para 195). While accepting, as I must, that this is to be regarded as a statement of the law as it now stands, I maintain all the reservations as to this proposition that I have expressed elsewhere (R. Higgins, *Problems and Process: International Law and How We Use It,* pp. 250–251).

34. I also find unpersuasive the Court's contention that, as the uses of force emanate from occupied territory, it is not an armed attack 'by one State against another'. I fail to understand the Court's view that an occupying Power loses the right to defend its own civilian citizens at home if the attacks emanate from the occupied territory - a territory which it has found not to have been annexed and is certainly "other than" Israel. Further, Palestine cannot be sufficiently an international entity to be invited to these proceedings, and to benefit from humanitarian law, but not sufficiently an international entity for the prohibition of armed attack on others to be applicable. This is formalism of an uneven-handed sort. The question is surely where responsibility lies for the sending of groups and persons who act against Israeli civilians and the cumulative severity of such action.

C. Tams, 'The Use of Force against Terrorists'
20 *European Journal of International Law* 359 (2009)

The key developments during the last two decades affect the rules governing the *unilateral* use of force against terrorists. Unlike with respect to the multilateral option, there has been a considerable body of practice—states exercising force against terrorists have, expressly or by implication, moved beyond the traditional regime.…

As noted above, ever since 1945, states have used force against terrorist threats; yet their practice for a long while was sparse, and typically critically received by the international community. The last two decades have seen a considerable shift. The number of states which claim a right to take forcible anti-terrorist measures has markedly increased, while the willingness of other states to condemn such measures has decreased. The situations in which force has been used (or a corresponding right has been asserted) vary considerably, but have almost exclusively been explained as exercises in self-defence.

(i) To begin with the most obvious piece of evidence, there was general agreement that the United States could resort to measures of self-defence in response to the 9/11 attacks. This it did from October 2001 by launching *Operation Enduring Freedom*. That operation has now been on-going for 7½ years and has served as a justification for forcible measures against Al-Qaeda and Taleban targets, but also includes a 'maritime component'. While initial debates about the conditions of self-defence have ebbed away, over the years there has been growing concern that Operation Enduring Freedom overstretched the limits of self-defence. Still, a series of international relations continues to underline the importance of the operation as part of the international efforts to stabilize the situation in Afghanistan.

(ii) The response against the 9/11 attacks is not an isolated incident. Quite to the contrary, in a variety of instances, states have reacted against terrorist attacks by using massive military force, including the invasion of states from which terrorists were operating.

Just as in the past, Israel has remained one of the most ardent supporters of a broad right to self-defence. In 2003, in response to a suicide bombing in Haifa it bombed Palestine camps north of Damascus. In the summer of 2006, following rocket attacks against it by the Lebanon-based Hezbollah, Israel responded first with bombardments and then an invasion of Lebanon. The international community's reaction to the raids of October 2003 as well as to the July War of 2006 was mixed. There was broad agreement (with respect to both conflicts) that Israel's use of force had been disproportionate. However, a considerable number of states, especially with respect to the July 2006 war, in principle accepted Israel's right to use force against terrorist organizations such as Hamas or Hezbollah. Israel itself was at pains to attribute Hezbollah's conduct to Lebanon and Syria, but did not claim that these states had controlled and directed Hezbollah's conduct.

Furthermore, since the 1990s, Turkey has repeatedly invoked a right to use force against Kurdish PKK bases in northern Iraq. The 1990s saw frequent incursions. A decade later, cross-border attacks of October 2007 led to an unprecedented escalation, culminating in 'Operation Sun', a ground offensive during which several thousand Turkish troops invaded northern Iraq in late February 2008. The international community's reaction was characterized by a 'mixture of sympathy and concern' for Turkey's conduct. Just as with respect to the July War, states stressed the need for reactions to be proportionate, and on that basis criticized the Turkish use of force. Most reactions however 'carefully refrained from formally condemning Turkey's behaviour'.

(iii) When looking at uses of force below the threshold of invasions proper, the number of instances in which states have used force against terrorist attacks increases considerably. Not all of them are well documented, but to support the argument made here, it may be sufficient briefly to refer to the following incidents:

- In 1998, in response to attacks on US embassies in Kenya and Tanzania, the United States bombarded a pharmaceutical plant in the Sudan (allegedly used by terrorists) and a terrorist base in Afghanistan. To justify its conduct, the United States referred to Article 51 UNC but did not allege any substantial involvement of Afghanistan and/or Sudan in the activities. The international community's reaction was mixed, ranging from condemnation (especially of the attacks on Sudan) to open or tacit approval. Similarly (though involving an instance of alleged 'state terrorism'), the United States had fired missiles on the headquarters of the Iraqi Intelligence Service in Baghdad in 1993, in response to an alleged assassination attempt on President Bush.

- From the mid-1990s, Iran on several occasions invoked Article 51 UNC to justify the use of force against bases of the Mujahedin-e Khalq Organization (MKO) on Iraqi territory. While Iraq denounced the use of force as an act of aggression, the international community did not condemn it. Equally 'uncommented' remained Iran's incursions into Iraqi territory in pursuit of Kurdish armed bands (labelled 'organized terrorist mercenaries'). There was little evidence suggesting that the conduct of the MKO (let alone that of Kurdish insurgents) could have been attributed to Iraq under the traditional 'direction and control' test.

- In 2000 and again in 2004, Russia asserted a right to respond extraterritorially to Islamic terrorists. In 2007, following attacks by Chechen rebels, it conducted air strikes against Chechen bases in the Pankisi Gorge in Georgia, claiming that Georgia 'had been unable to establish a security zone in the area of the [Russian–Georgian] border, continues to ignore Security Council Resolution 1373 and does not put an end to the bandit sorties and attacks on adjoining areas of Russia'. Responses were mixed, but again there was no principled condemnation that would have denied Russia's right to use force extraterritorially.

- In March 2008, Colombian forces moved into Ecuadorian territory in pursuit of rebels belonging to FARC (which it considers a terrorist organization). The OAS qualified the operation as a 'violation of [Ecuador's] sovereignty'; other international organizations were largely silent; the United States expressed support.

(iv) The examples mentioned so far involve the actual use of force by states. The new trend they reflect is confirmed by statements. Russia's assertion of a broad right to use force extraterritorially has been referred to already. Along similar lines, Australia claimed a right to use force extraterritorially against terrorists threatening to attack Australia or its citizens following the Bali bombings of October 2002. As for more principled statements, the 2005 African Union Non-Aggression and Common Defence Pact expressly qualifies the harbouring of terrorists, as well as any provision of support for them, as an act of aggression. Finally, the United States' 2002 National Security Strategy went well beyond these claims; it famously asserted a right of pre-emptive self-defence against non-imminent threats, in particular those by terrorist organizations.

(v) Finally, these instances seem part of a broader trend among states to exercise force against attacks by non-state actors—attacks which would have been difficult to justify under the traditional approach. While not specifically relying on a right to use force against terrorist attacks, states like Rwanda, Tajikistan, or Burma/Myanmar have all responded to cross-border attacks by insurgents or rebels. For that purpose, they have all moved troops into neighbouring states even though these, under the traditional rules of attribution, could hardly be said to have directed or controlled the insurgents.

The brief summaries provided in the previous paragraphs of course cannot replace a detailed assessment, but clearly point in one direction: the international community today is much less likely to deny, as a matter of principle, that states can invoke self-defence against terrorist attacks not imputable to another state. Instead debate has shifted towards issues of necessity and proportionality (i.e. the scope of self-defence measures). This is particularly clear in the international community's responses to Israel's repeated claims to use self-defence, in particular the July War of 2006. The vigorous and principled condemnation of the 1970s and 1980s has been replaced by concerns that Israel's actions should remain proportionate (which often they have not been). The traditional approach seeking to minimize the availability of lawful force in that respect has come under pressure—as Tom Franck noted already in 2002, assertions of a right to exercise self-defence against terrorist and other non-state attacks 'are no longer exceptional claims'. [Franck, *Recourse to Force* (2002), p. 64]

Letter from the Permanent Representative of the United States of America to the United Nations Secretary-General
UN Doc. S/2014/695, 23 September 2014

In the letter dated 20 September 2014 from the Minister for Foreign Affairs of Iraq addressed to the President of the Security Council (S/2014/691, annex) and other statements made by Iraq, including the letter dated 25 June 2014 from the Minister for Foreign Affairs of Iraq addressed to the Secretary-General (S/2014/440, annex), Iraq has made clear that it is facing a serious threat of continuing attacks from the Islamic State in Iraq and the Levant (ISIL) coming out of safe havens in Syria. These safe havens are used by ISIL for training, planning, financing, and carrying out attacks across Iraqi borders and against Iraq's people. For these reasons, the Government of Iraq has asked that the United States lead international efforts to strike ISIL sites and military strongholds in Syria in order to end the continuing attacks on Iraq, to protect Iraqi citizens, and ultimately to enable and arm Iraqi forces to perform their task of regaining control of the Iraqi borders.

ISIL and other terrorist groups in Syria are a threat not only to Iraq, but also to many other countries, including the United States and our partners in the region and beyond. States must be able to defend themselves, in accordance with the inherent right of individual and collective self-defence, as reflected in Article 51 of the Charter of the United Nations, when, as is the case here, the government of the State where the threat is located is unwilling or unable to prevent the use of its territory for such attacks. The Syrian regime has shown that it cannot and will not confront these safe havens effectively itself. Accordingly, the United States has initiated necessary and proportionate military actions in Syria in order to eliminate the ongoing ISIL threat to Iraq, including by protecting Iraqi citizens from further attacks and by enabling Iraqi forces to regain control of Iraq's borders. In addition, the United States has initiated military actions in Syria against al-Qaida elements in Syria known as the Khorasan Group to address terrorist threats that they pose to the United States and our partners and allies.

Memorandum to the Foreign Affairs Select Committee
Prime Minister's [David Cameron] Response to the Foreign Affairs Select Committee's Second Report of Session 2015–16: The Extension of Offensive British Military Operations to Syria, November 2015

It is the first duty of any Government to ensure the safety and security of the people they serve. This is a responsibility which this Government takes very seriously and which it will discharge by all lawful means it considers necessary. The Government has made very clear that when there is an identified direct and imminent threat to the UK and British interests abroad it will take action to counter that threat....

Effective action requires a full-spectrum response. At one end of that spectrum, the Government has made it clear that it is prepared to use force in accordance with international law where it is necessary to do so and there is no alternative. International law has long recognised the inherent right of individual and collective self-defence, which is clearly set out in Article 51 of the Charter of the United Nations.

Lethal action will always be a last resort, when there is no other option to defend ourselves against an attack and no other means to detain, disrupt or otherwise prevent those plotting acts of terror. The principles of necessity and proportionality underpin all our decision-making.

Legal basis

The legal basis for the Government's activity against ISIL in Syria is therefore the inherent right of individual and collective self-defence as recognised by Article 51 of the UN Charter....

Individual terrorist attacks, or an ongoing series of terrorist attacks, may rise to the level of an 'armed attack' for these purposes if they are of sufficient gravity. This is demonstrated by UN Security Council resolutions 1368 (2001) and 1373(2001) following the attacks on New York and Washington of 11 September 2001. Whether the gravity of an attack is sufficient to give rise to the exercise of the inherent right of self-defence must be determined by reference to all of the facts in any given case. The scale and effects of ISIL's campaign are judged to reach the level of an armed attack against the UK that justifies the use of force to counter it in accordance with Article 51.

It has been the long-held position of successive Governments that force may be used in self-defence, not only where an armed attack is underway, but also where an armed attack is imminent. Where the UK determines that it faces an imminent armed attack from ISIL, it is entitled to use necessary and proportionate force to repel or forestall that attack in exercise of the inherent right of individual self-defence.

Additionally, it is clear that ISIL are engaged in an ongoing attack on Iraq, and have been since 2014. On 20 September 2014 the Government of Iraq wrote to the UN Security Council seeking military assistance of other States to bring an end to ISIL's attack on Iraq, including through action against ISIL bases outside Iraqi territory. The US and other members of the Coalition (including the UK) have therefore asserted the right to take action against ISIL in Syria on the basis of the collective self-defence of Iraq. The UK asserted this right in its letter to the UN Security Council of 25 November 2014. . . .

Following the vote in Parliament on 2 December, the UK has extended its contribution to coalition efforts in Iraq and Syria. Specifically, our Armed Forces are now authorised to conduct air strikes against ISIL targets in Syria as part of the coalition effort. Such action will be taken in exercise of the inherent right of self-defence as recognised in the United Nations Charter.

Reyaad Khan

In the case of Reyaad Khan, who was targeted in an RAF air strike in Syria on 21 August, the legal basis for military action was the inherent right of individual and collective self-defence. There was clear evidence of Khan's involvement in planning and directing a series of attacks against the UK and our allies, including a number which were foiled. That evidence showed that the threat was genuine, demonstrating both his intent and his capability of delivering the attacks. The threat of attack was current; and an attack could have become a reality at any moment and without warning. In the prevailing circumstances in Syria, this airstrike was the only feasible means of effectively disrupting the attacks planned and directed by this individual. There was no realistic prospect that Khan would travel outside Syria so that other means of disruption could be attempted. The legal test of an imminent armed attack was therefore satisfied. The UK would not have acted had it not been necessary in the self-defence of the UK.

Additionally, the UK has supported and contributed to the US-led efforts to target ISIL in Syria as a necessary aspect of effectively bringing an end to ISIL's armed attack on Iraq, at the request of the Government of Iraq. Military action against members of ISIL in Syria that is necessary and proportionate to bring an end to ISIL's attack on Iraq is in accordance with the right of collective self-defence of Iraq. The strike targeting Khan was therefore also lawful in the collective self defence of Iraq.

As indicated above, any action taken under Article 51 must be both necessary to deal with the threat and proportionate to the threat, ie no more than required to deal with it. Care was taken in the planning of this operation to limit force only to what was necessary to disrupt the activities that Khan was planning and directing. No civilian casualties were sustained.

This was therefore a lawful use of force in the individual self-defence of the United Kingdom and the collective self defence of Iraq. The Government reported it to the Security Council on 7 September 2015, in accordance with the requirements of Article 51 of the Charter of the United Nations.

(b) Pre-emptive self-defence

In September 2002, the Bush Administration issued its National Security Strategy. This document, which built upon the strategies adopted by its predecessors, announced the Administration's doctrine of pre-emptive self-defence and is often known as 'The Bush Doctrine'.

The National Security Strategy of the United States of America 2002

41 *International Legal Materials* 1478 (2002)

The struggle against global terrorism is different from any other war in our history. It will be fought on many fronts against a particularly elusive enemy over an extended period of time. Progress will come through the persistent accumulation of successes—some seen, some unseen. . . .

We will disrupt and destroy terrorist organizations by:

- direct and continuous action using all the elements of national and international power. Our immediate focus will be those terrorist organizations of global reach and any terrorist or state sponsor of terrorism which attempts to gain or use weapons of mass destruction (WMD) or their precursors;
- defending the United States, the American people, and our interests at home and abroad by identifying and destroying the threat before it reaches our borders. While the United States will constantly strive to enlist the support of the international community, we will not hesitate to act alone, if necessary, to exercise our right of self defense by acting preemptively against such terrorists, to prevent them from doing harm against our people and our country; and
- denying further sponsorship, support, and sanctuary to terrorists by convincing or compelling states to accept their sovereign responsibilities…

For centuries, international law recognized that nations need not suffer an attack before they can lawfully take action to defend themselves against forces that present an imminent danger of attack. Legal scholars and international jurists often conditioned the legitimacy of preemption on the existence of an imminent threat—most often a visible mobilization of armies, navies, and air forces preparing to attack.

We must adapt the concept of imminent threat to the capabilities and objectives of today's adversaries. Rogue states and terrorists do not seek to attack us using conventional means. They know such attacks would fail. Instead, they rely on acts of terror and, potentially, the use of weapons of mass destruction—weapons that can be easily concealed, delivered covertly, and used without warning.

The targets of these attacks are our military forces and our civilian population, in direct violation of one of the principal norms of the law of warfare. As was demonstrated by the losses on September 11, 2001, mass civilian casualties is the specific objective of terrorists and these losses would be exponentially more severe if terrorists acquired and used weapons of mass destruction.

The United States has long maintained the option of preemptive actions to counter a sufficient threat to our national security. The greater the threat, the greater is the risk of inaction—and the more compelling the case for taking anticipatory action to defend ourselves, even if uncertainty remains as to the time and place of the enemy's attack. To forestall or prevent such hostile acts by our adversaries, the United States will, if necessary, act preemptively.

The United States will not use force in all cases to preempt emerging threats, nor should nations use preemption as a pretext for aggression. Yet in an age where the enemies of civilization openly and actively seek the world's most destructive technologies, the United States cannot remain idle while dangers gather.

M. Reisman, 'The Past and Future of the Claim of Preemptive Self-Defense'
100 *American Journal of International Law* 525 (2007)

The claim to preemptive self-defense is a claim to entitlement to use unilaterally, without prior international authorization, high levels of violence to arrest an incipient development that is not yet operational or directly threatening, but that, if permitted to mature, could be seen by the potential preemptor as susceptible to neutralization only at a higher and possibly unacceptable cost to itself. Preemptive self-defense differs from anticipatory self-defense in that those contemplating the latter can point to a palpable and imminent threat. Thus, anticipatory self-defense…is at least akin to the armed attack requirement of Charter Article 51, because there may be palpable evidence of an imminent attack. A claim for preemptive self-defense can point only to a possibility among a range of other possibilities, a contingency. As one moves from an actual armed attack as the requisite threshold of reactive self-defense, to the palpable and imminent threat of attack, which is the threshold of anticipatory self-defense, and from there to the conjectural and contingent threat of the mere possibility of an attack at some future time, which is the threshold of preemptive self-defense, the self-assigned interpretive latitude of the unilateralist becomes wider, yet the nature and quantum of evidence that can satisfy the burden of proof resting on the unilateralist becomes less and less defined and is often, by the very nature of the exercise, extrapolative and speculative. The evolution of weapons systems that are ever more rapid and destructive and that may be initiated without warning or with very narrow warning windows has been invoked as a justification for preemption. But ultimately the central issue is assessment by the risk-averse security specialists of one international actor of the intentions of another actor who has or may acquire the weapons. In an international system marked by radically different cultures, values, and, as a consequence, factual perceptions and their strategic assessments, an act of preemptive self-defense, based upon one actor's self-perceived good faith conviction, will often look like serious or hysterical misjudgment to some actors and like either cynical or self-deluded, naked aggression to others. When a major international actor claims a new right or its adjustment or termination, the implications for changing customary international law loom especially large, for, at every level of social organization, the making of law, much more than its institutional applications, is in great part political; doctrines of sovereign equality notwithstanding, the actions of a great power may be more generative of law than those of smaller states.

NOTES

1. Before the attacks on the World Trade Center in September 2001, States tended to adopt a criminal law, or law enforcement, approach to terrorism. There was a narrow view of the role of self-defence in response to attacks by terrorists and other non-State actors. A right of self-defence was only supported where the conduct could be attributed to the State. This approach may now have changed, and, as the above extracts suggest, there is increasing recognition (at least in the terrorism context) of a right of self-defence in response to attacks by non-State actors, even where the conduct may not be attributed to a State.

2. Neither the Security Council nor the General Assembly has criticised the United States or its allies for their initial military action in Afghanistan. Most States recognised the action as based on the lawful exercise of the right of self-defence, which is reflected in Resolution 1368 (2001), the Preamble to which recognises 'the inherent right of individual or collective self-defence'. What was more controversial was the ongoing nature of the military action in Afghanistan, with military forces still operational in Afghanistan many years after the initial attack. Were such forces relying still upon the justification of self-defence, or had the legal basis shifted, to intervention by consent for example (see Section 1G)? Certain activities undertaken by coalition forces have also been scrutinised; does a mission based on the exercise of collective self-defence support activities intended to prevent the opium trade in Afghanistan, a naval blockade or military strikes in neighbouring States?

3. The ICJ has not yet had to comment on the existence of a right of self-defence against non-State actors where the attack cannot be attributed to the State. As the extract from Judge Higgins in Section 1C shows, some have interpreted the Court's comments in the *Wall Advisory Opinion* as suggesting no such right exists. The Court avoided addressing this issue in *DRC v Uganda* (para. 147, extracted in Section 1B). The extract from Tams surveys the situations in which States have asserted a right of self-defence in response to an attack from a non-State actor. Even though the *Caroline Case* itself dealt with actions by non-State actors, there remains a question as to whether the practice set out by Tams fully justifies a new rule of customary international law. Is it consistent with the language of Articles 2(4) and 51 of the Charter?

4. More recently, the US and UK, with other States, conducted military operations in Iraq and Syria against Islamic State of Iraq and the Levant [ISIL], a terrorist organisation that started as an armed group in Syria and expanded to control large areas of territory in Iraq and Syria. ISIL is accused of committing serious crimes against civilians. The Security Council has adopted a series of resolutions concerning the response to ISIL, but has so far stopped short of authorising the use of force. For example, Resolution 2249 (2015) (see also Chapter14) 'Calls upon Member States that have the capacity to do so to take all necessary measures, in compliance with international law, in particular with the United Nations Charter ... on the territory under the control of ISIL also known as Da'esh, in Syria and Iraq, to redouble and coordinate their efforts to prevent and suppress terrorist acts committed specifically by ISIL' (para. 5). Iraq requested foreign military assistance 'for the specific purpose of targeting ISIL', including in Syria. Both the US and the UK have reported the involvement of their forces to the Security Council (see the US letter extracted above; for the most recent UK letter of December 2015, see S/2015/928), invoking the 'inherent right of individual and collective self-defence'. The UK legal position is set out more fully in the extract above. This confirms the emerging position in State practice that a right to individual self-defence exists in response to terrorist attacks, at least where the level and extent of such attacks amounts to an armed attack.

5. The Bush Administration adopted the National Security Strategy after the events on 11 September 2001 (9/11). The inclusion of the principle of pre-emptive self-defence was highly controversial, largely due to its potential for uncertainty and abuse. It was used by the United States as one of the justifications for the invasion of Iraq in 2003. The principle was reiterated in its National Security Strategy document issued in 2006, although the latter document also emphasises alternatives to military action. The United States itself attempted to limit the scope of the principle, stating that the right would only be exercised in situations of grave peril. The National Security Strategy issued by the Obama Administration in 2010 modifies the principle of pre-emptive self-defence, arguing that it is

possible to use pre-emptive strikes only when other options have been exhausted. Thus, the use of pre-emptive self-defence is to be taken only in extreme cases rather than as a matter of course. However, the Obama administration has used the doctrine of anticipatory self-defence to justify the targeting of suspected terrorists as a legitimate and necessary response to the threat of terrorism, in 'capture or kill' operations, including in the territories of other States. In 2011, the US relied on a policy of targeted killing to target and kill Osama Bin Laden for the attacks carried out on 11 September 2001 and potential future threats. The US has also dramatically increased the use of drone strikes to kill suspected terrorists, particularly in Pakistan, Afghanistan, Yemen and Somalia, arguing that the State in question is unwilling or unable to deal with the source of the threat. The legality of targeted killings—particularly the pre-emptive aspect—has been questioned by scholars and the policy itself has been criticised by UN Special Rapporteurs as being contrary to the use of force, human rights law and the laws of war (See B. Emmerson, *Report of the Special Rapporteur on the promotion and protection of human rights and fundamental freedoms while countering terrorism*, A/HRC/25/59, 28 February 2014).

6. Most other States have not adopted such a broad approach to pre-emption as the US, although some States, including Israel, Australia, China, France, India, Iran, Russia, Taiwan and North Korea, have adopted security strategies that could have a pre-emptive aspect. The United Kingdom did not rely on pre-emption as a legal justification for its intervention in Iraq (see Section 1F). Similarly, the UK memorandum on Syria, extracted above, is careful to refer to the attacks by ISIL against the UK as being imminent and does not invoke a right of pre-emptive use of force. The ICJ has not had cause to consider the legality of the principle, but its comments in *DRC v Uganda* (para. 146, extracted in Section 1B) suggest that it is disinclined to accept it.

7. Opponents of both a wider right of self-defence in response to attacks by non-State actors and the right of pre-emptive self-defence point to the role of the Security Council in a collective response to terrorist threats. The Council has indicated on several occasions that terrorism is a threat to international peace and security, and has been willing to exercise its powers under Chapter VII of the Charter (see next section) to impose sanctions against suspected terrorists and terrorist organisations, to establish tribunals and for other measures short of force.

8. It is also important to recall that any forcible measure taken in accordance with the right of self-defence, based on either an expanded right to self-defence or the pre-emptive use of force, must still comply with the requirements of necessity and proportionality.

D: Collective self-defence

Military and Paramilitary Activities in and against Nicaragua Case (Nicaragua v USA)
Merits, ICJ Rep 1986 14, International Court of Justice

The facts are set out in Section 1A.

196. The question remains whether the lawfulness of the use of collective self-defence by the third State for the benefit of the attacked State also depends on a request addressed by that State to the third State…

199. At all events, the Court finds that in customary international law, whether of a general kind or that particular to the inter-American legal system, there is no rule permitting the exercise of collective self-defence in the absence of a request by the State which regards itself as the victim of an armed attack. The Court concludes that the requirement of a request by the State which is the victim of the alleged attack is additional to the requirement that such a State should have declared itself to have been attacked.

200. At this point, the Court may consider whether in customary international law there is any requirement corresponding to that found in the treaty law of the United Nations Charter, by which the State claiming to use the right of individual or collective self-defence must report to an international body, empowered to determine the conformity with international law of the measures which the State is seeking to justify on that basis.…As the Court has observed above (paragraphs 178 and 188), a principle enshrined in a treaty, if reflected in customary international law, may well be so unencumbered with the conditions and modalities surrounding it in the treaty. Whatever influence the Charter may have had on customary international law in these matters, it is clear that in customary international law it is not a condition of the lawfulness of the use of force in self-defence that a procedure so closely dependent on the content of a treaty commitment and of the institutions established by it, should have been followed. On the other hand, if self-defence is advanced as a justification for measures which

would otherwise be in breach both of the principle of customary international law and of that contained in the Charter, it is to be expected that the conditions of the Charter should be respected. Thus for the purpose of enquiry into the customary law position, the absence of a report may be one of the factors indicating whether the State in question was itself convinced that it was acting in self-defence.

JUDGE JENNINGS (Dissenting Opinion): Another matter which seems to call for brief comment, is the treatment of collective self-defence by the Court. The passages beginning with paragraph 196 seem to take a somewhat formalistic view of the conditions for the exercise of collective self-defence. Obviously the notion of collective self-defence is open to abuse and it is necessary to ensure that it is not employable as a mere cover for aggression disguised as protection, and the Court is therefore right to define it somewhat strictly. Even so, it may be doubted whether it is helpful to suggest that the attacked State must in some more or less formal way have 'declared' itself the victim of an attack and then have, as an additional 'requirement', made a formal request to a particular third State for assistance. . . . It may readily be agreed that the victim State must both be in real need of assistance and must want it and that the fulfilment of both these conditions must be shown. But to ask that these requirements take the form of some sort of formal declaration and request might sometimes be unrealistic.

But there is another objection to this way of looking at collective self-defence. It seems to be based almost upon an idea of vicarious defence by champions: that a third State may lawfully come to the aid of an authenticated victim of armed attack provided that the requirements of a declaration of attack and a request for assistance are complied with. But whatever collective self-defence means, it does not mean vicarious defence; for that way the notion is indeed open to abuse. The assisting State is not an authorized champion, permitted under certain conditions to go to the aid of a favoured State. The assisting State surely must, by going to the victim State's assistance, be also, and in *addition* to other requirements, in some measure defending itself. There should even in 'collective self-defence' be some real element of self involved with the notion of defence. . . . (It may be objected that the very term 'self-defence' is a common law notion, and that, for instance, the French equivalent of 'légitime défense' does not mention 'self'. Here, however, the French version is for once, merely unhelpful; it does no more than beg the question of what is 'légitime'.).

NOTES
1. The issue here is whether collective self-defence is the joint exercise of individual rights (Jennings), or whether it is the exercise of a right by one or more States on behalf of the 'attacked' State (the Court). For example, after the invasion of Kuwait and the threat to Saudi Arabia, did the coalition deploy forces because it was also threatened in a way that gave *it* a right of self-defence, or did the coalition respond to assist Kuwait and Saudi Arabia in the exercise of their rights of self-defence?
2. The right was also relied upon in relation to Operation Enduring Freedom in Afghanistan, with NATO invoking Article 5 of its treaty (the provision on collective defence) for the first time. Similarly, the justification for the US action in Iraq and Syria in 2014 (extracted earlier) seems to rely both on the right of Iraq to individual self-defence, as well as a right of collective self-defence. A main concern regarding collective self-defence is whether it offers valuable protection for vulnerable States, or whether it may serve as a doubtful pretext for involvement in conflicts.
3. There is also the issue of the relationship between collective self-defence and collective security (see Section 2D), as shown by the first Gulf War. Clearly, States could have come to the assistance of Kuwait—which had suffered an armed attack—and repelled Iraq solely in reliance on the right of (collective) self-defence. Political motives and the need to build an international coalition clothed with the authority of the UN played a large part in why they did not and relied on the collective security system instead. However, the collective security system may be unavailable where a veto in the Security Council is threatened or used, as discussed in Section 2.

E: The right to protect nationals abroad

M. Akehurst, 'The Use of Force to Protect Nationals Abroad'
5 *International Relations* 3 (1976–77)

[A] broad interpretation of Article 2(4) [i.e., that it prohibits all use of force] does not necessarily mean that the use of force to protect nationals abroad is illegal, because Article 51, one of the exceptions to the ban on the use of force laid down in Article 2(4), permits members of the United Nations to use force in self-defence, and it could be argued that the use of force to protect nationals abroad is a form of self-defence....Even a narrow interpretation of Article 51, which would allow States to use force in self-defence only after an armed attack has occurred, would not necessarily be fatal to the view that it is lawful to use force to protect nationals abroad, because it could be argued that an armed attack on nationals abroad is equivalent to an armed attack on the State itself, since population is an essential ingredient of Statehood. However, most of the authors who adopt a narrow interpretation of Article 51 do not consider that it is lawful to use force to protect nationals abroad; they believe that force may be used in defence of a State's nationals only when they are present on the national State's territory...

It is further submitted that even the use of force for the protection of nationals abroad is contrary to the United Nations Charter. Virtually every example of the use of force for this purpose since 1945 has provoked protests from other States that such use of force is illegal. Admittedly some writers argue that the use of force for this purpose is permitted by Article 51 of the Charter, but that is not the only way in which Article 51 can be interpreted. Indeed, there are cogent reasons for interpreting Article 51 restrictively, so as to exclude the use of force in Article 51 is an exception to the prohibition of the use of force in Article 2(4), and it is a general principle of interpretation that exceptions to a general rule should be narrowly interpreted in order not to undermine the general rule. Moreover, to equate an attack on nationals abroad with an attack on the national State, as some writers do, is fallacious. Nationals cannot be identified with the national State for all purposes; for instance, a State possesses sovereign immunity in foreign courts, but its nationals do not.

Report of the Independent International Fact-Finding Commission on the Conflict in Georgia

European Union, September 2009

The Russian Federation invoked the need to protect Russian citizens abroad. Under Art. 61(2) of the Russian Constitution of 12 Dec 1993, '[t]he Russian Federation guarantees its citizens defence and patronage beyond its boundaries'. On 8 August 2008, in a statement on the situation in South Ossetia, President Medvedev said: 'Last night, Georgian troops committed what amounts to an act of aggression against Russian peacekeepers and the civilian population in South Ossetia....Georgia's acts have caused loss of life, including among Russian peacekeepers....In accordance with the Constitution and the federal laws, as President of the Russian Federation it is my duty to protect the lives and dignity of Russian citizens wherever they may be'. Foreign Minister Lavrov stated on 9 August, 2008: 'According to our Constitution there is also a responsibility to protect...This is an area where Russian citizens live. So the Constitution of the Russian Federation, the laws of the Russian Federation make it absolutely unavoidable to us to exercise responsibility to protect.'

2. State practice

The question is whether the protection of nationals abroad can justify a military operation. Since 1945, numerous states have led military actions on the grounds of the need to protect and rescue their own nationals abroad; but these interventions were often used only as a pretext for masking other objectives such as the overthrow of a government. And no international court or tribunal has pronounced on the question whether the objective to protect and rescue own nationals abroad can constitute a justification for the use of military force, and if so, under what conditions. In diplomatic practice, these actions have been followed normally by rather mild condemnations, or have even met with approval.

3. No stand-alone customary law exception to the prohibition of the use of force

Some scholars have argued that there is a customary law entitlement to rescue own nationals abroad. However, state practice and *opinio iuris* do not support a specific right to intervention in order to protect or rescue own nationals abroad as an independent legal title in itself. On the contrary, states have consistently rejected such a specific title to intervention. Those states which did undertake such actions in order to protect or rescue their nationals always relied on other grounds to justify their behaviour, e.g. on self-defence (see also below). Therefore, no specific customary law entitlement to protect or rescue own nationals abroad exists.

Such operations could therefore only be justified under a different legal heading. Here it is crucial to distinguish between full-scale interventions involving the occupation of territory from strictly limited and focused "Blitz"-type actions. If at all, only "Blitz"-type actions might be justified under international law. A "Blitz"-type action is legal if it does not fall under the scope of the prohibition on the use of force, because it remains below the threshold of gravity, and/or because it is not "directed against the territorial integrity or political independence" of a state, as formulated in Art. 2(4) of the UN Charter.

But as soon as a rescue operation exceeds a minimum intensity and thus falls within the scope of Art. 2(4), the protection of own nationals does not, according to the prevailing opinion of writers, constitute an autonomous, additional justification for the use of force. There is probably not one single instance in state practice where a state invoked an independent, stand-alone entitlement to rescue its nationals, without relying on one of the classic grounds of justification. In state practice, none of the arguments advanced by states in order to justify military interventions in favour of their nationals has been accepted by the entire community of states. The prevailing reactions were rather reprobation, e.g. in the case of the Congo, Grenada and Panama. From a policy perspective, the danger of abuse counsels against generous acceptance of such a principle. To conclude, the protection of nationals abroad does not constitute an independent exception to the prohibition of the use of force, and therefore does not provide a legal basis justifying a military intervention.

4. Rescuing Russians as a case of self-defence?

Sergey Lavrov, Foreign Minister of the Russian Federation, said before the Parliamentary Assembly of the Council of Europe: 'Protection of Russian citizens abroad, who stay in the territory of South Ossetia on a legal basis, *is a ground for the right to self-defence'....*

The basic argument here is that putting in danger and violating the rights of a state's nationals equals an "armed attack" on those nationals. According to one possible but unconvincing argument, because nationals constitute one element of statehood, an "armed attack" on nationals must be treated as analogous to an armed attack on territory and is therefore apt to trigger self-defence.

This analogy is not convincing, because putting in danger or even killing a limited number of persons is not comparable in intensity to an attack on the other state's territory. Unlike an attack on territory, attacking members of the nation is not apt to jeopardize the independence or existence of the state. The better view therefore is that self-defence can therefore not be invoked on the grounds of attacks on Russian nationals in Georgia.

5. Application to this specific case

Even if it were accepted that a Georgian attack on Russian citizens were in principle apt to constitute a case of self-defence, the legal conditions for self-defence were not met in the case at hand.

First of all, the Russian intervention in Georgia was not limited to a "Blitz"-type action and was not solely focused on rescuing and evacuating Russian citizens. Its intensity surpassed the minimum threshold of intensity required by Art. 2(4) of the UN Charter. It cannot be said that the military action was not "directed against the territorial integrity or political independence" of Georgia, because it did support the territorial separation of South Ossetia.

The constitutional obligation to protect Russian nationals (Art. 61(2) of the Russian constitution, quoted above) cannot serve as a justification for intervention under international law. Domestic law can in principle not be invoked as a justification for a breach of an international legal rule. At most, domestic constitutional law could be invoked as a defence against obligations imposed on a state by international law if those obligations contradict core elements of the national constitution. But this situation is not present here, because Art. 61(2) is not a basic principle of Russian constitutional law, which would be constitutive of Russian constitutional identity. Moreover, it is not clear that this provision required Russian authorities to take military action. Russia cannot argue that the international legal obligation to refrain from intervening in Georgia violates a core principle of its constitution.

Furthermore, a distinction must be drawn between those citizens who have possessed Russian citizenship for a long time, and those citizens who have only recently acquired Russian citizenship in the course of the broad Russian policy to confer Russian nationality in a simplified procedure....With regard to this latter group of "new" Russians, it seems abusive to rely on their need for protection as a reason for intervention, because Russia itself has created this reason for intervention through its own policy. This is especially the case if an effective or genuine link between Russia and those new citizens is lacking....In conclusion, the Russian intervention in Georgia cannot be justified as a rescue operation for Russian nationals in Georgia.

A. Cassese, *International Law*

(2nd edn, 2005)

On balance, it would seem that the objections of many States have not led to the obliteration of the general rule...However, this rule—which might be subsumed under the general notion of self-defence pursuant to Article 51 of the UN Charter—may only be resorted to *under very strict conditions*, dictated by the UN Charter system for the maintenance of international peace and security....The conditions to be fulfilled for the use of armed force to protect nationals abroad to be lawful, are as follows: (1) The threat or danger to the lives of nationals, due either to terrorist attacks or to the collapse of the central authorities, or to the condoning by those authorities of terrorist or similar criminal activities—is serious. (2) No peaceful means of saving their lives are open either because they have already been exhausted or because it would be utterly unrealistic to resort to them. (3) Armed force is used for the exclusive purpose of saving or rescuing nationals. (4) The force employed is proportionate to the danger or threat. (5) As soon as nationals have been saved, force is discontinued. (6) The State that has used armed force abroad immediately reports to the SC; in particular, it explains in detail the grounds on which it has considered it indispensible to use force and the various steps taken to this effect.

NOTES
1. As can be seen from the extracts above, the right to protect nationals can be justified on two grounds: either it is an aspect of self-defence, so that an attack on nationals is intended to equate with an attack on the State itself, or it is a right exempt from Article 2(4) because it is not (and does not compromise) 'territorial integrity or political independence'. An example of an allegedly lawful rescue of nationals was the Israeli operation at Entebbe airport, Uganda in 1976. The justification was also advanced (though not widely accepted) by the United States in respect of its invasion of Panama in 1989: see 84 AJIL (1990) 494 for a critical appraisal. There has, however, been more recent practice of certain States (predominantly France and the United States) sending troops to rescue nationals and others from dangerous situations (e.g. the US in Haiti in 2004 and France in Chad in 2006). A number of States evacuated their nationals from Lebanon in 2006 following the Israeli attacks. However, such missions appear to have been conducted with the tacit approval (at least) of the territorial State or where there is no operational government, and have not been characterised as a use of force.
2. One of the issues raised by the argument of rescue of nationals in the Russia/Georgia conflict was which individuals count as nationals for this purpose. The majority of the residents of South Ossetia and Abkhazia had acquired Russian nationality through naturalisation, as part of a massive scheme of 'passportisation' by Russia. The Fact-Finding Commission concluded that, for various reasons, including the lack of a sufficient connection to Russia, the scheme had violated international law, and that third States were not required to recognise the effect of the naturalisations (p. 180). For further discussion of nationality, see Chapters 8 and 11.
3. Some commentators, including Cassese, argue for the recognition of a right to rescue nationals abroad, albeit subject to strict conditions. It is questionable how many recent instances would satisfy the criteria set out by Cassese, not least as such incidents are very rarely reported to the Security Council. For example, Russia raised arguments based on protection of its nationals to justify its use of force against Ukraine in respect of Crimea. However, it is doubtful whether this can properly be characterised as a situation of 'rescue', as there was no suggestion that Russian nationals in Crimea faced a serious threat of harm. The assertion of such a right in the context of terrorist attacks may also be controversial (see Section 1C).

F: Humanitarian intervention

Many international lawyers argue for a right to use force to intervene in the domestic affairs of other States to prevent and suppress large-scale violations of human rights. If the intervention is with the consent of the territorial sovereign, there are few problems. However, if the intervention is 'non-permissive', it would appear to run counter to Article 2(4) of the UN Charter, as well being contrary to various pronouncements of the General Assembly. Accordingly, there have been suggestions made, by States and commentators, that customary international law supports a limited exception to the prohibition on the use of force in situations of extreme humanitarian crisis.

UK Parliamentary Select Committee on Foreign Affairs, Fourth Report
(2000), available at www.publications.parliament.uk

Kosovo was part of the Republic of Serbia, itself part of the Federal Republic of Yugoslavia. From early 1998 onwards, Serbian forces were engaged in widespread human rights abuses directed against the ethnic Kosovars and the Kosovo Liberation Army was engaged in an armed struggle against the Serbian forces. The result, in January–March 1999, was the displacement of over 300,000 people. Diplomatic measures either failed or were not pursued fully. Attempts to have the Security Council adopt a resolution authorising the use of force against Serbian forces were ultimately unsuccessful. On 24 March 1999, NATO, including the UK, began military operations against Serbian forces, both in Kosovo and in greater Yugoslavia. These ceased formally on 20 June 1999. This is the report of an inquiry by a Select Committee of the UK Parliament into the legal basis of the NATO action.

124. The Government has consistently asserted that the military action taken in the Kosovo campaign has been lawful, and that NATO would not have acted outside the principles of international law. Both Ministers told us that states had the right to use force in the case of 'overwhelming humanitarian necessity where, in the light of all the circumstances, a limited use of force is justifiable as the only way to avert a humanitarian catastrophe.' A number of difficult questions of law (as well as difficult questions of fact) arise.

125. These legal questions are not arcane. There is a need for a system of law governing the conduct of states, just as the internal affairs of states should be governed by the rule of law. An agreed system of law is particularly important where the use of force is concerned. It is in the national interest of the United Kingdom that an international order based on law should exist, and that individual states, or groups of states, should not be able to interpret the law perversely in their immediate interest. When the law is clear, there can be a consensus; when there is ambiguity, international stability and the mechanisms of collective security set up through the United Nations are threatened.

126. The Charter of the United Nations was described by Professor Simma as 'not just one multilateral treaty among others, but an instrument of singular legal weight, something akin to a "constitution" of the international community.' The Charter prohibits the threat or use of force except in self defence or when the Security Council determines that there is a threat to peace, breach of the peace or act of aggression, in which case the Security Council may determine (under Chapter VII) that force should be employed 'to maintain or restore international peace and security.' The NATO military intervention was patently not an act of self defence, nor was there any specific Security Council authorisation for the operation. As Dr Jones Parry told us, none of the three classic bases for intervention (a UN Security Council Resolution; an invitation to intervene; or self-defence) applied in the case of Kosovo.

129. International law is not, however, static. It develops both through the agreement of new treaties and other international instruments, and through the evolution of customary law. The Charter of the United Nations has been interpreted in different ways in the half century since it was written. As Professor Greenwood pointed out, some parts of the Charter have been conveniently ignored, while, since the end of the Cold War, the provisions of Article 2(7) which forbid intervention in internal affairs of states have been widened to allow such intervention on the grounds that what is happening internally in the state threatens international peace and security. Moreover, it is at least arguable that the preponderant will of the international community ought not to be held to ransom by the exercise of the veto (or threat of the exercise of the veto) by a minority, or indeed only one, of the permanent members of the Security Council. 130. Supporters of NATO's position argue that a new right has developed in customary international law—the right of humanitarian intervention. The argument in favour of the existence of this right was set out by Professor Greenwood. Dame Pauline Neville-Jones was clear that NATO action had been lawful, and Professor Lowe told us that NATO action (if a breach of a fifty year old Charter) was 'consonant with the way international customary law is developing.' Professor Reisman put it thus: 'when human rights enforcement by military means is required, it should, indeed be the responsibility of the Security Council acting under the Charter. But when the Council cannot act, the legal requirement continues to be to save lives.'

131. Professor Greenwood conceded that the right of humanitarian intervention was based on state practice, but that this was state practice which had evolved in the past 10 years since the end of the Cold War. Although the interventions of India in East Pakistan (1971), Viet Nam in Cambodia (1978), and Tanzania in Uganda (1979) had the effect of putting an end to massive human rights violations in each case, the intervening states relied ultimately on arguments of self-defence to justify their actions, even if reference was also made to the humanitarian situation. Only the interventions of ECOWAS in Liberia (1990) and the intervention by the USA, the United Kingdom and France in northern Iraq (1992) seem to have been unambiguously humanitarian in

their stated aims. Professor Greenwood told us that the very short time scale over which the new practice had been apparent was unsurprising in international law, where a custom could develop much more quickly than in domestic law. Moreover, he argued that customary law formed a much more important part of international law than it did of domestic law.

132. An entirely contrary view is taken by Professor Brownlie, who provided the Committee with an exhaustive review of the authorities, including jurists of twelve nationalities, three of whom had been President of the International Court of Justice. He concluded that 'there is very little evidence to support assertions that a new principle of customary law legitimating humanitarian intervention has crystallised.' We are persuaded that Professor Greenwood was too ambitious in saying that a new customary right has developed. We conclude that, at the very least, the doctrine of humanitarian intervention has a tenuous basis in current international customary law, and that this renders NATO action legally questionable.

C. Gray, *International Law and the Use of Force*
(3rd edn, 2008)

[T]he controversy over the legality of humanitarian intervention continues. Some regard the Kosovo action as a valuable precedent for unilateral action: other regard it as a counterproductive intervention, which had the perverse effect of increasing the displacement and persecution of the Kosovan Albanians in the short term. Many states in many different fora within the UN have subsequently made a point of stressing that they regard the NATO action as illegal. Others such as Germany and the USA, even though they supported the operation, argued that it was not to be seen as a precedent for future action. The USA has not itself developed a doctrine of humanitarian intervention….States are divided on treaty interpretation and on significance of state practice.

Does Article 2 (4) of the UN Charter allow humanitarian intervention? The states who argued in favour of this saw humanitarian intervention as an emerging right; this indicates that they saw Article 2(4) as open to changing interpretation over time and not with a fixed meaning. They did not argue that the right of humanitarian intervention existed in 1945. But the basis for the claim that this change in meaning has taken place is not clear. Apparently it rests in part on an argument that the law of human rights has developed since 1945 to such an extent that certain human rights are now *ius cogens* just as the prohibition on the use of force is *ius cogens*. But it does not follow from the mere fact that human rights may now be *ius cogens* that this overrides the prohibition on the use of force. For this further, crucial step in the argument it would be necessary to show, not only that human rights are accepted and recognized by the international community of states as a whole as a norm from which no derogation is permitted, but also that states have accepted the right to use force to protect them.

Those who opposed the interpretation of Article 2 (4) to allow humanitarian intervention saw it as a prohibition that cannot be altered without universal agreement. To confirm this view they also invoked the General Assembly resolutions on the use of force, which outlawed forcible intervention in absolute terms. They stressed the primary responsibility of the Security Council under Chapter VII in order to exclude unilateral action. This also seems to have been the final conclusion of the Secretary-General. In spite of the acceptance that human rights were not an internal matter, he wrote in his 1999 *Report on the Work of the Organization*: "What is clear is that enforcement action without Security Council authorization threatens the very core of international security system founded on the Charter of the UN. Only the Charter provides a universally accepted legal basis for the use of force. Therefore it seems necessary for those states and writers supporting humanitarian intervention on the basis that it is an emerging or a new right to show how the change in the law that they rely on has come about…The continuing opposition of China, Russia and the Non-Aligned Movement to intervention without Security Council authority means that the doctrine is far from warmly established in international law. The decision by states not to rely on humanitarian intervention as a legal jurisdiction for *Operation Enduring Freedom* against Afghanistan in 2001 or for Operation Iraqi Freedom is another indication of its controversial status. Although UK Prime Minister Blair in the run-up to the invasion of Iraq used the language of humanitarian intervention, in response to the widespread domestic opposition to the use of force, this doctrine was clearly not made part of the *legal* case for action. The UK Attorney-General acknowledged in his advice on the legality of military action against Iraq that 'the doctrine remains controversial'. In the USA President Bush openly called Operation Iraqi Freedom the legal basis presented by the USA was implied authorization by the Security Council rather than humanitarian intervention. It seems likely that express invocation of this doctrine by states will remain exceptional and that it will continue to be writers who are its keenest proponents.

General Assembly World Summit Outcome

UN Doc. A/RES/60/1, 24 October 2005

Responsibility to protect populations from genocide, war crimes, ethnic cleansing and crimes against humanity

138. Each individual State has the responsibility to protect its populations from genocide, war crimes, ethnic cleansing and crimes against humanity. This responsibility entails the prevention of such crimes, including their incitement, through appropriate and necessary means. We accept that responsibility and will act in accordance with it. The international community should, as appropriate, encourage and help States to exercise this responsibility and support the United Nations in establishing an early warning capability.

139. The international community, through the United Nations, also has the responsibility to use appropriate diplomatic, humanitarian and other peaceful means, in accordance with Chapters VI and VIII of the Charter, to help to protect populations from genocide, war crimes, ethnic cleansing and crimes against humanity. In this context, we are prepared to take collective action, in a timely and decisive manner, through the Security Council, in accordance with the Charter, including Chapter VII, on a case-by-case basis and in cooperation with relevant regional organizations as appropriate, should peaceful means be inadequate and national authorities are manifestly failing to protect their populations from genocide, war crimes, ethnic cleansing and crimes against humanity. We stress the need for the General Assembly to continue consideration of the responsibility to protect populations from genocide, war crimes, ethnic cleansing and crimes against humanity and its implications, bearing in mind the principles of the Charter and international law. We also intend to commit ourselves, as necessary and appropriate, to helping States build capacity to protect their populations from genocide, war crimes, ethnic cleansing and crimes against humanity and to assisting those which are under stress before crises and conflicts break out.

Chemical Weapon Use by Syrian Regime: UK Government Legal Position

Statement by UK government legal advisers, published 29 August 2013, available at https://www.gov.uk/government/publications/

1. This note sets out the UK government's position regarding the legality of military action in Syria following the chemical weapons attack in Eastern Damascus on 21 August 2013.

2. The use of chemical weapons by the Syrian regime is a serious crime of international concern, as a breach of the customary international law prohibition on use of chemical weapons, and amounts to a war crime and a crime against humanity. However, the legal basis for military action would be humanitarian intervention; the aim is to relieve humanitarian suffering by deterring or disrupting the further use of chemical weapons.

3. The UK is seeking a resolution of the United Nations Security Council under Chapter VII of the Charter of the United Nations which would condemn the use of chemical weapons by the Syrian authorities; demand that the Syrian authorities strictly observe their obligations under international law and previous Security Council resolutions, including ceasing all use of chemical weapons; and authorise member states, among other things, to take all necessary measures to protect civilians in Syria from the use of chemical weapons and prevent any future use of Syria's stockpile of chemical weapons; and refer the situation in Syria to the International Criminal Court.

4. If action in the Security Council is blocked, the UK would still be permitted under international law to take exceptional measures in order to alleviate the scale of the overwhelming humanitarian catastrophe in Syria by deterring and disrupting the further use of chemical weapons by the Syrian regime. Such a legal basis is available, under the doctrine of humanitarian intervention, provided three conditions are met:
   (i)   there is convincing evidence, generally accepted by the international community as a whole, of extreme humanitarian distress on a large scale, requiring immediate and urgent relief;
   (ii)   it must be objectively clear that there is no practicable alternative to the use of force if lives are to be saved; and
   (iii) the proposed use of force must be necessary and proportionate to the aim of relief of humanitarian need and must be strictly limited in time and scope to this aim (i.e. the minimum necessary to achieve that end and for no other purpose).

5. All three conditions would clearly be met in this case:
   (i)   The Syrian regime has been killing its people for two years, with reported deaths now over 100,000 and refugees at nearly 2 million. The large-scale use of chemical weapons by the regime in a heavily

populated area on 21 August 2013 is a war crime and perhaps the most egregious single incident of the conflict. Given the Syrian regime's pattern of use of chemical weapons over several months, it is likely that the regime will seek to use such weapons again. It is also likely to continue frustrating the efforts of the United Nations to establish exactly what has happened. Renewed attacks using chemical weapons by the Syrian regime would cause further suffering and loss of civilian lives, and would lead to displacement of the civilian population on a large scale and in hostile conditions.

(ii) Previous attempts by the UK and its international partners to secure a resolution of this conflict, end its associated humanitarian suffering and prevent the use of chemical weapons through meaningful action by the Security Council have been blocked over the last two years. If action in the Security Council is blocked again, no practicable alternative would remain to the use of force to deter and degrade the capacity for the further use of chemical weapons by the Syrian regime.

(iii) In these circumstances, and as an exceptional measure on grounds of overwhelming humanitarian necessity, military intervention to strike specific targets with the aim of deterring and disrupting further such attacks would be necessary and proportionate and therefore legally justifiable. Such an intervention would be directed exclusively to averting a humanitarian catastrophe, and the minimum judged necessary for that purpose.

C. Stahn, 'Between Law-breaking and Law-making: Syria, Humanitarian Intervention, and "What the Law Ought to Be"'

19 *Journal of Conflict and Security Law* 25 (2014)

The first fundamental question of the Syria crisis is whether the threat of force marked indeed a case of 'humanitarian intervention'. This concept has been defined in different ways. It is typically associated with use of force or threat of use of force by one or more states or an international organization to protect populations of the target state against widespread suffering, death or deprivation of fundamental human rights. The UK Memorandum, Bethlehem and Koh assume that the doctrine is applicable. But one may have doubts whether Syria falls squarely under the concept and whether it may be treated in one historical line with incidents such as Kosovo, Srebrenica etc. This analogy hinges. There are fundamental differences.

The primary norm breached in the Syrian context, that is, the ban of the use of chemical weapon in non-international armed conflict, is a fundamental norm of international law that is prohibited under different bodies of law, including international humanitarian law and international criminal law. The conduct, that is, use of sarin gas against civilians, qualifies both as a crime against humanity and a war crime. It meets the trigger of the R2P [Responsibility to Protect] concept, as embraced in paragraph 138 of the World Summit Outcome Document. But this does not necessarily imply that it gives rise to a 'right to intervene' under the 'humanitarian intervention' doctrine.

R2P and 'humanitarian intervention are distinct concepts. The two concepts coincide in their rejection of sovereignty as a shield against the principle of non-intervention. However, it is misleading to interpret R2P in support of a case for unilateral action, … R2P was adopted in response to the risks and failures of 'humanitarian intervention'. It seeks to strengthen collective security, rather than undermining it. Paragraph 138 embraces a changing conception of sovereignty as responsibility, but fails to connect this idea to the acceptance of new forcible response schemes. Reactions are addressed in the separate paragraph 139, which places the emphasis on UN mechanisms. It is thus a stretch to invoke R2P to limit constraints on the prohibition of the use of force.

It is further questionable whether doctrine of 'humanitarian intervention' offers a proper fit for the motives of intervention. The threat of strikes was linked to purposes of protection through preventive objectives. But given the conflicting views over the goals and roles of parties in the conflict, there was no clear strategy what to stop through 'intervention'. Unlike Kosovo, intervention was not directly aimed at ending atrocities and armed conflict as such. It was guided by other purposes, namely (i) shifting the military balance between the Assad regime and opposition forces and (ii) sanctioning an unlawful means of combat, that is, use of chemical weapons.

This reasoning differs from the necessity arguments and moral dilemmas that underpinned other interventions. There are two key differences. The case for intervention sought to remedy and deter a specific modality of action by one party to the conflict. Moreover, the proposed reaction was limited in scope. It was essentially framed as a response to an incident in a crisis, that is, the use of chemical weapons, rather than as a response situation as such. This incident represents only a small fraction of the violence committed in the Syrian conflict, as illustrated by the Independent International Commission of Inquiry on the Syrian Arab Republic, established by the Human Rights Council. A sustained international presence in and after conflict was ruled out.

The Syrian case differs also from the establishment of no-fly zones in Iraq as of 1991 by the USA, the UK and France, which is invoked as another precedent in support of 'humanitarian intervention'. The establishment of no-fly zones was preceded by a number of Security Council Resolutions and a recognition of protection needs by the Council under Resolution 688 (1991). It was technically a case of 'unilateral interpretation' of Security Council resolutions. The threat of strikes against Syria lacked any such basis. This makes it difficult to draw a direct historical comparison.

As I have argued elsewhere, the discourse on military intervention in Syria essentially turned this protective logic on its head. It used 'protection' as a means to achieve accountability through military force. Syria is thus to some extent a 'new' type of intervention. The justification is in line with the tendency to mix different rationales of intervention, as done in the cases of Iraq (2003) or Afghanistan. It illustrates a growing trend to merge different rationales (eg human rights, democracy, peace and accountability) into a case for military action. Typically, these objectives are not sufficient on their own to support a legal basis, but are weaved together in order to make the case for legality more acceptable.

NOTES

1. There is particular concern that alleged humanitarian interventions usually result in the overthrow of the incumbent government—Viet Nam in Cambodia, 1979; India in East Pakistan (Bangladesh), 1971; and also (eventually) in the extent to which the actions by NATO could be said to have led to the independence of Kosovo from Serbia.

2. Serbia (originally under the name of the Federal Republic of Yugoslavia) challenged the legality of the NATO action before the ICJ. In its request for provisional measures, it asserted that, by participating in the NATO action, each of the ten respondent States had violated the prohibition on the use of force and, by training and supporting terrorists (the Kosovo Liberation Army), had violated the obligation to refrain from intervening in the affairs of another State. Serbia stressed the unqualified nature of Article 2(4) and rejected the concept of humanitarian intervention. Alternatively, it argued that the facts of the case did not satisfy the conditions for humanitarian intervention. Of the ten respondent States, Belgium was the only State to address the legal justification for the NATO action in any detail, relying upon the doctrine of humanitarian intervention (although the UK also indicated its support for the doctrine). The Court did not comment upon the legal arguments in its decision when it decided to refuse provisional measures, although it did note with concern that States should comply with international law, including the UN Charter: *Legality of Use of Force*, ICJ Rep (1999) 124. It subsequently held that it had no jurisdiction to decide the cases (see Chapter 16): ICJ Rep (2004) 279.

3. The Kosovo action represented a turning point in the UK's attitude to the use of force for humanitarian intervention. There was a hint in respect of the UK's intervention to protect the Kurds and marsh-Arabs in Iraq in 1991 in that the intervention was said to be justified in order to prevent a humanitarian catastrophe, but the statements made at the time of Kosovo were the most explicit justification to date from the UK. However, even then, the UK government chose to stress the moral imperatives of its action as government statements directly addressing the legality of the action were few. However, as is discussed in the extract from Gray, it does not appear that other States have adopted the principle. The UK itself did not rely on the principle to justify Operation Iraqi Freedom in 2003 although it restated and refined its position on the doctrine in relation to Syria in 2013.

4. While Russia did not expressly rely upon the doctrine of humanitarian intervention to justify its armed intervention in South Ossetia in 2008, the Russian President did refer to the casualties in South Ossetia. The Independent International Fact-Finding Commission concluded that there was not as yet an accepted principle of customary international law permitting unilateral action for humanitarian purposes in the absence of a Security Council mandate. Moreover, the Commission considered that, even if such a principle had emerged, Russia's consistent and persistent objections to the justification of the NATO action in Kosovo would preclude it from invoking the principle in support of its own military actions (pp. 283–284). Russia's own interest in the region and the absence of a collective action were also viewed as precluding reliance on the principle of humanitarian intervention. Russia has expressly and consistently refused to accept the principle, commenting after the Kosovo intervention that 'the Russian side cannot accept attempts to introduce into international practice the concept of "humanitarian intervention", which allows the use of unilateral enforcement measures by a State or a group of States without the approval of the Security Council, in violation of the UN Charter. Such a policy contradicts the fundamental principle of

the UN Charter in accordance with which the Security Council bears the main responsibility for maintaining international peace and security. A policy of unilateral use of force is fraught with undermining the whole system of international security and can lead to chaos and anarchy in international relations' (Statement by the Representative of the Russian Federation at the session of the Special Committee of the United Nations on Peacekeeping Operations February 15, 2000).

5. This debate is also seen in the development of the concept of the responsibility to protect (or R2P as it has become known). Its adoption was a major development for those supporting the protection of human rights. However, the legal status of the concept is uncertain. R2P focuses on the responsibility of the territorial government towards its own people and the need of the UN system to respond to any failure to fulfil that obligation collectively. It does not address the question of whether there is a right to use force for humanitarian purposes where there is no authorisation forthcoming from the Security Council. Moreover, because it does not modify existing rules, it does not provide any additional basis for the use of force under international law. Thus any use of force based on the responsibility to protect must also be consistent with Article 2(4) of the Charter, although several States remain suspicious that R2P is simply humanitarian intervention in disguise. Finally, R2P is limited to responding to genocide, war crimes, crimes against humanity and ethnic cleansing. Thus it cannot provide the basis for intervention in other circumstances, as was suggested following the failure of the authorities of Myanmar to allow international assistance following a devastating typhoon in 2008.

6. The Security Council appeared to rely implicitly on the doctrine of R2P in its response to atrocities committed in Libya by pro-Gaddafi forces during political protests in 2011. Security Council Resolution 1973 authorised States to take all necessary measures to protect civilians. A coalition of states, which included 15 NATO States, implemented a ban on all flights in Libya's airspace, a no-fly zone through air strikes, and tightened sanctions on the Gaddafi regime (see also Resolution 1970). Yet disagreements quickly emerged as to what the authorisation 'to protect civilians' actually entailed, amid suggestions that excessive force had been used and that operations were in fact directed at supporting the emerging opposition forces militarily, with the ultimate aim of regime change.

7. The use of chemical weapons in Syria in 2013 by the Assad regime renewed debate about the justification for the use of force on humanitarian grounds. While the UK government justified the legal basis for military strikes 'under the doctrine of humanitarian intervention' subject to certain conditions being met (see extract above), the US used a mix of justifications, part of which included deterrence, threats of further attacks, collective self-defence and the enforcement of norms. However, Stahn (see extract) argues that it is doubtful whether a case for military action can be made by merging different rationales together to bolster the legality of military action. Ultimately, military strikes were not taken against the Syrian regime due to its willingness to cooperate to remove and destroy chemical weapons in its possession.

8. The actions of ISIL in Iraq and Syria pose a significant threat to peace and stability in the region and have resulted in the use of force by the US and its allied powers justified by multiple bases (see Section 1C on self-defence). The US and its coalition partners have responded to the humanitarian crisis in multiple ways, including targeted air strikes in Syria and Iraq, the supply of arms to Syrian rebels, and the provision of military support and training to Iraqi and Kurdish forces to enable them to fight ISIS. Yet States have not sought to rely on R2P expressly. While Security Council Resolution 2170, recalls that 'widespread or systematic attacks directed against any civilian populations because of their ethnic or political background, religion or belief may constitute a crime against humanity' and 'urges all parties to prevent such violations and abuses' does not contain an explicit reference to R2P and does not authorise the use of force. Instead, both the US and UK have justified the use of force on the basis of self-defence, exercised by invitation of the Iraqi Government. Russia based its military operations in Syria on the invitation of the Syrian government.

9. A few commentators have suggested that the use of force may also be justified where it is to protect or ensure democratic governance in another State (see, for example, Franck, 'The Emerging Right to Democratic Governance' (1992) 86 AJIL 46). However, there is little evidence of State practice in support of this assertion. While the Security Council has authorised the use of force to restore democracy in certain situations, most notably Haiti in 1991, it has not done so on the basis of the supposed right to democratic governance. Nor has it acted to support democratic governments in all situations. The right to democratic governance was not asserted by the US or the UK in support of the use of force in Afghanistan or Iraq, and the then UK Attorney General stated that a desire

for regime change does not justify the use of force. However, other developments, in particular the military intervention in Libya in 2011, have raised questions as to whether the use of force is being used to secure 'regime change' or, as raised by the conflict in Yemen, to prevent transition of power (see Section 1G).

G: Intervention by invitation of the territorial state

L. Doswald-Beck, 'The Legal Validity of Military Intervention by Invitation of the Government'
56 British Yearbook of International Law 189 (1985)

Since the Second World War, there have been numerous instances of troops being sent to another State allegedly upon invitation of its government. Many texts would support a principle unequivocally in favour of the legality of such intervention, and there is certainly no doubt that a State can legally send troops to another State upon invitation for certain limited operations.…However, certain recent texts express doubts as to the validity of intervention by invitation where foreign troops are to be used to quell an insurrection. The reasons given for such doubts are variously stated to be the inability of a shaky regime to represent the State as its government, a conflict with the principle of self-determination or a violation of the duty of non-intervention in the internal affairs of another State.

It is submitted that there is, at the least, a very serious doubt whether a State may validly aid another government to suppress a rebellion, particularly if the rebellion is widespread and seriously aimed at the overthrow of the incumbent regime…

With regard to the origin of the norm of non-intervention in internal affairs, this can best be seen, in this author's opinion, in the *travaux préparatoires* to Resolution 2131. The principle of non-intervention in internal affairs is, in effect, an attempt to limit outside neo-colonial attempts to influence events in other countries for the interests of the intervening country. The policy behind the norm is a recognition that countries intervene in practice for their own benefit and major powers have an interest in not allowing the influence of an adversary power to be strengthened in this way. The policy interest of weaker countries is self-evident as well as the general wish to avoid the escalation of violence. It is to be expected, however, that these norms will be broken when a State considers it imperative to do so in certain circumstances, or when it considers that it can be got away with, but this is quite normal with any legal system and does not in itself derogate from the norm when that norm is clearly expressed and not in doubt. It is submitted that this is the case with the law of non-intervention in internal affairs.

The effect of this new customary law is to revolutionize the traditional law, which held that a State can intervene to help a government suppress a rebellion unless belligerency is declared.…It is this that now regulates intervention in civil war and represents the modern law.

Military and Paramilitary Activities in and against Nicaragua Case (Nicaragua v USA)
Merits, ICJ Rep 1986 14, International Court of Justice

209. The Court therefore finds that no such general right of intervention, in support of an opposition within another State, exists in contemporary international law. The Court concludes that acts constituting a breach of the customary principle of non-intervention will also, if they directly or indirectly involve the use of force, constitute a breach of the principle of non-use of force in international relations.

246. …As the Court has stated, the principle of non-intervention derives from customary international law. It would certainly lose its effectiveness as a principle of law if intervention were to be justified by a mere request for assistance made by an opposition group in another State—supposing such a request to have actually been made by an opposition to the régime in Nicaragua in this instance. Indeed, it is difficult to see what would remain of the principle of non-intervention in international law if intervention, which is already allowable at the request of the government of a State, were also to be allowed at the request of the opposition. This would permit any State to intervene at any moment in the internal affairs of another State, whether at the request of the government or at the request of its opposition. Such a situation does not in the Court's view correspond to the present state of international law.

Armed Activities on the Territory of the Congo (Democratic Republic of the Congo v Uganda)
Merits, ICJ Rep (2005) 168, International Court of Justice

In response to the DRC's allegations of military activities amounting to the unlawful use of armed force, Uganda asserted that, at least for a certain period, its forces were present in the DRC by invitation of the DRC government. The DRC claimed that consent had been withdrawn.

45. Relations between Laurent-Désiré Kabila [now President of the DRC] and the Ugandan Government had been close, and with the coming to power of the former there was a common interest in controlling anti-government rebels who were active along the Congo-Uganda border, carrying out in particular cross-border attacks against Uganda. It seems certain that from mid-1997 and during the first part of 1998 Uganda was being allowed to engage in military action against anti-Ugandan rebels in the eastern part of Congolese territory. Uganda claims that its troops had been invited into eastern Congo by President Kabila when he came to power in May 1997. The DRC has acknowledged that 'Ugandan troops were present on the territory of the Democratic Republic of the Congo with the consent of the country's lawful government'. It is clear from the materials put before the Court that in the period preceding August 1998 the DRC did not object to Uganda's military presence and activities in its eastern border area....

46. A series of bilateral meetings between the two governments took place in Kinshasa from 11 to 13 August 1997, in Kampala from 6 to 7 April 1998 and again in Kinshasa from 24 to 27 April 1998. This last meeting culminated in a Protocol on Security along the Common Border being signed on 27 April 1998 between the two countries, making reference, *inter alia*, to the desire 'to put an end to the existence of the rebel groups operating on either side of the common border, namely in the Ruwenzori'. The two parties agreed that their respective armies would 'co-operate in order to insure security and peace along the common border'. The DRC contends that these words do not constitute an 'invitation or acceptance by either of the contracting parties to send its army into the other's territory'. The Court believes that both the absence of any objection to the presence of Ugandan troops in the DRC in the preceding months, and the practice subsequent to the signing of the Protocol, support the view that the continued presence as before of Ugandan troops would be permitted by the DRC by virtue of the Protocol.... The DRC has not denied this fact nor that its authorities accepted this situation.

47. While the co-operation envisaged in the Protocol may be reasonably understood as having its effect in a continued authorization of Ugandan troops in the border area, it was not the legal basis for such authorization or consent. The source of an authorization or consent to the crossing of the border by these troops antedated the Protocol and this prior authorization or consent could thus be withdrawn at any time by the Government of the DRC, without further formalities being necessary.

48. The Court observes that when President Kabila came to power, the influence of Uganda and in particular Rwanda in the DRC became substantial.... From late spring 1998, President Kabila sought, for various reasons, to reduce this foreign influence; by mid-1998, relations between President Kabila and his former allies had deteriorated. In light of these circumstances the presence of Rwandan troops on Congolese territory had in particular become a major concern for the Government of the DRC.

49. On 28 July 1998, an official statement by President Kabila was published, which read as follows:

The Supreme Commander of the Congolese National Armed Forces, the Head of State of the Republic of the Congo and the Minister of National Defence, advises the Congolese people that he has just terminated, with effect from this Monday 27 July 1998, the Rwandan military presence which has assisted us during the period of the country's liberation. Through these military forces, he would like to thank all of the Rwandan people for the solidarity they have demonstrated to date. He would also like to congratulate the democratic Congolese people on their generosity of spirit for having tolerated, provided shelter for and trained these friendly forces during their stay in our country. This marks the end of the presence of all foreign military forces in the Congo.

50. The DRC has contended that, although there was no specific reference to Ugandan troops in the statement, the final phrase indicated that consent was withdrawn for Ugandan as well as Rwandan troops. It states that, having learned of a plotted coup, President Kabila 'officially announced...the end of military co-operation with Rwanda and asked the Rwandan military to return to their own country, adding that this marked the end of the

presence of foreign troops in the Congo'. The DRC further explains that Ugandan forces were not mentioned because they were 'very few in number in the Congo' and were not to be treated in the same way as the Rwandan forces, 'who in the prevailing circumstances, were perceived as enemies suspected of seeking to overthrow the régime'. Uganda, for its part, maintains that the President's statement was directed at Rwandan forces alone; that the final phrase of the statement was not tantamount to the inclusion of a reference to Ugandan troops; and that any withdrawal of consent for the presence of Ugandan troops would have required a formal denunciation, by the DRC, of the April 1998 Protocol.

51. The Court notes, first, that for reasons given above, no particular formalities would have been required for the DRC to withdraw its consent to the presence of Ugandan troops on its soil. As to the content of President Kabila's statement, the Court observes that, as a purely textual matter, the statement was ambiguous.

52. More pertinently, the Court draws attention to the fact that the consent that had been given to Uganda to place its forces in the DRC, and to engage in military operations, was not an open-ended consent. The DRC accepted that Uganda could act, or assist in acting, against rebels on the eastern border and in particular to stop them operating across the common border. Even had consent to the Ugandan military presence extended much beyond the end of July 1998, the parameters of that consent, in terms of geographic location and objectives, would have remained thus restricted.

53. In the event, the issue of withdrawal of consent by the DRC, and that of expansion by Uganda of the scope and nature of its activities, went hand in hand. The Court observes that at the Victoria Falls Summit...the DRC accused Rwanda and Uganda of invading its territory. Thus, it appears evident to the Court that, whatever interpretation may be given to President Kabila's statement of 28 July 1998, any earlier consent by the DRC to the presence of Ugandan troops on its territory had at the latest been withdrawn by 8 August 1998, i.e. the closing date of the Victoria Falls Summit.

92. It is the position of Uganda that its military actions until 11 September 1998 were carried out with the consent of the DRC, that from 11 September 1998 until 10 July 1999 it was acting in self-defence, and that thereafter the presence of its soldiers was again consented to under the Lusaka Agreement....The Court will first consider whether the Lusaka Agreement, the Kampala and Harare Disengagement Plans and the Luanda Agreement constituted consent to the presence of Ugandan troops on the territory of the DRC.

99. The Court is of the view that, notwithstanding the special features of the Lusaka Agreement just described, this conclusion cannot be drawn. The Agreement took as its starting point the realities on the ground. Among those realities were the major Ugandan military deployment across vast areas of the DRC and the massive loss of life over the preceding months. The arrangements made at Lusaka, to progress towards withdrawal of foreign forces and an eventual peace, with security for all concerned, were directed at these factors on the ground and at the realities of the unstable political and security situation. The provisions of the Lusaka Agreement thus represented an agreed *modus operandi* for the parties. They stipulated how the parties should move forward. They did not purport to qualify the Ugandan military presence in legal terms. In accepting this *modus operandi* the DRC did not "consent" to the presence of Ugandan troops. It simply concurred that there should be a process to end that reality in an orderly fashion. The DRC was willing to proceed from the situation on the ground as it existed and in the manner agreed as most likely to secure the result of a withdrawal of foreign troops in a stable environment. But it did not thereby recognize the situation on the ground as legal, either before the Lusaka Agreement or in the period that would pass until the fulfilment of its terms.

105. The Court thus concludes that the various treaties directed to achieving and maintaining a ceasefire, the withdrawal of foreign forces and the stabilization of relations between the DRC and Uganda did not (save for the limited exception regarding the border region of the Ruwenzori Mountains contained in the Luanda Agreement) constitute consent by the DRC to the presence of Ugandan troops on its territory for the period after July 1999, in the sense of validating that presence in law.

Z. Yihdego, 'Ethiopia's Military Action Against the Union of Islamic Courts and Others in Somalia: Some Legal Implications'

56 International and Comparative Law Quarterly 666 (2007)

Somalia has been without government since 1991. A transitional government was established in 2004 under the presidency of Abdullahi Yusuf, with the backing of the United Nations, the African Union (AU), the Arab League and the Inter-governmental Agency for Development (IGAD). The Government sat in Baidoa in southern Somalia from June 2005 until December 2006. In June 2006 the Union of Islamic Courts (UIC) took control of much of southern and central Somalia, including the capital, Mogadishu, but not Puntland and Somaliland. They declared and tried to establish an Islamic State. Somalis were told to comply with stringent Islamic rules or face harsh punishment. In the meantime, efforts to achieve national reconciliation were ongoing under the auspices of IGAD, though without much success. It was reported that on 20 July 2006 Ethiopian troops crossed into Somalia. Ethiopia only admitted to having military trainers to help the Somali Government (estimated to be 400 military personnel). On 21 July, the UIC declared a 'holy war' against Ethiopia. In September 2006 the Somali interim President survived an assassination attempt in Baidoa. On 25 October 2006 Ethiopia said that it was 'technically at war' with the Islamic Courts. After few days the UIC claimed to have ambushed and killed Ethiopian troops near the Ethiopian border.

A Resolution of Ethiopian Parliament on 30 November 2006 authorized the Government to take all legal and necessary measures against any invasion by the UIC, subject to the prior exhaustion of all peaceful avenues—the effort to find a peaceful route turned out to be a failure. A Chapter VII Security Council resolution, Resolution 1725, condemned the Islamist bombings in Baidoa, and authorized IGAD and the AU to deploy a protection force to Baidoa. The UIC entirely rejected the Security Council's move, and on 8 December officially declared that it was fighting Ethiopian troops to the south-west of Baidoa. The UIC went on to give Ethiopia a deadline of a week to leave Somalia or face a 'major attack'. Ethiopia, on 24 December, for its part, revealed that it had launched a self-defence operation against the UIC and foreign fighters in Somalia. Ethiopian warplanes bombarded Mogadishu airport shortly after the declaration.

The Courts faced major ground and air force attacks and were forced to leave all cities and towns including Mogadishu and the port city of Kismayo, in one week or less, after the counter-offensive began. The UIC leadership stated before it left Mogadishu that the retreat was tactical and it had resorted to guerilla or Iraq-type attacks against the 'enemy'. Ethiopia claimed in December that 'the UIC has melted away'. Al-Qaeda's second figure, Ayman al-Zawahiri, urged world Muslims to join the *jihad* against Ethiopian and Somali Government troops.

Whilst Ethiopian and Somali forces were in pursuit of the escaping faction of the UIC close to the Kenyan border, Kenya closed its borders with Somalia. The US navy had been closely patrolling the Indian Ocean coast of Somalia, so that US-wanted 'terrorists' could not escape. Somewhat unexpectedly, the US air force launched an air strike on what it called Al-Qaeda operatives in Somalia on 8 January 2007, a measure welcomed by the interim President, but which caused considerable civilian casualties. Ethiopia officially declared the successful end of its military operation in Somalia on 9 January 2007, and its troops began withdrawing on 18 January 2007.

The situation is complex. Many countries, such as Eritrea, Iran, Syria and Egypt, and other groups like the Hezbollah militia, foreign fighters from around the world and Ethiopian rebels, supported by some rich individuals from Gulf States and Saudi Arabia, have helped the UIC. Ethiopia, Yemen and Uganda have assisted the internationally endorsed Government. The aid has ranged from arms, ammunition and financial provision to sending commanders, troops and fighters to the territory of Somalia.

Ethiopia relied on a number of reasons as justifications for its military intervention in Somalia…There are two separate but related issues we need to consider here. The first one is a question of intervention upon invitation. In principle, international law permits third-State intervention by force into another State if there is clear consent from the government of the State where the intervention takes place. If a State is encountering a foreign military attack or an attack from internal armed rebels who get assistance from foreign forces, it can lawfully be assisted by a third-State to repel the attack by way of collective self-defence. On the other hand, a military intervention by invitation into a civil war situation poses very problematic questions of fact and law. In most cases, these interventions are illegal unless the inviting government is a constitutionally installed government, which has made a clear invitation to the intervening State, the invitation is given on an ad hoc basis, the intervention is not contrary to Article 2 (4) of the UN Charter (the prohibition of the use of force) and the intervention does not run against peremptory norms, for instance, violations of humanitarian law.

Ethiopia justified its military presence in Somalia up until 24 December 2006 (until the major counter-offensive started) by the fact that the interim Government had asked it to intervene. The Somali Parliament, assembled in Baidoa, approved such an invitation. Though President Yusuf's Government is not constitutionally elected, it has enjoyed a support and recognition from the international community. However, it was very weak, with control only of a tiny area of the country until the beginning of the Ethiopian military offensive. It was the UIC which held control of much of central and southern Somalia. The UIC also managed to maintain stability in the capital and other major cities/towns which were under its control. In such a fragile situation and in a crisis mainly of an internal nature, military intervention by invitation may be very controversial indeed, in particular as a justification for the deployment of troops into the territory of sovereign Somalia. The UIC was not merely a Somalian force, as became clear in the course of the conflict by the capture of foreign fighters, notably Eritrean troops and officials, Arab fighters and some Ethiopian rebels and from reliable media reports. Taking into account the international and regional legitimacy of the interim Government, the concern about terrorism, the fact that Ethiopia's intervention was and is not contrary to peremptory norms including the prohibition of aggression…, Ethiopia's intervention based upon the invitation of the interim Government may be lawful. It has to be noted that unless there is a question of defending one's own sovereignty and security, global problems such as helping governments in transition and global terrorism have to be tacked collectively, either through regional or global frameworks. Unilateral intervention is often controversial and counter-productive for both the intervening State and the State where the intervention takes place.

Statement issued by the Kingdom of Saudi Arabia, the United Arab Emirates, the Kingdom of Bahrain, the State of Qatar and the State of Kuwait
26 March 2015

Saudi Arabia, the United Arab Emirates, the Kingdom of Bahrain, the State of Qatar and the State of Kuwait have followed with great pain and concern the dangerous developments in the Republic of Yemen. The security and stability of Yemen have been shaken by a coup that the Houthi militias carried out against the legitimate authorities. These developments also constitute a major threat to the security and the stability of the region, and a threat to international peace and security. Our countries have acted quickly and made every effort to stand with the Yemeni people as its strives to restore security and stability by building on the political process launched by the Gulf Cooperation Council initiative and its implementing mechanism, and to safeguard the region from the repercussions of this coup.…

We are mindful of our responsibility towards the Yemeni people. We note the contents of President Hadi's letter, which asks for immediate support in every form and for the necessary action to be taken in order to protect Yemen and its people from the aggression of the Houthi militias. The latter are supported by regional forces, which are seeking to extend their hegemony over Yemen and use the country as a base from which to influence the region. The threat is therefore not only to the security, stability and sovereignty of Yemen, but also to the security of the region as a whole and to international peace and security. President Hadi has also appealed for help in confronting terrorist organizations.

Moreover, the acts of aggression have also affected Saudi Arabia, and the presence of heavy weapons and short and long-range missiles beyond the control of the legitimate authorities poses a grave and ongoing threat to our countries. The Houthi militias have failed to respond to repeated warnings from the States members of the Gulf Cooperation Council and the Security Council. They have continued to violate international law and norms, and to build up a military presence, including heavy weapons and missiles, on the border of Saudi Arabia. They recently carried out large-scale military exercises using medium and heavy weapons, with live ammunition, near the Saudi Arabian border. The Houthi militias have already carried out a bare-faced and unjustified attack on the territory of Saudi Arabia, in November 2009, and their current actions make it clear that they intend to do so again. Our countries have therefore decided to respond to President Hadi's appeal to protect Yemen and its great people from the aggression of the Houthi militias, which have always been a tool of outside forces that have constantly sought to undermine the safety and stability of Yemen.

NOTES
1. As noted, the UN Charter provisions are directed at the use of force in inter-State conflicts. A legiti-mate government may invite the forces of another State on to its territory for any purpose lawful under international law, i.e. not for genocide, wars of aggression, or to prevent an exercise of self-determination. For example, in 2014, Iraq's Foreign Minister formally requested the US to launch air strikes against ISIL insurgents who had taken control of large parts of the country including stra-tegic areas containing oil refineries (see extract). The Russian Federation also based its intervention in Syria against ISIL on the invitation of Syrian President Bashar Al-Assad. However, intervention must be by the invitation of the legitimate government. Identifying the legitimate government may be problematic, particularly where there are two (or more) governments competing to be the legitimate government, as is demonstrated by the cases in Somalia and Yemen (discussed in the extracts above), the invitation by the former President of Ukraine to the President of Russia in 2014 and the differing views as to the legitimate governments in Libya and Syria (see Chapter 5).
2. Moreover, a request for intervention usually occurs in the context of a civil war. It is recognised that there is no right for the opposition in a civil war to request assistance from third States to overthrow forcibly the government. For a State to intervene in such circumstances serves only

to encourage unilateral interference and would constitute a violation of the principle of non-intervention (see extract from the *Nicaragua Case*). This was a concern raised regarding military intervention in Libya in 2011 and possible intervention in Syria in 2013. Yet such assistance may not be unlawful if the situation does not constitute a civil war. Thus the categorisation of the situation is important: does the violence amount to a civil war, with the opposition party(s) in control of territory, or is it merely civil unrest? This distinction can be very difficult to make in practice. The Independent International Fact-Finding Commission on the Conflict in Georgia noted that this principle of non-intervention also extends to intervention in a war of secession. It held that Russia could not lawfully use force in response to the invitation for military assistance from the authorities of South Ossetia (pp. 277–278). Similar concerns would apply to Russia's military intervention in Crimea.

3. There is also the problem of fabricated invitations, as with the alleged invitation made by the government of Afghanistan to the Soviet Union in 1979, and the alleged invitation made by the Governor-General of Grenada to the United States in 1984. Additionally, the use of force may be disguised; for example, the United States argued that its use of force in Colombia was actually law-enforcement assistance to the government of Colombia in tackling the drug cartels. As is also seen by the discussion of the intervention in Somalia, there may be some difficulty in establishing where intervention to assist against terrorism fits into this framework.

4. Consent to the use of force by a third State must be freely given, and cannot be obtained by duress. As is shown by the extract from *DRC* v *Uganda*, consent may be found in peace agreements or other instruments. Moreover, consent, once given, is not open-ended and may be revoked or varied at any time by the territorial State, and the terms of the consent must be complied with. In December 2015, the Iraqi Prime Minister indicated that he had not consented to the deployment of foreign ground troops in Iraq, but had made a specific request for air support, weapons, ammunition and training (statement, 3 December 2015). Consent may also follow from an international mandate. For example, when the Security Council authorisation for coalition personnel to remain on Iraqi territory expired in 2008, those States intending to remain in Iraq to assist with repressing the insurgency (mainly the UK and the US), did so at the invitation of the Iraqi government. The territorial government may impose conditions on the use of force and the presence of foreign forces on its soil, through the use of a Status of Forces Agreement, such as the agreement negotiated between Iraq and the US in late 2008 and the restrictions referred to in the extract from *DRC* v *Uganda*.

H: Reprisals

D. Bowett, 'Reprisals Involving Recourse to Armed Force'
66 American Journal of International Law 1 (1972)

Few propositions about international law have enjoyed more support than the proposition that, under the Charter of the United Nations, the use of force by way of reprisals is illegal. Although, indeed, the words 'reprisals' and 'retaliation' are not to be found in the Charter, this proposition was generally regarded by writers and by the Security Council as the logical and necessary consequence of the prohibition of force in Article 2(4), the injunction to settle disputes peacefully in Article 2(3) and the limiting of permissible force by states to self-defense…

In recent years, and principally though not exclusively in the Middle East, this norm of international law has acquired its own 'credibility gap' by reason of the divergence between the norm and the actual practice of states…

Clearly, if self-defense is a permissible use of force and reprisals are not, the distinction between the two is vital…

Reprisals and self-defense are forms of the same generic remedy, self-help. They have, in common, the preconditions that:

(1) The target state must be guilty of a prior international delinquency against the claimant state.

(2) An attempt by the claimant state to obtain redress or protection by other means must be known to have been made, and failed, or to be inappropriate or impossible in the circumstances.

(3) The claimant's use of force must be limited to the necessities of the case and proportionate to the wrong done by the target state.

The difference between the two forms of self-help lies essentially in their aim or purpose. Self-defense is permissible for the purpose of protecting the security of the state and the essential rights—in particular the rights of territorial integrity and political independence—upon which that security depends. In contrast, reprisals are punitive in character: they seek to impose reparation for the harm done, or to compel a satisfactory settlement of the dispute created by the initial illegal act, or to compel the delinquent state to abide by the law in the future....

This seemingly simple distinction abounds with difficulties. Not only is the motive or purpose of a state notoriously difficult to elucidate but, even more important, the dividing line between protection and retribution becomes more and more obscure as one moves away from the particular incident and examines the whole context in which the two or more acts of violence have occurred. Indeed, within the whole context of a continuing state of antagonism between states, with recurring acts of violence, an act of reprisal may be regarded as being at the same time both a form of punishment and the best form of protection for the future, since it may act as a deterrent against future acts of violence by the other party....

In fact, the records of the Security Council are replete with cases where states have invoked self-defense in this broader sense but where the majority of the Council have rejected this classification and regarded their action as unlawful reprisals. These cases are worth the study, for they illustrate the importance of this question—Is the legality of the action to be determined solely by reference to the prior illegal act which brought it about or by reference to the whole context of the relationship between the two states?

Weighing the advantages against the disadvantages, however, it would seem that the approach of the Security Council in assessing whether a case for lawful self-defense has been made out has been somewhat unrealistic. To confine this assessment to the incident and its immediate 'cause', without regard to the broader context of the past relations between the parties and events arising therefrom, is to ignore the difficulties in which states may be placed, especially in relation to guerrilla activities. The result is not only that the Council finds itself being accused of being 'one-sided' but it may also be forced to characterize as reprisals (and therefore illegal) action which, on a broader view of self-defense, might be regarded as legitimate. Or, even worse, the Council characterizes such action as an unlawful reprisal but, realizing the difficulties faced by the 'defendant' state, does not make any formal condemnation and thus appears to be condoning action which it holds is illegal.

Y. Dinstein, *War, Aggression and Self-Defence*

(4th edn, 2005)

Armed reprisals do not qualify as legitimate self-defence if they are impelled by purely punitive, non-defensive, motives. But the motives driving States to action are usually multifaceted, and a tinge of retribution can probably be traced in every instance of response to force. The question is whether armed reprisals in a concrete situation go beyond retribution. To be defensive, and therefore lawful, armed reprisals must be future-oriented, and not limited to the desire to punish past transgressions. At bottom, the issue is whether the unlawful use of force by the other side is likely to repeat itself. The goal of defensive armed reprisals is to 'induce a delinquent state to abide by the law in the future', and hence they have a deterrent function....There is no reason why the built-in time-lag between the original armed attack and the response of the victim State, which is an inevitable feature in all armed reprisals, should divest the counter-measures of their self-defence nature. The allegation that lapse of time by itself turns armed reprisals into punitive—as distinct from defensive—action is unfounded. The passage of time between the incidence of unlawful force and the activation of lawful counter-force is not unique to defensive armed reprisals. It is an attribute that defensive reprisals have in common with a war of self-defence undertaken in response to an armed attack 'short of war'....

In the final analysis, defensive armed reprisals are post-attack measures of self-defence 'short of war'. The availability of such a weapon in its arsenal provides the victim State with a singularly important option. If this option were to be eliminated from the gamut of legitimate self-defence, the State upon which an armed attack is inflicted would have been able to respond only with either on-the-spot reaction or war. On-the-spot reaction is dissatisfactory because it is predicated on employing counter-force on the spur of the moment, meaning that hostilities (i) erupt without any (or, at least, any serious) involvement of the political branch of the Government; and (ii) take place at a time as well as a place chosen by the attacking State, usually at a disadvantage for the defending State. War, for its part, requires a momentous decision that may alter irreversibly the course of history. Defensive armed reprisals enable the victim State to fine-tune its response to an armed attack by relying on an intermediate means of self-defence, avoiding war, but adding temporal and spatial nuances to on-the-spot reaction.

It would be incomprehensible for war to be acknowledged—as it is—as a legitimate form of self-defence in response to an isolated armed attack, if defensive armed reprisals were inadmissible. Taking into account that Article 51 allows maximum use of counter-force (war) in self-defence, there is every reason for a more calibrated form of counter-force (defensive armed reprisals) to be legitimate as well.

International Law Commission, Articles on Responsibility of States for Internationally Wrongful Acts (2001)

Article 50 Obligations not affected by countermeasures

1. Countermeasures shall not affect:
   (a) the obligation to refrain from the threat or use of force as embodied in the Charter of the United Nations;…

Commentary on the ILC Articles on Responsibility of States for Internationally Wrongful Acts (2001)

Official Records of the General Assembly, Fifty-Sixth Session, Supplement No. 10

(4) Paragraph 1 (a) deals with the prohibition of the threat or use of force as embodied in the Charter of the United Nations, including the express prohibition of the use of force in Article 2, paragraph 4. It excludes forcible measures from the ambit of permissible countermeasures under chapter II.

(5) The prohibition of forcible countermeasures is spelled out in the Declaration on Principles of International Law concerning Friendly Relations and Cooperation among States in accordance with the Charter of the United Nations, by which the General Assembly proclaimed that 'States have a duty to refrain from acts of reprisal involving the use of force'. The prohibition is also consistent with the prevailing doctrine as well as a number of authoritative pronouncements of international judicial and other bodies.

NOTES

1. The main issue concerning reprisals is the difficulty of distinguishing an armed reprisal (unlawful) from a legitimate act of self-defence (lawful). In the *Oil Platforms Case* (see Section 1B), Iran argued that the acts by the United States constituted an armed reprisal and were therefore unlawful. Iran argued that the US actions were unlawful because the attacks on the oil platforms occurred after the damage to the ships by the mines and missiles, they were both premeditated and disproportionate, and that the use of force complained of had not originated from the targets. While the majority of the Court did not answer this question directly (because it found there had not been an armed attack), several of the Separate and Dissenting Opinions suggested that the attacks were in fact reprisals, and had a punitive, rather than defensive, intent (see: Judge Simma, para. 15; Judge Kooijmans, paras 52, 55, and 62; and Judge Elaraby, para. 1.2).

2. Some commentators, such as Dinstein, suggest that armed reprisals should not be considered unlawful in all circumstances. However, practice shows that States have been reluctant to advance such arguments, relying instead on a more extensive view of self-defence. The instances of the use of force in relation to terrorist attacks (see Section 1C) demonstrate that many acts that, at least on the face of it, appear to be reprisals in that they are retributive rather than defensive, continue to be justified by reference to the right of self-defence.

3. Article 50 of the Articles on State Responsibility confirms that a lawful countermeasure under the law of State responsibility (see Chapter 11) does not include an armed reprisal. Similarly, lawful counter-measures under international economic law (see Chapter 13) are not reprisals.

I: Self-determination

H. Wilson, *International Law and the Use of Force by National Liberation Movements*

(1989)

One of the most common justifications of the use of force by national liberation movements is the plea of self-defence.…First, in some cases liberation movements and States supporting them have justified their use of force based on a right of self-defence against the original colonial invasion.…This argument is not particularly persuasive because of the principle of intertemporal law, by which the acquisition of a territory by force at a time when the use of force to acquire territory was not illegal confers good title.…

The more common argument made to support the plea of self-defence is that colonialism, by its very nature, is permanent aggression and any other conception of colonialism misrepresents its true nature. Therefore colonial peoples have a right, consistent with the Charter's norms, to defend themselves.…Such a liberal interpretation of self-defence was not in accord with the views of the Western Bloc nor with many of the Latin American States. In the first place, a number of countries were still of the opinion that Article 51 applied to the right of self-defence for States.…

Secondly, both the Western and Eastern Bloc States were sceptical about such a broad interpretation of Article 51 which, in their view, would undermine the prohibition of the use of force and return the idea of 'self-help' to international law. They supported the view that the important clause of Article 51 was that an *armed attack* must take place for there to be a right of self-defence....

There is a third argument posed for the legitimization of the use of force based on a right of self-defence which is less vulnerable to the criticisms of the Western powers although it still has failed to convince that group. By the 1970 Declaration on Principles of International Law, member States of the United Nations agreed by consensus that a people who have a right to self-determination have a status in law separate and distinct from that of the State administering them, and that every State has the duty to refrain from the use of force to deprive such peoples of their right of self-determination. If the colonial power initiates the use of force, some argue that the people, represented by their liberation movement, have the authority to use force in self-defence. In other words, national liberation movements have the same authority as subjects of international law as sovereign States. They are still prohibited from resorting to the threat or use of force in their relations with the colonial power, but they may defend themselves against armed attack in accordance with Article 51 of the Charter.

The Third World States have not been eager to embrace this limited justification because it does not legitimize the eradication of colonialism by force of arms if necessary....

The plea of self-defence was only one of the legal arguments proposed by the anti-colonial States. In a way, it was a justification within the bounds of the Charter of a more fundamental idea: that the denial of self-determination by colonial domination, alien occupation, or racism is so abhorrent that the use of force to eradicate these evils is justified irrespective of any prohibition of the use of force. In other words, wars of national liberation are an exception to the general prohibition of the use of force and anti-colonialism is part of a higher law.

Several Third World and Eastern Bloc States have argued that wars of national liberation are not prohibited by the Charter because Article 2(4) was referring to territorial aggrandizement. Wars of national liberation, in contrast, are fought to eradicate an agreed evil, and are therefore exempt from this prohibition.

Although the idea that wars of national liberation are exceptions to the general rule prohibiting the threat or use of force is widely accepted by Third World and Eastern Bloc States, it is not accepted by the Western States where sympathy for the ends of securing self-determination does not justify the use of force as a means. Many critics, quite rightly, have seen in this argument overtones of the medieval concept of a just war.

Finally, there is a third legal argument, less challenging of the traditional norms of international law than either the right of self-defence for peoples or the idea of a higher law. Quite simply, it is the explicit acceptance of a right of revolution by national liberation movements....The law as it stands is still not agreed upon. However, some conclusions can be made about the current state of affairs.

1. National liberation movements have an international legal personality unlike that of other non-governmental organizations. This status is based on the right of the peoples which they represent to self-determination.
2. There is general agreement that wars of national liberation are not strictly internal armed conflicts.
3. The use of force to deny the free exercise of a people's right to self-determination is contrary to the principles of international law.
4. The right of a people to self-determination may legitimize the recognition of a government which would otherwise be premature.
5. The authority of national liberation movements to use force is not agreed upon as a matter of international law. Such authority is actively supported by the newly independent States and the Eastern Bloc States, but has never been accepted by an established government confronting a liberation movement, or by the Western States. Practice in the UN, particularly the Declaration on Principles of International Law and the Declaration on Aggression, both adopted without vote, does not resolve the fundamental differences of opinion over the status of national liberation movements and the extent of their authority as a matter of law. However, the trend over the last four decades and since 1960 in particular has been toward the extension of the authority to use force to national liberation movements.

NOTES
1. The alleged right of 'national liberation movements' to use force to achieve self-determination, and the alleged right of other States to assist them with force to achieve this objective, is controversial. If permitted, both rights would seriously erode the prohibition on the use of force. For this reason, it is strongly resisted by some States, though favoured by the developing States in the General Assembly. See the discussion of self-determination in Chapters 5 and 6.
2. In the 2008 conflict between Russia and Georgia concerning South Ossetia and Abkhazia, it was suggested that Russia may have been entitled to use force to support the right to self-determination of the peoples of those territories. The Independent International Fact-Finding Mission on the Conflict in Georgia, established by the Council of Europe, concluded that the right to self-determination did

not confer on South Ossetia and Abkhazia the right to secede from Georgia. Thus it did not consider the argument that Russia's use of force was in support of the right of self-determination. In 2014, during civil disturbances in Ukraine, a dispute arose between Russia and Ukraine concerning control of the Crimean Peninsula. This followed pro-Russian protests in Crimea, leading to its annexation by Russia and a Russian-backed referendum held in March 2014, in which 97 per cent of the population of Crimea voted to join Russia. In defending its position, Russia claimed it was entitled to use force to support the right to self-determination of the peoples of Crimea. The secession vote was declared invalid by the UN General Assembly under Resolution 68/262 (see Chapter 5).

SECTION 2: COLLECTIVE SECURITY: USE OF FORCE UNDER CHAPTER VII OF THE UN CHARTER

In contrast to the unilateral use of force, a collective use of force occurs where the use of force (or other coercive measures) occurs under the authority of a competent international organisation, usually in promotion of international community goals. The actual force may be employed by one or many States acting under the authority of the international organisation.

There was an attempt to establish a tentative system of collective security under the Covenant of the League of Nations but it was not until the United Nations Charter that a legally effective system came into being. Essentially, if the UN Security Council makes a determination that there has been a 'threat to the peace, breach of the peace or act of aggression' under Article 39 of the Charter, it may exercise its powers under Chapter VII (Articles 40 to 42) and include both military and non-military measures. Prior to the end of the Cold War, this power was used sparingly but has been used more frequently since that time.

A: The Security Council

United Nations Charter

CHAPTER VII ACTION WITH RESPECT TO THREATS TO THE PEACE, BREACHES OF THE PEACE, AND ACTS OF AGGRESSION

Article 39

The Security Council shall determine the existence of any threat to the peace, breach of the peace, or act of aggression and shall make recommendations, or decide what measures shall be taken in accordance with Articles 41 and 42, to maintain or restore international peace and security.

Article 40

In order to prevent an aggravation of the situation, the Security Council may, before making the recommendations or deciding upon the measures provided for in Article 39, call upon the parties concerned to comply with such provisional measures as it deems necessary or desirable. Such provisional measures shall be without prejudice to the rights, claims or position of the parties concerned. The Security Council shall duly take account of failure to comply with such provisional measures.

Article 41

The Security Council may decide what measures not involving the use of armed force are to be employed to give effect to its decisions, and it may call upon the Members of the United Nations to apply such measures. These may include complete or partial interruption of economic relations and of rail, sea, air, postal, telegraphic, radio, and other means of communication, and the severance of diplomatic relations.

Article 42

Should the Security Council consider that measures provided for in Article 41 would be inadequate or have proved to be inadequate, it may take such action by air, sea, or land forces as may be necessary to maintain or restore international peace and security. Such action may include demonstrations, blockade, and other operations by air, sea, or land forces of Members of the United Nations.

Article 43

1. All Members of the United Nations, in order to contribute to the maintenance of international peace and security, undertake to make available to the Security Council, on its call and in accordance with a special agreement or agreements, armed forces, assistance, and facilities, including rights of passage, necessary for the purpose of maintaining peace and security.

2. Such agreement or agreements shall govern the numbers and types of forces, their degree of readiness and general location, and the nature of the facilities and assistance to be provided.

3. The agreement or agreements shall be negotiated as soon as possible on the initiative of the Security Council. They shall be concluded between the Security Council and Members or between the Security Council and groups of Members and shall be subject to ratification by the signatory States in accordance with their respective constitutional processes.

H. Kelsen, 'Collective Security and Collective Self-Defence under the Charter of the United Nations'

42 American Journal of International Law 783 (1948)

Collective security is the main purpose of the United Nations, just as it was the main purpose of its predecessor, the League of Nations. What does collective security mean?…We speak of collective security when the protection of the rights of the states, the reaction against the violation of the law, assumes the character of a collective enforcement action.…The difference between such kind of collective security and the status of self-help is relatively small.…The difference between the most primitive type of collective security and the state of self-help consists only in that, in the case of collective security, states not directly violated in their rights are obliged to assist the violated state; whereas in the state of self-help under general international law, they are only allowed to do so.

A higher degree of collective security is reached if the collective enforcement actions provided for in the constitution of the international community are centralized, that is to say, if these actions are to be decided upon and directed by a central organ of the community. Such centralization of the use of force may be combined with the obligation imposed upon the individual members not to use force on their own initiative in their mutual relations, to abandon completely the principle of self-help—the use of force being reserved exclusively to the central organ of the community competent to take enforcement actions against members. In case of such centralization of the use of force, the force monopoly of the community is much more evident than in case of decentralization.

Collective security reaches the highest possible degree when the obligation of the members to refrain from the use of force is guaranteed by their disarmament, when the force monopoly of the community is constituted not only by the exclusive right of a central organ to take enforcement actions against members, but also by the fact that only a central organ of the international community has armed forces at its disposal to be employed against delinquent member states, whereas the single members of the community are allowed only to keep a police force for the maintenance of law and order among their subjects, that is to say, for enforcement actions against individuals. By such a high degree of centralization, the international community is about to be transformed into a national community, the union of states into a state.

However, the centralization of the use of force—be it in a state or in a true international organization—is possible only with an important limitation. This limitation refers to the case of self-defense. Self-defense is not identical with self-help; it is a special case of self-help. It is self-help against a specific violation of the law, against the illegal use of force, not against other violations of the law. Self-defense is the use of force by a person illegally attacked by another. The attack against which the use of force as an act of self-defense is permitted must have been made or must be intended to be made by force. Self-defense is that minimum of self-help which, even within a system of collective security based on a centralized force monopoly of the community, must be permitted. As such it is recognized by national as well as by international law, within the state as well as within international organizations.

Security Council Resolution 678 (1990)

29 November 1990, Security Council

Noting that, despite all efforts by the United Nations, Iraq refuses to comply with its obligation to implement resolution 660 (1990) and the above-mentioned subsequent relevant resolutions, in flagrant contempt of the Security Council,

Mindful of its duties and responsibilities under the Charter of the United Nations for the maintenance and preservation of international peace and security,

Determined to secure full compliance with its decisions,

Acting under Chapter VII of the Charter,

1. *Demands* that Iraq comply fully with resolution 660 (1990) and all subsequent relevant resolutions, and decides, while maintaining all its decisions, to allow Iraq one final opportunity, as a pause of goodwill to do so;

2. *Authorizes* Member States co-operating with the Government of Kuwait…to use all necessary means to uphold and implement resolution 660 (1990) and subsequent relevant resolutions and to restore international peace and security in the area;

3. *Requests* all States to provide appropriate support for the actions undertaken in pursuance of paragraph 2 above;

4. *Requests* the States concerned to keep the Security Council regularly informed on the progress of actions undertaken pursuant to paragraphs 2 and 3 above…

S. Murphy, 'Contemporary Practice of the United States relating to International Law'

97 *American Journal of International Law* 419 (2003)

UN Security Council Resolution 1441, adopted November 8, 2002, decided that Iraq was in material breach of its disarmament obligations under Resolution 687, which was adopted following the UN-authorized campaign to expel Iraq from Kuwait and to restore peace and security in the region. Nevertheless, Resolution 1441 afforded Iraq 'a final opportunity to comply with its disarmament obligations' by submitting within thirty days 'a currently accurate, full, and complete declaration of all aspects' of its weapons of mass destruction programs, and decided that any false statements or omissions in that declaration, as well as any further failure to cooperate in disarmament, would constitute an additional material breach. The resolution directed the UN Monitoring, Verification and Inspection Committee (UNMOVIC) and the International Atomic Energy Agency (IAEA) to report immediately to the Security Council any interference by Iraq with their inspection activities. The resolution stated that the Security Council would convene to consider reports of Iraqi malfeasance and recalled that Iraq had been warned 'that it will face serious consequences as a result of its continued violations of its obligations'.

On December 7, Iraq submitted a declaration of almost twelve thousand pages to the United Nations. The declaration, which Iraqi officials asserted contained 'currently accurate, full, and complete' details about Iraq's chemical, biological, and nuclear programs, maintained that Iraq had no weapons of mass destruction. A senior Iraqi official subsequently challenged the United States and United Kingdom to produce evidence that Iraq has weapons of mass destruction or programs to develop them. In the meantime, UNMOVIC and IAEA inspectors had commenced daily inspections in Iraq on November 27. Three weeks later, on December 19, UNMOVIC Executive Chairman Hans Blix provided his preliminary assessment of Iraq's declaration. After noting that many of Iraq's prior declarations during the 1990s proved to be inaccurate or incomplete, he stated that the 'overall impression is that not much new significant information has been provided in the part of Iraq's declaration which relates to proscribed weapons programs, nor has much new supporting documentation or other evidence been submitted'. Moreover, 'In a few cases there is information in our possession that would appear to contradict Iraq's account.… [T]here are indications suggesting that Iraq's account of its production and unilateral destruction of anthrax during the period between 1988 and 1991 may not be accurate.'…

In further reports to the Security Council on January 9 and 27, 2003, Blix reiterated that Iraq had failed to provide adequate answers to questions about its arms programs–such as accounting for large quantities of anthrax and VX gas–but he also conceded to journalists that UNMOVIC investigators had uncovered no 'smoking gun' evidence that Iraq had resumed secret programs. With no such evidence, with UNMOVIC and IAEA inspectors operating without any restrictions in Iraq, and with Iraq professing its willingness to cooperate in resolving any alleged discrepancies in its declaration, support by other governments for the resort to armed force against Iraq weakened.' France declared that it supported full and effective disarmament of Iraq by peaceful means through use of the inspectors, but would oppose military action against Iraq and would veto any Security Council resolution authorizing such force. Within days, Germany joined France in opposing the resort to war prior to exhausting all efforts at inspections. Russia, too, announced that it was ready to use its veto power to block a Security Council resolution authorizing the use of force. A U.S. request that the North Atlantic Treaty Organization (NATO) provide military assistance for the defense of Turkey in the event of a war on Iraq was rejected, led by opposition from Belgium, France, Germany, and Luxembourg. The Turkish Parliament voted against allowing U.S. forces to use Turkish bases to open a northern front against Iraq, although it later voted to allow U.S. aircraft to fly through Turkish airspace. Protests broke out, both in the United States and elsewhere, in opposition to war. Other governments, however, supported the view that Iraq needed to be disarmed by force. The UK government was staunchly in favor of doing so. In a declaration published in European and U.S. newspapers on January 30, leaders of the Czech Republic, Denmark, Hungary, Italy, Poland, Portugal, and the United Kingdom endorsed the U.S. position on using force to enforce Iraq's disarmament obligations.

In an effort to bolster support for action against Iraq, Secretary of State Powell addressed the UN Security Council on February 6 and presented satellite images, intercepts of conversations between Iraqi military officers, and information from defectors, all indicating Iraqi efforts to evade its disarmament obligations. Most other members of the Security Council continued to believe, however, that prior to any use of force, the inspectors needed more time to do their work. [as did the Secretary-General]...

At a further meeting of the Security Council on February 14, Blix again faulted some aspects of Iraqi cooperation, but also credited Iraq with taking several steps 'indicative of a more active attitude'. Moreover, Blix challenged several of the conclusions expressed by Secretary of State Powell in his earlier presentation (which had been based on U.S. intelligence information), such as the contention that Iraqis had been tipped off to some impending inspections. Overall, Blix noted that the inspectors had conducted more than four hundred unannounced inspections in the eleven weeks that they had been operating in Iraq. In October 2002, Congress adopted a joint resolution, which was signed into law by President Bush, authorizing the use of military force to defend the United States against Iraq and to enforce all relevant Security Council resolutions regarding Iraq.

In mid-February, the United States and the United Kingdom embarked on a diplomatic campaign to win Security Council approval of a new resolution authorizing the use of force against Iraq. The U.S./UK position was that obtaining at least nine votes for the resolution (even if one of the permanent members cast a veto) would provide moral, if not legal, legitimacy to the use of force. On February 24, the two states circulated a draft resolution-cosponsored by Spain-in which the Security Council would decide 'that Iraq has failed to take the final opportunity afforded to it in Resolution 1441 (2002)'....

In early March, the United States and the United Kingdom engaged in extensive diplomatic efforts to obtain Security Council approval for their proposed resolution or an alternative version that would grant the inspectors a brief additional period of time to conduct their work. This alternative resolution would also have established "benchmarks" for judging Iraqi compliance. Since a French and Russian veto appeared likely, the United States and United Kingdom focused on obtaining the nine Security Council votes that they deemed necessary to provide increased legitimacy to the use of force against Iraq. By mid-March, however, it became clear that there was little support for a further Security Council resolution authorizing the use of force, even from Western Hemisphere neighbors such as Chile and Mexico. On March 17, the leaders of the United States, the United Kingdom, and Spain met in the Azores and stated that if 'Saddam refuses even now to cooperate fully with the United Nations, he brings on himself the serious consequences foreseen in UNSCR 1441 and previous resolutions'....

[In an address to the US people on 17 March 2003] President Bush stated that Saddam Hussein and his sons had forty-eight hours to leave Iraq; if they failed to do so, there 'will be military conflict'. Saddam Hussein immediately rejected that ultimatum. On the evening of March 19 (Washington time)—two hours after the 48-hour deadline had lapsed—President Bush announced that war had begun. [Armed attacks commenced the next day.]

Lord Goldsmith, UK Attorney-General, Parliamentary Statement on the Legal Basis for the Use of Force in Iraq

17 March 2003, quoted in 52 *International and Comparative Law Quarterly* 811 (2003)

Authority to use force against Iraq exists from the combined effect of resolutions 678, 687 and 1441. All of these resolutions were adopted under Chapter VII of the UN Charter which allows the use of force for the express purpose of restoring international peace and security:

1. In resolution 678, the Security Council authorised force against Iraq, to eject it from Kuwait and to restore peace and security in the area.

2. In resolution 687, which set out the ceasefire conditions after Operation Desert Storm, the Security Council imposed continuing obligations on Iraq to eliminate its weapons of mass destruction in order to restore international peace and security in the area. Resolution 687 suspended but did not terminate the authority to use force under resolution 678.

3. A material breach of resolution 687 revives the authority to use force under resolution 678.

4. In resolution 1441, the Security Council determined that Iraq has been and remains in material breach of resolution 687, because it has not fully complied with its obligations to disarm under that resolution.

5. The Security Council in resolution 1441 gave Iraq 'a final opportunity to comply with its disarmament obligations' and warned Iraq of the 'serious consequences' if it did not.

6. The Security Council also decided in resolution 1441 that, if Iraq failed at any time to comply with and cooperate fully in the implementation of resolution 1441, that would constitute a further material breach.

7. It is plain that Iraq has failed so to comply and therefore Iraq was at the time of resolution 1441 and continues to be in material breach.

8. Thus, the authority to use force under resolution 678 has revived and so continues today.

9. Resolution 1441 would in terms have provided that a further decision of the Security Council to sanction force was required if that had been intended. Thus, all that resolution 1441 requires is reporting to and discussion by the Security Council of Iraq's failures, but not an express further decision to authorise force.

NOTES
1. The Security Council has taken an expansive interpretation of what constitutes a threat to international peace and security and has determined that threats arising internally may constitute a threat to international peace and security. This includes civil wars, terrorism and large-scale human rights abuse. It has also, at least since the end of the Cold War, relied extensively on Article 41, authorising such activities as trade embargoes, economic sanctions and the freezing of assets, and the creation of international criminal tribunals.
2. The intention of the drafters of the UN Charter was that, where measures under Article 41 proved to be insufficient, the United Nations would itself be able to use force. Thus, in at least this one sense, the original scheme of the Charter for collective security has failed. No agreements have been concluded under Article 43 and there are no instances of the Security Council *requiring* States to use force against a State. However, the Council has assumed the power to authorise States to use force on behalf of the international community. As the UN does not itself have the resources required to support enforcement action, it has increasingly turned to 'coalitions of the willing' to fulfil its mandate.
3. Authorisation of the use of force by the Council may be express or implied. Resolution 678 (1990) is perhaps the only instance of the Council expressly authorising the use of force against an aggressor State. It has, however, authorised the use of force in other situations, including in internal conflicts, to secure implementation of measures under Article 41, to combat piracy and armed robbery at sea, and to ensure the delivery of humanitarian assistance. The phrase seen in Resolution 678 'to use all necessary means' is considered shorthand for an authorisation to use force. Security Council resolutions authorising force do not always state that the Security Council is 'acting under Chapter VII'.
4. States have relied on implied authorisations to use force, generally where States are unable or unwilling to obtain an express authorisation under Chapter VII from the Security Council. Implied authorisation was relied upon by some States in relation to Kosovo in 1999 and by the UK and the US to support activities in Iraq from 1990 to 2002. As is seen from the (controversial) UK Attorney General's legal opinion above, the UK relied on an implied authorisation to use force in respect of *Operation Iraqi Freedom* in 2003, based on the revival of the authority to use force contained in Resolution 678. States opposing the use of force in Iraq (for example, Russia, France, China and Germany) argued that it was for the Council, and not States acting unilaterally, to determine whether there had been a material breach by Iraq and that an express Council authorisation was required before resort could be made to force. The UK Government subsequently released a more detailed legal opinion (see (2005) 54 ICLQ 767), which noted the uncertainty surrounding the

arguments in favour of action. Australia and the US relied on similar arguments (for the US legal position see Taft and Buchwald, 'Pre-emption, Iraq and International Law', (2003) 97 AJIL 553; for the Australian position see Attorney General's Memorandum on the Use of Force against Iraq, 18 March 2003, (2003) 24 *Australian Yearbook of International Law* 415).

5. The uncertainty of the legal basis for the use of force in Iraq, and the general view of several international lawyers that it was unlawful, has led some commentators to speculate that the incident would shatter the collective security system (see, for example, Franck, extracted in the first section of this chapter). However, while there is certainly now a more cautious approach on the part of some Security Council members in drafting Resolutions to avoid future arguments based on implied authorisation, the system does not appear to have collapsed. Moreover, the US Obama administration has stated its willingness to work within the UN system to a greater extent than its predecessor. The use of force in Iraq has also been the subject of various national inquiries.

6. In addition to authorising the use of force (or peace-enforcement), the UN has also authorised the deployment of peacekeeping missions. While there is no express legal basis for peacekeeping missions in the UN Charter, the ICJ has determined that such missions are within the competence of the organisation (see the *Certain Expenses Case* in Section 2B). The factual matrix of peacekeeping—as opposed to peace enforcing—is that a United Nations force is interposed in a conflict with the sole purpose of observing, fostering, or perhaps maintaining by its presence (though not by positive use of force) a ceasefire or disengagement. As a legal concept, the essence of peacekeeping is that the UN force enters and operates within a territory only with the consent of the government, group or groups exercising sovereignty within it. It is a consensual operation and can be terminated by the withdrawal of the consent of the territorial sovereign. In a 'traditional' peacekeeping situation, peacekeepers are authorised to use force only for defensive purposes (i.e. in defence of their own safety and, more controversially, in defence of the mission objectives). While the mandate of a peacekeeping force can be changed by the Security Council into one of peace enforcement action that does not require the consent of the territorial sovereign and may authorise the use of force offensively, this step will not be taken lightly. In this respect, a consensual peacekeeping operation can be instigated by action of the General Assembly, Security Council, or even the UN Secretary-General, although it is most likely to be instigated by the Council.

7. It is only the Security Council that can formally terminate an enforcement action, be it military or economic. Thus the Council as a general rule tends to avoid 'open-ended' mandates and maintains supervision of the measures and missions it has authorised, usually in the form of regular reports prepared by the Secretary-General or by a committee of the Council.

B: The General Assembly

The apparent failure of the Security Council to take effective enforcement action during the Cold War (1948–1990) led some States to seek alternative methods of galvanising the international community into enforcement action. The General Assembly Resolution somewhat hopefully entitled 'Uniting for Peace' was the manifestation of these concerns. The resolution purported to confirm the Assembly's latent powers to recommend enforcement action in the event of deadlock in the Council. Not surprisingly, the constitutionality of this procedure generated considerable criticism, although the current approach of the Council has made the issue moot.

Uniting for Peace Resolution
Resolution 377 (V) 1950 3 November 1950, General Assembly

The General Assembly

1. Resolves that if the Security Council, because of lack of unanimity of the permanent members, fails to exercise its primary responsibility for the maintenance of international peace and security in any case where there appears to be a threat to the peace, breach of the peace, or act of aggression, the General Assembly shall consider the matter immediately with a view to making appropriate recommendations to Members for collective measures, including in the case of a breach of the peace or act of aggression the use of armed force when necessary, to

maintain or restore international peace and security. If not in session at the time, the General Assembly may meet in emergency special session within twenty-four hours of the request therefore....

7. Invites each Member of the United Nations to survey its resources in order to determine the nature and scope of the assistance it may be in a position to render in support of any recommendations of the Security Council or of the General Assembly for the restoration of international peace and security.

8. Recommends to the State Members of the United Nations that each Member maintain within its national armed forces elements so trained, organized and equipped that they could promptly be made available, in accordance with its constitutional processes, for service as a United Nations unit or units, upon recommendation by the Security Council or the General Assembly, without prejudice to the use of such elements in exercise of the right of individual or collective self-defence recognized in Article 51 of the Charter.

Certain Expenses of the United Nations
Advisory Opinion, ICJ Rep 1962 151, International Court of Justice

The General Assembly assesses members' financial contributions to the running of the Organisation under Article 17 of the UN Charter. A number of States refused to pay their contributions in respect of two peacekeeping forces created under the direction of the Assembly. They argued that the Assembly was not competent to levy contributions in respect of such bodies, because the Charter assigned the maintenance of international peace and security to the Security Council. The ICJ was asked for an advisory opinion.
   Article 24 of the Charter provides:

   In order to ensure prompt and effective action by the United Nations, its Members confer on the Security
   Council primary responsibility for the maintenance of international peace and security,...

The responsibility conferred is 'primary', not exclusive. This primary responsibility is conferred upon the Security Council, as stated in Article 24, 'in order to ensure prompt and effective action'. To this end, it is the Security Council which is given a power to impose an explicit obligation of compliance if for example it issues an order or command to an aggressor under Chapter VII. It is only the Security Council which can require enforcement by coercive action against an aggressor.
   The Charter makes it abundantly clear, however, that the General Assembly is also to be concerned with international peace and security. Article 14 authorizes the General Assembly to 'recommend measures for the peaceful adjustment of any situation, regardless of origin, which it deems likely to impair the general welfare or friendly relations among nations, including situations resulting from a violation of the provisions of the present Charter setting forth the purposes and principles of the United Nations'. The word 'measures' implies some kind of action, and the only limitation which Article 14 imposes on the General Assembly is the restriction found in Article 12, namely, that the Assembly should not recommend measures while the Security Council is dealing with the same matter unless the Council requests it to do so. Thus while it is the Security Council which, exclusively, may order coercive action, the functions and powers conferred by the Charter on the General Assembly are not confined to discussion, consideration, the initiation of studies and the making of recommendations; they are not merely hortatory. Article 18 deals with '*decisions*' of the General Assembly 'on important questions'. These 'decisions' do indeed include certain recommendations, but others have dispositive force and effect ... [In light of the fact that both forces were established only with the consent of the receiving state, and in view of the terms of the relevant Assembly and Council resolutions, the Court was of the opinion that neither action constituted 'enforcement' within Chapter VII of the Charter.]

C: Regional organisations

United Nations Charter

Article 52

1. Nothing in the present Charter precludes the existence of regional arrangements or agencies for dealing with such matters relating to the maintenance of international peace and security as are appropriate for regional action, provided that such arrangements or agencies and their activities are consistent with the Purposes and Principles of the United Nations.

2. The Members of the United Nations entering into such arrangements or constituting such agencies shall make every effort to achieve pacific settlement of local disputes through such regional arrangements or by such regional agencies before referring them to the Security Council.

3. The Security Council shall encourage the development of pacific settlement of local disputes through such regional arrangements or by such regional agencies either on the initiative of the States concerned or by reference to the Security Council.

4. The Article in no way impairs the application of Articles 34 and 35.

Article 53

1. The Security Council shall, where appropriate, utilize such regional arrangements or agencies for enforcement action under its authority. But no enforcement action shall be taken under regional arrangements or by regional agencies without the authorization of the Security Council, with the exception of measures against any enemy State, as defined in paragraph 2 of this Article provided for pursuant to Article 107 or in regional arrangements directed against renewal of aggressive policy on the part of any such State, until such time as the Organization may, on request of the Governments concerned, be charged with the responsibility for preventing further aggression by such a State.

2. The term 'enemy State' as used in paragraph 1 of this Article applies to any State which during the Second World War has been an enemy of any signatory of the present Charter.

Article 54

The Security Council shall at all times be kept fully informed of activities undertaken or in contemplation under regional arrangements or by regional agencies for the maintenance of international peace and security.

M. Akehurst, 'Enforcement Action by Regional Agencies with Special Reference to the Organization of American States'
42 British Yearbook of International Law 175 (1967)

Article 53 of the Charter states that no enforcement action may be taken by regional agencies or under regional arrangements without the authorization of the Security Council. What does 'enforcement action' mean?... Communist States argued that all sanctions imposed by a regional agency constituted 'enforcement action'; that sanctions might only be imposed in order to deal with a threat to the peace, a breach of the peace or an act of aggression (and not, for instance, in order to bring about the downfall of a Communist government in Cuba); and that they might not be imposed without the authorization of the Security Council.

The United States and its allies, on the other hand, maintained that 'enforcement action', necessitating Security Council authorization, referred only to military action, and that a regional agency could employ any non-military sanctions it liked, without Security Council authorization, against a member which presented a threat to the peace or which broke the rules of the organization. A number of arguments were put forward in support of this contention.

Firstly, it was said that enforcement naturally connoted force...

Secondly, it was urged that this interpretation reflected the basic principle of the Charter that military force was the monopoly of the Security Council and could not be used by States except in self-defence. It was only natural, then, that Security Council authorization was needed before regional agencies could use force, because otherwise it would be too easy to evade Article 2(4). But there was no corresponding reason why regional agencies should need Security Council authorization to do things which any State could lawfully do on its own.

This brings us to the third and principal argument used by the supporters of the OAS—that any State is at liberty to break off economic relations with another State at will and that groups of States are entitled to do the same on a concerted basis, whether the groups are regional or not...

There is one other possible argument in support of the OAS position...Under Article II(2) of the United Nations Charter, as interpreted in the *Expenses* case, the General Assembly cannot take enforcement action; the Security Council is the only United Nations organ which has that power. But the General Assembly has, from the beginning, claimed the right to recommend members to break off diplomatic or economic relations with particular States. If the General Assembly passes such a recommendation and members comply with it, no one would suggest that they are thereby infringing the Security Council's monopoly of enforcement action and acting illegally. Why, then, should States not be able to comply with a similar recommendation made by a regional agency of which they are members?

Report of the UN Secretary General 'An Agenda for Peace—Preventive Diplomacy, Peacemaking and Peace-keeping'

UN Doc. A/47/277, 31 *International Law Materials* 953 (1992)

VII. Cooperation with regional arrangements and organizations

60. The Covenant of the League of Nations, in its Article 21, noted the validity of regional understandings for securing the maintenance of peace. The Charter devotes Chapter VIII to regional arrangements or agencies for dealing with such matters relating to the maintenance of international peace and security as are appropriate for regional action and consistent with the Purposes and Principles of the United Nations. The cold war impaired the proper use of Chapter VIII and indeed, in that era, regional arrangements worked on occasion against resolving disputes in the manner foreseen in the Charter.

61. The Charter deliberately provides no precise definition of regional arrangements and agencies, thus allowing useful flexibility for undertakings by a group of States to deal with a matter appropriate for regional action which also could contribute to the maintenance of international peace and security. Such associations or entities could include treaty-based organizations, whether created before or after the founding of the United Nations, regional organizations for mutual security and defence, organizations for general regional development or for cooperation on a particular economic topic or function, and groups created to deal with a specific political, economic or social issue of current concern.

62. In this regard, the United Nations has recently encouraged a rich variety of complementary efforts. Just as no two regions or situations are the same, so the design of cooperative work and its division of labour must adapt to the realities of each case with flexibility and creativity. In Africa, three different regional groups - the Organization of African Unity, the League of Arab States and the Organization of the Islamic Conference - joined efforts with the United Nations regarding Somalia. In the Asian context, the Association of South-East Asian Nations and individual States from several regions were brought together with the parties to the Cambodian conflict at an international conference in Paris, to work with the United Nations. For El Salvador, a unique arrangement - 'The Friends of the Secretary-General' - contributed to agreements reached through the mediation of the Secretary-General. The end of the war in Nicaragua involved a highly complex effort which was initiated by leaders of the region and conducted by individual States, groups of States and the Organization of American States. Efforts undertaken by the European Community and its member States, with the support of States participating in the Conference on Security and Cooperation in Europe, have been of central importance in dealing with the crisis in the Balkans and neighbouring areas.

63. In the past, regional arrangements often were created because of the absence of a universal system for collective security; thus their activities could on occasion work at cross-purposes with the sense of solidarity required for the effectiveness of the world Organization. But in this new era of opportunity, regional arrangements or agencies can render great service if their activities are undertaken in a manner consistent with the Purposes and Principles of the Charter, and if their relationship with the United Nations, and particularly the Security Council, is governed by Chapter VIII.

64. It is not the purpose of the present report to set forth any formal pattern of relationship between regional organizations and the United Nations, or to call for any specific division of labour. What is clear, however, is that regional arrangements or agencies in many cases possess a potential that should be utilized in serving the functions covered in this report: preventive diplomacy, peace-keeping, peacemaking and post-conflict peace-building. Under the Charter, the Security Council has and will continue to have primary responsibility for maintaining international peace and security, but regional action as a matter of decentralization, delegation and cooperation with United Nations efforts could not only lighten the burden of the Council but also contribute to a deeper sense of participation, consensus and democratization in international affairs.

65. Regional arrangements and agencies have not in recent decades been considered in this light, even when originally designed in part for a role in maintaining or restoring peace within their regions of the world. Today a new sense exists that they have contributions to make. Consultations between the United Nations and regional arrangements or agencies could do much to build international consensus on the nature of a problem and the measures required to address it. Regional organizations participating in complementary efforts with the United Nations in joint undertakings would encourage States outside the region to act supportively. And should the Security Council choose specifically to authorize a regional arrangement or organization to take the lead in addressing a crisis within its region, it could serve to lend the weight of the United Nations to the validity of the regional effort. Carried forward in the spirit of the Charter, and as envisioned in Chapter VIII, the approach

outlined here could strengthen a general sense that democratization is being encouraged at all levels in the task of maintaining international peace and security, it being essential to continue to recognize that the primary responsibility will continue to reside in the Security Council.

Security Council Resolution 1631 (2005)

17 October 2005, Security Council

The Security Council,

Recalling Chapter VIII of the Charter of the United Nations,

Reaffirming its previous relevant resolutions and presidential statements,

Welcoming the adoption of the 2005 World Summit Outcome (A/RES/60/1),

Recalling its invitation of January 1993 to regional organizations to improve coordination with the United Nations, the Declaration of the General Assembly of December 1994 on the enhancement of cooperation between the United Nations and regional arrangements or agencies (A/RES/49/57), its meeting on 'The Security Council and Regional Organizations: Facing the New Challenges to International Peace and Security', held on 11 April 2003 under the Mexican presidency, and its debate on 'Cooperation between the United Nations and regional organizations in stabilization processes', held on 20 July 2004 under the Romanian presidency, *Welcoming* the Conclusions of the Chairman of the Sixth High-Level Meeting between the United Nations and Regional and other Intergovernmental Organizations (25–26 July 2005),

Reiterating its primary responsibility for the maintenance of international peace and security,

Emphasizing that the growing contribution made by regional organizations in cooperation with the United Nations can usefully complement the work of the organization in maintaining international peace and security, and *stressing* in this regard that such contribution must be made in accordance with Chapter VIII of the United Nations Charter,

Recognizing the necessity to support capacity-building and cooperation at regional and subregional level in maintaining international peace and security, and noting in particular the importance of strengthening the capacity of African regional and subregional organizations,

Acknowledging the resolve of Heads of State and Government of the 2005 World Summit to expand, as appropriate, the involvement of regional organizations in the work of the Security Council, and to ensure that regional organizations that have a capacity for the prevention of armed conflict or peacekeeping consider the option of placing such capacity in the framework of the United Nations Standby Arrangements System,

Welcoming the decision in the World Summit Outcome to establish a Peacebuilding Commission, and *looking forward* to it as an important opportunity for cooperation and close contact with regional and subregional organizations in post-conflict peacebuilding and recovery,

1. *Expresses its determination* to take appropriate steps to the further development of cooperation between the United Nations and regional and subregional organizations in maintaining international peace and security, consistent with Chapter VIII of the United Nations Charter, and *invites* regional and subregional organizations that have a capacity for conflict prevention or peacekeeping to place such capacities in the framework of the United Nations Standby Arrangements System;

2. *Urges* all States and relevant international organizations to contribute to strengthening the capacity of regional and subregional organizations, in particular of African regional and subregional organizations, in conflict prevention and crisis management, and in post-conflict stabilization, including through the provision of human, technical and financial assistance, and *welcomes in this regard* the establishment by the European Union of the Peace Facility for Africa;

3. *Stresses* the importance for the United Nations of developing regional and subregional organizations' ability to deploy peacekeeping forces rapidly in support of United Nations peacekeeping operations or other Security Council mandated operations, and *welcomes* relevant initiatives taken in this regard;

4. *Stresses* the potential role of regional and subregional organizations in addressing the illicit trade in small arms and light weapons and the need to take into account in the peacekeeping operations' mandates, where appropriate, the regional instruments enabling states to identify and trace illegal small arms and light weapons;

5. *Reiterates* the need to encourage regional cooperation, including through the involvement of regional and subregional organizations in the peaceful settlement of disputes, and to include, where appropriate, specific provisions to this aim in future mandates of peacekeeping and peacebuilding operations authorized by the Security Council;

6. *Welcomes* the efforts undertaken by its subsidiary bodies with responsibilities in counter-terrorism to foster cooperation with regional and subregional organizations, *notes with appreciation* the efforts made by an increasing number of regional and subregional organizations in the fight against terrorism and *urges all* relevant regional and subregional organizations to enhance the effectiveness of their counter-terrorism efforts within their respective mandates, including with a view to develop their capacity to help Member States in their efforts to tackle the threats to international peace and security posed by acts of terrorism;

7. *Expresses* its intention to hold regular meetings as appropriate with heads of regional and subregional organizations in order to strengthen the interaction and cooperation with these organizations in maintaining international peace and security, ensuring if possible that such meetings coincide with the annual high-level meetings held by the United Nations with regional and other intergovernmental organizations for better efficiency of participation and substantive complementarity of agendas;

8. *Recommends* better communication between the United Nations and regional and subregional organizations through, notably, liaison officers and holding of consultations at all appropriate levels;

9. *Reiterates* the obligation for regional organizations, under article 54 of the Charter, to keep the Security Council fully informed of their activities for the maintenance of international peace and security;

10. *Invites* the Secretary-General to submit a report to the Security Council on the opportunities and challenges facing the cooperation between the United Nations and regional and subregional organizations in maintaining international peace and security, *and encourages* the Secretary-General to explore with regional organizations the possibility of agreements establishing a framework for regional organizations' cooperation with and contributions to United Nations-led peacekeeping operations, taking into due consideration the cooperation guidelines already identified between the UN and certain regional organizations;

11. *Requests* the Secretary-General, where appropriate, to include in his regular reporting to the Security Council on peacekeeping and peacebuilding operations under its mandate, assessments of progress on the cooperation between the United Nations and regional and subregional organizations;

NOTES

1. The UN Charter does not define what constitutes a regional arrangement or agency for the purpose of Chapter VIII. Practice suggests that the UN now adopts a functional approach, where the key factors are the activity to be performed and the attitude of the Security Council, and not the nature of the organisation.

2. The question of whether a proposed action is lawful according to the constitutional instruments of the regional organisation is never usually considered, although many organisations do not expressly provide for the use of force or peacekeeping. In recent years, several regional organisations have amended their constitutional instruments or agreed new ones so as to recognise such a role, for example the African Union.

3. Thus the key issue is the legality of an action under the UN Charter. The right of the UN to utilise regional organisations for properly authorised enforcement action is not in doubt. The crucial question is the extent to which regional organisations can authorise the use of force against their own members when the Security Council has not authorised the action. Article 53 is quite clear that 'enforcement action' cannot be undertaken without Council approval and Article 103 establishes the primacy of the UN Charter over all other treaties. Hence NATO action in the Kosovo crisis does not become lawful simply because it was legitimate under NATO treaties. There was no UN authorisation in that case (see Section 1F). This limitation has led some members of regional organisations to claim that force can be authorised against a member provided it does not amount in a technical sense to 'enforcement action', e.g. in respect of the US-led invasion of Grenada in 1985, though this is of doubtful merit. It is also necessary to distinguish between peacekeeping, which can be conducted without an authorisation from the Council provided the host State has consented, and peace enforcement, which does require such authorisation.

4. In *An Agenda for Peace*, the Secretary-General set out the aspirations for the role of regional operations, working in cooperation with the UN, in the maintenance of international peace and security. This hope was reiterated in the World Summit Outcome document, which called for a stronger relationship between the UN and regional organisations. Security Council Resolution 1631 is the first Council resolution to consider cooperation between regional organisations and the UN. It

appears that the hopes of the Secretary-General have been fulfilled to an extent. Various regional organisations have taken a lead role in some conflicts. In particular, African regional and sub-regional organisations have established a number of peacekeeping missions in Africa. The African Union (AU, the successor to the OAU) has been more proactive, though recent experiences of AU peacekeeping forces in Somalia and Darfur highlight the problems that such missions may encounter. The AU has struggled to field sufficient numbers of troops and its missions have operated with limited resources, both financial and material. This has impacted upon the ability of the missions to perform their mandates effectively, and has led in Darfur to the deployment of a hybrid AU/UN force. The European Union has also assumed a more active role under the European Security and Defence Policy. It has been authorised to lead operations both within and outside Europe (e.g. the DRC, Chad and the Central African Republic).

16

Peaceful Settlement of International Disputes

An international legal order, as with any effective legal system, must have some rules in regard to the settlement of disputes. These rules are particularly necessary in an international community where States are not equal in terms of diplomatic power, access to weapons or access to resources, and where there is the potential for massive harm to people and to territory. That these disputes should be settled peacefully is a direct corollary of the prohibition of the use of force seen in the previous chapter.

The legal obligation to settle disputes peacefully, reflected in Article 33 of the UN Charter, may now have the character of *jus cogens*, at least if the non-use of force has that character (see Chapter 15). However, this obligation does not prescribe any specific method of peaceful settlement to be used, or that a dispute must be settled at all. Instead it provides that if an attempt is made to settle the dispute, it must be done peacefully. The means available for the settlement of international disputes are commonly divided into two groups: diplomatic means or non-judicial means that include, for instance, negotiation and mediation (see Section 2); and arbitration and judicial settlement (Sections 3–5).

In most instances States do comply with decisions of international judicial, quasi-judicial or other international supervisory bodies. This may be due to moral, economic, social or political pressure, or as part of an acknowledgement of an international legal order.

The International Court of Justice settles relatively few international disputes. Nevertheless, its position as a permanent international court and the wide impact of its decisions in clarifying and developing international law requires consideration of its structure and jurisdiction to a greater extent than its actual dispute-settling role would suggest.

SECTION 1: GENERAL OBLIGATION ON STATES

United Nations Charter

Article 2

3. All Members shall settle their international disputes by peaceful means in such a manner that international peace and security, and justice, are not endangered.

Article 33

1. The parties to any dispute, the continuance of which is likely to endanger the maintenance of international peace and security, shall, first of all, seek a solution by negotiation, enquiry, mediation, conciliation, arbitration, judicial settlement, resort to regional agencies or arrangements, or other peaceful means of their own choice.

2. The Security Council shall, when it deems necessary, call upon the parties to settle their dispute by such means.

Status of Eastern Carelia Case

PCIJ Ser B (1923), No. 5, Permanent Court of International Justice

It is well established in international law that no State can, without its consent, be compelled to submit its disputes with other States either to mediation or to arbitration, or to any other kind of pacific settlement.

NOTE: What constitutes an 'international dispute' was considered by the International Court of Justice in the Advisory Opinion of *Interpretation of Peace Treaties Case* ICJ Rep 1950 65. It held that 'whether there exists an international dispute is a matter for objective determination. The mere denial of the existence of a dispute [by a State] does not prove its non-existence'.

SECTION 2: NON-JUDICIAL SETTLEMENT PROCEDURES

A: General procedures

D. Bowett, 'Contemporary Developments in Legal Techniques in the Settlement of Disputes'

180 *Recueil des Cours* 169 (1983-II)

The principle of settlement of disputes by *peaceful* means is, of course, one of the principles basic to the whole structure of international society. Its juxtaposition in Article 2(3) of the United Nations Charter with Article 2(4) is no accident of drafting: for it is the corollary of the prohibition of the use or threat of force as a means of resolving international disputes. This emerges clearly from the Manila Declaration on the Peaceful Settlement of Disputes adopted by the General Assembly in 1982 at its thirty-seventh session: for there the constant reiteration of the obligation not to use force for the settlement of disputes emphasizes the fundamental link between these two Charter provisions.

Yet settlement of disputes by *peaceful* means is not the same as settlement by *legal* means. Realistically, we have to accept that the vast majority of disputes will be settled by political rather than by legal means. Settlement is normally achieved by negotiation, with or without the assistance of some third party. The third party may be a State or an organ of some organization such as the Security Council, or the Council of Ministers of the Organization for African Unity, or the Council, or the Arab League. And the third party involvement may be formalized good offices, or mediation, or conciliation; or it may be quite informal, and undertaken as a more or less routine part of the functioning of the many international organizations, or even the diplomatic function.

Yet, whatever its form, these techniques of settlement are rarely indifferent to the legal rights of the parties. Obviously, the relevance of the law will depend on how far the parties invoke legal arguments. In general, however, they will do so and the settlement process has to take account of them. The eventual settlement would, however, be normally expected to embody elements of a compromise: and, indeed, willingness to compromise is deemed something of a virtue.

Clearly, however, there are occasions when the parties prefer settlement by *legal* means, and by that I mean resort to either arbitration or judicial settlement. It is the characteristic of these techniques that they involve the application of law—to the exclusion of political discretion or, indeed, any other 'non-legal' factors—and result in a binding award or judgment. At least, that is the theory.

H. Wilson, *The Labour Government 1964–1970: A Personal Record*

(1971)

The Rann of Kutch is an area north-west of Bombay on the Arabian Sea, and was the subject of a territorial dispute between India and Pakistan which resulted in the use of force in 1965. The boundary was eventually judicially settled by a judicial tribunal in 1968.

We [the United Kingdom Government] were able to make progress with the Rann of Kutch dispute, which had become more dangerous with the outbreak of fighting on the Kashmir border. Mr Shastri [Prime Minister of

India] was at Chequers [a government house in the UK], President Ayub [of Pakistan] at Dorneywood [another government house in the UK]. After dinner, when my guests went … for coffee and drinks and informal discussion, I [United Kingdom Prime Minister Harold Wilson] took the chance of sounding out the Indian Prime Minister about the dispute, and we were soon looking at maps. 'Was this track essential? Could Pakistan move along that one? Suppose it were only police and not troops involved in this area, and guns moved back in that one?' Gradually the sticking-points became clearer. Meanwhile, a similar process was going on at Dorneywood. Each tentative advance or embryo concession was passed through private secretaries from one house to the other and we began to make progress.

On the next evening the roles were reversed. I took Ayub aside after dinner, Arthur Bottomley [UK Secretary of State for Commonwealth Relations] engaged Shastri.…We…passed on to the Rann of Kutch problem, again exchanging messages point by point with Dorneywood. By midnight, putting together the moves in both houses, we were moving towards a possible settlement. Both our guests accepted my proposal that, with the Queen's permission, we might retire for a few minutes from the Royal dinner for the Commonwealth prime ministers to see if an agreement could be worked out. Detailed briefing was prepared in the Commonwealth Office, and on the night of Tuesday, 22nd June [1965], when we were all at Buckingham Palace, by prior arrangement with Her Majesty we went to a prepared room and quickly reached the basis of a settlement. The two British High Commissioners followed this up with their host Governments and, a cease-fire was signed on 30th June and announced by me in Parliament.

NOTES
1. Article 33 of the United Nations Charter suggests a range of dispute settlement methods. Many of these methods are substantially non-judicial, for example, negotiation, enquiry, mediation and conciliation. States can decide for themselves how to resolve their disputes peacefully.
2. The distinction between legal and non-legal means of settling disputes is given in the extract from Bowett. As seen from the memoirs of Harold Wilson, a non-legal method was applied in the Rann of Kutch settlement. The settlement reached was then put into a legally binding agreement, which included an agreement to arbitrate the dispute—*Rann of Kutch Arbitration* 7 ILM 633 (1968).
3. The introduction of a third party into a dispute is often used once the parties are unable to resolve the dispute by negotiation. The extent of the role of the third party varies from being merely a channel of communication between the parties to an active promoter of solutions after undertaking its own investigations.

B: United Nations procedures

United Nations Charter

Article 36

1. The Security Council may, at any stage of a dispute of the nature referred to in Article 33 or of a situation of like nature, recommend appropriate procedures or methods of adjustment.

2. The Security Council should take into consideration any procedures for the settlement of the dispute which have already been adopted by the parties.

3. In making recommendations under this Article the Security Council should also take into consideration that legal disputes should as a general rule be referred by the parties to the International Court of Justice in accordance with the provisions of the Statute of the Court.

Article 37

1. Should the parties to a dispute of the nature referred to in Article 33 fail to settle it by the means indicated in that Article, they shall refer it to the Security Council.

2. If the Security Council deems that the continuance of the dispute is in fact likely to endanger the maintenance of international peace and security, it shall decide whether to take action under Article 36 or to recommend such terms of settlement as it may consider appropriate.

Article 38

Without prejudice to the provisions of Articles 33 to 37, the Security Council may, if all the parties to any dispute so request, make recommendations to the parties with a view to a pacific settlement of the dispute.

NOTES

1. Since the end of the Cold War the Security Council has been able to take action to settle disputes. Some of this action has been by force and some by peacekeeping operations, as was seen in Chapter 15.
2. The Secretary-General of the United Nations has used the 'good offices' function of the position to settle disputes, either personally or through an appointed representative. He can be involved in many ways, including reaching a negotiated solution. An example is the attempts by his representatives to forge a peaceful solution to armed conflict since 2011 in Syria. Regional organisations are also involved in settling disputes peacefully.
3. The interaction between the roles of the Security Council and the International Court of Justice in the peaceful settlement of disputes, as provided for in Article 36(3) of the United Nations Charter, is dealt with in Section 6.

SECTION 3: ARBITRATION

C. Gray and B. Kingsbury, 'Developments in Dispute Settlement: Inter-State Arbitration since 1945'

63 *British Yearbook of International Law* (1992) 97

In the post-1945 period, arbitration is best understood as a locus of activity rather than a highly precise category, recognised as distinct in practice but not separated by clear lines from adjudication on the one hand and conciliation on the other. Thus, for instance, while conciliation is traditionally distinguished from arbitration on the basis that the parties are not obliged to accept the recommendations of a conciliation commission, treaty provisions occasionally provide that recommendations are binding or at least must be considered in good faith. The United Nations Secretary-General in the 1986 *Rainbow Warrior* case between New Zealand and France functioned as both conciliator and arbitrator in producing a ruling which was 'equitable and principled', which 'respect[ed] and reconcil[ed]' the differing positions of the parties, which was informed by diplomatic consultations the Secretary-General had undertaken with each party separately, which did not contain explicit legal reasoning, and which the parties had agreed in advance to accept as binding. Arbitral tribunals have on occasion been asked to produce non-binding legal opinions on disputes, or to attempt to achieve friendly settlement of a dispute in the manner of a mediator or conciliator before issuing a binding ruling. The substantive differences between arbitration and judicial settlement have also become less precise; the ICJ has developed the chambers procedure so as to be comparable in many respects to the procedure of an ad hoc arbitral tribunal, although institutional and other differences remain important....

The three most obvious reasons for States to choose arbitration over settlement by the ICJ, particularly now that the modified and functional chambers procedure is established and has considerably increased the flexibility of that body, are the possibility of secrecy, the possibility of greater party control over the composition of the tribunal, and the ability to avoid an intervention in the proceedings by a third state. A fourth feature is the possibility of closer control by the parties of the questions actually addressed to the tribunal, although the International Court has also shown considerable deference to the parties in special agreement cases. Further possible advantages which have been relevant if not highly significant in practice include the possibility of recourse to the ICJ against a tribunal decision, and conceivably the non-application of provisions such as articles 94 and 102 of the UN Charter. Recourse to arbitration may also be a response of state discouraged by a particular experience with the ICJ. Finally where it is desired to entrust resolution of the dispute to persons with particular technical competence, arbitration by technical experts or by international adjudicators closely assisted by technical experts may be preferred to ICJ adjudication.

NOTES

1. Arbitration is a device for leaving the settlement of disputes as much in the hands of the parties as is possible. It can be conducted confidentially and can be quicker and cheaper than ICJ proceedings. When the parties conclude an agreement, they generally settle the law to be applied to the agreement, and also the method of settlement of any disputes which may arise, including the place where the dispute is to be settled, by whom and in accordance with what procedures. They have much more freedom of choice than in court settlement, where there is a standing panel of judges with its own procedural rules.

2. States may choose arbitration as the method to settle a dispute between them, even if the dispute concerns territorial boundaries or treaty interpretation. Examples include the *English Channel Arbitration Case* 54 ILR (1977) 6 (see Chapter 3), the *Air Services Agreement Case* 18 RIAA (1978) 416 and the Eritrea-Ethiopia Boundary Commission PCA (2002). In these situations, the States agree on the form of arbitration and the membership of the arbitration tribunal, usually with an arbitrator appointed by each State and the third arbitrator either appointed jointly by the States or by the already appointed arbitrators.

3. The Permanent Court of Arbitration (PCA) is an international mechanism established in 1899 to facilitate arbitration and other forms of dispute resolution between States. The PCA was established by the 1899 Convention for the Pacific Settlement of International Disputes, which was revised in 1907 at a second peace conference (see 1907 Convention for the Peaceful Settlement of Disputes). As at March 2016, 117 States have ratified or acceded to one or both of these conventions. The PCA is supported by a registry and secretariat, based in The Hague. It is not limited to hearing disputes between States, and may also arbitrate disputes between States, State entities, intergovernmental organisations and non-State actors. Though not widely used, the PCA has arbitrated disputes in a number of subject areas, including territorial disputes, investment disputes, use of force and treaty interpretation.

4. An international tribunal can be set up for a limited purpose in order to decide specific disputes between two States. Examples include the United Nations Compensation Commission (established by the Security Council following the invasion and occupation of Kuwait in 1991) and the Eritrea-Ethiopia Claims Commission (established pursuant to an agreement between the Governments of Eritrea and Ethiopia in 2000 following an armed conflict between the two States).

5. In international commercial arbitrations between a State and an international corporation, there are many arbitration agreements which are supervised by international arbitration institutions (see also Chapter 13). These agreements provide procedural rules which can be adopted by the parties if they consider them appropriate.

6. A major consideration in choosing arbitration as a means of settling a dispute between a State and an international corporation will be that the international corporation may not wish to be subjected to the courts of the State with which it has contracted. Agreements are made to limit a State's ability to interfere in, or to frustrate, an arbitration by, for example, claiming State immunity or giving diplomatic protection (e.g. Articles 26 and 27 of the ICSID Convention, see further, Chapter 13).

7. While there are certain circumstances where the decision of an arbitral tribunal may not be final, very often economic pressures, such as the desire for foreign investment—which usually demands a relatively stable legal system and confidence that law will be complied with—or pressures from other States often facilitate a State's compliance with an arbitration decision.

SECTION 4: SPECIFIC INTERNATIONAL TRIBUNALS

In 1946, the International Court of Justice (see Section 5) was the only permanent international court. However, there has been a vast growth in the number of international tribunals, both judicial and non-judicial, in the past few decades. There are now over 25 permanent international courts and tribunals. Higgins outlines practical suggestions for how to respond to possible issues of fragmentation, jurisdictional conflict and inconsistency within the international legal system.

R. Higgins, 'A Babel of Judicial Voices? Ruminations from the Bench'

55 International and Comparative Law Quarterly 791 (2006)

[The] 'intermingling' of legal regimes is in fact going on all around us. The intellectual debate began with expressed concerns about fragmentation arising from the now many judicial institutions, and what the less reverent may have perceived as 'judicial turf wars'....

One school of thought urgently proposes that a judicial hierarchy be established within our horizontal international legal order. The leading proponent is Judge Gilbert Guillaume, former President of the International Court of Justice...Judge Guillaume concludes that relations between courts need to be institutionalized to ensure harmony both procedurally (which tribunal should be seized of the case and development of principles such as *res judicata*) and substantively (consistency of rendered decisions). He argues that the ICJ should occupy a privileged position in the international judicial hierarchy for a variety of reasons: (1) It is the only court with a universal general jurisdiction; (2) it is the 'principal judicial organ of the United Nations'; and (3) its age and length of duration give it special authority. However, Judge Guillaume is unclear about how precisely to institutionalize this privileged position of the ICJ. He does not believe that there is sufficient political will actually to formalize the position of the ICJ as a supreme appellate body that has the capacity to review judgments rendered by other international bodies. Alternatively, he posits that a version of the preliminary reference procedure available under Article 234 of the EC Treaty in European Community law should be institutionalized so that Courts can refer new questions of general international law to the International Court of Justice.

My own views on these issues have been somewhat different. My starting point has been that the multiplication of intended legal institutions has resulted in a de facto decentralization of some subject-matter which the ICJ could in principle deal with *ratione materiae*. When one compares the tribunals established to deal with specialized areas of international law with the ICJ, one readily sees that the tribunals are more open to non-State actors, can respond more quickly, and are composed of experts in complex subject matter. I can see no reason why States who have deliberately chosen such new bodies to respond to their real-life needs should support the slowing down of the work of these specialist tribunals to allow some form of reference to the ICJ. And I find it ironic that the proponents of 'unity' in international law should think it possible for a specialist tribunal to retain full powers in 'specialist' areas of law while referring over to the ICJ the issues of 'general' international law. Are the particular and the general so easy to distinguish and slice up? And do we really want to do so?

Further, many of these specialist tribunals have what comes close to compulsory jurisdiction. There are not the same opportunities for non-participation in the judicial process, or the fashioning of reservations thereto, as there are under the International Court's Statute. Why should States who have declined to submit to the jurisdiction of the International Court of Justice agree to a reworking of the international system so that matters they have agreed to submit to particular specialized tribunals may in part still finish up with the ICJ? In sum, I have always regarded the 'hierarchical' approach to the risks of Babel as unworkable...

What, then, is to be done? There are no simplistic answers....We judges are going to have to learn how to live in this new, complex world, and to regard it as an opportunity, rather than a problem:

- We must read each other's judgments.
- We must have respect for each other's judicial work.
- We must try to preserve unity among us unless context really prevents this.

A: International criminal tribunals

There have been several international bodies established to deal with international crimes. These include the International Criminal Tribunal for the former Yugoslavia, the International Criminal Tribunal for Rwanda and the International Criminal Court. There is also a growing number of so-called hybrid and internationalised tribunals, including the Special Court for Sierra Leone, the Special Tribunal for Lebanon, the War Crimes Chamber for Bosnia and Herzegovina, the Extraordinary Chambers in the Courts of Cambodia and the Extraordinary African Chamber within the Courts of Senegal. These tribunals are discussed in further detail in Chapter 14.

B: Human rights supervisory bodies

International human rights law has a large number of bodies that supervise compliance with treaties protecting human rights. These are set out in Chapter 6, and include both global human rights treaty-based committees, that can consider both periodic State reports and individual complaints, and regional human rights courts. In addition, a number of these bodies, such as the Inter-American Commission on Human Rights, can seek to settle the matter prior to a final judicial or quasi-judicial decision. The impact of these international human rights supervisory bodies on the settlement of human rights disputes, including through national law and courts, is significant and growing.

C: International economic law

As explained in Chapter 13, a detailed dispute settlement procedure was created by the World Trade Organization (WTO). The Understanding on Dispute Settlement (DSU) was incorporated into the Agreement establishing the WTO and is designed to provide a unitary system for dispute settlement. There are also specific dispute settlement procedures for international investment disputes, including the International Centre for the Settlement of International Disputes (ICSID).

D: Other specific international tribunals

Under the Law of the Sea Convention 1982, dispute settlement occurs by a variety of methods, including the International Tribunal for the Law of the Sea, and its Seabed Disputes Chamber, though there are some issues that are expressly exempted from any form of compulsory dispute settlement (see Chapter 10). This Tribunal was formed in 1996, after the Convention came into force.

SECTION 5: INTERNATIONAL COURT OF JUSTICE

The International Court of Justice (ICJ) was created in 1945. It is substantially a continuation of the Permanent Court of International Justice (PCIJ), which was created in 1921. Article 92 of the United Nations Charter describes the ICJ as 'the principal judicial organ of the United Nations', with the Statute of the ICJ being 'an integral part' of the Charter.

A: General

Statute of the International Court of Justice

Article 2

The Court shall be composed of a body of independent judges, elected regardless of their nationality from among persons of high moral character, who possess the qualifications required in their respective countries for appointment to the highest judicial offices, or are jurisconsults of recognized competence in international law.

Article 3

1. The Court shall consist of fifteen members, no two of whom may be nationals of the same State.

Article 26

1. The Court may from time to time form one or more chambers, composed of three or more judges as the Court may determine, for dealing with particular categories of cases; for example, labour cases and cases relating to transit and communications.

2. The Court may at any time form a chamber for dealing with a particular case. The number of judges to constitute such a chamber shall be determined by the Court with the approval of the parties.

3. Cases shall be heard and determined by the chambers provided for in this Article if the parties so request.

Article 27

A judgment given by any of the chambers provided for in Articles 26 and 29 shall be considered as rendered by the Court.

Article 31

1. Judges of the nationality of each of the parties shall retain their right to sit in the case before the Court.

2. If the Court includes upon the Bench a judge of the nationality of one of the parties any other party may choose a person to sit as judge. Such person shall be chosen preferably from among those persons who have been nominated as candidates as provided in Articles 4 and 5.

3. If the Court includes upon the Bench no judge of the nationality of the parties, each of these parties may proceed to choose a judge as provided in paragraph 2 of this Article.

Article 34

1. Only States may be parties in cases before the Court....

Article 35

1. The Court shall be open to the states parties to the present Statute.

2. The conditions under which the Court shall be open to other states shall, subject to the special provisions contained in treaties in force, be laid down by the Security Council, but in no case shall such conditions place the parties in a position of inequality before the Court....

Judge Peter Tomka, President of the International Court of Justice, Speech to the Asian-African Legal Consultative Organization

ICJ, Press Release, 30 October 2013

As the principal judicial organ of the United Nations, the Court has been entrusted with the primary responsibility of delivering international justice between disputing States....We are witnessing a willingness among States to submit their disputes to pacific settlement options, with both judicial settlement and arbitral proceedings remaining viable avenues. After all, Article 33 of the UN Charter provides States with considerable freedom of choice in electing potential dispute resolution options: the overarching principle is that such settlement or adjustment mechanisms must provide for the peaceful resolution of disagreements. This obligation is mirrored in other provisions of the Charter, in particular to signal that Member States undertake to 'settle their international dispute by peaceful means in such manner that international peace and security, and justice, are not endangered'.

Unsurprisingly, the Court is increasingly turned to by States as an effective forum for the pacific settlement of disputes. This tendency may be best explained by the fact that parties to international disputes feel comfortable in putting their confidence in the Court and in the prospect that it will reach well-reasoned and just outcomes, on the basis of the evidence submitted to it and the arguments of the parties appearing before it, and in accordance with the rules and principles of international law. Since its inception after the Second World War, the Court has consistently and efficiently discharged its noble judicial mission. The Court's judicial output has been particularly impressive over the last quarter century: over the last 23 years, the Court has delivered more judgments than during the first 44 years of its existence. Other relevant figures confirming an enhanced confidence in the Court's work are equally eloquent: of the 70 declarations recognizing the jurisdiction of the Court as compulsory, more than a third have been deposited in the past 20 years, a large majority of those emanating from States which had never before accepted the Court's jurisdiction. What is more, some States have withdrawn their reservations to multilateral conventions precluding the jurisdiction of the World Court for disputes arising under their specific conventional schemes, thereby indirectly—but importantly—contributing to strengthening the jurisdiction of the Court....

The Court's regular clients include States from Africa, Asia, Latin America, Western Europe and America, and from a contingent formerly designated as Eastern Europe and the Middle East. Needless to say, the Court has been very active in the African context, having resolved several boundary disputes and other cases arising between African States. Sometimes, such disputes involve States from two continents such as the recent case concerning *Questions relating to the Obligation to Prosecute or Extradite*, opposing Belgium and Senegal, or the older but important *Continental Shelf* case opposing Libya and Malta, which was brought to the Court by way of special agreement. In fact, the Court has developed a solid reputation in matters of boundary disputes and maritime delimitation. Its resulting jurisprudence has not only illuminated the work of other international tribunals—such as the International Tribunal for the Law of the Sea and UNCLOS Annex VII arbitral tribunals—but has also informed governments, legal advisers and legal scholars. It is no surprise, therefore, that several African States have put their confidence in the Court to peacefully settle their disputes. Furthermore, at this time 22 African States have in force a declaration recognizing as compulsory the jurisdiction of the Court, in accordance with Article 36 (2) of its Statute. This represents roughly 40 per cent of the 54 States subsumed under the 'African Group' according to UN's Regional Groups of Member States.

Even a cursory glance at the judicial docket, since the inception of the Court, showcases the trust that African nations have afforded the Court in resolving their disagreements. For instance, 17 cases opposing African States have been brought to the Court, with only three of those disputes having been discontinued. As a result, several of the remaining 14 cases have generated at least one judgment by the Court, if not two or three judgments, be it at the preliminary objections, merits or compensation phase, or in some mixed configuration. Moreover, as I indicated earlier, other disputes before the Court have opposed one African State as a party against a European State. In total, nine such cases have been submitted to the Court for adjudication; of those nine cases, four were discontinued, although two of those were discontinued after the delivery of one judgment. Setting aside contentious proceedings for a moment, it is also interesting to underscore that six advisory opinions delivered by the Court have concerned—oftentimes very directly—African States.

By contrast, the litigation picture that emerges from Asian experience before the Court is one of perhaps more restraint. Among the 53 States falling within the rubric of the Asia-Pacific Group under the UN system, only seven States—or roughly 13 per cent of the broader contingent—recognize the jurisdiction of the Court under the optional clause (Article 36 (2)). Since the inception of the Court, eight disputes opposing Asian-Pacific States have been submitted to the Court, including a request for interpretation, namely the *Request for Interpretation of the Judgment of 15 June 1962 in the Case concerning the Temple of Preah Vihear (Cambodia v. Thailand)*....Of those eight cases, only one was eventually discontinued.

P. Kooijmans, 'The ICJ in the 21st Century: Judicial Restraint, Judicial Activism, or Proactive Judicial Policy?'
56 International and Comparative Law Quarterly 741 (2007)

Does the Court have a special responsibility towards the Parties relating to matters which—strictly speaking—are not, directly or indirectly, included in their submissions? Is it the duty of the Court not only to decide the case within the confines of the submissions but also to express its view on the future conduct of the Parties in implementing the judgment?...

I strongly believe that such a proactive judicial policy serves the interests of the Parties and enriches the Court's mission, provided the 'extras' given by the Court rest on a solid legal basis. It is not for a court of law to make moral recommendations or to suggest political measures. Both in *Gabčíkovo/Nagymaros* and in *Kasikili/Sedudu Island* the Court referred to existing legal obligations, thereby placing the relations between the Parties in a wider perspective. In the first case the Court explicitly referred to new norms relating to the environment and the utilization of international watercourses, in the second to obligations ensuing from a bilateral document. It can be readily admitted that not all cases lend themselves to such an approach. But whenever the possibility is there and the relations between the Parties make such an approach commendable, the Court should not shy away from using available opportunities which may contribute to an effective solution of the dispute....

This type of proactive policy differs from...[the policy that considers that] the function of the judge [is] to utilize those aspects of the case in hand which have a wider interest or connotation in order to make general pronouncements of law and principle that may enrich and develop the law. Such an approach seems to be diametrically opposed to that of Chief Justice Roberts of the US Supreme Court who said: 'Judges must be constantly aware that their role is limited. They do not have a commission to solve society's problems, as they see them, but simply to decide cases before them according to the rule of law'....

[I]t is judicial restraint that seems to characterize the Court's jurisprudence of the last 10 years. This was very clear in the Court's decision in the *Arrest Warrant* case, where it refused to deal with the issue of universal criminal jurisdiction in spite of the fact that it had explicitly stated that the *non ultra petita* rule (the Parties had not asked the Court to rule on the issue of universal jurisdiction although they had given it a great deal of attention in their written pleadings) cannot preclude the Court from addressing certain legal points in its reasoning, in particular the question whether the Belgian investigating judge, in exercising his purported universal jurisdiction, complied in that regard with the rules and principles of international law. By abstaining, however, from doing what it said it was entitled to do, and instead concentrating on the question of immunity, the Court made a logical mistake....

What is perhaps of even greater importance is that the Court wilfully abstained from using the opportunity (which does not come that often) to provide clarification on a matter which, while being of great topical value, is highly controversial. Such clarification would, as President Guillaume said in his separate opinion, have been in the interest of all States, including Belgium in particular. As a result we have an interesting clash of views between President Guillaume and the three judges who wrote a joint opinion, but no authoritative opinion of the Court.

This judicial restraint is also noticeable in the field of the legality of the use of force. The Court has had ample opportunity to expose its view on the way the prohibition of the use of force and the right of self-defence has to be interpreted in the beginning of the 21st century.... By refraining from dealing with it, the Court has foregone a precious opportunity to provide clarification on a number of questions which are of primordial importance in present-day international society but still are largely obscure from a legal point of view....

A court may have sound reasons not to rule on issues which are not strictly necessary for the determination of the *petitum*. One may wonder, however, whether this is the most meritorious attitude for a court which is the principal judicial organ of a world community which has to cope with a multitude of problems and where lawlessness is rampant and thus could benefit from guidance in the legal field.

The Court increasingly is dealing with cases concerning what President Higgins called 'cutting-edge' issues. This allows the Court to play a more preponderant role in delineating the law than it was able to do in the past.

I am certainly not in favour of judicial activism which may turn into a destructive trap. But neither am I in favour of a form of judicial restraint that closes windows which need to be opened and thus becomes barren.

NOTES

1. By Article 93 of the UN Charter, all members of the UN are parties to the Statute of the ICJ. Other States can become parties to the Statute on conditions determined in each case by the General Assembly on the recommendation of the Security Council. In this way, five States have become parties to the Statute, often prior to their becoming members of the United Nations: for example, Switzerland (1948), Liechtenstein (1950), Japan (1954), San Marino (1954), and Nauru (1988). As at March 2016, all States party to the Statute of the ICJ are also members of the UN. The ICJ may also be open to States that are not party to the Statute in accordance with Article 35(2) of the Statute of the ICJ, on conditions laid down by the Security Council (see Resolution 9 (1946)). This has enabled declarations to become parties to be filed by several States, including Albania (1947) and Cambodia (1952).

2. Cases are heard by the full Court of the ICJ, unless the parties to a case have requested to have a case heard by a special Chamber. The use of Chambers of the ICJ has, at least in the past, not proved very successful, mainly because there were some problems as to whether the parties should be able to choose the judges they wish for the Chamber, with certain judges regularly chosen and some never chosen. Moreover, there is a perception that much more weight was given to a decision by the full Court.

3. The judges of the ICJ tend to be appointed with the standard UN considerations of geographical distribution being taken into account, and in accordance with the convention that each of the five permanent members of the Security Council shall have a national as a judge on the ICJ.

4. There have been concerns about the apparent politicisation of the judges of the ICJ, with judges rarely voting against the claims of the State of which they are a national and decisions being seen as representing a particular cultural or political philosophy (see Posner and Figueiredo 'Is the International Court of Justice Biased?' (2005) 34 *Journal of Legal Studies* 599, estimating that judges vote for their home State 90 per cent of the time). The concern about politicisation is increased by the ability of each State that is a party in a contentious case before the ICJ to appoint judges ad hoc (under Article 31 of the Statute), usually being judges of that State's nationality, who are seen to represent the views of that State to the other judges of the ICJ. Judges ad hoc have to date almost always voted in favour of the appointing State (though see Judge ad hoc Bastid, appointed by Tunisia, voting against the request of that State for revision of the judgment in the *Continental Shelf Case (Tunisia v Libya)*). This may be the inevitable result of the nature of international law (or most

law), as it cannot be removed from the political realities or from the various theoretical concepts underlying it (see Chapter 1). The Court has suggested that no person should be appointed a judge ad hoc who has acted as an agent, counsel or advocate before the Court within three years of his/her appointment (Practice Direction VII, 7 February 2002). The extract from Kooijmans also raises the question of the proper role of ICJ judges in developing the law or responding to international issues.

5. The position of Serbia regarding its membership of the UN following the disintegration of the former Yugoslavia posed a unique problem for the ICJ. In its provisional measures judgment in the *Legality of the Use of Force* cases and its provisional measures and preliminary objections judgments in the *Bosnia Genocide Case*, the ICJ had avoided making a finding on the application of Article 35(1) of the Statute, choosing to base its decision on other grounds. In the decision in the preliminary objections phase of the *Legality of the Use of Force* cases, (*Case Concerning the Legality of Use of Force (Serbia and Montenegro v United Kingdom) (Preliminary Objections)* (2004), the Court considered whether Serbia had been a member of the UN, and hence a party to the Statute of the Court, at the time it filed proceedings in 1999. The Court concluded that Serbia itself was not a member State at that time and its membership could not 'back-date' to the disintegration of the former Yugoslavia or of the Federal Republic Yugoslavia, and therefore the ICJ could not exercise jurisdiction in the case. However, the Court appeared to adopt a more flexible approach in its decision at the preliminary objections stage in the *Croatia/Serbia Genocide Case* (*Case Concerning Application of the Convention on the Prevention and Punishment of the Crime of Genocide (Croatia v Serbia) (Preliminary Objections)* 18 November 2008), finding that the Court can look beyond the normal rule in certain cases and take into account jurisdiction that has subsequently been established.

B: Jurisdiction in contentious cases

Statute of the International Court of Justice

Article 36

1. The jurisdiction of the Court comprises all cases which the parties refer to it and all matters specially provided for in the Charter of the United Nations or in treaties or conventions in force.

2. The States Parties to the present Statute may at any time declare that they recognize as compulsory *ipso facto* and without special agreement, in relation to any other State accepting the same obligation, the jurisdiction of the Court in all legal disputes concerning:

    (a) the interpretation of a treaty;

    (b) any question of international law;

    (c) the existence of any fact which, if established, would constitute a breach of an international obligation;

    (d) the nature or extent of the reparation to be made for the breach of an international obligation.

3. The declarations referred to above may be made unconditionally or on condition of reciprocity on the part of several or certain States, or for a certain time.

4. Such declarations shall be deposited with the Secretary-General of the United Nations, who shall transmit copies thereof to the parties to the Statute and to the Registrar of the Court.

5. Declarations made under Article 36 of the Statute of the Permanent Court of International Justice and which are still in force shall be deemed, as between the parties to the present Statute, to be acceptances of the compulsory jurisdiction of the International Court of Justice for the period which they still have to run and in accordance with their terms.

6. In the event of a dispute as to whether the Court has jurisdiction the matter shall be settled by the decision of the Court.

Declarations Accepting Compulsory Jurisdiction of the International Court of Justice

The text of the declarations is available at http://www.icj-cij.org/jurisdiction/index.php?p1=5&p2=1&p3=3

As at March 2016, there were 72 Declarations in force under Article 36(2). The following are examples:

Haiti

On behalf of the Republic of Haiti, I recognize the jurisdiction of the Permanent Court of International Justice as compulsory.

(*Signed*) F. Addor, Consul.

India

I have the honour to declare, on behalf of the Government of the Republic of India, that they accept, in conformity with paragraph 2 of Article 36 of the Statute of the Court, until such time as notice may be given to terminate such acceptance, as compulsory *ipso facto* and without special agreement, and on the basis and condition of reciprocity, the jurisdiction of the International Court of Justice over all disputes other than:

(1) disputes in regard to which the parties to the dispute have agreed or shall agree to have recourse to some other method or methods of settlement;

(2) disputes with the government of any State which is or has been a Member of the Commonwealth of Nations;

(3) disputes in regard to matters which are essentially within the domestic jurisdiction of the Republic of India;

(4) disputes relating to or connected with facts or situations of hostilities, armed conflicts, individual or collective actions taken in self-defence, resistance to aggression, fulfilment of obligations imposed by international bodies, and other similar or related acts, measures or situations in which India is, has been or may in future be involved;

(5) disputes with regard to which any other party to a dispute has accepted the compulsory jurisdiction of the International Court of Justice exclusively for or in relation to the purposes of such dispute; or where the acceptance of the Court's compulsory jurisdiction on behalf of a party to the dispute was deposited or ratified less than 12 months prior to the filling of the application bringing the dispute before the Court;

(6) disputes where the jurisdiction of the Court is or may be founded on the basis of a treaty concluded under the auspices of the League of Nations, unless the Government of India specially agree to jurisdiction in each case;

(7) disputes concerning the interpretation or application of a multilateral treaty unless all the parties to the treaty are also parties to the case before the Court or Government of India specially agree to jurisdiction;

(8) disputes with the government of any State with which, on the date of an application to bring a dispute before the Court, the Government of India has no diplomatic relations or which has not been recognized by the Government of India;

(9) disputes with non-sovereign States or territories;

(10) disputes with India concerning or relating to:
    (a) the status of its territory or the modification or delimitation of its frontiers or any other matter concerning boundaries;
    (b) the territorial sea, the continental shelf and the margins, the exclusive fishery zone, the exclusive economic zone, and other zones of national maritime jurisdiction including for the regulation and control of marine pollution and the conduct of scientific research by foreign vessels;
    (c) the condition and status of its island, bays and gulfs and that of the bays and gulfs that for historical reasons belong to it;
    (d) the airspace superjacent to its land and maritime territory; and
    (e) the determination and delimitation of its maritime boundaries.

(11) disputes prior to the date of this declaration, including any dispute the foundations, reasons, facts, causes, origins, definitions, allegations or bases of which existed prior to this date, even if they are submitted or brought to the knowledge of the Court hereafter.

2. This declaration revokes and replaces the previous declaration made by the Government of India on 14 September 1959.

New Delhi, 15 September 1974.

(*Signed*) Swaran Singh, Minister for External Affairs.

Timor-Leste

On behalf of the Democratic Republic of Timor-Leste, I have the honour to declare that the Democratic Republic of Timor-Leste accepts as compulsory ipso facto and without special agreement, the jurisdiction of the International

Court of Justice in conformity with Article 36, paragraph 2, of the Statute of the Court, until such time as notice may be given to terminate this acceptance. This declaration is effective immediately.

The Government of the Democratic Republic of Timor-Leste reserves the right at any time, by means of a notification addressed to the Secretary-General of the United Nations, either to amend the present declaration or to amend or withdraw an[y] reservation that may hereafter be added.

Dili, 21 September 2012

(Signed) Kay Rala Zanana Gusmão, Prime Minister of the Democratic Republic of Timor-Leste

---

United Kingdom of Great Britain and Northern Ireland

British Yearbook of International Law 803 (2004)

1. The Government of the United Kingdom of Great Britain and Northern Ireland accept as compulsory ipso facto and without special convention, on condition of reciprocity, the jurisdiction of the International Court of Justice, in conformity with paragraph 2 of Article 36 of the Statute of the Court, until such time as notice may be given to terminate the acceptance, over all disputes arising after 1 January 1974, with regard to situations or facts subsequent to the same date, other than:

   (i) any dispute which the United Kingdom has agreed with the other Party or Parties thereto to settle by some other method of peaceful settlement;

   (ii) any dispute with the government of any other country which is or has been a Member of the Commonwealth;

   (iii) any dispute in respect of which any other Party to the dispute has accepted the compulsory jurisdiction of the International Court of Justice only in relation to or for the purpose of the dispute; or where the acceptance of the Court's compulsory jurisdiction on behalf of any other Party to the dispute was deposited or ratified less than twelve months prior to the filing of the application bringing the dispute before the Court.

2. The Government of the United Kingdom also reserve the right at any time, by means of a notification addressed to the Secretary-General of the United Nations, and with effect as from the moment of such notification, either to add to, amend or withdraw any of the foregoing reservations, or any that may hereafter be added.

New York, 5 July 2004.

(Signed) Emyr JONES PARRY

Permanent Representative of the United Kingdom of Great Britain and Northern Ireland to the United Nations.

Norwegian Loans Case (France v Norway)

ICJ Rep 1957 9, International Court of Justice

Both France and Norway had made declarations under Article 36(2) accepting the compulsory jurisdiction of the ICJ. Norway objected to France commencing the action, which concerned the rights of French holders of Norwegian bonds, as it claimed that the issue was essentially a matter within Norway's 'domestic jurisdiction'. Although Norway did not have such a reservation (often called an 'automatic' reservation) to its declaration, it submitted that it could rely on the fact that France did have such a reservation. The Court upheld Norway's submission. However, Judge Lauterpacht made a few comments about such 'automatic' reservations.

THE COURT: [I]n the present case the jurisdiction of the Court depends upon the Declarations made by the Parties in accordance with Article 36, paragraph 2, of the Statute on condition of reciprocity; and that, since two unilateral declarations are involved, such jurisdiction is conferred upon the Court only to the extent to which the Declarations coincide in conferring it. A comparison between the two Declarations shows that the French Declaration accepts the Court's jurisdiction within narrower limits than the Norwegian Declaration; consequently the common will of the parties, which is the basis of the Court's jurisdiction, exists within these narrower limits indicated by the French reservation....

In accordance with the condition of reciprocity to which acceptance of the compulsory jurisdiction is made subject in both Declarations and which is provided for in Article 36, paragraph 3, of the Statute, Norway, equally with France, is entitled to except from the compulsory jurisdiction of the Court disputes understood by Norway to be essentially within its national jurisdiction.

JUDGE LAUTERPACHT (Separate Opinion): I consider that as the French Declaration of Acceptance excludes from the jurisdiction of the Court 'matters which are essentially within the national jurisdiction as understood by the Government of the French Republic'—the emphasis being here on the words 'as understood by the Government of the French Republic'—it is for the reason of that latter qualification an instrument incapable of producing legal effects before this Court and of establishing its jurisdiction. This is so for the double reason that: (a) it is contrary to the Statute of the Court; (b) the existence of the obligation being dependent upon the determination by the Government accepting the Optional Clause, the Acceptance does not constitute a legal obligation. That Declaration of Acceptance cannot, accordingly, provide a basis for the jurisdiction of the Court. Norway has not accepted the jurisdiction of the Court on any other basis. The Court therefore has no jurisdiction.

If that type of reservation is valid, then the Court is not in the position to exercise the power conferred upon it—in fact, the duty imposed upon it—under paragraph 6 of Article 36 of its Statute.... The French reservation is thus not only contrary to one of the most fundamental principles of international—and national—jurisprudence according to which it is within the inherent power of a tribunal to interpret the text establishing its jurisdiction. It is also contrary to a clear specific provision of the Statute of the Court as well as to the general Articles 1 and 92 of the Statute and of the Charter, respectively, which require the Court to function in accordance with its Statute. Now what is the result of the fact that a reservation or part of it are contrary to the provisions of the Statute of the Court? The result is that that reservation or that part of it is invalid.

Military and Paramilitary Activities in and against Nicaragua Case (Nicaragua v USA)

ICJ Rep 1984 392, International Court of Justice

The United States had made a Declaration in April 1984 limiting its Optional Clause Declaration. It did this after it became clear that the dispute with Nicaragua was to be placed before the Court. The Court considered that the limitation had no effect on the present case.

59. Declarations of acceptance of the compulsory jurisdiction of the Court are facultative, unilateral engagements, that States are absolutely free to make or not to make. In making the declaration a State is equally free either to do so unconditionally and without limit of time for its duration, or to qualify it with conditions or reservations. In particular, it may limit its effect to disputes arising after a certain date; or it may specify how long the declaration itself shall remain in force, or what notice (if any) will be required to terminate it....

60. In fact, the declarations, even though they are unilateral acts, establish a series of bilateral engagements with other States accepting the same obligation of compulsory jurisdiction, in which the conditions, reservations and time-limit clauses are taken into consideration....

64. The Court would also recall that in previous cases in which it has had to examine the reciprocal effect of declarations made under the Optional Clause, it has determined whether or not the 'same obligation' was in existence at the moment of seising of the Court, by comparing the effect of the provisions, in particular the reservations, of the two declarations at that moment....

65. In sum, the six months' notice clause forms an important integral part of the United States Declaration and it is a condition that must be complied with in case of either termination or modification. Consequently, the 1984 notification, in the present case, cannot override the obligation of the United States to submit to the compulsory jurisdiction of the Court vis-à-vis Nicaragua, a State accepting the same obligation.

Legality of the Use of Force Case (Provisional Measures) (Federal Republic of Yugoslavia v Belgium, Canada, France, Germany, Italy, Netherlands, Portugal, Spain, United Kingdom and United States)

38 International Legal Materials 950 (1999), International Court of Justice

The Federal Republic of Yugoslavia (FRY) brought this case against ten North Atlantic Treaty Organization (NATO) States in relation to events that were occurring during the armed conflict between NATO and the FRY in Kosovo (being a constituent part of the FRY). The ICJ declined to order provisional measures against any of the respondent States and made some comments about the Court's jurisdiction.

18. Whereas the Court is mindful of the purposes and principles of the United Nations Charter and of its own responsibilities in the maintenance of peace and security under the Charter and the Statute of the Court;

19. Whereas the Court deems it necessary to emphasize that all parties appearing before it must act in conformity with their obligations under the United Nations Charter and other rules of international law, including humanitarian law;…

47. Whereas there is a fundamental distinction between the question of the acceptance by a State of the Court's jurisdiction and the compatibility of particular acts with international law; the former requires consent; the latter question can only be reached when the Court deals with the merits after having established its jurisdiction and having heard full legal arguments by both parties;

48. Whereas, whether or not States accept the jurisdiction of the Court, they remain in any event responsible for acts attributable to them that violate international law, including humanitarian law; whereas any disputes relating to the legality of such acts are required to be resolved by peaceful means, the choice of which, pursuant to Article 33 of the Charter, is left to the parties;

49. Whereas in this context the parties should take care not to aggravate or extend the dispute;

50. Whereas, when such a dispute gives rise to threat to the peace, breach of the peace or act of aggression, the Security Council has special responsibilities under Chapter VII of the Charter…

The Court Rejects the Request for Provisional Measures.

Armed Activities on the Territory of the Congo (New Application: 2002) (Democratic Republic of the Congo v Rwanda), **Decision on Jurisdiction of the Court and Admissibility of the Application**

ICJ Rep 2006, International Court of Justice

The Democratic Republic of Congo (DRC) brought a case against Rwanda concerning violations of human rights and of international humanitarian law committed on the territory of the DRC. The DRC invoked, inter alia, the Genocide Convention, in order to establish the Court's jurisdiction.

64. The Court will begin by reaffirming that 'the principles underlying the [Genocide] Convention are principles which are recognized by civilized nations as binding on States, even without any conventional obligation' and that a consequence of that conception is 'the universal character both of the condemnation of genocide and of the co-operation required 'in order to liberate mankind from such an odious scourge'.…It follows that 'the rights and obligations enshrined by the Convention are rights and obligations *erga omnes*' (*Application of the Convention on the Prevention and Punishment of the Crime of Genocide (Bosnia and Herzegovina* v. *Yugoslavia), Preliminary Objections, Judgment, I.C.J. Reports 1996 (II)*, p. 616, para. 31). The Court observes, however, as it has already had occasion to emphasize, that 'the *erga omnes* character of a norm and the rule of consent to jurisdiction are two different things' (*East Timor (Portugal* v. *Australia), Judgment, I.C.J. Reports 1995*, p. 102, para. 29), and that the mere fact that rights and obligations *erga omnes* may be at issue in a dispute would not give the Court jurisdiction to entertain that dispute. The same applies to the relationship between peremptory norms of general international law *(jus cogens)* and the establishment of the Court's jurisdiction: the fact that a dispute relates to compliance with a norm having such a character, which is assuredly the case with regard to the prohibition of genocide, cannot of itself provide a basis for the jurisdiction of the Court to entertain that dispute. Under the Court's Statute that jurisdiction is always based on the consent of the parties.

A. Llamzon, 'Jurisdiction and Compliance in Recent Decisions of the International Court of Justice'

18 *European Journal of International Law* 815 (2007)

It is important to recognize, however, that the ICJ's generally favourable compliance record in recent years (regardless of the mode of jurisdictional acquisition) should call into question some of the assumptions underlying these issues, as jurisdiction and compliance cannot be viewed with a strict cause and effect optic. The decline of the

Court's compulsory jurisdiction should not be taken as an indication that the ICJ is in irreversible decline. Indeed, the approach of states towards its jurisdiction over the years suggests that the world community has matured in its understanding of the potential and limits of the ICJ, and is moving closer to an equilibrium situation where, based on rational choice, most states have decided both to comply with the Court's judgments and further restrict its compulsory jurisdiction due to the uncertainties inherent in being unable to control outcomes. The Court's docket is increasingly being left open only for cases in which: (a) states that actually wish to settle present disputes through special agreement (because they have already discounted and are prepared to accept the consequences of an adverse decision); or (b) are undaunted at the prospect of resolving future disputes through international adjudication (those who remain committed to the optional clause or have signed treaties with compromissory clauses). This, in turn, is likely to lead to even greater compliance with the Court's decisions, thus strengthening the institution.

Avena stands out among recent cases as a predictor of what states' attitudes towards the ICJ may be in the future. As discussed, *Avena* was the third in a string of cases on the Vienna Convention on Consular Relations in which the ICJ required the United States, in increasingly mandatory tones, to review the convictions of foreign death row inmates whose consular notification rights were violated. Commentators had good reason to doubt that the ICJ judgments would result in US compliance, and were surprised when the President of the United States 'determined…that the United States will discharge its international obligations under the decision of the International Court of Justice in the Case Concerning *Avena*'. It was a pyrrhic victory for those hoping for a change in the US's attitude towards international adjudication, however, as it then promptly withdrew from the Optional Protocol to the Convention, thereby divesting the Court of jurisdiction over similar disputes in the future.

Without going into the minutiae of contemporary theories on why states obey international obligations, the US response to *Avena* does demonstrate that even the most powerful states are likely to comply with adverse ICJ judgments so long as the Court's jurisdiction and competence to rule upon the dispute is unquestionable. In order to foreclose further unpalatable judgments while simultaneously protecting the US's reputation as an international law-abider, however, one can expect that the US (along with some states with similar compromissory clauses and similar ambivalence towards international law) will, in the future, continue to prune down the Court's jurisdiction.

Whether this same type of unilateral withdrawal from ICJ jurisdiction (assuming its legality) will occur when other states find themselves in similar situations is an open question, as many multilateral treaties (unlike the Optional Clause) concern very narrow subject matter and states party may be less apprehensive about compulsory jurisdiction within those fields. It is quite possible, however, that further curtailments of the ICJ's compulsory jurisdiction will continue. Many states will not be satisfied until their agreements reflect an engagement with the ICJ only for cases wherein the worst possible adverse judgments against them have already been foreseen and discounted in advance. In that sense, future ICJ adjudication may not be unlike public international arbitration.

M. Wood, 'The United Kingdom's Acceptance of the Compulsory Jurisdiction of the International Court'

in O. Fauchald, H. Jakhelln and A. Syse (eds), *Festskrift Til Carl August Fleischer* (2006)

It might be useful to consider what a reasonable, or reasonably prudent, declaration of acceptance under the Optional Clause would look like. This might change over time, and vary according to the circumstances of individual states, but—based on the United Kingdom's practice—the following are among those reservations that may be considered legitimate.

a) A reasonable cut-off date, to exclude stale or purely historical claims. What is reasonable may vary according to the circumstances of particular States. In the case of the United Kingdom about 30 years may be thought to be reasonable. In the case of those just emerging from troubled times a shorter period, or none, would be understandable….

b) A twelve-month (or lesser period) reservation, to prevent "surprise" applications. Without such a reservation there is no equality of exposure: a State which has not accepted the jurisdiction can launch proceedings against a State which has done so, without exposing itself to any risk whatsoever (except possible counterclaims).

c) A right to terminate or vary upon reasonable notice or indeed without notice. Reservation of such a right seems now to have become a fairly common practice. Reservation of the right to terminate without notice remains, however, controversial, and some may think it reflects less than wholehearted commitment to the Court. But retention of such a right may be regarded as a political necessity for the time being.

d) An exception for disputes which the parties have agreed to settle by some other method of peaceful settlement. This would seem useful in order to maintain the priority of specific arrangements, such as those provided for in the Treaties establishing the European Communities, which are becoming more common in an era of proliferation of international courts and tribunals.

NOTES

1. The ICJ has jurisdiction to attempt to settle a dispute only if the parties to the dispute consent to the ICJ so doing. Partly for this reason, many international disputes never reach the ICJ. As is evident from the decision in the *Legality of Use of Force Cases (Provisional Measures)*, both the ICJ and States still have obligations under international law to settle disputes peacefully irrespective of whether the ICJ has jurisdiction in a particular instance. In *Armed Activities on the Territory of the Congo (Congo v Rwanda) (Provisional Measures)* ICJ Rep 2002, the ICJ reaffirmed that there is a 'fundamental distinction' between the Court having jurisdiction and whether an act is in violation of international law. As is seen in the above extract from the Court's admissibility in *Armed Activities on the Territory of the Congo (Congo v Rwanda) (New Application)*, even the fact that the act in question would constitute a violation of a *jus cogens* norm does not confer jurisdiction on the Court. Only consent can do so.

2. The main methods by which the ICJ has jurisdiction in contentious cases are where the parties specifically agree to submit a defined dispute to it (a *compromis* or special agreement), as was the case in the various *Continental Shelf Cases* (see Chapter 10); by a compromissory clause in a multilateral or bilateral treaty, where the treaty provides for reference of certain disputes to the Court (of which there are more than 300 such treaties), as in the *United States Diplomatic and Consular Staff in Tehran Case*, ICJ Rep 1980 3 (see Section 6); or where the parties have made a declaration under Article 36(2), known as the 'Optional Clause', accepting the compulsory jurisdiction of the Court in all matters not specifically excluded by the State, as the parties had done (or appeared to have done) in the *Nicaragua Case*. A number of these declarations were made to the PCIJ's jurisdiction and remain current for the ICJ due to Articles 36(5) and 37 of the ICJ Statute.

3. An application may also be brought which invites the respondent State to consent to the exercise of jurisdiction by the ICJ in relation to that specific case. This process is known as *forum prorogatum*. As such applications have tended to be made for political purposes, with no prospect of the jurisdiction of the Court being accepted, Article 38(5) of the Rules provides that such applications are considered ineffective for procedural purposes until consent is provided. This is not normally forthcoming. However, it is possible to establish jurisdiction on this basis. In the first case where jurisdiction was based on this form of jurisdiction, the Court emphasised that consent to jurisdiction must be clearly established. However, where established, consent may extend to matters other than those set forth in the main claim: *Case Concerning Certain Mutual Legal Assistance in Criminal Matters, Djibouti v France*, Judgment, 4 June 2008). The Court has held that merely participating in the proceedings for the purpose of challenging the admissibility of the dispute does not constitute consent to jurisdiction on the merits: *Armed Activities On The Territory of the Congo (New Application: 2002) (Democratic Republic of The Congo v Rwanda)* ICJ Rep 2006, paras 20–21.

4. It is argued that one difficulty of the Optional Clause method of accepting jurisdiction is that the State so declaring has perhaps little control over deciding whether the particular dispute is appropriate for settlement by the ICJ. There are few declarations which, like Haiti's, do not have any reservations. India's Commonwealth reservation was declared to be a valid reservation in *Aerial Incident of 10 August 1999* (Pakistan v India ICJ Rep 2000, para. 44).

5. The vast majority of States either have not made any declaration under the Optional Clause, or have significant reservations in their declarations, such as India's. Of the five Permanent Members of the Security Council, only the United Kingdom has a current declaration under the Optional Clause, and that declaration includes reservations (as seen above). This has the effect of reducing the ability of the ICJ to settle international disputes and decreasing the possibility of the ICJ clarifying and developing international law. There have also been suggestions, including by judges of the Court, that disputes in which jurisdiction is based on the Optional Clause declarations of the party are more likely to lead to compliance issues, as there is no will to resolve the dispute (see below).

6. The United Kingdom declaration extracted was deposited with the Secretary-General of the United Nations on 5 July 2004, replacing a declaration made in 1969, and is the ninth successive UK declaration. It was reportedly introduced in part in response to statements by Mauritian officials to the effect

that Mauritius may leave the Commonwealth in order to bring proceedings against the United Kingdom challenging its sovereignty in respect of the British Indian Ocean Territory.

7. The concept of reciprocity allows a State to rely on a reservation by another State party to the ICJ even if that reservation has not been made by the first State, as seen in the *Norwegian Loans Case*.

8. In many of the cases brought to the ICJ, one party objects to the jurisdiction of the ICJ at a preliminary stage and the Court has to decide the question of whether it has jurisdiction before proceeding to decide the merits of the dispute. However, the Court can leave the issue of jurisdiction until its considerations of the merits if the two are inextricably linked. A State objecting to the jurisdiction of the ICJ that has not raised its objection at a preliminary stage may still argue the objection at the merits stage, although it may have forfeited the right to suspend the proceedings on the merits: *Avena and other Mexican Nationals (Mexico v United States of America)* (ICJ Rep 2004, 29, para. 24). Note that the need to establish a basis for jurisdiction is in addition to the requirement that a party is entitled to have access to the Court. In any event, there is a distinction between there being a basis for jurisdiction for the Court and the Court deciding that the case is admissible.

9. It may be the case that a party relies on jurisdiction both under the Optional Clause system and arising under a treaty. Such distinct bases of jurisdiction may not be mutually exclusive, and one may confer wider jurisdiction on the Court. For example, the Court has held that a restriction on the jurisdiction to be exercised pursuant to a treaty provision did not extend to the Optional Clause declaration: *Territorial and Maritime Dispute (Nicaragua v Colombia) (Preliminary Objections)*, ICJ Rep 2007.

10. There appears to be a trend towards the Court interpreting texts conferring jurisdiction broadly. The Court's willingness to find jurisdiction in the *Oil Platforms Case* (see Chapter 15) has been criticised as over-extending the reach of its jurisdiction and having potential implications for judicial policy. In that case, the Court relied upon a compromissory clause in a treaty promoting trade and commerce between the two States to found the basis for the Court's jurisdiction. However, as was noted by several of the Separate and Dissenting Opinions, the dispute essentially concerned the use of force.

C: Absent third parties

On a number of occasions, States have submitted disputes to the ICJ, even though other States, which may be affected by any resolution of the dispute, have not been parties to the case. This can cause considerable difficulties for the Court.

Case Concerning Certain Phosphate Lands in Nauru (Nauru v Australia) (Jurisdiction)
ICJ Rep 1992 240, International Court of Justice

Nauru brought a claim against Australia, which had been one of the administering authorities of Nauru when it had been a Trust territory, for reparations for environmental damage caused by phosphate mining on Nauru. One of Australia's objections to the Court having jurisdiction of the matter was that the other two administering authorities—New Zealand and the United Kingdom—were not parties before the Court (due to their reservations about the Court's jurisdiction). The Court decided that it did have jurisdiction. The case settled before the merits were considered.

In the present case, the interests of New Zealand and the United Kingdom do not constitute the very subject-matter of the judgment to be rendered on the merits of Nauru's Application…In the present case, the determination of the responsibility of New Zealand or the United Kingdom is not a prerequisite for the determination of the responsibility of Australia, the only object of Nauru's claim.…In the present case, a finding by the Court regarding the existence or the content of the responsibility attributed to Australia by Nauru might well have implications for the legal situation of the two other States concerned, but no finding in respect of that legal situation will be needed as a basis for the Court's decision on Nauru's claims against Australia. Accordingly, the Court cannot decline to exercise its jurisdiction.

Case Concerning East Timor (Portugal v Australia)
ICJ Rep 1995 90, International Court of Justice

Portugal commenced these proceedings after the conclusion of a treaty between Australia and Indonesia concerning the delimitation of the continental shelf between Australia and East Timor. Portugal was then the administering authority over East Timor (being a non-self-governing territory). In 1975 Indonesian forces occupied East Timor and committed human rights violations. Portugal objected to Australia entering the treaty with Indonesia, inter alia, because it infringed the right of self-determination of the East Timorese people, which Portugal was meant to protect. Because Indonesia did not accept the jurisdiction of the ICJ, no case could be brought against Indonesia. The Court held (by 14 votes to 2) that it could not decide this case in the absence of Indonesia, as Indonesia's rights and obligations would have been affected by any judgment of the Court.

26. The Court recalls in this respect that one of the fundamental principles of its Statue is that it cannot decide a dispute between States without the consent of those States to its jurisdiction. This principle was reaffirmed in the judgment given by the Court in the case of the *Monetary Gold Removed from Rome in 1943* and confirmed in several of its subsequent decisions....

28. The Court has carefully considered the argument advanced by Portugal which seeks to separate Australia's behaviour from that of Indonesia. However, in the view of the Court, Australia's behaviour cannot be assessed without first entering into the question why it is that Indonesia could not lawfully have concluded the 1989 Treaty, while Portugal allegedly could have done so; the very subject-matter of the Court's decision would necessarily be a determination whether, having regard to the circumstances in which Indonesia entered and remained in East Timor, it could or could not have acquired the power to enter into treaties on behalf of East Timor relating to the resources of its continental shelf. The Court could not make such a determination in the absence of the consent of Indonesia.

JUDGE VERESHCHETIN (Separate Opinion): Besides Indonesia, in the absence of whose consent the Court is prevented from exercising its jurisdiction over the Application, there is another 'third party' in this case, whose consent was sought neither by Portugal before filling the Application with the Court, nor by Australia before concluding the Timor Gap treaty. Nevertheless, the applicant State has acted in this Court in the name of this 'third party' and the Treaty has allegedly jeopardized its natural resources. The 'third party' at issue is the people of East Timor.

Since the judgment is silent on this matter, one might wrongly conclude that the people, whose right to self-determination lies at the core of the whole case, have no role to play in the proceedings. This is not to suggest that the Court could have placed the States Parties to the case and the people of East Timor on the same level procedurally. Clearly, only States may be parties in cases before the Court (Art. 34 of the Statute of the Court). This is merely to say that the right of a people to self-determination, by definition, requires that the wishes of the people concerned at least be ascertained and taken into account by the Court.

NOTES

1. In a number of decisions by the ICJ, particularly on continental shelf delimitation, the Court has been careful to avoid deciding on aspects of a case which could overlap with claims of third States, for example, in the *Continental Shelf Case (Libya v Malta)* ICJ Rep 1984 3 (see Chapter 10), the Court did not decide on part of the maritime boundary which could have affected Italy (see also notes on intervention in Section 5E). See also the Court's decision in the *Land and Maritime Boundary Between Cameroon and Nigeria (Cameroon v Nigeria; Equatorial Guinea intervening)*, where the Court held that it was unable to rule on the parts of the claim that may affect the rights of other States with territorial and maritime claims in the disputed area.

2. As Judge Vereshchetin pointed out in the *East Timor Case*, there can be other interested parties (including non-States) which could be directly affected by a judgment of the ICJ but which do not, or cannot, appear before the Court.

3. There are also a very few instances of the absence of an actual party to the case, usually where that party objects to the Court taking jurisdiction of the matter. An example was the absence of the United States at the merits stage of the *Nicaragua Case*. This situation has occurred rarely since.

D: Provisional measures

Statute of the International Court of Justice

Article 41

1. The Court shall have the power to indicate, if it considers that circumstances so require, any provisional measures which ought to be taken to preserve the respective rights of either party.

2. Pending the final decision, notice of the measure suggested shall forthwith be given to the parties and to the Security Council.

Military and Paramilitary Activities in and against Nicaragua Case *(Nicaragua v United States)* (Provisional Measures)

ICJ Rep 1984 169, International Court of Justice

Nicaragua's main request was that the United States should cease and refrain from any action restricting, blocking or endangering access to or from Nicaraguan ports and, in particular, to cease the laying of mines. The Court indicated these provisional measures.

24. Where as on a request for provisional measures the Court need not, before deciding whether or not to indicate them, finally satisfy itself that it has jurisdiction on the merits of the case, or, as the case may be, that an objection taken to jurisdiction is well-founded, yet it ought not to indicate such measures unless the provisions invoked by the Applicant appear, prima facie, to afford a basis on which the jurisdiction of the Court might be founded;…

26. Whereas the Court will not now make any final determination of the question of the present validity or invalidity of the declaration of 24 September 1929, and the question whether or not Nicaragua accordingly was or was not, for the purpose of Article 36, paragraph 2, of the Statute of the Court a 'State accepting the same obligation' as the United States of America at the date of filing of the Application, so as to be able to rely on the United States declaration of 26 August 1946, nor of the question whether, as a result of the declaration of 6 April 1984, the present Application is excluded from the scope of the acceptance by the United States of the compulsory jurisdiction of the Court; whereas however the Court finds that the two declarations do nevertheless appear to afford a basis on which the jurisdiction of the Court might be founded;

27. Whereas by the terms of Article 41 of the Statute the Court may indicate provisional measures only when it considers that circumstances so require to preserve the rights of either party;…

40. Whereas the decision given in the present proceedings in no way prejudges the question of the jurisdiction of the Court to deal with the merits of the case or any questions relating to the merits themselves, and leaves unaffected the right of the Governments of the United States of America and the Republic of Nicaragua to submit arguments in respect of such jurisdiction or such merits;

JUDGE SCHWEBEL (Dissenting Opinion):…It is beyond dispute that the Court may not indicate provisional measures under its Statute where it has no jurisdiction over the merits of the case. Equally, however, considerations of urgency do not or may not permit the Court to establish its jurisdiction definitively before it issues an order of interim protection. Thus the Court has built a body of precedent which affords it the authority to indicate provisional measures if the jurisdiction which has been pleaded appears, prima facie, to afford a basis on which the Court's jurisdiction might be founded. Whether 'might' means 'possibly might' or 'might well' or 'might probably' is a question of some controversy. The nub of the matter appears to be that, while in deciding whether it has jurisdiction on the merits, the Court gives the defendant the benefit of the doubt, in deciding whether it has jurisdiction to indicate provisional measures, the Court gives the applicant the benefit of the doubt. In the present case, the Court, in my view, has given the applicant the benefit of a great many doubts.

The result is that States which have, by one route or another, submitted to the Court's compulsory jurisdiction in advance of a particular dispute, run the risk of being the object of an order indicating provisional measures even though (as in the *Anglo-Iranian Oil Co.* case) the Court may eventually conclude that jurisdiction on the merits is lacking. Thus the tactical disadvantage which the minority of States which has adhered to the Optional Clause generally suffers, as compared with that majority which has not submitted declarations under the Optional Clause at all, may be markedly greater than was conceived at the time declarations were submitted or has been perceived since.

A ready solution to this problem which comports with the maintenance of the Court's jurisdiction is not obvious. But one step which the Court itself can take is to ensure that the parties, at the stage of argument on provisional measures, are afforded the time required to prepare to argue issues of jurisdiction in depth. A second step is to ensure that the Court itself is afforded the requisite time to deliberate issues of jurisdiction in depth and to formulate its order in accordance with its internal judicial practice.

Case Concerning Application of the International Convention on the Elimination of all forms of Racial Discrimination (Georgia v Russian Federation) (Provisional Measures)

15 October 2008, International Court of Justice

Georgia sought provisional measures in order to protect its nationals from what it alleged were discriminatory acts by Russian armed forces and to prevent irreparable harm to the rights of ethnic Georgians. The Court indicated provisional measures, including that both parties shall refrain from any act of racial discrimination and from sponsoring, defending or supporting such acts; that they shall facilitate humanitarian assistance; and that they shall refrain from any action that might prejudice the respective rights of the parties or might aggravate or extend the dispute.

142. Whereas, nevertheless, the rights in question in these proceedings, in particular those stipulated in Article 5, paragraphs *(b)* and *(d)* (i) of [the Convention on the Elimination of all forms of Racial Discrimination(CERD)], are of such a nature that prejudice to them could be irreparable; whereas the Court considers that violations of the right to security of persons and of the right to protection by the State against violence or bodily harm (Article 5, paragraph *(b)*) could involve potential loss of life or bodily injury and could therefore cause irreparable prejudice; whereas the Court further considers that violations of the right to freedom of movement and residence within a State's borders (Article 5, paragraph *(d)* (i)) could also cause irreparable prejudice in situations where the persons concerned are exposed to privation, hardship, anguish and even danger to life and health; and whereas the Court finds that individuals forced to leave their own place of residence and deprived of their right of return could, depending on the circumstances, be subject to a serious risk of irreparable prejudice;

143. Whereas the Court is aware of the exceptional and complex situation on the ground in South Ossetia, Abkhazia and adjacent areas [of Georgian territory] and takes note of the continuing uncertainties as to where lines of authority lie; whereas, based on the information before it in the case file, the Court is of the opinion that the ethnic Georgian population in the areas affected by the recent conflict remains vulnerable; Whereas the situation in South Ossetia, Abkhazia and adjacent areas in Georgia is unstable and could rapidly change; whereas, given the ongoing tension and the absence of an overall settlement to the conflict in this region, the Court considers that the ethnic Ossetian and Abkhazian populations also remain vulnerable; Whereas, while the problems of refugees and internally displaced persons in this region are currently being addressed, they have not yet been resolved in their entirety; Whereas, in light of the foregoing, with regard to these above-mentioned ethnic groups of the population, there exists an imminent risk that the rights at issue in this case mentioned in the previous paragraph may suffer irreparable prejudice;

146. Whereas the Court, having found that the indication of provisional measures is required in the current proceedings, has considered the terms of the provisional measures requested by Georgia; whereas the Court does not find that, in the circumstances of the case, the measures to be indicated are to be identical to those requested by Georgia; whereas the Court, having considered the material before it, considers it appropriate to indicate measures addressed to both Parties.

JUDGE AL-KHASAWNEH, RANJEVA, SHI, KOROMA, TOMKA, BENNOUNA AND SKOTNIKOV (Joint Dissenting Opinion)

19. ... We consider that the majority has wrongly decided that the Court has jurisdiction prima facie to hear this case under Article 22 of CERD, in so far as it has neither succeeded in establishing the existence of a dispute over the interpretation or application of that Convention nor demonstrated that the precondition for the seisin of the Court has been satisfied.

20. Even if jurisdiction prima facie were established, according to the jurisprudence of the Court two further conditions, namely the existence of a risk of irreparable harm to the rights in dispute and urgency, have to be met.

21. In our opinion, the Order nowhere demonstrates the existence of any risk of irreparable harm to Georgia's right under CERD. The Court confines itself to a *petitio principii* when it states that 'the rights in question in these

proceedings…are of such nature that prejudice to them could be irreparable' (Order, para. 142), defining neither the precise manner in which they are threatened nor the irreparable harm which they might suffer. The Court thus appears to suggest that certain rights may automatically fulfil the irreparable harm criterion, without analysing the real facts on the ground or the actual threat against the said rights. With regard to the expulsions alleged by Georgia and attributed by it to Russia, they cannot in and of themselves be considered to constitute irreparable harm, since the Court, if it arrives at the merits stage in this case, can always order that the expelled individuals be allowed to return to their homes and be granted appropriate compensation. It is even more difficult to claim irreparable harm to the rights in dispute when the appropriate organs of the United Nations have reported that thousands of persons have, since the cessation of hostilities, returned to their homes in Abkhazia and South Ossetia, and when the ceasefire agreement of 12 August 2008 provides that negotiations will soon open in Geneva, on 15 October 2008, between all the parties, concerning *inter alia*, the progressive return of the displaced persons.

22. With regard to urgency, there simply is none, since after conclusion of the ceasefire agreement, European Union observers have now been deployed to monitor the ceasefire and the return of troops of both countries to their positions before 7 August 2008, and the observers from the United Nations Missions in Georgia and those from the Organization for Security and Co-operation in Europe will continue their missions in Abkhazia and South Ossetia respectively.

23. Therefore, one has no choice but to observe not only that the Court does not have jurisdiction prima facie to pronounce on the merits in this case, but the conditions established in the jurisprudence for the indication of provisional measures are obviously not met.

NOTES

1. The decision on provisional (interim) measures requirements in the *Nicaragua Case* has been repeated by the ICJ in a number of cases. Indeed, there is an increasing number of applications for provisional measures, including in the context of armed hostilities and the Court seems gradually to be liberalising its view as to what circumstances warrant the granting of interim measures. Prior to examining urgency and the existence of a real and imminent risk, the Court has to establish its *prima facie* jurisdiction and be satisfied that the rights invoked by a party are at least plausible.

2. In order to persuade the Court that an order for provisional measures is required, it is necessary to establish urgency. There must be a real risk that action prejudicial to the rights of the party affected might be taken before the Court's final judgment is issued. The Court must be convinced that there is a real and imminent risk that irreparable prejudice may be caused to the rights in dispute before the Court can give its final decision. The Court found that such risk was apparent in *Georgia v Russian Federation* (see extract). An undertaking to the Court that the action in question will not occur may remove the urgency and preclude the need for an order for provisional measures (see for example, *Case Concerning Questions Relating to the Obligation to Prosecute or Extradite (Belgium v Senegal), Request for the Indication of Provisional Measures*, 28 May 2009).

3. The decision in the *LaGrand Case (Germany v United States)* ICJ Rep 2001 466, para. 109, clarified that an order of provisional measures by the ICJ is a binding order and the measures indicated constitute an independent legal obligation. Failure to comply with the order is grounds for a claim by the affected State. The ICJ has confirmed the binding nature of an order for provisional measures in subsequent decisions. Provisional measures, being of an interim nature, lapse on delivery of final judgment, even where the orders made in the final judgment do not extend as far as the provisional measures: *Avena and other Mexican Nationals (Mexico v United States)* ICJ Rep 2004.

4. Due to the need for urgency, applications for provisional measures are generally made and heard very soon after the application to the Court is filed, before any objections as to the Court's jurisdiction have been resolved. This might be seen to be inconsistent with the principle of State consent, as an order may be made in circumstances where the respondent State is asserting that there is no jurisdiction. Indeed, the Court's recent approach to provisional measures, particularly the *LaGrand* decision, could be seen as limiting the role of State consent. The Court's approach is perhaps understandable where the protection of natural resources, the environment or human rights are in issue. It will be interesting to see what the effect of this approach will be on States' willingness to accept the Court's jurisdiction. It is also of note that in *Georgia v Russian Federation*, the Court addressed the provisional measures to both parties.

5. There is an emerging trend of the Court formulating recommendations to the parties at a preliminary stage, often where it has held that it cannot grant a party's request for an order for provisional measures. For example, in the case concerning the *Armed Activities on the Territory*

of Congo (Democratic Republic of the Congo v Rwanda) (Provisional Measures) ICJ Rep 2002 240), the Court declared that: 'Whereas, whether or not States accept the jurisdiction of the Court, they remain in any event responsible for acts attributable to them that violate international law…whereas, the Court wishes to stress the necessity for the Parties to these proceedings to use their influence to prevent the repeated grave violations of human rights and international humanitarian law which have been observed even recently' (para. 93). Such recommendations do not have binding legal effect, and their use has been criticised as being inappropriate, first, as the Court may not have established jurisdiction and second, as such recommendations may risk prejudging the merits of the case (see the declaration of Judge Buergenthal to the *Congo* v *Rwanda (Provisional Measures Order)* (para. 7)). Thirlway suggests that the number of recommendations may increase now that the Court has held that its orders for provisional measures have binding effect: H. Thirlway, 'The Recommendations Made by the International Court of Justice: A Sceptical View' (2009) 58 ICLQ 151.

E: Intervention

Statute of the International Court of Justice

Article 62

1. Should a State consider that it has an interest of a legal nature which may be affected by the decision in the case, it may submit a request to the Court to be permitted to intervene.

2. It shall be for the Court to decide upon this request.

Article 63

1. Whenever the construction of a convention to which States other than those concerned in the case are parties is in question, the Registrar shall notify all such States forthwith.

2. Every State so notified has the right to intervene in the proceedings; but if it uses this right, the construction given by the judgment will be equally binding upon it.

Rules of the International Court of Justice (1978)

Article 81

1. An application for permission to intervene under the terms of Article 62 of the Statute, signed in the manner provided for in Article 38, paragraph 3, of these Rules, shall be filed as soon as possible, and not later than the closure of the written proceedings. In exceptional circumstances, an application submitted at a later stage may however be admitted.

2. The application shall state the name of an agent. It shall specify the case to which it relates, and shall set out:
   (a) the interest of a legal nature which the State applying to intervene considers may be affected by the decision in that case;
   (b) the precise object of the intervention;
   (c) any basis of jurisdiction which is claimed to exist as between the State applying to intervene and the parties to the case.

Article 82

1. A State which desires to avail itself of the right of intervention conferred upon it by Article 63 of the Statute shall file a declaration to that effect, signed in the manner provided for in Article 38, paragraph 3, of these Rules. Such a declaration shall be filed as soon as possible, and not later than the date fixed for the opening of the oral proceedings. In exceptional circumstances a declaration submitted at a later stage may however be admitted.

2. The declaration shall state the name of an agent. It shall specify the case and the convention to which it relates and shall contain:
   (a) particulars of the basis on which the declarant State considers itself a party to the convention;

    (b) identification of the particular provisions of the convention the construction of which it considers to be in question;

    (c) a statement of the construction of those provisions for which it contends;

    (d) a list of the documents in support, which documents shall be attached.

    3. Such a declaration may be filed by a State that considers itself a party to the convention the construction of which is in question but has not received the notification referred to in Article 63 of the Statute.

Case Concerning Land, Island and Maritime Frontier Dispute Case (El Salvador v Honduras; Nicaragua Intervening)

ICJ Rep 1990 92, Chamber of the International Court of Justice

The dispute between El Salvador and Honduras concerned the Gulf of Fonseca. This lies on the Pacific coast of three States, with the north-west coast being the territory of El Salvador, the south-east coast being the territory of Nicaragua, and Honduran territory lying on the coast between them. By Special Agreement between El Salvador and Honduras the dispute was brought before a Chamber of the Court. Nicaragua sought to intervene in regard to the delimitation of the waters of the Gulf, the legal situation of the islands in the Gulf, the legal situation of the maritime spaces outside the Gulf, and the legal régime of the waters of the Gulf itself. El Salvador objected to any intervention, but Honduras did not object to Nicaragua being permitted to intervene for the sole purpose of expressing its views on the legal status of the waters within the Gulf. The Chamber, unanimously, decided that Nicaragua could intervene only in regard to the legal régime of the waters of the Gulf.

58. If a State can satisfy the Court that it has an interest of a legal nature which may be affected by the decision in the case, it may be permitted to intervene in respect of that interest. But that does not mean that the intervening State is then also permitted to make excursions into other aspects of the case. This is recognized by Nicaragua…In the Chamber's opinion, however, it is clear, first, that it is for a State seeking to intervene to demonstrate convincingly what it asserts, and thus to bear the burden of proof; and, second, that it has only to show that its interest 'may' be affected, not that it will or must be affected….Nevertheless, there needs finally to be clear identification of any legal interests that may be affected by the decision on the merits. A general apprehension is not enough. The Chamber needs to be told what interests of a legal nature might be affected by its eventual decision on the merits.…

90. So far as the object of Nicaragua's intervention is 'to inform the Court of the nature of the legal rights of Nicaragua which are in issue in the dispute', it cannot be said that this object is not a proper one: it seems indeed to accord with the function of intervention….It seems to the Chamber however that it is perfectly proper, and indeed the purpose of intervention, for an intervener to inform the Chamber of what it regards as its rights or interests, in order to ensure that no legal interest may be 'affected' without the intervener being heard; and that the use in an application to intervene of a perhaps somewhat more forceful expression is immaterial, provided the object actually aimed at is a proper one.…

92. In the light of these statements, it appears to the Chamber that the object stated first in Nicaragua's Application, namely 'generally to protect the legal rights of the Republic of Nicaragua in the Gulf of Fonseca and the adjacent maritime areas by all legal means available', is not to be interpreted as involving the seeking of a judicial pronouncement on Nicaragua's own claims. The 'legal means available' must be those afforded by the institution of intervention for the protection of a third State's legal interests. So understood, that object cannot be regarded as improper.…

96. …The competence of the Court in this matter of intervention is not, like its competence to hear and determine the dispute referred to it, derived from the consent of the parties to the case, but from the consent given by them, in becoming parties to the Court's Statute, to the Court's exercise of its powers conferred by the Statute. There is no need to interpret the reference in Article 36, paragraph 1, of the Statute to 'treaties in force' to include the Statute itself; acceptance of the Statute entails acceptance of the competence conferred on the Court by Article 62. Thus the Court has the competence to permit an intervention even though it be opposed by one or both of the parties to the case; as the Court stated in 1984, 'the opposition [to an intervention] of the parties to a case is, though very important, no more than one element to be taken into account by the Court' (*ICJ Reports 1984*,

p. 28, para. 46). The nature of the competence thus created by Article 62 of the Statute is definable by reference to the object and purpose of intervention, as this appears from Article 62 of the Statute. ... It is therefore clear that a State which is allowed to intervene in a case, does not, by reason only of being an intervener, become also a party to the case. It is true, conversely, that, provided that there be the necessary consent by the parties to the case, the intervener is not prevented by reason of that status from itself becoming a party....

100. It thus follows also from the juridical nature and from the purposes of intervention that the existence of a valid link of jurisdiction between the would-be intervener and the parties is not a requirement for the success of the application. On the contrary, the procedure of intervention is to ensure that a State with possibly affected interests may be permitted to intervene even though there is no jurisdictional link and it therefore cannot become a party....

101. The Chamber therefore concludes that the absence of a jurisdictional link between Nicaragua and the Parties to this case is no bar to permission being given for intervention.

C. Chinkin, 'Third Party Intervention before the ICJ'

80 *American Journal of International Law* 495 (1986)

One often repeated policy—reiterated by certain judges of the International Court—justifying a flexible attitude towards intervention is to promote economy of litigation for the efficient administration of justice. Certainly, the inclusion of the procedure in the Court's Statute stems from the recognition that international disputes rarely, if ever, fit neatly into a bilateral pattern. Rather, because of the interdependence of international relations, events that culminate in international adjudication will affect different actors in different ways and with varying intensity. Where this impact is upon the legal interests of other states, principles of economy and efficiency may require that pertinent submissions be presented along with the main proceedings.

In sum, by allowing third-party intervention, the Court could avoid the possible duplication of proceedings. It could also gain a wider perspective on the entire series of actions culminating in the litigation than that presented by the original parties and thus be better informed about all aspects of the dispute. Finally, easier access to the international judicial arena and the increased participation in international adjudication that could be expected to result would promote the peaceful settlement of disputes, recognized as one of the fundamental norms of international law....

Where states have brought a dispute before the Court, especially through special agreement, which precludes a jurisdictional conflict, the Court may well determine that it can best serve the interests of the international community by adjudicating that dispute without allowing intervention, as that may lead the original parties to withdraw their acceptance of the Court's authority. Admittedly, this represents a limited view of the Court's role, but it may be a realistic one, allowing the Court to resolve specific disputes between states that will accept its ruling. If other interests are affected by its decision, they can be resolved at a subsequent time and, possibly, in another forum. The Court may not want to risk jeopardizing the successful resolution of the original dispute by widening its ambit through the overready acceptance of intervention.

This latter view of the Court's role is supported by the concept of party autonomy in international adjudication and necessarily entails restricting intervention. It recognizes that facilitating intervention could prove counter-productive by discouraging states from initiating a contentious suit for fear that they might be unable to control its course and eventual outcome if the dispute were widened beyond their direct concerns. It is also argued that third-party intervention runs counter to other fundamentals of international law such as the equality of states, consent and reciprocity in international adjudication.

NOTES

1. Intervention pursuant to Article 63 was granted by the ICJ in the *Haya de la Torre Case*, ICJ Rep 1951 71, but the *Land, Island and Maritime Frontier Dispute Case* was the first case in the history of both the ICJ and the PCIJ in which a State has been accorded permission to intervene solely under Article 62, or its equivalent. In the *Land, Island and Maritime Frontier Dispute Case,* the legal interest was the legal delimitation of disputed seabed areas where the geographical aspects of the seabed may infringe the rights of another State; see also *Land and Maritime Boundary between Cameroon and Nigeria; Equatorial Guinea Intervening* ICJ Rep 2002 303. In any event, the intervention of a third party is strictly limited to its interest of a legal nature, as seen in *Jurisdictional Immunities of the State (Germany v Italy: Greece Intervening) (Order of 4 July 2011)*, where the Court gave permission for Greece to intervene only where its intervention concerned the decisions of Greek courts in similar

cases. In *Sovereignty over Pulau Ligitan and Pulau Sipadan (Indonesia v Malaysia) (The Philippines Intervening)* ICJ Rep 2001, the Court refused The Philippines' application to intervene because it considered that no interest of a legal nature was demonstrated, as the claims by Indonesia and Malaysia did not relate to the issue on which The Philippines sought to intervene. However, Article 62 gives the Court the discretion not to allow an intervention, even if an interest of a legal nature and an appropriate object are shown.

2. The finding of the Chamber in the *Land, Island and Maritime Frontier Dispute Case* that no jurisdictional link was required for an intervention which did not render the intervening State a party to the dispute has been confirmed by the full Court: see *Land and Maritime Boundary between Cameroon and Nigeria; Equatorial Guinea Intervening* ICJ Rep 2002 303 *and Sovereignty Over Pulau Ligitan and Pulau Sipadan (Indonesia v Malaysia) (The Philippines Intervention)* ICJ Rep 2001. In the *Whaling Case (Australia v Japan)* (2014), New Zealand intervened in the case without becoming a party; its written observations were very long and detailed, and so similar to that of a party's submissions.

3. When the ICJ gave its final decision in the *Land, Island and Maritime Frontier Dispute Case* (ICJ Rep 1992 92), it held that because Nicaragua was not formally a party to the case before the Court it was not bound by the Court's decision and similarly could not rely on the decision as against the original parties. This is consistent with the Court's view that no jurisdictional link is required for intervention, but, as Judge Oda pointed out in his Dissenting Opinion, this means that Nicaragua is not bound by the Court's lengthy determination of sovereignty over all the islands, maritime and other territory in dispute. This is not a good result if an international legal order for settling disputes is desired.

4. In a number of the cases where intervention has been sought, the Court has taken into account the arguments of the intervening State in its ultimate decision on the case. It has usually done so by limiting its decision so as not to infringe the potential rights of the intervening State, as with Italy's application to intervene in the *Continental Shelf Case (Libya v Malta)* ICJ Rep 1984 3 (see Chapter 10).

5. While the consent of the parties to a case before the ICJ is important and must be considered by the Court, the ICJ is meant to be a body whose purpose is to settle international disputes between States. Its decisions do have an impact wider than simply on the parties to the case, and most cases brought to the Court by two parties are formulated in a bilateral manner, which may not reflect the multifaceted interests involved. If the Court's decisions on principles of international law are to be based on a full appreciation of the legal situation, then interventions (perhaps including those by non-States) may have to be allowed more frequently. In this way the Court can operate more effectively as a means to settle disputes peacefully, to promote international peace and justice, and to further the development of international law.

F: Interpretation and revision of judgments

Statute of the International Court of Justice

Article 60

The judgment is final and without appeal. In the event of dispute as to the meaning or scope of the judgment, the Court shall construe it upon the request of any party.

Article 61

1. An application for revision of a judgment may be made only when it is based upon the discovery of some fact of such a nature as to be a decisive factor, which fact was, when the judgment was given, unknown to the Court and also to the party claiming revision, always provided that such ignorance was not due to negligence.

2. The proceedings for revision shall be opened by a judgment of the Court expressly recording the existence of the new fact, recognizing that it has such a character as to lay the case open to revision, and declaring the application admissible on this ground.

3. The Court may require previous compliance with the terms of the judgment before it admits proceedings in revision.

4. The application for revision must be made at latest within six months of the discovery of the new fact.

5. No application for revision may be made after the lapse of ten years from the date of the judgment.

NOTES
1. Requests for interpretation and revision of judgments under Article 61 of the Statute are made relatively infrequently. Requests for interpretation have been filed on only five occasions, most recently in relation to the Court's judgment on the merits in *Request for Interpretation of the Judgment of 15 June 1962 in the Case Concerning the Temple of Preah Vihear (Cambodia v Thailand)* ICJ Rep 2013. There the Court accepted the request for interpretation and declared that the Judgment of 15 June 1962 decided that Cambodia had sovereignty over the whole territory of the promontary of Preah Vihear, and that, in consequence, Thailand was under an obligation to withdraw from that territory all the Thai military and police forces, and other guards or keepers, who were stationed there.

2. Revision of a judgment of the Court is also seen as exceptional. Requests for revision are not restricted to decisions on the merits and can be made in respect of decisions made at a preliminary stage. The requirement in Article 61(2) for the existence of a 'new fact' has been problematic, and requires the fact to be unknown at the time of the judgment, and not to have occurred several years later. For example, the Court has held that the admission to the UN of Serbia in 2000, four years after its judgment, did not constitute a 'new fact': *Application for Revision of the Judgment of 11 July 1996 in the case concerning Application of the Convention on the Prevention and Punishment of the Crime of Genocide (Bosnia and Herzegovina v Yugoslavia), Preliminary Objections*, ICJ Rep 2003. The Court considers that the conditions in Article 61 are cumulative; once one condition has not been satisfied, the request must be rejected and there is no need for the Court to discuss the remaining criteria.

G: Obligations to comply with decisions

Statute of the International Court of Justice

Article 59
The decision of the Court has no binding force except between the parties and in respect of that particular case.

United Nations Charter

Article 94
1. Each Member of the United Nations undertakes to comply with the decision of the International Court of Justice in any case to which it is a party.

2. If any party to a case fails to perform the obligations incumbent upon it under a judgment rendered by the Court, the other party may have recourse to the Security Council, which may, if it deems necessary, make recommendations or decide upon measures to be taken to give effect to the judgment.

A. Llamzon, 'Jurisdiction and Compliance in Recent Decisions of the International Court of Justice'
18 *European Journal of International Law* 815 (2007)

It is unfair to compare the enforcement mechanisms available to domestic court decisions with the judgments of the ICJ. The institutional framework of the ICJ is complex, and the avenues available under the UN Charter for enforcement of its decisions reflect the disproportionate power bestowed by the Charter upon the Security Council. Under the Charter's framework, non-compliance is dealt with principally through Article 94(2) of the UN Charter, which offers the creditor state recourse to the Security Council in seeking enforcement of the judgment. Thus, the Charter views compliance as much more a political issue involving international peace and security than a legal one.

In its entire history, the Security Council has never employed its Article 94 powers even on occasions of clear non-compliance. It is understandable, given the discretionary nature of Article 92(4), for the Council to be inert in situations wherein the debtor state is a Permanent Member. More puzzling is the fact that creditor states themselves very rarely seek the Security Council's assistance in this capacity, even in the face of continued non-compliance....

While it is true that Article 94(2) has failed to play a significant role in practice, the reason has certainly not been for lack of non-compliance incidents. Why do creditor states not resort to the Security Council more often?

At least part of the reason for such paucity can be ascribed to the difficulties laid upon states seeking Security Council action. Because enforcement action under Article 94(2) is merely discretionary upon the Security Council, a finding that the ICJ judgment was defied does not, of itself, immediately trigger Security Council action; this uncertainty and potential for arbitrariness, in turn, nullifies much of the possibility that the Security Council can ever act as 'international enforcer' in the same way the Executive department does in most states. Moreover, the relationship between Article 94(2) and the Security Council's general enforcement power is unclear....

Another reason why Article 94(2) was never employed by the Security Council is that in appropriate cases, the mere threat of Security Council action was sufficient to trigger the desired response from the recalcitrant state. In the *Land, Island and Maritime Frontier Dispute* discussed above, for example, Honduras' letter to the Secretary-General was sufficient to trigger a more conciliatory tone from El Salvador, prompting renewed vigour in negotiations that diffused tensions and ultimately speeded up compliance with the ICJ's delimitation of their common border. Thus, when the debtor state does not have the power to block Security Council action, the possibility of Security Council action is often enough impetus for them to agree to a negotiated, less destructive solution in order to avoid Article 94(2).

R. Higgins, President of the ICJ, 'Statement at the UN Security Council's Thematic Debate on "Strengthening International Law"'

S/PV.5474, 22 June 2006

The Security Council, faced with the massive problems on its agenda, might be forgiven for wondering whether Judgments by a Court with no enforcement powers of its own—indeed, the Charter provides that enforcement of Court Judgments ultimately lies with the Security Council—will in fact be complied with. The answer is surprising to many that out of nearly 100 contentious cases that the Court has dealt with, no more than a handful have presented problems of compliance. And of this handful, the problems of compliance have mostly turned out to be temporary....

The Security Council will wish to know why it is that the question of compliance with the Court's Judgments is relatively rarely a problem. The reasons, I think, are various. First, the Court is the embodiment of the United Nations, being a major organ thereof. The potency of that factor should not be underestimated. Thus it is not for States to rewrite, to challenge, to approve of the way the Court functions. That is a 'given' in the Statute, itself a component part of the Charter. Second, the Court is stated in the Charter to be the primary judicial organ of the United Nations: this authority accorded to the Court has served the UN well over the years. Then there is the fact that the Court is indeed the Court of all the Members, in the sense that it is composed of 15 Judges elected by all the UN membership (Security Council and General Assembly)—judges of high expertise in international law, who represent the different legal systems of the world. The decision making process of the Court is such that all the Judges are engaged in all the cases (save in those occasional circumstances where the parties themselves request a reduced Bench, a chamber). It is not the Court of any region, or any personalities. It is the Court of the UN.

NOTES

1. In the *Territorial Dispute Case (Libya v Chad)* ICJ Rep 1994 6 the parties enforced the decision rapidly, with a treaty to implement the decision being signed by the parties two months after the decision, and, within less than two more months, the parties had acted to remove troops from the disputed area. Such quick enforcement is, however, rare, particularly where the judgment affects large numbers of people or land areas, or raises political or strategic considerations. Compliance in such circumstances may take several years.

2. Generally, as Higgins' notes above, the Court's compliance record is quite good, at least in relation to final decisions. Studies confirm that final judgments receive considerable deference, even though compliance may be partial or imperfect, take many years or be subject to other settlement measures. The compliance record regarding interim decisions is less impressive, although this may be explained by the confusion as to the binding status of orders for provisional measures that existed up until the decision of the Court in *LaGrand* (see Section 5D). It is also important to recall that submitting a dispute to judicial determination may have a positive effect on the dispute, leading perhaps to the settlement of the dispute by diplomatic means before a final judgment is reached.

3. Apart from the Security Council, there are still a number of alternative methods of enforcing decisions available to a State, of which diplomatic and economic pressures are used the most often. For example, the UK took a lead role in encouraging Nigeria to comply with the ICJ's 2002 judgment. The UN also assisted implementation by establishing, at the request of the parties, a commission to consider the implications of the judgment and to propose a workable solution.

4. The lack of the ability to ensure enforcement of international law is one of the principal difficulties of the international legal system. If legal enforcement measures are not available or are inadequate, then lack of complete resolution of the dispute can threaten international peace and security and it can diminish the development of an international legal order. If the peaceful settlement of disputes is customary international law (let alone if it has the character of *jus cogens*), then it must include an obligation to comply with any decision which aims to settle an international dispute.

H: Advisory opinions

United Nations Charter

Article 96

1. The General Assembly or the Security Council may request the International Court of Justice to give an advisory opinion on any legal question.

2. Other organs of the United Nations and specialized agencies, which may at any time be so authorized by the General Assembly, may also request advisory opinions of the Court on legal questions arising within the scope of their activities.

Statute of the International Court of Justice

Article 65

1. The Court may give an advisory opinion on any legal question at the request of whatever body may be authorized by or in accordance with the Charter of the United Nations to make such a request.

2. Questions upon which the advisory opinion of the Court is asked shall be laid before the Court by means of a written request containing an exact statement of the question upon which an opinion is required, and accompanied by all documents likely to throw light upon the question.

Article 66

1. The Registrar shall forthwith give notice of the request for an advisory opinion to all States entitled to appear before the Court.

2. The Registrar shall also, by means of a special and direct communication, notify any State entitled to appear before the Court or international organization considered by the Court, or, should it not be sitting, by the President, as likely to be able to furnish information on the question, that the Court will be prepared to receive, within a time limit to be fixed by the President, written statements, or to hear, at a public sitting to be held for the purpose, oral statements relating to the question....

Interpretation of Peace Treaties
Opinion, ICJ Rep 1950 65, International Court of Justice

A number of States, which were parties to the post-Second World War peace treaties with Bulgaria, Hungary and Romania, had claimed that those latter States had violated the provisions of the treaties concerning their human rights obligations. The treaties provided for commissions to decide disputes between the parties, with each party to appoint one commissioner and a third member to be agreed or, failing agreement, to be appointed by the Secretary-General of the United Nations. Bulgaria, Hungary and Romania refused to appoint any commissioner. The Court was asked to advise the General Assembly as to whether the Secretary-General could nevertheless appoint the third member. The Court answered this question in the negative. Bulgaria, Hungary and Romania had objected to the Advisory Opinion as they had not consented to it.

The consent of States, parties to a dispute, is the basis of the Court's jurisdiction in contentious cases. The situation is different in regard to advisory proceedings even where the Request for an Opinion relates to a legal question actually pending between States. The Court's reply is only of an advisory character: as such, it has no binding force. It follows that no State, whether a Member of the United Nations or not, can prevent the giving of an Advisory Opinion which the United Nations considers to be desirable in order to obtain enlightenment as to the course of action it should take. The Court's Opinion is given not to the States, but to the organ which is entitled to request it; the reply of the Court, itself an 'organ of the United Nations', represents its participation in the activities of the Organization, and, in principle, should not be refused....

Article 65 of the Statute is permissive. It gives the Court the power to examine whether the circumstances of the case are of such a character as should lead it to decline to answer the Request. In the opinion of the Court, the circumstances of the present case are profoundly different from those which were before the Permanent Court of International Justice in the *Eastern Carelia* case (Advisory Opinion No. 5), when that Court declined to give an Opinion because it found that the question put to it was directly related to the main point of a dispute actually pending between two States, so that answering the question would be substantially equivalent to deciding the dispute between the parties, and that at the same time it raised a question of fact which could not be elucidated without hearing both parties.... In the present case the Court is dealing with a Request for an Opinion, the sole object of which is to enlighten the General Assembly as to the opportunities which the procedure contained in the Peace Treaties may afford for putting an end to a situation which has been presented to it. That being the object of the Request, the Court finds in the opposition to it made by Bulgaria, Hungary and Romania no reason why it should abstain from replying to the Request.

Western Sahara Opinion

Advisory Opinion, ICJ Rep 1975 12, International Court of Justice

The details of the questions put by the General Assembly for an advisory opinion by the ICJ are set out in Chapter 7.

17. It is true that, in order to reply to the questions [put by the General Assembly], the Court will have to determine certain facts, before being able to assess their legal significance. However, a mixed question of law and facts is none the less a legal question within the meaning of Article 96, paragraph 1, of the Charter and Article 65, paragraph 1 of the Statute [of the ICJ]....

18. The view has been expressed that in order to be a 'legal question'...a question must not be of a historical character, but must concern or affect existing rights or obligations...the references to 'legal question'...are not to be interpreted restrictively.

19. ...It has undoubtedly been the usual situation for an advisory opinion of the Court to pronounce on existing rights and obligations, or on their coming into existence, modification or termination, or on the powers of international organs. However, the Court may also be requested to give its opinion on questions of law which do not call for any pronouncement of that kind, though they may have their place within a wider problem the solution of which could involve such matters....

23. ...In exercising this discretion [under Article 65], the International Court of Justice, like the Permanent Court of International Justice, has always been guided by the principle that as a judicial body, it is bound to remain faithful to the requirements of its judicial character even in giving advisory opinions....It has also said that the reply of the Court, itself an organ of the United Nations, represents its participation in the activities of the Organisation and, in principle, should not be refused. By lending its assistance in the solution of a problem confronting the General Assembly, the Court would discharge its functions as the principal judicial organ of the United Nations. The Court has further said only 'compelling reasons' should lead it to refuse to give a requested advisory opinion....

73. In any event, to what extent or degree its opinion will have an impact on the action of the General Assembly is not for the Court to decide. The function of the Court is to give an opinion based on law, once it has come

to the conclusion that the questions put to it are relevant and have a practical and contemporary effect and, consequently, are not devoid of object or purpose.

74. In the light of [these] considerations…the Court finds no compelling reason, in the circumstances of the present case, to refuse to comply with a request by the General Assembly for an advisory opinion.

Legal Consequences of the Construction of a Wall in the Occupied Palestinian Territory

Advisory Opinion, ICJ Rep 2004 136, International Court of Justice

The details of the question posed by the General Assembly are set out in Chapter 11.

41. Furthermore, the Court cannot accept the view, which has also been advanced in the present proceedings, that it has no jurisdiction because of the 'political' character of the question posed. As is clear from its long-standing jurisprudence on this point, the Court considers that the fact that the legal question also has political aspects, 'as, in the nature of the things, in the case with so many questions which arise in international life, does not suffice to deprive it of its character as a "legal question"' and to 'deprive the Court of a competence expressly conferred on it by its Statute' [*Application for Review of Judgement No. 158 of the United Nations Administrative Tribunal*, Advisory Opinion, ICJ Reports 1973, para. 14]….Whatever its political aspects, the Court cannot refuse to admit the legal character of a question which invites it to discharge an essentially judicial task, namely, an assessment of the legality of the possible conduct of States with regard to the obligations imposed upon them by international law [*Legality of the Threat or Use of Nuclear Weapons*, Advisory Opinion, ICJ Reports 1996, para. 13]…

43. It has been contended in the present proceedings, however, that the Court should decline to exercise its jurisdiction because of the presence of specific aspects of the General Assembly's request that would render the exercise of the Court's jurisdiction improper and inconsistent with the Court's judicial function….

46. The first such argument is to the effect that the Court should not exercise its jurisdiction in the present case because the request concerns a contentious matter between Israel and Palestine, in respect of which Israel has not consented to the exercise of that jurisdiction. According to this view, the subject-matter of the question posed by the General Assembly 'is an integral part of the wider Israeli-Palestinian dispute concerning questions of terrorism, security, borders, settlements, Jerusalem and other related matters'….

47. The Court observes that the lack of consent to the Court's contentious jurisdiction by interested States has no bearing on the Court's jurisdiction to give an advisory opinion….

48. As regards the request for an advisory opinion now before it, the Court acknowledges that Israel and Palestine have expressed radically divergent views on the legal consequences of Israel's construction of the wall, on which the Court has been asked to pronounce. However, as the Court has itself noted, 'Differences of views… on legal issues have existed in practically every advisory proceeding'…

49. Furthermore, the Court does not consider that the subject-matter of the General Assembly's request can be regarded as only a bilateral matter between Israel and Palestine. Given the powers and responsibilities of the United Nations in questions relating to international peace and security, it is the Court's view that the construction of the wall must be deemed to be directly of concern to the United Nations….

50. The object of the request before the Court is to obtain from the Court an opinion which the General Assembly deems of assistance to it for the proper exercise of its functions. The opinion is requested on a question which is of particularly acute concern to the United Nations, and one which is located in a much broader frame of reference than a bilateral dispute. In the circumstances, the Court does not consider that to give an opinion would have the effect of circumventing the principle of consent to judicial settlement, and the Court accordingly cannot, in the exercise of its discretion, decline to give an opinion on that ground…

51. The Court now turns to another argument raised in the present proceedings in support of the view that it should decline to exercise its jurisdiction. Some participants have argued that an advisory opinion from the Court on the legality of the wall and the legal consequences of its construction could impede a political, negotiated solution to the Israeli-Palestinian conflict. More particularly, it has been contended that such an opinion could undermine the scheme of the 'Roadmap'…which requires Israel and Palestine to comply with certain obligations in various phases referred to therein….

53. The Court is conscious that the 'Roadmap', which was endorsed by the Security Council in resolution 1515 (2003)…constitutes a negotiating framework for the resolution of the Israeli-Palestinian conflict. It is not clear, however, what influence the Court's opinion might have on those negotiations: participants in the present proceedings have expressed differing views in this regard. The Court cannot regard this factor as a compelling reason to decline to exercise its jurisdiction.

Accordance with International Law of the Unilateral Declaration of Independence in Respect of Kosovo

Advisory Opinion, 22 July 2010, International Court of Justice

The facts leading to this Advisory Opinion and the question posed to the Court are set out in the extract from Warbrick, Chapter 5, Section 1B.

39. … [I]t has been suggested that, given the respective powers of the Security Council and the General Assembly, if the Court's opinion were to be sought regarding whether the declaration of independence was in accordance with international law, the request should have been made by the Security Council and that this fact constitutes a compelling reason for the Court not to respond to the request from the General Assembly. That conclusion is said to follow both from the nature of the Security Council's involvement and the fact that, in order to answer the question posed, the Court will necessarily have to interpret and apply Security Council resolution 1244 (1999) [authorising the United Nations territorial administration of Kosovo] in order to determine whether or not the declaration of independence is in accordance with international law.

40. While the request put to the Court concerns one aspect of a situation which the Security Council has characterized as a threat to international peace and security and which continues to feature on the agenda of the Council in that capacity, that does not mean that the General Assembly has no legitimate interest in the question. Articles 10 and 11 of the Charter…confer upon the General Assembly a very broad power to discuss matters within the scope of the activities of the United Nations, including questions relating to international peace and security. That power is not limited by the responsibility for the maintenance of international peace and security which is conferred upon the Security Council by Article 24, paragraph 1. As the Court has made clear in its Advisory Opinion on *Legal Consequences of the Construction of a Wall in the Occupied Palestinian Territory*, paragraph 26, 'Article 24 refers to a primacy, but not necessarily exclusive competence'. The fact that the situation in Kosovo is before the Security Council and the Council has exercised its Chapter VII powers in respect of that situation does not preclude the General Assembly from discussing any part of that situation, including the declaration of independence. The limit which the Charter places upon the General Assembly to protect the role of the Security Council is contained in Article 12 and restricts the power of the General Assembly to make recommendations following a discussion, not its power to engage in such a discussion.…

43. It is true, of course, that the facts of the present case are quite different from those of the Advisory Opinion on *Legal Consequences of the Construction of a Wall in the Occupied Palestinian Territory*. The situation in the occupied Palestinian Territory had been under active consideration by the General Assembly for several decades prior to its decision to request an opinion from the Court and the General Assembly had discussed the precise subject on which the Court's opinion was sought. In the present case, with regard to the situation in Kosovo, it was the Security Council which had been actively seised of the matter.…

44. However, the purpose of the advisory jurisdiction is to enable organs of the United Nations and other authorized bodies to obtain opinions from the Court which will assist them in the future exercise of their functions. The Court cannot determine what steps the General Assembly may wish to take after receiving the Court's opinion or what effect the opinion may have in relation to those steps.… [T]he General Assembly is entitled to discuss the declaration of independence and, within the limits considered in paragraph 42, above, to make recommendations in respect of that or other aspects of the situation in Kosovo without trespassing on the powers of the Security Council. That being the case, the fact that, hitherto, the declaration of independence has been discussed only in the Security Council and that the Council has been the organ which has taken action with regard to the situation in Kosovo does not constitute a compelling reason for the Court to refuse to respond to the request from the General Assembly.

NOTES
1. It is rare for the ICJ to decline to give an advisory opinion for the reasons given in the case extracts above. The ICJ has, to date, never exercised its discretion to decline a request for an advisory

opinion on considerations of judicial propriety, or other discretionary grounds. It has indicated that it would do so only where there exists 'compelling grounds' to do so.

2. As is noted in the above extracts, the basis of the Court's jurisdiction to give an advisory opinion is not based on consent. This is because the Court's response to a request for an advisory opinion is not binding on States. Thus, even where the request for an advisory opinion concerns a bilateral dispute between States (or, as in the *Wall Advisory Opinion and the Kosovo Advisory Opinion*, a non-State actor), it is not necessary for the State party to the underlying dispute to consent. The Court in the *Wall Advisory Opinion* appears to have abandoned its dicta in the *Western Sahara Advisory Opinion* that 'lack of consent might constitute a ground for declining to exercise jurisdiction' (see para. 32).

3. The Court in both the *Wall Advisory Opinion and the Kosovo Advisory Opinion* found that the argument that another UN organ (in both cases the Security Council) was the more appropriate body to request the opinion was not a compelling reason to refuse to provide an advisory opinion. This was so even where the General Assembly had very little previous involvement in the situation in question and was unlikely to be able to take further steps based on the advisory opinion, due to the involvement of the Council (for the contrary view, see the Separate Opinion of Judge Keith). The Court also indicated that the motives of the General Assembly in requesting the opinion are largely irrelevant in determining whether the Court should provide an advisory opinion.

SECTION 6: INTERNATIONAL COURT OF JUSTICE AND THE SECURITY COUNCIL

As the ICJ indicated in the extracts from the *Western Sahara and the Wall Advisory Opinions*, the ICJ sees itself as an important organ of the UN and it has an obligation to offer its legal opinion when requested to do so. However, because the Security Council (as distinct from the General Assembly) can take decisions on legal matters that bind all States, there is an issue of the power of the ICJ in relation to the Security Council when the Security Council decides on matters of law.

United States Diplomatic and Consular Staff in Tehran Case (United States v Iran)
ICJ Rep 1980 3, International Court of Justice

This case arose from the occupation of the United States Embassy in Tehran (see further in Chapter 11), and was heard by the Court prior to the release of the Embassy staff. Iran, in a letter to the Court, had stated that the violations of diplomatic and consular law alleged by the United States could not be examined by the Court as they were part of a current political dispute, the dispute was before the Security Council, and the Secretary-General of the United Nations had established a Commission to settle the matter.

[L]egal disputes between sovereign States by their very nature are likely to occur in political contexts, and often form only one element in a wider and long-standing political dispute between the States concerned. Yet never has the view been put forward before that, because a legal dispute submitted to the Court is only one aspect of a political dispute, the Court should decline to resolve for the parties the legal questions at issue between them. Nor can any basis for such a view of the Court's functions or jurisdiction be found in the Charter or the Statute of the Court; if the Court were, contrary to its settled jurisprudence, to adopt such a view, it would impose a far-reaching and unwarranted restriction upon the role of the Court in the peaceful solution of international disputes...

Whereas Article 12 of the Charter expressly forbids the General Assembly to make any recommendation with regard to a dispute or situation while the Security Council is exercising its functions in respect of that dispute or situation, no such restriction is placed on the functioning of the Court by any provision of either the Charter or the Statute of the Court. The reasons are clear. It is for the Court, the principal judicial organ of the United Nations, to resolve any legal questions that may be in issue between parties to a dispute; and the resolution of such legal questions by the Court may be an important, and sometimes decisive, factor in promoting the peaceful settlement of the dispute...The establishment of the Commission by the Secretary-General with the agreement of the two States cannon, therefore, be considered in itself as in any way incompatible with the continuance of parallel proceedings before the Court. Negotiation, enquiry, mediation, conciliation, arbitration and judicial settlement are enumerated together in Article 33 of the Charter as means for the peaceful settlement of disputes. As was pointed out in the *Aegean Sea Continental Shelf* case, the jurisprudence of the Court provides various examples of cases in which negotiations and recourse to judicial settlement by the Court have been pursued *pari passu*. In that case, in which also the dispute had been referred to the Security Council, the Court held expressly that 'the fact that negotiations are being actively pursued during the present proceedings is not, legally, any obstacle to the exercise by the Court of its judicial functions' (*ICJ Reports 1978*, p. 12, para. 29).

Lockerbie Case (*Case Concerning Questions of Interpretation and Application of the 1971 Montreal Convention arising from the Aerial Incident at Lockerbie*) (*Libya* v *United States; Libya* v *United Kingdom*) (Provisional Measures)

ICJ Rep 1992 3, International Court of Justice

This case arose as a consequence of the explosion, caused by a bomb, of Pan Am Flight 103 on 21 December 1988, over Lockerbie in Scotland in the UK, killing all passengers and crew and some residents of Lockerbie. Investigations by American and British authorities (and, later, French authorities) came to the conclusion that two Libyan nationals were responsible. Requests, and demands, that these men be handed to American and British authorities were refused by Libya. Libya maintained that it would cooperate with enquiries but that it could not extradite its nationals under its constitution (such a provision being found in many States' laws). Libya then requested, on 18 January 1992, an arbitration of the matter under Article 14(1) of the Montreal Convention for the Suppression of Unlawful Acts Against the Safety of Civil Aviation 1974, as Libya claimed the matter raised issues of interpretation and application of that Convention.

On 21 January 1992, the Security Council passed a resolution (Resolution 731 (1992)) urging Libya to respond fully to the demands of those States to hand over the men. Before the expiry of the six-month period of notice of an arbitration request (as required by Article 14), Libya applied on 3 March 1992, to the ICJ for a declaration that Libya, in refusing immediately to hand over the men, had complied with the Montreal Convention. It also requested an order for provisional measure to protect its rights under international law. The ICJ heard the request for provisional measures from 26 to 28 March 1992, and began to prepare its judgment. However, on 31 March 1992, at the instigation of the US, the UK and France, the Security Council passed a resolution (Resolution 748 (1992)) imposing sanctions on Libya for non-compliance with its earlier resolution. The ICJ then gave its decision on 14 April 1992.

The ICJ decided, by 11 votes to 5, not to grant Libya's request for provisional measures. The decision given here is in the case *Libya* v *United States*, though the decision in *Libya* v *United Kingdom* was essentially identical.

42. Whereas both Libya and the United States, as Members of the United Nations, are obliged to accept and carry out the decisions of the Security Council in accordance with Article 25 of the Charter; whereas the Court, which is at the stage of proceedings on provisional measures, considers that prima facie this obligation extends to the decision contained in resolution 748 (1992); and whereas, in accordance with Article 103 of the Charter, the obligations of the Parties in that respect prevail over their obligations under any other international agreement, including the Montreal Convention;

43. Whereas the Court thus not at this stage called upon to determine definitively the legal effect of Security Council resolution 748 (1992), considers that, whatever the situation previous to the adoption of that resolution, the rights claimed by Libya under the Montreal Convention cannot now be regarded as appropriate for protection by the indication of provisional measures;

44. Whereas, furthermore, an indication of the measures requested by Libya would be likely to impair the rights which appear prima facie to be enjoyed by the United States by virtue of Security Council resolution 748 (1992);

JUDGE SHAHABUDDEEN (Separate Opinion): Whatever might have been the previous position, resolution 748 (1992) of the Security Council leaves the Court with no conclusion other than that to which it has come. This is the result not of imposition of superior authority—there is none—but of the fact that, in finding the applicable law, the Court must take account of the resolution in so far as it effects the enforceability of the rights for the protection of which Libya is seeking interim measures. The validity of the resolution, though contested by Libya, has, at this stage, to be presumed (see the general principle in *Legal Consequences for States of the Continued Presence of South Africa in Namibia (South West Africa) notwithstanding Security Council Resolution 276 (1970)*, ICJ Reports 1971, p. 22, para 20). Article 25 of the Charter of the United Nations obliges Libya to comply with the decision set out in the resolution (*ibid.*, pp. 52–53). By virtue of Article 103 of the Charter, that obligation prevails over any conflicting treaty obligation which Libya may have (*Military and Paramilitary Activities in and against Nicaragua (Nicaragua v United States of America)*, ICJ Reports 1984, p. 440 para. 107). Treaty obligations can be overridden by a decision of the Security Council imposing sanctions (Paul Reuter, *Introduction to the Law of Treaties*, 1981, p. 113. para 228, and Sir Gerald Fitzmaurice, *The Law and Procedure of the International Court of Justice*, 1986, Vol. 2, p. 431). Hence, assuming that Libya has the rights which it claims, prima facie they could not be enforced during the life of the resolution.

Several cases demonstrate, in one way or another, that the Court is not precluded from acting by the mere circumstances that the matter in contest is also under consideration by another organ of the United Nations (see, *inter alia*, United States Diplomatic and Consular Staff in Tehran, ICJ Reports 1980, p. 22, para. 40; and *Military and Paramilitary Activities in and against Nicaragua (Nicaragua v United States of America) Provisional Measures*, ICJ Reports 1984, pp. 185–186, and, same case, *Jurisdiction and Admissibility*, ICJ Reports 1984, pp. 433–436). In this case, it happens that the decision which the Court is asked to give is one which would directly conflict with a decision of the Security Council. That is not an aspect which can be overlooked. Yet, it is not the juridical ground of today's Order. This results not from any collision between the competence of the Security Council and that of the Court, but from a collision between the obligations of Libya under the decision of the Security Council and any obligations which it may have under the Montreal Convention. The Charter says that the former prevail...

JUDGE BEDJAOUI (Dissenting Opinion): 22...[I]f the simple but essential distinction...is borne in mind, between the quite specific juridical dispute submitted to the Court and the much wider political dispute brought before the Security Council, it becomes perfectly understandable that, given its functions, and powers, the Court has no alternative but to refrain from entertaining any aspect whatever of the political solutions arrived at by the Security Council. The Court's attitude in this respect continues to be defensible *so long as* no aspect of these political solutions adopted by the Council sets aside, rules out or renders impossible the juridical solution expected of the Court. It is clear that, in this case, it is the judicial function itself which would be impaired. Indeed, this is what is happening here in the area where these two disputes overlap, where the solution arrived at by the Council to the question of the extradition of two individuals deprives a solution found by the Court of all meaning.

23. Such a situation, in which, on the basis of the case, the Court should have indicated provisional measures solely in order to protect a right that the Security Council annihilates by its resolution 748 (1992) when the case is *sub judice*, is not satisfactory for the judicial function. It is even less so when one of the two Respondents, the United States of America, asks the Court quite simply to refrain from exercising its judicial duty and to bow to the Security Council 'in order to avoid any conflict' with it....In the past the Security Council awaited the Court's decision.

Case concerning Application of the Convention on the Prevention and Punishment of the Crime of Genocide (Bosnia and Herzegovina v Yugoslavia (Serbia and Montenegro))
Indication of Provisional Measures, ICJ Rep 1993 325, International Court of Justice

The Republic of Bosnia-Herzegovina instituted proceedings against the Federal Republic of Yugoslavia (Serbia and Montenegro) claiming that the latter were responsible for the commission of genocide in Bosnia-Herzegovina. The former Yugoslavia had previously ratified the Genocide Convention. Bosnia-Herzegovina also requested provisional measures to prevent on-going genocide. The Court made two decisions indicating provisional measures, in April and September 1993. Judge ad hoc Lauterpacht gave a Separate Opinion in the latter instance.

JUDGE LAUTERPACHT (Separate Opinion): 99. This is not to say that the Security Council can act free of all legal controls but only that the Court's power of judicial review is limited. That the Court has some power of this kind can hardly be doubted, though there can be no less doubt that it does not embrace any right of the Court to substitute its discretion for that of the Security Council in determining the existence of a threat to the peace, a breach of the peace or an act of aggression, or the political steps to be taken following such a determination. But the Court, as the principle judicial organ of the United Nations, is entitled, indeed bound, to ensure the rule of law within the United Nations system and, in cases properly brought before it, to assist on adherence by all United Nations organs to the rules governing their operations…

100. The present case, however, cannot fall within the scope of the doctrine just enunciated. This is because the prohibition of genocide, unlike the matters covered by the Montreal Convention in the *Lockerbie* case to which the terms of Article 103 could be directly applied, has generally been accepted as having the status not of an ordinary rule of international law but of *jus cogens*. Indeed, the prohibition of genocide has long been regarded as one of the few undoubted examples of *jus cogens*. Even in 1951, in its Advisory Opinion on *Reservations to the Convention on the Prevention and Punishment of the Crime of Genocide*, the Court affirmed that genocide was 'contrary to moral law and to the spirit and aims of the United Nations' (a view repeated by the Court in paragraph 51 of today's Order) and that the principles underlying the Convention are provisions which are recognized by civilized nations as binding on States even without any conventional obligation (*ICJ Reports 1951*, p. 22). An express reference to the special quality of the prohibition of genocide may also be seen in the work of the International Law Commission in the preparation of Article 50 of the draft articles on the Law of Treaties (*Year-book of the International Law Commission*, 1966, Vol, II, pp. 248–249) which eventually materialised in Article 53 of the Vienna Convention on the Law of Treaties and in the same Commission's commentary on Article 19 (international crimes and delicts) of the draft articles on State Responsibility (*Yearbook of the International Law Commission*, 1976, Vol, II, Pt. 2, p. 103). The concept of *jus cogens* operates as a concept superior to both customary international law and treaty. The relief which Article 103 of the Charter may give the Security Council in case of conflict between one of its decisions and an operative treaty obligation cannot—as a matter of simple hierarchy of norms—extend to a conflict between a Security Council resolution and *jus cogens*. Indeed, one only has to state the opposite proposition thus—that a Security Council resolution may even require participation in genocide—for its unacceptability to be apparent.

101. Nor should one overlook the significance of the provision in Article 24(2) of the Charter that, in discharging its duties to maintain international peace and security, the Security Council shall act in accordance with the Purposes and Principles of the United Nations. Amongst the Purposes set out in Article 1(3) of the Charter is that of achieving international co-operation 'in promoting and encouraging respect for human rights and for fundamental freedoms for all without distinction as to race, sex, language or religion'.

102. Now, it is not to be contemplated that the Security Council would ever deliberately adopt a resolution clearly and deliberately flouting a rule of *jus cogens* or requiring a violation of human rights. But the possibility that a Security Council resolution might inadvertently or in an unforeseen manner lead to such a situation cannot be excluded. And that, it appears, is what has happened here. On this basis, the inability of Bosnia-Herzegovina sufficiently strongly to fight back against the Serbs and effectively to prevent the implementation of the Serbian policy of ethnic cleansing is at least in part directly attributable to the fact that Bosnia-Herzegovina's access to weapons and equipment has been severely limited by the embargo. Viewed in this light, the Security Council resolution can be see as having in effect called on Members of the United Nations, albeit unknowingly and assuredly unwillingly, to become in some degree supporters of the genocidal activity of the Serbs and in this manner and to that extent to act contrary to a rule of *jus cogens*.

103. What legal consequences may flow from this analysis? One possibility is that, in strict logic, when the operation of paragraph 6 of Security Council resolution 713 (1991) began to make Members of the United Nations accessories to genocide, it ceased to be valid and binding in its operation against Bosnia-Herzegovina; and that Members of the United Nations then became free to disregard it. Even so, it would be difficult to say that they then became positively obliged to provide the Applicant with weapons and military equipment.

104. There is, however, another possibility that is, perhaps, more in accord with the realities of the situation. It must be recognized that the chain of hypotheses in the analysis just made involves some debatable links— elements of fact, such as that the arms embargo has led to the imbalance in the possession of arms by the two sides and that that imbalance has contributed in greater or lesser degree to genocidal activity such as ethnic cleansing; and elements of law, such as that genocide is *jus cogens* and that a resolution which becomes violative of *jus cogens* must then become void and legally ineffective. It is not necessary for the Court to take a position in this regard at this time. Instead, it would seem sufficient that the relevance here of *jus cogens* should be drawn to the attention of the Security Council, as it will be by the required communication to it of the Court's Order, so that the Security Council may give due weight to it in future reconsideration of the embargo....

106. While, of course, the principle thrust of a finding that paragraph 6 of Security Council resolution 713 (1991) may conflict with *jus cogens* must lie in the direction of third States which may be willing to supply arms to Bosnia-Herzegovina, that does not mean that such a conclusion could have no place in an order operative between Bosnia-Herzegovina and Yugoslavia in the present proceedings. There may well be advantage for Bosnia-Herzegovina (it is not for the Court to determine) in being able to say that the Court had identified a source of doubt regarding the validity of the embargo resolution which, though not directly operative by itself, requires that the Security Council give the matter further consideration.

Judge Peter Tomka, President of the International Court of Justice, Speech to the Legal Advisers of the United Nations Member States

ICJ, Press Release, 29 October 2013

The Court is one of the six main organs of the UN and constitutes its principal judicial organ pursuant to Article 92 of the UN Charter. Contrary to its predecessor, the Permanent Court of International Justice, which, while instituted by the League of Nations was not legally part of that entity, the ICJ was fully integrated into the institutional architecture of the newly created UN....While it is true that the Court's jurisdiction remains based on the consent of States appearing before it, with proposals aiming to institute compulsory jurisdiction having been rejected in San Francisco in 1945, the UN Charter nonetheless carves out an exceedingly important judicial function for the Court in adjudicating international disputes. This observation is particularly applicable to the resolution of disputes susceptible of endangering the maintenance of international peace and security, which constitutes the exclusive focus of Chapter VI of the Charter. It is imperative to keep in mind that Article 36 of the Charter vests the Security Council with the power to recommend appropriate procedures or methods of adjustment to States parties to an international dispute, the extension or aggravation of which are susceptible of jeopardizing international peace and security....

Indeed, the restoration of harmonious relations between States sometimes hinges on the judicial resolution of their disputes by the Court. This possibility becomes particularly compelling when seen through the prism of Chapter VI of the UN Charter, which addresses the pacific settlement of disputes likely to endanger the maintenance of international peace and security. Thus, the prospect of the Security Council recommending to parties to refer their dispute to the Court may have a stabilizing impact on the relations between the parties or defuse tensions between them, a feature that often characterizes proceedings before the Court. This is particularly true with respect to disputes involving competing claims to sovereignty or maritime zones. In the absence of fruitful avenues of resolution by means of mediation or negotiation, or where creative solutions such as joint management and exploitation régimes may not be devised, recourse to the Court remains a viable and peaceful settlement option for disputing States. The Security Council has not frequently used its power to recommend to the parties that they refer their dispute to the ICJ; the best known example is the seminal case the *Corfu Channel* (*United Kingdom* v. *Albania*)

The Security Council can also play a role ensuring compliance with the Court's decision, although such role is infrequently invoked given that the Court's decisions have generated a strong record of compliances by parties. The Court does not concern itself with enforcing its own judgments, as parties to a dispute before it undertake to comply with its decisions by virtue of Article 94, paragraph 1, of the Charter. In the rare event that such compliance is unfulfilled, a party seeking to enforce the Court's judgment may seize the Council of the matter pursuant to Article 94, paragraph 2....Alternatively, any UN Member State may bring the matter to the attention of the Council under Article 35 of the Charter, provided they are satisfied that a dispute or situation exists 'which might lead to international friction or give rise to a dispute'. I should also like to recall that the Security Council does not enjoy a monopoly over recommending compliance with decisions of the Court. Under the terms of Article 10 of the UN

Charter, the General Assembly may also put forward such a recommendation. This was one avenue Nicaragua pursued in 1986 regarding the Court's judgment in the case concerning *Military and Paramilitary Activities in and against Nicaragua*, after its earlier attempt to seize the Security Council of the matter resulted in two draft resolutions being vetoed by a Permanent Member. Ultimately, the General Assembly adopted a resolution urging immediate compliance with the Judgment....

The links between the Court's judicial function and the activities carried out by the other principal UN organs was further developed in the case concerning *Military and Paramilitary Activities in and against Nicaragua* (*Nicaragua* v. *United States*). At the jurisdiction and admissibility phase of the case, the Court reproduced the contents of Article 24 of the Charter to emphasize that, while the Security Council is vested with the primary responsibility for the maintenance of international peace and security within the UN system, that responsibility is by no means exclusive....[t]he Court went on to declare 'that the fact that a matter is before the Security Council should not prevent it being dealt with by the Court and that both proceedings could be pursued *pari passu*'. Furthermore, the Court recalled that it 'never shied away from a case brought before it merely because it had political implications or because it involved serious elements of the use of force' before again reiterating the organic links that bind the Court and other principal UN organs in the furtherance of common purposes and objectives: 'The Council has functions of a political nature assigned to it, whereas the Court exercises purely judicial functions. Both organs can therefore perform their separate but complementary functions with respect to the same events.'

Similarly, this time in the *Lockerbie* cases, the Court stressed that, should it have jurisdiction to entertain a dispute at the time the application instituting proceedings was submitted to it, subsequent Security Council resolutions and intervention would have no bearing on that jurisdiction, once established. The Court's conclusion on this front remained congruent with its earlier remarks in the *Tehran Hostages* case when it had observed that 'legal disputes between sovereign States by their very nature are likely to occur in political contexts, and often form only one element in a wider and longstanding political dispute between the States concerned'....This undoubtedly prompted the Court to reassert, in the 2004 *Wall Advisory Opinion*, that the political nature of a question submitted for its consideration would not constitute a bar to establishing its jurisdiction. In the Court's view, it followed that the fact that a legal question also had political aspects was insufficient to deprive it of its character as a 'legal question', or to prevent the Court from exercising jurisdiction over the matter.

NOTES

1. The decision in the *Lockerbie Case* above was on whether provisional measures should be granted and not on the merits of the case. However, as Judge Shahabuddeen indicates, a number of important legal issues could be raised when the merits of the case are considered. The second Security Council resolution had a direct impact on the decision in the case, as seen in a joint Separate Opinion by Judges Evenson, Tarassov, Guillaume and Aguilar Mawdsley, where it is made clear that, prior to the second Security Council resolution, Libya was within its rights to refuse to extradite its nationals and the United States and the United Kingdom were entitled to take any action consistent with international law. Eventually, the matter was settled by a trial of two Libyan men before a Scottish Court in The Netherlands.

2. Most of the judges in the *Lockerbie Case*, as indicated in the decisions of Judge Shahabuddeen and Judge Bedjaoui, as well as Judge Lauterpacht in the *Genocide in Yugoslavia Case*, seem to take the view that the ICJ could undertake judicial review of a decision of the Security Council, even though this review could be exercised only in limited circumstances. This view raises the issue of the constitutional structure of the international community, particularly as between the Security Council and the ICJ. The power relationship between these two organs is not made explicit in the UN Charter, except that Article 36(3) (see Section 2B) provides that the Security Council should take into consideration that legal disputes should be referred to the ICJ. The difficulty is that a political decision by the Security Council can have legal impacts. Hence, Judge Bedjaoui's view that any conflict of powers between the two organs would occur only where the Security Council has made a decision which renders judicial determination of a case futile.

3. There have been some decisions within the European legal system that have dealt with matters concerning the effect and legality of UN measures. In *Yassin Abdullah Kadi and Al Barakaat International Foundation* v *Council and Commission* ([2008] ECR I-6351), the European Court of Justice considered the legality of a European Union measure that was intended to implement a counter-terrorism sanctions regime adopted by the UN Security Council acting under Chapter VII of the United Nations Charter. The Court found that it had jurisdiction to review the European Union measure and hence, indirectly, it could review the relevant Security

Council resolution for compliance with, for example, European Union requirements of non-discrimination and fair trial. This decision was supported by the Court's later case law (*Kadi II* (Judgment of 18 July 2013)).

4. In order to settle international disputes peacefully, it is necessary that a variety of measures, legal and non-legal, are available. However, if international law is to exist as a properly functioning legal system then its institutions must abide by the rule of law, including the Security Council. This suggests that there perhaps should be a role for the ICJ to review whether decisions of the Security Council are in accordance with international law.

APPENDIX

Member States of the United Nations

The 193 Member States of the UN (as at March 2016) and the dates on which they joined are listed below. Details on any changes of status and/or of name are set out on the United Nations web page at http://www.un.org/en/members/index.shtml.

Afghanistan (19 November 1946)
Albania (14 December 1955)
Algeria (8 October 1962)
Andorra (28 July 1993)
Angola (1 December 1976)
Antigua and Barbuda (11 November 1981)
Argentina (24 October 1945)
Armenia (2 March 1992)
Australia (1 November 1945)
Austria (14 December 1955)
Azerbaijan (9 March 1992)
Bahamas (18 September 1973)
Bahrain (21 September 1971)
Bangladesh (17 September 1974)
Barbados (9 December 1966)
Belarus (24 October 1945)
Belgium (27 December 1945)
Belize (25 September 1981)
Benin (20 September 1960)
Bhutan (21 September 1971)
Bolivia (14 November 1945)
Bosnia and Herzegovina (22 May 1992)
Botswana (17 October 1966)
Brazil (24 October 1945)
Brunei Darussalam (21 September 1984)
Bulgaria (14 December 1955)
Burkina Faso (20 September 1960)
Burundi (18 September 1962)
Cambodia (14 December 1955)
Cameroon (20 September 1960)
Canada (9 November 1945)
Cape Verde (16 September 1975)
Central African Republic (20 September 1960)
Chad (20 September 1960)
Chile (24 October 1945)
China (24 October 1945)
Colombia (5 November 1945)
Comoros (12 November 1975)
Congo (20 September 1960)
Congo (Democratic Republic of the)
   (20 September 1960)
Costa Rica (2 November 1945)
Côte d'Ivoire (20 September 1960)
Croatia (22 May 1992)
Cuba (24 October 1945)
Cyprus (20 September 1960)

Czech Republic (19 January 1993)
Denmark (24 October 1945)
Djibouti (20 September 1977)
Dominica (18 December 1978)
Dominican Republic (24 October 1945)
Ecuador (21 December 1945)
Egypt (24 October 1945)
El Salvador (24 October 1945)
Equatorial Guinea (12 November 1968)
Eritrea (28 May 1993)
Estonia (17 September 1991)
Ethiopia (13 November 1945)
Fiji (13 October 1970)
Finland (14 December 1955)
France (24 October 1945)
Gabon (20 September 1960)
Gambia (21 September 1965)
Georgia (31 July 1992)
Germany (18 September 1973)
Ghana (8 March 1957)
Greece (25 October 1945)
Grenada (17 September 1974)
Guatemala (21 November 1945)
Guinea (12 December 1958)
Guinea-Bissau (17 September 1974)
Guyana (20 September 1966)
Haiti (24 October 1945)
Honduras (17 December 1945)
Hungary (14 December 1955)
Iceland (19 November 1946)
India (30 October 1945)
Indonesia (28 September 1950)
Iran (Islamic Republic of) (24 October 1945)
Iraq (21 December 1945)
Ireland (14 December 1955)
Israel (11 May 1949)
Italy (14 December 1955)
Jamaica (18 September 1962)
Japan (18 December 1956)
Jordan (14 December 1955)
Kazakhstan (2 March 1992)
Kenya (16 December 1963)
Kiribati (14 September 1999)
Korea (Democratic People's Republic of)
   (17 September 1991)
Korea (Republic of) (17 September 1991)

Kuwait (14 May 1963)

Kyrgyzstan (2 March 1992)

Laos (People's Democratic Republic of)
  (14 December 1955)

Latvia (17 September 1991)

Lebanon (24 October 1945)

Lesotho (17 October 1966)

Liberia (2 November 1945)

Libya (Libyan Arab Jamahiriya)
  (14 December 1955)

Liechtenstein (18 September 1990)

Lithuania (17 September 1991)

Luxembourg (24 October 1945)

Macedonia (former Yugoslav Republic of)
  (8 April 1993)

Madagascar (20 September 1960)

Malawi (1 December 1964)

Malaysia (17 September 1957)

Maldives (21 September 1965)

Mali (28 September 1960)

Malta (1 December 1964)

Marshall Islands (17 September 1991)

Mauritania (7 October 1961)

Mauritius (24 April 1968)

Mexico (7 November 1945)

Micronesia (Federated States of)
  (17 September 1991)

Moldova (Republic of) (2 March 1992)

Monaco (28 May 1993)

Mongolia (27 October 1961)

Montenegro (28 June 2006)

Morocco (12 November 1956)

Mozambique (16 September 1975)

Myanmar (19 April 1948)

Namibia (23 April 1990)

Nauru (14 September 1999)

Nepal (14 December 1955)

Netherlands (10 December 1945)

New Zealand (24 October 1945)

Nicaragua (24 October 1945)

Niger (20 September 1960)

Nigeria (7 October 1960)

Norway (27 November 1945)

Oman (7 October 1971)

Pakistan (30 September 1947)

Palau (15 December 1994)

Panama (13 November 1945)

Papua New Guinea (10 October 1975)

Paraguay (24 October 1945)

Peru (31 October 1945)

Philippines (24 October 1945)

Poland (24 October 1945)

Portugal (14 December 1955)

Qatar (21 September 1971)

Romania (14 December 1955)

Russian Federation (24 October 1945)

Rwanda (18 September 1962)

Saint Kitts and Nevis (23 September 1983)

Saint Lucia (18 September 1979)

Saint Vincent and the Grenadines
  (16 September 1980)

Samoa (15 December 1976)

San Marino (2 March 1992)

Sao Tome and Principe (16 September 1975)

Saudi Arabia (24 October 1945)

Senegal (28 September 1960)

Serbia (1 November 2000)

Seychelles (21 September 1976)

Sierra Leone (27 September 1961)

Singapore (21 September 1965)

Slovakia (19 January 1993)

Slovenia (22 May 1992)

Solomon Islands (19 September 1978)

Somalia (20 September 1960)

South Africa (7 November 1945)

South Sudan (14 July 2011)

Spain (14 December 1955)

Sri Lanka (14 December 1955)

Sudan (12 November 1956)

Suriname (4 December 1975)

Swaziland (24 September 1968)

Sweden (19 November 1946)

Switzerland (10 September 2002)

Syria (Syrian Arab Republic) (24 October 1945)

Tajikistan (2 March 1992)

Tanzania (United Republic of)
  (14 December 1961)

Thailand (16 December 1946)

Timor-Leste (East Timor) (27 September 2002)

Togo (20 September 1960)

Tonga (14 September 1999)

Trinidad and Tobago (18 September 1962)

Tunisia (12 November 1956)

Turkey (24 October 1945)

Turkmenistan (2 March 1992)

Tuvalu (5 September 2000)

Uganda (25 October 1962)

Ukraine (24 October 1945)

United Arab Emirates (9 December 1971)

United Kingdom of Great Britain and Northern
  Ireland (24 October 1945)

United States of America (24 October 1945)

Uruguay (18 December 1945)

Uzbekistan (2 March 1992)

Vanuatu (15 September 1981)

Venezuela (15 November 1945)

Vietnam (20 September 1977)

Yemen (30 September 1947)

Zambia (1 December 1964)

Zimbabwe (25 August 1980)

INDEX